REBRANDING Rule

REBRANDING RULE

THE RESTORATION AND REVOLUTION
MONARCHY, 1660–1714

KEVIN SHARPE

YALE UNIVERSITY PRESS
NEW HAVEN AND LONDON

Published with the support of The Paul Mellon Centre for Studies in British Art

For information about this and other Yale University Press publications, please contact:
U.S. Office: sales.press@yale. edu   www.yalebooks.com
Europe Office: sales @yaleup.co.uk   www.yalebooks.co.uk

Set in Minion by IDSUK (DataConnection) Ltd

Printed in Great Britain by TJ International Ltd, Padstow, Cornwall

Library of Congress Cataloging-in-Publication Data

Sharpe, Kevin (Kevin M.)
    Rebranding rule: images of restoration and revolution monarchy 1660–1714/Kevin Sharpe.
    pages cm
    ISBN 978-0-300-16201-1 (cl: alk. paper)
    1. Great Britain—History–1660–1714. 2. Great Britain—History—Stuarts, 1603–1714.
3. Great Britain—History—Restoration, 1660–1688 4. Great Britain—History—
Revolution of 1688. 5. Monarchy—Great Britain—Public opinion—History—17th
century. 6. Monarchy—Great Britain—Public opinion—History—18th century.
7. Political culture—Great Britain—History—17th century. 8. Political culture—Great
Britain—History—18th century. 9. Great Britain—Kings and rulers—Public opinion.
I. Title.
DA435.S53 2013
941.06—dc23
                                                                          2012042931

A catalogue record for this book is available from the British Library.

10 9 8 7 6 5 4 3 2 1

CONTENTS

ILLUSTRATIONS

FOREWORD

Kevin seemed to have made such a good recovery from his cancer and appeared so full of life that it was quite a shock that he sunk so rapidly in his final illness, dying without being able to see this book through to publication. Only three months earlier he had flown to Chicago where Trevor Burnard and I were running a summer school. He gave a virtuoso performance to the graduates and early career scholars there. Kevin's insatiable curiosity about ideas and people fused which his generosity towards those starting out on academic careers; and they were in turn a rapt audience with Kevin relished performing in front of and engaging with. Kevin always enjoyed the drama of an academic conversation and conveyed his message with style.

Indeed, he had clearly absorbed the lessons of his own trilogy, of which this is the last volume, examining the arts of presentation and representation practised by English rulers in the sixteenth and seventeenth centuries. In the preface to the first volume, covering the Tudors, Kevin talks about how the spin of New Labour set him thinking about the ways in which politics and power more generally were conveyed and cultivated through images and words. That engagement with contemporary concerns must, of course, have been a key motivating factor behind the work; but I also wonder how far his interest in representations was also an interest in how he packaged himself. At his memorial service we were treated to wonderful anecdotes about his flamboyant but carefully chosen clothes and exuberant hair-style as a student, about how he later had to wear the 'right' jeans or designer shirts that would exactly convey the image he wanted to create and impress those around him. He cultivated his own image, self-fashioned himself, with almost as much care as the Tudors and Stuarts whom he studied cultivated the cult of monarchy and shaped how it was projected to the people. It was perhaps surprising that Kevin did not do more TV work to disseminate his ideas – he could surely have given Starkey more than a run for his money; but he was, for all his sense of fun, always first and foremost a serious scholarly star, and he may have been uneasy about giving control over his own image to production and PR teams.

Kevin recognized that both in the past and in the present, in his own life and in the world of academia, cultivating an image was an art. That art required mobilizing all available tools, including the visual and the verbal (the ocular and oral) as well as ceremony and ritual. Studying this necessitated an interdisciplinary approach. Kevin's trajectory, from history departments to literature departments, and his increasingly sophisticated knowledge of art history, is suggestive of the restlessness that the early modern period so often condemned but which ran through almost everything Kevin did, in both personal and professional life, together with a methodological hunger for the appropriate way to interpret the multifaceted past. For Kevin interdisciplinarity was not an end in itself or something faddish (though he did like to set trends, as his early revisionism and later history of reading show); rather it was something essential to understanding a phenomenon that he saw as essentially multi-stranded. It was highly appropriate that, at Queen Mary, he ran a high-profile seminar series about the Renaissance, a movement that also refused to acknowledge strict boundaries of knowledge and saw the profit in moving across fields. 'The world of the Renaissance, early modern England,' he wrote in the preface to *Representing Rule*, 'was an intertextual world which we can only begin to comprehend, as contemporaries comprehended it, from multidisciplinary as well as interdisciplinary perspectives.' A model of how to write such a truly cultural history of authority is one of Kevin's most important legacies. It was that interdisciplinarity, the need for historians to reach beyond the confines of their own discipline, that Kevin was still urgently impressing on the participants of the Chicago summer school shortly before his death. I think he was largely preaching to the converted – and that may in itself be a testament to the success of his work – but there was no doubting the genuine passion and conviction with which Kevin delivered his message.

The various strands that demanded interdisciplinary treatment are laid out in all three of his books about the representation of power. The structure that he adopted in the first volume – an examination of royal speeches, sermons, royal ceremonies and rituals, royal images in paintings, engravings and on coins, and an assessment of criticisms of rule – can be found repeated in the second and now in this third volume. The structure gives coherence and allows us to follow developments in any of these themes and it also highlights the importance of genre, which was another of Kevin's abiding interests and another issue he wanted to impress both on our workshop participants and on the rest of the scholarly community.

Kevin remarked, in the preface to the first volume, that 'the early modern state as it developed under the Tudors and Stuarts was a representational state in which political crises were inevitably bound up with crises of representation.' Following such crises across three volumes, through reformation, civil war, regicide and revolutions, he underscores both the enduring importance of representation in the construction of authority and changes in genre, media and tone. These included but went beyond the absorption of print as an increasingly important tool to construct authority. Over the three volumes Kevin highlights a process of sacralizing and then de-sacralizing monarchy. This present volume charts the emergence of a 'state in which the mystification of majesty became less the programme of rulers and governments, and more the election and desire of subjects and citizens'. The volume takes him chronologically into new terrain but he sensed both that more work needed to be done on the later Stuarts and that important shifts in the representational culture that he had been charting took place then. Having started his career attacking Whig historiography in relation to early Stuart constitutional and religious conflict, his last work attacks the Whigs' neglect of kingship in the later Stuart era. Ironically, however, his conclusion that the mid-century revolution was demystifying and transformative, and that a need to appeal to a wide public altered the culture of royal representation, might fit within a Whig narrative so long as it is one that appreciates the power and poetry of the visual, of ritual and of words and literature.

To be sure, there are blindspots that I used to tackle Kevin about. His generic approach does sometimes cut across the desire stated in *Selling the Tudor Monarchy* to place a Holbein next to a sermon or a eulogy of William III next to a graphic satire – they are in the same volume but the reader sometimes needs to make his or her own links. More importantly, although alive to the reception of authority (as his work on reading shows), Kevin was also relatively uninterested in a social construction of authority. For him, rule and authority were resolutely wielded by monarchs and those in Whitehall and Westminster, rather than by and through the mass of office-holders emphasized in more recent accounts of the early modern period. But already running to almost 2,000 pages the trilogy would surely have swelled into an unmanageable monster had the remit run any wider. The task of examining the cultural and social construction of authority more generally in the early modern period remains but Kevin's work will make it much easier to see similarities and differences in the strategies adopted by those lower down the social scale. Words, ritual and images will remain important shared concerns across such histories.

Historians are more used to dealing with the papers of people they never knew and who died long ago than they are with the papers of recently deceased friends. So preparing Kevin's volume for the press has been an odd and slightly unsettling experience. When he was alive Kevin would frequently bounce into my office – usually not at the most convenient times – to see if I knew the answer to one of his many questions and that would set us going, talking about later Stuart culture, discussion that would almost inevitably morph into Kevin's tales of who was going for what job, or at least who ought to get it and who ought not! Academia for him resembled an early modern royal court, with some who were 'in' and some who were 'out', the rises and falls which it was his duty as a court observer to chronicle and gossip about. Now, the queries have been more sterile corrections to proofs – the ends of conversations, rather than the beginnings. But it has also been a fascinating experience, glimpsing the working practices of one of the most influential historians of his generation. When I received a message from Kevin's hospital bed, as he drifted in and out of consciousness, that he wanted me to see the book through to publication, I was struck by his sense of drama, for he could have asked me on many other occasions. Even in death, like the monarchs he studied, he had a sense of occasion and timing. This volume is Kevin's legacy. I am not sure it is his *Eikon Basilike*, but it was certainly written against the odds and is surely a worthy testament.

Mark Knights

PREFACE AND
ACKNOWLEDGEMENTS

Rebranding Rule takes me into historical territory which I had only begun to work on before writing this book. It is also a historiographical terrain that until recently was broadly neglected and which even today has vast areas uncharted by new scholarship. We have now good narratives of the politics – and not just the high politics but the politics of crowds and public opinion. And there have been excellent recent studies of Restoration and Augustan political culture which have begun to transform our understanding. Not least, the best of them recognize the need to pay address to poems and prints as texts of politics in a highly polemicized and partisan political culture.[1]

Yet the images of the monarchy and representations of rule from 1660 to 1714 remain largely unstudied. Where literary scholars, and art historians, as well as historians, have explicated aspects of Tudor propaganda, image making and ritual, and where students of the reigns of James I and (especially) Charles I have examined masques, portraits and buildings as texts of Stuart power, very few have shown any interest in the *styles* of post-Restoration and post-Revolution rulers. Though we now have an excellent account of the ceremonies of Charles II, there are no broad studies of his representation in words and visuals; and of those of James II, William III and Queen Anne we know even less.[2]

In part this omission has been due to a still-prevailing Whig historiography that, in characterizing this period as one in which parliaments at last won the initiative and established a 'constitutional monarchy', made focus on royalty less important, as well as (to many Whig scholars) unattractive. And while few would now, in the wake of important revisionist scholarship, simply rehearse those arguments, new studies have largely – and rightly – concurred in describing the king and court as less important than the capital and metropolitan society in the cultural life of the realm.[3]

What we need to ask is how those changes came about and whether they themselves reflect broader changes in society and state – or whether post-Restoration and post-Revolution rulers failed to impress themselves, as the

Tudors had so assiduously sought to do, on the lives, and the imaginations, of their subjects.

Such a question brings me to the central issue of first the Restoration – and then the Revolution. Did the civil war, regicide and republic fundamentally change the nature of the English state and constitution or was the clock put back in 1660 to the point where the hands were before the war? Historians have been divided in their answers to this, some identifying a transformed polity with the Restoration, others pointing to the replaying after 1660 of many of the same narratives and problems of pre-civil war England.[4] My sense is that the differences of opinion derive not least from the divisions among contemporaries themselves about whether the world had fundamentally changed or not. And those divisions were not just between people but also within their minds. For many, that is, the impulse was to try to erase the bitter memories of the civil war and Revolution and to behave as though these had been forms of interlude – even if they suspected that the legacy of war and republic was deeper than that. There was an ambiguity at the centre of Restoration England, which made the art of representing rule and embodying the nation more challenging than it had ever been.

The representation of royal authority faced other challenges in 1660. Most knew – even if they still disapproved of the fact – that England was now a divided realm and that there were fundamental differences over faith, the church and the polity, which undermined a traditional belief in unity and harmony. Traditional beliefs, however, were not easily or quickly surrendered and could certainly not be ignored. The challenge for a monarch was to represent both: to validate and stand for tradition and custom while recognizing and accommodating to change.

It was not the only challenge. In 1660, England had been ruled for thirteen years without a king; and the consequence, whatever the rhetoric of ardent royalists, had not been anarchy. Indeed, many had admired (and even some of his opponents had grudgingly respected) Oliver Cromwell's rule as Protector – an age which saw English successes abroad as well as relative order and peace at home. In 1660, a returning king had to again make the case for monarchy: to argue for rather than assume his authority. And because during the Commonwealth many of the old traditional discourses and signs which had validated monarchy had been disrupted – or appropriated for republic – the monarch had to re-establish and re-possess them. He had also, in his turn, to appropriate the other, sometimes radically different discourses and languages in which republican rule had been justified: languages, for example, of providence, of probity, of classical virtue, also of interest and commerce.

We talk – as did contemporaries- of monarchy being 'restored' in 1660. In reality, in large measure, it had to be reconstituted and refashioned. This was literally true of the regalia, much of which had been melted down to pay for wartime costs. But it was also true in the broadest terms: not only the ceremonial, but all the discursive, visual and performative aspects, the representational, indeed the psychological facets of royalty had to be re-formed and refashioned.

The story of the first part of this book, then, is of how Charles II and James II faced those unenviable challenges: how they represented their authority as part of reconstituting it; and how they responded to changing circumstances and problems. The fortunes of the last Stuart brothers were very different: Charles died peacefully in his bed; James lost his kingdoms and was driven into exile. We must ask whether the image and representation of the rulers, as well as their policies, were important in their fates and fortunes. Did Charles II, not least by skilful cultivation of his people, re-establish a monarchy which might have wielded more authority than even his father had dreamt of? Was James II's fate determined simply by his faith or did the failure of a once popular prince to convince his people of his best intentions cost him his throne?

The 1688 Revolution poses some not dissimilar questions. Was it, as has recently been argued, the first modern revolution which, in laying the foundations of modernity, rationalism and constitutional monarchy, transformed the nature of rule and regality in England?[5] Or was it, as some hold, a palace coup which replaced – for a time – a Stuart dynasty with an ambitious Dutch usurper without fundamentally changing the institutions or culture of politics?[6] To be specific, could William III have ruled in a similar manner to Charles II – or for that matter Charles I? And had he not prioritized his continental wars, would the decisive changes that did occur during his reign have taken place? Could Anne, the last Stuart, have reverted to an earlier style and form of rule? My particular concern is also to ask about how 1688 affected the discourse, style, image and representation of rulers; and, as much, to ask how the speeches, images and performances of William and Mary and of Queen Anne determined or changed the place of monarchy in the polity and in the perceptions of their subjects.

Because these matters remain understudied, and because more than ever the politics of Restoration and Revolution England are embedded in all forms of writing and material culture, I have drawn on – and studied in some detail – a very wide and eclectic range of texts in which monarchical rule was presented and represented. And – it is *essential* to recognize from the outset – contested. In my earlier volumes, *Selling the Tudor Monarchy* and *Image Wars*, albeit (as both I and some reviewers observed) space dictated too brief a discussion, I wrote of the criticisms of and opposition to authorized and official representations; indeed, in *Image Wars* I charted how increasingly the Stuarts found their words everywhere combated as well as critiqued. After 1660, however, and still more after the Popish Plot, the story of both representation and counter-representation is in no way (and had never entirely been) a story of government and opposition. The emergence of parties, even though they took time to acquire (and perhaps never in our period fully acquired) legitimacy, made both propaganda for government and opposition to it more than ever a complex political negotiation. Not least for historians, as it was for contemporaries, it becomes increasingly difficult to calculate the *impact* of any one locution, text or image in the bombardment of representations from all sides. What is certain is that parties changed the culture of royal representation – and the perceptions of rule. During the 1680s, the Charles II who had appealed to all his people in the 1660s and who had deployed a variety of representations committed himself to the Tories – and not only to a party but to a particular set of vocabularies and images that were (by now) distinctly partisan. From the 1680s onwards, though monarchs, with greater or less determination, tried to retain some independence of party (not least, I shall argue, in Anne's case through her speeches from the throne), even the representation of the monarchy had become a partisan business.

The shifting representations of regality and images of individual monarchs were then an important facet of the vital changes that took place in late seventeenth-century and early eighteenth-century England. In appealing to their people, the Tudors had involved them in the *arcana imperii*, the mysteries of state. Division, civil war, and then the emergence of party, frequent parliaments, elections and a fully developed public sphere of political news and gossip, increasingly enfranchised subjects to become citizens and made it imperative for kings and queens, as well as politicians, to appeal to a broad public beyond Whitehall and Westminster. How successfully individual rulers did that – and how effectively they represented themselves as the embodiment of the nation and national interest – helped decide how much authority they wielded. Charles II demonstrated (paradoxically) that an appeal to his people could provide a platform for sacred kingship. It is significant, however, that after 1688, no ruler (though at times I have suspected Anne might have wished to) emphasized or advertised divine right.

The Revolution, reviving what many would have preferred to forget had been a legacy of civil war and regicide, demystified royal authority and (at least in retrospect) transformed the monarchy and the representation and perception of monarchy. The course of English history was not determined in 1660. But the civil war, I have always thought, had revolutionary consequences (if not causes), not least in an altered psychology of power. *Rebranding Rule* attempts to analyze how early modern England's last monarchs fashioned their image in challenging, changed – and changing – conditions.

This is a long book, full of matter – for which, since it is the evidence that grounds the argument and many of the subjects here have not been adequately treated – I make no apology. Indeed, I rather apologize for subjects which I have omitted or only touched on: the representations of monarchs on playing cards and Delftware, the figuring of power and politics in Restoration theatre or the satirizing in poems on affairs of state (and other forms of scribal publication), to give a few examples. The organization also merits comment. As with my two earlier volumes, this book is structured into parts by reigns, into chapters by forms of representation; with attention to chronology and change, the chapters investigate genres – those on images taking in portraits, medals and prints, for example. This organization (like any) has disadvantages: themes and motifs are, of course, repeated across genres within a reign as well as over reigns and readers interested in topics across the period (such as divine right, or visions of imperial regimen) will need to follow cross references. But it has enabled me to examine distinct forms and genres in their (shifting) historical moments and I hope makes it possible for readers to pursue their interests in particular periods, or texts and modes of royal representation as well as to follow my larger story and arguments about the rebranding of post-Restoration and Revolution monarchy.

The research for this volume, more extensive and more difficult than for either of its predecessors, was made possible by a number of organizations and people. In particular I am most grateful to the Master and Fellows of my old college, St Catherine's College Oxford, for electing me to a visiting fellowship which enabled me to spend a year reading a wide variety of late seventeenth-century tracts. I would also like to thank the staff (especially Vera Ryhajlo) of the Bodleian Library where, over many summers, I continued research into poems as well as pamphlets, and the Sackler Library at the Ashmolean Museum where I investigated portraits, engravings, medals and coins on which I had begun extensive work at the Huntington Library in San Marino, California.

I began writing thanks to the generous award of a Humboldt prize which enabled me to spend a year at the Max Planck Institute for History in Göttingen. I would like to thank George Schutte, the Humboldt Foundation and Professor Hartmut Lehman for sponsoring and hosting me and the staff of the Max Planck and the Göttingen University Library which was especially rich in primary materials for late seventeenth-century England and where working conditions were excellent. The book was partially drafted in Germany, then edited, revised and completed during tenure of a Leverhulme Major Research fellowship (2005–8) – and since. I would again like to express my profound gratitude to the Trustees of the Leverhulme for making an award that enabled me to envision and advance this book, as well as to write my last two volumes. I would especially like to thank the Paul Mellon Centre London for a generous grant towards the cost of illustrations.

Over the many years this volume has been in the making, I have greatly benefited from the advice not only of old friends but new; and of scholars who have not only transformed our understanding of the late seventeenth century but welcomed a relative newcomer to their conversations. I would like especially to thank Julia Marciari Alexander, Tony Claydon, Tim Harris, Karen Hearn, Ronald Hutton, Anna Keay, Mark Knights (whom I have plagued with many queries), Catharine MacLeod, Annabel Patterson, Steve Pincus, Paul Seaward and Steven Zwicker (from whose suggestions and friendship I have as ever much benefited) who have joined George Bernard, Tom Corns, Peter Lake, Joad Raymond, and Greg Walker from whom as always I have had sound advice and feedback in a variety of forms.

To many (the above among them) I owe a greater debt that quite literally made this book possible. When in 2009 I was close to completing a draft, I was diagnosed with an aggressive lymphoma and forced to abandon work on it for a year. I do not know how to express my thanks to those who kept me alive, medically and in good spirits, during that difficult year or so; but to my consultants, Peter Johnson and Andrew Davies, and my family and dear friends I dedicate this volume as a small token of my appreciation for all that they did – and still do.

At Queen Mary, colleagues – with very few exceptions! (I am happy to provide names on request) – and friends remained supportive through difficult months of ill health. I am most grateful to the two press readers – one of whom (Mark Knights) generously broke his anonymity to give me invaluable advice – who helped me to reduce (but also expand), revise, qualify and sharpen key sections of the typescript; where I have not followed their advice, I can at least promise that I carefully considered it. I would also like to thank warmly my friend as well as editor (the right order after thirty years), Robert Baldock at Yale University Press, who accepted a book much longer than he would have preferred, and Peter Robinson who has never given up on me, even though we make less money with each new publication. For turning my handwritten drafts into a very neat typescript, I thank Liz Cameron, and for transforming a script into a handsome book my thanks to Richard Mason, to Candida Brazil and to Rachael Lonsdale. As before, Meg Davies provided an exemplary index.

INTRODUCTION
REPRESENTING RESTORED MONARCHY

Throughout the Tudor and early Stuart years, monarchs had encountered both challenges and opportunities in representing their regality. On his succession, Henry VIII had still to establish a dynasty, and after the Reformation had to assert his legitimacy; Mary and Elizabeth shared the difficulty of validating female governance and, for all their different positions, that of ruling a realm polarized by religion.[1] James I had to overcome the obstacle of being a Scot, as well as securing a new dynasty. And yet all these kings, even a minor and queens, were able to draw upon languages, symbols and rituals that sustained monarchy, and – increasingly over the course of the sixteenth century – enhanced it. Who can doubt – certainly not his successors themselves – that Henry VIII's children all drew strength from his legacy, not just to the processes of government but to the image of royal authority? And, after half a century of Elizabethan rule, James VI and I succeeded to a crown that had been elevated in the public imagination to celestial heights.

The cult of divine kingship, urged more insistently from Henry VIII's reign, did not, of course, preclude problems or opposition. Many – relatives, counsellors, noblemen, even citizens – sought to claim the authority of the monarchy for positions not favoured by the wearer of the crown. Even the most extravagant praise could constitute not only counsel, but pressure, as Elizabeth was made well aware. Edward VI and Mary, as respectively a minor and a Catholic woman, had to fight (literally as well as discursively in Mary's case) to appropriate for themselves the awesome majesty of Tudor monarchy. Indeed, the act of successful appropriation – of investing the body personal of the monarch with all the mystical power of the body sovereign – was the principal art of successful royal government. Not for nothing were the most successful early modern rulers those who had the largest impact on their subjects and those whose persons and portraits we can conjure in our mind's eye: those who, like Henry and Elizabeth, made the authority of the crown their personal authority.

Opposition and rebellion may evidence the vulnerability of even the strongest rulers, but they also, paradoxically at times, manifest their success and strength. For all the danger the leaders of the Pilgrimage of Grace in 1536 represented, they appealed to Henry rather than against him; and the many plots against Elizabeth's life bound her person – all too precariously in the view of her parliament – inextricably with the crown. The civil war itself was not – initially at least – the exception. Early modern Englishmen went to war in 1642 because they could not deploy a discourse of opposition sufficiently powerful to change royal decisions. And even when fighting broke out, both sides had to claim the validating languages and symbols of kingship – Scripture, the law, the scales of justice – to argue that they were the true supporters of majesty. To suggest that Charles I never quite lost the benefit, the ownership, of those languages and symbols may seem perverse: it is a pyrrhic victory that ends up on the executioner's block. Yet, though there were republicans among the ranks of Parliamentarians who through necessity led the opponents of the king (sometimes uncomfortably) to more radical claims, Charles was executed as king after a process of which many – and not just Royalists – doubted the legitimacy. As I have argued, the Commonwealth began its life as an illegitimate government; and from the very day of its birth, its struggle for legitimacy was damagingly undermined by a seemingly effortless reclamation of all the discourses of legitimacy for monarchy: the *Eikon Basilike*.[2]

But whatever the extent of its revolutionary causes, 1649 had profound revolutionary consequences – for the representation of rule, as well as for government itself. Because though the new regime deployed initially – and in some measure continued to deploy – traditional regal scripts, new terms and vocabularies, new symbols and ceremonies were devised to underpin republican government. And as the months passed, and the Commonwealth felt comfortable enough to pass an ordinance abolishing kingship, the fact of republican government, hitherto unimaginable to most Englishmen, effected a sea change in the discourses and perceptions of rule. Alongside, and against, the old languages of subjection to sovereign rule, a new lexicon of obligation to *de facto* government (whatever its origin) strengthened to form the argument of the most revolutionary text in the history of early modern political thought – and in the history of early modern representations of authority: Thomas Hobbes's *Leviathan*. And the divinity of rulers was not only countered by a new deployment of the language of providence, but also by utilitarian appeals to commerce, interest and contract. While scholars have recently rightly demonstrated that such alternative discourses and imaginings had for long been a (too little studied) subtext of monarchical culture, it was the fact and experience after 1649 of a Commonwealth (a term which itself audaciously appropriated a Tudor royal term) that gave these alternative languages some force and authority. That authority, I have argued, was not sufficient to secure republican government, which never quite freed itself from a culture of monarchy that, as Protector, Oliver Cromwell in large measure reconstituted.[3] But the republic, and the new languages it articulated, had, as Hobbes intuited, transformed for all time the texts and the culture of authority.

Language was not the most obvious problem facing Charles I's son and successor. On the day of his father's execution on the scaffold, his son claimed the throne as rightful heir and always dated letters and documents from his first legal regnal year, January 1649. Other rulers had faced rival claimants to the throne. Yet, in exile, Charles's problem was not only making good his claim to the throne, but reconstituting the legitimacy of monarchy itself. Not only was the king without his crown; England was for the first time without a monarchy. Charles's problems lay not only in England. In Ireland, before the first year of Charles's *de iure* reign was out, Cromwell stormed Drogheda and crushed the forces of the Duke of Ormonde who was hoping to secure the country for the king. Scotland, which had initiated the collapse of his father's regime, was willing to recognize Charles only on the most stringent conditions, chiefly his acceptance of the Covenant and the authority of the kirk. Charles's coronation as King of Scotland at Scone in January 1651 was characterized by very different language to that which had inaugurated English monarchs onto their throne. The sermon preached on 2 Kings 11 glossed the scriptural passage with references to a royal 'power limited by contract' with the people and, a justification of Scotland's proceedings against Charles I, an assertion of the power of the kirk.[4] But, for all the qualifications and conditions that hedged it, the Scottish crown gave Charles a legitimacy and, he hoped, a base from which to retrieve all his kingdoms. The hope proved forlorn. Charles's attempted invasion of England in the autumn of 1651 with the duke of Hamilton and sixteen thousand troops ended in a rout which nearly cost the king, who was a fugitive for six weeks in his native land, his life. The legitimacy conferred at Scone was another matter. After January 1651, but two years from regicide, Britain once again had a king and Charles one kingdom *de facto*, as well as *de iure*: even the Commonwealth and Cromwell referred to him as the King of Scots.[5] And whatever the practical limitations on his action, Charles II spoke and wrote and presented himself as a king.

As historians of the Royalists during the Interregnum have shown, the king's court in exile was, throughout the 1650s, divided over whether military plans and the quest for foreign military aid were the best means to restore Charles II to his kingdoms.[6] Edward Hyde, in particular, urged a waiting game, confident that time and argument would return England to loyalty. While Charles himself – sensibly – remained open to all options, often craving the resources or allies to launch an invasion of England, he did not fail to understand the importance of representing himself, and of writing and speaking, as a king. In letters, from those to his brother and family, to foreign princes and followers in England, Scotland and Ireland, Charles often wrote insisting on his authority to command as a *king*.[7] But circumstances also necessitated another tone: that of the supplicant and grateful friend who never took support for granted, and who, through his word, had to unite his divided followers and sustain the spirits of loyalists who had fallen on hard times. Though, as he reminded Hyde, he was by inclination averse to writing letters, Charles penned frequent missives, the frankness and 'cheerful good nature' of which helped to sustain a royalist community – and culture – in Britain and in exile.[8] But, especially as time went on, Charles found himself corresponding not just with loyal supporters but with those, like Admiral Montagu, who had served Cromwell yet whose support the king hoped – and needed – to attract.[9] 'We must not,' Charles told Lord Mordaunt, 'discountenance anybody who may be made to do good service.'[10] In such letters in which he both announced his authority and also pragmatically sought the means to establish it, Charles skilfully deployed traditional monarchical conceits with the appeals to 'Liberty' and 'Providence' which had been such a hallmark of Cromwellian oratory.[11] Such letters and lexicons helped in the end to gain Charles the allies he needed to recover his throne. No less, it was his more public declarations and representations that rendered him a powerful regal presence during the years of republic and presented him as a king who might fulfil the wishes of the nation.

Charles was brought powerfully to public attention in print on the day of his succession – in the letter from his father that closed some editions of the *Eikon Basilike*.[12] It was probably immediately afterwards that the Prince of Wales authorized and published, with his crowned arms prominent on the title page, his *Declaration . . . Upon the Death of His Royall Father* (1649).[13] In this his first proclamation as *de iure* sovereign, Charles claimed the languages of 'religion and reason' – of a king.[14] Calling all loyal Englishmen to arms, in defence of his 'lawful inheritance', the prince, charging regicides with blood guilt, yet expressed willingness to 'excuse' those 'which endeavoured the prevention of so great a mischief'.[15] Though he doubted the efficacy of 'any language but that of the sword' and denied any design 'to expostulate or gild my intentions with plausible oratory', Charles, in his appeal to the privileges of parliament and subjects' liberties rhetorically presented himself as his father's heir and fit successor, the protector of 'the ancient known laws' and the 'peace and . . . tranquillity' of England.[16]

From his 'court in Jersey' the following September, Charles issued the first of what were to be many volumes of prayers he 'recommended to be used . . . throughout his dominions' in a volume titled *A Fountain of Loyal Tears Poured Forth By a Sorrowful Son for the Untimely Death of His Royal Father* (1649).[17] Not only a painful reminder of the regicide and of the national sin that many felt it had perpetrated, the volume appropriated Old Testament scripturalism from – and against – those who had forbidden 'preaching and praying in that uniform way formerly agreed upon'.[18] The prayer, 'for all oppressed people', reminding readers that 'it is evident by thy word that thou never gavest any people a power over their king', identified atonement for regicide with obedience to the martyr's son 'whom thou [God] hath set over us'.[19] Another prayer asked the Lord to 'raise up we beseech thee a Moses to thy people and a Jehojadah to their king'; 'call in, we beseech thee, the heir of our vineyard'.[20] And a prayer for the king asked the Lord both to 'give him power and strength that he may regain his rights' and to 'us obedient and loyal hearts to him'.[21] Castigating his own enemies as rebels against the Lord, the *Fountain of Loyal Tears* endeavoured to lead a nation back to God and king.

If Charles had any hopes of an early revolt against the republic and a return to obedience, time swiftly brought home the hard reality of his situation. His next publication issued to his subjects of all three kingdoms in September 1650 was a product of a necessary compromise and represented an offer of concessions. Renouncing, as he was made to, his father's 'evil counsels' and opposition to the Covenant, Charles appealed beyond Scotland to offer oblivion to enemies and to announce his readiness to entertain proposals from England, especially regarding religion, and his willingness to follow the wishes of parliament.[22] Charles had subsequently to distance himself from any commitment to Presbyterianism; but his self-representation in letters and declarations as open to advice and compromise, as well as a rightful king, remained an important part of his image and, in time, of his appeal to the people of England.

After his Restoration, Charles attributed some importance in effecting the turn of his fortunes to the *Declaration to All his Loving Subjects* that he issued from Breda in April 1660, when the course of affairs in England was plunged into uncertainty.[23] Known as the *Declaration of Breda*, drafted by Hyde but titled 'by the Kings Majesty' and likely finalized as well as approved by Charles, it was a brilliantly crafted document. Charles left his subjects, who were readier than they had been to hear it, in no doubt that he regarded the crown as his by 'God and Nature'. Yet his prayer to Divine Providence was not only, he wrote, for his own right, but for 'all our subjects' that they 'may enjoy what by right is theirs'. The language of a king *and* people 'after so long misery' restored to rights skilfully made the royal cause that of the nation. And the *Declaration* also removed anxieties and obstacles to restored monarchy. Charles, as he had nearly a decade before, offered all subjects who returned to obedience a full pardon – excluding only those excepted from it by parliament. The king desired, he insisted, the end of recrimination ('all notes of discord, separation, and differences of parties') and 'a peaceful union'. So that religion were not the cause of animosities, Charles proposed 'a liberty to tender consciences' until parliament settled toleration by statute. All other contentious matters – land transfers, army arrears (for George Monck's soldiers) – the king left to be 'determined in Parliament which can best provide for the just satisfaction [of] all men'. At a time of near anarchy in London, the appeal to peace and unity, to the old harmony of 'king, peers and people' (not, we note, king, Lords and Commons) was well made. In its lack of specificity and detail, the *Declaration* wisely passed over myriad particular problems to evoke a mood of future well-being.[24] And in the willingness to refer the major issues to a parliament, as well as in the language used of the parliament, Charles offered himself as a future king-in-parliament. As he added in a letter to the Speaker of the House that was published with the *Declaration* (and with a large royal arms): 'we do believe [parliament] to be so vital a part of the constitution of the kingdom and so necessary for the government of it that we well know neither prince nor people can be in any tolerable degree happy without them'.[25] Charles posited a reciprocal notion of government: that as parliaments were necessary for the government, so 'we are most confident', he wrote to MPs, who again feared army coups, 'that the preservation of the king's authority is as necessary for the preservation of parliaments'.[26] Underlining the language of reciprocity and mutuality, Charles promised the Commons, and the nation, 'we are ready to give as you to receive'.[27] And, assuring them of his devotion to the Protestant religion and fundamental laws, he added a (I suggest) revealing claim to personal qualification for the throne: that 'affliction . . . observation and experience . . . in other countries' had made him 'the better for what we have seen and suffered'.[28]

The *Declaration of Breda* raises perhaps more questions than historians have asked of it. May we take the *Declaration*, though drafted by Hyde, as Charles's – as it was received by contemporaries? I think we should. If so, was this, whatever advice or assistance he received, a skilful rhetorical performance by a king who needed to write himself back onto his throne; or was it a genuine statement of Charles's beliefs – a true representation of himself? Clearly, it was the first: in April 1660, when John Milton was still passionately arguing for a revival of true republican government, Charles could not take anything for granted.[29] Even when he landed on English soil at the end of May, as he confided to his sister 'Minette', the joyous welcome 'overwhelmed' him: 'my head is so prodigiously dazed by the acclamation of the people'.[30] For all his hopes – and many had been dashed over the decade – Charles knew that he needed to win hearts and minds, as he did with the declaration which was celebrated on May Day in the streets of London.[31] But the style and tone of the declaration, like that of Charles's letters, suggest also a different style of monarchy: a king who recognized that, beneath the public acclaim, the nation was divided, that Monck's 'discreet conduct' and the political arts of compromise and co-operation would be needed.[32] Here we may begin to understand the oblique reference to the benefit to him of affliction and hard experience. Charles II was not going to be simply a traditional king of England and Scotland, his father's son, and divinely chosen heir. He had seen other polities – absolutist France, the German empire, the Dutch Republic; and he had had to negotiate the world of diplomatic *realpolitik* as European affairs and Commonwealth and Protectorate foreign policy turned a former host into an enemy, or vice versa. Still more importantly, affliction had shaped his character and perhaps too his sense of his position. During the 1650s, Charles had often to grapple with poverty, to meet men equipped not like a king but so scruffily dressed in 'rags and clouts' that he was unrecognizable.[33] He had also, especially during the weeks after his flight from Worcester in September 1651, while incognito, to suffer indignities, discomforts and taunts quite unbefitting a king and, most important, to depend upon and live with quite ordinary subjects: innkeepers, boatmen, servants, as well as Jane Lane who had assisted his escape by disguising him as her attendant. The reports of Charles's dealings with such ordinary subjects, as well as the king's letters to Lane, indicate a capacity to engage with commoners that was not a characteristic of many of his royal predecessors, especially his father.[34] And the frank, familiar tone of much of his correspondence suggests that in him a sense of majesty had been tempered by 'affliction and experience', indeed by a pragmatic need to take loyal assistance from whomsoever it was offered. Pragmatism was to be the hallmark of a very different style of monarchy from his father.

Whether the joy that greeted the publication of the *Declaration of Breda* owed anything to Charles's self-representation or was simply the occasion of a nation's relief that the confusion might soon be over, we cannot be sure. As events transpired, the compromises Charles so freely offered were neither necessary nor taken. The king was invited to return to his throne with no conditions, not even those his father would have accepted, attached. And he was greeted, as we shall see, in language of the most elevated panegyric: as a biblical King David, a Constantine, an angel, a God. Those who made the Restoration settlement, in their desire to erase the recent past, reinstated and revalidated all the old discourses and symbols of divine kingship. And Charles obliged by re-echoing them, and by touching to cure the King's Evil even as he progressed from the Low Countries to his capital. As we turn to examine representations of monarchy and of Charles from 1660, we will encounter all the familiar metaphors and modes – in words and visuals – of sacred kingship. Yet, Charles's own sense that all was not quite what it had been, that the clock could not simply be turned back, was incisive and right. One suspects that, more than most of his subjects, he sensed from the outset that the world, and the monarchy, had changed. It was to change yet more over the course of his quarter century on the throne.

Traditional political narratives of Charles II's reign tend to plot distinct phases: the period of the Restoration and Restoration settlement to about 1662; the beginning of disenchantment with the regime that culminated in the impeachment of Edward Hyde, Earl of Clarendon, in 1667; the years that saw the Declaration of Indulgence and Secret Treaty of Dover, 1668–73; the period of the rise of party and opposition that culminated in the Popish Plot and its aftermath, 1678–81; and the king's victory over his opponents and years of loyal reaction, 1681–5. Through times that sanctified monarchy to a crisis that brought the realm to the brink of renewed civil war, the languages and symbols of kingship had to be deployed very differently, as well as with consummate skill. As he had in 1660, Charles II had often to stand for stasis and tradition, while accommodating to change.

My study of the representation of Charles II, then, will perforce be a complicated, at times ambiguous story. As with earlier monarchs, I will examine the ways in which Charles represented himself, and was represented by others in published texts, portraits and images, processions and rituals, and in the theatres of court and household, the pulpit and tribunal of justice. But as well as traditional genres of representation – declarations, speeches and sermons – we must explore new genres of representation in travel narratives, treatises of empire, fictions. To the familiar languages of regality we must add the deployment in the representation of monarchy of the discourses of providence and of memory as well as history, of science as well as faith.

Importantly, we must consider the changing community and culture in which all these languages were received and performed: a culture not only of a near-industrialized expansion of print and informed public opinion but one of what scholars have recently characterized as an informed and institutionalized public sphere, of a society noisy with the buzz of political discussion and party contest.[35] Such changes, I will argue, transformed not only royal representation but criticism and counter-representation, complicating the very categories of government and opposition.

At the end of Charles II's reign, as at the beginning, the changes that circumstances had wrought were not always brought to public attention. After the national trauma of 1649, the traditional texts and mantras were more appealing to many than change or novelty. If the most successful of the Tudors, Elizabeth, owed so much to her brilliant capacity to combine a sense of mystery with a popular appeal, the skill of Charles II – perhaps the skill that secured his throne – was his ability to accommodate change and to represent tradition: that is, to embody the ambiguities of his age.

PART I

Re-presenting and Reconstituting Kingship

CHAPTER 1

REWRITING ROYALTY

I

In 'A Panegyric Upon His Sacred Majesty's Most Happy Return', the poet Thomas Forde wrote in praise of the king:

> You *Conquered* without *Arms*, your *Words*
> Win hearts, better than others *Swords*.[1]

Flattering Charles's own sense that he had scripted his own restoration, Forde depicted the royal word as the victor over violence. In his dedication of his *The Original and Growth of Printing* to Charles in 1664, Richard Atkyns appropriated the scriptural text to make the same point: 'where the word of a king is there is power'.[2] Talking and writing, however, had had no simple relationship to authority. After the noisy debates of his father's reign, Charles I had preferred a silence from which only the necessities of civil war had drawn him.[3] After the Babel of civil war, Charles II may have been inclined to his father's preference: he referred to his own reluctance to write at length, and it may be that the translation of *A Philosophical Discourse Concerning Speech* in 1668 had the English as well as French king in mind when the translator referred to 'the prudence you have to be silent'.[4] Charles II did not choose to repeat himself at length or at large in speech. But recognizing, with Hobbes, that the force of 'the word of a king' (as the *Declaration of Breda* put it) was an essential attribute of sovereign authority, Charles regularly spoke to his parliaments and to his people, and his speeches, throughout his reign, many of them printed, were directed at the maintenance as well as representation of that authority. Because those speeches were central both to Charles's self-presentation and to how others saw him, I shall analyze them across the reign, paying attention to how the king adjusted his words to shifting circumstances.[5]

Charles's first major speech to his parliament, to the House of Lords on 27 July 1660, concerned a matter of vital import to him and was delivered at a critical moment. Royalist and Presbyterian MPs, eager for revenge against their enemies, proved reluctant to pass the Act of Indemnity which Charles regarded as essential to his honour (the upholding of his word given at Breda) and to the stability of a peaceful settlement. After royal promptings eventually pushed the bill through the Commons, Charles addressed the Lords in a speech published to the nation, with a large royal arms on the title page.[6] It was to the nation as much as the house that Charles reaffirmed, lest any began to fear the contrary, that 'I have the same intentions and resolutions now I am here with you which I had at Breda.'[7] Thanking the Lords diplomatically for their persecution of regicides, Charles explained, lest any had read Breda as mere rhetoric, that 'I never thought of excepting any other'; and he proceeded to justify indemnity as the best interest of the nation.[8] 'This mercy and indulgence,' he began in the language of virtuous princes, 'is the best way to bring them to a true repentance.'[9] But widening the argument beyond his own concerns, he continued: 'it will make them good subjects to me and good friends and neighbours to you and we have then all our end ... the surest expedient to prevent future mischief'.[10] The clever use of the first-person plural pronouns, the invocation of peace and unity, but also the reminder of the risk of renewed conflict were carefully combined to construct the platform of Restoration: restored regal government over all subjects, former Parliamentarians as well as Royalists. Giving his consent to the Act he had secured on 29 August, Charles took the occasion of a speech to both houses to assert his severity now against any who refused his clemency, and his love for all others. 'Never king,' he told them, in strains that not for the last time echo Queen Elizabeth's speeches, 'valued himself more upon the affections of his people than I do; nor do I know a better way to make myself sure of your affections than by being just and kind to you all.'[11] In turn, the king felt, he told his auditors, 'so confident of your affections that I will not move you in anything that ... relates to myself' – though references to debts, the expenses, disbandment money and the Poll Bill meant that he did not pass entirely over his own needs.[12] Even here, however, in a delightful and masterly close, Charles bemoaned not his own wants: 'that which troubles me most,' he told them, 'is to see many of you come to me to Whitehall and to think that you must go somewhere else to seek your dinner'.[13] It is hardly surprising that the disarming reference, a reminder of the fitting bounty of a king but with all the familiarity of friends invited to supper, prompted a vote of supplies which, for all that it did not fall out so in practice, was reckoned to provide a handsome revenue for the crown.

Interestingly, as the foundation of settlement began to be laid, Charles began a different pattern of address to his parliaments: a brief personal speech followed by a longer, explanatory gloss by either his Lord Chancellor (and long time penman) Edward Hyde or subsequent Lord Keepers. Addressing both houses on 13 September, Charles, who even in adversity had taken pains over such gestures of gratitude, expressed his thanks for all the parliament had done for the king and kingdom, not least in a grant of supply of which, again with a flourish reminiscent of Elizabeth, he promised 'I will not apply one penny of that money to my own particular occasions . . . till it is evident to me that the public will not stand in need of it'.[14] Expressing a due concern that they now give attention to restoring parliament to its 'ancient rules and order', Charles handed over to Clarendon to speak in his name.[15] Ventriloquizing and reinforcing royal injunctions to peace and unity, in church as well as state, Clarendon urged his audience to follow the king's example and 'learn this excellent art of forgetfulness' so as not to reanimate divisions.[16] In an astonishingly hedged clause, he noted 'You know kings are in *some* sense called Gods' and, like God, the king extended his heart to all.[17] Then, moving to a rather different rhetoric, the Chancellor, underpinning the king's commitment to the 'public good', announced the royal intentions to establish a Council of Trade and another for the Plantations, very much in the spirit of Protectorial initiatives.[18] His speech closed with an adage of the king's 'own prescribing': 'continue all the ways imaginable for our own happiness and you will make him the best pleased and the most happy prince in the world'.[19] As the last words before a recess, one can hardly better them for instilling the 'feel good factor' on which Charles knew the stability of his throne yet depended.

Three months later, in December 1660, Charles was to address his first parliament – strictly speaking a Convention rather than a parliament – for the last time as, having resettled crown and kingdom, it had done its immediate work and the realm could await a normal assembly duly summoned by royal writ. The king's tone was fittingly personal and his speech full of first-person pronouns. And as well as a valedictory thanks to one assembly, it was spoken to future MPs and to the political nation. 'All I have to say,' Charles told both houses, promising brevity, 'is to give you thanks'; but, once more like Elizabeth denying any oratorical skills, the king regretted his deficiency in expressing the thanks he felt: 'ordinary thanks for ordinary civilities are easily given. But when the heart is as full as mine is', he opened himself to his auditors, 'it cannot be easy for me to express the sense I have of it'.[20] The king had met them 'with an extraordinary affection and esteem for parliament', but they had enhanced it. To those who might be concerned about a Convention that some might not remember as a true parliament, Charles promised them a place in history: 'let us all resolve that this be for ever called "the Healing and Blessed Parliament"'. Announcing that he would soon meet many of them again, Charles assured them that they would, even in absence, remain his counsel and guide. 'What', he would ask himself at every decision, he assured them, 'is a parliament like to think of this action or this council?'[21] Even, briefly without parliament, Charles II announced himself as always a king with parliament.

True to his word, Charles did not waste much time summoning his second parliament. But as he addressed it on 8 May 1661, the king opened with a half-apology that was also a clever reminder to newly elected MPs of the miracle of Restoration that had taken place exactly a year ago. Acknowledging that the assembly might have met a week earlier, Charles relished the fact that parliament had been delayed until the anniversary of his proclamation as king and noted 'the great affection of the whole kingdom' manifest on that day.[22] 'I dare swear,' he half admonished, half flattered the MPs, 'you are full of the same spirit.'[23] Personalizing the formality of the occasion and adding intimacy to the rhetoric of unity, Charles noted: 'I think there are not many of you who are not particularly known to me' and few, he added, about whom he had not heard such good testimony as to be confident of all their good endeavours for 'the peace, plenty and prosperity of the nation.'[24] Turning to business, Charles presented them with two bills for their confirmation from (the possessive pronoun implicates them fully in the deeds of the last session) 'our last meeting'. Above all he again pressed the Act of Indemnity as the 'principal cornerstone' of 'our joint and common security' and made it a test of personal loyalty that they enforce it.[25] The king then closed by confiding in them with news, indeed admitting his parliament to the most personal of state affairs: his deliberations over marriage and his choice of Catherine of Portugal as a bride. This, he made clear, had been no single personal decision; the king would not without advice, he observed, 'resolve anything of public importance'.[26] Privy Council concurrence he took as 'some instance of the approbation of God himself'.[27] Then, having advertised himself as a king of counsel, Charles sat down to leave his Chancellor to gloss his remarks.

Clarendon, taking up the theme of advice, reminded the houses that Charles had from Breda referred all to parliament, and the Convention ('called by God himself') had honoured the trust, as it was for their successors to do.[28] To the new members, 'the great Physicians of the kingdom', the Chancellor commended the Act of Indemnity and measures to settle the public debts and the king's revenues.[29] Warning them of seditious preachers who still vented their poisonous doctrines and of the late rebellion (by Thomas Venner and the Fifth Monarchists) in the city, Clarendon urged them to act to secure the preservation of a nation and a king who, as his marriage deliberations had demonstrated, 'took so great care for the good . . . of his people'.[30] Emphasizing the considerations of trade that weighed, along with the advancement of the Protestant religion, on the king's mind, the Chancellor again stressed the lengths Charles had gone to heed advice and closed reiterating how the king 'hath deserved all your thanks' for the matter and the manner: the choice of bride and the process of choosing.[31] The royal marriage (even to a Catholic bride) manifested the king's love for his people and his concern for the interests of the nation.

So commenced a long relationship with a parliament that was not to be dissolved for eighteen years – a relationship shaped in large part by the king's words and responses to them.[32] Though the parliament began as a staunchly loyal body, the elections had resulted in an aggressively Cavalier Commons that was more inclined to pursue vendettas than to follow Charles's preference for moderate courses in church and state. In his speeches Charles then skilfully had to woo and win the house (which early on set about pursuing more regicides), to persuade MPs to drop proceedings, and to pass a new Act of Oblivion; and, when he met with them, he judged well the occasion for thanks and reassurance. 'Let us,' he urged them in rhetoric very familiar to our jaded modern ears, 'look forward, and not backward.'[33] Only unity and affection for each other would secure the public peace against the disaffected and advance the nation abroad. Presenting settlement and oblivion as the way to future greatness, the king obtained his bills before the summer adjournment at which he assured members returning to their counties that 'you cannot but be very welcome for the services you have performed here', and adjourned them until November, when 'we shall come happily together again'.[34]

When the houses reconvened in November 1661, Charles was faced with the pressing need to plead his own case, while not appearing to pursue his self-interest. His opening congratulations to a parliament, now fully constituted of Lords spiritual as well as temporal and Commons, set the mood. Then adeptly Charles denied any necessity to ask anything for himself when he knew that, left to themselves, members would do all for his good. No, he insisted, it was not his particular need that brought him before them with a plea, but 'as I am concerned in the public'.[35] The revenue of the crown, he told them, was 'for the interest, honour and security of the nation' – for the fleet and its provisions.[36] Subtly alluding perhaps to earlier quarrels that had beset his father's levy of ship money, as well as acknowledging a new world in which even divine kingship was open to scrutiny and suspicion, Charles invited the house to 'thoroughly examine whether these necessities be real or imaginary', or whether the consequence of private royal profligacy rather than public need.[37] In an extraordinary gesture, he offered a 'full inspection into my revenue' that, he claimed, would dispel any false rumours of extravagance. For all the traditional rhetoric of the unity of king, parliament and nation, Charles II's speech early on in his own first parliament suggests – and helped to construct – a new openness, a new pragmatism, a different style of monarchy that was to emerge alongside the old discourses and symbols of state. In parliament, while rhetorically denying the need to do so, Charles understood that, more than his predecessors, he must argue and justify his case.

The address set the tone for subsequent speeches to the house: expressions of mutual affection, a recognition of their care, and pleas for supply and expedition, 'to advance the public service', when the Commons got bogged down with private bills.[38] As weeks and months passed, on 10 January 1662 Charles reminded new MPs of the 'miserable effects' caused by the necessities of the crown in the recent past, and warned them of a still-present republican threat that only a strong monarchy could quell.[39] Turning to their own concerns and discontents, Charles diplomatically thanked them for their solicitude with regard to the church, and – though he sensibly did not name it – his preferred policy of toleration. In a newly familiar vein, the king light-heartedly indulged a personal reference: 'I have the worst luck in the world,' he quipped, 'if after all the reproaches of being a papist whilst I was abroad, I am suspected of being a Presbyterian now I am come home.'[40] Charles asserted his devotion to the Book of Common Prayer and to uniformity which he had commended to the Lords; what he yet favoured, he told them by way of qualification, was 'prudence and discretion and the absence of all passion.'[41] Despatching the MPs, Charles closed with a reminder of the impending arrival of his betrothed and the major business of the spring, his marriage.

It was a skilful speech marked by reciprocity as well as familiarity, the king addressing the Commons' anxieties as much as he urged his own needs. What undercut its effectiveness was an action taken by the king after the prorogation in May – significantly during Clarendon's illness – in issuing *A Declaration to Tender Consciences* on 26 December.[42] The *Declaration*, dispensing with the penal laws against religious nonconformity, was clearly meant to temper the intolerance of the restored Anglican church that the Cavaliers were hurriedly resurrecting. But for the first time it presented Charles as a king ready to act outside of parliament and not with the consideration of their wishes, as he had earlier claimed was his constant rule of action. Charles, recognizing the need to assuage such concerns and to explain himself, squarely broached the subject when he met his reconvened parliament on 18 February 1663.

Endeavouring perhaps to counter any talk that his unilateral action had marked a shift in attitude to advice, the king greeted members telling them he had 'often wished you had been together to help me in some occasions which have fallen out.'[43] He had issued his *Declaration*, he continued, 'to cure the distempers' and trusted in that desire (the language made it hard for them not to concur) to 'have your concurrence.'[44] Cleverly attributing bloody punishments to 'popish times', Charles expressed his aversion to corporal penalties for nonconformity. And to any who feared that his intent was a restoration of Catholics to full public rights, the king, while acknowledging their aid to him and his father, insisted that papists remained barred from all public office; 'further, I desire some laws may be made to hinder the growth and progress of their doctrines.'[45] Underlining his zeal for the Protestant religion and church, Charles still hoped for toleration for dissenters who lived peacefully; and in a diplomatic step back from unilateral action or extravagant claims for his prerogative, he added, 'I would humbly wish I had such a power of indulgence' to prevent their being given cause to conspire.[46] The speech closed with a classical rhetorical conceit: 'it would look like flattery,' Charles began, as he proceeded to flatter MPs, to say that he was as 'confident of your wisdom and affection' and of their agreement concerning what was best for all. A consummately artful act of damage limitation ended with disarmingly homely salutation: 'I . . . bid you heartily welcome.'[47] The king's words sought to smooth over the anxieties raised by his actions.

Though the speech succeeded in avoiding confrontation, as did so many of Charles's speeches, it did not change minds. Careful not to push things to the brink, the king abandoned his indulgence, evidently genuinely optimistic that the houses would respond with affection and supplies.[48] Certainly, if he begrudged his defeat, the king displayed no hint of it in his speeches, in which he communicated with them 'as good friends ought to do' and endeavoured to extract advantage from the haste he had made to satisfy them.[49] Again, Charles flattered the members by praising electors who had returned such men of good principles and affections to the crown. Cataloguing all their marks of affection, how, he asked, would it be possible it should not continue between them: 'I am sure it is impossible.'[50] But, and after the introduction the shift of tone had great effect, he continued, 'You cannot take it amiss that I tell you there hath not appeared that warmth in you of late in the consideration of my revenue.'[51] Despite the mild admonition, Charles averted confrontation by inviting a dialogue of friends – 'you shall use as much freedom with me.'[52] Continuing concession and introducing compassion, Charles reissued his invitation to inspect the royal accounts and expressed his keen sense of the burdens the country had been under, as well as his unwillingness to add to them. But without supply – 'I must deal plainly with you' – he could not sustain the people's peace and security. His words were evidently effective. Though the Commons had not been much inclined to do so, the speech persuaded them to grant four (albeit inadequate) subsidies. Ever sensitive to the need to give as well as take in a changed political universe, Charles not only thanked them but announced and issued orders for a reduction of household expenses and pensions, before proroguing the parliament.[53]

What is important to note is that, though tensions had overtaken the euphoric mood of Restoration, Charles, not least by the style of his addresses to parliament, had, through conciliation, reciprocity, most of all a language of affection and love, managed to sustain the mood of harmony and mutual co-operation so essential to the establishment of the Restoration settlement. But three years had already been an extended honeymoon and it would take all the king's rhetorical skill to sustain harmonious co-operation as difficulties mounted at home and abroad. Before the parliament reconvened in March 1664, a rising in the North had advertised disaffection at home, while conflict with the Dutch was brewing in the struggle for naval and commercial supremacy. Charles welcomed his MPs back – the *Lords Journal* dates the speech on the 16th, the day they returned, the version printed 'cum privilegio' Monday 21st – at (a reminder that he was as good as his word) 'the time appointed', he noted: 'I have been so far from ever intending it should have been otherwise'.[54] This time the familiar strain of the king's love for parliament was more vital than ever; for some had begun to hint that parliament 'should meet no more'; and had the king's secret discussions with France been revealed, the suspicion would have been confirmed.[55] The crucial thing, Charles insisted, was that none be permitted to sow jealousies between them. In the rhetorical device of uniting by joining against unnamed others, Charles urged on them unity against 'whisperers'.[56] Here he used the late conspiracy to point up the danger that faced them as well as him. Providence (as we shall see, it was to be a recurring refrain of Restoration discourse) had revealed the plots of their enemies, but schemes were still afoot to recruit old members of the Long Parliament. From summoning these demons, it was not a difficult move for the king to recall an assault on the royal prerogative that still chaffed. The Triennial Act of 1641 was one of two statutes (the other the Act Against Dissolving Parliament Without Its Own Consent) that had heralded an outright assault on the constitutional prerogative of Charles I. Charles II cleverly made no specific request concerning it beyond that they give it a reading and 'then in God's name do what you think fit for me, and yourselves and the whole kingdom'.[57] It was a subtle move: mere reference to recent times inimical to the crown condemned the act to oblivion. But, just in case the desire was misunderstood, Charles repeated the 'I need not tell you': 'I need not tell you how much I love Parliament . . . nor do I think [he elevated present to eternal affection] the Crown can ever be happy without frequent parliaments'.[58] Such affection was, it was implied, a far stronger security than the statutes of a discredited time, from which all were anxious to dissociate themselves. And the king, appealing to his record of candour and enacting his promises, asked for that gift desired by any ruler – trust. 'Trust me', he appealed, 'it shall be in nobody's power to make me jealous of you'.[59] Finally, alerting them to (without blaming them for) a shortfall in the revenue they had voted – 'I am sure you would have me receive whatsoever you give' – Charles, as though despatching a sermon audience, prayed 'God bless your counsels'.[60] If action is the testimony of effectiveness, this was (as it was) a masterly performance that led to a revised and neutered Triennial Act which, with as speedy gratitude, the king, on 5 April, told the house, 'every good Englishman will thank you for'.[61]

Preparations for war with the Dutch consumed the months of the summer recess of 1664, a turn of events which was to change the political tide. Charles greeted his returning members in November 1664 for the first time with news of foreign events. The Dutch had forced him to make preparations for defence and war and, he uttered with pride, in the absence of parliament, by borrowing, he had managed to put a fleet to sea 'worthy of the English nation'.[62] But parliament, he promised, would be given a full account of what had transpired and of the expenditures necessitated. What he appealed for was the public demonstration of parliament's promise 'to stand by me' and the levy of speedy and adequate supplies. A barometer of a world altered from the encomia of 1660, the king sensed a need to counter rumours that, having been funded for war, he might use the money for his 'private occasions'.[63] Though he felt 'sure' that MPs would consider such a charge 'not to deserve an answer', the king had clearly – and rightly – felt the need, without advertising the need, to give it one. War, Charles informed them, lest the suspicion of dynastic aggrandisement enter men's minds, was not his inclination. But if war were necessary 'for the protection, honour and benefit of my subjects' (the trilogy of traditional and more nakedly mercantile considerations is noteworthy), he would not shrink from it.[64] And how would any king if the safety and benefit of the nation were at stake? Charles, he flattered as well as subtly cajoled them, was 'sure you will not deceive any expectation'.[65]

The king's words, at least on this occasion, translated into action. The outbreak of war led to an English victory in June 1665 off Lowestoft. But the battle, followed by minor skirmishes and campaigns, exhausted supplies and led to spiralling debts. Charles had to summon parliament to Oxford in October in the midst of the plague that was the first of the disasters to blight the next three years and provoke the first political crisis of his reign. In his opening speech, the king thanked them for their attendance and stressed the importance of their counsel. But the main issue was – unapologetically and especially since 'God hath hitherto blessed [us] with success in all encounters' – money.[66] Recognizing, in a way that less astute predecessors had often not, that ordinary MPs did not comprehend the vast and escalating costs of war, Charles explained to them that all was spent and more needed both to continue war and prepare defence, not least against other enemies who might ally with the Dutch. Freely disclosing what he might have shielded as *arcana imperii*, he informed them of some dealings with the French for a peace, which had hitherto come to nought. Clarendon added a long peroration on naval victories and the benefit to trade that had followed Restoration, as well as the threats of the Dutch to England's peace and prosperity and the speed of the king's response to merchant complaints against them, detailing all the costs he had incurred. In almost every paragraph he referred to parliament's declaration so as to involve the house fully in the conduct of, and payment for, war. And he particularized what was a clear appeal to interest by explaining that the only peace terms on offer would have destroyed the lucrative English trade in the East Indies and Guinea.[67] As he identified the insolent terms offered, and the general 'rudeness' of the Dutch ('suitable to the manner of a Commonwealth')

as affronts to the nation as well as the king, Clarendon advanced that development towards the monarchy becoming the focus of patriotism and nationalism
which (Linda Colley and others have argued) characterized the Augustan
state.[68] 'Noble indignation' was fired to warm loyalty and the willingness to
provide supplies.[69] It was a brilliant double performance by king and minister
of forensic skill, and desperately needed. At least some further aid was voted,
for all the parliament's own preoccupation with the Five Mile Act and other
legislation.

The challenges to sustaining harmony through royal rhetoric, however, were
great. Over the next year, fire followed plague, while war continued. To the
crown's financial problems was added the beginning of equally dangerous talk
that disasters implied divine wrath against the land, and – equally dangerously
– against the king, whose sexual profligacy, as we shall see, was anything but a
secret.[70] When he spoke to parliament in September 1666, it was vital for
Charles to use disaster to unify (as it so often does) the nation and to strengthen
his government, rather than allow the mutterings of godly disapproval to serve
the discontents. With his flair for a fresh but ever familiar salutation given
extra force by his personal role in quenching the flames, Charles welcomed
fellow survivors – 'God be thanked for our meeting together' – and with them
breathed a sigh of relief that their beloved Westminster was standing.[71] Far
from divine wrath, 'nothing but a miracle of God's mercy' had preserved men
and monuments.[72] God had also given English forces success that summer. But
two powerful enemies menaced; and, for all he had done or wished to do, the
king, as he explained, could not bear the costs of fighting them alone. Displaying
sensitivity to the hardships bequeathed by the recent plague and fire, the king
asked parliament to consider 'expedients for the carrying on this war with as
little burden to the people as is possible'.[73] Sounding a jingoistic note, Charles
informed them how foreign enemies had hoped to take advantage of domestic
disaster, and he made (as it were) a grant of supplies for the war almost an
antidote to further catastrophes at home: one cause that united king and nation.
Again, the Commons responded with a vote of nearly £2 million, even though
most of that was already committed.

As he prorogued the parliament in February 1667, Charles was frantically
seeking a peace that would ease his burdens. And not only his but the people's.
As he acknowledged, there were mounting complaints of 'oppression', and the
'malice of ill men' was working to fuel 'false imaginations in the hearts of the
people'.[74] The war had strained the culture of mutual affection which Charles's
speeches had done so much to foster and sustain, because he knew that on that
culture, that discourse, his authority rested. Soothing words had done much
but were not themselves enough. Peace was necessary for love as well as money.

Before peace could be secured, however, the Dutch ventured a bold strike. In
June 1667, Lieutenant-Admiral Michiel de Ruyter entered with a fleet right up

the Thames to the River Medway, burnt several large battleships moored there (not least because there was a shortage of funds to equip them), and humiliated the English by capturing their flagship. The peace that followed at the end of July was less humiliating than the defeat. But the political damage – and damage to the image of Charles II as well as his government – was considerable. Andrew Marvell, as we shall see, expressed the sense of many when he painted the defeat as a third visitation upon the nation, for which he squarely laid the blame on an effeminized court and a debauched king. The royal body was represented in 'The Last Instructions to a Painter' as the site of corruption and inappropriate passion, not as the icon of the people and nation; and royal desire was figured not as mutual love but selfish lust.[75] In 1667 it was Clarendon who paid the price – impeachment by parliament – for the disasters in public relations as well as policy.[76] With his own political honeymoon well and truly over, Charles had to work on his image and representation, and to re-present himself in changing times. Not least of those changes were in the king himself. The difficulties he had faced with the Dutch had inclined Charles more towards France – away from England's principal rival in trade but also away from a fellow Protestant nation and towards a popish ally whose style of kingship was very different to the way Charles had presented himself since Breda. A French alliance also held out the prospect of a subsidy to an impoverished king, especially if he could secure toleration for his Catholic subjects. While feelers were put out and secret negotiations conducted, parliament was prorogued for almost a year. When it finally reassembled in October 1669, a full eighteen months (the longest recess) since its last meeting, the house faced a monarch who had perhaps hardened in attitude and who, quite against all his earlier declarations of openness and honesty and his specific statements in his speech of 10 February 1668, harboured a major secret: a secret alliance that incorporated his willingness to convert to Rome.[77] As Patterson has observed, royal speeches responded to circumstances and from 1668 they represented Charles very differently.

It may be revealing that when he addressed both houses on 19 October 1669, Charles's speech was perfunctorily brief. And though the language was still of affection, the royal 'I am very glad to see you' sounds less effusive.[78] Charles offered little justificatory discourse or personal pleasantries: he asked for supplies and left all else to his Lord Keeper (Bridgeman) who, far removed from Clarendon's classical references and oratory, was likewise matter of fact.[79] Even on St Valentine's Day 1670, love was not much in the air. The king again requested supplies, 'with greater instance' and 'speedily'.[80] With regard to expenditures, rather than inviting inspection, he had 'fully informed myself'.[81] Though he reprised the language of interest, the speech was distant and more autocratic than reciprocal. Before parliament met again, Charles had concluded his secret treaty with Louis XIV, was again at war with the United Provinces, and issued what had years before got him into trouble, a declaration of indulgence.[82] Again the tone was crisp, even to the point of being blunt. The king announced in February 1673 that supplies had been inadequate and asked for more. Raising his Declaration of Indulgence, he explained that papists had only freedom of religion in private, but stood on his authority: 'I should take it very ill to receive contradiction . . . I am resolved to stick to my Declaration'.[83] Even the dangerous rumour that the forces the king had raised might be used 'to control law and property' Charles only touched on rather than answered.[84] The Lord Chancellor's comment that the king had spoken with such 'full weight' and that the royal words 'will have its effect with you' now rang hollow.[85] There had been rumours that parliament might be no more, so the Chancellor's reference to a happy marriage that would not be breached sounded strained. For its part, parliament voted an assessment for the war but insisted that the declaration be withdrawn and that penal laws in religious matters could be suspended only by parliament. It was the first real constitutional tussle between king and Commons since the Restoration and, diplomatically, Charles tried to retain his indulgence while renouncing any prerogative right of suspending 'any laws wherein the properties, rights or liberties of . . . his subjects were concerned'.[86] The Commons refused the royal answer, in a gesture that manifested that the rhetoric of royal authority had entered a new, more contestatory age, and overrode the indulgence by framing a bill for a test of orthodoxy to Anglicanism. If for the first time (at least obviously) royal words had failed to secure the royal wishes, it may be not least because Charles had devoted less attention to the royal script that had underwritten his authority. Yet, though he had become less good as a speaker, Charles retained a good political sense for knowing when to withdraw and for not appearing a grudging loser. Returning after withdrawing his indulgence to again request supplies, he promised lest 'any scruple remain', that what he had done 'shall not for the future be drawn either into consequence or example'.[87]

Supply, however, did not buy victory over the summer and Charles had to face his parliament in October 1673 in a weak position, having spent his grant, and run up debts with nothing to show for it. The king's rhetoric appeared to fail him. His 'hope that you need not many words to persuade you' now betrayed not the confidence of the early 1660s but a sense that no words would easily make the royal case.[88] Instead of turning to the issue of supply, the Commons criticized the king's maintenance of an army and his government; Charles prorogued them within a week.[89] When they returned in January 1674, Charles at least matched his plea that 'the evidences of your affection are become so necessary' with a more conciliatory tone.[90] The king involved the Commons fully in his peace negotiations with the Dutch, and he acted, giving orders to reduce his army to the level and numbers of 1663. But he took too an extraordinary gamble: offering to let a committee review the terms, he lied by

denying rumours of secret articles in his treaty with France.[91] Far from
sustaining harmony and authority, royal words were now distancing the king
from his MPs and subjects. The seeds of suspicion that would grow into the
Popish Plot had been sown.

The story of the origins of the so-called Popish Plot, which in 1679 so nearly
toppled the monarchy, does not usually include a chapter on royal speeches nor,
for that matter, forms of royal representation.[92] Of course the tide of uncritical
loyalty that had swept in the king in 1660 had ebbed with time and the normal
process of disenchantment with government. Yet, part of what made Restoration
political culture had been the behaviour, and not least the rhetoric and language,
of Charles II. The king had not only uttered what his parliament and (as most
of the speeches were broadly published) the majority of his people had wanted
to hear. His careful use of language and his tone had brilliantly negotiated the
ambiguities of a Restoration England poised between old and new worlds,
between traditional and transformed models of kingship – indeed, had negotiated these issues so successfully that many had not to confront them. As with
Queen Elizabeth, a communal language, a discourse of affect, a gesture of
familiarity had tempered, as they did with the first attempt at indulgence,
potential political, or constitutional, quarrels. Whatever the other factors, it was
also a shift in royal rhetoric, a lapse in attention to the art of his image, that
plunged Charles into a crisis – a crisis that was significantly manufactured and
sustained by texts and discourses that had run out of royal control and which
were accorded more authority than royal words.[93]

When, in April 1675, Charles recalled the parliament that had been
prorogued the previous February, it was on the advice of Thomas Osborne first
earl of Danby, who was still urging the king to work with the loyal MPs to
secure supply. Charles's own doubts are audible in an opening speech that
appeared to undercut Danby's strategy and to undo the good that calling the
assembly was meant to do. He opened well enough, by explaining that his principal end in calling them 'is to know what you think may yet be wanting to the
securing of religion and property'.[94] Putting the Commons' concerns first,
inviting them to set the agenda, was a shrewd move. But the articulation of his
own sense that it would fail, and his primary motive 'to give myself the satisfaction' of endeavouring an understanding, helped to ensure failure.[95] Moreover,
Charles's unsubtle hint that the 'pernicious Designs of ill men' might 'make it
unpracticable any longer to continue this parliament' sounded more like a
threat than a shared concern.[96] Marvell, for one, saw through it and reported
that the thanks of MPs were but grudgingly given.[97] Despite recommending
unity, the king had on this occasion spoken little to further it. Though he had
once more needed to speak for himself, he referred all other matters to his Lord
Keeper, Heneage Finch, the English Cicero known for his rhetorical skills.[98]
Finch tried to expand in more gracious terms on the royal words flattering the

members of 'this great Council'.[99] Though he asserted that 'the royal declaration of himself . . . carries so evident an assurance', he sensed that Charles had not done enough to calm nerves, and spoke with more rhetorical flourishes and classical and historical references.[100] Indeed, Finch asked MPs to contrast the miseries of Europe with England's felicitous state, which was reaping the fruits of peace, trade and expansion, under a glorious and divine prince: 'a prince whose style Dei Gratia seems . . . to be written . . . by the arm of omnipotence itself'.[101] The rhetoric of love and an exchange of hearts suggests that Finch was more committed to parliamentary courses than was, at this point, the king. But his language, which not long before would have but ventriloquized that of his master, now sounded a note of contrast to Charles's evidently irritated tone.

The session proved a disaster, as suspicions mounted of the king's involvement with France, and no supply was passed. Parliament was prorogued in November for a further fifteen months.[102] When the house reconvened in February 1676, Danby at least secured a payment for the navy; but, with French troops advancing through Flanders, the whole direction of the government's foreign policy came under criticism. Charles himself took fright at the imbalance of power and moved to check French hegemony by a marriage treaty with the United Provinces which also served to temper fears of his Catholic leanings.[103] When, therefore, he recalled parliament in January 1678, the opportunity was there again for the king to rebuild trust. It was perhaps a sign of a different approach, or return to an earlier style, that Charles spoke a little more himself and did not defer to his Lord Keeper. The king began by referring to his earlier promise that 'I would do that which should be to your satisfaction' and announced his alliance with Holland, for the preservation of Flanders, and his recall of troops, an earlier request of the house, from France.[104] Outlining the need for a fleet and men and the care he had already taken to provide them, Charles appealed for supply in the language of reciprocity that had earlier served him so well. 'I hope these things will need little recommendation to you . . . . I have not only employed my time and treasure for your safety but done all I could to remove all sorts of jealous[ies]'; in particular, he continued, 'I have married my niece to the Prince of Orange, by which I hope I have given full satisfaction that I shall never suffer his interest to be ruined . . . . Having done all this, I expect from you a plentiful supply . . . whereon depends not only the honour but . . . the being of an English nation'.[105] Events would argue that the speech was ineffective. Supply was granted but was inadequate and delayed; and, with threats of ministers being impeached, Charles again had to prorogue the parliament.[106] But what may have been vital about this speech 'published by His Majesties Command' was its signalling to a wider political nation the language of a king who, having listened and acted, could reasonably expect supply. Even on the eve of the greatest crisis of his reign, Charles's very speaking may well have begun to recover the support that enabled him to survive it.

In fact there is a clear sense that Charles, faced with an opposition that was a faction, had again begun to address the wider nation every bit as much as the parliament. His speech to both houses on 18 June 1678 was, as well as measured, once again personal and fond ('I shall open my heart freely to you'); and, narrating recent events and achievements, it was also blatantly patriotic.[107] 'Both you and I,' the king told them, '(as we are true Englishmen) cannot but be pleased and understand the importance of that reputation we have gained abroad' by brokering a peace through quickly raising a force.[108] The crown and the honour and interest of the nation were allied, as, requesting supply, the king promised to 'employ my whole life to advance the true and public good'. Charles could not have foreseen how timely his shift of style as much as policy would be. For when he next met parliament, on 21 October 1678, a veritable fever of anxiety had been generated by the revelations made to the Council by Titus Oates of a plot, and the opposition had every intent of taking full advantage of it.

If the crisis of the Popish Plot saw Charles II the adroit politician at his most astute, there can be no questioning that his oratorical skills returned to complement his political strategy. Not least, in the heated atmosphere, Charles spoke calmly, deferring reference to the domestic circumstances until he had reminded his audience of the part he had played in preserving neighbours and in securing Flanders and the 'honour and interest of the nation'.[109] Then, innocently as if nothing had been heard of the news that ran current on every street, he continued: 'I now intend to acquaint you (as I shall always do with anything that concerns me) that I have been informed of a design against my person by the Jesuits.'[110] In a brilliant move, the king withheld any opinion and resolved that 'I will leave this matter to the law'.[111] But, to check any plan to question his own Protestant credentials, Charles announced his care to halt the activities of any who sought to advance popery. Hardly touching on the plot, Finch, alluding to French support for the opposition, revealed pernicious designs by a 'correspondency with foreign nations' but otherwise called for loyalty and supply, for 'zeal' in the king's – and the country's – service.[112] Discursively pursuing the politics of isolating the king's enemies, the Lord Keeper reminded MPs of their affections for the king and the manoeuvres of a few 'malicious men' to 'raise a storm'.[113] It was for the loyal to check them, to give the king the 'glory of reigning in the hearts of his people', to ensure the people 'as much felicity as this world is capable of' and themselves the satisfaction of securing it.[114] The old rhetoric of love and unity had now to accommodate the harsh facts of difference, division and party. In Charles's calm words and Finch's oratorical cunning, the excitement that fed the opposition was tempered and the support of the majority that the king's opponents needed was eroded.

In accordance with a strategy of isolating his opponents, a week after Shaftesbury had proposed the dismissal of the duke of York from the Privy Council, on 9 November Charles opened his address to both houses with 'most hearty thanks' for the care they had taken for his preservation.[115] No less than any was the king, he assured them, concerned to establish the Protestant religion; and, he added, in a clever tactical move, 'not only during my time, of which I am sure you have no fear, but in future ages' – and here the language is apocalyptic – 'even to the end of the world'.[116] To secure the principle of hereditary succession, and to outmanoeuvre his enemies, Charles invited parliament to proffer bills securing Protestantism for the reign of his (Catholic) successor, along with measures against recusants, 'that the world may see our unanimity'.[117] Unanimity was not the hallmark of the next weeks in which the impeachment of Danby forced a prorogation, then in January 1679 a dissolution, of the 'Cavalier Parliament' that had sat for eighteen years.[118] It was a high-risk strategy that did not work, leaving Charles to face a new parliament packed with and controlled by Shaftesbury's followers who were bent on pushing through the exclusion of the king's brother James, duke of York.

The editor of several of Charles's speeches observes that the king met a hostile assembly in March with 'politeness'.[119] Indeed, in the most difficult of circumstances, Charles spoke to present himself as a champion of Protestantism and parliament. He catalogued his actions in excluding papists from the Lords and sending his brother out of the country to bolster his Protestant credentials. Lest any suspect, or fan the suspicion, that he retained an army for illicit purposes, the king informed them that he had disbanded troops as soon as he could afford to. Shifting suspicion from himself to others, he now asked all to consider whether 'Protestant religion and the peace of the kingdom be as truly aimed at by others as they are . . . by me'.[120] Even facing a hostile majority, Charles tried to isolate his enemies by painting them as men with 'private animosities under pretence of the public', and urged the house to curb such 'unruly spirits'.[121] To what he hoped, using a metaphor often applied to kings, would be a 'healing parliament', Charles held out a reciprocal vision of kingship which he had deployed successfully before.[122] He would with his life defend religion and the land: 'and I do expect from you to be defended from the calumny, as well as danger, of those worst of men who endeavour to render me . . . odious to my people'.[123] As Finch glossed the speech, he reinforced the wisdom of unity, of the 'king . . . seated in parliament . . . in the fullness of his majesty and power', the dread of the nation's enemies.[124] 'Calm and peaceable' proceedings, Charles had urged, 'great and orderly' Finch had added, would enable 'doing great things for the king and kingdom'.[125]

Ignoring a subsequent plea, Shaftesbury's followers pressed on with attacks on royal ministers and, in May, with a second reading of the Exclusion Bill.[126] James, Duke of York, now in exile, doubted his brother's moderate handling of the affair.[127] But it was not least the calm and moderation Charles maintained in direct opposition to the noise and extremism of his opponents that paid dividends. And in dissolving his third parliament and issuing writs for new elections, the king was calculating that he might have won over subjects and citizens. His *Declaration To All His Loving Subjects* in June was, as we shall see, a move to undercut popular support for those soon to be called Whigs.[128] Proroguing, then dissolving, his new parliament on several occasions, Charles played for time and a turn of the tide.[129] And, at Oxford in March 1681, as the crisis looked set to head towards civil war, he spoke to remind a nation all too conscious of recent experiences 'that without the safety and dignity of the monarchy, neither religion nor property can be preserved'.[130]

That memory was clearly a decisive factor in the nation pulling back from the brink of renewed civil conflict. We should not, however, underestimate the importance of the image of himself that Charles had been projecting with care in his speeches. Amid provocation and assault he had (he himself referred to his 'patience') sustained a calm eirenic, conciliatory tone which had made charges of autocracy harder to sell.[131] Gradually, through words as well as deeds, I would suggest, Charles II had begun to isolate and undercut his opponents and, mixing old tropes with rhetorical devices suited to a new age of party, to re-script the authority of the crown.

My argument that royal words and speeches played a part in the king's victory in 1681 has at least one powerful contemporary testimony. In 1681, Edward Cooke of the Inner Temple published with a large engraving of Charles II facing the title page, and 'dedicated to the Grand Council or Senate of this Kingdom', *Memorabilia or The Most Remarkable Passages and Counsels Collected out of the Several Declarations and Speeches That have been made by the King, His L. Chancellors and Keepers, and the Speakers . . . in Parliament since His Majesty's Happy Restauration.*[132] An introduction explained the purpose of the edition. 'Many abominable pamphlets' had come abroad with the malicious design of installing in the people fears and jealousies that would undermine their affections for a monarchy, which, they charged, threatened religion, laws and liberties. 'Never,' it continues, 'was this spirit of libelling more pregnant than it is now.'[133] The need was to restore the nation to its old humour, and preserve the king in his just prerogative that he might protect the religion, liberties and properties of Englishmen. And as the introduction made up almost entirely of quotations itself manifests, if any should question the king's affection for Protestantism or the rights of the subject, 'let him be pleased to *hear him give his own royal word for't*'.[134] Cooke gathered under headings (Protestant Religion, Popery, Liberty and Property, Parliaments) words spoken by the king and his Lord Keepers which evidenced, he argued, Charles's 'extraordinary' 'affection' for church and parliament.[135] Cutting and pasting extracts from speeches over twenty years (the appendix took the collection right up to 1681), and often highlighting royal words with a gothic typeface, Cooke, adding little else to make his point, expected that the royal word would settle all. 'Where the word of a king is,' he cited the familiar Solomonic adage, 'there is power.'[136] It was, of course, a partisan claim which we cannot finally verify. Yet, as within weeks or months of his publication Charles gloried not only in the power of his throne but, again, the adulation of his subjects, it may well be that readers followed Cooke's adage: 'Take his own words for your security'.[137]

Cooke's collection was a compilation of declarations as well as speeches. We have had occasion to observe that Charles's speeches to the Houses of Parliament often, especially at critical moments, read like addresses to the nation. They were. Members of Parliament returned to their constituencies to report royal words and a very high proportion of the royal speeches, for the first time, were published by the king's command, or *cum privilegio*, and widely distributed. Charles II, however, also took particular advantage of a mode of royal representation that had been used increasingly but still only occasionally before the civil war: a declaration issued to the people and often commanded to be read in the churches of the realm so as to create an impression of personal, oral delivery. While a few of these declarations were purely informative – such as that of 1665 declaring the Dutch aggressors and licensing subjects to seize their shops and goods[138] – Charles's declarations were in the main rhetorical performances: explanations and even justifications; appeals, at difficult moments in relations with parliament, to a wider political nation and a burgeoning public sphere. The declaration as a genre of royal representation may indeed have developed as a response to an informed public; and it risked, as we shall see, plunging royal words into the vast flux and flow of political texts and news that swirled through the capital and country during the Restoration. Yet, either because he felt the necessity (in a way that his father had for long not) of such an appeal to a broader public, or, perhaps because experience had led him to judge the people at large loyal friends to monarchy, Charles from the beginning to the end of his reign presented himself directly to his people in words: words that were quoted, copied, circulated, remembered – and contested.

At a time when everything depended on the right move, Charles calculated that his best course was a direct appeal to his (we note the effortless use of the term before the Restoration) 'subjects'.[139] The *Declaration of Breda*, as we have seen, is familiar to all historians; its rhetorics, however, remain curiously neglected. What Charles had to offer (pardon, toleration, consultation) was, of course, vital. But his words were, as he was fully aware, not just the first presentation of him to many, as their monarch, but a means whereby he might come to the throne in reality as well as by right. The *Declaration* 'to all subjects' opens with a simple self-description, not an argument, at a time when every possible political option was being argued: 'Charles, by the grace of God, king of England, Scotland, France and Ireland, Defender of the Faith, etc to all our loving subjects of what degree or quality soever, greeting'.[140] He was a traditional king, with all the titles of majesty but a different monarch – ready to speak to the humblest as well as the great. As he proceeds to lament the wounds that have kept the country 'bleeding' for years, Charles skilfully attributes no blame, only expresses his willingness to 'contribute' to (not, we note, control) the process of resolution.[141] His desire to take possession of his 'right which God and Nature hath made our due' leads him to pray for God's providence, not only for his restoration but one 'with as little blood and damage to our people as possible'.[142] Charles conjoins his right with his subjects' rights and his fervent desire that they may enjoy 'what by law is theirs'.[143] He conjures a 'perfect union' that he might establish by pardon and prohibition against 'all notes of discord'.[144] With regard to the contentious issues (religion, land settlement) that might undermine union, he referred all to the determination of parliament, leaving himself a symbol of unity above the debate and fray. Because he knew one of the crucial issues to be that of trust – there were many warning of what a restored monarchy might enact out of vengeance – Charles, 'after this long silence' urged all to 'rely upon the word of a king'.[145] Only trust in the royal word could restore Charles to his throne; yet his royal word was an essential medium for securing that trust. Because he believed that he owed his return to trust in his word, in the early years of the Restoration he was to reiterate time and again to parliament the importance of his promises, his words delivered from Breda, to which he was bound by honour: that is, by the word of a king. Though, as satirists and critics were quick to observe, during the course of his reign, the king's promises (on toleration, for example) were broken, and royal words concealed as well as revealed the king's person and policies, even misrepresented him, Charles remained committed to a belief in the power of his words spoken directly to his subjects and to the efficacy of those words in gaining, or regaining, the people's trust.

One of Charles's earliest difficulties after regaining his throne was presented by the old champions of monarchy who distrusted his advocacy of indulgence and toleration. In order to temper Cavalier prejudice, and probably judging the nation at large more sympathetic than his parliament, the king issued in the October of his first Restoration year a Declaration concerning ecclesiastical affairs to all his subjects.[146] Holding up as his objective the universal desire for peace, Charles drew on his experiences of the continent where Protestant divines, he told his people, lamented the schisms in England. Speaking person- ally, autobiographically, the king recounted his meetings in Holland with Presbyterians and his personal 'satisfaction' that they presented no threat to the church or episcopacy – the basis of the indulgence he proposed from Breda. Some, however, had taken the king's words (together with his earlier declarations from the 1650s) to raise questions about his plans for the Church of England. Identifying the problem as not one of belief but of 'passions and appetites', and positioning himself as the reasonable mediator, Charles presented it as his duty to God to bring together Christians who concurred in all fundamentals.[147] Assuring readers of his devotion to the old Church of England, he was ready to recognize that ceremonies 'of former times may not be so agreeable to the present'.[148] What mattered most was unity and peace and, he added, 'episcopal authority', which was 'the best means to contain the minds of men within the rules of government'.[149] The precise exercise of episcopacy, however, had differed over time and in relation to the needs of the kingdom. Charles therefore proposed an episcopacy modified by the advice of presbyters and ministers. And while underlining the importance of a set form of liturgy, in the Book of Common Prayer, he expressed his willingness to see change and to avow different practices by ministers and laymen not least in matters of ceremonies that had caused bitter divisions.

The declaration was Charles's personal intervention to sustain what he had promised at Breda. But it was a declaration too of a restored Supreme Head defending his authority in (what George Bernard has termed) a monarchical church and an effort to foster the unity on which in turn the security of his authority depended, as well as the peace of the nation.[150] In his detailed proposals, Charles, in a manner similar to Queen Elizabeth in 1558, tried to represent all his subjects and to make and represent the church of which he was head a national church, not that of a party. He endeavoured to do so because he feared (events bore him out) that without that his monarchy too might be the institution only of a party, not the realm.

Restoration re-established Charles on his throne, but by no means ended the discursive competition to gain support. In the wake of Venner's uprising, and the efforts of the old sects and commonwealthsmen to undermine the regime, Charles published a second Declaration 'to All His Loving Subjects' on 26 December 1662. Though the personal voice of the king, and bearing prominently his royal arms, the declaration was, the title page announced, published by the advice of his Privy Council, that is by a king who took counsel through the established constitutional means, not from favourites or intimates.[151] The king began by reminding the people of the hand of God that had restored him to his inheritance and them to peace and tranquillity, which he had sought to maintain by mercy and moderate courses. Presenting himself as the embodiment of the royal virtue of clemency, Charles expressed his regret that late treasonable designs had led, albeit with legal process, to executions and his determination to prevent more. The cause of trouble had had its origins in words and the purpose of the royal declaration was to counter, to subjugate, those words: as he put it, in the conventional metaphor of the royal physician: 'to apply proper antidotes to all those venomous insinuations, by which ... some ... endeavour to poison the affections of our good people'.[152] Turning to particulars, Charles identified four charges that were dangerously circulating: that having re-established his authority, he would ignore indemnity and leave all exposed to the revenge of Cavaliers; that he intended a military absolutism; that he planned to persecute dissent; and that he indulged papists. All the accusations, of course, amounted to a claim that the king had reneged or would renege on his word issued from Breda, breach his trust. Accordingly, for all the risks of a monarch entering the lists of charge and answer, Charles felt compelled to speak, to undeceive subjects, and to reassert and republish 'our steadfast resolutions in all these particulars'.[153] Once again, by solemn 'engagement on the word of a king', with repeated expressions of 'sincere profession' and quotations from the Declaration of Breda, Charles restated the principles on which he considered the Restoration was founded.[154] In a reiteration of terms like 'distempered', 'madly', he correspondingly sought to undermine the voices of his enemies – to isolate them from an increasingly more rational discourse of politics.[155] Moreover, without attributing blame to parliament, with which he needed as well as desired good relations, the king subtly indicated that the delay in establishing toleration lay more with the Commons than with him, who sought 'to incline their wisdom' in that direction.[156] And at length he endeavoured to counter any change that, in permitting them private exercise of their faith, he indulged papists, threatening, as the other hand of indulgent practice, 'to be severe' against proselytizers and priests.[157] The royal word was given, Charles concluded, to 'arm' subjects against detractors and to prepare them for a parliament that would help him perform his promises: a parliament for which, of course, this declaration was part of his own preparation. Indeed, in what might have been, as well as advertisement of his care for the realm, an attempt to stir public pressure on MPs, the king suggested bills: against licence and impiety, for the restraint of excess, for – a tactically selfless gesture – retrenchment in his household, and (a popular measure) for the advancement of trade for public plenty and prosperity. A risk though it was to answer accusers, Charles skilfully re-presented himself and his preferred way of indulgence as embodying the unity and prosperity of the nation; most of all he rewrote himself as a ruler true to his word.

With his throne established, Charles, sensibly, used declarations sparingly through most of his reign, and significantly at times of difficulty. Twice in 1666, however, he addressed his people, very much in the manner of a modern president or prime minister, on the occasion of a national disaster, the Great Fire which ravaged London. Though his declaration was directed to 'his city of London', it was published to the nation as a representation of a king who (as indeed he had) shared in the tragedies as well as joys of his subjects. Charles immediately announced his own sense of, his share in, the loss along with his solicitousness for rebuilding the city with expedition. The king praised the 'undaunted courage' of those who had suffered and offered his support to turn adversity into benefit.[158] Outlining rules for rebuilding (in brick or stone, not timber, with safe distances across streets, etcetera) that most would have regarded as sensible, Charles emphasized the need to appease divine displeasure by charitable donations for the reconstruction of churches – for which he promised encouragement by the example of his own bounty. Beyond that, the king (though he did not make the point that his revenue depended on it) promised at his own cost to rebuild swiftly a Customs House 'with the most convenience for the merchants' and, beyond, generously granted that on all royal land, 'we shall depart with anything of our own right and benefit for the advancement of the public service and beauty of the city', and waived the hearth tax for all new builders.[159] As for the victims, Charles publicized his 'princely compassion and tender care' for the homeless, and evidenced it with measures to bring bread to merchants in the city and on its peripheries (in Clerkenwell and Islington and Mile End); to store salvaged goods in churches; and to require other towns to take in London's workers, promising that they would not be laid to their charge.[160] Along with his actions – Charles stood with his people amid the smoke and flames working a fire wagon – the royal words presented him as of his people rather than over his people, as a king who with them was rebuilding not only the city but the nation. That today we have become jaundiced at the ritual appearance of leaders on our TV screens, or the statements from Buckingham Palace or Number 10 that follow tragedies, should not blind us to the importance of Charles's words. Though earlier monarchs had, in a proclamation say, referred to critical events, Charles II was the first to sense the importance of his role in embodying the nation's grief and distress, not least as part of a discursive and symbolic process whereby the monarch came to embody the nation.

While the Fire served to unite the capital in a fight against adversity, when the king next made direct address to his people he wrote amidst mounting division in parliament and the country. Charles's Declaration of Indulgence for Tender Consciences was unquestionably another salvo in his assiduous efforts to enact the promise he had made at Breda and, as he sincerely believed, to temper the religious divisions which were mounting and menacing. But it belongs, too, very much to a moment when, disenchanted with parliament, Charles, as we saw, was signing secret terms with Louis XIV which held out the prospect of his public conversion to Rome. With suspicions mounting, and his decision to take action quite contrary to parliament's wishes, Charles resolved to address the wider nation. But, as with his speeches to parliament at this time, the tone is quite different to earlier utterances and the king falls back on his authority to empower his words, rather than the opposite. The declaration does not seek to persuade; it announces a 'supreme power in ecclesiastical matters' which entitles the royal actions.[161] Though it gestures to popular concerns, notably trade, rather than explaining or 'selling' his action, Charles commands 'obedience' in a lexicon new to him of 'declare', 'express will', 'warning' and threats of 'severity'.[162] Far from the direct appeal to the nation and an authoritarian tone working, this was the only royal declaration that Charles publicly rescinded in a later (1675) declaration publicizing and enforcing a Council order for the prosecution of all recusants.[163] Charles had forgotten, or dangerously departed from, his own sense of the need in a changed political culture to speak with, not to, the people and to be seen to woo rather than simply command.

Indeed, the crisis that grew almost to overwhelm him stemmed from the erosion of popular support, especially in the capital, as well as parliamentary intransigence. The London crowds that had cheered so loudly for the king became by the late 1670s supporters of the opposition whose leaders fanned popular fears of popery and arbitrary government.[164] Charles II, in other words, lost the war of words to gain popular support. Whilst it has been argued that no advocacy could have rendered popular the royal policies of friendship with France and commitment to hereditary, that is Catholic, succession, such an argument should not be simply accepted. By the end of Charles's reign, James, Duke of York succeeded to his throne on a tide of popular support. Perhaps it needed the threat of civil war to turn the tide. But it was a revival of his skills in navigating turbulent waters that gave Charles the victory; and not least of those skills was self-presentation in words.

Charles's first address to his subjects after the Declaration of Indulgence seems a surprising one. *His Majesties Declaration for the Dissolution of His Late Privy-Council, and for Constituting a New One*, printed and published a Council order of 20 April 1679.[165] The Council order, following a move by which Charles tried to buy off leading opponents by bringing them into the government, announced that the advice of a small foreign committee had led to 'jealousies and dissatisfaction among his good subjects'.[166] In response, therefore, the king had resolved to dispense with private advice and to reconstitute a full Council of the best informed out of (the subtle reference to party or faction is arresting) 'the several parts this state is composed of.'[167] As well as royal officers and nobles, the new Council was to include commoners whose 'known abilities interest and esteem in the nation shall render them without all suspicion of . . . betraying the true interests of the kingdom'.[168] With this Privy Council and 'the frequent use of his great Council of Parliament', the king would govern in accordance with the 'true ancient constitution'.[169] The declaration lists the new Council, with Shaftesbury prominent as Lord President, and prints Charles's speech to the Lords and Commons reporting the change. Here is neither the king's own voice nor any prefatory matter. What the declaration does, however, is publicize as a free royal act what might have been represented as forced from the king; it advertises Charles's responsiveness to the people's concerns; and it brilliantly appropriates the language of counsel and the ancient constitution to re-present the monarch as the custodian of traditional courses, whilst at the same time he adapts to the new politics of party. Moreover, published to the people, this conciliar order involves the people in the business of government demonstrating what the order enacts: a king who does not govern secretly but for the public weal, who listens as well as speaks to all 'the several parts of this state'. The next year, Charles issued a declaration to undercut a rumour that he had married Mrs Walter, making Monmouth legitimate, by denying any contract or marriage with his former mistress.[170] In this document, too, Charles makes much of his registering in the Council book that he had not married Walter. The support for James as his successor was being advanced not least by an advertisement of proper constitutional courses.

As the crisis surrounding the Popish Plot destroyed session after session of parliament, Charles, who had at least again worked to nourish popularity, gambled on a greater measure of support in the nation than at Westminster. In the first three months of 1681 he dissolved two parliaments and issued an explanatory declaration 'to all his loving subjects' of his reasons for dispensing with them.[171] The moment was critical, as the Whigs had turned up at Oxford with armed support and talk of another civil war was widespread. Charles opened on a note of sorrow and regret, but also with a clear attribution of blame. For his part, he had offered to do anything to assuage fears about religion and liberties and to 'satisfy the desires of our good subjects'; he had met only with 'unsuitable returns' and illegal courses: votes against members of his government and arbitrary orders for their imprisonment.[172] In a nice move, he noted the Commons had taken the unconstitutional step of assuming a power to suspend the laws, in their tolerating Protestant dissent. Presenting himself as the custodian of the law and constitution at home, Charles emphasized his care for the interest of the nation abroad (in Tangier, for example) in contrast to a parliament that had not only failed to supply but blocked royal borrowing to reinforce the port. The declaration made the last Westminster parliament appear unpatriotic, its proceedings determined not by the good of the nation. The Oxford assembly, Charles continued, he had specifically urged 'to make the laws of the land their rule, as we did'.[173] The succession was part of that law, but the king, he emphasized, was ready 'to hearken to any expedient' for the preservation of religion and had offered that 'the administration of the government might remain in Protestant hands'.[174] Such offers were spurned by a house that insisted on exclusion, an unconstitutional course which – and here Charles played on fears of 1641 again – 'we cannot, after the sad experience we have had of the late civil war that murdered our father . . . consent to', lest it lead to 'another most unnatural war'.[175] Then cleverly branding the Whigs as revolutionaries ambitious for power, Charles hinted that even exclusion was not their ultimate goal which was, he put it obliquely drawing on all the contemporary fears of change, 'to attempt some other great and important changes even in present'.[176] The Commons clash with the Lords, 'a violation of the constitution of parliaments', manifested how far they pursued private ambitions 'to the disappointment of public ends'.[177] The king's act in dissolving them is here presented as a preservation of parliaments and of the wider public good they had violated.[178] Only those driven by 'ambition' and their own 'particular designs' or by 'old beloved Commonwealth-principles' could report Charles as ill disposed to parliaments, 'for we do still declare that no irregularities in parliament shall ever make us out of love with parliaments which we look upon as the best method for healing the distempers of the kingdom and the only means to preserve the monarchy in that due credit and respect which it ought to have both at home and abroad'.[179] The declaration ends with Charles's resolution to have 'frequent parliaments' and his desire to save the country from a 'relapse' into 'the late troubles and confusions' in which, along with monarchy, 'religion, liberty and property were all lost and gone'.[180] This was a brilliant rhetorical performance that powerfully presented Charles as the reasonable, moderate, open ruler, the guarantor of the constitutional order and established courses, and his Whig enemies as a cohort of hated republicans and self-interested aspirants. Emotively it evoked the fear of renewed civil war that haunted the Restoration age and hinted that the Whigs might relish renewed 'confusion'.

Charles's declaration was ordered to be read in all churches and chapels throughout the kingdom, and, published, was plunged into contest. *A Letter from a Person of Quality to his Friend concerning His Majesties late Declaration* attacked the arguments of the paper and restated in detail the Whig case for a popish plot and for the exclusion of the Duke of York.[181] But, paradoxically, the *Letter*'s attack revealed the strength and polemical effect of the king's declaration. Just as with Milton's response to *Eikon Basilike*, the author had been thrown onto the defensive and the need to answer general and emotive charges in tiresome detail.[182] Moreover, in denying royal authorship, and in objecting at several points to a new practice – that of 'without lawful authority' ordering the royal declaration used in churches ('which no doubt the blind obedience of our clergy will . . . see performed'), the *Letter* betrays the sense of the broad polemical appeal of the king's words.[183] Indeed, John Dryden, in his response, mocked anxious Whigs who had set many pens to work to answer the royal declaration and so 'to hinder the king from making any good impression on his subjects by giving them all possible satisfaction'.[184] Though Dryden's invective was no less partisan, he was on the winning side and he was right: the king's words had made an impression and done much to satisfy the people. As, following his declaration, over two hundred addresses of generous thanks to the king evidence, Charles's words had not only encouraged loyalists but (since the addresses attracted mass subscriptions) won over volatile public opinion.[185] Despite his expressed love for them, Charles called no parliaments after 1681; but he apparently ruled with most of the people's approval and affection.[186] He did not repeat the mistakes of 1672 of taking these for granted. Following the conspiracy to assassinate him and his brother at Rye House in the summer of 1683, Charles took full opportunity to milk the threat to his life so as to destroy any vestiges of Whig support and to elevate his own position. *His Majesties Declaration to All His Loving Subjects, Concerning the Treasonable Conspiracy Against His Sacred Person* was the second ordered to be read in all churches and it was marked by a new – or rather a revived – language of sacred kingship which served almost to render support for the crown again as an act of worship.[187] The *Declaration* economically constructed a narrative of the last few years from the king's viewpoint: a narrative of a seditious party plotting against the crown and misleading the people while Charles steadfastly upheld the Protestant religion and the laws. God, however, opened subjects' eyes to these 'villainous designs' and so forced the faction to plan armed insurrection and the murder of the king and his heir.[188] Had they succeeded, Charles proclaimed, they would have 'enslaved . . . the whole kingdom'.[189] But they were prevented by a higher power which oversaw the king and the nation. Alluding to the story of his escape from Worcester (which was published at this time), Charles wrote 'the Divine Providence which hath preserved us through the whole course of our life hath at this time in an extraordinary manner showed itself in the wonderful deliverance of us and our dearest brother and all our loyal subjects'.[190] With all the narrative skill of a novelist, Charles, as he had in recounting his escape from Worcester, now told the story of the plan to kill him and the providential fire which had led him to leave Newmarket ahead of schedule and so foil the assassin's plans. And, identifying the threat to himself with that to the nation, he vividly conjured images of guerrilla forces throughout London ready to mount 'a general insurrection'.[191] Having related the 'hellish conspiracy' and 'great deliverance', Charles urged his people to join him in a service of thanks to God and announced that he had appointed 9 September as the day for a national service of thanksgiving.[192] The declaration, written in a reappropriated vocabulary of providence and read in churches, closed with an invitation to divine service – to a service of thanksgiving to God, but a service of thanks also to and *for* the monarch who had, as the chosen agent of divine providence, saved the nation as well as himself from ruin. In those last months of his reign and life, whatever his behaviour, Charles rewrote his authority in sacred script, and in response another three hundred loyal addresses in the wake of the Rye House Plot resounded with loyal echoes of love for 'the darling of heaven'.[193]

The pamphleteer who criticized the royal declaration ordered to be read from pulpits alerts us to an important change in early modern royal representation through words. During the Tudor years, proclamations had been a

principal vehicle of royal public address and had often carried long explanations, even justifications, for royal actions, as well as advertising the monarch's
care for the common weal.[194] Proclamations remained important documents of
government authority: the Commonwealth and Protectorate regimes had
retained the elements of their form in gothic script, arms, the style of address,
etcetera. But during the course of the 1650s, proclamations became shorter and
more businesslike, not least perhaps, because the business of public argument
was carried on in pamphlets, gazettes and newsbooks on a scale not seen
before. What, then, of the role of the proclamation in the representation of
restored monarchy? Did the return of a single sovereign voice re-authorize the
royal proclamation as a primary site of royal self-publication, or had changed
circumstances rendered this, as the declarations we have examined might
suggest, an insignificant medium for representing the king? As well as being
inconvenient, it may be significant that, in contrast to the Tudor and early
Stuart years, we have no modern editions of royal proclamations for the
years after 1660. This may be an accident of historical scholarship and
fashion; or it may be yet another manifestation of the impact of Whig history
on the records as well as interpretation of the past: after 1649, it may have
been thought, historical attention was more fittingly turned to the records of
parliaments rather than of the crown. Interestingly, there seem to be few
contemporary collected editions of proclamations of the sort published before
and during the 1640s, though some later seventeenth-century collectors
evidently sought to compile their own.[195]

Charles II certainly used, and used conventionally, proclamations as an
instrument of government. Royal proclamations of Charles II deal with the
pricing of wines, assessing prices when the court was in progress, regulating
imports, promoting and protecting native industries, poor relief, the apprehension of criminals, the ordering of access to court for curing the king's evil,
registering knights, confirming pardons, coin, shipping and foreign affairs,
and a myriad of religious matters including profanity and the reverencing of
the sabbath. New conditions gave rise to new proclamations – for regulating
potteries, or most famously that of 1675 for the suppression of coffee houses.[196]
And from 1679, there was a flood of proclamations prompted by the Popish
Plot: proclamations for discovering the design, seeking out the murderers of
the prominent magistrate Sir Edmund Bury Godfrey, for securing and
disarming recusants, for hunting down Jesuits, for recalling English Catholics
from foreign seminaries, and the like. These, several for the suppression of
popery being repeated, advertised Charles's willingness to act to quell the
threats identified by his subjects. But few of these proclamations, even in times
of crisis, were texts of much discursive sophistication. The form of proclamations was reinstated – 'God Save The King' is imprinted with the royal arms on
every one. But what is notable is their brevity: Restoration proclamations were

usually a dozen lines or half a page, whereas Tudor and Stuart texts ran to pages. The ritual rhetorical gestures can be found, announcing a king 'watchful for the good of his loving subjects' or ever concerned for 'the suppression of vice and the advancement of virtue' and for the 'preservation of the true religion'.[197] In the early 1660s the language of providence and divine monarchy is heard in proclamations for commemorating 29 May, the day of the royal coronation, and for the better ordering of those who repair to court to be touched for the king's evil.[198] But we are left with a sense that the proclamation had diminished in importance as a text of royal representation, and that the royal declaration, with its similarities to speech and opportunities for greater familiarity, was seen as a more effective medium for publicizing the royal words.

The royal texts we have examined, speeches, declarations and proclamations, for all the continuance of form, are texts that reveal change and the king's own perception of change. If the language of these texts reads as belonging to a more modern world that may be because, certainly after the early 1660s, their tone sounds more secular. After the violent religious conflicts of the civil war and revolution, one senses in Restoration culture a need to lower the heat of religious language and, in some measure, to deploy a discourse of state not defined by sacred script. If so, the sense is only half accurate. One of the central ambiguities of Restoration society and culture was that between the secular and the sacred; and, as often, Charles II embodies the ambiguity. While in his speeches and declarations even concerning matters of religion, Charles could deploy a language of calm reason, in no way could he abandon the vocabularies of Scripture, faith, divine will and providence which validated both him and the monarchy. In the early years of Restoration, as we shall argue, there was a need for the monarchy to reclaim these discourses from puritan and Commonwealth appropriations: that is, to represent the king as God's appointed ruler of his chosen people. Queen Elizabeth and Charles I advertised their piety, as well as performed their Supreme Headship in prayers published to the nation.[199] Perusing the proclamations of Charles II, we note a number of fast days appointed by the king at which the nation was required to join with the ruler in prayers which he had authorized.[200] We need now to turn to these important representations of Charles to his subjects: to the sacred texts of royal discourse.

From the beginning, the Restoration was represented and heralded as a religious miracle and commemorated in a service of public worship. Charles ordered 29 May, the day of his entry into London, to be made a calendrical day of worship (as Queen Elizabeth's accession day had been). In 1661, accordingly, there was set forth 'by his Majesty's Authority' and published 'cum privilegio' by the royal printer *A Form of Prayer with Thanksgiving To Be Used of All the King's Majesties Loving Subjects . . . Yearly for His Majestie's Happy Return to his*

Kingdoms, it Being Also the Day of His Birth.[201] The service, which began with
a prayer for those in authority and a national confession of sin and absolution,
is worthy of our attention. For in this service, worship of the Lord, thanks to
the Lord, and worship of and thanks to the king, his lieutenant on earth, are
welded in a public ritual that took place in every parish church in the land, one
in which the people spoke as well as listened, and joined in the adulation and
exaltation. The reading, in the morning service, from Psalm 21 began with the
1st verse 'The King shall rejoice in thy strength, O Lord' and the first verses
from Psalm 85 followed, blessing the Lord for ending the captivity of Jacob.[202]
The first lesson for the day took the 9th verse of 2 Samuel 19: 'the King saved
us out of the hand of our enemies and he delivered us out of the hand of the
Philistines . . . why speak ye not a word of bringing the king back? And 'so the
King returned and came to Jordan. . . . And Judah . . . came to meet the King',
and so on, the biblical passage almost exactly paralleling the journey to greet
the returning exile.[203] After the first lesson a Te Deum Laudamus in English
praised the Lord. The second lesson, on a text familiar to all early modern
English people, must have been heard with striking freshness in the circumstances of restored monarchy. 'Let every soul,' the minister read from St Paul's
epistle to the Romans 13:1, 'be subject unto the higher powers. For there is no
power but of God: the powers that be are ordained of God.'[204] A Benedictus
followed the reading: 'blessed be the Lord God of Israel: for the Lord redeemed
his people. And hath raised up a mighty salvation for us in the house of his
servant David.'[205] Then the minister prayed 'O Lord save the King', and the
congregation kneeling responded 'Who putteth his trust in Thee'. The minister
continued with the prayer of thanks: 'O Lord God thou has dealt exceeding
graciously with this sinful land, who by thy miraculous providence hath delivered us out of our late insufferable confusions, by restoring to us our dread
sovereign lord, thy servant king CHARLES.'[206] Between the collects, prayers
asked that the land be delivered from conspiracies, that the Lord protect his
king, and 'let his people serve him with honour and obedience'.[207] Closing
prayers for the king and royal family reminded the people that the Lord had
brought home his servant, 'thereby restoring to us the open and public profession of the true religion' – 'the free profession', the priest repeated at the
communion prayer, 'of thy sacred truth and gospel together with our former
peace and prosperity'.[208] The last reading from the gospel was taken from St
Matthew 22: 21, the story of Christ responding to the question about tribute:
'Render therefore unto Caesar the things which are Caesar's', before final
prayers for Charles and his peaceful government.[209] The form of prayer (based
on an earlier June 1660 thanksgiving for Restoration)[210] remained the template
for the annual texts and services printed from 1662 with a large royal arms, and
with a royal command that it be read in all cathedral churches, colleges, parish
churches and chapels throughout England and Wales. There were minor

variations, but each year, even amid the flurry of pamphlet exchange and mounting political divisions, English people joined to praise God for his providence in restoring a king who led the church from sin and exile back to the Lord, as well as to their peace and prosperity. As through the minister, the authorized words were spoken, so the congregations of people responded ritually as the prescribed service scripted. Here, in the churches of the realm, as well as the words of the Lord, the word of a king had power.

The companion text to the service of thanks for the Restoration was, of course, the service devised, also in 1661, for the day appointed by parliament for fasting and humiliation to remember and atone for the execution of Charles I on 30 January. As the colophon and title page bearing the royal arms and command announced, the service was directed to 'implore the mercy of God' that he might not chastise the land for its guilt in delivering up the king to his enemies.[211] The service book is long and contains the scripts for morning and evening prayer. Here, of course, the usual opening confession and absolution took on a highly political resonance, as the sin uppermost in the congregation's mind was that against monarchy, and indeed against a particular king. After several readings from the Psalms, the first lesson took the passage from 2 Samuel 1 (where David laments the slaying of Saul), 'Ye daughters of Israel weep over Saul'. The second lesson, after the Te Deum, from Matthew 27, was the text for the day of Charles's execution, that account of Christ's Passion, an exegesis of which James I had dedicated to his son.[212] The minister drew out in prayer the comparisons between 'our late martyred sovereign' and a saviour who had suffered all indignities of his people.[213] After the collect and litany, the people prayed 'let his memory O Lord be ever blessed among us and his example powerful to work upon us.'[214] A reading from Matthew 21: 42 – 'the stone which the builders rejected, is become the head of the corner' – turned attention from the martyred to a living king, as the epistle of St Peter 2: 13 ordered 'Submit yourself to every ordinance of man for the Lord's sake . . . fear God, honour the King.'[215] And the subsequent prayers asked the Lord to favour 'especially thy servant CHARLES our King that under him we may be godly and quietly governed.'[216] The minister gave thanks that, though through the provocations of the people the Lord had taken away that beloved martyred king, 'yet thou wouldst not leave us as sheep without a shepherd but didst immediately invest our most gracious sovereign King Charles the second with sacred and royal authority; and by thy sacred providence did miraculously preserve him from his bloody enemies . . . to exercise that authority over us which . . . thou hadst committed unto him.'[217] The congregation praying for his long and happy reign, the morning ended with supplication that the Lord 'reconcile all our differences' under him. This official remembrance of the past, the memory of which was divided and contested, was, we shall see, an important strategy in securing support for the king in the present and future.[218] What the Lord had taken away, the Lord had restored. In leading the people in a service of atonement for the death of the father, Charles hoped he led them also to devoted obedience to the son.

Where these early official prayers for the memory of the father and the blessings of the son made Stuart monarchy an object and subject of worship, a text entitled *The King's Psalter* very much connected the person of Charles II with religious observance and religious education.[219] Despite its title, *The King's Psalter* was not by Charles II. It was, however, 'printed and published according to order with his Majesty's special approbation', and appeared, like Elizabeth's prayers, with an engraving of the king, surrounded by these lines:

First worship God, and his Command obey;
And next the King, who doth his Scepter sway:
Observe his laws, no Innovators trust
And for thy Neighbour, as thy self, be just.

The verse nicely summarizes the relations plotted in the *Psalter* between obedience to God and the king, and the practice of Christian virtues. The compilation of psalms, prayers and hymns (with antiphons), together with the Ten Commandments, and an alphabet of instruction for youth, contains prayers for each day, beginning with the letters of Charles II's name, and is scattered through with topical references and injunctions. Next to a father's advice, 'my son fear thou the Lord and the king', is an engraving of an earthly monarch; a gloss on the Fifth Commandment explains that, as well as honouring parents, 'in like manner . . . honour and obey the king . . . reverence his sacred power'.[220] A large royal arms of Charles II fills a page between prayers, and numerous scriptural passages ('curse not the king, no not in thy thought', 'keep the king's commandment and that in regard of the oath of God') enjoin obedience to a divinely appointed sovereign.[221] A prayer for the queen ('the nursing mother of our land'), the Duke of York and the king asks for the blessings of David and Solomon on the royal family.[222] In a lengthy chapter on meditation on kings, the *Psalter* quotes Scripture: 'A divine sentence is in the lips of the king'.[223] Though he may not have authored it, *The King's Psalter*, composed and sold as a successor to *The King's Primer*, advocated the king's divinity and presented the Christian life as one lived in obedience to kings.[224]

Like his father, Charles ordered fast days and services for particular occasions, and in Charles II's case, increasingly for political purposes. In 1661, the king ordered a form of prayers for the averting of dearth, and saving the realm from disease;[225] in 1665 and 1672, prayers were ordered for a blessing on the navy, as in 1665 and 1666 for naval victories.[226] In each case the text and service presented the king as the mediator between nation and God, and in each case the prescribed prayers took the opportunity to underwrite the divinity of the king and his orations. The prayers against disease and dearth, for example, presented Charles as another David to be honoured and praised unity and peace as the means to turn away God's wrath. The services of thanksgiving for victory bless the Lord for 'the abundance of Thy gospel, the honour of our sovereign . . ', and invoking God's providential favours on him, the people are led to pray: 'let all the blessings of heaven and earth be poured out upon the sacred head of thine anointed and from thence flow down even to the . . . meanest of his people in peace and plenty and prosperity'.[227] The form of Common Prayer for the day of fasting and humiliation in consideration of the Fire, set forth by royal command in October 1666, enabled Charles to give his own interpretation of the divine disfavour that it indicated, which some were suggesting was brought down by the licence of the court. Charles's service presented it rather as admonition to 'an unthankful and rebellious people' and, folding the text of his proclamation within the covers of holy writ, prayed to God for the preservation of 'thy servant Charles'.[228]

Several of the volumes of prayers issued with royal authority, like that at the time of dearth, include prayers 'for the high court of parliament under our most religious and gracious king'.[229] But in February 1674, the specific form of prayer for imploring blessing on the parliament may have represented a novel royal move in the mounting tension between crown and parliament.[230] The fast day and service in themselves represented Charles as a monarch committed to working with parliaments (at a time when some questioned it and his own foreign policy belied it). The people asked forgiveness for the sins of ingratitude against the Lord and prayed to Him 'to reconcile our differences and heal our breaches, to unite our hearts in the profession of the true religion . . . to which end we hereby beseech . . . thy blessings . . . upon the king's most excellent majesty and the high court of parliament'.[231] Prepared perhaps as the parliament was about to reassemble from recess after a frustrating stalemate, the prayers present Charles to his people as the king of union and harmony who implored God as well as his parliaments for reconciliation and settlement.

The use of fast days, services and texts of prayer to, as it were, put the royal case, or to present the king in the best light, is most evident during the crisis of the Popish Plot. As he was recalling his parliament in 1678, Charles also ordered for 13 November a fast day and a service 'to implore the mercies of almighty God in the protection of his Majesties sacred Person and in Him of all his loyal subjects, and the bringing to light . . . all secret machinations against his majesty and the whole kingdom'.[232] The language manifests Charles's attempt to recast the plot not as a consequence of his actions, as the opposition viewed it, but as a 'machination' by conspirators outside the community of the nation. Indeed, as the prefatory prayer announces, the purpose of the service was to 'knit together the hearts of all this people . . . in the defence of their king, their laws and their religion'.[233] In thinly veiled language, prayers, directed at opponents and nonconformist sects, asked God to cut off those who turned 'religion into rebellion and faith into faction' and to strengthen the king as the best preservation of true religion.[234] As the people turned to God in contrition for having disobeyed his precepts and shown unthankfulness for their deliverances, they were reminded of the greatest deliverance of their times: 'thou hast miraculously restored . . . the breath of our nostrils thine anointed servant and under his protection the solemnities of thy sacred ordinances, the establishment of our laws, and [the language moves to a different key] the enjoyment of our interests'.[235] 'Let not,' the prayer continued, 'the return of our iniquities call back thy judgements.'[236] Imploring God to protect Charles with his holy angels, the congregation also prayed God to 'blast the enterprises of all his enemies' and, in particular, to 'turn the wisdom of Achitophel to folly'.[237] The particularization, the pointing to the Earl of Shaftesbury, long before Dryden's famous poem identified the Whig leader with the biblical rebel, made the service almost a party pamphlet.[238] But the fast and service were an occasion and text in which the king, as he led his people in prayer, could effectively represent himself as the godly ruler of the chosen nation and cast his enemies into the darkness.

As the tensions over a plot mounted, and he faced ever more hostile sessions of parliament, Charles ordered another fast day the following April, 1679, 'to seek reconciliation with Almighty God, and to implore him that he would . . . defeat the counsels of the papists . . . and bestow his abundant blessings upon his sacred majesty and this present parliament'.[239] Like the prayer for a parliament, this service again demonstrated the royal wish to work with his Commons and moved to isolate the Whigs, whose nonconformist supporters would likely not have attended the parish church. The service was prefaced by a declaration of the Clerk of Parliament that Lords and Commons were convinced of a popish plot against the king, government and Protestant religion. In the text that follows, the king as Supreme Head of the Church responds to parliament's resolution. In the opening prayer, the minister led the people in thanking God that the plot had been revealed and asked Him to 'knit together the hearts of this whole nation in the defence of our king, our laws and our religion'.[240] A prayer taken out of the office for 5 November cleverly led the congregation to recall a former Stuart, an undoubted champion of the Protestant faith and patron of the Bible, who had stood against the bloody attempts of papists, as the service ended with blessings on the king and parliament.[241]

The last of the Popish Plot prayers, as we may call them, was published by royal command in December and ordered a fast day virtually on the eve of Christmas (the 22nd). The service was prepared once again to 'defeat the counsels of *our* enemies' (my italics) and pray for God's blessings on king and parliament 'and on all their consultations and endeavours'.[242] As the talk of renewed civil conflict was again in the air, we must wonder how, that Christmas, the congregation gathered to confess their sins to the Lord ('we have rebelled against him') and to ask Him to avert His anger; as they prayed for Charles II: 'clothe all his enemies with shame but upon himself *and his posterity* let the crown ever flourish'; or as they responded to the litany 'from all sedition, privy conspiracy and rebellion', 'Good Lord deliver us'.[243] Certainly the minister did not fail to point up 'the great dangers we are in at present' by divisions, and the congregation's obligation to God to pursue 'union and concord'.[244] Before the people departed, the customary prayers for 'our most religious and gracious king' and royal family (which named 'James Duke of York'), followed by prayers against the papists and for union, recalled the late 'bleeding wounds' and the need to implore God to avert 'the great dangers we are in at present'.[245] Their prayers were answered: the nation pulled back from the precipice of civil war.

To the obvious and vital question, what part these services and published texts played in restoring support to Charles II, there is no easy answer. It is even more problematic to assess the counter-factual case: how different things would or might have been had these texts not been published. What we can be certain of is that the king himself attributed importance to them as a medium of his representation and that he was at least correct in assessing that the people could be won back to loyalty. Nor should we underestimate the mantras of king, faith and law that these fast-day services made a regular national recital, or the memories of sin and regicide they invoked and the divinity of kings they preached. Where, increasingly over the 1660s and 1670s, royal speeches and declarations displayed a more secular, rational discourse of state, the very nature of the fast-day services and prayers represented monarchy – and Charles himself – as God's own script for His people to follow. Opposition to the monarch in these texts implicitly becomes one of the sins the nation confesses as its falling away from the Lord and its ingratitude at England's miraculous deliverance from confusion. If the Popish Plot prayers, following a whole series of fast days of prayer and thanks for the king and royal family, led the people to again equate resistance with sin, they would have made an invaluable contribution to the turning of the political tide that left the Whigs high and dry. As we shall see, the sacred strains of monarchical panegyrics that followed in the loyalist reaction to the Plot, echoing the language of prayer, suggest at least some recirculation of these discourses that most powerfully underwrote early modern monarchy.

Triumphant over the Whigs, Charles represented himself in more sacred garb in the last of the prayers he authorized for Sunday, 9 September 1683, a day of thanksgiving for the preservation of the king from the Rye House conspiracy, as the title page puts it, 'in due acknowledgement of God's wonderful Providence and mercy in discovering and defeating the late treasonable conspiracy against his sacred majesty's person and government'.[246] In this

service, instead of the collect for the day, both at morning and evening
prayer and in the communion service, the people were to give thanks for their
deliverance and 'unfeigned thanks and praise for the . . . wonderful deliverance
of our most gracious sovereign, his royal brother and loyal subjects of all orders'
from 'the fanatic rage and treachery of wicked and ungodly men'.[247] After the
usual collect for peace and grace and the litany, the congregation prayed again
to God for kings, 'the great instruments of thy goodness to mankind', and
thanked the Lord for 'thy many wonderful deliverances formerly vouchsafed to
thy servant, our dread sovereign, through the whole course of his life'.[248] In
particular, the people gave thanks for 'the late miracle of thy mercy whereby
thou didst rescue him *and us all* from those bloody designs'.[249] Confessing their
unworthiness of divine grace and promising no further ingratitude, the people
prayed for Charles: 'continue him a nursing father to this thy church, and thy
minister for good to all his people. And let us . . . look upon him not only as the
ordinance but also as the gift of God . . . with a religious obedience'.[250] Repeated
in communion prayers, these terms present a more sacred notion of kingship
than had been current for more than a decade. The final prayer for 'our enemies',
that we 'not . . . triumph in the disappointment of their wicked imaginations'
but pray for their conversion, only reinforced the return to prominence of the
Christ-like king: 'Oh Lord forgive them for they know not what they do'.[251]

The language of the 1680s, echoing as it does that of 1660, may tempt us to
see a wheel having turned full circle. Such would be too simplistic a judgement.
In Charles's self-representation in words, there was always a doubleness. For
all the different emphases and different circumstances and times, the king
deployed traditional discourses of divine right, elect kingship and providence,
along with new appeals to interest, a familiar style, and a vocabulary (and
metaphors) of shared authority. In words, as in so many other ways, Charles
opened himself up to his subjects more than he mystified his rule, while
never surrendering the language and symbols of the sacred. Different genres of
address – the service, the parliamentary speech, the public declaration –
enabled him to move between these different lexicons, at times simultaneously
to keep several in play. But it was his skill at deploying a variety of representations that was one of the principal political arts that enabled him not only to
survive the tensions and difficulties of his reign, but even to strengthen his
authority and develop it on the foundations of public affection.

Royal words, of course, had never been published into, nor read in, a vacuum.
Yet more than any of his predecessors, Charles II spoke and wrote in a culture
and public sphere shaped by print and a veritable Babel of texts and words. The
printing press was not a resource of only the king's friends, though some
dreamed of again making it so.[252] But in 1660, and even right on through his
reign, Charles did not want for loyal supporters ready to take up their pens to
publicize their sovereign in exalted strains. Even before he had landed on

English soil, royalist panegyrists were emerging to greet the restored monarchy at a critical moment in the restoration of the arts and letters. In traditional genres, odes and georgics, histories and political treatises, as well as newly emerging forms, such as narratives of empire and various fictions of power, writers wrote and (in a fully fledged literary market) sold texts that represented the sovereign in a variety of ways. Written by authors sometimes close to, sometimes distant from, the king and the court, not all these texts, even when intended to laud the monarch, presented him in terms that Charles II himself would have favoured. Yet they made the king, more than ever, the subject of print and publicity, an object, as well as author, of words. Because, along with royal words themselves, they presented and re-presented Charles to his subjects, lowly and elite, we must sample their own constructions and publications of royal images, some of which have remained to this day.

II

Wake dull Muse, the Sun appears[253]

In his verse 'Upon His Sacred Majesties Most Happy Return', Thomas Forde was one of many who coupled the restoration of the monarchy with the revival of poetry. As a dedicatory verse to Henry Oxinden's *Charles Triumphant* declared, poets who had been ready to abandon the muse 'and take leave of . . . Poetry' had been called back by God to proclaim the 'bless'd and halcyon times'.[254] The author of *The Restauration* thought poetry the only medium lofty enough to greet the king and prayed for the gifts of bards of the recent as well as distant past:

> Oh for the silver quill of *Quarles*
> To celebrate our Gracious CHARLES!
> . . .
> Oh for a Strain ascending quite
> 'Bove *Denham*, *Cowley* or the *Knight*!
> Oh for Muses Ninety Nine!
> Oh for a Fancy as Divine
> As *Virgil*'s, and as smooth and fit
> As *Ovid*'s . . .[255]

In the early days and weeks of Restoration, poets formerly associated with the court and royalist cause burst into print with panegyrical verses: Charles Cotton, Abraham Cowley, William Davenport and Edward Waller, to name a few. To the familiar names were added new panegyrists, most famously John Dryden, and indeed female poets like Katherine Philips, Aphra Behn and

Rachel Jevon who heralded, as well as the returning monarchy, a new age of female letters.[256]

This mixture of old and new was, I want to suggest, a feature of the vast outpouring of printed panegyrical poetry published in 1660 and 1661. Like Charles's own self-presentation in words, the poets who lauded him presented and re-presented the king in new terms of encomium as well as in the traditional metaphors of praise. There was no shortage of traditional metaphors, images and similes. In literally thousands of lines, poets revived familiar conceits that had validated monarchy: the king was the 'espoused' of what had been 'widow'd kingdoms'; a restored father; the good physician to heal the distempered realm; 'our glittering Sun' that dispelled the 'dismal clouds' and brought calm to rough seas; the spring – and here the date of Charles's birthday in May was opportune – that promised rebirth and re-creation.[257] Most of all, Charles was heralded as a divine ruler, a little god, as his grandfather had said of kings. Arthur Brett described Charles's restoration as a 're-surrection'; Rachel Jevon lauded Charles as a 'Terrestrial God, Off-spring of Heaven'.[258] Other poets who did not rise to such celestial comparisons freely compared the returning monarch to Constantine, the first great Christian emperor, or to biblical patriarchs: 'our Joshua' in the words of a volume of Oxford University encomia, the 'banish'd David' who returned in triumph in the lines of Dryden's *Astraea Redux*, as so many others.[259] In verses that seem to echo each other, poets anticipated the return of a golden age, in which a hereditary and divinely chosen king would rule in love a people who embraced him (ran into 'your princely arms', Charles Cotton put it), in Waller's verse, as the restorer of Faith, Law and Piety, Justice and Truth.[260] In *A Mixt Poem*, J. C. (John Crouch) blended several of these conceits to welcome a

> *Monarch of Hearts*, the summe of Heavens Expence,
> Heir by Succession, *King* by Providence.[261]

Perhaps evoking a famous Tudor predecessor, as well as Charles's personal circumstances, several poems depict him as 'our phoenix prince' risen from the ashes to nourish the people.[262] The restoration and the continuity of Stuart monarchy seem to be written in the very tropes of antebellum panegyric – in the old idioms and conceits of regality. But, as well as the new names of Crouch or Dryden, who had penned panegyrics for the Protectorate regime, the image of the phoenix risen from ashes drew attention to death as well as birth. And in many, perhaps most, of the poems greeting and praising Charles II, we encounter elegies and panegyrics on Charles I and, along with ubiquitous references to 'our martyr'd king', memories of rebellion, of civil war and republic. Indeed, the images and metaphors of Restoration verses – images of cloud, disease, storm, etcetera – though familiar in the representation of antebellum monarchy, performed differently in 1660, disclosing how the experience of revolutionary events still hung like a shadow over the land.

While much then of the verse, like so many of the texts, of Restoration culture sought to tie the present to the past in an unbroken chain, the experience of civil war and regicide broke through onto the page, complicating any simple representation of a return to old forms. Those who prayed in verse to the new monarch, 'Come then and bind us up', or praised him as did Brett for his recognition that not all men would or could agree, acknowledged implicitly that the world had changed, and that with it the monarchy needed to change too.[263] Those who dwelt on Charles's experience of adversity, as equipping him well for rule, as did the author of *Anglia Rediviva* and others, appear to have recognized that the capacity to tackle the 'worst' fortune might be a skill necessary in the new times.[264] This doubleness, a sense of things as they were but an apprehension that they had changed, is often to be found within the same text, even the same few lines. The welcome to Charles II from the master and scholars of Woodstock in *Votivum Carolo*, for example, deploys all the familiar tropes of the advent of spring, the calm after the storm, the light that follows darkness, in figuring restored monarchy. Here too a sacred language of 'a resurrection day', 'sacred majesty', the worship of kings as saints and gods, appears to reinscribe divine kingship.[265] When, however, the author (probably Francis Gregory) emphasizes the loyalty the nation owes to the new monarch, the language is mixed to the point of jarring:

> We owe him *Twelve yeares* duty; our *Arreares*
> Can ne'er be paid, except by *Prayers* and *Teares*
> His Principall must need be lost; pay the best
> We can, 'twill not amount to th' Interest.[266]

The discourse of credit and interest is sustained even as the poem describes the crowds gathered to witness the king's return to his capital:

> See, see what *crowds* are here! I dare to say
> Here is some *fair*, or *market* kept too day

When the figure of the king approaches, wonder is strangely mixed with unfamiliarity – 'Who's that yonder in an Ermyn gown?' – and though the verse exhorts all to bow down in homage, the memory of a very different response to majesty is brought onto the page:

> Sure, 'tis the *King*: peace, peace stand still, fall down
> I never saw such *Majesty*! I fear,
> It is *high treason* to approach thus near

Let's *worship* and *away*; fools were we, when
We thought that *Kings* and *Princes* had been *men*.[267]

Nor, despite the past tense, were such thoughts entirely eclipsed: the poem laments that those who rebelled might not yet be ready to obey. Here is monarchy divine and human, familiar and unrecognizable, unaltered but changed. While the stanzas of *Votivum Carolo* struggle with contradiction, other panegyrists seem more willing bluntly to proclaim that, far from simply becoming its old self again as some imagined, 'The old Realme of England is become a new'.[268]

In the panegyrics of 1660, indeed, new images jostle with the traditional in lauding and validating kingship.[269] The economic vocabulary of trade and commerce is only the most obvious: John Evelyn and Edmund Waller were only two of many who greeted the restoration of monarchy as the revival of commerce and 'The Cities Trade'.[270] What is just as important is a vision of the monarch as head of a commercial empire, the leader indeed of a national imperial vision and mission. Dryden in *Astraea Redux* moves swiftly from 'wealthy trade' to a new world order, which is also a new monarchical order, of a kingdom stretching from the West to East Indies, an empire that has no limits.[271] Numerous verses in 1660 describe the Restoration in the metaphorical language of empire, of the king bringing more than all the Indies;[272] and even a female poet like Katherine Philips imagined Charles's kingship as founding a new Rome, an empire to which all paid homage:

For *England* shall (rul'd and restor'd by You)
The suppliant world protect, or else subdue.[273]

Charles II was praised and presented then as, on the one hand, 'the living image of our martyr'd king', and on the other as a new monarch who would reform the realm, effect 'a reformation of times and manners', and lead it to new imperial glory.[274]

Poetry, I wish to suggest, as well as celebrating Charles's return in 1660, also refigured, re-presented and helped to reconstitute monarchy by reappropriating for kingship authoritative cultural forms. And throughout the reign, poets (not least, by any means, the king's bedchamberman and friend, the Earl of Rochester) engaged with and publicized the ambiguities of a Restoration monarchy in which the mystery of the royal body politic was, especially in Charles II's case, not always complemented by the representation of the body personal. For all the verse extolling majesty, the poetic publicization of the king's personal, sexual body (we perforce recall Rochester's memorable lines 'his sceptre and his prick are of a length') made verse central in the changing representation and perception of authority in Charles II's reign.[275] And for all Dryden's hopes that with the Restoration the names of parties might cease, poets became embroiled in the mounting political divisions of the reign and so in an increasingly contested representation of Charles in verse.[276] By the mid-1660s, the poetic representation of the monarchy had shifted. What had been, however complex, a largely spontaneous outburst of encomia at the Restoration gave way to more obviously partisan and particular validations, increasingly not only of monarchy in general but of specific royal acts.

It was, significantly, around the mid-1660s that a new poetic genre began its short life: the so-called 'Instructions to A Painter' poems. The first, by the arch-loyalist Edmund Waller, who had been banished during the 1640s for trying to secure London for the king, was entitled in full *Instructions to a Painter for the Drawing of a Picture of the State and Posture of the English Forces at Sea, Under the Command of His Royal Highness*.[277] Published at first as a broadside in 1665, a second, larger edition followed explaining that the poem celebrated the victory over the Dutch off Lowestoft in 1664.[278] Though the poem was modelled on the Italian poet Busselino's verses to the painter Pietro Libero in celebration of a Venetian naval victory, the deployment of the new genre responded very much to the English circumstances that also produced the *Gazette* and efforts to exert more control over the press. The very term 'Instructions' implies a direction of royal representation that had not before been so publicized. Though Waller's poem specifically lauded the English admiral, James, Duke of York, the references to 'his brother's glory' abound in the poem, which imagines the 'glad English' raising healths to their leader, as they had so zealously in 1660, and England's imperial destiny advanced by royal triumph over its rivals. That Waller's was not the only perception of the victory or state of England in 1665 is implicitly recognized in the poet's second version. This edition, published in 1666 by Henry Herringman who had published most of the Restoration panegyrics, celebrates the naval victory of 3 June 1665. But though reprinting the earlier verses, the poem is both much longer and of a very different register. In Waller's second poem, the extravagant praise of the Duke of York makes room too for the 'British Court' and its king, Charles. In these lines, the king's mistresses, 'the Beauties' of his court, embolden martial valour; and after the heat of battle, the poet asks the painter:

> Then Draw the Parliament, the Nobles met,
> And our Great Monarch, High above Them all,
> Like young *Augustus* let His image be
> Triumphing for that Victory at Sea
> Where *Aegypt's* Queen and Eastern Kings o'erthrown
> Make the possession of the World His Own.[279]

Here the promise of Augustan imperialism that had welcomed Charles in 1660 is revisited to re-present him, against the tide of criticism, as having fulfilled that destiny. Figuring a House of Commons 'pouring out treasure' to supply the glorious king, Waller ends with an address to Charles himself that, as well as ranking him among the gods, attributes to him the victory:

> Small were the worth of Valour, and of Force,
> If your High Wisdom Govern'd not their Course;
> You as the Soul, as the First Mover You
> Vigour and Life on every Part bestow.[280]

By 'Your Great Providence' as well as God's, Waller claims, the English were triumphant.

If Waller had intended to found a sub-genre of verse to buttress the monarch at a time of mounting criticism, his hopes were dashed. In the hands of the brilliant Andrew Marvell and, perhaps even more disturbingly for the government the formerly loyal John Denham, the *Instructions to a Painter* were re-deployed by critics of royal foreign policy, the court and the king, in sharp satires that excoriated licentiousness and corruption.[281] Waller himself was involved in the impeachment of the Earl of Clarendon and published no subsequent panegyrics on the king.[282] As England was beset by plague, fire, the humiliating defeat by the Dutch and mounting political conflict, it seemed that the panegyrists lost their voice. Cowley died in 1667, and with Denham's death in 1669 and Waller's retirement from public poetry, a trio of loyal supporters of Restoration had passed; and in Marvell and Milton (as we shall see) it was the opposition that wielded the sharpest poetic pens.

Poetry, however, was never the preserve of any party; and new poets emerged to represent the royal case, increasingly as the monarchy veered towards crisis. R.W.'s – Robert Wild's – *Panegyrique* addressed to the king 'on his most or his most auspicious meeting his two houses of parliament' was published in 1673 evidently with royal support and with a large royal arms on the title page and, together with Charles's speech to the houses, at a difficult time (as we have seen) in his relations with them.[283] The poem endeavours to render Charles's own words a poetry that 'ravisht' the nation with 'joy and wonder', and presents the royal voice as that which might reconcile the nation and lead it to greatness:

> Secure us from *Our selves*, and from the foe,
> Make us *Unite*, and make us *Conquer* too
> Those *Fiercer Factions* which Men's *Souls* did move
> Are by your Favour Reconcil'd in love.[284]

Recalling the English to the 'confusion' and 'strange madness' that Charles's restoration had reordered and cured, Wild proceeds to praise of a king who has raised the nation's honour abroad while ruling 'by sweet . . . politicks' (that is, gentle regimen) at home. Under 'the Greatest Sovereign', the poem argues, Britain has grasped commercial supremacy and 'a power great as old *Rome*'.[285]

In these lines, England is figured as a promised land, blessed with the fruits of silks and spices brought home by the king's ships. Answering critics of the government at home, the poem reminds them that there is 'no freedom like the rule of Pious Kings' and conjures Charles in his parliament in which the '*Illustrious body*' met their '*Dearest Soveraign*' with 'a loving *Awe*'.[286] 'Ah,' the poet sighs, endorsing the royal wishes that experience did not bear out:

> . . . blessed fruits! such happy *Union* brings
> *The Loyalist Subjects with the best of Kings*.[287]

He sees purses opened to support England's wars. Warning any who might rise to disrupt this idyll, Wild pronounces:

> Cursed be he, those *Sacred Bonds* that parts,
> *Kings greatest Treasures, are their Subjects Hearts*.[288]

With king, parliament and subjects united in love, W. R. predicts for Charles triumph ('Dazzling Majesty') and adulation, 'our *King's Honour*, and our *Countries good*'.

Signing his poem 'Iter Boreale', the author disclosed his identity – as Robert Wild – and recalled readers to a poem he had written on the king's birthday in praise of George Monck who had set the Restoration in train.[289] Wild, a 'loyal' nonconformist who praised Charles's 1672 Declaration for Liberty of Conscience, had his own reasons to hope that the king might find support from loyal MPs and people.[290] He died in 1679 in time to witness how forlorn those hopes were, but too soon to contribute to the encomia which again proliferated in Charles's last years.

As the discovery of the Popish Plot plunged the crown as well as the succession into crisis, poets, deceased as well as living, were summoned to aid the monarch and to buttress in verse the prerogatives of the king. In another salvo in the Painter series, an anonymous *Second Advice to the Painter* stridently countered criticism of the regime.[291] Damning the pope as a satanic figure, the *Second Advice* berated subjects who might use the pretence of a popish plot as a means to oppose the king:

> Had he been cruel or Tirranick grown,
> You had more reason to usurp his Throne;
> But to a Gratious and obliging Prince,
> 'Tis past all hopes of pardon or defence.[292]

Addressing the king, the poet hoped that with the Jesuits' plot revealed, 'The Cloud's blown over', and that

> May still your sacred Majesty give Law
> To all your Kingdoms, keeping them in aw,
> May your bright Crown, as beauteous rays disperse,
> As any Monarchs of the Universe.[293]

In 1679, however, neither the clouds nor 'mists' had blown away and, helpfully, female poets emerged to champion the crown. A broadside poem presented to 'his sacred majesty' on the discovery of the plot, evidently 'written by a lady of quality', greeted a prince who was 'the glory of Monarchical Powers' and who, caring more for his people's than his own safety, defied conspirators.[294] The author made the duty of subjects clear – 'Burst every *Heart* that dares but *Think* him ill' – and the poem imagines a people all ready to lay down their own lives for the king's, to express their love.[295]

In such poems, the threat to Charles's life exposed in the Plot is deployed to strengthen loyalty to the king as the focus of a glorious nation. Increasingly as the tensions heightened, loyal poets both conjured the spectre of renewed civil war and wrote to re-clothe monarchy in sacred raiment. *A Worthy Panegyric upon Monarchy* for 'information of the miserably misled Commonwealthsmen' traced regal sovereignty back to Adam and into Nature:

> The *Rational Soul* performs a *Princes* Part
> *She* rules the Body by *Monarchick* Art.[296]

There could be no other polity for a Britain that had, in emulation of heaven, been a regality since the beginning of time; and the poet warned the people that 'where *All* or *Many* bear the *Sway*/Such *Order*, to *Confusion* leads the way'. 'Kings', a panegyric to Charles published in 1681 declared simply in terms that had been increasingly contested, 'are like Gods'; and faith, it added, commanded obedience.[297] On Charles's birthday, a poetic essay on *The Glory of the English Nation* related his life story, his flight from puritans and the miracle of his second birth in the coronation, to reassure the people of the steadfastness of his faith and to remind them of their joy after the miseries the nation had suffered during the civil war. 'What hath bewitched you now ...?', the essay asked Londoners, to turn you 'from loyal subjects to ... Mutineers?' 'Is not the King the same God that day sent?' Did not the nation prosper in peace, the subjects enjoying their liberties? 'Summon your Reason', the people were urged, 'and your loyalty', as the verse closed with songs of praise of the king.[298]

In 1681, as a parliament dissolved in London gave way to another broken assembly in Oxford, loyalist poets fought against a tide of Whig satire and polemic to condemn resistance, to re-sacralize royal authority and to support hereditary succession.[299] *An Heroic Poem* branded the oppositionists as men who would again 'enslave' the nation; while the ballad *The Present State of England*, seeing in the Plot a ruse to revive the rule of the saints, urged 'let True Hearts Sing Long Live Charles our King/The Church, and the State to Cherish'.[300] As always, the precise role of these poetic representations of Charles's kingship in countering opposition and winning the people's loyalty is difficult to calculate. Yet the outpouring of these verses from 1678–9, the increasing deployment of the one-page verse broadside, the manipulation of memory (both of civil war and Restoration) all evidence at least the writers' own beliefs in the importance of their addresses to audiences, popular as well as elite. And one, the author of perhaps the most devastating piece of propaganda for the king in any medium, never doubted the power of verse. In the epistle to the reader that prefaces *Absalom and Achitophel*, Dryden acknowledged that he would never persuade the committed party men, the Whigs. 'Yet,' he proclaimed, 'if a poem have a genius, it will force its own reception in the world. For there's a sweetness in good verse, which tickles even while it hurts.'[301] Posing (as audaciously as improbably) as one of the moderates, Dryden ruthlessly exposed and brilliantly undermined the tactics of the Whigs and the character of their leader, Shaftesbury. As one by one the leaders of the faction are demolished in an epithet or line, the poem closes with the voice of King David, which in part reproduces the speech of Charles to the Oxford Parliament of March that year. As the voice of the laureate reproduces the words of the king, so the power of poetry helped to reinstate the authority of monarchy.

As the year came to its close, although the situation remained uncertain, it was poets who discerned the turn of the political weathercock, and (perhaps not unreasonably) claimed for themselves some part in the rising star of monarchy.[302] The author of *The Recovery*, either prescient or hopeful, discerned that

> Already with fresh Beames, the crown does shine
> Power sacred grows, and Majesty divine.[303]

And the author of *The Poets Address to His Most Sacred Majesty* assured Charles that 'Though scribbling factions are so saucy grown/To dart *Curst Libels* at your Sacred Throne', 'Yet mighty SIR the *Poets* are your own'.[304] As the king's victory became apparent, scores of verses were published celebrating the royal triumph, lauding the principle of hereditary succession, and praising James, Duke of York, the popular 'Jemmy'.[305] As congratulatory verses presented the people 'Drinking prosperity to the royal line', poets began to excoriate the Whigs who had, they now claimed, misled a loyal people almost into renewed civil war.[306] A paean on the Duke of York's *Entertainment in the City* presents London re-emerging to clear understanding from dark ignorance:

Loyalty so long banish'd from this Place,
Returns with greater Splendor, sweeter Grace
The late Dark Clouds of Ignorance are gone,
And faction that so spur'd the Rabble on.[307]

In the poetic process of glossing over the opposition to Charles, the Whigs were marginalized as a faction that had schemed to rupture the natural bond of love between king and people. Verses and mock elegies on the deaths of the Earl of Essex and Algernon Sidney urged readers to learn by their fate the lessons of the evils of rebellion and the divinity of kings.[308] John Dryden's once again was the most powerful voice. In *The Medal: A Satire against Sedition*, as well as a devastating personal assault on Shaftesbury, the laureate branded all the Whigs as deceivers who, under the name of loyal criticism, were the heirs of George Buchanan and Milton who promoted only sedition and republicanism. Vaunting the force of his own verse, Dryden taunted his opponents whom 'God hath not bless'd . . . with the talent of Rhiming.'[309] As a dedicatory poem rightly observed, Dryden had fought, in the king's name, 'the threatening Hydra-faction of the Age', and had emerged as the monarch of wit, like the 'poets king' triumphant over detractors.[310] Yet, though the best known, Dryden's was only one of the king's vatic champions, many of whom in the wake of the defeat of the Whigs extolled monarchy to ever greater heights. Where Dryden defended the balance of the English constitution and the moderate sway of monarchy ('Our Temp'rate Isle will no extremes sustain'), many others stressed 'the high Prerogative of Majesty' and heaven's 'vicegerent' protected by God, the 'celestial prince, descended from above'.[311] *A Choice Collection of 86 Loyal Poems* written during the two plots and gathered by Nathaniel Thompson gives some idea of the range and reach of the poetry supporting the royal cause and its role in the desperate battle for public opinion during the years of crisis.[312] From Pindaric odes and traditional litanies, the popular renditions of *Absalom and Achitophel* and similar cantos against the Duke of Monmouth and Whig leaders, the eighty-six verses bear out the editor's and the poets' own claims for the role of verse in sustaining Charles II's prerogative and throne. What the dedicatory verses to *The Medal* claimed for the laureate – the power of persuading men to return to loyalty – was the skill, the triumph, too, of many, albeit lesser pens.[313] As the editor of the loyal poems and of *A Choice Collection of 180 Loyal Songs* argued in the last year of Charles II's reign, 'Amongst the several means that have been of late years to reduce the deluded multitude to their just allegiance', these poems, ballads and songs had 'not been of the least influence. . . . While the . . . heads of the factions were blowing up sedition in every corner of the country, these flying choristers were asserting the rights of monarchy and proclaiming loyalty in every street.'[314] Thompson had no doubt of their effectiveness: 'The misinformed rabble began to listen; they began to hear to Truth in a SONG, in time found their errors, and were charmed into obedience. Those that despise the reverend prelates in the pulpit and the grave judge on the Bench ... will yet lend an itching ear to a loyal song and often become a convert by it when all other means prove ineffectual'.[315] Without the poet and the chorister, Thompson felt sure, the people would not have been brought to obedience or the monarchy restored to its glory. Though his emphasis on the poet's role in presenting and representing monarchy as the best government and Charles as a good king is not to be questioned, we must grant a higher importance than does Thompson to the representation of the monarchy in prose, even the prose of judges and divines.

III

In 1660 and the early years of Restoration, the panegyrical prose works that poured from the press in praise of monarchy and Charles sounded with lyrical strains as they competed with each other to demonstrate the nation's loyalty and to silence opposition and dissent. Where John Evelyn wrote in the manner of masque of 'dismal clouds' dispersed by a king on whose arrival 'the storm universally ceased', the sick rose from their beds, and women in labour delivered without pain, the chronicler James Heath wrote of the 'stunning and amazing ravishment' of the Restoration which 'no fable' could hope to capture.[316] Walter Charleton felt similarly the limitations of words: his significantly titled *Imperfect Portraiture of His Sacred Majesty*, though it heaped praise over pages on Charles II's humour and humanity, charity and virtue, wit and judgement, yet concluded that 'silence and admiration' were the most appropriate acts of homage.[317] In all their elevated rhetoric, treatises like these quite literally presented the new king to a people most of whom, given his absence since boyhood, knew quite little of him. Charleton described the king's 'delicate features' and 'dignity of presence', as well as his genial disposition and mildness, his piety and devotion to the law which, 'like Jupiter the Preserver', brought remedy to the nation's distemper.[318] And while Evelyn emphasized rather his intellectual passions and pursuits, his interests in sculpture, music, buildings, gardens and science, the author of *Ostenta Carolina* presented Charles as a Josiah to reform false doctrine and relieve oppression.[319] As another panegyric presenting the king put it: 'hic dei dignitus est' – here is the dignity of a God.[320]

Presentation and praise of the new monarch so dominate the literature of Restoration that these many texts at first reading seem to blend into one discourse of encomium and celebration.[321] Such an impression itself testifies to the important ideological task performed by these works in drowning the voices of discontent or dissent, but it is not the whole story. For, even from the moment of the Restoration, and still more as the years passed, writers loyal to monarchy recognized the need to argue the case for royal government and prerogative and for the policies and virtues of Charles II. In historical and political treatises and sermons, but also in heraldic and courtly books, in writings on travel and empire, in varieties of translations, fictions and novels, the literary culture of late seventeenth-century England argued for – and had to argue for – monarchy against the voices of republican apologists and political malcontents. In representing the case for the king and the monarchy, as well as in representing Charles himself (albeit often without his direct command or patronage), prose writers, no less than poets, validated and revalidated a monarchy the natural acceptance of which after 1649 could never be assumed.

Whatever the need to present Charles, as a new king, to his subjects, it was as important, if not more so, to announce him as his father's son, as a Stuart and as one of a long line of kings stretching back into time beyond memory. Like so many texts of Restoration culture, histories both chronicled the civil war and sought to erase it as an insignificant moment in the seamless continuity of the English past.[322] Evidently even before he knew of the Restoration, Richard Baker's *Chronicle of the Kings of England From the Time of the Romans . . . to King James* established the monarchy and the Stuarts as part of the movements and story of the nation. The 1660 edition carried an engraved frontispiece of Charles I, crowned and bearing a sceptre, between the figures of Roman and Saxon rulers, with a legend 'inter reges ut lillium inter flores' – 'among kings as the lily among flowers' (the lily was a symbol of purity, perfection and majesty) – and with the major cities of England, and of its regal history, surrounding him.[323] Baker's chronicle was published with a 'Continuation' to 1658 which is largely devoted to the transactions of Charles, king of Scotland, and (it is implied) to whom the whole volume was also dedicated.[324] Though the work was clearly commenced before even the regicide, publication in 1660 and the 'continuation' that followed the account of Charles I's reign and death very much placed Charles II in the long line of British kings. Written as well as published in more secure times, Edward Leigh's *Choice Observations of All the Kings of England from the Saxons*, dedicated to Charles, reminded him (and readers) that since Cadwallader, the last king of the Britains, he was the first born Prince of Great Britain. Presenting Charles II as a fit parallel with and heir to Queen Elizabeth, Leigh also praised Charles I and condemned the regicide and the doctrine of regal accountability as abominable and Jesuitical.[325] The Welsh chronicler Percy Enderbie deployed history to extol as well as to entrench the new king. Dedicating his *Cambria Triumphans*, a history of Britain with 'the succession of their kings and princes', to Charles, Enderbie dismissed as 'brain sick' any who might 'question or dispute the antiquity of kings and monarchical government'.[326] For, he assured his sovereign as well as readers, Scripture designated kings as gods and 'natural reason . . . first ordained them on earth by an unavoidable imitation of their creator's providence'.[327] Greeting the new monarch who had arisen like 'a morning sun', Enderbie promised that his lengthy tome would demonstrate how Great Britain's government was 'ever princely', indeed how Charles himself was descended from Cadell, the prince of South Wales who was crowned in 876. Reviving the long-questioned legend of Brutus's foundation of Britain, Enderbie traced monarchy back to the time of the prophet Samuel, over a thousand years before Christ.

So anxious were royalist writers to re-place and secure the restored monarchy in the continuity of history that some even read the very ancient monuments of Britain as arguments for kingship. Walter Charleton's *Chorea Gigantum*, a study of Stonehenge, which Charles had visited after his flight from the battle of Worcester, posited, after reviving various theories about the origins and purpose of the site, that it had been erected by the Danes as a royal court.[328] The import of Charleton's identification of the 'most famous antiquity' with the crown, and with Charles II specifically, was expressed in the author's own use of the term 'restoration' for both the stones and monarchy, and in the brilliant prefatory verses that lauded the new interpretation. Sir Robert Howard, who was to hold several government offices as a loyal supporter of the king, observed that Charleton's discovery that Stonehenge was not a place 'where gods were worship'd, but where kings were crown'd' underlined the 'great respects' due to a monarchy with which the realm was again 'so blest'.[329] Howard's brother-in-law, John Dryden, drew out the implications explicitly:

STONE-HENG, once thought a Temple, You have found
A *Throne*, where Kings, our Earthly Gods, were Crown'd
Where by their wondring Subjects they were seen,
Chose by their Stature, and their Princely meen.
Our *Soveraign* here above the rest might stand;
And here be chose again to rule the Land.[330]

In paying the visit that had prompted Charleton's study, Charles had restored the true meaning of Stonehenge; and in turn, in *Chorea Gigantum*, Charles's monarchy was not only traced back to Danish times but written onto the very stones and the landscape.

Histories remained of vital importance for the representation of Charles II's monarchy as the nervous euphoria over Restoration gave way to a much more divisive politics and divided political culture. Indeed, as a few years passed, the story of Charles's exile and restoration themselves became part of the long narrative of the English story, the 1665 edition of Baker's chronicle describing 'the wonderful restoration of his Majesty' as 'one of the most extraordinary actions that has ever been mentioned in story'.[331] As is often the case, histories were also where Restoration society explored its own identity and culture, and the nature of the polity. The anonymous *First Part of the History of England* extended only to the Roman conquest, but the long introduction rehearsed a very Hobbesian analysis of human nature and resounded with debates about kingship that were again beginning to resurface.[332] Though the discussion of monarchy was measured (the author considered that the voice of the people in parliament might better declare that law of reason than one man and argued that absolute government was good for neither prince nor people), the praise of hereditary monarchy, the need to supply kings and trust them, are strongly argued.[333] With a realism that began to characterize Restoration political discourse, the author freely described kings as 'but men, and may have their feelings'; but Charles II he described as a monarch of 'excellent endowments' who had led the realm to victory and would lead it to still greater power with the interests of the king and people, as Charles himself had proclaimed, 'inseparably entwined'.[334] The first part of the *History* looked forward to another age of greatness under a restored monarchy, the best government.[335]

Writers of history came forward as invaluable spokesmen for the crown while hopes gave way in the 1670s to suspicions of Charles and opposition to his policies of toleration and proximity to France. In 1675, for example, an ancestor of a famous twentieth-century historian, Winston Churchill, published his significantly titled *Divi Britannici . . . A Remark Upon the Lives of All the Kings of this Isle* to 1660. Bearing a title page image of Britannia and Neptune, with a tag from Horace – 'Divus habitatus Augustus adiectis Britannis imperio', the volume was dedicated to England's Augustus, as Charles had often been described.[336] Reminding Charles, and readers, of the times of civil war from which the realm was rescued by his miraculous deliverance, Churchill argued the gratitude that all owed Britain's second Augustus.[337] To further that end, his history presented the English monarchy as 'ancienter than the records of any time', its kings 'absolute princes' and as Christian emperors of a glorious realm.[338] To those MPs who had begun to act otherwise, Churchill's history maintained that parliaments had no authority to do anything without the king who himself could not be restrained.[339] The same year saw the republication of the work of a staunch supporter of Charles I, Peter Heylyn's *A Help to English History*, now continued 'to the present year'.[340] The general preface made the *Help*'s broader purpose clear: 'to satisfy the minds of those . . . that either are the enemies of regal or episcopal power, for whereas some conceive that kings were instituted by the people . . . these following catalogues will make it evident . . . that in this country there was never any other government than that of kings'.[341] On the pages of the updated Heylyn (reissued again in 1680), Charles II, 'miraculously restored' son to the second British king 'most impiously murdered', joins the races of Saxon, Danish, Norman and later kings, as the '65 monarch of the English and 46 king of England in descent from Egbert'.[342] *A Help to English History* in 1675 was also a help to English monarchy and to Charles II himself.

If histories such as Heath's *Chronicle*, republished in 1676, kept the memories of civil war very much alive, it was the events of the later 1670s that, in threatening a repetition of conflict, embroiled histories more deeply in the paper wars of charge and counter-charge. As civil conflict loomed, supporters of Charles II endeavoured to claim history for the king's cause – so as to make the past underwrite royal policy and undermine the critics of the crown. At times, the project was not obvious. The 1677 translator of Cornelius Nepos's *History of the Life and Death of Pomponius Atticus* seems to dissuade readers from any application of the lessons 'to any kingdom or state on this side Rome'.[343] But his story of how Rome descended from faction to civil war clearly sounded a warning, while the description of its 'perfect growth' to imperial government under Augustus seems a thinly veiled message.[344] Like Augustus, only Charles had secured the realm from 'ruin by civil dissentions' and only allegiance to him dispelled the rumoured threat of faction.[345] (It may be too that *The Life of Atticus* carried implicit advice to Charles to avoid engaging with any party, and to remain 'constant to his principles'.)[346]

A message that was oblique and allusive in the *Life of Atticus* could hardly have been more explicit than in the herald Francis Sandford's *Genealogical History of the Kings of England . . . from the Conquest, anno 1066 to the Year 1677*, in which it was published. Sandford's weighty folio, issued with royal approbation, came close to being an official history. In his dedication to Charles, Sandford explained his purpose in gathering and reproducing the coins, seals, monuments and arms, along with the histories, of English monarchs: addressing the king and 'the ocean into which all those mighty springs of royalty have, through the streams of so many several generations, discharged themselves', Sandford described the 'desired effects' of his labours as 'the convincing the people of the reasonableness of their obedience'.[347] He continued:

> For though kings ought to be honoured as the lively images of the divinity and God's vicegerents upon earth, yet it must needs be acknowledged that when their faith is strengthened by a descent from so many royal progenitors . . . and the blood of all these united in one person or family, to make their right indisputable, loyalty redoubles . . .'[348]

To any who doubted the sheer weight of genealogy, Sandford presented the Stuarts as a family blessed by God's providence and approval, never more powerfully manifested than in Charles II's own case. Only 'the most perverse of mankind' would not yield 'that to be right which heaven and earth proclaim to be so'.[349] As his massive, lavishly illustrated, seven-book history reached its denouement in the reign of Charles II, at the time when exclusionists were endeavouring to deprive the Duke of York of the succession and to reduce the king's authority, Sandford presented his monarch not only as the embodiment of history but also as the living monument to God's divine plan. As he closed, he warned the king's enemies, 'the Lord of Hosts who hath delivered him from the paws of the lion and the bear will also deliver him out of the hands of the Philistine'.[350]

As over the ensuing years the crisis of the Popish Plot re-opened questions about the succession, the extent of sovereign authority, the privileges of parliament, and the liberties and properties of the people, histories were ubiquitously deployed in the representation and counter-representation of the monarchy and the king. The period 1678–83 gave us not just the first truly party histories, but those heavily polemical collections of documents that still shape interpretations of the English past: John Rushworth's *Historical Collections* and John Nalson's *Impartial Collection*.[351] During this crisis period, histories from the age of Adam to near contemporary times, learned folios and more popular octavos, were part of the battle for power, and in some cases for survival. It was not the least of his good fortunes that in that contest to control history, Charles II was well represented and well served. In the thick of the fray, the 1679 edition of Baker's *Chronicles* continued its narrative of English monarchical descent from Egbert to 1662, and was published with a large oval engraving of Charles II opposite the engraved title page.[352] The title and form of *The Plain Englishman's Historian*, published the same year, were clearly aimed at a broader audience, readier to read romances than histories, whom the author sought to reach in his 'landskip'.[353] To these ordinary people, to whom the king was also appealing, H. C. described the purpose of his history that 'by recording the disastrous ends of rebellion, treachery, oppression' it might 'plant in us a just abhorrence . . . of such odious practices'. Moving swiftly to 'this pious prince' Charles I whom 'factious spirits' had destroyed, he arrived at Charles II, 'and with him happiness and order to these . . . kingdoms'.[354] H. C. concluded his history with 'hearty prayers that God would long preserve the monarchy of Great Britain [and] protect the person of our gracious sovereign . . . in spite of all public enemies or private confederacies whatsoever'.[355]

The next year, while the posthumous publication of the royalist Robert Filmer's *Patriarcha* argued an Adamic origin of kingship and divine right absolutism, new histories ancient and modern were published to support the monarchy and hereditary succession.[356] An extract taken from Lucius Annaeus Florus's *Epitome of Roman History* (Florus was also published in Latin the same year) made it plain, the editor 'Roger Trusty' maintained, 'that the liberty of the flourishing commonweal of the Romans destroyed all property and its own government turned to levelling, discord and diffusion'.[357] Where popular liberty and aristocratic faction brought on early ruin, Augustus emerged to bring justice and peace with imperial sway – 'which is a note to me', Trusty drew out the implied attack on the Whigs, 'that the absolute government of many interests or rulers in an aristocracy is a greater tyranny and oppression than single persons commonly are'.[358] Having concluded from Roman history that only hereditary crowns secured settlement, Trusty wished that 'we may all agree to strengthen our old fabric, since we may be knocked upon the head in the pulling it down'.[359] Moving to more recent times, Trusty hoped that the English Commonwealth which had destroyed liberty and property would teach all to stand by the hereditary principle and the king. Others took the argument for hereditary succession forward from Rome to the English medieval past.

In his *Brief Essay on The Long Reign of King Henry III*, Timothy Yalden of Gray's Inn reprised Sir Robert Cotton's old history to demonstrate that, at a time when 'every moment seems to threaten inevitable miseries', it was 'the interest as well as duty of every subject to pay an entire obedience to the government . . . and that without murmuring or grumbling'.[360] Rising to tyrannical strains, Yalden affirmed 'The king in his turn is like the Sun in the firmament' and called upon his countrymen to display loyalty.[361]

In *The White Rose, or, A Word for the House of York, Vindicating the Right of Succession*, W. B. argued passionately for succession and divine right kingship: 'A king,' he reasserted, 'is the animate image of God . . .'; 'surely none but the same superintendent power (by which kings reign) ought or can dispossess or disinvest princes'.[362] As well as ancient and medieval histories, accounts of the civil war and of the birth and early life of Charles II rammed the royalist case home with more recent examples. *The Northern Star*, the third edition of *Boscobel*, and a new account of 'His Majesty's Happy Restoration', all published in 1680, made Charles's personal story part of a history of God's providence, as well as of a continuous English past.[363] In the year that Charles took the risk of dissolving two parliaments in order to sustain the hereditary principles, perhaps his most powerful historical advocate was appropriately the Physician in Ordinary to the king and Keeper of Records in the Tower, the loyalist Robert Brady whose later *Complete History of England* was to do such devastating damage to the Whig view of the past.[364] In his brilliant tract on the succession, turning against the Whigs the charge that questioning hereditary succession was popish and Jesuitical (he recalled Parsons' 1594 tract), Brady reviewed English history from Saxon times to demonstrate that nothing could be 'clearer than that the succession to the crown of England was always thought, judged, had, taken and reported to be from nextness of blood'.[365] Lineal succession was English law and Brady reminded readers, positing Charles as the champion of the law, 'nolumus leges angliae mutare' ('we do not want the laws to be changed').[366] Edward Cooke made the same point differently and graphically: his history of the succession ended with the 'wonderful deliverance' of Charles and an elaborate genealogical tree with James next to his brother as the only male successor to the crown.[367]

Given the Whigs' appeal to right and religion, the force of those loyalist histories presenting Charles as the defender of church and law should not be underestimated. As Brady (who dwelt on the case of Queen Mary) intuited, the English people were not easily led to break hereditary succession, especially when they were reminded of the dire consequences of doing so. Loyalist historians, then, presenting Charles as the champion of traditional courses, as embodying continuity, helped secure his throne. Others helped to make Charles's a triumph not just for monarchy but for Stuart dynasty. Drawing together in his *Memoirs of the Family of the Stuarts*, 'the remarkable providence of God towards them', the editor of the papers of John Watson followed the 'signal preservations' of Stuart kings, 'all of them so good, so virtuous and wise', to prove not just the folly but 'the impiety of all attempts against a throne of divine establishment attested by so many miraculous deliverances'.[368] 'Grant,' the preface prayed, 'that there may never want one of that family to set upon his throne so long as the sun and moon endure'.[369] In the wake of the king's triumph, loyalist historians did not neglect to turn on the Whigs and to write into history the lessons that the Popish Plot had taught the nation. The translator of Jean Baptiste de Rocoles's *The History of Infamous Imposters* used his preface for a blistering assault on Shaftesbury – a deceiver who, having enjoyed royal favour, had endeavoured to stir the people against the crown by groundless fears and specious pretences.[370] Debasing the Whig leader to the ranks of sodomites, forgers and tricksters, and predicting his story would soon appear a Rabelaisian farce, the author sought to write him out of memory. And finally, as one after another of those Whig leaders was led to the executioner's block, an historical account of rebellions in England from Edward the Confessor to contemporary times drew the appropriate lesson from their fate and extolled royal authority. Suggesting even that no societies or clubs should be tolerated unless licensed by the government, *The Rebels Doom* deployed the extravagant language that had welcomed Charles in 1660: 'the majesty of lawful authority scatters the threatening tempests . . . as the sun consumes the gloomy fogs of winter'.[371]

Histories had, since antiquity and never more so than in the Renaissance, been political discourses and, in famous cases such as Camden's *Annals* of Elizabeth, major texts of royal representation.[372] Though political conflict in early and mid seventeenth-century England had sharply polarized arguments from the past as precedents in political disputes, histories remained vital in representing and validating, as well as (as we shall see) in contesting, authority. The civil war, however, had given rise to less historicized, sometimes anti-historical, discourses of authority and state. Though there had always been political argument, Thomas Hobbes – whose 1668 *Behemoth*, a history of the civil wars, was published in 1681 – has been, understandably, described as the first political philosopher in England. The English Revolution prompted, indeed necessitated, discussion from first principles of the nature of obedience and loyalty, the reach of authority, the liberties and rights of subjects; and neither such questions, nor the texts that debated them, came to an end with the cessation of conflict. Whilst most, including Charles himself, preferred in 1660 to revive shared languages of history and law and eschew (especially radical) theoretical reflections, the regicide and revolution had rendered monarchy itself an institution that required theoretical argument. Even as the sun shone down on Charles's coronation day, the shadow of Hobbes – and a rationalist theoretical discourse of politics – fell over Restoration. And as political disputes again excited fundamental questions, the monarchy, and Charles II, depended upon advocates who supported the crown in treatises of politics and discourses of state.

Though his *The Dignity of Kingship Asserted* was published in 1660, Gilbert Sheldon's treatise, written just before the Restoration, acknowledged the need to engage with a whole genre of writing that had questioned monarchy.[373] Contesting specifically Milton's *Ready and Easie Way to Establish a Free Common-wealth*, and John Harrington's *Oceana*, Sheldon admitted that 'the poison of such books . . . creeps far' and that they were 'dangerously insnaring'.[374] Although he endeavoured to respond by traditional appeal to history and Scripture ('the glory of Israel was never complete but under kingly government'), Sheldon also reviewed the apologia for commonwealths and argued, along with other royalists, that neither the Dutch state nor Venetian differed much from monarchy, which all Europe evidently regarded as the best polity.[375] He had in his dedication to Charles assured him that 'your majesty nor your royal father neither of you need vindication', yet it was vindication that Sheldon had delivered as a necessary step to re-establishing the throne.[376]

In the early years of Restoration it may be significant that several treatises defending monarchy were republications of earlier works written before revolution: Richard Mocket's *God and the King*, a defence of monarchy and allegiance, originally published in 1615, was reissued in 1663 by the royal command, while 1662 saw the republication of Bishop Griffith Williams's *Jura Majestatis, the Right of Kings both in Church and State*, first published in (royalist) Oxford in 1644.[377] Both were, as their titles imply, theological as much as political treatises on kingship written before divine right theory had confronted the executioner's axe.

Within a few years, arguments for monarchy were made in rather different forms and genres. In his discussion of kingship in his 1669 *The Present State of England*, the writer Edward Chamberlayne, albeit he claimed the divinity of monarchy, and the miracle of Charles II's in particular, freely deployed the language of 'civil policy' and 'prudence' and argued for the benefit of British monarchy to the industry and wealth, as much as liberty, of the subject.[378] Chamberlayne knew that the Restoration world was not that of antebellum

England – 'no man . . . can reasonably hope to see . . . the like blessed days again'; and he knew that even a 'great monarchy' was changed from the one 'before the late unparalleled rebellion', such that in *The Present State of England* he had both to revalidate as well as describe it.[379]

For some time, to some extent throughout the reign, both traditional arguments and more pragmatic rationalizations of kingship appeared along-side each other: 1671, for example, saw the publication of Fabian Philipps's *Regale Necessarium*, which upheld the royal prerogative from precedent and 'the principle of nature', and (perhaps less surprisingly in the republican) Slingsby Bethel's *The Present Interest of England Stated*, in which the 'mysteri-ousness' of government being put aside, the monarchy – and Charles II – were praised principally for their advancement of trade.[380] But it is significant that even Phillips, whom we shall encounter again as an acute analyst of his age, feared that recent events had 'brought forth a sort of . . . men whose humours . . . makes them unwilling to submit to laws and . . . government, unless their understanding . . . may be convinced and satisfied with the reason thereof'.[381] The revolution in thinking and writing about government heralded by Hobbes presented a fundamental challenge to the traditional arguments for the king. Revealingly, as religious and political tensions revived criticism of the crown, royalist apologists took Hobbesian views head on.[382] In his *The Creed of Mr. Hobbes Examined*, published in 1670 and 1671, the future archbishop Thomas Tenison, seeing that Hobbes's teachings were 'injurious to the right of his present majesty' as well as the church, set up a fictional dialogue in which a divine countered the philosopher with the 'kingly power of Christ' and the divine authority of the king.[383] In 1673, one J. Shafte published *The Great Law of Nature or Self-preservation Examined, Asserted and Vindicated from Mr. Hobbes His Abuses*. Shafte acknowledged two important facts: that Hobbes had taken away the moral basis of government, and that he was 'well approved of by many' who rejected the 'doctrine and pedantry of moralists and divines'.[384] Seeking, therefore, to answer him 'out of . . . his own principles', Shafte endeav-oured a defence of law and government as natural and divine, *and* at the same time posited that duty to government was 'inseparable from our interest'.[385] Drawing the application, he concluded, 'the well compounded government as that of England is the best under which it is most manifest that the people live most royally' on account of the moral and legal foundations of the English monarchy.[386] Not surprisingly, another combatant, an architect of the Restoration, engaged directly with the implications of Hobbes's politics. Writing in exile, his *A Brief View of the Dangerous and Pernicious Errors to Church and State, in Mr Hobbes's Book, Entitled Leviathan*, Edward Hyde, Earl of Clarendon, confuted, chapter by chapter, the idea of a social contract and the foundation of government on force, 'so pernicious to the sovereign power of kings and destructive to the affection and allegiance of subjects'.[387] In reaffirming against Hobbes, that 'all power was by God and Nature invested into one man', the king, Clarendon indeed fulfilled his hope to be 'of some . . . service to your majesty' even while out of government.[388]

In the furious pamphlet exchanges of the Popish Plot, however, most varieties of civil war and republican theories were re-circulated. In the works of Henry Neville and Algernon Sidney, for example, the republican arguments of Milton and Harrington were rearticulated as the intellectual arm of Shaftesbury's politics.[389] Whig history has established those figures in the national memory, and even, in Sidney's case, in the ranks of political martyrs. What we need to appreciate is that, in the 1670s and 1680s, Charles II did not want for spokesmen who answered them and revalidated discourses of royalty. In 1678, the historian John Nalson, editor of the vast collection of state papers collected towards a royalist history of the seventeenth century, entered the lists of political argument with a substantial treatise entitled *The Common Interest of King and People*, published with a large van Hove engraving of Charles II opposite its title page.[390] Hobbes is again Nalson's target, and he rejects the argument for the origin of civil society in fear. But it is the 'stiff republicans' against whom he directs the bulk of his labours which are devoted to re-asserting the foundations of kingship in 'Nature, Law, Reason, Providence and Religion'.[391] A critical review of republics, which, he claims, 'can never be for the general good of any community of men', opens into a discussion of monarchy as that polity designed by God and Nature for the happiness of mankind.[392] Monarchy, Nalson argues, is in the public interest and in language reminiscent of Hobbes, he continues: 'the remotest sphere of the populace is animated . . . from the primum mobile of royal authority'.[393] Instructing the people that 'there can be nothing wanting to complete the happiness of all sorts . . . of men who live under this admirable government but the knowledge of it', Nalson catalogued those benefits and discredited its critics by associating them with Calvinist writers (Knox and Buchanan), Presbyterians who had sought to tear down all government.[394] Calling upon readers not to be misled again into ruin, Nalson urged 'unity among ourselves and loyalty to our prince' as the key to 'peace, prosperity and happiness'.[395]

As the cloud of revolution loomed once again, apologists for monarchy re-emphasized the natural, paternal and sacred, rather than utilitarian, argu-ments of kingship.[396] *The Divine Right of Kings Asserted in General: Ours in Particular; Both by the Laws of God and this Land*, published in 1679, both heralded that shift, and in its brief four-page format, crystallized divine right theory for an audience not willing to read hundreds of philosophical pages.[397] As well as a reiteration of *iure divino* kingship, the text defends the dispensing power and the principle of 'perpetual succession'.[398] Another 'briefly collected' volume of arguments was Robert Constable's *God and The King*, to which the long subtitle provides accurate summary: 'monarchy proved from holy writ to be the only legitimate species of politic government and the only polity constituted and appointed by God ...'[399] And John Brydall added to his historical defence of the crown a treatise *Jura Coronae*, on the rights and prerogatives of the king, which was published with a large royal arms facing the title page.[400] Although he denounced despotism, Brydall made a powerful case for the divinity of kingship, the indivisibility of sovereignty, the legal basis of the prerogative and the inalienability of the succession. 'To obey, revere and love our prince,' he instructed readers, 'we are bound by the laws of God and man', and the nation should pray for a king 'to whom we owe, under God, all the peace, liberty, justice, property and prosperity we have enjoyed since his Majesty's restoration'.[401]

The publication of Henry Neville's *Plato Redivivus* in 1681 raised the Whig challenge to monarchy to new theoretical heights. An old associate of Harrington, Neville revived, in his dialogues on government, the Harringtonian model of a Venetian-style polity, with the powers of any single figure, if one there was, circumscribed and subordinate to a senate.[402] The anonymous *Antidotum Britannicum* took up the challenge Neville presented, offering 'A Counter-pest against the distinctive principles of Plato Redivivus' by an assertion of the prerogatives of the crown.[403] In a dialogue between Platophilus and Britannicus, it is Britain who defends the English monarchy as ancient, paternal and 'successive by inherent birthright', divine, 'the most absolute and perfect form of government', the safeguard of the subjects' liberties and property.[404] Arguing the king's authority over parliament, and the people's duty of subjection and obedience, Britannia persuades Platophilus that Neville's doctrines are 'pernicious' as well as erroneous, as the author also hoped to convince the reader that divine monarchy in England 'is the most sure basis of the people's liberties and the only staple of their happiness'.[405] The dedication to Charles II made the abstract arguments particular and personal: 'Your majesties just rights are the best preserver of the people's liberties; they are an impregnable bulwark against all popular invasions and arbitrary powers. If once your royal authority suffers any diminution, tyranny will become a law, oppression will become a law, fanaticism will become a law'.[406] Not only the monarchy but Charles himself was the cause of 'Britain'.

Though not mentioning Neville by name, a posse of other writers joined the author of *Antidotum Britannicum* to fight for the king. *Britanniae speculum* (1683) incorporated a defence of monarchical government to which the author felt impelled by 'the audacious scribbles of certain profligate wretches [Neville was a notorious libertine] who make way for the overturning of this famous monarchy and the introducing of popular tyranny'.[407] Against them, the treatise argued the divine origins of kingship, the absoluteness of paternal authority and the blessings of the Stuart family. Similarly from Scotland, George MacKenzie's *Ius Regium or The Just and Solid Foundations of Monarchy* attacked Milton and Hobbes (among others) to underpin the prerogatives of kings, argue their freedom from accountability, and urge the duty of obedience.[408]

In the act of answering the republican challenge, advocates of monarchy in the 1680s exalted the position and power of the crown to heights not, at least hitherto, claimed by Charles himself. After more than a decade of more pragmatic, rationalist arguments, faced with the resurgence of a theoretical critique of regality, as well as with Whig opposition, spokesmen for Charles II, the crown and the succession, with – or without – official support and sanction represented monarchy as sacred, natural and absolute. At the end of Charles II's reign, it seemed that a battle of ideas as well as parties had been won and the panegyrics that greeted Charles's triumph over the Whigs echo the claims of the apologists for prerogative. Not long before Charles II died, to be succeeded by his brother, A Discourse of Monarchy by John Wilson was claiming for the king the prerogative of being the sole maker and interpreter of the law, loosed from obligation to the laws himself; and a king to whom parliament and people were subject.[409] By 1685, such claims had been sufficiently repeated that it may not be surprising that, when he finally ascended his throne, James II literally believed he owed no account to any but God. Thanks to those who had so powerfully defended the crown and the Stuarts in philosophical, legal and religious discourses, the theoretical foundation of an English absolutism had, perhaps, never been firmer.

IV

Since at least the assumption of the royal supremacy, and the establishment of a Church of England and what has been called a 'monarchical' church, the pulpit had been a vital medium for the representation of the king, as well as the faith. Despite, and also on account of, religious divisions and opposition, loyal clergy had preached and published sermons extolling the prerogatives of the crown, sometimes (as in the case of Mainwaring and Sibthorpe in Charles I's reign) to degrees that discomfited MPs and lawyers.[410] The experience of republic, when the sects had seemed to threaten the breakdown of social order, had made the restoration of the church every bit as popular as that of the crown and bound the interests of bishop and king even more closely. Although Charles II personally preferred toleration, churchmen, for the most part, were ardent advocates of the authority of the king and crown. And that was not least because both confronted challenges of cynicism, scepticism and unbelief that undermined the sacred foundations of kingship as well as episcopacy. Though our more secular priorities, as well as disciplinary distinctions, have seldom led us to study them as such, Restoration sermons were political treatises and representations of the Supreme Head of the church, the king. Those delivered to Charles and/or published by his command were doubtless read, alongside royal declarations and prayers, as 'official' representations and advertisements of kingship. Beyond those, from the bishops to the parish clergy, sermons, especially on calendrical days of commemoration and thanksgiving, represented both Charles II and the Stuart family to congregations and, via the press, to readers. The published sermon literature of Charles II's reign is vast – sermons were perhaps the most popular of all publications – and a rich corpus of material that still awaits a study we cannot offer here.[411] However, no understanding of the public representation and reception of Charles II can be written without a brief glance at the ways in which, over a quarter of a century, the discourse of sermons helped to reconstitute and revalidate monarchical rule and to sustain the authority of the king in difficult times.

Certainly in 1660, the pulpits of the restored church appeared to be platforms for the celebration of the monarchy. And, it is in the sermons, unsurprisingly, that we encounter an important strain in the early representation of Charles II: that of the Davidic king returned to his throne. On days of thanksgiving in May and June 1660, from pulpits in London and the provinces, sermons told the story of Restoration as a biblical story of Israel, God's chosen nation, and its rulers returned. Robert Mossom, the vicar of St Peter's, Paul's Wharf, in a sermon he delivered on 10 May and dedicated to Charles, took Psalm 75 as his text from which to expound on the parallel with David and God's protection of the king.[412] At Oxford on the 27th, the Woodstock schoolmaster, Francis Gregory, preached his sermon, *David's Return*, which, published by the university with the insignias of the rose and thistle, welcomed the new king as one whom God himself had numbered among the gods.[413] Banishment, Gregory argued, for Charles, as for David, had led him to know suffering and better equipped him to rule, as God now brought him back to reign over his people. In All Saints, Northamptonshire, a month later, Simon Ford, preaching on 2 Samuel 19: 30, delivered an even more elaborate exposition of the David parallel and an almost sacrilegious praise of Charles. Indeed, he claimed, 'in point of mercy and miracle, King David's restitution came short of King Charles's'; and he anticipated a reign of love between the returned parent and a people whose 'genius' inclined them to receive the king with joy, as Mephibosheth had David.[414] With the return of Charles, Ford preached, 'we are returned to ourselves again', and the chosen nation might be united.[415] In Aberdeen, John Paterson, at the request of the provost, preached and published his thanksgiving sermon, *Post Nubila Phoebus*, on the return of the sun after darkness. The return of the king, he knew, was the Lord's work because Christian kings were God's vicegerents.[416]

As with the verse panegyrics we examined, between the lines of these sermons of celebration we can discern anxieties and concerns. How could God have permitted the ruin of the kingdom and the death of his vicegerent?

How had He permitted the Philistines to triumph? The preachers knew too that, for all the appearance of universal rejoicing, the realm was still divided: Ford acknowledged the suspicions and fears that Royalists and Covenanters, bishops and Presbyterians still had of each other; and Paterson described with blunt accuracy the situation of the restored king: 'never any of his royal ancestors did come to their crown in a more difficult time. Never a king had more variety of tempers to deal with . . . never any of his royal predecessors had more enemies, some known and some veiled, who can very slyly and subtly drop out words for his disadvantage'; the 'evil spirit' that brought down his father, he continued, 'is not yet banished away'.[417] It was the role of the loyal preacher to counter it, to sustain the image of the king as God's chosen, the protector of the faith and the people.

The sermons preached on the day of the king's coronation, 23 April 1661, and published by the royal command, provided a semi-official script for the pulpit representation of the king. In his dedication to Charles, whose engraved image faced the title page, Bishop John Morley admitted that some had found his sermon too political, too harsh against the rebels and traitors, but made no apology for his theme. Preaching on Proverbs 28: 2, on 'the transgression of a land', Morley damned those who had rebelled against God as well as the throne.[418] God's judgments had taught them that there was no alternative to monarchy which was 'natural and . . . according to divine institution'.[419] Turning to Charles himself, and his comeliness, courtesy, affability and understanding sharpened by experience, Morley thanked God for his miraculous preservation at Worcester and the day of celebration which he hoped might annually be remembered. The day the king in fact chose to have remembered was not his coronation day – perhaps because it was St George's Day – but the day of his entry into London on 29 May. By a royal proclamation and a parliamentary statute, 29 May was appointed a day of thanksgiving for God's mercy and favour in dispelling treason and effecting the king's return and became an annual occasion for a series of authorized sermons delivered and published by trusted clerics close to the court, from whom, it was hoped, the parish clergy might take their cue.[420] On the first thanksgiving on 29 May 1661, two sermons from the centre of the Restoration ecclesiastical establishment provide excellent examples of the representation of Charles II's monarchy, as the king himself approved it. Peter Heylyn could hardly have been closer to the monarchy: a chaplain to Charles I, he was restored to his position in 1660 as one of the prebendaries of Westminster where he preached on 29 May to a large audience on 2 Samuel 19: 14. Once again drawing the parallel with the history of David, Heylyn also drew attention to the bishops and loyal clergy driven into exile for their allegiance to the crown and welcomed, with the return of the king, the re-establishment of the church in the beauty of holiness. Reminding the king perhaps of the loyal support of churchmen, Heylyn's sermon underlined the symbiosis of church and crown which was to be an important theme of Restoration political discourse.⁴²¹ At Whitehall on the same day, Henry King, restored Bishop of Chichester, preached the first sermon to the king: a sermon which was published 'by his majesties command' with the king's crowned initials on the title pages. 'Pleased is he that comes in the name of the Lord', King expounded his text (Ezekiel 21), as he thanked God that the nation again enjoyed a king. Not wanting to dwell on those who 'entertain it not . . . with the same affection as we do', the bishop led the congregation in a day of 'comfort and rejoicing' for a king of piety, fortitude and justice who would be a 'nursing father' to church and nation.⁴²²

In the early 1660s, it would seem that these themes – of God's deliverance manifested in the restoration of his chosen, of light after darkness, and of joy at a monarch blessed with all virtues and qualities for rule – were rehearsed not only in the cathedrals and palaces but the counties and parishes of the land. Anthony Walker, the minister of Fyfield, Essex, preaching (several times he tells us) on 'these productions of deep and astonishing providence', lauded the return of the king and true religion.⁴²³ At Maidstone, on coronation day, the vicar of Yalding expounded verse 50 of Psalm 18 ('great deliverance gaveth he to his king') to give thanks for 'clouds of rebellion dispersed', a church delivered from 'a Babel of confusion', and for England's David miraculously restored after God had dashed the forces of his enemies.⁴²⁴ At Ely in Suffolk, Edward Willan, delivering a sermon on the eve of the election of MPs, denounced the sects and 'Protectorean mushrooms' that had brought woe and unchurched as well as unkinged the land.⁴²⁵ Now, he assured his flock, the realm again had a shepherd, a sovereign by birth and upbringing, the son of the martyr, Charles the Good, in thanks for whom he led them in prayers. The official thanksgiving day spurred a flood of loyalist sermons. In Suffolk, Henry White's sermon, printed by means of a bookseller in Norwich, offered a thanks to the Lord for his work in restoring without bloodshed the true religion and a king now 'enthroned in the hearts of his people'.⁴²⁶ In the parish church of Waltham Abbey, meanwhile, Thomas Reeve preached a sermon which, when published as *England's Beauty*, he dedicated to the king. The Lord, he told Charles, 'hath restored you to your father's throne to be looked upon as a glorious spectacle'.⁴²⁷ And in the text he re-presented to his auditors the king in all the traditional metaphors of regality: 'a king in a commonwealth is like the head in the body, the root in the tree . . . the sun in the firmament'.⁴²⁸ Depicting Charles as an 'object of miracle', he asked his congregation: 'An hereditary king, an orthodox king, a complete king, what can the eye of the nation look upon with more satisfaction?'⁴²⁹ As with the official sermons, many who preached in the parishes in the early months after Restoration knew that not all the clouds had been dispersed. Edward Willan prayed to be spared from 'the mutability of the many'; John Lynge, the vicar of Yalding, knew that there were 'some who show themselves not so much pleased with the deliverance'.[430] Sermons in fact sought by reiterating the themes of divine deliverance and royal virtue not only to describe but to inscribe restored monarchy and to bind a still divided nation into one church and polity. Presenting the king as the nursing father of the church and clerics as the best support of monarchy, the clergy reappropriated from the Commonwealth sects the language of Scripture and providence, and anointed the monarchy with what a preacher at the Warwick assizes described as 'the oil of the sanctuary that is used in the fial of government'.[431] With the onset in the following years of problems and tensions, as well as a more secular discourse of mutual interest, the regular reiteration of the sacred nature of regality and obedience was an essential prop to monarchy.

Over the decade or so that followed the coronation, the relations between the king and the church were not without some tensions. Charles's publicly profligate lifestyle with his mistresses drew oblique criticism in a number of sermons, including some presented to the king himself and published with his approval. Loyal clergy like Bishop George Hall of Chester, Edward Stillingfleet and Richard Perrinchief all preached in 1666 against the sins of luxury and lust corrupting the nation; and Charles either failed to discern any implied criticism of his own behaviour or brushed it aside.[432] More serious, the king's persistent flirtations with toleration might have eroded the support of the church and clergy as well as the Anglican gentry.

However, though sermons against freedom of conscience were regularly preached and published, the clergy's tactic was more one of persuading Charles than of attacking him. In a sermon preached to the king on 12 March 1665, for example, the Bishop of Lincoln, Benjamin Laney, specifically engaged those who advocated opening the doors of the church by offering freedom of conscience. Such freedom, Laney reminded Charles, chief among his auditors, 'destroys the very foundation of government' as it had in 'our late times when the conscience was loose for a while [and] some would think hell had broke loose'.[433] Princes, he asserted, to a monarch very ready to hear this, had as good authority as conscience and a greater one than that of private judgements.

Overall, whatever the difficulties, churchmen remained staunch advocates of the crown not least perhaps because, in the wake of the disaster of the plague, the Fire and the humiliating defeat by the Dutch, criticism of the king was accompanied by a revived nonconformist assault upon the church. Laney himself revealed his fear in 1665 that the sects 'still keep their quarters and leagues within doors with more secrecy but no less danger' and saw schismatics planning another breach of the peace in church and state.[434] Nathaniel Hardy, vicar of St Martin-in-the-Fields and Chaplain in Ordinary to the king, worried that the Fire was making a 'fit season' for 'those cursed incendiaries . . . who delighted in division' and in 'breaches in church and state'.[435] The Dean of St Paul's, William Sancroft, imparted that the 'ill spirit, this restless fury' of 'disobedience' 'walks about day and night'.⁴³⁶ Faced with the resurgence of the sects, then, the clergy closed ranks behind the king, Perrinchief reminding the House of Commons that 'government is the soul of society, and magistrates in church and state are ... the ... intellectual faculties to guide the whole to safety and honour'.⁴³⁷ The days of prayer or thanksgiving appointed for the blessings on the fleet or thanks for victories provided a platform indeed for loyalist clergy to be virtual media spokesmen for the government. John Dolben, the Dean of Westminster and Clerk of the Closet, in a sermon before the king, pausing to remember the 'beauty and order' which the Restoration had brought out of chaos, delivered a jingoistic address against the Dutch (who had 'shame-fully fled ... broken and shattered') in what was a glorification of a royal triumph.⁴³⁸ At the public assizes in Northamptonshire, meanwhile, on the day of thanksgiving for the victory, Simon Ford, in a sermon published as *The Lord Wanders in the Deep* and dedicated to James, Duke of York, clearly identified triumph with God's favour to the Stuarts.⁴³⁹ Not least, he related to his congre-gation, the survival of the brave duke when three standing next to him were blown to pieces, splattering him with their blood, was another remarkable sign of God's providence. Victory at sea, Ford knew, strengthened the king at home, just as defeat would have let loose 'unquiet spirits' ready to seize any opportunity to assault the crown.⁴⁴⁰ Alongside the official *Gazette* reports of naval expeditions and successes, victory sermons rendered the pulpit a vital medium of representation for the monarchy.

Perhaps not coincidentally, the period after 1667, in which Charles II faced most criticism from parliament and people, was also one of difficulty for the church. The failure of the king to sire a legitimate heir was increasingly associ-ated with his debauchery, which also compromised his authority as head of the church. An increase in scepticism and atheism undermined not only religion but, as the clergy were to remind Charles, the sacred foundations of authority.⁴⁴¹ And the mounting fear of popery consequent on Charles's closer relations with France provided ammunition to nonconformist critics of church and state who again linked popery and absolutism in their polemics against the clergy and the king.⁴⁴² In their efforts to sustain the alliance between church and monarchy, preachers counselled as well as praised the king. John North's sermon to Charles at Newmarket on the danger of intemperance and debauchery to 'ordinary policy', and the link between reverence and modesty, hints at the political consequences of moral failings.⁴⁴³ And the sermon presented by the Dean of Bangor, William Lloyd, on Romans 8: 13 ('if you live after the flesh ye shall die') suggested, perhaps not just with the afterlife in mind, that those who did not renounce such sins did disservice to themselves. You 'run out', Lloyd told the king and congregation at Whitehall, 'of your estate, your credit, your health, in pursuit of a momentary pleasure'.⁴⁴⁴ No less, the clergy brought to the king's attention the danger of scoffing at religion and urged action against unbelievers. Those who rejected Christianity, North told the king in carefully chosen political language, thereby hoped for 'freedom from rule'.[445] In a sermon before the king, William Cave, a royal chaplain, asked his sovereign to consider, if religion were subordinated to natural rights, 'what becomes of obedience to natural parents or civil powers?'[446] In the main, however, the clergy knew that the best way to secure royal protection of the church was through demonstrating their loyal service to the state. And, as criticism of Charles mounted from the late 1660s, sermon after sermon took up the themes of the necessity of authority and obedience. The 29 May became a regular occasion for sermons to celebrate a monarchy which was facing in other media a more hostile press. In 1668, for example, the Master of the Savoy, Henry Killigrew, preaching at Whitehall, returned to the Davidic theme to present kings as preserved by God. Giving thanks and exhorting the people to festive commemoration, Killigrew also seriously reminded them not to forget 'the days of silence and sadness when we had no king' and, he added, coupling church with the monarchy, when 'to be orthodox [was to be] an enemy to the state'.[447] Two years later on the same occasion, John Lake, rector of St Botolph's, expanded Psalms 2: 6 ('Yet have I set my king upon my holy hill of Zion') to re-emphasize the divinity of monarchy against 'some unquiet spirits [who] are still ready to cry out . . . we will not have this man to reign over us'.[448] Preaching at the visitation at High Wycombe the following spring, the royal chaplain Samuel Gardner urged his fellow minister to stand by the crown: 'in the fear of God let us give all due obedience unto authority'.[449]

The 1672 Declaration of Indulgence clearly threatened to damage the unity of church and monarchy and to deprive Charles of valuable support. The most loyal clergy warned Charles against the consequences for his position of toleration of Catholics or dissenters. 'The pretentions are as high and as great at Rome for this monarchy as ever they were,' Stillingfleet proclaimed from the pulpit at St Margaret's, Westminster; by contrast, 'it is the honour of our church of England that it accepts the rights of princes so clearly and so fully'.[450] At the Guildhall, Richard Meggott identified the risk to monarchy from the sects as well as from Rome. 'So many as there are among us of dissenters from the Church of England,' he told the mayor and aldermen, 'so many there are who are more or less unsound in tenets concerning magistracy'.[451] Against both – and in another prompt to the king (he was a royal chaplain) to know who his loyal supporters were – Meggott underlined the benefits of royal government and the attendant ruin that faced people who challenged it. 'The commodities of government are great,' he argued, against any revived discourse of resistance, that even 'a very froward [sic] and rigid father of the country is better than none at all', and the rule of Charles II a blessing to all.[452]

The king's retreat, under Danby's influence, from promoting toleration may not have succeeded in winning the Commons, but it undoubtedly firmed the support for monarchy from the church and clergy at a moment when it was never more needed. 'We have,' John Meriton wrote in praise of the renewed partnership, 'the best religion . . . with one of the best churches . . . under the protection of our most religious and gracious sovereign.'[453] The sheer volume of loyal sermons representing the king's cause from 1676 to 1677 is itself testimony to the value of the pulpit in countering charges and challenges in opposition pamphlets. To take a few examples, James Duport, Dean of Peterborough, preached one of the three sermons he delivered and published in 1676, on 29 May, on the text 'Fear God. Honour the King' (1 Peter 2: 17). Damning schismatics or any who claimed the authority of conscience, Duport presented kings as God's lieutenants whom the word of God bound subjects to venerate. In an unsubtle rebuke to recent parliaments, he warned that if royal rights, 'their iura regalia, their regalities or revenues of the crown be clipped . . . the reverence of their persons will not long continue'; and he called on all to rise 'by fighting . . . or uniting in defence of his royal person.'[454] Among the many who followed his call to unite was the Dean of Ripon who in his sermon before the assize judges at York on 17 July 1676 presented monarchy in lofty terms. 'Our breath of our nostrils,' he addressed the assembled, 'is not more necessary for our being than our princes sovereignty is to our well being', for the king was a 'universal influence' for life 'as is the Sun.'[455] Touching on the late rebellion, led (he argued) by the false claims of conscience, Cartwright hoped that 'this nation lies under no disloyal temptations for a second holy war.'[456] Condemning all those who had again 'deflowered' the beauty of the crown by libels and 'satirical invectives', the dean delivered an axiom of church and state that echoed the words of Charles the martyr: 'they who do not obey the king, who is a visible God, will never obey God who is an invisible king.'[457] If not all rose to his lofty strains, around the country, in countless sermons, preachers taught congregations to shun what Thomas Sprat called 'mad enthusiasm' and to re-learn, as William Pindar put it, in a sermon at the Guildhall chapel in March 1677, 'the duty of submission and obedience.'[458]

The depositions to the Council concerning a supposed Catholic plot laid the next autumn by Titus Oates presented a blow to the church as well as the king, and, in the wake of the scandal, the clergy made even greater efforts to defend Charles against Whig attacks. Preaching weeks after Oates's revelations, on that year's highly charged anniversary of the Powder Plot, the Bishop of Exeter, Thomas Lamplugh, moved swiftly to try to check the advantage that the enemies of the government and of hereditary succession looked to take from the events. Papists, he admitted, had indeed threatened the king and the realm. But, he went on, an equal if not greater danger came from those who 'pretend to new revelations, raptures, or voices from heaven', those 'who raise tumults, abet rebellions'; and only measures to preserve the king's 'sacred person' could undo that danger.[459] At the funeral of Sir Edmund Bury Godfrey, the supposed first victim of the Plot, the Dean of Bangor, William Lloyd, sought similarly to emphasize the danger to the king and his care for the safety of the nation.[460] The proclamation of a fast day in November to pray for deliverance from danger provided an official opportunity for other loyalist sermons, such as that of Benjamin Camfield, rector of Aylston, near Leicester. Published with the Bishop of London's imprimatur, Camfield's sermon did not downplay the threats from Romish enemies. But he used the Plot to stress the need for loyalty to the king as 'the head of order and the very life and soul of law', and to argue the godliness of a monarch, again preserved by providence, who led the nation in confession and prayer, as a true head of the church.[461] This was (necessarily) to be the tactic and refrain of the loyal clergy, as of the king himself. Only weeks before his murder, the Archbishop of St Andrews preached to the Commons on another fast day, urging temper, moderation and a stop to 'scandalous schisms', that 'by your means, not only the person of his sacred majesty and the rights of his crown may be secured against all wicked attempts whether of papists *or others*: But also that upon his head the crown may be supported and so flourish'.[462] In a sermon on 5 November, James Bedle, a royal chaplain as well as vicar of Great Bursted, contrasted the unity of the papists with the divisions among Protestants, all of whom he urged to join in loyal allegiance to the supreme magistrate, 'his majesty's most sacred person and government'.[463]

What all the preachers hoped and believed was that, as Simon Patrick put it, 'the fidelity of subjects will be firm and unmovable when it is incorporated into piety and accounted a part of religion'.[464] Accordingly, as the crisis over the Plot came to the brink, they reiterated both the sacred nature of kingship and the sin of resistance, hoping to win the argument of conscience, while pamphleteers were battling to win that of reason. In a sermon he published in 1681 to persuade the mayor of London, Sir John Moore, to help cool 'the immoderate and unchristian amongst the several parties', Joseph Goodman, preaching on Matthew 19: 16, reminded his congregation to think of eternal life and obey God's commandments and those of his vicegerents.[465] 'Some,' he ended, 'are placed in a magistracy and authority; these are called Gods because they represent his divine majesty in the world'.[466] Two other sermons to the mayor and aldermen illustrate the battle for support as well as souls in the capital. Glossing his text from 1 Kings 18, Charles Hickman warned his congregation that the choice they faced was between following the Lord or Baal and 'no man did or can follow the Lord to the tents of rebellion; he always leads his people by the hands of Moses and Aaron and has given us kings to go in and out before us and whoever forsakes them forsakes also the commandments of his God'.[467] Dedicating to Clayton his sermon delivered on 19 September, the rector of Northill recalled that his purpose in preaching had been to stir men to their duties. Countering the argument of *Leviathan*, that the obligations of

subjects lasted only as long as the power of rulers, Robert Hancock had emphasized the Christian duty to oppose the 'spirit of sedition and division that is
working among us'.[468] 'You have,' he told those assembled in the Guildhall
chapel, 'the Scriptures in your own language and if you read them without
partiality and prejudice you will soon learn those indispensable duties of peace,
humility and obedience'.[469] Moreover, the Church of England, in contrast to
Rome, supported the rights of princes, so 'no man can be true to the Church of
England whilst he is false to his Sovereign'.[470] In Putney church the next April,
on the day Charles's declaration of his reasons for dissolving parliament was
read, the minister Edward Sclater took the opportunity to meld royal with
divine words. Every government, Sclater agreed, was subject to discontent; but
to seek to divide the people from David was also to divide them from God.
Citing the classical as well as biblical past to prove the ills of rebellions against
rulers, Sclater recalled to the congregation the words of Solomon, 'speak not
evil of the king', and prayed for their own David, a nursing father to the church
who had preserved them, and would go on preserving them, from the wicked.[471]

Preachers took the same message of the dangers of resistance to the provinces, in a series of sermons presented in 1681 at the assizes. At the Salisbury
assizes in July, for example, the rector of Stanton Quintin delivered a sermon,
quickly published as *The Necessity of Subjection Asserted*. Expounding the
familiar text of Romans 13, John Byrom reasserted the divine and natural
foundations of civil government and the agreement of all reformed churches
on the need for subjection to magistrates. Only papists and those who had no
claim to be true Christians condoned rebels, Byrom argued, as he prayed
that the realm might be spared from 'the fury of Rome and Enthusiastic rage'
and all honest Protestants might honour their king.[472] In the same month at
Reading, the vicar of Shinfield, John Okes, taking St Mark's gospel, chapter 12,
verse 17 ('Render unto Caesar'), explained how Scripture commanded not
simply the passive obedience to kings but outward acts of fidelity and love.
Reverence, he maintained, was due to monarchs as well as to God whose deputies they were: 'a contemptuous thought of a king or lawful authority is a sin of
a high nature'.[473] Every suitable occasion was used to press the case: at a funeral
of alderman Sir Thomas Bludworth, Samuel Freeman, rector of St Anne's,
Aldgate, interjected into his encomium on the deceased his 'mighty affection
and zeal for the king and the church of England', a church that 'asserts the
rights of princes against all usurpations'.[474]

As well as bringing the full force of Scripture to argue the divine authority of
rulers in general, the clergy took pains – it cannot have been an easy move after
years of public sexual scandal – to represent the British monarchy, and Charles
II personally, as sacred. William Clifford's October 1681 sermon at Wakefield
indeed was titled *The Power of Kings, Particularly the British Monarchy Asserted
and Vindicated*, and in his dedication to 'all loyal subjects' he lauded 'ours

(without doubt the best of governments)' and urged all 'to stand by our prince with our lives and fortunes'.[475] Charles's birthday and the day of thanksgiving for his return also provided the occasion for personal support for the king as well as advocacy of divine monarchy. On 25 May 1682, at Bow church in London, Benjamin Calamy, a royal chaplain, re-evoked all the rhetoric and memories of Restoration to represent to the mayor and citizens a Charles who had lately been described in far less favourable terms. The day, Calamy reminded them, was one of thanks for God's 'wonderful train of Providences' which had without bloodshed restored 'our most gracious sovereign, the light of our eyes', and 'with him', he added, coupling what Whig polemicists had sundered, 'our equal laws and just liberties', our 'true reformed religion'.[476] Evoking those happier times, he asked those old enough to have witnessed them, 'shall we ever forget the triumphant shouts and joyful acclamations that greeted the king?'[477] But lately, he shifted his tone to dramatic effect, men had forgotten both that joy and the miseries it had dispersed. It was not a time to forget. 'This glorious restoration doth lay an eternal obligation upon us all of continuing true and faithful'; and, he warned, 'God may next time deprive us of our king and never restore him again'.[478] Rather than carping, therefore, Calamy called on the congregation to pray for Charles and 'to praise God for him and those manifold blessings which he hath been the happy instrument under God of transmitting down to us': his mildness, equity, and fatherly care of the people.[479] 'Blessed', he closed, on this birthday 'be the day wherein he was born' and, he added, 'blessed by God that hath given the king to the hearts and affections of all his people'.[480]

In May 1682, Calamy's last blessing might have seemed more hopeful than realistic. But the political current had by then clearly begun to flow in a different direction and within a year Calamy was able to add to the list of remarkable providences that God had shown towards Charles His 'blasting' of the conspirators and his preservation of his chosen.[481] In the so-called Tory reaction that followed the defeat of the Whigs, the Church of England and its pulpits were to be in the forefront.

How important had the preachers been in helping Charles II to secure his victory? As well as difficult, the question is multifaceted: for it asks us (among other issues) to weigh the relative importance of religious texts in relation to a myriad of other writings and to assess the effectiveness of sermons in particular. Though there can be no easy answer to the first, the repeated iteration of divine kingship and the sin of resistance, and the representation of Charles as a providential prince, constituted a powerful argument; and one that ballads and popular verse suggest percolated down from the elite philosophical and legal debates about government into popular culture. Attended by most parishioners and heading the bestseller publications of the age, the sermon remained an unrivalled platform for disseminating a message both in performance and in print. By no means did the loyalists monopolize the pulpit; and several preachers, citing their reluctance to be published, referred to the critical reception they faced, or expected. John Okes told the Earl of Clarendon that he feared exposure to 'a critical and censorious age'; John Byrom knew that 'censure abounds' and that he faced the opposition of 'restless men'; John Bennion, preacher of *Moses's Change*, looked for protection from 'such variety of censure' as ''tis likely enough to meet withal'.[482]

Some even questioned the impact of sermons at all: the Earl of Northampton said of Lord Chief Justice Scroggs, after a speech he had given, that he had 'told the king that he had, since his happy restoration . . . caused many hundred sermons to be preached, all which taught the people not half so much loyalty'.[483] The preacher William Cave feared the same impotence: he had been reluctant to publish his sermon, he told Sir Patience Ward, 'because I had seldom seen printing of sermons attain the desired effect, being generally thrown aside'.[484] The sheer number of published sermons, however, and the command of those, from the king to mayors, who ordered them published, suggest that Cave's pessimism may have been misplaced. All of the sermons we have examined were sold, and were presumably a commercial proposition. Their ubiquity in modern libraries, and the survival of bound collections, suggest too that, for some at least, sermons were anything but ephemeral. Moreover, we should note that Cave's remarks relate to the act of publishing, rather than preaching. Clearly the explosion of print in Restoration England left sermons to find their way amid a veritable bombardment of publications. In the coffee house they mingled on the table with tracts, newspapers and the latest verses. The occasions of sermons, however, gave them a special significance and impact. In metropolitan and parish churches on Sundays and perhaps especially on days of fast and thanksgiving, the congregation was a captive audience removed, for a time, from the influence of other scripts and voices. And, for all the tendencies of modernizing narratives to emphasize what was more secular, rational and scientific about the Augustan age, salvation, faith and sin were still central to daily life, and the prescriptions of the clergy were not lightly disregarded.[485] If we may take some measure of what the loyal Anglican clergy contributed through sermons on divine kingship to the survival of Charles II, compared to the fate only a few years later of his brother, then it would appear that the preacher had been vital to the representation and the validation of the monarchy and the monarch.

On 9 September 1683, in the cathedral church at Winchester, the Dean of Windsor, Francis Turner, preached to the king a sermon on verse 10 of Psalm 144: 'thou hast given victory unto kings: and hast delivered David thy servant from the peril of the sword'.[486] Charles II, we recall, appointed the day as one of 'public thanksgiving for the delivery of his sacred majesty's person and government from the late treasonable conspiracy'; but it became as near as a day of worship can come to a victory parade for the king, with the clergy leading the march. It was, of course, a day of victory for the churchmen too and in the sermons that were delivered cleric after cleric savoured it and used Scripture not only to advertise church and king but to launch an assault on the Whigs and their nonconformist allies. Turner, pressing home the point that the king had had God on his side, denounced commonwealthsmen and 'murderous fanatics' along with those who sought 'a deformed mass of all religions'.[487] At Petworth the same day, John Price, underpinning the divinity of kings, hinted at the need to punish those who, in the words of his text, were 'murmurers' in Israel, those whose 'indiscreet zeal' had almost led to the 'drawing of swords'.[488] Over in Worcestershire, Samuel Scattergood, vicar of Blockley, praising 'the best religion under the happy government of one of the best of kings', cursed the sons of Belial, the dissenters and especially the Absalom and Achitophel who had plotted to murder their David.[489] In rural Sussex, that September, Dr John Harrison named the Achitophel as the Earl of Shaftesbury (along with his co-conspirators Jenkins and Russell) and gave thanks that the storm had fallen on their heads. Identifying the preservation of the bishops with that of the crown, Harrison's sermon carried on its title page a reminder of the role the clergy had played in defeating the conspiracy: 'tantum religio potuit suadere maiorum' – 'so much has religion done to persuade most people'.[490] Though with different levels of specificity in the application and exposition, the Absalom and Achitophel story was evidently common in thanksgiving sermons. In *The Religious Rebel*, the published version of the sermon he had preached at South Marston in Wiltshire, Charles Powell felt no need to explain it: 'I hope,' he told his congregation, 'you do not suspect that I am going about to draw that parallel which is obvious to every eye'; indeed, the story of Absalom 'is now grown so stale a theme that you cannot but think it superfluous . . . to mention him'.[491]

What was important, as much as identifying and pillorying the rebels, was to learn the larger lessons of the Plot. For, John Fitzwilliam reminded his congregation in Cotenham, Cambridgeshire, the rebels against God and the king had come close to taking the people with them to perdition. 'Did you not,' he asked in a series of painful rhetorical questions, 'greedily swallow down the lies they fed you with against the government?' 'Have you not had,' he challenged, 'their persons in the greatest admiration?'[492] Had they not all but considered themselves absolved from allegiance? The Lord had delivered David, but it was vital now to keep the nation 'fully convinced' of the dangers of the conspirators. And to achieve that, it was up to priests, like himself 'zealous' for the government, to defend the nation and to be 'the people's mouths'.[493]

For the rest of Charles's reign the clergy were the king's and the people's spokesmen, extolling him and the monarchy in sermons that were, if George Hickes's belief is correct, 'bought and read by common people'.[494] The defeat of the Whigs secured the king's immediate objective: the loyal clergy enunciated the principle that, in the words of John Turner, 'a successive monarchy is without all question the best form of government upon the face of the earth . . . the best fitted to procure the peace and happiness of the world'.[495] But the crisis had re-opened fundamental questions about the church and religion, about the nature of government, the extent of royal prerogative, and about the character of the king – all questions which the Anglican preachers sought to counter and silence. Some clergy, like George Hickes or Richard Pearson, endeavoured to repair the fractures and reunite a loyal nation in peace under one king and church. Preaching at Easter 1684 before the mayor and aldermen of London, Hickes, Dean of Worcester, delivered a sermon on charity and community: 'for every man is of the blood of every other, we have all one common alliance'.[496] In his aptly titled sermon, *The Study of Quietness*, Pearson, rector of St Michael's Crooked Lane, preached on 1 Thessalonians 4: 11 to urge that men renounce 'licentious tongues and pens' and 'keep close only to [their] particular voca-tion', in quiet obedience to authority.[497] But, in sermon after sermon during Charles's last months, the monarchy and king were represented from the pulpit as sacred, inviolable and unaccountable to any human power. Royal chaplains and provincial preachers alike, through popular sermons that sacralized his image, made a powerful religious argument for an absolute rule that neither Charles, nor even his father, had imagined.

Before we leave the sermon as representation and proclamation of monarchy, we need briefly to examine a group of sermons that deserve consideration as a genre of their own. Following the proclamation of 1661, 30 January, the day of the regicide, was instituted as a day of commemoration of, and atonement for, the death of Charles the martyr.[498] Though they may seem to belong – and do belong – to the history of the posthumous image of Charles I, the 30 January sermons from the beginning were also texts in the representation of a son who, for all his considerable differences, drew much of his own representation from his father. Charles II commemorated his restoration on 29 May, but the day of regicide was (of course) also the day that the king succeeded to his throne. The 30 January sermons were, then, a discourse of the son as well as the father; and they present a revealing case study of the shifting representation of Charles II over his quarter century on his throne.

In the early years of Restoration, the 30 January sermons were directed at sanctifying Charles I as a means of underlining the sins of rebellion and republic. Though these were essential for the restored monarchy in re-appropriating Scripture and God for the crown, they made few references to Charles II himself or his own circumstance. By 1664, however, perhaps as criticisms of the monarch again began to be voiced, Bishop Henry King, in a 30 January sermon, preached at royal command, closed with a prayer that the king not only inherit the martyr's virtues 'but that those virtues may never be put to the cruel test that' his father's were.[499] It was the hint of the way in which 30 January sermons would become as much about Charles II as Charles I. Joseph Glanvill's sermon, published after the plague and Fire and amid mounting political tension, with a crown on the title page and taking up a text against resistance (Romans 13: 2), opened with a warning that 'we yet feel the smart' of the late wounds.[500] Observing that the Fire should convince all of the sinfulness of any resistance, to which people who had once rebelled were prone, he used the occasion of commemoration to reassert that 'kings wear God's image and authority', and none more than their own prince, restored by a 'miracle of providence'.[501]

From the late 1660s, the 30 January sermons became ever more particular and topical texts of Charles II's representation, and increasingly party polemic. In 1670, for example, Thomas Lambert, a prebend of Salisbury Cathedral, pre-faced his sermon with an attack on the sorts of MPs being elected to serve in parliament for the corporations and a prediction that the nation might 'come into the same state . . . that it was in anno 1642', if the lesson of obedience were not learned.[502] By 1676, the Dean of Peterborough, James Duport, was engaging with very contemporary issues in his attack on sectaries and malcontents in church and state – 'that universal neglect and contempt of authority' which he saw raising its head again.[503]

During the crisis of the Popish Plot, the clergy recruited the martyr directly for their fight against the Whigs. On 30 January 1679, weeks after Oates's revelations, Edward Pelling used his sermon to warn against renewed miseries, to argue against limited monarchy and to urge that the nation (even those too young to have been involved) expiate their sins against the father by unqualified obedience to the son.[504] To his 'country audience', John Cave moved swiftly from the martyr to the 'dangerous times' that now faced Charles II and instructed them that Scripture proscribed even 'murmerous complaints' against kings: 'They are accountable to God and to none but Him . . . those who arraign them at any other bar invade the divine authority and do encroach upon God's prerogative as well as the king's'.[505] The 30 January 1681 followed on the crisis provoked by the first dissolution of parliament that year. Sermons by Samuel Crossman and Francis Turner, to take but two, countered the view that the king owed an account to the people and presented Charles as the father, the physician and the husband of the realm.[506] The next year, 30 January sermons accused the Whigs of repeating the tactics and charges deployed to murder Charles I, and desperately appealed to auditors and readers not again to be tricked out of their duty of loyalty. Edward Pelling hoped, he told the Duke of Somerset, that by his preaching on Lamentations 5: 16 ('the crown is fallen from our head'), on the miseries of the Commonwealth, the people might be 'disciplined into wisdom for the future'.[507] It seems that they were. If, as we shall later suggest, the memories of Charles I and civil war were instrumental in Charles II's survival, then the sermons on 30 January that carefully evoked and glossed memories were powerful Tory weapons in the polemical war.[508]

It was a war waged to the very last days of Charles's reign. James Ellesby's 30 January sermon, though sent to the press the Monday after it was published, appeared in print only after the death of the king on 6 February 1685. Ellesby's text had been the 31st verse of Proverbs 30: 'a king against whom there is no rising up'; and, in expounding it, he rehearsed the divinity of kings, the judgments of God on rebels, and the Christian obligation of subjection which no objections 'drawn from interests and reasons of state' could dissolve.[509] By the time it was published, he was writing of James II, whose succession the preachers had done so much to effect. The new king had declared his intention to govern as his brother: 'let us then perform the duty of good subjects in yielding that obedience and subjection which we owe to our lawful prince, and of good Christians in praying for a blessing upon his royal person . . . that he may reign long and happy over us'.[510]

V

Panegyrics and pamphlets, histories and sermons had throughout our period been texts concerning the representation of, and debate about, monarchy and the person of the ruler. There can be no doubt, however, that in the circumstances of 1660, after violent revolution and regicide with their legacy of political division and party, these genres of writing became more specific, more topical and more partisan. This same process of overt polemicization and particularization marked other literary genres, both established and newly emerging, making the entire culture of writing, publishing and reading in Restoration England inseparable from its political culture and political contests. As well, that is, as carrying the traces of recent events and civil conflict, texts – many that we do not think of as overtly political – performed to shape the contours of a new political realm as well as a new aesthetic and literary culture.[511] Though it may not go too far to suggest that, in some ways, all Restoration texts presented and represented the monarchy and Charles II, space permits only a small sample of the genres, old and new, which, more or less overtly, performed to reconstitute, and refigure, the monarchy, and even the public 'person' of Charles II. To begin with a genre inextricably associated with early modernity, books on genealogy and heraldry, honour and courtesy had, since at least the early sixteenth century, served to fashion as well as represent an aristocratic and regal system of values. During the 1640s and 1650s, the crises over loyalty, as well as regicide itself and the abolition of the House of Lords, disrupted all the prescriptions of genealogy and honour which no less than the monarchy itself had to be rewritten in 1660. Though the subject awaits

its historian, it appears that after Restoration, texts of genealogy and honour overtly asserted the need for loyalty and obedience to the king, and reaffirmed the mutual interest and relations of crown and nobility.[512] Moreover, as the succession emerged as the central political issue and conflict, heraldic and genealogical works underpinned Charles II's insistence on the hereditary principle and presented the virtues as well as lineage of his brother as qualities suited for rule.

Matthew Carter's *Honor Redivivus* set out in 1660 to reacquaint even ordinary readers with the codes of honour and armory, but it also did much more. As well as listing the nobles created by Charles II (since 1649) and tracing the origin of monarchy to an age before the Flood, Carter's section on 'The King' was uncompromising in its assertions. The king, he tells readers, is 'subordinate to no sublunary power'; he is 'the true fountain from whence all these rivulets and swelling streams of honour spring', and, he added, 'he is God's vicegerent ... to be obeyed accordingly both in church and state'.[513] The discussion of royal prerogative and obedience, an important move in 1660, served Charles perhaps still more effectively when repeated in 1673 in a third edition, published at a time when the Declaration of Indulgence had reopened debates about regal powers which Carter resolutely defended.[514] William Ramsay's *The Gentleman's Companion*, first published anonymously in 1672, though a guide to virtuous and honourable bearing, was similarly also 'an epistle ... admonitory' from the times. Reminding gentry readers of the contempt for their class fostered by the late rebellion, the guide counselled the need for unity and loyalty, arguing that 'nothing [is] more unbecoming a gentleman than to oppose his sovereign, the fountain of gentility'.[515] Continuing the instruction that the essence of gentility was 'obedience, allegiance', Ramsay advised gentlemen to avoid 'gests' or discourse about the monarchy to whom they owed 'all that thou hast or art'.[516] On his pages, courtesy became synonymous with loyalty and new as well as established gentlemen were tutored into obedience.

Over the next years, when that obedience was tested in the mounting crisis over popery and the succession, courtesy books and genealogical and heraldic works again appeared in print to defend the king. In 1677, John Logan's *Analogia Honorum, or, A Treatise of Honour and Nobility* soon unfolded into a loyalist treatise and polemic for the king. For, as well as praising monarchy as the divine, most ancient and best government, the author singled out Charles II and his brother for encomium.[517] Countering Hobbesian arguments with a reassertion of the sacred blessing of kingship, Logan gave thanks that 'God hath ... restored our ancient government and seated our sovereign in the throne of his ancestors, giving him a power just and absolute'.[518] Expressing his hope that the king would be obeyed as God's chosen, that all traitorous tenets would be discredited, and that the yeomen too would sense their obligation to a prince under whose power and government 'their rights and privileges are preserved', Logan cited the glorious deeds of the Duke of York whom he prayed might live long 'to support the grandeur of the British monarchy in the person of his sacred majesty' and then to succeed to a throne from which no law or act could debar him.[519]

The same year, in a *Genealogical History* of the monarchy, 'encouraged' by the king's appreciation, the Lancaster herald Francis Sandford explicitly set out, as he told the king, to argue the case for obedience.[520] 'Kings ought', the preface proclaimed, 'to be honoured as the lively images of the divinity', especially when 'their title is strengthened by a descent from so many royal progenitors'.[521] 'Never,' he continued, had the arm of God more plainly appeared 'than in that miraculous preservation and Restoration of your majesty' to a throne, he reminded readers, that had passed 'by a continued succession of near twelve hundred years'.[522] If Charles II is presented in Sandford's history as 'flesh of the flesh . . . of every one of us', his brother by implication must continue the narrative of history and God's providential determinations.[523] The re-inscription of honour as loyalty and the argument for succession made genealogies and courtesy books into loyalist texts of Stuart kingship beyond the dynasty itself. In Charles's last year, a genealogy of the prince and princess of Denmark traced Stuart descent and the dynasty's providential victories over enemies, and prayed for its triumph over 'all factious opposers whatsoever'.[524] As the author, Henry Keefe, hoped that 'all abhorrers of monarchy [be] . . . brought to condign punishment' and the Stuart line be continued, Charles was basking in his triumph over the Whigs and his brother was looking to the succession.[525] Although eschewing 'overlong and tedious harangues', the genealogist had played his part in securing that triumph.[526]

Where Restoration genealogies tied Charles and monarchy to history and ancient empires, travel writing linked the king to new imperial sway, to national destiny, unrivalled riches and the prospects of world power. Travel literature has always been, and remains, as much a representation of and meditation on the home country as on other lands; and as we recall the famous names of Hakluyt and Raleigh, there can be no doubting the place of early modern travel texts in domestic politics and power.[527] Not least, in Charles II's case, the rise of England as a trading and colonizing nation, and the acquisition of Tangier that came as dowry with the king's marriage to Catherine of Braganza, fostered imperial ambitions. But travel literature also drew from the Virgilian, the Augustan tropes of Restoration discourse, to present England's king as the chosen heir of empire: as a leader who would bring peace and (increasingly, it was claimed) civility to the rest of the world. In so presenting the restored king as a global emperor, travel writings, both through devices of comparison and contrast, represented to English readers the special virtues as well as strengths of their own kingdom – and of their own king.

Indeed, early texts of travel and empire clearly interpreted and represented miraculous events of 1660 as the sign of a chosen nation's imperial destiny. Having surveyed the kingdoms of Europe, noting the deficiencies of their governments and constitutions, the author of *Europae Modernae Speculum* came to England 'the fortunate island' which was, he posited, 'in its Restoration a miracle and its settlement a wonder'.[528] With a unity settled at home, and under 'an excellent prince' whose right is as undoubted as his succession but who 'reconcil[ed] his prerogative and his people's liberties', England, the author boasted, was placed to 'give the law to Africa and Europe'.[529] And, the treatise suggests, the reverse was true: empire and trade depended upon unity, loyalty and obedience to a monarch, who was the life of the nation. Whatever any mounting difficulties or tensions at home, travel writers were able to present English governance in a favourable light, by looking to less fortunate nations abroad. In his description of *Africa*, for example, the deviser of Charles's entry pageants, John Ogilby, in a dedication to the king, rehearsed how Charles had restored peace to a ravished land and so laid the foundations too for a restoration of the arts and sciences, wealth, splendour and reputation that England now enjoyed. In Ogilby's survey of Africa, Tangier is placed as the seat of the new empire of a second Augustus who would bring civilization to barbarity – abroad, as he had at home.[530] Paul Rycaut's study of the Ottoman empire, where he was English consul at Smyrna, led him to conclude that all was barbarous 'which are differenced from us by diversity of manners and custom', as all were unfortunate to live subject to any other government than England's, 'the most free and just in the world' under 'the most gracious of all the princes of the universe'.[531] Comparison with foreign servitude, Rycaut argued, comparing the Muslims with the puritans, taught Englishmen 'to know and prize thy own freedom . . . that thou mayest ever bless God and the king'.[532] The same emphasis on English civility and benign monarchical rule contrasted with cruel tyranny and barbarity abroad characterizes accounts of Russia, West Barbary and Japan, all published in the early 1670s.[533] Not only England, but King Charles, Fage's *A Description of the Whole World* suggests, is a model for all nations.[534]

By the early 1670s, as we have seen, not all at home saw Charles in such terms and it is noteworthy that travel writers such as Lancelot Addison increasingly often refer to the late internecine wars in England while recounting foreign conflicts: indeed, the author of a *History of Muscovy*, published in 1674, found such clear parallels between the wars there and the civil wars in England that his account of Demetrius and his recovery of his murdered father's throne reads like an allegory of Charles II.[535] As conflicts intensified in England, we even discern domestic differences translated onto foreign soils, as travel writers reflect on how difficult it is to 'maintain such a form and order of government as will prove a sufficient security from the common good and public safety'.[536] And, as civil conflict again loomed, we hear articulated the view that, rather than renewing fighting at home, the English would do better to advance colonial acquisition and power abroad.[537] No more than the history of domestic regimen was the story of England's expanding empire one without troubles and tensions.

Yet, in the main, the literature of travel presented to the English an England, and a monarchy, in favourable light. Editing and revising a famous survey of Britain in a new age of empire, the travel writer and cartographer Richard Blome felt confident in asserting both the unique 'perfect and happy composition of England' and the special virtues of its monarchy and ruler.[538] England was, he assured readers, 'a monarchy so free and happy, that as industry is cherished, liberty and happiness enjoyed, so the king is no way eclipsed of those royal prerogatives due to so great a monarch as would not have his subjects his slaves'.[539] In its early manifestation in travel writing, the Whig myth of the perfectability of the English constitution, far from a discourse of opposition, presented kingship and the restored king as the best regimen and ruler, and a model for less civilized, less fortunate peoples. Empire and civility, in short, were royal as well as English attainments.

While contemporary domestic affairs increasingly invaded histories and genealogies, courtesy books and travel literature, politics also became ubiquitous in the imaginative literature of Restoration England.[540] Imaginative writing, power and politics had in early modernity always been in close, if often tense, relations; and literary texts, as we have come to appreciate, yield at times the profoundest contemporary insights into political negotiations and imaginings. Yet the changes effected by the events of mid-century are everywhere apparent in Restoration literary culture: in publication and print, poem and novel, habits of writing and reading.[541] For one, as students quickly observe, Restoration poems are dominated not only by the large question of power and subjectivity, but by particularities: the details, events, most of all the names of ministers and administrators, noblemen and mistresses, courtiers and rakes. As the newly recognizable genre of poems on affairs of state testifies, literature became a site of political debate and contest, a legacy of civil war which had rendered all literary performances, all choices of style, form and genre, not only political but partisan. While the topical development of this politicization resulted, in Charles II's reign, in the official laureate and party hack, from the outset literature played a large role in the political process of representing and reconstructing the monarchy in the imaginings and emotions of readers.

Not least the publications and republications of pre-civil war poets and playwrights, especially those closely connected to the court, served both to stress continuity and to reconstitute a royalist system of values which had been exiled with the cavalier poets themselves. The work of Thomas Carew (for example) was published in 1670, Sir William D'Avenant's in 1673, and Herbert's

The Temple in 1667.[542] But the re-impression of regality on the literary imagination went well beyond that. Mark Kishlansky demonstrated some years ago how, after Restoration, Aesop's *Fables*, especially that of the frogs desiring a king, were re-read as royal apologia; and in the edition by James Ogilby there is little surprise in that.[543] Indeed, Ogilby directs us to how other translations were re-read and rewritten in the wake of the Restoration to strengthen the argument for monarchy over republic, and to support Charles II in particular. Ogilby's 1665 edition of the works of Virgil, as Annabel Patterson has argued, appropriated classical text for royalism, not least in its gendering of the 4th book of the *Georgics* and the bees' loyalty to their king, and the 9th book of the *Eclogues* with its account of how 'swords make oppression'.[544] Ogilby summarizes the argument of the first *Eclogue* in lines directly evocative of the experience of Charles II as well as of the nation:

> Sad Milebaeus, banished, declares
> Those miseries attend on Civil Wars;
> But happy Tityrus, the safe defence
> People enjoy under a settled Prince.[545]

The licence taken by the translator opened into the full liberty of imagination for authors of romances such as *The Princess Cloria*, who freely used the genre to allegorize recent and contemporary events and to teach the lesson of the blessings of monarchy and the need for obedience.[546] Because we find among the list of (newly fashionable) romances rushed into print soon after Restoration a work by the king's Advocate, George MacKenzie, or his Master of Ceremonies, Charles Cotterell, we sense a whole genre of writing that merits further study as a discourse of politics.[547] As Charles Cotterell wrote, in an address to the reader of his translation of *Cassandra* (dedicated to the king): 'neither can the strange success of the Grecian conqueror, the fatal destruction of the Persian monarchy . . . nor any other passage in it seem improbable to us, whose eyes have in as short a space been witnesses of such revolutions, as hardly any romance . . . can parallel'.[548] Romances, in other words, and proto-novels, not only revived as the genre suitable to a restored court and aristocratic culture, but they drew renewed popularity and, as several prefaces suggest, broad readership from the history of the royal family itself.

The relationship between such fictions, historical truths and the politics and polemics of royal representation is nowhere better demonstrated than in the story that circulated long before Restoration and which was all but ubiquitous after 1660: the story of Charles's escape from the battle of Worcester and his hiding in the famous 'Royal Oak'. The established facts of the story – of a monarch, on the run, in disguise, hiding in houses and woods, before finally effecting an escape incognito on a boat to France – were enough to blur the boundaries between history and fiction. But as it was told, in various versions, the fictional devices of suspense, the near discovery, the comic interlude that relieved tension, were so fully deployed that the story of the Royal Oak indeed became a romance. As the author of the third edition of one of the earliest versions described it in 1680, the world had proved more greedy for the story 'than ever young ladies were to read the conclusion of an amorous strange romance'.[549] Though Charles II himself evidently enjoyed telling the story, he did not commit his own account to paper until 1680 when he dictated a version to Samuel Pepys at Newmarket.[550] Before then, as A. M. Broadley, Richard Ollard and most recently Brian Weiser have shown, the accounts of the various participants in the drama – Lane, Wilmot, Penderell and others – differ in the authors' relations and emphases in accordance with their different ideological perspectives, as well as their respective interests in highlighting their own service.[551] Accordingly, where John Danvers's *The Royal Oak* makes no reference to Catholics who aided Charles and stresses Protestant providentialism, *Whiteladies* and *Boscobel*, perhaps to argue the case for toleration, stress the recusants' contribution to the royal escape and the sacral nature of the king, evident even through his disguise.[552] Such differences underline the extent to which the story, indeed the representation of Charles himself, was available for diverse causes and parties. For our purposes, however, it is the image of the king that the texts constructed and circulated which is arresting. For, from the various accounts, Charles emerges as both strong and vulnerable, Christic and human, sacred and yet still familiar, even ordinary. Here we have both the king whose hair, cut off to effect a disguise, is treasured as a holy relic and the monarch who in disguise as a servant is scolded, indeed boxed on the ear, by a mere maid who laughs at him. The story of the Royal Oak helped to enable Charles to perform the negotiation required in 1660 between the mystical and the rational or demystified.[553] Though he did not publish his own account of the story, it textualized the dual characteristics he embodied and deployed in his own acts of speaking and writing.

And the story resounded with both elite and popular audiences. While Abraham Jennings's two-hundred-page, complicated Anglican narrative *Miraculum Basilikon* (1664) 'probably attracted few readers', and those learned in law and astronomy like the author, Danvers's *The Royal Oak* ran to four editions in 1660 alone and, it has been estimated, eleven thousand printed copies.[554] Although less spectacularly successful, Thomas Blount's *Boscobel* went into two editions in the first two years of Restoration, and (as we have seen) a third later in the reign. Beyond these narratives, the story of the Royal Oak was the subject of hundreds of sermons, broadsides and ballads, as well as the cause of so many visits to Boscobel that souvenir hunters threatened to strip the oak bare.[555] History and legend, multiple hands as well as his own oral accounts, Catholic emphasis on sacred icons and Protestant narratives of providentialism, the tradition of aristocratic romances and popular tales of adventure and disguise melded in the story of the Royal Oak to represent Charles to all his subjects, to forge an affective bond of community between author and readers, between the king and his people.

Those bonds, as we have seen, became strained with the years, and if the story of the Royal Oak may be taken as a barometer of Charles's standing, it may be significant that there appear to be no accounts or editions of the story for a decade after the publication of *Claustrum Regale* in 1667. A renewed interest in publicizing and publishing the adventure emerged in 1680, at the time of the Popish Plot, and was initiated by no less a person than Charles II himself, who instructed Pepys to take an official version in shorthand. B. Weiser rightly argues the comfort Charles may have taken in a crisis from the memory of his earlier escape, and the value of the oak story in validating his policy towards Catholics; the adventure too had a popular appeal at a time when the king sought to command the loyalty of his ordinary people. Charles's own account plays down the language of providence and figures the king as less a passive victim, more in control of events, in a manner that 'emboldened and empowered' his representation.[556] Charles's own version was, as Weiser says, dexterous and astute – like his dealings with his exclusionist enemies. But in 1680, Charles was not alone in retelling his story, nor in reconstructing the romance of authority more generally. The third edition of *Boscobel*, published in two parts, was republished in 1680, the preface announced, with extra details and observations. Thomas Blount's text now observed more pointedly 'that in this persecution much of his Majesty's actions and sufferings have run parallel with those of David'.[557] And, at the close of his narrative, Blount prints a speech of Clarendon delivered to parliament on 29 December 1660: 'we may tell,' the Lord Chancellor pronounced, 'those desperate wretches who yet harbour in their thoughts wicked designs against the sacred person of the king in order to the compassing their own imaginations, that God Almighty would not have led him through so many wildernesses of afflictions of all heads ... but for a servant whom he will always preserve'.[558] As Clarendon's words were reprinted, Charles faced the second major crisis of his life: in invoking the story of the first, Blount hoped that his new edition might be called 'the second stage of the royal progress'.[559]

In that moment of crisis, as well as poetical panegyrists like Dryden, novelists and romance writers stepped forward to support the royal cause. The novel *Grimalkin*, published the same year as *Absalom and Achitophel*, testifies to the full politicization of all literary forms, famously articulated in Dryden's preface. *Grimalkin, or, The Rebel-cat* was a Tory novel, 'representing the unwearied attempts of the beasts of his faction against sovereignty and succession'.[560] Using an animal allegory, the author narrates the plots of creatures to bring down the lion by spreading rumours of his threat to consume all, and the need to respect the lion's position and authority. With its close allusions to Charles, James, Duke of York, and Monmouth (and his 'prostitute mother'), the allegory was thinly veiled.[561] Yet it underlines not only the role of Restoration fictions in presenting Charles's monarchy, but the participation of all literary genres and forms in the politics of contest and party.

The full politicization of literary culture made it impossible for Charles II to control his representation in any genre or words. Indeed, some scholars have suggested that he did not seek to do so: that in contrast to his father he preferred a laissez-faire attitude to the control of his image, at least until the last years of his reign.[562] One new genre of royal writing, however, very much represented the government's desire to direct its textual representation. During the 1630s, faced with the criticism of his foreign policy in newsbooks and with Cardinal Richelieu's *Gazette* as a model, Charles I had been advised to issue an official newspaper to counter parliamentary, then Commonwealth papers.[563] At the Restoration, Charles appointed the cavalier Sir Roger L'Estrange as Licenser of the Press; and, as well as acting as a vigorous censor of news, he established in 1663 an official government organ, *The Intelligencer*, which was succeeded in 1665 by the London *Gazette* and *The Public Intelligencer*.[564] At first glance those newspapers look to be brief factual accounts, principally of foreign campaigns or fleet engagements. But they include poems, as well as reports from the fleet, and use emotive language to stir patriotic support for government policies. The *Current Intelligence* for June 1666, for example, reprints a Waller poem on a battle with the Dutch and concludes the month's reporting with the admonition 'if there be any heart in that island that is not influenced with indignation and resolution at this news, it must be of a French or Dutch temper and inclination'.[565] As well as whipping up support against foreign enemies, the paper was prone to print a favourable gloss – it is not inappropriate to say 'spin' – on the situation at home where, it reported in July 1666, not entirely accurately 'such a harmony there is between the head and heart of this kingdom'.[566] Reports of small victories, often against the odds, of heroic deeds, of good progress, the taking of booty, a relative silence on setbacks, the odd humorous retort, the mixture, that is, of report and literary device that is a feature of the modern newspaper, were all deployed in the 1660s to rally support for the king. As with modern reporting in wartime, defeats only exacerbated the tendency to present a glossy impression and by the 1670s a series of *True Relations* was published alongside the *Gazette*. Here emphasis was laid on the 'heroic behaviour' and 'fearless courage' of the Admiral, the king's nephew Prince Rupert, and on countering the negative representations, 'told only as ... the other faction ... would have it'.[567] As the language of party indicates, domestic politics was never far below the surface. For, as *An Exact Relation* explained in 1673, the king had replaced the Duke of York as commander, in accordance with the Test Act; and while not all had gone well, under a prince zealous for the reformed religion, God, through his providence, had brought home the royal fleet without serious loss.

The polemics and literary techniques of Restoration newspapers, and their role in the emerging politics of party, await their own full study. In our discussion of the representations of monarchy they both epitomize what we have been reviewing through other genres of textual representation and make a statement of their own. The *Intelligencer, Gazette* and various *Relations* in their mix of news with history, verse and literary tropes exemplify the textuality of Restoration politics as well as the full politicization of its literary culture. But they suggest too a conscious artfulness in the act of representation, the use of terms and techniques to sell a message or to counter another version. The Restoration official government newspapers, for all their language of unity and nationhood, were, and were increasingly, partisan. And they announce as well as further a shift in the representation of kingship to a recognition that, in a divided realm, the king might need to seek the support of a party.

Though for a time in 1660 many tried not to recognize it, the civil war, we can see, had made all the languages and texts of representation partisan. And increasingly, we sense, contemporaries themselves discerned that those languages – and all the texts and arts of royal representation – were, and had to be, constructed and polemical. This is not (quite) to argue that representation had become propaganda – a concerted and cynical readiness to communicate (possibly false) information to persuade; but it is to acknowledge a greater self-consciousness in the deployment of vocabularies and languages at particular moments, a recognition in fact by contemporaries of what one called the 'poetical and rhetorical flourishes' in the representations of authority.[568] The history of the discourse of providence over Charles's reign provides a good example of both that sense of strategy and that self-consciousness. In 1660, the language of providence pervades almost every text, poem and treatise, as well as sermon, because there was a perceived need to reappropriate from the puritans an argument that had so much damaged the royal cause: the argument that God had not favoured the Stuarts. Where some preachers, like John Paterson, sought to dismiss as a 'Turkish argument' the notion that success was a sign of external providence, others like Francis Gregory tried to reinterpret the message of providential scourge as a sign of love, and then to reverse the position by asking 'if the cross Providence of God which once befell our king might be looked upon as so many frowns from heaven, why may not the successful Providence of God that now attends him be looked upon as smiles'.[569] There is artfulness as well as anxiety here and, with the crown settled, most writers, including Charles himself, played down the sacral and providential. By 1667 Thomas Sprat, though as historian of the Royal Society not a typical commentator, was freely describing 'the wild amusing men's minds, with prodigies and concerts of providence' and urging new languages and texts of politics, as well as learning.[570] For more than a decade, the lexicons of commerce, reason and interest dominate social and political debate – until political crisis from 1678 saw the noisy resumption of a language of providence to support what is by now a party as much as a royal cause. During the heated polemics of the Popish Plot, Whig polemicists charged the king and government with manipulating the language of providence, with inventing, with misrepresenting.[571] And, for all the royal victory, and the near universal acclamation of kingship, by the end of Charles's reign even the king and his supporters would have acknowledged the charges. That the tenets of sacral kingship, that is, were knowingly rather than naturally deployed, and if not directly disbelieved, believed most passionately and conveniently when they were needed.

The history of the representation of Charles II in words is complex and ambiguous. Across the quarter century of his reign, texts – his own, and those of others – figured him as traditional and new, sacred yet ordinary, his rule natural yet in need of justification. To some extent different genres, the history and the sermon, for example, allowed for very different images to be kept simultaneously in play; but the ambiguities beset at times all the genres of the king's representation. Yet in their very ambiguity, such representations saved and sustained Charles's kingship, as he intuited. For a nation that could not in 1660 fully accept the realities of division, demystification and political conflict, the mix of older vocabularies and tropes with new languages helped to reconstitute the polity. Gradually textual ambiguity and contest enabled an accommodation of non-violent difference, ultimately the rise of parties, formed not least out of different discourses that had remained in play. At some point in Charles II's reign – perhaps from the outset – the business of representing authority had become a political art, every bit as much as authority depended upon texts, images and acts of representation. Not least of Charles II's skills was that he knew it, and intuited the need to deploy ambiguity at times, to adopt different genres and tones in shifting circumstances, and, for the most part, when to represent his own cause and when to allow others to speak for him.

After the Babel of civil war and republican pamphleteering, Hobbes's vision of a sovereign signifier, in control of words, was no more than a fantasy. But as we analyse the rhetorical and literary tropes of royal speech and writing and the traces of words and figures of royalty in all the genres of Restoration writing, we might suggest that fantasies and fictions could lend authority their own power, even in a divided realm.

CHAPTER 2

REDRAWING REGALITY

I

The visual culture of the reign of Charles II has not attracted much scholarly attention. There has been no major exhibition of the paintings of that age for over forty years, with the splendid exception of female portraits.[1] The last exhibition of Sir Peter Lely's male as well as female portraits was over thirty years ago, and the last biography of the artist who succeeded Sir Anthony Van Dyck is over half a century old.[2] As for other major figures in the painting of the age, many like John Michael Wright, Jacob Huysmans, Antonio Verrio, John Riley and William Wissing have received little notice, and we lack reliable catalogues of their oeuvres.[3]

At first sight this neglect seems as puzzling as it is regrettable. The age of Charles II saw a vibrant cultural flowering: in science, theatre, aristocratic life and in architecture, gardens and habits of collecting. Moreover, Charles II himself was, infamously, a 'colourful' character and his dark skin, full mouth and luxuriant hair made him a striking figure, whose image is today instantly recognizable by many who have only a passing acquaintance with the details of the history of the time. If Charles II made a visual impression on his subjects and on history, why, we need to ask, has his own image remained in the shadows of art-historical scholarship?

At the most general level, the history of later seventeenth-century England (relative to the period from the Reformation to the civil war) has suffered from a scholarly neglect from which it is only slowly being rescued. Only over the last couple of decades has the political narrative of this age been revisited and revised so as to free it from the prejudices of a Whig historiography which was virulently hostile to the last Stuarts.[4] This, however, offers at best a partial explanation for the indifference displayed towards the art of the age. The literary culture, after all, of the age of Dryden and Bunyan, Behn and the later Milton, has been richly illuminated by successive schools of critics from the formalists to modern historicist literary scholars. We are left with the most likely explanation: a sense among the art-historical establishment, that, by contrast with a preceding age and indeed with the literary giants of Restoration letters, the painters of the age of Charles II were not particularly good. Though some powerful claims have been made for his brilliance, there remain differences concerning Sir Peter Lely's skills and few scholars have conceded him the accolades heaped upon Van Dyck. And, as the 2002 *Painted Ladies* exhibition displayed and argued at London's National Portrait Gallery, if Lely has a claim to be the equal of his former master, that claim is best upheld by his female portraits – though even here contemporary criticisms of a formulaic, repetitive style still resonate in modern scholarship. Lely's portraits of court and aristocratic women, writes Dr Catharine MacLeod, so drew on repetitive poses and drapery that it becomes 'difficult for the twenty-first-century viewer to distinguish one from another'.[5] If such has been the verdict on Lely's women, his portraits of men seem to lack the vitality and command of Van Dyck's. And his portraits of the king, certainly when contrasted with the luminescent images of Charles II's father, appear prosaic and workmanlike. Charles himself, despite appointing Lely principal court painter in 1661 with an annual pension of £2,000 ('as formerly to Sr Vandyke'), seems not to have held him in high regard and – remarkably – as Sir Oliver Millar observed, 'seems to have owned no finished portrait of himself by Lely'.[6]

But whatever Charles's own opinion (which may anyway not have been an aesthetic judgement) or those of modern art historians, Lely's contemporaries eagerly acquired originals, versions and studio copies of his portraits. Few country houses fail to display a Lely, or more often an 'after Lely', of one of the king's mistresses or a courtier, or an image of the king himself: the artist had seventeen copies of portraits of Charles in his studio at his death, and these were presumably painted for sale.[7] Indeed, the almost industrialized production that Lely went in for, with an efficient team combining to churn out copies of portraits, clearly suggests, as well as commercial acumen, a large demand at the time for canvases that do not impress us much today. And we encounter the same experience with other artists, lesser known to us than Lely. Wright's and Wissing's and Kneller's portraits, and those attributed to them or their school, turn up frequently in provincial galleries, country houses and private collections, indicating that there was no small interest among Charles II's contemporaries in owning and displaying images of the king and his court. Furthermore, as we shall see, engravings and mezzotints distributed such images to a broad public which showed an even larger appetite for acquiring such reproductions, often (as framed and varnished copies suggest) to adorn their walls.[8]

When the evidence of contemporary taste seems so different to modern critical judgement, we face a series of interesting questions: were late Stuart painters and collectors undiscriminating? Was it a historical accident that no artists of greater brilliance presented themselves? If these portraits were, as they were, both appreciated and popular, by what criteria, different to ours, did they evaluate them? In short, how does one read the portraits? Reviewing *The Age of Charles II* in 1961, the editorial to the *Burlington Magazine* observed that 'the painting . . . of the period is of abundant historical interest but of sadly little aesthetic consequence'.[9] Such a decontextualized emphasis on 'aesthetic merit', judged presumably by trans-historical standards and values, was once also the dominant approach to works of literature, our understanding – and our appreciation – of which has been transformed by various schools of historical criticism concerned to explicate how texts performed and were received in their times.[10] Such historical approaches – often initiated by scholars outside the discipline of art history, as well as leading figures within it – have recently illuminated and revised our understanding of the visual culture of, say, the German and Italian fifteenth century or the English eighteenth century.[11] If we are to understand the portraits of the age of Charles II, and their vital role in representing the king, we need to restore them too to their histories: to all their moments of conception, execution, consumption, reproduction and circulation.

Central to that historicization is the history of the royal portrait. As we know, motifs recur, but the Tudor royal portrait responded to personal circumstances – such as Henry VIII's emphasis on procreation, dynasty and Supreme Headship, and Elizabeth's move from allegorical goddess to iconic genre.[12] As I have also observed, there were in the 1620s and 1630s relatively few portraits of Charles in royal robes or with the regalia, the canvases instead highlighting an innate majesty that rules the family, the landscape and the viewer by a representation of personal command. In Van Dyck's symbolic portraits of Charles and the royal family, the man gives authority to the crown, as well as draws his authority from it; and monarchic rule is figured as paternal and affective.[13] If the image of effortless personal majesty became harder for Charles I to sustain as opposition gave way to civil war, military defeat and imprisonment, it was certainly not a mode of representation available for his son, when he succeeded *de iure* in January 1649. During the years of the civil war and Commonwealth, images of Charles II, in armour, with regalia and arms, were needed to keep the cause of Stuart monarchy alive and to display the king as legitimate heir, ready to fight for his rightful inheritance.[14] And with an adult life and reign shaped by military conflict, defeat and flight, even at his triumphant moment of Restoration, Charles faced the problem of how to reconstruct and represent the visual symbols and images as much as the vocabularies of kingship.

Like the discourses of Restoration, the visual images of the king harked back to, and yet simultaneously were distanced from, the past. Indeed, in considering the place of the past in Restoration visual culture, we might fruitfully begin with a portrait not of Charles himself but with the copy he commissioned Remigius

Van Leemput to make of the Hans Holbein group portrait of Henry VII, Elizabeth of York, Henry VIII and Jane Seymour.[15] In its original form, this was a proclamation of dynasty and succession by Henry VIII who was the first son to succeed peacefully to his throne in over eighty years.[16] There can be little question that behind Charles's ordering of the copy in 1667 lay some similar advertisement of descent, lineage, family and legitimacy. The king's commission, as well as the artist's name, is inscribed with the date 1667 on the copy, and the portrait was probably displayed with other portraits of royal predecessors. The French visitor Charles Patin, viewing Whitehall in 1671, described the group portrait and what he felt was its purpose: 'Dans l'antichambre de Roy, il a sur le pignon de la croisée de la main d'Holbein, le portrait d'Henry VIII et des Princes ses enfans, dont le Roi a fait tirer une excellent copie, pour en etendre la posterité . . . et n'abandonner pas une si belle chose à la fortune des temps'.[17] We might suggest that it was not only objects that Charles II wished to preserve from the ravages of time but, after the experience of the 1650s, monarchy and dynasty. The various other copies Leemput made of the portrait of Henry VIII suggest that images of dynastic continuity appealed not only to the king.[18] But this was not the only Henrician gesture in the visual culture of the Restoration court. As we shall see, John Michael Wright's state portrait of Charles owed a stylistic and iconographic debt to Holbein and Henry VIII; and it may, in this context, be worth recalling that Charles was the first adult male monarch born in England since Henry.[19]

Most of all, however, during the 1650s, Charles had presented himself as his father's son, as the successor to the martyr, and countless engravings and woodcuts during the Commonwealth years had figured him with images evocative of, and emblems associated with, Charles I, some derived from William Marshall's famous engraved frontispiece to the *Eikon Basilike*.[20] Restoration panegyrics, as we have seen, celebrate and represent Charles as the son of the martyr and the royal word made flesh. No less, there were ubiquitous visual evocations of Charles I, and indeed of his representation on the canvases of Van Dyck. Several of the Lelys and 'after Lely' (or 'Lely circle') portraits of Charles II in armour standing by a table with the crown and sceptre and a baton in his right hand evoke the Van Dycks of Strafford, Northumberland, Warwick and others, which Lely knew well and may even have worked on or copied for the master.[21] In the early 1660s, to which period these have been assigned, such images surely recalled a pre-civil war court and community, and an aesthetic, that were re-embodied in Charles II and revived with the restored monarchy. A portrait now in the government art collection makes a direct reference to Charles and a famous image. Dated as *c.*1661 and thought to be from Lely's circle, the equestrian portrait of Charles II on a white horse with a baton held in his right hand almost exactly follows *Charles I on Horseback* (fig. 1).[22] Though, unlike his father in this case, Charles is not in armour, the

1 Circle of Peter Lely, *King Charles II on Horseback*, c. 1675.

pose, and that of the horse (though reversed) caught in exactly the same motion, could not but have recalled the halcyon days of the Caroline regime. The reverse direction of the portrait might even gesture to a return to such days. Like the fashion for portraits in Greenwich armour, by the Restoration over sixty years old, these visual echoes of Henrician and early Stuart times helped to re-establish a visual sense of historical continuity and to displace republic into the shadows.[23]

Portraits, especially royal portraits, also participated in the reconstitution of a monarchical culture in England. What is immediately evident are the many portraits of Charles II in royal robes, or Garter robes, with the (newly made) royal regalia and displaying the emblem of the Garter, not only the greater George but that Garter Star badge based on the Order of the Holy Spirit, adopted by Charles I and worn in his portrait by Van Dyck now in Dresden.[24] Van Dyck's portrait of Charles in robes of state with the collar of the Garter, standing beside a pillar with the crown and orb, was clearly a model. But whereas the representation of Charles I in royal robes is rare, in the case of Charles II, the Garter, crown and sceptre are ubiquitously figured and the king's favoured official portrait depicts him in both coronation robes and Garter insignia, holding the orb and sceptre and wearing St Edward's crown.[25]

Not only do such images represent monarchy, and all the symbols of a monarchy; they return us to the reality that in 1660 a recently fugitive Charles *needed* these symbols to express his regality and authority, whereas his father did not. That these props of majesty appear less commonly in later portraits strengthens the suggestion that they may have been part of the process, not merely the representation, of Restoration.

For all their evocations and reconstitutions, however, Restoration portraits are different from earlier royal representations in ways that should not simply be explained in terms of the change of court artists. For one, Charles II is not the dominant image we take from this period: in terms of sheer quality, the capacity to evoke life, movement, character and passion, Lely's female portraits still surpass *any* portrait of the king. Indeed, Lely was patronized principally by the Duke of York whose first wife, Anne Hyde, commissioned the series we know as the Windsor Beauties. Moreover, the images of Charles II, while they recall poses and objects, appear to carry very different symbolic freight to those of his father. After the Restoration we do not encounter the Neoplatonic references and *topoi* that are fundamental to readings of Van Dyck's portraits: the *topoi* of the king as the father of the realm, the focus of reason, a Christ figure to be adulated, a romantic chivalrous knight. Nor, in the words of Sonia Wynne, was any 'family romance' a theme of Restoration portraiture.[26] Whereas Charles I commonly represented his loving regimen through symbolic paintings of himself with Henrietta Maria and various of their children, indeed sometimes through portraits of his children alone, Charles II was seldom painted with his wife and had no legitimate heir.[27] Indeed, Catherine of Braganza's favouring of Huysmans (who styled himself 'her Majesty's Painter') over either Wright or Lely suggests distinctions of taste that underlined the royal couple's separateness.[28] Even when Restoration royal images do evoke earlier Caroline themes, as with the Garter, we encounter now no image quite like that of Peter Paul Rubens's *St George* which draws on a whole panoply of discourses, symbols and associations to fold Charles I into Christian history and eschatology.[29]

Indeed, Restoration portraits, rather than rendering visual complex Neoplatonic philosophies and Christian Neoplatonic conceits, seem rather to play with them, as though to advertise a dissociation from an older world of ideas and forms and a scepticism, easily understandable after 1649, about their authority.[30] Witty playfulness is very much a feature of Lely's female portraits in which sitters are figured as saints, and mistresses as Madonna, in a manner that, especially in this last case – the Countess of Castlemaine with Lord Fitzroy – disrupts the association between the timeless symbol and the sitter.[31] Paintings of aristocratic women, and court whores, with the attributes of chastity (the rose, for example), seem similarly to play with symbolic conventions; and Lely's canvas of Barbara Villiers seated by the Venus fountain comes close to mocking both symbolic conventions and the representation of those conventions.[32] Even in the portraits of Catherine of Braganza as St Catherine, a conceit copied by several courtly women, the signifiers of sainthood – the broken wheel and palm – appear more as fashionable props and puns than invocations of the female martyr.[33] While this playfulness did not extend to the king's own portraits, it suggests a changed culture of the visual in which the numinous has given way to the witty and ironic. And if Charles himself does not appear here, these images of his mistresses, still more the emblematic references to the king in the King Charles spaniels sometimes idly fondled on their laps, distort sacral images of kingship, as well as biblical conceits and Christian symbols generally.[34] As we will suggest, the art of Restoration England was by no means divorced from the religious issues and controversies of the age – for one, Catherine's choice of Huysmans as her painter may have owed much to his Catholicism; but Christian symbols and biblical conceits are here appropriated for quite novel purposes, just as in the Earl of Rochester's poems the language of Scripture is now deployed in graphic, some would say pornographic, verse.

Indeed, the Restoration evocation of old themes and associations and yet their deployment in new, sometimes audacious ways, is exemplified in the Windsor Beauties which almost became a mock-dynastic gallery. Not only were the portraits viewed as a set by the late 1660s, satires like 'The Fifth Advice to A Painter' referring to the 'gang' of mistresses, describes them as 'a parody of the sets of kings and queens that had been collected' by earlier rulers and patrons.[35] In Lely's canvases, then, to revise Sonia Wynne, we do encounter a family romance; but, in the repeated images of royal bastards, it is an illegitimate family: a parodic reversal of Charles I's paternal representation, just as the explicitly sexual references are dramatically opposed to the Platonic love by which he and Henrietta Maria presented their marriage and rule.[36] In all these Restoration portraits, the king is present, as well as absent: as the lover (not the husband), as the sire (but not the present father) and, in the portrait of the Countess of Castlemaine as Madonna and her son, as – boldly, sacrilegiously – God.[37] It is royal as well as female representation that is audaciously refigured here.

As well as radical redeployment of the traditional, Restoration royal portraits are, in the most obvious and less apparent ways, also new. The most obvious novelty was the depiction of the king, as well as other sitters, in Roman dress. While James I was represented on coins and medals wearing a laurel and a Le Sueur bronze of Charles I (at Stourhead) features Charles I in pseudo-classical armour, earlier monarchs were not usually painted in Roman dress unless depicted as performing a role, as in a court masque.[38] While Diana de Marly is undoubtedly right in suggesting that the Restoration move to classical dress responded to a need for clothing that would not date a picture by fashion, the argument neither explains the timing nor goes far enough. The appearance of

Roman dress in regal portraits and busts was not peculiar to England: Louis XIV was painted during the 1660s as a Roman hero, and portraits, engravings, sculptured busts and statues, medals and coins all presented Charles II, and his brother James, Duke of York, in Roman garb. It is surely no coincidence that both Louis XIV's and Charles II's depiction in classical dress followed periods of civil war. Rome stood for the peak of civilization and accomplishment in the arts military and civil, and in the figure of Augustus for empire and peaceful new beginnings. We have encountered both Augustan motifs and imperial themes in Restoration panegyrics and travel literature; and we shall meet with them again.[39] The adoption of Roman dress after 1660 should surely then be interpreted as a claim to all these associations – and, not least, as an appropriation for monarchy of classical symbols which had been used to validate republic. Under Charles II the imperial theme was displayed on the body of the king.

Other innovations, or emphases, are evident in genre. While allegorical and actual landscapes formed an important background to Van Dyck's royal portraits, there were few landscapes commissioned by Charles I. By contrast his son appointed, following his return to England about the same time as the king, Hendrick Danckerts as a painter of 'prospect pictures and landskips'.[40] As well as classical landscapes, Danckerts painted 'by the king's command' a picture of Hampton Court Palace around 1665–7, shortly after Charles's restoration work on the grounds. If this advertised the mortar and monument of old royalty, his *View of Tangier* from the south-west, with the union flag and St George's flag flying, unquestionably proclaimed a new British imperial, and regal, power, which was gestured to also in the views of Falmouth and Portsmouth harbours, the seats of naval might, with their defensive castles and batteries.[41] Narrative paintings represent another innovation in royal taste and representation after 1660. Robert Streeter, appointed the King's Sergeant Painter in 1663, painted for Charles a huge canvas of Boscobel House and Whiteladies which, by contraction of distance even within its vast scale, framed the story of Charles's flight in two stages – first to Whiteladies, and subsequently to Boscobel (fig. 2).[42] The right foreground, with the royal oak in which Charles hid and which, as we saw, became a symbol of providential kingship and a folk legend, conceals two figures; and numbers on the composition not only identify, but lead the viewer sequentially through, the stages of movement, the logical end of which was where the viewer stood – at Whitehall, in the palace of the restored monarch where we know the painting was hung. Extending that narrative across five canvases (which we shall examine in some detail), Isaac Fuller also painted the various stages of the king's flight from Worcester to France.[43]

Such narrative canvases point up the topicality and the specificity of much of Restoration royal portraiture. Just as students of later Stuart literature encounter a new world of names, events and texts, the appreciation of which depends on

2 Robert Streeter, *Boscobel House and Whiteladies*, c. 1670.

identifying them, so the comprehension of these images, as their keys indicate, requires identification and specification. Where the symbolism of earlier paintings was more often generalized, subtle and allusive, the specific association left to the viewer, the portraits of Charles II and his reign figure and follow events, moments and men, state affairs and affairs of state. The 'advice to a painter' poems which we find among the collections of poems on affairs of state remind us how contemporaries viewed the visual culture of Charles II's reign as inextricably interwoven with the fabric of politics.[44] The king's use of his desirée Frances Stuart as a model for Britannia on the Peace of Breda Medal exemplifies and embodies the congress between art and political events, just as Andrew Marvell's satire conjuring her naked body and her representation takes its force from the interplay between visual aesthetics and statecraft.[45] And, perhaps more than before, topical events appear to have determined the artist's subjects whether or not by official commission. A representation of the Battle of Lowestoft may have been a royal commission in 1665; and certainly James, Duke of York, commemorated the victory with a use of thirteen portraits of the flag officers and commanders (now in the National Maritime Museum).[46] In 1678, to take another example, an artist (possibly Lely) painted Sir Edmund Bury Godfrey whose murder sparked off the crisis that produced the Popish Plot.[47] Given a culture in which works of art, like literature, were so closely interrelated with politics and events, to begin to understand the paintings we must – as now we shall – return them to their specific moments.

The dating of undated paintings and portraits, often based on style, is an inexact science. But in the case of some of the portraits of Charles II we know, or can confidently assess, the dates and therefore examine the king's pictorial representation at various points, and in the different circumstances of his quarter-century on the throne. Let us begin with a painting that is not a portrait but the picture of a procession: Dirck Stoop's depiction of Charles II's cavalcade through the City of London on 22 April 1661, the night before his coronation on St George's Day (fig. 3).[48] We cannot be sure who commissioned the work. The Utrecht painter and etcher Stoop, son of a stained-glass artist, was in Portugal in the period 1659–62 where he was known for landscapes and battle scenes. He painted a portrait of Catherine of Braganza and travelled with her when she journeyed to England in the spring.[49] It may be that he executed the painting for the queen, but the subject makes it more likely to be a work for Charles, and, if a recent suggestion about its association with Isaac Fuller's Boscobel paintings is right, it is most probable that the king himself commissioned it.[50] Stoop, who did not arrive in England until May 1662, had clearly not been a witness to Charles's coronation. But John Ogilby had published a detailed account of the proceedings with a full description of the triumphal marches in 1661, and the next year (the licence is dated June) issued a lavish folio illustrated with detailed engravings of the procession and the pageants.[51] It seems likely that Stoop had access to these; what seems certain is that, a year after his coronation, Charles II desired a painting that would commemorate the occasion of his entry into his capital.

In his Declaration from Breda, Charles made a direct appeal to the people of England who, he believed, were keen to see him returned to his throne. For much of his reign he sought, and in cases relied upon, popular support. In 1660,

3 Dirck Stoop, *Coronation Procession of Charles II to Westminster from the Tower of London, 22nd April 1661*, 1662.

when he had landed at Dover, and the next year as he processed to his coronation, Charles had been greeted by much public acclamation and festive euphoria.
The painting of the cavalcade records that moment and the scale of the reception. It also records permanently on canvas the temporary arches which, as we
shall see, laid out a complicated iconographic narrative of welcome to the triumphantly returning king.[52] And a triumph is what this painting stages. Charles,
more or less at the centre of the canvas, the only figure on a white horse, has just
ridden through a triumphal arch that bears his name. The long procession, in
orderly ranks, with all attendants in finery, snakes its way through a further four
arches into the distance, as if to suggest the long road that had led to Restoration,
almost a pilgrimage. But most importantly, Charles is here figured not as an
isolated figure but as part of a procession, a community: the dress of some of his
attendants even appears to meld with that of the king who is distinguished principally by his tall hat and Garter badge. With the king, on this canvas, returns,
along with the monarchy, the proper order of rule and officers of state, the aristocratic order, the symbolic order after years of the world turned upside down.
The triumph is not just the king's but the nation's – every man's.

It was probably shortly after the event recorded by Stoop that the king's
favourite painter in large, John Michael Wright, painted Charles II in his coronation robes, full length and seated under a canopy of state embroidered with the
royal arms (fig. 4).[53] The king wears St Edward's crown and holds in his left hand
the orb and in his right the sceptre – all of which had had to be re-made by the
royal goldsmith at a cost of over £30,000, the originals having been destroyed
during the Interregnum. As Sir Oliver Millar observes, the portrait is not just a
representation of Charles; it 'is as much a demonstration of restored monarchy
and an illustration of the revived royal ceremonial apparel of the new Garter
costume, and of the new regalia.'[54] It is, of course, an image of both – the regalia
and the man. Charles sits with his legs wide apart and the viewer is directed to
the royal loins: to the prospect for progeny and dynasty. The pose should not
pass without remark for, though seated, Charles's stance and gaze straight to the
viewer recall Holbein's Henry VIII (which, as we have seen, he had had copied).
Moreover, the king is seated in front of a tapestry, the figures represented on
which appear to attend Charles. The subject of the tapestry has been identified
as the Judgement of Solomon; and with that in mind, we recall Holbein's delicate
miniature of *Solomon and the Queen of Sheba*, with Solomon given the features
of Henry VIII.[55] Solomon/Henry VIII sits in the same swaggering pose as
Charles. Holbein's picture of the encounter of Solomon with the Queen of Sheba,
who has arrived from the east to pay homage to the king of wisdom, has been
read as an allegory of the submission of the church to the crown, effected in
Henry VIII's assumption of the Supreme Headship. We cannot know whether
Charles intended, or others viewed, Wright's portrait as a reprise of the same
themes. But the Solomonic motif seems unquestionable and, as Millar notes, the

4 John Michael Wright, *Charles II, c.* 1661–2.

sceptre and orb with the cross 'represent the king's temporal power under the blessings of the Cross'.[56] What we have then in Wright's portrait is Charles as successor to the Tudors, as Solomon, and as Supreme Head of the Church founded by Henry VIII, a church now again restored with the king.

But after the early 1660s, as the monarchy became established, portraits of Charles II less frequently depict the king with the trappings of monarchy. Lely and Lely studio works figure the king frequently in Garter robes, but a famous example which appears to be a template for several copies features Charles now standing with his plumed hat on a table beside him, with only the large fluted column behind signifying regal authority.[57] Similarly later works by Wright or his studio feature no other allegorical canvases; while the picture of Charles painted with a pineapple depicts the king, apart from the kneeling John Rose, almost as a lord at ease on his country estate (fig. 5).[58] Whether the gesture from Rose, chief horticulturist to the king, was freighted with symbolic meaning – the presentation of the fruits of the season, or more likely, since pineapples were probably not yet growing in England, of foreign lands (Columbus gave the first account of the fruit) – we cannot be sure.[59] The association of the pineapple with

5 Hendrik Danckerts, *John Rose the King's Gardener, presenting Charles II with a pineapple, supposedly the first grown in England at Dorney Court in Berkshire*, seventeenth century.

exotic places and welcoming hospitality may not be irrelevant to a reading of the painting, but more topically in 1667 Father Duterte, author of the *General History of the West Indies*, described it as 'the king of fruits since God placed a crown upon its head'.[60] But if this painting was a representation of majesty, it was a majesty far more at ease than in 1660.

If there is in the Danckerts picture a hint of the fruits or homage of empire, other portraits of Charles II proclaim Augustan imperialism in no uncertain terms. In particular the Catholic artist Antonio Verrio, who was taken into royal service almost on his arrival in England, was evidently commissioned for works with imperial themes. One head and shoulders of Charles in armour within an oval frame of palm branches has been identified as probably part of a ceiling decoration in the Presence Chamber at Windsor with Mercury 'showing the monarch to the four quarters of the world'.[61] If Verrio here gestured to an Augustan triumph of peace, his portrait of *The Sea Triumph of Charles II* probably celebrated a treaty, the Treaty of Westminster that in 1674 ended the war with the Dutch who yielded to England's dominion of the seas (fig. 6).[62] Sovereignty of the seas had long been a preoccupation, some might say a dream,

6 Antonio Verrio, *The Sea Triumph of Charles II*, c. 1674.

of the Stuarts (Charles I had named his flagship the *Sovereign of the Seas*), and the yielding of honour to the English flag was seen to symbolize that suzerainty.[63] The portrait of Charles, in classical armour, driven through the water by Neptune, may allude to earlier Caroline proclamations and representations of naval victory. The canvas has masque-like properties, but as well as an evocation of earlier ambitions, is a work very much of its time, and of England's emerging dominance of the seas. Charles's shell-like chariot, drawn by white horses as well as Neptune, is flanked by three female figures bearing crowns of the three kingdoms. Above the king, Fame with her trumpet carries a scroll inscribed *Imperium oceano famam qui terminet astris* and other figures gesture to bestow on him a wreath and a helmet. 'In the sky Envy is struck by lightning and chased by putti with the attributes of Peace and Love, and two more putti carry the royal arms on a shield'; below two dark-skinned putti carry a map inscribed, over an apparently erased earlier inscription, *pacatamque reget* – 'may he rule having established peace'. 'Beyond are Minerva and Venus looking down at the British fleet at anchor, with the royal standard flying on a warship.'[64] The proclamation of naval victory, peace and imperial grandeur as the fruits of royal wisdom is obvious. But if this canvas did commemorate the Treaty of Westminster, we should recall that it was a treaty to which Charles was driven by shortage of funds to sustain a war and the terms of which fell far short of his dreams of eradicating the Dutch as a naval rival. Moreover, it followed a parliamentary refusal of supply.[65] Were Verrio and Charles together making the most of at best a half-hearted triumph? And did the Envy pursued by Peace and Love figure English detractors as well as foreign foes? We cannot be sure. But what is clear is that, as well as again underlining Augustan imperialism, this canvas presents Charles as the person with Time (she offers the wreath), the forces of Nature, the gods and destiny on his side – one recognized by Nature as a mighty leader who would carry all before him. In the increasingly tense circumstances of the king's relations with parliaments and a mounting public suspicion of his policies, it was an audacious representation indeed.

As we have seen, domestic tensions heightened to the point of crisis in the later 1670s, so it is worth our reviewing how (if at all) the royal image was represented in difficult and dangerous times. Any such discussion begins with the first portrait of the king by Godfrey Kneller, who arrived in England from his native Lubeck (via Rome and Venice) in 1676. Charles commissioned him for a Garter portrait in 1678 or 1679, but evidently soon after he painted a second full-length portrait of the king which has, significantly, been described as 'more of a state portrait than any surviving earlier picture of the king' (fig. 7).[66] Oliver Millar observes that the portrait presents us with 'a stiffened derivation of Van Dyck's portrait of Charles I with the regalia placed in the same relation to the figure'. Charles stands in an ermine robe (what looks like coronation robes) with his right hand on the orb which stands, with the St Edward crown and sceptre, on a solid oak chest. It is the first portrait since the coronation so presenting the king and one which, as well as proclaiming authority, appears to reach for it, for the symbols of regality as a defence against challenge. If such a representation reasserts royal authority at a time of opposition, an anonymous portrait in the Government Art Collection of Charles and his brother the Duke of York holding hands either manifests the king's determination to hold on to the succession or

7 Isaac Beckett, after Sir Godfrey Kneller, *Carolus IIdus D.G. Mag: Brit: Fran et Hiber: Rex*, c. 1680–5.

celebrates his triumph in overcoming the Whig movement to exclude the Duke (fig. 8).[67] Nothing is known of the painting, which is undated as well as anonymous. But Charles, in Garter robes, and his brother are already well on in years and the depiction of the king owes some debt to Kneller.

The suggestion that this little-known portrait makes a claim to succession at the moment of the Exclusion crisis may gain credence from another portrait of James, Duke of York, with his first wife and children.[68] Though the painting was begun by Lely, probably in the 1660s, research indicates that the children were either finished or added when around 1680 Benedetto Gennari (who painted devotional pictures for Catherine of Braganza) was commissioned to complete Lely's unfinished work. Critical evaluation of his work has not been favourable, like the portrait of Charles and James, however, Gennari's completion of Lely's canvas – a depiction of progeny in a crisis of disputed succession – may suggest much about strategies of royal representation in the difficult political circumstances of the late 1670s and early 1680s. As might a rather different portrait that we can fairly confidently assign to the later part of these years: William Wissing's

8 Unknown artist, *King Charles II and King James II*, seventeenth century.

three-quarter-length portrait of Charles II in armour.[69] Wissing, who came to London from Amsterdam in 1676, found immediate favour with both Charles and James, but was a committed Protestant and a member of the Dutch Reformed Church in London. His portrait of Charles, at Windsor, presents the king not only in armour but with a baton in his right hand, and in a pose evocative of a Van Dyck portrait, with a cavalry engagement in the right background. Though this has rightly been described as 'a standard martial pattern that Wissing was to use', it was by the 1680s not at all a familiar image of Charles II who had not been commonly painted in armour since the 1640s. Peace and love find no place here. On Wissing's canvas, we encounter instead a king perhaps ready to fight – as his father had done – for his cause in a gesture of defiance against those who hoped he might yield as the nation a second time faced civil war.

Certainly portraits that have been assigned to the very last months of the reign again strike a different, and, if not relaxed, less militant mood. Thomas Hawker's portrait, of uncertain date but not before 1680, though described by the National Gallery as presenting Charles as 'lascivious' and 'glum', harks back to Wright's coronation portrait with Charles in rich silks posed with legs apart under a canopy before a tapestry depicting Solomon.[70] Kneller's final portrait of the king dated 1685 may, as the Walker Gallery describes it, depict an 'aging and even lonely figure', but Charles in full length sits in garter robes with the crown and orb in the shadows behind him, now symbolizing the continuity of succession he has secured.[71]

The most interesting late portrait is that by the French artist Jacques Parmentier, whose image of Charles may even have just been posthumous. In this small oil on copper, an owl-helmeted Minerva on a cloud holds aloft an oval portrait of an armoured Charles, framed in laurel leaves, above a view of Windsor. The warrior king has triumphed through wisdom and ascends to heaven with the crown safe. Here, interestingly, we discern not only a proclamation of Charles's political victory and divinity, but reference too to his visual representation, the Minerva and twined leaf frame featuring in and around later portraits of the king.[72]

To this period too we should assign an image that, while not in any sense a portrait of Charles II, must surely be interpreted as a representation of him. Antonio Verrio's painting of *Christ Healing the Sick at Capernaeum* was evidently executed as a modello in the early 1680s when payments to him for work on the state apartments at Windsor mention 'painting and adorning of the ceilings, side walls, end walls . . . in the King's Chapel'.[73] The painting by the artist who executed the allegorical *Sea Triumph* figures Christ not (as in the text of St Mark 2: 1–2) in a house but in a lavish classical columned hall, open to the sky. The *Christ Healing the Sick* was part of a series of illusionistic ceiling paintings in the baroque style glorifying Charles. In this case, surely, the king who, as we shall see, had touched more than any other monarch to cure the king's evil, is symbolically represented through the Christ figure and a scene that may have adorned the royal chapel.[74] Not since Restoration had the divinity, the apotheosis, of the monarch been so boldly figured in a style that brought the Italian and French baroque to England. With these images, the visual representation of Charles II looks to have moved some distance from the prosaic portraits of the 1660s and 1670s. Here is no toying with the sacred: the gods, Christian and classical, are summoned to the support of monarchy. Charles himself, however, remained very visibly human, and even later portraits of him have been described as looking decadent and 'lascivious'.[75] Though, as with verbal representations, periods of uncertainty and crisis – 1660 or 1680, for example – appear to highlight sacred motifs and tropes, in different images, sometimes the same image, artists seen to be negotiating the ambiguities of the king's two bodies, mystical and corporeal, and the representation of a king who touched to cure as well as publicly touched up his mistresses. The problem of visually representing a monarch whose body personal fitted ill the mystical body public was not new – unlike Elizabeth I or Charles I, James VI and I never radiates on canvas the divinity he claimed so vociferously in words. But the problem after regicide was fundamentally different. And for Charles II, the problem was in 1660, and perhaps remained: 'how does an artist depict a king who has successfully disguised himself as a peasant?'[76] In a brilliant essay pursuing that question David Solkin turns our attention to, and must take us back to, the narrative series of paintings by Isaac Fuller depicting Charles II's escape after the Battle of Worcester.[77] The five enormous canvases (7 feet high and between 6 and 10 feet wide) were probably painted in the early 1660s, and Solkin suggests they may have formed part of a narrative scheme in a room that included Stoop's cavalcade of Charles II. Though Lord Falkland may have been the patron, these were clearly canvases close to Charles, painted for him and most probably hung at Whitehall. The first pictures trace the story of Charles at Whiteladies, in Boscobel Wood, hiding in the oak, on Humphrey Penderel's Mill Horse, and finally riding with Jane Lane to Bristol. As Solkin observes, though these depict a monarch, they appear like folk art of a low genre; and, as well as disrupting normal subject-genre relations, they constitute a 'highest form of narrative art'.[78] For, as Solkin brilliantly demonstrates, though scenes (such as William Carlos and Penderel with Charles seated on a tree stump) evoke scriptural images, for example the adoration of the shepherds, the figure of Charles changing into Penderel's clothes is that of a very ordinary (not even socially exalted) man (fig. 9c). Moreover, though

9a Isaac Fuller, *King Charles and Jane Lane Riding to Bristol*, 1660s.

9b Isaac Fuller, *King Charles II and Colonel William Carlos in the Royal Oak*, 1660s.

9c Isaac Fuller, *King Charles II in Boscobel Wood*, 1660s.

many of the symbols in these canvases are timeless, their deployment here is both topical and ambiguous. Solkin notes how the oak, the tree sacred to Jove and an enduring symbol of authority, also evokes the tree figured in several satirical Commonwealth engravings as a symbol of the world turned upside down.[79] Similarly, while Charles is presented as the father of the nation, there is in the scene of his riding with Jane Lane a sexual frisson which not only presents him as the husband but perhaps too as the rake that he was already known to be.[80] And while (what Solkin does not observe) the progression conjures Christ's entry into Jerusalem (see John 12: 12–20), it also plays on images of the prodigal son. Such multiplications and ambiguities make this series 'a highly unstable confluence of meanings', and Solkin astutely compares the mixed genre to the tragicomedies devised in the Restoration theatre to handle the pathos and triumph of the royal story.[81] In this 'pastoral tragicomedy in paint', the dejected peasant slowly makes his progress to return as a monarch. But from these images that are not very transcendent, the viewer is left with an impression not only of the monarch who always underlay the humble clothes of the ordinary man but the reverse: the ordinariness of the king.[82]

Charles, as we have seen, enjoyed telling his Boscobel story and retold it throughout his reign.[83] The Streeter canvases of Boscobel now at Hampton Court hung at Whitehall where, on the ceiling of the king's bedroom, Wright's *Astraea Returns* depicts putti carrying the royal oak into heaven.[84] But, as the king himself must have gauged, the story, whether in words or pictures, was an ambiguous representation and, indeed, represented the ambiguity at the core of Restoration kingship. Fuller's canvases, then, grappling with a political and a representational instability, brought together the sacred and secular, the old and the new, the rational and the mystical, most of all the regal and the popular. Viewing them we may begin to wonder whether the prosaic, workmanlike quality of many Restoration royal portraits, so lamented by critics was, rather than aesthetic 'failure', a necessary response to changed times.

Those changes as much affected the nature and authority of visual aesthetics as the visual representation of authority. Indeed, what regality and the visual arts had shared for much of the early modern period was privilege and mystery. Artistic objects were often themselves sacred objects and secular portraits tended to hang in privileged spaces and places that themselves often had quasi-sacred functions: churches, royal palaces, aristocratic chapels and tombs. Art collecting for the period up to the civil war was a minority taste even among the aristocracy, with the Earl of Arundel and a few others emerging as spectacular exceptions to English noble habits and taste.[85] At the other end of the social spectrum, among the illiterate, woodcuts had for long illustrated cheap print, ballads and broadsides; but such images were usually generic types and, though they played their part in cartooning and contesting social norms and figures of authority, they neither distributed nor democratized the elite arts of the age.[86] It was towards the end of Elizabeth's reign that the first series of engraved images of monarchs were published and sold, and perhaps almost another four decades before the first shops specializing in prints were a viable commercial business.[87] From 1640, however, visuals, in ways that have yet to be studied, fully participated in that explosion of print culture that accompanied the political crisis of civil war. Subjects were eager to see and own images of new figures emerging into power as well as of the eclipsed monarch or martyr. Engravings and woodcuts of Charles I and II, and of the royal family as well as aristocrats and generals, circulated unhindered in the 1650s free from any censorship of the sort Queen Elizabeth had tried to enforce, prohibiting the distribution of unauthorized images of her.[88] Like the secrets of state, images of the king were promiscuously distributed both by print and revolutionary politics.

Just as many followed Thomas Hobbes in the belief that the reconstitution of political authority necessitated control over the promiscuous Babel of words, so there were those in 1660 who bemoaned the prostitution of the royal image.[89] John Evelyn was not alone in lamenting, in the early 1660s, 'that the deeds of Kings and heroes should be permitted to hang for signs . . . at the first pleasure of every tavern and tippling house';[90] in his 30 January sermon for 1664, Bishop Henry King, contrasting the martyr's words with his enemies' declarations, uttered that 'they looked like Tintaret's or Holbein's pieces compared to a painter of signs'.[91] Whatever the laments or hopes of such individuals, however, images of authority, royal images, had become part of a broader popular culture, as had the visual arts themselves.

One of the interesting developments in late Stuart England is not just the growing fashion for commissioning and collecting portraits and *objets d'art*, which was a feature of polite society, but what we may, at the risk of using an anachronistic term, call some democratization of the aesthetic. The author of *The Glories of London* described the hordes that came up to the Guildhall in London to view paintings – 'all the Countrey multitude drew nigh' – and, whilst images of royalty still instilled some reverence in the onlooker, it was a respect forged by a sense of contact and involvement rather than distance:

But when their ey'es the King and Prince survey,
They blush, look down and softly steal away
And in their country brag that they were where
His Majesty, the Duke and Judges were.[92]

And, some felt and feared, as well as observing, even common people were beginning to judge works of art, to the point where, rather than being the preserve of an elite, the visual arts had become a 'universal mystery'.[93]

The oxymoron is revealing. For neither the universal nor the publicized and democratized can long retain mystery. And if this was the fate of regal authority, it was also the case of the visual arts which were being demystified in the process of becoming better known.[94] In a poem or song dedicated to the principal Restoration engraver Thomas Faithorne, on his publication of a book of his drawings, Thomas Flatman (whose own engraved portrait faced his title page) wrote 'Those mysteries . . . thou dost unfold in every friendly page'.[95]

Many user-friendly pages in late seventeenth-century England began to unfold the mysteries of the visual arts. The 1668 translation of the treatise by R. F. Sieur de Chambray, as *An Idea of The Perfection of Painting*, began the process of explaining in laymen's terms the language of the arts and to interpret some images – not least the *Lord's Descent from the Cross* – for readers.[96] The same year a manual entitled *The Excellence of The Pen and Pencil* offered sound practical advice to would-be artists on everything from processes of observation to all the practicalities of engraving, including where to find the tools and copper plates and how to have them prepared.[97] The author, at the end of this quite brief but wide-ranging guide, certainly lived up to his claim that 'in a plain style I have given you an account of the whole mystery of engraving'.[98] The lengthy title of William Salmon's *Polygraphice* (1672) accurately described the text that followed as 'the art of drawing, engraving, etching, limning, painting, washing, varnishing and colouring . . . the drawing of men and other animal creatures, landskips, countries and figures of various forms'.[99] Beyond that, the author unpacked all the emblematic attributes of figures in art, such as Time, Fortune, Peace and Providence; instructed readers how to recognize allegorical and classical figures; and somewhat debased the ancient gods by his 'how to' guide on their representation: 'Jupiter . . . paint with long black beard curled hair, in a purple robe . . . and sitting on a golden throne'.[100] If the gods could be so simply modelled by everyman, it was not long before the monarch too was the subject of the common brush.

Indeed, in his *Ars Pictoria*, the engraver Alexander Browne (who dedicated his treatise to Lely, 'Painter to his Majesty') included amidst all his sound advice help towards depicting sovereignty: 'as in a king, to express the greatest majesty by putting or designing him in such a graceful posture that may move the spectators with reverence to behold him'.[101] There was surely a danger here that mysterious majesty would become little more than a construct of the artist – and of the ordinary amateur artist at that: a danger illustrated perhaps in a popular poem on a picture of King Charles drawn by Mrs Lane, which so moved the viewer that he felt 'I am i'the Presence whilst I spy him here'.[102] What he was in the presence of was not majesty itself but a woman's construct and artistic power, the political implications of which resonate in the language of praise for the artist: 'You can make Kings, and get them Subjects too'.[103]

There may well have been a backlash against a tendency to publicization and demystification of the arts no less than, after Exclusion, there was of the state. William Aglionby's *Painting Illustrated*, which received its imprimatur on 8 December 1685, seems in places to have yearned for older times when the arts of painting were tied in with patronage and privilege and revered authority and regality. Aglionby castigated 'those barbarous rebels whose quarrel was as much to ... the liberal arts as to monarchy and prelacy' and lamented that England lacked a historic painter to capture (royal) heroic scenes.[104] Yet it was too late. The vulgar had entered into the mysteries of painting as well as politics, and even Aglionby conceived his purpose as to 'make painting familiar and easy'.[105] Albeit his address was to 'the nobility and gentry of this nation', and his book long, the text opened with a surprisingly popular form: a dialogue in which a traveller explained to a friend terms and techniques of art such as foreshortening. As he listens to expositions on *chiaroscuro*, painting in oils and techniques of distemper, the student companion responds: 'I find that by little and little I shall penetrate into the secret of this art'.[106] His sovereign James II similarly was to experience the effects of such a 'penetration' into the mysteries of majesty.

As these guides (written to sell) reveal, the arts, as well as writing about the arts, had become part of a commodity culture and so been further demystified by the harsh realities of commerce. Books advertised not only other books but materials and paints. The appendix on limning to Browne's *Ars Pictoria*, for example, carries on page 39 'Advertisements' for Browne's own colours for limning, which plays out all the modern tricks of proffering the best, home-made goods which only this special opportunity has made available 'at a reasonable rate'.[107] Indeed, increasingly in this period, artists were advertising themselves, as did Edward Pickering who beckoned customers to his house on King Street near Guildhall 'where you may have drawn and painted according to the arts of painting ... arms on designs, standards, funeral escutcheons ... drums', etcetera.[108]

The publicization and commodification of the arts appear to have fostered a politicization of the visual aesthetic. For decades, of course, qualities of visual taste and preference had divided the nation – into Catholic and Protestant, Royalist and Roundhead, to cite the most obvious. But after the Restoration, one senses artistic taste being fully implicated in the politics of partisanship and party. In 1660, Bishop Matthew Wren had startlingly – and presciently – related aesthetic to political differences. His difference as a Royalist with the republican James Harrington, he wrote, was 'no more a wonder than that two men viewing the same object by various lights should judge it to be of various colours'.[109] The reverse implication – that matters of taste would be shaped by political affiliation – may be evident in the associations of artists with factions and faiths about which we as yet know too little. Critics of Charles's sexual and political morality, like Marvell, however, clearly little valued the visual aesthetics of Lely's female beauties, while those who (especially for female portraits) patronized Wright, Catharine MacLeod suggests, may have 'wished to distinguish themselves from court society'.[110] If they nothing like so explicitly prefigured Dryden's comments in *Absalom and Achitophel* on the politicization of litera-ture, Evelyn's words in the preface to *An Idea of the Perfection of Painting* are revealing when he speaks of modern artists having 'introduced into their cabals I know not what kind of licentious painting'.[111] The word 'cabal' of course was used to describe the junta of the five magnates who formed the most powerful Privy Council committee in 1667; so Evelyn's language conjoins artistic with political association. The world of the visual arts was becoming, and was under Charles's successor more to become, a divided polity and another source of division.

II

By the end of his reign, then, Charles's pictorial representation – an emulation of his hero Louis XIV whose portrait (perhaps not coincidentally) he sent Kneller to France in 1684 to execute – had become a Tory representation.[112] The complex ambiguities we have discovered in early Restoration images, the combination of the sacred and the popular, gave way increasingly to baroque aggrandizement and apotheosis. At his court, Charles could wield considerable control over how he was depicted, and how and where his image was displayed and observed. Even in royal palaces, however, as the *Last Instructions* suggests, there was no control-ling how works of art were interpreted or received. Beyond the court, in the polite (and not so polite) society of post-Restoration England, the royal image was circulating in communities more than ever interested in the visual, in portraits of power: communities better informed about the arts as politics, communities of collectors and consumers, communities formed, and distinguished, by politics and partisanship.

After eleven years of republican rule, the visual reconstitution of monarchy was not simply a matter of portraits. Though these were, after the Restoration especially, increasingly seen by provincial as well as metropolitan gentry, and by classes below the elite, and widely copied and distributed; and though the image of Charles II was thereby publicized, Restoration required the re-establishment also of the material monuments of monarchy – in buildings, statues and sculptures, for instance: forms that announced permanence, solidity and continuity. Even with most royal palaces escaping the fate of demo-lition that some revolutionaries had advocated, and whilst at Hampton Court and Whitehall, Oliver Cromwell repaired some of the damage when he took royal buildings back from private ownership to government use in 1654, Charles II and his followers recognized in 1660 the need to remake those historic buildings as royal domains and as monuments to monarchy.[113]

The first step was the re-establishment of the Office of His Majesty's Works and the appointment of a Surveyor and Clerk of the Works for each of the principal palaces. Under the surveyorship of first Sir John Denham, then, after 1668, of Christopher Wren, Charles II planned an ambitious programme of repair and rebuilding. At Whitehall, the king planned a radical reconstruction of the rambling old buildings, based around the Banqueting House designed by Inigo Jones for James I.[114] In 1664, Charter planned a new palace at Greenwich and, towards the end of his reign, initiated work on a new palace at Winchester, a city with a long tradition of loyalty to the crown. As Simon Thurley has shown, the king planned at Greenwich not to replace the dilapidated buildings with a new standing house or regular residence but a 'ceremonial gateway to his kingdom', a place for the reception of envoys and dignitaries before their conduct to London.[115] Financial stringency led the king to abandon the grandiose scheme, but not before the King Charles Block was completed by the summer of 1669.[116] The palace at Winchester, far advanced by Charles's death, was, like Greenwich, abandoned by his brother.[117] But while finance and contingency checked his grand plans, Charles II's programmes of architectural work and royal display were by no means negligible. In the preface to de Chambray's *A Parallel of the Ancient Architecture*, translated in 1664, John Evelyn praised the king for having in three or four years effected more in terms of architectural splendour than had been seen in the previous twenty.[118] Cataloguing the royal accomplishments, he listed paving at Whitehall, work on Westminster Hall and St Paul's, the additions and improvements to the Queen Mother's quarters at Somerset House to make it 'a structure becoming her royal grandeur'.[119] 'The promoting of such public and useful works,' he opined, was 'a certain indication of a prudent government' and he looked forward to further development.[120] Edmund Waller and John Webb similarly lauded Charles for his architectural interests, plans and accomplishments in lines that cannot be dismissed as empty flattery.[121] When he abandoned Greenwich to concentrate resources on Whitehall and especially Windsor, Charles, with his Comptroller of Works, Hugh May, effected refurbishments which, in the words of the historian of the royal works, 'provided . . . the grandest suite of royal apartments that any English monarch enjoyed before the reign of George IV'.[122]

Indeed, for all the repairs and extensions that the king ordered for Whitehall – work on quarters for the royal family, the Queen's Chapel, on the Volary garden, on the hall 'for masking plays, and dancing', and on the royal bedchamber ceiling adorned with an allegory of the Restoration by Wright – it was at Windsor that Charles showcased restored kingship.[123] His decision to concentrate resources there was neither arbitrary nor purely aesthetic. Windsor was a garrison; it was the headquarters of the Order of the Garter that was prominent in representations of the king (and his courtiers), and it was the burial place of the royal martyr Charles I on whose memory, as well as lineage, his son drew in his representation in words and in visuals. After minor refurbishments, including a new organ for St George's Chapel in the 1660s, Charles from 1674 embarked on a rebuilding programme to make Windsor the principal royal residence and headquarters of restored monarchy. [124] In two phases, new apartments for the king and queen and the Duke and Duchess of York were constructed, and the chapel and St George's Hall entirely rebuilt. Though May retained not only ancient Norman and fourteenth-century towers and the Henry VII Tower and Queen Elizabeth's Gallery, not least as signifiers of historical continuity and Tudor lineage, a new building dominated the west range and view. Here Charles himself was figured in the Star Building which, with its 12-feet diameter star, recalled the star that had appeared on the king's birthday and which was a subject of many Restoration panegyrics and prognostications.[125] Internally, Ionic and Corinthian columns provided a suitable backdrop for England's Augustus and for those who progressed through the public rooms to the royal bedchamber. The internal carvings and decorations, though much of these are now lost to us, were clearly of equal importance in refashioning the settings of majesty. Thistles, harps, roses and crowns mentioned in the accounts quite literally repainted the old emblems of regality and dynasty.[126] But the ceiling paintings executed by Antonio Verrio laid out a pictorial panegyric of restored monarchy of the sort not seen since Rubens's Whitehall ceiling for Charles I. We have encountered the image from the Presence Chamber of Mercury showing the portrait of Charles II to the four corners of the world. The ceiling of the next room, the Privy Chamber, depicted 'a most lively representation of the re-establishment of the Church of England on the restoration of Charles II' in which the three kingdoms were shown attended by Faith, Hope and Charity, while Religion triumphs over Superstition and Hypocrisy.[127] The themes of restoration and imperial grandeur were reiterated in the Withdrawing Room and the now semi-public Great Bedchamber, decorated with scenes of the four continents bringing their tribute to a Charles elevated among the clouds, the whole scheme effecting a glorification of Stuart monarchy that clearly emulates (as Charles increasingly was inclined to do) Louis XIV.

The year that Verrio completed the ceilings, 1678 – the year of the revelation of a Popish Plot which nearly destroyed the monarchy – was also the year that Charles 'made provision . . . for enhancing the ceremonial and dynastic associations of Windsor castle' by ordering for St George's Hall a new throne carved with the figures of Prudence and Justice, and the year he planned a monument in memory of his father, depicting Charles I trampling on his enemies and with the figure of Fame atop the cupola.[128] On 31 October of the same year, exactly a month after Titus Oates appeared before the Privy Council with his revelations, a royal warrant authorized the 'glorious redecoration' of St George's Hall and the King's Chapel.[129] Here, the painting of *Christ Healing the Sick* gestured to a monarch who had more than any predecessor touched for the king's evil, while the ceiling painting of the Resurrection echoed the Restoration allegories shown in the state apartments. Grinling Gibbons's carvings of the pelican in the wall niches not only reprised a Christian symbol of sacrifice (the pelican feeds her young from her own blood) but one very much associated with the royal martyr in 1649.[130] In the refurbished chapel, Charles II was symbolically represented in dynastic and sacral images that re-mystified Stuart monarchy. In St George's Hall, meanwhile, Verrio's decorative scheme, echoing Rubens's canvas of Charles I, depicted St George and the dragon above the royal throne, presenting Charles II as the embodiment and custodian of chivalry, honour and Christian virtue.[131] Finally completed not long before his death, the rebuilt and redecorated Windsor Castle represented the triumph of monarchy over the revived threat of republic. It may even have helped effect it.

As so often with Charles II, however, the sacral was by no means the only (though it was significantly the last) representation of the king in stone, wood and paint. Moreover, as well as with his palaces, the king was very much involved, and associated, with public spaces and buildings. St James's Park, indeed, became very much a public space after the Restoration, where the king could be sighted (or petitioned) as he promenaded in the newly refurbished gardens, with their aviary and ornamental waterworks and canal.[132] But it was after the Great Fire of 1666 that Charles took a leading role in civic activities as a symbol of monarchical munificence and glory. As we have seen, in his declarations in the wake of the disaster, Charles stressed the opportunity presented for orderly rebuilding, offered tax incentives to those who embarked upon it, and set a national example by his offer to rebuild the Customs House destroyed by the flames.[133] In the new Great or Long Room, as well as carved crowns, a large 3 ft × 4 ft royal arms (carved by the Master Carver to the Works) memorialized the king's generosity as well as his authority; and it is clear that contemporaries associated Charles with the rebuilding in general, and with, we might say, the politics of architecture.[134] A poem on the rebuilding of London, praising the royal commission, runs:

The Buildings thus shall uniformly stand,
Each diff'rent magn'tude in a divers Sphere:
Such Uniform'ty does our King command.[135]

Similarly, a 1676 edition of Heath's *Chronicle of the Late Intestine War* reports Charles ceremonially laying the first stone of the Royal Exchange which, as its name fully manifests, connected Charles to the symbol of trade and commerce as well as to a building that had taken its regal title from Queen Elizabeth I, who had opened it in 1566.[136] Royal generosity and the role of the architect Sir Roger Pratt and the king's Surveyor General, Christopher Wren, in rebuilding St Paul's not only revived royal association with the principal church of the City, but would surely have evoked memories of Charles I's patronage and the important work, then financed by the crown, of Inigo Jones on the west portico of the cathedral.[137]

Towards the end of his reign, at a time when the Windsor refurbishments were extolling his glory in his principal palace, Charles II also patronized, and partly financed out of the Privy Purse, a magnificent monument to his kingship for which in 1682 he laid the foundation stone. By contrast with Windsor, the Royal Hospital at Chelsea was conceived in 'monastic austerity'.[138] Though the idea of a provision for invalided soldiers and veterans was taken from Louis XIV (who a decade earlier had founded the Hotel des Invalides), Charles's chosen site for his charitable erection was that of a Jacobean educational foundation, Chelsea College, the title of which still heads some late seventeenth-century engravings of the new buildings (fig. 10). The building has been described by our leading architectural historian as in spirit 'more akin to homely Holland than to pompous Paris' and as notable for 'intimacy and friendliness'.[139] Though the design might have owed something to the Greenwich Palace project abandoned fifteen years earlier (Greenwich was symbol of England's naval might and triumphs), Charles's last architectural bequest to his people (its hall painted later by Verrio with images of the king) stood not for absolutist grandeur but charity and community: for the gratitude of a king and nation to its veterans and for the victories and conquests achieved in the king's name and reign. As he excitedly watched the progress of his palace at Winchester that would have offered him a safe refuge from the wavering politics of his capital, the Charles who had in the midst of crisis relied on his people, erected in the heart of London and on a site of former Stuart beneficence what was to become, when it admitted its first occupants in 1689, a living monument to this king who took such care of his subjects.

Though palaces and public buildings themselves represented monarchy, they were also the stages for more particular and personal representations of the individual monarch in statuary of stone or bronze. Throughout history, as Nicola Smith has recently demonstrated, statues of rulers have been seen to have an iconic status; their erection is the most public advertisement of a ruler's virtues or memory; and their destruction, as recent events on our own TV screens bring home, is the most common symbol of the fall of a regime. Such was certainly the case during the civil war. Though many royal statues – not least those carved on funeral monuments – survived the iconoclasm of the 1640s and 1650s, in part thanks to Royalists who removed them to safety, the most prominent statues of Charles I were destroyed. In a famous ritual moment following regicide, for example, the statue of Charles I that adorned the Royal Exchange was pulled down and in the space a single inscription, 'Exit Tyrannus', proclaimed parliamentary victory and republican government.[140] Given this symbolic freight, it was vital in 1660 that the image of the king be re-placed in prominent public spaces and places to represent restored monarchy. Or rather

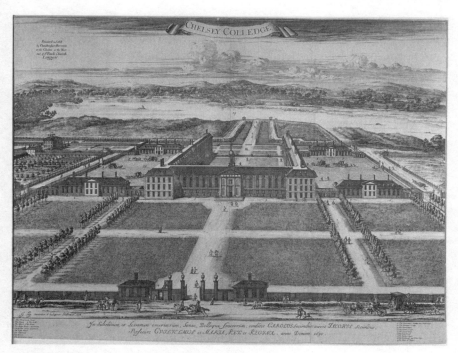

10 Johannes Kip, *Chelsey Colledge*, 1694.

the image of two kings. If, as we shall see, the memory of Charles I was essential
in the representation of his son, the resurrection of the martyr in statues
of stone and bronze was seen to be important in the revalidation of his rule
and in underpinning Stuart succession and effacing republic. In his account
of *The Glories and Magnificent Triumphs of the Blessed Restitution of His
Sacred Majesty King Charles II*, amid a narrative of the manoeuvres and entertainments that brought the king from Holland to his throne, James Heath
(chronicler of the civil war) paused to dwell on this symbolic moment:

> The Royal Exchange of London had been deprived and forsaken of one of its
> tutelar angels. . . . It was therefore most pious, most dread, a most just venera-
> tion and reverence (as it was of the greatest glory among the Romans) which
> the City of London did to both Princes together. The statue therefore of King
> Charles the first which the malice of his rebels had first decollated and . . .
> [after] taken it wholly down, was now replaced in the same niche, in its full
> proportion, with a sceptre in the right hand, a Church in his left arm, a globe
> at his left foot and on his shield MAGNA CHARTA. On the back stood this
> inscription: Carolus Primus Monacharum Magnae Britanniae Secundus
> FRANCIAE ET HIBERNIAE Rex Martyr ad Coelum Missus penultimo Jan.

Anno Domini 1648. And the statue of Charles the Second supplied the vacancy of the next vault or nick [niche] being erected with a sceptre in his right hand, a globe in his left hand, and on his shield Amnestia OBLIVION Carolus Secundus Monacharum Magnae Britanniae Tertius FRANCIAE ET HIBERNIAE Rex Aetatis suae anno tricessimo, regni duodecimo, Restaurationis primo: 1660.[141]

The statues almost stand before us telling the complicated history of Restoration and its representation. At the renamed Royal Exchange, the two bronzes announce the simultaneous impulses to remember and commemorate and to forget and forgive; the continuity of kingship, but the recognition of its interruption and the need for its reconstitution; the narrative of British history (Charles has for twelve years been the third emperor of Great Britain) but the new start that the year of Restoration, significantly the date carved here as opposed to 1649, represents. Interestingly, too, though the two statues stand side by side, that of Charles II holds no church – perhaps because in 1660, it was unclear, and a contentious issue, what the restored church would be. Whatever the reason, the statue of the son was more a dynastic than regal image, and the representation of a king willing (in both senses) to forget the past (which is inscribed on his father's shield) and to start anew. Pepys's brief entry for 29 March 1660, 'the king's effigy was new making to be set up in the Exchange again', may have articulated more than he appreciated.[142] The re-establishment of the monarchy in statuary complemented Robert Vyner's equestrian bronze at Stocks Market, Cornhill, of Charles II as St George trampling a dragon – a dragon with the features of Oliver Cromwell (fig. 11).[143]

If the immediate politics of Restoration offered the first stimulus to representations of the monarch in statuary, the fire that levelled much of London presented opportunities for the adornment of new buildings which might bear the figure of a king who had expressed his determination to new make his imperial capital. The Exchange itself was destroyed and the aforementioned statue with it. When it was rebuilt in the late 1660s new statues of Charles I and Charles II (along with Sir Thomas Gresham) were commissioned from John Bushnell who had just returned to England from Venice.[144] Bushnell's Charles I was now sculpted in a Christ-like pose with a hand on his breast, drawing attention to his suffering, and his eyes raised to heaven. Charles II, by contrast, sculpted in Roman armour and holding a scroll, is presented as a heroic figure perhaps, both to commemorate his bravery in the Fire and his statesmanlike resolution to rebuild the capital after it.[145] Certainly the erection of Temple Bar after the Fire not only gave Charles II the opportunity to complete in stone a new gateway to the city (the original had been devised as a temporary arch to welcome the first Stuart), it also offered a magnificent setting for sculptures – the first in Roman dress – of himself with his Stuart predecessors and Queen

The Statue of KING   CHARLES II. at the Entrance of Cornhill.

11 Unknown artist, equestrian statue of King Charles II at the entrance of Cornhill in the Stocks Market, Poultry, *c.* 1740.

Elizabeth, which still overlook the boundary between the Cities of London and Westminster.[146] That it became later in the reign a site of popular demonstrations serves only to emphasize the symbolic importance of the statuary at Temple Bar, albeit it was, during the Popish Plot, the figure of Elizabeth that was venerated.[147] Temple Bar marked London as a royal capital, the capital of Charles II, and the criticism of his regime staged there, via an appeal to another popular, Protestant monarch, describes a sophisticated popular sensitivity to the politics of symbols as well as the symbols of power.

The Fire also produced another enduring memorial to Charles II: the Doric column known as the Monument, designed by the King's Surveyor, Sir Christopher Wren, with the assistance of Robert Hooke, and built between 1671 and 1677. [148] Wren preferred that a statue of Charles II should top the column, rather than the flaming urn chosen. But the bas-relief carved on the west side of the pedestal by Caius Gabriel Cibber (Bushnell's rival for the Royal Exchange commission) lacks nothing in panegyrical representation of Charles II and his brother, both of whom had won plaudits for their public-spirited actions amid the disaster.[149] On the panel, the king with a baton and the duke in Roman dress, flanked by Fortitude, Justice and Liberty and accompanied by Architecture and Science, descend steps to aid a disconsolate figure of London languishing amid broken pediments and comforted by Time (fig. 12). Below the king, a figure

12 Cajus Gabriel Cibber, *Allegory of the Great Fire of London*, relief on the Monument, London, 1671–7.

representing the Fire breathes the flames that have destroyed the city but which are now controlled by the king's arrival. Though complicated, the symbols are clear. Here Charles II is not only represented, as his father had presented himself, as the liberal builder, and rebuilder, of an imperial capital; but his government, with the benefits of justice and liberty it bestowed, and his personal qualities of liberality and fortitude, are figured as bringing in their train the fruits of Peace and Plenty who hover above the scene, gesturing to Charles on the one part and scattering their munificence to the citizens on the other. Though the monstrous figure beneath the king's and duke's feet stands for the Fire, the identification in a (later) engraving with Envy should not pass without comment.[150] Envy might stand for the jealousy of the world for a London which was emerging as an international city of trade and opulence. But Envy was a stock character in civil war engravings of Charles I, which seem to be an influence here on the pose of the king. Charles tramples over not only the City's enemy but the enemy of monarchy – and of the virtues and civilized arts that follow in monarchy's train – the arts of liberty and justice, the arts of knowledge and reason, in contrast to Envy's ignorant and destructive violence. That the representation of Charles with his brother should not be read as simple testimony to their fraternal bravery is borne out by a later engraving that sought to erase the figure of the Duke of York.[151] In 1679, when the Monument was completed, Charles was making a statement not only about himself and monarchy but the succession. James, helmeted but carrying a laurel wreath, stands between Charles and Fortitude as a defender of monarchy and its benefits as well as of the city. And, as he stands firmly above the Fire, James triumphs over his detractors while the new London rises behind him. Not only 'the most elaborate piece of sculpture which had been produced in England since the Middle Ages', the Monument was a polemic for Stuart monarchy and succession as it faced its second moment of crisis.[152]

The king's triumphant emergence from the Exclusion crisis not surprisingly gave a final impetus to his representation in sculpture. Indeed, it was in 1684 that plans were revived for (the first time since its rebuilding) a statue of Charles in the middle of the Royal Exchange. The artist chosen was Grinling Gibbons, not only (in the estimation of Aglionby) the best of sculptors, but the person chosen by Wren to execute the aborted monument to Charles I proposed in 1678, for which, interestingly, drawings show the king with four virtues pressing down the figure of Envy.[153] Working with his collaborator Arnold Quellin, Gibbons sculpted Charles in the Roman habit of the Caesars, with a baton in his hand and wearing a laurel of victory, as the Augustus who had triumphed through peace.[154] Though the statue was lost in a fire of 1838, we yet have not only contemporary descriptions of the work but contemporary testimony to its impact. In his address to the artist before a poem, 'On Mr Gibbons his carving the Matchless Statue of the King', Samuel Philipps declared that 'any person who reveres his Prince must necessarily have a peculiar regard for you', for Gibbons had captured and immortalized the royal virtues of heroism and clemency in marble.[155] Beyond that, in Philipps's estimation, the statue enacted a vital political performance: 'look upon this royal figure,' he invoked, 'and who will not be steadfast in his loyalty? Look upon this ye disobedient, and who again dare rebel? A soft yet powerful Voice seems to issue from it, that cheerfully encourages the one, and formidably deters the other.'[156] Phillips hoped for more, that the 'plastique power' of Gibbons's stone 'will do many a wondrous thing', not least reconcile a divided nation:

> Which when set up, the Nation's Wounds shall heal
> As the Brass Serpent those of *Israel*.[157]

Paid for by the Merchant Adventurers, probably to reassure the king of London's loyalty after a period of Whig dominance in the capital, Gibbons's statue may not have succeeded in doing that. But it was not the only representation in statuary erected by a grateful nation at the end of Charles's life. The Grocers Company funded in 1685 yet another statue (by Quellin) of Charles for the Royal Exchange, and Gibbons's own work was repeated by Tobias Rustat in a bronze sculpture of the king for Chelsea Hospital.[158] For King's Square (now Soho Square), laid out in French style in honour of Charles in the 1680s, Cibber was commissioned to do a stone of the king in modern armour on a pedestal decorated with figures representing the Thames, Severn, Tyne and Humber, as a representation of the reach and beneficence of royal rule (fig. 13).[159] As a recent historian of royal monuments has observed, some of these statues resemble a figure of Louis XIV presented to the king in 1683, which opened a veritable campaign of public statues glorifying the Sun King.[160] In 1685, it must have seemed that there was no reason why the stones and bronzes of Charles II and his father should not similarly stand as the heralds of a beneficent new Stuart absolutism.

13 Caius Gabriel Cibber, statue of Charles II, 1681.

Sculpted portraits, it has been argued, were 'the way in which the image of the monarch was customarily presented in the most striking, immediate, tangible and permanent form on a large scale in the public arena'.[161] As well as the statues still standing in the public spaces of our built environment, or known to have stood, statues and busts of Charles, like that by Bushnell now in the Fitzwilliam Museum in Cambridge and bought from private owners, were probably displayed (along with paintings after Lely, Wright or Cooper) in the houses and gardens of ministers and courtiers.[162] Such representations need to be studied in their specific moments of construction and display, since, increasingly after the Restoration, these images responded to specific political circumstances.

III

The images of the king that were most obviously distributed to mark political occasions were the medals that themselves owed much to the baroque busts and bronzes of Bushnell, Cibber and Rustat.[163] The issuing of medals and badges had proliferated during the civil war to mark events, the lives and deaths of Royalist ministers and heroes, or military victories; during the Commonwealth, medals and badges, small enough to conceal when not worn, circulated among the Royalist community as tokens of loyalty and hope.[164] Gold and silver medals were issued to mark Charles's coronation at Scone in 1651, with the crowned king on one side within an inscription describing him as King of Scotland, England and France, and on the other the royal lion brandishing the Scottish thistle with the motto 'Nemo Me Impune Lacessit' – 'Let no one attack (or asperse) me with impunity'.[165] Throughout the 1650s, small badges figuring Carolus Secundus, often featuring the crowned Charles, or with crowns (in some cases a phoenix) on the reverse, were important for circulating as 'indications of affection to the monarchy upon the prospect of its speedy restoration', though the small size and often coarse workmanship did not make them very exact likenesses of the king.[166]

But from 1660, it is clear that Charles took pains over the representation of himself on medals, which he used to commemorate the landmarks in his restoration and to reward many who had assisted, in a variety of ways, in effecting it. Before he left Holland, medals were struck consisting of two embossed plates figuring Charles I and II on the obverse and reverse, both wearing the Garter badge and with Charles II in armour.[167] Other Dutch medals, by Peter Van Abeele, commemorated the royal embarkation on 2 June, from Scheveningen. Above are the ships topped with the royal pennant, an angel with a trumpet proclaiming 'Soli Deo Gloria' – to underpin the providentialism of Restoration – and, around the inscriptions, 'In Nomine Meo Exultabitur Cornu Eius' – 'in my name may his strength be raised up'.[168]

Jan Roettier, who accompanied the king to England, struck his first medal in his new country to commemorate the landing at Dover on 26 May. The medal features the Royal Charles with a star (the sign that had appeared at Charles's birth in 1630) leading the new king to English shores on which three devoted figures (like the Three Wise Men) wait to bestow their gifts; the religious theme was underpinned by the motto 'If God is my guardian who will be my enemy' (fig. 14).[169] On the other side, a finely struck portrait of Charles, within twisted olive branches of peace, presents the king as protected and restored by the mercy and providence of God. Days later, a second elaborate medal celebrating Charles's birthday and arrival in London presented the monarch in Roman costume with, on the reverse, 'Felicitas Britanniae' enjoying once again the fruits of justice, peace and plenty.[170]

Medallic representations also display the ambiguities we have discerned in the Restoration moment. In two, both by George Bower, Charles is presented respectively as Jupiter defeating his foes, and as the king grown stronger by adversity who, not stooping to petty revenge, will pardon and reconcile.[171] And the theme of the many medals struck that Restoration year, like the panegyrics, is that of not just Royalists' but a nation's celebration as Peace, Commerce, Prudence and Plenty – and all the gods – unite in restoring Britain to greatness.[172] One medal, now thought to be by Thomas Rawlings, compares Charles (with an oak leaf) to a second Moses who led his people from oppression to the promised land.[173] Similarly, the medallic representation of 29 May disseminated the image of a providential king, a merciful ('clementissimus') king (also with an oak leaf), preserved by God to rule His people.[174] Whoever was responsible for the designs, which echo the conceits of royal speeches and religious services commemorating Restoration, the medals formed an important part of a programme of representation, essential to the re-establishment of Charles II on the throne.

The constitutional and ritual occasion of that re-establishment, the coronation, was not only marked by the issue of medals but, perhaps for the first time, by their free distribution among the spectators of the ceremony.[175] Whether the more elaborate medals given to dignitaries, or badges more hurriedly executed for the populace, many of the coronation medals feature Charles on one side crowned, on the other enthroned with the sceptre in his right hand and an angel crowning him; while others present the new monarch as the shepherd of the nation's flock – 'the people's pastor', in Waller's words – or figure the flourishing oak and crowned sun, evidently widely recognized symbols of rebirth, befitting the spring ceremony.[176] The next spring, Charles's marriage to Catherine of Braganza saw the casting and distribution of several medals and badges heralding, as must have been expected, a fertile union and secure Stuart dynasty. Taking as their inscriptions and themes Maiestas at Amor, medals represent Charles and Catherine (sometimes both on the obverse) with the

14 Hawkins, *Medallic Illustrations*, plate XLIII, 3.

figures of Jupiter, Venus and Cupid, accompanied by legends taken from Ovid and Virgil suggesting the imperial sway that will be the consequence of their union; one reads:

> Hinc Progeniem Virtute Futurem
> Egregiam et Totum Quae Viribus Occupet Orbem.[177]

Several badges and counters of poor-quality metal and workmanship were, it has been suggested, 'probably made for sale in the streets at the time of the king's marriage and . . . worn as ornaments', suggesting that the Restoration had fuelled as well as reflected a popular love of royalty and a desire to own some keepsake of these momentous events.[178] As the survival of pairs of dies suggests, medals of Charles and his bride were in great demand and had become a genre through which carefully crafted representations of regality could (in their cheaper materials) reach a wide audience.

Not surprisingly therefore, Charles used medals to mark important triumphs and to put a favourable gloss on not so glorious occasions. After the Battle of Lowestoft, medals were issued to all who had served with distinction in battle – the first military honours granted and financed by a sovereign.[179] On the signing of the Peace of Breda, Roettier was commissioned to cast a medal which, quite different from those distributed in Holland showing images of English ships burning in the Medway, presented Charles as the Augustus who had secured peace.[180] It would appear also that Charles endeavoured to promote his policy of toleration by means of a medal struck in 1672 announcing his declaration for liberty of conscience, on the reverse of which the figure of

Liberty holds in her right hand a cornucopia to signify the fruits of toleration and in her left hand the book of faith inside an inscription describing Charles as not merely defender of the faith but specifically Protector of the Reformed Religion (fig. 15).[181]

But, like most forms of representation, medals became not only more explicitly political, but also more blatantly partisan. During the later 1660s and 1670s, Dutch medals circulated in England very different representations of naval engagements and England's place in the European power struggles. And in 1678, in what is a remarkable testament to their significance and wide reach, some poorly designed and worked medals were issued depicting the murder of Sir Edmund Bury Godfrey as the work of the devil and the pope, and the figure of a heroic Titus Oates disclosing the Popish Plot.[182] These medals were advertised in the *London Gazette* and evidently sold.[183] Still more dangerously, Whig supporters presumably financed a medal in 1681 celebrating the acquittal (from a charge of high treason) of the Earl of Shaftesbury, who led the opposition to the king in parliament.[184] Interestingly, during three years of crisis, the official medallic images commissioned and distributed appear to be more often of the Duke of York (whom the Whigs were seeking to exclude) than of the king. A fine medal issued in 1680 features James and his second wife, Mary of Modena, respectively on the obverse and reverse, while another presents him with on the reverse Britannia and a legend used in Charles's early medals – 'Nullum Numen Abest' – underlining divine support for his rule.[185]

The image of Charles himself makes its medallic return in 1683 with a piece struck by George Bower to commemorate the defeat of the Rye House Plot and a rise in the king's fortunes (fig. 16).[186] In a medal that almost seems to enact what Dryden imagined in his poem, *The Medal*, Charles is figured as Hercules,

15 Hawkins, *Medallic Illustrations*, plate LVI, 6.

16 Hawkins, *Medallic Illustrations*, plate LXI, 8.

reclining on the lion's skin, repelling with his raised left hand the six-headed hydra of rebellion (here with the features of the conspirators Monmouth, Russell, Hampden, Sidney, Essex and Howard, and the devil supporting them), beneath the inscription 'Peribunt fulminis' – 'they will be destroyed by his thunderbolts'. On the reverse, as rebel wolves hang on a gibbet, Charles, beneath the dove of peace, appears as the shepherd attending his flock, with an oak tree in the right foreground and an inscription attributing the defeat of conspiracy to God. An undated medal assigned to the same year, and to an artist working under the duke's patronage, praises Charles for 'always standing firm' ('Semper Adamas') and shows on the reverse a crown raised aloft beneath a shining star, or, in another version, a radiant sun.[187] As his medals proclaim, only Time, not his enemies, would bring the end to Charles's reign – and even Time proffers a laurel (a laurel of victory as well as restful peace?) – as Time decrees that 'All Heads Must Come to the Cold Tomb'.[188] His head on countless medals may have saved Charles from an earlier grave.

In the case of several of these medals, there has been some confusion and there remains uncertainty (itself further evidence that many medals may have had a wide distribution) whether the die was cast for a medal or coin. The same engravers at the Royal Mint, Thomas Simon, John Roettier and others, worked on medals and coins, and there was a close relationship in the iconographic themes and programmes. But, if anything, coins were of the greater importance and not only on account of their universal distribution. The right of coinage had been an uncontended prerogative of the crown, and counterfeiting or clipping or marking the royal coin was a treasonable offence because the image on it was held to represent the royal authority. Having lost control of the London Mint, the Royalists had continued to mint and use their own coin; and

Charles had, as a fugitive, issued coins with his father's legend 'Dum Spiro Spero', and the claim to be God's chosen one.[189] In *A Royal, Loyal Poem* published in 1660, Thomas Saunderson celebrated the return of king, church and liberty and knew that all would be restored to order 'when our new coyne (all that is mine is gone)/Shall bear the King's Face and Superscription'.[190] In his entertainment for the king at the Guildhall in July the same year, John Tatham used numismatic language to express the union between Charles and the people: 'You have new Coyn'd all hearts, and there Imprest/Your image'.[191] Contemporaries remarked that in republican Venice, coin did not bear the Doge's image.[192] It was the special power of a monarchy that made coin what it was: in the words of Thomas Bayly in *The Royal Charter Granted Unto Kings by God*, 'though it be true that such a piece of silver is but a piece of silver; yet as it bears Caesar's image and superscription upon it, it is more significant'.[193] Because the face and superscription of the king on coin were the most public manifestations of authority, it was vital for Charles to quickly replace Cromwellian and republican coinage with his own. The reminting of coin had, throughout the early modern period, often been a slow process, with old coin from a previous reign circulating long after the decease of the sovereign. Charles's government's efforts to replace republican with royal coin were assisted by the development from 1662 of the milling, or machine production, of coin as an alternative to hand stamping. And the broad distribution of the royal image on coin was greatly furthered by the resumption, in 1672, of the production of low-denomination coins (halfpennies and farthings) which parliament had ended in 1644.[194] After 1672, the various 'town pieces', bearing inscriptions and symbols of the cities and towns that minted their own small change for the poor (Woodbridge's 1670 halfpenny was called 'The Poores Advantage'), or the private coins, like those manufactured by the Cambridge chandler Thomas Ewin as change for his customers, were replaced by royal coins, the images and later inscriptions on which did not significantly differ from the finer gold and silver pieces.[195]

Thomas Simon's pattern piece for the Restoration crown piece figures a well-cut likeness of Charles's bust in profile to the right, in classical dress and wearing a laurel, with the inscription 'Carolus II Dei Gra' and with, on the reverse, the crowned arms of England, Scotland, Ireland and France, with entwined letter Cs, around a Garter badge and motto 'Honi Soit Qui Mal Y Pense'.[196] This so-called 'petition piece', bearing on the edge Thomas Simon's invitation to the king to review the quality of his work, was adopted and from 1662 became the type for the first milled crown which now bore on its edge 'Decus et Tutamen', as British coins still do. For the half crowns, and smaller silver-hammered and later milled pieces, however, the portrait of the king, now in profile left, was crowned and lacking the Garter badge; the reverse carried the inscription 'Christo Regno Aspice', underlining the link between the crowned and divine lord.[197] Perhaps it was felt that for coin circulating more broadly the image of a crowned sovereign constituted an important statement about restored monarchy. If so, it is interesting that later half crowns and (as early as 1663) silver shillings and sixpences – but *not* coins of lower denomination – abandoned the crown and followed the laureate Roman model of the Restoration coin.[198]

Thereafter, throughout Charles's reign, the hammered (till 1662) and then milled gold coins and higher denomination silver coins followed this pattern, some from 1662 with the legend 'Concordia Regna Florent' ('Through concord kingdoms flourish').[199] Pattern pieces for small copper coins reveal a range of types under consideration before their reissue. All those that featured the king's head depict it crowned, some with a legend in English, 'Such God Loves'.[200] Some prototypes display a crowned Tudor rose, three columns supporting the emblems of the three kingdoms, or a ship bearing the cross of St George – perhaps a reminder of the *Royal Charles* bringing the king from Scheveningen.[201] On these patterns, Latin legends boast the royal conquest of all the four oceans, as well as the royal title; one has the inscription 'the poors relief'. The actual coins milled depart from these models. By the 1660s coins of lowly denomination, even halfpennies and farthings, represent Charles not crowned but laureate (from 1672 with Britannia on the reverse), with the legend 'Quatuor Maria Vindico' ('I claim the four oceans'), 'Carolus a Carolo' or simply 'Britannia'.[202] We cannot be certain whether this was just an aesthetic preference, or a change in taste after Thomas Simon was succeeded at the Mint on his death in 1665. But if, as is almost certain, all coins received royal approval, the abandonment of the crowned image from the mid-1660s may indicate a greater assurance on Charles's part of the stability of the monarchy and the loyalty of the lower orders.

Throughout the rest of his reign it was the laureate classical image that survived even on the Maundy pieces traditionally given by the monarch at the occasion of the washing of the feet of the poor, in emulation of Christ. The introduction of Britannia (first used in 1672) may begin to unfold another story.[203] Along with the inscription proclaiming imperial rule, on these popular objects the monarchy was being represented as the embodiment of the nation and popular patriotism was subtly being directed as devotion to the sovereign. If Charles's fine-quality regal copper farthings helped effect that identification, they had given the monarchy a very good return indeed.

Coins circulated the royal image universally, as statues stood in public places regardless of the interest of passers-by in them. But, as we have seen, in the case of medals, there is evidence that citizens were buying mementoes of royal occasions, with images of the king; and that the circumstances of a popular Restoration of the monarchy fostered a public desire to see and possess some image of the king and royal family (fig. 17). This was nowhere better demonstrated than in the full emergence of a trade in engravings, mezzotints and prints which accelerated rapidly after the Restoration, creating a native industry for the first time. While the general link between the print trade and civil war politics is evident but difficult to specify, the specific contribution of Prince Rupert in developing the art of mezzotint is crucial. Mezzotint with its capacity to render light and shadow, not just by a thickening of lines, enabled engraved versions of paintings and portraits to reproduce the original far more clearly and pleasingly. Rupert brought his knowledge back to England, and the first mezzotint made in Britain, by William Sherwin and dedicated to Rupert, was a portrait of Charles II.[204]

Doubtless recognizing the potential for a wider market, Lely appears to have entered into an understanding with printmakers and publishers through the likes of Abraham Blooteling and Jan Van der Vaart, Alexander Browne and Richard Tompson.[205] Reproductions of portraits of Charles, Catherine of Braganza, the Duke and Duchess of York, and a posse of royal mistresses and bastards, poured off the presses to find a ready and rapidly growing market. Even Pepys was not averse to acquiring an engraving, which he framed and varnished, of his favourite, Barbara Villiers; and the habit of collecting engravings is evidenced by the numbers of printmakers setting up shop and by the

17 Coronation mug, Delftware, 1661.

tendency to a standardization of forms and frames, enabling collectors to compile and display a set.[206] During the reign of Charles II, as well as the already established business of Peter Stent, we have evidence of print shops at the Globe in the Poultry, the Bishop's Head in Cornhill, the Crown in St Paul's Yard, the White Horse 'without Newgate', the Angel in St Paul's Yard, the Golden Duck in Fleet Street, to name a few.[207] While some of these businesses may have sold books as well, Alexander Browne's own shop, the Blue Balcony in Little Queen Street and The Oval Frame in Bishop's Gate Street, appear to have been specialist shops for engravings and mezzotints.[208] The rapidly expanding market gave work to a host of new immigrant and native engravers who joined the familiar names of Hollar, Stent and Faithorne: namely Richard Gaywood, David Loggan, Edward Rixon, Pieter Van Gunst, Michael Burghers, Isaac Beckett, P. Williamson, Robert Williams, Edward Cooper, John Smith and Richard Tompson.

The popularity of engraved portraits obviously follows what contemporaries recognized as this very English artistic preference and taste, but manifests too a broad desire for images of the restored monarchy and court, the new king, his bride, the royal family and, increasingly, the new ministers and figures prominent in public life.[209] What often distinguished engravings from canvases are the inscriptions and verses printed beneath them, which of course direct an interpretation of the image and sometimes render it specific and topical by relating the engraving to another text or incident familiar to the purchasers. In consequence, engravings sometimes yield evidence to the historian of the moments of the production and circulation of (otherwise undated) images, and of the contexts in which the image was distributed and performed.

We know that images of Charles II circulating from the moment of the regicide in 1649 were seen as important in the campaign to secure him his father's throne. Hollar engraved a portrait of him after Van Dyck in 1649 with his right hand on a cane, in a pose not unlike that of Charles I in *Le Roi à la chasse*, and with what appears to be a palace in the background; while Richard Gaywood, Hollar's student, etched Charles being crowned at Scone in 1651.[210] While, understandably, most of the engraved images of Charles during the 1650s were executed abroad and by foreign artists, it seems likely that we should assign to a period before the Restoration a large William Faithorne image of Charles, published with the following verse:

The Second Charles, Heire of ye Royall Martyr,
who, for Religion and his Subjects Charter,
spent the best Blood, yt uniust Sword ere dy'de,
since the rude Souldier pierc'd our Saviours side:
who such a Father had'st; art such a Son;
redeeme thy people and assume thy owne.[211]

Whether it anticipated or celebrated Charles's restoration, the engraving clearly presented Charles, as we have seen with so many texts, as the son of the martyr whose portrait Faithorne, the principal pre-war artist in this genre, had often engraved.[212]

Though most simple engraved portraits are not dated, many of the scores of Charles II by Sherwin, Gunst, Gaywood and others appear to be productions of the early Restoration years. The depiction of the king laureate was a post-Restoration fashion; and the portraits of the king in Garter robes, with the Garter badge and motto and the royal regalia, indicate, like canvases, early efforts to publicize the restoration of the crown and its traditional symbols and associations.[213] In several cases, the iconography announces the Restoration moment. Frederik Hendrik van Hove's complex image of the king, for example, very much presents Charles as the heir chosen to make Britain great again, in the spirit of some of the panegyrical poetry of the early Restoration years (fig. 18).[214] Though standing (with his left foot on the globe of Britannia and his right on an orb inscribed 'Pacificus'), Charles is placed in a setting almost identical to Marshall's frontispiece to the *Eikon Basilike*. Brandishing a sword, inscribed 'Fidei Defensor', and standing (as had Charles I) before a book with the text 'in verbo tuo spes mea', the king reaches with his left hand towards a heavenly crown on which is written 'Carolus ad Carolum', while an angel crowns him with laurel. Behind, where on Marshall's engraving stood the palm suppressed by weights, an oak tree holds the crowns of the three kingdoms and a small crowned figure of Charles himself. Around it, on a calm sea (as opposed to the tossed seas of the *Eikon* image) we see a flotilla of grand vessels – perhaps those that brought Charles home. From the hem of the royal ermine, a scroll reads 'Europae Arbiter', expressing Britain's imperial claims under restored monarchy. As with many texts we have reviewed, the clear gestures to the past and the looking to a magisterial new present are powerfully combined. Another engraving, headed 'By Peace not War' not only celebrates the Restoration as a providential blessing rather than military conquest, its purpose was evidently to introduce the English (and Irish) to their monarch. For accompanying the image, a verse reports Charles:

> His person's such as he for that alone
> (His birth a way) deserves the Royall Throne;
> His Statur's Tall, & of the comeliest male,
> His visage oval, his Heyr thick and black,
> In ample Curles, on's Shoulders falling down,
> Adorning more his Head than any Crowne.[215]

Moving from merely physical attributes, the poem continues to announce the qualities of this king, blessed by nature, for rule:

AUGUSTUS ANGLICUS.

F. H. Van Houe. sculp.

18 Frederik Hendrik van Hove, *King Charles II*, seventeenth century.

His Eyes are lively, full of flame and Spirit,
And of that colour, most delights the sight
Royall, and largly featur'd all the rest,
Declaring largnesse of his Royall Brest;
Which with long Travail, h'as improved so
He knows what e're befits a Prince to know.

A magnificent engraving that seems to belong to Restoration is an anonymous work featuring Charles in armour with a baton firmly grasped in his right hand, beside a table on which stand the crown and sceptre (fig. 19). Behind his right side, a Roundhead army flees before a god hurling thunder and lightning after it.[216] On our right behind the crown and sceptre shines a star in the sky and the sun rises above a peaceful horizon; on a cliff a phoenix rises from the ashes to announce the rebirth of kingship and the restoration of peace after republic and war. Beneath the image, in which Charles's central position places him as an agent of transformation, an inscription on a plinth flanked by abandoned arms and cornucopia explains how as a phoenix arises,

19 *Redivivo Phoenici.*

Charles, King of Britain, France and Ireland expels the forces of evil while, like the star that greeted his birth, as a sun rising he dispels darkness to stand as the light of his people. A complex combination of Christian and classical allusions, the engraving also gestures to Caroline, Elizabethan and earlier Tudor images and emblems (especially the phoenix) in ways that advertised Charles's divine and dynastic claims and the beneficial fruits of his assumption of rule.

Other engravings present attributes of restored kingship old and new. An engraving of Charles II touching to cure the king's evil, depicting the king under a canopy, with the clergy standing to his right while the sick line up to be touched, and titled *The Royal Gift of Healing*, records Charles's extensive exercise of the royal touch, which he performed especially often during years of his reign (fig. 20).[217] Hollar's engraving for the frontispiece of Thomas Sprat's *History of the Royal Society*, by contrast, conjures very different associations (fig. 21).[218] Here a bust of Charles stands on a column inscribed 'Carolus II Societatis Regalis Author & Patronus' with Fame about to crown it with a laurel. On the left and right of the bust, respectively, William Viscount Brouncher, the first president, points to the inscription, and Francis Bacon gestures to his left, or perhaps to the instruments and insignia in the background. Surrounded by

20 *The Royal Gift of Healing.*

books and instruments, and with a palace or country house in the background, the bust of Charles is placed at the centre of old and new learning and directly beneath the arms of the Society that he is praised for inaugurating and which bears the royal name.

As well as his image and attributes, engravings recorded key moments in the restoration and reign of the king. The brothers Philippe (David and Pierre) engraved early scenes of Restoration: David's depicting of the landing of Charles II on English soil to streets crowded with coaches and ordinary citizens clambering on rooftops to catch a glimpse of the sovereign, whom angels descend from heaven to crown, represents the popularity as well as divinity of the restored Stuart.[219] In Pierre Philippe's plate, before a group that watches the royal procession, Fame descends with the royal arms while aloft angels bear the laurel, and a cherub holds a globe in a sky filled with the signs of the zodiac to reveal the divine will and – since this is likely to be the king's birthday – the

21 Wenceslaus Hollar, after John Evelyn, frontispiece to *The History of the Royal-Society of London* by Thomas Sprat, 1667.

providential significance of his birth moment and sign.[220] As well as the elaborate illustrated John Ogilby's 1662 edition of the royal coronation, and engraved images by and after Stoop, Richard Gray engraved the coronation procession for a print sold at the Globe in St Katherine's.[221] In this depiction of Charles on horseback, crowned and bearing the sceptre and orb, processing past an inn displaying the sign of the oak, an alphabetical key identifying the figures (from the king = A) suggests an audience not of the best informed. Though there was likely some correspondence between the popularity of the occasion of Charles's restoration and the distribution of these images, we do not know just how widespread they were.[222] But there can be little doubting the popularity of engravings of the royal wedding that took place in May 1662, almost exactly a year after the coronation. As well as several engravings of the new queen, there were double portraits of the royal couple by Peter Stent, P. Williams and others, and one anonymous but simple depiction is titled 'Married May 1662', indicating that this was a memento piece (fig. 22).[223] One image of the royal pair, with the queen

King Charles the Second and Queene Catharine

22 Unknown artist, *Catherine of Braganza and King Charles II*, 1662 or after.

proffering a garland of roses to Charles who takes it with his right hand, while he holds a sceptre in his left, and an angel hovers above them, recalls the double portrait of Charles I and Henrietta Maria, engraved by Van Voerst after Van Dyck.[224] The allusion here may be not only to the martyr and to dynastic descent but also to the prospect of royal progeny, which in 1662 made this a popular marriage – and evidently these engravings a good business proposition. For this image indeed was printed for two outlets: John Williams's shop at the Crown in Paul's Yard and the entrepreneurial Peter Stent at the White Horse in Giltspur Street, near Newgate. Hollar's 1672 engraving of the Grand Procession of the Sovereign and Knights' Companion of the Garter indicates both the king's desire to represent himself as Garter knight and a public interest in the ceremonial.[225] Indeed, an engraving of the inside of St George's Hall, showing the Garter dinner and with a key pointing out the position of the king and officers, suggests an opening of these former royal mysteries, very much in Charles II's spirit, to public view and gaze.[226] Through such representations in print, many partook of the spectacle of majesty.

In the representation of monarchy, as well as images of the restored king, portraits of the Stuart royal family were important in announcing that continuity between past, present and future. Engravings of the Queen Mother Henrietta Maria by William Faithorne and Robert Walston were probably issued to mark her return to England in October 1660, or July 1662, to Somerset House, where she resided before returning to France in 1665; and to represent the reconstitution of the royal family and the link with past.[227] Several prints of the armoured portraits of James, Duke of York, were 'made public' – or sold – and were popular perhaps on account of his military prowess abroad during the Interregnum, and later his naval victory at Lowestoft.[228] Portraits of the duke's first and second wives (Anne Hyde and Mary of Modena) and their daughters, and of Prince Rupert, displayed to the nation Stuart progeny in the secondary branches of the family.[229]

In the case of Charles himself, the impossibility of a representation of legitimate succession resulted in a remarkable profusion of images of royal bastards and their mothers, the king's mistresses. While the market for images of royal mistresses doubtless responded to public curiosity and titillation, these engravings usually followed official portraits which Charles was evidently not averse to publicizing. Engravings, by Blooteling after Lely, of Charles's son by Lucy Walter, the Duke of Monmouth, present the duke in his Garter robes with all his titles and offices; and images of the Dukes of Richmond, Grafton, Southampton, Northumberland, and St Albans, the Earl of Plymouth and other royal offspring were freely circulated and sold.[230] How these portraits, some published 'cum privilegio', with endless prints of the Duchesses of Cleveland and Portsmouth, performed as images of Charles II's monarchy it is not easy to determine.[231] But before we deduce from Marvell's *Last Instructions* a general moral outrage against the king and court, we should recall that those portraits were in demand and that Charles's popularity with his people appears to have been little damaged by them. Indeed, in some quarters it may have been enhanced as the new monarch, by the publicization of his sexual life, not only dispelled puritan cheerlessness but manifested a fecund masculinity – rather as did the conspicuous codpiece in Holbein's portrait of the monarch whom Charles evidently admired: King Henry VIII.[232]

It seems likely that, as increasingly with all forms of royal representation, such engravings met with very different responses among different (indeed opposed) factions and faiths.[233] Like poems, prints during Charles II's reign became fully implicated in the politics of party, though more research is needed before we can begin to identify clearly any affiliations of engravers and publishers with party patronage and politics. From virtually the moment of Restoration, engraved portraits of ejected ministers, former republicans and Cromwellians, had circulated, presumably principally among the disaffected and critics of the regime.[234] John Bunyan's portrait, for example, was advertised for sale at the Bible in Newgate Street – probably a nonconformist business – where all of Bunyan's works were advertised, along with 'Dr Merwood's ink powder'.[235] But during the Exclusion crisis one senses not only a wide use, but polemical glossing, of engraved portraits to score party points. Several images of Sir Edmund Bury Godfrey were sold with accompanying verses and tags describing him as a Protestant martyr, hero and patriot;[236] a 1680 engraving of Shaftesbury by White depicts the leader of the opposition with the motto 'Love Serve';[237] and the portrait of Rye House Plotters, both those who were executed and those who escaped, from Lord Russell to the likes of the Stepney preacher Matthew Meade, were probably sponsored and purchased by sympathizers.[238]

On the other side, the 1680s saw a second wave of engravings of Charles I and the late engravings of Charles II appear, like the portraits from which some were taken, more propagandistic and overtly partisan.[239] Indeed, as well as frustrating, it is revealing that in the case of many anonymous and undated engravings, the principal uncertainty is whether they belong to the very early or later part of the reign, both periods in which several images of Charles and the monarchy were devised to shore up the sanctity and continuity of monarchy in uncertain times. But we know that the Alexander Browne mezzotints were later – Browne was not working in the 1660s – and interestingly figured Charles, after Lely, in armour, before a huge column, representing authority, and bearing a baton of command.[240] About the same time, Browne engraved portraits after Van Dyck of Charles as a prince with his father and siblings to advertise Stuart dynasty and to rally support for continuing Stuart succession.[241]

Engravings by John Smith, William Shearwin, John Beckett, Edward Rixon, and Vanderbranc, several after Kneller, to which we can assign a late date on account of the biography of the artist, recirculate images of Charles in armour, and coronation robes, with the royal regalia and, in the cases of a Vanderbranc, with a Tudor rose worked into the Garter badge beneath the royal portrait.[242] An engraving by Michael Burghers, who was not working in England until the later 1670s, can similarly be dated later, and portrays Charles enthroned with, on his right, the blindfolded figure of Justice leaning on the royal arms (fig. 23).[243] From the heavens a pair of hands reach down with the crown, illustrating the legend 'Per Me Reges Regnant'. Nobles gather on the right, attentive to the king, and beneath the image is written 'Sibi, et successoribus suis legitimis' – 'for the king himself and all his legitimate successors' – the only divine rulers and defenders of Justice for all. The 1681 edition of *The Wars in England, Scotland and Ireland*, a loyalist call to obedience, has an engraved frontispiece depicting Charles II enthroned in parliament, as a constitutional sovereign, and with the Armada tapestries visible in the background, recalling the victories which the author urged Englishmen to pursue in preference to civil disputes.[244]

23 Michael Burghers, *King Charles II with Justice and twenty unknown men*, c. 1660–79.

Engravings and mezzotints of quality, replacing the older woodcuts, issued in multiple copies, advertised in newspapers, sold and purchased in businesses sometimes specializing in visual prints, and collected and displayed, publicized the image of the king and the monarchy, his family, ministers and mistresses. Increasingly, political crisis also stimulated prints and cartoons critical of the king, royal family and court.[245] As a genre they were deployed by loyalists and critics, and enabled both the sacralization and demystification of regality as they passed into a consumer culture and public sphere increasingly divided over religion and state affairs. Yet in the fashion for collecting engravings, along with porcelain commemorating the restored king, we may discern the origins of our own experience of royal souvenirs which still, in our more democratic age, indicates some desire for connection with authority.[246] Charles II, more than many of his predecessors, encouraged that desire and enabled that sense of connection. It is a truism to say that, for all the importance of printed words and images, the most vital representation of monarchy was the monarch himself; but in the case of Charles II, the king's style of government, self-presentation and ultimately his personality shaped not only the royal image but the very nature of monarchy.

CHAPTER 3

RITUALS OF RESTORED MAJESTY

I

It may seem paradoxical that the reign of one of the most familiar and informal monarchs in British history was also a reign marked by some of the most magnificent ceremonies and rituals of the early modern age. As we shall see, Charles II's coronation outdid all his predecessors in its splendour; he touched to cure the king's evil more than any before him; he devised schemes for the building and decorating of grand palaces and stages for the performance of majesty; and he remained a stickler for ceremonies throughout his reign. The paradox takes us to the heart of Charles's experience and times. Rituals of state had, as we have seen, taken on enhanced importance following the Reformation and court ritual reached its elaborate sacred heights in the reign of Charles I.[1] Unsurprisingly, the noble appointed governor to the prince and heir, the Duke of Newcastle, had sought to impress on his young charge the centrality of ceremony in the exercise and sustenance of sovereign authority: 'Ceremony though it is nothing in itself yet it doth everything. For what is a king more than a subject but for ceremony and order?' On Charles's restoration, Newcastle repeated his counsel: 'there is nothing keeps up a king more than ceremony and order, which makes distance and this brings respect and duty and those obedience'. Though he advised the king to be 'courteous and civil to everybody', Newcastle urged Charles never to countenance over-familiarity or insubordination in his bedchamber or court: 'you cannot put upon you too much king'.[2]

But ritual and ceremony had not only failed to sustain the monarchy and bind the nation, in a symbolic parody of royal ceremonial, Charles I had been publicly executed on a scaffold at Whitehall, turned towards the Banqueting House which had been a principal site of state festival. During the 1640s for Prince Charles the elegant ceremonial of his courtly youth was exchanged for the hardships of the campaign site and battlefield. During the 1650s, the king, though lodged in foreign courts, was an impoverished guest often bound by alien modes of etiquette; while, famously, the events of his escape after the

Battle of Worcester read like a mock or inverted royal ritual, with the king figured as the victim, the hunted, the servant and the 'booby', or clown. Ritual, however, did not pass with the fall of the executioner's axe in 1649; in exile Charles went to lengths to maintain, as far as he could, rituals and proprieties; the Commonwealth instituted its own ceremonial practices, and the longer he wielded power the more Oliver Cromwell's court began to resemble and emulate the customs of royal Whitehall – not least because the Protector recognized the popular associations of ritual with legitimate authority.[3]

Restoration, then, both did not – and did – require a reconstruction of state rituals and ceremonies. That is, state rituals needed to be recast and re-presented as monarchical occasions; and royal rituals needed to overshadow those of the Protector to mark not just the grandeur but the legitimacy of regal government. Moreover, rituals were needed both to express the divinity of the sovereign and to re-bind a divided Commonwealth into a united kingdom. Those who made the Restoration settlement had no doubt of the vital importance state ritual would play in restoring obedience and affection for monarchy. As James Heath, the historian and son of the king's cutler, wrote perceptively in 1662: "'tis not in the power of reason or force of words to charm people and subjects into that veneration of their princes which the silent yet awful majesty of their magnificent public appearances can most undoubtedly conciliate and command'.[4] 'By these glorious distances,' he continued, 'the regardful subject is kept within his bounds; and by such pomp the throne is raised from the level of plebeian encroachment to its due height and most sacred imperious ascent.' Deploying a more Machiavellian vocabulary, Heath adds: 'Love and fear [are] the great props of government being never more equally attempered in men to the harmonious conservation of the peace than by these State Grandezzas, true policy being like true religion which once denuded of its decency and ceremonies is quickly profaned by the malepert vulgar and invaded by sedition.'

Ritual for Heath both sacralized power and fostered the love as well as awe that subjects felt for the king; spectacle promoted the subject's regard (in both senses) towards sovereignty. Preaching on Isaiah 33: 17 ('Thine eyes shall see the king in his beauty') at his parish church in Waltham Abbey, Essex, Thomas Reeve economically made a similar point when he instructed Charles in his dedication: God 'hath restored you to your father's throne to be looked upon as a glorious spectacle'.[5] It was for the king to play his part.

Rituals of royal restoration commenced long before Charles's coronation and even before he set foot on English soil. On 1 May 1660, having received Charles's letters and declaration from Breda, the parliament read them 'with the greatest expressive submission in the world, standing bare-headed', and promptly voted to send Charles a payment of £50,000 and to reward Sir John Grenville, who had delivered the letters, as a royal envoy.[6] As the letters from Breda were published and news of a likely Restoration spread abroad,

Londoners commenced their own celebrations, taking a 'perfect vacation from all business', as they made the capital 'a theatre of pleasure'.[7] While the Estates General in Holland conveyed their formal congratulations, and made all preparations for Charles's departure as a sovereign of England, Scotland and Ireland, on 8 May the clerk of parliament proclaimed that 'immediately upon the decease of our late sovereign lord King Charles, the imperial crown of the realm of England, and of all the kingdoms and rights belonging to the same, did by inherent birthright and lawful and undoubted succession descend . . . to his most excellent majesty, Charles the Second'.[8]

The process of proclamation was the first truly regal ritual of the Restoration. Having read the proclamation in parliament, the Lords and Commons took their coaches and processed, followed by troops of officers, trumpets, heralds and nobles, to Whitehall where the king was proclaimed a second time before arriving at Temple Bar; there, following established ritual of succession, the gate was closed so that the King at Arms could knock and request admission to proclaim the new monarch. From Temple Bar, along streets lined, as if for a royal procession, with a militia guard, the assembly marched to Chancery Lane 'where at the word Charles the Second in the proclamation, the King at Arms lifting himself up with more than ordinary cheerfulness, and expressing it with a very audible voice, the people presently took it and on a sudden carried it to the Old Exchange, which was pursued with such shouts that near a quarter of an hour was spent before silence could be made to read the rest of the proclamation'.[9] At the fourth reading – at Cheapside – the shouting was so loud it drowned the bells as a 'numberless number' celebrated in the streets.[10]

Though his royalist account is biased, Heath was insightful about the significance of these events. The ceremonies of reading the proclamation antedated that feature of the coronation ritual in which the king, in Westminster Abbey, was presented on all four sides to the people: it conferred on Charles public acceptance and recognition; and the joyous public response reciprocated the royal letters from Breda in affirming the people's love for their sovereign. Beyond that, the readings of the proclamation were what anthropologists call a liminal moment: they constituted a key moment of psychological response. Heath spoke of a multitude released from 'mad tumults . . . at that very cross' at Cheapside; of a people restored to reason 'by the magic of his (Charles II's) excellent name'.[11] And, significantly, he described their behaviour as 'an atonement'.[12] In demonstration of that atonement, at the same time as the new king was being proclaimed, in a ritual that reversed a key moment in the founding of the republic, 'the martyred king's statue was re-erected at Guildhall, and the arms of the Commonwealth everywhere pull'd down and defaced and his majesty's set in their places'.[13] Re-erected in courts and churches, often with local ceremonies, the royal arms reconstituted a monarchy which now awaited only the king's presence.[14]

As his English subjects filled their churches on Sunday, 13 May to give thanks to God for his return, Charles was commencing his journey home to present himself as the 'spectacle' for the sight of which his people longed. At The Hague a state reception was held with all the grandeur the Estates could manage in the short notice of time they were given. Here a number of rituals were performed before representatives of the states of Europe as well as the English parliament. The royal family began to be reconstituted as Charles was met by his aunt Elizabeth, his brothers the Dukes of York and Gloucester and his sister the princess dowager of Orange; international recognition was ceremonially affirmed in a series of grand banquets; and the rituals of atonement and pardon were theatrically played out in the submission and request for pardon of the parliamentary commissioners who publicly made in the king's chamber 'a very low and most submissive reverence'.[15] The Dutch paid attention to symbolic detail, ensuring that more dishes were provided at the king's table than at those of the Estates.[16]

Amid all, Charles played his part on the stage of the ceremony with consummate skill. When the delegate of the States General came to address him, Charles, it was observed, 'never offered to be covered, as was thought to show that he would do something more for them than he would do for an ambassador'.[17] When he was entertained at dinner, he displayed 'good spirits', stayed late, and expressed his appreciation of his magnificent entertainment.[18] Though an attempt on his life was rumoured, Charles refused to allow his guards to draw swords lest it give offence to his hosts.[19] When Oliver Cromwell's envoy George Downing craved pardon of the king for his past disloyal service, Charles graciously, and wittily, excused it and knighted him.[20] Charles appointed Sunday 20th as a sermon day, to show his religious zeal and, following it, made public show of his divine election by touching for the evil – even though there was a shortage of 'angel' coins to give to the sick – speaking the words as he did so, 'I touch thee but God heal thee'.[21] As he prepared to embark, Charles had through ritual displayed royal divinity, mercy, liberality and an exact sense of protocol – news of which flew back to England ahead of him.

The embarkation itself was a ritual performance. Not only did a reputed fifty thousand people spend the night taking up places on the Downs for a view, the ships had to be made ready to convey the king. Going aboard the fleet, the Duke of York summoned all the captains to take the oath of allegiance; Admiral Edward Montagu changed the flags of the Commonwealth to the Royal Standard and removed the republic's arms from the stern; the flagship that Cromwell had named the *Naseby*, in commemoration of a parliamentary victory over the Royalists, was ceremonially renamed the *Royal Charles*.[22] Doing their part, meanwhile, 'the estates of Holland had caused one of the greatest barks of the place to be fitted for the royal persons. The body of the vessel was garnished with tapestry, its mast carried the royal flag and its yards were loaden with garlands and crowns of verdure and flowers, among which there was one fastened . . . with a streamer which carried for its device Quo fas ab fata, to denote that the king embarking himself went to the place where his right and Providence of God called him, attending to the ordinary motto of the kings of England, Dieu et Mon Droit.'[23] After a final dinner shipboard and a last feast at The Hague, the royal flotilla set sail – the journey itself constituting a symbolic safe return of the ships of state, for so long tossed (we recall Marshall's frontispiece to the *Eikon Basilike*) on stormy waters. In Heath's words, 'The Lord of the ocean now kept his court upon it in all his regalities and gave law to its unruly floods.'[24]

When he landed at Dover, in a theatrical gesture Charles went down on his knees to kiss the ground.[25] George Monck kissed the king's hand and conducted him to the principal cathedral city of the realm as nobles and gentlemen drawn up on the Downs provided a guard of honour. At Canterbury, the streets were strewn with flowers and hung with garlands as the mayor welcomed Charles on the eve of a service the following day. Charles then progressed to Rochester, taking leave on his birthday, 29 May, for London. As he passed through Deptford, in a welcome ritual symbolic of purity, rebirth and fertility, 'about 100 maidens clothed in white . . . stood ready and having prepared baskets full of flowers and fragrant herbs strewed the way before him.'[26] At St George's Fields, where the mayor waited to present the sword of the city as the sign of the king's sovereignty over all, Charles again displayed a magnificent – and magnanimous – grasp of these rituals as a first representation of his rule. Having knighted the mayor, he permitted him to carry the sword before him 'which had not been done any other public entry but when the late king of blessed memory returned from Scotland anno 1641'.[27] Symbolically returning to the last peaceful days of his father, as well as displaying a humility that dispelled any fear of triumphalism, Charles II between his two brothers was then led by a cavalcade of troops and livery companies, in velvet, white and pink lace and gold, through the city (here when offered a Bible, in a gesture reminiscent of Elizabeth I, he promised to make religion his first care) to Whitehall, where, in the Banqueting House, the Lords and Commons waited to do obeisance and the clergy met to sing a Te Deum, often a prelude to a royal coronation.[28]

Once again all these rituals of affirmation were accompanied by ceremonies of ritual denigration. Following the often elaborate popular 'roastings of the Rump' in mockery of the republic, which had taken place all over London in February, now in May bonfires were lit across the city.[29] 'Among the rest, a costly one was made' (presumably not by the common people) 'in the City of Westminster where the effigy of Oliver Cromwell was set upon a high post with the arms of the Commonwealth, which having been a while exposed there to public view, with torches lighted, that every one might take notice of them, were both burnt together'.[30] The fire, Heath hoped and believed, 'did . . . purge and expiate' the Protectorate and Republic; and he noted how, while Cromwell's effigy burned, the ambassador of his erstwhile ally Sweden threw money to the people, to ingratiate himself with a new mood and a new regime.[31]

As a sign of the world being turned back the right way, on 1 June Charles went to parliament to assent to statutes, where he appeared 'in his proper and full orb . . . constituting the parliament more by his presence than by his . . . assent'.[32] And across the kingdoms, though Charles could not be present in person, rituals were devised to mark his symbolic presence, the representation of his royal authority. In Edinburgh, within a rail by the cross, almost like an altar, 'was placed a large table cover and with a rich banquet served up in glass and representing divers forms and devices, as his majesty's arms . . .', and food was distributed to the people as a sign of royal beneficence.[33] In Duldachin, Ireland, even the return of the rooks was celebrated as 'an auspicious' blessing.[34]

As attention turned to planning the principal ceremony of state, the coronation, the rituals affirming the new and overturning the old regime were played out with careful symbolic detail. On the one side ten regicides were hanged with their faces turned (as Charles I's head had been) towards Whitehall, and the carcasses of Cromwell, Ireton and Bradshaw were exhumed, drawn on the sledge to Tyburn, and there hanged until sunset to publicize their treason and their failure to merit the honourable death by the sword. On the other, the bodies of Montrose, who had ignobly suffered the traitor's death, and Sir Charles Lucas and Sir George Lisle, Royalists executed at Colchester, were reinterred with full military honours, the coffins of the last being 'accompanied with at least ten thousand gentlemen'.[35] Such rituals were not simple acts of righting wrong – important though they would have been as a sign of justice restored; they also announced the return of an honour society, and of the due punishments and rewards bestowed by a king who would be the champion of justice and honour and the exemplar of good lordship.

Charles II's coronation was, in every sense, extraordinary. No monarch in British history had before followed a republican regime. No monarch before was crowned on St George's Day, 23 April. Sir John Reresby was not alone in believing the ceremonies for Charles 'richer than was ever known'.[36] Edward Walker described the clothes and trappings as 'so great as no age has seen the like before', and predicted that such great solemnity was unlikely to 'ever be again in this kingdom'.[37] James Heath reported that 'foreigners acknowledged themselves never to have seen among all the great magnificences of the world any to come near or equal to this'.[38] Even – it was taken as a sign of God's favour – the sun shone 'gloriously all that day and the next . . . not one drop of rain falling in all that time, as very much had done at least ten days before and as many after these . . . great solemnities'.[39]

As was customary, the organization and planning of the event were the work of many people, from within the city as well as the court. John Ogilby's *Relation* mentions both commissioners, appointed by the crown, and a committee of the City.[40] While we do not know the details of the distribution of labour from conception to execution, it is evident that the king himself was involved from the beginning of the preparations.[41] On 26 September 1660, Charles resolved in a full meeting of the Privy Council to begin preparations and directed the new making of the regalia for the event.[42] Directions to the Master of the Jewel House for making crowns, sceptres and orbs, rings, spurs and chalices, and to the Master of the Great Wardrobe for tunics, coats of cloth of gold, palls, shirts, sandals, gloves, mantles and robes are detailed and precise.[43] And the crown commissioners met all those who by virtue of their tenure were obliged, or claimed by right, to attend or perform service at the coronation.[44] If Clarendon's testimony can be trusted, Charles's personal involvement may have extended to the very conception of the entertainment, for he informs us that the king urged that 'the novelties and new inventions with which the kingdom had been so much intoxicated for so many years altogether might be discountenanced and discredited in the eyes of the people'.[45]

In large measure, the City of London companies, which paid for the lavish spectacle, took their cue from the king's wishes, and staged a neo-Roman triumphal entry to mark the end of 'a dismal Night of usurpation, and oppression'.[46] Yet, as with all the texts of Restoration, the complex symbolism of the coronation pageant did not represent simply the old kingship returned but also visions of a new monarchy, a new nation and a new British empire.

The entertainment through the City of London before the actual coronation in Westminster followed a processional narrative, which unfolded at a series of classical-style arches, the sites of pageants, which are visible in Stoop's painting and engravings after it.[47] The theme, devised by John Ogilby, drew on a festival organized for Ferdinand the Infante of Spain by Rubens in 1635, but ultimately on Virgil's *Aeneid, Eclogues* and *Georgics*, to represent Charles as an epic hero: as both Aeneas who, wandering after the fall of Troy, founded the city of Rome; and as Augustus who, following the turmoil of republic, presided over the empire's longest period of unity, peace and prosperity.[48] The Augustan theme, which we have encountered in many panegyrics and portraits, gestured back to James I and forwards to imperial ambition; but there can be no doubting the immediate topicality or polemics of the conceit. Ogilby, whose own translation of Virgil (as well as of Homer and Aesop) had in key terms rendered it a royalist text, was not just reproducing but representing Roman history for monarchy, by writing Augustan imperialism over republic.[49] Within an overall Roman conceit, the processional narrative, the arches and pageants, and the speeches delivered, engaged with specific and topical English circumstances and proffered a strong vision of monarchy which was to shape expectations of Charles' reign.

As he processed from the Tower towards Whitehall, Charles drew up at the first arch erected at Leaden Hall Street. Here on the north side was the figure of a woman, 'begirt with serpents' signifying Rebellion attended by Confusion, with torn crowns and broken sceptres in her hand. On the south side, two women figured Britain's Monarchy supported by Loyalty, both with emblems of the three kingdoms. On this same side, a painting of Charles's landing at Dover was titled above 'ADVENTUS AUG' ('on the arrival of Augustus') and carried below verses (derived from Virgil) on Fortune's restoring the crown.[50] On the north side, a painting and tags from Virgil and Horace represented and announced God's vengeance on rebels. Over the middle arch, flanked by statues of James I and Charles I, a painting of Charles II on horseback depicts him routing Usurpation; above which stands a statue of the king, crowned and in coronation robes before a leafy oak bearing crowns and sceptres. Beneath the king's statue, an inscribed tablet describes him (with gestures back to the inscription the republic placed at the Royal Exchange) as the extinguisher of tyranny and restorer of liberty.[51] Other paintings recorded the mayor delivering the keys to the city and the transformation from disorder to order effected by the royal arrival.[52] As Charles drew near, Rebellion addressed him with defiant boasts of her power, her fomentation of 'late unnatural Broils' and her determination to 'tread down *Monarchy*.'[53] But confronted by Monarchy and Loyalty, she skulks away as the figure of Monarchy invites Charles to enter in triumph as 'our *Sun*, our *Comfort* and our *Life*.'[54] On the first arch, then, almost as if in a masque, as the king approaches, confusion is transmuted into order, rebellion into loyalty and republic into monarchy. Charles is represented as the imperial Augustus, the rightful Stuart descendant, the beloved of the people and the monarch protected by Providence, while in a niche above an oak tree (a symbol of the king's providential deliverance) angels hold a celestial crown (fig. 24).

The cavalcade moving forward, at the East India House in Levant Street the company staged a welcome pageant of loyal thanks. Here a youth in Indian garb on a camel with panniers of jewels, silks and spices, sang of the riches of their joys at the phoenix-like restoration of the monarchy. And, as was customary in civic festivals, the company took the opportunity to express their hopes: of victory over Dutch rivals, a trading empire under England's Augustus, and colonial acquisition and expansion.[55] The second arch took up the imperial theme. This naval arch erected in Cornhill, near the Exchange, bore an inscribed tablet to 'Neptuno Britannico Carolo II Cuius Arbitrio Mare Vel Liberum Vel Clausum', which referred to the fulfilment of the British monarchy's long-standing claim to be the sovereign of the seas.[56] Adorned on its south and north sides with paintings of Neptune, Mars and (above them) two London scenes, the Tower and the Exchange, the arch carried a large portrait of Charles I

24 The first pageant arch, engraving from J. Ogilby, *The entertainment of His most excellent Majestie Charles II . . .*, 1662.

with Prince Charles (now the king) viewing the flagship the *Sovereign of the Seas*, and (on the west side) a portrait of the Duke of York, Lord High Admiral, dressed as Neptune. On the pedestals and in the niches, actors representing Europe, Asia, Africa and America, and Arithmetic, Geometry, Astronomy and Navigation, figured the four empires of the world and the arts that might make England triumph over them all. Thames addresses the king:

> Hail Mighty *Monarch*! Whose Imperial Hand
> Quiets the Ocean and secures the Land.[57]

and gives the thanks of London for the restoration of wealth and trade under Stuart naval might. And sailors sing of their anticipation that, under England's Neptune, France, the Dutch, the Spanish and the Turks will be eclipsed as Charles, 'from strand to strand' rules the oceans, aided by 'our Royal Admiral' the Duke of York.[58] As he rode beneath the arches, Charles represented restored monarchy as the new learning, as naval empire and as the means to lead England to imperial destiny.

At Cheapside, where in the traditional symbol of liberality, the fountains ran with wine, close by the spot of the famous cross was erected the third arch dedicated to the theme of Concord (fig. 25). Atop a Corinthian arch inscribed 'Concordia Insuperabilis', flanked by figures of Peace and Truth, was built a large temple of Concord with, on its cupola, the figure of Concord treading on the serpent of division and rebellion. Around the temple, eight figures with pennons represented the four cardinal virtues (Prudence, Justice, Temperance and Fortitude) and, with an attendant within the temple, a figure representing a citizen of London presented the king (over whose head is written 'Pater Patriae' – 'the father of his country') with an oak garland. Beside them, Truth

25 The third pageant arch, engraving from J. Ogilby, *The entertainment of His most excellent Majestie Charles II . . .*, 1662.

and Love stand with other figures. One bears a shield with a 'King of bees', followed by a swarm, inscribed 'Rege Imcolumi Mens Omnibus Una' – 'all of one mind makes for a safe and sound king(dom)'; others represent love, unity, counsel, and a bright star, a reference to that which shone at Charles's birth.[59] When Charles drew up to the middle of the temple, Concord, Love and Truth in song lauded the 'long foretold' 'king of peace' who 'Brings healing Balm . . . To close our Wounds'.[60] As all are reminded of the rich fruits of peace and unity, Charles is represented as 'the King of Truth, and Peace' who resolves divisions and restores love and harmony, the sacred figure to whom the Temple of Concord is dedicated.[61]

The fourth and final arch in Fleet Street near Whitefriars represented the Garden of Plenty. On a tablet over the main archway the inscription announces that the temple was constructed in honour of him who had put an end to civil strife and destruction. To left and right respectively Bacchus and Ceres represent abundant vineyards and harvests, the fruits of peace. On the second Ionic storey of the arch stand the goddesses Flora and Pomona, garlanded with roses and fruits, and the figures representing the four seasons; on top of all the figure of Plenty, crowned, holds a palm and a cornucopia.[62] From a stage adorned like a garden, another actor representing Plenty addressed the king. Describing the royal absence as a 'sad winter' that blasted all, Plenty heralds the return with Charles of a golden age, as Nature herself welcomes him:

> Thus Seasons, Men, and Gods their Joy express
> To see Your Triumph, and our Happiness.[63]

Before he processed onwards therefore to his palace at Whitehall, which he reached about 3 p.m., Charles had performed in what was virtually a masque in architecture.[64] Only his presence gave life to the symbols and voice to the mute figures of the pageants. And, as each of the arches dedicated to him announced, only his presence banished rebellion, re-established peace, concord and plenty, and promised a rich imperial future for the city and the nation. Each structure constituted a complicated iconographical tableau, combining classical texts and scriptural allusions, figures from myth, ancient and recent British history, emblems well known from iconographic literature, and symbols personal to Charles like the star, or the oak. Charles II, that is, was represented both as a public body – as the embodiment of the continuity of kingship, and especially of Stuart kingship – and as a man, Charles Stuart, who had experienced displacement, exile and danger. The procession, as it wound through the arches, traced, as it were, the narrative of both his and the nation's experiences and quite literally joined the city, the nation and the monarch through a human chain that (like Stoop's painting) displayed reconstituted royal government: the Lord Chancellor and Lord Steward, judges and Privy Councillors, Gentlemen of the Privy Chamber, Sewers and Quarter waiters. Those who devised the entertainment endeavoured not only to represent restored monarchy but to reconstitute it through ceremony.

Evidently both the city and the king considered the spectacle of such importance and such a success that they authorized an official account of the entertainment, with detailed descriptions of the arches, pageants and spectacles. John Ogilby's *Relation of His Majesties Entertainment* was published, probably soon after the day, with the royal arms, a royal imprimatur, and a grant of monopoly. The next year Ogilby issued a lavish folio, with a full-page royal arms, fine engravings of the arches, fuller explanations of the classical references and symbols, and detailed illustrations; this edition also contained a multi-image engraving of the procession with the royal officials and officers and noble ranks identified.[65] Ogilby's text, the first of its kind, going into two editions in both its 1661 and 1662 formats, was evidently a sought-after souvenir of the spectacle. But what of the impression made by the occasion on contemporaries? Roger Coke, author of *A Discourse of Trade* (1670), protested at the cost, while Sir William Petty celebrated the opportunity given to craftsmen who worked on the constructions, and the stimulus to the economy.[66] Clearly the pageants made a powerful impression on the national memory, for twenty years later, in his opera *Albion and Albianus*, Dryden had constructed a simulacrum of the triumphal arches onstage – presumably on the assumption that they would be immediately recognizable.[67] Certainly, too, the enemies of monarchy viewed them as a powerful symbol: the Fifth Monarchist Thomas Venner and his co-conspirators had planned to burn down the arches as part of their rising against monarchy.[68]

As for the citizens and common folk, did the entertainment and appearance of the king, as Heath had hoped, 'charm them' into 'veneration' of 'awful majesty'?[69] There can be no doubt that, as well as nobles and gentry, ordinary people who had weeks earlier taken to the streets to celebrate the end of the Rump or cheered the proclamation of the king, flocked out onto the streets to witness the spectacle. Heylyn vividly conjured the two days 'when all the bravery of the nation seemed to be poured into the city and the whole city emptied into some few streets, the windows in those streets to be glazed with eyes, the houses ... to be tiled with men'.[70] And while more prosaic in his description, Edward Walker offered testimony that it was a crowd of all classes and degrees: 'innumerable multitudes of people of all ages, conditions, and sexes, who came from all parts of England'.[71] The author of *A Brief Chronicle* described the assembled in terms that resonate with the language of modern crowd psychology as 'in a kind of ecstasy'.[72]

In recent years, historians have expressed scepticism concerning the impact of performances rich in complex classical and symbolic allusions which Ogilby delighted in expounding.[73] But these were only part of the entertainment which also drew on popular emblems and, it has been shown, on ballads, or imagery (like that of spring after winter) that was a popular commonplace. According to Heath there was a maypole, with a stage for Morris dancers erected at the Strand; and it is evident that for many the restoration of the monarchy signalled the restoration of pleasure, as well as trade and wealth.[74] As well as Delft chargers, the first coronation mugs I have seen suggest a popular desire for mementoes of a memorable day.[75] As the texts of the third arch had articulated, the authority of the king rested on the unity and love of the people. Those who filled the streets, as Charles's cavalcade wound its way to Whitehall, did not merely observe the spectacle; they made it and gave it meaning, their presence realizing the end of rebellion and the return of concord which the pageants symbolized. In time, in chronicle, history and in many material evocations of memory, their participation was represented to them, as the evidence of their joy and adulation.

The entertainments of 22 April were only a magnificent prelude to the occasion of the next day: the king's coronation on St George's Day. As we shall see, the great solemnity that preceded the coronation was the restoration of the Order of St George, as well as the creation of Knights of the Bath, so that all traditional ceremony and attendance were in order.[76] At about seven in the morning, the king went by barge from Whitehall to the parliament stairs where, in the Princes Lodgings, he was arrayed in his ermine, while the nobility prepared themselves in the Painted Chamber. At about 9.30, the nobles processed through the Court of Requests into Westminster Hall, to align themselves on each side of the throne of state. As the king was sat, 'under a glorious cloth of state', the dean and prebends of Westminster, who had carried the regalia from the abbey, entered Westminster Hall, preceded by the gentlemen of the King's Chapel, the choir and the heralds, and ceremoniously laid them on the table beside the king.[77] Charles II entrusted the regalia to the privileged nobles: the crown to the Duke of Ormond, the orb to the Duke of Buckingham, the spurs to the Earl of Pembroke, and so on. And at 10 a.m. the procession filed into the Palace Yard to the west end of Westminster Abbey, walking all the way on a blue cloth, the king supported by the bishops of Bath and Durham.[78] In the abbey, two galleries had been built at the upper end of the choir for the aldermen and judges, on the one side, the Knights of the Bath and Gentlemen of the Privy Chamber on the other.[79] The nobles were seated on the benches, with the heralds close to the altar. As an anthem was sung, from Psalm 122, the king entered, knelt, uttered 'private ejaculations', then proceeded to what Ogilby revealingly calls 'the theatre between the quire and the altar', where the throne of state was placed, and sat beside it on a chair covered with cloth of gold.[80]

At this point, amid the sanctity of the moment, the Bishop of London, with the great officers of the royal household, went to all four sides, to perform what in 1660 must have been a moment charged with drama and emotion. The bishop

> acquainted the people that he presented to them King Charles the rightful inheritor of the Crown of this Realm; and asked them if they were willing to do their Homage, Service, and bounden duty to him. As this was doing, the king rose up, looking towards the people, to whom the bishop spake: Who by their shouts signified their consent. The like question was put to the nobility.[81]

After the affirmation of the nobles and people, Charles descended from the throne to the altar, at which he knelt with an offering while the bishops said grace. After the sermon (on Proverbs 28: 2 – 'for the transgressions of a land, many are the princes thereof but by a man of understanding and knowledge, the state shall be prolonged'), the oath was administered – 'to confirm the laws to the people and franchises to the clergy' – and sworn by Charles before the altar.[82] Then, as the choir sang an anthem, he was anointed, invested with the surplice and given the sword of state, whilst prayers were said for blessings on his rule and person. At the moment the crown was placed on his head – the moment not witnessed (even at Cromwell's inauguration) for nearly forty years – the people cried out 'God Save The King'.[83] After the placing of the ring on the king's finger and his receiving the sceptre, prayers were said and a Te Deum sung before the bishop and the nobles did homage, swearing to 'be faithful and true . . . unto you, our Sovereign lord, and your heir as kings of England', and to be the king's 'liegemen'.[84] While, led by the Duke of York, all the nobles stepped up to touch the crown, the Lord Chancellor went to all four corners again to proclaim the royal pardon, and the Lord Treasurer of the Royal Household threw gold and silver medals made for the occasion to the assembly 'as a princely donation or largesse among the people'.[85]

Charles II, king of England, then proceeded in all the regalia of state to St Edward's Chapel. He was there arrayed in purple and, having taken off St Edward's crown and been crowned with the imperial crown, made his return, with the two sceptres in his hands, to Westminster Hall attended by all the bishops and nobles, to dinner.

The coronation service, far more than the entertainments staged for the king's progress through the city the day before, represented the sacred origins, the sacred powers and the sacred obligations of kingship; and – visibly and audibly – it underlined the symbiosis between monarchy and the church, after two decades of the dissociation of secular government from any religious hierarchy. In the service and especially in the accounts of the service, the symbolism of the regalia (the sceptre with the dove was a signifier of virtue and equity) and the ceremonies (the bestowing of the mantle formed of four corners was a reminder of God's mighty power) was explained.[86] And it appears that efforts were made to make the coronation a public ritual not only for the court and the nobility. As well as the galleries for the city aldermen, the herald Edward Walker informs us that 'upon the north and south side in the cross of the church without the stage were scaffolds provided for *persons of all conditions* to sit and behold the great and sacred solemnity'.[87] There is even some suggestion that Charles, in Elizabethan manner, played to the gallery: when he was presented for the affirmation, Charles 'standing from his chair turned himself to every of the four sides of the throne and at every of them spake to the people'.[88] Commentators also remarked how, in accordance with the spirit he had displayed in his declaration from Breda, the king's pardon 'far exceeded the precedents of all former coronations'.[89]

Not all went to perfect, choreographed plan: as the barons of the Cinque Ports were conducting the king to dinner under a canopy, some of the royal footmen 'insolently and violently seized on the canopy' and a scuffle broke out, which upset the placing at tables.[90] But in the sanctum of Westminster, subjects had again witnessed the annointing of a king, the taking of sacred oaths, and the swearing of homage and fealty to a feudal overlord. Britain's imperial Augustus had there been presented to his people as St Edward's successor and as the protector of the church and the law.

Unlike his father and brother, in staging a royal entry the day before, and on the coronation day itself, Charles presented himself (as we have seen he did in speeches) as both a sacred and a popular monarch. The popularity of coronation souvenirs (as we saw, the first coronation mugs were made for Charles II's coronation), as well as the festivities, evidence the impact of the spectacle; and the early rush of ordinary folk to be cured of the king's evil suggests that the re-presentation of sacred kingship had made its impact after years of republic. Over two days, unique in early modern British history, as well as healths drunk and fires lit to celebrate his coronation, there were prayers and blessings said for King Charles.[91]

Nor did the new king's subjects have long to wait for another occasion of public ceremony and public rejoicing. Charles's bride, Catherine of Braganza, arrived hardly more than a year after the solemnities of St George's Day, and James Heath was not alone in including the festivities of her reception in August as part of the history of the 'magnificent triumphs of the blessed restitution' of the king.[92] Though she was Catholic, the marriage was popular. By it Charles not only appeared to complete the restoration of hereditary Stuart monarchy, he secured for his country a valuable commercial alliance, and (by dowry) Tangier, a post which promised the enhancement of trade and empire in the East and West Indies.[93] A further testimony to the success of the king's coronation, the original plan was for the new queen to make a royal entrance through London while Ogilby's triumphal arches of wood and canvas were still standing.[94] Evidently it was Charles himself who decided otherwise and favoured a different public display – an entrance on the water – though whether to preserve the memory of his own coronation, or in recognition of the impact of a novel ceremony we do not know.[95] For the second time in months, therefore, the city companies were faced with devising and financing, probably under royal supervision, a series of pageants on which some of the same craftsmen (the joiner Thomas Whiting, for example) who had built the arches now worked for the spectacle on the Thames.[96]

The conception and planning were entrusted to John Tatham, a London playwright who made a career organizing mayor's festivals in the late 1650s and early 1660s and who had in 1661 staged a water pageant to greet Charles's return to Whitehall after his progress from the Tower.[97] Tatham commandeered each of the livery companies' barges to stage 'something of affection and loyalty'.[98] Accordingly, on the Mercers' barge, a virgin was seated under a canopy of state, and on the Drapers' stood a Roman magistrate with a sceptre and crown, these two symbolizing the royal pair, attended by Loyalty, Truth, Fame and Honour, each presented with the emblems and arms of both England and Portugal. As the Lord Mayor awaited the arrival from Putney of the royal couple at Chelsea, three pageants were put in place to mark their river passage to Whitehall.[99] In the first in a sea chariot, Isis, wife of Thame, greeted the royal couple as a divine pair and as lovers whose union promises a spring of Plenty for all. As watermen sang in celebration of revived trade and blessed the king and queen in earthy, familiar but loyal speech, the royal barge came to the second entertainment, a floating island with a large royal arms and a figure representing the River Thames, attended with nymphs. In his address, Thames lauds the providential marriage of two mighty realms which will increase the fame of each and lead other nations to fear England's new strength. Finally at the landing stairs at Whitehall, in a chariot of scallop shells, attended by two tritons, Thetis, with a crown of a star and silver crescent (to represent the king and queen), heralded the 'mighty ... conjunction' of Braganza and 'England's Charlemain' who quell the storm-tossed waves, so that ships might sail in safety, and boasted their strength founded in their union and 'your people's love'.[100]

The praise of Plenty, Fame and Peace took up the themes of the Restoration arches, but Tatham's water pageant emphasized the pregnant fruits of union. Interestingly, two years after the Restoration, the entertainment still discloses the anxieties as well as hopes of the king and his subjects. Thames's speech, for example, refers to thrones nearly lost, to 'false pretenders', 'eclipses'; while Thetis's address is replete with references to recent conflict and continuing concerns.[101] In these lines, the realm was beset by 'rebell' waves, and her wish for the king is that he may 'out-live the Malice of your Foes'.[102] Counselling the monarch while echoing Charles's own rhetoric, Thetis sees the future safety and strength of the crown in 'Your Peoples Love/Which will Your Treasure, and

Your Amour prove'.[103] And in Tatham's pageant, for all the mythological and classical references (carefully glossed for non-elite readers), it is the representation of the love and loyalty of ordinary subjects for the king and queen that is striking.[104] In a speech far removed from the mysteries of Westminster Abbey, for example, a humble waterman dared to address their majesties in bold terms:

> Haul in, haul in for the honour of your calling, and be hang'd, do you know your fellows no better? I have something to say for the good of ye all. God bless Thee King CHARLES, and Thy Good Woman there, a Blest Creature she is I warrant thee, and a True: Go thy wayes for a wagg. Thou hast had a merry time on't in the west, I need say no more . . . dost hear me, don't take it in dudgeon that I am so familiar with thee, thou maist rather take it kindly, for I am not always in this good humour; though I Thee Thee and Thou Thee, I am no Quaker, take notice of that; he that does not love Thee in his heart, may be drawn in a cart.[105]

In a speech remarkable even in a pageant, the waterman, after apparently alluding to Charles's pre-marital sexual escapades, defends his blunt, familiar style as a mark of simple love and loyalty – that 'people's love' which will be the best support of the crown.[106] As we sense that no such speech could have been delivered to Charles I – or to Queen Elizabeth – we are perhaps led to the very new world of Restoration, in which, for all the re-presentation of old forms, recent history, changed circumstances, and the king's own style were also constructing a different political culture and style. As well as the awe inspired by the mystical rituals of majesty, king and subjects were forging, and representing, affective bonds which Charles's failings and foibles never quite severed.

Indeed, it was an unusual combination of the familiar and debauched on the one hand, and the concern with ritual and ceremony on the other, that marked Charles II's reign. As we know, and shall examine more closely, Charles was open and familiar in his manner, was often seen strolling abroad in St James's Park, and publicly paraded – and sometimes openly pawed – his mistresses.[107] Yet a sense of the importance of proprieties on ceremonial occasions, which he had been so careful to display in exile, remained with him and may even have enhanced towards the end of his reign when (to some degree) he retreated behind the office of kingship.[108]

From the very beginning of his reign – in this he was very much his father's son – Charles attributed great importance to the festivities of the Garter. Representation as sovereign of the Order, as saint and chivalric knight, had been central in Charles I's image on canvas, and in procession and public ceremonial.[109] The Order, of course, had been destroyed by the civil war and regicide, 'derided', according to Heath, 'by the most abjectest . . . people', albeit the cult of St George did not fade from public, or indeed popular, memory.[110] By no means coincidentally, the revived interest in the Garter was coterminous with the move to restore monarchy and was heightened by the fortuitous name of the architect of restoration, George Monck. Already in 1659 a pedigree of Monck traced his descent to Edward III, the founder of the order of the Garter; and popular verses and songs collected in *The Rump* figure Monck as St George slaying the dragon of the rebellious Commonwealth which had swallowed churches and palaces.[111] But it was the king who was the Sovereign of the Order; and even as Charles sailed from Scheveningen, William Pestell imagined his ship followed by dolphins bearing streamers with the inscription of the Garter motto: Honi Soit Qui Mal Y Pense.[112]

In 1661 an anonymous publication, *The History of that Most Famous Saint & souldier St George of Cappadocia*, set out explicitly to 'redeem St George from the jaws of such phantastick oblivion and to establish a fitting reverence to that most noble order of knighthood which is dedicated to his memory and of which our gracious king is sovereign'.[113] The treatise catalogued the names of the knights during the reign of Charles I, and of those to be instituted on 17 April 1661. Though anonymous, the author was obviously well informed. As the herald Edward Walker makes clear, the king considered the restoration of the Order of the Garter an essential prelude to his coronation, and the reconstitution of a culture of aristocracy and divinity an essential support to the re-establishment of a monarchical society and state. The restoration of the Order of St George, Walker writes, 'would no other wise be effected than by installing all the Companions elect as well strangers as his majesty's subjects either by themselves or proxies, who in regard of his Majesty's long absence could not be fully invested'; so it may be that the preparation of these ceremonies delayed the coronation itself which the king, having considered for February, put off until 23 April – St George's Day.[114] Charles held a chapter of the Garter at Whitehall and announced the ceremony of installation to be held on the 17th, a week before the coronation, while letters were meanwhile sent to foreign members of the Order to send their proxies. On 18 April, Knights of the Bath were created with full traditional ceremony, underlining the importance the king attached to his role and representation as a chivalric knight and champion of aristocratic orders.[115] A catalogue of the newly installed Garter Knights (and all their predecessors) in 1661, probably compiled with the assistance of Elias Ashmole, who had assiduously preserved all the records of the Order during the Commonwealth, reminded readers how, since King Arthur, godly kings had rewarded those of special virtue; and in citing the Book of Samuel (2, 23: 13), he alluded to that David who had freed England from the Philistines.[116] Charles himself ordered a hymn for the installation taken from Psalms of David.[117] And in the preparations for the coronation, as Ron Knowles has shown, Ogilby went to lengths to associate Charles (now rather than

Monck) with St George. Days before the entry into London, tracts celebrating Charles II as the sovereign of the Order were sold on the streets of London; and, as well as several scholarly histories of the Garter published in 1660 by Richard Johnson and anonymous authors, a popular song, 'St George for England', was distributed to be sung 'to the tune of Cook Laurell'.[118]

Both as a regal and a popular cult the Garter and St George were re-established during the early years of Charles II. The market for books about the saint remained strong and official government interest unabated. Thomas Lowick's *History of the Life and Martyrdom of St George*, licensed by Sir Roger L'Estrange, in June 1664, related the life of the 'titular patron of England' and his killing of a dragon and delivering the king's daughter. In a prefatory dedication to Charles II, Thomas Lowick explained his purpose in publishing, associating the royal cult with a growing patriotism, and 'for King, for Patron and four Countrie's Sake'.[119] He advised Charles: 'in my judgement never English King had greater cause than you to honour him'.[120] In a work of a very different nature, the 1670 volume of crude, sexual anti-republican and (what we would call) racist songs and verses, *Merry Drollery*, a poem 'St George for England' manifests how the saint had become a symbol for the nation – indeed almost for nationalism – as well as for monarchy.[121]

Charles II also patronized and directed the work for the full recovery and publication of the history, laws and ceremonies of the Garter that was carried out by the antiquary Elias Ashmole. Ashmole's massive folio, *The Institution, Laws & Ceremonies of the Most Noble Order of the Garter* announced its regality in its magnificent folio form as well as on its first page where a licence by Charles granted the scholar a monopoly over printing the book, including its numerous engravings.[122] Opposite, an engraving of Charles full-length in Garter robes presents him as sovereign of the Order as well as king of Britain, France and Ireland. Under royal patronage, Ashmole gathered all the materials he had collected when he feared the end of the Order under the republic; and his full descriptions of the history, statutes and ceremonies, as important as the engraved images of Windsor and St George's Chapel, reassembled and re-presented all the aspects of an Order that Ashmole throughout describes as an ornament of British kingship. Describing the martyr Charles I as 'the greatest increaser of the honour and renown of this most illustrious order', Ashmole praises his son for his assiduous attention to 'the augmentation of the honour of this renowned order', symbolized in Charles's ordering 'the irradiated cross of St George encompassed about with the royal garter to be stamped in the centre of his silver coin' in 1662.[123] Associating the fortuitous preservation during the Commonwealth of the king's lesser George set in diamonds, with the providential preservation of Charles II himself, Ashmole made the Garter a Stuart order: one associated with the bravery of Prince Rupert and James, Duke of York, as well as the king himself.[124] Ashmole also records the innovations ordered by Charles II, notably the replacement of the litany with a hymn which drew on the books of Exodus and the Psalms. After the choir sang in praise of the Lord 'Thou hast rebuked the rebellious' and 'Great deliverance gaveth he to the king', the choir returned 'The Lord will give strength unto his people'.[125] It is important to note – and typical of his style – that Charles also sought to publicize the Garter festivals and to connect the regal ceremonies with the popular cult of St George. A spectacular firework display, for example, was staged for the investiture of the king of Sweden in 1668; and Charles revived the grand procession of the sovereign and knights' companions, Wenceslaus Hollar engraving the event in 1672 as well as a magnificent dinner in St George's Hall.[126] Hollar's engravings complete with a key identifying Charles, the knights sitting at dinner, and the officers, all published with royal imprimatur, further document Charles's desire to publicize the Garter ceremonies as a religious and spectacular representation of his kingship.[127] That another account of Garter ceremonies, published by royal command, went to a second edition within three years suggests wide interest in the festivals.[128]

If Charles II, for all his easy familiarity, retained a sense of the importance of ritual in sustaining majesty, that sense was sharpened by political crisis. Just as in 1660 the king had personally directed the plans for a coronation procession that was intended to efface and erase the signs of republic, so with the looming crisis sparked by the Popish Plot he knew that a display of majesty might be the best prop to beleaguered monarchy. And not just majesty but dynasty. Ritual had marked not only Charles's restoration in 1660 and his marriage in 1662, but the deaths of members of the royal family throughout the reign. The Duke of Gloucester was given a state funeral in 1660, and the king's sister Elizabeth of Bohemia in 1661; James, Duke of York's son James was buried in 1667.[129] In 1678, however, Stuart dynasty was threatened not by death but by the campaign to exclude James, Duke of York, from the throne. Amid the mounting crisis, Charles arranged an entertainment of the duke in the Whig heartland of the capital at Merchant Taylors' Hall. The entertainment was clearly stage-managed by the court. Several stewards of the Artillery Company, who hosted the event, were courtiers, and James himself was rumoured to have paid for the feast.[130] Attended by a troop of guards, the duke rode to Merchant Taylors' Hall for a grand feast, after prayers and a sermon at Bow church. The public procession, service and dinner were planned to present James as legitimate heir; according to the official report, healths were drunk at dinner to hereditary succession, while, for his part, James swore to defend the religion of the Church of England and the laws. 'The entertainment was', the author of *The True Account* had no doubt, 'designed to retrieve a little in the eye of the nation that reputation the York interest lost in the late choice of parliament men', that is, in the recent elections.[131] But, significantly, in the midst of crisis, the author doubted the display had worked. Though James himself was said to be pleased and some evidently swallowed the official line, other citizens who had paid for tickets 'not being willing to give the countenance of their presence to that entertainment, when they understood the Duke of York was there . . . tore them to pieces' or 'gave them to their porters or other mean [that is, common] men'.[132] As James on his return from Merchant Taylors' Hall passed through the Poultry, cries of 'no papist' were heard, while as he came to Temple Bar, 'the people began to hiss'.[133] The episode underlines our strong impression that even carefully orchestrated rituals could not, especially in the sophisticated and highly contested public sphere of Restoration London, resolve bitter political divisions and religious anxieties. But James's own sense of success should not be entirely discounted. Albeit not to the hard-core committed exclusionists, public procession and entertainment displayed and affirmed the duke as heir to the throne and represented the symbiosis of king, court, city and nation on which the survival of monarchy depended.

II

If, in a personal monarchy, the most important representation of rule lay in the personal style and personality of the ruler, these were never more important than in the case of Charles II. It was, as Oliver Cromwell had discerned, a regal style of government that the people hungered after and, as Restoration loomed, it was the character of the new king that was the subject of news and gossip. Though the monarchy was restored essentially by others, in 1660 Charles II had to re-establish a regal style – in government, at court and in his behaviour – that distinguished his from republican regimes and publicized England once again as a hereditary monarchy.

The royal court and household were the visible expression of a monarchy, and in 1660 Charles moved swiftly to reconstruct a court that resembled that of his father. In October, Charles himself ordered that the court establishment be based on that of the sixth year of his father's reign and the next month revived the full diets for dinners in the Great Hall which had been the ceremonial public face of monarchy before the civil war.[134] In Clarendon's words, Charles 'resolved . . . to settle his house according to former rules . . .' and 'He directed his own table to be more magnificently furnished than it had ever been in any time of his predecessors'.[135]

Not only were the old forms and customs revived, many of the old personnel returned to take up the posts they had lost during the upheavals of civil war and interregnum. Though death had taken its toll of Charles I's servants, Sir Edwin Griffin returned to the position of Treasurer of the Chamber (to which he had been appointed in 1642), Sir Henry Herbert resumed office as Master of the Revels, which he had exercised since 1623, and Nicholas Lanner took up again his post as Master of the King's Music, which he had held since the beginning of Charles I's reign.[136] Such appointments, along with less high-profile returns to office of kitchen clerks, represented continuity as well as familiarity. Similarly the appointment to household offices of those who had held reversionary grants by Charles I, or by Charles II in exile, as well as rewarding royal followers, underlined the royal authority which Charles had claimed from his father's death.[137] As the late historian of the king's servants has authoritatively demonstrated, the 'themes of continuity and resumption of places which had been lost in the 1640s and 50s', and which characterized the Restoration court, were reflected in the age of office holders in 1663, at which date nearly three hundred had been born before 1630.[138]

Not all was as before. The statutes abolishing purveyance and feudal tenures, passed in 1641, were not rescinded and, as we shall see, some observers felt that the magnificence of the court was straitened and the majesty of kingship undermined by such change.[139] Certainly Charles soon had to face the reality that, within a short time, the costs of his restored household were running into substantial arrears and that some reforms and cuts were necessary. Accordingly in 1662, he embarked on reforms which Clarendon and others had advocated from the outset: notably the replacement of diets for all but the senior officers with board wages and a consequent reduction in servants below stairs. Though interested parties reacted with outrage – the Earl of Anglesey thought 'the splendour and dignity of the court is taken away' – the reforms were neither draconian nor permanent.[140] While the reality was that Charles II could not afford a court of the size and scale of that of his predecessors, there were sound reasons, other than financial stringency, for some reduction in personnel, and no one doubted after 1660 that regal splendour had returned. As Edward Chamberlayne observed in the third edition of his *Angliae Notitia, or, The Present State of England* (1669), though Charles II had, following the example of his father, reduced the numbers who attended at court, still 'The court of the King of England for magnificence, for order for number and quality of officers, for rich furniture, for entertainment . . . for plentiful tables, might compare with the best court of Christendom and far excel the most courts abroad'.[141] Along with elaborate ceremonies for receiving envoys and processing to chapel, Charles revived the formal dining of the monarch in public both in the Banqueting House and Presence Chamber and, as a signifier of restored Stuart dynasty, often sat with his brother and sisters as well as his wife – before an audience of those 'of good fashion and good appearance that have a desire to see us at dinner'.[142]

Moreover, for all his reputation for familiarity, Charles was a stickler for forms. His father's son in this respect, Charles sent the Marquis of Dorchester and Duke of Buckingham to the Tower for a scuffle at court and refused to readmit them to the Presence after their return until they had formally begged the royal pardon for their infringement.[143] (Similarly when the second Earl of

Clarendon forced his way past a porter to see a play after admission had been closed, Charles sacked him from his post.)[144] Charles, in the words of his biographer, was 'pedantically conscious of the dignity which was due to monarchy'.[145] For his own part, Charles always received deputations, not only from envoys but his own subjects, with 'solemn majesty'.[146]

The king also attached considerable importance to the ceremonies of touching to cure the king's evil. We have remarked on the Verrio canvas in the royal apartments alluding to Charles's emulation of Christ curing the sick and the engraving of the ceremony of healing showing people queuing to be touched.[147] After a decade of interregnum, there appears to have been a massive demand from subjects to take the benefit of royal curative powers, and Charles went to lengths to oblige. Records for the period 1669 to 1684 kept by Clerks of the Closet disclose that Charles touched nearly 29,000 persons over this period, that is over 1,800 a year.[148] Royal proclamations published elaborate regulations governing those who came up to court to be touched.[149] And an engraving from 1676 depicting 'The Manner of His Majesties curing of the disease called the King's Evil' shows a very orderly assembly with the sick men, women and children in a queue behind yeomen of the guard and the king, under a raised canopy and flanked by kneeling divines reaching out to a supplicant.[150]

Such scenes of ceremony and protocol, however, are not the best known images of Charles II's court or the king himself. Contemporaries spoke of a courtly world of intrigue, dissimulation and disguise. Though such were stock tropes of anti-court literature, and often the discourse of courtiers themselves, Restoration court culture, as Steven Zwicker has argued, was characterized by 'the arts of disguise' as secret policy, factional intrigue and the emergence of parties raised the competitive struggles of early modern court life to new heights.[151] As John Evelyn wrote as early as 1667 in his treatise on *Public Employment*, 'the Court is a stage of continual *Masquerade*, and where most men walk *incognito*; where the art of dissimulation ... is avow'd'.[152] More famously – or infamously – Charles's court was most known, and is most remembered, for sex. Sex, of course, was not new to the Restoration court. Love and sex were intertwined with dynastic and social relations, and amorous language was a discourse of politics throughout early modernity.[153] But the case of Charles II was novel and different. The king was well known to have had affairs and sired bastards while on the run or in exile. Almost immediately on succeeding to the throne, he began an affair with the married Barbara Palmer, which soon became public. Even after his marriage in 1662, Charles continued the affair, fathering a second child with his mistress. And, as his relations with his new wife rapidly descended to formal compliments, Charles virtually set up house with Barbara and was more often seen in her quarters than those of the queen.[154] Such became the pattern for the rest of the reign. Charles's mistress the Duchess of Portsmouth was given lavish apartments at Whitehall where the king was often seen at cards or dinner.[155] Nor was she the sole concubine. Charles fathered bastards with Kate Pegge, Elizabeth Killigrew and Moll Davies. Though he did not lodge her at court, the actress Nell Gwynn was a regular companion of the king and visitor to his bedchamber. After 1675, smitten by Hortense de Macini, Duchess of Mazarin, Charles provided her with an establishment at St James's and often, having gone through the formal ceremonies of retiring to his bedchamber, stole away to spend the night with her.[156]

For all the occasional effort, perhaps for the queen's sake, at subterfuge, these sexual relationships were both public and publicized. Charles was seen with his mistresses and their illegitimate offspring; they were painted by the court artist Peter Lely; the offspring were given ducal titles and names (like the thinly veiled Fitzroy, and four sons were called Charles) that announced their royal descent. Moreover, the intimacies Charles enjoyed with his lovers was not confined to private quarters: Pepys and others report the king dallying with and fondling his mistresses in public, while popular ballads as well as court verse freely circulated explicit details of the royal affairs.[157] The king's bedchamberman and friend, the poet John Wilmot, Earl of Rochester both celebrated and satirized Charles's relentless quest for 'cunt', and his sexual prowess and equipment: 'His Scepter and's Pricke are boeth of one Length'.[158]

Rochester's line, linking sex and politics, encapsulates how central were the king's sex life and mistresses to the image of the court and the government. Libertinism in early modern England had often been associated with political failings and corruption – not least in royalist attacks on republican figures such as Henry Marten.[159] As we shall see, after some years of a king's barren marriage and foreign defeats, Charles's critics lambasted the extravagant expenditure on mistresses and bastards, the dissipation of royal energies, and the undue influence believed to be wielded by mistresses, especially Catholic concubines.[160] Libels and satires freely spoke of the king as a whoremonger; Marvell figures him ready to rape the realm to satisfy his lust.[161] Unquestionably, Charles's sex life provided ammunition to his opponents and the discourse of sex became a language of opposition. Yet, for our study of the royal image, the story is not so straightforward. For one, Charles II was not ignorant of the force of charges of sexual incontinency and corruption. And loyal writers close to him – Dryden as well as Rochester – appear to have celebrated as well as publicized and gently satirized royal promiscuity.[162] Possibly, they were making the best of a bad situation: putting, we would say, a positive spin on behaviour that the king would not change. Such an explanation, however, risks underestimating the political skills and canniness of Charles. For whatever damage it came to do him in some quarters, the sexual freedom of the Restoration court also served the image of the new regime.[163] Those who roasted the Rump in celebration of the downfall of the Commonwealth associated the republic with puritanism and the prohibition of pleasure.[164] For years not only were Christmas and other festivities – maypoles, dancing, Sunday sports and the like – proscribed; from 1655 with the appointment of the major-generals, the counties of England had been governed by military ayatollahs who often policed morality as stringently as security.[165] Though the populace had an ambiguous attitude towards promiscuity and there was unquestionably a code of morality among the communities of early modern England, there had been little affection for strict moral regimen imposed from above in a society used to more local regulation – and negotiation. Certainly, in 1660, the restoration of monarchy was widely heralded as the restoration of pleasure. Initially at least, the free sexual congress at court may for many have symbolized the overturn of republican and puritan constraint – and perhaps even freedom and self-determination itself. In the early 1660s, courtiers such as Pepys (a good Cromwellian, we must recall) seemed more fascinated than repelled by the king's mistresses; his diary entries about Castlemaine, his fantasies, and purchase of pornography, could even be read as the documents of psychological release.[166] Rather than sexual profligacy itself, it appears to have been the disasters of the Fire and Plague, then the humiliating Dutch invasion of the Medway, that drew criticism, as some saw crisis as the judgment of God on an immoral land. As for the people, though a mass of salacious libels and the apprentices' attack on the bawdy houses of London evidence a moral politics antagonistic to sexual libertinism, Charles's popular personal image and reputation nevertheless seem to have remained high.[167] That the affectionate popular nickname for the king, 'Old Rowley', was the name of a racing stallion at Newmarket with a reputation for breeding suggests, perhaps, that Charles's sexual activities, no less than his love of horseracing, may – at least in some quarters – have raised his popular profile.

The suggestion that sex and pleasure could become positive royal representations gains some support from the evident concerns of Charles's opponents. John Milton, for one, appears to have sensed the danger to godly politics of a royal appropriation of sexual pleasure. As James Grantham Turner has so well demonstrated, though he continued to condemn illicit sex, Milton abandoned the sage and serious doctrine of virginity of his youthful work to, in *Paradise Lost*, celebrate the full sensual sexuality of Adam and Eve in paradise.[168] As Dryden was to show with brilliant polemical prose, sexuality – royal sexuality – could be represented as patriarchal abundance. And, of course, Charles's sexual foibles and exploits – some with common women such as Nell Gwynn – underlined the humanity of the new king. To his advantage as well as discredit, Charles's court presented an image of sexual promiscuity and libertinism.

III

The royal household and court, especially after a decade of interregnum, represented restored regality. In a monarchy in which the king was the highest legal authority in the land and Supreme Head of the Church, so did the workings of justice and the Church of England. Justice was traditionally held to be the principal royal virtue: the epitome of good kingship. Justice involved the impartial upholding of the laws, due process, legal trial and prescribed punishment; and a measure of mercy. From the beginning of Charles's reign (whether we date it, as he did, in 1649, or from 1660), the exercise of justice and a reputation for justice were problematic. Many of the old Cavaliers longed for what they, not entirely unreasonably, viewed as proper justice against traitors to and enemies of Charles I; to others that was revenge. As his declaration from Breda manifests, Charles recognized the danger such pressures presented and the need (for the stability of his kingship as well as that of the realm) to be seen as a just and merciful, rather than vengeful monarch, as a ruler who protected justice for the nation, not merely for a party. Charles's inclination to forgiveness was not just a personal attribute; it was an essential image of restored kingship.

In a realm, however, divided by civil wars, justice had become embroiled in party politics; and ex-Royalists and ex-Parliamentarians all carried into Restoration bitter memories of injustices done, and justice not done. The growth of parties revived and sharpened grudges and memories; and during the crisis of the Popish Plot the processes of royal justice – of evidence, witness, impartial juries and judges – were all threatened, and in some cases subverted, by political hysteria and partisan allegiance.[169] To Charles II's credit, and to the benefit of his image and reputation, whatever the accusations of his opponents, the king himself neither cynically deployed the judiciary as a political tool nor gave way to the pressures for party revenge. Though Whig hagiographers attributed the death of Shaftesbury to royal vindictiveness, Charles has (rightly) never been branded with the reputation for judicial ruthlessness earned by Henry VIII's arbitrary removal of former spouses and ministers, or James II's bloody assizes. In 1660, in a move befitting his quest for moderate settlement, Charles abandoned his father's practice of appointing judges at the royal pleasure, and permitted at least some to enjoy independent tenure, as the Long Parliament had desired.[170] Significantly after the fall of Clarendon, and the first political setbacks of the reign, from April 1668 judges were again issued patents 'at pleasure'; and amid the crisis of the early 1680s, as the Whigs attempted to control London elections and juries, there can be no doubt that Charles sought to appoint loyal judges, notably the Tory Judge Jeffries; though in 1683 his appointment owed as much to his sharp legal brain as to politics.[171]

When we impartially review the state trials of Charles II's reign, it is hard to concur with the Whigs' insistent accusation that the king used the courts to pursue vendettas. For sure there were bloody scenes of judicial punishment in 1660, as ten regicides were hanged, with their faces to Whitehall, drawn and quartered – the traditional death for traitors. Symbolically on 30 January the next year, the corpses of Cromwell and Bradshaw were exhumed, their carcasses drawn in a grisly parody of the traitor's end to Tyburn, where they were hanged and their heads set on stakes at Westminster Hall.[172] Such trials, executions and symbols, though distasteful to modern sensibilities, were a necessary demonstration of justice: of the king's prosecuting the treason against his father and the realm and his re-establishing of royal justice, overthrown by the trial and execution of Charles I in 1649. Though recognizing the need to make such a symbolic display, Charles, against the inclinations of most ex-Cavaliers, proceeded against few – only those directly involved in regicide – pardoning hundreds who had unquestionably committed legal treason, not least prominent figures like John Milton. Though Colonels John Okey, John Barkstead and Miles Corbet were arrested in 1662 in Holland and executed, followed by Sir Henry Vane, by the summer of 1662 the rituals of justice consequent on the civil war were all but concluded.[173]

The efficacy of the scaffold in representing royal justice, however, was seriously compromised by the behaviour of the victims, more by a still-divided nation and sympathizers to the Good Old Cause. Several of the condemned defended the cause they died for and went to their deaths bravely, even, as a royalist admitted, 'readily'.[174] Though some accounts, like that of the trial of Vane, come closer to hagiography than reportage, even sources loyal to the king acknowledged their stoical deaths, and lamented that 'not any of these at his death expressed any sorrow or repentance . . . but justified the authority by which they did it'.[175] Worse, their demeanour drew some popular sympathy and support. As Vane passed through the streets on his way to execution, the crowds, we are told, 'used such means and gestures as might best discover . . . their respects and love to him'.[176] The trumpets' efforts to drown out his dying words brought 'great . . . dissatisfaction'.[177] The author of A Brief Chronicle observes that the victims' 'party highly magnified this their obstinacy for Christian courage and printed their prayers and speeches' – which indeed survive in multiple copies.[178] The king's licenser, L'Estrange, was left in little doubt about the damage these scenes and texts had done: in his Proposals for regulation of the press published in 1663, he noted that 'scarce any one regicide or traitor has been brought to public justice since your Majesty's blessed return whom either the pulpit hath not canonised for a saint or the press recommended for a patriot and martyr'.[179] Even amid the euphoria of the early years of Restoration, the theatre of justice was by no means an uncontested site of royal representation.

For much of Charles's reign, after the early 1660s, the image of a just king was not tainted by any judicial causes célèbres whether overtly political, such as the trial of Prynne, Burton and Bastwick, which so much damaged Charles I, or those of Castlehaven or Overbury, which publicized scandal.[180] Tracts such as An Exact Account of the Trials of the Several Persons Arraigned . . . in the Old Bailey, published in 1678, and sold in Goat Court, Ludgate Hill, indicate a general public interest in crime, the law and punishment, and a traditional moral message concerning just retribution, but no sense that justice was harsh or contentious.[181] The events of the next years changed that as the full emergence of party politicized all the facets of royal justice. The dispassionate account of the execution in 1679 of Henry Bury, one of the murderers of Sir Edmund Bury Godfrey, followed a list of thieves and felons condemned at the February sessions.[182] But the suspicion, soon to be hysterical rumour, was that Godfrey had been murdered for his knowledge of a popish plot which, for the rest of the reign, sank justice under religious and political conflict, charges and counter-charges.[183]

Throughout, however, the king's government and judges, while establishing a strict concern for the safety of the crown, endeavoured to maintain the norms of justice and to present Charles himself as a just and merciful ruler. Accounts of the trials and executions of William Staley, John Grove and William Ireland extol the 'benign rays of indulgent majesty', and the 'justice and mercy' of 'our most gracious sovereign'.[184] But to Catholics then as now (Grove was sanctified by the Pope in 1929), these figures were martyrs to their faith and victims of a travesty of justice and manufactured evidence.[185] Amid the confusion as to the reality or the extent of a plot, the royal judges appear to have endeavoured to hold to firm evidence and due procedure. At the trial of Edward Coleman, for example, the Lord Chief Justice and King's Solicitor laid out the evidence (which problematically included Oates's testimony) in full defence; and in 1679 Scroggs warned that justice could not simply follow popular suspicion – 'to find what is not and stretch one thing beyond what it will bear'.[186] As his personal doubts about the credibility of Oates and Dangerfield grew, leading him to acquit the accused queen's physician, Sir George Wakeman, Scroggs was vituperatively attacked in print, as a vast literature replayed all the trials, from Catholic and Whig viewpoints, in a heated public sphere. Indeed, Scroggs was himself arraigned (before the Council) but was acquitted.[187] Throughout the next three years, the trials of the likes of Viscount Stafford, Edward Fitzharris, Stephen Colledge, Elizabeth Cellier and Lord Russell were all the subject of public controversy and bitter party contests.[188] Though he persistently urged that 'there is nothing more necessary than that such trials as these should be entire and public . . . for the satisfaction of the world that it may appear no man receives his condemnation without evidence', Scroggs was perceived to be partisan – and was so, if a concern to defend the king against the charges of the Whigs that he promoted popery and tyranny was a party position.[189] Unquestionably, during the Popish Plot, as the Commons denounced all the judges as time servers, the image of the king as the custodian of justice was damaged.[190] But, partisanship was as much a failing of juries during the Plot as judges, and of the king's opponents as well as supporters, and even after dismissals and replacements several of the judges continued to exhibit 'considerable independence'.[191] In the words of the historian of the Restoration judiciary, 'the conduct of the judges was morally and intellectually above the general level of politics'.[192] And as politics had damaged it, it was a turn in the political tide that restored the king's reputation for justice. As the true intent of the Whigs became clear, and a plot to murder the king and duke at Newmarket became public, public opinion rallied to Charles, and juries (admittedly some packed by newly resurgent Tories) readily convicted those who had conspired against him.[193] Together with a bench remodelled to promote the royal interest, growing popular support for the king robbed the Whigs of support for their charges of illegal courses. Against Whig accusations, a modern historian concludes that William Russell's trial for treason was conducted by the new Lord Chief Justice Pemberton with 'exemplary' regard for procedure; and while Algernon Sidney, who met with less fair treatment, was heralded as a martyr in Whig circles, he did not sustain a popular following.[194] John Hampden, convicted in 1684 of complicity in the plot to murder the king, but spared, never entered the list of champions of the public cause like his ancestor, who restored ship money. Though in 1689 a triumphant Whig party roundly condemned Charles II's judiciary and the abuses of royal justice, historians have concluded that, for the most part, the charges against the judges 'cannot be substantiated' and that Charles himself behaved with steadiness and 'restraint'.[195]

IV

The role of, and expectations of, the monarch as the protector of church and faith was at least as old as the royal duty to secure justice. Medieval monarchs who quarrelled with the papacy or their own churchmen were usually weakened by the conflict; by contrast the church was the most powerful ally of the crown against opponents abroad or at home. Henry VIII rightly felt strengthened by the pope's conferment on him of the title Defender of the Faith. After his break from Rome, he regarded assumption of the Supreme Headship of the church as *the* essential prop to his authority in a divided Europe and, increasingly, a dividing nation. Though Mary had renounced the title and, as a woman, Elizabeth had instead taken that of Supreme Governor, the early Stuarts were quick to re-establish the royal supremacy as a vital attribute and image of their regality. For all their different ecclesiological preferences, James I and Charles I regarded their headship of the church as the cynosure of their kingship.[196]

The abolition of episcopacy by parliamentary ordinance in 1646 ruptured the link between church and state; indeed, though this has not been adequately explored, the rupture may have been an important factor in the downfall of the republic and the fragility of the Protectorate. Government, as astute observers discerned, required some element of the numinous. In 1660, it would appear not only that the restoration of the Church of England was as popular as that of the monarchy, but that the reconstitution of their relationship – of a state church and royal supremacy – was the widely heralded as the essential foundation of political society. Because Charles II was welcomed as the head of the church as well as the realm, the perception of his rule would be inseparable from evaluation of his exercise of the Supremacy and of the nature and vitality of the church under his governance.

In 1660, however, such expectations presented insuperable problems. Though from late in Henry VIII's reign division had rendered the notion of a church which incorporated all the commonwealth a fiction, and one ever more strained as the Tudor century advanced, the wars of religion of the 1640s and 1650s had openly exposed the fiction.[197] Moves towards toleration acknowledged the fact and future of religious differences and division. Charles II acknowledged it too. Whatever his personal faith (to which we shall return), his experience during his escape and exile of the loyal support of Catholics and Presbyterians only confirmed his personal inclination to, and political sense of the benefit of, an accommodation of faiths, at least of those that did not threaten royal authority.[198] As his declaration from Breda evidences, Charles thought that a 'liberty to tender conscience' was not only the best policy, but a popular one.[199] The disjuncture between his political preference, on the one hand, and the desires of most of his powerful subjects, on the other, was to make the exercise of the supremacy a near impossible art and the image of the church and its head ever the subject of controversy and contention. Although we cannot here rehearse the religious history of the reign, some sense of the conduct and perception of the royal supremacy is essential to an assessment of the image of the king.[200]

Assessments of the Restoration church and royal supremacy have been bound up with assertions about the religion of the king. Charles II, it has traditionally been held, was publicly cynical but was a private Roman Catholic; and the charges of both popery and worldliness have been levelled at the Church of England during his reign. As revisionist histories have latterly powerfully demonstrated, the 'evidence' on which assertions about the king's faith has been based is highly unreliable.[201] Whatever the status of reports of a deathbed avowal of Catholicism, Charles II took seriously – and repeated – his father's advice to keep faith with the Church of England.[202] And though – also for politic reasons – he dabbled with indulgence for other confessions willing quiescently to accept his authority, the king kept sight of the value of church support and ultimately, to preserve his authority, wholeheartedly endorsed its position.[203] For its part, the Church of England also faced seemingly insurmountable problems: from 1660 it had to be reconstituted and throughout the reign faced the challenges and threats of dissent, secularism and scepticism, a supposed Catholic resurgence and, in the eyes of some, especially high church clerics, a king whose support could not be relied upon. The inseparability of religious and political issues and divisions also exposed the church, as the crown, to the attacks of party. Too much of the ecclesiastical history of the Restoration has been written from such partisan polemic. What we shall suggest is that, through all the difficulties, and despite attempts to enact tolera-tion, the Restoration church emerged by the end of Charles's reign firmly as the established church of the nation and the partner of the crown.[204] And, whatever his differences at times with the Anglican establishment, by 1685 Charles had cemented that partnership and so strengthened the royal supremacy and the monarchy.

Contrary to Charles's early beliefs, what most of the gentry who had experi-enced interregnum feared in the early 1660s was the continuing threat of Puritanism, or dissent, to the ecclesiastical and social order. Though its latest historian describes a broad church in the 1660s, the Commons feared the puri-tans and the 'disorders brought upon us . . . [by] emotion, raptures and swelling words of vanity' – that is, by godly enthusiasm.[205] Charles's own inclinations to comprehend moderate Presbyterians and dissenters within a settlement of the national church probably sprang from the same concern but a different strategy: one that assumed some indulgence might win nonconformists from separatism and opposition. If so, the abortive rising known as the Yorkshire Plot in 1663, in which Presbyterians and sectaries were involved, shifted the royal position.[206] Throughout the next decade, the cry of conscience was casti-gated as 'the great palladium of sedition', and government and church enacted legislation to hunt out nonconformist 'scorpions'.[207] The problem, however, did not go away; nor by any means were all in the church, or nation, as Gilbert Sheldon recognized, convinced of the need for strict conformity.[208] Though strict Anglicans like William Assheton condemned any toleration as incompat-ible with stability, and predicted that liberty of conscience would result in the dissolution of all government, the merchant and MP Slingsby Bethel, in *The Present Interest of England*, argued passionately for a grant of liberty to tender conscience to advance trade.[209]

If Charles was still wavering, the situation in Europe led him back to support for toleration. Charles was negotiating an alliance with Louis XIV, and suspen-sion of the penalties against Catholics was essential to it. As we have seen, the king's Declaration of Indulgence of 1672 met with immediate and fierce oppo-sition, not least from within the church.[210] As well as his authority as king, Charles's supremacy was compromised. Moreover, suspicion of his pro-Catholic stance damaged his reputation – and, since (for all the tensions) church and crown were bound together, came to taint the church too. Recognizing his error, Charles followed the advice of a new minister, the Earl of Danby, and embarked on a strict execution of laws against both Catholics and nonconformists, in alliance with the bishops. Whether the Catholics or the old puritans presented the greater threat increasingly divided the nation; and, especially after the publication of the Duke of York's conversion, it bound religious positions with attitudes to monarchy. Throughout the 1670s, contesting polemical treatises warned the church and the king of the dangers of popish superstition or of Calvinist teaching, to magistracy as well as episcopacy. The revelation of the Popish Plot and the Exclusion crisis threatened to sink the church in party conflict; as *A Dialogue between Whig and Tory* versed it in 1681:

> When shall sweet Concord and lost Peace Repair?
> When Covenant agrees with Common Prayer.[211]

In 1681, there seemed little prospect of that. Yet, though divisions raged, amid them, and now under a Supreme Head who abandoned toleration, the Church of England developed an identity and strength as a church independent of Rome and Geneva. Though as divisions sharpened and conformity was pressed harder, the Church of England was no longer (what Charles might still have hoped in 1660) the church of all the nation, it was, in the heat of controversy, becoming the national church – and the best guarantee of peace and order.

Importantly for Charles II, it was by the time of the Exclusion crisis widely seen as (what a historian of pre-civil war England has called) a 'monarchical church'.[212] As a preface to a 1682 republication of Hooker's *Laws of Ecclesiastical Polity* reminded the king, the 'inseparable happiness and interests' of 'this church and kingdom . . . are bound up in the monarchy'; the church, as it protected the crown, so it depended upon royal protection.[213] Benjamin Calamy's sermon on the king's birthday the same year took up the same theme: religious divisions ruined civil states, and church and king needed to extol each other.[214] The religion of the Church of England, a sermon put it in 1683, 'was not a thing of talk and noise and tumult, but a quiet, calm peaceable thing', a church that stood by England's David against both 'the bloody Romanist and . . . the deceitful Enthusiast'.[215] As, in the wake of the Rye House Plot and discrediting of the Whigs, countless sermons praised an Anglican church 'placed between the two extremes of popery on the one hand and fanaticism on the other', so they denounced all plotters, rebels and opponents of the king as outside the fold of the church.[216] The preacher John Scott in a 1684 sermon argued succinctly 'when men live in dissent from the established religion it is impossible but their minds should be . . . prejudiced against the government'; 'the honest principles of our religion,' he affirmed, are 'loyalty, both to God and the King'.[217]

In 1660 the re-establishment of relations between church and state had widely been held as the foundation of restored monarchy. By now a loyal member of the church and a staunch supporter of the crown and royal supremacy, William Prynne warned Charles that 'whoever steers the helm of subjects' consciences will easily give checkmate to his king'; and argued for supremacy in matters ecclesiastical as a historic and indispensable attribute of sovereignty.[218] As the vicar of St Martin's and future archbishop Thomas Tenison argued in his refutation of the creed of Thomas Hobbes, without God and the church there was no government.[219] In his *Discourse of Ecclesiastical Polity*, Samuel Parker expressed the point even more fluently: 'take away the divine institution of government and the obligation of conscience to obedience and then all government is usurpation . . . and princes have no other right to their crown but what is founded upon force'.[220] As Charles II sought to establish his supremacy independently of the church as well as the Commons, divines such as Edward Stillingfleet reminded him that it was the Church of England that most asserted the rights of princes – against, for example, the views of the Quakers who regarded church government as distinct from royal government.[221] In following their counsels and (finally) aligning himself with the bishops, Charles – as his brother's reign was to demonstrate – tied the supremacy and the monarchy itself to Anglicanism. But in so doing he massively strengthened his kingship and re-vested majesty in sacred garment.

Having countered the assertion that by his Catholicism and indulgence Charles undermined the royal supremacy, what of the other common charge that, not least through his own debauchery and cynicism, he presided over a church that was 'sordid and godless', lukewarm in its spirituality and consequently weakened?[222] Unquestionably Charles was at times coarse, publicly profligate, and (perhaps understandably after the experiences of the 1650s) exhibited more cynicism than his father. Yet, as Ronald Hutton has well demonstrated, he was by no means indifferent to religion: 'in exile he heard services twice a day and enjoyed a good sermon' and every Friday fasted in memory of his father.[223] Moreover, from his first steps on English soil, he promised to advance the Word and to prohibit profanity 'that we shall be all godly'.[224] What as much threatened Restoration spirituality was a more secular, sceptical spirit fashionable among the court wits (admittedly many of them the king's friends) and metropolitan society. Though the early modern clergy had long lamented the worldliness of their flocks, the Bishop of Rochester, John Dolben, discerned in 1665 a new world when he opined that 'many of us believe the articles of our faith as we do the antipodes or the story of the Trojan war; we care not whether they be true or no.'[225] The new science and Hobbesian rationalism had fostered a more secular worldview as preachers who strove to counter them evidenced. By 1667, as ranting and scoffing at the mysteries of faith became almost the mark of wit, Stillingfleet warned the king that divine religion ought not to be 'the sport of entertainments, nor the common subjects of plays and comedies'.[226] Perhaps heeding the lesson, Charles ordered the sermon published, as he did too Miles Barne's sermon at Newmarket denouncing 'a sceptical age . . . apt to strike at the very foundation of all religion'.[227] In his *Discourse of Ecclesiastical Polity* of 1670, perhaps in a move to gain royal support, Samuel Parker directly identified scepticism as a threat to the monarchy no less than the church: 'there is no man that laughs at the folly of religion who is not angry at the superstition of government'.[228] And throughout the 1670s, often with royal imprimatur, divines preached and published against the tide of scepticism and atheism and the benefit of lively faith. The rise of nonconformist opposition to the church and their alliance with the Whig opposition to the government drove the point home. As Benjamin Calamy told the mayor of London in 1682, 'they were absolute enemies to the government that should free men's minds from the dread of invisible powers'.[229] Though the scoffers and sceptics remained (within court circles as well as the nation), from the later 1670s we sense a retreat of the rakes – even Rochester repented in 1680 – before a resurgent Anglican church that lauded the spiritual life.[230] As John Spurr has demonstrated, by the end of Charles II's reign, the Church of England had acquired not only remarkable unity and a strong Anglican identity and piety, which was anything but lukewarm, but a revived spiritual authority.[231] Not only did that authority benefit Charles II, it enabled the Church of England to survive a royal regime that was to rupture the partnership of church and state that Charles II had rebuilt.

V

From the beginning of our period, besides the traditional duties of upholding the church and the law, the monarch was expected to be a patron and a figure of learning. Queen Elizabeth and King James had relentlessly advertised their classical and religious learning as qualifications of rule; the image of Charles I had been directed by a king who was the leading connoisseur and expert in the visual arts of the England of his age. Learning, civility and cultivation are not the first attributes historians have identified when describing the court of Charles II. As even a generous biographer of the king concludes, 'Charles was not as great an aesthete as his father and not as much an intellectual as his grandfather James'.[232] That, however, is to judge by exceptional standards. Though, not least on account of his early penury, Charles never emerged as a major patron or collector of art, he inherited from his father a love of beautiful objects. As we shall see, his reign saw the full reconstitution of the theatres, which had been closed for twenty years, frequent royal attendances making play-going an essential social event of the beau monde. And the court patronized and staged masques and developed the operas with which William Davenant had experimented during the Protectorate.[233] Though Charles's own musical tastes were restricted, the king not only re-established the royal music, he enlarged the violins in imitation of the French court orchestra.[234] From the Chapel Royal emerged one of the greatest composers of the baroque period and one of the greatest of all English composers, Henry Purcell, whose chapel and theatre music, composition of 'semi operas' and the opera *Dido and Aeneas* made Charles II's reign a high point in English music history.[235] It was as a member of the twenty-four violins that Purcell composed birthday and welcome odes and symphony anthems for the Chapel Royal: the symphony anthem 'owed its existence to the personal faith of Charles II'.[236] In 1660 Charles also made several attempts to establish an Italian opera company in England and sent Nicholas Staggins, Master of the Music, to France and Italy in 1676 to study practice there.[237] The royal interest probably provided Purcell with the stimulus to write *Dido and Aeneas*.

Yet when all these were considered, Charles's own learning was 'of a scientific rather than a literary bent'.[238] Though he made efforts to learn French, Italian and Spanish, by his own admission he never mastered them. And, though endlessly curious about the world, Charles was not known for being bookish. A man of relentless energy who enjoyed all the vigorous outdoor sports – riding, hunting, hawking, sailing and swimming – he was more given to practical than contemplative learning.[239] Indeed, an important representation of the king was as the patron and enthusiastic fellow of the Royal Society – or to give it its full title the Royal Society of London for the Improving of Natural Knowledge. Certainly Charles's patronage was no mere formal gesture: he enjoyed learning of scientific projects and observing experiments. Praising his new sovereign in 1661, the virtuoso and scholar John Evelyn drew attention to Charles's 'rare collections of all your kinds', his 'curiosity' and 'your curious enquiries about the load-stone and other particulars which concern philosophy'.[240] Referring directly to the Royal Society, he added: 'for you is reserved the being founder of something that may improve practical and experimental knowledge, beyond all that has been hitherto attempted, for the augmentation of science and universal good of mankind'.[241] Illustrated (as we have seen) with a bust of Charles II amid all the instruments of the old and the new learning, Thomas Sprat's official *History of the Royal Society*, in its dedication to the king, articulated what was also the royal sense that 'a higher degree of reputation is due to discoveries than to the teachers of speculative doctrines.'[242] In praising the king for being an experimenter, and for installing a 'perpetual succession of inventors', Sprat also observed in arrestingly topical political language that 'to increase the power of all mankind and to free them from the bondage of errors is greater glory than to enlarge empires'. Indeed, the *History* offers clues as to what, as well as his practical curiosity, attracted Charles II to the scientific project. For Sprat made clear that the Royal Society originated in a resistance to (puritan) enthusiasm and 'the passions of the sects'.[243] Echoing the Restoration discourse of healing and unifying, Sprat promised that 'the contemplation of Nature draws our minds off from past or present misfortunes' and 'gives us room to differ, without animosity: and permits us to raise contrary imaginations . . . without any danger of civil war'.[244] Not only, Sprat continued, did science proffer 'mathematical plainness' to the potential abuses of lofty rhetoric or cant, the very meetings for experiments brought men together: 'from enduring each other's company, they may rise to bearing of each other's opinions'.[245] Presenting scientific knowledge as the solution to conflict and division, Sprat added that 'by such a gentle and easy method our several inter-ests and sects may come to suffer one another with the same peacableness as men of different trades live one by another in the same street'.[246] All the work needed was the assistance of a prince who had already promised 'all the kind influence of his power and prerogative'.[247] Sprat's co-founder of the society, John Wilkins, argued a similar case in his 1668 treatise presented to the Society advocating a more scientific language: 'this design,' he claimed, 'will . . . contribute to the clearing of some of our modern differences in religion by unmaking many wild errors that shelter themselves under the disguise of affected phrases'.[248]

Sprat's and Wilkins's promise may seem vain in an age that witnessed pamphlet wars, bitter religious disputes and party divisions. But gradually scientific learning and philosophical discourse did temper the heat of religious war and contribute to an acceptance of civilized difference that was to pacify English society after its century of upheaval and revolution. If Charles were attracted to the Royal Society for such reasons, and contributed by his own style to a more civil resolution of difference, his patronage of the new learning was of the first importance. Whatever those lofty claims and ambitions, Charles as patron of the Royal Society sustained the image of the monarch as the promoter of learning and fulfilled John Webb's prediction that 'new discoveries make the lives of princes famous'.[249]

Ever since Queen Elizabeth's reign, as royal language itself acknowledged, monarchy had been represented on the stage. Though we should never forget that theatre was entertainment, its rise owed much to a growing public interest in performance and display. In turn royal performance and display both informed and drew from the theatre, the most popular repertoire of which was plays about kings, princes and courts. The close association of theatre with regality – never an unambiguous or uncomplicated association – seemed to be confirmed by the closing of the playhouses at the outbreak of civil war and the king's flight from London; and, as we have observed, no few panegyrists in 1660 heralded restored monarchy as the signal for a revival of the theatre: of the royal companies of players as well as plays about princes.[250] Not only were they right to do so; after 1660 the monarchy and theatre were in closer affinity than before the civil war. As Susan J. Owen writes, 'the creation of the Restoration theatre was an act of state', and the theatres were integral to a campaign to reconstitute monarchy and rebuild a political culture.'[251] Charles II was by no means in the wings. The king discussed with dramatists the subjects of plots and with theatre managers what should be staged; and plays complained of by courtiers were taken off.[252] This is not to suggest that the Restoration theatre was a simple tool of royalty. As recent revisionist studies have shown, there was a vigorous tradition of oppositionist, later Whig, drama; and even plays patronized from within the court were not averse to critical commentary on the failings of the government or the foibles of the king. For all that, however, not least because they were addressed to audiences more aristocratic and courtly than those ante-bellum, 'most plays and more sharply, most prologues and epilogues, were Tory' – or to put it less anachronistically, were loyalist.[253]

The loyalism of the early Restoration stage was manifest in genre, as well as subject and language. Nancy Klein Maguire has demonstrated how a new mixed genre of tragicomedy was forged to accommodate the ambiguities of loss and mourning, restoration and celebration that characterized the 1660s.[254] And the royalist heroic plays have been read as deliberate attempts to paper over the cracks of Restoration political culture: to constitute a united and harmonious polity through acts of representation.[255] While by no means devoid of contradictions (intended or read) and anxieties (consciously or unconsciously disclosed), Restoration theatre was an important site – and perceived to be an important site – not only of the representation but of the reconstitution of kingship.[256]

In the early 1660s, theatre was a principal means of invalidating through mockery the republican regimes and their leaders. John Tatham's *The Rump*, for example, performed at Dorset Court and published in 1661, discredited the Commonwealth in scatological language as a government of ambition and interest, while Cromwell's wife is degraded by vulgar references to her work in Sodom.[257] Even as late as 1668, a play like Edward Howard's *The Usurper* presented a thinly veiled allegory of Cromwell's illicit exercise of office and the need for the nation still to expiate the crime.[258] Though, even from early in the reign, playwrights were prepared to echo some of the nation's disappointment with the new king – the anonymous *Unfortunate Usurper* (1663) featured a carousing king who 'did the lately seem as if / He were made up of Sanctity' – in the main, the politics of theatre remained loyalist: 'True Monarchy's supported by our play'.[259] As criticism of the government mounted in the second half of the decade, in fact, figures on the stage spoke up for the 'chiefest Right belonging to the Throne'.[260]

The importance of these representations should not be underestimated. Re-established, the theatres became a regular place of congress, and conversation, for the political classes. Though the Restoration audiences were more restricted (if only by price), humbler folk did go to the theatre, and there was clearly a ready market for a large repertoire of published plays.[261] In his

Theatrum Triumphans, or, A Discourse of Plays, Richard Baker considered the stage an 'epitome of the world's behaviour' and thought plays 'the schools of such as cannot study'.[262] Fittingly compared to the modern BBC, theatre represented government and politics to a broad public. The value of the stage to the monarchy became especially apparent during the years of political crisis. In an entertainment of 1678, for example, a pastoral setting provides the playwright with an opportunity to lampoon the heated London world of coffee houses and political criticism, and to urge that 'love, peace and unity' that 'reign' in the countryside.[263] Warning explicitly of the danger of renewed rebellion and pressing the need to support the king as the defender of the country, a loyal lord Sir Jeoffrey Do-Right advises, 'we have a brave King, brave Peers and a brave Community; nothing but intestine factions can make us unhappy'.[264] And the noble lords are counselled:

> You cannot wear your Arms t' better end,
> Then to serve your King and th' Country to defend.[265]

Appropriating the countryside, the locus of virtue and honesty, often of anti-court criticism, for the court, *Huntington Divertisement* presents an ideal kingdom only menaced by city – that is, Whig – vices and grumblings. There is no greater testimony to the force of such texts and performances than the Whigs' sense of the need to enter on the stage as well as into the lists. As well as the political theatre staged on the streets – of pope burnings and Catholic plots – the theatre itself graphically rehearsed the villainies of Rome. J. D.'s *The Coronation of Queen Elizabeth*, acted at London fairs in 1680, depicted the pope seducing a nun before leading the Armada, against which England was saved only by the staunch Protestantism of Elizabeth who is throughout called a 'king'.[266] As Susan Owen has shown, there was a vibrant Whig opposition drama in the later 1670s and 1680s, and Nathaniel Lee's tragedy *Lucius Junius Brutus* acted at the Duke's Theatre was censored for 'scandalous . . . reflections upon the government'.[267] Indeed, for a while, the regime became so sensitive that even basically loyalist texts, such as Tate's *History of Richard II*, were banned.[268] But it is important to note that there was no shortage of Tory playwrights or plays to press the king's cause during the Exclusion crisis; and in his 1682 *The Ingratitude of a Commonwealth*, Tate this time made the message of his play explicit: 'the moral . . . of these scenes', he informed the Marquess of Worcester, 'being to recommend submission and adherence to established lawful power'.[269] Though in a divided realm, the enactment of such messages on the stage presented its difficulties, loyal playwrights claimed a role for theatre in sustaining monarchy. The prologue to Tate's *Ingratitude*, spoken at the Theatre Royal, associates enemies of monarchy with critics of theatre and has it:

From Kings presented, They may well detract,
Who will not suffer Kings Themselves to Act.[270]

The playhouse, the epilogue concluded, 'is the Nation's Weather-Glass', and the very presence of the audience after revolutionary weeks suggested a return to normality – that is, to regality:

Methinks this Company's a blessed Sight,
And shews the Realm's disorder coming Right.[271]

Although some have attempted to read Banks's *The Unhappy Favourite* as a critical oppositionist text, Dryden's prologue to the play, addressed to the king and queen, pressed home the loyalist message of peace through obedience to a good king.

All that our Monarch would for us Ordain,
Is but t'Injoy the Blessings of his Reign
Our Land's an *Eden*, and the Main's our Fence,
While we Preserve our State of Innocence . . .
. . .
What Civil Broils have cost we knew too well,
Oh let it be enough that once we fell,
And every Heart conspire with every Tongue,
Still to have such a King, and this King long.[272]

On his return from Scotland to London, the Duke of York appeared in the Duke's Theatre, and a series of prologues and epilogues to plays performed in 1682 by Dryden and Aphra Behn celebrated his return and the restitution of Charles's authority.[273] Loyalist drama in the crisis of 1678–81, as throughout the reign, represented monarchy as the natural order of the realm and opposition to it as not only doomed by providence but by theatre itself. As the royal chaplain John Fitzwilliam put it, in a sermon delivered on 9 September 1683, the day of thanksgiving for the king's deliverance: 'Rebellion, though it prospers on the stage through four acts, is generally plagued in the fifth'.[274]

The principal actor, of course, on the stage of majesty remained the king – and so we return to what, still after some very good studies, remains the enigma of Charles II.[275] Whatever the trappings of majesty, monarchy still remained personal. As a preacher put it towards the end of the reign, 'magnificent titles, triumphs and arches, honourable attendants, crowns, thrones and sceptres are all requisite and suitable to the grandeur of a king; and apt to beget awe and reverence in the hearts of the vulgar; but alas that is but the outside and ceremony of that sacred majesty whose representative the king is'.[276] What sort of king, then, was Charles II? And, as importantly to our study, how was he perceived by his subjects as a 'representative' of majesty?

Modern historians have presented Charles as both a puzzle and a set of contradictions. John Miller called him 'the most slippery of kings'.[277] In a broad brushstroke essay on the royal style, Richard Ollard describes a figure who was courteous yet coarse, vigorous at activities and assiduous in attending meetings but lazy at dealing with memos, a king who stood by a loyal servant – as he did Clarendon at the time of Anne Hyde's illicit marriage to the Duke of York, but who deserted him later. A king who was open, affable and loquacious, but who tightly controlled his temper and rarely showed his feelings in public.[278] To these paradoxes, Ronald Hutton's typically incisive summary adds the contradiction of physical bravery and, often, moral cowardice, as well as a persuasive suggestion that, for all his voracious sexual appetite, Charles was not ruled by, and probably did not love, his mistresses.[279]

Contradictions and inconsistencies are, for better and worse, the essence of humanity. Yet in Charles's case they may have been shaped or exaggerated by experience and by strategy. From the complex negotiations in which his father, and he, were involved, and the diplomatic intrigues of the 1650s, when he suffered exile and impoverishment, Charles was schooled in the danger of trusting and of revealing his hand. Though his father's son (he once declared that he 'looked on falsehood ... as the greatest of crimes'), manoeuvre in the world of international diplomacy, and domestic civil conflict, necessitated not laying all one's cards on the table.[280] If experience taught Charles the need for circumspection and disguise in dealing with others, the exception was his encounter with ordinary people. After his near escape from death at the Battle of Worcester, on the run, Charles was forced sometimes to deploy disguise (verbal and sartorial), but sometimes to reveal himself and trust to the loyalty of a succession of ordinary men and women. That none broke that trust, that with nothing immediately to gain and at considerable risk to their lives, they aided his escape, made a lasting impression on the man and monarch. Charles's oft-cited greater ease with strangers may owe something to those years; his trust in the loyalty of his common subjects – not least in the Exclusion crisis – certainly does. If Charles judged that the politics of the ruling classes were more characterized by calculation, such was but another instance of a shrewd political intelligence that he brought back to England in 1660. In a world still divided by the issues and memories of civil war, Charles discerned that the images and discourses of unity and harmony – even his own – were, in part (necessary) fictions. Like his affability, these fictions were not 'falsehood': they expressed ideals and were devices by means of which such ideals might be realized.

In 1662, the chronicler James Heath reports the nervousness of Sir George Downing, Cromwell's ambassador to the United Provinces, when he went to ask his pardon of the king about to embark to England. Charles knighted him 'and would it should be believed that the strong aversions which this Minister of the Protectorate had made appear against him on all occasions . . . even a few days before the public and general declaration of all England, proceeded not from any evil intention, but only from a deep and honest dissimulation where-with he was constrained to cover his true sentiment, for fear to prejudice the affairs of his majesty'.[281] It is a revealing moment that expresses more than Charles's moderation and willingness to forgive. Though he knew that Downing had acted in accordance with his own interest, the favourable gloss the king placed on his motivation sustained the fiction, and in Downing's case effected the reality, of loyalty to the crown. Even more revealing – if his words were reported accurately – is Charles's language of 'should be believed' and 'deep and honest dissimulation'. Cynicism, with which Charles has often been charged, seems too simple an explanation for this language. Rather the king sensed that at times, to effect a good end, it might be necessary to disguise one's beliefs, especially in difficult circumstances. And he knew that appearances and perceptions (what was believed) could be as important in the exercise of monarchy as what was.

Early impressions of Charles were nothing but favourable. All who met him found him courteous, affable and charming. Walter Charleton rose to lyrical strain describing how none departed from the king's presence sad – 'so powerful in their operation . . . are the beams of majesty'.[282] Hutton aptly calls Charles a seducer, in other than the most obvious sense; and it is clear that he had, and used, that (Bill Clinton-like) ability to make the person he was talking to feel the sole focus of the royal attention.[283] Though he could be politically ruthless, Charles was known for 'gentleness both in the tone and style of his speech'.[284] And contemporaries appreciated that, after the heated rhetoric of revolution, such may have been a strategy as well as a trait. As *A Character of Charles II* put it in 1660, 'as the common father of his people, he endeavours that we should reconcile'.[285] An easy manner was politics as well as personality.

Contemporaries also grasped that the experience which had forged the character well equipped the monarch for rule in what they were occasionally prepared to acknowledge were new circumstances. Several observers noted that afflictions and Charles's stoical bearing had strengthened him for kingly office. Arthur Brett suggested that experience of different peoples abroad made Charles suited to govern a still divided realm where ' 'tis impossible that we/ Should here in all things all agree'.[286] And suffering made kings, many said, more merciful and less remote.[287] Indeed, for all the nation's rejoicing in the pomp and mysteries of restored monarchy, Charles was not the only figure to recognize that the regicide and republic had transformed the nature of the relations between the king and subjects. As an analyst of another polity observed,

'Nothing takes more with the multitude than to see their prince accommodate to their customs and bear a part in their recreations'.[288] Charles was – or, perhaps more accurately, presented himself at times – as very much the people's man. He participated in many popular as well as elite recreations and athletic pursuits;[289] during the Great Fire he, to the amazement of some, 'laboured even at the pump' to quench the flames;[290] on his walks he doffed his hat and had a civil word for all;[291] even his sexual profligacy, I have suggested, appealed to certain ideas of robust masculinity – his later critics saw it as a ploy to gain popularity.[292] Charles could be a stickler for authority and ceremony, but usually eschewed mere pomp.[293] Aurelian Cook only slightly exaggerated when he wrote of the king that he was 'not afraid of degrading himself into the likeness of a subject', and that 'in his most illustrious days he seemed to be a private citizen'.[294]

Again, the 'seemed' in the description should not pass unremarked. Charles had a clear sense of his descent, his dynasty, his authority and his divinity. But, like Elizabeth but with greater reason, he understood that while pomp awed subjects, it was the behaviour of the ruler that made them love him. Charles deployed both awe and love throughout his reign and as fitted the circumstances. At the time of the Popish Plot, it was noted that he suspended the ceremonial procession to parliament 'thinking that pompous ceremony no way suitable to the melancholy temper of those distracted times'.[295] After the Exclusion crisis and Plot, whether out of disenchantment or a sense of ease, we cannot say, Charles tended to withdraw from public congress.[296] This adjustment of style to circumstance, which I have traced in speeches, was very different from Charles I who, at least until the civil war, stood fast to clear principles that both governed his private life and fashioned his public representation. If historians have found it difficult to find and fix the man, that is not least because Charles II did shift and change, and was a performer of various roles in the masquerade of Restoration politics. Whatever his contradictions or human weaknesses, Charles II, Ronald Hutton concludes, 'in the theatre of kingship in the age of Baroque . . . was a star'.[297]

The star may have carried the performance but another character, especially in the later scenes, played a major role in the presentation and reception of monarchy. With all the risks and threats to life in early modern England, the heir to the throne stood only a little less in the spotlight than the monarch, whom illness or a bullet could remove at any time. In 1660, none – least of all Charles – could have predicted that the heir would be the king's brother. Charles was healthy, thirty, a notorious womanizer, and a known father of illegitimate offspring. But a barren marriage soon directed attention to James, Duke of York – Clarendon was charged with marrying his daughter to the duke in order to elevate her to the throne – as the king's likely heir.[298] Hindsight would suggest that James was a liability in the politics of royal representation and the image of monarchy; but, at least initially, nothing could be further from the truth. At the Restoration, James, who had served with distinction in the armies of the continent, was greeted with popular joy as, in Ogilby's words, 'the second Glory of our Nation'.[299] Indeed, James's reputation and popularity survived the early 1660s rather better than the king's. Though James too had his mistresses, they were less the subject of public comment and none could charge the duke, as some were beginning the king, with being dissipated or effeminized by lust.[300] As admiral of the fleet at the Battle of Lowestoft, James was widely credited with the victory which, we recall, he commemorated by commissioning Lely to paint all the flag officers.[301] Not only a victorious leader, James had the double benefit of having had a narrow escape from death as two beside him were shot, their blood bespattering the duke's face and body.[302] Sermons and verses on the remarkable protection of providence for one of God's chosen rehearsed for James the language that had praised Charles in 1660. In 1666, Waller's 'Instructions to a Painter' lauded this beneficiary of divine protection and example of courage as a national hero:

> What wonders may not *English* Valour work,
> Led by th'Example of Victorious YORK[303]

James's reputation for martial valour and military skill survived the setbacks and defeats of the following years; and it was not until his public conversion to Catholicism – which disqualified him from office but not the succession – that his position was compromised. Still, however, in 1677, in his catalogue of honour, John Logan compared the Duke of York's triumphs to those of Caesar and Alexander and prayed that he might remain 'to support the grandeur of the British monarchy in the person of his sacred Majesty'.[304] As, however, suspicions of royal foreign policy exploded in the story of a Popish Plot, James became a risk and a liability and Charles sent him to Scotland. There, James impressed many by his 'industry and tact' and won the praise of the Scottish Privy Councillors and others.[305] W. B. used masque-like language in a letter from Scotland praising 'the benign influence of this generous prince', which he compared to the 'welcome approaches of the Sun'.[306]

Even while James was being denounced in Whig polemics, he was, according to report, being fêted 'with all . . . expressions of joy imaginable' in Scotland.[307] An anonymous *True Narrative* of the duke's reception, printed with the approval of the Council, claimed that, on his journey from Leith to Holyrood, James was escorted with the 'whole body of the people universally shouting with great joy'.[308] Another account of his progress to Linlithgow and Stirling similarly describes 'one continued crowd of people all blessing and praying for the duke' and the public manifestations of 'affection' in every town and village.[309] Though 'official' accounts may have embellished the facts, James was well received in Scotland. Charles was sufficiently satisfied concerning his standing to appoint him commissioner to the Scottish parliament.[310]

Nor was the Duke of York's popularity confined to the northern kingdom. Whatever his enemies, he did not entirely want for popular support in England. Many congratulatory verses were written to welcome James and his wife Mary back to London; and if some emerged from official circles, it is clear that they had a market as volumes set to song were sold 'at John Smith bookseller in Russell St Covent Garden' 'at reasonable rates'.[311] In these verses and songs James was praised for his military prowess and victories as an admiral, as one born, a poem puts it, for the defence of the crown and realm.[312] Perhaps following rather than leading the tide, the playwright Thomas Otway welcomed the couple back to London saying 'Our mighty Blessing is at last return'd'.[313] The affectionate nickname ubiquitously used of the duke, 'Old Jemmy', suggests, as well as his Scottish identity and success, a popular affection, akin to that enjoyed by his brother, 'Old Rowley'. One panegyrist indeed, setting forth 'Royal Jemmy's praise', thought that the Duke of York alone might 'keep the Crowd in Peace'.[314] As the Whigs, pushing the realm to the edge of civil war, lost popular support, the tide of praise for the Duke of York swelled. A loyalist poet, Caleb Calle, felt able in 1682 not only to praise James as a 'Great Son of Triumph, Son of Martyrdom' but to return to the conceit of providential protection: 'Heav'n made the Royal Prince its tender care'.[315] As James and Mary were fêted by a city restored to order and obedience, a multiplicity of poems celebrated their return: 'To loyal subjects hearts,' one told the Duchess, 'you gladness bring'.[316] 'London's Joy and Loyalty' looked for a happy future:

Great JEMMY's happy
RESTAURATION here
Makes a new day[317]

'The right successor,' the verse continued, 'Is Returned Again'. These paeans were unquestionably Tory. But by 1682, the people were represented as – willing to appear – Tory too. And James, Duke of York and Charles II were popular as king and heir. Charles's belief in – and his careful cultivation of – the loyalty of his people had been triumphantly vindicated.

The cultivation of popularity in early modern England had also required the display of monarchy – in the capital and around the country, traditionally, on the royal progress. Queen Elizabeth I was famous for her long annual peregrinations; and, though the early Stuarts have been charged with paying inadequate attention to being seen, both James I and Charles I partook of regular summer progresses through southern England, not to mention (unlike Elizabeth) long journeys to Scotland with visits and entertainment en route.[318]

Though he did not venture himself to Scotland, Charles twice sent his brother there. As for the king himself, he was by no means a stationary ruler. Charles regularly undertook, sometimes lengthy, spring and summer progresses. In 1663, for example, he journeyed to Bristol and Bath via Newbury and Reading, and then went on to Cirencester and Oxford.[319] The summer of 1664 saw him visit Salisbury, Marlborough and Weymouth.[320] In July 1671 Charles went on progress to Plymouth, where he touched many for the king's evil; later, in September, he travelled east to Norwich and Yarmouth.[321] When he re-visited Plymouth in 1677 the king resolved to go there at least every other year, and it is likely that only political crisis prevented him.[322] For Charles was so fascinated by ships and dockyards that he made very frequent visits also to Portsmouth, Chatham and Sheerness, as well as the nearer Deptford and Greenwich.[323] In addition horse racing, and evidently cock fighting, took him regularly to Newmarket (he spent most of the spring there in 1682) from where he made other expeditions, in 1676 to Chippenham for example.[324] Add to this the royal moves between palaces – Whitehall, Hampton Court, Windsor and, increasingly towards the end of the reign, Winchester (where we recall he designed a grand new residence) – and one comes away with a sense of a king always in transit, and often making several moves in a relatively short time.[325]

Though the sight of the monarch with his train on the road was still important for the representation of reconstituted monarchy, it was less important than before the civil war. By the second half of the seventeenth century, London had grown exponentially more than before, and become a magnet for the provincial squirearchy as well as gentry. Travel to the capital became ever more common. And in London, Charles II was seen – and made sure that he was seen. It was the king himself who had helped to plan his entry into the capital on the eve of his coronation because he appreciated the need and benefit of such display. Charles, however, in what was a major shift in royal practice, believed in the importance of being seen when not in state – as the ordinary man whom Pepys famously realized the king was when a royal spaniel shat in the royal barge.[326] Charles was seen at the theatres frequently; and he went there to be a spectacle, as to a much smaller and more restricted audience, did Charles I to a masque. Famously he also took a walk most mornings for an hour or more in St James's Park, which if Rochester's verse is reliable was a place of promiscuous social miscegenation.[327] On his strolls, Charles was accompanied by guards (we have a painting of him ambling in Horse Guards' Parade), and was open and affable to those who passed or greeted him (fig. 26). At Newmarket, according to Sir John Reresby, 'He mixed himself among the crowd [and] allowed every man to speak to him that pleased; and ordinary subjects took advantage of royal accessibility to press suits.'[328] Though, as has recently been argued, Charles strategically regulated access to his person at the

26 Unknown artist, *Charles II in Horse Guards Parade*, seventeenth century.

political hotbed of the court, he opened himself to his people and courted encounters with ordinary subjects.[329]

Charles II was the first monarch to pursue popularity by means of an image of ordinariness – an image proffered and used since, with mostly less success, by the royal family to this day. It was an image and style he publicized not merely out of personal preference and experience, but one he cultivated from and with a shrewd political sense. Charles II intuited, often before and more incisively than his subjects, that English society, polity – and monarchy – had been irrevocably transformed by the events of civil war, regicide and republic. He adjusted his rule and his representation to what he discerned to be changed circumstances, and in so doing he accelerated (in ways that would not have pleased him) social and political change and the recognition of change. New experience, conditions and developments were rapidly transforming the modes, and the reception, of royal words and images; by corollary, the images of king and court helped to fashion new responses to regality in a fully formed public sphere. As we turn to assess the reception and legacy of Charles II's representations, we need at least to sketch the changed social sphere in which the royal image circulated and performed.

CHAPTER 4

A CHANGED CULTURE, DIVIDED KINGDOM AND CONTESTED KINGSHIP

I

In 1660 what preoccupied the social sphere, indeed the social psychology, of the nation was memory of recent bloody conflicts, or rather memories – different, passionate and contested memories. We have briefly reviewed some of the 30 January sermons that officially enshrined the memory of Charles I and their important role in supporting the monarchy of his son and successor. Memories of the civil war, however, were, and remained, complex, ambiguous and ambivalent, an impetus to both reconciliation and division, and a back-drop to the performance and representation of restored kingship. For all Restoration society's grasping of the modern – science, empire, a more secular spirit, sexual liberation – the second half of the seventeenth century was overshadowed by a past which dictated the course of events and the fates of ministers and kings.

In proposing a policy of forgiving and forgetting, Charles II and his closest advisors were in a minority. Even in their cases, it is impossible to believe that they actually forgot. Charles's memory of events during his exile remained sharp and detailed, even as late as 1680 when he again narrated his escape story to Pepys.[1] In 1660 Dryden praised Charles, writing ' 'tis our king's perfection to forget'; in a speech the same year, Clarendon (who was to write volumes on the civil war) urged 'the excellent art of forgetfulness'.[2] An art it was. Oblivion and indemnity was a strategy designed to assist the process of healing and unifying which, Charles hoped, would bind the nation under his rule. It was not to be. On both sides of the civil war conflict, memories had shaped identities and values. For all the official and ubiquitous gestures to oblivion and reconciliation, memories sustained divisions and differences and were later instrumental in forging the political parties that took their very names from civil war polemic.[3]

The policy of indemnity from the outset confused as well as dissatisfied many loyal supporters of the crown. In the published version of his coronation sermon at Westminster, the Bishop of Worcester, George Morley, expressed his dismay that some had accused him of meddling with affairs of state and, in particular, with having 'trespassed against the act of Indemnity'.[4] Surely, he asked, to make men appreciate regal government, it was necessary to remind them of the 'miseries' that befell the land under republic.[5] And, though he vigorously supported indemnity as the king's sacred promise as well as the wisest course to compose the realm, did not indemnity 'suppose confession and repentance of a fault in him that receives it?'[6] Morley's question exposes indemnity for what it was: a politic course (he refers to Henri IV of France) that did not penetrate the conscience. And, even for this staunch loyalist, it evidenced the ambivalences about forgetting and remembering that character-ized the regime. In a sermon preached at Suffolk, on the eve of the elections in March 1661, Edward Willan, vicar of Horne, mentioned Charles II practising 'the art of forgetting', which he praised; yet throughout his sermon the refer-ences to 'Protectarian mushrooms', 'Jesuiting puritans' and to the martyr Charles, who 'yet speaketh' sustained the bitter memories of the war.[7] Though some tried to insist that 'what has been done is gone and past', a flood of publi-cations overwhelmed them.[8] In the epistle dedicatory to his history of *The Civil Wars of Great Britain*, John Davies, though claiming to write with 'an impartial pen', told the Duke of Lennox:

> we might in some sense wish they [the wars] might be forgotten, but because posterity is always most conscious of such actions, where their predecessors have been involved in war and trouble, because such examples of the ruin that followed may deter men from attempting such future evils, because the memories of rebellious regicides . . . may be continually odious . . . And because the renown and evaluating fame of those . . . who lost their lives in their king's and country's service might be eternally sounded with praises . . . those transactions may likewise be thought fit to be transmitted to future times.[9]

The publication (often in several editions) of, and the market for, works such as *The History of the Commons War of England* (1662), of Heath's *A Brief Chronicle of the Late Intestine Wars*, most of all of Richard Baker's *Chronicle*, support Davies's claims about the curiosity of readers, which did not quickly fade.[10] Indeed, Thomas Sprat argued in 1667 that an official history of the late civil wars was much needed to meet public demand and to 'give them a full view of the miseries that attended rebellion'.[11] Still in 1674, Richard Meggott, a royal chaplain, could on the one hand 'abhor the barbarous cruelty of tearing open wounds which time is closing up' and on the other caution 'let not the distance of time since these things were done make us fancy ourselves more secure'.[12]

As criticism and suspicion of Charles II grew and the fear of popery revived memories of the start of the old troubles, 1641, always in the shadows, came back into the spotlight of contemporary observations. At a sermon at York in 1676, for example, Thomas Cartwright, Dean of Ripon, warned his congregation: 'I hope this nation lives under no disloyal temptations to a second holy war, because we cannot yet have forgot what a vast expense of blood and treasure the first cost us'.[13] To remind them, the 1676 edition of Heath's *Chronicle* was published with a frontispiece abstract of the vast sums drained from the public purse by the Long Parliament.[14]

These long-lasting ambiguous memories were sustained not only by histories and sermons but by biographies and panegyrics of, and diatribes against, leading figures in the conflict. Both sides in the conflict, of course, had their heroes, martyrs and *bêtes noires*; as so often, such figures and personalities sustained and polarized memory. Cartoons and engravings added the power of visual culture to the arts of memory. George Bate's account of the lives, actions and executions of the regicides was illustrated with engravings of the infamous signatories to the king's death, while in his *Loyal Martyrology*, William Winstanley presented a visual tableau of the Royalist martyrs who, he hoped, 'would make a volume as big as Foxe's martyrology'.[15] Even within Royalist circles, however, the memories of leading figures were not uncomplicated or shared. While, especially in 1660, most writers excoriated the old Rumpers, memories of Charles I and Oliver Cromwell were ambivalent as well as divided. Many in office in the 1660s, of course, had fought against Charles I and served Cromwell; and even Clarendon was the voice of a Royalism that little favoured the prerogative courts or fiscal schemes of the personal rule. Because Charles I became a sacred text, there was little room for overt criticism; but evocations and images of the king's ministers, Laud and Strafford, doubtless prompted mixed memories even in loyal circles. And, as Andrew Lacey has shown, whatever the official sermons, prayers and injunctions to observe 30 January, some were lukewarm in their observance.[16] By the time of crisis in 1678, Charles I was more the symbol of a party than the nation. Where Cromwell was concerned, even Royalists appear ambivalent from the start. Even as the Protector's remains were being hung on the gibbet, loyalist writers were publishing rounded, even generous assessments of Oliver's rule. Though works such as *Cromwell's Conspiracy* present the Protector as another Macbeth, playing out evil and murderous intent on the stage of state, Baker's *Chronicle* of 1660 offered a more balanced portrait of 'the Mighty Man of the three kingdoms' – a figure of courage and resolution who was able to make men and the times follow his designs.[17] Personal vilifications of Cromwell's morals and appearance manifested a royalist unease about his reputation, quite understandable when, even in a collection of *Heroic Portraits* dedicated to Charles II, the playwright Richard Flecknoe (who had earlier written a work of praise, *The*

Idea of His Highness Oliver) described Cromwell as 'bold and resolute'.[18] The poet Abraham Cowley captured the loyalists' doubleness on the subject of the Protector when in his *Vision Concerning . . . Cromwell*, a testament to the Protector's hold on the poet's imagination, he admitted that though 'sometimes I was filled with horror and detestation of his actions . . . sometimes I inclined a little to reverence and admiration'.[19] For those Royalists who had esteemed Cromwell's military and naval successes, admiration only grew as, by contrast, Restoration forces suffered setbacks and defeats. By 1668, writing *The World's Mistake in Oliver Cromwell*, the republican critic of the Protector, Slingsby Bethel, acknowledged the 'undeserved approbation and applause that Cromwell's memory seems to have . . . amounting to little less than idolatry of him', which, Bethel felt sure, was a critical reflection on contemporary times.[20] Only as the monarchy itself was again threatened, was Cromwell wholeheartedly demonized in loyalist circles; by then, like his opposite Charles I, he had become a totem in a tribal war.[21]

Party conflict sharpened contested memories but also grew out of them. In 1662 the Archdeacon of Coventry, John Riland, wondered what, if the French civil wars had produced thirty thousand witches and a million atheists, 'the effects of ours hath been'.[22] An immediate answer was the indelible imprint on the national culture of difference and division.[23] The same year, the author of *The History of the Commons War of England* lamented that it was, for all his efforts to be faithful to his materials, almost impossible now to write 'by reason of the diversity of relations framed by the passions of different parties'.[24] Though he had endeavoured to reconcile different factual reports, he knew that was 'a thing not manageable as to their judgements'.[25] The anonymous chronicler of *The Late Intestine War* judged that the civil war had so marked those born during it (as much as those who fought it), he feared that a generation might not be resettled in 'unity and allegiance' 'which was a stranger to their nativity' – in other words that they had not known.[26] Divided and contested memories of the wars bequeathed to England permanent ideological fissures which belied the Restoration discourse of unity.

Not surprisingly, therefore, the opening salvos of the polemical war that was launched with the 'discovery' of a popish plot used ammunition forged from civil war memories. Loyalists and Tories especially responded to Exclusionists by evoking the threat of renewed civil conflict and by branding the Whigs as republicans and sectarians. Three texts from 1678 will serve as illustrations. In his *Common Interest of King and People*, John Nalson tarred the Whig 'faction' with the aims of 1642 and hoped that 'we have seen revolutions enough to make us wiser'.[27] A response to Marvell's *Account of the Growth of Popery*, entitled *An Account of the Growth of Knavery*, directly connected 'the reformers of 1677 and those of 1641 in their . . . designs' of using false rumour to bring down royal government.[28] The same year *Oliver Cromwell's Ghost* was revived to warn rebels of the fate of traitors and the divine retribution that awaited rebels.[29] The Whigs, however, had their own take on the connections between the 1640s and 1670s, the radical Whig Charles Blount arguing that in both moments it was Catholics and Royalists who fatally manipulated fears.[30] As the polemical combat intensified, two massive Whig and Tory histories of civil war were published: Rushworth's *Historical Collections* and Nalson's *Impartial Collection*, as well as texts of their moment, were also monuments to long-divided memories and their relationships to party politics.[31] As the Tories gathered around the martyr Charles I and republished the *Eikon Basilike* in 1681, Whigs appealed to Queen Elizabeth's days, as well as echoing the arguments of civil war reformers and Commonwealth republicans.[32] Both revived the words and images of civil war, a 1682 Tory pamphlet redeploying the old engravings of the king defending the tree of religion against Roundheads who came to hack it down and images of the devouring dragon of the Commonwealth.[33] In the 1682 pamphlet *History of Whiggism*, Whig and Tory define their positions not least through their views of the civil war and of its histories, the Whig locutor citing Rushworth as his authority.[34] Though the defeat of the Whigs for a time exalted the memory of the martyr, history and memory remained – and of course remain – contested cultural terrain.

It was Charles II's sense of the divisiveness of civil war memories that had led him to favour oblivion. Though he instituted 30 January as a day of remembrance for his father, the king adopted a very different style to Charles I, almost a counter-image; and for much of his reign distanced himself from tendencies to rake over the past: even his account of his flight from Worcester seems free of bitterness or venom. As I have suggested, Charles used a new, and mixed, language in his speeches and declarations, just as he appointed his ministers from the ranks of Parliamentarians as well as Royalists.[35] Reconciliation required the putting of the past behind and in his own self-representation Charles II often attempted it. But the ghosts of civil war could not be laid to rest, even in the king's consciousness. Memories of the 1640s and 1650s re-fashioned the political culture and the nature of government, and with them the monarchy itself.

Historians are still passionately debating the causes of the English civil war or revolution. But of the revolutionary consequences of the eighteen years that followed the outbreak of conflict there can be little doubt.[36] After civil strife, the trial and execution of a king, and reasonably stable republican government, without a House of Lords or bishops, English society and state were fundamentally transformed. In 1660 institutions were reconstituted, but the culture and the psychology that underpinned them were not. In the case of the monarchy, for all the rhetoric of full restoration, there were even important legal changes that reflected, and exacerbated, changed attitudes. Though all the legislation passed after the expulsion of the bishops from the Lords in January 1642 was rescinded, the statutes of 1641, outlawing the prerogative courts and ending feudal dues, were not. Schemes to replace old feudal revenues – wardship and purveyance especially – went back to the beginning of the century and the formulation of the Great Contract.[37] Cecil's plan failed then not least because councillors such as Francis Bacon warned James I against surrendering essential prerogatives of the crown.[38] In 1641 they were surrendered and in 1660 not restored. The financial loss was not the main issue: parliament intended to compensate the king fully. But in 1660, Fabian Philipps offered an incisive analysis of the other consequences for kingship of the ending of feudal tenures and dues. In an epistle dedicatory to the Lord Chancellor of his treatise on the necessity of preserving knight service, Phillips argued passionately that 'the exchanging of the tenures in capite and by knight service for a constant yearly payment . . . will level the regality and turn the sovereignty into a dangerous popularity'.[39] Homage and fealty, he added, were, in a personal monarchy, 'the essence of sovereignty', essential 'to sustain the fabric of our ancient and monarchical government', and he urged that they be 'rescued'.[40] Three years later, in a treatise on purveyance, Philipps returned to the theme: purveyance was an ancient feudal levy which sustained the royal household on progress and expressed the principle 'that the members of the body politic should . . . be willing to . . . contribute unto the good and well-being of the head'.[41] Phillips continued: 'by taking away the king's purveyance and compositions . . . [they were] levelling him and his officers and servants and ranking them in the business of markets amongst the . . . plebeians'.[42] Monarchy, as the embodiment of virtue, should, Phillips argued, be free from 'the oppression of the markets'.[43] The language of these analyses is arresting. Was the crown, without feudal dues, placed in a different and uncertain relationship with subjects? And was regality itself now plunged into the market economy that seventeenth-century England had rapidly become?

Certainly Philipps, for all his antiquarian instincts, was not the only one to deploy a language of commerce and commodity when writing or speaking of monarchy. Edward Hyde himself described in 1660 the bill for removing feudal tenures as 'a bill of exchange' (both a reciprocity and a banknote); and one panegyrist figured Charles II himself as a commercial vessel: 'Your SELF, the ship return'd from foreign Trading'.[44] The talk of trade and commerce that had grown louder during the interregnum came to prominence in the Restoration; and by 1671 Slingsby Bethel was freely discussing the relationship between trade, the national interest and monarchy.[45]

The language of interest articulated other fundamental changes.[46] In 1660 Gilbert Sheldon tried to assure Charles II 'that your Majesty nor your royal father neither of you need vindication'; but his words were a prefatory epistle to his book *The Dignity of Kingship Asserted . . . In Answer to Mr Milton's Ready and Easy Way*.[47] Matthew Wren had similarly written his *Monarchy Asserted* in answer to John Harrington's *Oceana*.[48] As these debates forcefully remind us, monarchy had been questioned, examined and rejected; its restoration *did* need vindicating or arguing; and the tropes and terms of argument had shifted. Though the old conceits of regality as natural and divine were insistently revived in Restoration discourse, the belief that they expressed a truth was not. Regicide did not only sever the connection between the head and body of the king but between the language of regality and truths of nature. In a sermon he preached at Waltham Abbey in 1661, Thomas Reeve, reviving all the metaphors of kingship (heart, spring, eye), yet acknowledged that 'when a king hath lost his dread and reverence he is but a painted Sun'.[49] A 'painted sun', artificial, constructed not an analogue to the sun – the source of light, warmth and sustenance. Many intuited that (in both senses) the natural reverence for monarchy had been destroyed. Even those well disposed to regality and to Charles sensed it: Pepys in that epiphany when he realized the king was but a man 'just as others are', a panegyrist when he recalled the civil wars when 'we thought that kings and princes had been men'.[50]

In 1651, Thomas Hobbes, recognizing that after 1649, divine right and nature would not be the basis of authority or allegiance, set out to devise a rationalist theory of rule and obedience. Though he never quite succeeded in removing religion and conscience from consideration, Hobbes was part of (and prompted) a larger discourse of state formed on rational, utilitarian principles.[51] Though his teachings were officially discredited, Hobbes transformed the nature of thinking about authority; transformed, that is, the nature of kingship – and its representation. Scores of editions of, works by, lives of and engagements with Hobbes were published over the course of Charles II's reign: the notorious *Leviathan* was republished in 1676 and sparked off another round of debate.[52] Hobbes, by no means universally contemned in royalist circles, was actively revived by Whig critics of the crown and publishers. As an elegy at his death accurately claimed, it was

> With ill success, some fond disputers strove
> What doctrines he had planted to remove.[53]

Hobbes had set the mystery of power aside to subject it to rational scrutiny. While monarchy was reconstituted, it was no easy task to re-endow it with the mystery that had been pared away. In a revealing scene in one of the mock processions of the pope that became frequent during the Exclusion crisis, a street pageant figured Antichrist, led before a statue of the king, dressed in scarlet and gold with the word MYSTERY blazoned in capitals on its crown.[54] Mystery here is presented as superstition; and for all that the context is anti-Catholic, the implications are clearly political. During the party exchanges of Exclusion and Popish Plot, polemicists rehearsed old civil war arguments pro and con about the very basis of royal authority. Subjects freely discussed whether the power of kings stemmed from God or the people and one casualty of the exchanges was the numinosity of monarchy. Indeed, amid the heat of crisis, some were willing to expose the fictions of state for what they were – constructions, stories and performances. In 1681, for example, the Whig historian Thomas Rymer, in his *General Draught and Prospect of Government*, analysed the ways in which poets and divines attributed authority to God:

> Though the whole operation and train of causes and proceedings be never so natural . . . the images they *make* [my italics] are often taken in the grossest sense and worshipped by the vulgar; any many times the statesman is willing to contribute to their idolatry.[55]

But, he added, quite definitely at the time of writing, 'now in an age of history and human reason, the blind traditions go hardly [that is with difficulty] down with us. So that iure divino at this day makes but a very litigious title'.[56] In a dialogue between Whig and Tory, in answer to the Tory's use of these 'images' (of the king as sun, for example), supporting Rymer, the Whig snaps: 'these are poetical and rhetorical flourishes . . . surmises not argument'.[57] Furthermore, Rymer took the traditional metaphor of the king on the stage to suggest that monarchy was – well, simply that, a performance; and ventured to add that often the right actor was not chosen for the role.[58] In the arguments of Whig pamphleteers, monarchy was at risk of becoming an artifice, the king a figurehead, a *mere* symbol rather than locus of authority; in Dryden's sneering words, 'the only use that can be made of such a monarch is for an innkeeper to set upon a signpost to draw custom'.[59]

Rymer, however, had recognized that many believed – or chose to believe – in the images constructed by poets and divines. In 1660, not least in revulsion against the cold utilitarianism of Hobbesian argument, many had chosen to believe in them again. And in the 1680s they did so once more. The mysteries of power, as we have begun to see, express the desires of subjects as well as rulers. But throughout his reign, Charles was faced with deploying, and making believable, images of his authority in which many (he was surely among them) did not place full credulity. To different audiences at different times, he had to perform as a god, a monarch and an ordinary man. It was not least that he crafted his diverse representations so as to enact all these roles that he sustained royal authority during an age when the 'conceits' that had sustained it were threatened by scepticism and when no other firm foundation for it had been laid.

The changes in the nature of monarchical government were part of broader social and cultural shifts which were important to royal representation. As John Evelyn almost casually described it, empire and colonial acquisition had become as normal a facet of public life as the exercise of government at home.[60]

And at home, men were beginning to accept that government was not just about the exercise of conscience but a matter of policy – to recognize that Machiavelli had not been entirely wrong to identify a sphere of politics with its own codes and values. As we have seen, not least because they did not want to fight again, men began to accept the necessity of differing peacefully, of accepting others' views.[61] Such changes were a long time coming and not complete in Charles's reign. Yet already at the beginning of the reign, the astute discerned that the old polity could not simply be reset upon its foundations. As Chamberlayne wrote nostalgically of the world ante bellum: 'no man . . . can reasonably hope to see . . . the like blessed days again.'[62] Obedience and deference, whether to government or social superiors, had been loosened. Where Philipps lamented how 'unhappy times have brought forth a sort of reasonless men whose humours . . . make them unwilling to submit to laws and the necessary and just means of government', Nalson feared one legacy of war was the greater inclination of the people 'to be curious in discovering anything which may lessen their superiors.'[63] Like the mystery of regality, social privilege during the revolution had been scrutinized and vilified by radical sects and, though a structure of order and class was reconstituted with remarkable success, more than ever privilege had to be defended and deference maintained by force. The herald William Dugdale for one felt that 'the marks of honour called arms are now by most people grown of little esteem'; trade and money now competed with land in securing stature.[64]

The questioning of authority extended from rank to matters of taste. Men and women of modest standing felt free to air opinions about literature and art which, among other subjects, were the talk of the coffee houses. Some even thought that Hobbes taught his contemporaries that 'vice and virtue both were our opinion and varied' according to circumstances.[65] Like the sceptical questioning of faith, the dilution of moral absolutes opened the most fundamental of beliefs and values to discussion and difference.

Indeed, the greatest challenge facing Charles II was perhaps the exposure of just about every assumption and action to broad public investigation and judgement. Throughout my earlier volumes, I have argued for the impact of an increasing output of printed material on the political culture in which images performed. Indeed, counts of publications and pamphlets reveal a steady and rising increase in print production, especially from Elizabeth I's reign through the early Stuart decades. But the largest explosion of print came with the outbreak of civil war, and our military metaphor is one contemporaries freely used as they analysed the move from paper quarrel to armed conflict.[66] As George Thomason's collection manifests, from 1641 to 1660 more items were printed than in all periods before; and every political question and issue was argued in print: in books, pamphlets of many genres, newspapers and dialogues.[67] And, as the rise in advertisements for (and in) books suggests, print became part of a commodity culture that reached far into metropolitan society – and beyond.[68] The significance of these developments for monarchy is suggested not least in the advertisements for other books (plays, works on mechanics and drawing) that are found at the end of James Heath's account of the restoration of Charles II.[69]

In 1660, all who welcomed the king's return were aware of the damage that print had done to Charles I and its potential danger to peace and stability, but there was uncertainty about the best course. Richard Brathwaite, in his verse address to Charles in 1660, hoped that, if corantos (News-sheets) continued, they would carry more 'honest' news than before – in other words be supportive of the crown and government.[70] Others could not escape from the memory of the pen as the incitement to 'skirmishing', as the instrument of violence in 'a war-like world'.[71] In his *The Dignity of Kingship Asserted*, Gilbert Sheldon recalled those who had 'done more mischief with their pens than the soldier with his weapons', especially republican writers like Milton and Harington.[72] Accordingly, though many loyal supporters of the crown saw the necessity of using print to re-establish the monarchy – Sheldon, after all, published against republican writers and Ogilby memorialized the coronation pageant on the page – most regarded regulation of the presses as essential to stable government. In 1662 a new printing act, instituting a new office of Surveyor of the Press, passed onto the statute book.[73]

Whatever the intentions of this legislation, the Licensing Act neither suppressed publications critical of the government nor satisfied those who sought to exercise control of the press.[74] Two works published in 1663 and 1664 address the failings of the act specifically. In *Considerations and Proposals in Order to the Regulation of the Press*, published in June 1663, Roger L'Estrange, the appointed Licenser, detailed the problems of still-unregulated publications.[75] In an epistle to the king, L'Estrange warned Charles of the hundreds of pamphleteers who attacked the church and crown as popish and claimed that at least thirty thousand sermons had been printed in breach of the Act of Uniformity.[76] In particular, the farewell sermons of ejected ministers were selling in tens of impressions, while libels, justifications of regicide and other treasonous and seditious works were still freely circulating. The Stationers and printers, L'Estrange concluded, could not be trusted – as the Act of 1662, reviving earlier practice, trusted them – to regulate the press. He pressed for direct royal control and firm punishments of delinquents.[77] L'Estrange had his reward in his appointment as surveyor of the printing presses the same year.[78] Richard Atkyns's *The Original and Growth of Printing*, published in 1664 with an engraved portrait of Charles above the legend 'Scriptura et leges sunt fundamenta coronae', expanded an argument he had made in a Restoration broadsheet that control of printing was a flower of the crown.[79] Reminding Charles that a free press had brought down his father, that words and 'paper pellets', as dangerous as bullets, had 'begat blows', Atkyns argued that the danger was far from past.[80] Like the tongue, he argued, 'the quill . . . is of a flying nature in itself and so spiritual, that it is in all places at the same time, and so powerful . . . that it is the people's deity'.[81] Such a force was too mighty to be entrusted to the Stationers, who were motivated by profit more than loyalty and who had, Atkyns claimed, prosecuted none under the late Licensing Act. Like L'Estrange, therefore, Atkyns advocated an examination of the charter of the Stationers Company, greater royal control of the press, and regulation of the swelling numbers of the printers and booksellers who, he observed, did not get their business from licensed publications.

As well as their advice, however, both L'Estrange and Atkyns acknowledged (the latter in religious language) the reach and power of the printed page. L'Estrange, as we have seen, instituted an official organ to publicize the government's cause and Atkyns appreciated the potential value of a medium that 'flies into all parts of the world without weariness'.[82] Quite simply, print had become not only part of the nation's life, but in many ways the medium through which men and women experienced and viewed the world. As Edward Howard observed, there were few plays that did not go into print, 'the press being . . . the stage's tiring house'.[83] Catalogues of recent books published, more common after 1660, indicate a full entry of the book into commerce and commercial society. The author of *Troia Redeviva* was not the only author to 'read' London as if the city were a book; in his sermon after the Great Fire, Nathaniel Hardy, vicar of St Martin's-in-the-Fields, lamented his city 'this large volume in folio abridged almost to an octavo'.[84] The book had become not only part of the cultural imaginary, but also an intrinsic facet of the political culture. Ogilby regarded his account of the coronation as a 'shining trophy' of majesty and described the success he had with his translation of Virgil as a royal progress in print: 'from a mean octavo a royal folio flourished'.[85]

The reach and depth of print into Restoration culture made L'Estrange's project of royal control impossible. With the Stationers responding to the market, increasing literacy and, as well as popular pamphlets and plays, the burlesquing of 'elite' texts (such as Virgil) in popular form, print became the medium of everyman. Indeed, if the civil war could be said to have bequeathed a cultural legacy of ubiquitous, and politicized, print, the near-revolutionary crisis of Charles II's reign was initiated, manufactured and escalated by, and contested on, the printed page: the Exclusion crisis and Popish Plot, that is, were above all a battle of text and print.[86]

From the first revelation, the Popish Plot involved a fevered exchange between oral rumour and print, a contest over the reliability of testimonies and texts, and a battle for credibility and authority.[87] As earlier commentators who had judged Charles I's fate as determined by loss of control of the press, the royalist John Nalson traced the onset of the new troubles to a similar cause. On the eve of the

Plot, in a survey of the dissenting party, published in 1677, Nalson regretted how in 'a scribbling age' the defences of the church had been too expensive and too long to draw a broad audience and had been suspected of partiality, whereas the dissenters had commended the pulpit and the press for their pernicious doctrines.[88] The next year, in *The Common Interest of King and People*, he declaimed against those who 'boldly print and spread abroad in public their seditious pamphlets' as he sought to undo their hold on readers.[89] But once the Plot was revealed, all parties took to print: the Jesuits and Catholics to counter the false allegations, the Presbyterians to insist on the truth of them, then the loyalists to argue royal authority and hereditary succession, the Whigs to call for limited government and a Protestant rule. Not only was the status of the evidence at trials compromised by misinformation and false witness, the accounts of the trials, turned into print, threw the processes of justice into the public marketplace of print and the competition to win readers' allegiance.[90] During the Plot the titles of pamphlets – *The Just Account, True Relations, The Impartial Considerations*, the 'Answers' and 'Antidotes' and 'Animadversions' – abundantly illustrate the interplay of print, the contest of credibility, and politics. Though Justice Scroggs, initially a believer in the Plot, tried desperately to win support against 'libellous pamphlets' – not least by arguing that 'if men can . . . write and print whatever they please, the papists will be sure to put in for their share' – the years 1679–82 saw a flood of publications to rival 1642 and a series of new newspapers, the *Weekly Packet*, the *Friendly Intelligence* and the *Domestic Intelligence*, for example.[91]

As pamphlet after pamphlet sought to undermine the reports and claims of each other, as works like *The Compendium* and *The King's Evidence Justified* hurled accusations of 'fiction', perjury and contrivance, print not only proliferated but led readers to a new relationship with the page, to a recognition both of the need to consume yet more print and yet not be consumed by it.[92] Several contemporary bound collections of a plenitude of Popish Plot polemics evidence readers garnering works from all sides of a debate, so as to better argue their case, or indeed to determine truth for themselves. In one instance of Anthony Wood's copy of *The Trial of Nathaniel Reading*, marginal notes suggest an effort to evaluate disputed evidence in a text that was itself party to dispute, while in a copy of the dying speeches of five Jesuits another hand first records with certainty that they were 'feigned . . . to get money', only to come to the view that 'It is false as I have since understood', and the originals were found in Newgate.[93]

As print served more to confuse than inform, from many sides came audible views that print had become a problem rather than a resource. In 1680, John Rushworth, the Whig, opined that 'the press seems overcharged' and the author of *The Disloyal Forty and Forty One* expressed the view that 'it were happy for the nation if the great heats . . . of scribbling pamphleteers were laid aside and that both parties would seriously weigh things in the balance of equity'.[94] The author who depicted Whig and Tory alike as 'scribbling duellists' who fought with the weapons of lampoons, pamphlets, histories and plays, cursed both for a combat in which 'sense and law and history are slain'.[95] *Britanniae speculum* urged an end to the debauchery of the press 'whose prolific womb teeming with new monsters fills every corner of the nation with seditious pamphlets.'[96] Doubtless there was a weariness of the fray in print, as there was a fear of armed conflict. But in this last case, as often, the call for restraints on the press came from loyalists and Tories. For, as Dryden was succinctly to put it, the arena of print was levelling the monarch: 'sovereign princes when they enter into the lists of disputation may be answered as well as private men: for then they command not, but only argue, speak their opinion'.[97] After the dissolution of the parliament at Oxford, a contemporary historian noted, 'all the weekly intelligences and the factions and scurrilous libels which the press had vomited out in great numbers whilst they expected impunity from the parliament were suppressed and easily brushed into silence by an order of Council'.[98] It was a judgement excessive in its optimism. No more than the Licensing Act (which was reissued in 1685) could a Council order silence the presses. Print had helped to fashion political parties; still more it had transformed subjects into citizens who were freely debating and formulating their own judgements.

A community of free debate and independent judgement is almost the definition of the public sphere as outlined in its first formulation by Jurgen Habermas.[99] I have suggested that as far back as Elizabeth's and even Henry VIII's reigns, and increasingly thereafter, there was a broader discussion of *arcana imperii* than historians have assumed.[100] Rumour and news, I have argued, helped to forge a political consciousness. Yet, though we see glimpses of this consciousness, in commonplace books and private correspondence, sometimes the report of tavern talk, public meetings to discuss state affairs, especially of those below the elite, were dangerous and infrequent. Political news circulated orally, in manuscript and through illicit presses; but to a large extent it was an underground network, albeit one to which governments paid close attention. The civil war transformed the discussions of state affairs: by the fact of division freeing debates about fundamental principles, by the effective collapse of censorship, and by the arrival during the 1650s into England of the coffee houses as centres of news and open discussion. From the beginning, coffee houses appear not to have been the exclusive presence of a party of faction. During the Interregnum, Anthony Wood tells us, a group of young royalists met regularly at a coffee house in Oxford. But, as Steven Pincus has shown, coffee houses became associated in many minds with the Commonwealth, and with that vulgar intrusion into the secrets of state that had turned the world upside down and threatened the overthrow of social and political order.[101]

At the Restoration, some expressed the need to draw the boundaries, as well as lower the heat, of public debate about government. In 1661, for example, the physician and Anglican royalist, Walter Charleton, advised that 'silence and veneration are the most proper expressions subjects can use' in their relations with government; detestation of the opposites (noise and critical debate) characterized the Restoration high churchmen and was a frequent refrain of sermons.[102] The coffee houses, however, had become, in every sense, popular (there were said to be eighty in London by 1663) and the appetite for news and discussion, across the political spectrum and differences of class, was as strong as that for the new beverage.[103] A couple of hours with coffee, a newspaper and a discussion – of literature, philosophy, science, but most of all politics – had become part of London life. And not only life in the metropolis. By the end of the first decade of restored Stuart rule, coffee houses had been opened in Oxford and Cambridge, York and Bristol, Harwich and Yarmouth, as well as in Scotland and Ireland, and the numbers of businesses grew quickly over the course of the reign.[104] So popular were they that many lamented the business they took from the taverns and alehouses; and though doubtless some such comments were special pleading, in the third edition of *Angliae Notitia . . . The Present State of England* (1669), Edward Chamberlayne judged that there was 'generally less excess in drinking (especially about London, since the use of coffee)'.[105]

The special popularity of the coffee house, its place as a mart of news and talk, was the subject of endless fascination and comment. Shortly after the proposals for a tighter regulation of the press, John Dolben, Dean of Westminster, referred in a thanksgiving sermon on the naval victory in June 1665, off Lowestoft against the Dutch, to 'those who frame commonwealths in coffee'.[106] Later, at a dinner for the newly appointed mayor of the Draper's Company, a song presented a graphic picture of the London coffee house. According to Thomas Jordan's entertainment, the clientele consisted of those who were curious:

And love to hear such News;
That come from all parts of the Earth,
Turks, Dutch, and *Danes* and *Jews*
I'll send ye to the Rendezvouz,
Where it is smoaking new;
Go bear it at a Coffee-House,
It cannot but be true.[107]

In his gentle mocking of the coffee houses, Jordan describes how these experts claimed to know the outcome of a battle before it had been fought and continued:

There's nothing done in all the World,
From Monarch to the Mouse;
But every day or night 'tis hurl'd
Into the *Coffee-House*.[108]

There men and women talked of fashion, books ('so great an university', he calls it), most of all the ups and downs of politicians and ministers.[109]

Interestingly, though many had advocated a politics of silence and reverence, there was no clampdown on the coffee houses. Not until the failure of the second Dutch War was there any discussion of closing them, and not until 1675 did the king issue a proclamation for their suppression.[110] While some argued that coffee houses fostered political divisions and diminished the traditional English virtues of good fellowship in the alehouse, and even smacked of puritan sobriety more than cavalier ale-healths, it may be that Charles II did not share their views. We have more than a sense that L'Estrange and others had to persuade the king to greater regulation of the press, and Charles's openness to witty criticism from the likes of Rochester suggests a more relaxed attitude than that of his advisers. Steven Pincus argues that the move to suppress the coffee houses by proclamation followed on the gaining of influence and position by the high-church party who associated freedom of discussion with claims to personal conscience and reason.[111] If, however, it was they who persuaded Charles to act, the king quickly withdrew the prohibition, and within weeks the proclamation was rescinded.[112] Still, in the mid-1670s, there were many – and the king may have been one – who did not see the coffee houses as sites of opposition. Some, recalling the Royalist meetings during the Interregnum, described the coffee houses as 'a friend to monarchy'; some expressed the belief (one that ultimately validated parties) that debate and disputation over coffee might save England from armed conflict on the battlefield.[113] In a work, for example, licensed by L'Estrange in 1678, W. M. presents an entertainment in which the coffee house is a subject of discussion.[114] Though the news that comes into Huntingtonshire from London is that 'no body is free from a Coffee-House lash', the local JP, Sir Jeffrey Do-Right is measured in his assessment. While he agrees that 'it seems every man there thinks himself to have brains enough for a statesman', he felt too that such a claim was 'excusable', 'since his aim is for the public good and by such innocent discussions the state may the better judge of what is most rationally conducible to the interest of the body politic'.[115] Later in their broad discussion of state, Sir Jeffrey repeats his point: 'I see no harm in these discussions; so long as people keep their ears loyal and their tongues only nimble in such innocent discourses; good may come out of it for the public profit'.[116] Danger came not from discussion but from 'intestine factions' and disloyalty.[117]

If Charles II in 1675 was inclined, unlike the high churchmen, to share the view that honest critical debate need not threaten government, the Popish Plot and Exclusion crisis forced a rethinking. The crises were born of discussion and rumour as well as print; and there were distinct Whig coffee houses which became organizational headquarters of opposition.[118] During the confusion over the veracity of the Plot, with news, like all print, increasingly partisan, some coffee shops emerged as places where convictions were simply confirmed, others

27 *The CoffeHous Mob*, frontispiece to *The Fourth Part of Vulgus Britannicus: or the British Hudibras*, 1710.

doubtless where, with all the latest pamphlets on the table and a gathering to review them, opinions and allegiances were formed – and where sometimes quarrels flared (fig. 27).[119] In some cases they appear to have functioned as an archive: the Whig author of an account of the Duke of Monmouth's progress, on which he touched to cure the king's evil and so advertised his right to the throne, challenged that 'whoever doubts the truth of this relation may be satisfied thereof by sight of the original at the Amsterdam Coffee-House in Bartholomew Lane near the Royal Exchange'.[120] Here the public sphere is itself set up, in a radical move, as the arbiter of truth; but, as the name of the Amsterdam coffee shop, with its evocation of toleration, dissent and republic, indicates, it was a public sphere now rent by religious and political division. Though they had their own favourite places, Tories lambasted the coffee houses as the meeting rooms where Whigs and dissenters planned treason. Where the *Complaint of Liberty* characterized the coffee-house clientele as dissenters and conventicles, Tom Tell-Truth's *Letter to the Earl of Shaftesbury* accused the leader of the Whigs of a plot: 'what divided interests and factions have there been for seven years last past ... to bring the king and governors into disgrace, by frequent clubs at coffee houses and taverns, on purpose to break the bonds of unity among us'.[121] The author of *Ursa Major & Minor* further charged that, as provincial coffee houses imported and discussed news from London, they spread factions to country farmers.[122] And Dryden, dismissing the Whig's complaint that the king had his reasons for dissolving parliament read from the pulpits, retorted that the Whig 'introduces it [his case] into conventicles and coffee houses of his faction, besides his sending it in post letters to infect the populace of every county'.[123]

Though the representation of coffee houses as Whig enclaves of sedition was a party-polemical charge, there can be no doubt that the Whigs sought to take advantage of a fully formed public sphere to subvert the regime. And Tory loyalists, as well as the king, saw the need to address it. The Tory newspaper *Heraclitus Ridens*, for example, cursed 'Dissenting-Coffee-House statesmen' and posted a mock advertisement inviting any who 'out of natural curiosity desire to be furnished with ships or castles in the air or any sorts of prodigies ... to persuade them to ... seditions, let them repair to Ben Harris at his shop'.[124] In reality, as the author and all knew, coffee houses were not simply frequented by the naïve and credulous; they had fashioned a broad public often very well informed and able to discriminate. In their 1680 pamphlet dialogue over a 'dish of coffee', the humble Tom and Dick ranged widely over matters of religion and government; and most who published pamphlets addressing the people assumed their familiarity with debate about state affairs.[125] Accordingly, Thomas Rymer, in his epistle to *A General Draught ... of Government*, addressed readers 'thoroughly informed';[126] on the other side, even the author of *The Deliquium* acknowledged that evenings with coffee were 'lac'd with long Argument/of the King's Power and Rights of Parliament';[127] and, defending the king, John Brydall felt the need to 'return you solutions to those objections that have been stated at coffee houses'.[128] As both sides knew, public opinion was now determining the fates of ministers and even monarchs.

For many high church Tories, however, the fevered public debates during the Plot only confirmed the risks to church and state when authority was not veiled in mystery and subjects were not confined to their rightful place of reverent obedience. In his sermon to the mayor and aldermen on 29 May 1682, Benjamin Calamy, urging that each 'keep his own proper rank' in quiet obedience, observed 'it hath ... never been well with us in this nation since this itch of hearing and telling public news hath so notoriously infected all sorts of men'.[129] 'Matters of policy,' he continued, 'the arts and methods of government are things too sacred to be profaned by every unhallowed hand. They are like the mysteries of religion.'[130] In the wake of the (failed) Rye House Plot to assassinate the king, the dangers of coffee-house debate and the need for unquestioning obedience were pressed more forcefully. In his sermon on *King David's Deliverance*, preached in September 1683, Thomas Long damned the 'treason' that was 'the familiar discourse of coffee houses and taverns' and re-sanctified Charles as the biblical David.[131] As other thanksgiving sermons demonized coffee houses as nearly again the cause of civil war, John Harrison, rector of Pulborow in Sussex, decried the coffee shops as 'nurseries of rebellion, drunkenness, debauchery of every kind'.[132] Over in Salisbury, Paul Lathom, a prebendary of the cathedral, lamenting the 'unhappy age' when men took 'to arguing pro and con . . . whether the nation might be as happy or more under a republic than a monarchy', advised his auditors not to enquire into the mysteries of government: 'it is better,' he told them, 'to comfort ourselves in the practical use of a piece of clockwork than to puzzle our heads with speculative enquiries' into its workings.[133] Thinking about the mysteries of state, John Scott proclaimed in his sermon at the Guildhall, and discoursing in coffee houses led men to perdition.[134] And the plotter John Rowse's scaffold speech confirmed Scott's prediction: running from the coffee house to the tavern, he confessed, had led him into treason and, warning others 'to take notice of it', he had come to see coffee shops as 'the debauchery of this age'.[135] A history of conspiracy, *The Rebels Doom* cited Isocrates's sage counsel that there should be no societies or clubs except those licensed by the state.[136]

In the wake of the high-Tory reaction, coffee houses and the debates they hosted were demonized, just as the monarchy was re-mystified and re-sacralized. And mystery meant silence. In his sermon to the mayor of London on 1 Thessalonians 4: 11, published as *The Study of Quietness*, Richard Pearson, recalling the damage done by words, enjoined all to follow St Paul: to 'study to be quiet and to do their own business'.[137]

The call to suppress dispute found willing support as the nation reviewed how close it had come to civil war. But, whether from a sense of the impossibility of closing them or an unwillingness to do so, Charles II issued no further proclamations against coffee houses. Still, at the end of his reign, though for now the voices of opposition were subdued, *A Character of London Village* described the popular 'Coffee House, the Rendezvous of Wits/Is a Compound of Gentlemen and Cits'.[138] The monarch played now on the stage of majesty before a public sphere that sat in judgment on his performance.

II

Memories of civil war, changes in the nature of monarchy, the full commercialization of print and emergence of a public sphere, most of all the gradual acceptance of difference and division and the appearance of political parties, not only refashioned royal representations, and the performance and reception of regality; they transformed the modes and perceptions of counter-representation and of opposition to the monarchy and government. Though at first sight this may seem a contentious claim – the coups attempted and the discourses of opposition often appear familiar moves and tropes – I shall argue that the post-Restoration opposition, rather than illustrating the continuity of seventeenth-century politics, heralds the change to a different politics of rule and representation. Just as, even more than his predecessors, Charles II was faced with representing himself in a contested culture and public sphere, so his opponents had to counter royal representations in contending for the support of the public.

What had been all too familiar to early-modern monarchs were plots and planned coups and uprisings, and Charles II's reign was by no means free of these. The fear of uprisings, of course, was central in shaping the Restoration settlement and Charles's own attitude to it; but when the first resistance appeared in the opening days of 1661, only forty men supported the Fifth Monarchist cooper, Thomas Venner, though it took three days to suppress them.[139] The next year, in the wake of the repressive religious legislation, Thomas Tonge, George Phillips, Francis Stubbs and other 'satanical saints' attempted a coup to seize the Tower, murder the king and restore the Commonwealth. Though they were said to have planned risings in Mansfield, Nottingham, Bristol and Essex, nothing came of the affair and there is some evidence to suggest that the plotters were drawn into a trap by government agents.[140] During the summer of 1663 there was another scare: a rising in the north. Again, despite extravagant claims by loyalists of a conspiracy to secure Newcastle and Boston, obtain foreign aid, descend on Whitehall and reinstate the Long Parliament, the handful who gathered at Durham and in Yorkshire were (in Ronald Hutton's words) 'the dupes of over-enthusiastic diehards and agents provocateurs'.[141] Indeed, for all the government paranoia and almost monthly reports of planned insurrections, what is striking about the first decade of Restoration government is the quiescence of old republicans and the sects, especially given the religious intolerance imposed against the king's wishes and promises. In 1666 a motley group of old commonwealthsmen under the names of Rathbone, Saunders, Evans, Miles and Cole were indicted for plotting to set fire to the city and seize the Tower.[142] More seriously, in November a small army of Scottish Presbyterians swore the Covenant and marched from the south-west towards Edinburgh, but they were routed by Lieutenant-General Dalzel and the survivors were tortured.[143] Other than these fracas, there was no armed resistance to Charles II before the Popish Plot: and then, whatever the fear of uprising in England, it was again eighty Scottish rebels who rose in the west, marched on Raglan and, there proclaiming the Covenant, burned the acts of parliament for the royal supremacy and for a day of rejoicing on 29 May, the anniversary of Restoration and the king's birthday.[144] When they attempted to move into Glasgow, they were beaten off, and then roundly defeated by Monmouth. In England, it had already become clear, opposition to the regime was being conducted by other means.

Some of the discourses of opposition deployed in the late seventeenth century were traditional modes of criticizing the government. Histories provide one good example and it is no coincidence that the Exclusionists, who were putting forward new and revolutionary claims, sought the protection of the past.[145] From 1678 a multiplicity of old texts were republished, at times with new prefaces, to argue the powers of parliament (Elsynge's *Ancient Method* and Cotton's *Antiquity and Dignity of Parliaments*),[146] the dangers of popery (*Memoirs of Queen Mary's Days* and *A Brief . . . Life of Mary, Queen of Scots*)[147] or arbitrary rule (*The Life and Reign of King Richard II*)[148] and the benefit of moderate Protestant monarchy (*The History of the Glorious Life . . . of Queen Elizabeth*).[149] Prophecies too had long been a genre for criticism and more so after the split from Rome; despite the discrediting of enthusiasm after the Restoration, they continued to perform to counsel and question the monarchy.[150] In 1680, for example, the pamphlet *Strange News from Bishop-Hatfield* in Hertfordshire reported the vision of one Elizabeth Freeman in which she had, it was claimed, been instructed to ask the king not to break with his parliament.[151] And *The True and Wonderful Relation* of a vision in the sky over Carmarthen of pikemen and combat in 1681 was probably intended to stir the godly to armed conflict.[152]

The civil war, however, had fundamentally changed the languages of criticism and opposition. During the 1640s and 1650s earlier attacks on evil counsellors or oblique criticisms of the sovereign had transmuted into a rejection of not only the monarch but the institution of monarchy. Despite the discrediting in 1660 of republican voices and an apparent national amnesia concerning radical debates about the fundamentals of government, these voices and texts could not be forgotten, not least because some did not wish them silenced. While he may have been exceptional in his stridency, L'Estrange expressed the fears of many when he warned Charles that the 'same arguments, pretences, ways and instruments that ruined your royal . . . father' were still menacing the crown.[153] By the late 1660s obliquely and by the 1670s explicitly, questions about the respective virtues of monarchy and republic were being freshly aired again, Nalson exaggerating only slightly when he observed in 1678 that it had 'grown to be but too popular . . . among us to entertain very kind thoughts of the democratic way of government'.[154] In 1680–1, for example, Henry Neville's *Plato Redivivus* and the first edition of Henry Care's *English Liberties, or, The Free Born Subject* rehearsed the dialogues and debates of the civil war and even the Leveller language of each man's 'fix'd fundamental right born with him'.[155] However, though these texts and arguments reveal the survival of a republican caucus and, more broadly, the legacy of republican arguments in the cultural memory, the actual number of republicans, and the supporters of them, were few. Charles's victory in 1682 manifests that, as they moved from denunciations of the government to possible restoration of a republic, his enemies lost the support of the people.

In terms of opposition to royal words and images, the civil war bequeathed a legacy more enduring and more difficult for rulers: permanent divisions and differences. As we have seen, relentless efforts were made, especially by Charles II, to gloss, temper and deny them, to advertise unity and harmony.[156] Yet those who passed in the streets old enemies, or perused their books, or simply remembered, knew that profound religious, political and cultural differences had emerged out of the civil wars and revolution. For all the prohibitions against name-calling, many like Charles Hammond, author of *The Cavalier's Case*, wrote that 'he that cannot swear and swagger, drink, rant and rogue is looked upon (by some) as a pitiful fellow . . . these vices . . . are looked upon to be the only badge to distinguish a cavalier from a sectary'.[157] Drinking and wenching were ubiquitously figured on the stage as the pastimes of a party, of men quite removed from sobriety, abstinence, industry, that is, the old puritan virtues. If they were not to fight again, such groups would have to learn to live together in peace. But though not devoid of some truth, these stereotypes too simply delineated the nation. For many old cavaliers had served the Protector with admiration for his government; and, on the other side, no few puritans (Prynne was an obvious one), after the extremes of the 1650s, were ready to raise a health to the new king.[158] Divisions and differences, that is, not only divided people from each other; they became embedded in the consciousness of many subjects, with important consequences for the political culture. In short, I would suggest, both the tenets of difference and division and a social psychology shaped by them came to render criticism of, and opposition to, the government not (or not just or primarily) an underground, illicit activity but an acceptable, even normal, feature of public life. Together with the development of print, and of new genres of writing, these changes stimulated different expressions of, and attitudes to, opposition – changes that were to make it a normal condition of government and of the representation of rule.

The literature of criticism and opposition offers one example of the transformation. Verse satires and libels, of course, were not new to the late seventeenth century; those circulating during the Overbury affair had been mordant and pornographic.[159] In Restoration England, however, these emerged from the underground to become part of the culture of the court they lampooned. And just as the monarch openly publicized his sex life, explicit satires on pox-ridden ministers and avaricious royal mistresses freely circulated (albeit some in manuscript) and were copied, imitated and talked about, largely with impunity. Nor did the genre spare the king himself. Rochester more than hinted that Charles was more devoted to sex than to good government, and while in his case the criticism is in some measure affectionate, the language is sharp and

Rochester's view of his master, and of monarchy, is, to say the least, equivocal.[160] Others, from a position of antipathy, not only deployed the verse satire as critique, they countered a form of panegyrical representation that had emerged from court circles: the 'Instructions to A Painter' Poems.[161] While the first of these appeared to celebrate royal victory, in 1667 John Denham, a former staunch royalist, penned and published a bitter mockery of the genre and of Waller in his *Directions to a Painter*.[162] Blaming Charles's lax regimen for disasters that had befallen England, Denham directly charged that 'women have grossly snar'd the wisest Prince'.[163] Importantly he also discredited the 'Court-gazettes' that misrepresented the truth with accounts of 'empty triumphs'.[164] The same year, Marvell's savage mock-heroic 'Last Instructions to a Painter', with its title announcing the death-knell to a mode of representation – and possibly also again to monarchy – dared even to enter imaginatively the king's bedroom and to envision Charles II about to rape a bound virgin: Britannia.[165] It is surely a sign of very altered times that Pepys's reaction to such satires was that they were 'too sharp and so true'.[166] Moreover, more than ever before, whether published or not, they were in the broad sense public. As one commentator observed regretfully, 'there was never any age or time like this for the itching of people's ears'.[167]

It was not only the inherited discourses and divisions of civil war but a familiarity with and acceptance of sharp public criticism of the crown that made possible the opposition to Charles launched by the Popish Plot. While the stance of loyal counsel was still taken in many texts, it was (and was read as) more artful, whereas opposition itself was no longer everywhere regarded as treachery or even as disloyal. The years 1678–82 witnessed a bitter contest for representation, to gain the support of public opinion, and this time there was no prospect of the king standing above the fray. During the years of the Plot, all – royal judges as well as midwives – struggled to sell their own version of the truth.[168] Royal organs, such as the *Gazette*, were directly attacked as mendacious, an account of the Duke of York's poor reception in Scotland being published 'because I believe you will not be told it in your gazette'.[169]

Interestingly, during the late 1670s, opposition was displayed with impunity on the streets and in popular forms that appeared to parody the rituals of royal representation itself. In 1679 and again in 1680, there were pope-burning processions staged on Queen Elizabeth's coronation day that unfolded a mock regal pageant through London. In the first, as the procession wound from Moorgate, to Leaden Hall, the Royal Exchange, Cheapside and Temple Bar, the route of royal entries, a dead body representing Sir Edmund Bury Godfrey was carried before Jesuit priests, Carmelite friars and the pope in 'a lofty glorious' chair of state, attended by 150 flambeaux.[170] Coming to Temple Bar where there were four statues of monarchs (Elizabeth, James I, Charles I and II), the figure of the pope was brought before the statue of Elizabeth, which was especially garlanded 'with a crown of gilded laurel' and a shield inscribed 'The Protestant Religion and Magna Carta', 'in regard of the day'.[171] Having been, as it were, judged by the queen, the 'pope' was placed on a bonfire before cheering crowds. Here not only is King Charles II symbolically replaced by the figure of Elizabeth (who, we note, wears the laurel of Charles's representation), the king's judgement and faith are both questioned, for all the loyal acclamations. Moreover, the published account of this procession almost directly borrows the language of Charles's coronation to describe the attendant crowds: 'Never were the balconies, windows and houses more numerously lined or the streets more thronged with multitudes of people' to the number, it was claimed, of two hundred thousand.[172] The same ritual the next year virtually re-staged a royal entertainment. In 1680 the *Solemn Mock Procession* recounts the nine pageants at which the cavalcade halted – pageants of 'the lies and monstrous actions' of friars and Jesuits, of popish bishops, of the emperor crushed by the papacy, and of papal 'courtesans in ordinary' – all an inversion of the coronation pageants and paeans to church and monarchy.[173] And on this occasion, in a gesture that could not but have recalled Ogilby's volume, the published account advertises for readers that 'the full manner of their procession is hereby represented to the eye on copper plate and to be sold by Jonathan Wilkins at The Star in Cheapside next to Mercers Chapel'.[174] The very texts and modes of royal representation were being overturned on the streets.

Closer still to the throne, and novel for early modern England, was the opposition to the Duke of York and to the principle of hereditary succession. During the 1640s there had been discussion of Charles renouncing the throne for his nephew, but the arguments and personal assaults on the heir by the Exclusionists were unprecedented. Thomas Hunt's *Great and Weighty Considerations, Relating to the Duke of York* assaulted the fundamental axiom of English monarchy and insulted the king's heir. 'Every form of government,' he argued, 'is of our creation and not God's and must comply with the safety of the people'; 'the succession of the crown is the right of the whole community'.[175] Turning to the king's brother, the treatise suggests he be banished to a monastery 'before he hath filled the land with blood and slaughter'.[176] Others repeated the case and the abuse: 'there was never anciently . . . any fundamental or unalterable law of succession', asserted James Tyrell; James, Duke of York, it was widely charged, was hand in glove with popish conspirators.[177] Moreover, in a radical move that served almost to legitimize opposition, and which looked ahead to what in the eighteenth century would be called 'the reversionary interest', the opposition to James and Charles was fronted by the king's illegitimate son, the Duke of Monmouth. In putting himself forward as a Protestant successor, Monmouth not only opposed Charles's clear policy and James's right, he directly countered the truth of the king's words and, like the pope burners, he appropriated royal ritual to advance his cause. In claiming his legitimacy and the lawful marriage of his mother Lucy Walters, Monmouth explicitly defied Charles's denial, in particular his speech in Council and declaration to his subjects of 2 June 1680 that 'there was never any marriage or contract of marriage had or made'.[178] In order to press his claim to legitimacy, Monmouth embarked on (what was as defiant as inappropriate) a royal progress, attended by Shaftesbury, to which crowds of people flocked. At Chichester, where the report had it, he was met by five hundred horse, Monmouth was given a great reception which was understandably taken as a public validation.[179] More audaciously still, on his progress round the west, Monmouth performed the ceremony of touching for the king's evil. As one account of a cure by Mrs Fanshaw, Monmouth's sister and a converted former Catholic, argued, the cures established Monmouth's 'legitimacy' and, it was implied, his capacity to bring others over from Rome and cure the popish sickness that corrupted the nation.[180] Again opposition to Charles took the form of counter-representation, thereby robbing not only James but in some measure Charles himself of legitimacy and authority.

In the divided world of late seventeenth-century England, especially during the Popish Plot, all the texts and symbols of monarchy had been plunged into party contest. Despite its title, that fact is well illustrated by *An Impartial Enquiry into The Administration of Affairs in England with Some Reflections on the Kings Declaration of July 27, 1683*.[181] In that declaration, Charles attacked his enemies for the 'tumults and riots' they had staged and for the '*misrepresenting*' his actions in which they had engaged.[182] By way of reply, the *Impartial Enquiry* both repeated the charge of 'misrepresenting' ('insincerity' and 'falsehood') that Charles referred to and attacked the royal declaration.[183] The king's account of a plot to kill him was false, the pamphlet charged; the fire at Newmarket that allegedly saved him was contrived. Why, the author asked, should readers place any trust when the king had been insincere in his former declarations and broken the promises he had made in them? 'What faith,' he taunted, 'can be given to a person who is a Protestant in the chapel and a papist in the closet?'[184] The people were urged not to swallow a royal word without also reading the words of Lord Russell alongside them: though he was not a king, he 'may yet . . . be put in balance with him for truth and sincerity'.[185] It was Russell who here was the 'blessed soul' commended to heaven – Russell the conspirator against the king's life.[186]

Charles escaped the violent opposition that overcame his father. Though historians depict the crisis of 1678–82 as a narrow escape, the people in general had little appetite, as Charles rightly gambled, for civil war. Opposition, however, to the king himself, had become virulent, public and almost legitimate; and opponents of the king appropriated, mocked and countered all the genres of royal representation in contesting royal actions and programmes. In the aftermath of the crisis, as Charles was re-sacralized in paeans to divine monarchy, opposition appears for a time to be discredited. Charles, however, survived because, against his earlier wishes to head a nation united in love and obedience, he made himself the king of a party.[187] In finally validating party, he ultimately helped also to validate opposition politics and a political culture in which no royal image or word would go unanswered or uncontested.

III

In a stimulating recent essay on the historiography of Charles II and the difficulties in writing his biography, Ronald Hutton suggested a different model for the next study of Charles.[188] Faced with intractable or ambiguous sources that at key points obstruct definitive judgements about the man, Hutton advises three considerations: of the stereotypes of good and bad monarchs, of the image Charles projected of himself, and of the receptions of and responses to those representations. Such, in this, as in earlier chapters, has been our project. Professor Hutton's conviction, however, that such analyses 'would permit an objective conclusion as to the overall success or failure of the reign', seems over-optimistic.[189] The difficulties that biographers face in the character of Charles – the ambiguous attributes of charm and ruthlessness, energy and laziness, openness and secrecy, loyalty and infidelity, sincere beliefs and opportunism – were also contradictions of the political culture, bequeathed by civil war and fostered by mounting public debate and division.[190] As much as being responsible by his duplicitous actions for fostering dissimulation and mistrust, Charles had to perform the role of monarch and present himself in a world which was already characterized by intrigue and artfulness, that is, the world of politics. True, his own clandestine behaviour in signing the Secret Treaty of Dover aroused suspicions that hugely damaged him; but in doing so the king more likely acted from a politic sense of the need to have options (abroad and at home) than out of any Catholic or absolutist agenda.[191] If keeping his options open, if need be by secrecy and dissimulation, was a failing in a king, it was one of an age and most of its political players. Charles was committed to some principles: he staked his life on hereditary succession; if he appeared less committed to them than his father (who did lose his life for them), it was not least because his survival and preservation of his authority in a changed world was his first principle.

Charles II's image, like his character, is also ambiguous and multiple. As his coronation was celebrated with the greatest pomp, he licensed stories and displayed images of his humiliation in exile; as he touched to cure the evil, he publicly fondled his mistresses.[192] These contradictions of self-representation, I would suggest, were not simply contradictions: they were images crafted to give the king room for manoeuvre, to enable him to negotiate the contradictions of a polity torn between old and new values and perceptions, and to permit him to speak to different audiences. Professor Hutton draws clearly and tries to resolve the very different reputations that Charles has had in the largely negative academic biographies and the more positive and romanticized popular lives of him.[193] While clearly these differences disclose different genres of writing history, and different audiences, they also stem from the type of contemporary sources that writers prioritize. Popular songs, ballads and anecdotes convey a positive and affectionate picture of 'Old Rowley' – one that Charles himself did much to construct.

What then did contemporaries make of him? Hutton's question, though obvious and important, is also complicated. For contemporary observers also had to grapple both with the contradictions of the character and the changing values of an age which they could not always acknowledge or, perhaps, discern. Certainly Hutton and others are right to identify the disillusion that set in by the later 1660s, after the near universal acclamation with which Charles was welcomed at the Restoration. Yet even that seemingly universal joy concealed very different hopes and expectations that time would perforce open into disappointments and divisions, for which Charles was by no means solely responsible. Not least his subjects' disillusion was mirrored by Charles's own frustration that a national rhetoric of healing and harmony dissolved into recriminations and factions. Whatever the inconsistencies of his own personality might have been, Charles had to refashion his language and image through changed circumstances, or at least to shift the emphasis from providential ruler to patron of science, from but-a-man to god-like king, from a champion of unity and comprehension to head of a party. Because he had to perform differently in a series of different moments, even 'the image of the king' is too static a model for an understanding.

Many near-contemporary appraisals of Charles were understandably and overtly partisan. They highlighted, in some cases possibly manufactured, a feature of the royal image for polemical ends. This is most obviously the case with efforts to portray Charles as a sincere Catholic: *A True Relation of the Late King's Death*, for example, related his sending for Father Huddleston who had preserved him in the oak tree and who he 'now hoped would preserve his soul'.[194] Dismissing, the report goes, the bishops who tried to enter his bedchamber, Charles took extreme unction and commended 'so good a brother' whom he had left to rule. Whatever the dubious veracity of that account, we should note the author's effort to make a neat pattern of the king's life from 1651 to 1685, from adversity to a triumph that reaches its zenith in public conversion and Catholic succession.[195] On the other side, especially after 1688, staunch Whig and nonconformist biographies sought to demonize Charles. To take a case, the 1694 *Eikon Basilike: The Portraiture of His Sacred Majesty King Charles II* depicts a king who uses religion only as a trick to dupe his subjects, who flirted with Presbyterians and courted Catholics only out of political expediency, and who used lust as a means to enhance his power.[196] Once again, though worth little as a portrait of Charles II, the *Eikon Basilike* reveals an anxiety about the image of both Charles I and II, and especially the popularity of the latter who by a reign of 'jollity and pleasure' had drawn that majority of the people naturally inclined to lust and corruption.[197] The impersonation in the text of Charles's voice and the attribution to him of words he never spoke suggests too a perceived need to counter the actual words and image of the king. Ironically, in presenting him as a figure moved by 'policy', 'interest' and 'reason of state', the author may have undermined his own assault in a 1690s' world in which such values were progressively being validated.[198] Yet though they sometimes unwittingly disclose cultural contradictions, these polemical appraisals on each side had a clear agenda and offer a one-sided image of the king.

Many Tory panegyrists of Charles focus on a particular virtue of the king or offer a frankly idealized sketch of him. The author of *Suspiria*, for example, singles out 'that Clemency/which sav'd three Kingdoms from a fatal Yoke'.[199] Thomas Flatman gave the king the memorial title 'Charles the merciful'; and Nahum Tate's ode on the 'Sacred Memory of our late Sovereign' called him 'All-forgiving CHARLES' to mark the Christian, indeed Christ-like, quality of mercy.[200] Understandably, poets praised in Charles that other traditional virtue of rulers, his patronage of learning. Observing 'to what vast heights did learning rise', *A Pindaric Ode* lauded Charles's support for science; Sir Francis Fane summed him:

> Great Lord of Wit, Patron of Arts he was,
> Learning's strong Atlas, Poetry's best friend.[201]

If clemency, liberality and learning were traditional royal virtues, other verses singled out traits in Charles valued in a modern world. One praised a king who 'established our commerce so universally'; another raised a poetic monument to him 'whose Empire reached throughout the wealthy Seas'.[202]

Those who penned the most extravagant panegyrics on the whole man had to gloss difficult areas, and at times their artfulness seeps to the surface. Fitzmorris Wood's claim that Charles '*said the word*, and all Obey'd' must have sounded strangely to all who had experienced the pamphlet wars of 1678–82; and the description of the king as a 'dear lov'd Husband' must have been read differently by any with more sense of irony than the panegyrist.[203] John Phillips was one of many to revive the language of 'Terrestrial Gods' to describe monarchs in 1685, but some would have recalled his service as secretary to Milton.[204] Aphra Behn called Charles 'such a God', 'Sacred Sir', but her lines suggest a contrivance that might have occurred to those familiar with her plays.[205] In Dryden's lines, the gestures to a king of 'godlike mind', who led his people to the promised land, appear not merely artificial but compromised by praise of a king who, like the poet, 'Art to Rage . . . didst oppose'.[206] Surely faith, rather than art (with its hint at artfulness), was the true weapon of the church against 'rank Geneva Weeds'.[207]

Indeed, some poems explicitly raise some of the culture's uncertainties about a religious language of representation and an association of kings with gods. If, an elegy by Thomas D'Urfey asked, heaven opened to welcome Charles, why was not the earth shaken by winds?[208] Now Charles was dead, Sir Francis Fane's ode wondered:

> . . . why no Prodigy at all?
> No Beacon-Comet fir'd above?
> No *Monstrous* Births, no *storms*, no *Whale*
> Or to presage Great CHARLES thy fall.[209]

An age beginning to doubt the influence of the supernatural world in the natural was questioning too the numinosity of kings. Edward Arwaker's vision of a divine commissioner calling his vicegerent home feels disrupted by an advertisement for another book.[210] Though perhaps it is only appropriate that the memory of Charles should be so immersed in the commerce of print, that, in the words of Flatman, 'what He has done shall to a volume swell'.[211]

The disruptions, anxieties and ambiguities of the age that we read between the lines and in the margins of these texts appear on the centre of the page in two encomia to Charles, both published immediately after his death. *Musa Praesica the London Poem* presents 'An Humble Oblation on the Sacred Tomb of our late Gracious Monarch . . .' by 'a loyal apprentice of the City'.[212] In this poem, the author moves from contemplation of 'the sacred image of the deity' to the reflection that 'kings are only born to reign and die'.[213] More radically he asks, reviewing Charles's experience of exile and plots:

> What real Essence is there in a Crown,
> When Monarchs thus are tumbl'd down?[214]

As the poem continues, we cannot but be struck by the uncertainties as to whether Charles was saved by providence or 'preserv'd by a woman's hand', whether he enacted his elected divine plan or performed in 'the regal theatre'.[215] As for his successor, James has already been 'Martyr'd in Effigie': as a marginal note explains, 'his picture in Guildhall cut from the legs downward'.[216] Henry Anderson's *A Loyal Tear Dropt on the Vault of the High and Mighty Prince, Charles II* recalls the title of a memorial to Charles I by his son, but the sensibilities of the text belong to a new age.[217] For sure the vicar of King's Somborne seeks to sacralize Charles, whom he compares to Moses, Solomon and David,

and calls 'Britain's Josiah'.[218] However, the sheer humanity of Charles is acknowledged and embraced and praised to the point that his very ordinariness
becomes a virtue of his kingship. Praising his clemency, candour and open
nature, Anderson continues: 'His converse gave his nobles a pattern of harm-
less and inoffensive mirth, a sweetness and familiarity that at once gained love
and preserved respect in all his subjects; a nobility and grandeur safe in its own
worth, not maintaining itself by a morose distance.'[219] He was, Anderson put it
with no evident irony, 'an angel clothed in flesh'.[220] Nor was this praise of the
humanity of Charles simply a positive gloss on his very public life of the flesh.
It was praise for a new type of king: one who was humble, who did not soar on
the wings of pride and ambition, a monarch who knew that he would die like
other men, and that 'he was cast of the same mould with those of a lower
species'.[221] Paradoxically, the praise comes close to the satire that figures Charles
reflecting that 'English kings are but a sort of royal beggars'.[222]

After Restoration, the English, though they would not have acknowledged it,
wanted their monarch to be a man as well as a god, of flesh as well as celestial
matter. Charles had to craft his image, as his actions, out of the ambiguities
of his age. In every sense – and it was no small accomplishment in the arts of
representation – he literally embodied them. In his essay on the life of the
king, Aurelian Cook predicted that 'posterity shall come to see and show their
children the cottage where he rubbed off his martial dust and the sacred tree
wherein he lay hid'.[223] If not all his subjects, let alone future historians, paid that
homage, there can be no doubting that Charles remained a figure of affection
in the popular memory and, as one of the most common pub signs in England
testifies to this day:

> The *Royal Oake* a story still will tell
> To the World, of wonders, and so will *Boscobell*.[224]

PART II

CONFESSIONAL KINGSHIP? REPRESENTATIONS OF JAMES II

PROLOGUE

A King Represented and Misrepresented

Every bit as much as Queen Mary Tudor, the image of James II that has passed into history is one crafted by others – by his enemies. While no single work pillorying him found its way into every parish church, as did Foxe's *Book of Martyrs* which indelibly stained Mary, James was systematically demonized as a popish absolutist bent on subordinating English liberties, property and Protestantism to Rome. James II, in fact, entered our history books as the monarch who threatened the peace, prosperity and progress of the nation, as one whom destiny itself had condemned, as it rendered also his supporters, the Jacobites, a lost cause, standing in the path of English progress.

It is often argued that history is always on the side of winners; and at first sight we might be tempted to explain James's reputation simply by reference to his failure to repel William of Orange's invasion in 1688 or to regain his throne by force. The case of Charles I, however, reminds us that the power of an image, and of words, can, as contemporaries did not doubt, vie with arms; that even a vanquished ruler can remain an effective political force. The *Eikon Basilike*, we have suggested, may have done more to sustain Stuart monarchy than any other of Charles I's acts.[1] Did, then, James, unlike his father, fail to put his case, to attend to his representation in words and images, and so fail in those arts increasingly central to the exercise of rule?

Again, the king's historical reputation would seem to suggest a swift and straightforward answer: that James either could not or little heeded the need to present himself in the languages that underpinned authority or misjudged his representation, surrendering the battle for hearts and minds to his enemies. Later we shall examine the massive efforts – a veritable political industry – the Whigs deployed across all discursive and cultural forms and media to vilify James: how, as it were learning a lesson from the failure of their republican predecessors of the 1650s, they recognized the need to inscribe a new regime in all the texts of politics and literature, history and memory.[2] For the moment, we should observe that such a polemical industry, though it secured a Whig cultural dominance, also suggests an anxiety about James II's self-presentation and the need to make and reiterate the case against him. Indeed, the stakes were high. Recent revisionist scholarship rescuing Jacobitism from both the condescension of some polemicists and scholars and the romanticization of others has demonstrated the real threat to the stability of the regime that the Stuarts continued to pose, until the defeat of Bonnie Prince Charlie in 1745, over half a century after his grandfather's deposition.[3] Nor was James II himself silent in his own case and cause. Before he succeeded to the throne, during his three-year reign, and after his flight to St Germain, James took pains to represent himself as the son and brother of a king, as a legitimate and divine king, and as the father of a rightful king. Though the modes of his representations changed with shifting circumstances no less than those of his father and brother, from both of whose own words and images he borrowed, James endeavoured to validate and underpin his authority through speeches, declarations and prayers, portraits and rituals. In fact James's concern with his self-presentation and his place in history may have outstripped that of most of his predecessors. Why, then – and how – did it fail to sustain his authority? Was it because by the end of the century there were limits to the force of a ruler's self-representation? Or did James simply lose the contest for representation to more skilful opponents?

CHAPTER 5

A KING OF MANY WORDS

I

Though James's has been a voice and pen lost to history and overwritten by his enemies, it is hard to think of a monarch who wrote so much, and at every point of his reign. As a recent biographer of his early years observes, 'Among British monarchs only his grandfather, James VI and I and Alfred the Great could come close to matching him in terms of the volume of work produced.'[1] As well as letters, speeches and declarations, carefully crafted, James wrote nine volumes of memoirs that were evidently intended, John Callow writes, as a 'record . . . for future generations of his thoughts, words and deeds', papers of devotion and a treatise of advice to his son.[2] They were mostly not published in his lifetime, but there are indications in James's writings from the earliest that these were intended for circulation and publication, and possibly for contemporary audiences as well as 'future generations'. A mixture of memoir, history and autobiography, they convey – and surely were meant to convey – a clear image, or rather over the half-century they were written, images, of the king. Though they have received no critical attention, the writings of James II need to be considered as representation: that is as self-publicization and advocacy as well as source material for the king's life and reign.[3]

The problem that immediately arises is that James's original memoirs have been lost, and are believed to have been burned during the French Revolution by Madame Charpentier, wife of an emissary of the Benedictine Order of Paris, who feared that the volumes would incriminate her. It would seem to be an insurmountable problem. However, in the century or more before their destruction, these memoirs were seen and used by a variety of actors and scholars, including James II and his son themselves, some of whom claimed to be reproducing them, at least in part, in the original words. It appears that from the beginning James used editorial assistants, among them his first wife Anne Hyde and Dryden, to help turn his notes, often hastily taken amid events or battles, into an official memoir or narrative.[4] Probably on his father's death in

1701, his son commissioned a formal life to be prepared from the papers. Though James himself had by warrant dated 24 March of that year entrusted the originals to one Lewis Innes (or Louis Innesse), principal of the Scots College in Paris, the task of writing the life was assigned on royal orders to William Dicconson, a clerk at St Germain.[5] From early in the eighteenth century, therefore, there were at least two versions of James II's memoirs: the 'originals', themselves a mix of notes, some almost a continuous narrative, others only disconnected jottings; and the *Life* which was based on them but supplemented and made into a history by the use of other records, including speeches and declarations of the former king. Visitors therefore to the Scots College over the course of the eighteenth century would have had access to both James's 'originals' (some holograph, some revised by others) and Dicconson's *Life*. Most importantly, they were used by Thomas Carte, the Anglican historian, Jacobite sympathizer and biographer of James, Duke of Ormonde, who had planned a study of James's reign, and by Charles James Fox who researched in Paris towards a full study of James II which proceeded only as far as his *History of the Early Part of the Reign of James the Second*, published in 1808, two years after his death.[6] Both Carte and Fox evidently had access to and used both James's original writings – or at least the fair copy of them by Dryden – and Dicconson's *Life*, and would have been able to have made an exact comparison and assessment of the relationship between them.

Though if they did so, they made no effort to distinguish the manuscripts, another figure did. In 1775, James Macpherson published his *Original Papers Containing The Secret History of Great Britain, from the Restoration to the Accession of the House of Hanover to which Are Prefixed Extracts from the Life of James II As Written by Himself*.[7] In this work, the author claimed to have used James's own memoirs and published fragmentary extracts as the prefix to his *History*. Macpherson, however, was a scholar of dubious repute who in 1760 had claimed to have discovered fragments of epic poetry relating to the legendary Fingal and Ossian, which in fact he had forged.[8] His claims about James's memoirs have therefore been treated with scepticism, and Winston Churchill for one (in his *Life of Marlborough*) asserted that Macpherson had seen only Dicconson's *Life*.[9] However, comparison of Macpherson and that *Life* reveals considerable discrepancies, leaving at least the possibility that on this occasion Macpherson had faithfully reported and in part reproduced some of James's memoirs. Though in using Carte's notes, Macpherson sometimes disrespected the antiquary's distinction between the *Life* and the memoirs (perhaps Dryden's version), he evidently used both as well as transcripts of his own, and John Miller concludes that 'the standard of editing and degree of authenticity of the extracts … are much higher than his dubious reputation would lead one to suspect'.[10]

Early in the next century, the story and text of James's *Life* returned to royal hands. During the Napoleonic Wars, the Prince Regent, later George IV, bought from the estate of the Duchess of Albany, a descendant of the Stuarts, a copy of Dicconson's manuscript that had originally belonged to the Young Pretender. The prince commissioned an edition of the text and appointed as editor the naval chaplain and biographer of Horatio Nelson, James Clarke.[11] Unlike earlier scholars whose interest in the memoirs was as source material, Clarke focused on the text itself, and endeavoured to check its provenance. Though his edition is essentially that of Dicconson's *Life*, Clarke prints the marginal references to what are thought to be the original papers used to construct the narrative. What his edition made manifest was the extent to which Dicconson's *Life* was cobbled together from very different originals, produced for different purposes. At the core were undoubtedly James's own writings, with other works brought in to supplement them, bringing us back to the problem of what was James's own, and how he wanted to present himself.

The edited manuscript provides the most extensive marginal references for the period up to 1660 (with continuous pagination), from 1678 to 1685 (with frequent notes to 'original memoirs tomes 7, 8 and 9'), and correspondingly few for the period thereafter.[12] This is not in itself certain evidence for Dicconson's own editorial practice, but it is suggestive; and, at least for the earliest part, we are able to check the *Life* against an independent and unimpeachable source. In 1695, Cardinal de Bouillon, meeting with James II at St Germain, asked the king whether he could provide him with a record of his service in the French armies under the command of the cardinal's uncle, the Vicomte de Turenne. James replied that he had already written his memoirs of these experiences and offered to make extracts from them and have them translated into French for Bouillon.[13] On 27 January the next year, he fulfilled his promise and presented the manuscript. However, he had originally thought of translating only those parts of his own memoirs that concerned Turenne in Bouillon's manuscript is found a certificate signed by five members of the Scots College at Paris where James's papers were deposited which states that 'these memoirs . . . conform to the original English memoirs written in H. M's own hand'.[14] In 1954 the Bouillon manuscript was discovered in a private collection in France and edited by A. Lytton Sells. Not only does this provide us with an authentic account by James himself; the very close approximation, in many places identity, between the Bouillon manuscript and Dicconson's *Life* proves that, for this period at least, the *Life* was not only factually based on James's original memoirs but that it is largely the king's own narration.[15]

At the other end of the spectrum of James II's life, another independent source comes to our aid. During the last decade of his life, in order to advertise his faith and to strengthen converts, James compiled devotional papers. Some are included in Dicconson's *Life*, as edited by Clarke. But in this case the original manuscript escaped the destruction of the French Revolution. Preserved by James's grandson, Cardinal Henry Stuart, the papers were purchased in

1842 by a priest from Drogheda and were edited for the Roxburgh Club by Godfrey Davies in 1925.[16] These alone survived in James's own hand and in their original form and offer some indication of his (random) working methods at this stage of his life. Once again, too, the manuscript presents an opportunity to check Dicconson and 'as the two sources match up very well', we have reason to believe that here, as with the earlier military memoirs, Dicconson closely followed the original memoirs.[17]

What we can begin to suggest, then, is that, at least where the king's originals were full, the *Life* very probably gives us not only their sense but the royal words. Though for the period 1660 to 1678 we have no such check, and the sparsity of marginal references in Dicconson's originals might indicate a stronger editorial hand, we should not assume that here the *Life* departs from James's own materials. Miller, cautious in his use of the *Life*, conjectures that this period was covered by volumes 4–6 of the nine volumes of memoirs which James wrote.[18] Clearly James kept memoirs of some sort for the period after 1660. Moreover, the suggestion that the predominance in the *Life* for these years of the third-person pronoun indicates the loss of James's own account is complicated, to say the least, by Innesse's statement that 'in the original Memoirs His Majesty speaks always of himself in the third person', and that it was only in the 'copy of M Dryden he is made always to speak in the first person'.[19] What seems most likely is that, other than the full account of his naval victories, James's interest in the memoirs flagged, and he left the details of political developments to others. In other words, the deficiencies of the record as a source may speak not only to James's priorities but to the image of himself that he was most anxious to convey: that of a prince skilled in arms, courageous yet chivalrous and merciful.

Indeed, whatever their (considerable) value as evidence for the life and times, James's memoirs, the devotions and indeed Dicconson's *Life* all await study as texts of royal representation. The form and fate of the manuscript suggest that James not only attached great importance to his memoirs, but that he at some point intended them for publication – and probably originally in his lifetime. We may as historians be frustrated by what appear to be in part informal jottings, scraps and occasional notes, but we should note that James went to great lengths, as his own memoirs relate, to secure his papers. His resolution to flee his kingdom having been taken, 'there was nothing His Majesty was more in pain for than to save his papers or memoirs of his life from whence all that is material in this account or relation of it is in a manner taken'.[20] Fearing for his life, he had only just time 'to thrust them confusedly' into a box which he entrusted to the Count de Therese, the Duke of Tuscany's envoy, who transported it to Leghorn and then France.[21] Moreover, whatever the status of their contents, the nine volumes of memoirs were, as we know from Charpentier, bound in leather and embossed with the royal arms – which may suggest

psychological connection between writing and regality, as well as their importance in the king's mind.[22] In 1696, when he presented a translation of his
campaign memoirs to Bouillon, James specified that they should not be shown
to any during his lifetime.[23] But whatever discretion dictated in the condition
of exile, secrecy had evidently not been part of the king's original purpose in
compiling. Bishop Gilbert Burnet recalled in his history of his times that as
duke, James had 'kept a journal of all that passes, of which he showed me a
great deal'.[24] References throughout the memoirs, either directly to the reader
or that imply concern for readerly comprehension, indicate that James wrote
for an audience from the outset.[25] And in a letter of 1740, Thomas, the brother
of Louis Innesse, and his successor as principal of the Scots College, informed
the secretary to James's son that, the originals had been perforce hastily assembled – 'written upon paper of different sizes such as his late Majesty had about
him or at hand during his campaign' – but in 1686, Dryden 'the famous poet'
transcribed a neat copy, which James then checked and corrected, ready for
publication.[26] Innesse adds: 'There are besides some other marks upon this
copy of Mr Dryden by which it would appear A.D. 1686 when it was making
ready for the Press and probably it had been published, if the unhappy
Revolution had not soon after fallen out.'[27]

The assumption that the famous poet Dryden was the laureate's son Charles,
who was just twenty in 1686, must be erroneous. Rather James entrusted to an
established and loyal Catholic laureate the honour and important responsibility of rendering in clear prose narrative the memoirs for which he had twice
risked his life. The use of Dryden as editor as well as scribe nicely returns us to
the complexities of the memoirs and to Callow's sage comment that 'commentators have been led astray in searching for a complete, authoritative and original text which was authored solely by James'.[28] As we have learned, from the
case of Henry VIII onwards, royal 'authorship', like most forms of royal representation, was the work of many hands; not until long after James began his
memoirs was there any statutory notion of authorial copyright.[29] What James
did, however, was to supervise and finally authorize Dryden's version. If the
king took such pains to preserve and prepare for publication the memoirs of
his life, they must have an important place in our essay on his self-presentation.

What was their purpose or role in constructing and disseminating an image
of the duke and then the king? The text of the *Life* states unequivocally that the
memoirs would be a model for future princes and a monument for a king who
displayed resignation while a subject and moderation as a king.[30] But this was
clearly a (probably posthumous) afterthought. To gain some sense of James's
own self-representation, we must return to the memoirs themselves, especially
those where we can be most confident that we have his own words. The
passages of James's early life may at first seem of little relevance to the representation of his kingship, but if, as is likely, what we have in the *Life* was based on

the Dryden version of the memoirs, then the narrative of those years is that which James later, in 1686, approved as the record of his youth. There is little doubt that what he records offers insights not only into the formation of his character, but also into those qualities he came to regard as essential for strong and effective monarchy. The *Life* begins with an act of defiance against Charles I, which had obvious personal resonance for the nine-year-old prince. James in 1642 had been sent to Hull; when Charles I came to join him and to take charge of the town and its arsenal, Sir John Hotham closed the gates against his sovereign.[31] James's personal safety was not in question – he was released to join his father – but the incident was formative. James observed that Hull should have been taken by surprise and that this first blow to the royal cause in the civil war was due to irresolution and ill management. Whilst the ordinary soldiers had not been ill-intentioned, a failure of leadership squandered an opportunity. By contrast, when the nobles rode to their sovereign's standard at York, James took it as a sign of 'what might be performed when men well born and rightly principled undertake to serve their prince with diligence'.[32] From these opening moments of the war, James's record of events is dominated by the detail of military engagement (especially Edgehill), in observations on 'the natural courage of Englishmen', or brave deeds, but also on opportunities lost for lack of daring.[33] James praises his father's personal bravery, but hints at a criticism of the king's reluctance to take Prince Rupert's advice after Edgehill to march on London.[34] Indeed, whether they reflect views he held (precociously) at the time or those he formed later, James's memoirs manifest his own clear views on military tactics and his contempt for those who, by disobeying an officer or by unjustified fear, compromised a victory or diverted vital resources. The implication of all is that the civil war could and should have been won. When it was lost, the young duke kept a 'settled resolution' not to disclose his cipher when interrogated by his jailers; and then by ingenuity (he pretended to play in 'the childish sport' of hide and seek) he effected his escape.[35] Within a day or two of reaching Paris, he heard the news 'of the most horrid murder of the king his father; and what impression that made both on the queen and the duke may be more easily imagined than expressed'.[36]

Like Edward VI's chronicle, James's memoirs hide emotion in order to represent the writer as in command of the passions, strong and regal.[37] James contrasts the treatment he received by Parliamentarian custodians in England who denied the young boy even the company of his dwarf and threatened him with the Tower, with the hospitality of the French who bestowed on him 'all the majesty due to his quality'.[38] The memoirs portray James as one who, knowing that he was a subject, was always ready to obey his brother's and mother's commands (even when he was inclined otherwise) and as a prince with a clear understanding of the symbols of protocol.[39] When ambassadors from England were received at The Hague, not wishing to add any validation to an illegitimate regime by his presence before regicides, he withdrew for days to Breda.[40] James was sure of the natural authority of regality and had a sense that the common people knew it too. Though, after his brother's defeat at the Battle of Worcester and flight from Cromwell's Ironsides, James experienced 'dreadful apprehension for the King', he knew that God watched over his lieutenant on earth, and that Charles's escape was literally 'miraculous'.[41] Even after regicide, James believed in the natural and divine authority of kingship, but more than ever he believed in the need for decisive action.

Shortly after Charles's defeat at Worcester, James, Duke of York, enlisted in the French army under Marshal Turenne; and, as we have seen, his account of these years, which survives in a manuscript independently of the *Life*, was almost certainly his own words. The war memoirs of James II have attracted little attention since they were edited over forty years ago. Some use of them has been made as a record of the campaign, but no commentator has considered them as a text of representation, both of the time when they were written and of the 1690s when James 'translated' them for Bouillon. It has been remarked that, 'entirely free of emotion', the memoirs appear a prosaic catalogue of battles and manoeuvres. Despite disparaging comments made about his prose, James attempts to enliven bare military chronicle with anecdote and arresting episodes and the memoirs are clearly concerned both with audience and readership and with values and ideas.[42] For all that they may seem detached from politics, we must recall that the campaigns in which James was enlisted involved a civil war in France in which the princes threatened the survival of the monarchy there, no less than it was under threat in England.

James's contempt for the rebels in France is not disguised. He maintained a soldier's respect for enemies who fought for their country, but those who rose against their monarch, on whatever pretence, deserved only odium: it was, he doubted not, the work of God that more Frondeurs than loyalists were killed in a battle.[43] For rebels interposed between a king and most of his subjects in whose loyalty, in France – and England – James believed a good ruler could trust: when, on Turenne's advice, the king and queen risked entry into Paris, as James reports, they were greeted with popular joy.[44] James therefore believed that his commander, Turenne, fought a noble cause; and in these memoirs he emerges as the hero who all but single-handedly saved the French state from ruin, by his skill and ferocity. To James, Turenne 'acquired immortal fame through saving the monarchy several times by his counsel, his conduct and his valour'.[45] Turenne's service, of course, lay most in his military brilliance.[46] But in James's memoirs, Turenne's armies are figured almost as little commonwealths and the commander's role is seen as not dissimilar to that of a prince. Division and disobedience, Turenne and James concurred, were the principal threats to success, which usually followed resolution.[47] Turenne, however, also fully understood his duty always to 'consider nothing but the public good', to care for his men, and, while taking decisions, also to heed counsel.[48] James made especial note of his habit of 'familiar conversation with several officers' whereby 'the General does not only instruct them much better . . . but is ready at the same time to answer any of their objections, and to clear any doubt which may arise.'[49] Effective leadership, care for his charges and counsel were, of course, the qualities of a good king as well as a good captain, so Turenne appears a model for, as well as saviour of, monarchy.

As for James himself, the modesty with which he relates his own role has rightly been remarked; but it should not be exaggerated. James makes clear his pride in being a senior officer and the youngest with such a commission; his own full involvement in the fray and the danger – he was shot in the boot; and his loyal resolute service to two masters, first Turenne, then Don Juan.[50] Nor does he fail to remind readers of his royal status and the respect for regality shown him by friends and even foes. At the siege of Mousson, the governor 'knowing me by my star', evidently his Garter badge, forbade his men to fire; while when he fought with the Spanish forces, his enemies and former French colleagues, recognizing his greyhound, asked to converse with him, which they did for nearly an hour.[51] Subtly, then, James represents himself as a great warrior and a virtuous prince, one who, though for now he fought to save a Bourbon king, was qualified by character and experience to champion the Stuart cause. For all his respect for the civilities the continental armies maintained – perhaps in contrast to what he knew of the British civil wars, he noted that 'I never knew any inhuman act committed either by French or Spaniards all the time I served amongst them' – James pauses in his narrative (as he does often in the *Life*) to praise the courage of the English.[52] England and the fate of his brother (to whom Turenne was to offer military aid) float across the pages of these memoirs.[53] And when they were revised in 1686 and translated in 1695, their advertisement of military training and proficiency, leadership and resolution, were by no means irrelevant to James's circumstances.

We do not know how widely James's memoirs were known during the 1650s. But his reputation as a martial prince trained in the military school of the Thirty Years War, was firmly established; and it was as a military man that James returned to England at his brother's Restoration in 1660. The differences of personality and style of the two brothers certainly owed something to their experiences during the Commonwealth: Charles of military defeat, squabbles in royal councils, complex diplomacy, and the need ever to deploy cunning to keep options open; James's of the battlefield, with its lessons that victory came to the bold and firm. What is more important for our purpose is that in the memoirs in which he crafted his own representation, James chose to highlight those differences and to continue to emphasize, even in peace, his martial prowess.

As we have seen, the memoirs for the period 1660–78 may have undergone a degree of editing that means they must be used with caution. Not least there

is a sense of those being written or rewritten after the event and from a knowledge of what transpired later. Nevertheless, what is evident are James's concerns
and perceptions and his desire to present himself as a loyal brother, and, later,
a fit heir to Charles II. From virtually the time of Restoration, James evidently
had misgivings about aspects of the settlement: the failure to repeal some statutes forced upon his father, the inadequacy of the royal revenue and, most of
all, the neglect of providing the king with a guard.[54] The duke notes, whether
from hindsight we cannot be sure, that those who failed the king in those
respects also caused him to break his solemn word given at Breda that he would
extend liberty to tender consciences.[55] If he held these views, as the memoir
implies, prior to his conversion, we may see James – and evidently he wished to
be seen – as interested above all in the strength of the crown which, he hints,
was not the objective of even counsellors close to the king. Even when first-
person narrative suggests James's originals, the memoirs appear to lose interest
thereafter in domestic events. 'I have not much to say,' he wrote, 'from this time
till the beginning of the Dutch war, all things then continuing quiet, at least in
outward appearance.'[56] James, however, makes apparent that he suspected a
republican plot to destroy the government from early on – one that owed then
nothing to his conversion or imminent succession.[57]

The memoirs come to life when James again has the occasion to present
himself as a warrior, this time as admiral in the wars against the Dutch. The
account details battle tactics, the odds against which his forces triumphed, the
small losses and not only the courage but chivalry of the English who risked
their own safety to save drowning Dutchmen from the sea.[58] In arms again, he
wants the reader to know, James was himself; his zeal to press on being thwarted
by his brother's concluding a peace.[59] Yet even in peace he battled for his
country, having when the Great Fire struck 'no little share of toil and danger in
exposing himself day and night to stop the rage' of the flames.[60] The duke's
bravery, resolution and martial spirit, however, were not shared by all, any
more, he implies, than was his zeal for the service of king and country. The
memoirs seem to conjoin the parliamentary reluctance to vote supply for
continuing the war, the humiliating Dutch invasion of the Medway and the fall
of Charles's chief minister, Clarendon, which James considered an ill precedent
for the crown.[61] As he saw it, a party was resolved on reducing royal authority;
and, significantly, it is at this point that they begin to scheme against the duke
and to promote Monmouth as a legitimate heir.[62]

Two years at least, then, before James discussed with Father Simons his
doubts about a Church of England that he had held 'long in his thoughts . . .
was the only true church', a Commonwealth faction, or so he believed, set about
dividing the royal family as a device to weaken the crown.[63] In reporting the
death of Henrietta Maria and the visit from France of Charles's beloved sister,
Henrietta Stuart ('Minette'), the memoirs draw attention to the importance of

family and dynastic unity.[64] And, as he relates it, the death of James's own wife, a recent convert to Rome, directed the spotlight to him, and his need, at a time when Charles had no heir, to remarry to secure the succession.[65] From this moment, indeed, James's memoirs seem to present him as a future king, and to set out his agenda for rule. The duke returns to war and the relation of an extraordinary naval battle (Solebay), from which despite their advantage the Dutch did not emerge victorious.[66] He underlines his concern for trade, the 'great interest of England', opposing the proposal that there should be an embargo during the war.[67] And, he believed, that as a prelude to renewed war, it was essential to have 'an union amongst ourselves' which he thought best attained by the Declaration of Indulgence that Charles issued in March 1672.[68]

In James's memoirs, 1672 is presented as, in several respects, a turning point. When, that Christmas, Charles II (whom James implies was himself already a convert) requested him to take Anglican sacrament so as to disguise his faith, the duke replied that he was 'not to be moved in his resolution of not going against his conscience'.[69] His famous quality of resolution, when now moved from the field of battle to the religious arena, also transformed the duke's standing with a parliament which, having earlier rewarded him for courageous service, sought now to remove him from office. From the time his Catholicism became public, the memoirs relate more or less accurately, the duke who had been 'looked upon as the darling of the nation for having so freely and so often ventured his life for the honour and interest of the king and country', was regarded as 'a common enemy'.[70] Nor did James credit his critics with sincerity. The expressed antagonism to 'popery', he believed, was but the stratagem, as it had been before, of those 'discontented with the government'.[71]

From 1672, James's *Life* traces a parallel conspiracy against his person and the monarchy itself by 'the factious party', encouraged now by Monmouth and William of Orange whose ambitions emerged from darkness into view.[72] Against their machinations and shady intrigues, James posits, as well as 'his unshaken courage', his 'Christian patience and magnanimity' as conversion adds fortitude of spirit to his self-image as brave warrior.[73] The revelation, however, of a supposed Popish Plot brought all to a head – and, interestingly, re-enriches James's memoirs, with what was probably a self-contained volume far more detailed than the sketchy account of the years since 1660.[74] From 1678 onwards, James's *Life* highlights the different responses of the duke and the king to crisis. Where Charles took the course of politic concession from the outset, advising his brother of the need to leave, James felt certain – and does not hesitate in his revision to underline his correctness – that concession only fostered more trouble.[75] Yet though he disagreed with his brother, James is keen to demonstrate his obedience, 'never putting his own satisfaction or advantage in balance with his majesty's interests' or against his command.[76] Knowing he had right, and God, on his side, the duke and his duchess left for Brussels, 'to wait there the design of Providence to which they always bore an entire submission'.[77]

In exile, the memoirs claim, James acted as the voice that, opposing less loyal counsels, urged Charles not to temporize, but to be resolute and break the opposition.[78] Offering his life for the king's service – a hint that things might come to armed conflict – James also advised that, if Charles took a tough line, the ordinary people might more likely turn their displeasure on 'those violent members of parliament'.[79] To the duke's regret, however, Charles was 'not yet disposed to follow those vigorous counsels' and moved to buy off his principal opponent, Shaftesbury, by bringing him into his Council – 'a method', James observes tartly, 'which seldom succeeds'.[80] As Charles continued in his 'yielding temper', even to the point of sending innocent men, supposed plotters, to the gallows, James pressed for the deployment of troops.[81] The contrast between the two is made starkly clear. When Charles's illness necessitated James's recall in August 1679, the duke's very appearance, he proudly noted, cowed his enemies: 'for his person always forced an awe and respect from those who were worst affected to him'.[82]

As the memoirs relate the process leading to Exclusion, James reveals his doubts about the resolve of a brother whom he needed to remind of their father's 'mistake in the like condescensions'.[83] Against all, even the horrible charge that he sought to murder the king, the duke stood firm, convinced that the greatest danger to monarchy was, once again, 'want of steady resolutions'.[84] Though he recognized the king's tactics – letting parliament make itself unpopular by extreme measures – James criticized Charles for his failure to see the 'juggling', the politicking of his closest admirers and his mistresses, and the 'dark designs' of Orange.[85] Even when Charles displayed 'unexpected vigour' in dissolving parliament in March 1681 (a course that won him 'exceeding great reputation'), the two brothers held different views.[86] Where Charles, resisting James's wish to return immediately, urged 'patience', James thought his brother's 'excessive love of ease' – another contrast with his own bustling activity – explained the delay.[87] So while James summoned a parliament in Scotland that, under his management, loyally asserted prerogative and succession, Charles dallied.[88] Having triumphed in the northern kingdom, the Duke of York, by a skilful ruse, won over the Duchess of Portsmouth to support his recall.[89] Having shown by example the best course, and again at his brother's side to press his advice, James was at last able to persuade Charles II to act sagely and, trusting that memories of 1641 would prevent most subjects running 'into the same errors', deal with the rebels.[90] Though desperate, the faction planned a last attempt, the Rye House Plot to murder Charles and James; they were defeated and the Stuarts were victorious.[91] Restored to the Admiralty, James, to display his tolerance, married his daughter (Anne) to the Protestant Prince George of Denmark. Charles, meanwhile, happier than at any point since the Restoration, sought (or so James reports) comfort at last in the bosom of the Catholic church, with the assistance of the duke.[92]

What is remarkable here is not the familiar events, but James's gloss on them. Though his portrayal of Charles is affectionate, the king appears as lazy, misled, somewhat naïve, unperceptive and weak. The duke himself, by contrast, is decisive, brave and resolute. These are the qualities he advertised in his military memoirs; in his account of the Popish Plot, he adds to them his (as he sees it) acute understanding of politics: of the interests and intrigues of all the players and of the need to deploy guile and make alliances. Moreover, James does not only present himself as a model of how to behave in a crisis, but as an example of moderation and grace in victory. The *Life* relates how he offered pardon to Shaftesbury if he would return to loyalty; and in Scotland he gave parliament its head to present public bills and country grievances.[93] James's self-portrait, in short, is the image of a good and wise king: not a bigot or an absolutist; but an astute, brave man who had saved the Stuart monarchy and the state, just as had Turenne whom he had served and admired three decades before. James's memoirs for those years are an elaborate response to Exclusionists in the form of autobiography. Of course we cannot know how much of the relation was penned in the moment: reference to later events meant that hindsight coloured, and may have shaped, the narrative. However, given the recurrence of phrases and ideas heard in the military memoirs, and what we know from other sources, much of the *Life* may contain James's contemporary reactions to events. What is certain is that in commissioning Dryden in 1686 to prepare a relation for publication, James planned to open his reign with a representation of himself as a true king: a monarch bold and determined, but tolerant and moderate too. It is a self-representation, as we shall see, from which he did not depart.

For the period after James's succession to the throne, the more sporadic references to original memoirs and the text itself suggest that this was a relation heavily edited by, and probably in large part compiled by, Dicconson rather than the king himself. It is of course justificatory; and, written up after 1688, it is concerned with identifying what triggered the Revolution. Nevertheless, not least because they follow from the earlier volume that was desperately close to James's own originals, some themes emerge that it would appear James desired to highlight in his defence: either to his subjects or before the tribunals of God and history.

The first theme that runs through the memoirs of the years 1685–8, as of the Popish Plot, is James's conviction that steady adherence had gained more than temporizing, not least in winning the respect of the people who greeted him with 'such universal acclamations of joy, such inexpressible testimonies of duty and affection'.[94] This belief in the need for steadfastness and resolution is again related to the experience of Charles I's reign, James recalling that 'the yielding temper . . . had proved so dangerous to the king his brother and so fatal to the king his father'.[95] Where the author (possibly Dicconson) seems prepared to concede that prudence might have suggested concessions and negotiations, James's own inclinations were not to budge.[96] Resolution, however, was by no means incompatible with moderation. The *Life* narrates James's early concern to put the people's minds at rest concerning the style of his government, to reassure all-over religion and property, and to continue Charles's tenderness towards his people, even former opponents most of whom were continued in their posts.[97] The *Life* goes to some lengths to distance James himself from the cruelties and severities of Judge Jeffreys: where, it is recorded, the king in London pardoned several of the guilty before issuing on 1 March a general pardon, in the west Jeffreys sent scores to the gallows, 'his imprudent zeal . . . carrying him beyond the terms of moderation and mercy which were always most agreeable to the king's temper'.[98] Though this may have been an editor's *post hoc* defence of the king, the reference to James's mistake in later promoting him as well as the language itself suggest that these may well have been James's views – or at least a view he, as well as a later editor, wished to convey.[99] Moderation and mercy were certainly in his vocabulary of self-representation. So was a concern for the wealth and welfare of the realm and the people. The memoirs record MPs' joy at the king's own references to his 'English heart'; and frequently mention the king's solicitude for the public good, not least the trade which he hoped to engross for the enrichment of England.[100] And finally what emerges from the account of those years is James's belief that liberty of conscience was itself in the interest and for the good of his subjects. James, the memoirs rightly state, believed that consciences should not be forced, and that toleration was both beneficial to trade and to securing peace and unity.[101] Though the *Life* here admits that the exercise of the prerogative of royal indulgence raised discontent, James did not believe that the policy of toleration in itself was unpopular with most; and was so convinced of its rectitude that he reasserted it in the face of Anglican opposition.[102] As for the issue of his own faith, the memoirs completely distinguish James's Catholicism from his advocacy of toleration. And though they present James as making no secret of his worship, they record his surprise and dismay that his word, that he would not force it on the nation or weaken the Church of England, was not trusted.[103] The blame for the mistrust that rendered all his good intentions suspect or odious, James lays not on the people – faith in whom continues to flit across these pages – but on ambitious men who were themselves untrustworthy: ministers like Sunderland, some Anglican clergy, Monmouth and William of Orange.[104] The portrait we are left with of James's three-year reign is of a king, just, moderate, upright and solicitous for his subjects, who was misadvised, poorly served and, most of all, *misrepresented* by schemers who sought to poison his good relations with his people.

We shall have occasion to return to James's memoirs or *Life* for the period after his flight from England.[105] What is worth noting even here is the debt that these records owe to other texts of self-representation, not least those of Charles II and particularly Charles I. James not only knew the story of his brother's escape from the Battle of Worcester and his wanderings incognito and in grave danger before he escaped; he prompted the king to gather his reminiscences into a tale.[106] Throughout the Duke of York's own life, we have accounts of accidents in which he nearly lost his life, and occasions on which his disguise was penetrated and he was forced to trust to the loyalty of a humble subject who proved worthy of the trust.[107] James was evidently not willing to leave to his brother alone an image of adventure, heroism and a capacity to deal with ordinary people. But more, the memoirs owe a debt to the writings of Charles I, not least the *Eikon Basilike*. James's relation, for instance, of the fate that befell Sir John Hotham after betraying his sovereign in Hull echoes the account in Chapter 8 of the *Eikon*, as, more generally does his stand on the integrity of his conscience and intentions, the affection for the king of the people, and the belief in a conspiracy.[108] For the many differences of their faith, James all but repeats Charles I's words when he notes that 'it is not religion they drive at so much as the destruction of monarchy'; and his summoning of an assembly of the nobles in 1688 'in the nature of a Great Council' follows his father's example of 1640.[109] Where James differed from his father, as his brother, was in learning the lesson that concession was treated as weakness and in laying emphasis on military support and loyal officers. When, however, they too deserted, James resumes a role taken up by both Charles I and II: that of the unjustly persecuted divine king who had to place his trust in God, not men. James, or his editor, forged such an image, as we shall see, in exile, where the king's devotions follow the form, if not the faith, of Charles I's.[110] But, even before 1688, the memoirs present James 'in the like circumstances with holy David', as alone in his holy rectitude.[111] Long before he had given up his throne, James was portraying himself not only as the warrior but as the man of conscience who submitted himself to God's providence.

Though he evidently intended to publicize them as a self-representation of his kingship shortly after succeeding to the throne, James's memoirs were not published and we do not know whether, beyond court circles, they were known. Like Edward VI's diary, however, they testify to the king's concern to construct and disseminate his authority in a text, in which selection and narration are determined by his authority (we recall he corrected Dryden's work) and through which clear values and virtues emerge.[112] Whatever their reliability as a historical record, in a study of royal representation, they provide a framework for what must now be the focus of our chapter: the king's self-presentation in public texts, images and rituals, and yet his failure to win the battle for hearts and minds – the contest for representation.

It was, we need remind ourselves, a contest that had begun in earnest from at least 1672. Before then, the image of James had been almost entirely positive. He was known to have been an accomplished soldier on the continent; he was greeted at the Restoration as 'the second glory of our nation'; he rendered noble, some thought glorious service at the Battle of Lowestoft where he stood at his command while the blood of the dead beside him splattered over him.[113] Though he also had mistresses (a sin to which the memoirs refer and for which he later expressed penitence), James was never pilloried as a whoremonger and was probably more popular than his brother a decade after Restoration.[114] Two factors transformed his public image: his public conversion, and, as importantly, his emergence as the likely heir to the throne. Had Charles had legitimate issue, James's faith would have remained, if not a private, at least not a prominent matter. From the early to mid-1670s, a party concerned by Charles's foreign policy, policy of toleration and the prospect of a popish succession, systematically set out to render the Duke of York anathema. Others, as we have seen, in Scotland and in England, in panegyrics and ballads, continued to praise 'Royal Jemmy' and to view him as a fit successor to the throne.[115] James, and his Catholicism, came to personify all the divisions of the nation: over religion, foreign policy, the powers of the crown and the sanctity of hereditary monarchy. When Charles, who had for long endeavoured to heal or surmount those divisions, threatened to be deluged by them, he threw in his lot with a party. And in the struggle that took place, the king and the Tories – just – won. Charles, however, knew that the realm remained polarized. For all the paeans to his divine rule, after the Popish Plot he sought a retreat (in Winchester) away from a capital the loyalty of which he did not cease to distrust.[116] If he were already a committed Catholic, he felt the need to keep his faith private. James was faced then, as his brother had been in 1660, with the challenge of presenting himself to divided subjects, but subjects now whose differences had refashioned political life and were embedded in a culture of rival Tory and Whig publications and plays, coffee houses and societies. It is too simplistic to conclude from the outcome that from the outset he failed to meet it.

II

Immediately on the death of Charles II, James made a declaration to his Privy Council. 'I have,' he acknowledged, 'been reported to be a man for arbitrary power', and he added, 'that is not the only story that has been made of me'.[117] In reality, he assured them, he intended to follow his brother in his clemency and tenderness towards his people and to preserve the government in church and state as it was by law established. James reassured his auditors that 'I know the principles of the Church of England are for monarchy and that the members of it hath shown themselves good and loyal subjects and therefore I shall take care to defend and support it. I know likewise that the laws of England are sufficient to make the king as great a monarch as I can wish. And therefore as I will never depart from the just rights and prerogatives of the crown, so I shall never invade any man's property.' As an opening address, it was a masterstroke. The new king acknowledged the criticisms and representations made of him by others, and in the language of their own concerns, re-presented himself as a man of moderation, while leaving the Tories in no doubt that, whatever his Catholic faith, he knew his interest lay in alliance with them. It was probably more because the Council saw the value of publicizing the royal words than from any distrust that they requested James print his words – which he readily did.[118]

Indeed, James repeated them soon afterwards to his first parliament that met on 11 May 1685. The new king had, it seemed, managed the assembly in Scotland to good effect and the acclamations of joy at his succession led him to expect a loyal parliament in England. For all his scattered comments about the emptiness of oratory, James carefully crafted his opening speech to MPs. God, he reminded any still inclined to question his legitimacy, had brought him to 'peaceable possession of the throne of my ancestors'.[119] On succeeding, his first thought had been to call a parliament so that his reign might begin as he meant it to continue, 'easy and happy for you'.[120] What he had told the Privy Council, James repeated and amplified. Members of the Church of England had 'showed themselves so eminently loyal in the worst of times, in defence of my father and support of my brother of blessed memory, that I will always take care to defend and support it'.[121] Reprising his words about government, prerogative and property, he reminded them that 'having here before ventured my life in the defence of this nation, I shall still go as far as any man in preserving it in all its just rights and liberties'.[122] The repetition was unequivocal. James reiterated words that were not 'spoken . . . by chance', but the words of a king that might be relied upon as a 'promise solemnly made'.[123] It helps to understand how James perceived later events to note that in his view a royal promise given commanded reciprocity: trust, service and support.[124] Cleverly James argued the need for the maintenance of the customs revenues paid to his brother (the benefit to trade, the navy, the monarchy and the realm) whilst rhetorically denying the need to argue: 'I am confident your own consideration of what is just and reasonable' will effect all.[125] More than niggardliness, he promised, generosity would incline him to call them often. Then, after honeyed words, James informed them of Argyll's rebellion and declaration charging the king with tyranny. After his declaration to Council and parliament, that could only appear all the more outrageous and James knew that his trust in their support against the traitors was well placed.[126] It was an excellent opening address: the house, having cheered throughout, at the mention of a traitor cried out 'Long live the King' and voted all Charles's revenues to his successor.[127]

When he next addressed the house on 30 May, James kept up the mood of harmony and reciprocity. Silent on a petition proposed by a Commons committee requesting the persecution of all non-conformity, James thanked the house for its supply and added, in a gloss worthy of Queen Elizabeth, 'I assure you the readiness and cheerfulness that has attended the dispatch of it is as acceptable to me as the bill itself'.[128] Confident, James even requested extraordinary supply: to pay Charles's debts, provide security and equip the navy, 'the strength and glory of this nation'.[129] In tones of rousing patriotism, the former Admiral of the Fleet assured them: 'I have a true English heart as jealous of the honour of the nation as you can be; and I please myself with the hopes that by God's blessing and your assistance, I may carry the reputation of it yet higher in the world than ever it has been in the time of my ancestors'.[130] Supply, James told them, was not for his private good but for the public and would be used with good husbandry for the purposes he had outlined. It was a speech that could not be – and was not – denied. James had strengthened the loyalty of the English Tory parliament with skilful oratory and tact.

Nor, though absent, did he neglect his Scottish parliament, to whom, on 28 March he wrote a letter that was read at the opening of the assembly the next month. James, again skilfully, thanked 'our ancient kingdom' for the loyalty it had shown Charles and him 'when amongst you' and which, he trusted, it would confirm now, in the wake of 'fanatical contrivances' of wild traitors.[131] For, he reminded them, nothing more sustained their properties and privileges than royal power, which he intended to maintain in order to protect their rights and religion that were threatened by Argyll and the rebels. In his following speech, expounding on the king's words, Lord Commissioner Queensbury continued the flattery of the Scots by pointing out that on the very day of his coronation in England, James was 'no sooner placed on the throne of his royal ancestors than he inclines to have your advice', confident that it would be for his good.[132] Queensbury repeated the royal promises about preserving religion and property and added that the king would readily assent to bills for the public good and the improvement of trade. Now it was for parliament to strengthen the monarchy with action against conspiracy and supply freely given in the knowledge that what was granted was bestowed on the king, but for themselves.[133] As he sat, the Lord High Chancellor rose to underline the obligations Scotland owed to a king who as duke had found them in disorder and division but through 'easy, gentle ways' had established peace and unity. In particular, he called on 'honest Scotsmen' to suppress Covenanters and support a king saved by providence and equipped to rule by experiences of hazards and conflict, courage and industry, clemency and sobriety.[134] The parliament vowed to serve and maintain the honour of the king's 'sacred person'; Argyll was swiftly suppressed.[135]

Much had happened before James met with his first, and as it turned out his only, parliament again. When he re-summoned MPs to Westminster for November, James had faced Monmouth's rebellion and the 'bloody assizes' had despatched scores and hundreds of his supporters.[136] Clearly James hoped and felt that treason might, in England as it had in Scotland, reinforce the loyalty and compliance of MPs. After the storm, he told the house on the 9th, 'I am glad to meet you all again in so great peace and quietness'.[137] But, in contrast to Argyll's revolt, Monmouth's had not been swiftly suppressed. Reflecting therefore on the risks to his safety and that of the realm, and manifesting his 'concern for the peace and quiet of my subjects', James argued the inadequacy of the militia and reported that he had increased the number of troops to safeguard him and the country, for which he now sought supply.[138] Though such a move flew in the face of England's long trust in a (local) militia and detestation of a standing army, James, as a military man, appears to have anticipated no real opposition.[139] Where he did foresee criticism was over his appointment, in breach of the Test Act, of some Catholic officers on whose loyalty he knew he could rely. Though some, he knew, would seek to make this an issue, he believed that his good understanding with parliament would prevent any opposition, especially as he renewed his promise to venture his life, if need be, for the safety and interest of the country.[140] It was a speech of an entirely different order to that of the spring: as well as to concerns about a large army, James seemed insensitive to the persecution of the Huguenots in France, and the fear that would be excited by Catholic officers.[141] And he said nothing on this occasion about the laws or the church. It is likely that, having been startled by Monmouth's easy advance and then having triumphed through God's protection, it seemed to him so right and sensible a course that it needed no argument. As probable is James's belief that, having given his solemn promise to preserve the church and law, he should and would be trusted. If so, within twenty-four hours, he was disillusioned, as the house refused to vote supply before enquiring into the king's measures.[142] A brilliant beginning to the reign had been squandered, not only by James's actions but by a more combative mode of address that failed to calm anxieties. The king took no opportunity to speak to his MPs again.

James's frustration at the response to his speech may have been compounded by a declaration that he had issued to the people in August, the first of several addresses directly to his subjects in which the king sought to present himself as what he had announced to his council: a protector of the laws and liberties of the nation. The king announced that he had found it necessary 'for the preservation of the peace of this our kingdom' to maintain an army.[143] But to ensure that no disorders occurred and that subjects had no cause for complaint, the declaration ordered troops to pay for all provisions and announced that no subject was to be compelled, or threatened, to quarter soldiers in private houses without consent. If the declaration revealed a commander's understanding of the hostility that undisciplined troops could evoke, it was silent on the army itself and on its Catholic officers, despite the rumours that were beginning to circulate. It was not simply that James had an autocratic temperament and sense of his authority. The welcome he had received (not least in response to his early promises) had led him to believe that his people knew that he intended no programme of Catholicization or absolutism and that it hardly needed reiterating; it did.

Forced, however, by mounting opposition to his policies and from a church whose unqualified loyalty he had counted on, James, like his brother, came to use declarations as a means of appealing to the people (whom as his memoirs reveal he had always trusted) and as a platform for explaining his intents. The first, and most famous, is *His Majesty's Gracious Declaration to All His Loving Subjects for Liberty of Conscience*, published in April 1687.[144] Here, James returns to an understanding of the need to explain and argue as well as to assert. Through reminding his subjects of God's favour to him, His preserving him and bringing him to his throne 'by a more than ordinary Providence', James did not simply claim divine authority.[145] Rather he explained an 'earnest desire . . . to establish our government on such a foundation as may make our subjects happy and unite them to us by inclination as well as duty'.[146] The means to such unity and love, James discerned, was a grant of toleration, to which he cleverly linked 'the perfect enjoyment of their property' that (he noted) 'has never been in any case invaded by us since our coming to the crown'.[147] Explaining his antipathy to constraints on conscience in a language of national interest, James catalogued how intolerance discouraged foreigners, depopulated countries and damaged trade. Worse, as the history of four reigns made manifest, persecution secured neither unity nor peace. To those with scruples about such a use of royal authority, James communicated his confidence that what he did out of affection by prerogative his next parliament would ratify by law. Reassuring those who feared other motives that he adhered to his promise to protect the church, he sensibly added the specific guarantee that he would preserve all in their properties 'as well as church and abbey lands', the estates of the dissolved monasteries, 'as . . . any other'.[148] If the suspension of the Test Acts raised concern about Catholics, in the declaration's promise of pardon to all nonconformists James sought wide support and popularity which, other circumstances being different, he might have secured.

Though his Declaration of Indulgence, read in some circles and represented as a subtle device for Catholic proselytization, only added to his troubles, James apparently did not (and his memoirs confirm the impression) lose his faith in the people or in his capacity to persuade them of his true intentions for their welfare.[149] On 27 April 1688 the king issued a further declaration aimed at correcting and countering misrepresentations of him that he believed had eroded the people's support. Beneath the royal arms, the declaration opens with both assertion and yet persuasion. 'Our conduct has been in all times,' James declares, 'as ought to have persuaded the world that we are firm, and constant to our resolutions.'[150] Since, however, 'crafty, wicked men' had set out to abuse the people, the king announced that his intentions were unchanged from 4 April of the previous year; his declaration for liberty of conscience he now reissued. Then glossing his own earlier words, James claims both his impartial application of and the popularity of the indulgence, witnessed by 'multitudes of addresses' from subjects.[151] Restating some of his earlier beliefs that toleration might help his kingdoms towards 'commanding the trade of the world', James sought to explain his need to employ about him only those who shared his belief in it and his care 'for the general good of the whole kingdom'.[152] Finally, in an appeal to his people to 'reflect on their present ease and happiness', James stood on his record that was quite at odds with how others presented him. Reappropriating traditional metaphors to validate himself and to demonize critics, he closed: 'We have not appeared to be that Prince our enemies would have made the world afraid of, our chief aim having been not to be the oppressor but the father of our people.'[153] Then, fulfilling an earlier promise, the king announced his resolution to call a parliament, which he hoped might disperse the 'private animosities' that alone threatened the nation's happiness.[154]

Later events have completely overshadowed this royal declaration. Those events, however, may offer some testimony to what supporters believed and what opponents feared was its polemical effectiveness. A broadside defence, for example, analysed the declaration clause by clause and, mocking the critics who spread rumour of a design to bring in popery, argued that a true representation of it showed the king's aim as only 'the enlargement of his people's happiness'.[155] Those who opposed the royal injunction being read from the pulpit, the pamphlet parries, feared that in dispelling 'prejudice', it would strengthen support for the king, not least from the forthcoming parliament. Though partisan, the author may have had a point. Those clergy (they were a majority in London but they may not have been in the country) who refused to read it were not only reluctant to endorse it but were perhaps also concerned at the extent of support for the policy from dissenters.[156] Whatever his feelings about his authority and right, James was taking his case to the people, and any who recalled the recent events of 1681 must have wondered whether, in the end, the people would not prefer to trust the king, as he was asking, than risk the alternatives.

Because James at least made that calculation, he continued the firm resolution he had always advocated with words and measures intended to gain or cement popular support. On 8 September 1688, for example, the king, reacting to abuses arising from the quartering of soldiers, repeated his declaration of 25 August 1685 and strengthened the procedures of complaint, giving authority to civilian magistrates (the JPs) as well as army officers to deal with abuses.[157] On the 21st, as an invasion from Holland was expected, he issued a broadside declaration, the page topped with the royal arms in a Garter inscription and bearing the motto 'God Save The King'.[158] Announcing that he was issuing writs for the parliament to meet in November (and so proving good to his word of 27 April), James expressed his hope to establish toleration by statute and to reaffirm the church by confirming the Act of Uniformity. To leave no doubt of his good faith, 'and to remove fears and apprehensions', the king offered the extraordinary concession of disabling Catholics from serving as MPs.[159] Whether or not it expressed a desperate attempt to re-secure Tory support (and the adherence to indulgence throws doubt on that), James was not only re-presenting himself as a king who 'will always take care of his people', he was publicizing his commitment to established (parliamentary) courses and his willingness to respond to concerns. Though we cannot gauge how the declaration was received, those who were in league with William of Orange were not prepared to risk losing a war of words.

William's invasion, however, by no means put an end to the contest of discourse. As we shall see, William took great pains over how he presented himself in words and symbols; and it is likely that he, and those who invited him, intended that the army itself be used more as a show of force than for actual battle.[160] Nor did James, though a soldier, underestimate the need for words as well as troops. When the first copies of William's carefully crafted manifesto were discovered at the end of October, James, as well as fortifying his garrisons, issued another (counter-) declaration.[161] Published, again as a broadside, on 8 November, the declaration condemned the invasion in emotive language as an assault on the bonds of religion, nature and family: 'We cannot consider this invasion of our kingdom by the Prince of Orange without horror, for so unchristian and unnatural an undertaking in a person so nearly related to us.'[162] Playing the patriotic card, James warned of the 'mischiefs and calamities which an army of foreigners and rebels must unavoidably bring upon *our* people'.[163] Cleverly acknowledging the 'plausible pretences' in his declaration, James subtly re-invoked the spectre of Oliver Cromwell in revealing Orange's real design as one of usurping the crown, as was evident in his adoption (like the Protector) of a regal style. Only 'immoderate ambition', the Faustian quality in all rebels, explained the prince's actions and his questioning the legitimacy of James's prince and heir, sent by God's providence. Orange's statement had promised that he would submit all to a free parliament. But James, who we recall had recently issued writs for one to meet that month, endeavoured to turn it against him, observing – and again the memories of Commonwealth parliaments destroyed by the New Model Army are prompted – that 'nothing is more evident than that a parliament cannot be free, as long as there is an army of foreigners in the heart of our kingdoms'. By contrast, the parliament

James had summoned, though now obstructed by Orange, was (it was claimed) indeed free and the king, he now announced, had restored all borough and corporation charters and privileges to ensure free elections and to provide the sovereign with an opportunity to heed and respond to the grievances of his 'good subjects'.[164] As well as their duty of 'natural allegiance', such considerations, James expected, would lead most subjects to join him in suppressing the invasion. Though brief, in repeating assurances about religion, liberties and properties, making new concessions, anticipating a parliament, and portraying Orange as a Machiavel, James attempted to publish a skilful riposte that sought to unite – his use of inclusive pronouns is noteworthy – 'our' people against the foreigner. The crowds who greeted him when he later returned to London suggest that it did not entirely fall on deaf ears.[165]

By the time James's declaration was published, William had landed at Torbay and attention turned to tactics. But plans to take the campaign to the enemy failed as officers and troops deserted, and William marched on London with little opposition.[166] James, remembering the fate of his father, having sent his wife and son ahead of him, decided to flee. After one failed attempt, he escaped, to the relief of William who helped to arrange it, from Rochester, but not without pausing, amid the turmoil, to pen a final declaration on English soil, to which he hoped he would before long return.

Apprehending that his departure (significantly he uses the word 'withdrawing') might weaken his position, James published his *Reasons for Withdrawing Himself from Rochester* on 22 December. Cataloguing William's actions (such as imprisoning his messenger) as 'against the practice and law of nations' and hinting at a possible design to murder him, James condemned Orange's words as no less violent in denying the legitimacy of his son and making 'me appear as black as hell to my own people'.[167] Though brave (James reminded his subjects of how he had ventured his life on several occasions), the king – in the very language the Whig polemics were using – wrote of precious liberty, to preserve which he was forced to remove himself. To withdraw, however, was not to desert the people but to be free to serve them, 'to be within call whensoever the nation's eyes should be opened, so as to see how they have been abused and imposed upon by the *specious pretences of religion and property*'.[168] James hoped for and awaited, unlike William he implied, a 'legal parliament' which might serve what he now describes, shifting the emphasis from Catholics, as 'liberty of conscience for all Protestant dissenters'. Far from seeking to advance popery, the king hoped only that 'those of my own persuasion' (he does not use the name Catholics) might live in peace 'as Englishmen and Christians' rather than being compelled, as the king himself now was, to leave the country they loved. Once again asserting his conviction that toleration might make England great, James hints at the Dutch commercial rivalry that may lie behind opposition to him: 'some of our neighbours dread it'.

Whatever historians have written of his autocratic temperament, in this, as other declarations, James argued, 'appealed' and conceded; and he cast himself as the guarantor of freedom, law and peace. Had he dared to remain and met the parliament to which he could have addressed these words in person, it is not at all clear that he would have failed. Instead, as we shall see, James continuing to argue his case from exile, at least made it more difficult for his Orangist and Whig opponents to secure legitimacy.[169] Had his speeches and declarations not, in important respects, appeared to be undermined by his actions – and indeed by other representations – they might have been more effective still.

Certainly James paid more attention than had his predecessor to royal proclamations not only as an instrument of government but as a vehicle of communication and representation. And though not as long as many Tudor or early Stuart texts, James's proclamations echo with the rhetoric of public welfare and the common good. Royal proclamations prohibiting the export of English inventions, such as a knitting frame, or banning the import of cheap foreign wares (such as needles and buttons) that undercut domestic products, rehearse the 'royal intention to encourage manufactures' and to promote the trade and wealth of the realm.[170] Similarly, decrees dealing with social dangers or ills announced the monarch as the caring father of his people. James, the proclamations inform subjects, attended to the regulation of hackney coaches and the trade in selling insurance policies to remove inconveniences and abuses 'for the benefit of our subjects'.[171] Proclamations banning wool exports and promoting tillage by duties on imported corn demonstrated 'our own princely care for the welfare of our kingdom'.[172] In such proclamations, the king often advertised his listening and responding to grievances brought to his attention by subjects, as he also frequently mentioned the advice of his Privy Council which, as the mark of a good king, he had sought and followed. Indeed, James's proclamations represent him, far from his historical image, as a moderate and merciful prince. Though, naturally, they call attention to the king as God's chosen protected by his providence, James goes to lengths to persuade his subjects of his good intentions and good government. In the wake of rebellions in Scotland and England, proclamations announce royal indemnity and pardon, to manifest that clemency which 'has shined in the whole line of our royal race'.[173] Indeed, in a rhetoric that endeavoured to sustain a discourse of unity and harmony, James, expressing belief in the love and loyalty of most subjects, commiserated with those few who were 'drawn and seduced' into rebellion 'by the subtle and crafty insinuations of some ill-disposed persons'.[174] Long before crisis overtook him, James in a variety of proclamations, sought to persuade his people of 'the benign influence of our most clement government' and of 'our fatherly care of the peace, quiet and prosperity of all our subjects'.[175] Echoing that of his father, his proclamation announcing the queen's pregnancy gave thanks not only for God's favour to the royal family but for a 'public blessing' which promised 'great security of peace and happiness to this kingdom'.[176] Royal proclamations of 1688, therefore, though they perforce responded to extraordinary circumstances, did not mark an abrupt shift in James's language of self-presentation. Announcing the expected invasion on 28 September, James, as he had in 1685, cast the rebels as a small cabal of 'restless spirits' with 'desperate designs', who, despite the 'former intestine distractions which should make us value peace', to further their ambitions were prepared to deceive the people and embroil them in war.[177] Though he had been offered foreign aid to repel the invaders, James announced that he had declined it, choosing to 'rely upon the true and ancient courage, faith and allegiance of our own people, with whom we have often ventured our life for the honour of this nation'. Against enemies who expected a realm divided, James presented, and in uniting tried to reinforce, a people united behind him. Even as, to deprive the invading army of provisions, he gave orders to remove livestock from the coasts, he made sure to clarify his 'will and pleasure that the respective owners may suffer as little damage and loss as may be consistent with the . . . public safety'.[178] And, as only days before his flight, he announced a parliament to meet in January, James's proclamations for pardon and free elections anticipated, it claimed, 'the reconciling of all public breaches'.[179]

However his proclamations were received, James, far from deploying a divisive rhetoric, clearly sought – and, as importantly, laboured to represent himself as seeking – the unity and love of the people. Few of his royal proclamations are concerned with religion, and of those that are, several prescribed services of thanksgiving for victory over rebels, or for the king's birthday in which all were to join in 'demonstrations of joy'.[180] Official services devised at royal command and prayers prepared with royal approval had been throughout our period, and especially since the reign of Charles I, important occasions and texts for the broad representation of the ruler as godly prince and Supreme Head, sometimes for polemical ends.[181] Here then we might expect the Catholic James to use an established genre to promote his faith and in the prescribed services he authorized texts from which we can perhaps trace the alienation of the king from his people. The new king was certainly quick to revise and publish 'by his majesties special command' forms of service and prayer, in the first year of his reign. As he declared in the preface to a new service of thanks for the end of rebellion and for the Restoration, the form of the day's worship on the death of Charles was 'necessary to be altered'.[182] The alterations, however, announce no major changes. Prayers give thanks for the deliverance of the realm, from the 'unnatural rebellion of . . . ungodly men' and for God's providence which restored the king and along with him – significantly – 'true religion and worship'.[183] Though the new prayers had the congregation promise their dutiful allegiance to God's servant now reigning over them, there was no departure in that. Similarly, in the prayers he commended for victory over Monmouth's rebellion, while reference was made to a 'deluge of sects and heresies', the theme of the service was the blessings of 'a quiet and peaceable life'.[184] Indeed, so little did James depart from Anglican tradition at this time that in the services for 5 November, prayers still give thanks for the deliverance of James I and the royal family from 'popish treachery', as well as for the preservation of James II.[185] In December 1685, James personally revived, as his preface indicates, the service of commemoration for the succession of the monarch which had been interrupted by the death of Charles I and, amid prayers for his long reign and the obedience of his subjects, the congregation prayed that the new king may 'be always a religious defender of thy holy faith and church'.[186] As the service of 30 January would have reminded all, that was the Anglican faith and the Church of England.[187]

James issued no controversial prayers before the last year of his reign in England. The service he ordered for 12 September for 'the prosperity of the Christian arms against the Turks and especially for taking the city of Buda' was an oecumenical text that enjoined prayers for all Christian princes and governors joined in concord against the 'abominable superstition' of the infidel.[188] Only in the summer of 1688, and then surely without a sense of their reception, did a royal service turn out to be a spark for a conflagration, and then the occasion could hardly have been more traditional. The thanksgiving James commanded for the safe delivery of his queen and birth of a prince praised God for the blessing he had given the royal family in granting their 'hearts desire' and the nation in the gift of 'stability . . . the thing O God, that thou hast wrought among us'.[189] Thanking the Lord for his protection of the king, the service offered prayers for the long life of the prince, his preservation for the happiness of the nations, and the establishment of the Stuarts for ever.[190]

James's apparently sincere belief in the love and support of his subjects has been described (rightly as events were to show) as naïve. But at least as far as his addresses to his people are concerned, he had been as good as his initial promise. Other than his commitment to toleration which he appears (whatever his opponents claimed) to have held as a sincere principle (though he disliked them he objected to the religious persecution of French Huguenots) and argued for in a language of trade and national interest, it is hard to find in his speeches, declarations or prayers obvious Catholic discourse or advocacy.[191] The textual representation of monarchy, however, was not the work only of the king. We must therefore turn to those who wrote his kingship, in panegyric, pamphlets and histories, and to the tropes deployed in figuring and supporting the new reign.

III

James II's succession and then coronation were greeted by a flood of verse panegyrics. Though they were anti-Exclusionist and anti-Whig, there was no evident outpouring of Catholic paeans for the new reign. It is too simple even to describe the poems as Tory. After 1682, at least on the surface, a majority of the nation had appeared to welcome Charles II's victory or at least the re-establishment of peace after the threat of renewed civil war. With a new king, and queen, most hoped to bury the recent past, to enjoy continued peace and perhaps greater unity, and to see the nation advance in glory abroad and prosperity at home. As rightful successor, a Stuart, a monarch who promised to continue his brother's mode of government in church and state, who was brave and virtuous, James (at least initially) appeared to fulfil all the hopes and desires of the nation.

Three years after the defeat of Shaftesbury, the memories of Exclusion were still powerful, and they were dramatically revived in the rebellion of the Duke of Monmouth in June. But, at least in so far as poetry reveals the mood of the nation, there was apparently no appetite for reviving other claims to the throne. In his pindaric ode on the coronation, for example, John Wilson, the loyalist playwright and son of an archdeacon of Exeter, announced, with pardonable exaggeration, 'Ev'ryone/Has washt his Hands of *Your Exclusion*'.[192] Where the Tory Aphra Behn might not surprise us with her attack on the 'stiff neck'd crew' who by their 'blind Sorcery' had tried to keep James from the throne, even the ex-Whig Elkanah Settle, in a heroic poem on the coronation, dismissed the 'Republic owles and Bats of Night' dispelled by the 'ravishing scene' of James's arrival.[193] In his monument to the late king, dedicated to James, Thomas Otway imagined a painting of Charles, with his brother by his side, dispelling the furies of treason.[194] As for Monmouth, elegies on the duke after his execution compared him to Icarus and other over-ambitious subjects 'who durst against the best of Kings Rebell'.[195] One poem believed his rebellion might complete the nation's happiness by entombing faction itself with the duke, as 'Heaven and Great JAMES' restored 'sense' to the nation.[196]

James was lauded in 1685 as a Stuart. *A Loyal Tear Dropped on the Vault of . . . Charles II* celebrated James as brother to that illustrious prince, as son of Charles the Martyr and as one who ascended the throne 'by an unquestionable right and lineal succession'.[197] Tracing that succession further back, Wilson thought he saw the shapes of Henry VII, the founder of the Tudor dynasty, and Henri IV (the first Bourbon king of France) in James.[198] Most panegyrists, however, were content to emphasize more immediate Stuart descent and the intimacy between James and his brother, John Crowne comforting himself for the loss of Charles by the knowledge that 'He lives in Royal JAMES, they both were one', and by a sense that 'SUCCESSIONS golden Chain' would now in 'These Floating Isles for ever fix't remain'.[199] Indeed, even beyond adhering to his brother's good courses, James was represented in many verses as the hope of and means to a renewed unity in the nation that might erase the names and bitter invectives of party. A pindaric verse prognosticated that James 'will the

Great Healer of our *Breaches* be', while R. Mansell's poem on the coronation hoped that the '*Healths* crown'd with *Huzzahs*, heals each factious Wound'.[200] The viper of sedition having been trampled, others looked to James as another St George, the symbol of a nation, not a party.[201] *A Loyal Subject's Loving Advice* prayed 'God Bless King JAMES, and all Dissensions Cease/That we at last may have Eternal Peace'.[202]

After all the republican theory of the Exclusion crisis, during his last years, as we saw, Charles II was heralded again in sacred language as God's lieutenant.[203] And from the moment of his succession, James too was greeted as a divine ruler, singled out and preserved by God. In his *Humble Offering*, the poet John Phillips asserted, as though it were no longer disputed, 'Sovereign Kings are our Terrestrial Gods'; though absent from England, as he imagined the coronation, Edmund Arwaker saw the 'mystick oyle prepared' to anoint a sacred monarch – an 'earthly GOD' in Aphra Behn's words.[204] Now, the hazards he had run and setbacks he had suffered were read as making James a part of God's providential design. Poets, recalling his being saved from shipwreck on a voyage to Scotland or from the plot to murder him at Newmarket, represented him, like the Messiah, as 'a Sacred Promis'd Prince', 'A Prince, in whose each Act is clearly shown,/That Heaven design'd him to adorn a Throne'.[205] Under such a prince, England might again become 'another Eden', God's promised land.[206]

A rhetoric of promise and rebirth suffuses the paeans to the coronation of James and his queen. The election of 23 April, St George's Day, as coronation day not only invoked the nation's saint and the spectacular coronation of Charles II on that same day a quarter century before, the date enabled a language of spring, sun and regeneration that, though traditional, was applied to James's particular circumstances. Like spring, James was depicted as God's gift and light after a season of storm and darkness.[207] 'See', one poem on the coronation summons readers, 'where Great JAMES our second Sun does rise'.[208] Sun imagery – not uninterestingly at a time when Louis XIV had established himself through a programme of representation as 'Le Roi Soleil' – pervades the verse of Phillips and Behn, and James is figured as 'the Monarch of the Day', the king who ruled like nature and 'with one united Ray'.[209] Under James, poets foresaw Britain 'wake' to a new age, 'the Blest Golden Age again'.[210] 'From this coronation,' one author spoke for the nation, 'He our lives renew'.[211]

Nothing in this verse speaks directly of James's Catholicism, any more than does his own textual self-presentation. Most of the authors were not Catholic, but Anglicans or even Quakers.[212] And in so far as the religious issue that had nearly destroyed the monarchy resurfaced, it was – at least in these poems – neutered by James's promise to, like his brother, protect the church. The author of *A Loyal Tear* quietly affirmed that all might rely on the king's word when it came to religion, but, lest others were inclined to doubt it, the anonymous author of *Suspiria* spelled it out:

Away Suspicion! Here's the Royal Word;
What greater surety can Mankind afford?
That Publick-Sacred-Obligation binds
The Royal Breast to leave things as he finds.[213]

James's own speech to his Council and parliament, published to the nation, was echoed in verses that reminded readers how the king 'declares He will/Press narrowly, His Predecessor's Ways Supporting, Church and State establish'd still.'[214] Because kings were like gods, 'what they do say/Is like the oracle'; because, they argued, nothing James had said raised doubts, the predominantly Tory panegyrists urged trust in his promise to be 'Our Faith's Defender and our Liberty'.[215]

Rather, James had many attributes and virtues that made him a fitting subject for praise. The reputation for bravery and martial accomplishment, to which the king himself so frequently alluded, was often rehearsed in laudatory verse. Aphra Behn recalled for readers, in an address to the monarch, 'Your *Glorious Deeds* in arms when yet but Young'.[216] John Wilson celebrated the succession of a king of military prowess; a 'congratulatory poem' dwelt on the more recent 'naval victories'; and John Baber's poem greeted a sovereign who was 'Admiral . . . no less than king'.[217] His military and naval record and accomplishment rendered James, in verse, as the hope of a new imperial sway – at which he had himself hinted in arguments for the promotion of England's trade. A poem that linked James II to the first of his name who 'joyn'd the kingdoms' to forge 'Great Britain's Glory' may have anticipated a new empire under British rule.[218] Dryden certainly foresaw 'a conquering navy proudly spread' in the new reign; songs published in 1685 and 1686 had James as 'the ocean's lord' outvying all Europe's monarchs; one poem celebrates in its title the 'All Conquering Genius' of James II; Behn explicitly addresses the king as 'you, oh sacred Sir, for Empire born'.[219]

Panegyrists were as concerned to advertise James's clemency, tenderness and justice as his militarism, and to present him as the nurturing father of the realm. Perhaps recalling James's own early acknowledgement of a reputation for absolutism, the author of *Suspiria* assured the nation that, despite the death of Charles II, there would be 'No Inter-Regnum of that/Clemency/Which sav'd three kingdoms from a fatal Yoke'.[220] The new monarch was, *The Poets Address to King James II* claimed, aptly 'surnamed the just'; and his royal justice was merciful.[221] In Baber's poem, though a prince of justice, James, who as duke had been (the feminine noun reinforces the gentle regimen) a 'True Mother' to his country, as king 'To Us a Father's tenderness he shows'.[222] James's own representation of himself as moderate, as a lover of law and freedom, is supported in a range of verse, some published after Monmouth's rising and the harsh suppression of the rebellion.

In view of later events, and even of the anxieties that had surfaced during Exclusion, it may surprise us that of the many virtues for which he was praised, James's marital status and (as was hoped) fertility were prominent. The new monarch's coronation, along with that of Mary of Modena, was the first double coronation of a husband and wife since the reign of James I. And, not least after the sexual profligacy and unhappy, barren marriage of the previous reign, the opportunity to celebrate the royal couple was readily taken. 'In History it never did appear', a poem on the coronation vaunted, 'where King and Consort better coupled were'.[223] In another poem the couple are presented as 'This pair of Suns, their double deity'.[224] And, as in the reign of Charles I and Henrietta Maria, the apparently happy royal marriage lent support to a representation of the larger marriage between the king and the realm. As the lines of Settle's *Heroic Poem* on the coronation put it:

> . . . 'tis Britannia's Sacred Nuptial Day
> The Royal Bridegroom puts the Diadem on,
> And Weds a Kingdom when he wears a Crown.[225]

Not least in the context of a spring double coronation and a language of (re) generation and renewal, poets expressed their hopes of progeny that would secure an heir and Stuart succession. 'May your God-like Persons', Baber prays for the king and queen, 'many more/Years Reign together, than ye liv'd before':

> Our Hopes are great, but I should little say
> of Sons, from you, which shall great *Britain* sway.[226]

In *Tears Wip'd Off* or *The Second Essay of the Quakers by Way of Poetry Occasioned by the Coronation of James and Mary*, W. P. [William Penn] prayed for the king and his consort:

> That God would great Increase unto 'em give,
> That a long Race of Kings might them survive
> That from their Loyns a Prince of Wales may come,
> To Conquer Foes abroad, win them at home.[227]

The last line reminds us that there were still 'foes', opponents of the king, in what remained a divided polity; but initially it was panegyric that dominated the succession. After 1685, however, panegyrics, as is often the case, began to fade as succession and coronation gave way to the ordinary business of government. Whether in James's case, Tory poets began to feel disenchanted, from a sense of hopes dashed and promises not kept, and retreated into silence, we cannot be sure. But, such as it is, the evidence does not unequivocally support such a hypothesis. In 1687, for example, an edition of *Aesop's Fables* by Aphra Behn wrote the moral tales as stories of the 'false ambition' of a 'young usurper', a thinly veiled reference to Monmouth, and as a lesson in the ills of rebellion and the benefits of Stuart rule.[228]

The year 1687 saw yet more audacious and more controversial verse apologia for James II: an anonymous pindaric poem *Upon His Most Sacred Majestie's Late Gracious Indulgence*, and another better known fable of power, John Dryden's *The Hind and the Panther*.[229] In a preface to the first, the author acknowledges controversy, that the Declaration of Indulgence published in April 1687 'has been a subject sufficiently bandied about by all parties', but feels that it was appropriate that the indulgence had 'a poet's talent in its praise'.[230] Opening with an allusion to James's defeat of the rebels, 'returning from the conquer'd coast', the poem introduces 'the noblest Monarch . . . that th'English Scepter e'er did sway'.[231] As the lieutenant of providence, James, in these lines, stands guard over a people living 'with Plenty and Delight'.[232] To destroy England's peace, the devil endeavoured to plant discord in the familiar form of religious divisions, fears and recriminations – the clarions of rebellion. 'Now', however, 'no more shall that ill-boding sound . . . Our happy Isle confound'.[233] By his indulgence, the poet claimed, James had united the people in 'one inclosed Paradise'.[234] Although, the poem runs, the sway of the English monarch was divine and absolute, James believed that the conscience should be free not forced. So that, as he had vowed, he gave authority to the church, and he gave 'free Liberty . . . That all Religions may live', securing for the realm harmony and peace.[235] In establishing the 'sweet calm' of peace, the pindaric verse figures James as another Augustus whose 'goodness is almost too great for to be prais'd'.[236] The text itself, printed for J. S., offers no clues as to authorship. However, despite its welcome support for monarchy, the writer seems no friend to the Church of England with its 'partial laws', 'engrossing' of 'publick Priviledge and Right'.[237] Whilst the figuring of Christian conversion as the slow 'yielding sense' rather than the assault on the will may imply some antipathy to Calvinism, there is no firm indication of Catholic sympathies.[238] The poet appears rather to write from painful memory and experience of civil war and republic and a desire to remove religion as a pretended cause for conflict 'in this loose unquiet age' than from any clear denominational advocacy.[239] James is lauded as a fit lieutenant of God, 'the Prince of Peace'.[240]

The Hind and the Panther is the work of a (by now) avowedly Catholic poet as it is very likely that Dryden converted in 1685. He was charged with opportunism but his conversion probably owed as much to his own reading and reflection as to the succession of James II.[241] The poem is complicated in itself and its performance in the historical controversy it invokes and enters is neither simple nor easy to determine. Part II, rehearsing Reformation debates over the authority of Scripture versus tradition as well as passages about the eucharist and transubstantiation, suggests the laureate's dialogue with himself, and the careful weighing of theological and historical arguments before conversion. But this is in every line a public, indeed a polemical text that makes myriad direct references as well as gestures to recent and contemporary events and debates. *The Hind and the Panther* speaks for, respectively, the Catholic Church and the Church of England, and follows their relationships from the Henrician Reformation to the moment of writing – Dryden informs us that the royal declaration appeared just two weeks before he completed the poem.[242] Throughout their discussion, the relations between the two beasts remain civil. The Hind offers the Panther hospitality and at the close bestows on him 'the peace of heaven' and the two eschew, for the most part, 'sharp debate'.[243] But both speak forcefully and neither persuades the other. What has united them for long, and what is a clear theme of the poem, is a firm belief in the authority of monarchy. In the first part, the sects are castigated for fomenting civil war, regicide and anarchy in church and state. While their origin is traced to Protestantism and the Reformation, the Church of England itself is spared the vitriolic satire reserved for those wolves and bears that devoured all noble crea- tures. It is their attitude to monarchy that begins to divide them in the third part of the poem, in which both beasts review the fortunes of their faith and co-religionists in the reign of James II. The Panther articulates the concerns of the Church of England and in a sub-fable of the swallows implies that, with a monarch of their faith on the throne, the Catholics might attempt to extend their sway and to usurp Anglican positions and privileges. The Hind, whose own modest abode lends strength to his argument, answers that the Catholics sought no such aggrandizement. In his own counter-fable, of the pigeons, he accuses the Anglican clergy especially of misplaced envy and points up the absurdity (and hypocrisy) of their inclination to dispute with a king whom conscience bound them to obey. It is James who is, as it were, the hero of the poem, the Adam whose reason surpasses that of all brute beasts, and who offers the best prospects for peace and harmony. Evoking James's military and naval reputation, *The Hind and the Panther* yet presents the king as a moderate man who sought the good of *all* his subjects. Whatever fears some had harboured, on his succession, the poem observes, James did not repeal the Test; and, true to his promise, he preserved the Church of England in all its authority and property. Nor did he endeavour to proselytize. All he insisted upon was that his co-religionists, indeed all who believed differently from the Anglican faith, be free of repression and persecution. For the church to oppose him in that was not only to renounce the duty of obedience but to squander the prospect of peace among Christians.

The Hind and the Panther, written over the winter and spring of 1686/7, speaks to circumstances very different from the panegyrics of only a little more than a year earlier. A reminder of the divisions hardening beneath the surface of panegyric, the rhetoric of unity gives way in this poem to sharp disputation: to a world, as the address to the reader puts it, in which 'all men are engaged either on this side or that'.[244] Here already the laureate fears that the discontented within the church might join forces with dissenters and even seek to supplant the king with another 'high potentate' invited 't' accept the government'; and the warning against such courses is clear.[245] In the end, however, Dryden's purpose, 'in the body of the poem' as he tells us, is the averting of confrontation.[246] Through discussion, the Hind and Panther try to dispel the misrepresentations of their respective faiths, that Protestants were radical sectarians or that Catholics were ultramontane Jesuits. The poem is positioned against extremes and the swallow and pigeon fables offer each party counsel about avoiding them. Though a Catholic poem, as well as the work of a Catholic, in the end Dryden's fable is 'aimed only at the refractory and disobedient on either side'.[247] Like James II's, Dryden's belief in toleration is expressed not as a Catholic interest or device, but as rational principle and 'the spirit of Christianity'.[248] England was dividing, but its laureate had not surrendered hope that indulgence 'being granted to all the sects' might be received 'thankfully' as 'from a Christian king, their native sovereign'.[249]

As King James ascended the throne of his brother, prose authors were as forward as verse panegyrists in loyal support for the monarchy in general and James in particular. The path to a smooth succession was prepared virtually from the defeat of the Whigs; and the attempt on the life of the Duke of York as well as the king at Rye House caused a swell of public support and sympathy for both.[250] Indeed, a life of James published in 1683 reads almost as a campaign document for his succession. *Some Historical Memoires of the Life and Actions of His Royal Highness, The Renowned and Most Illustrious Prince James Duke of York* presented him as, in every respect, an 'inestimable treasure' of the realm.[251] Here was a future ruler who, brave and victorious in wars, 'valued not his life as too dear to purchase honour and safety for his king and country'; a prince of 'mercy and bounty' loved by the people of Scotland and, until a mad folly overtook the nation, of England; and heir apparent again welcomed back to London with acclamations of joy after the rage had subsided.[252] Lest any remnant of opposition should rise to question or limit James's kingship, treatises restated the divinity of regality and the rights of kings. The year 1685 saw the republication, for example, of *The Excellency of Monarchy* originally published in 1658 'for information of the miserably misled Commonwealthsmen' concerning the religious and rational foundation of kingship.[253] And the next year, dedicated to James II, Nathaniel Johnston's *The Excellency of Monarchical Government* reviewed the attributes and benefits of regality and 'the inconvenience of commonwealths'.[254] Lauding just monarchy as 'like the Sun [that] ever dissipates all the mists', Johnston, rising to hyperbole, claimed that English monarchy exceeds even the ideals of Utopia.²⁵⁵ And, having demonstrated the evils of sedition and of the libels that fed it, Johnston underlined the duties of subjects to obey, pointedly arguing that 'religion qua religion should neither influence the succession nor their obedience'.²⁵⁶ In 1686 Edward Pettit issued a second edition of a work first published two years earlier, *The Visions of Government wherein the Antimonarchical Principles and Practices . . . Are Confuted*.²⁵⁷ With a new preface written in the wake of the Western Rebellion against 'the monsters of the age', the book presented a series of visions condemning fanatics, conspirators, libellers and rebels, and praising English monarchy and the rule of Charles and James.²⁵⁸ 'God be thanked,' the author concluded, 'the government is so well settled under our most gracious sovereign King James the Second and the high court of parliament . . . that, relying on his royal declarations . . . we may have reason to hope that there will be no fanatics left.'²⁵⁹ Though, after the defeat of Argyll and Monmouth, James's reign seemed securely settled and fewer defences of monarchy appeared, some apologia for royal power were published throughout the reign. At least until 1687, James did not want for authors willing to extol his authority and right.

As well as treatises on kingship, histories wrote James II into the continuities of the past, both English and imperial; and historians presented a gallery of glorious English monarchs to support James's lineage and right and to highlight his virtues. Joshua Barnes's *The History of that Most Victorious Monarch Edward III*, licensed by authority and dedicated to James, associated with the founder of the Garter and glorious victor in war a monarch who manifested 'the lively resemblance of all those virtues which he so eminently possessed'.²⁶⁰ Towards the end of his reign, defenders of James endeavoured to sacralize the king by associating him with England's only saint-king, Edward the Confessor. In *Edwardus Confessor Redivivus*, for example, John Gibbon, a herald and antiquary, found 'the poetry and virtues of holy Edward the Confessor reviv'd in the sacred Majesty of King James the II', especially the qualities of piety, justice, mercy and gentleness.²⁶¹ More recent history was also appropriated to support the rule of James. In 1686, Thomas Manningham's *A Solemn Humiliation for the Murder of Charles I* reiterated, as a whole series of 30 January sermons continued to do, the doctrine of non-resistance; and the next year a second edition of *The Works of Charles I, With His Life and Martyrdom*, with a large royal arms facing the engraved oval of the martyr, clearly associated James, as he did himself, with his father's cause and right.²⁶² More recent history yet re-emphasized the lessons of civil war and the benefits of monarchical, that is Stuart, rule.²⁶³ As his own monarchy became less popular, supporters of James even called to memory the happier history of his own first entry onto the throne. Francis Sandford's richly illustrated history of the coronation of James II and Queen Mary was published by 'his majesty's special command' in 1687.²⁶⁴ A full and lovingly detailed account of the preparations and preliminaries, the rooms, tapestries and regalia, the symbols and ceremonies and the processions that together made the coronation, Sandford's volume provided a massive testament to the historicity and sanctity of monarchy at a time when some were beginning to question it. As his preface to the king put it, this literal souvenir of, this act of remembering and commemorating the coronation, magnificently displayed 'the boundless antiquity of your imperial descent, through so many ages, the splendour of your kingly progenitors . . . and all these transcendent blessings and advantages made yet greater by that series of miracles that have been still wrought in favour of your Majesty's life and government; in despite of all practices and conspiracies against your person.'[265]

Perhaps even in 1688, as troubles mounted, the author of *The Historian's Guide: or Britain's Remembrancer* yet hoped that history and memory might sustain his sovereign. In a text that, if the title page is to be trusted, went to several impressions, the author charted all events 'worthy notice' from 1600 to the time of publication.[266] Coming to James's reign, the chronicle traces from 'the coronation of their sacred majesties', the just fates of rebels, the smooth course of government and acts of royal beneficence up to 'his majesty's gracious declaration to all his loving subjects for liberty of conscience'.[267] Ending with the royal summer progress, on which he 'met with very dutiful acknowledgements in all places' and the king's dining at the Guildhall with the newly appointed mayor, *The Historian's Guide* suggests a peaceful regimen and popular king – which was already far from the whole story.[268] History and memory were soon to become the battlegrounds of Whig, Tory and Jacobite as they fought to have the past serve their cause. For much of his reign, however, historians had been the allies of Stuart monarchy and protagonists of James's right to rule.

Given the breakdown in their relations that precipitated his downfall, we should note how for much of the reign none spoke in support of James II's kingship more frequently and insistently than the clergy. From the very first Sunday after his brother's death on Friday, 6 February, sermons across England and in Ireland and Scotland lauded the new king and preached the duties of obedience to sovereign authority. In Suffolk, for example, the rector of Worlington, Erasmus Warren, preached on *Religious Loyalty, or, Old Allegiance to the New King* in a sermon on Proverbs 24: 21 ('My son, fear then the Lord and the King . . .').[269] Reminding his congregation of the Tory axiom that 'Kings [God] affirms to be Gods on earth', Warren identified 'true loyalty' as the 'true religion'.[270] Recalling James's deeds of bravery for the nation, he praised him as a king who would protect the people, their religion, laws, liberties and property: 'he is,' he closed, 'father of his country', so people should banish 'all unreasonable doubts with all . . . fears'.[271] In Dublin, the Bishop of Cork enjoined the flock to peace, obedience, and trust in the king's word which, he assured them, was worth a thousand times more than any other's.[272] In his sermon at Leicester,

Benjamin Camfield, rector of Aileston, as well as asserting the 'compact and agreement of society to be subject to kings', expounded his text (2 Chronicles 13: 5) to emphasize the rightful succession and to praise the son of the martyr and faithful brother to Charles II, who had given his word to protect the Protestant faith.[273] Not far away in Market Harboro, the minister Thomas Heyrick sought specifically, as he told the Earl of Rutland, to reassure the congregation concerning the change that had taken place. 'God,' he preached, 'stamps something great and excellent on the souls of princes', so the people could trust all to God and to a king protected by God who had assured his people that he would not violate their faith or liberties.[274] 'We have,' he told the flock using a metaphor that evoked a succession of Protestant princes, 'another phoenix sprung out of the ashes of the former.'[275] 'What,' he asked, 'may we not hope for from the son of a martyr?'[276] The murmurings and anxieties to which Heyrick alluded were addressed directly in John Curtois's sermon delivered at Branston near Lincoln and published as a discourse showing that kings had their authority from God.[277] 'What if,' the rector raised the question on many minds, 'our king should actually endeavour to destroy the religion that is now by law established?'[278] His answer was intended to be unequivocal: 'it is an unseasonable question now', for, he assured them, God whose providence should not be questioned had ordained the Stuarts to govern and James had given his word, of which 'a distrust would be an odious suspicion of his want of the sense of conscience and honour.'[279] The 30 January sermons delivered a week before the succession were, when published, issued with prefaces to make the same points: the duty of obedience to a king who was the son of the martyr and who had sworn to continue the religion of his father.[280] Dedicating his sermon to the king himself, Dr Benjamin Woodroffe, praised a monarch who had 'carried the glory and terror of the English nation to the remotest parts of the world', and predicted ' 'tis only treachery . . . can disturb your Reign.'[281]

The sermon delivered at the royal coronation on St George's Day took as its text the theme of continuity. Preaching on 1 Chronicles 29: 23 ('Then Solomon sat on the throne of the Lord as King instead of David his father'), the Bishop of Ely, Francis Turner, presented to the congregation a king whom 'I presume to style . . . the very similitude and picture of Charles the martyr.'[282] Countering any remnants of a belief that the throne of England might be (as ironically it not long after turned out to be) elective, Turner argued that God gave kings their title and right and that the happiness of the people depended on their recognizing it. For where other nations had been embroiled in wars, for want of a clear title, in England none could 'pretend such a successive title to his estate as his majesty can show to his crown.'[283] Moreover, in James, England had a sovereign bred in affliction, one who 'understands . . . that in a hereditary monarchy tis the great peculiar advantage of the prince as well as people that their interest is one and the same.'[284] With the king having given his word and the first months of his reign happy, Turner asked all gathered at Westminster to give 'strict adherence . . . to your oaths of allegiance' and to honour and obey their sovereign.[285]

The church's willingness to trust in James's word and to reinforce his king-ship with the underpinning of Tory political theory was if anything enhanced by the rebellions that threatened the new reign. Argyll's rebellion clearly provided a backdrop to some of the sermons preached on 29 May to commem-orate the Restoration. Delivering the sermon for the day at Norwich Cathedral, for example, William Jegon preached on the 'damning nature of rebellion' and the 'unlawfulness of resistance', presenting James as a worthy successor to the late king they had lost.[286] After the defeat of Monmouth's rising, the day estab-lished to give thanks for victory over the rebels (26 July) offered a platform for a series of loyal sermons extolling James's rule. Edward Pelling's sermon at Westminster Abbey on Psalm 124 set out a theme that was to be reprised around the country: the deliverance of David and a second providential pres-ervation of the crown 'as it had been before in the Restoration of the prince himself'.[287] Answering the fear rebels had fostered that a prince of another communion might seek to alter religion, Pelling recalled James's solemn assur-ance, now manifested by 'real demonstrations of his sincerity'.[288] While in the same spirit at Oxford, Charles Allestree, as well as attacking Monmouth directly, celebrated the first half year of James's government which had fulfilled all the royal promises, at Newbury, the rector John Hinton returned to the story of Absalom and Achitophel to damn rebels and praise God for his deliv-erance of David.[289] In the capital, at St Margaret's Fenchurch Street, Thomas Wagstaffe denounced the rebels as 'state atheists' and, coupling 'our religion and our king', urged that all give thanks for the king and parliament and 'let not a mutinous and ungovernable thought be found among us'.[290] Meanwhile at the geographical centre of Monmouth's bid for the throne, in the west, in the parish of Up-Lyme, the minister Charles Hutton, in a sermon published as *The Rebels Text Opened*, thanked God for the miraculous defeat of a large army of rebels by a handful loyal to James who 'fought from heaven'.[291] Finally, in Exeter Cathedral, one of the prebendaries Thomas Long, preaching on rebellion as the sin of witchcraft, gave thanks for God's rout of the rebel host, and for the security of the monarchy: 'The king,' he declaimed, 'hath another glorious inauguration, the crown being a second time fixed on his head by God's own hand: the church appears fixed on that rock, against which the gates of hell cannot prevail'.[292]

The honeymoon between the Catholic James and the Church of England outlasted those early weeks and months. On 6 February 1686 a series of sermons offered thanks on the anniversary of the king's succession to the throne and the texts that have survived suggest no obvious disenchantment or retreat from the loyal support of Stuart monarchy. To take a couple of examples, at York Cathedral, William Stainforth, a canon, describing monarchy as most like heaven's own regimen, argued for the Christian duty of subjection to all princes, while in neighbouring Richmond, Christopher Wyvill outlined the duties all subjects had to esteem and honour the king who had been saved from 'that black bill of Exclusion'.[293] In London, at Bow church, Thomas Staynoe reaffirmed the principle of subjection to higher powers and dismissed any claims to withhold that duty from argument of conscience.[294] But a faint sense that such homilies on obedience were now being delivered to congregations growing disaffected is confirmed by a sermon of Thomas Cartwright, a royal chaplain, who explained his purpose as opposing 'those rebellious principles . . . which renders too many among our people . . . unclean'.[295] From the outset, Cartwright's sermon set out to reassure and persuade. 'Do we not,' he asked those gathered in the collegiate church at Ripon, 'enjoy Peace, Plenty and Liberty; nay and the best religion in the world?'[296] Had not God blessed the realm with a prince not inferior to Solomon? Why then, he continued, addressing the mounting unease at the recruitment of Catholics to office, did they murmur if the king 'favour some few of them of whose good services he hath so long experience'.[297] Since James had ascended the throne, he reminded them, 'the ark of God was not shaken, as many feared it would have been'; fears of popery had proved 'groundless'.[298] It was not therefore for subjects to 'call [the king] to account for his religion, nor question him for his policy in civil matters'.[299] The church held a rightful king answerable only to God and, Cartwright insisted, 'our religion will never suffer us to dispense with our loyalty'.[300]

The inaccuracy of his assertion may be suggested by the absence of surviving sermons for 6 February, the next year, for which only Thomas Codrington's sermon before the Queen Dowager on 'the anniversary of his late majesty', Charles II, survives.[301] Codrington, an ex-Douai priest and a royal chaplain, had returned to England from Rome less than two years before and was attempting to introduce into England an institute of secular priests, with the assistance of Cardinal Howard.[302] Though in Scotland, John Mackqueen was still, on James's birthday, damning fanatics and celebrating the peaceful reign of a king to whom the church owed loyalty, in England the only sermon that remains for the same day is that preached to the king and queen in their Catholic chapel at St James's.[303] Much of the text sounds familiar: the description of kings as 'a sacred race', the injunction to loyalty and the curse on Absaloms who tried to subvert the rule of God's chosen.[304] But the preacher now was not a pillar of the church of which James was Supreme Head, but William Cuthbert Wall, a Benedictine monk.

From the moment of his succession, James made his word the representation of his rule. Although a Catholic, he promised that he would uphold and do nothing to undermine the Church of England. Until he issued his Declaration of Indulgence in April 1687, nothing he said or wrote broke that promise. The king in speeches and declarations undertook no programme or proselytization. And the churchmen, true to their religion of loyalty and obedience, greeted a Catholic monarch with abundant paeans and made lofty arguments for his right and powers in sermons, services and treatises. At least for the first two years of his reign, what James said and wrote neither excited noisy discursive contestation nor seems to have alienated most of his subjects. If, then, we are to understand that breakdown of trust that left James isolated, we must turn to those other modes of representation which figured the king as, increasingly, other than his word: as not the protector of the religion and liberties of Englishmen, but as a threat to them.

CHAPTER 6

A POPISH FACE?
IMAGES OF JAMES II

I

By comparison with that of his father and his brother, the portrait of King
James II is not one that most people today would easily recognize. But if that is
the case, the explanation does not lie in James's indifference to the arts or to
visual modes of representation. As Duke of York, James, together with his first
wife, Anne Hyde, had been an enthusiastic patron of Sir Peter Lely who worked
more for them than for the king. As we have seen, the famous Windsor Beauties
were commissioned by the duke and duchess and were hung, according
to Pepys, in the 'duke of York's room' at Whitehall, before being removed to
Windsor on his succession to the throne.[1] James had also commissioned, to
commemorate his victory, portraits of his flag officers of the fleet at the Battle
of Lowestoft.[2] And, as well as finished canvases, at least three portraits of James,
unfinished by Lely at his death in 1680, were inventoried at St James's Palace
and probably executed for the duke.[3] As monarch, James continued to be an
active patron of artists who had served his brother – Vignons, Gascar, Verelst,
the decorative painter Verrio, Kneller, Wissing and Riley – and he favoured the
French portraitist Nicolas de Largillière and patronized the landscape painter
Jan Loten.[4] In 1688 the king also commissioned an inventory of his pictures
and statues; and, while entries are too brief to identify many of the objects,
headings such as 'A List of His Majesty's Pictures that were not the late King's
in Windsor Castle' and 'Pictures in Whitehall of His Majesty's that were not the
late King's' give some indication of works commissioned by James perhaps
after, as well as before, his succession.[5]

During the long reign of Charles II, the royal portrait evolved in response to
changing circumstances. As we have seen, the early canvases figuring the king
in coronation robes and with the regalia as symbols of restored monarchy gave
way to less formal, more relaxed images, before political crisis revived representations of Charles in state robes and in armour, as the rightful king fighting
to preserve his authority and the succession.[6] Before his succession, portraits of

28 Henri Gascar, *James, Duke of York*, 1672–3.

James, following his self-image and representation, most commonly figured the duke in armour, as military and naval commander.[7] In some of these, begun if not finished by Lely, of James bearing a baton in his right hand, we discern a debt to Van Dyck's portraits of Wentworth and Northumberland as lord lieutenant and admiral respectively.[8] Though very different in style, Henri Gascar's baroque portrait of James as Mars not only presents him, with the fleet in the background, as admiral, but with the armour of Prince Charles or Henry and in a pose with a cane and attendant page that evokes two famous Van Dycks of Charles I (fig. 28).[9] Shortly before his brother's death, James was painted by Godfrey Kneller full length and again in armour with a sceptre in his right hand and the crown and orb on a table or pedestal on his right; behind James's left and right a shield and anchor join the armour to signify military and naval command.[10] Kneller's is a warrior-king, a prince of action. The image of James as duke was martial and dynastic, the image of a warrior and a Stuart. What then of his image as king?

While it is not always easy to date paintings, two canvases unquestionably give us early representations of James as monarch. Presumably on St George's Day 1685, the naval and seascape artist Willem van de Velde the Younger made the graphite and ink drawing of the river procession at the coronation of the new king and queen, perhaps as a preparation for a commemorative canvas, in the manner of Stoop's painting of Charles II's cavalcade.[11] And certainly before she died in June 1685, the artist Anne Killigrew, daughter to Henry, chaplain and almoner to James as duke, executed a full-length portrait of James standing in a glade at the steps of a terrace wearing the badge of the Garter. Beside the king, a stone surmounted with a crown is carved with the royal arms and 'JACOB II REX'.[12] Killigrew had painted James as duke and his second duchess, and her royal portraits evidently made as great an impression as her poetry on Dryden who penned an ode to the young Anne on her death aged twenty-five. She, he praised,

> . . . With bold erected Look
> Our martial King the eye with reverence strook;
> For, not content t'express his outward part,
> Her hand call'd out the Image of his heart:
> His warlike mind, his soul devoid of fear,
> His high-designing *Thoughts* were figur'd there.[13]

In this case, however, despite Dryden's reference to a martial king, Killigrew's pastoral canvas makes a significant break from a military representation of James. Rather, the new king stands in a glade at ease beneath a calm sky, wearing a richly embroidered coat, with only the crowned arms gesturing to his regality. Here, for all the differences of style, Killigrew gestures more to portraits, like that of Charles I (*Le Roi à la chasse*) depicting a realm at peace and effortless majesty.

We have it on good authority that Wissing and Riley painted portraits of James (and his family), however, none of James as king survives in the royal collection or any other major repository, other than in engraved form.[14] And while Kneller, who succeeded as principal royal portraitist, especially in full length, was high in favour with James and Mary, executed state portraits, and boasted that the king and queen sat for him 'about thirty six times a piece', few have survived as paintings.[15] Kneller evidently followed his full length of James in armour, executed just before the succession, with an oval bust.[16] It seems likely that a full length of the king in state robes (which now survives only as an engraved head and shoulders by Kneller's friend and collaborator, John Smith) was the first state portrait that Kneller executed; of the many others the only two that survive, and have been authenticated, belong to the end of the reign, to 1688.[17] The two canvases present James very differently. One, now at

Guyzanze Hall, figures James full length in Garter robes, with both the Garter badge on his cloak and a greater George worn on a chain.[18] As with his left hand the king holds aside his cloak to reveal a finely shaped leg, almost about to step out of the canvas, with his right he grasps the crown on a table beside him, bringing the person and the ultimate symbol of majesty into one. However, again, and significantly, the portrait gestures to a Van Dyck of Charles I in Garter robes, the pose is more animated and the grasp of the crown (that replaces Charles I's hand) is defiant.[19] The other portrait, painted in 1688 and now in Munich, returns to an earlier model of James in armour, with a sword and, grasped with his right but between both hands, a baton of command.[20] Though the portrait is said to have been executed for Pepys, it is likely that James sat for, and approved, this military representation. Whilst we cannot be certain of the exact moments of those images, James's visual self-representation in 1688 was assertive and defiant. As the portraits by Kneller and by Nicolas de Largillière (which became the template for many contemporary engravings) confirm, the predominant image of James as king was, as he constantly reminded his subjects, that of a brave fighter for his country – and for his crown.[21]

While they owe little to the visual representations of Charles II after Restoration, the portraits of James, as we shall have further occasion to remark, do make gestures to images of his father: to both the Van Dycks of the 1630s and the portraits of an armoured Charles I of the civil war.[22] A traditional concern with lineage and dynasty, doubtless sharpened by the threat of exclusion, not only shaped James's own portraits. The king had Gennari complete a Lely painting of his family with his first duchess and their children; immediately after his succession, he sent Wissing to Holland to paint his daughter Mary and the Prince of Orange; James had several portraits of his wife, Mary of Modena, the royal princesses and their consorts (the princes of Orange and Denmark) and a portrait of his brother that were not inherited from Charles.[23] (He was later to have the Prince of Wales painted by Kneller at just a week old.)[24] But lineage and dynasty were not the only subjects of James's patronage. He commissioned and collected naval scenes and other 'sea pieces' by Van de Velde, and landscapes by Jan Loten.[25] More importantly, it would appear that he commissioned a number of devotional portraits which would have done little to assist his subjects who preferred to forget the intensity of the king's Catholic faith.

Though a leading authority has asserted that 'the accession of James II led to no profound changes in the character of painting in England', the religious art did mark a departure from the playful irreverence of Lely's handling of Christian tropes and traditions in the reign of Charles II.[26] James did not embark upon an obviously Catholic visual self-representation (at least not before his flight in 1688); he continued to favour the artists of his brother's reign, Dutch Protestants like Wissing and Kneller as much as French and

29 Sir Godfrey Kneller, *Abraham Simon*, c. 1685–90.

Italian Catholics like Largillière and Verrio. But James's inventory reveals that he owned several depictions of the holy family, saints, some with angels, and Capuchin monks, who, as we shall see, began to be a visible presence at court.[27] Moreover, though they remained only 'a small fraction of his total output', Kneller in James's reign turned his brush to devotional works and in that vein executed for the king some of his most famous portraits.[28] One of these is a large portrait of a semi-reclining male, bearded, and with his right arm across a large folio book (fig. 29).[29] While the figure has been identified as the medal-list Abraham Simon, descriptions of the canvas as the representation of a 'Hermit Saint' or specifically 'St Jerome' appear fully understandable, given the portrait's debt to depictions of that saint with the Scriptures by Pierfrancesco Mola, Rubens, El Greco and others, as well as to the Apostolado recently painted by Carlo Maratta for Cardinal Barberini.[30] Two other Kneller canvases take up the subject of piety and meditation. One, also often mistaken for the representation of a saint (St Anthony of Padua), depicts an unknown Franciscan monk contemplating the cross which he holds in both hands (fig. 30); the second figures one (otherwise little known) Mrs Anne Knight, as Mary Magdalene, with a crucifix hanging from her waist, kneeling in adoration, in an austere setting, before a cross with Christ.[31]

30 Sir Godfrey Kneller, *Unknown Franciscan ('St Anthony of Padua'),* c. 1685. Private collection.

Though these, especially the portrait of Simon/St Jerome, are likely to have been commissioned by the court, we cannot be sure of James's direct patronage. But with the portrait that Horace Walpole considered the best of all Kneller's work there is no question.[32] *The Chinese Convert* was painted for James II in 1687 and placed in the king's Presence Chamber. The canvas depicts Michael Alphonsus Shen Futsung who came to Europe with Father Philip Couplet, Procurator of the China Jesuits in Rome, and who himself entered the Society of Jesus in 1688. Described as 'striking . . . in its naturalness, simplicity and gentle sincerity', the portrait presents Fu-Tsung in a sober interior holding a crucifix in his left hand, to which he gestures across his body with his right (fig. 31).[33] The light that enters from the opening (or window) falls on the sitter's hands and on his face, turned towards the heavens in contemplation. As a model of austere Catholic piety and the promise of conversion the portrait had evident personal importance to James, who told Bodley's librarian in September 1687 that he had the picture 'hanging in his room next to the bedchamber'.[34]

31 Sir Godfrey Kneller, *Michael Alphonsus Shen Fu-Tsung, 'The Chinese Convert'*, 1687.

Such images were far removed from the Lelys of Charles's court or, for that matter, the Duke of York's court. Together with (as we shall see) Verrio's work on James's Whitehall Chapel, the circulation of Catholic books and the presence of Capuchins, Franciscans and Jesuits at court, such images firmly advertised a new – and Catholic – spirituality and aesthetic. Indeed, in the year that James commissioned *The Chinese Convert*, the Catholic polemicist John Gother, a leading figure in attempts to counter the misrepresentation of 'popery', published *A Discourse of the Use of Images* in which he argued, controversially, the close agreement between the churches of England and Rome.[35] Pointing out the similar images in English churches and the king's Catholic chapel and drawing on the provocative High Anglican writings of the controversial Caroline divine Richard Montagu, Gother dismisses the charge of superstition directed against the Roman Church.[36] Images, he asserted, were essential aids to devotion: 'they force from the beholders an interior love and honour' and serve as 'helps to piety'.[37] Such arguments with their implicit attack on the efficacy of the word and gestures towards a Catholic theology of grace would have done nothing to dispel Protestant anxieties. It was Montagu's *Appello Caesarem* that had fired the controversy over Arminianism which had persuaded (fatally as it happened) many of Charles I's subjects that England was heading towards Rome.[38] If the portraits of James himself announced no fundamental changes in the royal image, the representations of Catholic and monastic piety he patronized doubtless led many to fear that, rather than his faith remaining private, the king would return the nation to idolatry and superstition.

The paucity of portraits of James, especially in the royal and other national collections, raises the question – all the more so if he indeed gave Kneller thirty-six sittings – whether, after 1688, the efforts ubiquitously to present William III as the legitimate heir and saviour of the nation were accompanied by a programme of erasing James's representation as well as right.[39] That neither of his daughters displayed a portrait of their father as king, nor of their stepbrother, the Prince of Wales, suggests at least some sensibilities concerning the king's image and the difficulties encountered at the highest level with what might have been read as declarations of allegiance to the Stuart cause.[40]

By the late seventeenth century, however, engravings were produced in huge numbers, artists like Kneller worked closely with their favourite engravers and printers, and images of royalty were distributed broadly – in this case in a form that could (but need not) involve public display. Though, not least on account of his short reign, we have fewer engravings of King James than of his brother, and, moreover, several were appropriated and contested in cartoons, several versions of (now lost) portraits were published from 1685 as engravings and mezzotints. While it is not always possible to date these exactly, and while many, perhaps revealingly, post-date the death of James – and William III – some images produced in England can be confidently dated or bear a date. Robert White's engraving of James (after an unknown artist) may have been executed during his reign;[41] and Robert Williams's mezzotint, published by Edward Cooper after a portrait by Wissing, is thought to have been issued shortly after James's succession.[42] A full-length portrait of James in Garter robes engraved by David Loggan and 'sold . . . at the Angel in Paul's churchyard' may well have commemorated the king's first Garter feast.[43] And Michael Van de Gucht's print, after Kneller, of James framed by a rose and thistle may similarly have marked the king's succession to the thrones of England and Scotland.[44] We know for certain that in 1685 the Dutch engraver Peter Vanderbanc executed after a portrait by Kneller a large plate ($21\frac{1}{2} \times 15\frac{1}{2}$ inches) that may have been intended to commemorate James's succession.[45] In an oval frame of engraved roses and thistles, James is depicted in armour, with long hair, a fine lace collar and wearing a lesser George. At the foot, an orb is flanked, on the left and right, by a lion and unicorn, while below are the arms of Ireland and Scotland; above the oval is a crown and the inscription 'Dieu et Mon Droit' (fig. 32). The engraving, conjoining the arms and

32 Peter Vandrebanc, after Sir Godfrey Kneller, *Jacobus II Dei Gratia Magnae Britaniae, Franciae et Hiberniae Rex Fidei Defensor*, 1685.

emblems of the kingdoms and the king, proclaims the triumph of dynasty and divine right after the battles over the succession. However, the portrait that James evidently most favoured for engraving was that by Nicholas de Largillière, painted in 1686. In that year both Isaac Becket, who had engraved portraits after Van Dyck, Lely and Kneller, and John Smith, Kneller's favoured mezzotinter, published prints after Largillière, with royal licence.[46] Smith's for example, depicting James in armour with a lace collar, with bowed sash, was issued 'cum privilegio regis' and 'sold by Alexander Browne at the Blue Balcony in Little Queen St';[47] a companion piece, of Mary of Modena, suggests that these were more or less 'official' images of the new king and queen of which there were evidently several printings.[48]

As with the portraits, engravings of James emphasize his military accomplishment, prominently display his Garter badge and jewel (a greater George in some cases is not only worn but engraved, with the Garter motto, along with the portrait) and proclaim his succession to the thrones of three kingdoms.[49] Other than straightforward portraits, we have an anonymous simple engraving of James, in the style of earlier equestrian images, mounted in armour with a

baton in his left hand and a sash blowing behind, titled 'James the Second by
the Grace of God King of England, Scotland, France and Ireland, Defender of
the Faith'.[50] Two frontispieces to the composer Godfrey Finger's *Sonatae* of
1688, dedicated to the fame of a munificent and virtuous king, also featured, as
well as James's arms and supporters, a bust of the monarch being crowned by
angels, evidently on a pedestal reminiscent of that on the title page of Sprat's
History.[51] The Moravian Gottfried Finger had come to England to serve as a
musician in James's Catholic chapel in 1687, and his frontispiece evidences the
adulation of James by his Catholic household servants.[52] In similar vein, the
frontispiece of John Michael Wright's 1688 account of Roger Earl of
Castlemaine's embassy to Innocent XI depicts Roger kissing the pope's foot
while angels hold aloft an oval of James II (fig. 33).[53] But for his own part,

33 Frontispiece of John Michael Wright, *An Account of His Excellence, Roger Earl of
Castlemaine's Embassy from His Sacred Majesty James IId . . . and Now Made English*, 1688.

James's engraved image – at least at this stage – eschewed religious symbols and themes and emphasized Stuart dynasty and continuity.

Indeed, as with commissioned portraits, James patronized, authorized and licensed mezzotints and engravings of his family and sons-in-law. In 1687, for example, Smith engraved, 'cum privilegio regis', a Wissing of Princess Anne that was sold at The Three Pigeons in Bedford Street, along with another Smith (after Kneller) of Prince George and another Wissing of the Prince of Orange – the latter also sold by Edward Cooper at The Three Pigeons.[54] The importance James attributed to such representations of fecundity and lineage is surely nowhere better demonstrated than by the engraved images of his son, the Prince of Wales, born in June 1688.[55] Though opposition to the king was mounting and James had much else to preoccupy him (his battle with the fellows of Magdalen College had escalated to strengthen the church's defiance), he commissioned engravings of his baby son after the portrait by Kneller.[56] As well as Smith's mezzotint depicting the baby bathed in light on a silk cushion that must have almost immediately followed the portrait, other engravings depict the infant prince alone or with his mother.[57] Where Smith's mezzotint after Kneller pictures the baby beneath a crown ringed with laurels, in another engraving by William Vincent angels hold a crown over his head;[58] one executed by Bernard Lens showing the baby in a cradle adorned with Prince of Wales feathers joined the other royal portraits for sale at Cooper's shop, The Three Pigeons; others displayed the royal arms.[59] Given the muttered suspicions about legitimacy that immediately followed Prince Charles's birth, then the direct accusations concerning the delivery of an impostor in a warming pan to the birthing room, these images of the baby prince – unprecedented in the history of Stuart royal representation – had an important task to perform.[60]

Not least, 'engraved images were a vital means by which the infant's physical resemblance to his parents, memorably affirmed by Sir Godfrey Kneller could be judged by a general audience'.[61] Like James's own portraits, they proclaimed and published a Stuart with his crown and title as heir to the empire of Great Britain. As with the battle of words, the speed with which Dutch and Whig cartoonists moved to contest these images – which they captioned the 'pretended Prince of Wales', adding devils and cardinals to suggest a Catholic conspiracy to dupe and subjugate the nation – testifies to the authority they could carry.[62] As we shall observe, no Stuart monarch more encountered a systematic programme of visual opposition in engraving and cartoon than James II, for whom a loss of the contest over his image led to the loss of his crown.[63]

James, however, had his supporters as well as opponents even among the circles of Dutch engravers who still dominated the emerging English industry. As we shall see, the herald Francis Sandford arranged for the history of James's coronation, in a series of elaborate plates illustrating the clothes and regalia of majesty (including details of the coronation ring as well as crown and orbs) and the procession to Westminster – the subject of no fewer than nineteen images, the seating within the cathedral, and all the stages of the coronation service through to the feast in Westminster Hall.[64] In this volume, illustrations not only memorialized the coronation, they advertised majesty and the social and political hierarchy of which the monarch was the head. One engraving dated 1687 and entitled 'Unanimity in Variance' figures James seated on his throne, rather like Henry VIII in the frontispiece to the King's Bible, with the bishops to his left and dissenters on his right clutching the royal Declaration of Indulgence, the king's key text of the year.[65] We do not know whether James authorized the image, or indeed anything about its provenance or circulation; but the title renders in axiom the king's argument for toleration and offers one instance at least that the case was advocated in visual as well as verbal media.

II

For his seal, James II followed the imperial style of his brother, adding a clear proclamation of his divine right to rule.[66] On the obverse the king, enthroned with a sceptre and orb, is placed between the lion and unicorn, while aloft two angels hold the arms of the kingdoms. Around an inscription proclaims James 'Jacobus Secundus D. Gra. Mag/Bri Fra et Hib Rex Fid Defensor, King of Britain, France and Ireland and Defender of the Faith' – a reminder perhaps to all who received a royal seal of the promise James had made to his Privy Council concerning his protection of the church. On the reverse, the king is mounted in classical dress, bearing a sword in his right hand with a laurel (of peace and victory) in his hair. Behind a view of London displays an imperial capital, the seat of a new British empire. Though there was nothing particularly controversial about its design, this became perhaps the most controversial royal seal in English history when James took it as he fled in 1688 and even cast it into the Thames, as a symbol of the illegitimacy of the Orangist government that was forming in London.[67] During the reign of Charles II, medals had been issued in large numbers first to celebrate the return of the monarchy, then to mark the major events and triumphs of the reign – the royal marriage, victories, treaties – also the Fire, the Declaration of Indulgence and the marriage of members of the royal family. As we saw, during that reign medals also entered party contest as the Whigs struck medals to celebrate the acquittal of Shaftesbury and to proclaim the reality of a Popish Plot.[68] Indeed, before his accession, two medals struck to celebrate James's survival of a shipwreck en route to Scotland in 1682, and another of the same year with the motto 'nullum numen abest', commending his prudence and the divine protection, clearly formed part of the royal programme to assert his right to and qualification for the throne.[69]

As king, James wasted no time in deploying the genre to advertise and sustain his regal authority. His first medal was, as the inscription on the obverse tells us, issued on the day of his accession; and the inscription rendered his past and future in a few words: 'Ferendum Sperandum': the king had borne adversity, now he succeeded with hope. On the reverse, inside an inscription 'Experientia Fulcitur' ('Trial strengthens'), a legend 'Maiora Minoribus Consonant' ('the greater are in harmony with the smaller') suggesting the affinity of king and people embraced a crown beneath a simple proclamation of divine right – 'A Deo'.[70] Issued in a variant, with James's portrait bust laureate, and as well as silver, in a crude and cheap copper version with an English inscription, the accession medal was obviously intended for broad distribution.[71] One example, with the inscription 'Tuebitur Omnes', on an altar-like pedestal, expresses the solemn promise James had made to protect the church.[72] As well as publicizing his authority, James was using medals to reassure his subjects, to promise continuity, protection and good government.

The coronation, only weeks after his succession, offered another opportunity for medallic representation of the new king and his queen, Mary of Modena. An official medal distributed to spectators on 23 April presents James, in Roman armour, wearing a laurel, with on the reverse a laurel with a crown held above by a hand from heaven, and with the inscription 'A Militaria Ad Regiam' – from military service to a crown.[73] The medal not only again emphasizes James's military victories, it implies that through them he had come to rule, the crown perhaps the prize of determined struggle at home as well as against foreign enemies. The medal of Mary, distributed as a companion piece the same day, figures her as no less than a goddess ('O Dea Certe'); while a fine silver medal, with a double portrait by George Bower, likens, on the reverse, the splendour of James and Mary to the midday sun which dazzles beholders.[74] These coronation medals, as well as proclamations of beneficent divine rule, carry specific political freight. A medal issued in Scotland on the day of James's English coronation and the opening of his Scottish parliament, with a sturdy crowned lion, its paws firmly grasping the regalia, and with the motto 'No one provokes me with impunity', clearly sounds a message of defiance to the Covenanters who were already plotting resistance.[75] Perhaps, too, on the reverse of the double medal the inscription after Pliny – 'Who is now the sea eagle?' – was directed as a warning to Monmouth who was already under royal suspicion.[76] For in his *Natural History* Pliny relates how the sea eagle forces its young to regard the sun and, if they resist, throws them out of the nest.[77]

Certainly when Monmouth rose in rebellion, James countered him with a series of polemical medals, as well as with arms. One medal, mocking Monmouth's pretensions to defend faith and liberty, depicts him vainly struggling with the royal lion, the true defender of faith and freedom.[78] A second, issued on the day of his rout at the Battle of Sedgemoor (in a visual gesture to

Marshall's frontispiece to the *Eikon Basilike*), has the gods laugh as Monmouth stumbles to his death in the sea, while trying to seize three crowns.[79] And a third, crudely executed in copper as well as silver, perhaps for more popular distribution, shows the improvident duke falling headlong from a column of majesty topped with crowns protected by providence (fig. 34).[80] As well as using the rebellion to increase his standing army, James took advantage of his victory to repeat his oft-made claim to providential protection, as the sea, from which he had been saved in 1682, threatens to claim his illegitimate nephew.[81] In fact, Monmouth fell not to the waves but the axe; and in what must have been a gesture of derision, a medal by the courtier George Bower shows his decapitated head in the clouds while angels hold the crown secure.[82] And lest any question the justice of the proceedings, an elaborate medal, probably cast in the summer, figured James as the protector of king and kingdom and on the reverse Justice, beneath a resplendent sun, holding a sword and crown above the severed heads of Monmouth and the rebel Earl of Argyll, who followed him to the scaffold at the end of July.[83] As well as denigrating the rebels, James issued medals of reward which were distributed to the commander of the royal forces sent into the west and to Scotland.[84] Though the visual record and memory of Monmouth and Argyll were not uncontested (at least one medal commemorated Monmouth as a martyr), the Monmouth medals enabled James to publicize the traditional warning about ambitious traitors and the personal security guaranteed only by God's chosen king.[85]

Over the course of the next three years, James encountered opposition to his policies and proclamations through the medium of medals, usually struck in Holland, as well as pamphlets and prints. In particular, as we shall see, the imprisonment of the seven bishops prompted a whole series of pieces which

34 Hawkins, *Medallic Illustrations*, plate LXIV, 8.

attacked motifs of royal representation and that were defiantly worn by opponents of the king.[86] But with the birth of the prince, James hastily commissioned a series of medals not only to proclaim his son and heir but to answer
his critics and reassert his authority.[87] In the one struck to commemorate the
birth, on the reverse of an obverse with the arms of the kingdoms crowned, the
baby prince seated (after the portrait by Kneller) on a cushion gestures to
angels who hold aloft a crown and a banner (inscribed 'veniat centisimus
haeres) – announcing the certainty and security of Stuart dynasty (fig. 35).[88]
More provocatively, a medal by Bower, struck in silver and copper, depicts the
infant prince as Hercules despatching the monsters of opposition inside the
inscription 'Cunae Monstris Funera Dant' ('the child inters the monsters')and
saving three kingdoms.[89] As well as medals in cheap copper and lead as well as
silver, for distribution in England, royal ambassadors, to Holland and Denmark
for example, gave out medals that represented the prince as the rising sun
dispelling the storms from all the British realms, as the harbinger of public
contentment.[90] As with engravings, depictions of the baby, on the birthing bed
with his mother, were clearly intended to counter rumours and doubts about
the delivery.[91] The course of events might lead us to conclude that, as generally
with James's royal representation and image, the king's efforts to persuade were
a failure. But the struggle to persuade James's subjects that his son was no true
heir was fierce and long. Certainly, the Orangists took no chances: as well as
satirical medals, cartooning the 'pretender' and a supposedly infertile king and
queen, Whig medallists joined artists, engravers and pamphleteers in what
amounted to an industrial output of artefacts arguing William and Mary's right
and legitimacy.[92] It was nearly half a century after both their deaths before the
battle was finally won.[93]

35 Pretender medal, Hawkins, *Medallic Illustrations*, plate LXVI, 9. Hartley Library,
University of Southampton.

Somewhat surprisingly, though he took full advantage of medals as a medium of representation and polemical statement, James's coins tend to follow a type across all the denominations. While the milled coinage minted from about 1663 tended to favour a stereotyped design, Charles II had used a variety of inscriptions and patterns before settling for a laureate profile – on coins of low denomination, with Britannia on the reverse.[94] Where coin was concerned, the reign of James II was certainly not one of inactivity: in 1685 the king started production of a plugged tin halfpenny, which continued until 1687.[95] Being less expensive than copper, tin yielded a higher profit to the Royal Mint, but as public opinion turned against the low intrinsic value, James restored a heavier weight. The changes in metal and intrinsic value, however, were not followed by changes in design. The king's silver coin featured a laureate bust, profile left rather than Charles II's right; and on the reverse a cross consisting of four shields, carrying the lions of England and Scotland, the French fleur-de-lis and the Irish harp (fig. 36).[96] The inscriptions merely announce the royal titles and the king's position 'Dei Gratia'. The tin farthings with copper plug repeated the bust, though now with the profile to the right, but reverted to a crude image of Britannia.[97] With coin, unless we are tempted to read significance into the reversed bust on the silver coin, James appears content to have simply proclaimed his title.[98]

During the last years of Charles's reign, one demonstration of loyalty in the wake of Exclusion had been donations for, and the erection of, statues of the monarch to stand as symbols of the triumph and durability of royal government. Charles's victory was inseparable from that of his brother and, in 1685, Tobias Rustat, Yeoman of the Robes to Charles II, donated to a London grateful for the opportunity to reassure the crown of its fidelity, statues of Charles and his brother.[99] The *Gazette* for 1685 reports the 'free gift' and the erection

36 Silver crown of James II, 1687–8.

of statues of Charles at the Royal Hospital, Chelsea, and that of James at Whitehall.[100] Cast in bronze, the statue of James (now at Trafalgar Square) probably came from the workshop of Gibbons whose figure of Charles in Roman armour it follows (fig. 37).[101] Though it presents the new monarch laureate and in Roman armour with a baton of command, the stance and extended leg evoke portraits of James by Kneller. John Bushnell also carved a statue of James for the front of Southwark Town Hall.[102] Nor was London the only city to endeavour to ingratiate itself with the new regime in statuary. At Gloucester, the city's (Roman Catholic) mayor John Hill commissioned a figure of the king to stand at the conduit near Holy Trinity church.[103] If that were likely a controversial benefaction in a city with a long history of Puritanism and dissent, we know that the scheme for a bronze at Newcastle emerged from factional rivalry and party conflict.[104] Here, to gain the upper hand in a local conflict, the mayor, Sir Henry Brabant, petitioned the king, informing him of his desire 'that your Majesty's statue on horseback (like that to your Royal father at Charing Cross) should be

37 Statue of James II, 1685, Trafalgar Square, London.

made and set upon the market place', and noting the opposition of his rivals to such a gesture.[105] The bronze, the only equestrian monument to James, did indeed evoke that of Charles I; and if a 1742 engraving can be taken as a reliable guide, William Lawson (who had a workshop at Charing Cross) created a magnificent figure of James armoured and laurelled, skilfully managing a rearing horse in the style of the great equestrian portraits and bronzes of the seventeenth-century's commanders (fig. 38).[106]

Just as James ascended the throne, public statues of Louis XIV – crowned with victory, or mounted – were being set up in Paris and the major towns of France.[107] By contrast, it has been claimed, 'there was certainly not the will to honour the Roman Catholic James II in that way'.[108] This may be too confident an assertion. Though for all his own polemical purposes Brabant claimed the opponents of his statue said it 'looked like popery', and though it was removed after 1688, there is no reason to believe that in 1685 the nation was unwilling to celebrate the peaceful succession of a king who promised to continue his

38 Joseph Barber, *Statue of James the Second, which stood on the Sandhill,* 1742.

brother's popular policies.[109] Indeed, statuary seemed to announce continuity and stability, especially as the Roman figures of James – in stone at Oxford as well as in bronze in London – closely followed the Gibbons of his brother.[110] Even loyalist Oxford, however, was to find cause in James's short reign for that discontent and opposition that almost certainly obstructed any further monuments to Stuart rule. But in such statues as were erected, private and municipal benefactors reflected to passers-by the king's self-image: as emperor and commander.

III

Finances may have rendered no more than a dream their desires for a new palace that would be a monument to their dynasty; but each of the Stuarts perpetuated the dream and, within the limitations of reality, put his mark on royal buildings, be it through small projects, extensions or decorations. Charles II, as we saw, built at Whitehall and refurbished Windsor, before turning his energies and purse to a planned baroque palace at Winchester as a new seat of majesty.[111] Though James had evidently been party to his brother's plans, it is worthy of note that one of his first acts as king was to cancel, or suspend, them.[112] It may be that the new king wanted to review the costs, but John Evelyn felt sure that 'his new Majesty did not seem to encourage the finishing'; and in 1687 James signalled the abandonment of the project by selling off unused timber and preparing to sell back land.[113] It would seem that a seat of government and a residence, at remove from London, planned (we recall) shortly after the Popish Plot when the capital had favoured Whig politics, did not appeal to him. Charles's other projected lodge, at Greenwich, James intended for Trinity House, a building 'to be fitted for the service of impotent sea commanders and others', and a project realized in the next reign.[114]

James focused his attention on a few traditional royal residences. He appears to have little favoured Hampton Court.[115] By the time of his death, Charles had all but completed his restoration programme at Windsor and James commissioned no new building works there, though Gibbons executed altar pieces for the king's and queen's chapel, and Verrio painted a magnificent baroque ceiling painting of James enthroned among allegorical figures.[116] As for St James's, when the king succeeded to the throne, he gifted the palace to the queen who commissioned Wren to provide her with a council room and other facilities.[117] James retained an apartment in his former palace and planned to move the Royal Mews there; accounts of the Office of Works show work on the chapel at St James's including a font and 'two confessing seats' for the king and queen.[118] But St James's remained for the most part the queen's project and residence, after she replaced the Queen Dowager who removed to Somerset House. 'For James II', writes the historian of the king's works, 'Whitehall remained the centre of government and the usual home of the court'; indeed, more so than it had for his brother.[119] While we do not know his motives for focusing attention on Whitehall, it is worth speculating whether James had not concluded that a powerful and visible presence in his capital was essential to sovereignty, and that the palace before which his father had met his death should again be a monument to Stuart majesty.

The last British monarch to live at Whitehall, James effected changes to the ancient palace, small and large. In keeping with his military image, for example, James ordered a refitting of the Guard Chamber in the Tudor state apartments, so that arms and armour could be hung on the walls. To carry their weight, 69 feet of cornice were strengthened and a pedestal was set up at the Presence Chamber door 'for the cap-a-pe armour', perhaps a sign, as one entered the room, of the symbolic presence of the martial king.[120] Major work was commissioned for Mary of Modena. Where Charles, who had spent liberally on quarters for his mistresses, had left Catherine of Braganza in cramped Tudor rooms, James – perhaps to underline the centrality of his marriage and the hopes of succession – immediately set about a relocation of the queen's apartments to the Privy Gallery range which, as Simon Thurley observes, 'was, since 1682, a vestigial part of the palace'.[121] The king's plans involved a two-storey building, with apartments and a chapel, a council chamber and a stair behind the Banqueting House, running from the Holbein Gate (to the west) to the east boundary of the Privy Garden. The king's sense of priority was expressed in the workforce assigned to the project and the speed of completion: by January 1687 Evelyn reports Mary in her new apartments. These completed, James turned attention to the queen dowager's privy lodgings next to the water and ordered a new building for Mary with suites of rooms, lavishly appointed.[122]

James's new buildings were not simply for the comfort and convenience of his consort; both in design and execution they made large political statements. As Howard Colvin remarks, the rebuilding of the council chamber within the new Privy Gallery range 'would accord with the primacy of Whitehall as the seat of government of a king who intended . . . to be seen to govern'.[123] Moreover, within the constraints of not building an entirely new palace, the additions changed the appearance and performance of Whitehall. In planning the queen's apartments, Wren, under James's direction, sought to complement and follow the design of Inigo Jones's Banqueting House which, it had once been hoped, would be the foundation of a new classical building.[124] The height of the first floor of the new buildings followed Jones's, and Wren chose a plinth of the same depth. The great staircase on the north of the new apartments and at the south end of the Banqueting House not only connected the buildings, but 'effectively became the principal entrance to the palace for the king and queen', as it were sidelining the old Tudor apartments which all had traversed after entering the Holbein Gate.[125] As the historian of Whitehall explains, the new staircase gave the

Banqueting House a grand entrance suitable to its magnificence, and made it the new centre of the palace. From July 1686, accordingly, James commissioned internal redecorations, regilding all the cornice and architrave and a relining of the Rubens ceiling canvases, which were also rearranged so that the view from the throne, moved to the north after the new staircase provided a southern entrance, retained a privileged view of royal apotheosis.[126]

With the focal points of Whitehall moved to the east, James came the nearest he could to having a classical palace as the principal residence of his imperial rule. More dangerously, he also made it appear a Catholic palace: a building that came to monumentalize the anxieties of his subjects. James did not ignore the sites of Protestant worship. Improvements were made to the old Chapel Royal at Whitehall for James's daughter, Princess Anne, who remarried a Protestant.[127] But attention focused on the building of a Catholic chapel from virtually the moment of James's succession, the second Sunday after which the king heard mass in his oratory publicly with the door open.[128] The Catholic chapel at Whitehall was a similarly public site, 'the most lavish ecclesiastical building built by an English monarch since the Reformation'.[129] Work began in May and the chapel was first used for midnight mass the Christmas of the next year; but improvements and alterations continued almost to the end of 1687, meaning that it was in use for hardly a year.[130] The first stage of the work evidences both the magnificence of the concept and the close identity the king and queen sought with the liturgies of their faith. On a raised platform, a splendid gilded throne, decorated with putti, a tasselled canopy, a crown and sceptre, the symbol of an earthly god, faced, according to Evelyn, 'just opposite to the altar', the site of a heavenly god.[131] But, for all the magnificence, the chapel did not satisfy James or Mary. Wren's design, which, it has been suggested, may have incorporated deliberate ambiguity and a possible future use for the chapel for Anglican worship, rendered it unsuitable for Catholic liturgical devotions. New work therefore involved the addition of a side chapel, which also accommodated the great organ, steps before the great altar at the east and a staircase that provided the king and queen with a processional route to the altar.[132] The altarpiece, designed by Gibbons and Quellin, filled the width of the east end and was nearly 40 feet high. Initially, it framed a large painting of the Annunciation by Gennari (who had completed Lely's canvas of the duke and his family), but late in 1687 this was replaced by 'a picture representing the nativity of our Lord' by the same artist.[133] As well as figures of two apostles, the virtues of Faith and Hope and angels, John Gother informs us that 'over the altar at his Majesty's chapel at Whitehall . . . [was] a pelican feeding her young ones with her blood; to signify what Christ gives to the faithful . . . in the sacrament, that he feeds them with his blood'.[134]

In this case, the sense of James's daughter Mary that what had been built was a 'popish chapel' cannot be dismissed as partisan polemic.[135] The chapel at

Whitehall shocked Evelyn and must have shocked all Protestants who entered it. Indeed, it represented a reversal of the Reformation in the very palace that the first head of the English church had taken from a cardinal (Wolsey). Undoubtedly, there had been Catholic chapels before – of royal consorts and the duke and duchess themselves; and Wren's design owed much to the baroque chapel built for Charles II at Windsor. But as James's new chapel, the first Catholic chapel since the Reformation, eclipsed the old Chapel Royal in the Tudor apartments, Whitehall could easily be regarded as the palace of a Catholic king. For many of those who had rallied to James in the 1680s, the hope had been that the new king would keep his faith, insofar as he could, private. Whatever his restraint with his image in other media, in his architectural innovations at Whitehall, James appeared – dangerously appeared – to represent his Catholicism not only as personal faith but as the religion of state.

CHAPTER 7

STAGING CATHOLIC KINGSHIP

I

As well as expressions in marble and stone, palaces were the stages on which the rituals of monarchy were performed. Rituals of state were, of course, inextricably interwoven with religious liturgies and, after the break from Rome, with those of the Church of England. Since Mary's reign, England had not been ruled by an avowed Catholic monarch. And though Catholic consorts had raised problems – Queen Anne of Denmark declined to receive the sacrament in 1603 and Henrietta Maria refused to be crowned by a Protestant bishop – royal coronations spectacularly presented the monarch as a son and servant as well as Head of the church. After a decade of republican rule, Charles II had gone to great lengths over all the stages of his coronation: the entry into the city, the procession to Westminster the next day, and, not least, the liturgy which provided all the sanctity that was absent from the civic entertainment of the previous day.[1] In Westminster Abbey, on St George's Day 1661, whatever his private faith or lack of it, Charles made a 'publicly avowed commitment to Anglicanism' that 'was an effective strategy of legitimation and re-presentation of the Stuart monarchy'.[2] In almost exactly following the service devised for his father's coronation in 1626, Charles, as he did in other ways, presented himself as the son of a martyr to the Anglican church, its theology, liturgy and hierarchy.

The continuity of policy that James promised on the day of his brother's death was not entirely lacking in his coronation. James entrusted the preparations of his coronation to a committee of all Privy Councillors, who had served his predecessor; and in the preparations the Clerk of the Wardrobe was required to attend with abstracts of particulars pertaining to the coronation of Charles II and heralds were asked to bring their books, especially those relating to the reign of James I.[3] Indeed, the republication in 1685 of accounts of *The Ceremonies, Form of Prayer and Services Used in Westminster Abbey at the Coronation of King James the First and Queen Ann*, and *The Complete Solemnity of . . . the Solemn Coronation . . . of his Late Sacred Majesty Charles II* may have been prompted by these meetings and discussions, though there is no indication of official licence or approval.[4] If Sandford's account is to be trusted, the committees, in making plans, scrupulously followed precedents: in according offices and privileges (such as the right to carry the canopy or the king's towel), in determining matters of rank, and in the arrangements required by a joint coronation.[5] Most obviously, and surely strategically, in selecting St George's Day for the event, the Council and James sought not only to associate the new reign with England's patron saint, but to evoke memories of Charles II's coronation the same day, and the joy and acclamation that accompanied it.

In one matter, James himself requested a change. On 21 February at the committee, 'his Majesty having declared that his royal consort the Queen should be crowned with him, the said officers of arms produced a ceremonial of the coronation of Queen Anne . . . whereupon His Grace the Lord Archbishop of Canterbury was desired to view the forms of divine service used at former coronations, and (keeping to the essentials) to abridge, as much as might be, the extreme length thereof; and to bring a draught or formulary thereof to the Lords of the Committee, as well for the coronation of the Queen as of the King'.[6] Was James desirous of avoiding a full Anglican service, or was his suggestion that a double coronation required some shortening of the 'extreme length' of the proceedings genuine? The committee of the Council remained in charge, but the king's wishes could not lightly be ignored. A hint that the nature of the service may have been long in discussion and possibly the subject of difference is provided by a marginal note in Sandford's account. Reporting the meeting of 19 March, among the things agreed upon, he listed among the items 'to be laid ready upon the altar in the choir', 'A silk towel to be held before the king at the communion by two bishops'; the margin note adds: 'This was not prepared because there was no communion'.[7] The coronation was to be a Church of England service without the Anglican communion.

As the event came near, the committee ordered the proclamation of the new monarch by the heralds at all the traditional stations, at the Temple and Exchange for example.[8] The hangings organized to decorate the rooms combined classical and biblical themes, and the medals to be distributed were approved by the king.[9] In April, reviving the plans for the procession, James expressed his preference 'that the queen should go even with him' (that is, alongside him) unless the passage were too narrow and the king participated in final decisions concerning the ranking and dress of the nobles.[10]

The coronation itself was not, as Charles's had been, preceded by any state entry into the city. Ogilby's spectacular entertainment had been unprecedented, and Charles I, whose example James followed in many matters, had had no civic entry to London; but the reasons for not repeating what had been such a success a quarter century earlier elude us.[11] One partial explanation of course was time. James moved swiftly to arrange his coronation immediately after his brother's death and may, after the Exclusion crisis, have regarded a speedy inauguration as a prudent move to undercut any attempt by challengers, notably Monmouth. The coronation day itself, however, incorporated what its chronicler called 'several performances', and even an element of military parade.[12] Troops of Horse Guards, with grenadiers and foot guards, took up station at five in the morning in the piazza at Covent Garden, at Haymarket, in Lincoln's Inn Fields and St James's Park, where they made ready to march to Westminster, bearing the royal standard and initials with an imperial crown of gold.[13]

The night before the coronation, James and Mary spent at St James's, 'for the greater conveniency of performing their devotions', presumably, that is, so as to have the use of Catherine of Braganza's Catholic chapel for worship and perhaps to avoid Whitehall.[14] On the morning, therefore, James had to pass through St James's Park to Whitehall to take a barge to the parliament stairs at Westminster, whence he was conducted to the Princes Lodgings for robing, while the queen made her way to the Court of Wards.[15] Having processed into Westminster Hall, the king, 'attended only by the Great Officers and the two Archbishops', ascended the stage to his chair of state on the right hand of the queen, for the ceremony of presenting the regalia, brought in by the dean and prebendaries of Westminster.[16] Afterwards, supported respectively by the bishops of Bath and Wells and Durham, and the bishops of London and Winchester, the king and queen prepared for the grand procession to the abbey.[17] At the head, behind the trumpets and drums, the royal chaplains, canons, deans and archdeacon of Canterbury, Windsor and St Paul's, Salisbury, Winchester and Norwich in their doctor's scarlet, displayed the affinity of church and crown and their pre-eminence in the hierarchy. Along a route from Westminster Hall, through New Palace Yard into King Street, to the west door of the cathedral, the passage railed on both sides and spread with 1,200 yards of blue cloth, the cavalcade made its way into the church where an anthem composed by Dr Childs, organist of the Chapel Royal, from Psalms 61 and 132 greeted them: 'O Lord, grant the king a long life'; 'He shall dwell before God for ever'. 'As for his enemies, I shall clothe them with shame. But upon himself shall his crown flourish'.[18]

At the moment the king and queen entered, the choir of Westminster sang an anthem from Psalm 122 ('I was glad when they said unto me, we will go into the House of the Lord . . .') before they entered the choir and ascended to their thrones.[19] In front of his chair, James knelt and 'made some private adoration', the bishops on either side of him.[20] After the recognition, when on all four sides the Archbishop of Canterbury presented the king to the assembly asking if they would do him homage, the ceremony proper began. With both their majesties kneeling opposite the altar, the archbishop prayed for them, before the bishops of Oxford and St Asaph sang the litany.[21] After the sermon from the 29th chapter of Chronicles (which lasted half an hour), James took the solemn oath, to keep 'the laws, customs and franchises granted to the clergy by the glorious king St Edward . . . the true professions of the gospel established in this kingdom . . . and the ancient customs of the realm'.[22] To the bishops he swore 'to protect and defend . . . the churches under their government', sealing his promise by kissing the Bible.[23] Then, as the archbishop said a collect for a king called and protected by divine providence, the anointing began, followed by the investing with tunic, spurs and sword, and finally the crown.[24] The service clearly involved changes. Obeying his brief to reduce the length of the proceedings, Sancroft cut long prayers from the beginning of the service, and the communion was omitted, causing other changes: the place of the litany, for example, was moved from after the oath to before the sermon.[25] In addition, as Sancroft's manuscript draft of the service reveals, some prayers were altered so that the blessing on the ornaments became a blessing of the king invested with them; and two anthems were introduced from the 89th Psalm (20–30, 'I have found David my servant') and Psalms 45 (10, 14–16) and 147 (12).[26] But in many respects the coronation followed familiar Anglican rites. The service was conducted by the archbishops and senior bishops whom the king 'vouchsafed to kiss . . . as they kneeled before him', to do homage.[27] A final anthem looked to a long Stuart imperial future ('thou shalt have children, whom thou mayst make princes in all lands') and the progeny of a king and queen who would be nursing fathers and mothers to the church.[28] Then, 'there being no communion', the archbishop pronounced the benediction (fig. 39).[29]

As the procession filed back from the abbey to Westminster Hall, 'all the way . . . the drums beat, the trumpets sounded, and the vast multitude of beholders, filling the air with loud acclamations and shouts, and hearty prayers for their majesties' long life and prosperity, expressed . . . the utmost height of joy and satisfaction'.[30] Evidently James believed that the proceedings had passed off well – and he may not have been wrong. The plan to commemorate the occasion, as Ogilby had Charles II's entry, with an official account, illustrated with engravings, went ahead with royal approval, and Francis Sandford, Lancaster herald, laboured, over the next two years, to publish a lavish folio, printed by a royal printer and 'by his Majesty's special command'.[31] In his eulogistic preface to a king of martial virtues, descended of emperors, delivered by providence and chosen by God, Sandford recalled the 'magnificent ceremony', the 'art, ornament and expense . . . of the spectacle' which had been 'as welcome to the hearts of your people as it was to their eyes'.[32] As the grant of royal privilege made clear, however, Sandford had incurred 'great expense and charges'; his intended audience for a costly folio was not the crowds who had looked on in awe, but the nobility.[33] Sandford, indeed, appears to have prepared a souvenir volume for the participants in the spectacle: the details and the fine engravings that carefully delineated the features of all the office-holders and magnates in

39 William Sherwin, *A Perspective of Westminster-Abby from the High-Altar to the West end, Shewing the manner of His Majesties Crowning*, 1685–7.

the procession add to an impression that the herald hoped to recoup his costs, and perhaps profit, from the pride, or vanity, of the establishment. Much has been made of the failure of his hopes and of a project that helped to bankrupt him.[34] But we should not too easily take that failure as evidence of the unpopularity of the event that his history memorialized. Though the two years spent in production radically transformed attitudes to the king, Sandford's project, as conceived and initiated in 1685, only makes sense if most of those he expected to buy it had been happy with the coronation and with their participation in it. Perhaps, too, in his detailed explanations of the symbolism, maps of Westminster, diagrams of the abbey and reproductions of the regalia, he was seeking a larger market of those gentry and merchants who had not secured entry to this all-ticket ceremony but whose fascination with regality was enabling a lively commerce in royal engravings and artefacts.

Certainly Sandford was not alone in believing there was a public desire for some record of the day (again, a belief explicable only if it had passed off without controversy or discontent), for soon after the coronation, by the order of the Duke of Norfolk, the Earl Martial, a one-page account of 'the ceremonial at the coronation of their most excellent majesties' was published and printed by the royal printer Thomas Newcombe.[35] Barely describing the procession and proceedings, the account merely reported the solemnity 'performed . . . with all imaginable splendour and expressions of joy'. There were other fuller accounts, in prose and verse, while one broadside, 'published by authority' and sold at the Wine-Bell in Thomas Street, tried to convey more of the rich spectacle in words and in a simple engraving of the procession, complete with a crude image of the king and queen under their canopies.[36] In this account, poetic praise of a queen who moved 'like an angel' and a king, 'the wonder of the eye', elevated the factual narration to a paean to James and Mary.[37] The panegyrical verses that poured out to celebrate the day suggest both elite and popular audiences. Where a Latin verse proclaimed joy for 'his reign begun', Behn's pindaric poem followed the procession person by person.[38] A poem by 'a person of quality' commemorated the 'Triumphant Sight' of a day 'design'd by Destiny/To remain Saved to Posterity', while a 'new song' on the coronation was written 'to the tune of King James's jig'.[39] For England's Royal Renown in the Coronation, the printer provided some bars of the music of the tune 'The Cannons Roar', to which new verses provided patriotic paeans to the martial James:

> Loyal hearts both rich and poor,
> Now our Gracious Prince adore
> Drink his Health Boys ten times o're.[40]

Remembering the day when 'many hundreds there beheld/the KING in all his glory', the author looked forward to a long reign and 'princely heir'.

The wealthier subjects, who according to the song paid a guinea for the best view from the windows of the top floor of buildings along the route, also collected more enduring mementoes of the day. Following the first production of coronation mugs, issued to commemorate King Charles II's inauguration, it would seem that souvenir pottery was produced for the coronation of James and Mary. The Fitzwilliam Museum in Cambridge, for example, has an English Delftware dish, from the pottery at Brislington, Somerset, with inside a blue floral decorative border, a bust of James, crowned and in coronation robes, with 'J.R.2' each side of his head (fig. 40).[41] It may well be that the tin-glazed earthenware plate was part of a larger set that has not survived. For the less well-heeled, as well as the broadsides, a crude medal or illustrated pack of cards had to serve as a keepsake.[42]

Despite the absence of a state entry, James's coronation was not lacking in a spectacle for the common people. Indeed, the original plan had been to 'have closed the grandeur of the great day' with a firework display in the evening; but with the royal couple wearied, the show was postponed to the next evening.[43] Delayed it may have been, but the 'wonderful and stupendous' display was the next day duly 'done beyond all thought'. As the royal couple entered onto the

40 Dish depicting James II, Brislington Pottery, *c.* 1685–8.

galleries at Whitehall, just after 9 p.m. the show began. On a platform measuring 180 × 50 feet, between two pyramids were placed a brass sun, cross and crown, with, in front, two statues 7 feet high of the 'two giants of Guildhall', all stuffed with fireworks.[44] As the shouts of the crowd fell silent, suddenly a 'stupendous torrent of fire' burst upwards 'like a summer sun' before breaking into 'a shower of ten thousand of stars'. Then, for nearly an hour, the crown, cross and the sun burst into resplendent flame, while on a smaller lighter, fireworks burned, jumping over the river, hissing and flying on the water.[45] From the engraving in Sandford's history, we can better grasp the iconography of the display (fig. 41). Beneath the sun, and an imperial crown, the royal cipher of James and Mary was illuminated. On the right above the statue bearing a scroll with the motto 'omnibus unus', the word 'MONARCHIA' was spelled out in flames, while above the left in fire was 'PATER PATRIAE'. On the water, from machines pageant swans burst forth bearing the ciphers of the king and queen, as letters in flame spelled out 'SOL OCCUBUIT NOX NULLA SECUTA EST' ('The sun has set but is followed by no night' – a reference to James shining after his brother's death).[46] In a show that truly awed a crowd that had waited for hours to see it (some cried 'Lord have mercy' at the thunderous noise and great cascade of fire), James was represented as the sun that brought light even

41 *A Representation of the Fire-Works upon the River of Thames, over against Whitehall, at their Majesties Coronation Ao. 1685*, 1685.

to darkness, as the father of his people, as the source of wonder. To the German 'master artists' who engineered the spectacle, the king gave a pension of three hundred pounds, 'to encourage their art'.[47]

The coronation and fireworks were the only major state spectacles of the reign of James, whose brother's funeral was 'privately solemnised' (with the Prince of Denmark as chief mourner), perhaps to avoid upstaging the coronation.[48] But, as we have seen, the London entertainments annually provided for the inauguration of the new mayor often represented royal as well as civic government and the symbiosis of court and city. In Charles's reign, particularly during the Popish Plot, such pageants reveal the strain of party and opposition, before again heralding kingship in the wake of Charles's victory over the Whigs.[49] The accession of James coincided with the succession to Thomas Jordan (who died early in 1685), as laureate of the lord mayor's shows, of the city poet Matthew Taubman, who had penned loyal verse on the Duke of York's return from Scotland in 1682 and who had gathered a volume of anti-Whig songs.[50] Taubman's first commission for the inauguration in October of Sir Robert Jeffreys was not restrained in its praise of the new king, who was described as the 'most judicious and most discerning prince in the world'.[51] In the first pageant, the figures of Victory and Triumph bore the king's banner and Victory's speech celebrated the new ruler's triumph over passion.[52] Similarly in the third pageant, a triumphal arch decorated with a rose and crown was inscribed 'Jacobus Imperator' and Concord, bearing white and red roses, represented the 'union of king and people, the court and city'.[53] As in a physical performance of the theme of the entertainment, the king and queen dined with the new mayor, a song welcomed a 'halcyon calm' after a storm and the victory of James over Monmouth and the rebels of the west.[54]

In its reprise of official panegyrics and texts, the mayor's show cautions us against too hasty assumptions about the initial impact of James's reign on his people. The entertainment the next year for Sir John Peake, the mayor chosen from the Mercer's Company, was hardly less adulatory.[55] As Triton addressed the new mayor, the honour of the day was due 'first to illustrious JAMES, and next to you'.[56] For the second pageant, on a platform of three architectural orders, the figure of Monarchy, crowned and with a sceptre, stood attended by Principality (with a banner of St George), Nobility, Honour and Obedience, and by Mars and Minerva, Victory and Knowledge.[57] In their address to Peake, the god and goddess of war remind him that it is the monarch who gives the city law 'And Britain's King, who keeps the Gods in awe'.[58] In the magnificent third pageant, a richly jewelled triumphal chariot, bearing the banners of the king and the company, carries the virtues and the muses, supporters of crown and city, before final songs praised loyalty and damned Whigs who, along with Jews, were figured as the enemies of a 'Christian monarchy'.[59]

As opposition to James mounted, over the next year, the city of London remained publicly loyal, if only because royal influence was used to promote as mayor Sir John Shorter of the Goldsmiths, whom 'contrary winds' had endeavoured to keep out.[60] James, Mary, the queen dowager, and the Prince and Princess of Denmark attended the spectacle that year in what may have been a display of force; and Taubman responded with a pageant that was unequivocally loyal in a highly charged political atmosphere. Here once again Courage (and beautiful young negroes with the royal banner) signified James's imperial sway.[61] But on this occasion, the verse provided obvious apology for the royal faith and policies. In the second pageant, for example, the patron saint of the company, St Dunstan, mitred and holding a crosier, pronounces: 'These pontifical ornaments I wear,/Are types of Rule and Order all the Year.' And he continues:

In these white Robes none can a fault descry,
Since all have liberty as well as I:
Nor need you fear the Shipwrack of your Cause,
Your loss of Charter or the Penal Laws,
Indulgence granted by your bounteous Prince,
Makes for that loss too great a Recompense.[62]

In one of the most specific political references in a mayoral entertainment, then, Taubman validates Catholicism, advocates toleration and indulgence, and answers voices critical of the royal policy. In the final pageant, the figure of Liberty bears, with a banner of the king, a shield inscribed 'Liberty of Conscience'.[63] In the Guildhall, to which James rode 'with a large guard to attend him', the king joined the royal family, archbishops, bishops and principal officers of state, where he was addressed in song:

> How great are the Blessings of Government made,
> By the excellent Rule of our Prince.[64]

Chief among them, or so the city loyally claimed, was the freedom of indulgence or religious liberation – 'each Man his own way'.[65]

Though faction and discontent break out between his lines, Taubman's *London's Triumph* represents James as he had begun to present himself by 1687: as a Catholic but also a sincere advocate of toleration of 'each man his own way'. His *Anniversary Festival* the next year proved to be not only the poet's last for the king, but the king's last.[66] Carrying on its title page lines adapted from Virgil's *Aeneid*, Book VI, the account of the pageant was prefaced by recognition of crisis – 'the present impending storm, the dread of foreign invasion'.[67] But boldly Taubman celebrated the restoration of the city's charter and liberties, which coincided with Sir John Chapman's inauguration and, more boldly yet, the 'unspeakable act of royal bounty' that he claimed it was.[68] While the fevered atmosphere proved inimical to a full pageant, Taubman penned a panegyric to both mayor and monarch which, reminding all that 'The God and Winds fight for the English crown', called on London to stand in loyal resistance to the Dutch as it had to Spain an exact century earlier.[69] After the usual description of the procession, with its royal and city banners, the account ends with the song sung at dinner, 'To the son of the Martyr, Who Restored us the Charter'.[70] Raising a health to 'Mighty James' in 'loyal song', London, 'the Royal Chamber', pledged her support. Within weeks, James had fled. But, in this case to the last, the city authorities had represented the king to the citizens and spectators as mighty and beneficent, the protector of capital and nation. Though the realm was divided, James even now did not want for supporters who were willing to present him as he represented himself. The image of England's sun king was contested and shadowed but not eclipsed.

II

In the reign of James's father, a preacher had opined that it was 'the court of a king' that was an 'image of the ruling of their states'.[71] Though this was as true after the Restoration as before, little research has explicated the late seventeenth-century court and there has been no full published study of that of James II.[72] Before he fashioned his own, James's experience of royal courts had been diverse and often unhappy. The 'halcyon days' of his father's splendid and punctilious court during the prince's childhood in the 1630s had given way to dislocation and crisis; and in exile in France, factional rivalries and religious disputes between Anglicans, Catholics and Presbyterians had made court life acrimonious. Indeed, some to promote their own ends had endeavoured to foster division between James and his brother, Charles II, and to sow dissension within the royal family. It would appear that the memories and lessons of those years shaped James's attitude to his household, as so much else.[73] Like the French king's younger brothers, James as Duke of York at the Restoration court had his own establishment at St James's, as well as apartments at Whitehall. 'By 1662, James had over a hundred servants, plus thirty for his Duchess. He had his own Groom of the Stole and Master of the Horse, his own Attorney General, Solicitor General and revenue commissioners.'[74] Later in Charles's reign, the duke's rising revenue (from post office and wine licences) enabled him to enlarge the establishment, but money was evidently not wasted. In 1677, Paul de Barillon, the French envoy, reported, 'his household is very well regulated, all his servants are paid punctually and he owes nothing.'[75]

The history of James's household and court as monarch has been obscured by myths that have only recently been dispelled in a regrettably unpublished study by Andrew Barclay. Rather than an abrupt turn that opened a new path to inevitable disaster, Barclay demonstrated authoritatively the continuity that James pursued from his brother's reign in his household, as in other aspects of his rule. Of the 1,051 appointed to office in the household by James II, Barclay computes, 646 had served his predecessor and a further 55 had been part of his own establishment as duke.[76] Though he raised his loyal supporter, Laurence Hyde, Earl of Rochester, to be Lord Treasurer (and effectively First Minister), James in the main reappointed most of Charles's household officers. And even in the Privy Chamber, of the thirty-eight gentlemen appointed in 1685, only six had not served in the previous reign.[77] Though the Gentlemen of the Bedchamber were reduced, from twelve to eight, James similarly continued in office former servants of his own or his brother's court.

Moreover, in making appointments, James (as his brother) exhibited an extraordinary willingness to forgive former opponents – or an astute understanding of the role of the court as a point of contact with diverse groups and, by now, parties.[78] The new king advanced several supporters of exclusion: Sir John Baker to the Privy Chamber, for example. Other former Whigs, such as Newport, or men like the Earl of Huntingdon or Henry Savile, who had 'political records to which James might have taken exception', were retained; as late as 1688 the former Whig Edward Nosworthy was appointed to the Privy Chamber.[79] At his succession, then, far from conducting any political purge,

James constructed 'a remarkably diverse alliance of courtiers': Tories, ex-Whigs and exclusionists who had been reassimilated to the court and were willing to serve the new king.[80]

For all the continuity of personnel, however, James clearly resolved to effect changes in the royal household, some of which suggest attitudes to kingship that have been little recognized. Almost immediately upon his succession, the king set about streamlining the royal household. In the efficiency review, numbers were cut, board wages were abolished and mergers were effected to save jobs. Deciding no longer to serve diets on a large scale, James was able to halve the numbers in the bakehouse, the cellar, the larder and the pantry.[81] And through transferring their duties to the Gentlemen Ushers Quarter Waiters, the Gentlemen Ushers were paid off. It has been estimated that eighty-five Chamber posts were cut and that overall James reduced his household by a third or more.[82] The changes are notable not least because the most obvious and usual explanation for retrenchment cannot simply be summarized. James, that is, was not impoverished. By the 1680s, royal revenues were healthier than at any point since the Restoration and, in Barclay's words, 'had the will existed, James II could have, with little difficulty, returned the household to the pre-1662 retrenchment level of expenditure'.[83] Indeed, some of James's changes cost rather than saved money. The abolition of board wages, because it involved compensatory payments, initially raised the bill for even the smaller household.[84] James and his Lord Treasurer Rochester may, like Danby earlier, have been looking to find long-term savings that would give the king greater financial security and independence. But a suggestion that the reforms marked James's recognition of an altered role for the royal household is persuasive and worth pursuing.[85] Along with the retention at the Restoration of other republican innovations, such as boards and a more professional civil service, James may have felt that a smaller court better suited the times, without compromising royal dignity.

Like his father, and to an even greater extent than his brother, James paid attention to etiquette and ceremony. Yet in his personal manner, he was (often to the surprise of visitors) affable and even familiar, in recognition perhaps that, more than ever, charm was an essential component of majesty.[86] Where he departed radically from his predecessor was in the tone he sought to set at court. Charles II's court, as we have remarked, remains infamous as one of the most debauched in early modern history; and in the sexual shenanigans that made it notorious the Duke of York had hardly been less indulged than his brother. On his succession, however, James – perhaps responding to the satirical attacks on Charles's behaviour – signalled a shift from the indulgence in pleasure. He spent more time at business and seems to have resolved, not with complete success, to renounce mistresses and affairs. Very much in the spirit of his father's reforms (after what he had perceived as a debauched predecessor),

James 'declared that he would not employ drunkards, blasphemers, gamblers
... He warned that anyone who came to court drunk would lose his place and
admonished husbands to be faithful to their wives'.[87] Some of these resolutions
and instructions were (literally) pious hopes. James's court still consisted
largely of the same men as his brother's; moreover, of those he promoted,
Rochester was an inveterate drunkard. Yet, what Miller calls, even allowing for
his uncontrolled sexuality, James's 'natural puritanism', does appear to have
effected some change, if only in perception.[88] For all the bitter attacks on him,
James's court never drew the charges of, nor had the reputation for, the
debauchery we to this day associate with the court of Charles II. James endeavoured to conceal his own affairs and represented himself very much as a
married man; as important, no mistress in his reign wielded the (inappropriate,
as it was thought) influence that the Duchess of Portsmouth had exercised.
Moreover, though his Catholic faith aroused other suspicions, James's obvious
piety, contrasted with the cynicism and irreligion of Charles's court, which
many were inclined to blame for its loose morals. The new court, at least in
announcing a reformed king, serious and diligent, presented – in the changed
circumstances and reaction to the debauchery of his brother's court – a potentially positive image of James, which later events should not obscure.[89]

The fundamental question of course, is: was it a Catholic court? Whig propaganda might suggest that this is a non-question or one to which one can
provide a swift answer. Barclay's researches, however, confirm that, initially,
James's household appointments reflect his promise to sustain the privileges of
the Anglican establishment and his sincere commitment to toleration.[90] James,
we have seen, appointed Presbyterians as well as Anglican Tories to high office.
By contrast, there were few prominent Catholics elevated in his household and
many of those who held a post had already served Charles. Verrio, for instance,
who had executed decorative paintings at Windsor, succeeded Lely as principal
painter and was also appointed Keeper of the Great and Privy Gardens; and
Balthasar Reading was made part of the royal musical establishment. But
overall, there was a signal 'absence of an influx of Catholic servants' with the
new monarch.[91] Barclay's researches uncovered only three such appointments
in the whole of 1686, two of them Gentlemen Ushers Quarter Waiters. James
may well have been hoping for conversions to provide him with an entourage
of co-religionists; and it may be that when they did not appear, he changed his
tack. It was the year 1687 that 'seemed to make the most decisive shift towards
a more Catholic court'.[92] That year James dismissed Rochester and brought in
Lord Thomas Howard and James Porter as vice chamberlains. Perhaps seeing
which way the wind was blowing, the Earl of Peterborough, Groom of the
Stool, announced his conversion.[93] Yet, even then, rather than heading a pro-
active campaign to build a Catholic court, James may have been reacting to the
staunch opposition that he encountered over his Indulgence and seeking

support for toleration rather than Catholic evangelism. Even with the growing number of Catholic appointments in the last months of his reign, the total may not have exceeded two dozen, with a mere handful of converts in addition.[94] Indeed, though he was much later to advise his son of the importance of some Catholic officers in the army, contrary to rumour, quite few were appointed, still fewer in the navy.[95] The advice James later gave his son on a politic balance of religions in his household was not contrary to his own practice. As Barclay concludes, 'insofar as [James's] household was a reservoir of support, it was [to the end] still a predominantly Anglican one'.[96]

Where it was not – understandably but fatally – was in the royal religious establishment. Here James probably pursued a policy he regarded as a *modus vivendi* between himself and the Tories, but one that turned out to be a miscalculation. James left the old Chapel Royal at Whitehall and St George's Chapel at Windsor to the Protestants, while he worshipped at St James's and in the chapel adjacent to St George's Hall.[97] Once, however, his new Catholic chapel at Whitehall was consecrated, James staffed it predominantly with Catholics: musicians, confessors and priests, monks and Jesuits.[98] Conspicuously, James appointed Cardinal Howard to replace Bishop Francis Turner as almoner, which meant that the distribution of alms became a Catholic service, even if it was not for certain restricted to Catholics.[99] James also used Catholic priests as assistants when touching for the evil.[100] Against the wishes, and hopes, of those who expected that he might keep his faith private, in his appointments as well as the religious art he commissioned, James proclaimed publicly that he was a Catholic king. As a consequence, though Anglican sermons and services continued, the Anglicans felt sidelined in the religious affairs of the court. Such a policy does not merit the description 'bigotry'. In exile, James was to struggle to secure the rights of Protestants to worship publicly in Catholic France and was not inconsistent in refusing to hide Catholic worship in Anglican England.[101] As James counselled his son, the basis for a king and his subjects being happy was if both were 'at ease' and not disturbed in their conscience.[102] In his will he added, 'we as a father advise and require him never to molest his subjects in the enjoyment of their religion'.[103] But if there is little evidence of a royal campaign of proselytization or pressure (and John Spurr tells us only ten clergy converted), James's chapel and its Catholic personnel stood as a symbol, as provocation and a threat of what might follow.[104] Reconstructed in 1660 after its destruction during the civil war, the Church of England had not felt secure against the surviving cabals of dissent nor the rising tide of atheism and Catholicism in Charles II's court. But at least all the symbols of an Anglican state, and monarchy, had been sustained, especially after 1672, and from the later 1670s Charles had advertised himself as a son of the church. In making his new chapel and its staff a centrepiece of his court, James, whatever his intentions or lack of them, led many to ask whether the future of their church was secure. As John Spurr writes, the very identity of the Church of England 'was bound up with the royal supremacy'; but it was now a supremacy that seemed more to invade its jurisdiction than uphold it.[105] Perhaps coincidentally when Anglican opposition began to form, James's former almoner, replaced by a cardinal, was at its centre.[106]

James's core belief that if his subjects knew him and understood his faith they would embrace rather than eject him was borne out not only in royal declarations but in the royal progress that he undertook in the summer of 1687. He had already made an excursion to Bristol the previous year and, during April 1687, planned an extensive tour of his realm, evidently to promote his policy of indulgence and to meet the leading gentry of the shires.[107] The progress took in Portsmouth and Winchester in the south, Bath and Bristol in the west, Oxford, Banbury, Gloucestershire and Shrewsbury in the Midlands, Ludlow and Newport on the Welsh border and Chester in the north.[108] Though he dispensed with the attendance of the militia, James requested that the Lords Lieutenant, their deputies and the sheriffs meet him at each place; and it would appear that, confirming a sense that this was a public relations exercise, critics as well as supporters of the king followed the news of his travels attentively.[109] On 1 September, for example, a correspondent informed the Prince of Orange, who was weighing up plans to invade, that 'I hear in all the king's progress very few of the gentry waited on his Majesty'.[110] A few days later, Halifax assured the prince, as James returned to Oxford, 'we do not hear that his observations or his journey can give him any great encouragement to build any hopes upon, as to the carrying on some things which appears every day to be more against the grain'.[111] Despite these reports, the accuracy of which we cannot gauge, James continued his progress west for a further two weeks.[112] And he evidently held on to his belief that he could sell his policy of indulgence – presumably the 'thing' carried on – to his subjects. One reporter noted, for all the poor attendance on the king, his conviction that the corporations would return a House of Commons ready to endorse his policy.[113] Whether or not he misjudged, like his brother, James trusted in the loyalty and support of his people and reached out to them in person as well as in print.

III

On his succession, James had acknowledged that he suffered from an image problem and, as we saw, took pains to reassure his people that he would defend their laws and religion. The maintenance of justice and the protection of the church were traditional royal duties, the performance of which was vital for the representation and perception of a reign. In the case of the first, James's reign unquestionably got off to a bad start and ended even worse. The 'bloody assizes' of 1685 and the trial of the seven bishops remain among the most famous legal proceedings in popular memory; and, though later Whig propaganda is largely responsible for that, even James recognized the damage they did to his reputation – and to his representation.[114] It should not have been so. If anything, Monmouth's rising in the west increased the support for a James who had been greeted with popular demonstrations of joy. Sunderland reported the gentry of the west 'very affectionate and loyal', and while the south-west had shown support for Monmouth in the Exclusion crisis, the people did not rise for him in June.[115] He was easily defeated, most of his followers but for 'some particular obstinate scythemen and clubmen' fleeing before a fight.[116] Though a nasty shock, the rebellion provided occasion for parliament to display its loyalty, and might have given James an early opportunity to demonstrate that royal tenderness to his people which he had vowed to continue.[117] James, however, made two mistakes: in his dealings with Monmouth himself and his followers. Seized on 8 July disguised as a shepherd, Monmouth threw himself on his uncle's mercy.[118] Whether or not the king should have granted it is debatable: not least because some believed the story of Lucy Walters's (Monmouth's mother's) marriage to Charles, the duke remained a threat.[119] Once, however, James agreed to see the duke, who begged for his life before the king and queen, the refusal of a pardon breached unwritten codes of mercy and, even though the normal traitor's sentence was commuted to beheading, savoured of revenge rather than justice.[120]

A breach of etiquette in dealing with Monmouth was followed by severe proceedings against his hapless supporters. Even before the judges arrived, peasants who had proclaimed Monmouth king were summarily put to the sword, though the threat was over. At the next assizes of the Western Circuit, Lord Justice Jeffreys was vitriolic in denouncing the rebels and harsh in his sentencing. Probably three hundred were executed and more than one thousand transported as slaves to the colonies in Jamaica and Barbados.[121] It has rightly been observed that, though severe, the punishments were not unprecedented and that there appears to have been no criticism of the proceedings voiced by the gentry.[122] But possibly even before James's flight, an opposition account of the 'bloody assizes', representing the convicted as 'Protestant martyrs', assumed some public revulsion at the proceedings.[123] Certainly in 1685, many official accounts went to lengths to explain the legality of the proceedings, to assert the need to deal sharply with traitors, and to publicize the lessons of the ills of rebellion.[124] Looking back, James evidently believed that he had suffered by them.[125] The compiler of James's Life, indeed, sought partially to excuse the king and to place the blame on Jeffreys, his 'imprudent zeal, and as some say avarice, carrying him beyond the terms of moderation and mercy which was always most agreeable to the king's temper'.[126] Where Jeffreys in the west hanged even those the king would have pardoned, in London, the Life argues, James showed mercy to the guilty.[127] A suspicion that this was special pleading on behalf of the king appears to be confirmed by James's approval 'entirely of all your [Jeffreys'] proceedings'.[128] On the other hand, Jeffreys warned the king not to be 'surprised into a pardon to any man, though he pretend much to loyalty'.[129] Whatever the truth, justice was royal justice and when he elevated Jeffreys to the Lord Chancellorship, though it was a post for which his legal skills qualified him, James would have been seen to endorse all his judge had done in his name.[130]

Monmouth proclaimed his devotion to Protestantism, but few, as even the author of *The Protestant Martyrs* acknowledged, regarded the trials as part of a religious campaign. In the case of the second legal *cause célèbre* of the reign, royal justice appeared to be subordinated to proselytization, and due process to arbitrary courses and to popery. The case arose from the refusal of the Archbishop of Canterbury and six other bishops to read the royal Declaration of Indulgence in their dioceses, on the grounds that the dispensing power was illegal.[131] Though even the loyal Jeffreys wanted no part in it, James decided to commit them for trial for seditious libel.[132] And albeit James had endeavoured to appoint a compliant bench, the judges displayed their independence. Two, favouring the bishops, even departed from the strict remit, to consider – and rule illegal – the royal dispensing power.[133] Not surprisingly, the jury returned a verdict of not guilty. The rebuff to the king, both in the verdict and the larger matter of his prerogative, occurred in a full blaze of publicity. As we shall see, engravings, medals as well as pamphlets and newsbooks, presented the bishops as heroes and martyrs as they were committed to the Tower.[134] The trial itself 'drew a great concourse of people to see one of the greatest sights that had ever been known'; and they made their sympathies clear.[135] The people hissed when evidence was given against the bishops, and there were cheers in court for half an hour when the verdict was returned.[136] Celebrations spilled on to the streets and the crowd, in a replay of Exclusion, burned an effigy of the pope outside St James's.[137] The Seven Bishops Case, rather like the trial and punishment of Prynne, Burton and Bastwick half a century earlier, marked a turn of the tide.[138] Not only had the king lost a show trial, as the bishops were feted, he had lost his authority and trust in his promise to uphold the law and the church.

What then of James's performance of that vital role and representation of early modern monarchy, headship of the church? Unless we interpret the promise he made on his succession as blatantly cynical, it would seem that in effect he planned to live with two churches, that of the nation over which he ruled and that of his own faith.[139] James's Catholicism, however, was not private, so, as the various royal chapels testified, the Church of England was faced with the effective establishment of a Catholic church alongside it. On a small scale, such a situation was not new: earlier royal consorts had had their Catholic priests, retainers and chapels. But in the case of a Catholic monarch – the first in a truly Protestant England – the situation was tense from the outset. It would appear that in 1685 the Church of England establishment still hoped, perhaps naïvely, that James would keep his faith as private as possible, and some even interpreted the promise he gave as meaning just that. As the lines of John Baber put it in 1685:

> Safely on him may *England's* Church depend,
> Pious he is, and will the Faith defend:
> The Faith I mean of our Progenitors.[140]

Anglicans reminded James of the staunch support of the church for monarchy and, in the wake of Monmouth's rebellion, sermons like that by Thomas Long on *The Unreasonableness of Rebellion* underlined that the crown was established and 'the church appears fixed on that rock against which the gates of hell cannot prevail'.[141] But members of the church also took the precaution of reasserting its identity for the new reign. Celebrating the king's peaceful succession in a sermon at the Guildhall, John Goodman expressed pride in a Church of England founded on reason and distinguished from a Rome whose doctrines of transubstantiation a man could 'confute with his fingers ends' and that of Geneva, with its theology of 'fatal security'.[142] And the republication of several works by James Usher, along with Richard Parr's life and letters of the primate, as well as reviving a model of Anglican piety, publicized the church's history and antiquity, which Usher's scholarly researches had been devoted to elucidating.[143]

As with just about every new regime in early modern history, those outside the church also had hopes and expectations of the change of ruler. The leader of the Quakers, William Penn, was quick to celebrate James's coronation, and over the next months his influence on the king grew.[144] What Quakers and other dissenters sought was toleration; and by the end of 1686, James, in response to their petitions, effectively suspended persecution, as he similarly quietly allowed some Catholics to take up offices despite the Test, before proceeding to issue a formal Declaration of Indulgence on 4 April 1687. Dissenters extolled the king and the act: *The Dissenter's Description of True Loyalty* argues:

> His Declaration shews them well
> No Prince in Wisdom doth Excell
> . . .
> For *Liberty* to this land he brings
> And fames his Name above most *Kings*.[145]

Others, and they included some Anglicans, though less ecstatic, could see the benefits of peace and the pragmatic arguments for some relaxing of persecution.

STAGING CATHOLIC KINGSHIP 305

Thomas Cartwright, Dean of Ripon, asking his auditors: 'Is it not possible for men of two minds to be of one heart?' and defended James's favouring some whose loyalty he had experienced.[146] Others, echoing the arguments of the Declaration, hoped that it would put an end to 'jarring factions', cement unity and benefit trade.[147] As the Recorder of Gloucester put it in an address to that city, there were only two roads to peace: one was the submission of all Christians to one authority – 'no more need be said of that'; the other 'bearing with one another's differences in religion', which was what the king had wisely proposed.[148] Many, however, feared that Indulgence in 1687, as in 1672, opened – worse, may have been intended to open – the door to popery; and increasingly defence of the dispensing power and toleration, not only by dissenters but Tories like Roger L'Estrange, had to answer the charge of a design to destroy Protestantism. The king, Roger L'Estrange argued, had vowed to maintain the authority of the church and its bishops and there was no need for indulgence to undermine that assurance.[149] From the provinces, the loyal address of Leominster made the same point: 'should we admit of the least doubt or scruple of the sincerity of your Majesty's intentions, we must become more stupid than Brutes'.[150]

James's intentions may indeed have been sincere. Though he believed that the Reformation had instigated a series of schisms that had undermined the unity of the state as well as church, though he held Calvinist views dangerous, and though he hoped that what had led him to Rome might in time bring subjects over to him, he harboured no secret design to destroy the church.[151] Indeed, in 1686, the king had reprinted, with a large royal arms, the thirty-nine Articles agreed in 1562 'for the [e]stablishing of content touching true religion'.[152] His Majesty's declaration prefixed, following Charles I and II, asserted the royal belief that it was 'agreeable to this our kingly office and our own religious zeal to conserve and maintain the church committed to our charge', and that the articles contained true doctrine. Moreover, in a visible and symbolic gesture, James re-established the commission for the rebuilding of St Paul's Cathedral which Charles II had instituted after the Fire, and expressed his wish to see the work hastened.[153] As Charles II in 1672, James saw no necessary contradiction between his headship of the church, his faith and his genuine belief in toleration. But the anxieties others felt were exacerbated by what was widely, and rightly, perceived as a rise of Catholic influence and teaching that compromised royal words and promises and struck at the core of the church.

From the beginning of their reigns, James and Mary licensed for publication the sermons delivered in their chapels at St James's and Whitehall, often by monks and Jesuit priests. If the publicization of the event were not itself disturbing enough, the contents of the sermons would certainly have been. On the day of 'the annunciation of our mother' of Christ, Dr John Bethan of the Sorbonne preached on the 'miraculous mother' of Christ, urging that 'devotions to Our Lady . . . will engage her efficaciously in our protection and invite her powerfully to use that grace and favour she has with her divine Son'.[154] If such an emphasis on an intermediary questioned the Protestant belief in a direct relationship with Christ, worse was to follow in Father Philip Ellis's sermon on the Feast of All the Saints of the Holy Order of St Benedict, where, in a text larded with Latin, Ellis praised the monastic life and state and, though acknowledging that 'they can by no law . . . be wrested out of the hands of the present possessors', hinted at a regret that monastic lands could not be restored.[155] In other sermons, on texts taken from the Vulgate rather than the King James Bible, Catholic preachers invoked the mediation of saints, celebrated the monastic life and clerical celibacy, and struck at the core doctrines of Protestantism.[156] In a sermon before the queen dowager, at Somerset House, for example, the Franciscan Father James Ayray directly countered predestination, asserting 'no man can tell whether he deserves love or hatred'.[157] Only the church of Rome, the Jesuit Lewis Sabran preached in a sermon at Chester that provoked massive controversy, offered a reliable guide to the Scriptures and to faith.[158]

Printed by the royal printers, Henry Hills and Thomas Newcomb, and 'published by His Majesty's Command', such sermons publicized doctrines, beliefs and lifestyles not authorized since Mary's reign. Nor was the promotion of Catholic doctrine confined to the published court sermons. Hills, printer to the king for his household and chapel, supervised the publication of a number of Catholic treatises, published by royal command, including a translation of Bossuet's *An Exposition of the Doctrine of the Catholic Church* and the *Kalendarium Catholicum for the Year 1686*.[159] Encouraged by such official patronage, other Catholic authors did not hesitate to rush into print.[160] An edition of Henry VIII's *Assertio Septem Sacramentorum* against Luther was, the title page claimed, 'published by authority', and books on the cult of the Virgin, the Catholic doctrine of images, clerical celibacy and of the Jesuit Father Bridoul's *The School of the Eucharist Established* (with a preface on miracles) were freely sold.[161] *The State of Church Affairs in this Island of Great Britain under the Government of the Romans and British Kings*, published by Nathaniel Thompson, offered an alternative Catholic history written around virgin martyrs and the relics of saints.[162]

Understandably, many suspected that in questioning the very foundations of the Church of England and Reformation, such literature was published in order to bring about conversions to Rome.[163] Though almost certainly only few, the converts there were seemed to confirm that suspicion by themselves publishing to win over others. For example, *Consensus Veterum*, the reasons of Edward Sclater, minister of Putney, for his conversion to the Catholic faith (published by a royal printer), relating how Sclater had come to believe in the real presence and other Roman doctrines, was clearly intended to persuade others.[164] Not only did James's chapel, imprimatur and printer appear at the centre of Catholic proselytization, it was the king himself who advertised what was claimed to be the most spectacular conversion – that of his brother, King Charles II. In 1685 and 1686 James licensed and had published copies of papers 'I found in the late King my Brother's strong box, written in his own hand'.[165] The papers upheld the authority of the Catholic apostolic church, rejected the claims of the Church of England to be the true church, and lamented the schisms caused by the break from Rome. It is far from certain that these were authentic: a contemporary manuscript note in a copy in the Huntington Library suggests 'these two next following papers (in my apprehension) seem rather to be written to King Charles ye 2nd and after transcribed by him, than to be endited [set down in writing] by him'.[166] Published, however, with the king's arms, they proclaimed either a long Stuart design to bring in popery or a trick of James's to add strength to his cause. In spite of his verbal assurances, Catholic publications and conversions made James II appear to subjects not merely as a Catholic king but a ruler determined, by all means, to rule a Catholic nation.

CHAPTER 8

COUNTERING 'CATHOLIC KINGSHIP' AND CONTESTING REVOLUTION

I

It was this Catholic literature that was countered by a barrage of texts that were (perhaps inevitably given how James had connected them) to turn opposition to Catholicism into direct resistance to the king.[1] Initially, some efforts were made to separate the king from the advance of Catholicism. In a sermon preached at St Giles in Edinburgh and published in both Edinburgh and London, the Selkirk minister James Canaries urged his hearers to trust in the king's promise to the church while he attacked 'Rome's additions to Christianity' as the superstitious accretions of a false church.[2] By 1686 the presses were pouring out sermons and tracts against Catholic doctrine and defences of Protestantism and the church. *A Discourse Concerning the Worship of the Blessed Virgin and the Saints*, answering books that 'the gentlemen of the church of Rome have been pleased lately to send . . . amongst us', denounced prayer to saints as near idolatry, as whorish behaviour.[3] *A Brief Discourse of the Real Presence* and other works exposed the subtle plans to revive belief in transubstantiation, which was rejected as 'one of the most bombast pieces of pageantry the world ever saw'.[4] *A Defence of the Exposition of the Doctrine of the Church of England Against the Exceptions of Monsieur de Meaux* [Bossuet] restated the church's position against Rome in all the major controversies of doctrine and the authority of the church.[5] In a hint of the anxieties that were mounting, *The Protestant Resolution of Faith* announced that 'we will never countenance any rebellion against our lawful sovereign', but identified the threat posed by Roman emissaries who were seeking to corrupt the people and the need to instruct the people concerning their errors.[6]

As the perception of a threat heightened, anti-Catholic, that is oppositionist, treatises became sharper in tone and were increasingly directed to a broader audience. *An Answer to a Dialogue between a New Catholic Convert and a Protestant* derided the 'absurd' doctrines of the mystery of the trinity and transubstantiation; a *Discourse Concerning Penance* mocked the practice as a 'mere phantasm'.[7] Samuel Freeman used brevity and a popular pamphlet form to provide *A Plain and Familiar Discourse by Way of a Dialogue Betwixt a Minister and His Parishioner Concerning the Catholic Church*.[8] As the author explained in his preface to the reader, 'the design of this tract is to furnish thee with answers to the many captious questions of the Romanists'.[9] Clearly the concern was that Catholic writers were winning over members of the church, at times by blurring the distinctions between Rome and London and representing the Church of England but as a diluted version of the true Catholic church. Anglican writers, therefore, had to underscore the historic differences, to argue again that reconciliation was 'impossible as long as the doctrines of each of them stand as they do'.[10] And, as one treatise recognized, since the Romanists' great seduction tactic was 'to persuade them they can have no certainty of their religion without a fallible judge and that there is no infallibility but in the Church of Rome', the scriptural foundations of Protestantism and the church needed restating.[11] Accordingly, in 1687, Chillingworth's famous *The Religion of Protestants* was reissued in a new edition, 'made more generally useful' and, as an advertisement hoped, 'of a lesser bulk and an easier purchase' than before.[12] In this copy, parts were omitted to 'make the reading of his book more pleasant' and beneficial, as 'his defence of the Protestant doctrine' and the cause of the Reformation were highlighted by editing.[13]

Most of the anti-Catholic published works were (though it has mostly not proved difficult to trace authors) published anonymously, but often with the imprimatur of the archbishop and senior bishops of the church. This of course meant that, though on the one hand they were performing their duties, on the other the bishops and clergy who licensed or authored these books were directly opposing positions authorized by their head of the church, who was behind many of the Catholic publications. James did not help the situation when he issued the two papers allegedly found in Charles II's study.[14] As the preface to one anonymous *Answer* to 'Some Papers Lately Printed' put it, 'a due respect to the name they bear would have kept the author from publishing any answer to them' had they 'not been so publicly dispersed'.[15] Religious controversy, as was so often the case in early modern England, was becoming inseparable from the issue of authority. Indeed, in 1687, a series of works by a figure who personified the willingness of the bishops to take on the king as well as the Catholics reopened old political as well as religious sores and divisions. John Tillotson, Dean of Canterbury, published that year not only a treatise against transubstantiation, and sermons attacking 'idolatry' and 'the gross follies of superstition', but also an edition of the works of Isaac Barrow, who had written a powerful treatise against Rome.[16] Tillotson, the son of a puritan clothier, had married a niece of Oliver Cromwell. In 1683, even at the height of the Tory reaction, he had attended the Whig Lord Russell on the scaffold.

James made his authority the core matter when he both issued his Declaration of Indulgence and then commanded that the bishops and clergy read it from the pulpit. While many had been willing to turn a blind eye to the non-enforcement of penal laws against Catholics, the public policy of indulgence, and the defence of the dispensing power it involved, unravelled not only the support of the church but of the Tory laity for the crown.[17] In the wake of indulgence, the religious clashes spread from the pages of sermons and theological treatises to popular pamphlets and broadsides. A ballad 'on the late toleration' ran:

> Dissenters countenanced, Church-Men Cashiered
> Now what th'event will be is greatly feared.[18]

The author foresaw Jesuits and fanatics combining to destroy 'the glorious beauty of this Church and State'. The anti-popery that Dryden identified as endemic among the common people broke out too in pornographic verse, reminiscent of civil war satires.[19] A ballad, entitled *The Explanation*, for example, revived old popular radical tropes as prophesying that religious houses could be restored; it sang of friars fucking nuns under an abbess who 'has f..cked and b..gger'd three score years'.[20]

Sharp pamphlet exchange and popular satirical ballads were an unpleasant reminder to the king that, for all the elevation of divine monarchy that had followed in the wake of the Rye House Plot, the post-Restoration monarchy lived in the demystifying world of print and publicity. Soon after the king's succession to the throne, the rector of Worlington, Suffolk, Erasmus Warren, had warned James that there were subjects who deemed the king 'no better than a mere superfluity, an over grown wen, a monstrous excrescency rather than the head of the body politic'.[21] And Catholics in particular, perhaps, including James himself, were inclined to see a connection between contempt for the mysteries of the faith and for those of monarchy. In a sermon, published in 1687, the Benedictine Father Wall told James and Mary in their majesties' chapel at St James's: 'sceptres have lost their awfulness and strangely lessened in that state and grandeur with which kings heretofore did prop their sovereignty'.[22] As the next year another explosion of print saw divine right interrogated and denied, elective monarchy reasserted, the language of contact revived and the king roughly received by his own subjects, the hard political realities beneath the 'painted rays' of majesty became all too evident.[23] Not only was James's beloved faith scorned, his word was called deceit, his sincere love of toleration a conspiracy to advance popery, and defences of royal sovereignty were 'speculations'.[24]

One development in the opposition to James and his royal representation was the broad use of visual media by his critics and enemies. Almost since the beginning of print, of course, and particularly from the Reformation, woodcuts had joined words in attacks on authority; during the Popish Plot prints had been used not only to oppose royal policies but to satirize both the king and Duke of York: in his trial for treason, Stephen College was charged with publishing a print against Charles II.[25] But it is in James's reign that we discern a systematic programme of visual opposition to royal policies and positions, in genres both elite and more popular. As Charles's brother, James (as we have seen) regularly issued commemorative medals to celebrate triumphs, and to proclaim his divine kingship.[26] Towards the end of his reign, however, a series of anti-royal medals began to circulate, directly opposing royal policy and under- mining the symbols of royal power. One, known as 'The Religious State of England', for example, countered all of James's claims by representing him 'desirous of trampling on liberty of conscience, disowning his coronation oath, and renouncing the Test and Penal Laws, which sealed the safety of the country'.[27] The imprisonment and trial of the Seven Bishops provided the subject for at least half a dozen opposition medals. One, with a depiction on he obverse of the Tower, describes their imprisonment as honourable and in God's cause, while the reverse, balancing the sun and moon equally, symbolizes king and people – as polar and equal opposites (fig. 42).[28] Others, some of coarse workmanship so probably for broad distribution, boldly appropriated images and legends from the *Eikon Basilike* to present the bishops rather than the crown as the rock on which the church rested, or represented the seven as the Pleiades, stars that shone as the light of faith in the midst of darkness.[29] Evidently the medals were in great demand and it is believed that, in a direct parody of the loyal habit of wearing miniatures of Queen Elizabeth or Charles I, they were hung from the

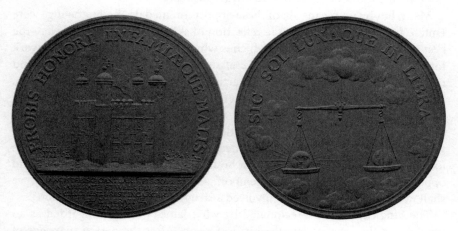

42   Bishops medal, Hawkins, *Medallic Illustrations*, plate LXV, 9.

neck by clergy and laymen to announce their defiance of royal policy and authority.[30]

It was, however, through the medium of engravings and prints that opposition to James in visual form was broadly publicized. Though, as we shall see, most of these probably post-date James's flight, the programme of visual opposition began earlier and served to undermine the king's cause. An engraving that we can tentatively date to early in James's reign consists of ovals of eight nobles who were executed, with Monmouth at the centre – perhaps as a paper monument to the Whig heroes Russell, Sidney and Argyll, who had plotted or rebelled against the king.[31] But again it was the trial of the Seven Bishops that turned engravings into a powerful medium of opposition. A large print, for example, presents ovals of the bishops arranged in a pyramid with Archbishop Sancroft at the head, on an altar, on which is inscribed Revelation 1: 20, the text of which in the King James Bible reads: 'the seven stars are the angels of the seven churches'.[32] Other versions of this form of the image of the seven carry different inscriptions – 'the unmoveable rock' signifying their defence of the church, or 'we are overcome but not broken', announcing their and their supporters' resolve.[33] Not only do the similar motifs between medals and engravings (in the case of the Tower medal, an exact replication)[34] suggest a carefully orchestrated programme, the number of these images (of the seven and of each of the individual bishops) indicates a market for opposition figures represented as martyrs and heroes. Other engravings, of the bishops' legal counsel and the Lord Chief Justice who presided over their acquittal, confirm an impression of a broad interest in collecting these images – a habit that itself constituted a defiance of authority.[35] On the other part, engravings of Father Edward Petre, the king's confessor, in the company of devils, literally demonized not only the Catholic cause but the royal cause too.[36]

Many, but by no means all, of these opposition medals and engravings were Dutch. In part this was a simple reflection of skill. Dutch medallists were the best in the seventeenth century, which is why they had been recruited to work for Charles II; and, though native craftsmen were emerging, engraving and mezzotint were dominated by Dutch artists, again several working in London. But increasingly the Dutch had an interest in the image of James II, and their dominance of the engraving industry was to have major political as well as aesthetic import. However, it was not the Dutch medallists or engravers alone who turned against the king. English medallists like George Bower or engravers like David Loggan worked openly for both the Stuarts and for their critics and opponents. As the final crisis came upon James, the fight for his authority, we shall not be surprised to learn, involved a struggle over his representation.

The king's crisis was precipitated by what James probably regarded as an occasion of the greatest joy: the birth of a son. After the barren marriage of

Charles II and Catherine of Braganza, and Mary of Modena's miscarriage, an heir was a powerful representation of God's blessing and legitimate kingship. The prince symbolized and represented the security of the dynasty – and (given that James's daughter Anne was Protestant) the Catholic religion. For exactly those reasons, those most alarmed at the course of James's reign had to find some means to respond swiftly; as we know, their solution was to deny and to spread doubts about the legitimacy of the prince, and to argue that an impostor child had been imported into the birthing room in a warming pan, as a Catholic conspiracy to ruin Protestantism. Just as during the year of the Popish Plot, the last months of James's reign were dominated by a struggle: a battle as much about what could effectively – and persuasively – be represented as the truth, as well as what was the truth. Like the Popish Plot, the struggle concerning the Prince of Wales was one that revolved around words and witnesses, and the reliability of depositions and testimonies.[37] But it was also a contest conducted in visual culture, from both sides a multimedia contest to persuade a people and to secure a throne.

For his part, James took the opportunity of the occasion of the prince's birth for a representation of majesty. James Francis Edward, Prince of Wales, was born on 10 June 1688. Immediately the king ordered a form of service of thanksgiving 'for the safe delivery of the queen and the happy birth of the young prince' to be drawn up for use in London churches the next Sunday, the 17th, and on 1 July in worship throughout the rest of the country.[38] The theme of the service was God's continuing providential blessings on his chosen king, James. The congregation intoned prayers of thanks for having protected their king from the dangers of war, the rage of the sea and 'the madness of the people'.[39] Having set his lieutenant safely on the throne, the prayers stated, God now enlarged his blessings: the Lord 'showeth loving kindness to David his anointed'.[40] God's gift to the king, the service emphasized, was also a benefaction to the people. 'Thou hast given our dread sovereign his heart's desire,' one prayer ran, 'and hast not denied us the request of our lips, in blessing him and our gracious Queen with a son and all his subjects with a prince.'[41] The people prayed for the infant's long life and the preservation of his house for the happiness of three nations: 'O Lord save the King/And let his seed be mighty upon the Earth.'[42]

With England's long history (endlessly re-enacted on the stage) of the turmoils of disputed successions, the birth of a new prince was inherently an occasion of popular joy, and James took advantage of a new medium of royal celebration to make it so. As with the king's own coronation, the prince's birth was marked with an extravagant and dazzling fireworks display which again symbolically represented the king as the light of the nation. On 17 July, perhaps after a delay required to prepare the extravaganza, thousands gathered along the Thames to enjoy the spectacle engineered by Sir Martin Beckman and financed by 'princely generosity'.[43] Once again, on the river between two pyramids erected on lighters and topped with pennants of England, a large sun was suspended, with below it an imperial crown and the monogram 'JMR' of the fertile royal couple. Three other figures, filled with fireworks, joined the royal symbol and cipher: a Bacchus astride a large barrel, a woman representing Peace and Plenty, and another female figure with a coronet and emblems of 'firmness', representing 'Stability of Empire'.[44] As the display began, the sun with the imperial crown and cipher was first fired so that 'all appeared as glorious as at noonday' before, from and around the other figures, and rockets flew into the air, accompanied by sounds like guns representing 'a sea fight'. Almost like a masque in fireworks, the display not only reminded spectators of the king's post as admiral and represented James as the sun and the source of peace and prosperity, it also associated the royal couple, through the figure of Bacchus, with popular joy and revelry, for which the birth of the prince gave occasion. The continued shouts and 'huzzas' of the crowd attested to their delight. Whatever his deficiencies in the political arts, James II did not fail to grasp the need to present himself, in a variety of forms, to his people.

As well as official pronouncements and rejoicing, the birth of the prince was heralded in the first verse encomia to the birth of a male heir in half a century. Oxford University used the occasion of celebrating the prince to remind the king of

> ... those days well try'd
> When we 'mongst others, stem'd that swelling tide
> That would have turned Successions course aside.[45]

Now, with the royal birth, all doubts about the dynasty were allayed:

> Hail Infant Prince! The Messenger of peace,
> At thy approach all our Confusions cease.[46]

With 'pleasing smiles' the university bards looked forward to 'A Golden Age/ From Thee, Auspicious Babe' and to a new emperor of Britain who would give the law to Europe.[47] For all the tensions arising from James's religious policy, Tory panegyrists were not slow to welcome the royal birth. Thomas D'Urfey, a dramatist and songwriter who had been close to Charles II, hoped that the happy event would finally dispel 'Enthusiastic Schism' and that the faithless spouse, the City, would now unite in love with the fertile husband and father of the realm.[48] And, at a time when some were wavering, the king reasserted the principles of non-resistance that were the traditional doctrines of his church and party:

Since Kings can do no wrong, what strange decree
Is that, which can Allegiance backward draw?
Duty Chief Point should of Religion be,
And an Obedience Passive should be Law.[49]

Aphra Behn rose to loftier strains. Comparing the birth of Prince James to that of 'the sacred infant', she greeted 'A young APOLLO, rising from the gloom;/ Dressed in his Father's brightest Rays . . . ', and, like D'Urfey, she hoped that a settled succession could temper division and dissension:

Now join their *Int'rests*, and no more dispute,
With sawcy Murmurs, who is *Absolute*;
Since, from the Wonders of your Life, 'tis plain
You *will*, You *shall*, and *must* for ever Reign.[50]

Medals issued to commemorate the royal birth figured the infant James as another Hercules.[51] Official mezzotints by Smith and others of Kneller's portrait of the week-old prince on a velvet cushion, beneath a richly embroidered crown, or by Lens of the infant in his cradle with the Prince of Wales feathers, were distributed within weeks of the birth; and it seems likely that William Vincent's mezzotint of the prince attended by angels, who (as we have seen) hold a crown over his head, was published soon after.[52] James's unusual haste in distributing portraits of his son (it is hard to think of another early modern royal offspring depicted within days) may have its explanation in his sheer joy: at the news he fell on his knees and cried for most of the night.[53] The baby's fragile health may also be relevant: a diet of boiled bread and canary wine almost ended his life. More likely, however, was the king's shock at, and immediate sense of the need to counter, the rumours that began to circulate almost as soon as his son entered the world.

For many, the birth of the prince could hardly have been more unwelcome. Passive obedience to James while they awaited the succession of his Protestant daughter Mary was one thing; the prospect of a continuous Catholic rule another. For some, the stakes were even higher. By the late spring of 1688, William of Orange, suspecting that James might divert the succession, was planning an intervention in English affairs.[54] Some Englishmen, Burnet chief among them, had long been in contact with him, in anticipation of his wife's succession.[55] The birth of James not only dashed their hopes but rendered some liable to a charge of treason. Moreover, the birth may have caught them off guard. Though there had been rumours of the queen's pregnancy, it may genuinely not have been believed, or, given her history – it was five years since she had given birth – might have been expected to end in miscarriage.[56]

The immediate reaction to the birth could hardly have delivered the king's opponents any comfort. For, though, in their invitation to William, they claimed that the news of the queen's pregnancy had been 'a matter of laughter and derision amongst the people and a subject of poets lampoons', when the prince was born, the response had in fact been rather different.[57] Not only had the poets sung their laudations, from around the country loyal addresses of congratulations were sent to the royal couple.[58] York, the city reported, was 'transported with joy' at the news; Sudbury described the prince as a reward for his father's virtue; Bridgwater vowed 'we will bear all faith and true allegiance to this illustrious prince'; Durham regarded the birth as 'the greatest blessing that could possibly descend upon these your kingdoms'.[59] Rochester not only conveyed its 'congratulations for the inestimable jewel you have bestowed upon us' but regarded the birth as a sign of 'the propitious conduct of heaven over your sacred majesty, as your majesty over us'; the city hoped that the forthcoming parliament would support the king in all his designs.[60] It may well be, though we should not be too quick to assume it, that such declarations were formulaic and politic rather than sincere. The point remains that they would have disturbed the Orangists in England who were also alarmed to discover that the prince was permitting prayers for James's son in his chapel.[61]

Whether or not they believed it, therefore, the Orangists had to deny the legitimacy of the baby prince and to persuade others of that doubt. First, they needed to provide ammunition to Orange himself, which they did in a full account of the suspicious nature of the pregnancy that little fits with their alleged disregard of false reports of the queen's condition.[62] In detail hitherto unseen about a royal birth, those who invited William into England reported the absence of reliable witnesses at the delivery, the queen's slim shape, continuing menses and lack of breast milk when she was supposed to be pregnant; and artfully observed that the onus of proof lay not on him but on the king and queen.[63] The 'evidence' sent to Holland became the basis of opposition pamphlets distributed in England. *An Account of the Pretended Prince of Wales* folded doubts about the legitimacy of the prince into a larger narrative of an assault on Protestantism, complete with an appendix claiming that the Whig Earl of Essex had been murdered rather than taken his own life.[64] Adding to the stories about the queen's weight, lactation and menstrual cycle, the tract evoked an atmosphere of secrecy around the place and time of the birth and asserted that another newborn baby (and indeed its afterbirth) had been smuggled in to a curtained room by papists. Satirical medals were hastily produced to counter the image of a Stuart prince born as the hope of his dynasty and nation. In one, the king's confessor Father Edward Petre hides in a cabinet, from which, it is implied, he emerged with a baby, here presented on the cushion in parody of the (official) Smith mezzotint.[65] Inscriptions on the Dutch medal hint at the desperate need that led James and Mary to trickery – 'Sic Non Heredes Decunt' ('Without heirs they fail') – and ask whether Britons could be so credulous as to believe the falsity. In another, a directly personal attack, the reverse shows a withered rose bush (figuring the infertility of the royal couple) with a young shoot springing not from their infertile stock but growing at a distance from them.[66] In the same spirit, an engraving of Prince James in his cradle, drawn from Lens, adds a foreign priest with his dark arm around the queen in what may be meant to suggest a lascivious and adulterous embrace (fig. 43).[67]

Faced with such powerful counter-representations, James, who had initially dismissed the warming-pan rumours, took action. On 22 October, he summoned his full Council and the mayor and aldermen to a meeting at Whitehall to report what he knew were connected events: the poisoning of subjects to doubt the legitimacy of his son and the planned invasion of Orange.[68] Announcing his determination to fight any incursion, James then produced depositions of the women from the queen dowager downwards and the men who had been witnesses to Mary's labour and parturition.[69] Maids and midwives like Isabelle Wentworth avowed to feeling the child in the womb; Mrs Elizabeth Bromley 'saw the milk constantly fall out of her Majesty's breasts'; Mrs Judith Wilks testified to

43 James II as an infant.

the queen's waters breaking; Mrs Pears confirmed her condition from 'the washing of her linen'; Mrs Delabadie saw the blood of the prince's umbilical cord given him in cherry water, a practice believed to avert fits.[70] The men, 'at the bed's feet' or at further remove, testified to the travails of labour, to the cries of the queen 'wearied and panting'.[71] James ordered all the signed depositions to be enrolled in Chancery and had them published in versions ranging from forty- to four-page formats, hoping that they would confirm the prince, in Dryden's words:

> Born in broad Day-light, that th'ungrateful Rout
> May find no room for a remaining doubt.[72]

It was a hope quickly dashed. *The Several Declarations Together with the Several Depositions Made in Council*, spuriously claiming to be 'published by His Majesty's special command', repeated some depositions, marking with an asterisk those made by Catholics.[73] Accordingly, it was argued, the testimony of the midwife Judith Wilks was undermined by a supposed account of her confession to her papist cousin and her flight to France.[74] Meanwhile, *The History of Queen Mary's Big Belly* revived memories of an earlier, actually phantom pregnancy and of an unpopular monarch and reign demonized by Foxe.[75] Among the people, 'satires and lampoons in verse and prose, like rude serpents ... flew about, not sparing the queen's petticoats', including near-pornographic mockery of the depositions.[76] As one entitled *Father Pete's Policy* goes:

> Another great lord both Grave and Wise
> Stood peeping between Her Majesties Thighs.[77]

The struggle over the legitimacy of the prince was not resolved by testimony. Though the debate continued, it was overtaken by events – by realpolitik and force.

On 28 September, William of Orange informed the States General of the United Provinces of his decision to invade England, to rescue the people from popery and arbitrary rule. On 20 October the Dutch fleet set sail; after being delayed and driven back by a storm, it passed Dover on the 3rd and William landed on British soil at Torbay two days later.[78] Within a month, Orange was marching towards London and James had resolved to flee.[79] It may be thought that the bare facts tell the story of military force determining a major historical outcome. The 1688 Revolution, however, like other early modern crises, was not simply decided on the battlefield. During and after, as well as before, William's invasion, the crucial battle was that for support – a battle between the representation and reception of two kings, each of whom recognized the importance of words and symbols as well as arms. In sheer military terms, the advantage lay with James.[80] In early modern Europe an invasion by sea was always hazardous.[81] The English fleet was equal to William's, and James's army was twice or three times the size of his. William, therefore, was banking on the support from England which those who had urged him to intervene had promised. Though there were to be minor military encounters, the outcome was not decided by arms, but by a battle of wills and for minds.

William commenced that campaign before he set off from Holland. Given the struggle between the Orangists and republicans in the Netherlands, he had to persuade his own countrymen of the benefits of his proposed action; but his address to the Estates was couched in language intended too for English ears and eyes.[82] The letter of invitation to William (promising the support of nineteen out of twenty Englishmen) had provided him with the script of religion, liberties and properties threatened.[83] On 30 September, therefore, William published from The Hague his declaration of his reasons for a descent on England, 'for preserving of the Protestant religion, and for restoring the laws and liberties' of the three kingdoms.[84] Using the familiar conceit of the 'evil counsellors' who had led James to break his promises to protect the church and the law, the declaration catalogued the grievances of the realm: the dispensing power, the promotion of Catholics, the ecclesiastical commission, the violation of the rights of Magdalen College and so on – and hinted at further threats to the 'honours and estates' and privileges of Protestants.[85] 'To crown all', the declaration continued, those promoting such evil designs had publicized the birth of a prince, concerning which there were 'visible grounds of suspicion'.[86] In the absence of a parliament, and with no prospect of a free parliament, William announced that 'a great many lords' had 'earnestly solicited' his aid, which his affection had dictated he could not deny.[87] His intention, he affirmed, was 'no other design but to have a free and lawful parliament', elected on the basis of the old corporation charters, that would restore the church and 'just and legal government', which, once secured, Orange would send back his forces.[88] Closing with a prayer for God's assistance and the support of the people, Orange announced his sole wish to see the 'peace, honour and happiness' of three kingdoms re-established on lasting foundations.[89] In addition to this general address to the English, intended to strengthen the support of which he had already been assured, William directed a manifesto to the officers and seamen of the English fleet, calling on them to assist rather than obstruct him:

> You are only made use of as instruments to bring both yourselves and your country under Popery and Slavery . . . . And therefore we hope that God will put it in your hearts at this time to redeem yourselves, your country and your religion.[90]

As he set sail, Orange equipped his flagship with English colours bearing the motto 'The Protestant Religion and Liberties of England', with beneath 'And I will Maintain it'.[91]

The importance at this critical juncture of words and symbols, of representations, was not lost on James, who issued a proclamation even as William's *Declaration* was going to press at The Hague. On 28 September, informing his subjects of the advice he had received of an imminent invasion, James warned them against 'false pretences relating to liberty, property and religion, contrived or worded with art and subtlety' that 'may be given out' to bolster the unlawful attempt on England.[92] For, his proclamation continues, the reality behind the pretences was the design of 'an absolute conquest of these our kingdoms and the utter subduing and subjecting us and all our people to a foreign power'; and it was a design even supported by some in England. To counter the invasion, James made it known that he had been offered foreign assistance; but he had declined, choosing rather to rely upon 'the true and ancient courage, faith and allegiance of our own people', with whom the king would again, as he had before, venture his life against the nation's enemies and 'their rash and unjust attempt'. Finally, reminding subjects of the parliament due to meet in November, James regretted that the invasion (William's principal reason for which was a parliament) forced him to withdraw the writs. In what was a short rhetorical performance, James cleverly (and it has been suggested effectively) played the patriotic card and branded the Orangists as foreign usurpers and, not least by carefully deployed pronouns and memories, tried to bind his subjects to him, describing the planned parliament as a symbol of their union.[93] A further proclamation restoring to all corporations their ancient charters and franchises sought to confirm the king's good faith.[94] Whatever its impact on subjects, the royal response appears to have rattled William: just as he was about to sail he was forced to issue a supplementary declaration on 14 October/24 October denying any design of conquest and emphasizing his dependence not on foreign troops but the support of the true lovers of England who had invited him.[95] It was on the persuasiveness of such exchanges that the outcome of events would depend.

Before Orange had landed, a royal proclamation of 2 November had threatened severe punishments of any guilty of distributing Williamite propaganda.[96] Having marched for four days through Devon, however, Orange ensured that the first impression he made as he entered Exeter (where his declaration was read aloud) would itself proclaim his case.[97] Conducting what was more a ceremonial procession than an army, the Earl of Macclesfield led two hundred cavalry 'the most part of which were English gentlemen' to demonstrate English support.[98] Attending them, two hundred 'blacks brought from the plantations of the Netherlands in America' with white feathers proclaimed William's imperial sway. Behind a troop of Finns and Laplanders, fifty gentlemen bore the

Prince of Orange's banner 'bearing this inscription, GOD and the PROTESTANT RELIGION', after whom rode Orange himself 'on a milk white palfrey', armed but clad in the colours of innocence, purity and faith. The author of the broadside description of the public entry surely exaggerated when he claimed that 'since the foundation of monarchy . . . there was never any that exceeded this of the most illustrious hero the Prince of Orange his entrance into Exeter'; but the extravagant relation, like the entry, was intended to represent William as what he claimed to be: a Protestant champion and deliverer of the English people. Though the numbers who came over to him were (to him) disappointingly few, an Association of those who did was also published vowing allegiance to Orange and 'this common cause' against papists.[99]

With the strategic advantage on his side, James determined to move against the invaders and rode to join his forces at Salisbury. A bold decision to fight – of the sort he had taken scores of times in his military career – might then have seen James victorious; because for some reason, whether it be ill health, mental exhaustion or some other failure of nerve, he did not take it, the king's reputation as a martial hero was damaged and the advantage, psychological as much as military, passed to William.[100] The battle for support, however, was far from over. On 6 November, James had issued an artful declaration in which he revealed how William's regal style exposed his true design to seize the crown and in which he promised a free parliament.[101] On his return from Salisbury to London, he turned words into actions and issued writs for it to meet on 15 January along with a general pardon to his subjects.[102] Probably surprised and temporarily outmanoeuvred, William issued from Sherborne on 28 November yet a third declaration, also promising a free parliament that would extract real concessions and an amnesty even to papists who did not oppose him.[103] The concession suggests some nervousness on William's part that James had regained the initiative. Certainly one pamphlet, *The Common Interest of the King and Kingdom* foresaw a parliament which might dispel doubts about the legitimacy of the prince and settle the differences between James and his subjects: 'let his crown flourish', it concluded.[104] William could hardly oppose it, but had reason to fear that it could indeed 'do his majesty more service in this conjuncture, than . . . an army' and check his own plans.[105]

In other respects, however, it was James's position that was weakening. After the king's retreat, and the withdrawal of his troops, from Salisbury, William was unopposed in his move towards London. Moreover, the defections to his cause about which he had been earlier hopelessly optimistic, now began in earnest. There were risings in Yorkshire and Nottinghamshire when the nobility, gentry and people assembled issued a declaration asserting that no trust would be placed in any concessions offered by the king and that resistance to a tyrant was not rebellion but necessary defence.[106] As defections increased, and even his daughter Princess Anne went over to William, who now insisted that he should attend the parliament in London with his guard, James, fearing he faced the fate of his father, resolved on flight to France.[107] In taking such a course, James – against the advice of the Earl of Ailesbury – publicly announced that he did not trust his people – an acknowledgement that he had lost the struggle to win support.[108] Was he right? Had he lost the propaganda war? Again the simple answer appears too simple. For when, after a bungled attempt to flee, he was brought back to London, he was cheered by crowds.[109] Bishop Burnet was not the only one to fear the fickleness of the people.[110] Orange, who had tried to prohibit the king's return to the capital, with veiled threats ordered James to withdraw, and was then complicit in his slipping away to France, saying 'nothing was so much to be wished for'.[111] By fleeing his capital twice, James undermined the effect of his skilful declarations. When he destroyed the writs for the forth-coming parliament and jettisoned the Great Seal into the Thames, he abnegated his duty to govern and left his people in chaos.[112] When he took ship to France, he appeared to confirm the fears of an international papist conspiracy to subvert Protestantism that his enemies were claiming.[113] Most of all when he fled, leaving an interregnum, James forced others to take actions that they may not otherwise have favoured and to place the government under the administration of William, whom the king had long suspected of desiring it.[114]

Over the weeks immediately before and since William had landed, it was not only James and his son-in-law who had contended in words and symbols. Amid the heat of the polemical pamphlet exchange, the like of which had not been seen since the Popish Plot or the civil war, supporters of both James and William subjected the king's and prince's declarations respectively to critical scrutiny. To take just two examples, Orange's first and supplementary declara-tions showing why he 'invaded' England were dissected and answered in 'animadversions' that questioned all his charges against James, his motives and his right.[115] 'He comes,' the author argues, 'for himself not us', and he came to seize the crown not establish a free parliament.[116] On the other side, glosses and reflections on James II's *Reasons . . . for Withdrawing Himself from Rochester* represented royal defences and apologies as sinister and cynical, rendering James's boast that he had ventured his life for his country as but 'needless wars for the destruction of the Protestant religion'.[117] In turn, such critical animad-versions were themselves answered in 'reviews of the reflections' and in answers to the refutations.[118] Such exchanges underscore the issue of the authority of royal words and the combat over representation that were decisive in 1688. Indeed, though in December actions and events appeared to have overtaken words and symbols, the representation and image of James II were to remain central to the politics of the rest of the century – and beyond.

On the day, 18 December, that James, this time successfully, embarked for France, William of Orange entered London as if in triumph. An engraving by

Romeyn de Hooghe shows a long cavalcade attending William in his coach drawn by six Flanders horses and winding its way into the capital, in a manner reminiscent of Stoop's painting of Charles II's civic entry (fig. 44).[119] Both the engraving and the entry were intended to make a case: that with James having abdicated his kingdom, authority had passed to the Prince of Orange who, 'accompanied by persons of quality in coaches and on horseback' and cheered by crowds, some with oranges on sticks, enjoyed the full support of the people.[120] Like most state rituals, William's entry was intended as a display of power and also of unity. The very different reality was captured by observers even on the day: the Tory Edmund Bohun believed the nation divided; Clarendon questioned the official account of popular joy – 'what a damp there was upon all sorts of men' – and (rightly as it turned out) suspected that James's expulsion had 'moved compassion even in those who were not very fond of him'.[121]

From the moment that the Dutch army had landed, and perhaps before, James's subjects had differed over what was the desired outcome of Orange's intervention. While a few radicals had hoped for a coup to supplant Stuart rule, most had desired that pressure be brought upon James to reverse his policies.

44 Romeyn de Hooghe, *The Reception of His Royal Highnesse the Prince of Orange at his entring London*, 1688.

When James issued writs for an assembly, many expected it would mark the end of William's involvement; some hoped it would bring about the deposition of the king. James's flight, far from resolving those differences, exposed them. Though necessity dictated the establishment of some government to prevent anarchy, especially in the capital where mobs were running riot, a stark question presented itself: where lay legitimate authority? Related to that fundamental question were several others: had James wilfully abdicated or been expelled by force from his realm? Was there an interregnum or did his writ still run? What was the position of the Prince of Orange, and his troops? And what was to be the future for the church, the monarchy and the state? Over the next weeks and months, as events led a Convention to effectively govern and propelled William and Mary to the throne, the questions (and hence divisions) only multiplied: by what right would they rule? Was England now an elective monarchy?[122] What were the implications of these changes for the doctrines of divine right and nonresistance, that is, for the constitution, the law and the Church of England? The manner in which these questions were put, the anxieties they raised and the responses to them, reopened and exacerbated long-standing differences, hardened and sharpened party divisions, and finally exposed as an illusion the rhetoric of unity in the commonweal and the church. As Jonathan Israel writes, the legacy of the events of November and December 1688 was 'profound, almost hopeless division'.[123]

The following twelve months saw the publication of some two thousand pamphlets and treatises that endeavoured to negotiate that division or to press a case for one side, or position, or another.[124] In recent years, historical and other scholars have stripped away the Whig historiography and rhetoric that presented 1688 as a national deliverance, to study the arguments and contestations over the constitution, the church, the law, theology and toleration, philosophical and political ideas, history and memory.[125] Only now, however, is attention being directed to the contest for legitimacy and the struggle over royal representation and image. In the early months of 1689 especially, the issue of who would be king was also one of who could most effectively represent himself, or be represented, as king. Though the full story of that contest, because it touches all the history of the time, cannot be told here, we must examine briefly some principal exchanges in the representation of rule and competition to establish authority.

As circumstances led him to ascend the throne, William had to be represented – indeed sold – to the nation as a king. Not least because in the justifications for his invasion, he had denied any such ambitions and claimed to desire only a restoration of Protestantism and due legal process, this proved by no means an easy task.[126] It seems likely that, even before the end of 1688, the publication of works such as *The History of the Most Illustrious William Prince of Orange* may have been intended to promote and present him as a 'noble and heroic prince' of the house of Nassau, 'one of the greatest and most ancient in all Germany'.[127] Here in two hundred pages, readers were given a portrait of a prince of a renowned descent, martial courage, one who combined the qualities of his blood with the virtues of his country, to make him 'a prince of many virtues without any appearing mixture of vice'.[128] Thomas Rymer's poem on *The Prince of Orange His Expedition* similarly prepares William for kingship by representing him in all the traditional symbols and figures of regality: as Hercules, Phoebus, Jove, the sun, the Messiah, 'The God-like Power, that now begins to reign'.[129] Thanks to the work of Tony Claydon, we have begun to understand the process by which William was refashioned from leader of an invasion into the instrument of providence, to God's chosen ruler.[130] In our next chapters we will examine all the texts, portraits, medals and rituals which were deployed after their coronation to underpin William and Mary's de facto rule and to argue even their right.[131] Nothing short of the most prolonged and systematic cultural campaign across all the media of representation and argument placed and (? just) preserved William III on the British throne, and the strategies of that campaign still await full explication. But the ubiquitous, even relentless, publicization of Orange in print and paint should not occlude – indeed it evidences – the power of the image of James II. During the celebrations of the tercentenary of the 1688 Revolution, one historian observed how James II had been all but ignored.[132] Whatever the long-term effects of their success for the historiographical marginalization of the Stuarts, however, in 1688 the Whigs could by no means ignore James. Indeed, a systematic programme of counter-representation, of the demoniza-tion of James Stuart, was essential to the process of establishing Orange and preventing civil war.

The attacks on James ranged over all genres of writing and visual culture, from the specific to the general, the subtle to the vituperative. Burnet's *Enquiry into the Present State of Affairs* and the question of allegiance, recognizing that the inconstant multitude might yet run to James because 'the name and title of a king carry a sound with them', endeavoured to undermine James by arguing that his desertion acquitted them of all ties to him.[133] Stripping him of a powerful and affective metaphor, Burnet insisted that obedience to a father ended when he ceased to act as a father 'by becoming an enemy'.[134] Other tracts made the same argument, drawing specific attention to the 'highly dangerous' threat presented by Irish and French power and by a James who only invited England to surrender.[135] While several treatises presented James's wilful abdi-cation as a sign of his abnegation of his duty towards, even as a breach of his contract with, his people, on the other side those more willing to talk of his expulsion argued the need to 'bolt the door after him', since he had been provoked too far to return with anything other than vengeance in mind.[136] The catalogue of specific charges levelled against him in 1689 included embezzling to sustain a troop of Irish ragamuffins, his dishonesty, his subterfuges, most of all his arbitrary actions and his religion; or, as one pamphlet put it frankly, 'being a papist he could not be king of England'.[137] A play, *The Bloody Duke*, implied that he might have poisoned his brother, while *An Account of the Transactions of the Late King James in Ireland* described the seizure there of land, money and plate, and the fate of Protestants 'robbed and plundered . . . enslaved and subjected'.[138] Vituperative biographies and histories, such as *The Anatomy of an Arbitrary Prince* or *The History of the Late Revolution*, brought together all the charges into a catalogue of indictment against James;[139] the author of *Quadriennium Jacobi* presented him as a king who had done all he possibly could to lose his crown.[140] Some, perhaps in the hope that a longer historical perspective might temper the heat of present circumstances, vilified Charles II as well as his brother as fomenters of popish absolutism; another *Secret History* condemned all the Stuarts as despots and tyrants.[141] Charles Caesar, though certain that James was 'the principal engineer that sapped the foundations of our happiness', nevertheless suggested that history showed the second of all kings by a name (Richard II, Edward II and so on) had proved unfortunate or disastrous.[142] In the midst of this mass of publication against him, moves were made to erase James's name from public memory: on 2 February 1689 by order of the Lords, the observation of 6 February, as a day of thanksgiving for James's succeeding to the throne, was abandoned.[143] One writer took a more drastic course to remove him: in 1689 he published a 'full and true account' from 'unquestioned and undeniable intelligence' of the king's death.[144]

Rumours of James's death, however, were not just exaggerated; they were wishful thinking. For, though in France, the king personified the problems of England and continued to draw support. As Burnet recognized, it was notions of loyalty to James that led men to 'dislike such a complete settlement as the present exigence of our affairs requires', and many remained discontented on that score even after William and Mary were crowned.[145] Though thousands of pages were devoted to arguing that, in the title of one of Daniel Whitby's several attempts, 'obedience [was] due to the present king notwithstanding our oaths to the former', many subjects could not be brought to agree or so rapidly renounce oaths taken.[146] Far more than those who publicly refused the new oaths of allegiance to Orange, the so-called non-jurors, were the numerous subjects who were plagued in their consciences that the nation had sinned as well as breached the law.[147] Publications aimed at exacerbating their discomfort argued powerfully that James had not abdicated, that in consequence the throne was not void, that allegiance was still owed to God's lieutenant and that William had no legitimate authority.[148] One pamphlet, *A Justification of the Whole Proceedings*, staging a dialogue between Miner and Counter-miner, though apparently supportive of the new regime, gives voice to a view that many shared: 'I fancy there might have been ways to have settled all things quiet, and yet kept the king on the throne'.[149]

The most important advocate of the king's cause was, of course, the monarch himself. When he fled England, timidly, James had not only left a political vacuum, he also left unanswered William of Orange's supposed *Third Declaration*, published on 4 December, which struck a devastating blow against James.[150] The *Declaration* warned of a Catholic uprising in London, backed by French troops, to extirpate Protestantism. Though William later refuted it as a forgery, the declaration was received as his and in the panic it fostered, James's flight to France could all too easily be taken as confirmation of the king's own part in a grand international Catholic plot.[151] When, however, faced with William's troops James decided on flight, he had no intention of abandoning his throne: he resolved to 'reserve himself safe for a better juncture', in the hope that Orange, when he appeared in his true colours, might prove unpopular.[152] From exile, James quickly resumed the battle to win hearts and minds: to represent himself as the rightful, divine and fit sovereign over his people. On 4 January (English style), James wrote from St Germain to his Privy Council in England a 'letter in vindication of himself' which was 'industriously . . . dispersed' in London and beyond.[153] The letter itself of course underlined that James was king: far from abandoning government he was, as he had been when he left, issuing orders to his Council. Now he wrote to warn the nation against the 'imaginary grievances' which had been alleged and by means of which the people faced being 'cheated into a certain ruin'.[154] The letter reminded the Council and the wider reading public that James had voluntarily redressed all the alleged causes of discontent and pretences for invasion and had summoned a parliament to take the counsel of MPs. It was the wide expectation that this would resettle the realm that had forced Orange to reveal his true ambition to take the crown, to put off the parliament and to confine the king. By skilful repetition of verb and noun, James reiterated his 'confinement' and so refuted any notion that his actions had been voluntary.[155] And in a clever evocation of the martyr (whose memory no faction or party could denigrate) he compared the danger he faced to that of his 'royal father of blessed memory' who had observed that the prisons swiftly led to the graves of princes.[156] James's concern for his life and safety, however, was not just a natural preservation of himself. His treatment at his nephew's hands exemplified a wider threat to laws and liberties, which it was his duty as king to sustain. The king had removed himself therefore the better to serve the 'true interest of the English nation' and to secure those liberties for the maintenance of which he called for a free parliament that might 'undeceive our people', and to which, once called, the king promised he would hastily return to give attendance.[157]

The letter was carefully written to draw attention to the violence of Orange, to hint at the dangers of a civil war and to represent James, in contrast to his son-in-law, as the true defender of law, liberty and parliament. There was evidently a concerted effort to counter it. Endeavouring to convey some feeling of compassion for James's 'misfortunes', if only out of respect to his daughter, the remarks on his paper, published in several versions, attacked all the king's claims.[158] Where James used the language of force and confinement, his critic spoke again of 'desertion' and 'retirement'; against his representation as protector of the law, the 'remarks' assert that 'he has been pleased to trample upon . . . more laws and privileges in the four years of his reign than his predecessors for fourscore years made for our preservation'. As for his calling a free parliament, a metaphor of a card game figures James as only playing a game, as his 'sudden departure' before a parliament could meet confirmed.[159] Reminding readers of the 'repeated breach' of his word, and alluding again to the illegitimacy of the newborn prince, the respondent defends William from any charge of ambition and represents him as the true defender of religion and the laws.[160] It was a nervous response that, while appreciating the need to answer the king's letter, reads as though it recognizes also the danger of replying. Indeed, when James sent his letter, together with his declaration from Rochester, to the Convention that assembled on 22 January, it was 'refused to be opened'.[161] In his letters to the Lords and Commons, James drew attention to efforts to suppress his papers and intercept his letters.[162] In contrast to censorship and secrecy, he urged a full and open inquiry into the birth of his son and a free parliament and promised a free pardon to restore happiness, peace and the 'ancient government' that Orange had dissolved. In an additional despatch to the army, James called on the officers and men to see through Orange's designs and return to their natural loyalty and allegiance.[163] A parallel letter to the parliament in Edinburgh, which attempted to appeal to the nationalism of 'true hearted Scotsmen', promised to defend them against 'the workers of iniquity' and 'any foreign attempt'.[164] While the Convention deliberated, James's interventions had raised the military as well as constitutional stakes.

As even his critics acknowledged (and feared), James, through January, was still writing as a king. Moreover, there was a party in the Convention that either did not wish to or could not conclude that James was no longer king or could be deposed, and favoured a regency which left his title inviolate.[165] As debates in the Commons revolved around the pamphlet disputes over whether James had abdicated, a motion for 'a regency with the administration of regal power under the style of King James the second' failed in the Lords by only three votes.[166] Eventually, however, the Lords, after some wrangling, voted to agree that the throne was vacant and that the Prince and Princess of Orange should be declared king and queen. In a ceremony on 13 February at the Banqueting House, that symbol of Stuart triumph and tragedy, William accepted the crown.

From that day on, the historical record tells us, James II's reign was at an end, and with it our study of his royal representation. We will not, however, end it here; for if to consider his words and image after 1689 lays us open to the charge of Jacobitism, the opposite course simplifies and even misrepresents the politics of representation. During those early weeks of 1689, a veritable barrage of Williamite apologia had endeavoured to reassure subjects of the lawfulness of allegiance to a new regime, and to persuade them of the advantages of the present settlement, the dangers of division, the need for obedience and the virtues of the new ruler. The titles of the pamphlets and treatises testify to bitter divisions and the struggle for support: they are 'justifications', 'vindications' and 'absolute necessities', as well as 'reasons' and 'full answers'.[167] Such divisions were not dispelled overnight by the work of the Convention. Into the 1690s, writers of all sympathies admit to the 'animosities' fuelled by the Revolution and not yet cooled.[168] When many among the episcopacy, including some of the seven bishops who had challenged James, refused the oath of allegiance, together with other public non-jurors, they pricked the consciences of many who had been unhappy with the pragmatic solution to – we might say the fudge of – a thorny religious and legal issue.[169] As Robert Beddard argues, when the words 'rightful and lawful' were removed from the oath of allegiance to William and Mary, 'dynastic equivocation was ... built into the very foundations of the revolutionary regime'.[170] As a consequence of this equivocation, what many regarded as the *de iure* King James would still hope to press his case against the *de facto* King William.

II

Established in a magnificent court at St Germain, James determined to regain his throne by two means that we might think of as contradictory but which he regarded as complementary: by armed invasion with foreign support and by continuing efforts to represent himself as rightful king. An army might not conquer England but provide loyal subjects with the opportunity to resist their oppressors; and words and images continued the argument for the re-establishment of the Stuarts. Even as William was preparing for his coronation, Louis XIV, who was anxious to weaken or neutralize Britain, proposed an invasion of Ireland where James's Lord Lieutenant, Tyrconnell, still held sway.[171] For James, Ireland was but a means to the end of regaining England; from Dublin in May accordingly he issued *A Declaration ... To All His Loving Subjects in the Kingdom of England*.[172] Emotively describing the 'slavery' that England was being reduced to, James again sought to expose and answer the negative misrepresentations of him that circulated to make him appear 'odious'. His conduct since arriving in Ireland, the declaration asserts, offered proof of the king's sincere intentions and real designs – the defence of the religion, rights and properties of Protestants there, as much as his own rights. From resolutions in the Irish parliament, the king hoped 'our subjects in England will make a judgement of what they might expect from us'. Finally, hinting at an imminent attempt on England, he offered pardon to all who would join with him. William III answered with reissues of his earlier declarations and with troops, which on 1 July 1690 routed the poor Franco-Jacobite force at the Battle of the Boyne.[173] It was two years before the Jacobites could persuade Louis to consider support for another attempt. Having convinced his cousin of a growing opposition to William in England, an army was prepared and James moved to Normandy, issuing a declaration to his English subjects.[174] In it, the king, reiterating his trust in the loyalty of his people, announced that the troops provided by France were 'abundantly sufficient to untie the hands of our subjects and make it safe for them to return to their duty', but were deliberately not so numerous as to 'raise any jealousy' (fear of a Catholic invasion) or to deprive loyal Englishmen of a role in restoring their monarch.[175] Appropriating the tactics and language of his nephew from 1688, James claimed to sail as a deliverer. Rehearsing his earlier assertion that he had not abdicated, James warned of the consequences of the coup that had supplanted hereditary monarchy. William had squandered the nation's riches on European wars, which, initiated only to advance his ambitions, could not end until the Stuarts were restored. Calling for passive resistance until he landed and the submission of all magistrates once he was on English soil, James added to his promises arrears for the soldiers, restoration of the navy, and action (perhaps against the Dutch) to re-establish England's trade and wealth, along with the greatness of the monarchy.

Though Louis and even some of James's (Protestant) English supporters thought the Declaration was too harsh and offered too little, it sufficiently disturbed the regime in England to prompt a number of replies.[176] The anti-Catholic (but then by no means Williamite) William Sherlock's *A Second Letter to A Friend Concerning the French Invasion* counters James's declaration sentence by sentence: it repeats all the grievances against his arbitrary government; it revives the warming-pan story; it defends Orange's motives in entering England and his integrity; it argues that James vacated his throne; it warns that he sought only the restoration of popery, and so on.[177] In burlesque verse, rather than argumentative prose, *The Jacobite's Hudibras* mocks the royal declaration, implicitly satirizing James as another Cromwell in arms against the church and monarchy; but its twenty pages of couplets manifest a seriousness behind the humour, a sense of the need to repel threat by ridicule.[178] Even after the defeat of the French fleet at La Hogue ended any prospect of a French invasion, the anonymous *Reflections Upon the Late King James's Declaration* went to lengths to answer the manifesto.[179] Though claiming to write a response 'only for fashion's sake', and denying any need to take the declaration seriously, the author seeks to answer all of James's assertions, often in vitriolic language; significantly, despite his title, he seeks to deny royal authorship (referring to the penman) in the very year that controversy also surfaced over the authenticity of the *Eikon Basilike*.[180] The same denial of authorship greeted James's more conciliatory declaration issued, under pressure from France, in April 1693, the work ('a phantom', one Orangist called it) 'appearing in the likeness of a declaration from King James'.[181] The author James Welwood, who almost made it his business to respond to James II's pronouncements, doubted it would be the last: 'it seems we are yearly to expect a new declaration'.[182] Such responses remind us of the danger James continued to present. He had been defeated – answered by providence, as his critic put it; and there was to be no further attempt on England before his death.[183] But in England, no one could count on that, especially while the court at St Germain reminded them of the proximity of a king across the water.

The Jacobite court at St Germain was, until 2004, largely ignored by historians.[184] Whig writers tried to mock it as impoverished and insignificant, as well as paint it as an enclave of popish fanatics; the failure to re-establish the Stuarts all but confined it to oblivion. The defeat of the Jacobite cause is, unquestionably, an historical fact. But as historians have demonstrated, that fact should not lead us to underestimate the force, or rather the threat, of Jacobitism, which cast its shadow over the first half of the eighteenth as well as the last decade of the seventeenth century.[185] Thanks to Edward Corp's authoritative study *A Court in Exile*, we can now understand how the court at St Germain acted as the headquarters and symbol of the Jacobite movement. Not only did the court in exile orchestrate military attempts on Britain and efforts to infiltrate Hanoverian governments. It presented and represented James II and his son as legitimate king and prince, recognized as such by European rulers and living as British monarchs.

Far from suffering poverty, at St Germain, James and his family lived in spectacular surroundings, with far more money to dispense on pensions and patronage than Charles II had had during the 1650s.[186] St Germain had been Louis XIV's royal palace from 1666 to 1682; and with extensive refurbishment to accommodate the royal family, it provided the Stuarts with some seventy-eight apartments, sufficient to lodge household officers and servants. James and Mary were served by over two hundred servants and perhaps attended at their court by as many as a thousand.[187] St Germain was, in every sense, a regal establishment and the Stuarts were publicly accorded royal privileges: Louis walked a pace behind James and the two monarchs were regularly together at Versailles and at Fontainebleau.[188] For all its intimacy with the French royal family, however, the court at St Germain remained – and appeared to visitors – very English. James, his wife and son (who from 1695 had his own establishment) were served primarily by English servants who had waited upon them at Whitehall; many of them never learned French and most married within the Jacobite community.[189] There was an Anglican chapel and establishment, as well as Catholic chapels. James adopted English ceremonial and protocol, dining in public as he had at Whitehall, and the Stuart diet of beef, pie and ale advertised the essence of Englishness.[190]

Those who visited St Germain did not find a Stuart court that had become, as Whig propaganda presented James as being, entirely French. Nor was it, as it was depicted, a haven of Catholic bigotry. Though, in contrast to his English household, James was attended by far more Catholics than Protestants, he maintained Protestant services, tolerated, employed and protected Anglicans and dissenters, and sought to persuade the French king to permit them free public worship.[191] The court at St Germain was not only itself, as all royal courts, a representation of the king; it was an argument for his (and his son's) rights and restoration.

The culture of the court at St Germain displayed and publicized Stuart dynasty and legitimacy. Jacobite verse, not least in that seventeenth-century genre of exile, the epic mode, presented the Stuarts as classical and biblical heroes; especially themes from and Jacobite translations of the *Aeneid* associated James with epic triumph and the panegyrics that had greeted the Restoration and Charles II.[192] Paintings of the story of Joseph in the royal bedchamber enfolded the royal family into biblical narratives, while all who approached the royal chapel saw the large 'Triumph of David', another motif of Stuart restoration. Initially James and Mary commissioned no new portraits of themselves in exile; those painted by Gennari and Wissing were circulated as engravings to sustain an image of continuity.[193] The case of the Prince of Wales was very different. As we have seen, James ensured, not least as a consequence of the rumours already circulating, that his son was painted within days of his birth and that Kneller's portrait of the infant was engraved and widely distributed.[194] In France he commissioned a series of canvases of the prince, the purpose of which was directly political: to counter the warming-pan myth of a surrogate child, to show the likeness between the infant and his parents and, again, to emphasize the continuity of the Stuart dynasty.[195] Though these paintings have recently been helpfully identified and catalogued, they have not been closely studied, and cannot be here; but the aesthetic and stylistic evocations that serve their political purpose should not pass without notice. When James left France with an army for Ireland, either he or Mary commissioned portraits of the young prince who, in the event of James's death in arms could be – and so needed to be represented as – the heir to the throne of Britain. One, a double portrait by Gennari of the queen with her son, has not won critical acclaim (fig. 45).[196] The figures indeed appear stiff, but not only do the horizontal lines connect mother and child, and the raised positions of the infant and his position facing a column gesture to his royal authority, in pose and colour the canvas evokes images of the Madonna and Child (as well as the Lely of the Duchess of Portsmouth with one of Charles II's bastard children).[197] A second

45 Benedetto Gennari, *Queen Mary of Modena with her son*, 1692/3.

portrait of the prince, executed by Largillière in 1691, appears also to hint at dynasty, as the naked infant rests his right hand on, and points with his left towards, a spaniel, a dog long connected with the Stuarts and especially with Charles II who gave his name to the breed.[198]

In the 1690s, James acquired a copy of Van Dyck's *The Three Eldest Children of Charles I*, in which he, as Duke of York, stands beside the prince, and his sister, incidentally with two 'King Charles Spaniels'.[199] The painting may have been the inspiration behind family groups that James and Mary commissioned in 1691 and 1692, at the time of the planned Franco-Jacobite invasion of England. The first of these, by Largillière, has not survived; the second by Pierre Mignard, painted after the birth of Princess Louise-Marie, is worthy of comment (fig. 46).[200] For though the French style renders this magnificent canvas different in many ways, it is replete with aesthetic and political references to Stuart history and rule. On the left of the painting, the seated figure of Mary with her son (attended by a kneeling black servant) recalls the Van Dyck 'Great Piece' of Charles and Henrietta Maria with their two eldest children.[201] Here, however, rather than on a table beside, a small crown and sword are placed on a cushion at the queen's feet and Prince James points directly to

46 Pierre Mignard, *James II and Family*, 1694.

them, as does his mother's hand that holds her robe. On the right, the little princess sits on a table, below which is (again) a spaniel and behind which rises a column (a traditional symbol of regality). Louise Marie, whose right hand is held by her mother, points with her left to her father, seated to the right and wearing the regalia of the Garter and the greater George. Grouped around the dog – an emblem of fidelity as well as a Stuart spaniel – the family is linked by touch or gesture. If Mary, rather than James, is centred, this may be to display the very evident likeness of mother and son, and so to reassert the prince's legitimacy in the wake of the birth of his sister. Similarly, the presentation of the prince with the Garter, in an armour breastplate, associates him with his father, and his military reputation; and, together with the small sword beside the small crown, hints at an inheritance he may have to, and will, fight for – Stuart inheritance.

Between 1691 and 1694 four other portraits of Prince James were painted by Largillière, who also did a double portrait in 1695 of the prince with his sister.[202] Here, the princess points with her right hand to a brother who proudly wears over a red coat his blue Garter sash and who rests his right hand on a large hound. The presentation of Prince James (whose own household was established that year) again evokes a Van Dyck of Prince Charles, with his younger siblings, also painted when that prince was seven.[203] Perhaps the suggestion was that a second prince, born to majesty and forced into exile, would, as his uncle, return in glory.

Indeed, following the Peace of Ryswick, yet more portraits of the prince were commissioned, seven by François de Troy before James II's death, of which some exist in several versions.[204] In one the prince wears armour, in another he points across the Channel to England. Copies of these 'private cabinet pieces', and of paintings and miniatures were given to Jacobites who visited the court at St Germain, as tokens of reward for loyalty and for distribution, or copy, in England.[205] But the publicization of the portrait images of the prince and royal family was not confined to St Germain. James had, in 1688, commissioned and distributed medals of his son, and production of these in France continued throughout James's life and beyond.

Medals tended to be issued to commemorate specific events and, as we know, were also issued to satirize official commemorations. In that spirit, on the signing of the Peace of Ryswick, which recognized William III as *de facto* king, James II commissioned Norbert Roettier, son of John the engraver and medallist to Charles II, to design a group of medallic portraits of the prince, to remind the people of the rights of his son.[206] One, depicting James on the obverse, has on the reverse a dove with an olive branch and affirms that there can be no real peace in Europe without the restoration of the Stuart prince.[207]

More important than medals was the broad distribution of the Stuart image in engravings and mezzotints. Smith's engravings of the portraits of James, Mary and Prince James were by no means the last to circulate in England. As well as the home of some of the best portrait painters, working for the court of Louis XIV, Paris was the centre of the print trade and some of the best engravers of the age, and James took full advantage of their skills.[208] As well as being reproduced in replica, Gennari's and Largillière's portraits of the prince, and the double portrait of him with Mary, were engraved, and it may even be that the latter was intended primarily for an English audience.[209] As well as diplomatic presents, several of those were sent in multiple copies to England and Scotland; Largillière's 1692 portrait of the prince was almost certainly commissioned to be engraved and distributed, perhaps as a forerunner to a military campaign.[210] Later portraits by de Troy were similarly executed, in multiple copies by studio assistants, and engraved and sent to Britain where, it would seem, they proved impossible to censor.[211] Indeed, between the flight and death of James II, thirty new prints were published of the king, along with twenty of the queen and several family groups.[212] Individual portraits grouped in ovals on one plate continued to promote the powerful dynastic image, not least by recalling the old woodcuts and trees of monarchical descent we encounter in the sixteenth century.[213] And, more easily than with paintings, engravings could be, and were, issued with text making explicit their political message of Stuart lineage and legitimacy.

It is not easy to evaluate their effect as propaganda. Generally, however, we can be sure that portraits painted in France, engraved, then copied in England and collected by supporters preserved the Stuarts in the visual imagination of England, and helped to sustain the Jacobite community. No one could have failed to know the image of the Prince of Wales: it was even reported that William III asked to see it.[214] Beyond that, it may be that paintings and engravings did the even more effective propaganda work that James had hoped. John Evelyn for one, no Jacobite, on seeing a picture of the prince thought it 'in my opinion very much to resemble the Queen his mother, and of a most vivacious countenance'; while Kneller remarked as late as 1697 that the prince was 'so like' his parents 'that there is not a feature in his face but what belongs to father and mother'.[215] As well as resembling her brother, the princess, completely discrediting the stories that Mary of Modena was infertile, only added to the likelihood that James was lawful issue. Defeated James II may have been; but the representation of his family made it impossible for the British to forget that not only a king, but a dynasty, awaited its moment to reclaim its right.

The last painting we know of James II, commissioned in 1698, from de Troy, depicts him in armour in a manner that returns to early images.[216] By this time, James was preoccupied far less with martial pursuits, and may have intended to leave a very different image to posterity. While the characterization of James as 'a guilt-ridden depressive' may owe more to Whig and Protestant lies than reality, increasingly James turned to examining his soul, and commenced a text of spiritual self-examination and instruction which may have been intended as his testament.[217] It appears that he had begun to see his life – from military glory, through majesty lost as a consequence of sin, to reconciliation with God through penitence – as a text.[218] Not long before he died, he left instructions for his memoirs to be reissued to form a narrative of his life.[219] The last part of that life contains excerpts from devotional papers, a separate and complete manuscript of which was discovered early in the last century.[220]

The manuscript at first sight belies any attempt to read it as a testament, a final self-representation by James II. There are blank pages and unfinished sentences. The prose is full and even eloquent in places, scrappy in others. There is a section almost certainly not by James. Overall the volume reveals a binding probably, made immediately after the king's death.[221] As with the *Eikon Basilike* (and this is not the last reference back we will make to that), it would seem that loose papers by James were brought together with some additions and paginated and bound; a smaller volume appears to have been broken up and inserted into this larger one. As if the form of the manuscript did not present enough difficulties, it is near impossible to classify in generic terms. Part spiritual autobiography, part a

COUNTERING 'CATHOLIC KINGSHIP' AND CONTESTING REVOLUTION   337

manual for converts, part advice to his son, part meditations and prayers, the devotions are repetitive and move between the personal and public world, in places erratically. Yet passages ('I could say if I had more time . . .') imply an audience, and the wider address to converts would suggest publication.[222] It was by his devotions that James II finally wished to be remembered.

As much as the devotions are folded into the last section of James's life, the life itself, past, present and beyond death, is the subject of those meditations. James the military man of his youth makes his appearance: 'I come from seeing the camp at Compiègne, a sight that was more worth seeing than anything of that kind of our age'.[223] Now, however, the commander gives way to the devout Christian: 'at the same time I cannot hinder myself from making this melancholy reflection how very few amongst this great and formidable army, thinks of their duty to the king of kings'.[224] War he sees now as the heavy hand of God and the prospect of general war a dismal outlook for Christendom.[225] James the monarch is very much present on the page. He writes of the duty owed to king and country; he presents himself as chosen by God to rule; he thanks God for restoring the monarchy and protecting him to inherit his title; he prays that his son will succeed.[226] But even kingship takes second place now to salvation; and James comes close to the belief that only the loss of his realms secures his eternal life, as he prays, 'thou wert pleased to have taken from me my three kingdoms by which means thou didst awake me out of the lethargy of sin'.[227]

James believed that the providence which had saved him from civil war and foreign battlefield, fire and the madness of the people, had also taken his throne as a punishment for his sin of incontinence and to give him the opportunity to repent and atone before death, to secure a heavenly kingdom. The devotions then are a declaration, a manifestation of Christian faith, 'the fear of the Lord is the beginning of wisdom'.[228] James explains his conversion to Catholicism, and his regret that in breaking from Rome the Church of England began an unending process of fracture and schism; and prays for the conversion of three kingdoms.[229] He proclaims his belief in core Catholic doctrines and practices.[230] In those pages we eavesdrop on the king as he delivers prayers of thanks to God for His goodness in teaching him 'the duties of Christianity' or confesses – in English and French ('O mon Dieu, je me présente devant la Trône de votre miséricorde tout couvert de crimes').[231] The reader here sees James, the penitent, instructing himself in those duties – taking the sacrament, early rising for prayer, reading devotional works, meditation, fasting, acts of charity – which pages marked 'for myself' suggest was a continuing process.[232] James repeats his admiration for the simple piety of primitive Christianity personified in the lives of the monks at La Trappe, which made such an impact on him that, he tells us, he returned annually for a retreat from the 'vanity of all worldly greatness';[233] as, at several places the pages indicate explicitly, James was contemplating and preparing for death and working hard to be ready to meet God.[234]

The intensely personal nature of these devotions, however, should not lead us, as they did their editor, to conclude that James, in exile, had retreated from public presentation to personal introspection. For the king makes clear that his purpose in writing them is public: 'my chief design of writing this papers is to give some advice to new converts, and to such whose hearts are touched and have inclination to find out the truth'.[235] As his grandfather James I had written exegeses of Holy Scripture, James II writes an instructional manual for the Christian Catholic life, urging converts to amend their lives and all to devote themselves to Christ with complete 'resignation', to remove pleasures of the senses, and to advance every day in piety through a programme of prayer, confession and contemplation, and a life of humility and charity.[236] As James's own journey and self-instruction become an example – a text for others of the way to salvation, the devotions present the king as priest.

The spiritual advice, however, as well as general, is specific and personal: it is advice to a son, or sons and children, for as well as James and Louise, two of his illegitimate offspring were still alive and one, James Fitzjames, First Duke of Berwick, is addressed and also referred to by name.[237] James instructs his son (here presumably Prince James) to assist in the chapel, to avoid plays and opera, 'except it be with the Most Christian King and even to avoid that as much as one can without affectation'.[238] As a father whose principal duty it is to promote the welfare of his children, he commands them to find God while young and to repair past faults, remembering that death could come suddenly at an opera or ball.[239] He chides his son for failure to take communion one Christmas, for pursuing the pleasures of the world and not devoting himself to Christian duty.[240] Along with his *Advice to His Son*, James's devotions were a manual for the preparation of his heir to be a good Catholic prince – and, it is hoped, the Catholic ruler of three kingdoms.[241] For though the fate of princes, he knew, lay in the hands of God, James counselled his heir to 'make use of all lawful means to preserve what one has or to recover what has been taken unjustly from one'.[242]

In his own case, though his devotions evidence retreat, they are not a proclamation of defeat. While he admired the life at La Trappe, James did not in the end advocate solitude: 'I cannot be so partial to it, as to think one may not work out one's salvation in the world'.[243] And even as he instructed his son on how to work out his salvation as a prince, James harboured hopes that he might join the ranks of those, with callings in the world, who had yet become regarded as great saints – as, in fact, his father already was.[244]

What are now edited as the *Papers of Devotion of James II* were published in 1704 as *The Pious Sentiments of the Late King James II of Blessed Memory Upon Divers Subjects of Piety*.[245] Part autobiography, part prayer manual, part advice to a son and part self-representation as exemplar of piety, the text recalls the *Eikon Basilike* of Charles I.[246] Like his father, James even prays for his enemies (including William of Orange) in a gesture of magnanimity in victory as opposed to defeat.[247] Like the *Eikon*, the devotions are silent on most of the matters that alarmed James's subjects: his exile is attributed to his sin, and it is an exile that has ended in the ultimate triumph – sanctity. As we have observed, the *Eikon Basilike* was republished in 1692, with a flurry of controversial pamphlets concerning its royal authorship.[248] As Andrew Lacey discusses, the cult of the martyr was deeply embroiled in party conflict and Charles's image as saint and Christ-figure was inherently anti-Whig. In 1692 the Jacobite *Imago Regis or The Sacred Image of His Majesty . . . Written During His Retirement in France* directly appropriated the *Eikon* to present, this time, James as Christian martyr.[249] The frontispiece depicts James, the patient bearer of affliction – his head appears circled with a crown of thorns – reading at a table with, by him, the crown on a cushion and a dog by his side (fig. 47). The volume, which reproduces all the speeches and messages of James, carries on its title page a

47 James II, frontispiece to *Royal Tracts. In Two Parts. . . containing Imago Regis*, 1692.

quotation from Psalm 132: 'O remember David in all his afflictions'. In his own devotions, begun in the 1690s (the earliest dated section is 1694), James similarly wrote and represented himself: as another David, another Stuart, another martyr whose afterlife might too perform as a powerful political text.[250]

'A new David has appeared in our days'. With these words the funeral oration for the 'most mighty, most excellent and most religious prince James' opened in the church of St Mary de Chaillot, where the king's heart was interred.[251] The oration, published in England in 1703, followed James's life and conversion and made explicit parallel with that of Charles I. Like his father, brought down by the cajoling arts of Cromwell, James and with him the peace of Europe had been sacrificed to the ambitions of a foreign prince who had destroyed lawful government. *The Generous Muse*, a funeral elegy sold at The Angel at Lincoln's Inn Fields, mourns the son of a martyr, who should be placed by his father's side, who had reminded his own son: 'Stewart Blood dilates thy Veins.'[252] Even the Williamite *The British Muse* regretted the large numbers of commendatory elegies that followed James's death.[253] An account of James's collapse, after fainting in his chapel, relates his death taking place on the same day and at the same time as the crucifixion of Christ.[254] Another oration, after narrating his life warns: 'Woe unto you if the words of this great prince seconded by such a holy life and death do not cause you to return to your duty and renounce your unjust prejudice.'[255] Many more, it was claimed, would hymn his memory were it not for gain and interest that bought them off from support of the Stuart cause.[256]

Far from his Catholic piety being presented as disengagement, Jacobite orations and elegies, aided by the image and memory of Charles I, combined the Christic image with the dynastic cause. Some in England even read them as a call to arms. A gloss on a funeral oration published in France calls on fellow Englishmen, on the eve of a parliament, to provide for the defence of the religion and liberties of the realm.[257] And as part of that defence, the tract attacks the image and representation of James and the perception still of some that he had been expelled 'upon mere suspicions'.[258] Some, the author feared, still sought to disturb the peace and to bring over the Pretender.[259]

James II did not join his father in creating a cult that remained a powerful political force into the nineteenth century. But his image and final prayer that 'all his subjects would acknowledge his son for their lawful king' sustained serious divisions in English politics for over half a century and bequeathed historiographical and ideological differences that remain with us to this day.[260]

PART III

REPRESENTING REVOLUTION

PROLOGUE

AN IMAGE REVOLUTION?

Perhaps no historiographical interpretation of a period or reign had such a near monopoly for centuries afterwards as the so-called Whig interpretation of 1688 and the reign of William III.[1] For nearly three centuries, school and college textbooks and popular histories depicted – some still depict – William as the deliverer of the British nations from the popery and absolutism of the Stuarts, as the ruler who secured Protestantism, liberty and property, and as the prince whose reign witnessed the establishment of a limited monarchy and annual parliaments as the bedrocks of a British constitution which became the envy of the world. In this historiography, William, the Dutch invader, was depicted as a true English sovereign who rescued his people from subjugation by a foreign French power. His costly wars against France were heralded as the beginning of England's emergence as a major power in Europe. And initiatives such as the Toleration Act, the creation of the Bank of England and the development of a system of public credit have been viewed as the building blocks of a modern state, indeed of modernity itself.[2] Most histories of the Enlightenment or the eighteenth century have begun with 1688; indeed, historians often write of a 'long eighteenth century', wrenching the last two decades, from the seventeenth century as though they had little connection to what went before.[3]

The success of the Whig interpretation of English history is a complex story: of ancient myths of Saxon freedoms; the need after 1688 to play down rupture and change and stress continuity and nationalism at a time of foreign threats; vested economic interests; the military defeat of the Stuarts in 1715 and 1745; and later, importantly, the adoption of Whig ideology and history by the American colonies in their struggle for independence. The triumph of William and of Whig history was also a consequence of a systematic endeavour at the time to effect a Whig dominance of England's political, literary and visual culture.[4] The 1688 Revolution, as Lois Schwoerer observed, involved the most relentless and organized propaganda campaign that England had ever witnessed.[5] And the propaganda justifying the Revolution and lauding William and Mary continued unabated throughout the reign. Speeches, sermons, histories, political treatises, panegyrical poems, broadside ballads, and portraits, prints, medals and ceremonies were all deployed to underpin the Revolution, William and Mary's tenure of the throne, royal wars abroad and policies at home. In large measure, the Whig success in establishing a revolution in 1688 where the former commonwealthsmen had failed to secure a republican government in 1649 was a consequence of insight and effort – of a recognition that authority rested in cultural forms and of the readiness of supporters to argue a case to different audiences, in different ways and forms.[6]

What, however, more recent research has taught us is how far from inevitable the Whigs' triumph was and how powerful was the opposition and the challenge that they faced. Though they were later defeated and marginalized (albeit in some circles romanticized), we now recognize that the Jacobites were by no means a negligible force after 1688 or throughout William's (and Anne's) reign.[7] After he fled to France, James II from his court in St Germain established and maintained links with active supporters in Ireland, Scotland and England and, with at least the prospect or promise of French aid, was able to galvanize English subjects to arm, rise and plot on his behalf.[8] What perhaps presented greater difficulties for the Williamites than militant Jacobites was the much larger number of Englishmen and women who felt a considerable anxiety that what had taken place in 1688 had been not a providential deliverance, as Whig propaganda presented it, but a coup or invasion against a rightful – and even divinely appointed – monarch. As we have seen, though he was worsted in the contest for hearts and minds during the later months of his reign, from France James and his supporters issued declarations and letters and circulated portraits and engravings that argued the Stuarts' cause and ensured that James and his son remained very visible, and by no means universally unpopular, in England.[9] Such pro-Stuart propaganda, together with rumours of invasions and plots, and a mounting unease among many, especially the Anglican clergy, about the wrong the nation had done, ensured that, far from fading from memory, the figure of James II dogged the reign of William to the end.[10]

Indeed, the unpopularity of the king and regime fostered by the record high taxes needed to fund the vast cost of continental wars, the foreignness of William and many of his courtiers and ministers, the perceived corruption of officers, pensioners and MPs who had profited from the war and the financial initiatives instituted to fund it – all these combined to stir a nostalgia for and heightened affection towards James, who often spoke and wrote skilfully and diplomatically to take advantage of and nurture resurgent support. At the other end of the political spectrum, the army, big government, heavy taxes and (as they were perceived) arbitrary actions, which were consequences of England's first full engagement in modern continental wars, revived a republican or Commonwealth party and revitalized, even in an age of parties, a country critique of the court and regime.[11] While not slow to exploit these discontents, supporters of James II also represented such attacks on the monarchy, as on the church, as the inevitable fallout from 1688 and, increasingly as the years went on and William and Mary had no heirs, argued for the restoration of James as the means to heal the ills of the nation and protect its ancient institutions and constitution.

From 1688, in other words, there were two kings of England and a bitter contest to secure authority and what was now widely discussed as the best source for legitimacy: the support of the people. Williamite propaganda was organized, systematic and ubiquitous because it needed to be: to deter invasion and internal insurrection, to obtain supplies and co-operation for the government, and to secure the Revolution, the political settlement that was its bequest and the Protestant succession that was vital to its supporters. An important recent study has demonstrated how the representation of William as the agent of providence was a central concept of Williamite propaganda and has paid fruitful attention to the sermons delivered at court, principally by those close to the king such as the Bishop of Salisbury and historian Gilbert Burnet.[12] In the space we have, we will attempt to extend the study of pro-Williamite sermons and to read them alongside the regular services of prayer ordered for festival days and fast days instituted to implore God's blessing on the king's armies and fleets, or to give thanks for victories. Other genres of verbal support have received less notice and must engage us here. The scores, indeed hundreds, of panegyrical verses, from epics and pindarics to popular doggerels and ballads, have been largely neglected by historians and literary critics alike. Critical neglect of often mediocre or poor poems, which are repetitious and stylized, is aesthetically comprehensible. But, as we have seen throughout this study, poetry was an important genre of royal representation, and the legitimacy conferred by great literary forms or lofty authorial representations was never more vital than in the age of Milton, Marvell and Dryden. As the 1688 Revolution saw the Stuart laureate Dryden lose his post, his less talented successors, Thomas Shadwell and Nahum Tate, led a phalanx of minor versifiers to compose lyrics and lines in praise of the king and queen. Though many did not rise to the greatest vatic heights, verses commemorating victories, hymning royal virtues and the fruits of William's regimen played a part yet to be fully investigated in the Whigs' cultural as well as political triumph.[13] The virtually continuous wars waged from 1688 also refocused attention on a form of propaganda first effectively deployed during the civil war: the war report. As we shall see, more than bare factual reportage, the published accounts of military and naval manoeuvres, even setbacks as well as victories, served to involve the nation in what were William's wars, and served to boost morale and sustain public support.[14] Along with poets and military reporters, William's cause was supported, often against Jacobite or Commonwealth opposition, by a wide range of prose writers who in historical and legal treatises, surveys, reflections and animadversions, and topical polemical tracts, urged allegiance and obedience to the king, queen and government.[15]

Visual propaganda was hardly less important in a society in which most noble and gentry families and many in the ranks of the wealthy traders, stock jobbers and merchants, were collecting and taking an interest in paintings and engravings. As we saw, during James's reign and the events of 1688, Dutch engravings and cartoons had given a considerable advantage to William and his supporters.[16] In France, James II was able to call on the considerable experience and talents of French artists and engravers to represent his cause, so it was essential for William III to be represented visually as the rightful ruler, appointed by the will of God and his people especially, given the long absences of the king necessitated by campaigns. Long absences also deprived the people of the frequent sight of the king – in procession, in Garter festivals, or on other ceremonial occasions, and so made it important for Queen Mary to maintain a ritual calendar and presence and a magnificent court in her husband's absence, and for William to make himself as visible as possible when he was in England. With English subjects fully informed of the splendours of Versailles and even of the stateliness of the Jacobite court at St Germain, William's performance of majesty – at court, on ritual occasions, on progresses – and, no less, the representation and publication of those performances, were essential to the maintenance of his regal authority.

As with our discussion of earlier rulers, we will, therefore, study the representation of William in genres and forms of speech and writing, in portraits, on medals and coins, and in rituals and ceremonies. Throughout aware that official and other loyal representations were directed at countering opponents, especially supporters of the Stuarts, we will close with a brief examination of the counter-representations of William and the competing addresses and images of, and the apologia for, James II and his son. Given the triumph of Whig history, with which I began, it may be expected that the narrative of this section will be the story of how victory and security were secured by 1702. On the contrary, my argument will be that, far from a gradual stabilizing of William's regime, the threats and challenges, anxieties and insecurities lasted to the end and coloured all the modes of his representation. Though the propaganda for William was relentless, its eventual triumph was by no means inevitable at the end of his reign, as the uneasiness of many funeral panegyrics makes evident.

The reign of William III was throughout shaped not only by war but by the presence of James II who, of course, was at least a key pawn in the chess game between William and his allies and Louis XIV. Even significant military victories did not settle the question of William's legitimacy; and at key points, a threat, plot or crisis necessitated another round in the unending campaign to argue the rights and benefits of the Revolution. For the first few years after 1688, public debate was overwhelmed with discussion of the justification of what had taken place. The hundreds of pamphlets and tracts, as well as keeping a difficult and (for many) painful episode in the public eye, in making a myriad of different arguments on behalf of the new regime, ironically frustrated efforts to unite the people in obedience and loyalty to William's government. After three years' hard struggle, the king's military successes in Ireland effectively neutered a dangerous Jacobite base, but by 1692 there were widespread rumours of James II planning an invasion from France, and declarations issued from St Germain were crafted to raise support for the exiled king in England at a time when William was absent for long periods.[17]

The invasion threat seen off by 1693, William faced not only a deeply felt personal loss but a potential political crisis with the death of his queen, Mary, in December 1694. A Stuart and the daughter of James II, Mary's joint rule with William established by the Convention in 1689, enabled at least some of those deeply uncomfortable with the deposition of James and the break in the succession, to indulge a credible (if fictitious) belief in continuity. Though William had declined to rule as consort to Mary, the exercise of royal power in their joint names gave him some figleaf of legitimacy. In practice, too, given his absences on campaigns, it was Mary who visibly represented the monarchy at home and who (as we shall see) was more the subject of praise and the people's affection.[18] Mary's death, in exposing William's claim as one that rested on conquest, coup or the act of a convention (of questionable constitutional validity), revived uncomfortable questions about what had taken place in 1688 and, of course, focused attention on the succession to the throne of a childless widower whose own life was daily exposed to danger on the battlefield.[19] Relations between William and his designated successor, Mary's younger sister Anne, had been frosty – not least because the princess was suspected of contacts with her father, James; and, though she and William were reconciled publicly in January 1695, for his part William remained suspicious of the princess and jealous of her popularity, while 'on the other side, the princess's intense hatred of William continued'.[20]

The year 1695 was a high point in William's military fortunes: on 1 September the confederate forces took the fortress at Namur, a garrison that many had considered the strongest in Europe. Taken by Louis XIV in 1692, Namur's fall was symbolic of a change in military fortunes which passed the initiative to the allies and left France with little choice but to pursue a truce. As scores of panegyrical poems and thanksgiving sermons testify, the capitulation of Namur – the first definitive victory in a protracted campaign – also changed the mood at home, making it easy for the supporters of the government to justify the war and to paint the king, once again, as a hero who saved Europe from the threat of popery and absolutism.[21] Moreover, the move towards a truce held out the prospect of a peace and some abatement of the unprecedentedly heavy taxes which had fuelled discontent. In many respects 1695 was the zenith of William III's reputation. Yet, even amid the celebrations, intelligence discovered an attempt to assassinate the king and French preparations for an invasion.[22] Though William used the foreign threat and domestic plot to his advantage – when he informed the Commons they voted for an Association to swear the support and avenge any attempt against their 'rightful and lawful king' – they provided powerful reminders that victory had not resolved the problems of James II, William's legitimacy or the uncertainties about the future and the succession.[23]

Peace too was not for the government an unmixed blessing. In the first place the expected abatement of burdens was less dramatic and slower than the people had hoped. Debts had accumulated, fleets, armies and garrisons had still to be paid, and William, as we shall see, still had to ask each of his parliaments for subsidies. Still more damaging, peace refocused attention on domestic priorities and problems that had necessarily taken second place to fighting and winning the war. William himself endeavoured to seize the initiative by – in the spirit of his Revolutionary representation – championing the cause of moral reform and spiritual rejuvenation of the nation. Others, however, took the opportunity to raise uncomfortable questions about corruption in the government and to point the finger at Treasury and Naval Commissions, Excise officers and other officials who had got rich from the war and on the backs of the taxpayer. That many who had benefited were also MPs raised larger questions about the threat to the independence of the representative and the potentially corrosive consequence for the rights of parliament and people of a government with vast resources of patronage on a scale never seen before. A perception that many who had benefited from the spoils of war were foreigners, mainly Dutch, not only raised the temperature of an ever-simmering English xenophobia, it gave ammunition to critics of the regime who had, more or less from the start, protested that William's wars were not England's wars or in England's interest: that in fact England had been made to bear a disproportionate cost of the confederate campaigns while at the same time the Dutch, long-time mercantile rivals, had used the opportunity to take England's wealth and trade. Such accusations were not as effectively countered as they might have been by a ministry that was divided by jealousies, rival ambitions and personal animosities. Increasingly during the last years of the 1690s, a country opposition called publicly for inquiries into venality, fiercely opposed the maintenance of a standing army, and began to challenge excessive governmental powers.[24]

At one extreme end of the political spectrum, opposition charges and the language and tone of opposition polemics led to a discernible revival of an old Commonwealth faction advocating either republic or a monarchy which resembled, as Charles I had famously put it, no more than the Doge of Venice. As we will see, in the late 1690s old civil war and Commonwealth voices were again heard and works republished; and, even if their numbers of supporters were small, government apologists were forced on to the back foot by a perceived need to respond to them.[25] The re-emergence of the protagonists of the Good Old Cause caused yet further problems for William's government. The new freedom taken by the commonwealthsmen to discourse publicly against monarchy and kings in turn prompted a response from the champions of divine kingship and indeed of the monarch who had been a martyr for sacred monarchy, Charles I. Ever since the Restoration, the sermons delivered to mark the regicide and martyrdom of Charles I on 30 January had shown the potential to revive bitter disagreements and differences – and (as we shall see) never more than in 1692 when the figure and memory of Charles I re-emerged into the spotlight of public debate and pamphlet controversy.[26] However, it was at the end of the decade and in reaction to republican apologia that Charles I, and the question of whether and how he should be remembered, became the subject of many sermons, pamphlets and histories. Republican and Royalist apologists, stirring memories of the bitter divisions of a half-century past, made it harder for the government to unite the nation behind William and to maintain a state of preparedness for war in what remained a volatile and tense European situation. More particularly, the public discourse and rhetoric of both parties seemed to posit extremes at a time when the government, in the spirit of the Revolution, was claiming to maintain the virtue of a balanced constitution and moderate rule. Moreover, a renewed focus on, and apologia for, Charles I could not but, as many pamphlets acknowledged, cast their reflections on the fate of James II and on the Revolution which had deprived Charles's son of his throne, if not his life. One discerns, amid the mounting disenchantment with William's government, a growing nostalgia, even sympathy for James whose life of quiet piety and devotion in France was widely reported in England. Perhaps, many beyond militant Jacobite circles began to wonder, James had been harshly treated and did not present the danger that Williamite propaganda had claimed.

If there was mounting sympathy for James II, the death of Princess Anne's only son, Prince William, the Duke of Gloucester, in 1700, could hardly have come at a worse time. Gloucester, settled at court since 1698, just before his tenth birthday, was given Queen Mary's apartments in Kensington Palace in 1700, in a move that was surely intended to publicize him, as well as educate him, as a future sovereign. The death of the vigorous young prince, the last living child of his mother who had miscarried yet again earlier in the year, drew immediate attention to the fragility of the succession. With the prospect after William and Anne of the prolonged rule of a foreign dynasty, the presence over the water of one who was, though in exile, an English king, became the subject of feverish debate. Indeed, there was widespread discussion of proposals that James's son, the Pretender whose legitimacy had been denied, might be raised as a Protestant and so groomed to succeed his father – in place of William's preferred option of the heirs of Sophia, Electress of Hanover, the youngest daughter of James I's daughter Elizabeth, wife of the Elector Palatine.[27]

The likely resumption of continental war when Carlos of Spain died leaving his crown to the Dauphin of France and the prospect unfolding of an unassailable Franco-Spanish monarchy, heightened tensions at home and abroad. During 1701 rumours of Jacobite plots, relatively quiescent for some years, resurfaced. Some within the government were reluctant to see a resumption of war and may have dallied with restoring the Stuarts.[28] At this juncture, the God whom William had so often claimed as his protector manifestly intervened for his advantage. The death of James II benefited his nemesis in a number of ways. Obviously it terminated any talk of the former king's own restoration. And when Louis XIV immediately recognized the prince as James III, it made it possible to represent the twelve-year-old James Francis Edward, against those who might have been warming to his future succession, as a pawn in Louis XIV's design to be universal monarch of all Christendom. Once again the Stuarts could be – and were – represented as un-English; and William III was able to present himself in his favoured image as the protector of the nation's liberties, property and Protestantism. French ambitions and the death of James II enabled William the year before his own death to build the political support that ensured the Protestant succession to the throne – and with it the triumph of the Whigs and of his own reputation.

William outlived James by almost exactly six months. Had he predeceased him, it is by no means improbable that a campaign to promote James's restoration, and that of his son, as alternative successors to the childless Anne and foreign Hanoverians, would have gained momentum. That is to remind us that in 1701 William had still not fully established his legitimacy; and the next year, though the succession of a woman led to anxiety about England's military command in Europe, the accession of Queen Anne, James's daughter, who knew her heart to be 'entirely English', unquestionably helped heal bitter discussion and enabled her to commence her rule with a popularity that her predecessor had probably never enjoyed.[29]

It is then, against the grain of Whig history, the weaknesses of William III's government that we need to keep in mind in our study of his image and representation. And it is the need of his spokesmen and supporters to *respond* to other perceptions and representations that, we must appreciate, helped to fashion the royal image. Only when we admit those challenges and responses will we be able to evaluate the success of Williamite propaganda, both in the king's lifetime and in the longer-term history of his reputation and memory, and the story of the contest to write England's past. Like the regicides and republicans four decades before the Revolution, Williamites faced the challenge of persuading subjects of the legitimacy of a regime which had been brought to power by a violent coup. I have argued – and Milton suggested – that the English Commonwealth failed to survive because it neglected to address the presence of a king over the water and fell short in constituting and communicating new discourses and signs that might have represented and sustained a new form of government.[30] The Whigs after 1688 certainly did not neglect to argue the king's case, nor fail to represent or advertise William's virtues. It is to be hoped that our brief introduction in this section to the means and modes by which, and the genres and forms through which, they did so might encourage a full study of the images of the king in literature, art and artefacts, and of their contribution to a Whig political culture that secured the Revolution.

CHAPTER 9

SCRIPTING THE REVOLUTION

I

William III has been rightly characterized as a man of action: as a brave commander who led his troops into the thick of battle, narrowly dodging enemy bullets, and a man of daring who did not, as in 1688, shrink from taking risks. We tend not to think of such men as the great orators or writers: actions, the proverb says, speak louder than words. But, as since classical times great commanders have appreciated, leading armies and military enterprises involved persuasion as well as accomplishment at arms. Throughout his youth William had had to struggle politically to attain the Captain Generalship held by the Orange family since the Dutch Revolt and in 1688 had certainly displayed deft political tactics as well as military daring.[1] As we have seen, in advance of his invasion of England, he issued a carefully crafted *Declaration* of his reasons for appearing in arms and his intentions, and one of his first acts on landing was to set up a printing press.[2] William III, in other words, was aware of the need, even when at the head of an army, to make a case, to explain and justify himself.

The need for the arts of justification and persuasion did not end when he ascended to the English throne. William's principal objective in 1688 was to bring England into the war against France and into its first major involvement in continental campaigns for well over a century. Almost every year of his reign he had to make a case for the continuation, extension or resumption of war and for the unprecedentedly high taxes needed to fund it. Unlike other kings and queens, William did not write lengthy treatises or translations, commentaries or exegeses, poems or personal memoirs as representations of his rule. He was not, like Elizabeth I or James I, given to long speeches or flights of learned oratory. Yet, I wish to suggest, William's speeches, and William and Mary's declarations and proclamations, were important in enabling the king to secure support and advance his wishes and in representing him as a virtuous ruler with the interests of his people at heart. Though valuable study has examined his 'tirelessly repeated' injunctions to moral reformation, William's speeches and other pronouncements have received less notice or analysis than they deserve.[3] As is the case with other early modern monarchs (and modern rulers), William did not compose all these speeches himself.[4] But, delivered by him and published under his name by the royal printer, they represented William to his parliaments and people through changing circumstances.

William's early speeches to his first Convention Parliament set the tone of royal addresses and they also disclose some of the tropes and rhetorical moves of the king's oratorical style. After the difficult negotiations that finally secured him the throne, during which William had insisted on full sovereignty, as newly installed monarch he adopted a conciliatory style, but one that was no less assertive for being so.[5] Assuring the assembled lords and gentlemen on 18 February, 'how sensible I am of your kindness and how much I value the confidence you have reposed in me', William informed them that his purpose in speaking was to further 'assure you that I shall never do anything that may justly lessen your good opinion of me'.[6] Having begun with affectionate familiarity, the king turned to business: the difficult circumstances the allies, and especially the Dutch, were in. Without in this first meeting directly mentioning supplies, William deftly represented his assessment of financial need as one that his auditors shared (the phrase 'you yourselves must be sensible' repeats his opening lines) and, by assuming concurrence, clearly hoped to secure agreement 'that a good settlement at home is necessary, not only for your own peace but for the support of the Protestant interest both here and abroad'. William closed by leaving the Lords and Commons to determine how best to avoid delays, avert dangers, and order what was necessary 'for the good of the nation', to which he was 'confident' that, like him, they were devoted. It was a brief address but cleverly deployed a language of existing consensus to attempt to persuade men to support policies they had not yet resolved upon. And, by not mentioning supplies in so many words, William left the Commons to, as it were, volunteer them rather than respond to royal command.

In the early months of 1689, supply to secure the Revolutionary regime from foreign threats was not the only priority. Hinting at the instabilities that the nation still faced, William told the Lords and Commons 'I shall put you in mind of one thing which will conduce much to our settlement, as a settlement will to the disappointment of our enemies'.[7] The king needed to fill posts and places vacated by those who would not accept the change of regime and, he urged, a new oath was required to ensure their allegiance. Probably right in his confidence that they would act against papists, William glossed over often sharp differences about the treatment of dissenters when, in the second half of the same sentence, he hoped 'you will leave room for the admission of *all* Protestants that are willing and able to serve'.[8] Though the relation of dissenters to the Church of England had been a divisive issue since the Restoration, the king made his policy of comprehension all his MPs' interest. 'This conjunction in my service will tend to the better uniting you amongst your selves, and the strengthening you against your common adversaries'.[9] Contentious royal policies were represented as common interest in the hope of persuading the parliament that they were so. William failed to secure civil employment for dissenters; but bills for their comprehension or toleration were debated and a Toleration Act, though less than he had wanted, passed into law in May.[10] William still lacked confidence in his English, but was conscious of his need to preside in person, and gradually – as the Convention at last voted supplies for the navy and a land tax – saw some fruits of his exhortations.[11]

But with war declared against France on 7 May, it was not enough. Facing the difficult task of asking for more from a parliament that had already introduced a land tax, William combined demand with gratitude and concession. 'I am very sensible,' William told them (his favourite term had affective connotations), 'of the zeal and good affection which you gentlemen of the House of Commons have showed to the public in giving those supplies you have done already'.[12] The need for such supply having been recognized, William (who must in reality have doubted it strongly) continued to opine that 'I do not doubt but from the same inducements you will be ready to give more as the occasions require'.[13] The determination of those 'occasions', the speech made clear, lay with the king who was better informed of the costs and knew the expenses 'will much exceed the sums you have provided'.[14] But to avoid the appearance of autocracy and to attempt to see off criticism from the outset, the king offered an extraordinary concession which few of his predecessors had entertained: 'That you may make the truer judgement,' he insisted, meaning a judgement that would agree with his own, 'I am very willing you should see how all the moneys have been hitherto laid out', and informed them that accounts were already being prepared to reassure any sceptics that 'very little' of the revenue had been applied to any other purpose than the forces and ships needed for the nation's defence.[15] In traditional crown-parliament barter, one concession suggested another: having offered accountability and openness, the king asked therefore for 'a fitting reserve settled for myself', as well as for expedition of supply for Holland. William vowed his commitment to 'the preservation of all that is dear to us' and expected a similar 'vigour' from his parliament.[16] It was, we would say today, a 'something for something' speech, which may, given the imminent summer recess, have been meant for communication by MPs to their constituents.

When the MPs reassembled on 19 October, William, while apologizing that 'I am forced to ask such large supplies', again pressed the necessity for urgent action for the 'public interest'.[17] The wars for which they were needed, he told them, were not his; they were wars entered into with parliament's advice and blessed by God as the means of securing religion and liberties. For the greater good, William had been willing to venture his life, so it was incumbent on them to make the (lesser) financial sacrifice. Promising that expedition might reduce the charges, he also held out the carrot of 'in a little time . . . a lasting and honourable peace by which my subjects may be freed from the extraordinary expenses of a lingering war'.[18] The speech, it was reported, was received with 'universal applause', and a testy Convention voted £2 million for Ireland and promised vigorous prosecution of the war against France.[19] It was by no means all that William had wanted; but, as the Commons debates suggest, his speeches had begun to persuade some of the need to fund wars on a hitherto unimaginable scale. If royal words had contributed to that (and William's speeches were carefully debated) in the Convention, then they had done much to secure William's position and to enable him to embark on his larger goal.

From 1689, the challenge for the king was to persuade MPs, year after year, to vote supply and his personal addresses presented his best opportunity to make the case. Because they often had to reprise the same theme – the urgent need for money – the speeches were repetitious; and it may be for this reason that they have been neglected. However, William's adept combination of gratitude and exhortation and his adjusting of his pitch to changing circumstances and varying military fortunes had no small importance in sustaining the war and maintaining some faith in his judgement and rule.

During the early 1690s most of William's speeches to parliament opened with thanks for not just supply but the MPs' 'zeal and cheerfulness' – terms he used to underline the affection between them.[20] Indeed, the 'affection' between them, the king suggested, was as important as supply in the struggle against their enemies who would be quick to exploit any 'restlessness' at home.[21] The best argument, of course, for money was success, which both showed funds fruitfully spent and progress to a final victory and peace. Like modern regimes' careful management of reports from the theatre of war in order to sustain morale and public support, William was a master at using the half-victory, as well as the victory, as ammunition in his own rhetorical campaign. In his speech to the second session of his second parliament of 2 October 1690, for example, the king informed them of his progress towards restoring Ireland 'into such a condition this year, as that it might be no longer a charge to England'.[22] In a well-directed appeal to MPs just up from their localities where the burdens of war were already causing murmurings, William also claimed the support of, and almost a direct mandate from, the people. Their 'good inclinations' and 'demonstrations of affection' in his passage to and from Ireland left him, he told MPs, with 'not the least doubt, but I shall find the same from their representatives in parliament'.[23]

The rather mixed, not to say disappointing, campaigns of the early stages of the war were 'spun' by William to sustain the belief in progress towards victory that was essential. Addressing the MPs on the opening day of the fourth session, on 4 November 1692, William urged all to 'rejoice in the happy victory which, by the blessing of God, we obtained at sea'.[24] Alas, he continued with considerable understatement, since Namur had fallen to France that summer, the 'success at land' (the avoidance of a negative formulation was subtle) had not lived up to it, for all the bravery and courage of English soldiers. Their 'honour' dictated the need for an even greater supply. Though, the king was, he assured them, 'very sensible how heavy this charge is upon my people', evoking the bugbears of absolutism and popery, he explained that it was 'not possible to be avoided without exposing ourselves to inevitable ruin and destruction'.[25] As his speech at a difficult moment closed with a reminder of the personal risks he had taken for the nation, the Dutch king played the patriotic card exhorting MPs and the people to 'contribute to the honour and advantage of England'; or, as he rephrased it at the close of the session, 'the honour and interest of England'.[26]

William's military fortunes had not improved when he met the fifth session of his parliament. In his first speech since a bloody campaigning season he faced a now desperate situation and an urgent need for money, not only to continue the war but to enter the peace negotiations proffered by France from a stronger position.[27] Rather than lowering morale by speaking of setbacks, William referred to the 'disadvantages' that his troops and ships had met with in the last months.[28] While acknowledging that the fleet had not been well managed and promising to rectify and punish failings, the king, informing the house that 'the great number of our enemies . . . exceeded ours in all places', requested yet greater levies for increases in troops, ships and sailors to match the enemy.[29] Despite the political difficulties, William was sufficiently persuasive to be able to make a substantial addition to his forces during the winter of 1693–4 and so to check any further French advances. 'In 1694, for the first time since 1690, the king had reason to be pleased with his summer's work'; so when he met his parliament on 12 November for its sixth and final session, William was able to convey good news as his argument for supply.[30]

'I am glad to meet you here,' William opened as usual, but added 'when I can say our affairs are in a better posture both by sea and land than when we parted.'[31] The king used both 'the prospect of another success' and the hope, revived by recent successes, of a secure peace as arguments for 'such supplies as may enable me to prosecute the war with vigour'; and his speech was evidently well received.[32] The Commons 'went cheerfully on with the supply' and raised a heavy land tax to furnish over £2 million each for the army and navy.[33] The summer of 1694 was to prove the turning point in the campaign and the reign. Greatly strengthened by supplies, William was emboldened to attempt to retake Namur which, though heavily fortified by Louis's legendary military engineer Vauban, capitulated in September. It may be that his first decisive victory determined the king to make a new start at home. For no sooner had he landed back in England than he dissolved the parliament prorogued in May and issued writs for elections to his third parliament, and first since 1690.[34]

Just as he returned to popular acclaim, which had been demonstrated everywhere on his short royal progress, so the elections returned a clear majority of MPs willing to prosecute the war to victory.[35] William welcomed his new MPs on 23 November 1695, 'assured of a good disposition in my parliament when I have had such full proofs of the affection of my people'.[36] Observing (not entirely accurately) that he had been engaged in war by his first parliament and assisted with cheerfulness by his last, he made clear that he expected zealous commitment to the cause from the newcomers. Somewhat surprisingly not mentioning by name the victory at Namur, which was (as we shall see) the subject of scores of thanksgiving services, sermons and panegyrical poems, William alluded only to the 'advantages we have had this year' which promised the hope of further success.[37] Appealing to what must have been a patriotic mood, the king praised 'the courage and bravery the English troops have shown . . . which . . . has answered their highest character in any age'.[38] Though part of a confederacy, it was, he implied, English valour which had halted France – and it was English valour that merited the supply for continuing the war. Astutely, in meeting a new parliament, William turned to domestic issues and recommended parliament consider the reform of the coinage and prepare bills to advance trade, before closing with an appeal for prompt action. Though the parliament was by no means to prove entirely compliant, the king's opening speech was received with a hum of approval and a congratulatory address from both houses, which also voted more than £5 million in supply.[39]

During the winter before the campaigning season was underway, news came in of French preparations to invade England and of a Jacobite plot to assassinate the king. The opportunity to take political advantage from this news was too good to be missed. Untypically summoning the Lords and Commons in mid-session, on 24 February 1696 William spoke to explain the 'extraordinary occasion' that had brought them there.[40] After outlining an invasion and conspiracy 'disappointed by the singular mercy and goodness of God' and providence, the king underscored the warning it had given the nation to provide for security against still dangerous enemies, abroad and at home. Parliament's loyal response was immediate: the king's speech led both houses to wait on William at Kensington House the same evening with an address expressing wholehearted thanks for his deliverance, for taking them into his confidence, and vowing revenge on any who attempted against him. To give substance to their promise, the Commons immediately resolved to sign a document of Association which pledged all to defend him (or avenge him in the event of his death) as 'rightful and lawful king of these realms'.[41] The clause could hardly have been more significant, as the revisions in the Lords and the refusal of some Tories to subscribe to it soon evidenced. Since 1688 there had been a large question and bitterly contentious debate over whether William was merely king *de facto* or by right and law. In February 1696, therefore, it might have seemed that, after his address on the conspiracy, the king had never stood higher in the estimation of his MPs and subjects at home or in his prospects to dominate in Europe. William closed the first session with a warm response of his thanks for all their care of his person and government, and his assurance of 'all the returns which a prince can make to his people'.[42]

For all the honeyed words, however, William was prevented from continuing the war by a desperate financial crisis which led him to suggest a devaluation to raise funds for a starving army and to seek a peace with France.[43] Peace, however, could only be negotiated from strength. When he resummoned parliament on 20 October, the tone of William's opening speech was cooler and more admonitory than in the previous spring. The king opened by informing any complacent at the quiet since the thwarting of the invasion and conspiracy that this was not to be taken for granted.[44] Supplies, he chided, had been disappointing; the re-coining of money difficult. In a tense address, William pressed the urgent necessity of supply to clear debts and provide for next season's campaign. Recognizing that the case might not be as easy to make with rumours of a peace circulating, the king volunteered himself 'to acquaint you that some overtures have been made for a general peace'.[45] But stoking the fears concerning the French, he was 'sure' he told them 'we shall all agree in opinion that the only way of treating with France is with our swords in our hands', a safe peace depending on adequate preparation and supply for a vigorous war. William also cleverly targeted Protestant solidarity by mentioning 'the miserable condition of French Protestants'.[46] In closing, re-emphasizing the need to show unity, the king appealed to MPs' patriotism and sense of their importance: 'there is not one good Englishman,' he told them, 'who is not entirely convinced how much does depend upon this session . . . for the safety and honour of England'.[47] Albeit they reminded the monarch of the vast costs of the war and large supplies voted over eight years, the Commons yet replied with a promise of their continued support and proceeded 'with great alacrity' to bills to tackle the problems William's speech had identified and a vote of supply.[48] Dismissing them to leave for the continent, William, as he was good at doing, rewarded their loyal co-operation with gratitude, promises and flattery of 'the wisdom and zeal of so good a parliament'.[49] Thanks to their 'prudence, temper and affection', their entering on the business cheerfully and unanimously, the king's expectations were 'fully answered'. Provisions had enabled the king to put pressure on France to make a satisfactory peace, and the Commons' action to make good debts promised to restore credit. Instructing them to carry their affection back to their counties, he held out the prospect 'in a short time' of the 'universal ease and satisfaction of my people'.[50]

On 20 September 1697, after four months of negotiation, a treaty was signed at Ryswick which, it was believed, finally put an end to a nearly twenty-year war. If not everything he would have desired, the terms were very favourable to William and the allies. On his return to England in mid-November, he was greeted with a victory parade in the city and the cheers and bonfires of the people.[51] It was reported that William rejected the plan to erect triumphal arches that would have recalled the spectacular tableaux staged for the entry of Charles II. If in that he may have lost an opportunity to give the nation at last a real occasion of celebration after years of uncertainty, one cannot but feel that in his final speech to his third parliament, the king misjudged the moment and the mood. Without any (now fitting) words of triumph, or of affectionate greeting, William announced to the MPs that the war he had entered 'by the advice of my people' had 'by the blessing of God' been brought to an honourable peace.[52] The speech made no reference to the terms, not even to Louis XIV's recognition of the 1688 Revolution or the security of the throne. Somewhat clumsily, while explaining that he had pursued peace to free the kingdom from burdens, William dashed hopes by warning: 'I am heartily sorry my subjects will not at first find all that relief from the peace ... they may expect'. Worse, he continued, higher taxes would be needed to make good deficiencies and pay debts, and to maintain the fleet and army at existing strength. Peace, the king promised, did give him the opportunity to rectify corruptions in the administration of which the Country opposition (those critical of court power) had long complained; and enabled him to champion a moral reformation and so reassume his leadership of godly reform. Finally, William permitted himself a reference to all he had done to rescue the nation's religion and liberties. But overall, the speech seems a low-register, disappointing performance in which a (misplaced) sense of realism occluded the achievement of Ryswick and robbed the people of the triumphal reward of their sacrifices.

The Commons' response, far more positive about the end of war, the prospects of peace and the restored honour of England, confirms our sense that a more triumphal discourse would by no means have fallen on deaf ears.[53] However, William's desire, that he might be able to retain a standing army as a security, was dashed by a coalition of opponents in the house which proceeded to vote for a disbandment and forced the king's Lord Chamberlain, Sunderland, to resign.[54] Disappointed by his failure to persuade MPs to finance a standing army of twenty to thirty thousand men the king also aired his frustration that 'people in parliament now occupy themselves with private animosities and party quarrels and think little of the national interest'.[55] But, whatever his frustrations, recognizing the need to sustain publicly good relations with parliament, William dismissed the last session of his third assembly with warm words for 'so good a parliament' and 'the great things' it had done.[56] Listing its achievements (reform of the coin, restoration of credit, paying debts – most of all 'the happy uniting of us'), he promised the members who had sat for three hard years 'a lasting reputation', that they 'will be a subject of emulation to those who shall come after'. The tone of unity, gratitude and affection was carefully judged in the circumstances. Within a fortnight of the dissolution, William had again to leave to treat with France and 'peace and good order' at home needed to be safeguarded.

The peace gave way to an uneasy cold war as Louis XIV broke the terms of the Treaty of Ryswick and the prospect loomed of the Dauphin succeeding Carlos II on the throne of Spain, which would have created a superpower.[57] While William headed the negotiations that led to two partition treaties intended to divide the Spanish empire and limit French acquisitions, the parliament initially called for July did not meet until December 1698. During William's absence, his ministers heard rumours of 'complaints of taxes and offices' at the hustings, but the former Secretary of State, Nottingham calculated that the constituency of the new assembly was better than the last, and William evidently met his fourth parliament with hope.[58] The speech, drafted by Lord Chancellor Somers, who had been involved with the partition treaty, was a careful quest for unity.[59] Reprising an old formula, the king opened: 'My Lords and Gentlemen, I have no doubt but you are met together with hearts fully disposed to do what is necessary for the safety, honour and happiness of the kingdom.'[60] What (without naming it) he made clear he thought necessary to sustain security and to preserve England's 'weight' in Europe was a substantial force that the previous parliament had opposed, but for which it may have been hoped the new circumstances made a stronger argument. Along with supply, the speech recommended reform – specifically popular bills for advancing trade and manufactures, employing the poor and discouraging vice and profanity. Making the whole package one of 'common concern', William, perhaps with some optimism, hoped for 'unanimity and dispatch'.[61] This time he was to be bitterly disappointed. For not only did the Commons lay aside supply and insist on disbandment, they insisted on native Englishmen in the army in what amounted to a snub to the Dutch king.[62] Given that he was so offended that for weeks he spoke of leaving England, William's speech of acceptance of the bill for disbanding was a model of restraint and of a noble attempt to secure something in defeat.[63] With a remarkable understatement that was clearly more tactical than heartfelt, William observed that, in the Commons' insistence in removing his countrymen, 'I might think myself unkindly used'.[64] Yet, he continued, certain that nothing could be worse than any 'distrust or jealousy' between him and his people, he had passed the bill, leaving it now to MPs to ensure that the nation was not too much exposed and that the peace might be preserved.

Once again, William's speech had some effect and prompted a glowing address of thanks.[65] But the Commons remained resolute on the removal of the Dutch guards and proceeded to criticism of the management of the navy which opened a broader anti-court attack on placemen.[66] Along with a frosty rejection of the king's last-ditch effort to save his Dutch guard, the actions of the new parliament had been hostile and William's speech ending the first session on 4 May (1699) only thinly veiled the frustration and anger he felt. Virtually none of the measures he had proposed or recommended, he observed, in a curt and brief oration, had, despite their sitting for months, been advanced.[67] Indicating at least that they would be recalled in the winter, he tartly closed: 'I wish no inconvenience may happen in the mean time'.[68] Understandable as it was, the speech evidently soured relations for months so that even when the members reassembled in November, it was the May address rather than the king's more conciliatory words that dominated discussion and provoked a remonstrance, which heralded the worst parliamentary session of William's reign, one that scotched most of the legislative programme he had hoped to implement.[69] Revealingly, for the first time dissolving the parliament, William delivered no parting speech.

Following the death of Anne's son, the Duke of Gloucester, and Louis's accept-ance (in defiance of the partition treaties) of Carlos II's will bequeathing Spain to the French king's grandson, William met his penultimate parliament on 11 February 1701 convinced of the need to resume war and again persuade MPs to finance it. On this occasion, we are not left to guess at the tactics behind his opening speech. For William informed his absent ally in the United Provinces, Anthony Heinsius, that 'I thought it best simply to propose the problems for their deliberation, without expressing my own opinion for the moment, thinking that this will have more effect'.[70] In that spirit, the king simply laid out the prob-lems 'for the consideration of a new parliament'.[71] Since the parliament was divided and the Tories tended to be opposed to war, it was a risky strategy but one that produced what the king had wanted. The Commons voted to support the king and his joint negotiations with the Dutch and resolved on the succes-sion in the next Protestant line after Anne, albeit with serious limitations to the future king's sovereign powers.[72] As well as these, parliament's criticism of the partition treaties displeased William; but he had secured his main objectives – supply for war and the succession – and William, ending the session on 24 June, spoke with renewed warmth. 'I return you my hearty thanks', he opened, 'for the care you have taken to establish the succession to the crown in the Protestant line'.[73] 'And', he emphasized, 'I must not lose this occasion of acquainting you that I am likewise *extremely sensible* of your respected assurances of supporting me in such alliances as shall be most proper for the preservation of the liberty of Europe and for the security of England and Holland'.[74]

As war loomed, William felt the need to explain the dangers to a new parlia-ment in order to gain their support for another round in the struggle against France. His address on 31 December, the day after the houses assembled, was the longest of his reign and one of the most effective in making his case. William opened by reminding his auditors of the loyal addresses that had come in from the people on the news of Louis's support for the Prince of Wales. Not only did the French proclamation represent 'the highest indignity offered to me and the nation', William asserted connecting his with the patriotic cause, 'but does so nearly concern every man who has a regard for the Protestant religion or the present and future quiet . . . of his country'.[75] Moving from the powerful old evocations of Protestantism and patriotism, the king explained the consequence of the succession to the Spanish crown of the Duke of Anjou, grandson of Louis XIV. By endorsing the duke, he summarized, 'he [Louis] has made [Spain] to be entirely depending on France . . . and by that means he has surrounded his neighbours', creating a stranglehold and threat that made nonsense of the peace. Lest there be any minded to consider these as noises far off, William insisted, 'This must affect England in the nearest and most sensible manner': in its trade, peace and safety. Out of interest – always a persuasive language – as well as honour, England, he explained, needed to take its role in preserving the liberty of Europe: 'the eyes of all Europe,' he told them rising to lofty rhetoric, 'are upon this parliament' and it was incumbent on them to 'exert the ancient vigour of the English nation'. Offering to open all his negotia-tions with allies and accounts to their scrutiny, the king exhorted a divided Commons to lay aside party animosities for a greater cause. For his part, he told them, he was no king of a party, but – the deployment of an old metaphor was well judged – 'the common father of all my people'. It was for them, in the face of the threat of popish French rule, to unite 'for the Protestant religion and the present establishment', while the opportunity remained.

It worked. Tories vied with Whigs only to express their loyalty and support for supply, and even urged no peace to be made until Louis made reparation for recognizing James III.[76] Other than a brief message, it was William's last speech to parliament. Not unreasonably it has been described as 'the most eloquent'.[77] It was printed in Dutch and French as well as English and, it was claimed, 'hung up in frames in almost every house in England'.[78] Certainly the circumstances, the outrage at French perfidy, were favourable. But the clarity of William's exposition, the heights of patriotic rhetoric, the use of language and syntax to bind a divided parliament and people, an appeal to honour and a call for England to take its rightful place as the arbiter of Europe, present William (even if some of the words were his draughtsman's) in a very different light to the awkward, dour performer, ill at ease in English, in England and with his English subjects, of so many histories.

I have devoted considerable space to William III's speeches because these were some of the only occasions on which the king directly presented himself to his parliaments and, through their publications, to his people. The speeches were not long, like, say, those of James I, or memorable like those, say, of Queen Elizabeth I or Oliver Cromwell. Many were repetitious, even formulaic. Yet they were not without art. Repetition kept William's objectives at the centre of debate; and he was practised at in evoking memories, stoking anxieties, exciting fears and promoting patriotism. His use of old and new language, appeals to honour and interest, his deployment and manipulation of reciprocity and mutual affection were essential in an early modern discourse of authority and often expertly pitched. Were they effective? William faced problems – of his legitimacy, of bitter religious and party division, of an English aversion to continental war and high taxes, which he did not solve – and opposition from commonwealthsmen, Jacobites and an emerging 'Country' critique, which did not go away. Whatever his expressed wishes, or call for unanimity, he never united his parliament or people. However, he succeeded in establishing the Revolution, his throne and Protestant succession. Most of all, he persuaded his subjects to enter and sustain the longest, costliest land and naval wars in England's modern history and to pay unprecedented levels of taxation to finance them. Virtually every year, he was faced with trying to secure supply – by means of apology, explanation, or imprecation; and though they fell short of his needs, he secured funds adequate to maintain the confederacy, check French advances, secure some spectacular victories, and change the balance of power in Europe. In February 1701, informing Heinsius of his decision not to express his opinion to the new parliament, he observed 'they have paid very little attention to it hitherto'.[79] It was too negative a self-assessment. Whatever the difficulties and criticisms he faced, as the proceedings of parliament document, many of William's speeches were often greeted with addresses of thanks as well as grants of supply unprecedented in scale and frequency.[80] They deserve a significant place in the story of his representation and reign.

One of the decisive factors in securing English support for the Dutch invasion and then the Convention's offer of the crown were William's various declarations outlining the reasons for his appearing in arms and his intentions to rescue three kingdoms from slavery and popery.[81] Given this it may seem surprising that, once on the throne, William made little use of them, and after 1690 none. Of a handful of early declarations issued in the joint names of the king and queen and mainly dealing with minor matters (the pay and quartering of troops, for example) only one stands out: *Their Majesties Declaration Against the French King*, published on 7 May 1689.[82] As he embarked upon the course, unprecedented in modern times, of a war with France, William perhaps considered it politic to appeal to the nation. He did so by explaining how the threat Louis was posing to Europe affected English overseas territories, her trade and subjects too. Emotive references to Englishmen's houses burned or others 'inhumanely killed' and other 'notorious' crimes, and to his 'strange and unusual cruelties' against English Protestants in France, were accumulated so as to direct Protestant and patriotic zeal towards a crusade against an enemy who, it was claimed, plotted to overthrow England. 'Relying on the help of Almighty God in our just undertaking', William called on all subjects to support 'so good a cause' at a time when support in parliament was hedged and uncertain. It was his last direct address to the people. Though the king often referred, as we have seen, to manifestations of popular support and directed his MPs to carry his words to their constituencies, after 1690 he issued no declarations. It may be that the annual parliaments necessitated by war made royal declarations (which had often been used in long intervals between sessions) redundant. But abandoning this genre of royal representation may also have been a little unwise, especially during a decade when James II issued periodic declarations to his English subjects which attracted public attention and debate.[83] Whatever his reasons, William, as we will see, preferred other modes of communicating to his people – the court sermon, the official services of prayer and thanksgiving. But it remains the case that in surrendering a genre in which in 1688 he had scored polemical success, he failed to speak directly – and with what was still the voice of regal authority – to his subjects.

Compared to their length and highly rhetorical prologues and justifications in Tudor and early Stuart times, royal proclamations, while retaining their functions as instruments of business, lost some of their importance in representing majesty in the late seventeenth century. That acknowledged, we cannot discount them. Proclamations were not only printed by the royal printers in large numbers, they were republished in the *London Gazette*, the official government newspaper.[84] In the (less literate) provinces, they were still read out at Quarter Sessions, market crosses and sometimes from pulpits. In the words of one historian, during the 1690s they remained 'central to the court's self-presentation'; and, we would add, because they appeared with the royal arms and above the king's and queen's names, particularly central to the representation of the new monarchy.[85] William and Mary issued at least a hundred proclamations jointly from 1689 to the queen's death in 1694, William perhaps only half that number thereafter. Like nearly all early modern proclamations they have received little historical attention and no analysis as pro-Williamite polemic. Their importance, however, starts with their form and appearance. From the very beginning William and Mary used traditional gothic script that signified both authority and continuity. With a large royal arms above 'By the King and Queen', the initial letter of the text of the proclamation figured beneath an imperial crown and, amidst fruit and verdure, a tablet with a capital W – which also looked like an M (fig. 48). At the end of the text, above the names of the royal printers, each proclamation ended: 'God save King William and Queen Mary'. Proclamations, that is, visually as well as verbally proclaimed a joint rule, and William's supremacy, as well as the continuity of their rule and the legitimacy of the Revolution.

William and Mary's joint proclamations tended not to be long, like those, say, of Henry VIII or Charles I. Many simply enact business, be it proroguing parliaments, collecting arrears of taxation, or dealing with the coinage. In a decade of constant war, several were directed at regulating troops, encouraging

48 *By the King and Queen, A Proclamation . . ., 1690.*

and recruiting sailors, and ensuring supplies of munitions materials, such as saltpetre.[86] Williamite proclamations, however, were not lacking in polemic. Many refer to the advice of the Privy Council or parliament or, as the proclamation for dissolving the Convention expressed it, publicized how 'desirous we are to meet our people and have their advice in parliament'.[87] In the spirit of Tudor proclamations, William's often explained the motivation behind royal action as the 'good and welfare of the people or (as a proclamation regulating the price of coal put it) his 'tender compassion and care for our good subjects'.[88] Though the rhetoric was familiar, its reiteration during times of hardship and high taxes represented the king as a caring ruler – a stance he even adopted in a proclamation collecting arrears of the Hearth Tax by reminding subjects of his 'unparalleled grace and favour to his people' by repealing it.[89] Support for war, of course, was William's highest priority and he did not fail on occasions to use a proclamation to advance his argument for it. Let us take, for example, the proclamation of 1 May 1689 prohibiting the import of commodities from France. As well as pointing to the prejudice done to English manufacturers, the proclamation referred to 'the injuries, aggressions and dangers' done by the

French king and 'the just and necessary war' embarked upon 'with the help of Almighty God . . . to deliver this kingdom'.[90] In similar vein, a proclamation of April 1691, referring to 'a necessary war against France by sea and land' asserted that on the success of arms, 'the common safety of this realm . . . doth depend'.[91]

As well as several orders for apprehending traitors, including the non-juring Bishop of Ely, Francis Turner, William's proclamations helped sustain an anti-papal rhetoric that was important in keeping the nation together and resisting Jacobite propaganda.[92] In their May 1689 proclamation removing Catholics from London and Westminster, the king and queen stoked fears of papists' 'wicked and mischievous designs . . . tending to the ruin and destruction of all Protestants and restoring popery into these kingdoms'.[93] A year later, a further such proclamation, branding all Catholics as 'ill affected . . . restless spirits', represented them as in constant colloquy to plot against the government, or as an order confining them put it, 'endeavouring to corrupt and seduce their majesty's subjects and them excite to sedition and rebellion'.[94]

Most innovative, as well as important for William's self-representation as godly ruler, were the many proclamations published to order a fast, to implore God's blessing on the king's person and endeavours. In no reign before were so many issued, the annual campaigns providing the occasion for William to advertise his godliness and piety. The first such, issued on 23 May 1689, having again underlined the necessity of war, announced that the king and queen placed their trust in a God 'who hath . . . wonderfully preserved and blessed their majesties hitherto'.[95] To ask the Lord now 'that he will vouchsafe a special blessing to this their righteous undertaking', the proclamation commended a fast and service which (we will see) served as propaganda, and morale boosting, for the war. Almost every year, royal proclamations required subjects to join in fasts and prayers 'in most devout and solemn manner, for supplicating Almighty God for the pardon of our sins, and imploring his blessing . . . in the preservation of their majesties' sacred persons and prosperity of their arms both at land and sea'.[96] In such proclamations, not only was William presented as godly, and as God's agent; God himself was figured as a Williamite.

Proclamations for fasts to implore the Lord's blessing were often followed by proclamations ordering thanksgiving for victories secured by divine favour upon the king. The first of these, issued in October 1690 after the Battle of the Boyne and victory in Ireland, thanked God for 'his power and mercy in giving us success' and ordered a public service of thanks and the reading of the proclamation 'in all churches and chapels' preceding the service.[97] While the next year's military stalemate offered no such signal victories, a proclamation of October 1692 announced a public thanksgiving to God for having preserved their majesties at home and abroad, checked the French at sea, and defeated the conspiracy against the king 'for taking away his sacred life by assassination'.[98] During the seasons of setback, royal proclamations sustained morale – and the vital sense that the war was God's cause – by regularly ordering public services of thanksgiving for the safe return of the king from expeditions, in answer to their prayers. As the war dragged on with little to show for it, William made everything he could of the small gains secured on the continent. The thanksgiving appointed for 2 and 16 December 1694, for example, praised God that it had pleased Him 'to grant such success to his Majesty's arms both at sea and on land and to the forces of the confederate princes and states in several parts of Europe, as to put a considerable stop to the rage and fury of the enemy'.[99]

The announcement of a thanksgiving for William's most signal victory over the enemy at Namur came in a proclamation issued on 29 August 1695 by the Lords Justices who constituted a Council of Regency after the death of Mary in William's absence.[100] Indeed, from the death of Queen Mary in December 1694 far fewer proclamations were issued under the king's name, as the Lords Justices were left to superintend the administration of affairs at home.[101] However, the king did not entirely fail to continue to use the opportunities of proclamations to represent himself to his subjects. In several proclamations summoning parliaments, William emphasized his affection for them and confidence in their advice, and in 1695 commanded a fast to implore God's blessing on the parliament, 'we being deeply sensible how much the happiness of our kingdom depends on the good success of these consultations'.[102] In proclamations for fasts and thanksgivings, he continued to demonstrate his piety, trust in providence and the special protection he enjoyed of a God who, for instance, delivered him from a 'horrid and barbarous conspiracy' in 1696.[103] Indeed, after the death of Mary who was (we shall see) heralded as a model of godliness and piety, the king may have felt it all the more important to manifest that he was no less committed to godly reformation.[104] Accordingly, William reiterated his ready support for 'pious' motions, his love of 'divine goodness' and his desire to cleanse the nation of the 'manifold sins' which threatened divine judgment.[105] Most importantly, as has been observed, William, especially after 1697, used proclamations to spearhead a national campaign for godly reformation. Royal action had commenced shortly after the formation of the first Society of the Reformation of Manners, which Queen Mary had been invited to sponsor.[106] A proclamation of the next January duly required all judges, JPs and constables to enforce the laws against immorality and profanity, and encouraged all subjects to support them.[107] Mary continued to campaign by example and encouragement. But, not least perhaps, because some had indicated that William himself did not do enough, the king, especially after the Peace of Ryswick, turned his attention to further proscriptions and proclamations against vice and profanity. In a royal proclamation of 29 February 1698, expressing his duty to God and care for his subjects, William announced his determination to see 'religion, piety and good manners flourish' under his rule, and harsh measures against offenders: drunkards, blasphemers, the lewd and profane.[108] Reissued in 1699, the proclamation, along with William's injunctions to reform in his speeches, not only enabled the king to lead the campaign for moral reform, it went some way to neutralizing criticism that a corrupt government was itself to blame for the decayed morals of the nation.[109] It had always been an essential facet of William's rhetoric that he was a godly redeemer. In the face of criticisms and the initiatives of others, royal speeches and proclamations championing godly reformation were, as he recognized, important props to government. A significant plank of his ongoing campaign for legitimation, 'the king's patronage of legal reformation formed an impressive claim for royal authority'.[110]

The royal proclamations for fasts and thanksgivings instructed the bishops to devise an order of service for the day to be held in all the churches of the realm. As with many speeches and proclamations, these services were not penned by the king or queen; but, along with the likelihood that they were submitted for royal approval, they represented a sovereign who was Supreme Head of the Church; and the loyal prayers of the congregation legitimated a monarch who was, from the outset, described as a saviour and redeemer.[111] These services (as we have seen) were not new. But their regularity and frequency after 1688, and the questions about William's rightful authority as king and head of the church, made them important elements of an ideological programme to persuade subjects of the king's legitimacy, and though we cannot offer here the full study they deserve, we must sample them as a popular medium of royal representation.[112]

Even before he was offered the crown, the first of the many services led the nation, on 31 January 1689, in prayers for 'the glorious instrument of the great deliverance of this kingdom from popery and arbitrary power'.[113] As well as readings from Psalm 111 ('He sent redemption unto his people'), the service replaced the collect for the day with prayers of thanks for the 'late great and happy deliverance', and for William 'a mighty Deliverer by whom thou has wrought this great salvation without the effusion of blood'.[114] As if erasing James II, after a prayer for the royal family a prayer for his highness the Prince of Orange asked for God's blessing on his chosen instrument to restore religion and law.[115] From the beginning of 1689, prayer not only justified the Revolution in the powerful language of providence; it was polemic for the appointed king.

Once they were on the throne, services instituted by William and Mary made full use of prayer to claim divine approval, to underpin their right and to counter the charges of enemies and those afflicted with conscience. A Form of Prayer for 12 March 1689, prepared, as the title page announced, 'by their Majesties Special Command', folded within a full service of worship (confession, absolution, collects, creed, the litany, Lord's Prayer and lessons) prayers for 'abundant blessings upon our gracious king and queen', and on their fleets and armies.[116] A new prayer for the king, 'to be constantly used during his majesty's expedition', implored God to protect 'him whom thy gracious providence hath made the happy instrument of our preservation' and to instruct subjects 'in dutiful subjection to their majesties whom thou has set over us'.[117] Repeated at evening services, prayers for the king and queen and for Princess Anne sacralized a new dynasty and underpinned a new succession. Their power as propaganda in 1689 simply cannot be overstated.

As Tony Claydon has remarked, it is not possible to know what each worshipper actually took away from the compulsory services.[118] But the likelihood that the regular intonement of prayers *by* the congregation was even more effective than polemical addresses *to* them is supported by contemporary testimony. Writing in 1691, the rector of Great Mongeham in Kent felt sure that 'the thanksgiving days and fasting days, and the collects and prayers read, and the saying Amen by all the members of the congregation is a justification of what hath been done in this Revolution'.[119]

The justification of the Revolution was by no means accomplished by 1691: even as the rector wrote, William was fighting Jacobite resistance in Ireland and every Wednesday and Friday during the campaign, official prayers asked for divine blessing on their arms, protection of their persons and their safe restoration to advance true religion.[120] Several times a year, thereafter, official prayers were drawn up for the success of the king's campaigns against France and recited at every service.[121] Congregations prayed, in memory of the Protestant wind of 1688, for favourable winds for the royal fleet;[122] they prayed that the king may be preserved 'from all secret and treacherous practices' as well as enemy bullets;[123] they prayed: 'Let it appear that thou the Lord art with us to help us and to fight our battles'.[124]

As anxieties and setbacks at last gave way to some progress, services of thanks duly recognized, as William commanded, the hand of God in England's fortunes. The year 1695 gave occasion for two such celebrations. In April a service of thanksgiving was held 'for discovering and disappointing a horrid and barbarous conspiracy of papists and other traitorous persons to assassinate ... his most gracious majest[y] ... and for delivering this kingdom from an invasion'.[125] Thanking God 'for the wonderful deliverance of our most gracious sovereign', the congregation prayed: 'Let us never forget how often and how wonderfully thou hast preserved thine anointed and his people'.[126] As the service helped to forge through such language the unity that the government sought, all prayed to God to frustrate the designs of enemies who sought only to enslave them and to 'protect and defend our sovereign lord'.[127] The second service, appointed for 8 September, was a service of thanks for the 'great success in taking the town and castle of Namur, and for protecting his Majesty's sacred person from the many dangers to which he was ... exposed'.[128] To underline William's piety and humility before God in victory, the prayer began with the words of Psalm 115: 1 'Not unto us, O Lord, not unto us, but unto thy name give the praise.'[129] Before the collect for peace, a prayer for the king beseeched

God to continue William 'under the merciful care and protection of thy good Providence . . . to cover his head in the day of danger; to bless him with good success'.[130] After the litany and collect, the minister led prayers of thanks for victory and for blessings on the 'sacred head of thine anointed', his allies and 'all those that fight his battles'.[131] In the communion service, further prayers for the victory of the king and his allies presented them as fighting a holy battle and 'taught . . . to war' by God himself.[132] Against the background of murmuring discontent at monies syphoned into Dutch pockets in a war waged for the interest of foreigners, the service of prayer presented the conflict as a holy war and the Confederates as Christian soldiers.

The representation in prayer of William as God's chosen instrument, protected by his providence, was furthered by the miraculous revelation of another assassination plot against the king.[133] As well as the service of thanks for God's care of the prince, ordered by the Lords Justices in June, two very short prayers were published and perhaps sold for use in worship at home as well as in churches.[134] *A Form of Prayer and Thanksgiving To Be Used . . . After the General Thanksgiving* thanked God for all the favours he had shown King William, 'especially for thy late great mercy towards him, in discovering the designs and disappointing the attempts of malicious and bloody men', and prayed: 'convert his enemies, increase and prosper his dutiful subjects'.[135] Another short prayer, published 'by his majesty's special command', asked God to preserve the king from 'all secret and treacherous practices', to 'go forth with his fleets and armies' and 'to make him in thy good time the happy instrument of establishing peace and truth in these and our neighbouring nations'.[136]

The next year the 'happy and honourable peace' was the occasion of a service of thanks for the end of the 'miseries of war' and the safe return of the king.[137] Ascribing the blessing of peace to God, the service also lauded a sacred king 'whom thou hast made the happy instrument' of 'restoring peace', as 'so many mercies'.[138] In the communion service, a special collect spoke of a king who still had God's work to do: 'Finish, O Lord . . . the great work thou has begun by him. Grant, that under him, we may long enjoy the blessed fruits of peace and true religion; and that destructions may come to a perpetual end.'[139] Short prayers for the king again published separately from the text of the full service implores 'give us all grace under him to lead quiet and peaceable lives in all godliness and honesty'.[140]

Our argument that prayer was not only a representation of a godly king but a direct form of war propaganda gains some support from the fact that, after the Peace of Ryswick, there were virtually no official services or prayers published by the government or the royal command. In 1699 the king authorized a fast and service of prayer for the comfort of persecuted Protestants abroad.[141] In prayers which contrasted the fate of afflicted brethren with the special favours shown to England, the congregation was led to repent their sins and pray for 'new and contrite hearts'.[142] And prayers for the parliament and king, lamenting 'the great dangers we are in by our unhappy divisions', beseeched God that 'under our most religious and gracious king', 'we may be godly and quietly governed'.[143] A service for a fast day appointed for 6 April 1700, to bless the parliament, included collects in which the people prayed the Lord 'to remove the evils we now lie under . . . to reconcile our differences, and heal our breaches to unite our hearts'.[144] Imploring God's blessing on 'William, our King and Governor', in the spirit of all he wished for, they asked 'that we and all his subjects (duly considering whose authority he hath) may faithfully serve, know and humbly obey him in thee and for thee, according to thy blessed word and ordinance'.[145]

As revisionist scholars have argued, there is a danger that we exaggerate the secularism of post-Revolutionary England.[146] Since the Reformation, the king's position as Supreme Head had given the monarch, if not complete control, considerable influence over what was a major medium of propaganda.[147] The pulpits were commandeered to read proclamations and announce royal policy; court sermons often preached royal programmes; and liturgical ceremonies expressed royal preferences, in some cases, a broader ideology of rule. If anything, church services and prayers were even more important. In services of congregational confession, communion and prayer, rather than just the passive auditors, people (of all social classes) *participated* and *joined together* to recite as their own the words drawn up by bishops at the command of the king. Whatever the divisions of party or the discontents in the church, they prayed together for a monarch whose legitimacy was questioned and for a government the integrity of which many disputed. Most of all, they together prayed for victory in a war some opposed and for allies some viewed as grasping rivals. The rhetoric of prayers – prayers which often echoed William III's speeches and programmes – could not resolve those doubts and divisions. But the weekly recital through all the parishes of the land of prayers for a godly king and a Protestant crusade surely strengthened the resolve of William's supporters and won over sceptics. Certainly one supporter of the regime thought so. In his sermon preached on the day of thanksgiving for the deliverance of the king from the plot, John Strype preached on the power of prayer: 'Great is the efficacy of these frequently repeated repetitions.'[148]

Through speeches, proclamations and prayers, William III did more to represent his legitimacy, enhance his authority, and argue for his foreign policy than traditional accounts of this taciturn, remote ruler have acknowledged. William, however, was invited to England and elected to his throne, by willing supporters who, after the events of 1688, were no less invested in arguing the right course of the Revolution and the legitimacy of the king than Orange himself. Yet just as the civil war had indelibly politicized all cultural forms, so the Revolution rendered all those forms, all texts, signs, social spaces and sites as arenas of party discourse, debate and contest. The institutionalization of political difference in parties and social practices meant that, whatever his appeal for unity or attempt to build non-party administration, William could not secure the fidelity of all MPs or subjects. Though as yet far from being an official, legitimated 'his Majesty's Opposition', opposition to the administration of the day was, in the age of party, inevitable. However, the corollary of party opposition was party loyalty. And though the complexities of the Revolution, William's policies, the war and shifting circumstances belie any simple relationship between a party and loyal support for the king, William and Mary never wanted for advocates with pens and presses ready to praise and support them in every polemical genre and literary form. It is to the writers who created a Whig literary culture that established the Revolution and the post-Revolutionary monarchy that we now turn.

II

Judging by the attention they have received, it would be tempting to assume that few panegyrists lauded William and Mary in verse. Literary scholars have until recently taken little notice of Whig poetry and, for all the new interest in post-Restoration Britain, even in Williamite propaganda, historians have ignored the poetry. As Abigail Williams has recently argued, the neglect owed something to Tory disparagement of Whig literary forms.[149] The former laureate John Dryden asserted after 1688 that 'Poetry is curs'd', and Alexander Pope was to excoriate Whig poets as brain-crazed enthusiasts or dunces.[150] Their attacks, however, as well as evidencing a party battle for literary and aesthetic forms, should lead us to suspect an anxiety in Tory circles about the contribution of Whig poetics to the Revolution and to Whig politics. Certainly it is only in the circumstances of Revolution, party contest and contemporary events that the verse of the period can be fully appreciated. And it may be for this reason that Whig poetry is still 'tarred with the label of "bad poetry"'.[151] For though poets such as Charles Montagu (a leading member of the Whig junto and Kit Kat Club and an important patron of Williamite poets) enjoyed considerable standing at the time, none of the Whigs – as they sometimes seemed aware – enjoyed Dryden's reputation; and for whatever reason, none has acquired admission to the canon, to the club of the greats of English letters, those who are ever republished and studied in colleges and schools.

Critical and historical neglect of Whig verse, however, has overlooked a vital dimension of post-Revolutionary culture and politics. For to many Whigs, the securing of English Protestantism, property and freedom in 1688 opened an opportunity for a new literary culture, a new aesthetic and sublime which was inseparable from recent history and politics. Indeed, many Whig poets not only enjoyed patronage from the Williamite government but held offices in the Treasury or diplomatic service, the poet and literary patron Montagu becoming

Chancellor of the Exchequer in 1694. As Williams argued, 'the ties between statesmen and authors, between state ideology and literature are so tight that the association of party and poems becomes self-evident'.[152] And it is evident on a massive scale. From 1688 there were literally hundreds of verses published defending and praising the Revolution, William and Mary, and the Whig government. Throughout William's reign poets loyally lauded the king's accession, his birthdays, his military victories, his escapes from foreign bullets and domestic conspiracies, and his triumphant peace. As importantly, they countered and tried to override the voices of criticism, discontent and opposition. Closely tied to the ideology of Revolution and to government patronage, Whig poets were in the van of the battle for cultural supremacy that was vital to the legitimacy and stability of William's rule. Through representing William and Mary's monarchy, they did much to establish it: to endow a usurper with the authority of cultural forms which were inseparable from authority itself.

While, as we shall see, a number of *topoi* and themes were reprised in verse panegyrics across the reign, Whig poetry was, above all, occasional; and Whig poetry, crucially for the regime, responded to the needs of the occasion. In 1688–9 those needs could hardly have been greater. The nation, even those who had welcomed his invasion, was divided over William's right to the crown and the nature of his authority; and the presses poured out pamphlets interrogating and arguing over the invasion and the Revolutionary settlement. By their very form, coronation verse panegyrics did what polemical pamphlets could not: they recognized William and Mary as legitimate monarchs and placed them in a history of former sovereigns lauded by poets on their accession to the throne. In 1689 the two universities in volumes of coronation verse not only endowed the fragile regime with the authority of learning and history, they carefully underpinned the Revolution and the new monarchy. Oxford University expressed the nation's gratitude for a Revolution which, through God's providence, had, with little loss of blood, restored religion, liberty and peace to the nation.[153] Praising a king and queen who had delivered the people, and 'Scatter'd Joy and Freedom thro the land', the Oxford poets cleverly engaged the question of right and title.[154] Employing emotive language and tactics rather than consistent logic, verses on the one hand dismissed the 'misguided chance' of hereditary right and praised a pair who acceded 'By merit, not by dull succession', while, on the other, they emphasized William and Mary's pedigree which they traced not to Stuart forebears but to the best of rulers:

Our Edwards, and our Henrys fill his Veins
In her the fair, and Chast Eliza Reigns[155]

Though acknowledging the discontents and 'murmurers' discomfited by events, the Oxford poets contrasted the recent past 'of Jesuited Tyranny', 'arbitrary power' and 'baffl'd Justice' with the hopes for peace, religion and trade, and prayed that God bless William, another divine hero like Alcides, with success and long rule.[156]

Writing, like their Oxford peers, in Greek, Latin, Hebrew and Arabic as well as English, Cambridge University scholars offered a pindaric ode 'on the late Happy Revolution' which had rescued a wounded church and nation.[157] Evoking memories of earlier victories over popery and drawing attention to William's landing as God's instrument ('by heaven for miracles designed'), on 5 November, verses urged all to 'Hail above all ye Royal Pair!' and a 'Great Restorer' who had come as the 'Defender of our Faith, and Guardian of our laws'.[158] Like the Oxford scholars, the Cambridge poets also addressed the question of William's right to the throne. Again, contrasting the king with those – that is, Prince James – of 'dubious birth' and comparing William to Alcides whom God, they wrote in language that was deeply controversial, had called to a *vacant* throne, the verses attended to hereditary right whilst at the same time defending Revolutionary action:

The Longing Nation cou'd not wait with fear
Your slow advancement by Succession Here;
But strait Enthron'd You in the Vacant Seat,
And justify'd by You so Great a Change of State.[159]

As another Alcides, Constantine or Caesar, as another Moses or Joshua, as the father of the people and 'Blest instrument of heav'n', the 'Great Nassau' was presented in university verse as a ruler with 'the Godlike Pow'r of doing Good' and his queen as one in whom 'Eliza lives again'.[160] In language that is both historical and apocalyptic, the Cambridge poets, while claiming continuity, heralded a new age in which, delivered from oppression and popery, England, under its victorious new king, might 'hold the Ballance of all Europe's Fates'.[161]

Many other poems published in 1689 celebrated the accession of William and Mary and praised the Revolution that had brought them to the throne; space permits us to consider only a few. *An Ode Upon the Glorious Expedition of the Prince of Orange* directly connected political deliverance with poetic opportunity.[162] Praising another David who had freed an enslaved people, the author believed that, silenced under tyranny, 'now the Muses and Graces reign again' and prophesied that 'the Golden Age may yet appear agen'.[163] A *Panegyric to William and Mary* heralded 'Britain rescued' and lauded a 'half Divine', 'Heroick WILLIAM' who had brought the state at last to perfection.[164] Thomas Shadwell, who succeeded Dryden as Poet Laureate, in his *Congratulatory Poem* on the Prince of Orange's coming to England, after outlining a Whig view of English liberties and religion corrupted by priests and James II, presented 'the Glorious Orange' as the 'Glorious Deliv'rer' who restored 'beauteous order' to 'dark chaos'.[165] Where some poems, and collections of verse, 'against popery and tyranny' justified the Revolution by rehearsing the ills the nation had suffered, others in loftier strains hymned an 'Augustus', an Alexander or 'our other Moses' appointed to lead the people to the promised land.[166] *A Poem on the Accession of Their Royal Highnesses* raised panegyric higher still by paraphrasing the 45th Psalm in praise of the king and queen.[167]

Though poetry could replicate the debates that dominated pamphlet literature – *A Poem in Vindication of the Late Proceedings*, for example, staged a dialogue between a high Tory and a Trimmer – the value of vatic support for the regime was that it could at least *appear* to rise above narrow party polemic and fold contentious events into classical and historical forms and languages which had long validated authority.[168] In verse more than in prose, William's legitimacy was not relentlessly argued; it could be, and was, figured as the fulfilment of history, as redemption and deliverance, as the will of providence. Panegyrical poets in 1688 and 1689 sometimes disclosed the bitter struggles that underlay their lofty prophecies of glorious rule and a golden age. But in clothing William in the garb of ancient heroes and biblical patriarchs, they not only gestured towards a Whig sublime, they represented William and Mary as legitimate, divine sovereigns to whom subjects owed duty and love.

Pamphleteers, as we will see, continued to grapple with the issue of William's right to the throne, and the related issues of James's desertion and the right of resistance, more or less throughout the reign.[169] Significantly, by contrast, Whig poets, though they used occasions such as the king's birthday to recall his deliverance, rather than defending the Revolution of 1688, celebrated the key moments and achievements of the new reign, as though arguments about legitimacy had been resolved.[170] They had not. And whilst the Whig George Stepney (somewhat disingenuously?) wrote of 'The Humour of the Times/(Inclin'd for business, and averse to Rhimes)', poetic praise of William and Mary remained vital forms of support and deeply partisan.[171] Indeed, Stepney's lines come from his verse epistles to Charles Montagu on the occasion of William III's voyage to Holland.[172] Stepney praises 'William's glory' in his victory over the Jacobites at the Battle of the Boyne and presents a heroic king who has become the subject of discourse – of 'ev'ry Tongue and ev'ry Pen'.[173] As William headed home to his native Netherlands to a triumphant welcome, Stepney looked ahead to further and greater victories – against France, and 'o'er the Continent' – as the armies and princes of Europe prepared to 'combine' under William and 'center all their Interests' in his.[174]

Other poets followed Stepney in seeing William's voyage to Holland as the dawn of a new era of English victories on land and sea.[175] The former Tory poet and playwright and convert to Revolution, Thomas D'Urfey, for example, in a pindaric poem on the royal navy dedicated to the king and queen, pictures a British fleet, of revived force and 'improved state', disdainful of any foreign power and redeeming the nation's honour under 'Royal Nassau' the 'Deliverer', whose 'chief delight' was glory.[176] Despite divisions and factions at home in church and state, D'Urfey saw the revival of the 'Martial Genius' in 'great Nassaws illustrious Reign' and a new age of English empire.[177] William's triumphant reception in Holland appears to have shifted others' attention from the domestic to the European stage. In his *Congratulatory Poem on His Majesty's Happy Return*, Thomas Brown heralded a royal victor who surpassed Caesar and Alexander and recalled the mighty Edward III, and, hoping that 'no Distractions more shall us dismay', foresaw an England which might soon 'make Empires shake' and 'Search out new Worlds'.[178]

The only obstacle to England's dawning greatness, Brown suggested, was a 'foolish Jacobite Crew' which he urged to join William's and God's cause.[179] In reality, the Jacobites were preparing an assassination plot. During 1692, therefore, panegyrical poets turned to countering Jacobite propaganda and answering attacks on the king.[180] In his satire on *The Jacobite Convention*, Richard Ames attacked the 'state blockheads' who raised discontents and urged loyalty to a good king.[181] One anonymous bard parodied and satirized the declaration which James II issued from St Germain 'to all his loving subjects', while the new Poet Laureate Nahum Tate made a valiant effort, in an ode on William's birthday, to rally support for a 'CAESAR, still surviving'.[182]

William's fortunes, however, began to revive and with each small victory loyal poets appeared to boost morale and celebrate the king as a hero. Richard Bovet's congratulatory poem for Admiral Russell on his victory over the French fleet was dedicated to King William and 'your Majesty's glorious undertakings', and held out the hope again of England taking 'The *Oceans Sovereignty*' and reviving national glory.[183] A popular broadside poem on the 'happy proceedings of their Majesties royal army' similarly praised the unparalleled glory of a king who was the son of Mars; it celebrated the Revolution and attacked the 'insulting Jacobites', friends to the enemy France.[184] The optimism of such loyal poets was finally rewarded with the decisive victory at Namur that turned the tide of military fortunes. The loyal bards wrote to rally William after the death of Queen Mary to press home his recent gains. Matthew Prior, a poet and a diplomat at The Hague, summoning William from his grief to lead the 'Embattel'd Princes' of Europe, promised his monarch: 'to Thy Fame alone 'tis given/Unbounded thro' all worlds to go';[185] while another, urging the king to mourn no longer but 'Rouze, Rouze to Arms!', foresaw 'marshal glory' and conquest.[186] Namur fulfilled all such hopes and promises and gave rise to myriad verses of epic heroism. The poet and clergyman Thomas Yalden emphasized the measure of the victory by informing readers of the formidable strength of the fortress that had been forced to yield. And, while giving due praise to those generals who led the assault, the poet highlighted 'fam'd William's Valour' as he who, braver than Achilles or Ajax, was found in the thick of danger as 'Th' informing Soul that animates the War'. Proclaiming William as 'the glorious theme' of poetry, Yalden called on other bards to prepare 'Solemn Paeans' to the victor.[187]

Loyal Whigs rushed to answer his summons. The poet, playwright and client of Montagu, William Congreve, in a pindaric ode to the king, sang of the triumph of a William who had stood 'undaunted' amidst the fire and shot.[188] In another *Poem to His Majesty* presented to the Lord Mayor, Joseph Addison, fellow member of the Whig Kit Kat Club and an excise officer, heralded this great and latest in a string of conquests which 'Freedom the World afford'.[189] One Mr Denne, also underlining the formidable difficulties of the siege and William's personal leadership and bravery, praised 'The *British* Genius and the God of War' who had toppled the Gaul and succeeded to Louis's supremacy.[190] As William returned to England in triumph, Charles Cole spoke for many in welcoming home a 'Triumphant Augustus', 'the Noblest Soul that ever reign'd as yet!'[191] Inviting all Britannia to 'sing the Encomiums' of this prince, Cole asked them: 'Can we do less, than truly him adore?'[192]

That there were still some who did not adore the king was made dangerously evident only months after victory at Namur. The attempted assassination of William in February 1696, perhaps not least because it underscored the vulnerability of the regime even in victory, prompted almost as many poems as had the taking of Namur. Richard Bovet, who had praised naval victories, sought to contrast the noble deeds of 'England's greater Caesar' with the 'sordid attempts' and 'feeble treacheries' of 'ruffians' who resorted to poison to effect what their French allies could not do in war.[193] Counselling William to dispense with notions of cross-party government, Bovet advised the removal of any who questioned William's *de iure* right to the throne and praised the Association (by which parliament and people swore an oath of loyalty), rather optimistically, as 'approv'd by All'.[194] Where Bovet grappled with the threats of '*Home-bred Foes*', the Earl of Suffolk took up a pastoral mode in order to denigrate the cruel men who had sought to kill 'the righteous Pan' 'whom *Gods* and *Nymphs* so love' and ruin a land of Canaan enjoying plenty and 'glorious times'.[195] Another poem, anonymous, on the plot against a 'Godlike Prince' recalling his victories and virtues, praised a 'wond'rous deliverance' by providence which had safeguarded the king: 'Great reason then has *Europe* to rejoyce,/And sing his safety with exalted voice.'[196] As William, with the conspirators taken, again headed for the continent, the loyal Matthew Prior, claiming that his enemies' acts made William's glory even greater, called on England to cherish 'That Sacred Life on which all ours depend'.[197]

If the attempted assassination saw a poetic discourse of bravery and heroism shift somewhat to a new emphasis on William as sacred, it was the peace (of Ryswick) for which a war-weary nation had longed that invited another outpouring of vatic encomia. Regretting that he would not rise to the Virgilian heights his subject deserved, J. W. welcomed a monarch who, having secured victories, now brought the great gift of peace:

> But see, He comes Triumphant o're the Main,
> The Seas grow Calm, the Heavens are all Serene.[198]

Several poems described the peace as William's crowning victory.[199] And – whether knowingly idealistic or not – loyal poets expressed the belief as well as hope that peace would, at last, reconcile the whole nation behind the king. ' 'Tis done', John Glanvill wrote in his *Panegyric to the King*: 'Contention and Debate are o'er,/And Arms and warlike Honours are no more'; now, he closed, 'The Golden Times shall once again commence'.[200] Now he had united Europe, Joseph Browne, agreed, William would be the 'Monarch of all Hearts' at home and envy and opposition would cease.[201] Or, as another panegyrist put it, 'Our Different Factions You shall Reconcile'; and with peace 'A Series of new Time shall now begin'.[202]

Panegyrists on the peace, as well as drawing attention to the benefits of the cessation of hostilities, hint at a new direction for the king and government and a new attention to domestic reform. Along with enhanced trade, wealth and luxury, poets promised that William, who had always cared for it, would pursue 'the Publick Good' and look into abuses in the court and state.[203] Along with reform of the government, the law and the coinage, Glanvill hinted at what was to be a priority of the years after peace: a wider reform of behaviour – 'Our ancient *English* Manners to regain' – and of the morals of the nation.[204] A sense that such hints had official sanction is strengthened by the birthday ode presented to William III in December by his laureate Nahum Tate. Welcoming the peace along with 'Caesars day', Tate announced as if an official spokesman:

> Nobler wars he now will wage,
> Against Infernal Pow'rs engage,
> And quell the *Hydra-Vices* of the Age.[205]

In the same vein, Matthew Morgan, celebrating the peace, focused a new spotlight on a sovereign who set 'rules of conduct' for his people; while in *Albion's Blessing*, Thomas D'Urfey, promising that William's peace would 'all our ills redress', posited the king as an exemplar of moral reformation:

> Strict Morral Vertue do's his Breast controul,
> And there Reigns in him a true Kingly Soul.[206]

The title of D'Urfey's 'poem panegyrical' on the peace and the king's return described the undoubted happiness of the nation in 1698. If not quite what one congratulatory poem claimed – 'In Peace and Love, as we all ought to be' – the nation enjoyed renewed trade and the prospects of an alleviation of the very considerable costs of war.[207] A broadside verse of 1699 proclaimed confidently that William 'now Restores us joys again', and John Guy at last felt it timely to publish what he claimed was a poem written on the accession of William and Mary, to which he now added a preface in which he wrote: 'for Reformation of manners and restoring the laws to their due administration could Augustus or any other prince take more effective care than his Majesty?'[208] Not only did such partisan proclamations veil what were still sharp divisions in the nation, problems loomed for William and the government and also presented a challenge to panegyrists who promised security, wealth and domestic harmony. Far from permanently settling the peace of Europe, Ryswick gave way to an armed truce that looked increasingly fragile in the face of the impending question of the succession to the Spanish empire. More locally, but related, was the question of the succession to William which was brought starkly to the fore with the death of William, Duke of Gloucester, the only surviving child of Princess Anne and heir to the English throne.

The ever loyal Matthew Prior in his *Carmen Saeculare for the Year 1700*, presented to the king, flattered a prince of heroism and virtue who surpassed Brutus and Scipio, Augustus and Charlemagne, and praised his justice, moderation and freedom from faults.[209] But, though he prayed 'keep the dismal mischief [death] long away', Prior acknowledged that 'of the Demi-God, the Earthly half must die' and knew that at fifty William's death was not as 'long away' as he wished.[210] John Hopkins in *Gloria, A Poem in Honour of Pious Majesty* similarly lauded 'Immortal *Nassau*'; but as the words 'immortal' and 'mortal' in the verse disclose, there was anxiety as well as encomium in Hopkins's line 'A future World this Monarch holds in view'.[211] Poems on the death of Gloucester were more forthright: an ode that praised a William whose 'Virtues Rhetorick cannot Raise', who after victories secured 'quiet slumbers' gave way to a lament that the young prince had not lived to secure his legacy.[212] Fears about the vulnerability of the king and the nation – 'apt to fall' as one consolatory poem frankly put it – were heightened if anything by the death of James II in 1701.[213] For not only did poems praise (and even those by enemies soften the criticism of) the exiled king, his death forced a focus of attention on his son, whose legitimacy had been denied in 1688, and who was again being talked about – and beyond Jacobite circles – as a successor to the English throne. Loyalist Williamites as well as radical Whigs like John Tutchin wrote verse to counter the 'lying poems or elegies' on James II.[214] And when Louis XIV recognized James's son as heir to the British thrones, a poet made an address on behalf of others to William praising all the achievements of his reign and assuring him that his subjects would admit only those he and they favoured.[215] 'You,' the author told William, 'are the King that reigns in *English* Hearts.'[216]

During a reign of insecurity abroad and bitter political division at home, the Whig poets had indeed laboured loyally to make William a king loved and recognized by his subjects. Through all the vicissitudes of the Revolution, the wars in Ireland and on the continent, threats of invasion, assassination plots, victory, peace and renewed uncertainty, it was the poets who did not simply argue William's case but represented him as redeemer, hero, biblical patriarch, favoured son of providence and reformer. From the beginning, William was frequently described as 'our Moses and David', as Joshua Israel's champion against its enemies, and still in 1701 he was figured as a Moses and David who freed the land from the popish and tyrannical pharaoh James Stuart.[217] A parallel motif was the representation of William as a Roman hero or emperor: as Augustus or Alexander, as Julius Caesar.[218] And, of course, through all his narrow escapes from the enemy's bullet and the assassin's plot, he was depicted as a prince favoured by providence, and protected by a guardian angel who looked over him as God's chosen.[219] The typologies of the biblical patriarch, classical hero and providential ruler had been vital to royal representation, and the poets performed a major service in appropriating these for a king who was not hereditary, was of doubtful legitimacy, and was foreign. Indeed, to ameliorate that last disadvantage – which was ammunition to William's opponents and critics – panegyrists also took pains to figure William as a truly English king and fitting heir to the greatest sovereigns of England. Not only was he compared to Edward III and his victories to those of Crécy and Poitiers, the king was figured as chivalric knight, long after the great age of chivalry had passed.[220] A poem on William's invasion described his passage to the English throne as like that of a 'Romantic Knight' of old; an ode of the same year praised 'his Chivalry'; and, as has been observed, Sir Richard Blackmore's *Prince Arthur: A Heroic Poem*, published in 1695, was a 'transparent political allegory with the pious Arthur representing William III'.[221] The poets, that is, strove to present William as a truly English king, tied into national history and legend. In his victories, they persistently claimed, England's ancient honour was again revived after years of pusillanimity; under William 'England once more is England'.[222]

Yet as well as an English warrior king, the poets fashioned an image of William as a constitutional monarch, an image that was important in countering charges that the war and expansion of the army and bureaucracy had made him more powerful and arbitrary than his predecessors. Thomas Shadwell, as we observed, in a congratulatory poem of 1689, contrasted the recent tyranny of the Stuarts with the regime of a William who revived 'ancient usages', 'customs' and freedoms.[223] Throughout the reign, Whig loyalists praised a moderate rule where 'Empire and freedom are . . . Reconcil'd';[224] or, as William Colepeper put it in a *Heroic Poem* of 1694, 'A KING that Governs and is Great by Law'.[225] In lauding William's 'Easie . . . Rule' and in figuring him as the redeemer of ancient liberties, poets made an important contribution to that Whig interpretation of history which was so central to their political victory.[226]

But it was the affective bond between ruler and subjects that had long been vital to the success of a reign – never more so than in the years after civil war – and a discourse of love that was vital to royal representation. Though (as we have seen) by no means unskilful with words, William was not a ruler who radiated or naturally attracted warmth in the way that Charles II or Queen Elizabeth had. What was lacking in reality, however, the poets invented, verse after verse inviting the king to enjoy the people's love, to be the 'monarch of all hearts', as he showed his care of and love for his people.[227] For many and for much if not most of the time, that discourse and language of mutual love was a fiction; but it was a fiction of no small importance to the survival and stability of William's government.

For all the importance of poetic panegyric, it has been argued that ultimately Whig poets failed to convey a convincing sense of the heroic and that the reader discerns 'signs of strain' in all its forms.[228] Ironically, despite the sheer quantity of Whig verse, several poems lament the inadequacy of encomia and the absence of great bards to sing William's praise. 'Can your Muse be silent?' Montagu had asked his fellow poets after the victory at the Boyne; and others were to ask it till William's death, and beyond.[229] As Addison in 1695 appealed for 'Some Mighty Bard' to memorialize William's victories, Sir Richard Howard sounded less than confident when in 1696, in the preface to the reader of his poems, he wrote: ' 'tis now to be hoped that the praises of our prince, who so much merits it, may be received willingly by all'.[230] Even, that is, after Namur, it was felt that William had not quite won over his people; and between the lines of paeans to unity and concord, references to factions, 'jarring discord' and 'our now Divided Isle' prick the ideal and acknowledge that William remained, in some measure, the king of a party rather than the nation.[231] As we shall see, William was assaulted by a barrage of opponents and critics deploying verse satires in elite verse and popular ballad forms.[232] The Whig poets, who looked back to Milton, did not succeed in forging a new sublime that placed the king above the need for legitimation or united a nation under William and Mary. But as – for all Dryden's denial – they succeeded in forging a Whig poetry of praise, they performed a vital service to Whig politics and to the partial process of legitimation of the king and queen.[233]

III

It will not have escaped notice that my discussion of panegyrics has, like so many histories of the period, focused on William and ignored Queen Mary. Mary, however, was joint ruler with her husband and, as James II's daughter, had (albeit a tenuous one) a better claim to the throne. With William absent on campaign for much of the reign, Mary took charge of domestic government, but her importance for the image of the regime and the monarchy was greater still. As the daughter of an English king, Mary tempered the alterity of a Dutch prince and her descent enabled some to view 1688 as less of a revolutionary usurpation than it had been. Moreover, the royal marriage was a decided benefit to the image of William. The queen's femininity was seen to soften as well as complement the king's martial demeanour, while her gentle nature, piety and charity evidently made her a more attractive figure to her people than her husband.[234] Representations of Queen Mary were also part of the image of joint rule, part of William's image; and while they deserve fuller consideration, can only be touched on here.

As early as 1689, Oxford poets outlined a role for Mary as the guardian of peace and prosperity at home, while her husband waged war abroad:

> May you under the downy wings of peace
> Advance the Kingdom, and their trade increase,
> Whilst our Great King abroad his fame persues,
> Raises his Friends and triumphs o'er his foes.[235]

One poet expressed his hope that she might fulfil that other duty of a queen and provide an heir – 'a young Ascanius', the son of Aeneas and Creusa who, according to Virgil, had a role in founding Rome.[236] Though no such heir was born to the royal couple, Mary's own descent was the theme of several panegyrics on the queen. Cambridge scholars, for example, compared her to her Plantagenet ancestors as well (as was common) with Queen Elizabeth I.[237] 'In her', John Dennis observed, 'The Royal Ma[r]tyrs Blood runs *pure*.'[238] And Mary's blood as well as sex appears to have licensed the Tory loyalist and opponent of Revolution, Aphra Behn, to pen a congratulatory poem of welcome to a Mary who was the 'Illustrious Daughter of a King'.[239] As well as the queen's 'free and generous nature', Behn praised her piety and virtue which early made an impression on her countrymen.[240] Thomas Rymer similarly foresaw for Mary in 1689 'the Glorious Power of doing Good'; and for the first half of the reign it was Mary who was presented as the champion of the reform of religion and manners.[241]

Mary's death occasioned an outpouring of odes and elegies that bear testimony to her place in the image of the post-Revolutionary monarchy.[242] Mary's superintendence of domestic government and administration was widely presented as exemplary. While William was abroad, one elegist simply put it, 'Mary at home the gentler Scepter sway'd'.[243] George Stepney described her as 'form'd by Nature for Supreme Command' and praised her care for justice; others concurred that 'Above the Reason of her Sex' she displayed an aptitude for government and politics; William Walsh spoke for many in observing that

'The Nation flourish'd under Her Command'.[244] Yet, though for all the recognition that 'the royal helm, though steered by a female hand, was never better provided', as important in Mary's representation was her readiness as a woman and wife to return the reins of government to her husband as soon as he returned.[245] As well as a 'Courage Masculine', Mary was praised for 'A Female Sweetness' and for that due subordination that ensured that 'while the Queen govern'd, still the wife obey'd' – or as Defoe put it, the queen was proud to wear 'the humbler feminine badge even of . . . domestic housewifery'.[246] Not only then as a good queen but as a good and obedient wife, Mary served to represent the royal marriage (so often, and still, central to the image of monarchy) as a perfect union. Burnet's observation on the king and queen that 'both seemed to have one soul' advertised the perfect partnership of what another panegyrist described as that of 'William the Conqueror and Mary the Deliverer'.[247]

While she was heralded as queen and wife, and frequently compared to 'divine Eliza', it was Mary's personal virtues and piety that were the principal motif of encomia.[248] In a Pindaric ode on her memory, Samuel Cobb listed her virtues of patience, clemency, humility and charity.[249] Others incorporated all, presenting her as 'the Epitome' 'of Virtues Catalogue' or as 'a princess in whom all the virtues were united'.[250] Particularly highlighted were her piety and virtue. No less a figure than Samuel Wesley depicted Mary as 'formed by Heaven to shew/ To What *undissembled Piety* cou'd do,/To what a height *Religion* might be rais'd'.[251] Others described her as 'This Great Exemplar of a Pious Life', as one who 'Liv'd by Prayer' and who 'spread a spirit of devotion among all that were about her'.[252] Sir Peter Gleane's *Elegy* claimed that

> Those that have her Devotion seen,
> Thought her an Abbess, not a Queen.[253]

Some raised the queen to even more elevated rank: as a 'Dear Saint' or even an 'Earthly Goddess'.[254]

Even allowing for rhetorical tropes and flights of fancy, it is evident that the queen, unlike her husband, was popular with her people. When she lay ill, James Talbot informs us, crowds anxiously awaited news of her at the palace gates; on her death, the author of *The Mourning Poets* put it with pardonable exaggeration, 'all the World runs mad with Elegy'; and even the queen's political enemies mourned her sad death.[255] Though to the nation's sorrow not a mother to an heir, Mary was represented and regarded as a loving mother to her people, just as Elizabeth had been; as a queen who did 'Govern by the milder laws of love'.[256] Poets promised William, who suffered an emotional breakdown on Mary's death, that all the affection the queen had drawn towards her would now flow to him. 'So will Thy People's Love, now Mary's gone,/Unite both streams and flow on thee alone', Stepney assured the king, as another promised 'his People's Hearts more closely joyn'd/By New Espousals of Address'd Affection'.[257] Their optimism was misplaced. Even victorious in battle and as an architect of peace, William did not enjoy the affection or love of most of his subjects, many of whom continued to perceive him as a usurper, a foreigner who promoted Dutch interests, and as corrupt and aloof. To the advantage she enjoyed as James II's daughter – she 'was herself an Apology for the Revolution', Jacques Abbadie nicely observed – Mary added virtue, piety and charm.[258] As her recent biographer concludes, Mary not only reconciled most Tories to 1688, her campaign of moral reformation did much to ensure the permanence of the Revolution and to endow the monarchy with an image that contrasted post-Revolutionary rule with Stuart excess.[259] Mary's (exemplarily pious) death undoubtedly weakened William III and presented him with the challenge, which he never quite successfully met, of connecting with his people.

That said we should not discount the role even of party poets in securing the Revolution and sustaining William's position and campaigns. Clearly many poets were virtually agents of the regime: many of those who penned verse celebrating the king served in his governments and administration or received patronage from ministers. And the corollary of course is also true: ministers like Montagu and Dorset took time to write verse as well as serve the administration. They did so because they discerned, as had earlier statesmen – and monarchs – that poets and kings (both 'makers') had an affinity, and that accordingly poetry was a discourse of power. Moreover, and importantly, in this divided reign, not only did poetry often veil its party polemic, poetic conceits continued to rehearse values of sacred rule, obedience, love and unity which, albeit they were fictions, inscribed a usurping king with legitimizing languages and forms. Reflecting back on William's reign and the role of poets and playwrights in securing the Hanoverian succession, Horace Walpole described the wits of the Kit Kat Club (patronized by Lord Chamberlain Dorset) as 'the Patriots that saved Britain'. For all his apparent hyperbole, he may not have exaggerated their role.

Where the poetical panegyrics on William and Mary have been neglected, undoubtedly much more attention has been paid to the various forms of prose support for the Revolution and the king and queen. A modern study of Williamite propaganda has in particular focused on sermons as a genre of representation that the regime made its own.[260] As Tony Claydon states, the church was a 'great medium of mass propaganda' and, both delivered and printed and published, the sermon became a major vehicle for disseminating propaganda for the regime, the monarchs and government policies.[261] During William's reign – though too many assumptions about a more secular age once led scholars to assert otherwise – sermons dominated the book trade; and under a king and queen who relentlessly promoted and used a language of providence and godly reformation, 'the single paper-bound sermon was to become the most important unit of courtly . . . propaganda'.[262] While from the time of William's accession Gilbert Burnet and his circle ensured that the court sermons, published en masse, and those preached by the bishops closely followed William's aims, pressure was also extended to parish ministers who, as well as being instructed to read royal proclamations and letters, were strongly encouraged to toe a government line.[263] Perhaps to a degree greater than in any previous reign, the Williamite pulpit was used to garner support: for the Revolution, for the king and queen, and for war against France.

Burnet's early sermons set the tone for much of the preaching in 1689. The first, preached before the still then Prince of Orange in St James's Chapel, on Psalm 68 ('It is the Lord's doing'), looked back at 'this extraordinary revolution'.[264] Hailing the defeat of a king (James II) who had ravished religion and liberty, Burnet, who clearly wanted to make the case for William to be given the crown, heralded Orange as 'our great deliverer' and God's instrument to carry out His work: 'we ought not to stop the course of it till it has had its full effect'.[265] Preaching at the coronation he had helped secure, Burnet argued for a form of government that respected subjects as 'free and reasonable beings' and presented William as a ruler who would advance order without tyranny, champion true religion and be 'the glorious reverse of all cloudy days'.[266] Taking his cue from Burnet, who recommended him for election, John Tillotson, in a sermon of thanksgiving on 31 January, repeated the themes of a 'wonderful revolution', providential deliverance – 'the finger of God was visibly in it' – and the securing of religious and constitutional freedoms.[267] In similar vein, Simon Patrick, future Bishop of Chichester and then Ely, told his congregation at St Paul's Covent Garden, 'salvation is come to us by the help of that illustrious prince whom God hath made the great instrument of our deliverance'; the Lord, he added, in William 'hath put us into a way of settling the English liberties which were sealed by the blood of . . . our . . . ancestors'.[268]

Nor were such sermons confined to the capital. In his sermon to the assizes at Hertford, for example, the clergyman and Whig historian John Strype informed his congregation of what God had done for the nation, how justice and moderate rule had been secured, and how they now enjoyed 'one of the best constituted governments in the world'.[269] Before the judges and others at the Nottingham assizes and on another occasion before the mayor, aldermen and Common Council of the same town, William Wilson, rector of St Peter's, gave thanks for the nation's deliverance from popery and arbitrary power, praised a pious and just king, and urged obedience to monarchs whose possession 'is settled upon so fair a foundation'.[270] At York on 5 November, William Perse, comparing the late deliverance of the nation to an earlier providential intervention, advocated an annual day of remembrance for William's invasion as well as the discovery of Guy Fawkes's Plot.[271]

At a time when many were uneasy about the course of the Revolution (which few had desired to remove James II) and uncertain about William and Mary's rightful claim; at a time when pamphlets pro and con were published daily, the significance of these sermons can hardly be overstated. Whatever the disputes among men, the sermons assured, providence had effected the course of events; whatever the discussion of his loyal right, William was God's instrument; whatever the unease and uncertainty, a new dawn – of virtuous, pious, moderate, 'easy and truly English government' – was promised.[272] And it must have appeared marvellous in many people's eyes. Moreover, as well as preached to large congregations in London and the provinces, these Revolution sermons were published promptly and distributed widely. A 'divine in the north', for instance, had no doubt that even so far from London, Burnet's sermons were 'almost in every man's hand' so needed no repetition; while Perse's and Wilson's sermons were evidently published and sold respectively in York and Nottingham, where the bookseller Joseph Howe sold copies of the text printed for Awnsham Churchill, publisher of John Locke's works, at Amen Corner.[273]

In 1689 official sermons turned to an emphasis on godly reformation and a battle against atheism and irreligion, profanity and vice. Far, however, from this signalling a move from pulpit polemic, as Tony Claydon has shown, the representation of 1688 as the opportunity for moral reform, and of William and Mary as reformers, was fundamental to a spiritual view of recent history and to the sacralization of the Revolution settlement and the king.[274] As well as marking a distance from the profligate court of Charles II, Burnet saw a discourse and programme of reformation as a component of the military campaigns in Ireland against the Jacobites, and as a cement for the unification of (what he knew was) a divided nation into 'one church and one body, as it has one head'.[275] The same year saw a veritable flood of sermons by, as well as Tillotson and Patrick, John Sharp, another clergyman recommended by Burnet to the deanery of Canterbury; Charles Hickman, a royal chaplain and future bishop; and William Lloyd, royal almoner and future Bishop of Worcester, who preached and wrote widely in defence of the Revolution. As their posts and positions might lead us to expect, all connected the cause of reformation to the providential deliverance of the nation, presented the king and queen as examples of piety who might lead others to godliness and the country to its 'ancient piety and virtue', and called upon all to repent their divisions and unite behind a sovereign who desired to lead a righteous nation as another Israel singled out by God as a chosen nation.[276] The themes of reformation and righteousness were preached on fast days and days of thanksgiving for military success or the king's safety. Preaching on the thanksgiving day for victory in Ireland, Burnet referred back to the deliverance of 1688 as he also celebrated the return of a godly prince whom providence had protected as an instrument of the Lord.[277] Similarly in Newcastle, George Tullie, sub-dean of York, took as his text

Proverbs 29: 2 ('when the righteous are in authority, the people rejoice') to portray the victorious William as God's instrument to be the scourge of popery overseas, as at home.[278] Indeed, sermons played a key part in securing support for William's war against France. In a sermon to the mayor and aldermen of London in April 1692, for example, William Fleetwood, future royal chaplain and Bishop of Ely, preached one of his earliest sermons 'concluding the defence of . . . country and religion as very justifiable ground of war'.[279] Lauding a government at home that secured liberty and 'the best religion in the world', Fleetwood encouraged his City auditors to support the king's 'just and honourable' war in which 'all we have that is near and dear to us is at stake'.[280] In an even more direct defence of the supplies, Samuel Slater, a big-seller in the sermon business, urged a nation with 'a praying king', to whom they did 'owe our being a nation', to love and support 'our dearest and most renowned king' as he went out to defend them.[281] Slater acknowledged the 'discontent because of the taxes' but exhorted his countrymen to assist with their persons and purses: 'Can a war be maintained without charge? . . . Do you pay more than the Gospel is worth?' he asked before insisting, 'do not you expose their majesties to danger by your follies'.[282]

As well as support for supply, preachers were part of a propaganda campaign conducted in military reports, newspapers and pamphlets to put the best spin on the progress of the war, so as to sustain morale. Preaching at Whitehall on the occasion of the king's return from the continent in November 1693, Sharp, now Archbishop of York, admitted what everyone knew – that the campaigns had not been attended with 'the successes we desired' – yet, he comforted the congregation and nation: 'Tho' the king had not the victory being overpowered by numbers; yet he gained more honour and sustained less loss than those that boasted of the victory'.[283] Most importantly, God had favoured the people at home with peace and protected a king who was an example of the piety that alone would lead them to victory. Several others directly connected the nation's willingness to reform with military fortunes.[284] 'Our religion,' the author of *The True Interest of a Nation* preached at the Buckingham assizes, 'is very much bound up with the safety of our prince and his armies.'[285]

As war costs escalated and opposition mounted, loyalist clergy became all but official spokesmen for the government as it struggled to sustain supply and support for the war. Countless sermons repeated extravagant praise of the king and queen – 'such a nursing father and such a nursing mother', as Burnet described them, who had secured English religion, liberty, trade and wealth.[286] In a sermon before the allied forces in Flanders, published in London and sold at St Paul's Yard, a chaplain to a regiment of the Queen's horse, taking praise of William and Mary and the 'brightness of [their] imperial majesty' to heights, asked whether the people could 'conceive any princes more gracious' than those who so richly merited the subjects' love.[287] If the wars had not brought success, several sermons implied, that was because a sinful people had not followed their monarchs in reforming profanity and vice, and so had alienated God.[288] Others attributed setbacks abroad directly to divisions and opposition to the government at home. The Canon of Exeter Cathedral., Lancelot Blackburne, observing that William and England's enemies abroad were strengthened by 'continual division either about religion or about government' at home, appealed to the people to lay aside animosities and unite.[289] Murmuring against the government, Samuel Carte told his congregation, provoked God as well as obstructed the king and queen.[290] The Israelites, Carte recalled, had complained about costly wars and resented their leader as a usurper; but, with God's aid, Moses had delivered them.[291] As the allies attempted another push against France in the summer of 1694, a preacher at the camp (whose sermon was printed for Jacob Tonson in London) defended a holy war which Christians were duty-bound to support.[292]

Just as churchmen, quite literally, raised the spirits of a war-weary people for William's crusade, so they were swift to greet victories when they came at last as signs of God's favour to a chosen king and nation. To begin with the first of three examples from many, preaching on 8 September, the appointed day of thanksgiving for the taking of Namur, John Adams, rector of St Alban Woodstreet, decried the ingratitude of a nation that enjoyed liberties and laws 'under a wise and gracious administration' and a prince who 'preserved by divine providence' had now checked the torrent of French might.[293] On the same day at Westminster, the dissenter Vincent Alsop told the assembled, 'we are here as a people, and I hope really a people that would recognise the divine favours to our king', rather than, as too many had, murmur against him.[294] Discerning a better appreciation of William in the wake of victory, Alsop urged 'that we lend the king all our power and give thanks to God for a prince' who, having championed reformation at home, had, with his aid, 'broken the rod of the oppressor'.[295] A fortnight later, at Newcastle, as other towns on that day, a preacher gave thanks to the deliverer God had appointed and whom the ungrateful were now bound to esteem, love and support, with 'no charges . . . to be spared'.[296] Victory at Namur gave occasion and credibility to the theme of a godly prince and nation doing God's work and recast criticism as sin. For all the rhetoric of liberty and moderate government, sermons in the mid-1690s publicized a form of divine right kingship and sacred rule.

The assassination plot the next year underlined the sermon discourse of sacred kingship. In his sermon at St James's, Westminster, on the day of thanksgiving 'for the preservation of his majesty from the late horrid conspiracy', William Wake, the rector, figured William as another David whom Saul had endeavoured to destroy but whom God had safeguarded as 'the preserver of true religion' and the people.[297] Along with many making the Davidic parallel, in his sermon at Hackney, John Strype not only damned the plotters but acclaimed 'the justice and happiness of our present government under King William' and 'that settlement that by God's Providence is now settled amongst us'.[298] Taking advantage of the providential deliverance of the king that was widely being heralded as miraculous, William Stephens (rector of Sutton, Surrey) in his sermon to the mayor and aldermen, contemned any who would now, against God, dispute William's title and held up the king's life 'as dear to us as the breath of our nostrils'.[299] Preaching a similar sermon that was printed for two printing houses and went into at least two editions, the Presbyterian and prolific writer John Shower encouraged his flock – that 'the discovery of the design and the preventing of it . . . will help to unite the nation'.[300] All around the country, preachers repeated the motifs of divine deliverance of a godly prince, the Lord's hostility towards enemies and critics of the king, and the prospect of, and need for, the nation uniting under William. At the parish of Hambledon in Buckinghamshire, the rector Francis Gregory hoped that with God's disclosure of the plot having demonstrated beyond doubt that 'our present king is his and his anointed', men would accept that it was no longer possible to dispute his title but necessary 'to acquiesce under his government, to submit to his laws, to furnish him with supplies, to pray for his life, health and property and to obey his just commands'.[301] Standing for many more such sentiments, a revived high church polemic preached by Theophilus Dorrington and published as *The Honour Due to the Civil Magistrate*, asserted that all owed taxes and a virtually unquestioning obedience and acquiescence even 'when we do not know the particular grounds and reasons' of royal orders.[302] Such Tory strains in loyal sermons were not the exception in 1696. Victory at Namur and the king's providential escape from assassination had provided the loyalist clergy, in response to official thanksgivings, with the opportunity to extol the king and regal authority in language loftier than had been heard since the 1680s. William III may have been the Whigs' king but he was being clothed in the raiment of divine kingship and presented as above human reproach.

The Peace of Ryswick presented official and loyal preachers with a third great occasion for encomium. The date of 2 December was appointed as an official day of thanksgiving for the peace the nation had so long craved; and fittingly Burnet, who had led the official sermons for a decade, delivered the thanksgiving sermon before the king at Whitehall. Burnet used the occasion (as he often did) to make larger arguments about the Revolution and the subsequent course of events.[303] William, he told his auditors, and the reading nation, 'has indeed the blood of sovereigns in him but his crowns are the gift of heaven'.[304] Reminding all of the 'train of amazing providence' that had favoured and safeguarded the king, Burnet used religious language to describe the war and a king who was 'the soul of the whole alliance'.[305] Passing over the political struggles of the last years, Burnet also attributed the triumphant peace to the people: 'nothing but the certainties of the faith given by the body of the nation could have created the credit that was necessary in such unusual supplies'.[306] Acting together, the king and people had, under God's favour, emerged from danger to be leaders in Europe. At home, Burnet continued, the people enjoyed liberty, a prince whose priority was their happiness and one 'who descends oft to the equalities of friendship with his subjects'.[307] It was now for them to show gratitude and love to him who had again delivered them: 'may he be long the delight of his people, the arbiter of Europe, the patron of justice, and the maintainer of right all the world over'.[308] Published by His Majesty's special command, Burnet's sermon was a rhetorical masterpiece that used a moment of national relief and euphoria to endeavour to gloss a decade of doubts, criticisms and discontents; to answer opponents who had charged William's government with being arbitrary; and to fashion (by claiming that it already existed) a loving relationship between the king and his people.

Around the country, carefully appointed preachers followed Burnet in celebrating the peace and the king who had delivered it and the nation. At Durham Cathedral, for example, the dean and royal chaplain, Thomas Comber, described, in the most exalted language, a country 'ravish[ed] with delight' at the peace secured by the king which ended the miseries of war and brought trade, riches, the advancement of the arts and sciences for all.[309] Heaven had protected William, Comber preached, and 'our happiness and his preservation are . . . linked together'; indeed, he added, without the people's gratitude and prayers for the long life and safety of the king 'our peace will scarce endure long'.[310] In the parishes, whether through official direction or spontaneous joy, similar sermons were preached, heard and published. At Highgate Chapel, the minister proclaimed how 'fame has winged great William's name throughout the world' and praised 'the best and greatest monarch of the world' who had, under God, obtained it.[311] Urging all to unity and gratitude, the unknown 'R. L.' advocated the outlawing of all books and pamphlets critical of the state and admonished 'we should hear no whispers against the present auspicious government of great Caesar'.[312] James Gardiner, rector of St Michael Crooked Lane, recalling the terrible state of the nation before William's deliverance, reminded his congregation 'if ever subjects had cause to glory in a prince, we are the men' and, denouncing enemies and critics as 'sinful' or 'mad', instructed, 'if he be the minister of God for our good . . . let us love him affectionately'.[313] Peace, the preachers concurred, was a second deliverance that offered a new beginning: one in which, along with foreign threats, all domestic animosities could be laid aside in a nation united under a beloved ruler.

The last years of William's reign saw fewer official sermons trumpeting the king and a shift in the pulpit to advancing the cause of the reformation of manners that William more actively championed after the death of Queen Mary and still more after the Peace of Ryswick. Sermons like those preached before the king at Newmarket on the need for faith and reform or that by

Thomas Knaggs exhorting the nation to repentance, because they read so differently from the celebrations of victory and peace, may at first sight seem apolitical.[314] But because William had so identified himself with the programme of reformation, because he had represented himself as the pious instrument of God, sermons on this theme were encomia on the king to the end of his reign. As Thomas Knaggs put it in his sermon against profanity and immorality at the Kingston assizes: 'We live under the government of a most religious and gracious king who has not only delivered your bodies but endeavours ... to save your souls'.[315] In his sermon at Winchester Cathedral, Robert Eyre made the political point explicitly: the vicious and profane scoffers alienated God and were 'traitors' to William and 'the peace and welfare of his government'.[316] Before the assizes at Bedford, the minister of Wroxall, Warwickshire, Matthew Heynes, integrated the royal proclamation for reformation into the whole ideology of the Revolution and Whig cause. William, he observed, had not only secured the liberties of the nation, he had endeavoured its reformation as part of his sacred duty to and love for his people; and 'by reforming us to keep it from being in vain that he rescued for us the liberty of professing a religion'.[317] By making himself 'a minister of God', Heynes added, William took a course to 'establish his just authority' and to render it 'the more absolute'.[318]

Indeed, as Knaggs's phrase about saving souls attests, the royal championing of godly reformation was a claim to Christic kingship, a claim that had, at least since Henry VIII assumed the headship of the church, underpinned all advertisements of absolutism. Perhaps not coincidentally at a time when William was, after the resignation of the Whig junto, negotiating with the Tories, the discourse of divine kingship complemented, indeed shifted emphasis from, the traditional Whig rhetoric of constitutionalism. That such a suggestion should not be pushed too far is nowhere better cautioned than in the high churchman Francis Atterbury's praise, in a sermon to the House of Commons, of moderate and mixed government and the Saxon constitution.[319] Loyalist sermons, however, enabled and sometimes advanced a language that, in persistently representing William as God's instrument and head of a chosen nation, figured him not as the elected ruler following a Whig coup but as the sovereign of a new Israel by divine right.

If the loyalist sermons had been intended, as they surely were, to temper division, neuter opposition and extol William as a legitimate monarch of a united realm, one sub-genre always threatened to disclose bitter political rivalry and to evoke painful and (especially for the Whigs) awkward memories. Ever since 1660, the day of the regicide had been commemorated by sermons delivered to teach the lessons of civil war: the need for obedience, the divine right of monarchs, and the sin of resistance. Such memories and lessons posed challenges to a regime and king who had come to power as the consequence of another (albeit in England bloodless) episode of resistance; and 30 January had the potential to gift the Jacobites – or indeed any uneasy about the removal of a hereditary king – with occasion to attack Williamite rule. Though, over the course of William III's reign, some more extreme Whigs were to argue for setting aside the anniversary, Charles I had, thanks to the *Eikon Basilike*, attained an iconic status and the cult of the king had transcended old divisions: as one Whig sympathizer put it, accounts of the martyr's trial and execution were 'in every bookseller's shop'.[320]

It was therefore a triumph of the loyalist preachers that they not only with some success deflected criticism on this count, but with a measure of conviction appropriated Charles the martyr for the cause of the Revolution and for William and Mary. It was surely not happenstance that led Gilbert Burnet, amidst all the busy polemics of 1689, to republish his sermon, preached on 30 January 1675, entitled *The Royal Martyr Lamented*.[321] First published in 1675 by Richard Royston, the bookseller to whom Charles II had granted a monopoly of publishing his father's books, Burnet's sermon had condemned the regicide as a sin the guilt of which the nation needed to expiate and praised Charles I as a Christ-like figure, blameless and wronged by a seditious faction.[322] In reissuing the sermon in 1689, Burnet evidently sought to advertise his earlier loyal credentials and to suggest – perhaps as a comfort to the Tories – that 1688 had not been a repetition of 1649 or 1642 and that the monarchy would be preserved under William III, as under his grandfather. Such a signal that the post-Revolutionary regime would seek to claim the martyr was also sent by a 30 January sermon preached by William Stainforth, Canon of York, in the cathedral there; Charles was described as a Josiah and a king whose indulgent government might have made the nation happy had not an ungrateful people failed to countenance their blessing.[323]

As the Revolution became embedded and more secure, preachers of various sympathies came forth to claim the martyr as a supporter of the new regime. In 1692 an original non-juror and convert to William's *de facto* rule, preaching before the House of Commons on 30 January, denounced the principles of accountability that had led Charles I to trial, asserted that 'the late Revolution has made no alteration at all in the principles of government and obedience', and used the lesson of the day to underpin the authority of William and Mary as monarchs to whom obedience was owed no less than to Charles.[324] The argument was important, for, as Charles Blount put it, what had made many opposed to the Prince of Orange had been 'the black idea of resistance against sovereign power formed in their minds by that rebellion against King Charles the First'.[325] A successful Whig recruitment of Charles I, a distancing of the Revolution from the regicide and civil war, were vital in securing support for recognizing William's legitimacy.

The appropriation of Charles I for William's rule was, however, complicated by the discovery in 1690 of the so-called Anglesey Memorandum, a paper found in a copy of the *Eikon Basilike* in which Charles II himself denied his father's authorship of the book.[326] The revelation reopened party wars as some Whigs sought to use it to discredit the martyr (whose image was founded on the *Eikon* being his authentic testimonial), and Tories reacted with outrage to what they dismissed as a forgery produced by enemies of monarchy. The memorandum also exposed divisions among the Whigs. John Gailhard took the opportunity to advocate that 'there ought to be an end' to the 30 January commemoration which only occasioned trouble; and he found support from others, enemies to the high church party, who also wrote against 'a yearly commemoration'.[327] But William and Mary themselves continued to observe the day 'solemnly', and Williamite preachers tended to have no truck with the assaults on the martyr, calculating that they weakened the king.[328] In his sermon at St Sepulchre's in January 1694, which was published with the archbishop's imprimatur, Richard Newman, referring – without mentioning the controversy over authorship – to Charles's 'grandeur of language and . . . fluency of style', lauded his virtues, ranked him 'among the chiefest of Christians', and argued that the lesson of regicide did 'abundantly justify the annual solemnity of this day'.[329]

Indeed, official sermons tended to bypass the controversy over the Anglesey Memorandum and to continue to use 30 January as an occasion to represent William III as heir to the martyr. John Hartcliffe, for example, whom the king had appointed Canon of Windsor, in his 30 January sermon to the House of Commons in 1695, published with imprimatur, explicitly represented William as a monarch of Charles's blood 'with all the heroic virtues' of his ancestor.[330] Connecting the overthrow of the martyr with the zeal of the sects, Hartcliffe described William as a king 'designed by divine providence [and] . . . qualified by divine wisdom', as one whom religion as much as law obliged all to obey.[331] Addressing the Lords in tones that echoed the increasingly sacred discourse of politics in the mid-1690s, John Humphreys the Bishop of Bangor insisted, against those who dismissed 30 January as an 'antiquated solemnity', that the blood guilt of the regicides had left a 'deep and lasting stain'.[332] As he argued for the religious foundation of all government and the importance of pious and religious kings, Humphreys implicitly underlined the divine authority and piety of his own king who led 'a general reformation among the people'.[333]

The attempted assassination of William invited even closer comparison with the martyr, which the Bishop of Chichester (John Williams) eagerly identified in a sermon before the king at Whitehall. The date of 30 January, he observed, 'should be a warning to all' who engaged in designs against good princes, which were also against the welfare of the nation.[334] As we have seen, in the wake of the plot against William's life, loyal preachers extolled the king in lofty terms, and it may have been a reaction to a growing tendency to resacralize royal authority that prompted more radical Whigs, such as John Toland, to reiterate opposition to 30 January.[335] The establishment clergy, however, continued annually to draw the lesson from regicide that regal authority was derived from God and that, as Samuel Bradford (who secured promotion for the sermon he preached before William) put it, subjects owed 'reverence' to governors and had a duty to 'cherish good thoughts of them'.[336] The Archbishop of York, John Sharp, was even more outspoken. In his sermon on 30 January 1700 he told the assembled MPs that the business of the day was to 'press obedience and subjection to the government we live under'; for, he continued, kings were God's vicegerents and could only be passively resisted.[337] Though he knew that some would be uneasy with his case, Sharp took the memory of Charles I to argue the sanctity and inviolability of regal authority.

Time, and the passing of a generation that had experienced civil war and regicide, perhaps did as much as Whig attacks on the date of 30 January to diminish the importance of the occasion: in 1700, Edmund Hickeringill expressed disappointment at 'the little attendance on this day's celebration in this populous city who can, at other times throng in a crowd'.[338] Even more damaging, one commentator on recent sermons saw no reason why it mattered that men held different views of the martyr.[339] Yet in Queen Anne's reign, the figure of Charles I was to be central in the party struggles in church and state.[340] In William's case, whatever the reservations of some of their low church fellows, the established clergy readily preached on Charles I, and in recruiting his name and memory to support William III's authority did much to enhance that authority.

IV

While study of them has by no means been exhaustive, sermons have received attention as a principal genre of Williamite literary propaganda. Curiously ignored, by contrast, have been the war reports which, for the first time since the civil war, because of William's annual campaigns, became regular and frequent during the 1690s. The accounts of foreign battles and victories were especially important for a king whose image was that of a warrior and commander. Moreover, where the official newspaper, the *Gazette*, in the main confined itself to the 'drily factual', war reports could – and did – put a definite spin on the progress of allied arms and consequently played an important role in securing support for William's wars.[341]

The reports, some written with official direction, some not, were published as early propaganda for the Revolution as William established his authority and defeated Jacobite resistance in Ireland and in the Highlands. *A Full and True Account of the Two Great Victories Lately Obtained before Lymerick* gives a flavour of many that were to follow in relating the scale of victory, against the odds, over a cruel popish enemy that treated Protestants with barbarity.[342] In the form of a letter, the anonymous author, responding as he claimed to 'the longing desires of everyone in England to hear an account of the daily progress of our heroical prince's arms', reported the king's 'daily success in his glorious undertakings' and promised the conquest of Ireland and the protection of the Protestant Irish from the 'inhumane and barbarous French' and their Jacobite allies.[343] Another Irish relation, 'published by authority', emphasized, as so many later reports were to do, William's personal bravery in battle. 'His majesty receiving a shot in his right shoulder,' the broadside reports, 'as soon as it was dressed . . . took horse and continued on horseback for four hours'; along with lists of enemy prisoners, arms and baggage seized, the author closed with the good news that James was being driven back and was close to defeat.[344] When Limerick surrendered the next year, the author of a thirty-page journal reviewed the campaigns highlighting (improbable) stories of victories by small numbers, with negligible losses against large numbers, 'the superior valour and conduct of the English', and the (even more unlikely) 'compassion' of their officers towards the vanquished.[345]

As warfare moved from the suppression of resistance in Ireland and Scotland to full engagement with the French at sea and on land, and as William suffered setbacks, war reports (like William's speeches) were increasingly directed at making the best of minor gains and even defeats, so as to sustain morale and encourage parliamentary supply. From 1691, more and more William was presented as a 'matchless hero' and warrior prince prepared to deliver Europe as he had rescued England.[346] And the smallest gains were published as advances that promised further victories. A relation of the expedition in the Caribbean, for example, listed successes in Barbados and St Christopher, and promised the expulsion of the French from the West Indies.[347] Closer to home, several broadside accounts were published of naval skirmishes against the French in which the king's ships had the day.[348] With France planning to support an invasion and developing strength at sea, one author advised 'it is obvious in what condition the rest of Europe had been in but for the powerful opposition England has made, being influenced by their heroic king, which sufficiently shows the necessity there was for the late Revolution'.[349] 'From that time,' he continued, spurring the English to support the war, 'may Louis the fourteenth date the destruction of his project and the rest of Europe their enlargement from the slavery he designed.'[350]

When William's land campaign entered stalemate followed by a long period of setbacks, war reports put the very best face on the state of affairs.[351] The Battle of Landen, in which William's army was driven from the field, produced several accounts more notable for optimism than accuracy. One, published specifically to counter circulating reports of French victory, and 'to undeceive the public', tried to persuade readers that 'though the French kept the field, they were really losers'.[352] Others emphasizing William's personal bravery and tactical skill tried to make light of the losses ('much less than we thought') and likely exaggerated the French deaths too.[353] The Jacobite sympathizer who argued that biased reporting adorned William's war record with 'swelling elegies' was unquestionably *parti pris*, but he was not wrong.[354]

We will not be surprised therefore that a clear victory in battle gave rise to hyperbolic military reports, as we have seen it did in odes and verses. The official notification of the surrender of Namur, published from Whitehall on 29 August 1695, was sparsely factual.[355] But a full narration of the campaign in Flanders with an account of the siege wrote of 'the greatest courage and undauntedness that was ever seen', described William in the thick of the battle 'appearing everywhere', emphasized especially the role of the British troops in the allied assault, and thanked God for 'preserving our most sacred king who exposed himself in all places of the greatest danger'.[356] Moreover, the author clearly intended that Namur should stand as a justification of the war and a powerful argument for its continuation. In a preface he opined extravagantly that 'there never has been a war of greater consequence than the present between the confederates and the French king', because it was a war 'for the liberty or slavery of Europe'.[357] Against the might of a France without 'the providential accession of his glorious Majesty William the third to the crown of England and head of the most royal confederacy that ever was, we must soon have felt ourselves under the most absolute and lasting tyranny that ever Europe was subject to'.[358] Namur had finally demonstrated that God was on the allies' side, and authors of the accounts represented 'our sacred king' as poised to win the fight against the forces of darkness. After Namur, war reporters gave way to paeans to peace. However, the image of the king as a brilliant general and brave warrior lived on, reinforcing his representation as a deliverer of the nation.

Though historians freely write of a Whig view of history there has been remarkably little study of the histories published in the wake of the 1688 Revolution and during the reign of William and Mary.[359] Histories, however, were vital to the acceptance of the settlement and the king's legitimacy; and, perhaps more systematically than ever before, Whig sympathizers sought to construct and embed an interpretation of the past that buttressed their ideology and their monarch. This subject is worthy of a major book and cannot be treated here, but we need to appreciate how in histories of the Middle Ages, the early modern and recent past, in compilations of records as well as narratives, scholars loyal to William wrote him into British history and fashioned a view of the past that marginalized opposition.

Not least because the Revolution was a rupture with tradition and hereditary succession, a flurry of histories appeared in 1688–9 to win over those who weighed arguments by the scale of precedents. For example, the polemic behind *A Brief History of the Succession*, published in 1689 by Baron Somers, who had argued powerfully for William in the Convention, announced on the title-page declaration that it was 'written for the satisfaction of the nation'.[360] For those who were agonizing over broken succession, Somers's history, beginning with the Saxon heptarchy, demonstrated how kings had been rejected, elected and chosen by parliaments and people over natural heirs; and argued that, far from immemorial, hereditary succession was 'a new discovery' – an implicit support, of course, for William's title from a parliament which had, Somers argued, 'an unquestionable power' in settling succession to the throne.[361] *A Short Historical Account Touching the Succession*, perhaps drawn from it, listed the many broken successions in two short pages for a broader audience, while *A New History* faced 'how disjointed the hereditary succession became' from the days of King Edred.[362] Several histories evoked Kings Edward II and Richard II to underpin the argument that monarchy might be deposed or resign their crown; pursuing a different tactic, chronicles and histories of Britain from Julius Caesar to William and Mary, with frontispiece illustrations of each ruler, placed the king and queen in a lineage, as though there was nothing contentious about their succession.[363]

Because part of the controversy in 1688–9 was the presence and fate of James II, Whig historians wrote also to undermine him. Charles Caesar's *Numerus Infaustus* (licensed in June 1689) presented a short view of the 'unfortunate reigns' of William II, Henry II, Edward II, Richard II, Charles II and James II to make the case that destiny had never favoured 'the second of any name', before proceeding to a history of James's failings and an account of his 'voluntarily ... abdicating government'.[364] The anonymous author of the (also officially licensed) *Quadriennium Jacobi*, asserting that no other king had 'laboured ... so industriously to lose a crown' (rather than having it taken from him), similarly described James's 'desertion' as he also praised William as a 'preserver'.[365] An early example of the popular genre of secret histories, perhaps by Milton's nephew John Phillips, disclosed the scandal and corruption of the last Stuarts so as to contrast 'the furberies and tyranny of those times' with the 'sincerity and soundness of their present Majesty's reign'.[366] In a bolder polemical move, some wrote histories of the late Revolution both to establish an interpretation of recent events and to fold them into the story of England's national past. *The History of the Late Revolution in England*, published anonymously in 1689 but attributed by a contemporary hand in the Yale University Library copy to Burnet, traced the history of 'the greatest revolution in the world' from the beginning of 'a nation born to freedom as the English nation is' to a detailed account of James's misgovernment and abdication and William of Orange's arrival to popular joy and installation as monarch.[367] Two years later, Guy Miege's *Complete History of the Late Revolution* emphasized the growth of popery in Charles II's reign that led in turn to the prospect of ruin under his successor and 'our wonderful deliverance' by the Prince of Orange.[368] Together with histories of the Revolution, historical biographies of the princes of Nassau and of William himself assured English readers that their new dynasty and king were illustrious defenders of Protestantism in the mould of Queen Elizabeth.[369]

Though their Whig authors unquestionably wrote to attempt to unite the nation, histories remained contentious throughout the reign. Williamite loyalists, however, continued to publish histories which, chronicling distant and recent events, discredited James II and represented William as the fulfilment of England's happiness and destiny. Negative and 'tragical' histories of James II and (sometimes) Charles II were printed in 1693 and 1694 by Titus Oates, the discoverer of the alleged Popish Plot, and in 1696 and 1697 by the prolific historian (and spy) David Jones.[370] On the other side – and sometimes by the same authors – histories of the House of Orange lavished praise on a prince who had restored English laws and freedoms. William was compared by the royal historiographer and Whig apologist Thomas Rymer to the triumphant King Edgar and with the fabled, pious King Arthur, as well as (frequently) to Queen Elizabeth.[371] Narratives of the whole course of English history were written like John Seller's *History* to present William as the true heir of Julius Caesar, or like William Pudsey's *Summary Review of the Kings . . . of England since the Norman Conquest* to justify the Revolution as 'the most glorious . . . cause that hath appeared upon the stage of human actions'.[372] Lord Chancellor Somers's *History* told the story of the English past as that of constitutional, limited monarchy, re-established by William.[373]

More artful still – and decisive in the eventual triumph of a Whig view of the past – were the Whig historians and editions that published, *apparently* innocently and without gloss, selected documents of English history. James Welwood, an admirer of Burnet, appended to his Whig *Memoirs of the Most Material Transactions in England* over a hundred pages of carefully selected texts; more famously, John Rushworth completed his *Historical Collections* which, for all the claim to an 'impartiality which runs through the whole', was a deeply partisan edition that has coloured our view of history to recent times.[374] Whig histories (as we shall see) were by no means uncontested.[375] But because the ownership of the past was still so vital to political legitimacy and argument, their role in securing the Revolution and representing William as not a foreign usurper but a truly English ruler was vital. More successful than the poets who struggled to create a Whig sublime, a Whig interpretation of history not only came to dominate other views but remained for centuries the favoured interpretation of the national past.

If any Whig poets or historians harboured hopes that in such literary forms they might place themselves above debate and division, the pamphlets – some by the same writers of verse and history – acknowledged the folly of any such optimism. For not only did the vast numbers of Whig pamphlets bear witness to a perceived need to argue a case and to respond to Jacobite and Tory denunciations, countless Whig titles with words such as 'justification', 'defence', 'vindication', 'argument', 'answer' or 'animadversions' recognized that, for all the boasts about a bloodless Revolution, there was a fierce battle of words over 1688 and the right of William and Mary to rule. At no time since the civil war was the nation so divided; at no time since the 1640s or the Popish Plot – and perhaps not then – were so many pamphlets published pro and con, attacking or defending a case, and a king. The polemical pamphlet battles of the 1690s for some reflected the rage of party printers, publishers, booksellers and readers formed by partisan identities and commitments.[376] William III did not wish to be dependent upon, still less be the prisoner of, any one party; and the shifts and turns of events certainly complicated consistent party positions. Yet, whatever the appeals for unity, there was no escaping a culture of fundamental ideological conflict. In that divided society, in a world in which the affairs of state were more than ever the daily talk of coffee houses and clubs (which were themselves developing strong party affiliations), William depended upon the support of party pens, whether they operated under government patronage or not. Still more he depended upon those who sought to persuade his ordinary subjects of his legitimacy and to represent him to them as a lawful, good and pious king. Of the over twenty thousand works published in England between 1688 and William's death, next to religious titles the political pamphlets, many still neglected, loom largest. In the final pages of this chapter, I will discuss some examples of the hundreds I have sampled to convey a sense of how apologists presented the king in changing circumstances.

We will not be surprised to learn that the published output for 1689 was about two-thirds higher than the annual average for even the prolific 1690s.[377] The Convention that met in January of that year, and which offered William and Mary the crown, had been bitterly divided; division had led to a fudge about the precise justification for the Revolution and the foundation of royal authority, and left subjects to wrestle with their own consciences along with the multiplicity of arguments being aired.[378] No less an architect of the Revolution than Burnet acknowledged in his *An Enquiry into the Present State of Affairs* that the multitude were disturbed, were predisposed to James II, and would need to be persuaded to obey the new government.[379] The process of persuading involved what Thomas Long admitted were 'many very difficult arguments', not all of which were consistent with each other.[380] Some who justified William's invasion and his elevation to the throne argued the community's right of resistance when a tyrannical ruler broke his contract with the people and their right to elect another to his place.[381] As Burnet put it, using a familiar political metaphor for radical new ends, children were absolved from obedience when a father ceased to be a father, a position argued more abstractly by several who maintained that injuries done to subjects cancelled their allegiance.[382] Others, Edmund Bohun, for instance, took the line that James II had not been evicted but had deserted or voluntarily abdicated, leaving parliament to appoint a successor.[383] In such a circumstance, Francis Fulwood (who boasted of being quick in print 'to persuade my brethren to recognise this happy government') argued that the Convention acted 'to maintain the hereditariness of this monarchy' and 'allow the right of the next heirs William and Mary'. [384] Like Fulwood, others passed over the uncomfortable questions about the legitimacy of the Prince of Wales or William's claim to joint rule with his wife, to argue their right as hereditary successors on James's desertion of the realm.[385] But there were perhaps as many who did not press the hereditary argument. Of those some insisted, as had the author of *A Brief Justification of the Prince of Orange's Descent*, that 'the succession . . . is not to be governed by proximity of blood but by weighing what is expedient for the benefit of the community'.[386] More, however, favoured the argument that the events of 1688 and William's succession were determined by providence, and so beyond human agency – or blame. Though this was, as we saw, the theme of countless sermons, it was widely rehearsed also in pamphlets such as Defoe's *Reflections upon the Late Great Revolution*, or in *Allegiance Vindicated* in which the author wrote of God 'providentially reject[ing] a Saul' and installing a David.[387] In a more secular, Hobbesian vein, a few controversially maintained, as did Charles Blount, that William's authority rested on conquest.[388] And, while for most this proved a step too far, many advanced the so-called *de facto* argument: that obedience was owed to whomever was in power, irrespective of the means by which it had been obtained or the nice legal rights of the case. Advocates of William's *de facto* authority ranged from the argument of Daniel Whitby (a confidant of Burnet) who stated that 'we are bound to none beside the person in possession' or the more strident assertions of a divine who insisted that 'he is to be owned as supreme and God's minister who actually possesseth the throne', to the more pragmatic invocations not to rock the boat or disturb a government that was now peacefully settled.[389]

Quite different though they were, these justifications were written expressly to persuade subjects anxious about their uncancelled allegiance to James, to take an oath of allegiance to William, without which the new monarchy enjoyed no legitimacy or security. 'This is the great scruple,' admitted the author of one attempt, 'which I find cannot easily be shaken off by men even of greatest learning and greatest integrity'; less temperately, the Quaker Richard Claridge feared the issue exerted in some 'a frenzy and madness against the present lawful government'.[390] To help subjects deal with scruples, writers attempted tortuous arguments about how the oath to William only required acceptance of his *de facto* (as opposed to *de iure*) authority and so, being what the author of a *Vindication* of those who took it called an oath 'in a lower construction', supposedly left the original oath unviolated.[391] When it came to securing compliance and outward allegiance, writers were willing to indulge an equivocation and sophistry that recall some Reformation arguments. Moreover, amid the subtle and difficult negotiations with law and conscience, writers were not averse to making the case for William from a more straightforward comparison – or rather contrast – of personality and suitability for rule. A *Defence of Their Majesties*, for example, stated that as a papist James could not be king; the author of *The Advantages of the Present Settlement* catalogued his vices highlighting his untrustworthiness; *The Anatomy of an Arbitrary Prince*, revealing James's (alleged) plans to convert England and murder Protestants, warned that only 'he that designs to be a papist and a slave ... may be supposed to fight for the restoration of King James the Second'.[392] Quite other than James, as several brief characters and defences described him, William was a sound Protestant, a pious, devout, just and 'incomparable prince', another Constantine, and Mary a religious reformer, under both of whom the nation might be secure and prosperous.[393] As Whitby put it, gratitude done to such a heroic prince who had come to the people's rescue when they were deserted ought to be sufficient cause for allegiance: 'we have no liberty left us either to dispute the king's title or to deny him our duty'.[394]

Unfortunately for William (and the Whigs), the 'liberty' of dispute by no means ended and, in addition to the non-jurors, there remained an unquantifiable many who harboured doubts about their duty to the regime. Faced with continuing misgivings and disputes, apologists for William tried a number of polemical tactics. Pamphlets, for example, pointed up the dangers to England of division and appealed for unity.[395] Some sought to find it through the traditional humanist dialogue that ended in agreement. For example, *A Modest Attempt for Healing the Present Animosities* staged a discussion between a dissenter, a bigot and a moderate in which the Trimmer (the voice of moderation) pressed the others to reconcile and unite against their common enemy, France.[396] Adopting a personal tone, *A Letter to a Dissenting Clergyman of the Church of England, Concerning the Oath of Allegiance and Obedience to the Present Government* endeavoured to reassure the recipient (and all doubters) that, unlike the civil war, the recent events had done no harm to the late king; arguing that the logic now dictated taking the oath or leaving the country, the *Letter* observed that since James could no longer protect the people, 'your business is only to enquire which you may safely do'.[397] Probably the cleverest tactic, still highly effective today, was use of a political conversion narrative. In his 1691 *The Case of Allegiance Due to Sovereign Powers*, a work that went into six editions, the clergyman William Sherlock accurately reported how he had long refused to take the oath to William and Mary, but Scripture had brought him to an understanding that 'by what means soever any prince ascends the throne, he is placed there by God' and that the 'direction of Scripture is to submit to those in authority'.[398]

While the various arguments made in defence of William and the Revolution were reiterated, events and circumstances dictated different polemical moves and responses. After his defeat in Ireland, James II began a propaganda campaign to rebuild support in England beginning with a carefully worded declaration (published from St Germain in April 1693) which promised his 'loving subjects' that he would do all to reconcile them to their duty and re-establish the unity, peace and prosperity of the nation.[399] The potential effect of this on the consciences of all who remained uneasy necessitated that Williamite loyalists rush to answer it, which several did – Defoe point by point.[400] The responses focused mainly on negative portrayals of James as untrustworthy, but there was an awareness too of a renewed need to make the best argument for William. The question remained, however, what was the best argument. The author of *Some Short Reflections upon King James's Late Declarations* favoured the pragmatic argument: that it was the national interest to support William's government because any change now would involve bloodshed, an argument given only slightly more theoretical gloss by the naturalized clergyman Pierre Allix whose *A Letter to a Friend* was one of his several treatises in defence of the Revolution.[401] Yet, though such writers hoped that 'the argument from interest ties the subjects of England in the fastest bonds of duty and allegiance to their present majesties', the title of the pamphlet from which this quotation is taken, *An Enquiry into the Nature and Obligation of Legal Rights*, makes clear that pragmatism and interests alone were not making the case: as the author admitted, 'how advantageous soever the late Revolution may prove', if it is presented as 'founded in injustice' nothing would keep James out or secure William five years; therefore, after 1688 old arguments were reopened about the right of parliament to appoint the king, about the obligation to existing authority, about James's abdication and so on.[402] If William's situation was not helped by the reopening of painful debates, the loyalists' case was weakened by publicized disagreement among themselves. Charles Blount's thesis that William and Mary had a good title as conquerors was countered by several who feared that such an argument had the potential to suggest absolute monarchy when the virtuous William was 'contented with a plain English limited monarchy', his title rooted in the 'donation of the people'.[403] Renewed efforts were made to represent the Revolution as providential and William as God's instrument; the second edition of Miege's *The New State of England*, for example, contained an extravagant encomium of William as a prince with all the qualities that made him 'best qualified for a throne'.[404]

However, as Blount lamented, 'notwithstanding all that hath been written, a great many do yet remain unsatisfied'.[405] Dissatisfaction and doubts about his authority at a time when William was absent from the country and embroiled in continental war were problems enough. What exacerbated them was the poor progress of the early campaigns, which made it harder to present William as a hero blessed by providence, and the financial burdens which fostered discontent and charges of waste, mismanagement and corruption. Worse still the death of Queen Mary, as we observed, starkly laid bare the question of what legal right a consort had to rule after her death. During his most difficult months since 1688, spokesmen for William valiantly struggled to put the best face on the state of affairs. Matthew Tindal, a lawyer and government supporter with an annual salary from the crown, reiterated the grounds of obedience to present power and praised the good government that protected them; in *The Present Aspect of Our Times*, Robert Fleming, who was to take up a ministry at William's wish, nobly ventured that the last year had delivered 'a new testimony ... to the repute and honour of the king', praised William as a leader 'ready to sacrifice his nearest concerns on the altar of the nation's safety', and urged all to unite behind him for the common good.[406] The ever-supportive Defoe, brushing aside the burden of taxes, compared William to Gustavus Adolfus as a 'deliverer of oppressed nations' and, asserting that the national good was inseparable from William and the war, asked how any would dare to call themselves patriots who opposed one of the best princes; acknowledging that there was still ambiguity and equivocation concerning the king's right, he pressed for 'an oath of fidelity', 'an oath which will have no loophole'.[407]

On Mary's death, with rumours circulating that James would take the opportunity to call for his restoration, Williamites turned their attention to vilifying and mocking the king in exile. A mock *A Dialogue between the King of France and the Late King James, Occasioned by the Death of the Queen* stages James confessing that he had hired Jesuits, destroyed parliament and wiped his arse with Magna Carta, while (doubtless to reduce fears of invasion) Louis XIV is depicted as mocking the Stuart and offering him only a mackerel boat for his invasion of England.[408] (*A Secret History* of life at the court at St Germain scurrilously portrays and undermines James cuckolded by a queen who fucks priests and abbots while saying her rosaries and who dallies with Louis himself.)[409] A one-page broadside for popular consumption, illustrated with portraits of William and Mary, rehearsed all the vices that had led to James's expulsion, celebrated in its title *England's Deliverance from Popery and Slavery*, and reasserted – to check any claims from that quarter – the illegitimacy of the Prince of Wales whose real mother, the government agent William Fuller alleged in print, was an Irishwoman now in a French convent.[410]

After the gloomiest period, 1692–5, William's pamphlet spokesmen, as we would expect, extracted all the polemical capital they could from the victory at Namur and the discovery of the assassination plot which was to give rise to the new oath that Defoe had asked for. Along with the numerous verse panegyrics, sermons and campaign reports we have examined, pamphlets greeted the return of a hero. The author of *Anglia Grata* garlanded a commander who surpassed Alexander and Caesar, Edward III and Henry V, and now subjected the might of France.[411] With dominance in Europe, indeed 'o're the world' in prospect, the panegyrist looked back to the origins of this new age in 'the stupendious Revolution here at home' and promised William: 'you are the joy of our hearts'.[412] Though the attempted assassination made it all too clear that William was still not the joy of everyone's heart, the plot offered Williamites a chance to brand all Jacobites as traitors and the timely apprehension of the plotters a renewed occasion to represent the king as the favoured son of providence. In his *Remarks Upon the Horrid and Barbarous Conspiracy*, the author of *Simeon and Levi* claimed to be confident that, God having 'preserved us all by his mighty hand', Louis and James had been weakened by the plot and, predicting (or hoping?) that 'the wiser Jacks will quit their party and learn again to love their native country', rallied readers to assist William 'in person and with our purses'.[413] Others, such as Thomas Percival and the Williamite espionage agent John Macky emphasized the miraculous pang of conscience that had led a plotter to confess, and reminded the 'malcontent Protestants' that they had little to hope for from James and how 'unreasonable it is to be a Jacobite'; rising to apocalyptic strains, John Bundy saw in the revelation of the plot Babel finally defeated and 'king William proclaimed the second time'.[414]

Talk of a second proclamation was not entirely misplaced as, in the wake of the plot, MPs voted for a bond of association to the king which was entered into the Commons Journals and for a new oath which, going beyond the *de facto* loyalty that had hitherto been all that was required, referred to William as 'rightful and lawful' king. The Whigs' hope was that the oath and Association would unite all but the most hardened Jacobites; and, in an effort to isolate them, pamphleteers demonized the plotters as men infected by Jesuits, and James as a puppet of the cruel Louis XIV, as 'a prince abandoned to his sanguinary passions'.[415] Complementary to the denunciation of 'the blackest and most barbarous design that was ever set on foot' came proclamations of the new affection felt towards William who was, in the words of Jacques Abbadie, 'endeared to his subjects by the greatness of the common danger and receiving new assurances of their ... fidelity'.[416] Cleverly associating criticisms of William's wars and taxes with the plotters, Abbadie sought to render all opposition unpatriotic and insisted that 'never was the interest and happiness of a prince so inseparably united to that of his people'.[417]

The Association, however, as well as expressing unity, re-exposed, indeed created further, division. For some who since 1688 had been willing to acknowledge William as *de facto* king, the oath's requirement to recognize him *de iure* was a step they would not take. Abiel Borfet, minister for Richmond, for example, in his published *Reasons for Refusing to Subscribe the Association*, expressed his reservations about the words 'true and lawful' king.[418] In response, therefore, Williamites, such as the anonymous author who responded to Borfet and the government propagandist William Atwood, tried to castigate equivocation and trimming as aids to conspiracy.[419] In his *Reflections upon a Treasonable Opinion . . . Against Signing the National Association*, Atwood argued it was the duty of all to sign, a duty, the author of *A Free Discourse* concurred, that was owed 'for the enjoyment of life, liberty and property'.[420] But if Atwood accurately calculated that Borfet and others had led many to refuse the oath, the Association may have been an instance of ardent loyalists shooting themselves in the foot. Certainly the author of *A Free Discourse* considered it inadequate for purpose as, he reported, some of the clergy were forming 'anti-associations' that would retain the distinction between *de facto* and *de iure* and so mean that 'King William does not reign secure'.[421]

The fragility of William's security, even after the wave of support that followed the plot, was again exposed by a second manifesto issued by James II in which he endeavoured to rally the princes of Europe to his side and the cause of his son.[422] To prevent the declaration overshadowing the Peace of Ryswick, Williamite loyalists stepped forward to answer James's protest and discountenance any prospect that the Pretender would occupy the English throne.[423] Louis, another mocking dialogue observed, had made peace, recognized William as rightful king and shown nothing but contempt for his Stuart cousin.[424] In general, Williamites hoped that the peace would more firmly establish the king at home, as abroad; and one author took the occasion of the peace to publish *The Revolution Justified* in which he revived familiar arguments in new circumstances to urge that 'he that is so great and glorious abroad ought justly to be admired and revered at home', and his right to the crown recognized as 'greater . . . than any other'.[425] In a personal letter form, favoured in Williamite polemics, another pamphlet invited former Jacobites to join with loyalists in the benefits of peace – to be 'fellow sharers in this general joy', now that James's cause was 'at an end, the French king having . . . promised never to aid or assist him any more'.[426] Closing with the statement that 'now is the seasonable time of yielding' to a William who was returning a king of peace, the author of *Ratio Ultima* summoned them to 'full compliance with the present government' in peace and happiness.[427]

Because even the peace did not end controversy about the king's legitimacy, William's supporters sustained a campaign of argument that continued to the end of the reign. In 1699, for example, the turncoat government pensioner Richard Kingston, in his tenth pro-government publication, returned to a Whig narrative of the reigns of the last two Stuarts to justify the Revolution.[428] 'I am endeavouring,' he stated explicitly, 'to beget a good opinion of our present settlement, to help men in a quiet obedience to the government' by reminding readers of James's tyranny and by praising a king who 'knows how to gain power and how to make it pleasant and durable', a monarch who merited 'cheerful obedience'.[429] Someone even arranged the republication of the Benedictine Thomas White's *The Grounds of Obedience*, which, as a note on the flyleaf of the British Library copy records, was originally written 'to persuade people in general and the popish party in particular, to acquiesce in the new settlement' of Oliver Cromwell.[430]

The hope, however, that Louis XIV's recognition of William had permanently neutered the Jacobite threat proved illusory when the French king, on the death of James, recognized his son as king of Britain. The Whigs and Williamites had for much of the 1690s been quiet about the Prince of Wales, whom propaganda had denounced as an impostor in 1688. Occasional notices after the death of Mary bear testimony to mounting concern about the succession. But the death of Princess Anne's son, then Louis's recognition of James Francis Edward, again threatened the security of not only William but the whole Revolutionary Protestant settlement, necessitating in the last years of the reign yet another move in the unending campaign to secure it. The government agent William Fuller, following his revelations about the prince's true mother, published again in 1700 further details of the imposture.[431] If the Prince of Wales succeeded, *A Letter to a Minister of State* warned, the French would rule and Englishmen would, like peasants, be reduced to wooden shoes.[432] John Toland, not always a friend to the regime, rose to counter any claims for the prince and vigorously defended the Hanoverian succession favoured by the king as the best solution towards a settlement and for preserving the religion and constitution.[433] As so often, Defoe appeared in print twice to support the king. Observing in *The Succession to the Crown of England* that the issue was 'so much the general subject of discourse', Defoe dismissed the prince's pretensions ('the people of England ought not to trouble their heads about him') and asserted that 'the House of Hanover . . . is the only line which with an undisputed right of descent stands fair to claim the crown of England'.[434]

After Louis's reneging on the terms of Ryswick and the partition treaties, however, few loyalists doubted that the Protestant succession would be secured without the defeat of France, so, in William's last years, his supporters again published to encourage support for a war which was presented as a necessity in the face of the French snub to the nation, as much as its king. The best-known career diplomat of William's reign, George Stepney, in his *Essay upon the Present Interest of England* (1701) carefully explained the tangled European politics that necessitated a resurgence of war; the author of *The Present Disposition of England Considered* appealed for support and supply for alliances and war, remarking of William III that ' 'tis the length of his days must establish our prosperity and save us from gunpowder and blood'.[435] Still, at the end of the reign, the war William was about to re-embark upon was sold as a war for liberty as much as for the king.

Months before William's death, the loyal Defoe, taking 'my hero' William as 'the darling subject' of his satire against his countrymen, his bestselling *The*

True-Born Englishman, lamented that William had not received from his subjects the gratitude and love he deserved.[436] Indeed, it may seem a paradox that for all the panegyric verse of Whig poets, the hundreds of officially sponsored sermons, the Whig histories and the loyal battalions of pamphlet polemicists, William, as biographers concur and he himself intuited ('I see I am not made for this people'), was never warmly embraced by his people; and there remained subjects – beyond the avowed Jacobites – who were never willing to recognize his right to the throne.[437] Did then the champions whose names have recurred, government pensioners and agents, Whig clients and independent supporters, write and represent William and Mary in vain? To that question the response must be 'no'. For despite the revolutionary nature of his coup, his slim claim to rule as a partner with his wife, and the constant threat of challenge, invasion or plot, William remained on the throne. More than that, he was able – yes, in the face of difficulty and discontent but able nevertheless – to conduct a decade of continental campaigns of a type and on a scale that England had never witnessed before; and able to raise the supplies to maintain fleets and armies at a cost unprecedented in English history. His victories and political success owed much, of course, to military and parliamentary tactics. But in a political culture of party division and the relentless reiteration (as we shall see) of Jacobite, Tory and Country opposition, it was the power of Whig arguments that contributed to winning supply. And in the country at large, it was the Whig poets, preachers and pamphleteers' capacity to be dominant in the bookshop or coffee house, in the debate within the public sphere, that was vital to William's authority and campaigns. At no time did his supporters have an easy task. The sheer output and repetition of arguments for the Revolution and the king themselves testify to a battle that was never decisively won. Yet it was the loyalists' very persistence, their repetition, their response to every attack, their relentless programme of propaganda that helped to ensure the Revolution settlement was not undone – and that put, even in difficult times, the best spin on events and presented the best face of the king. It is time for us to examine how other artists of government propaganda represented that face in portrait and stone, on engravings, on medals and coins.

CHAPTER 10

FIGURING REVOLUTION

I

For all that Whig propaganda tried to present it as a continuation, 1688 represented a dynastic revolution. Mary was, of course, James II's daughter, a Stuart; but William, the effective ruler (to whom Mary always surrendered authority on his return from campaigns), was, albeit the son of Charles I's daughter, little known and foreign. Indeed, Dutch. Though for long allies in the wars against continental Catholicism, by the mid-seventeenth century the England and Holland were commercial and naval rivals and the Commonwealth government had gone to war with the Dutch. Under Charles II, a Dutch fleet had inflicted a humiliating defeat on the English in the Medway and even though, after three wars, England made peace with Holland, anti-Dutch feeling and rivalry persisted. Yet, as Lisa Jardine has recently reminded us, England and the Netherlands, even in times of conflict, had sustained a cultural exchange which had seen a convergence of taste, especially in the arts.[1] Pieter van der Faes, from Soet, had under his adopted name, Peter Lely, succeeded Van Dyck as the most prominent portraitist in England and was appointed Charles II's Painter in Ordinary in 1661. The Dutch also dominated the English engraving industry and the manufacture of porcelain, which was becoming an increasingly important medium for the representation of monarchs, so beginning our own tradition of coronation mugs.[2]

This ambivalent relationship between England and Holland thus presented William with a necessity and an opportunity. As a foreigner and Dutchman with no valid claim to the throne, he needed to represent himself: to make himself a visible, national, English king rather than, as some charged, a usurper who exploited the resources of England to fight a war in his own and the Netherlands' interest. The authors of panegyrical verse, histories and pamphlets, as we have seen, as well as William himself in his speeches, sought to present the king as a British patriot who, having rescued the English church, English liberty and property, as another Edward III or Henry V, heroically battled to defend them against the foreign popish threat of France. However, as the 1688 Revolution had manifested, visual propaganda was as important as words. Dutch cartoons had played a key role in the popular demonization of James II; in exile James himself grasped the importance of keeping his face and that of his son in the public eye by commissioning portraits and engravings that were sent to and circulated in England.[3]

James's host and ally, Louis XIV, was the master when it came to systematic orchestration of visual propaganda.[4] Acting on the conviction that royal control of the arts was an essential aid to royal absolutism, Louis had founded in 1648, in the wake of the rebellion known as the Fronde, an Academy of Painting and Sculpture, which was later followed by academies for letters, the sciences, dance and architecture, all of which recruited writers and artists for state service.[5] Not merely the communicators of Louis's glory, artists and architects helped, as Peter Burke brilliantly demonstrated, to fabricate the Sun King: to construct authority out of signs and symbols, as well as to represent it. Moreover, Louis's court at Versailles and the carefully constructed image of the king were designed for a European as well as a domestic audience.[6] Louis took artists with him on military campaigns, and victories were the theme of numerous paintings which figured the triumphant king as another Hercules and glorious conqueror.[7] In peace as in war, Versailles stood as a symbol of French European dominance, as European princes (many of them enemies) vied to emulate an acknowledged French supremacy in architecture, portraiture, and other forms of spectacle and display. A war to check the might of Louis XIV's France, that is to say, was one that necessitated a cultural as well as military campaign, a visual as well as verbal display of glory and power – both abroad and at home.

In England there had been developing since the earlier seventeenth century both habits of collecting and a more refined aesthetic and political appreciation of the arts.[8] Collecting spread beyond the aristocracy to the gentry and, through copies, mezzotints and engravings to classes beyond the elite. During William's reign, art auctions in coffee houses expanded greatly.[9] From the Restoration, as we have observed, books (often translations) on the art of painting began to appear frequently, evidencing as well as helping to create a community of amateur critics and artists.[10] The trend was to continue in William's reign with the publication in English of Charles Dufresnoy's *De Arte Graphica, The Art of Painting*, which, with a preface by Dryden, discussed the merits of painters; while a number of guides, such as Marshall Smith's *The Art of Painting According to the Theory and Practice of the Best Italian, French and German Masters*, John Smith's *The Art of Painting in Oil*, or *Art's Master Piece*, offered simple, practical instruction on drawing, painting, japanning (lacquer-working), and on the materials and techniques used to attain effects.[11] Such guides and histories discussed royal portraitists, Louis XIV's academy, and the contribution of the arts to the 'glory of princes'; in his *Epigram upon the Paintings of the Most*

Eminent Masters, for example, John Elsum assessed critically and ideologically portraits of Charles V, Charles I and Oliver Cromwell, as well as paintings by Tintoretto and Titian, Raphael and Rubens.[12] Alongside learned texts like the 1698 translation of Longinus's treatise upon the sublime, we should note one of the discussions reported in James Wright's *Country Conversations*, which, among other debates about 'painting and painters', features three characters conversing about architecture and art.[13] Though England still lagged far behind its continental neighbours, there was an informed market and audience for visuals, which presented the monarch with a further opportunity and incentive to represent his rule and his policies in and through visual media.

It was for long conventional to assert that, despite the compelling need and opportunity to project himself visually, William showed little interest in the arts. In his 1702 *History* of the king, for example, Abel Boyer observed that, though he had some admiration for pictures, William did not encourage artists.[14] Horace Walpole more tartly asserted that he 'contributed nothing for the advancement of the arts' and Mary little more.[15] The visual culture of the age remains one of the under-explored subjects of the seventeenth century. Since the 1970s, however, both in general surveys and scholarly catalogues and volumes, there has been a greater recognition of William's appreciation and patronage of the arts, and of his understanding and use of visual propaganda.[16] William had collected paintings from age fifteen and even amid military campaigns in the 1670s, had taken time to visit Antwerp dealers and to meet artists.[17] On his march to London from Torbay in 1688, he paused at Wilton to view the Earl of Pembroke's Van Dycks and immediately on assuming the throne sought advice about the royal collection.[18] During the 1690s, the diplomat Huygens frequently refers to William's interest in pictures and his removal of several canvases to Kensington House.[19]

Indeed, for all the opposition between their religious and political creeds, William's succession did not mark a revolutionary departure from that of James II in the arts. In his court as Stadtholder, William had followed French fashions even amid wars against Louis XIV and had employed the French-born architect and decorative designer Daniel Marot and Gerard de Lairesse, whose paintings so closely emulated French styles that he was nicknamed the 'Dutch Poussin'.[20] On his accession to the English throne, William retained the services of most of the artists employed by James with the exception of Antonio Verrio who, as a committed Jacobite, refused in 1688 (he was later to relent) to work for the new regime.[21] On Verrio's resignation, William gave the post of Principal Painter jointly to John Riley and Godfrey Kneller, who had worked for Charles II and his brother since the late 1670s.[22] On Riley's death in 1691, Kneller enjoyed sole possession of the post and further royal favour was shown in his appointment as a Gentleman of the Privy Chamber and his election the next year to a knighthood.[23] Such honours, together with William's later gift of a gold medal of himself on a chain, recall Charles I's relationship with Van Dyck.[24] It would appear that the king and queen saw in Kneller, who after a flirtation with French style had settled to painting in the tradition of Van Dyck and Lely, an artist who represented continuity and who could represent them to their English subjects in ways that emphasized both Englishness and the place of Dutch artists (Kneller had moved to Amsterdam from his native Lübeck) in English portraiture.

Even more than Van Dyck or Lely had done, Kneller served his royal patrons by concentrating on a series of portraits of the king and queen. These commenced with two state portraits for which, according to the Dutch diplomat and poet Constantine Huygens, William and Mary sat in March 1690, virtually as soon as the artist had taken up his post.[25] Though a recent state portrait of Charles II (by Wright) had depicted the restored monarch enthroned, crowned and wearing the regalia, Kneller's of William figures the king, standing by a table on which are placed the regalia, in a stance that recalls Van Dyck's of Charles I painted in 1636 (fig. 49).[26] The companion portrait of the queen placed her to the right of the table (on which were placed the crown, orb and sceptre), her pose and the position of her hands recalling the less official Van Dyck portrait of Henrietta Maria standing by a table and resting her hand on two roses placed next to her crown.[27] As Kneller's biographer remarks, the two canvases, 'though soundly constructed and well painted . . . are unoriginal'; unoriginality seems to have been the point.[28] In harking back to Van Dyck and Charles I, William and Mary advertised their common descent from the second Stuart and appropriated, as we have seen they were anxious to do, the martyr, while erasing their two immediate predecessors who were regarded as having favoured popery.

There can be no doubting the importance of these portraits to William. No royal images before this date were so much copied and distributed as these. Royal warrants for payments for copies (at £50 compared with £200 for the originals) are dated 1693 and 1694, 1697 and 1700.[29] As well as those the king sent to foreign princes, governors and ambassadors, noblemen were given permission to copy them and further copies of that of the king were made for the Guildhall, the Inner Temple and the Merchant Taylor's Company, and, as we shall see, were broadly distributed as engravings. 'It was,' writes J. Douglas Stewart, 'as though the king felt he could occupy and hold, by means of his portrait, the lands and loyalty of subjects over whom his purely hereditary claims were so questionable.'[30]

Nor were the state portraits Kneller's only homage to earlier artists and times. In 1690–1, he executed a series of female aristocratic portraits that has come to be known as the 'Hampton Court Beauties'.[31] The sitters were described by Defoe as 'the principal ladies attending upon her majesty', so the paintings

49 Sir Godfrey Kneller, *William III, c.* 1690.

represented the new queen who was, of course, James II's daughter as well as Charles I's granddaughter, and were hung in the Water Gallery at Hampton Court, which was redecorated for the queen. The title that has been given the series and a first sight of the canvases recall Lely's Windsor Beauties, a set of twelve like Kneller's.[32] But it is the differences rather than similarities that are striking. In contrast to the eroticism and, in some, explicit sexuality of Lely's portraits, the Hampton Court beauties, as well as being painted full length (as opposed to Lely's three quarters), are more formally dressed and of a more reserved, modest demeanour, with the Duchess of Grafton's downward glance, for example, presenting a meditative figure quite different from the audacious and inviting looks of Lely's figures.[33] In fact rather than from Lely it was from

Van Dyck, who had created the baroque full-length English female portrait, that Kneller drew for both specific gestures and, importantly, a broad ideology. Where Lely had daringly played with neo-Platonic conceits, Kneller's beauties, like Van Dyck's, suggest, along with their beauty, their control of the passions, that self-regulation central to Caroline representations of regality.[34] Kneller's beauties similarly do more than 'reflect the moral change which occurred in English society from the nineties'.[35] The king and queen – and Mary especially – were represented as making a break with the lascivious corruption of the Stuart court and as champions of a moral reformation of society. By association the Hampton Court beauties, the queen's attendants, represent Mary as what the prologue to Purcell's *Dido and Aeneas* (1689) called her – 'the Sovereign Queen of Beauty' – and as the heir to Henrietta Maria, the chaste queen of the uxorious martyr, whom even the puritan Lucy Hutchinson had praised as a king of moral rectitude.[36] Where, that is, Lely's Windsor Beauties symbolized a reign that, kicking off the traces of puritanism, celebrated pleasure as Charles II so publicly did, the Hampton Court beauties signified a morality and a politics of restraint, but one that looked back not to the (unpopular) puritan republic but to a virtuous royal couple and loving marriage – an image central to William and Mary's monarchy.

Kneller continued to remain in favour with and work for William and Mary jointly, then William alone, for the rest of the reign: the king sent him to Brussels to paint an equestrian portrait of his ally the Elector of Bavaria, commissioned him to paint the visiting Russian Tsar Peter, and the artist was in the royal entourage to the Low Countries when the Peace of Ryswick was signed in September 1697.[37] But there is no evidence that William sat for Kneller after the state portrait which remained the template for numerous pictures of the king. Whether on account of William's long absences on continental campaigns or the mixed fortunes of war, it was not until the later 1690s that the king again commissioned Kneller to paint him. A portrait dated to the period 1695–1700 (once attributed to Verrio) was evidently executed by Kneller as part of a redecoration of St George's Hall, Windsor, and is in oil on plaster (fig. 50).[38] Elias Ashmole records seeing 'at the upper end of the hall . . . the picture of King William III, seated on a throne, ten steps high . . . and above this St George killing the Dragon'.[39] The description and the fragment that remains (an accomplished half-length portrait of the king in Garter robes with a very prominent Garter George) suggest that the illusionist decoration might have been a celebration of William's victory, the dragon representing defeated France and Catholicism. What is probable is that in 1697 Kneller began a new series of royal portraits, almost certainly commissioned by the king, that depict William as triumphant warrior. Though it does not survive, except in a mezzotint by John Smith, Kneller painted William in armour with his cloak knotted on his left shoulder above a Latin description that proclaimed him king of

50 Sir Godfrey Kneller, *William III in Garter robes*, 1695–1700.

Britain and France.[40] If an inscription on the back of a now destroyed painting can be trusted, Kneller may also have painted an equestrian portrait of the king in 1697, presumably to mark the Peace of Ryswick and William's triumphant entry into London on his return.[41]

   While, since it no longer exists, we cannot be sure how, this painting, once at Gatschina Palace near Leningrad, is clearly related to *William III on horseback*, now at Hampton Court and a work signed and dated by Kneller 1701 (fig. 51).[42] At the centre of this allegorical canvas, William, in armour and wearing the collar of the Garter, rides a white horse along a coast, with ships visible in the background. Beneath William's horse lie – appropriately, if this was conceived to celebrate Ryswick – the weapons and emblems of war, over which the king now rides as triumphant peacemaker. In front of him Ceres kneels with a cornucopia offering an olive branch and Flora attends with a boy carrying flowers, significations of peace, plenty and pastoral tranquillity. Behind the king, in his shell chariot, Neptune attends, perhaps symbolizing the English mastery of the seas. Above William's head in a cloud the figure of Peace holds

51   Sir Godfrey Kneller, *William III on Horseback*, 1701.

in one hand William's helmet, in the other a palm (a symbol of victory, peace, abundance and happiness), and is attended by a putto who also holds the helmet.[43] Together with her and two other putti, Mercury, bearing his caduceus as messenger of the gods, looks down on the king, as if bestowing divine bene-faction. Immediately above the king's head, one putto holds a scroll on which is written 'Pacatumque Regit Patriis Virtutibus Orbem' – 'He reigns over a peaceful world with the virtues of his ancestors'. The sentence comes from the fourth of Virgil's *Eclogues*, which relates how 'justice returns . . . with a new breed of men sent down from heaven' and how under a second Apollo a new golden age of peace and justice will arise that 'shall free the earth form never-ceasing fear'.[44] William, in other words, is heralded as a classical hero who changed (literally by peace) an age of iron to one of gold. The eclogue, proph-esying the return of Astraea, also associated William with Queen Elizabeth I whose memory he often (and indeed visually) invoked and recalled Verrio's *Sea Triumph of Charles II* which alluded to the same quotation.[45] As well as general allusion, it has also been suggested that William was directly figured as

Aeneas, the Trojan hero of Virgil's *Aeneid*.[46] In historical legend, the founding king of Britain was Brutus, the grandson of Aeneas. In 1697 a new edition of Dryden's translation of the *Aeneid* had taken Ogilby's plates from the original 1654 version but altered them to give Aeneas the features of William III, suggesting that, at the time of Ryswick, the comparison was being made visually and directly, as it was in literary panegyrics.[47]

The complex Hampton Court portrait, therefore, draws on many conceits and makes many claims. William is presented as a heroic commander but as one who gifted the people a triumphant peace; as a monarch descended of a long line but as one who renewed and promised a new age; and as a British king yet an ancient emperor; a classical hero and yet – the white horse imparts a spiritual, indeed apocalyptic meaning – a Christian knight and son of providence who had triumphed over the forces of darkness to bring in the age of Christ.[48] Kneller's equestrian portrait has not received critical acclaim and he has – rightly – been compared to his disfavour with Van Dyck who, in contrast to Kneller's busy allegory, in his equestrian portraits evokes a natural authority and more subtly alludes to sacred and imperial themes.[49] But if William's 'warrant' and 'order' for this portrait indicate royal direction of the subject – and the recurrence of the iconographical motifs on medals is suggestive – then the king was clearly embarking on a new self-glorification in his visual representation.[50] It may, therefore, be no coincidence that on 12 February 1698 the annalist Narcissus Luttrell reported that 'his Majesty is resolved to settle an academy to encourage the art of painting', in emulation of Louis XIV.[51]

The shift towards a greater visual glorification of William – which at least qualifies the poet and diplomat Matthew Prior's quip that 'the monuments of my master's actions are to be seen anywhere but in his own house' – may also help to explain the return of Verrio to royal service at the end of William's reign.[52] The Catholic Verrio, whose son supported James II in Ireland, had refused to work for William in 1688; after ten years working at Burghley House, for John 5th Earl of Exeter, his patron, it is said, persuaded him to return to work for the king.[53] What needs remarking is William's eagerness to commission, for new state apartments at Hampton Court, a Catholic ex-Jacobite whose baroque decorations had adorned St George's Hall and James II's chapels at Whitehall and Windsor. Having fully established military supremacy over Louis, William, it seems, not prepared to cede cultural supremacy to the French royal house, was determined to proclaim his authority in the modes and forms favoured by absolute monarchs.

William's plan for an Academy in England recognized the visual absence of indigenous artists qualified to depict the nation and its ruler's glory to a domestic and international audience. Beside Riley, the only English painter, who died in 1691, the other artists at William and Mary's court were the Dutch Jan van der Vaart who copied Kneller's state portrait for aldermen, the German John Closterman and the Swede, Michael Dahl, neither of whom (though they painted courtiers and royal servants) executed portraits of the king or queen. Other than portraits by visiting artists – such as that by Godfried Schalken of William armoured and holding a candle, or battle scenes by Jan Wyck and others of the Boyne and Namur, with William visible as commander – the image of William on canvas, from the early state portrait to equestrian triumph, was the work of Kneller and the assistants, copyists and emulators who constituted what was a virtual factory production of his portraits.[54]

Even more of an industrial output were the numerous prints and mezzotints after Kneller, principally by John Smith. The artist and engraver first worked together before William acceded to the throne; but it was during the 1690s that they formed a friendship – each executing the other's portrait – and close business relationship, with Smith enjoying a virtual monopoly of engravings after Kneller.[55] Raising the standard of mezzotint to new heights, Smith's engravings became collectors' pieces themselves, and both the quality and sheer volume of his output made him a rich man.[56] There had been numerous Dutch engravings of William as Stadtholder and, as king, William doubtless appreciated the importance of this form of royal representation: one of Smith's mezzotints of the king was published 'cum privilegio regis' and sold at the Three Pigeons in Bedford Street.[57] There were various versions of Smith mezzotints of William after Kneller:[58] one of a painting evidently now lost of the king in armour sold from Smith's own rooms in the Lion and Crown in Russell Street, Covent Garden;[59] another an oval of the king wearing a large Garter George.[60] Though the engraver closest to Kneller, Smith was not the only one to make prints after the artist's portraits. William Faithorne, most likely the Younger, executed, also with royal privilege, the Kneller state portrait which, like Smith's, was also sold at the Three Pigeons, the business of the leading printseller Edward Cooper.[61] Several other anonymous engravings after Kneller were published: one with an inscription flattering the king stated that the love of one's country was more powerful and worthy than any other consideration, while another very large print (by Gerard Valck) figured William above a large crown with the motto 'Je Maintiendrai' ('I will maintain, or preserve'), the motto of the House of Nassau, and the words 'Vox Populi Vox Dei' ('The voice of the people is the voice of God'), alluding to the popular as well as divine support for William's kingship.[62]

As well as mezzotints after Kneller, English engravers etched prints after other artists, known and unknown. Smith himself executed a mezzotint of a portrait by Wissing[63] and Van der Vaart, Robert Williams and Bernard Lens, who both worked for Cooper, engraved portraits of William and Mary.[64] Robert White, a former apprentice to the master David Loggan, as well as doing a line engraving bust of William, also engraved the king and queen as a royal couple: his print consisting of two portrait ovals beneath a crowned canopy and above a large royal arms appears likely to have been intended to represent and naturalize a joint rule which was, of course, a constitutional anomaly (fig. 52).[65]

52 Robert White, *King William III, Queen Mary II*, 1689 or after.

Among the many anonymous engravings that survive, there may be the hand of other unidentified English artists. But, unsurprisingly, a large number of Dutch engravers continued to execute and publish portraits of William, some with royal privilege, and it is likely that these circulated in England as well as the Netherlands. Among the standard portraits engraved by Adams Frans Meulen, Pieter Van Gunst, Romeyn de Hooghe, Pieter Schenck, Jacob Gole and Gerard Valck, some officially commissioned, we find more representations than in English work of William in armour and as a military commander as well as king.[66] On one print by Cornelius Vermuelen, for example, beneath an oval of William in armour, crowned by an angel, French verses proclaim how all Europe is indebted to William for its liberty,[67] while Gunst and Van Hove depict the king at the campsite, and Abraham Haring places him, in a complex allegorical print, with a fleet visible in the background.[68] In the tradition of Dutch militant anti-popish satirical prints, the engraver Hendrick Hocken figures William as another Hercules crushing the popish whore of Babylon.[69]

Rather than English artists, it was Dutch engravers who issued prints to mark key episodes and victories in William's reign. It is not surprising that it was a Dutchman, Jan Luyken, who in 1691 etched a plate depicting William's triumphant entry into The Hague, but the relative absence of English engravings of William's celebrated victories is remarkable.[70] It was Dutch artists such as Dirck Maas who etched (as well as painted) William's victory at the Boyne, and the Huguenot *immigré*, Simon Gribelin, who did a line engraving to celebrate the taking of Namur.[71]

Amid the repeated portraits and foreign prints, there were, however, a few engravings that deserve to be discussed as English propaganda. In 1690 Bernard Lens, the English son of a Dutch family, who set up a drawing school in St Paul's churchyard, executed a commemorative mezzotint of the firework display in Covent Garden that was staged to welcome William's victorious return from Ireland in September.[72] Here the brilliantly illuminated monogram of William and Mary with a crown shining on the facade of St Paul's associates royal victory with divine favour, while the scene of popular rejoicing around the burning effigy of Louis XIV represents the king and his cause as enjoying the acclaim and love of his subjects (fig. 53).[73] The same year saw the publication (in a fifth state) of a print first issued in 1658 for Oliver Cromwell.[74] The complicated

53 Bernard Lens II, *A Perfect Description of the Firework in Covent Garden . . .*, 1690.

engraving figured William in armour with a sword and book (inscribed 'I take up, I lead and protect) beneath a tetragrammaton, the Hebrew symbol of God (fig. 54). Between two pillars William stands victorious over the figure of popish superstition, while on the right column kneeling figures representing England, Scotland and Ireland offer victory wreaths, and on his left Fame blows her trumpet. On the left column, topped with the head of Queen Mary, inscriptions connect the king with English law and liberties. The comparison of William with Cromwell was not unproblematic: by the later seventeenth century the former Lord Protector was often vilified as a hypocritical dictator. But in the circumstances of 1690, with the Jacobites defeated in Ireland, the appropriation for William of an image that represented a protector of religion, law and liberties, victorious over popery thanks to divine favour, made an effective statement to those doubtful about the Revolution and the new king. A more popular print, published by Randal Taylor, also commemorated a victory in Ireland – the

54 William Faithorne, after Francis Barlow, *The Embleme of Englands Distractions As also of her attained, and further expected Freedome, & Happines*, 1690.

surrender of Limerick – which effectively ended Jacobite resistance.[75] Against a background of battalions arrayed for battle, and amid cannon and other weapons of war, two crowned oval portraits of William and Mary are placed at the root of a large tree, the Royal Orange Tree (fig. 55). On its branches leaves contain the names of allied commanders and officers; from the branches hang illustrations of the forty-three sieges and battles won in Ireland since 1689. Itself a proclamation of victory, the print was issued, as its inscription put it, as 'a thankful remembrance of God's merciful deliverance of those three kingdoms of England, Scotland and Ireland from popery by the prudent conduct of his Illustrious Highness'. The victory in Ireland, a nervous people were here assured, was a triumph and a salvation for Britain and the beginning of a settled peace under 'our gracious king'.

An obvious propaganda piece is another engraving by Bernard Lens, who after his depiction of the firework display issued a plate celebrating Namur.[76] At

55   Randall Taylor, *The Royall Orange Tree*, 1691.

some point between 1689 and 1694 (more probably nearer the later date) Lens executed a mezzotint of the royal family, consisting of four oval portraits of William, Mary, George, Prince of Denmark, and Princess Anne.[77] The seemingly simple image asserted much. To Jacobites, of course, neither William nor Mary were (as they are described on the print) 'king' or 'queen'. Moreover, there were some beyond the circle of Jacobites who had not abandoned the thought of the restoration of James II, or indeed the future rights of his son, whose legitimacy had never been resolved. In addition, there were increasingly strained relations between William and Mary and the queen's sister Anne, who had given up her right to the succession after Mary to William and any heirs of his marriage; after 1692, the two sisters did not meet and 'Princess Anne in effect presided over an opposition court'.[78] Far then from a portrayal of a harmonious family and uncomplicated succession, Lens's engraving erases the Jacobite claim and advertises a secure line, even with the failure of William to beget an heir. No less than his portrayal of a victorious and popular king in 1690, Lens's *The Royal Family* was propaganda for the Revolutionary settlement at a difficult time at home and abroad.

A final example I shall examine is an engraving of *c.* 1697–8 that survives in only one known copy. The broadsheet, *The Pillar of Europe*, depicts an oval of William (above which putti hold a crown) atop a large pillar around the base of which are scattered armour, cannon, pikes and other weapons of war (fig. 56).[79] On the pediment of the pillar, an inscription declares how the Emperor of Russia (Tsar Peter) had come to visit William from afar to see 'A Moses, Joshua, Solomon'. Down the length of the pillar William's roles and virtues are inscribed, as defender of the faith, suppressor of tyranny, champion of the oppressed, darling of heaven; as one who governed with justice, maintained religion without persecution and sustained greatness without pride. *The Pillar of Europe* appears almost as a sketch for a monument to a sovereign who was, as a prayer on the base describes him, God's instrument. If it was, no such physical monument was erected. But the engraving, dedicated to the loyalist Mansel family, constituted its own memorial to William the 'Generalissimo of the Lord of Hosts, Prime Minister of the Prince of Peace'.

By the late seventeenth century free-standing mezzotints and engravings were being bought and collected by an expanding class of consumers; they were traded, displayed and debated in coffee houses in London and in urban centres beyond. Images of the king and queen, however, were also among the most common frontispieces to books and broadsides, and the visual representation of regality in books situated the image of the king and queen in the full commerce (and contestation) of the expanding print trade. Not least because A. F. Johnson's *A Catalogue of Engraved and Etched English Title Pages* ends with the death of Faithorne in 1691, frontispiece portraits of William and Mary (let alone illustrations within the body of books) have not been listed, or even

56 J. Jones, *The Pillar of Europe*, c. 1697.

studied.[80] My own sample, however, suggests that this is a subject in need of systematic research. In 1689 it was already important to depict the new king as the legitimate ruler of the nation as well as to argue for his right, and it is noteworthy that *An Historical Account* of William, written to celebrate his deliverance of England, published, facing its title page, a well-executed oval portrait of William in armour and wearing a prominent Garter star.[81] Images on some popular broadsides contributed to the establishment of the Revolution: *Great Deliverance*, for example, against the backdrop of a battle which had defeated popish forces, had a crude woodcut of William and Mary enthroned and flanked by angels, while a similar image of the king and queen in coronation robes illustrated *The Court of England or the Preparation for the Happy Coronation* of 'our faith's Great Defender'.[82] Such simple generic representations of the king and queen enthroned are not remarkable for their artistic qualities or even likenesses; but they did signify continuity and legitimacy in ways that hundreds of pages of text could not.

Engravings and woodcuts continued to support as well as figure William and Mary through the changing circumstances of the 1690s. *The History of the Wars in Ireland*, for example, depicted William at the centre of nine oval portraits of the generals and allies, or 'Great Britain's David & His Worthies', while *A Congratulatory Poem* on the king's victory and triumphant return figured William between two pillars (symbols of empire) and the emblems of war crowned with laurel.[83] Images of the royal couple also adorned books the subject of which was not overtly polemical. A work on language, for example, published in 1693, was illustrated opposite its title page with a remarkable double portrait of the king and queen above an anagram of William Henry Nassau's name: 'Heaven will save him'. Above them an inscription praises them 'who did restore Great Britain's rights and broke the Roman whore' and predicted that they would be 'the world's commander both by land and sea'.[84] As the arguments about legitimacy and obedience continued to rage, illustrations, like those to the broadside *Short History of the Succession of the Kings and Queens of England*, erased contention by simply depicting William and Mary as the last of twenty-eight figures of rulers since William the Conqueror.[85]

The death of the queen at a difficult time in the king's military fortune saw, as well as the verse panegyrics we have examined, several images of Mary adorning histories and lives of her, one broadside taking the occasion of her death to revisit the story of *England's Deliverance from Popery and Slavery* and to praise the 'piety and justice' of the royal couple.[86] At the time of the queen's death, when William's tenure of the throne was more exposed, a double portrait at least served to remind readers of the royal descent. Perhaps taking advantage of the wave of support that followed the assassination attempt on the king, John Seller, the royal hydrographer, illustrated his *History of England*, an account of plots, conspiracies and rebellions, with a woodcut of William above a mighty fleet surrounded by a Roman, a Briton, a Saxon, a Dane and a Norman king crowned by laurel as the head of a new empire.[87] Other book illustrations, like so many verses, figured William and Mary with a more recent English legend, Queen Elizabeth I.[88]

Curiously there were no engraved portraits in books or on broadsides celebrating William as a military hero following the successful siege of Namur. In so far as frontispieces were concerned, it was on works related to the reformation of manners that William's image most frequently appeared, announcing his patronage of a cause championed by Mary and vital to his claim to be a favoured agent of providence. Josiah Woodward's best selling *Account of the Societies for Reformation of Manners*, with a list of those 'zealous and diligent' in promoting it, carried opposite the title page a large and crowned portrait of William whose proclamation for preventing immorality and profaneness opened the text.[89] Already going to five editions by 1701, Woodward's history literally figured William as a champion of reform, while Sir Edward Dering recalled the 'incomparable virtues' of

Queen Mary in a life illustrated with a portrait inscribed 'Excellentissima Maria Cognata reditta Caelo' – the most excellent Mary, a fellow spirit returned to heaven.[90] At the very end of the reign, when war resumed and there was renewed talk of the succession, William's image reappeared in histories and biographies. J. A.'s *Princely Excellency*, for example, an account of the king's heroic actions, represented William in armour to signal to his successor the need to continue the fight against France; and the nineteenth edition of Edward Chamberlayne's 'monarchist panegyric', *Angliae Notitia* was published with a prominent three-quarter-length portrait of William (after Kneller) in coronation robes.[91] At the front of this topographical and historical survey of England's counties, government, customs and laws, William stands as – what he never was – the essence of an English sovereign.

Today one of the best-known representations of William III is not on paper but in stone: in a bust in the Temple of British Worthies (Alfred, the Black Prince, Elizabeth and William) that Viscount Cobham erected at Stowe in 1734 as a monument to Whig history.[92] About the same time, various cities, Hull and Bristol, for example, commissioned public statues of William (Hull's a grand equestrian bronze of the king in Roman armour), and other Whig grandees and supporters of Walpole erected statues of the king at Wrest Park, Bedfordshire, Walton Hall, Lancashire, Normanton Park, Rutland, and Hartwell House, Buckinghamshire.[93] Somewhat surprisingly, however, given the numbers of statues of James II and Charles II, 'only one public statue of William III was erected in England during his lifetime'.[94] Possibly to mark the death of the queen, the City of London commissioned a statue of William in Garter robes from John van Nost and another of Mary, which earned admiration from contemporaries, for the Royal Exchange.[95] Nost went on to work for the king at Hampton Court, but his (indeed the) only other contemporary royal bust (now at Portsmouth) was also likely a City of London commission, though its location during William's lifetime is unknown.[96] Given the growing fashion for public statues following the example set by Louis XIV, and both the official and local initiatives to erect them under Charles II and James II, the absence of tributes in stone or bronze to William is striking – and, since many were erected of his successor, Anne, during her lifetime, evidence perhaps of the fact that, whatever the efforts of Whig panegyrists and pamphleteers, the English people never took the Dutch king into their hearts – or communities.[97] In his poem on the Peace of Ryswick, Matthew Morgan called on his countrymen to honour the king in metal:

Let *Gibbons* his *Corinthian* Image cast
Which time's corroding Venom may outlast
The Hero mounted on a flaming Steed[98]

But it was not until a systematic campaign under Walpole that his wish was fulfilled and William was promoted in statues as a hero of the nation.

II

William's reign saw no grand new palaces built to mark Britain's new pre-eminence in Europe. The Stuarts had entertained grandiose plans to rebuild Whitehall, the rambling and outdated palace of Henry VIII; but James I's and Charles I's fantasies about making Inigo Jones's spectacular Banqueting House the centre of a new classical royal residence were scotched by shortages of money. The prodigious difficulties in raising supplies for war would itself have dictated the impossibility for William and Mary of grandiloquent architectural ambitions. But it has recently been argued that William, 'bred in a domesti-cated and small-scale environment', displayed no taste for such grandeur and that his architectural projects were characterized by modesty and restraint, that they were in that representations of his rule.[99]

While the argument holds in general, it risks understating William and Mary's interest in, and their sense of the importance of, palace architecture and even their role in reviving programmes abandoned by Charles II. William, who was asthmatic and found residence in central London detrimental to his health, favoured (as we shall see) other residences than Whitehall. Yet that did not mean he lacked an appreciation of the symbolic significance of the old Tudor palace which had been for a century and a half the principal royal residence and centre of government.[100] After the Revolution, the king and queen completed the construction of new privy lodgings (which James II had initiated for Mary of Modena) for Mary II. To the original plans, Mary added a 'fine terrace walk' on the river side and new stairs to the water.[101] Other alterations, to connect the two royal bedchambers, suggest an architectural advertisement of joint rule and it may be that had Mary lived her influence might have effected further changes.[102] What necessitated attention to the palace, even had William not been inclined to give it, was the fire of January 1698 that destroyed the royal lodgings, along with the Presence and Guard Chambers. Though lodged at Hampton Court and Kensington Palace, William immediately expressed his resolve to 'rebuild [Whitehall] much finer than before', 'if God would give him leave'.[103] As the diarist Narcissus Luttrell commented, however, it was not only God's leave but parliament's purse that was required; and, though Christopher Wren was commissioned to draw up plans for a grand rebuilding inspired by Versailles, the vast cost of war meant that they could not be afforded and, as the court moved to St James's, the ceremonial and business aspects of royal government were separated for the first time.[104]

The historian of Whitehall has speculated whether, had Whitehall not burned, the development towards a constitutional monarchy with a more modest establishment could have proceeded as it did.[105] In fact, though the symbolic royal presence remained crucial, William had almost from his succession retreated from residence at Whitehall which, on Mary's death, he offered as a home – though perhaps with a shrewd calculation of how it might underpin their succession – to Princess Anne and Prince George of Denmark. Just over a week after their coronation, William and Mary had elected to make Hampton Court, removed from the smog of London, their residence and thereafter they commuted to Whitehall only for Council meetings.[106] Not merely a residence for health and convenience, however, William and Mary sought to make the neglected Henrician palace a representation of their rule and a monument to Revolution.

While decorations and furnishings were arranged immediately to provide lodgings in the old Tudor apartments, Wren was commissioned to prepare plans for a new building suitable for a new centre of monarchical government.[107] It has been suggested that there was an early idea of demolishing the existing building and constructing an entirely new palace at the west end of Hampton Court. If so (and no drawings for such an ambitious project survive), costs must have quickly scotched the idea. But to a William concerned to emphasize continuity, there may have also been symbolic reasons for retaining much of the old palace and Henry VIII's Great Hall as its centrepiece. The final adopted plan combined novelty with this respect for Tudor history. As Simon Thurley has shown, the unprecedented symmetrical design of the new apartment for the king and queen was intended to recognize spatially the equality of William and Mary as joint rulers. Moreover, though Wren was influenced by both Versailles and the Louvre, 'it could be argued that Hampton Court sprang from a native school of design' for English country houses.[108]

During William's absence on the continent, Mary, overseeing the work in the royal apartment, decided to emulate Louis XIV in building a Water Gallery at the riverside as a private retreat.[109] The queen regularly inspected the works and was actively involved in plans as they developed. With her death in 1694, work ground to a halt, as William, first paralyzed by grief then preoccupied with the war and burdened by debt, had little time or resources to spare for Hampton Court.[110] The Peace of Ryswick, however, enabled building to recommence and the fire at Whitehall added impetus and urgency to the completion of the new work. In October 1699 it was reported that 'the king's apartment is finished' and William was able to focus on supervising decoration and furnishings.[111] The next spring the entire court moved to a palace that William perceived as his own Versailles and as a monument to his triumphant peace. Indeed, from 1700 the king received ambassadors at Hampton Court.[112] Though financial restraints prevented him doing so on equal terms, Hampton Court manifested William's determination to rival Louis XIV in architecture as well as on the battlefield.

William's decorations at Hampton Court also say much about how he wished the palace to represent his rule. We have discussed Kneller's large canvas of *William III on Horseback*, painted in 1701 for the Presence Chamber at Hampton Court as a celebration of the triumphant peace the king had attained.[113] Though different in its iconography, the painting recalls, of course, Van Dyck's equestrian portrait of Charles I painted for the gallery at St James's; and the decoration of the new royal apartments confirms an impression that William was seeking at Hampton Court to display his Stuart descent. In 1699, for example, William moved to his new palace several of the Mortlake tapestries commissioned by Charles I and selected from the royal collection predominantly dynastic portraits of Charles I, Elizabeth of Bohemia and the Duchess of York, Anne Hyde.[114] As we have noticed, William also returned to royal service for work on the king's staircase of his new palace the Catholic baroque artist Antonio Verrio, who had worked for both Charles II and James II. Though Verrio had not finished by the time of William's death, the substance of his commission is clear. Based on a design he had employed for Charles II's chapel at Windsor, Verrio planned a mural that glorified William as another Alexander the Great, attended by Victory and triumphing over the Caesars.[115] It has been argued that the figure of Julian the Apostate in the mural also represents William's stand for toleration and freedom, while that of Hercules replicates numerous references in the architecture of the palace (the twelve labours were painted on medallions in Fountain Court) and medals and emblems of the king.[116] Turning his skills to celebrate a Protestant and Whig triumph, Verrio executed 'a fitting and magnificent entrance to the king's apartments'.[117]

Hampton Court may have been intended and developed as a representation of William's kingship and victory, but for most of the reign while it was being built, it was not the king's actual residence. It may be that William never intended that it should be: that he planned to refurbish Hampton Court *as a representation* rather than a daily dwelling. For very soon after his accession William also showed interest in the acquisition of the Earl of Nottingham's house at Kensington to provide a London base, closer to the business still conducted at Whitehall but still then a village removed a couple of miles from the centre of the capital.[118] Having purchased it, the king commissioned Wren to improve and extend what was known as Kensington House. Pavilions were added and royal apartments, a Council chamber, a gallery and a chapel, and a fitting entrance was erected by new north and south wings that flanked the approach.[119] But, though not negligible, the changes were dictated more by pragmatism than a quest for grandeur. Kensington House – significantly not called at the time a palace – was 'designed to be simply a residence with no provision for entertainment, receptions or business'.[120] It appears that William and Mary may have chosen to separate their domestic quarters from the business and ceremony of monarchy. If so, that was to divide the two bodies of the king and to represent a different kind of monarchy in England from that of the dynastic predecessors he in other ways evoked.

Kensington House may have been William's attempt to provide in England a version of his beloved residence near Apeldoorn in the Netherlands, known as Het Loo. Commenced in 1684, Het Loo both made gestures to Versailles and yet asserted its modesty and domesticity as a house (again it was not called a palace) suitable for a substantial gentleman or burgher as much as a prince. John Dixon Hunt has suggested that Het Loo 'served as a model for William and Mary's post 1688 plans at Hampton Court' but, other than with respect to the gardens, it is as much Kensington that emulated the Dutch residence of which the king remained dearly fond and to which he transported pictures from the English royal collection.[121] It may seem inappropriate to discuss Het Loo in a study of the image of William and Mary in England. As well, however, as helping to understand the careful compromise between majesty and restraint that he sought in his English building, Het Loo was evidently known to, and fascinated, English subjects. There is evidence also that William and Mary favoured their English subjects having some acquaintance with their Dutch home; for it was the royal physician Walter Harris who, at the instigation of the queen, published with illustration *A Description of the King's Royal Palace and Garden at Loo*, in 1699.[122] Even making allowance for the fact that it was written by a doctor, Harris's description of William's palaces (and especially Het Loo) combines assurances of their stateliness and yet their freedom from the 'pleasures and vanities of the world' with the setting they provided for 'retirement and contemplation'.[123] In keeping with the latter, in his description Harris took the reader swiftly through the courtyard, hall and rooms of state to the gates that opened into what dominates the account, the garden. Harris provides a painstakingly detailed description of the king's and queen's gardens with their gravel walks, arbors, canals, fountains and statuary – including the Hercules Fountain behind the palace; but politics is by no means absent. Comparing the water works (a device that symbolized the control of nature) with the less impressive engines at Versailles and the 'ill stench' there to the 'sweet' water of Het Loo, the description is intended to convey 'a work of wonderful magnificence most worthy of so great a monarch', completed during the wars with France.[124] With their canals making the patterns of William's and Mary's cipher, in their magnificence, ingenuity and tranquillity, the gardens represent the Dutch king and queen, and the Dutch nation itself. In the second part of his book, the author moves from the gardens at Het Loo to 'A short account of Holland', the story of their bravery and William's victory at Namur. Holland, Harris informed his readers, was a 'paradise' of 'fine houses and fine gardens', a land of freedom, justice and security, of people 'grave and free from levity'.[125] Commending the 'good government' of the Dutch and their moderation in religion, Harris closed by urging Englishmen to be their close ally in the cause of defending the Protestant interest.[126] In Walter

Harris's description, Het Loo stands, I would suggest, as a synecdoche of the nation, its prince, its values and of a virtuous mean between 'gay decorations' of superstition and 'mean and homely addresses to divine majesty'.[127] It symbolized a religious and aesthetic moderation and a polity that secured liberty. And it did so as much in its perfectly ordered gardens as in the house itself.

'Buildings of themselves, however great and noble,' Harris asserted, 'do appear very deficient without the ornament and conveniences of a garden,' which 'conduces to the obtaining a cheerful tranquility of mind'.[128] William and Mary sought to construct in their new country such gardens and perhaps to express the ideology that Harris gestures to describing at Het Loo. When William and Mary came to the English throne, they had not yet completed the gardens at Het Loo, but they quickly turned their attention to the gardens at their planned residence at Hampton Court. As early as June 1689, William appointed a Superintendent of the Royal Gardens in England, William Bentinck, the Earl of Portland, who was his favourite and who had been principal adviser on gardens in the Netherlands.[129] The early plans for the gardens at Hampton Court were 'in . . . scale and ambition unprecedented'.[130] Under the supervision of the queen, a keen gardener, Daniel Marot designed for the area between the canal and palace what may have been the largest parterre built in the seventeenth century. As at Het Loo, elaborate water systems (including over 3,000 feet of new piping) manifested a control of nature, with a statue of Arethusa (one of the Hesperides) gesturing to England as a new paradise or blessed island, and to William as Hercules who was sent to the garden of the Hesperides to retrieve the sacred apples.[131] Mary's collection of rare plants from the east, Barbados and Virginia, as well as reflecting her personal passion, also signified the imperial reach of an England that was colonizing the furthest corners of the world and of a monarchy that sought to display imperium at Hampton Court.[132] From their new Privy Garden, the king and queen looked out over a parterre that symbolized a world ordered by their beneficent rule (fig. 57).

After Mary's death, William's absence and perhaps financial exigencies (the queen had spent £12,000 a year on the gardens at Hampton Court), there was less progress; but from 1698, William, as well as advancing plans for the palace, determined to complete the gardens which were always central to the overall design and, we might say, to the ideology of the palace.[133] After intensive planning, William extended his Privy Garden to the river with views and perspective over the grounds, as if to underline his own authority and sway, and installed fountains (traditional symbols of regality) and statues of Apollo (god of light), Vulcan, Pan and Orpheus, gods of spring and the harmony of nature, and symbols of contentment and harmonious government.[134] Spending as much on the grounds as the interior of the palace, William personally oversaw and amended the designs that reflected his 'personal vision': a vision that was as much political as it was architectural.[135] As critics as well as supporters of the Dutch horticultural

57 Leonard Knyff, *Hampton Court, c.* 1702.

style confirm, William and Mary's project to oppose Louis XIV's Catholicism and bid for universal monarchy 'can be and ... was read into their work as gardeners'.[136] As the designer and writer Stephen Switzer wrote of William: 'Gardening seems to be reserved amongst many other great actions ... of that prince to eternize his memory and make him appear to the world as great a gardener as he was soldier.'[137] In its gardens as much as its building Hampton Court was meant to, and was seen to, represent Revolution.

During the tumultuous events of the 1688 Revolution the symbolic power of the Great Seal as the sign of royal authority had been demonstrated with more than usual force. For as William approached the capital, on the night of 10 December, James summoned his Lord Chancellor to surrender the seal.[138] Taking it on a ferry from Westminster to Lambeth, James dropped it into the river, hoping, according to Lord Campbell, that 'he had sunk with it for ever the fortunes of the Prince of Orange'.[139] However, a fisherman recovered the seal in his net and delivered it to the Council.[140] It was later to become the template for William's own. In 1689, though, it was vital for the new king and queen to publicize their joint authority, and a seal was hastily prepared within a couple of weeks after their acceptance of the crown. The only recent model for the seal of the joint rulers William and Mary was that of Philip and Mary. The new seal went to lengths to figure shared sovereignty by depicting the two enthroned in coronation robes, with each resting a hand on the orb placed on a pedestal bearing the initials G. M. between them. Above them the arms of Nassau were added to the royal arms. On the reverse, the two are depicted mounted, in classical costume, the queen behind the equestrian figure of William carrying a short sword, with a view of the Thames and London behind them (fig. 58).[141] Though conventional, the inscription presenting them as

58 Seal of William and Mary, from Francis Sandford, *A Genealogical History of the Kings and Queens of England, and Monarchs of Great Britain*, 1707, p. 548.

'Fidei Defensores' doubtless resonated with the people in 1689. It underlined that quite unlike Philip and Mary, William and Mary (who also unlike their Tudor predecessors were mounted riding right) were protectors and restorers of Protestantism in all the kingdoms of Britain, and defenders of the faith against France over which, as always, the legend on the seal claimed rule.[142] The seal continued in use for some time after Mary's death in December 1694; for his seal as sole sovereign, William directly copied the images on that of James II on both the obverse and reverse, and so both advertised an uninterrupted succession and, as it were, erased his predecessor James who was again pressing his claim.[143]

Remarking on the unoriginality of William and Mary's seal, Wyon observed that 'no period of English history is so completely illustrated by contemporaneous medals'.[144] During a period of unprecedented continental wars it may not be surprising that many more medals than ever were issued. But, from even before William acceded to the throne, medals formed an important part of his political (as much as his military) campaign to secure England. In the summer of 1688 a medal was issued in Holland to commemorate the invitation from English nobles to William and Mary to protect Protestantism and liberties.[145] With its obverse of the Stadtholder and Mary, its legend ('For the Liberty and Faith of our ancestors') and its reverse with Religion trampling popery, the medal was clearly intended as part of the propaganda campaign to bring William to the throne (fig. 59). Indeed, as he set forth with his fleet from Helvoetoluys, another Dutch medal, depicting William in armour, between the figures of Providence and Valour, was issued with the inscription: 'May he triumph over the waves'.[146]

The medallic campaign was intensified as William reached English shores. At least seven medals were issued to mark his landing at Torbay on 4 November.[147] While some seem more directed at a European (or indeed Dutch) audience – and show the liberties of Europe upheld against the threats of Louis XIV's France[148] – most were clearly addressed to securing English support against James II, as William began his march to London. On the reverse of one medal (which on the obverse has a classical bust of Gulielmus Magnus armoured and laureate) a fleet is depicted landing, with, displayed prominently, the king's flagship which bore on its ensign the words 'The Protestant Religion and Liberties of England'.[149] Other medals made the argument that William had not come with force but by invitation to restore justice and show him welcomed by Britannia as James flees with his son (wearing on his head a windmill as a sign of his illegitimacy) and Jesuit confessor.[150] One medal makes a powerful visual case for the claim that became the theme of countless sermons: that of providential deliverance. On the obverse of this medal (which on the reverse depicts a Belgic lion coming to the rescue of religion and Magna Carta – the symbol of England's freedom), beneath an orange tree Britannia leans on a folio Bible placed on an altar and holds in her right

59 Hawkins, *Medallic Illustrations*, plate LXVII, 7.

hand a lance on top of which is the cap of Liberty. Though part of the inscription is in Dutch, the Latin legends ('Soli Deo Gloria' – 'For the glory of God alone' – and 'In Tuitionem Relig. Protes' – 'In defence of the Protestant religion') underline piety and altruism as the motives for Orange's expedition that has secured Britain.[151]

As the Convention met and debate raged over exactly what to do now William had arrived, several medals executed in Holland depicted the flight and abdication of King James. On the reverse of one (which on the obverse bears a bust of James with his hair tied to facilitate flight), a column destroyed by lightning from heaven and the legend suggest that it was both divine will and James's voluntary flight that made the way for William (fig. 60).[152] Another medal with the same obverse of James commemorates the offer of the crown to William in a simple juxtaposition of a broken oak and flourishing orange tree, with an inscription stating that it was the king's wilful flight that had conferred the crown on the prince.[153] The formal conferring of the crown by the Convention on 13 February was marked by an important medal by Anton Meybusch. On the reverse of an obverse bust of William alone, laureate and in armour, a figure representing him, in Roman costume, holds out the cap of Liberty to the three kneeling figures of England, Scotland and Ireland, who hold the British shield as a symbol of the kingdoms over which he is now to rule and to which (the inscription declares) he has restored freedom.[154] Where the theme here is Liberty secured, several other medals, some in cheap copper for broad circulation and one at least by an English medallist, celebrated the church restored and popery defeated. One, for example, by George Bower, who had designed medals for Charles II and James II, on the reverse of a double portrait of William and Mary, features a statue of the king on a pedestal holding under his left arm a

60 Hawkins *Medallic Illustrations,* plate LXIX, 3.

61 Hawkins *Medallic Illustrations,* plate LXX, 5.

model of the church while resting his right hand on a sword (fig. 61).[155] Above the king, rays from heaven illustrate the legend from Virgil's *Eclogues*, 'He comes down from lofty heaven', while on the edge an inscription describes the couple as a 'double constellation' that banished tyranny and superstition. In another example, depicting a church on a rock assailed by winds and seas, the inscription 'Immota Triumphans' alludes not only to the medal issued by Archbishop Sancroft, one of the seven bishops who defied James II, but also to the famous Marshall frontispiece to the *Eikon Basilike* of Charles I.[156] If here medallists were both figuring William as the restorer of the church and also representing him as the heir of the martyr, then they deserve a place of the first importance in the campaign to establish the legitimacy of the Revolution and Williamite kingship.

Nearly thirty medals were struck to commemorate the coronation and continue the propaganda for the Revolution. The official medal executed by Jan Roettier was struck in gold, silver and in lead for broad distribution among the spectators.[157] On the reverse of dual portrait busts of William and Mary, in a cloud Jove is depicted hurling thunderbolts against Phaethon who had wanted to drive his father the Sun-god's horses but who was thrown from his chariot. Though Jacobites were quick to read it as a symbol of William and Mary's wrongful assumption of their 'father's' power, the medal was meant to figure God evicting James Stuart before (as the legend read, 'that it may not all be consumed') he destroyed everything in his path.[158] Bower's medal for the occasion, almost exactly repeating the portraits of the king and queen, taking its legend from Ovid's *Metamorphoses*, a series of transformation stories, illustrated the myth of Perseus rescuing Andromeda from the serpent, an obvious allusion to William's saving Britannia from popery.[159] Other coronation medals, less technically accomplished, were issued to score polemical points. Some depicting an eagle ejecting from the nest one eaglet while retaining two others implicitly rejected the Jacobite claims made for Prince James and asserted the succession (through the daughters Mary and Anne) that had brought William to joint rule with his wife.[160] Some medallists, perhaps to press the divine authority of the royal couple over those who argued for *de facto* rule, depicted them with two bishops holding a crown above their heads.[161] Many repeated the propaganda themes of 1688 and represented William and Mary as providential deliverers and as protectors of justice, law and liberty.[162] As well as medals cast and issued to commemorate celebrations, several coronation medals were struck on the continent – in Germany as well as Holland – and we cannot be certain about their circulation in England. However, the repetition of conceits across Dutch and English medals (by Bower and Smeltzing, for example) at least suggests that the medals were commissioned as part of a European campaign to represent William as not only England's deliverer but as the defender of Europe from the oppressions of France. In one, perhaps the work of Jan Luder, with the legend 'Caetera Lustrabit' ('He will shed his light on the others'), a globe floating under a lustrous sun on the sea is inscribed London, Edinburgh, Dublin, Paris, as if to promise triumph over all and the defeat of Louis XIV.[163] In many cases, as well as emblems and allusions, medals promoted the brand image of the new king by arms, orange trees and oranges (for William) twined with roses – for Mary and England – thistles and Garter insignia, the advertisements of British monarchy.[164]

As we have seen, from Elizabeth I's reign onwards, and increasingly from the Restoration, medals were issued to mark major events or victories, such as naval action against the Dutch, the Peace of Breda or the foiling of the Rye House Plot.[165] In William and Mary's case, not only from the coronation onwards was every occasion taken as an opportunity to issue a medal, hundreds

of medals that did not commemorate any particular event were issued as tributes to the new king and queen and, in many cases of production in cheap
metals, circulated their image broadly. Again many of those struck in Holland
or Germany figured William now he was king of England, as another Joshua
fated to stop the sun – that is the Sun King Louis XIV – in its tracks.[166] The
passing of the Toleration Act in England in May 1689 gave medallists another
opportunity to celebrate the preservation of religion and liberty, and also to
conjoin England and Holland, the country where religious liberties had long
been established.[167] On one, with an orange and rose tree signifying the dynastic
alliance of the two, the legend 'she [Religion] flourishes in their garden' also
alluded to the Dutch and English gardens which, as we have seen, the royal pair
were developing as signifiers of Protestantism and liberty.[168]

It was about the same time as the passing of the Act that numerous tribute
medals – some to William, some to Mary, some to both – were issued in silver
and pewter and copper and lead, in England and Holland. While some of these,
such as Luder's tributes to Mary, bore emblems and legends from Scripture,
most simply depicted the monarchs with their titles as king and queen and
defenders of the faith.[169] The term 'simply' should not imply insignificance. At
a time when pamphlets were still firmly contesting their right, endless images
on cheap as well as more expensive medals (some the patterns for coins) of
William and Mary, crowned and bearing the sceptre, publicized continuity and
legitimacy in a medium where they were less easily challenged.[170] The sheer
volume of medallic images, in other words, may have helped to establish the
new king and to (literally) outface and efface James II and Mary of Modena.

As William began to prepare for a campaign to eradicate Jacobite opposition
in Ireland, and the Regency Act of 1690 was passed giving Mary authority to
exercise power in the king's absence, no fewer than eleven official medals were
issued to represent Mary as the effective ruler of the nation, while subtly
conveying that when William returned authority would be reinvested in him.[171]
Though Mary is shown on one medal as a lioness guarding three cubs representing the three kingdoms, the suggestion is that the lion will return; similarly
several medals figured the queen as the moon, perhaps a subtle reference to
Elizabeth I but a reminder, too, that Mary's was a lesser light only borrowed
from the sun – the English king.[172] Medals of the queen continued to be issued
throughout her regency until her death in 1694 and, as well as keeping her in
the public eye (some of the medals were copper), drew attention to her role in
defending the people. In July 1690, for example, medals depicting Mary with a
trident praised her prompt action in ordering the refitting of the navy after the
battle of Beachy Head.[173] Nearly two years later, as William again set off for the
continent, other medals were issued, as the legend ran, to show gratitude for
Mary's 'cheerful clemency and prudent government'.[174] Holding a palm branch
in one hand and resting her other on a rudder, against the background of a sea

with ships and a high fence, the queen is represented as the defender of England from invasion and the mild ruler at home. Her death in January 1695 was marked by the execution of nearly forty medals representing her as God's handmaiden, a saint, the delight and deliverer of the nation, as a pious princess translated to heaven, but lovingly remembered for her virtues.[175] For the first time in English history, funeral medals cast in copper and lead as well as silver were issued 'as cheap memorials of the queen ... for distribution at the time that the body of Mary was lying in state' at Whitehall, and on its interment in Westminster Abbey.[176]

While scores of medals kept Mary in the public eye and praised her peaceful regimen, an unprecedented outpouring marked virtually every moment in William's military campaigns, first in Ireland and then on the continent. Medals issued in June 1690 as he set sail with his fleet depicted the king as an eagle, a symbol both of imperial power and the triumph of the gospel.[177] The king's major victory at the Battle of the Boyne occasioned several popular medals, some showing the decisive cavalry charge led by William himself, in the background of the triumphant figure of Bellona, goddess of war.[178] As well as signifying William's bravery and, like campaign reports, making full capital out of the victory, medal illustrations and inscriptions announced the Irish defeated and Dublin (to which James II fled) open to conquest. When the king took the Irish capital, the next month medals represented the entry into Dublin as a liberation, William with one hand on an altar presenting a cap of liberty to kneeling Hibernia or as Hercules destroying the hydra of rebellion.[179]

One of the Boyne medals vaunted on its inscription on a bust 'William III King of Great Britain, over James and Louis triumphant'.[180] As we have seen, triumph over Louis was to take more than a battle in Ireland, involve political as well as military struggle, and even then elude the king. What has not been remarked is how medals, as well as military rewards, were central to that political struggle: to William's quest for supply and the support of his people, especially during setbacks and periods of hardship. When the king crossed to the Netherlands early in 1691 to begin his campaigns and was welcomed with a triumphal entry into The Hague, as well as the multitude of Dutch commemorations, medals by F. D. Winter and bearing the initials of the Master of the Mint, Thomas Neale, were issued in England in lead as well as silver and pewter.[181] At The Hague in February, a Congress of the allies (celebrated in German medals which may have circulated in England) assembled to plan concerted military resistance to Louis XIV. As French advances continued, F. D. Winter designed a medal contrasting the French with the English king. Where Louis is presented as a 'decrepit oppressor', William is figured beneath the beneficent rays of heaven (an emperor with a Christian standard and cap of Liberty), as protector and 'successful liberator' expelling the harpies of discord from Britain.[182] If the claim to have established harmony at home was more wishful thinking than reality, the implied triumphalism was misplaced at a time when French forces had just captured Mons. But, not least perhaps because Louis XIV was doing the same, Dutch and English medallists marked every and any small advance so as to sustain morale and (we would say) 'talk up' the progress of the campaign. Accordingly the relief of Liège and Coni were celebrated in medals depicting the sun, the emblem of Louis XIV, fading, while further Irish victories – at Aghrim, Athlone and Sligo – were widely published on medals as victories over the French who are shown fleeing before the might of Hercules, the most common figure for William.[183]

The end of the war in Ireland certainly removed the immediate Jacobite military threat to William's throne, and the dozen medals that celebrated it were probably aimed at persuading Stuart supporters to accept that the game was up.[184] However, James II did not cease his efforts to sustain support for his cause and, in exile at St Germain, was well placed to secure French assistance for any planned invasion or coup. It was likely for this reason that so many medals were commissioned to proclaim what was not a major but a symbolic victory over the French fleet at La Hogue in May 1692.[185] For, albeit the odds had favoured the English and Dutch, the destruction of French ships enabled the allies to claim supremacy at sea and reassured English subjects of the strength of the nation's naval defences. Among the dozens of medals cast and distributed (some by Queen Mary herself) taunting Louis XIV over his claim to empire over the seas, some, such as those designed in England by Roettier and Winter, represented the victory as a larger triumph, a toppling of the French power in Europe.[186]

The medallists who depicted the French cock fleeing to land before the mighty English lion were soon brought up short by a major French victory on land in the successful siege of Namur, which was commemorated by many French victory medals that mocked William III and the allies who had stood as powerful spectators on the opposite riverbank as the citadel fell.[187] In similar commemorations of his success at the Battle of Stein Kirk, Louis taunted Orange by appropriating emblems used on English and Dutch medals, in what was an international medallic competition as well as military contest.[188] At a time when the fortunes of war were not favouring the allies, medallists working for the king had to extract all the propaganda advantage they could from even minor advances. In July 1693, for example, Winter designed two medals (both issued in lead) to mark what was at best a draw at the Battle of Landen.[189] Though the French under Marshal Luxembourg took heavy losses, their eventual victory made the inscription on the English medal (which claimed French forces, inferior in courage, were 'conquered') outright propaganda that masked an actual defeat.

During the campaign season of 1694, allied medallists had little to celebrate but still medals were issued, publicizing the bombardment of Dieppe and Le Havre, Dunkirk and Calais, some again extravagantly claiming that the French were emasculated by such attacks.[190] Indeed, one medal, struck in Germany, but probably in international circulation, reminded recipients that the allied cause was the cause of Protestant Christianity and that, as providence favoured them, eventual victory was assured.[191] It came, as we have seen, at last with the recapture of Namur by William and the Confederate forces in August 1695, a victory commemorated by a flood of medals. William (always in armour) was represented as Europe's avenging warrior against France. Such victory medals proclaimed his personal courage and advertised him as the new champion of the world whose arms flew on the flag of fame.[192] Issued in copper and lead and with at least one variant (and probably several of those whose artists remain anonymous) by an English designer, medals for the first major defeat inflicted on the forces of the Sun King, the siege of Namur, joined the panegyrics and broadsides to represent to the people their own king as a heroic Hercules whose labours had accomplished success.[193]

Victory at Namur went some way to raising William's stock at home as well as abroad. What brought further support and sympathy was the attempted assassination which branded Jacobite opposition as treason and enabled William to be represented as the embodiment of patriotism. Like poets and pamphleteers, medallists sought to extract every iota of propaganda value from the plot and the National Association for defence of the king proposed by parliament in its wake.[194] A silver medal by the Dutch engraver Jan Bosham made close reference to the conspiracy of Sir George Barclay to kill the king, which is shown as being thwarted by the special intervention of providence.[195] On the obverse of a reverse of conspirators restrained by heaven, before a bust of William a shield bearing the name (in Hebrew) Jehovah carries the legend: 'He is not injured whom I protect' (fig. 62). In contrast to the providential protection of the English king,

62 Hawkins, *Medallic Illustrations*, plate CIV, 1.

various medals figured Louis XIV and James II (who is visually foregrounded as the instigator of the plot) bribing agents with money and consorting with priests, as Herod and Pilate had combined to murder Christ.[196] As medals in lead and copper were distributed announcing the National Association and representing William as another David, recipients were encouraged to join, as the inscription on one put it, 'to preserve so precious a life'.[197]

The Peace of Ryswick, signed on 20 September, was commemorated on over two dozen medals struck or cast in England and Europe. While most of the signatories to the peace (Louis XIV as well as the allies) issued medals, the greatest number were dedicated to or featured William III. On several of these the bust of William, rather than (as commonly before) armoured, is shown as laureate – the sign of victory – with a wreath of rose and olive branches or with corn growing in a discarded helmet: a symbol of plenty, the fruit of peace.[198] In some instances medals explicitly claim the peace as an English victory: that, for example which features on the reverse of a handsome bust of William, a lion crowned with the British crown and resting its paw on the globe of Europa, above an inscription 'The Glory of England under King William III 1697', proclaims *imperium* as much as peace.[199] Though warfare had been suspended, Williamite medallists continued the battle for supremacy and countered the boasts made by their counterparts in the French Academy that France had brought about Ryswick 'by the valour of her arms and the justice of her nations'.[200]

In England it was proposed to commemorate the peace by erecting arches of triumph in William's honour.[201] When the king refused the idea, medallists substituted for the pageants that many had wished to see. Three very elaborate medals, issued in pewter and copper, depicted on the obverse William, holding an olive branch and crowned by Victory, conducted in a chariot through a succession of arches of triumph, bearing abbreviated inscriptions that announce the king's virtues and achievements. At the foot of the image an inscription reads: 'Amidst the acclamations of the people' (fig. 63).[202] On the reverse, inside a wreath of olive, the medal announces: 'he delivered his country, acquired a kingdom for himself, preserved his allies, bridled licentiousness, and restored peace to the world, 1697'. Executed by Nicolas Chevalier of Amsterdam, the subject and inscription of the medal suggest an English audience and the issue of copper and lead versions an intended popular one. In England itself, the assistant engraver to the Mint, John Croker, executed and issued in copper as well as silver a medal with, on the reverse of a laureate bust of the king, a simple image: of Britannia with her trident and shield seated by a broken yoke and a book (probably standing for the Bible) with an olive branch of peace lying on it. The one-word Latin inscription 'To the Restorer' is Britannia's – the nation's – expression of gratitude to their monarch.[203]

Though the Peace of Ryswick had finally secured French recognition of William's right to the throne, it by no means ended Jacobite opposition:

63 Hawkins, *Medallic Illustrations*, plate CIX, 2.

James II, as well as publishing a protest against the treaty and seeking to gather support for a Stuart restoration, also commissioned medals and medalets affirming the legitimacy and rights of his nine-year-old son, which were evidently sent in large numbers to London.[204] Not least because, like Jacobite written propaganda, some of these medals suggested that the Stuarts were the national dynasty (and Orange an interloping foreigner), Williamite medals took pains to brand him as an English sovereign.[205] One, which was part of a projected series of medals illustrating the history of William and Mary to rival those issued by Louis XIV, featured (on the obverse of a reverse of the royal arms of Britain with the Nassau motto 'Je Maintiendray') beneath rays from heaven a fruit-laden orange bush with the legend 'The golden tree bears golden fruit.'[206] As well as alluding to the favour of providence and the prospect with peace of a golden age of plenty, the medal was, at a time when talk of a future restoration of the prince was in the air, making the Orange brand English (the tree was set in a distinctly English landscape of gentle hills) and royal.[207] In medals as much as in pamphlets, William's campaign to establish his legitimacy was – necessarily – waged to the end of his reign.

III

For all the large increase in the issue and circulation of medals, in base metals as well as fine, coins remained (as they still remain) the medium that most distributed the royal image to the people, elite and common. From the beginning of William's reign, for all the distraction of settling and fighting the French in Ireland, the government paid attention to the coin of the realm. In May 1689 a parliamentary committee was appointed to consider abuses of the coin and efforts were made to prevent the exportation of gold and silver.[208] Even from his camp at Finglas near Dublin in June, William issued a proclamation putting a stop to debased money and returned to the topic in several further proclamations and speeches to parliaments.[209] In November 1695 the king urged parliament to address the counterfeiting, clipping and debasement of the coin and, consequently, the clipped silver coin was recalled and a new coinage resolved upon.[210] Measures were taken to furnish the Mint with a supply of bullion by banning exports except for the supply of the royal armies.[211] William III clearly kept a close watch on the recoinage, raising further questions about problems in his speech to parliament in October 1696.[212] Though there were continuing difficulties, including an inadequate supply of bullion to the Mint, a 'great recoinage' replaced decrepit and debased English hammered coin with milled money of due weight to value.[213] To produce it, auxiliary mints at Bristol, Chester, Exeter, Norwich and York were provided with dies from London.[214] Millions of the new coins were struck, especially crowns, half-crowns and sixpences.[215]

Like earlier kings before him, William evidently regarded a sound currency not only as necessary for trade, international exchange and crucially war finance, he regarded the quality of bullion as intrinsic to his authority and reputation. In 1694 no less a figure than the royal chaplain and future Bishop of Ely, William Fleetwood, in a sermon against clipping had reminded his auditors that it was kings who were trusted with the care of coinage and that it was their heads that did 'publicly . . . vouch the true intrinsic worth of every piece'.[216] After the recoinage was under way, a minister took the reform of the currency as a step towards the larger spiritual reformation that William championed. Just as, he preached, the corruption of coin was allied to the sinful corruption of the nation, when the government resolved to reject debased coin, the king's image was restored again and the prospect was opened for 'greater purity in church and state'.[217] In sermons like these William's recoinage represented his campaign for moral reformation.

Turning to the representation of the king *on* the coins, on the gold coins (and early silver half-crowns) a large single shield replaced the four crosswise shields of the previous two reigns and later incorporated the lion of Nassau in a central frame, along with the royal initials 'WM' interlinked.[218] On the obverse, high-relief double busts closely replicated that on the coronation medal and may, like that, have been designed by the Roettiers. The importance of the double portrait to the representation and establishment of the joint rule saw it replicated on all early coins – groats, pennies, tin halfpennies and farthings as well as silver coins.[219] On the lower denominations, the reverse of coins often depicted Britannia seated holding an olive branch and spear, and so directly associated the royal couple with what had become since 1672 a national symbol. On Mary's death, the coinage had to be redesigned and a fine laureate bust of William, of the type seen on later medals, replaced the ubiquitous double portrait with a cruciform shield (without the 'WM' cipher) returning on silver coins, while copper halfpennies and farthings continued the image of Britannia.[220]

The great recoinage clearly presented an opportunity for new designs but, though there are minor variations in the portrait busts of the king, the new engraver John Croker largely followed the work of Roettier and no major changes were made.[221] From 1695, William's coins closely resembled those of Charles II, and it may not be accidental that for his solo bust he adopted the pose to the right favoured by Charles rather than the portrait bust turned left that was depicted on most of James II's coins. Perhaps most important of all to our review of his representation, where earlier monarchs had had to tolerate the coin of their predecessors circulating for some time into their reign, William III saw some seven millions of silver money coined and new copper (to replace the earlier tin) halfpennies and farthings produced in such quantities that there was no need for additional coppers to be minted during the reign of Queen Anne.[222] Both in sheer volume and in the weight and worth of his reformed currency, William's image was widely represented on the coins of his reign.

Fashion also brought the royal image of William and Mary into the homes of their subjects in another material form: that of porcelain. The earliest souvenir plate bearing a royal image that I have seen is that of Elizabeth I.[223] From Charles II's reign onwards, plates and mugs with a portrait bust of the monarch appear more frequently and a series of tiles illustrated the Popish Plot, but it is with the reign of William and Mary that souvenir artefacts of the monarch became commonplace.[224] Mary introduced to the court a fashion for collecting porcelain and Delftware, which she displayed at Hampton Court.[225] As so often the fashion spread from the court and, at the popular level, blended with that increasing desire to own some representation of the ruler that had earlier fuelled the vogue for engraved and mezzotint portraits of kings and queens. Jugs, dishes and plates depicting William and Mary together with their initials, some with the Batavian lion, the symbol of Orange, survive in English (and Dutch) collections, a residue of what was probably a large production.[226] One scholar discovered that half of the dishes known as 'blue dash chargers' depicted the king and queen and recorded at least twenty of the two together and sixty of William alone, most probably after Mary's death (fig. 64a).[227] Many, showing the king crowned and on horseback, were based on prints. Less fine in execution and detail, numerous surviving plates and some mugs are decorated with rough portraits of the king and queen, and it has been estimated that they must have been made 'in enormous quantities'.[228] Such artefacts do not only provide important (and still largely unexplored) evidence of the representation of the royal couple in the everyday objects of decoration and consumption.[229] They at least suggest that, despite what has been written about the discontent at a

64a William and Mary plate, London, c. 1689–95.

foreign prince and burdensome war, and for all the absence of statues commemorating them, William and Mary could be the objects of popular affection, at least in some quarters, as champions of Protestantism.

Today, William III is not one of the kings of England most immediately recognized. We may therefore understandably be tempted to conclude that he was unsuccessful in superintending and distributing his image. As we have seen, the king was not renowned as a patron of artists and sat infrequently for his portrait. However, on medals, coins and everyday household objects, as well as in engravings and mezzotints, the portraits of William and Mary, then of William alone, were more broadly disseminated than those of any predecessor. In the circumstances of the 1690s, those less aesthetically elevated forms were probably more important than portraits. For at a time when James II and his supporters were campaigning for a Stuart restoration, and (as we saw) commissioning and sending to England engraved and medallic images of the royal family in exile, the distribution through everyday objects of representations of William as the legitimate king could hardly have been more important.

The sheer numbers of surviving medals and porcelain objects bearing images of William and Mary may suggest that the couple could have been more popular than is usually assumed.[230] As important, they may help us to

64b William plate, London, c. 1690–1710.

understand how a ruler who had only a tenuous claim to the throne, and whose legitimacy was doubted by large sections of the population, not only remained on the throne but was able to raise vast sums in taxation to fight long costly campaigns against France. William III secured his throne in large measure by military strength, alliances and naval defences. However, his tenure depended on the Jacobites not building wider support for their opposition or a planned coup, and on his subjects – ordinary folk as much as the gentry and others who made up the political nation – acknowledging his right to rule. In that process, though it is hard to quantify, the circulation of the image of William as king, with the arms of Nassau, orange trees, and with legends and inscriptions proclaiming his divinity, piety, justice and protection, may have played a significant part.

It has recently been suggested that towards the end of the seventeenth century, the age of the great dynastic regal portrait was passing: that, as portrait artists resorted to standardized formats (in David Piper's words, 'the polite mask of the Augustan age'), royal portraits themselves became more bourgeois, more ordinary.[231] In a changed commerce of culture where taste was increasingly being determined by new aristocratic and gentry collectors, as importantly in a political culture of broader public participation, prints and medals, though they have received little attention from modern scholars, may have been some of the most effective genres and forms for communicating representations of the king. By the criteria of connoisseurship which favours the master portrait or the bronze over the everyday object, William III may not have succeeded 'in imprinting his image on our collective consciousness'.[232] But his and Mary's image, circulating in the material culture, was on the wall, on the shelf or table, and in the homes of the subjects who more than ever were beginning to share authority with the monarch. It was in the gardens, interior decorations, and on pottery, on medals and coins as much as in portraits, that the Revolution was visually represented and the claims of Williamite legitimacy argued and asserted.

CHAPTER 11

A KING OFF THE STAGE

I

For all the importance of the representation of regality in words and images, the personal performance of kingship remained vital to the exercise of rule. On ritual occasions, the public and personal bodies of the king became one: the mysteries of majesty were given a human face and the person of the monarch was endowed by ritual forms with the divine authority of the office. If ritual and performance were always essential arts of majesty for any ruler, they were still more vital at times of crisis (such as the Reformation or at the Restoration) or in cases where the claim, or the legitimacy, of a particular sovereign was contentious or disputed. Henry VII went out of his way to be seen by his subjects, his long progress north being undertaken to establish his position not least by showing himself to his subjects as king.[1] James I, as another first ruler of a new dynasty, and Charles II, reassuming a throne after a decade of republic, both performed in elaborate coronation entries that placed them in a series of mythological and historical tableaux which helped to construct, as well as represent, their authority as part of the customs and traditions of the realm.[2] As we have seen, Charles II had an acute sense that, after the civil war and republic, it was more important than ever for the monarch to perform on the public stage: to be accessible and affable – most of all to be seen. Whatever his other failings James as Duke of York had shown some skill in public relations and, though he did not process from the Tower to Westminster Abbey, the king ensured that his coronation day was a splendid affair accompanied with public rejoicing; and he commissioned, as had his brother, a lavish souvenir account of the occasion.[3]

There has been surprisingly little study of the rituals of kingship in the reign of William and Mary. As well as the larger historiographical neglect of the period, the explanation may lie in the often repeated remarks about William's character, reserve and lack of any common touch, or in the assumption that the king was more concerned with military power than symbols and rituals. In reality, William had taken pains over his image and performance as well as his military tactics from the moment he embarked on his expedition to England. The choice of 5 November for his landing at Torbay was probably elected to underpin his claim to be the deliverer of Protestantism from popery. William's entry into Exeter on a milk-white palfrey, accompanied by plumed riders and guards, gestured towards an apocalyptic triumph as well as a pageant of state, as the royal banner proclaimed 'God and the Protestant Religion'.[4] From Exeter, where one narrator compared his entry to 'the triumph of the Caesars', William's march towards London appeared more like a progress than an invasion. Holding court at cities and towns along the way, visiting magnates such as the Earl of Pembroke at Wilton, and responding to the crowds that gathered to greet him, on his journey towards London, William grew in authority and, even before the Convention had met, began to appear like a king. At Salisbury, for example, having entered the city 'attended with the mayor and aldermen in their formalities', he addressed the people telling them 'that he came (being invited) to restore their liberties and preserve their religion'.[5] Before he made his entrance into the capital, William manoeuvred to ensure that James II left, so avoiding the risk of another surge of popularity for the Stuart that might have undermined his triumphant progress. Indeed, the important contrast between a defeated king's departure and Orange's victorious arrival was spelled out in a broadside 'account of the arrival of the high and mighty Prince William Henry of Orange and Nassau at St James's with the king's retirement down the river'.[6] As he merely mentioned in passing James's slipping away to Rochester, the author gave a full description of William leaving Windsor with his magnificent train of nobles to arrive for a sumptuous entertainment at Sion House. Thence with his cavalcade and in a calash drawn by six Flemish horses, Orange entered London, flanked by mounted gentlemen on each side. When the train passed Arlington House (the old seat of Charles II's leading minister) it was met at Hyde Park by the sheriffs of London and Middlesex in their coaches who, 'with a great train of gentlemen on horseback', attended the prince through Knightsbridge to St James's.[7] With a white cloak over his shoulders and preceded by the sheriffs bearing a white wand, William was conducted through the park to the palace where he was greeted with cries of joy and welcome, and with bells and bonfires. If not quite the ceremonial entry of a crowned king, William's progress to and through the capital represented – and was surely orchestrated to be – a ritual form of legitimation of his expedition, a display of his popularity, and an advertisement of his virtues and qualifications for kingship.

The proclamation of William's kingship was of more than visual significance, for in this case the traditional ceremony of proclaiming the new monarch at key symbolic points in the city made appear routine what had been a highly contentious departure from the succession and constitution.[8] In an important respect it was not a routine event, as a Convention parliament was in session and involved in the rituals of proclamation. As the official account informs us, having presented William and Mary with an instrument declaring them king and queen and having received their acceptance, preceded by their Speakers, the Lords and Commons came to Whitehall Gate where the Earl Marshal was waiting with the heralds. There, the trumpets having sounded three times, the Garter King at Arms read the proclamation which was 'answered by several shouts of the people', affirming the king.[9] From Whitehall, with the High Constable and Head Bailiff of Westminster clearing the way, preceded by trumpets and pursuivants, the four heralds and Sergeant at Arms, with the Garter carrying the proclamation, led a procession of all the peers and MPs to Temple Bar. There the traditional ceremony of the heralds requesting that the gate be opened to them symbolized the new king's and queen's authority, which was proclaimed a second time. At Cheapside, near where the old cross had once stood, the proclamation was made again before a final pronouncement at the Royal Exchange. In this familiar ritual, William and Mary's authority was not only represented in a time-honoured form, it was invested with the symbolic freight of city locales and customs, and acknowledged by 'the vast multitudes of spectators who thronged the streets, balconies and windows', and who 'filled the air with loud and repeated shouts . . . of joy'. By sergeants in 'rich coats of the royal arms' and by the citizens of London, a foreign usurper and his wife were presented and represented as England's lawful king and queen.

The emphasis on normality, tradition and history characterized William and Mary's preparations for their coronation. On 16 March the king and queen published, in gothic script with an initial letter containing their cipher, a proclamation regarding their coronation in language that seemed crafted to obscure the revolutionary events that had taken place. Referring to the 'ancient customs and usages of this realm' and the feudal tenures that conferred privileges and duties on their holders at coronations, the king and queen proclaimed their commitment to following 'times precedent' in hearing petitions from tenants of the crown.[10] As well as confirming custom and privilege, the proclamation advertised William as an English king, to whom many subjects were bound by tenurial ties and to whom, as a feudal overlord rather than an elected interloper, obligations and fealty were due. At a time of ferment in the nation about the question of allegiance to James, about the legality of the Convention, and about the unresolved issues in church and state, traditional forms characterized plans for the coronation which would (it was hoped) settle William and Mary on their thrones.

'It is a near certainty', Lois Schwoerer concluded, 'that the new government looked to the coronation to assist in legitimating the Revolution and in reassuring domestic and foreign observers of the government's stability'; and it was for this reason that preparations were made with more than usual expedition.[11]

Though the unusual constraints of time led to some slips, considerable care was taken by William and Mary and their councillors to make the succession an opportunity to appropriate traditional forms for a new set of royal priorities and programmes. Henry Compton, Bishop of London, who was charged with arranging the ceremony, carefully advertised the differences between the new rulers and their Catholic predecessor. Beyond simply restoring the Anglican communion service which James had omitted, he gave a more noticeable place in the ceremony to the Bible, which had been the symbol of reformed Protestantism since the reign of Henry VIII and which had featured prominently in Queen Elizabeth's coronation entry pageant.[12] Accordingly, the Bible was placed among the regalia presented to the king and queen, carried in the procession, and re-presented to them after they were crowned as the symbol of rulers who had rescued Protestantism. Careful steps were also taken to express ritually the delicate compromise by which William and Mary had been appointed as dual monarchs while royal authority was invested in him alone. A special chair was supplied for Mary next to the St Edward's chair in which kings or queens had traditionally been crowned; but in other minor ceremonies precedence was given to William, who alone was girt with the sword and who was crowned first.

The coronation ceremony also cleverly negotiated the need to evoke history but to recognize changes. Prayers for Queen Catherine of Braganza connected the ritual to the reign of Charles II, whose effigy was on display in Westminster Abbey, and elided James II and Mary of Modena.[13] But the new realities of a parliamentary monarchy were also repeated in the presence of MPs at the anointing and William's inviting them to dinner afterwards in the Exchequer Chamber. The oath taken, what one described as the 'very touchstone and symbol' of the government was also revised to emphasize that the laws were not the king's and that he was obliged to govern in accordance with them.[14]

Preparations for the coronation apparently involved consideration of an audience beyond the capital as well as the many spectators who were expected to witness the event. On 5 April a licence was granted for the publication of *The Form of Prayers and Services Used in Westminster Abbey at the Coronation of the Kings and Queens*.[15] By not mentioning William or Mary by name and not remarking the unusual dual monarchy, the text again veiled the differences and ruptures that had been brought about by the Revolution. Similarly the re-publication in 1689, by the royal cosmographer, of John Ogilby's description of the coronation of Charles II invoked happy memories of Restoration and implicitly suggested the continuity of Anglican kingship under William and Mary.[16] *The Form of the Proceeding to the Coronation*, authorized by the Earl Marshal, listed the order of the procession of the members of the royal household, Privy Councillors, peers and bishops.[17] First of the royal family, Prince George of Denmark led those carrying the king's and queen's staff, sceptre, orb and sword, along with the Bible. Sixteen barons of the Cinque Ports carried a canopy over William and Mary, who were supported respectively by the Bishops of Winchester and Bristol. As much as a coronation, the procession manifested the Anglican church restored to its authority in the state.[18]

In this case, the moment in the service of recognition (of a king and queen who had not succeeded normally) was of particular importance. Conducted by the Bishop of London, it was 'concluded with a mighty shout of all the people present', before the litany and communion service.[19] As Burnet, Bishop of Salisbury, preached on 2 Samuel 23: 3–4 ('The rock of Israel spoke to me'), their majesties were reported as 'hearing the same with great attention'.[20] After the investiture and benediction, the king and queen kissed the bishops, then received homage as the Treasurer of the Household threw coronation medals for the assembled. After being arranged in their robes of purple velvet, and crowned, the royal couple processed back to Westminster, their cavalcade in the same order as before, with 'an infinite number of spectators . . . expressing their great joy by shouts and acclamations'.[21] At dinner, as was customary, Charles Dymock performed the ceremony of the challenge, offering – this time perhaps with apprehension – to take on any who denied their claim to be rightful rulers. For all the bonfires, fireworks and healths drunk, there were many who still doubted their right.

No magnificent illustrated folio like Ogilby's for Charles II commemorated the coronation of William and Mary. But a somewhat crudely illustrated broad-side 'licensed according to order' was sold by George Croom at the Blue Ball in Thames Street. Beneath an illustration of the procession, ending with the virtu-ally unrecognizable figures of William and Mary under a canopy, the *Description of the Ceremonial Proceedings at the Coronation of their Most Sacred Majesties* printed a shortened version of the Earl Marshal's order of procession and the service in the abbey (fig. 65).[22] If, in some respects, the woodcut appears from an earlier period as well as being unsophisticated and crude (especially compared to the fine engravings that illustrated Ogilby), it is possible that that may have been the point. As well as a display of magnificence and of a restoration of tradi-tional forms, the coronation of William and Mary (incorporating, we recall, MPs at the service of anointing) was – and perhaps more than usual needed to be – an occasion which involved the people in the rituals of recognition, legiti-mation and sanctification. In early modern England rituals were always part of a culture of legitimation; but in the case of a king and queen elected to their throne, ritual was especially needed to proclaim – and hopefully build – national support for a coup and to ease troubled consciences. Intended to give 'the impression of unanimity and wholehearted support for the new regime' and to integrate the Dutch and Calvinist king into the nation's dynastic tradition and Anglican ritual, the coronation combined traditional forms with changes that subtly acknowledged a shift in the nature of monarchy itself.[23]

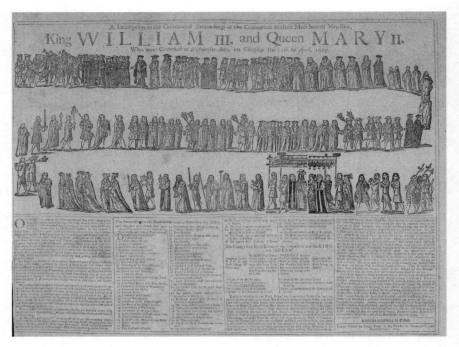

65 *A Description of the Ceremonial Proceedings at the Coronation of their Most Sacred Majesties, King William III. and Queen Mary II. . . , 1689.*

It would appear that, probably with official encouragement, ritual celebrations of the coronation were not confined to the event itself or to the capital and that in some cases their polemical purposes were overt. In Bath, for example, on 11 April, the coronation day, 'a great number of the best quality of the city . . . in testimony of the greatest joy, satisfaction and gratitude for their happy deliverance from popery and slavery by their Majesties universal care and protection', organized their own ceremony.[24] In a procession led by one hundred young men with swords, two hundred virgins with crowns and sceptres carried banners with the mottoes 'God Save King William and Queen Mary and Let Their Enemies Perish' and 'This Is a Joyful Day'. Behind them twenty-four women dressed as Amazons marched with a banner proclaiming 'Rather Than Lose the Day We'll Fight'. After a march twice round the town with arms and colours before spectators who had flocked in from the surrounding villages, the party sat down to a sumptuous banquet followed by dancing. The expenses were 'great'; but the civic authorities had evidently felt them justified and had clearly wanted to display their allegiance – and perhaps unite behind the new regime. Though Narcissus Luttrell noted celebrations at other places, such as Coventry, Exeter, Lyme, Oxford and Worcester, we do not know what form they took.[25] It seems likely, however, that several provincial corporations (as well as London) took coronation day as an occasion for ritual and communal affirmation of the Revolution and for bonding divided communities together in support of the new government.

After the coronation, there were for some years few ritual occasions in which William appeared on the stage of state before his subjects. In part his decision to leave Whitehall for Hampton Court and Kensington Palace somewhat isolated him.[26] But most of all the urgent need to tackle opposition in Ireland and Scotland necessitated the king's immediate departure and, while she managed affairs at home with quiet efficiency, Mary was not inclined, in her husband's absence, to pageantry or display. An aversion in both the king and queen to triumphant celebrations may have been a miscalculation. As we have seen, the Williamite regime issued official morale-boosting military reports on the campaigns in Ireland and on the continent, and an unprecedented number of medals; but military victories were not marked by festivals or civic entries that might have made the wars appear less remote, and made them more a national rather than (as critics charged) a personal campaign. Local initiatives add to the sense that William might have gained from staging a number of triumphs or entries on return from his campaigns. From an engraving we know that on 5 November 1690 Southwark erected a triumphal arch in William's honour.[27] As well as commemorating his landing at Torbay two years before, the arch was also a tribute to the king's defeat of James II at the Boyne. Decked with orange trees, banners proclaiming the nation's deliverance and prosperity, and a picture of the Boyne, the arch appears like one of that series of pageant arches through which Charles II had passed on his coronation entry into London; and crowds are shown gathered round it, suggesting that it was the site of at least local festivity and celebration. We recall too that, even after his victory over the French at Namur, William declined a triumphal entry on his return, leaving medallists to design a representation of what did not in reality take place.[28] Whatever his own motives for eschewing rituals and triumphs, it would appear that his subjects might have welcomed them and William might have enjoyed an opportunity to connect with and be fêted by his people.

Such an impression is confirmed by the obvious interest in England in the magnificent triumph that was staged by the Dutch for William's return to his home country in 1691 for the first time since 1688, to orchestrate the campaign against Louis XIV. There were several accounts published in English of the triumph which, albeit vicariously, involved English readers in a spectacular ritual. *An Exact Relation of the Entertainment of His Most Sacred Majesty William III . . . at The Hague* narrated for readers William's entry on 26 January over the Loosduyn bridge, with a vast multitude of spectators greeting his arrival.[29] Having noted the pictures of the king and queen on the Stadthouse, the author described the series of triumphal arches through which William passed, with their tableaux, emblems and inscriptions referring to his victories as Prince of Orange and King of England. The *Relation* closes with a description of the fireworks display in which the crowned cipher of William was flanked by the figure of Hercules, whose labours were here represented as William's achievement in settling government, advancing the interests of the people and establishing religion and liberty.[30] Two other accounts provided richer detail and illustrations. *The Triumph Royal Containing A Short Account of the Most Remarkable Battles . . . and Famous Achievements of the Princes of the House of Nassau . . . Described in the Triumphal Arches . . . Erected at The Hague in Honour of William III* was a translation of a work published first in Dutch and French.[31] Containing sixty-two copperplate engravings of the arches with detailed explanation of the emblems, *The Triumph* was dedicated to Queen Mary who was, along with English readers, assured that William exceeded Roman heroes in his accomplishments and 'had no other aim in all his enterprises but [to] advance the glory of the king of kings'.[32] In words that were clearly intended to answer opponents of the Revolution, the dedication asserted that William was 'never capable of unjust ambition or desire of rule' and only motivated by a desire to free Europe from tyranny.[33] As the epistle to the reader further explained, William had restored liberties and religion to England and Ireland, as he had earlier to the United Provinces, and the 'glorious . . . spectacle' staged for him expressed the gratitude of many princes and nations, not only the Dutch.[34] *A Description of the Most Glorious and Most Magnificent Arches Erected at The Hague for the Reception of William III* selected for a briefer account the main features of the arches and translated the Latin mottoes into English, presumably for a less educated, less elite readership.[35]

Many of the pictures, emblems, devices and inscriptions on the arches referred, of course, to Orange's Dutch victories, but some clearly celebrated the Revolution and defeat of the Catholic James II. Figure 16, for example, in *The Triumph Royal*, as the author explained, represented 'the willing submission of the kingdom of England to King William and his conquest of Ireland', and signified his intention in taking the throne 'to deliver the Protestants of those kingdoms from the tyranny under which they groaned'.[36] Similarly, figure 322 was an illustration of the Battle of the Boyne at which, the text explained, William did not hesitate 'to expose his life to the greatest dangers when he deemed it necessary for the welfare of his subjects'; and the meaning of figure 46 (in which William returns from Ireland to be met by maidens presenting him with the crown) was explained as showing that 'he was no less beholden for the procession of the kingdoms to the good will and affection of his people as to his conquering arms', and that the crowns were 'but a due reward of his merit'.[37] Neither was Queen Mary forgotten. In one illustration from the arches, she is figured standing with a cap of liberty in her hand under an Irish harp and an inscription 'with equal power the wife of Jove commands'.[38] One of the tableaux may have been intended in illustration to encourage support for William's continental war. Depicting Hercules trampling on the dragon, figure 28 in *The Triumph* was 'to show the preparations of the King of England to suppress the tyranny of the common enemy that threatens the destruction of all Europe'.[39]

English citizens did not get to see William's triumphal procession through the magnificent arches of the festivities – 'the like was never seen' – at The Hague.[40] But through the accounts translated, published and sold, they at second hand got to see their king feted by the princes of Europe as a mythological and conquering hero, as a providential redeemer, and altruistic defender of religion and liberties. There can be little doubt that those who published the English accounts, with dedications to Mary, intended them as justification of both William's right to the English throne and as support for his policy of committing England to the confederate war against France. One suspects too that those who published would have welcomed similar triumphal processions in England that William eschewed and the actual presence of the king as the embodiment of all the victories and virtues represented in the Dutch tableaux and richly illustrated in the English texts.[41]

At home, however, one sad event necessitated a grand state ritual: the death of Queen Mary on 27 December 1694. Stricken with a grief that virtually paralyzed him for weeks, William did not attend the funeral for the queen. Though panegyrists tried to make the best of his absence – 'In pity to his people' whom he did not wish to see him grieving, wrote the author of a poem on the funeral, 'he's not there' – William again may have miscalculated by not attending and receiving (at a difficult political time) the sympathy of his subjects.[42] Despite his absence, however, the funeral was a magnificent public occasion that drew the people to pay respects to a queen who (English, a Stuart and easier of manner) was more popular than her husband. The Duke of Norfolk, the Earl Marshal, organized, and licensed publication of, the form of the funeral proceeding from Whitehall to Westminster on 5 March 1695.[43] Preceded by trumpets, household officers and chaplains, members of the Lords and Commons, and heralds, the queen's body was drawn on an open chariot with two of the queen's bedchamber women in attendance and with sceptre, orb and crown on a velvet cushion. Followed by the chief mourner and eighteen assistants, the body was conveyed into the abbey mausoleum, where six ladies of the bedchamber attended, three on each side.

Contemporary observers praised the 'order and harmony' of the funeral: the 'costly', 'august cavalcade' which accompanied the hearse designed for the queen by Christopher Wren, with (as Defoe wrote) 'infinite more splendour than I can pretend to describe'.[44] Nahum Tate, whose poem *Mausoleum* had a frontispiece engraving of the structure, described it as reaching almost to the abbey roof, as he imagined the Protestant churches and nations paying tribute at the tomb.[45] Preaching shortly after the event, the minister John Howe recalled 'we have had this last week a public solemnity that was becomingly great and magnificent' and praised 'a most august funeral solemnity' 'which you have many of you so lately seen, and no doubt all of you heard of'.[46] Mary's funeral was indeed an occasion of popular commemoration as well as magnificence. Broadsides were published of the queen lying in state;[47] *The Mourning Court, or, The Solemn Representation of the Royal Funeral* printed, beneath a crude image of the procession, verses in praise of 'good Queen Mary';[48] the author of *The Royal Funeral* set popular verses commemorating the occasion to the tune of Hope's farewell;[49] and at least one enterprising character sold effigies ('cunningly done to the life in wax and drest in coronation robes') in London.[50] In sermons, odes and popular verses, Mary's death was met with 'an extraordinary outpouring of grief'.[51] While in several, sympathy was expressed for William who, it was said, 'more endeared himself to his people by that tenderness which he expressed' at her death, one is left with a sense that William's absence was a lost opportunity to bond with his people in grief over a queen who had asked nothing more than that 'his subjects might all love him as she had done'.[52] If, unlike his wife, William never enjoyed the love and affection of his people, it was not least because he failed to perform before them on ritual occasions of sadness or celebration.

The proposed celebrations for the victory at Namur, which some had sought and even planned, were, as we saw, declined by the king, though the Earl of Romney put on a fireworks display in St James's Square.[53] In the time between his return to England in mid-October and the meeting of parliament towards the end of November, William, at leisure, decided on a short progress but might have been better advised to have, in the wake of Mary's death and the victory at Namur, staged some public event to connect with his people after a long absence and to raise support for the next stage of the war. The wave of popular sympathy that followed the assassination attempt on the king and the formation of the 'General Association for King William' provided another opportunity when William might have refashioned himself as the embodiment of national sentiment and as the people's prince.[54] Instead he itched to get back to the continent to check any resurgence by the French.

On this venture, however, William secured not a victory but a prize that was yet more precious to his burdened subjects: a peace signed on 20 September 1697. On this occasion he either agreed to – or was bamboozled into – a state entry into the capital. That the initiative came from others is suggested by the reports that preparations for various forms of spectacle were being made while William was making his way to Margate. On the day after peace was signed, in fact, a newsletter writer informed Sir Joseph Williamson: 'we are preparing here against the king's arrival. Lord Romney has ordered "a firework" in

St James's Square for which £5000 is allowed.'[55] In addition to Romney's fireworks, he continued, 'St Paul's choir is making ready to celebrate the thanksgiving'. Another missive the same day, remarking that 'the news of the peace has been received in all parts of the kingdom with great demonstration of joy', implied it was public feeling which was dictating that the nation's joy should be 'expressed in a more solemn manner when the king returns from Holland'.[56] Reporting that the pyrotechnician and military engineer Sir Martin Beckman was in charge of the fireworks, this anonymous writer added: 'they intend to erect several triumphal arches in London'.

While the initiative came from the Corporation of London (which customarily staged such royal entries), the Lords Justices, in charge of affairs after Mary's death in William's absence, were clearly behind the plan. Meeting on 1 October with Sir Robert Clayton and a committee of aldermen to discuss the proposal, 'their excellencies told them the dutiful demonstration of their affection to his Majesty would be very acceptable to him'.[57] Despite the encouragement, however, there were doubts about William's interest in spectacles, and the language and tone of the Justices' meeting suggest that on this occasion they felt it appropriate to pressure him somewhat, ordering 'that it be laid before the king that, at some time or other, he will please to undergo this trouble' and asked 'whether he would avoid it at his first arrival'.[58] The City's plans to welcome William 'with all possible demonstrations of loyalty and affection' proceeded apace and the trained bands were forewarned to be ready in arms for such a day.[59] On 18 October, a few days after William reached Falmouth, the City aldermen were summoned to be informed that 'the king had accepted the reception they intend to make him'.[60] When, ten days later, they reported back on their plans, the proposed triumphal arches had gone, along with the usual cavalcade.[61] It may well be that the exigencies of time did not permit the scale of event originally conceived; and it has also been suggested that some citizens opposed the triumphal arches because they would block the spectators' view from many windows.[62] But, not least since he had been so close to the king, we should not lightly pass over Bishop Burnet's explanation that 'some progress was made in preparing triumphal arches, but he put a stop to it; he seemed, by a natural modesty, to have contracted an antipathy to all vain shows; which was much increased in him by what he had heard of the gross excesses of flattery to which the French have run'.[63] Whatever the explanation, the city scaled down plans so that William, in his coach, would be escorted by the mayor, carrying a sword, the aldermen and a retinue of two hundred through streets lined with the militia, to Whitehall.[64]

On 4 November, the king's birthday and the eve of the day on which he had landed in 1688, the citizens celebrated and the assistant Secretary of State reported, 'the people's thoughts [were] turned towards expecting his majesty and making preparations for his reception'.[65] William finally made his entry on

16 November. Setting out from Greenwich about noon, accompanied by Prince George of Denmark, the principal officers of state and 'a numerous concourse of the lords spiritual and temporal, the privy council, judges, and divers other persons of quality', all in coaches with six horses, William began his procession to Whitehall.[66] At St Margaret's Hill in Southwark, he was received by the aldermen and mayor who presented him with the city sword which, returned, was then carried before the king for the rest of the entry. In the city, the Recorder made a speech of welcome and one Isaac Crew, an orphan of Christ's Hospital grammar school, delivered a speech of congratulation to William 'the Palladium of our present liberty'.[67] Praising him for having rescued religion, laws and liberties, Crew promised that his glorious achievements would fill histories and blessed the 'best of princes', praying 'may you long sway the sceptre of those flourishing kingdoms'.[68]

From Southwark, a hundred of the trained bands in buff coats led the coaches to Charing Cross, with the Lord Mayor and city officers and the city and royal banners following.[69] Attended on each side by equerries, the king rode in a rich coach of state accompanied by Prince George, followed by his Life Guards and the long train of coaches of members of the royal household and nobility. On the route to St Paul's, the streets were lined with the livery companies 'with their banners and ensigns displayed'; the conduits ran with wine. As the procession moved on towards Whitehall, only the mayor, accompanied by Garter and Black Rod, attended the king to the stairs leading up to the Grand Chamber, before going to supper with the Lord Steward.

Observers gave mixed accounts of the spectacle. Robert Yard informed Williamson:

> The whole day has been spent on his Majesty's reception and passage through London, attended by the nobility in their coaches and by the Lord Mayor and corporation, with the heralds at arms on horseback. The Lord Mayor carried the sword before the king to Whitehall; the houses were all adorned with tapestry and rich hangings and filled with vast crowds of people, as were the streets also. Repeated acclamation attended his majesty as he passed. The cannons were fired from the Tower, and the King's Guards gave three volleys. In the evening there were bonfires, illuminations and great rejoicings.[70]

Others concurred that the royal entry was made 'with much magnificence and all the demonstrations of public satisfaction that possibly could be'.[71] A poet, dedicating to William verses on the king's return and entry to the city, praised the order and enthused: 'how great your entry and how gay the show!'[72] James Vernon, who was within days to become Secretary of State, agreed that 'there were very hearty demonstrations of the pleasure people had in the sight of the king as the author of this peace', but considered 'there was nothing

extraordinary in the show'.[73] In Burnet's words, it had been not a lavish spectacle but 'a sort of triumph, with all the magnificence that he [William] would
admit'.[74] William himself was clearly pleased with the day, the festive supper he
partook of before retreating to Kensington House, and especially with 'the
affectionate respects that were paid to him'.[75] As we read Burnet, the City's original proposals and accounts of the people's eager anticipation, we cannot but
suspect that the citizens would have welcomed more. Whatever his preference
for a different, less ceremonial style of kingship to that of his enemy, on this
occasion William might well have been advised – and, as we saw, there is a hint
the Lords Justices counselled him – to emulate Louis XIV with a grand triumph.
But at last he had presented himself before his subjects and behaved with grace,
receiving their compliments and toasting their healths. Had he done so earlier,
even the reserved, choleric Dutch king might have established a greater rapport
with Englishmen and women who then, as now, placed great store by watching
their monarch on the pageant stage of state. Not least on account of the death
of Ashmole, the historian of the Order, in 1692, we know little about the history
of the Order of the Garter under William and Mary. But the impression is that,
after the renewal and reinvigoration of the Order by Charles II and James II, its
importance lapsed in the reign of William, as the Dutch king showed less
interest in the ceremonial aspects of English monarchy than his predecessors.
William had been granted the Garter in 1653 (when he was only two and a
half) and was one of the early knights invested by Charles II in 1661. Portraits
show that he wore prominently a greater George on a gold chain, as well as the
Garter itself.[76] As monarch, William was quick to fill vacancies and obviously
had a sense of the political importance of elections to a prestige honour that
vied with the Habsburg Order of the Golden Fleece and the French Order of
the Holy Spirit. The list of the knights elected under William and Mary
evidences that in part the English monarch used the Order to reward allies and
cement alliances with the likes of the dukes of Schomberg and Brunswick, the
Marquis of Brandenburg and the Elector of Brunswick, and to prepare the way
for the succession of the Duke of Gloucester and Prince George, Elector of
Hanover.[77] At home William awarded the Order to close friends and political
allies against his opponents in all three kingdoms: in England to his friend (and
probable lover) William Bentinck, Earl of Portland, to the Dukes of Devonshire,
Shrewsbury and Newcastle, who had all been ardent supporters at the
Revolution; in Ireland to Ormonde whom William sought to bribe away
from support of James I; in Scotland, to Argyll who had been in the Scottish
delegation sent to offer William the crown.

It was, however, the spectacle of the Garter, the procession through London to
St George's Chapel, that had made it an important calendrical ritual in the
performance of monarchy before the people. From the little we know, there were
ceremonies of installation in William's reign, some evidently of considerable

grandeur. On 25 July 1696, a newsletter reported that 'there was yesterday a very great concourse of nobility and gentry at the Duke of Gloucester's installation at Windsor. There was afterwards a great entertainment in St George's Hall and a ball at night.'[78] On that apparently grand occasion, however, William was absent abroad. The king was present for the installation of the Duke of Newcastle in 1698, but we hear nothing of his role in the 'splendid entertainment' the Duke gave the knights 'and other persons of quality who assisted at the ceremony'.[79] Silence is not in itself evidence; but an impression that William was less interested in spectacle than his predecessors came from no less a source than Princess Anne. Writing to William to request that he fulfil his promise to grant the Garter to the Duke of Marlborough, Anne recounted the duke's service before closing: 'I am sure I shall ever look upon it as a mark of your favour to us. I will not trouble you with any ceremony because I know you don't care for it.'[80] The princess may have been referring to the king's dislike of compliment; but aversion to ceremony appears to have characterized William's overlordship of the Garter – and indeed his reign. It was, as I shall argue, an aversion that brought about a change not only in the representation of kingship but in the nature and exercise of monarchy.

As he made his way to and from his ports of embarkation and landing, such as Gravesend, Harwich and Margate, on his campaigns in Ireland and on the continent, William was probably seen by many of his subjects in the guise in which he was most comfortable: as a soldier and commander.[81] The king evidently also took his occasional leisure at Newmarket.[82] However, long absences overseas, insecurity in the months after the Revolution, and a love of privacy meant that William and Mary never undertook a formal progress together. Though the press of circumstances makes this understandable, this further neglect of the performative aspects of kingship – the display of majesty, the encounter with provincial cities and subjects, the receiving of petitions and intelligence on progresses – may again have been a miscalculation, especially by a ruler who needed to persuade his people of his legitimacy and claim to the throne. It was not until 1695, and nearly a year after Mary's death, that William resolved on a progress which, though short by the standards of earlier monarchs, offered an opportunity for the king to make himself familiar with more of his country and subjects. The progress followed the king's return from the victory of Namur and we might be tempted to think of it as an extended victory parade, were it not for William's disinclination to undertake a state entry into his capital. His biographer, noting the hiatus between the king's return and the assembly of the next parliament, suggests that this was a rare period where the opportunity of free time was presented, which the ever-energetic Orange was keen to fill.[83] In a letter to the Grand Pensionary Anthonius Heinsius, however, William outlined his own, rather prosaic reasons: 'Nowadays everybody in the provinces is busy on account of the new elections, and, all being absent, there is little business to take care of, and I am resolved to leave the coming Thursday on a journey to the country to divert myself somewhat and to see some of the country, since I have not been there yet. Perhaps this might not be bad for me either.'[84] Despite the language of recreation and diversion, the last sentence suggests the king had some political motivation: that of securing good will on the eve of the elections and assisting the return of MPs who would vote supplies for war. If that was the rationale, it seems from another remark that William did not much relish his planned encounter with his people, for he told the Prince de Vaudmont 'mon divertissement sera médiocre'.[85]

We have an account of the progress in *A Diary of the King's Journey* written by 'a person of quality' in the entourage.[86] William left Kensington on 17 October and reached Newmarket the same evening, whither several gentlemen came to congratulate him on his victory. After spending a couple of days hunting, the king received a delegation from Cambridge University and assured the vice chancellor and dons of his favour on this first meeting with one of the universities, which had once been regular stops on royal progresses. On the 21st, William left for Althorp House in Northamptonshire to stay a week with the Earl of Sunderland who had been first minister to James II but whose advice was increasingly sought by William after 1692 and who, according to Burnet, 'had the king's confidence to the highest degree' and was appointed Lord Chamberlain in 1697.[87] The king stayed at Althorp some days longer than planned; as well as enjoying hunting and other rural sports, he dined at Castle Ashby with the Earl of Northampton and at Broughton House with the Earl of Montagu, the former a signatory of the invitation to William in 1688, the latter Master of the Great Wardrobe. Montagu was a noted connoisseur and renowned host so 'here his majesty was splendidly entertained and was attended with a great member of the nobility and gentry of this country'; 'there was', our diarist informs, 'hardly anybody of note that did not come'.[88] On this occasion William displayed a rare charm and, receiving them 'very kindly . . . told them their county was in his opinion the finest in England and perhaps in the whole world'.[89] Leaving Althorp on the 28th, William travelled to Stamford and on to Welbeck Abbey, close to Burghley House, the county residence of John Cecil, fifth Earl of Exeter. The earl was absent – strategically it has been suggested, since he had never taken the oath to the regime – but William visited the house with its fine paintings, frescoes by Verrio and carvings by Gibbons.[90] At Stamford the mayor and aldermen attended on the king and celebrations with bonfires and fireworks gave a popular welcome. Having dined at Belton House with Sir John Brownslow, High Sheriff of Lincolnshire and MP for Grantham, the royal entourage came on the 29th to Lincoln 'being attended by a mighty concourse of people'.[91] As he made his way to Welbeck, William was met at Dunham Ferry, seven miles out, at the entrance to Nottinghamshire by the Duke of Newcastle, a staunch Whig and Williamite loyalist, whom the king had been keen to re-court, along with other old Whigs. The notice Newcastle received was short but the entertainment he provided was of 'great magnificence, having kept open house all the time his majesty was there, and tables being spread for all comers'.[92]

While based at Welbeck, William made a visit to Thoresby Hall, the home of the fourth Earl of Kingston, where he again used gracious compliments to his hosts, praising the excellent hunting, 'with a great deal more commendation of Nottinghamshire'.[93] The next day the mayor and aldermen of York attended on the king, who knighted the mayor, while the archbishop and clergy also attended to congratulate William on his safe return and to express their gratitude for his care of the church and to petition him for his continuing protection. Members of the corporations of Newark and East Retford also came to Welbeck to kiss the king's hand and to congratulate 'his Majesty's glorious success at Namur . . . which his Majesty took very kindly from them'.[94] After four days, the king left (on 3 November), arriving at night at Bradgate House, the residence of Thomas Gray, second Earl of Stamford, one of the old loyalists and influential Whigs whose support William very much needed in 1695. On his birthday the next day, the anniversary of the day before his landing, William came to Warwick where he was 'received with great acclamations, ringing of bells, illuminations, fireworks and other expressions of joy and respect'.[95] The mayor and aldermen escorted him to the castle where Lord Brooke provided a magnificent feast, not forgetting the ordinary townspeople for whom he provided 120 gallons of festive punch, which doubtless helped to ensure that 'great were the acclamations of the people here'.[96]

Brooke and his men escorted the royal train from Warwick the next day. After the king had dined with the Duke of Shrewsbury, his Secretary of State (who had just received his dukedom and the Garter), at Egypt House, a small private retreat where William happily felt himself 'out of the world', by evening the king reached Burford, where he was to remain for three days, hunting.[97] En route from Burford to Woodstock on 8 November, he paid a short visit to Queen Mary's uncle, the second Earl of Clarendon, at Cornbury Park, which William may have been interested in purchasing as a hunting seat for himself or his favourite, William Bentinck.[98] The next day, the royal visitor matched his compliment to the dons of Cambridge by coming to Oxford where he was met at Woodstock by the university chancellor (Ormonde), vice chancellor and doctors and the city magistrates.[99] On his entry into the university city, a grand ceremonial welcome was arranged at the Sheldonian Theatre, still the site of such occasions. But, far from merely ceremonial, this occasion has been described as a 'diplomatic mission'.[100] Oxford was still considered a stronghold of James II's supporters and was a centre of an Anglicanism to which William was not inclined. In the university chancellor Ormonde, however, William had an ally, and both the duke and the king appear to have used the visit to improve relations. As well as a splendid entertainment with music, a Latin oration of thanks was delivered and Ormonde presented William with a large Bible, a prayer book and 'the cuts [statutes] of the university, all richly bound and presented in folio . . . with a pair of gold-fringe gloves.'[101] For the townsfolk, the city conduits ran all the while with wine. Though Oxford had prepared a banquet, William stuck to his plan to leave; and, explaining that 'this was a visit of kindness not curiosity', did not on this occasion tour the colleges.[102] If this spoke still to some tension, it was not obviously evident as the dignitaries kissed the king's hand and escorted him to his coach.

By 7 p.m. William was back at Windsor, where the next day he held a Council meeting (after lunch with the financier and Treasury Commissioner Sir Stephen Fox) before returning to Kensington House. The king was pleased with his twenty-six days' progress, writing that he had met with 'a great deal of affection of the people everywhere'.[103] The diarist reported 'hearty English demonstrations of respect, zeal, affection and fidelity', and indeed that the royal progress would have real political benefits:

> This progress will have happy and glorious effects by engaging the hearts of all those of his Majesty's subjects who before had only heard what great things the king had done for them and all Europe, but now had the honour and happiness to see that excellent prince that was destined by heaven to make this renowned kingdom of England flourish beyond what it ever did in current times; and to retrieve her reputation and make her fame as lasting as time itself; and to crown all, to establish us in an honourable and durable peace.[104]

William raised England's wealth and reputation, and Ryswick, if not 'durable', was an honourable peace, but he never engaged the hearts of his people. If, as episodes on this progress hint, he was capable of rising above his surly reserve, his mistake may have been, for most of the country and most of his reign, in leaving subjects only to 'hear' of his actions. Over three weeks in 1695, a few of his subjects had 'the honour and happiness' of seeing the king. William had needed to do more to 'introduce himself to his new subjects and get himself liked'.[105]

Over the course of the sixteenth century, the court had emerged as both the headquarters of royal government and the showcase of personal monarchy. While administrative developments during the Interregnum, such as boards of state and standing committees, had reduced the place of the (royal) household in government, as Protector Oliver Cromwell had a clear sense of the political and symbolic importance of the court as a centre of patronage and a representation of authority, but his establishment was smaller than that of Charles I.[106]

On his Restoration in 1660, Charles II, who clearly regarded his court as *the* symbol of restored kingship, re-established a royal household as large as his father's, swearing in over twelve hundred officers and servants by October 1660, the bulk of them in the Lord Chamberlain's department which was responsible for ceremonies. Financial stringency forced him by 1662 to cut back the size of his establishment and to end diet (the right to take dinner at court) for all but high-ranking officers and further economies were made during the Exclusion crisis.[107] James II, as we have seen, reduced the household still further and enacted other reforms while re-emphasizing formality as a sign of his departure from his brother's fiscal and moral profligacy.[108]

William and Mary 'had an even more pressing need to maintain the royal state and, with it, an appearance of legitimacy'.[109] Soon after ascending the throne they announced their intention to reverse James's cuts and to restore the household establishment which again numbered over one thousand by 1690 – the largest after Charles II before 1837.[110] Financial difficulties also beset William and Mary, all the more so due to a less favourable financial settlement and the costs of war.[111] But, significantly, unlike Charles (and James), William, rather than cutting back, permitted debts to accumulate; even after, in the wake of the 1698 Civil List Act, a late concerted effort to pay arrears, it is estimated that he died owing his household servants over £300,000.[112] The conclusion must be that William and Mary regarded the court and royal household as of too great a political and symbolic importance to permit economies. Indeed, their court was 'easily the most expensive' of the later Stuarts.[113]

Shortly after their succession, the king and queen purged the personnel of James II's household – by no means all of them Catholic – and issued ordinances specifying the diets and board wages of all their servants.[114] Orders were also drawn up to regulate expenditure and accounts, and for preventing the sale of offices, and vetting for suitability all who held positions.[115] Under Mary, and after her death William himself, the court also became the centre of, and model for, moral reformation and Protestant rectitude, which was intended to mark a conspicuous break with the popish debauchery of the last two Stuart courts.[116] The 'virtuous court' of William and Mary was constructed to represent the virtues of 1688 and the new regime: to advertise the queen and king as pious, incorrupt and – against the facts – frugal.

However, for all that William and Mary recognized the centrality of the court in representing their rule, the verdict must be that their court failed to endow them with legitimacy or even to enhance their image among their subjects. In part, the explanation lies in the fact that William replaced (fully half) the officers of James's court and many of the new appointees were Dutch, making this the first conspicuously foreign establishment since the unpopular Scots took positions on the accession of James I – but this time in larger numbers that attracted greater odium. As with James I, those holding offices closest to the king, such as his favourite William Bentinck (who became Groom of the Stole) and Arnold Joest van Keppel (who became Master of the Robes), were foreign and their influence (albeit exaggerated) was highly resented. That they were also suspected (probably rightly) of being sexual as well as political intimates fuelled resentment and reinvoked suspicions of broader moral corruption that had ultimately undermined the first Stuart. Indeed, along with homosexual lovers, William's mistresses tarnished the court's self-image as an exemplum of moral virtue, for all the piety of the queen.[117]

Nor did suspicion of corruption arise only from sexual shenanigans, damaging as they were. The very presence of the Dutch in high places made the Williamite court an easy target for Jacobites and others who fanned innate English xenophobia to argue that, under William, foreigners were acquiring riches at the expense of the English – and of English taxpayers. Accusations of corruption gained credibility as the reality of corruption became all too evident. Those Whigs brought in after 1688 had been out of favour and excluded from office for the last two reigns and now saw an opportunity to seize the spoils that they had been denied. As they usually do, wars greatly increased the opportunities for such spoil and the almost perpetual wars of William's reign saw many courtiers rise to riches through corrupt contracts, backhanders and favours, as well as legitimate profits. Not least because William was so much of the time abroad and focused on the war, and because the turnover of personnel had removed many senior courtiers experienced in management, extravagance and corrupt practices went largely unchecked – at least until the Peace of Ryswick. Increasingly during the 1690s, a Country opposition joined Jacobites in denouncing the royal household and government as centres of profligacy and venery rather than virtue.[118] By the time that William, temporarily able to focus on domestic affairs, vowed to take action to reform, the political damage was done. The court which he had intended to stand as contrasting with his corrupt predecessors', as the court of a virtuous Protestant king and nation, was widely derided as the enclave of foreigners, favourites and a party of aficionados licensed to feather their own nests while true English subjects were asked to suffer austerity to finance the war.

As important as the failure to establish the royal court's reputation as the household of virtuous rulers, the Williamite court did not effectively perform its vital symbolic function: as a place where the abstract mysteries of monarchy were complemented by social relations with the person of the ruler, where shared rituals and entertainments tempered political rivalries and enmities, and where, in his own 'house', the monarch displayed his qualities to govern the larger family of the realm. It is no coincidence that the monarchs most remembered as successful rulers – Henry VIII, Elizabeth I and Charles II – in their very different ways structured court rituals and entertainments not only to secure the support of political elites but also to appeal to their common subjects.

That such were still the expectations in the 1690s is evident in contemporary observations that 'a king is more eminently present where his court is than where he himself is alone in person'.[119] 'Courts', a 1694 edition of *A Discourse of Government* insisted, 'must not want their splendour, for that is part of their majesty'.[120] While there was no shortage of expenditure on the household, the court of William and Mary did lack splendour and majesty.

One must be careful not to exaggerate. The king's and queen's ordinances for 1689 refer to receptions, masques and balls; there are several references in state papers and in Queen Mary's memorials to celebrations and entertainments, for the king's birthday for example.[121] William even entertained members of the House of Commons in 1701.[122] Yet there can be no doubt that after 1688 such occasions were reduced in number and scale and, more importantly, changed in purpose. William's annual absences from spring till autumn on campaigns, of course, meant that he was less well placed to make the court the centre of ceremonial and social life; but – and we note that he found time to socialize at Het Loo – it was by no means the only reason.[123] The king cut back on balls and dinners, being more often a guest than a host; he did not much like horse racing, seldom went to the theatre and, overall, 'showed great reluctance to participate in the social round which had traditionally cemented English monarchs to the political elite'.[124] While he did dine with friends and favoured nobles, William preferred to retreat to relative privacy and even kept his first Christmas not at Whitehall or Hampton Court but at one of the houses of the Duke of Ormonde, his major general.[125]

Reference is often made to Queen Mary's greater charm and sociability. The queen organized the king's birthday celebrations, occasionally attended plays and played cards with her courtiers.[126] Yet, despite this, Mary seems to have been little inclined to orchestrate a full court social life in her husband's absences. As she wrote to William in 1690, 'I must see company on my "sett days", I must play twice a week; nay, I must laugh and talk though never so much against my will. I believe I dissemble very ill to those who know me.'[127] Even allowing for the rhetoric of a dutiful wife assuring her spouse of her pining for him in his absence, the sense is that of a woman who preferred to be 'alone' and who had to make a reluctant effort to socialize. It is an impression confirmed on almost every page of Mary's memoirs in which she frequently writes of her 'inclination . . . to a retired, quiet life'.[128] Though she hosted a ball for the king's birthday, she had reservations about doing so; whenever she could she retreated from Whitehall (where she lived among 'perfect strangers') to Kensington; she declined to dance, found visitors 'troublesome' and resented any intrusions on her private devotions.[129] From almost the day she entered Whitehall, Mary had confided to friends that she saw small prospect of ever being as tranquil or as happy again as she had been in the Netherlands.[130] In matters social, as well as in her supervision of domestic government, Mary did her duty. But there was little gaiety or feminine sparkle at the court of a queen who was remembered for her lack of ostentation and the plainness of her dress.[131]

More important than the reduced social life of the court was William's scant concern for those courtly rituals which communicated the mystery and numinosity of monarchy. Before the civil war, these had been perhaps the court's primary contribution to representing sacred kingship and had reached their apogee under Charles I. The civil war and regicide had irreversibly punctured the royal mystique and claim to sanctity and Charles II intuited rightly that the clock could not simply be turned back. However, while pursuing a more down-to-earth style, he continued, even while only half believing in them, to perform the rituals of sacred monarchy, such as attendance at chapel, the Maundy service and touching to cure the king's evil; and he paid increasing attention to them as political crisis loomed.[132] William did, as well as attending some thanksgivings, gather the court for chapel where he made offerings, and continued Maundy services (he was the last to do so).[133] But, famously, he ceased to touch to cure the king's evil, describing the practice as 'a silly superstition'.[134] Though even some of his Whig advisers urged him not to show contempt for a popular custom, William recommended when faced with subjects coming to be cured: 'give the poor creatures some money and send them away'; and he even referred petitioners to the exiled King James in France.[135]

As a consequence, for all the increase in the size of the household, as a political centre and symbol, the court was diminished under William and Mary. 'Whereas the royal household had been, under Charles II, the very centre of an open, attractive, and vibrant court culture . . . it had become, by the death of William III, the residence of a secluded Royalty.'[136] Contemporary observers wrote of the diminution of the court and, looking back, even described the magnificence of earlier feasts and ceremonies as 'a little ridiculous now they are so antiquated'.[137] Social as well as political changes were reversing the development of the sixteenth century and making the aristocratic London scene more than the royal court the centre of fashion and taste.[138] Yet, more than his predecessors, it was William III who hastened those developments and whose reign saw the decline of the court as a social, political and symbolic centre of divine monarchy. In that he transformed not only the representation of regality, but monarchy itself.

II

The year 1688 had powerfully demonstrated how the role of the monarch as head of the church was central to both the image and authority of the king. The memory of Charles I was inextricably tied to his championship of the Church of England, and the Anglican laity as well as clergy deserted James II because of a personal threat to the church. William of Orange was welcomed initially by Anglican Tories as well as dissenters – welcomed as a saviour of the church as well as of Protestantism. However, the perception of William as saviour of the church began to fracture even before he ascended the throne. As John Spurr writes, once James II had left, 'the unity of the Church of England began to collapse'.[139] Some bishops and clergy had hoped to pressure James rather than to depose him and sought to bring him back rather than see Orange as king. The Archbishop of Canterbury, William Sancroft, refused to serve William, and headed those loyalist clergy, known as non-jurors, who felt that they could not take the oath of allegiance to the new king. Though William left Sancroft's and other non-juring bishops' dioceses vacant for a time, in hope of a reconciliation, the church proved to be permanently divided over the right of William and Mary to rule.[140] Because the non-juring bishops maintained that they were the true church and their replacements were uncanonical, 'for the first and only time in its history, the Church of England found itself condemned to a protracted contest for legitimacy between two rival hierarchies'.[141]

Not only was William not, in the eyes of many, a rightful king or head of the church, he was suspected of being ill qualified to be a defender of the faith. Since the Restoration, the church had distanced itself from continental reformed Protestantism and resisted any attempts at comprehension or toleration of dissenters. Orange, however, was a Dutch Calvinist, sympathetic to a more reformed theology and less ceremonial liturgy, and to toleration, for which the Dutch were famous. While he was able to find within the church, and promote to senior bishoprics, clergy who were sympathetic to his preferences, probably the majority of Anglican clergy and laity were opposed to either comprehension or toleration. From his very succession, then, William III was not accepted by a significant party within it as legitimate Head of the Church nor as a spiritual head. As within weeks of his coronation the Earl of Danby warned the king, 'he did all things to encourage Presbytery and to dishearten the Church of England, and that he would absolutely prejudice himself and government by it'.[142]

Faced with an opposition that rendered his supremacy impotent, William was forced to abandon a bill for comprehension of dissenters and accept a limited Toleration Act. The proposals of a royal commission to review the church's liturgy, canons and courts were ignored by Convocation, and 'any prospect of a formal rapprochement between the church and moderate dissent' was 'killed stone dead'.[143] Yet, for all its limitations, the Toleration Act, along with the Revolution, transformed the church and with it the place and perception of the king as head. For the first time since the Reformation, the Church of England was, in Spurr's words, reduced from being the national church of all to being merely the established church in a nation of religious pluralism.[144] Such a change was to profoundly alter the position of the ruler too.

The defeat of his proposals for comprehension and the abolition of the test for office effectively left William with a church with which he was not in sympathy and of which many members remained suspicious of, if not hostile to, him. The retention of the test for office also meant that the king could not appoint even to government positions those who would not conform. The stand-off between king and church led William to dispense with a sitting convocation, rightly suspecting that it would be a forum of opposition to his policies.[145] Relations between the church and monarchy deteriorated further with the death of Queen Mary in December 1694. Mary had been brought up an Anglican and, though sympathetic to a latitudinarian church, evidently retained – and, as importantly, was perceived to retain – an affection for the English Church, its liturgies and ceremonies.[146] During William's absences, and possibly as a consequence of a strategic decision, it was Mary who took charge of ecclesiastical patronage and policy, as well as championing godly reformation. After her death, William, anxious to conduct his war and avoid a bruising conflict at home, left control with a commission of bishops, while he remained Supreme Head in name only.[147] In a power vacuum and divided church, Tory Anglicans seized the opportunity to reverse even the concessions they had made to dissent and to revive convocation as a weapon against nonconformists – and indeed as a challenge to the royal authority. In his 1697 *Letter to a Convocation Man*, Francis Atterbury, a high church Oxford don, argued for an autonomous authority in convocation and its right to convene whenever parliament sat, irrespective of royal will or the absence of a royal summons.[148] Charging William with neglect of the church, Atterbury insisted a convocation meet to rectify it; in 1700, with Tories dominant in his ministry, William was forced to concede and a convocation proceeded to attack the Revolutionary church establishment.[149]

After the hostility to his early proposals for comprehension and reform of the liturgy and canons, William, in order to buy Tory Anglican support for his wars, more or less surrendered control of the church. His policy of 'virtual invisibility' has been described as a success in that it prevented bitter religious divisions disrupting the regime at home, while providing just sufficient toleration for William to maintain a continental Protestant alliance against Louis XIV.[150] Contemporary supporters indeed praised the king for striking a balance between 'popish thraldom' and 'frantic zeal' and for restoring the church to a 'happy condition'.[151] The price William paid for political expediency, however, was high. When he 'abdicated his role as spiritual governor', for all his invocation of providence, William (as he did in other ways) surrendered some of the sanctity and mystery of monarchy.[152]

Moreover, more limited though it was than what he had sought, toleration transformed both church and state. As has been suggested, pluralism reduced the role and authority of the Church of England – and the *raison d'être* of its creation – as a *national* church. Beyond that, the non-juror Charles Leslie identified a further loss of authority: the Toleration Act, he maintained, meant 'that we must give up our jure divino right' and so 'divested us of all our authority over the people'.[153] *Parti pris* though he was, he was right; and, if the church lost its *jure divino* right, then there were clearly implications for the right of its Supreme Head: not just William III, but every head, every monarch. Certainly seen from retrospect, the Toleration Act not only contributed to the acceptance of party and division that transformed politics, it also contributed to a decline of spiritual authority and mystery that was to change the nature of regality.

Anxiety about scepticism and atheism had always been present in the church and had been much articulated in a Restoration culture of the Royal Society, irreverent wit and debauched morality. It was, however, and probably because the church itself had been part of it, the Revolution that contemporaries identified as fostering a retreat from faith. As well as the king and queen, loyal Williamite bishops such as Edward Stillingfleet and Thomas Sprat attempted to counter the tide of irreligion and scepticism.[154] In his sermon at St Paul's, Covent Garden, on the thanksgiving day for the victory at Namur, John Swynfen explicitly castigated the irreligion and 'infidelity of the age' and blamed 'the late Revolution since which . . . atheistic notions and practices,' he added, 'have taken foundation from the very Revolution'.[155] Swynfen went on to give thanks to God for a king who had delivered the nation, but understood that there had also been regrettable consequences.[156] The divisions over 1688, the accommodations made by some clergy, and the denunciations of them by non-jurors had weakened the church and with it spiritual authority itself. In leading campaigns against deism and debauchery, first Mary then William endeavoured to (differently) re-establish pious example and spiritual leadership, not least because they were traditional expectations of rulers and intrinsic to monarchy. For all those efforts, however, William never secured recognition as a trusted Head of the Church and so, in abdicating his role as spiritual governor, surrendered his spiritual authority. As controversy raged over the memory of Charles I who, for all William's attempts to claim a descendancy from him, contrasted with the king as a saint of the church, Anglicans penned apologia for high church clerics such as Archbishop Laud who had taken a hard line against nonconformity and uncompromisingly asserted the spiritual authority of the church and king.[157] William's successor, Queen Anne, was to invoke that tradition as part of her own quest (she also revived touching for the king's evil) to reclaim sacred authority as Supreme Head.[158] Yet, as the bitter wrangles of her reign manifested, after 1688 and as a consequence of William's indifference, whatever the relentless claim to providential authority, the Supremacy would not be the same again. Indeed, the church and sacred

authority had become mired in the contest of party, with profound consequences for both the image and exercise of monarchy.[159]

III

The maintenance of the laws and the protection of justice had been vital to the
image and exercise of kingship since the Middle Ages, and it was the widely
held perception of a miscarriage of justice, notably in his prosecution
of the seven bishops who defied his Indulgence, that undermined James II.[160]
In 1688, as well as a deliverer of the church from popery, William of Orange
was welcomed as a protector of justice and the laws and, in his bid for
the throne, he promised restoration of, and respect for, legal courses. On
ascending to the throne, William and Mary accepted the Act Declaring the
Rights and Liberties of the Subject which listed James's illegal courses, unjust
prosecutions and excessive punishments, specified reforms and expressed
'entire confidence' in the Prince and Princess of Orange as rulers who would
preserve the laws.[161] Indeed (despite severity against Jacobite opponents in
Ireland and England), the king and queen presented themselves and were
represented by supporters as not only just but merciful rulers, in contrast to
the previous reign and the memory of the Bloody Assizes that followed
Monmouth's rebellion in the west.[162]

William III did not, like James, face an armed uprising to unseat him, but
throughout his reign Jacobite plots and conspiracies led to a series of trials for
treason which themselves undermined a rhetoric of unity and harmony
between the king and queen and their subjects. More importantly, and damagingly for the government, because there were many beyond Jacobite circles
who nursed doubts about the Revolution and its legitimacy, the trials were not
regarded by all as the due processes of English justice but as political and
partisan. While the government sought, therefore, to make its case against
conspirators as traitors against the nation, Jacobites used the courtroom and
the scaffold (as well as the press) to keep the case for James II alive, to attack the
legitimacy of the king, and to question the justice of an illegitimate regime's
judicial proceedings. So often in the history of early modern England, treason
trials and executions, which were intended as public demonstrations of royal
justice and authority, were used by opponents and the accused to undermine
that authority. In the case of William and Mary, in a divided political society,
those opponents were guaranteed a sympathetic audience; in consequence
the theatre of justice became a forum not simply for the performance of just
kingship but for a public dispute over where justice lay and who was its most
trustworthy custodian.

One of the earliest trials was that of John Ashton and others who planned in
1690 to exploit disillusionment with William III so as to restore James II to the

throne. With Richard Graham, Viscount Preston, former Secretary of State to the exiled king, Ashton travelled to St Germain to urge James to publish proofs of the Prince of Wales's legitimacy and to lay them before parliament.[163] As they set sail, however, they were apprehended at Tilbury and rapidly brought to trial as traitors in January 1691. Though the prosecution failed to prove Ashton's involvement in drawing treasonable documents, he was found guilty by a biased jury; despite advice to pardon him, Queen Mary accepted the verdict and sentence of death, albeit remitting the traitor's penalty of drawing and quartering.[164] Ashton's execution – the first show trial of the reign – drew 'a multitude of spectators' and the Jacobites clearly resolved to take advantage of the occasion for publicity.[165] Behaving with scrupulous decorum, even giving five guineas to his executioner, Ashton passed to the sheriff a paper, subsequently published, which testified his innocence and reasserted his principles.[166] In it Ashton, to avert any charge of popery, proclaimed his orthodox Anglicanism which, he reminded many troubled consciences, had obliged him to regard his sovereign James as accountable only to God. Having broken its oath, he continued, the nation now found itself in misery and the church likely to be destroyed, to which ills the only remedy was the restoration of the 'true father' of the people. Coupling the 'hard' and 'unjust' treatment James had received to his own case – and hence intimating that all were exposed to arbitrary courses when not even a king had been immune from them – Ashton protested against his conviction. The 'hasty and violent proceedings' and the 'severe charge given by the judges,' Ashton insisted, had denied him justice; and, contrary to Sir Edward Coke's opinion, he had been found guilty by presumption not proof. 'I am,' he declared, making his into a case of major historical import, 'the first man that ever was condemned for high treason upon bare suspicion.' Having made his point, Ashton forgave judges and jurors; but, as well as insisting on the rights of his king and queen and the legitimacy of the prince, he urged his countrymen to 'restore them all' and so re-establish the church and the law.

Not surprisingly, the government moved swiftly to counter Ashton's accusations. Edward Fowler, a royal chaplain and intimate of Burnet, was appointed to publish an *Answer* to Ashton's paper, with official imprimatur.[167] Recognizing the artfulness of the tract (which he attributed to others), Fowler saw the need to defend in detail the Revolution as well as the justice of the proceedings against Ashton. But in printing Ashton's original paper and even in answering at such length, Fowler gave publicity to the deceased and some credibility to Ashton's accusations concerning the unjust proceedings against him. Certainly, Ashton did not want for sympathy or support: copies of his paper were circulated in print in variant forms; and in a 'reflection' on Fowler's *Answer*, one defender of Ashton accused the government of having 'learnt to practise those methods of trial which themselves formerly complained of as arbitrary and illegal'.[168] Recalling both Orange's own declaration and the Declaration of Rights, *The Vindication of the Dead* showed how far short of them the trial had fallen and how the proceedings smacked of 'arbitrary power'.[169] Though a nervous government probably lay behind the mock *Elegy Upon the Death of Major John Ashton*, which branded him as a Catholic traitor, its author feared – probably rightly – that 'some in the Town will Swear he was Martyr'd'.[170] A year after their accession to the throne, William and Mary's reputation as custodians of justice was already appearing tarnished.

It was further stained, in the eyes of some at least, by the trial of the printer William Anderton in June 1693, for printing Jacobite pamphlets. While there was evidence against him, it was, his biographer observes, circumstantial and an informer's fabricated charges that he had insulted the king.[171] Conviction was obtained by the judges, led by the new Chief Justice Treby, bullying the jury, and Mrs Anderton's appeal to the queen was rebuffed. An official *Account* of the proceedings, 'licensed according to order', was published to persuade the public of Anderton's guilt in printing 'the rankest, vilest and most malicious treasons' and to advertise the time he was given 'that he might want nothing for his defence'.[172] Moreover, to counter a growing perception to the contrary, the *Account* praised 'their majesties' incomparable clemency' in taking the life of only one when so many others who had printed treasonable works had been punished for the lesser charge of misdemeanour. The official government account, however, had to contend with Anderton's own paper which, like Ashton's, connected a miscarriage of justice in his own case with a broader threat to the rights of the subject. The government, he charged, 'designed not to try but to convict me': the court refused counsel, made treason what was not, and when the jury could not agree, the judges instructed them it was 'their business ... to find me guilty'.[173] 'Now I pray consider,' Anderton asked his readers 'where [are] the rights and privileges of the subject' which had been 'the pretence of our present deliverers?' 'Nay, where the very laws themselves ... what are those proceedings but arbitrary ... and such as no reign ever produced before?' Anderton was supported by the non-juror Samuel Grascome (who may have penned the vindication of Ashton), who unpicked and denounced the sham trial and a regime 'more lawless and cruel than papists'.[174] Nor entirely inaccurately, Grascome informed his readers that the queen and Council 'no matter whether the law was strained or not ... had caught a man whom they thought fit should die, if not for his crimes, yet for example. And thus we have bravely secured our lives, liberties and estates, when men were hanged for reasons of state and for offences against law.'[175] Anderton proclaimed his loyalty to James and few would have been ignorant that Grascome's anonymously published *Appeal* was partisan. However, the charge against William and Mary of unjust, arbitrary courses appears to have stuck and progressively undermined their image as deliverers and protectors of laws and rights.

It seems that some official efforts were made to improve the reputation of royal justice and the image of the king as just. In a licensed account of the arraignment and trial of Sir John Friend on the charge of procuring forces from France to depose William, the Lord Chief Justice is reported as telling the accused that 'we are obliged to be indifferent between the king and you' and assuring Friend that he could call in his own time any witness in his defence.[176] But probably the best opportunity for the regime came with the attempted assassination of the king, which removed any doubt about the treason some Jacobites were prepared to commit and elicited sympathy for an unpopular king. Just as pro-government accounts of the conspiracy were published to blacken all Jacobites (and even non-jurors) and laud the virtues of William, so accounts of the arraignments and executions read as stage-managed propaganda for the regime. Judges' speeches made much of the king's providential delivery from the assassin's hand, declared that he was 'necessarily and rightfully placed upon that throne', and praised 'the wisdom and courage of his present Majesty (who) has rescued this kingdom from . . . slavery and oppression'.[177] In official accounts of the 1696 trials, it was the accused who were depicted as endeavouring to subvert the course of justice: Friend by trying to discredit reliable witnesses, others by endeavouring to pack the jury.[178] Moreover, concerted efforts were now made to persuade the public of the integrity of the court's proceedings. Accordingly, the author of *The Rye House Travesty*, a servant of the Bishop of Rochester, professing an 'utter abhorrence' of mere suspicion, boasted of the unequivocal evidence, unimpeachable witnesses and 'the whole proceedings . . . managed with all imaginable integrity'. [179] 'The trials that are already published,' another apologist asserted, 'carry in all the steps of them a fairness that former times was not acquainted with.'[180] William himself, his subjects were told as the trials proceeded, did not seek revenge, only 'a regular course of . . . justice'; for the king was a 'most clement and most excellent prince'.[181]

The convicted conspirators were by no means silent. Captain Thomas Vaughan delivered a last dying speech in which he avowed his Catholic faith and allegiance to James, maintaining he thought he was 'obliged to do it'.[182] On his scaffold, Charles Cranborne, who 'seemed very composed and little concerned', proclaimed his loyalty to the Church of England and to James II, Mary of Modena and their son, for whom he publicly prayed and hoped that 'he would be returned to his throne in God's good time'.[183] The sheriff interrupted him; more generally, official publications were commissioned to limit any damage done by last dying speeches. *Observations Upon The Papers Written By Mr Rookwood and Mr Lowick* (who shared the scaffold with Cranborne), 'published by authority', acknowledged that men's dying words were often believed.[184] Opposing their defences and charges, the author advised readers that 'little regard is to be given to whatever is said in these papers, either in defence of the late king, or for the justification of their own cause'.[185] With regard to James, he urged: 'I hope we do not easily forget what we then thought of him'.[186] As for the charge that William was guilty of bloodshed following the conspiracy, the author asked all to compare 'what is now done with what was done some years ago in the West' by Judge Jeffreys and King James; and to acknowledge William's 'clemency in abating the rigour of the law'.[187] More opponents of the regime were executed in 1696 than in all the previous years of William's reign. But just as in political terms the assassination plan was a 'godsend' for the king and the Whigs, and enhanced the popularity of both, it helped to take the sting out of opposition accusations of fixed trials and, whatever was the reality, to preserve the king's image as a just ruler threatened by a 'desperate crew' of papists out to subvert the church and law.[188]

IV

Despite the development of a more bureaucratic administration by boards of state, the person – and personality – of the monarch remained central to both the exercise and image of monarchy in England. Indeed, Charles II appears to have deliberately fostered what we would call a cult of personality which helped to secure an enduring measure of popularity for the king and the monarchy. Though he became unpopular for his Catholicism, James too culti-vated and won support in England and Scotland as a general and admiral. Both, of course, were Stuarts and sons of Charles I and both, especially Charles, were blessed with striking physiques and looks, were not averse to pleasure and could exude charm.

William of Orange enjoyed few of these advantages. He was, of course, known in England as a formidable military leader who had rescued the Netherlands from being overrun by France and as a champion of Protestantism. He was also the nephew and son-in-law of James and so by blood and marriage linked to the Stuarts whose cause the Orange dynasty had supported. Yet, though he visited in 1670 and 1681, Orange evidently made little impression on, and developed little affection for, England. What made him attractive to a desperate nation in 1688 was less who he was than who he was not; and the fact that, as well as a committed Protestant who had skilfully promised to uphold church and law, he was married to James's daughter and heir. As we have seen, in 1688 William was welcomed – by most Tories as well as Whigs – as a deliverer of the nation. And, as well as the plethora of sermons and panegyrics depicting him as the son of providence, some supporters wrote to present the character of their new king to his English subjects in a favourable light. In 1689, for example, there was published 'with allowance' a *Character of His Royal Highness, William Henry, Prince of Orange* which provided background infor-mation on and a character sketch of the Dutch prince who was now king.[189]

The *Character* related William's taking on the mantle of Maurice of Nassau as a defender of his country and his valiant victories over enemies. As well as a brilliant soldier, William was figured in the *Character* as a statesman who had, in his native Holland, reformed the government and re-settled a confused polity. Describing his physiognomy as masculine and martial, the author also singled out his 'charming sweetness' and presented him as a man mild, constant and temperate, who was tempted neither by women nor wine.[190] 'The charms of his valour, justice, temperance and the sweetness of his disposition makes him triumph not only in battle but by a more powerful conquest over the hearts of his opponents, as the nobility and gentry of England must acknowledge.'[191]

The reality was somewhat different. For a start, the new king was not very handsome. As even a supporter recalled with tactful understatement, his 'outward man' was 'not so magnificent'.[192] As well as being very short, William was remarkably awkward (Pead referred to 'the unhappy craziness' of his body), spectacularly ugly, hunchbacked, hook-nosed and afflicted by asthma.[193] Possibly as a consequence of physical disabilities and frailties, he was shy and reserved, even cold. When Princess Mary met her husband for the first time – 'an invalid in unusually weak health, hunchbacked, half a head shorter than herself' – she wept for a day and a half; and it is not likely that on appearance at least, William's subjects were any more attracted to him.[194] The king, it has to be said, did little to make himself more attractive. William had wanted to secure the English throne in order to bring the country into an alliance against Louis XIV. Naturally haughty, he held his new country and its people in little regard, and, as we have seen, withdrew from social gatherings and surrounded himself with Dutchmen.[195] In so doing, William not only excited an endemic English xenophobia (and not least dislike of the Dutch as commercial rivals), he gave ammunition to critics who argued that, rather than in England's interests, his continental wars were the means through which monies had been transferred to Holland while English taxpayers were fleeced and oppressed. For all the presentation of the king as a Stuart, William, who never mastered conversational English, remained very Dutch and – not least because he made no secret of his preference for his homeland – was seen to be Dutch.[196]

Nor were the virtues outlined in the *Character* evident in the man. For all his advocacy of reform of profanity and debauchery, William was not as unseduced by the pleasures of the flesh as his panegyrist claimed. In Holland he had publicly commenced an affair with one of Mary's ladies, Elizabeth Villiers, who, described by contemporaries as ugly, lacked even the essential attribute of a royal mistress.[197] In England, the perception and gossip were of worse sexual transgressions in William's alleged sodomitical relations with his Dutch favourites, William Bentinck (who was raised to the Earldom of Portland) and Arnout Joest van Keppel, who was created Earl of Albermarle – relations which cannot but have recalled the reign of another 'foreigner', James I, whose homosexual affairs had exposed him to damaging charges of corruption. If nothing else, such gossip reinforced a sense of excessive Dutch influence and, moreover, compromised both the moral image of the court and the representation of the happy partnership between king and queen that was a theme of courtly poetry and praise.

Queen Mary, as is often remarked, was in every sense more attractive, more gracious and better liked than her husband. Praise of her manners as well as her piety and charity appears to have been heartfelt; and there was sincere public grief at her death.[198] As we have seen, Mary was no more enamoured of her new country than her husband, felt herself (she confided to her friend) damned to perpetual unhappiness in England, and only reluctantly participated in hosting and attending social occasions from which she retreated with relief to the privacy of Kensington.[199] Whatever her preferences, however, Mary seems to have recognized the importance of putting on an *appearance* – the importance of public performance and image. If she did not bring sparkle to the court, she retained the affection of most, other than those Jacobites who could never forgive her for what they perceived as treachery against her father. She did not owe her relative popularity only to her character. Unlike William, for all the time she had spent abroad, Mary was English, a Stuart, a – or at least it could be held – natural successor to the throne and a champion of the Church of England. In addition, for all her short reign, where her husband was long absent, she was present as the visible face of monarchy, as the queen who ruled.

William III, it has to be admitted, ascended the throne with the disadvantage of a hard core of committed opponents and a larger number of subjects unconvinced of the legality of his rule. Yet the verdict must be that he also squandered the opportunity of his initial popularity and by his own actions, and lack of attention, became an unpopular figure, criticized for what had once been seen as virtues. Where he had been praised as a brilliant general and deliverer, William came to be characterized as a Cromwell-like usurper too fond of military rule. Where he had represented himself (and had been widely represented) as the servant and saviour of a grateful nation, he began to be perceived as an ambitious deceiver who sacrificed English blood and resources for his own self-interest and aggrandizement. While he cannot be blamed for military setbacks that for several years compromised his image as providential victor, the king did not do enough in person to perform the role of father of the nation – or indeed to develop those affective relations with subjects which were evermore a vital component of authority at a time when frequent elections were involving more ordinary people in the business of government. No less a supporter than Burnet lamented that 'he took little pains to gain the affection of the nation; nor did he constrain himself [that is, make an effort] to render his government more acceptable'.[200] Only the king's public and palpable grief at the death of Mary temporarily bridged the distance and connected him to his people. In a sermon of 1694, William Sherlock, the Dean of St Paul's, perhaps intending to publicize the more human side of a cold personality, spoke of 'such soft and tender passions in such a warlike, fearless mind'.[201] Archbishop Tenison even more directly opined that the king 'endeared himself to his people by that tenderness' which manifested a personality 'made up of courage and humanity'.[202]

But any such emotional connection (and we recall that William did not attend the queen's funeral) was short-lived. As we have seen, he eschewed triumphs and festivals, refused to touch for the king's evil, and only once went on a progress beyond his palaces and hunting lodges. If anything, after Mary's death, the king became even more invisible and more of a recluse. Conscious perhaps of an ever greater gulf between himself and his subjects with Mary dead, he was also exposed all the more to the antagonism of those who doubted his right to rule and were suspicious of his loyalty to the church.[203] The Peace of Ryswick, though it was welcome and celebrated, robbed William of his principal role as military commander, removed him from the continental stage, and focused attention on the domestic ills and problems he had neglected and on the pent-up discontents which destroyed his junto administration. With the failure of the partition treaties indicating that the triumphant peace was to be only fleeting, with his health failing and without an heir, William appeared, towards the end of his reign, an isolated figure faced with challenge from every quarter, even a resurgent Jacobite party.[204] Before he died, William secured the Protestant Hanoverian succession he favoured and reassembled the coalition that would eventually lead to the final defeat of France. But not least on account of his character and his failure to present himself and connect with his people, he did not, as one admirer claimed he did, reign 'in the hearts of his subjects'.[205] Given what he achieved abroad and at home – and he has been credited with no less than the elevation of England as a great power and the creation of modern English government – it might be thought that William's failure as a performer on the stage of monarchy mattered little; that party politics more than personal charisma now determined all. Such a conclusion would be too simple, if not wrong. For all the achievements of his reign, William III underlines the importance of the personal image and performance of monarchy, which he neglected to his cost – and still more to the cost of the monarchy that was diminished not least by his neglect of the theatre of majesty.[206]

CHAPTER 12

RIVAL REPRESENTATIONS

I

In any political society in which the image of the government constituted an important element of its authority, opposition to official representations, as well as policies, was (and of course is) inevitable. The more, from the Reformation onwards, that early modern English monarchs projected themselves and represented themselves as divine in words, visuals and rituals, the more opponents and critics contested their image: in pamphlets, cartoons and popular festival or carnival. The English civil war was as much a contest for representation as a military conflict.[1] And, though the Restoration understandably tempered for a time the language of political division, Charles II was in no doubt that support for his kingship could not simply be assumed but in a divided polity had to be cultivated. Indeed, the growth of print and the expansion of a literate, politically aware citizenry made it necessary for any seventeenth-century government to persuade subjects – and increasingly ordinary subjects – of its authority. The first emergence of party in Charles II's reign made this an even greater challenge for any monarch, since in reorganizing and institutionalizing political divisions, parties made it harder to secure – or even claim – unity and threatened to make opposition (for most of the period contemned as faction) respectable. It was not the smallest of Charles II's achievements that he checked, or as importantly appeared to have checked, some of these developments. While he threw in his lot with the Anglican-Tories, he discredited his opponents and was credibly able in the last years of his reign to *claim* to rule with national, popular support. The succession of his brother was a tribute to Charles's representational as well as political skill, as James II acceded to his throne with no outpouring of vocal opposition, indeed with rebellion the only resort left to Monmouth and his supporters. James, as we know, by threatening, as was widely perceived, the church and constitution, legitimated opposition. Yet, because he alienated the Anglican establishment more than any others, his short reign did not – because there was no need to

– legitimate party. Few disagreed with the need to bring the king to account, or even with the need to appeal to Orange as a means of putting pressure on him. It was less the course of James II's short reign than the events of 1688 and the Revolution themselves that transformed both the monarchy and the political culture and, along with the legitimation of parties, brought a contest between representation and counter-representation to the centre of government and public discourse.

The bitter religious divisions of the sixteenth century are enough to remind us that William III was not the first monarch to face ideological opposition to his legitimacy or questions about his divine right to rule. But he was perhaps the first early modern English monarch who had, from the moment of his succession and throughout his reign, to contend with a rival whom many considered the rightful king; an opposition that was organized as a party and socially legitimated; and significant numbers of subjects who were uncertain of their obligation or allegiance to him. William determined not to govern as head of one party; but he could not escape the fact that he ruled in a new condition of parties: of rival organizations, allegiances and identities that began to shape literary, cultural and social life as well as politics. During William's reign, while polemical efforts were still sometimes made to castigate opponents as factious, or as traitors, in the new circumstances of party, official images and representations were (more than ever) fashioned and disseminated as part of a dialogue with counter-representations and opponents. Parties, as Mark Knights put it, brought 'a new version of the political game' in which the exercise and representation of monarchy were now part of a culture of public participation and partisanship.[2]

For all the appeals to unity, Williamite propaganda itself freely recognized the state's divisions. In 1689, for example, the loyal Thomas Long, in *A Resolution of Certain Queries*, acknowledged that 'almost in every parish there are persons of different persuasions' about the legitimacy of the new government.[3] In his sermon of 30 January 1695, the canon of St George's, Windsor, John Hartcliffe, praising the Revolution, lamented the divisions in the realm, those who 'list themselves in parties', or who gave their allegiance to 'dishonest parties'.[4] The next year a preacher at the public fast at Hexham in Northumberland feared the consequences of the divisions that beset the realm, and the Association that followed in the wake of that year, it was recognized, exacerbated them.[5] As the government was well aware, it was not just the political elite that was divided but the ordinary people too. In 1695 the licensing of works prior to publication lapsed and effectively with it any censorship.[6] As many loyalists complained, print fostered as well as reflected divisions in the state and exposed them to common readers and public discussion. In the coffee houses, if the author of the *School of Politics* paints an accurate picture, common sailors and barbers sat down with knights and lawyers to argue about the very nature of William's authority – 'Of Kings de facto and de iure' – while Whigs and Tories publicly aired their differences at their designated tables where

> *One* would affirm that no pretence
> Could *Salus Populi* make Sense;
> T'other affirm'd the *Royal Line*,
> Could never be of *Right Divine*.[7]

As disputes and quarrels mounted over religion and taxes, over who was the rightful king, fights broke out, rupturing what the author nostalgically called the old 'regular society'.[8]

Along with divisions, opposition, though often regretted and denounced, was now freely acknowledged by the regime as a fact of political life. Himself a warm supporter, the anonymous author of *The History of the Late Revolution* freely admitted in 1689 that there were many opposed to the 'happy' change, as did the contributors to the Oxford University volume of verse presented the same year to the king and queen.[9] In 1690, Archbishop Tillotson confessed in a fast sermon that on account of the animosities to William's government the nation was 'very far from being happy'.[10] Nor did the passage of time much abate those animosities. In his Thanksgiving Day sermon preached in October 1692, Samuel Slater, urging his flock to love the king, nevertheless noted the 'discontents', the 'malice' against the government.[11] Analysing in 1693 the 'miserable estate we are fallen into from the happy and glorious prospect of things which we had in 1688', Daniel Defoe concluded that William was doomed to face opposition even within his ministerial ranks when Whigs were critics of monarchy and the Tories supporters of prerogative but opponents of Orange.[12] As he reviewed *The Present Aspect of Our Times* five years after the king's coronation, Robert Fleming could (though he passionately wished it were not so) only see opposition escalating to the point where he 'did not question but that many in this day may be too deeply engaged in sad and cross designs to the present settlements'.[13] If William's victory at Namur and the assassination plot brought some support and sympathy for the king, they apparently did little to diminish a sense of unabated opposition. In the preface to his *Political Essay* of 1698, William Pudsey, who announced himself as an early supporter of the Revolution, unhappily concluded that 'I do not find that men are less apt to talk against the government now than they were seven or eight years ago'; and there is enough testimony to suggest that he would not have found otherwise later in the reign.[14] As Pudsey's term 'talk' might imply, as well as the partisan polemics of disgruntled Tories or disappointed Whigs, there was widespread opposition to William's government which apologists for the regime often described as 'murmuring' – giving voice to discontent. In a poem, for example, on the memory of Queen Mary, written after the victory at

Namur, the satirist Robert Gould castigated the 'murm'ring People . . . That grudge . . . Caesar. . . his due'.[15] Similarly, at his thanksgiving sermon for the victory in September, Vincent Alsop regretted that instead of praying for a prince 'so tender of his subjects', they were 'murmuring at them upon any little tip'.[16] The opposition of both party and public did not just exist; it was recognized, indeed was part of the culture of representation in a partisan society.

The principal counter-image to William and Mary was, of course, James Stuart and his son. In that respect, William was placed in the position of Oliver Cromwell: of exercising power while a rival claimed legitimate authority and garnered support for that claim. James may have fled England in fear for his safety, but from exile he ensured that he remained a real presence as well as a memory in English political life, distributing (as Edward Corp and others have shown) portraits, engravings and medals of himself and his son, the true and legitimate heir after his father (and before Mary) to the English throne. Indeed, the sheer number of published engravings and mezzotints of Prince James Francis Edward seem intended to persuade English subjects of his legitimacy in both senses of that word: as, against the warming-pan stories, the natural child of his father and mother, and as the rightful heir to the British kingdoms.[17] As for James II himself, in exile he continued plans for military invasion with an active propaganda campaign of declarations written to his English subjects, insisting on his right and their allegiance and denouncing his daughter and son-in-law as usurpers. Such a threat was James's very existence that Williamites tried on occasions to convince people that he was dead. As early as 1689, a pamphlet thought 'fit to publish to the world the full and true relation of the death of King James as we have received it from unquestioned and undeniable intelligence', and other such rumours were repeated.[18] James, however, was not only very much alive, he was publishing and distributing declarations in Ireland, letters to the Convention in Scotland, and a 'letter in vindication of himself' to all his kingdoms.[19] The letter, interestingly republished by Williamite loyalists who rushed to answer it, reminded English people that, before he had fled, James had redressed ills, restored forfeited borough charters and resolved on a parliament.[20] It was Orange, he argued, who had resorted to force against his person and against the laws which (he sharply observed) the precedent case of his father suggested boded ill for all. It was he, James insisted, who was the rightful king and the king with (here appealing to xenophobia) the true interest of England at heart.

As the response indicates, James's protestations and charges, including his own alleged harsh treatment, caused anxiety in official circles. Nor was the power of his propaganda much reduced by the defeat of the Jacobites in Ireland. In 1692, as well as orchestrating renewed plans for invasion, James bombarded his three lost kingdoms with letters and declarations against William's government.

A letter to Privy Councillors calling them to come to St Germain to witness his wife's labour both advertised her fertility and suggested the legitimacy of the prince;[21] a broadside, *The Most Gracious Declaration to All His Loving Subjects*, offered all who had supported William an amnesty if they did not oppose James's endeavour to regain his throne and promised the removal of burdensome taxes and the referral of all to parliament.[22] Taking advantage of the mounting discontent, James cleverly coupled the vindication of his own right to the re-establishment of the liberties of the people. In the larger declaration, commanding his subjects' assistance, he expanded on the deceit that the ambitious Orange had perpetrated against a too credulous people, denied that he had willingly abdicated, and catalogued the ills that had followed Dutch rule: the loss of ships and trade, the draining of subjects' money to Holland, and tyrannical government. Recalling the Wars of the Roses to argue that without his restitution England faced prolonged civil conflict, James assured readers of his support for the law, parliament and the Church of England, and his commitment to a monarchy founded on 'the united interest and affection of the people'.[23] Apostiled as written 'per ipsum regem manu propria' ('by the king's own hand') 'in the eighth year of our reign', the very form of the declaration, in presenting James as the king, fundamentally challenged William's position and ensured that the opposition of those who questioned his legitimacy was sustained. That James authorized the same year the publication of all his *Royal Truths*, together with an *Imago Regis* and engravings that evoked the *Eikon Basilike*, strengthened his claim to royal authority and reminded subjects of both his Stuart descent and their sin of rebellion.[24] The government licensed, and may well have commissioned, the response which answered James's declaration clause by clause.[25] But, rather as with Milton's attempt to discredit *Eikon Basilike*, the length of the response made it seem defensive and, rather than limiting the damage, the reprinting of the declaration and rehearsal of old arguments reopened a wound which the government needed to be closed.[26] Curiously – and perhaps not wisely – the response left James the last word and his royal signature from St Germain as the last line on the page.

Indeed, there is some evidence that the Williamite government was concerned that James II's *Declaration* resonated with some subjects. In his charge to the Grand Jury at Chester in October 1693, Henry Booth, Earl of Warrington, delivered an attack on James, fearing that some had 'lately conceived a better opinion of him'.[27] If anything (as was the case with Booth himself) the 'better opinion' probably grew as William's popularity declined. After the death of Mary, as we have noted, there was increasing talk of a restoration of the Stuarts; and, while the assassination plot of 1696 discredited the Jacobites, James II remained a dangerous focus for resistance to the regime. In the wake of the Peace of Ryswick, by which Louis XIV at last recognized William as king, James issued a manifesto urging the Protestant princes of Europe (and his English subjects) to restore him.[28] Appealing to the sanctity of oaths, James argued that 'the Protestant princes are by the principles of their own religion obliged to acknowledge' that Orange was a usurper and that rightful authority remained in the exiled king and his son whose legitimacy he again asserted.[29] Recalling the Restoration, he confidently predicted that, since the late (1688) Revolution resembled the civil war, 'there is all the reason in the world to believe that the nation will return to its ancient laws and true masters, as it has twice done within 37 years past'.[30] It was, to any who had lived through two revolutions, a powerful argument. Though Titus Oates endeavoured to dismiss James's *Manifesto* with a derisive 'do you think that scribbling will ever bring you back?' the government felt the need to counter it clause by clause.[31] Rumour about a possible Stuart restoration dogged William to the end of the century, if not quite to the grave; and, albeit there was never sufficient military or political support for him, James II remained a figure who by his words as well as actions was a focus of opposition to the regime.[32]

Certainly James did not lack for vocal supporters who sustained a campaign directed at destabilizing the Revolution settlement. The Jacobites, of course, led the opposition to the conferment on William of the crown and to any recognition of his right to rule. In his 1689 *The Desertion Discussed*, for example, the non-juring Bishop Jeremy Collier denied that James had abdicated, dismissed arguments against him as a sham, and derided the monarchy of William and Mary: 'Like plate without the royal impression they ought not to be obtruded for current coin.'[33] Behind the similar argument of many anonymous pamphlets were the pens of Jacobite authors who kept the issue of legitimacy alive. Indeed, James's supporters remained quite willing to be identified as a party, as though claiming a parity with Whigs and Tories. In his *The Jacobite Principles Vindicated*, published in 1693, perhaps to coincide with James's declaration, Charlwood Lawton praised the exiled king and, indicating that he would be advised to forget and forgive the past, promised readers that 'a good and settled monarchy you may have', if they restored James.[34] The next year the scion of a Catholic family, Alexander Irvine, in a staged dialogue concerning the Revolution, attacked the contradictions in the argument used to justify the removal of James and catalogued the ill consequences for the church and nation of what had unjustly been carried out.[35] The same year, a defender of James's 1693 *Declaration* answered the riposte to it by the government respondent James Welwood and, castigating a foreign regime for robbing the English, predicted that in the end the English people's love for their legitimate ruler would overcome allegiance to a usurper: 'that the king [James II] will be restored,' he closed, 'I don't at all question. The follies, faults, the unsuccessfulness . . . of the Prince of Orange make way for his restoration.'[36] Jacobites, as might have been anticipated, took the death of Queen Mary as an opportunity to concentrate attacks on William's legitimacy and even gained support from surprising quarters, the former radical Whig Robert Ferguson agreeing that William was a usurper and that James should be recalled.[37]

If there was a lull in Jacobite propaganda with the discovery of the assassination plot, it was but temporary. In 1698, for example, a Jacobite tract, *The Fidelity of a Loyal Subject*, admonished readers that 'the righteous God who restored King Charles the Second can as easily restore King James the Second' and, threatening renewed civil war, urged William to see right done and the Prince of Wales recognized and restored.[38] With James himself retreating from active engagement to preparation for the restoration of his son, Jacobites in England turned their attention to pressing the Pretender's call for support against William's manoeuvres to secure a Hanoverian succession.[39] In 1700 it seems probable that it was Jacobites who published a collection of the old addresses to James II congratulating him on the birth of his son, to undermine the old charge that he had not been legitimate offspring; and the high church Tory, William Pittis, urging that 'no Foreign Lion mount the Regal Throne' of England, argued for the Prince of Wales against the succession of a distant cousin with no defensible claim to the throne.[40] As the death of James in 1701 saw Jacobite obituaries that praised the virtues of a misrepresented monarch and attacked the Revolutionary regime, so the same year birthday odes to the Prince of Wales celebrated the beauty and intelligence of a 'darling PRINCE' who, it was argued, alone held out the prospect of peace and settlement.[41] Lives of James II published in the immediate aftermath of his death contrasted his patriotism with a government that had subordinated England to the Dutch, praised his generosity and accessibility in implied contrast to William's reserve, and represented him as a man of conscience unlike the ambitious Prince of Orange.[42] Publication of James's *Memoirs* and *Last Dying Words*, as well as evoking the *Eikon Basilike*, endeavoured to win sympathy for a king who 'has been the most abused of all mankind', a Christ-like king who declared on his deathbed, at the moment of truth, that 'I have never entertained a thought that was not levelled at the good of my subjects.'[43] The empathy inspired by such portraits of the dying James was clearly intended to benefit a son whom his father had schooled always to remember that 'kings are not made for themselves but for the good of the people', and to see his subjects as his children.[44] The author of *A Letter to a Minister of State, Concerning the Pretended Prince of Wales Being Proclaimed King* nervously acknowledged that, far from fading away with James's death, the Jacobites were reinvigorated by the prospect of support for his son.[45] Even non-Jacobites were willing to express admiration for a prince who was handsome, witty, vigorous and 'performs all his exercises to perfection'; and the non-juror George Hickes only slightly exaggerated when, rehearsing again the case for his legitimacy and right, he reported that the claim of the Prince of Wales 'is the great talk of the town'.[46] If the figure of James II dogged William III almost to the end of his reign, Jacobite opposition continued unrelentingly to challenge the Revolution and the king – to his grave and beyond.

Jacobitism was a minority opposition movement. But Jacobite propaganda did damage to the Williamite regime by vocalizing and sustaining doubts that many beyond Jacobite circles had about the rights of the king and queen. Whether his title accurately reflected his own agenda or not, the author of *An Impartial Disquisition* carried many with him in denying that a just title to the throne could be secured by conquest or the deprivation of a rightful king or his heir.[47] Nor did time, as the government might have hoped, settle doubts. Rather, as the burdens of war mounted, it was increasingly argued that the 'mischievous' justification of events, based on James's alleged abdication, had caused all the subsequent problems.[48] Before the Convention declared a vacancy in the throne and elected William and Mary to fill it, *The Price of the Abdication* insisted, England had enjoyed peace and plenty: 'the very source of all . . . our fatal ruins was the expulsion of the king.'[49] While we cannot know the numbers who held such views, it is noteworthy that a government apologist still in 1693 acknowledged 'the loud clamours about right which disquiet so many men's minds', to the point of threatening trouble.[50] As the anonymous author of the allegory, *Antiquity Revived: Or The Government Of A Certain Island Antciently Called Astraea*, put it, 'whensoever there is an unjust or forcible intruder into a throne, he may by violence possess the room of a paternal monarch' but is not 'deemed a rightful father of people.'[51]

It was, of course, the government's own cognisance of the reservations harboured by many that led them to accept a half-hearted *de facto* recognition of William and Mary in 1689. Still in 1693, the loyalist Bishop of Worcester, Edward Stillingfleet, renewing the case for a fresh oath to the king and queen, rejected the proposal for a so-called oath of abjuration because he feared it would 'discover the nakedness of the land' and expose those who still harboured doubts about swearing allegiance.[52] The next year, at a day of thanksgiving for William's preservation from a planned French invasion, preaching at Sutton in Surrey, Henry Day traduced those who continued to question the legality of the government and bitterly regretted that 'those seven years we have been disputing the right of King William and the honesty of our establishment.'[53] For all that it in some measure benefited the government, the assassination plot of 1696 again stirred up the opposition of those not willing to swear to William as monarch *de iure*. In his treatise defending the new national Association formed to protect the king in the wake of the plot, the Whig lawyer William Atwood felt the need to counter the 'treasonable opinion' of not only those who refused to subscribe to the clause, 'declaring his majesty to be rightful and lawful king', but of some who still 'object novelty against this Revolution.'[54] Though exploited by Jacobites, reservations about William's right by no means translated into active Jacobitism. But, perhaps more damagingly, they did undermine William's self-representation as the providentially appointed ruler of three nations and consigned him to being a king without the full allegiance of many of his subjects.

Jacobitism and questions of right were not the only forms of opposition to William and Mary's self-representation as virtuous king and queen, devoted to their English subjects. Soon – for the government disconcertingly soon – after they had succeeded to the throne, discontents were articulated and coalesced into what historians have described, and what contemporaries recognized, as a cross-party 'Country' opposition to royal policies and powers. Recalling the pre-civil war language of a patriotic 'country' opposed to a corrupt and aggrandizing court, their opposition grew in William's parliaments and spread outwards into public print and talk which charged that the ideals and principles of the Revolution had been abandoned by a regime that pursued self-interest, greed and power at the expense of the nation.[55] Along with references to 'murmuring' that we have examined, talk of general 'discontent' began early, the 1690 *School of Politics* regarding the patrons of the coffee houses as 'no friends to the government' – indeed as disaffected and disenchanted.[56]

It was the war, however, and the growth of bureaucracy, patronage and corruption that was a consequence of massive military preparations, the establishment of a national debt and all the apparatus of what has been called a fiscal-military state, that provoked violent suspicion of and opposition to the government. Tories were quick to exploit such discontent which only grew as the vast expenditure of money and men was not matched by success on the battlefield, fuelling the suspicion that resources were misappropriated. And opposition was targeted not only at the Privy Council or royal ministers but directly at the king. In 1693, for example, Thomas Wagstaffe (a bishop of the non-juring church) published a polemical *Supplement to His Majesty's Most Gracious Speech Directed to the Honourable House of Commons*, delivered on 14 March. Addressing the Commons, Wagstaffe criticized William for glossing over the 'misfortunes' and 'miscarriages' that had taken place.[57] Observing that trade was in danger of being lost, that the merchants were not protected at sea, and that 'our money is gone abroad already', Wagstaffe pointed the finger not at 'misfortune' but at misdirection by the government.[58] Dismissing the king's request for yet more funding when the navy had shown itself little better than a 'pasteboard fleet at a mayor's show', Wagstaffe hinted at the need for government accountability: 'if you make provisions for the navy,' he advised MPs, 'we beseech you to begin at the right end, to provide us just and skilful ministers of state.'[59] From criticisms of the failings of the fleet, Wagstaffe proceeded to urge questioning of how large armies had suffered terrible defeats in Flanders and Piedmont and yet again suggested that, rather than a lack of resources, a failure of strategy and command had been to blame.[60] For all this, it was when he moved to problems at home that his critique was most devastating. Reminding

MPs who had increasingly to answer to their electorates, that families had starved to provide taxation, he accused the government of 'misemployment' (a euphemism for embezzlement) of treasure: 'our money is spent contrary to the ends for which you gave it'.[61] Wagstaffe also targeted the debt as a further opportunity for corruption: observing that 'by a strange paradox, the more you give the more you owe', he solved the paradox by claiming that monies were hived off to government pensioners and pressed the Commons to examine the account to track embezzled funds.[62]

Nor, Wagstaffe charged, was corruption confined to the Treasury. In an accusation that stands close to the king himself as traditional custodian of justice, he alleged that, rather than impartial, the judges were stooges of the regime who subordinated law and justice to favouritism and party, and who browbeat juries to obtain spurious convictions of innocent opponents of the government.[63] Finally, in a work that was addressed to a broad public as well as the Commons, Wagstaffe exploited a mounting xenophobic hostility to a foreign ruler. If corn had been scarce, he argued, it was because, even at a time of poor harvest, it had been exported to Holland by a government that 'let the Dutch have our plenty . . . and it is no matter if our poor be starved'.[64] Appealing to histories which had always shown examples of foreigners acting against English interests and recalling the oppressions of the Danes, Wagstaffe warned 'Lord Dutch may become as formidable to us as Lord Dane was to our ancestors.'[65] More sinisterly, he reminded MPs and readers 'that a great part of the military force of this kingdom is in the hands of foreigners' – Dutchmen – and 'give them power to defend us and they have power to ruin us,' even to overthrow the lives, liberties and estates that the Revolution had supposedly secured.[66] Wagstaffe closed his address to the house with advice that they re-enact the old Country insistence on redress of grievance before supply: 'our grievances must be remedied first or never . . . apply effectual remedies to the respective miseries we groan under; and then we will more cheerfully part with our money'.[67] Wagstaffe was a non-juror appealing to wider discontent; his critique of the conduct of war and government was devastating and exemplifies the strength of Country opposition to the court (Wagstaffe employs those very terms) that developed in the early 1690s.

Wagstaffe, though a non-juror, strategically confined his critique to the king's and government's failures and miscarriages, and refrained from fundamental questioning of their legitimacy. In other pamphlets, however, Country discontents extended to a larger, more fundamental questioning of the Revolution. One 1693 treatise, for example, listed as 'the exorbitant price of the abdication' of James II wars, the cost of which had exceeded all Queen Elizabeth's expenditure, debts that would burden the nation for two centuries, high taxes, the corruption of free parliaments by pensioners and eighty thousand English lives sacrificed to an unnecessary conflict.[68] The same year, the

Jacobite printer William Anderton, appealing to the discontented, published a broad-ranging attack on the government under the title *Remarks Upon the Present Confederacy*. Again listing the huge expenses of the war, loss of the nation's wealth and trade, 'isolation of justice', and invasions of liberties and properties, the tract concluded that in 1688 the nation had been deceived and 'gulled out of all those real blessings of government they formerly enjoyed'.[69] Indeed, so unpopular had the government become that the author of *New Court Contrivances* felt he could persuade readers that the discovery of supposed plots was merely a cynical device to strengthen an unpopular regime and enable it to tyrannize over the liberty of the subject.[70]

Opposition to the war and the growth of corruption was directed against the king personally. Striking to the heart of William's personal reputation – and representation – a pamphleteer described him as, rather than a pious king, one who 'plays tricks and juggles with religion'.[71] The many reports of William's personal bravery on the battlefield the author dismissed as 'all silly nonsensical stories made on purpose to keep up the hearts of the king-making rabble'. It was William, *The Remarks* charged, who had damaged trade, violated justice, destroyed the church and dissimulated; only now could the nation see that he had never intended to secure religion, liberties and properties but, as 'a true Machiavellist', had plotted 'to execute the design of the Confederates and to serve his own ambition'.[72] In 1694 the author of *An Honest Commoner's Speech*, probably a country Whig, answering a royal speech, depicted William as 'a stranger to our constitution' who needed to be checked.[73] Urging MPs not to vote supply for armies and continental wars ('what have we to do there?'), the author stuck to the core of the king's authority: 'remember he is a king of your making and should be of your influencing'.[74] As well as personal abuse of William's appearance and homosexuality, opposition pamphleteers increasingly made the most unflattering comparison with predecessors, especially Oliver Cromwell, another unpopular figure afflicted (as was William) with an ugly nose.[75] In a verse *Parallel Between O.P* [Oliver Protector] *and P.O* [the Prince of Orange], for example, the author unfavourably contrasted with a Cromwell who at least had not fleeced the nation the 'Grand Thief' William, under whose 'cursed Reign' the Dutch had taken all: 'of the two [he] is far the worst Evil'.[76] The extent to which such personal attacks had crossed party lines is illustrated by a pamphlet written by the moral reformer and supporter of Revolution, Edward Stephens. In 1695, in his *Old English Loyalty*, dedicated to William and Mary, Stephens criticized a king who had fallen prey to flattery, permitted corruption and taken poor advice, all of which had contributed to the failures abroad and mismanagement at home.[77] Stephens warned that 'we cannot rationally expect any better success this year than we had last' and forecast no improvement in the king's or country's fortunes 'unless public grievances be duly redressed and notorious criminals duly punished'.[78]

Victory at Namur rendered Stephens's gloomy predictions about the next year false prophecy. But it is far from clear that the favourable turn in William's military fortunes significantly abated the suspicion of the government or the Country opposition to it. The year after William's victory, in what might have seemed an inappropriately titled tract, *England's Calamities Discovered*, the broker James Whiston criticized the government for promoting favourites, selling offices and tainting justice.[79] The same year, 1696, one Robert Crosfeild launched a campaign against government corruption in a series of pamphlets with titles such as *Brief Observations Upon the Present Distresses of the Public, with Some Account of the Causes Thereof, viz. the Corruptions in the Government*.[80] Charging a corrupt cabal of wilfully perpetuating continental conflict for their own ends – 'to turn the war into a trade' – Crosfeild presented a petition to parliament 'complaining of the aforesaid corruption'. In his longer *Dialogue Between a Modern Courtier and an Honest English Gentleman*, he detailed venality in the Admiralty, Treasury, Council of Trade and Post Office, which the government had concealed, though 'everyone knows their wickedness'.[81] Warning that such corruptions strengthened the Jacobites, Crosfeild presented himself as an honest, loyal critic who sought to save the king from his ministers and the nation from slavery.

Even the Peace of Ryswick did not abate the criticism. While some reflected on a period during which 'all men in public employment have been let loose to their own appetite', others found new cause for concern in William's desire to maintain a standing army, which led to 'the climax in the history of protests against maintaining professional soldiers'.[82] As Lois Schwoerer has demonstrated, the king's wish to retain an army in an uncertain peace was interpreted – by radical and country Whigs as well as Tories – as a bid to enhance his prerogative and as a danger to English liberties.[83] While Robert Harley led opposition to the Dutch Guard in parliament, a plethora of tracts appeared denouncing William's proposal to retain an armed force.[84] In a series of pamphlets, beginning with *An Argument, Shewing That a Standing Army Is Inconsistent with A Free Government and Absolutely Destructive to the Constitution of the English Monarchy*, John Trenchard 'initiated . . . an eventually successful paper war against William III's standing army', a paper war that recruited writers from across the political spectrum.[85] At what might have been expected to be a time of respite if not triumph for William, the king who had presented himself as protector of the constitution was attacked as representing a risk of revived absolutism and as a threat to liberty.

The opposition to a standing army from 1697 highlights how, at the extreme end of the Country opposition to the court, William faced radical challenges to his royal authority and even a resurgent republican opposition to monarchy itself. Republicanism, of course, had not died in 1660 or 1688. Indeed, some saw the 1688 Revolution as another opportunity to remove not just a particular monarch but monarchy itself, the author of *Now Is the Time*, for example, rejecting 'barely to change our Master' and proposing a senate of eighty, not unlike the model Milton had advocated in *The Ready and Easy Way*.[86] While such republican hopes were dashed by a Revolution settlement that did not greatly reduce the powers of the crown, radical Whigs and republicans continued to seek to take advantage of opposition to make William's monarchy more accountable.[87] The fact that, as the *Honest Commoner's Speech* had reminded readers, William was a king of their 'making' unquestionably encouraged and aided those who wished further to curtail royal powers.[88] William's need for money for war itself necessitated frequent parliaments; but this did not prevent critics advocating them as a check on the monarchy. In 1693, for example, in *Some Reasons for Annual Parliaments*, N. N., criticizing heavy taxes and other abuses, and reminding readers that William did not have his crown by 'ius divinum', argued that 'a limited is preferable to a despotic monarchy' and proposed annual parliaments as the best means to secure it.[89] The death of Queen Mary, as well as exciting Jacobite opposition, was also taken as an opportunity by radical Whigs. In 1695, as we saw, the former Whig Robert Ferguson attacked the government in a pamphlet asking *Whether the Parliament Be Not in Law Dissolved by the Death of the Princess of Orange*; and at least one observer on the state of affairs on the death of the queen perceived republicans as manoeuvring to step in to prevent Queen Anne succeeding to the throne.[90]

It was the mid to late 1690s that saw a resurgence of republicanism and the republication of some famous, or notorious, republican treatises.[91] During 1694 and 1695, for example, the republican Henry Neville's translations of Machiavelli's *Discourses* and *Works* were reissued, followed in 1698 by Neville's Harringtonian treatise, *Plato Redivivus*.[92] In 1700 the republican John Toland republished Harrington's own model for a commonweal, *Oceana*.[93] In addition to those works of republican political theory, the 1690s saw the reissue of Exclusion crisis tracts, including Shaftesbury's speeches and the publication of Algernon Sidney's *Discourses Concerning Government* and Milton's *Paradise Lost*, and editions of his works were issued in 1697–9.[94] Toland, in his preface to *Oceana*, posed as a loyalist and did not directly recommend the re-establishment of a Commonwealth, but the government supporters were not taken in. Writing in 1702 on 'the common interest of our king and country', one apologist identifying a band of 'antimonarchical Williamites' judged that 'the most obstinate Jacobites are not near so destructive'.[95]

In fact the problem was that William faced opposition throughout his reign from both Whigs and Jacobites; and at times from both acting in concert. In 1688–9, neither the Jacobites and a fair number of Tories who had hoped to see James brought to account but not expelled nor the radical Whigs wanted the monarchy of William and Mary. Non-jurors were never reconciled to it; many Tories harboured reservations about it; 'true' or Country Whigs were

increasingly alienated by the expansion of government powers and bureaucracy as a consequence of the war. As William was told, though he was their
man, the Whigs were not supporters of the prerogative; and he was not the
Tories' king.[96] The costs of the war and the early years of military disappointments sharpened the hostility of both, and the death of Mary reopened questions about by exactly what right he sat on the throne now that James's daughter
was deceased. From the time of the Peace of Ryswick, opponents joined forces
to check William's ambitions to retain a large peacetime army. Jacobites (as we
have seen) pressed strongly the case for Prince James to succeed to the throne
on William's death, and with the death of the Duke of Gloucester, Princess
Anne's only heir in 1700, the issue of the succession again became a political
battle. William defeated attempts to recognize the Pretender and secured, after
Anne, the succession of the Protestant Hanoverians. But Tory and Whig opponents ensured that the powers of a future foreign dynasty would be significantly limited and checked. In 1701 the author of *The Claims of the People*
protested that the hopes of the Revolution had not been fulfilled, and that
subjects had remained 'only spectators' in the business of government.[97]
However, The Act of Settlement, passed in June that year, did much to alter the
constitutional balance of power.[98] While meeting William's wishes for a permanent Protestant settlement and excluding Catholics from any future succession, the Act represented a triumph for those who had opposed William's own
government. For the Act specified that in the event of a foreign sovereign, no
wars could be waged for territories that did not belong to the English crown
without the consent of parliament and, indeed, that no monarch could leave
the realm without such consent. Along with a direct prevention of any repetition of William's actions and priorities, the Act prohibited any foreigner (even
naturalized) from being a Privy Councillor, officer or MP and made judges
accountable not to the king but to parliament, provisions which echoed charges
of undue foreign influence, bribed parliaments, and corrupt justice. If, for all
the divisions over 1688, William succeeded to the throne with little constitutional diminution of regal powers, the Act of Settlement demonstrated the
strength of opposition he had aroused and which had developed over the
course of his reign.

My brief discussion here has only given a glimpse of the range and scale of
opposition to the image of William III. In truth, perhaps more than for any
earlier reign, opposition shaped and defined the king's own representation. For
where earlier rulers had met with opposition to specific policies, none –
certainly in the seventeenth century – had from the outset faced a significant
party that refused to recognize their legitimacy. While the political nation had
more or less united in welcoming his intervention, as king William was the
king of a party, whatever his efforts not to be tied to it. Though employing
Tories in his administration, William never fully won their loyalty, while in

doing so he alienated Whigs who expected a monopoly of office and spoils in return for their support. William was also the first king to face parties, and therefore an opposition that was organized both in and out of parliament. While most still lamented divisions, parties organized to petition, influence elections and propagandize made opposition, if not fully respectable, a recognized fact of political life and a new and difficult condition of monarchical rule. As clubs and coffee houses, as well as printers and bookshops, increasingly developed party associations and identities, so subjects too acquired loyalties other than to – and perforce at times opposed to – the government.[99]

William, it has been suggested, helped the process of recognizing and legitimating opposing voices.[100] Because his priority was building cross-party support for his war, he accepted what was a half-hearted Tory recognition of his rightful authority. In so doing, he condoned any who still felt that he was not the *de iure* monarch and, in the process, alienated Whigs for whose own position it was important that he was. As so often, a compromise that was intended to mute contention probably enhanced it, and certainly weakened William's position in the face of it. William's compromises and employment of Whigs and Tories secured his immediate ends and may have prevented insurrection; but they meant that he always faced discontents within the government and parliament, as in the nation. Moreover, William further legitimated dissension by – whichever party dominated in his administration – maintaining a dialogue with its, and the government's, opposition.[101]

Importantly for our story, the king's openness to both parties and his complex and frequent shifts between them, with most of his administrations some mixture of both, complicated, and perhaps dulled the force of, his image and representation. In not hitching himself to one party in a partisan world, William perhaps never enjoyed supporters who were throughout spokesmen for all *he* sought or himself endeavoured to represent. At various times, though they were Williamite government spokesmen and propagandists, Whig or Tory writers were also propagandists for their own parties which, even when in office, did not follow all the king's wishes; the Whigs by no means supported a standing army and the Tories in 1700 refused to re-enter war over the breach of the Partition Treaties. William, of course, was absent for much of his reign and, even when present, not given to long speeches. It was not these reasons alone, however, that led to the king's own voice being somewhat drowned out. The sheer scale and noise of party polemic came to override royal utterance. That, as a monarch devoted to action, William did not much mind only exacerbated the tendency.

In the reign of William III, then, opponents and opposition became – differently as well as to a greater extent than before – part of the institutions of political life, part of royal government, even a facet of the image of the king who did not cast permanently into the wilderness those who had, or would, oppose him. William inherited parties, but it was his reign that saw them become an accepted and regular part of social, cultural and political life, and with that changed both the exercise of monarchical government and the image of the monarch.

William III, the great military commander, cut a sad figure in the last years and months of his life. Leaning heavily on a cane when he walked, sometimes needing to be carried, his legs swollen, and suffering from gout in his hand, he appeared older than his years and unlikely to live to see the problems in Europe or England resolved.[102] The king, however, recovered enough to meet parliament in February 1701 and, with unusual grace, even entertained MPs at Kensington until the early hours. But the house was not in a co-operative mood and, as well as insisting on clauses in the Act of Settlement that represented an insult to William, they cut back on supply.[103] A new parliament the next year and some improvement in his health might have opened a last chapter of William's campaign against France. Instead a fall from his horse and a broken collarbone led to a fever and his death.

II

'There is,' a preacher had said at Mary's funeral in 1694, 'no certainer indication of the justice or violence of a reign past than the concern that is shown at the prince's death.'[104] William's death was mourned in a plethora of sermons that extolled him. The author of *The Essay for a Comprehension*, preaching on Psalm 82: 6 ('I have said you are Gods . . . but you shall die like men'), praised a ruler whom 'it had pleased God to raise up . . . to be under him our Saviour and Defender'.[105] Lauding his military prowess, his balancing of prerogative and liberty, his political skills and personal piety and morality, the author characterized William as 'the person designed by Providence to accomplish the salvation he had begun by setting us upon the lasting foundation of peace and righteousness'.[106] Preaching at St James's, Clerkenwell, the chaplain to the Duke of Newcastle, Devel Pead, singled out William's heroic actions and figured him as another David sent to protect and lead a chosen people: 'he was exalted to be our king and his exaltation was by the will of God'.[107] In what was clearly a very popular sermon, preached and published in several editions, by John Piggott, William, contrasted with a predecessor who had ruled arbitrarily and illegally, was celebrated as the deliverer of Protestants and 'the common father of his people'.[108] 'He was the darling of Providence,' Piggott wrote, 'the very man that God delighted to honour.'[109] In his *Sermon Preached on the Sad Occasion of the Death of the Best of Kings*, Thomas Goodwin told his congregation that William's 'whole life was a constant course of doing good to the nation'.[110] Reminding his parishioners at Morefields in London of William's piety, tolerance, mildness and kindness, Joseph Jenkins judged that 'he came purely to serve us in our distress' and 'he was the joy of our heart'.[111]

Around the country, as well as in the capital, William did not want for loyal preachers who delivered sermons lauding his virtues. At Cobham in Surrey, William Tucker lamented the loss of God's vicegerent who had delivered the people from slavery and popery.[112] Himself eminent in piety and goodness, Tucker preached, William had throughout directed all his endeavours for the welfare of his subjects. Taking as the text of his sermon at Richmond 'the memory of the just is blessed' (Proverbs 10: 7), Thomas Wise painted a biographical portrait of a hero pious, just and kind, the best of husbands who sacrificed his own interest for the public and 'ruled as a subject', rather than ostentatiously or solitarily.[113] William, he prophesied, would forever live in the temple of memory.[114] At St Mary's church in Nottingham, the vicar, Edward Clarke, compared William favourably to Saul, presenting him as a prince wiser and more equitable.[115] At Andover and Portsmouth, the minister Samuel Chandler, praising a king who had pursued the public good and moral reform, called William 'the good genius of England', 'our English Josiah'.[116] Also taking as his comparison Josiah, Richard Norris recalled a glorious reign in which victories had been won, religion and plenty secured, and the best constitution in the world safeguarded.[117] To him, William was simply 'the greatest man that ever was'.[118] For William Bentley, the king had been a Moses, 'the most considerable prince in Europe' who had raised Britain to glory.[119]

Not to be outdone by the Whig preachers, poets also went to press to memorialize in verse the deceased king. The author of *The Mournful Congress: A Poem on the Death of the Illustrious King William*, a 'sincere lover of his prince and country', figured William abroad as another Augustus, 'EUROPA's Bulwark and its Chief Defence', and at home as the prince who 'Came Timely in to save the Sacrifice/Made of Religion – And their Liberties/To a *Despotick, Arbitrary* Sway'.[120] The author of *Britannia's Loss*, recalling a Caesar and other antique heroes, praised a king who had pursued the common cause, the public good and the nation's liberty: '*Augustus*-like, his Country was his Care' and '*Lycurgus*-like, our Manners he refin'd'.[121] A 'True *Pater Patriae*', the poet concluded 'has our *Caesar* been'.[122] While Cambridge University issued a volume of Greek and Latin poems commending the king, in his *Pindaric Poem Sacred to the Glorious Memory of King William III* Marshal Smith asked readers to think back to the ruin that had faced them when laws and religion were trampled on and what 'Great William' had done for them.[123] Comparing Orange's deliverance of England to Christ's redemption of fallen man, the poet insisted 'our Great Monarch' restored 'halcyon days' to England, and security to Europe: 'This was our Prince our Saviour first, our Guardian Angel now'.[124] The author of *The Mournful Muse* similarly penned an elegy on 'William the Great, the most Magnificent/God's *High-Commissioner*' 'who bore a virtuous Soul and Pious

Mind'.[125] The Whig panegyrist John Oldmixon, in his *Funeral-Idyll, Sacred to the Glorious Memory of King William III*, penned a pastoral dialogue in praise of England's Caesar, 'Great *Nassau*' whose 'vertues and his Deeds of Arms, shall live/To all Posterity recorded down'.[126] Two poets, perhaps in the hope that they would inspire some testament in stone, offered monuments to William's memory in verse. Robert Fleming's *Fame's Mausoleum* was a 'pindaric poem with a monumental inscription sacred to the glorious memory of William the great', which sought to memorialize 'Great William's Name', 'A Name that fills the World, and that will last as long'.[127] Narrating William's life and 'galland [*sic*] and heroick Deeds', as redeemer of both the Netherlands and England, Fleming urged readers:

> Let's then immortalise our *David's* Name
> To be the Wonder and Discourse of Fame.[128]

The Whig poet and critic John Dennis constructed as his *Monument* 'A Poem Sacred to the Immortal Memory of the Best and Greatest of Kings'.[129] Dedicated to the Duke of Devonshire, William's Lord Steward, Dennis's blank-verse poem paid tribute to 'The Grand, the Great, the Godlike William', the 'Great Soul that watch'd the Christian World':

> So WILLIAM did, and seem'd design'd by Fate
> T'assert the awful Government of God,
> And Liberty of Man; and ne're did Heav'n
> Nor fate do more for mortal Man than him.
> . . .
> AND never was it known that mortal Man
> More Noble, more Heroick Deeds perform'd
> Than WILLIAM in the Cause of God and Liberty.[130]

Dennis's *Monument* concludes:

> WILLIAM the Great, the Good, the Just is gone;
> Yet never, never shall He die entire,
> But his Immortal Memory shall last
> As long as lovely Liberty remains.
> For WILLIAM was the Greatest, Best of Kings.[131]

While the Whig poets endeavoured to ensure that paeans to William's life and memory eclipsed the numerous poems commemorating James II, in prose historians and statesmen rushed into print with lives and times of Orange to secure, as they hoped, his historical reputation and, with his, that of the

Revolution and the Whig Party. Fittingly, Bishop Burnet, William's propagandist in 1688 and for much of his reign, was quick to the press with *A Complete History of the Glorious Life and Actions of That Most Renowned Monarch William the Third*.[132] At only sixteen pages long and illustrated with a simple portrait of William crowned and bearing the sceptre and orb, Burnet's history traced Orange's career from 1672 when he emerged into public life to save the Netherlands from French invasion. From there the *History* moves within a few pages to present Orange as a saviour again – of England in 1688. Briefly listing William's victories (and passing over setbacks and defeats), Burnet described the 'noble actions, worthy achievements and glorious undertakings' of William 'from the happy times of his proclamation to the day of his much lamented death'.[133] Burnet's brief account was amplified in *The Glorious Life and Heroic Actions of . . . William III* than whom, the author insisted, 'none more claims the admiration of the intelligent world and the homage and pious respect of mankind'.[134] Containing a full account (and justification) of the Revolution, this longer *Life* emphasized all the providential blessings on, and memorable actions of, England's king, who 'made so great a conquest to his own glory and honour of his kingdom'.[135] 'His glorious actions will be remembered', it concluded, 'and his name will be kept sacred to posterity'.

As well as these accounts, there were other histories and lives of William published the year of his death. In *Princely Excellency*, the anonymous J. A. offered 'an exact account of the most glorious, heroic, and matchless actions' of 'this most illustrious potentate', William III, proclaiming that 'such instances of prudence, courage, magnanimity and heroic virtues are scarcely to be paralleled'.[136] Writing on the grand scale, the annalist Abel Boyer published a three-volume *History of King William III*, the greatest commander and politician of his time, who 'aimed at making himself great by freeing nations from oppression and by preserving to all Christians the liberty of serving God'.[137] Boyer acknowledged that William had faults but, as a ruler who rescued three nations and revived the honour of England, the author concluded that 'he may be ranked among the greatest men and vie with the most celebrated heroes of antiquity'.[138]

Such histories, along with hostile lives of James II and accounts of 1688, laid the foundations of what we now call the Whig view of history: the argument that the 1688 Revolution set England on the road to constitutional monarchy and modernity. Similarly, Brady's sermon praised a king who had by reconciling the royal prerogative and the subjects' liberties re-settled the ancient constitution.[139] And poets, declaring their own commitment to constitutional monarchy, praised William for his 'moderation', his reconciling of prerogative and liberty as

Defender of the Liberties of Man
And Great Protector of the Rights of Kings.[140]

Such characterizations of William in 1702 were inextricably tied not only to a Whig view of the recent past but to visions of the future. As William Fleetwood, Bishop of St Asaph, put it in his 1702 sermon on the king: 'for our own sake we should glorify his noble acts and pursue his memory . . . to satisfy the world abroad how much we value our religion and our Liberties, and how closely we will abide by them by showing how we valued, loved and honoured him . . . whom we esteemed the great precursor of them both'.[141]

Yet even as they endeavoured to control history and memory, in the service of Whig political hegemony, these writers, as they had throughout the reign, acknowledged the divided opinions about the king – and hence about the Revolution – and the opposition that had never abated. One preacher of a funeral sermon lamented the 'divisions and animosities which reign amongst us' and which, he suggested, may have been the cause of William being taken from them; Thomas Goodwin agreed that factions and parties had helped to bring about this calamity.[142] In the preface to his *History*, Abel Boyer admitted that, for all his efforts to be impartial, he could not please all readers when 'people differ so much in opinion about the prince' – some viewing him as an angel of providence, others as an ambitious absolutist.[143] Others admitted, even as they regretted, the extent of ingratitude and antagonism shown towards the nation's deliverer. Pead denounced the 'ungrateful, slandering, contradictory and self ruinating subjects' of William and hoped that malice would not taint his memory; while he wanted to claim that William 'reigned a MONARCH in all Hearts', the author of *The Mournful Muse* decried the ingratitude he had met with.[144] Mr Lewis lamented that during William's reign, '*England* proved a factious, murm'ring Isle'; in similar language, John Dennis criticized those who 'murmur'd at their Great Deliverer' and asked opponents of the king:

> Why dost thou murmur then, ungrateful Isle?
> What dost thou envy to the Best of Kings
> That Happiness which waits upon a Crown
> That thru thy self so freely hath bestow'd.[145]

Even, he lamented,

> His loyal'st supporters too divided were,
> Too factious grown to take just care of him
> . . .
> How few, alas, he found entirely true![146]

More bitterly, Defoe denounced 'an ignominious crowd' of men who openly rejoiced at William's death:

Insult the Ashes of their injur'd King;
Rejoyce at the Disasters of his Crown;
And Drink the Horse's Health that threw him down.[147]

Such opposition and divisions exacerbated the anxieties and doubts expressed by many on the king's death. 'What shall become of us now he is gone,' Edward Clarke asked aloud in his sermon at Nottingham, as he contemplated France poised to take advantage of England's loss.[148] 'What champion,' the poet Marshall Smith asked, 'have you now that can withstand/The Storms which threaten your unguarded land?'[149] With the fate of Europe again about to be decided, he was not alone in fearing for England and her allies now they were bereft of their commander. 'But who shall for us wield the Military?' asked Defoe: 'Who shall the growing Gallic Force subdue?'[150]

The Whigs' anxiety was not merely about the loss of Europe's commander. There was uncertainty about the policies that would be pursued by William's successor, Queen Anne, who was rightly suspected of inclining more to favour the Tories and the church party. Still in 1702, that is, the fate of the Revolution and William's legacy and memory were open to doubt and contest. For all the efforts of preachers and panegyrists, the image and perception of William III remained embroiled in the struggles of party.

III

William's biographers have expressed surprise and disappointment at the contrast between what the king achieved and how he has been regarded and remembered – both by his contemporaries and by later commentators and historians. In what remains the standard life of the king, Stephen Baxter, though not uncritical, credited William with saving his native Holland and with delivering England, reforming its system of government, and leading it to new strength and supremacy, while preserving liberties at home. Writing in the shadow of the two great twentieth-century wars and very much still in the Whig tradition, Baxter praised William's bequests of a strong state and a constitutional monarchy, and for making England 'a better place in which to live'.[151] Yet he had to acknowledge that, at least among the political classes, William was not appreciated – and in some quarters was despised. Four decades on after a period which, despite the tercentenary of the Revolution, saw little reappraisal of William, his latest biographer in brief, Tony Claydon, points up a similar contrast. William, he observes, secured notable achievements – the defeat of a foreign enemy, upholding Protestantism and promoting parliament – which 'have usually led to the British Pantheon'.[152] Yet, William was quickly forgotten after his death (a monument planned was never built) and has received little attention since. Even the 1998 commemorations of 1688 did little to enhance his reputation. As the editor of a major collection of essays celebrating the tercentenary observed, William was – and remains – regarded as an invader and 'the national detestation of William was an intense and remarkable historical phenomenon'.[153] In the words of the *ODNB* entry, 'William went for 300 years with few champions, and the king remains a shadowy figure in British perceptions in the early twenty-first century'. Featuring nowhere in the BBC's list of 100 Great Britons, William, the corporation observes, is most remembered today for his victory at the Battle of the Boyne commemorated by the Orange Order, which has played a prominent part in the troubled modern history of Northern Ireland.[154]

Baxter, Israel and Claydon explain the contrast between William's achievements and his image or reputation in terms of his nationality and English xenophobia. William, writes Baxter, 'remained throughout his life Dutch'.[155] 'The British,' Claydon expands, 'were happy to be rescued from French popery and arbitrary power, but were embarrassed to have received deliverance from a Dutch man. Quite rapidly they wrote William out of the story. They transformed 1688 into a victory for Britain's own moderation and love of Liberty; they retold his war as an apprenticeship for Marlborough – an appropriately British hero.'[156] It would be foolish to deny the significance of either William's foreignness or English prejudice: even the Scottish James I battled to be accepted as a Scot on the English throne. They are not, however, the whole story.

For, not unlike James I, but unlike say the Welsh Tudors, William drew attention to his foreignness and did little to accommodate himself to English ways. As we have seen, he filled his armies with Dutch officers, had Dutch intimates and confidants and, in large measure, withdrew from English courtly and social life which had over centuries accommodated so many foreign princes. William, to take up Baxter's phrase again, not only 'remained throughout his life Dutch', despite being king of England for the last fifteen years of it; he *presented himself* as Dutch. He was often absent – for longer even than campaigns demanded – and, as not least his triumphal entry into The Hague and retreats to Het Loo evidence, he was more comfortable with a Dutch style and mode of rule. The problem of William's perception and reputation, that is, was one not only of his nationality but of his image and representation: of how he presented himself to his English subjects.

The circumstances of his election to the throne meant perhaps that the image and representation of William and Mary, and especially William, would necessarily be different from that of their predecessors. It was for a time fashionable to argue that the 1688 Revolution brought about relatively fewer constitutional changes than was once thought – a view vigorously rejected in the latest account of 1688.[157] When we focus on the image and perception of the monarchs, the altered circumstances of the Revolution are vital. William was not, and he was by no means widely regarded as, a legitimate king; moreover, in not pushing for recognition of his *de iure* rule, he did not even claim to be or insistently present himself as the rightful ruler. While only a minority regarded William as a usurper, it is likely that most accepted him as a convenience: as one who had solved the problem of James's rule and re-established stability without bloodshed. Pragmatism, as so often, solved political problems; but the pragmatism of 1688 unsettled principles – of succession, legitimacy and dynasty – and, as important, traditional discourses of monarchy. Secondly, for all the insistent rhetoric of providential deliverance, William was not – or not in the same way – a king by divine right. God may have secured him victory over James, but it was very obviously human beings and institutions, the aristocratic politicians and the Convention, who and which gave him the crown. Because neither William and Mary nor their subjects forgot it (we recall the reference to subjects 'making' him), the representation and perception of their kingship was bound to be different.[158] Thirdly, as we have remarked, in 1688 William was the monarch of a party. The political nation may have been united in opposition to James II, but by no means all concurred in the decision to place William and Mary on the throne. More than their predecessors, they faced from the outset opposition to their rule which made a continual discourse of unity and harmony transparently a fiction. Whig propaganda, as we have seen, sought to address all these new conditions and problems: to claim continuity, divine intervention and legitimacy. William himself, however, seemed less involved and less concerned than his Whig advocates to promote himself as a legitimate successor. Indeed, sceptical of the claims of his Stuart predecessors, he abandoned many of the discourses and symbols of their monarchical representation, and in the process transformed the image of monarchy.

It has often been argued that, more than the events of 1688 itself, it was the course of William's reign that led to profound changes in the English state and constitution. William's wars required heavy taxation, the development of a bureaucracy, a national debt and bank and frequent parliaments to secure them.[159] The king's preoccupation with fighting Louis XIV meant that he was willing to compromise his prerogative and, as long as supplies came in, to give more power to parliament – to inspect accounts, for example. What has been less remarked are the real changes William's reign effected in the *image and perception* of monarchy. At the simplest level, the most important image and performance of kingship involved the royal presence; and William was very much absent, leaving after the death of Mary in 1694 no visible face of monarchy for many months of each year in England. When he was in his kingdom, both what William did – and did not do – had little effect on ameliorating the problem of long absences. The king did not speak English fluently, did not (other than once) go on progress, did not participate often in ritual ceremonies, and did not make his court the cultural and political focus of the nation. William was not an unskilful speaker and was not oblivious to the power of images. But, in his self-presentation, as in his policies, his priority was securing support for a continental war rather than for his domestic authority or for himself.

Most importantly – and its importance has been understated – William ceased to touch to cure the king's evil and, moreover, mocked the practice. [160] In an age when people still flocked to be cured, the abandonment of the royal touch changed the image and perception of the king as being (since the Reformation monarchs had claimed) a priest as well as a sovereign, as a mediator between the people and God. William may have insistently claimed the favour of providence and led a programme of moral reformation; yet (again for pragmatic reasons as well as out of disinclination) he did not advertise his headship of the church or his faith. For all his Protestantism, abroad William forged alliances with Catholics, was willing to tolerate them at home, and was only strategically drawn to popular anti-popery.[161] A culture of scepticism and atheism has been traced back to the civil wars, the rise of the new science, and to a Restoration court infamous for immorality and irreligion. It was, however, more William's than Charles II's reign that saw anxiety about irreligion rise to a crescendo, perhaps as a consequence of the 1688 Revolution, the Toleration Act, and William's own indifference to the church and suspicion of the Anglican establishment. Whatever his private beliefs, Charles II came to see the importance for his kingship of the Church of England, the opposition to which cost James his throne. In effectively severing his kingship from the headship of the church, from an Anglican confessional state, William not only weakened the church, he made kingship too less sacred, less numinous. If, by the end of the seventeenth century, monarchy was perceived as less sacred and mysterious, one factor was the behaviour and image of William who had placed little emphasis on mystification. It seems fitting, as well as novel, that on the king's death, there was published a *Report of the Physicians and Surgeons, Commanded to Assist at the Dissecting the Body of His Late Majesty*. The report, describing a body emaciated, with swollen limbs and diseased lungs from which 'issued forth a quantity of purulent ... serum', graphically publicized the deceased king's natural body as divorced from its mystical counterpart, the body politic.[162] It may be that it marked the end of a 'theology' that had conjoined them.[163]

The course of William's reign also witnessed a decline in the popularity of the monarchy. This may seem a paradoxical or perverse statement given the popular welcome Orange received as a deliverer and saviour of Protestantism. Popular support for his replacing James as king, however, was another thing. Since the abortive coup of Lady Jane Grey against Mary Tudor, the English people had displayed a loyalty to rightful rulers over rival claimants and, on his return to London from his first aborted flight to the continent, James II received an enthusiastic welcome and retained some popular sympathy and support throughout his life.[164] For his part, William did not have the character, nor did he make much effort, to bond with his ordinary subjects. Disliked as a foreign usurper, William added to his unpopularity by his scant respect for the church to which the people were fiercely loyal, most of all by the heavy taxes which were seen as lining the pockets of foreigners and toadies. Where predecessors such as Elizabeth I and Charles II had tempered the unpopularity of imposts or policies by a charismatic common touch that won them affection, William III remained distant from the English people and they from him. It was a distance that the Jacobites were able to exploit at the expense of the king.

By the end of William's reign it was not only the mystery of monarchy and the affective bond between king and people that had been eroded. In addition – and partly as a consequence – attention had shifted from the person of the king and the monarchy itself. In *Selling the Tudor Monarchy*, I traced the ways in which, necessarily, Henry VIII and his successors had striven to publicize themselves, to make themselves the focus of the nation and of the popular imagination.[165] By the end of the sixteenth century, theatre, print, artefacts and consumer culture all bore witness to the central place of the monarchy in the society and psyche of English subjects. While the Stuarts had struggled to sustain that central place in the popular imagination and affection, the failure of the republic was due in part to the enduring hold of monarchy. Both the memory of Charles I and the figure of Charles II remained dominant, for all the emergence of a vibrant culture and social life beyond the court, in the life and culture of the metropolis and, increasingly, in provincial cities. It may be the case that the exigencies that led to a smaller court and the rise of London as a cultural centre would inevitably have seen a shift of cultural focus from court to capital city. It was William's reign, however, that saw attention move decisively from the court and king to other avenues of cultural and political life.

Writing under the influence of Jürgen Habermas, several historians have described this shift as part of a move from a representational state to a public sphere.[166] While Habermas's thesis has rightly been criticized and challenged, much remains that is persuasive, but more attention needs to be paid to the reign of William III in the process Habermas identified in England. In pursuing foreign priorities and military power, William's rule saw a decline in the *symbolic* authority of monarchy and the growth of parliament and the press, of party and the public, as not just political forces but as arbiters of taste. Rather than being the author of his discourse and representation, William – and the very questions of his right and authority to rule – became the subject of party pamphlets and polemics, satires and coffee-house talk. No early modern monarch, of course, had been able to control their image or representation. But where most had laboured to be or remain a dominant voice in the debate, William, in order to maintain his armies, proved willing to permit the 'public' to become the determinant of the fate of parties and regimes. His reign marks an important phase in the shift from a monarchical 'representational' state to a polity in which the government drew its authority from representing (in our sense) the people. Indeed, in subordinating the *image* of monarchy, William altered and diminished the exercise and *authority* of monarchy. On his death in 1702, he was succeeded by an English queen who did not share his cool indifference to the country, the Church of England, or the authority and image of the crown. It remains for us to examine her efforts to re-present and re-mystify sovereign authority and to consider how – and with what success – her representations were directed to those ends.

PART IV

Representing Stuart Queenship

PROLOGUE

SEMPER EADEM? QUEEN ANNE

Queen Anne has what we now might call an image problem. Today few of us would recognize her image or even be able to pick her out from the portraits of any number of Augustan aristocratic women. Though she adopted Queen Elizabeth's motto, unlike the Tudor monarch's her words have not resonated through the ages. After the drama of the seventeenth century, when a succession of monarchs faced the civil war, Popish Plot and the Revolution, Anne's reign has appeared unexciting, even uneventful. Even those who recognize her twelve years of rule as important in the establishment of a constitutional monarchy at home and in England's emergence as a superpower on the world stage tend not to give the queen a starring role in these stories. Whereas there have been several lives of Charles II, James II and William III, the last scholarly biography of Anne is more than three decades old.[1] Unlike other early modern queens – Anna of Denmark as well as Elizabeth I – she has attracted little interest from feminist historians. Caricatured in *1066 and All That* as a 'dead queen' and described on a popular website as 'somewhat lacklustre in comparison to the rest of the Stuart line', Anne is now remembered most not for her self but for an architectural style to which she contributed little.[2] She came nowhere in a BBC poll of great monarchs or great Britons which found a place for the demonized Richard III.[3]

Anne, however, ascended the throne in 1702 with very distinct advantages and with many of the attributes that made for a favourable image. First, she was, as she was to underline in her very first speech, English. The Dutch William III had grown increasingly unpopular as suspicions mounted that the protracted wars which had cost Englishmen unprecedented payments of taxation had been waged more in Dutch than English interests. Just as significant, Anne was, unlike the widower William, married; and, though a succession of still-births and children who died in infancy indicated reproductive problems, the queen's fertility at least was not in doubt; at thirty-seven she was still technically capable of producing an heir to replace the loss of the Prince of Gloucester, on whom the hopes of the nation for a secure succession had been placed.

Most important perhaps, Anne was – again unlike her brother-in law, from whom she had stood aside on the death of Queen Mary – the legitimate hereditary successor to the throne: a Stuart daughter of James II and granddaughter of Charles I. Since 1688, as we have seen, the national political culture – it is not too much to say the national psyche – had been fractured by the events and decisions that followed the Revolution. Many who had been willing to *oppose* James II had not been at all happy to *depose* him. Though the fiction that he had abdicated salved some consciences, many, even some Whigs, had been disturbed by the breach of the succession. The question of the rights of the king over the water had dogged the reign of William III. From planned French invasions and Jacobite plots to party and pamphlet warfare, throughout his reign the opposition to William had been inseparable from the issue of his own doubtful legitimacy. Anne, as succession panegyrics underlined, by her legitimacy, promised the possibility of healing the rupture in the succession and so of settling, it was hoped, the divisions that had rent the polity and people. Her rapturous welcome and popularity stemmed above all from that.

But Anne came with other reputations that made her popular. Since her youth – and not least through her rejection of any attempt to convert her – she had given plentiful evidence of her Anglican piety and commitment to the Church of England. William may have paid lip service to the church over which he exercised the supremacy but his Dutch Calvinism inclined him to different devotions and the bishops he elevated or favoured were, like himself, those tolerant of dissent. Given the national devotion to the church, Anne was welcomed as a queen who would support and reinvigorate it.

If in this she recalled her grandfather, Charles I, like him Anne was also inclined to religious ceremony. Where William had, we remember, directed those subjects who petitioned him to be touched for cure of the king's evil to go to James II in France, Anne revived the ceremonies of royal touching, which underscored the supremacy as a spiritual headship.[4] The claim to cure scrofula also, of course, suggested the divine status of the monarch as God's lieutenant. Much has been made by Anne's biographer of her readiness to jettison 'any belief in divine hereditary right in favour of a monarchy based on parliamentary statute', but we should not leap to conclude from her support for the Hanoverian succession her lack of interest in divine right.[5] Anne endeavoured to rule independently of any party, but Tory hopes that she represented a view of monarchy as well as church more their own and that she rescued England from a drift back towards a Commonwealth were by no means entirely misplaced.

Another striking difference between Anne and her predecessor was her daily presence – not only in England but in parliament and at the Council table, at prayers and thanksgivings. Whereas William had been (necessarily) willing to hand over domestic government so that he could lead allied armies on the continent, as well as return to his native Holland, Anne worked assiduously at the business of ruling: holding daily meetings with ministers, presiding weekly at cabinet and giving audience to envoys.[6] For all her alleged dependence on others – ministers and favourites – Anne, who attended more cabinet meetings than any predecessor, was visible at the centre of the body politic.[7] By her very birth and position, and her attitudes and actions, there was good reason to suppose that Anne would be a dominant figure both in the practice and the image of her government.

The historian of Anne's reign, however, comes away with a different impression; and, whatever the evidence of her devotion to business, the queen appears somehow less central than her predecessors to the course of ruling and to our perceptions of her reign. Even her biographer, while urging that she be given greater prominence, drifts into a narrative of campaigns and party manoeuvres that all but obscures Anne herself. The reasons for this apparent paradox are complex and still not entirely clear. But our talk of campaigns and party machinations may begin to provide some answers. The central matter of Anne's reign – not least to the queen herself – was the securing of victory in a war against France that had been waged since 1689. William had been the champion of that war and his identity as king had been inseparable from his military fortunes and prowess. As a woman, Anne could not lead armies. While she chose ministers and officers, lobbied (very successfully) for supply to continue the struggle, organized prayers for her troops and thanksgivings for victories, the queen's role was by definition secondary to that of her generals, notably Marlborough. Even as they endlessly represented her as Augusta, as heroine, champion and warrior, panegyrists struggled to figure Anne as the focus of the war – and therefore of the reign.[8]

Another obstacle to her appearing prominent – in historiography and history – was the full development during Anne's reign of party. Parties, in an inchoate form, were the legacy of civil war, still more of the Popish Plot. It might be thought that the 1688 Revolution had cemented them – as in some measure it did; but when we recall that it was most Tories as well as the Whigs who ousted James II, we will not be surprised that the history of Williamite politics is not easily related simply as one of two-party conflict. Whig and Tory certainly defined attitudes to key issues, such as religious toleration, but as (some) Whigs pressed for a standing army and greater powers for the monarchy, lines and clear principles were blurred and parties themselves divided by court and country wings. By the end of William's reign, however, the political landscape had become clearer: 'the pattern of politics after 1701 was not the same . . . as that which persisted during the 1690s'; the 'lifeblood' of early eighteenth-century politics was 'the existence and conflict of two major parties'.[9] Anne, like William, sought to remain independent of party and to form mixed ministries. But ultimately she was dependent on them, and party fortunes were every bit as much the news of the day as were royal actions.

The solidification of parties was related to another development of the 1690s that is important for our understanding of Anne's position. In his readiness to sacrifice anything to the cause of advancing the war with France, William had required frequent parliaments and surrendered prerogatives to them. Together with the king's need for unprecedented supply, frequent parliaments and elections led to a need for management of the Commons. William may have sought to remain independent of party and to choose any minsters who could secure his ends; but his reign witnessed change to a politics in which management of parliament – and the winning of elections – was shaped by parties. Frequent elections and party organization further enhanced the importance of the public sphere and gave at least the enfranchised a key role in the determination of Commons majorities and ministries – in government.[10] From the reign of Henry VIII and especially Elizabeth I, the relentless publicization of monarchy had increasingly involved the people in the performance as well as representation of rule.[11] It was, however, regular parliaments, frequent elections and the solidification and organization of party that formed an electorate on which increasingly the monarch was dependent for the enactment of his or her will. As Mark Knights has demonstrated, the Augustan period saw the emergence of politics as public participation and public dialogue – and not merely for the enfranchised but for a wider public that participated through increasing numbers of petitions and addresses. Frequent elections, an expanded electorate, party conflict and print created a culture in which appeal to the public became a vital art of politics, a polity in which partisan politics became a contest for popularity. In part because Anne, like Elizabeth I, combined a strong sense of her authority with popular appeal, she was able to retain the affection of her subjects and draw on her popularity to strengthen her position. Increasingly, however, royal authority itself was being *derived* from popularity, and the monarch as well as parliament was becoming representative of the people.

Queen Anne was – and was seen and welcomed as – a conservative figure, one who, many hoped, might put the clock back and temper the bitterness of divisions.[12] Yet she ascended the throne in quite new and changed political circumstances which her reign saw further develop. We meet this ambiguity everywhere in the politics and political culture of the reign and, despite herself, in Anne's own actions and behaviour. Whatever her tactical reasons (keeping them as far as possible safe if not on side), Anne flirted with Jacobites while promoting the Hanoverian succession. She permitted the impeachment of Henry Sacheverell while probably being sympathetic to many of his views – though not the divisive manner in which he pronounced and publicized them. She had a keen sense of her ancestry and the Stuart past yet came to accept (without any overt sign of discontent) a constitutional monarchy that her predecessors would neither have recognized nor applauded. Rather than simple inconsistency, these ambiguities may have been necessary negotiations of a monarch with the new realities of powerful parliaments and parties. It may even be that through acknowledging and accommodating change, Anne helped to secure her – and regal – authority in a new political order. But it was a diminished authority she exercised and bequeathed.

Political changes and such ambiguities very much complicate the story of the image and representation of the queen. Albeit certain policies remained constant and were promoted by loyal supporters – the war, for example, for most of the reign – shifts of ministries meant that the emphases of royal policy (on toleration, for instance) would alter; and what had been loyal support could appear under different circumstances as criticism or opposition. Importantly, ministries dominated by a party also make it more difficult to distinguish the representation of the queen from polemic for party. And, though it was not yet respectable or officially instituted, opposition was an undoubted and widely recognized aspect of the party system, sometimes a device for obtaining influence and power rather than subverting it. We will need to consider how party complicated all the modes of royal representation, and disturbs any simple binary of panegyric and opposition. We will need to think about how others – ministers and their rivals and opponents – used the image of the queen to advance their own ends. We must study how and with what success Anne was able to represent herself in her effort to avoid being the pawn of a party. We might ask, in fine, whether her reduced visibility was not itself the representation as well as reality of a new politics, a new polity in which monarch and court would loom less large as centres of patronage, taste and image.

As our only modern biography of Queen Anne suggests, the image of the queen was and is inseparable from the key political issues which dominated parliaments and pamphlets. The largest issue, the war against Louis XIV, was not of the queen's making but was one she wished as well as had to pursue, not least because her own position depended upon it. Other initiatives and emphases were more obviously her own. Advocated by William III (who foresaw the dangers for the succession of an independent Scotland), the policy of union was pushed forward by Anne. Though she staked her personal authority on it and regarded it as her proudest achievement, Union became embroiled in party and factional as well as national conflict. No less, while almost all applauded her piety and charity, Anne's commitment to the estab-lished Anglican church and also to some measure of toleration embroiled her reign in its most interminable party quarrels and instabilities. Moreover, the row over Sacheverell's sermons exposed the faultlines in the queen's own atti-tude to the succession as well as exacerbating a public division which might (had the Tories not thrown in their lot with Hanover) have disrupted the growth of political stability.

That stability and the Hanoverian succession owed not a little both to the actions, popularity and image of Queen Anne and, paradoxically, to her relative lack of prominence. In part by not often imposing or advertising her authority, she came to be not just the symbol of a new style of monarchy – one which was to change the politics of representation as well as the constitution – but to be lauded as Augusta, the empress of a new Britain and a new British empire.

CHAPTER 13

A Stuart's Words

Queen Anne and the Scripts of Post-Revolution Monarchy

I

William III had made extensive use of declarations to justify his invasion of England and to press his claim to the throne. After 1690, however, he issued no more and a genre of royal representation that had become increasingly important over the course of the seventeenth century lapsed. Queen Anne did not revive it. On 4 May 1702, just weeks after her succession, she published a declaration of war against France. Reciting the treaties that Louis XIV had broken, his retention of Spain and invasion of territories, his designs to overturn the liberties of Europe, and his support for the 'pretended Prince of Wales', the declaration justified England's joining with her allies in renewed war 'for maintaining the public faith, for vindicating the honour of our crown, and for preventing the mischiefs which all Europe is threatened with'.[1] While titled a declaration, rather than a proclamation, there was little to distinguish the format; indeed, the Scottish version was issued as a proclamation and both texts, though justificatory, were but a page in length.[2] Very early in her first year of rule, Anne also commanded the publication of orders for the inclusion of Princess Sophia in prayers for the royal family and a declaration of her hostility to the sale of office.[3] These advertised the new queen's commitment to the Hanoverian succession and her determination to choose servants on the basis of 'virtue and true merit' but hardly constituted public pronouncements of major impact. Where Charles II had taken advantage of declarations, often to appeal directly to the people at times of crisis in relations with parliaments, Anne, like William, dispensed with them, not least perhaps because war, frequent parliaments and elections and an emerging party system had made royal appeals to subjects over the heads of parliaments anachronistic and redundant.

The queen also issued fewer proclamations than her predecessor, averaging only just over four per annum throughout her reign compared to the hundred published by William and Mary in the first five years of their joint rule and the

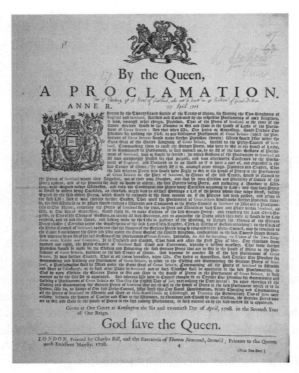

66 *By the Queen, A Proclamation. Anne R. Whereas by the twenty second article of the Treaty of Union, for uniting the two kingdoms of England and Scotland . . ., 1708.*

fifty or so issued by William III alone. As had become the trend, Anne's proclamations, particularly when contrasted to the early Stuarts, were brief (virtually all just a page) and businesslike more than rhetorical or explanatory. However, whoever actually drafted them – and however much the dominance of party ministries limited royal independence, the appearance of the proclamations clearly announced them as the queen's: starting out with a large royal arms, the English proclamations after 1705 were printed with Anne's personal motto 'Semper Eadem' as well as a subscription that they were 'given at our court at St James's' or 'given at our court at Windsor' or at Kensington, along with 'God Save the Queen' (fig. 66). Interestingly, too, several proclamations were printed with a listed price of one or two pennies, which suggests a market for royal proclamations and perhaps implies that these once-hallowed royal texts were now just another genre in the teeming commercial world of late seventeenth-century print culture, as likely to lie next to pamphlets and squibs on a coffee-house or tavern table.[4]

Though not as long or rhetorical as before, however, these royal proclamations (full of personal pronouns) were by no means insignificant in representing the queen as well as dealing with business. In even some of the apparently most businesslike, for example, Anne manifested her personal commitment to all aspects of the war. Her proclamations from 1702 were concerned with the recruitment of soldiers and sailors, recalling men from service abroad; and with supplies of ordnance, hemp, pitch and tar.[5] In 1705 she issued letters patent to encourage subjects to contribute by loans to Prince Eugene of Savoy, not doubting that her loving subjects 'when they consider of what importance the supply of the said money will be moved to contribute'; her proclamation of 1711 regarding the establishment of a general post office assigned a weekly sum from its profits to the war.[6] Just as significant as her material support, Anne's procla-mations also consistently justified and underlined the legitimacy and necessity of the war. Year after year proclamations for fasts and thanksgivings repeated the mantra of 'this just and necessary war' waged 'for the common safety of our realms and the liberties of Europe'.[7] A 1711 proclamation, for example, reminded critics of the war that campaigns were continued 'for the common safety of our realms and for disappointing the boundless ambition of France'.[8] But as time went on, not least to disarm critics, royal proclamations also ordered prayers to God 'for restoring and perpetuating peace, safety and prosperity to us'.[9] When peace became government policy, the queen's proclamation justified a cessation of arms, the wisdom of which some questioned, as 'for preventing the effusion of Christian blood' and 'putting an end to this long and expensive war'.[10] Clearly royal forms were appropriated by successive ministries for their own ends; but to observe that is to be reminded of the continuing force of those royal forms and locutions. During a war which, perhaps more than any other issue, defined parties and divided the nation, the queen's own words, repeated in these procla-mations, helped to sustain support; by adding the voice and authority of the crown to the cause, they made it harder for (both Tory and Country) opponents to claim that the war was prolonged only to favour corrupt interest groups who had benefited by it.

Anne also used proclamations to demonstrate her commitment to policies dear to her own heart: the union with Scotland and the Hanoverian Protestant succession. In one of September 1708, for example, prohibiting unlawful intrusions into churches and manses in Scotland, she reassured subjects that all its 'immunities and liberties' were guaranteed by the Treaty of Union.[11] Advertising her personal oversight of that treaty, she also issued proc-lamations to set in motion the procedure for electing the sixteen Scottish peers to sit in the Lords at Westminster and promptly ensured a replacement for one, the Duke of Hamilton, after his murder in a duel in 1712.[12] Printed in Edinburgh, given under the signet at Edinburgh, or issued from Holyrood, Anne's proclamations helped to reassure nervous Scots that she was truly their queen and a nursing mother to them as well as the English.[13] To secure the Hanoverian succession, at a time when it appeared threatened by planned invasion, Anne used a proclamation to warn off any subjects of her British kingdoms against support for James Francis Edward Stuart. Dismissing James II's son, as she had at his birth, as an imposter 'pretended to be Prince of Wales', she denounced him emotively as but a stooge 'instructed to introduce the French government into all our realms'.[14] Declaring the (we note the repetition) 'pretended prince' and all his accomplices to be traitors and rebels, Anne ordered that they be apprehended. Given the rumours that she herself might have done a deal for a future Jacobite succession, such proclamations (importantly) presented the queen as an unequivocal backer of future Protestant and Hanoverian monarchy.[15]

Her proclamations also subtly represented Queen Anne as a monarch who exercised her sovereignty as a constitutional or parliamentary monarch – indeed beyond that as a queen who understood the new power of the people and embraced the new politics of elections and the public sphere. In virtually every proclamation proroguing or dissolving a parliament, Anne expressed her desire to meet with them – or another – quite soon. Such sentiments, even if not always acted upon, had been expressed by predecessors; but there was a new language in Anne's proclamation of July 1702 expressing her resolve 'to meet our people and have their advice in parliament'.[16] Dissolving parliament in April 1708, her proclamation promised the imminent issue of writs for a new one 'to the intent our good subjects may perceive the confidence we have in their affection and how desirous we are to meet our people and have their advice by their representatives in parliament'.[17] Often referring to her 'loving subjects', Anne issued orders, like that for quarantining ships coming from the Baltic, 'out of a tender care of our people' and desire to preserve them from plague.[18] In 1703 a royal proclamation published just two days before Christmas and in the wake of a violent storm, announced the queen 'highly sensible', that is aware, of the sufferings (the 'deplorable condition') of widows and children of deceased seamen, and her support out of 'princely compassion' for alms and 'charitable benevolence' throughout the kingdom.[19] Albeit not the most important medium of communication and representation, Anne's proclamations assisted in representing her as a nursing mother to her people and in sustaining her personal popularity throughout her reign.

Her proclamations also made clear the queen's sense of her authority and absolute intolerance of any popular political action that spilled over into disobedience or disorder. Early in her reign, under the influence of high churchmen, Anne issued a longer than normal proclamation forbidding the spreading of false news, the writing and printing of blasphemous and irreligious works or treasonable and seditious books.[20] Expressing a conviction that this reproaching of temporal and ecclesiastical government 'requires our public care and is of great concernment', Anne threatened (at a time when the statutes on censorship had lapsed) to proceed against offenders with the utmost vigour, 'being resolved as much as in us lies to suppress the said enormities by a most strict and exemplary punishment'. She continued to spearhead a campaign against libels and unlicensed pamphlets by offering rewards to those who revealed the author or printer of seditious works, such as *Legion's Humble Address to the Lords*, and issuing a proclamation for the apprehension of those behind such publications.[21] Six years later, in a proclamation of March 1710, the queen was to vent her anger against the perpetrators of popular disorder. Published at the height of the furore generated by the Sacheverell trial, Anne's royal proclamation vilified the 'loose, idle and disorderly persons' who crowded the streets of London and Westminster, attacking coaches and obstructing the business of the courts and parliament.[22] Identifying among them papists of uncertain allegiance, the queen expressed her 'detestation of those who had stirred them up'. The queen, she made clear, would tolerate no popular 'defiance of our regal authority'.

Most of all it was her piety and care for the Church of England that Anne advertised to her subjects in proclamations, as in other ways. From the first year of her reign almost annually, the queen issued orders for services of thanksgiving for victories that, she made clear, she attributed above all to God. The proclamation of 30 December 1708, for example, observing that 'it hath pleased Almighty God who directeth and ruleth all things . . . to afford us his assistance in this just and necessary war', praised him for protecting her people from treacherous designs and blessing the allies with victory at Lisle.[23] The same year, emphasizing her own devotion, she ordered: 'we most devoutly and thankfully acknowledge the great goodness and mercy of the Almighty God who has continued his protection and assistance in this just and necessary war', and attributed to God the 'late wondrous success' in Flanders.[24] When, as in October 1709, Anne repeated how it had pleased God 'to continue to *us* his protection', it was to herself as well as the armies or the nation she referred.[25] Whilst not trumpeting divine right, the queen represented herself as a pious lieutenant of God who led the nation in devotions; as we shall see, no few panegyrists were to ascribe the victories to the queen's personal piety.[26] Proclamations also gave concrete evidence of the queen's devotion to church and faith. On 3 November 1704, in one of her longest proclamations, the queen and (as she reminded) Defender of the Faith, explaining that since her succession 'the welfare and support of the Church of England . . . have always been our greatest care', announced her intention to redress the miserable condition it, and the clergy, were in.[27] Having discharged the arrears of tenths due to the crown, she now made 'a grant of our whole reserve arising out of first fruits and tenths' and ordered the establishment of a corporation called the Governors of the Bounty of Queen Anne for the Augmentation of the Maintenance of the Poor Clergy, whose task it was to assess the maintenance of every vicar and enhance that of the poorest. After years of monarchs who had more plundered the church than endorsed it, Anne's was a remarkable personal initiative and one which, long known as Queen Anne's Bounty, represented her charity and care of the fabric of the established church. In Scotland the queen also lent her support in a proclamation 'for encouraging the design of erecting schools for propagating the knowledge of Christ in the Highlands and islands', in which she declared her 'approbation of an undertaking for so good and pious an end' and gave authority to commissions to erect a corporation.[28] Read aloud in every parish church in Scotland, the proclamation also recommended the queen as a monarch of unusual piety, charity and virtue. Indeed, the same month in England, Anne issued a proclamation 'for the encouragement of piety and virtue' by the 'preventing and punishing vice, profaneness and immorality'.[29] Proclaiming her keen sense that it 'is an indispensable duty upon us to be careful above all other things to preserve and advance the honour and service of Almighty God', she indicated her determination to suppress vice and profanity, which as well as 'so highly displeasing to God' and 'so great a reproach to our religion and government', had also 'so fatal a tendency to the corruption of many of our loving subjects'. Declaring that she would punish all profane or immoral acts and seek out persons of piety for favour and place, Queen Anne presented herself as the worthy successor to William III who had made moral reformation his own. To demonstrate that these were not mere words, Anne acted the next year to order the removal from the fair at Brookfield in St Martins-in-the-Fields of the stalls and booths which had been erected there 'for entertaining loose, idle, disorderly people with plays, interludes and puppet shows, gaming and other disorderly pastimes to the great encouragement of all manner of vice and debauchery'.[30] A champion of church hierarchy and ceremony, in ways that pleased the Tories and clerical establishment, in acts of charity and her campaign of moral reformation the queen could also represent herself as a nursing mother to all those, including Williamite Whigs and dissenters, who deplored the mounting atheism and immorality of the age. Royal proclamations on religion contributed to what we will see was Queen Anne's careful self-positioning as Supreme Head of the Church in a realm bitterly divided over religion. They contributed, that is, to her exercise and maintenance of that authority.

There can, however, be no doubt that Queen Anne most impressed herself upon her subjects by her speeches from the throne. More than even with her predecessors we should not assume that those words were always her own: party ministries set agendas (we have drafts and annotations of speeches by Godolphin, Nottingham and Harley) and Anne was, more than earlier monarchs, obliged to work with them.[31] But the reverse was also true; contending parties needed the authority of the queen's voice and, given the continuity of themes and language over changing ministries, it is probable that what she published and spoke reflected her own as well as party priorities. Importantly, the queen's words –

certainly if addresses presented to her in response to them are a guide – were *received* as her own and as an expression of her will, not just that of the government of the day.[32] And, those addresses also evidence, whatever the divisions among the public, Anne evidently impressed her subjects as a speaker. To those who regard her as rather colourless and bland, an argument that she was an effective orator must seem unpersuasive. Yet, even allowing for the conventions of praise, there were many contemporary testimonies to the queen's effectiveness as a speaker and to the impression that her words made on auditors in parliament and her subjects beyond Westminster. As early as 1706 a poet implicitly compared her oratory to the biblical prophetess Deborah: several preachers and pamphleteers quoted Anne's words; the bookseller John Dunton, having quoted her addresses to convocation and the universities as well as parliaments, concluded that the queen 'conquers with her gracious speeches'.[33] Nahum Tate opined that those who heard her speak felt blessed.[34] As well as individual speeches, two editions of the queen's speeches were published, in 1712 and 1714, evidently as commercial propositions, and sold for 6d by the booksellers of London and Westminster.[35] With her motto 'Semper Eadem' prominent on the title page, they evidently were seen to represent Anne's policies and person to her people and parliaments.

The new queen's first speech – to her Privy Council – was delivered on the very morning (8 March 1702) of William's death. Not published until later, the speech was an important act of reassurance: a declaration of the queen's values, her commitment to the war and (of no little importance in the case of a new legitimate Stuart monarch) her readiness to take advice. Opening with an expression of 'the unspeakable loss' the kingdom had suffered with the death of William (from whom she had been estranged), Anne assured her councillors that she was fully aware of and ready for 'the great burden' of monarchy. Her first concern, she continued, was 'for the preservation of our religion and the laws and liberties of my country', which were 'as dear to me as they can be to any person'. No pains would be wanting on her part 'to defend and support them', more specifically, 'to maintain the succession in the Protestant line; and the government in church and state, as it is by law established.'[36] Having demonstrated, by inclusive pronouns as much as promises, that she shared the views of her ministers and subjects, the new queen stressed her firm commitment to continuing the war against France: 'nothing shall be wanting on my part to pursue the true interest of England . . . for the support of the common cause'. In all her actions, she promised them, 'I shall always be ready to ask the advice of my Council and of both houses of parliament'; there was nothing to fear of a return to Stuart autocracy or clashes with parliaments.[37] In her maiden speech, Anne did more than acknowledge the constitutional changes that were the legacy of William's wars; she seemed to celebrate them and dispel any concern that things might alter.

Three days later, in her first address to parliament, Anne repeated her sadness at the loss of a king who had been 'the great support not only of these kingdoms but of all Europe' and her recognition of the 'weight and difficulty' now upon her.[38] Rehearsing again her concern for the religion, laws and liberties of her realm, the queen held out the hope (after a long, wearying war which had seen many setbacks) that they might be 'successful by the blessing of God and the continuance of that fidelity and affection of which you have given me so full assurance'. From warm words, Anne proceeded to urgent business. Somewhat optimistically claiming a 'unanimous concurrence' in support of the war against France, she made a clever appeal for supply. Rather than bully or harangue, she told the Commons, 'I rely entirely upon your affection for the supplying . . .' what was needed for 'the honour and dignity of the crown'. If the rhetoric here evoked memories of Queen Elizabeth I, Anne also adopted a language of reciprocity and business to describe how she saw her relations with her future parliaments: 'It shall be my constant endeavour to make you the best return for the duty and affection which you have expressed to me by a careful and diligent administration for the good of my subjects.' Her peroration again evoked Elizabeth but had an appealing topical resonance when spoken by a successor to the unpopular, and Dutch, William. 'As I know my own heart to be entirely English, I can very sincerely assure you there is not anything you can expect or desire from me which I shall not be ready to do, for the happiness and prosperity of England.' Nor, she vowed, were such sentiments empty rhetoric: 'you shall always find me a still and religious observer of my word'. Published by the 'printers to the Queen's most excellent majesty', the speech – and in particular the phrase about her English heart – was widely quoted, establishing Anne as the most popular sovereign since the Restoration, also as (though a woman) a fit monarch to lead a nation at war.

To quicken supply but also to demonstrate her acceptance of the need for accountability and her recognition of the difficulties the burdens of war caused, Anne, having assented to a statute establishing a commission to audit the public accounts, emphasized her willingness by telling the parliament (and nation) on 30 March that 'nothing is more reasonable than to give the kingdom the satisfaction of having those great sums accounted for'.[39] The reciprocity now was that such a willing concession implied parliament's agreement to 'continue great taxes'. And to make refusal all but impossible, the queen, adding to Elizabeth's similar rhetoric and firm performance, offered 'while my subjects remain under the burden of such great taxes', to abate 'my own expenses' so as to contribute £100,000 from her own reserve to 'the public service'.[40] Anne's gesture and self-representation as a monarch who shared her people's sacrifices could not but direct MPs to similarly give 'all possible despatch to the public business'. As a modern political orator might say, the message was 'we are in this together'. The speech helped to effect the queen's, and government's,

wishes: war was declared on France and Spain in May.[41] In her speech that
month dissolving what had been William III's last parliament, Anne – and it
was to be typical of her – did not withhold her gratitude and thanks: 'my hearty
thanks to you all for your great care of the public' and 'affection to me'.[42]
Probably heartfelt, the gratitude was also strategic. In expressing her especial
appreciation that the Commons had given supplies not just for the war but to
pay off some of William's debts to sustain the 'honour and credit' of the nation,
she urged them 'to prevent such inconveniences for the future'. As she
dispatched the MPs to their constituencies, Anne had already determined on a
different ministry and direction, and her speech has also been fittingly
discribed as 'the new government's election manifesto'.[43] The Tories Rochester
and Nottingham may have pressed the queen to include it, but Anne could
genuinely inform MPs and the electorate that 'my own principles must always
keep me entirely firm to the interests and religion of the Church of England,
and will incline me to countenance those who have the truest zeal to support
it'.[44] Such a recommendation of the Tory Party, however, was tempered by a
moderation and appeal to unity that Anne reiterated throughout her reign and
which was important in saving her from total dependence upon party. For all
her love of the church (which appealed to Tories and many uncommitted
voters), she assured Whigs and dissenters that she would be 'careful to preserve
and maintain the act of toleration'. As one who often favoured mixed ministries, the queen told voters that she believed that those of different opinions
could be 'equally attracted to my service' and expressed the hope that all might
eschew 'heats and animosities among themselves'.[45] As well as government
patronage, Anne's speech helped to secure a substantial Tory majority in the
summer election; but the queen had also signalled that she would not be the
creature of one party, not give the Tories completely free – and divisive – rein.

Anne addressed her own first (and Tory) parliament on 21 October. Having
expressed her pleasure at their meeting, she subtly reminded MPs of the affection she had met with from her people when on progress, that is, of the popularity which had helped secure their election. Turning specifically to the
Commons, she began directly – 'I *must* desire you to grant me . . . supplies' for
war – but reminded them of her own contribution and repeated the offer to
inspect accounts, this time encouraging them to report any guilty of corruption for punishment.[46] To manifest her care for her kingdom, Anne personally
recommended specific bills to prevent the exportation and improve the manufacture of wool, the historic business of old England. She closed with an old
Elizabethan flourish which was perhaps now the statement of a new political
reality: 'I am firmly persuaded that the love and good affection of my subjects
is . . . the truest and greatest support of the throne'. 'My interest and yours are
inseparable,' she asserted (as much as promised), 'and my endeavour shall
never be wanting to make you all safe and happy.'

Despite traditional Tory suspicions of the long land wars initiated by William, the new Commons speedily voted the supply the queen had requested along with a pension of £100,000 for her husband, Prince George. Anne returned her 'hearty thanks' for both, promised, along with further royal contributions to the cause, that all monies voted would be 'strictly applied to the uses for which you have designed them', and held out the hope that the sums granted would translate into success on the battlefield.[47] Then, turning to domestic matters, the queen took up the question of the church. The Tories had introduced, almost certainly with her approval, a bill to prevent occasional conformity, a tactic whereby dissenters bypassed the proscription against their holding office by taking the sacrament occasionally in an Anglican church whilst regularly worshipping in their chapels.[48] It was a controversial bill and, given the decisive Tory majority, it was likely that it was Anne herself who was concerned in her speech to lower the heat of controversy and allay anxieties among dissenters while enacting measures to protect and preserve the Church of England to which, unlike her predecessor, she was devoted. It was not only the moderation of her language that was notable. The queen expressed her hope that those of her subjects who 'have the *misfortune* to dissent from the Church of England' would 'rest secure and satisfied in the Act of Toleration which I am firmly resolved to maintain'.[49] To those who have – and we note the inclusive possessive pronoun – 'the happiness and advantage to be of *our* church', she conveyed assurance that, as she had run risks to preserve it in the past (not least during her father's reign), so she would maintain it in all its privileges, favouring for promotion those who were zealous for it.[50] If by such judicious language she hoped to secure the bill, Anne failed – at least in this session.[51] She succeeded, however, in preventing a violent division that would have impaired the war effort, while signalling her own religious commitment and preferences. Still determined, with a predominantly Tory ministry, not to rule a country riven by party feud, the queen closed by recommending 'peace and union' and in particular the renewal of laws against the publishing of scandalous pamphlets and libels which were the ammunition of party warfare.[52]

During the summer of 1703 progress with the war had been disappointing.[53] When she addressed both houses at the start of the second session of parliament in November, however, Anne – perhaps necessarily to keep supplies coming – struck an upbeat note. The money they had voted in the previous session, she reported, had helped secure a treaty with Portugal (which gave the allies a base in the Iberian Peninsula) and the assistance of the Duke of Savoy, developments which she (somewhat precociously) told them held out 'so fair a prospect . . . of bringing it [the war] to a glorious and speedy conclusion'.[54] To strengthen the case for more and urgent grants, Anne again announced that, despite hardships, she had 'contributed out of my own reserve towards some public services', in particular to Swabia. Once again the queen advertised her care for her subjects, recommending measures to deal with the high price of war which hit the poor, and her 'earnest desire' to see all in unity. A few weeks later, intelligence of a plot in Scotland gave Anne a further opportunity to press the quickening of supply 'to defeat the malicious designs of our enemies'.[55] Alluding to her personal safety as well as the security of the nation, she told MPs 'I depend entirely on your [supply].' Chivalry and honour now argued for the war effort, which Anne's speeches helped sustain among MPs and subjects alike. As she spoke to prorogue her first parliament in April (1704), Anne thanked them for their effectual and 'early dispatch of supplies, while lamenting that her appeals for unity had not met with the like success, though 'nothing, next to the blessing of God, can so much contribute to our success abroad and to our safety at home'.[56]

During the summer of 1704, Marlborough secured a decisive victory for the allies at Blenheim; at home, the high Tories, Nottingham and Seymour, were replaced by Robert Harley, a moderate who endeavoured to build a mixed ministry more loyal to the queen than to a party.[57] When she delivered her speech at the opening of the third session of parliament on 24 October, Anne took full advantage of the summer's news. 'The great and remarkable success with which God has blessed our arms in this summer,' she began, 'has stirred up our good subjects in all parts of the kingdom to express their unanimous joy and satisfaction.'[58] The victory, she explained, in calling for more supply, provided an opportunity for further gain that should be speedily taken. Recalling the unanimous joy of the people, Anne also used the occasion, as she sought to free herself from one party, to urge unity at home and 'no contention among you but who shall most promote the public welfare'. Indeed, she made her appeal personal: 'This would make me a happy queen, whose utmost endeavours would never be wanting to make you a happy and flourishing people.' The appeal to unity was topical as well as general. In this final session of Anne's first parliament, the Tories attempted to 'tack' a third Occasional Conformity Bill (which the queen herself now regarded as divisive) to the Land Tax Bill – a move that was finally defeated by Harley's men voting with the Whigs.[59] In her final speech proroguing the parliament before its dissolution on 5 April 1704, as well as giving her customary (and genuine) thanks for their 'cheerful assistance' in prosecuting the war, Anne reflected on a divided session and sent a clear signal regarding where her support lay in the forthcoming elections.[60] They had all, she observed, only narrowly escaped in the previous weeks the fatal effects of party 'animosity'. With elections looming, she instructed all 'to carry themselves with the greatest prudence and moderation'. It may have been intended as a hint – or coded message – to the electors. For all the energy and virulence of the Tory campaign, the results of the election, in which the Tackers were defeated but neither Whigs nor Tories secured an absolute majority, were 'something of a personal triumph for the queen' as well as Harley.[61] Again her personal plea from the throne, printed and circulated, may have helped secure the monarch's wishes and independence. Anne must have been optimistic that the moderation she had enjoined might characterize the new Commons and that, in Harley's words, 'persons or parties are to come in to the queen, and not the queen to them'.[62]

Party wrangles, however, continued throughout the summer, in particular over a Tory plan to invite the Electress Sophia of Hanover to reside in England with her son, a move to which Anne (and George) were opposed, not least because it was bruited in some circles that this was a plot to disrupt the Hanoverian succession by fomenting divisions.[63] In one of her longer speeches to the new parliament, delivered on 16 March, the queen skilfully laid out and argued for what would seem to be her own objectives: the war, the union with Scotland, and the abatement of party warfare. Passing over the doubts still raised in some quarters, Anne told the houses that she interpreted the high turnout (MPs traditionally straggled to Westminster, often arriving well after a session had begun) to the fact that '*all* are convinced of the necessity of prose-cuting the just war'.[64] To new MPs she explained that French mastery of the Spanish empire upset the balance of power and risked their dominance (here she appealed to the self-interest of the commercial classes) of trade and wealth. Lest interest did not persuade, the queen invoked patriotism: 'no good Englishman' could, she took it for granted, acquiesce in such French hegemony; especially when the prospects were clear for restoring Spain to Austria, the consequences of which would be 'glorious for England'. Repeating her offer (to new MPs) to make a contribution from her own reserve, Anne presented a powerful case for supply. No less important to her was the succession; and as a childless queen, she appreciated that the security of the succession depended upon a full union with Scotland which, if it remained independent, might well support a Stuart heir to the throne. Anne announced her commitment to union; yet only allusively referring to the 'many inconveniences' it would prevent, 'which may otherwise happen', she argued more generally for the 'peace and happiness' it would bring to both nations.[65] Her third topic – or instruction – related to her concerns to hold the balance and prevent divisions destroying her government. Another union, she told MPs, which she commended 'in the most earnest and affectionate manner', was a union of minds and affections among her people. Perhaps in an appeal to the uncom-mitted, she (optimistically) claimed that only a few stirred animosities and that the majority could defuse them. With marked restraint Anne confessed her anger – or as she put it, 'warmth' – against those (high Tories) who had insinuated that she was failing to protect the church. Denouncing such accusers as 'enemies', she even hinted that they might have Jacobite leanings ('designs which they dare not publicly own').[66] To appease loyal churchmen, she reiterated her support for the Church of England whilst warning high Tories 'I will inviolably maintain the toleration.' Should royal words and wishes not be sufficient to secure co-operation, the queen closed with a promise – and veiled threat: it was those who 'concur zealously with me in carrying on these good designs' who would find favour (and receive royal patronage); others would be left in the cold.[67] The repetitions and pleasantries in this important speech should not lead us to underestimate it. Anne took the opportunity to announce her wishes to new MPs as much as to convey information. She also had the skill of making seemingly general remarks address specific and topical issues and, especially in this speech, of communicating frustration sweetened with honied words of affection. As with Elizabeth, the effect was in the tone as much as the content, in a capacity persuasively to make royal wishes appear the desires of all.

To quash plans to invite Sophia, Anne (unusually) attended debates in the Lords where the force of her presence was seen to sway opinion against it.[68] Instead, the queen backed a bill to establish a regency council to exercise government until her Hanoverian successor arrived. In a parliamentary session aptly described as one of the 'smoothest' of her reign, Anne also helped the rejection of a Tory motion that the church was in danger and secured the nomination of an equal number of commissioners from Scotland and England to prepare a treaty of union.[69] The objectives of her speech had largely been secured when the first session of parliament ended in March. In her address closing the session, she acknowledged as much. Thanking the Commons (as she did, never taking it for granted) for supply, on this occasion she expressed her especial pleasure that divisions had been avoided and her happiness 'to find how entirely your sentiments have agreed with mine'.[70] As she dispatched the MPs to their constituencies, Anne encouraged them to be an example to discourage others from faction, to be, in fact, ambassadors to communicate her wishes.

During the recess the Battle of Ramillies (fought on 23 May 1706) delivered the greatest blow France had yet suffered; at home in July the treaty of union was concluded. For all these successes, however, Anne faced the hostility of the Tories and pressure from the Whigs to increase their hold on the highest offices, while the queen remained (as she said) determined not to be 'in the hands of a party'.[71] On the very eve of the second session, she was forced to appoint the old Junto, Lord Sunderland, Secretary of State to guarantee Whig support for the war.

In her speech on 3 December to the returning MPs, Anne seized the occasion to report, as if to justify the supplies she had requested, the 'glorious successes' that God had given.[72] This time the request for further supplies to press home the allies' advantage was accompanied by the future prospect of a durable peace and a balance of power that secured the liberties of England and

Europe. The queen was also able to report the success of the commissioners in drawing up a treaty which she hoped would soon be ratified by the Scottish parliament. After the Christmas break, she commended the union treaty, very much her personal project ('particular happiness'), to her English parliament as 'a lasting blessing to the whole island, a great addition to its wealth and power and a firm security to the Protestant religion'.[73] When opposition was overwhelmed in both houses, in no small part thanks to Anne's promotion and advocacy, the queen congratulated her parliament on effecting what a hundred years of attempts (since James VI and I's succession in 1603) had failed to achieve. 'I make no doubt,' she exhorted them with words chosen to ensure their place in history, 'but it will be remembered and spoke of hereafter to the honour of those who have been instrumental in bringing it to such a happy conclusion.'[74] Fluently, she moved from flattery to admonition, observing that the treaty required all her subjects to live in respect and kindness to one another. As the session neared its close, she allowed herself a boast: 'I cannot but look upon it as a peculiar happiness that in my reign so full a provision is made for the peace and quiet of my people, and for the security of our religion by so firm an establishment of the Protestant succession throughout Great Britain.' As well as a (rare) vaunt, it was also a notice to either party or any who disrupted it that they, not the queen, would be held accountable.

Royal speeches to parliament had always been addressed to the wider political nation, whether they were communicated by returning MPs or published in print. During Anne's reign, frequent elections, the consolidation of the party system and a well-informed and active electorate made it imperative for the queen to speak to those beyond Westminster. Her response to that need is well demonstrated in her speech at the close of the second session of this parliament. As was her custom, the queen thanked MPs for generous supplies. But, on this occasion recognizing that more money had been voted than ever before in one session of a parliament, she added: 'I am very much concerned that the public occasions require the raising of such great sums from my people.'[75] Then reminding MPs that when they returned they would come back to Westminster as members of the first parliament of Great Britain, she effectively asked them to promote the union, and the 'great and lasting benefits' it would bring, to their constituents.

After a truly triumphant year, however, England and the allies suffered severe military setbacks in the spring and summer of 1707: Marlborough failed to capture Toulon, the largest French port on the Mediterranean, and the allies suffered a decisive defeat at the Battle of Almanza in Spain.[76] When she addressed her parliament on 6 November (at the beginning of a session that all expected would be its last), the queen knew that she faced a difficult challenge and that more than warm words were needed to sustain the war. Her speech opened with a welcome to the first parliament of the union which, she assured them, would better enable the prosecution of the war.[77] Then she moved to put the best possible spin on the bad news. The failed attempt on Toulon she only half conceded, with considerable understatement, 'had not wholly its desired effect', before claiming that the attempt had nevertheless gained (unspecified) advantages for the allies' cause. Downplaying the terrible defeat at Almanza ('the French have gained ground upon us in Spain'), she highlighted the good news that their forces had been driven out of Italy – which, she added, would strengthen the king of Spain. Finally, though she acknowledged that things had not gone well in Germany, she promised that Hanover's taking command would remedy those setbacks in the next campaign. Anne spoke of the various theatres of the war in more detail than before. But, as we are familiar from news management by our own governments, the apparent openness was itself a way of presenting things in the best possible light. The war desperately needed further funds and Anne used words like 'just' and 'plain necessity' to argue for them, as well as appealing to the 'honour of the first parliament of Great Britain' and holding out the 'reasonable prospect' of an end to hostilities. Probably in reality quite doubtful, she deployed and repeated the rhetorician's 'I make no doubt' in stating that these were 'sufficient arguments' for augmenting supply. She added, however, one further argument. Her subjects, she observed, had been happy with her government and willing to support the war; so, she implied, opposition in parliament would fly in the face of popular opinion and opponents might well be punished at the next hustings by voters who regarded the interests of queen and subjects as one.

Despite her admonitions, however, in this session there were inquiries launched into mismanagement in the Admiralty, Tories criticized the conduct of the war in Spain (backed by country Whigs), and Whigs proposed and secured the abolition of the Scottish Privy Council, threatening further Scottish dissatisfaction with the union and fear of the loss of national independence.[78] Moreover, the Whigs effectively forced the queen to part with Harley and his supporters. Faced with unusual difficulties, Anne addressed the session more often than previous meetings, speaking twice in December to encourage augmented funds for the war and making it clear that only those who supported her might hold out any hopes of future favour.[79] What assisted her was an attempted Franco-Jacobite invasion of Scotland. Anne cleverly used the threat to argue that enemies had taken heart from hopes of less vigorous prosecution of the war and divisions within her kingdoms and made an appeal for unity in the face of a common enemy.[80] Her statement, however, that 'I must always place my chief dependence upon those who have given such repeated proofs of . . . support of the Revolution . . .' indicated how the crisis had exacerbated her dependence on the Whigs. Her closing address to parliament on 1 April 1708, as well as evidencing her anxiety at the invasion, adopted a less moderate and more partisan language that echoed the discourse of many Whig pamphlets and so reflected the Whigs' new influence.[81] The blessings of her government, she told them, would be irrecoverably lost 'if ever the design of a popish pretender, bred up in the principles of the most arbitrary government' were to succeed. Yet, she continued, some (unnamed) of her subjects had encouraged just such an enterprise. Accordingly all were enjoined on their return home to enforce the laws against papists and other disaffected. Whether or not from reading the hint in the queen's speech, the electorate voted in a clear Whig majority (of sixty-nine).[82] The need to sustain the war and the course of events had forced the queen into addresses that departed from the supra-party orations she had delivered to maintain her independence and promote her policies. In the spring of 1708 she sounded like – and looked likely to be – a Whig queen.

In the wake of their decisive election victory, the Whigs pressured the queen to give more ministerial posts to Whig grandees to the point of their taking over the Cabinet. During the summer of 1708, Anne struggled to resist a Whig monopoly of government, with only limited success.[83] At least good news came from the continent. Marlborough's third great victory, at Oudenarde in July, effectively destroyed the French army in the southern Netherlands, and the captain general went on in October to take Lille, the second and most fortified city in France.[84] In normal circumstances, Anne would have taken the opportunity of such successes in her opening speech to her new parliament the next month. However, the month of victory abroad was one of personal tragedy at home as Anne's beloved husband of twenty-five years died on the 28th. Paralyzed by grief, the queen lost the strength to hold out against Whig pressures. As Anne evidently felt too distraught to deliver a speech to the second session of parliament, an address was instead made by the Lord Chancellor, the Whig Earl Cowper. Cowper's speech of 18 November reads, when compared to the best of Anne's, as flat and workmanlike; and, of course, his use of the third person (Her Majesty) renders the delivery more distant, less intimate and less effective and authoritative.[85] By November, Anne had recovered sufficiently to deliver the queen's speech herself, but one commentator informed a correspondent that 'she spoke it in a much fainter voice than she used to have and her manner was more careless and less moving than it has been on previous occasions'.[86] The suggestion that her heart was not in it, that she spoke others' words, must remain suggestion. What is worthy of note is that contemporaries had been struck to date by the care and force of her speeches and discerned a real change.

During the winter and early spring months of this second session (November 1708 – April 1709), the spotlight fell on domestic politics as the sermon delivered by Henry Sacheverell and his subsequent impeachment by the Whigs excited popular support for the church and the Tories who also sought to make political capital out of mounting weariness with the war.[87] Though she had apparently approved Sacheverell's impeachment (she was incensed at the suggestion she did not protect the church), Anne would have been acutely aware of the popular support he garnered and was willing to use the changed circumstances at last to free herself from a Whig stranglehold with the assistance of Harley.[88] (With county petitions calling for an election making it clear that a Tory victory was in prospect, the Duke of Beaufort told the queen: 'Your majesty is now queen indeed'.) Anne was more than willing to free herself of the Junto but had no desire to make herself a pawn of the Tories. In that spirit we should read her speech of 5 April 1710 proroguing a parliament which was, in fact, not to meet again. After the usual thanks, Anne came to the 'occasion' that had consumed so much time, without naming Sacheverell.[89] To appease public opinion she reiterated her 'tender concern' for the welfare and prosperity of the church and her willingness to support measures against immorality or to promote piety. On the other hand she openly condemned (again without naming them) those who used such concerns as a 'pretence' to 'insinuate' that the church was in danger. 'I could heartily wish,' she continued, 'men would study to be quiet' rather than revive disputes. She had, she closed, herself brought about the union and now hoped to be the instrument to unite her subjects. It was a coded warning to the Tories that they should not, as the Whigs had, endeavour to hijack the government; it was a personal affirmation and a device to enhance her authority.

The summer reconstitution of the ministry, in which Harley secured the dominance of his followers on the Treasury Board, broke the power of the Whigs and initiated peace negotiations with France, was followed by the dissolution of parliament in September. After a campaign of unprecedented heat, the ensuing elections produced a Tory landslide which resulted in the largest majority of the reign to date – 151.[90] It was greater than Anne or Harley had anticipated – or desired. Not only that, among their ranks were a group of high Tories who were in no mood to follow Harley in his (and the queen's) natural moderation. In her opening address to her fourth parliament, the queen made her usual pitch for supplies, but to Tory MPs less committed to prolonged war she asserted that 'the carrying on the war in all its parts . . . with the utmost vigour is the likeliest means, with God's blessing, to procure a safe and honourable peace for us and all our allies'.[91] Also possibly appealing to the Tories who had often advocated blue water policies, she drew attention to naval debts, which she asked them to remedy. As she turned to home, Anne told them 'in the plainest words' her 'intentions'. She would – she assured Tories by making it her first priority – support the church; and she would preserve the British constitution established by the union. But, she made it equally clear in the wake of the Sacheverell furore and the Tory landslide, she would 'maintain the indulgence by law allowed to scrupulous consciences'; and, she warned any high Tories looking towards St Germain, 'I shall employ none but such as are heartily for the Protestant succession in the House of Hanover; the interest of which family no person can be more truly concerned for than myself.' Anne closed with an uncharacteristically assertive tone: 'these are my resolutions'. Printed and sold for a penny, her speech bore a large royal arms with the motto she had added to them, 'Semper Eadem' – 'Always the same'. Her ends were in most respects the same: moderate courses, the crown's freedom from dependence on party, peace and unity at home, the successful conduct of war abroad until a secure peace. But the pitch was different. The queen was direct and acerbic because she needed to signal that, despite the large Tory majority, there was a royal agenda, and what she claimed was 'the interest of the country', which was to have priority over party.

Despite her admonitions, the Tories tried to capitalize on their electoral success to reduce their rivals: in the Lords they censured the Whig conduct of the war in Spain after allied defeat at the Battle of Brihuega; they introduced a bill to repeal the Naturalization Act, a Whig measure to enable Protestant immigration; hard-line Tories embarked on an anti-Whig vendetta which they sought to force on Harley.[92] Anne manifested her support for Harley (by creating him Earl of Oxford and appointing him Lord Treasurer) and continued to consult with Whigs, such as Somers and Shrewsbury, in private.[93] An attempt on Harley's life (by a French refugee) strengthened the Lord Treasurer (and the queen) as they pursued negotiations for a peace which Anne had become determined to secure.[94] By no means all went smoothly; but when she prorogued the first session of this Tory parliament on 12 June 1711, Anne was genuinely able to give her usual thanks for unprecedentedly large supplies when, as she hinted, enemies (and perhaps the queen herself) had thought they would not be forthcoming.[95] Considering her predominantly Tory auditors, Anne gave particular thanks for a 'supply for building many new churches' from a parliament that had manifested zeal for church and state. The queen used, too, rather different language, words that would have pleased high churchmen, in referring to her own 'power with which God has entrusted me', and in commending the more moderate Tories for the 'temper' (moderation) they had shown, 'which I hope will convince those who have the misfortune to differ from our church that their liberty is not in danger'. Finally, again adopting the rhetorical device of refutation (claiming as given what is not), Anne told them that 'it was needless' to reiterate assurances about the Hanoverian succession – which by no means all Tories endorsed. Not for the first or last time, Anne was using her speeches to find a space independent of party to posit her own views.

Peace preliminaries were signed between England and France on 27 September.[96] Not all were happy with the terms and, of the Tories, Nottingham joined the Whig opposition. Against the background of mounting opposition to her government, the queen was apprehensive about the reconvening of the parliament in which a majority could not be assured, especially in the Lords. Public opinion, however, was clearly for peace, and the queen and her ministers took advantage of it. In her speech of 7 December, Anne reported the opening of a treaty 'notwithstanding the arts of those who delight in war' – a demonizing of the critics of peace without Spain as warmongers.[97] Claiming (somewhat cavalierly) Dutch support, the queen reminded the MPs that her 'own subjects' were fully behind the terms which secured Protestantism, the Hanoverian succession and (a sop to the Whigs?) 'your interest in trade and commerce'. As she came to a close, the queen held out to ordinary subjects the prospects of an ease in the burden of taxes, stronger manufactures, lower costs of poor relief and (an appeal to the Country wings of both parties) redress of the abuses that had 'crept into any part of the administration during so long a war'. Critics of the peace she castigated as aids to the enemies of all the English, who 'delivered from the hardships of war . . . may become a happy and a flourishing people'.

More than any other this was a speech of unashamed spin – of selective and (in part) misleading information to persuade the houses to the ministry's and queen's desired goal. In the days immediately after, it looked to have failed. Nottingham's opposition motion that the peace was not honourable unless Spain were detached from the Bourbon was carried in the Lords, prompting a crisis which was headed off only by the creation of a dozen Tory peers.[98] Yet the spin also did its work. Not least because the people believed that the allies also supported the peace, Harley was able to get an endorsement from both houses before the end of the session in June 1712.[99] In her long speech on the 6th the queen, who began by reminding all (in a tone reminiscent of early Stuart kings) that 'the making peace and war is the undoubted prerogative of the crown', outlined all the terms of peace which, she promised, would make some amends for the burdens the people had borne, and Britain glorious and great.[100] A fortnight later she spoke again to underline the serious disadvantages that would follow if the peace failed and advised MPs to support it against any who designed against it in their localities.[101] A clever mixture of appeal to the people, half-information and misrepresentation, the queen's speeches helped to secure support for the peace which was formally signed at Utrecht during the recess of parliament in March.

The third (and last) session of Anne's fourth parliament in 1713 opened as the treaties were being signed. The queen, as she told them, had deferred their meeting until she could, as now, announce the successful outcome.[102] Simple report, however, was not the only business of the speech. There had been strained relations between England and Hanover (which had favoured continuing the war), and rumours had circulated that Anne was inclined to the Pretender. Denying any difficulties and scotching rumour, she vaunted 'the perfect friendship there is between me and the house of Hanover', and her commitment to the succession, perhaps also to send a warning to those who were flirting with the Stuarts.[103] Then, as if demonstrating the fruits of peace, the queen outlined domestic measures to improve manufacture and trade, especially the fishing trade, to check libellous and blasphemous publication and to outlaw duelling. It was a partisan speech, probably drafted in part by Harley to wrong-foot the Whigs on the eve of an election; but, according to Swift, though her voice was 'a little weaker' from ill health, 'the queen delivered her speech very well', closing with her own usual plea to all to avoid, now that England was at peace abroad, 'party rage' at home.[104] Peace among parties was not obtained, but at the close of the session in July Anne was (genuinely as well as strategically) able to praise the Commons for the 'remarkable services you have performed'.[105] Along with supply, parliament had assisted with an honourable peace. On 2 March, after a serious illness but speaking 'very distinctly', the queen was able to welcome her last parliament with news of final ratifications of commercial treaties with Spain and the prospects under her leadership of 'the settlement of Europe'.[106] England's true interests, trade and naval power, she stated prophetically, were now assured. More personally, possibly with intimations of mortality, Anne reflected on her achievements and legacy. The joy of the people at her recovery touched her; by contrast she was wounded by factious designs and suspicions that she was not committed to the Hanoverian succession. The queen made her customary appeal for peace and unity. With greater than usual use of personal pronouns, moreover, she asserted her own authority as the best security for her subjects: 'I must hope you will all agree with me,' she closed, 'that attempts to weaken my authority or to render the possession of the crown uneasy to me, can never be proper means to strengthen the Protestant succession.' Anne was publicly dissociating herself from those Tories (even in her government, including Harley) who were now entertaining Jacobite sympathies; in the wake of her speech, both houses voted (albeit narrowly) that the Protestant succession was not in danger. It was a vote of confidence in the queen. As she approached death, there was talk of a likely civil war as the cabinet was split and the nation divided between Hanoverians and Jacobites. Just days before her death, Anne made a final personal appeal to end divisions and for all 'to show the same just regard for my just prerogative . . . as I have always expressed for the rights of my people'.[107] It was a last protest against party; albeit it failed in that, on the queen's death, the Election of Hanover was peacefully proclaimed as George I.

I have analysed Queen Anne's royal speeches at some length not merely because they have received almost no notice. Speeches were the principal medium through which Anne represented herself to her MPs and her subjects, the medium through which she also negotiated the delicate balance between being a constitutional monarch in a new age of parties and yet asserting her royal prerogatives and personal opinions. Certainly, many were drafted for her by ministers attached to a party. But the repetition of themes, the echo of phrases and conceits across different ministries, suggests that Anne advanced her own policies: we have seen in several speeches her subtle and skilful manoeuvres to express her own opinions and wishes, at times against, or at least in modification of, those of a party ministry. Today the Queen's Speech is read as the government of the day's manifesto; it was not so simply the case in Anne's reign. In his 30 January sermon in 1714, the rector of St Paul's Covent Garden, Robert Lloyd, quoting some, stated that 'these several incomparable speeches of her sacred majesty from the throne sufficiently demonstrated the true sense of the legislature'.[108] Lloyd did not discuss whether that was because Anne set the agenda which parliament followed or whether she was the mouthpiece of her ministry. However, in *A Dialogue Between a New Courtier and a Country Gentleman* (published in 1713), the country gentleman made a clear distinction between party (or ministerial) and royal utterance: 'I know of no way to judge of the sense of the Queen concerning matters but by such declarations as she is graciously pleased to make to her people from the throne'.[109] 'We country gentlemen,' he added, 'have no other opportunities of knowing the opinions of our princes but by their speeches in parliament, which I always read with the most profound respect and pay such an entire deference to whatever her majesty is pleased to say'.[110]

In 1703, Defoe had told Queen Anne that 'the speeches your Majesty is pleased to make in Parliament are looked upon as words spoken to all the kingdom, and their influences are . . . universal'.[111] Anne had a full appreciation of Defoe's point that through such speeches she could 'let all the world know' that she pursued the good of her people and demonstrated 'princely care and love'.[112] The country gentleman in the dialogue, however, suggested a more specific impact: 'whenever I see any measure taken contrary to the Queen's express declaration, I think it my duty rather to dispute and disapprove such proceedings than presume to call in question anything that has the sanction of our sovereign's royal word'.[113] Published to, and so read by, her people, Anne's speeches had, as addresses to the queen suggest, the power to influence popular opinion and hence elections, and so to enhance the queen's influence and independence: as Burnet put it in 1702, as well as direct patronage and influence at the hustings, the sovereign's inclinations 'wrought on the . . . multitude'.[114] Though much had changed since an age when (even in theory) the king spoke and it was done, Anne's 'sovereign royal word' was an important representation of her person and her sovereignty in a new age of constitutional monarchy and party.

Through the course of the seventeenth century official prayers authorized by the sovereign for use in services on fast days, days of thanksgiving and other commemorative occasions had been important texts through which the monarch might (as it were) address the people from the pulpit of every parish. Especially during the long wars of William's reign they had become more frequent as services were held to implore god's blessings on the allied armies of each campaign or to give thanks for victories. Such prayers and services advertised the ruler's piety and enabled the monarch to lead the nation as a spiritual head. As a sovereign who attributed far greater importance than her predecessors to the Church of England and her royal supremacy, Queen Anne issued numerous proclamations for fasts and thanksgivings; typically in each year there were two or three occasions when her subjects were required to attend services of official prayers which, as the title pages proclaimed, were published by the queen's printers and 'by her majesty's special command'.[115]

Indeed, within a month of succeeding to the throne, the new queen authorized a short prayer 'to be used after the prayer in the time of war and tumults' throughout England and Wales at morning and evening services.[116] The prayer led all to implore God's blessing 'upon her majesty and her allies engaged in war' and asked the Lord 'in thy own good time' to 'vouchsafe them such a peace' as might provide for the safety and glory of England 'and the common welfare and happiness'.[117] Like her opening speeches to Council and parliament, the short prayer was a manifesto of Anne's wishes for her reign, no more evidently so than in the closing prayer to 'give us all grace to lead quiet and peaceable lives'.[118] Before the first campaigning sermon of her reign had got under way, the queen commanded by proclamation the devising of a full service to ask God's blessing on the armies 'engaged in the present war against France and Spain'. In this full forty-page service, the congregations were enjoined to pray God: 'pour out . . . abundant blessings on our gracious queen, direct and bless her in all her consultations'.[119] As well, therefore, as asking the Lord 'to fight our battles', the services contained numerous prayers that presented Anne as (what in reality her sex prevented) the leader of the wars.[120] 'Strengthen her,' an evening prayer for the queen implored, personalizing the conflict, 'that she may vanquish and overcome all her enemies'; while during communion all prayed 'that we and all her subjects (duly considering whose authority she hath) may faithfully serve, honour and humbly obey her'.[121] If this prayer expresses Anne's hope that her people might mend their divisions and unite under her, morning and evening prayers for the Princess Sophia of Hanover, daughter of the Elector Palatine and (by the 1701 Act of Settlement) heir to the English and Irish thrones, underlined Anne's commitment to the Hanoverian succession.[122]

As befitted a pious queen, imprecations were also accompanied by prayers of thanks. Anne ordered by her special command services on 12 November and 3 December to thank God for the successes he had bestowed: 'we adore thy gracious and wonderful providence,' the people prayed, 'in the late eminent successes vouchsafed to her majesty and her allies whereby thou hast given such remarkable disappointments to the ambitious and cruel designs of the common enemy'.[123] Asking God, and so holding out for the people the prospect of – 'attaining . . . a just and lasting peace', the prayers represented Anne as God's favoured daughter and the war as a holy war, which, with God on their side, could only be won by England and her allies.[124]

These prayers imploring blessing and giving thanks set a pattern for the reign. At the dawn of the next campaigning season, for example, official prayers led the people to appeal to 'the God of battle for help against our enemies' as also for his blessing on the fleets and armies preparing to set out.[125] An occurrence in 1703, however, also reminds us of the extent to which Augustan England still attributed what we would consider natural disasters to divine intervention. The great storm of November which resulted in severe loss of life, and of thirteen naval vessels, was widely interpreted as a sign of God's anger at a sinful nation.[126] The Queen (who had herself to take shelter) hastily ordered a form of prayer to be drawn up which led congregations across the nation to ask God's forgiveness 'lest a worse thing come unto us'.[127] At a time of war when many feared that the storm did prognosticate worse afflictions, Anne's prayers reminded the people of God's providences to England as well as of the need for repentance. The fast day in January was appointed not only for seeking God's blessing on the war effort but 'also for the humbling of ourselves before him in a deep sense of his heavy displeasure showed forth in the late dreadful storm'.[128] The prayers sought, after a summer of military disappointments, to sustain morale for the war and admonished those who had suffered in the storm to attribute it to God and not 'murmur or repine' at a government or queen who, above all, sought the Lord's glory.[129]

To publicize the blessings of her government, in February 1704 Anne expressed her own 'will and pleasure' that an annual service be held on 8 March to give thanks for her accession to the throne.[130] Like those that celebrated William III's arrival, the prayers give thanks for the queen's care of church and nation, wish her long life, and urge the obedience and love of her subjects. Anne's own voice is surely audible in the prayers to banish profanity and religious divisions, perhaps too in those asking God to make her the happy mother of children – and successors.[131] If that last were to prove but a pious hope, the inauguration of annual services of thanks for the queen proved auspicious in a year that at last brought news of major victories. Perhaps out of a sense of the need to signal a success as well as out of genuine piety, Anne ordered a public thanksgiving for Marlborough's success at the Battle of Schellenberg near Donauwörth on 2 July. As she was always to do, she attributed the victory to God – 'it is thou that didst tread down our enemies'; but at a time when the Tories were critical of a war in which Marlborough had yet to win a victory, it was also politically vital to advertise an allied – and government – success, albeit there had been costly casualties.[132] The prayer that Anne personally commissioned on 6 July ordered thanks 'for the late great success vouchsafed to the forces of her Majesty . . . under the command of the Duke of Marlborough'. Using the words of (Shakespeare's) Henry V after Agincourt, the prayers conveyed the hope that this significant (but not major) victory might open the way to the destruction of France – and peace.[133]

Within less than a month, as events turned out, a more decisive victory did indeed deliver the allies a crushing blow against France. The official service ordered by Queen Anne could now justifiably publish a thanksgiving for a 'glorious victory' at Blenheim; and the prayers were written to justify the government's conduct of the war and praise the queen and her commander-in-chief.[134] Thanking God for a victory that exceeded all expectations, the text led all to pray 'with the help of our God we have put to flight the armies of the aliens and scattered the people that delight in war'.[135] Such mercies, it was implied, obliged subjects to obey the queen who had been favoured by providence and to join together with her so as to 'prosper all her pious designs and endeavours, for the good of this church and nation, the common welfare of Europe and the preservation of the Protestant religion'.[136] After a collect for the queen, a prayer repeated thanks for *her* victory and the promise it held out of more. As a pamphleteer observed the same year, such public prayers represented the queen as God's minister exercising his authority.[137]

As with her speeches to successive parliaments, Anne used the occasions of official services and prayers to sustain support for the war. The title of the form of prayer she ordered for a fast day on 4 April 1705 itself made the argument. The fast was 'for imploring the *continuance* of a blessing from almighty God upon her majesty and her allies engaged in the present war', yet ultimately for 'restoring and perpetuating peace'.[138] While reminding worshippers (and readers) of late successes given by God, the prayers upbraided those who, by licentiousness and strife, had shown themselves unworthy of God's favours and in particular those who obstructed the queen who, as God's instrument, championed pious designs. Praying for the queen and her allies, the congregation asked God's aid 'for the carrying on and perfecting of that great work they have begun' – God's work.[139] During the summer, Anne ordered another service of thanksgiving for what was described, with some exaggeration, as another 'glorious success' of her armies under Marlborough in the Spanish Netherlands.[140] Nor, the prayers that congregants spoke in place of the first collect declared, had war brought the hardships other nations had suffered; England still enjoyed 'peace and plenty'.[141] As she was about to meet her second parliament, comprising almost equal numbers of Whig and Tory MPs, Anne's prayers were ordered and published to try to unite all behind the war and behind the monarch.

The parliamentary session of 1705–6 was, as we remarked, one of the smoothest of Anne's reign. The Whigs co-operated with the court, and a Tory motion that the church was in danger was defeated.[142] However, in March 1706 the queen still ordered a service to implore the 'continuance of God's blessing . . . on the arms of her Majesty'.[143] In this service, along with numerous prayers that the Lord protect his 'chosen servant Anne', 'prosper her in all her under-takings; and compass her with . . . favour as with a shield', there was a warning to potential troublemakers, such as those who had tried to stir up divisions over the church.[144] 'Let not', the people were led to pray, the queen's 'pious endeavours for the advancement of thy glory, the prosperity of this church and nation, and the common welfare and happiness be disappointed by any unrea-sonable jealousies and divisions.'[145] By May, news of a decisive victory in Brabant, after months of little progress, led the queen hastily to order a collect to be used in all churches at morning and evening prayer.[146] The next month the victory at Ramillies, which crushed French power in Flanders, was commemorated by a thanksgiving. The published form of service relayed to all that this 'signal and glorious victory' had restored most of the Spanish Netherlands to Austria.[147] Thanks to God's favour and care, the 'arms of her Majesty and her allies' had checked the 'cruel designs of the common enemy' and destroyed them.[148] On the very last day of 1706, which had seen in the wake of Ramillies the greatest allied advances, a final service, ordered and printed 'by her majesty's special command', combined a thanksgiving with supplications to God for the continuance of his blessings in the New Year. In particular in a communion prayer, the people prayed that God, 'who hast been pleased to make the reign of our most gracious queen exceedingly happy and glorious and to bless her arms', continue to protect her, assist her just war, and enable her to be the instrument of restoring peace, safety and prosperity.[149]

Fast days with prayers for continuing God's blessings on the queen's and her allies' arms became annual; from 1707, perhaps in recognition of national war weariness, they include more prayers for peace. Though those services and prayers focused on the war, injunctions to unity at home and admonitions against opponents of the government or critics of the queen suggest also that they were as much addressed to domestic agendas and politics. Such address became more obvious in official services and prayers of 1707–8, beginning with that ordered to be used on 1 May 1707 'for rendering most hearty thanks to Almighty God for the wonderful and happy conclusion of the treaty for the Union' of England and Scotland.[150] Passing over the difficulties and opposition that had bedevilled the union negotiations, the congregations were instructed to pray: 'We bless thy holy name for all the signal providences by which the union of this island is brought to a happy conclusion.'[151] Representing the union as God's will, the prayers also made clear that it was Queen Anne herself who had enabled the Lord's will to be done: 'Thou hast given the queen her heart's desire.'[152] Now all that was needed was for all subjects in both kingdoms to unite in love and charity to each other for the happiness of 'this great united nation'.[153]

The hope expressed in the prayers that the people would be united and the kingdoms stronger was dramatically tested within months of the union celebrations. Jacobites, taking advantage of Scottish discontent at the union and rumours that Anne might even favour the succession of her half-brother, planned, with French support, an invasion of the northern kingdom.[154] In part owing to delays, the invading fleet was blocked by English and Dutch vessels and no landing was even attempted. The failed attack, however, highlighted the dangers of Jacobitism and disunity, and Queen Anne, in official prayers as well as other pronouncements, sought to make political capital out of the undoubted scare. In April and May 1708, official prayers were devised and ordered to be inserted in church services after the general thanksgiving prayers. In 'all . . . places throughout England and Wales', parishioners thanked God for 'the happy success of her majesty's counsels and forces against the late insolent and unjust attempt to invade her kingdom of Great Britain'.[155] In August, after the campaigning season brought new advances, the queen authorized a service of thanksgiving both for her escape from the Pretender's planned invasion and for Marlborough's victory near Oudenarde on 11 July.[156] Against any who held out hopes that the queen might indeed be brought to look favourably on the claim of James Francis Edward, the prayers denounced the 'unjust Pretender' and appealed to all, perhaps especially the moderate (non-Jacobite) Tories, to unite against the 'common enemy'.[157] By manifesting His providence to the queen, God has given subjects 'fresh motives to our duty' – to Him and to the sovereign.[158]

Prince George's illness, then death, probably explain why Marlborough's storming Lille (in October) was not commemorated by a service of thanksgiving until February 1709. Then in a collect reviewing the previous months, the people thanked God: 'Thou hast crowned this year with thy goodness, having most visibly protected our gracious sovereign against the treacherous designs . . . of her enemies, and given to her and her allies many glorious successes in this just and necessary war'.[159] At the close of the litany, together they prayed: 'thou hast been pleased to make the reign of thy chosen servant Queen Anne exceedingly glorious, crowning every year thereof, especially this last, with great and signal blessings on her arms . . .'.[160] As further victories indicated the clear turn of the tide against France, it was prayers for peace at home – 'that no sedition may disturb this state, nor schisms distract this church' – that articulated the government's hopes and fears.[161] The year 1710 saw more domestic distractions and divisions than any year of Anne's reign, as the impeachment of Sacheverell reopened deep ideological fissures and split the entire nation. Accordingly, along with prayers to implore God's blessing on the war effort and his assistance towards a peace abroad, official services also led the people to pray: 'and let not her [the queen's] gracious government be disturbed by any unreasonable jealousies and divisions'.[162]

Fast days continued to be held to implore god's blessing on the queen's and allies' arms, and in November a thanksgiving for the recent victories in Spain instructed all to pray for further successes.[163] Overtures for peace from France, however, and the Tory landslide in the October elections reoriented prayers as well as policy; accordingly now the congregations were led to pray 'that after the miserable calamities of a tedious [we note the term] and bloody war, thy people may reap the fruits of a just, honourable and lasting peace, together with a general increase of all Christian virtues and graces'.[164] 'Make, we pray thee,' they implored after the litany and collect, 'our gracious queen the blessed instrument of bringing destructions to a perpetual end.'[165]

During the thirty months of peace negotiations, from the autumn of 1710 to the signing of the Treaty of Utrecht in April 1713, there were virtually no official services of fast, thanksgiving or prayer ordered. A month after the conclusion of the peace, a royal proclamation (of 18 May) appointed a thanksgiving to be observed on 16 June – later deferred to 7 July to allow more time for preparations – 'for the conclusion of a just and honourable peace'.[166] Not for the first time, the title of the service glossed over discontents and divisions, notably protests that the government had abandoned its allies without securing the terms agreed. Yet peace was popular in the country and the queen and her government sought to enjoy the fruits of popularity. In place of the collect for the day, it was ordered that the parishioners pray to God: 'We bless and magnify thy holy name for that thou hast restored to us the voice of joy and thanksgiving and made peace in our borders.'[167] Lest any questioned who, under God, had brought it to pass, they cautioned: 'We praise thee that thou hast strengthened the hands of our sovereign Lady Queen Anne, and raised her up to be the glorious instrument of this great work.'[168] The service closed with prayers that under her, all 'may long enjoy the blessed fruits of a lasting peace', laying aside 'unhappy divisions', prejudice and hatred.[169]

The frequent occasions of official fasts, prayers and thanksgivings instruct us that the queen and her government attached importance to them. Traditionally, 'royal' – or official – prayers had reminded subjects that their ruler was a spiritual as well as secular head; while it has, with some exaggeration, been argued that the claim to divine rule little interested Anne, we should not entirely discount her frequent self-representation in these prayers as the instrument of God's will and work. In 1704 the Tory feminist writer Mary Astell, responding to Whig arguments for authority residing in the people, observed that 'in the communion service we are taught to own in our very prayers, that the queen is God's chosen servant, God's minister . . . that she has God's authority; that it is God's word and ordinance that we should faithfully serve, honour and humbly obey her.'[170]

Beside such claims, which of course unquestionably placed the queen above party, royal prayers, like royal speeches, in some measure enabled Anne to speak to the people as well as to the political nation and to outline her own policies, hopes and discontents. As with speeches, the services were not written by her and changes in tone suggest the shifting priorities of different ministries; yet imprimaturs and royal command make it probable that she approved them before authorizing publication: several indeed make clear that the services were published at the queen's pleasure. As with speeches, what is important is that these imprimaturs and expressions of pleasure meant the prayers were received as royal. Preaching his own sermon at Footscray in Kent on a Thanksgiving Day in June 1706, the rector John Whittle evidently saw the queen as the driving force behind such commemorations which had been 'visibly stamped in great letters ... by her majesty's special command'.[171] Certainly we can discern the personal voice of the queen in and across many of the texts: in the praise of union, the repeated injunctions to unity and peace, in admonitions against murmuring, divisiveness and intrigues.

Most significantly the prayers sustained the (increasingly burdensome and unpopular) wars by representing the conflict as just and providential, by claiming them as god's will, and by giving occasions of thanks for the celebration of victories. Numerous contemporary commentators bear witness to what they perceived to be the importance of these prayers in sustaining morale, retaining support and even obtaining victories. 'Oh how many myriads of prayer', the rector of Hesterton, Yorkshire, exclaimed in his thanksgiving sermon, 'have been sent up to heaven ... to supplicate the divine assistance in all our warlike preparations.'[172] In his sermon on the same day, Joseph Stennett opined that 'the pious method her majesty has taken to open each campaign with public prayers has received a signal approbation from heaven by the many wondrous successes'.[173] A pindaric ode of 1708 made the same claim succinctly in verse:

> ANNA is Providences Darling Care
> Nothing so infinitely Good as Her;
> Can Pray, or Ask, of Heav'n in vain,
> Her Prayers obtain Our Victories.[174]

Anne's prayers for blessing on her armies and of thanks for victories helped to represent a queen who whilst she could not head troops, was yet the leader of 'her armies', or of the nation's wars.

In several ways, in fact, prayers enhanced Anne's independence, position and authority. For, as several contemporaries suggested, the thanksgiving days often became thanksgivings for the queen and the blessings of her government, as much as for victories. When he preached on 19 August 1708, on the day of thanksgiving for the victory at Oudenarde, Thomas Coulton, urging all to obey a queen whom God had manifestly favoured, argued that 'every thanksgiving for victory should be as a fresh coronation day to the queen' – that is, a day to celebrate her.[175] Preaching before the queen on the March fast day of 1710, her chaplain Robert Moss regarded one purpose of such occasions as 'that the queen's empire may be firmly seated in the hearts of all her people and the people's duty solidly founded both upon principle and affection'.[176] In the eyes of many auditors and readers, Queen Anne's prayers had been efficacious not only in leading England to victories but in securing her the obedience and affection of subjects. As the preacher Samuel Wright was to reflect in his sermon preached on the first Sunday after the Hanoverian succession, prayers to God for sovereigns had 'not been in vain'.[177] The presence of George I on the throne after the defeat of French forces and Jacobite invasions confirmed that Anne's own prayers had not been in vain either; indeed, that they had helped establish the king for whom the nation was now joined in prayer.

II

Even more than that of her predecessors, the reign of Queen Anne was characterized, even defined, by the battles of party. For all the queen's determination to remain free of dependence on one party, to continue to choose her servants from both parties, and to speak her own mind, politics, ministries and government were fashioned by party. The same is true of the literary culture of the age. The legacy of civil war and the 1688 Revolution was, as we have seen, the politicization of literary forms. More than ever it was in Anne's reign that literary patronage and production were inextricably tied to party; and that poetry and prose were often published to conduct party struggles by other means. The partisan nature of all genres and forms of writing unquestionably complicates the representation of the queen in verse and prose. However, the ministry in office always had writers ready to praise the victories and attainments of the regime. Harley maintained a large network of writers; while even those in opposition, whatever their willingness to vilify their opponents, were anxious to court favour with the monarch.[178] For all the bitter party divisions in the literary culture of the age, most writers spared criticizing the queen herself and figured her (at different times with more or less enthusiasm) as the champion of the nation. Not least, as we shall see, poets and pamphleteers laboured to depict Anne, who as well as female was sick and frail, as a military heroine who by her leadership and choice of commanders secured the allies' military advances and England's glory.[179]

Late seventeenth-century English verse has not met with a favourable reception among modern critics and, as we saw, Abigail Williams has suggested that Tory disparagement of a dominant Whig poetics shaped the subsequent reception of the verse. During Anne's reign, however, poets Whig and Tory appear both to have lamented the standard and quality of literary production and to have been grappling to find literary models or modes suitable for the new circumstances and England's remarkable military victories. The massive quantity of published verse, contemporaries complained, produced too little of quality. The editor of a 1705 *New Collection of Poems Relating to Affairs of State* advertised his volume as having purged much of the 'dross' of other compilations.[180] Though they used less extreme language, others voiced similar negative judgements: in 1706 John Chase expressed his difficulty in writing when others had so conspicuously fallen short; in 1707 the panegyrist Samuel Cobb asked in the preface to *Poems on Several Occasions*: 'what has the battle of Ramillies produced? What battles usually do: bad poets and worse critics.'[181] Even the Williamite physician and writer, Sir Richard Blackmore, revealed little enthusiasm for the bards who 'their weekly work rehearse'.[182] Heroic victories, all concurred, were not matched by epic verse or great poets. To create a mode fitting the events and times, indeed to fashion an aesthetic, many especially Whig writers looked back to Milton and Spenser, as did, for example, Matthew Prior, Charles Gildon, John Dennis and John Paris. Yet not even all Whigs thought that a fit new poetic lay in imitations of Milton; in the absence of a new great poet like Dryden (though a Tory, he was better, Cobb conceded, than the Whigs' own 'laborious laureat'), Blackmore advised writers like Prior, Congreve, Granville, Stepney, Hughes, Walsh, Summers and Montagu to combine in 'united Strength' to write lines 'worthy of *Anna*'s Arms, of *Marlboro*'s Fire'.[183]

However, while we must concur with those contemporaries who judged the verse of Anne's reign as failing to memorialize the dramatic events and military successes of the age, we cannot discount the role of poems and panegyrics in promoting the war, in representing the queen, and in praising her government at home and campaigns abroad. Various collections of poems on affairs of state, or for and against Sacheverell, demonstrate that, as the subtitle of one collection put it, there was 'wit on both sides' and (at various times) on both sides poets ready to serve and celebrate the queen.[184]

In early modern England, the accession of a new monarch was traditionally greeted by a flood of panegyrical verse, all the more so when there were anxieties about the accession. The death of William III and succession of Queen Anne (who had stepped aside from claiming the throne earlier) was widely celebrated in verse, albeit in different ways. The Tory poets naturally celebrated the succession of a Stuart, a queen devoted to the church and a legitimate heir; but Whigs too heralded a Protestant queen committed to the war against France; and the people at large welcomed a native sovereign who had emphasized her Englishness the day she succeeded. A Tory agenda was announced in the very title of *The Church of England's Joy on the Happy Succession of Her Most Sacred Majesty, Queen Anne* and the poem indeed praised 'a Native Queen', 'within our church's bosom bred', 'the Church's Champion of the Martyr's

Race'.[185] Published on the day of the coronation, the verse expressed the reasonable hope that '*England* to ANN with one consent is joyn'd' and praised a queen who loved her country, in whom the virtues of Elizabeth I were revived, and from whom the nation might hope for 'a goodly Race of Kings'.[186] Anne, the anonymous author believed, would heal and unite the people; but in urging obedience he did not perhaps simply conventionally advocate loyalty to the monarch but hinted at a Tory political philosophy to be promoted in verse:

For he that listens to Poetic Songs,
Learns thence the duty which to Crowns belongs.[187]

The author of the *English Muse* was yet more overtly partisan. With Anne's succession the poem claimed, the church would be free of the 'sectaries' who had attacked it and England would be spared the designs of commonwealthsmen and republicans who plotted to destroy monarchy and ruin the constitution, and freed from 'hungry Dutchmen' who had purloined the nation's wealth under William.[188] Now 'A Stewart's English heart supports the Crown', monarchy and state would both revive.[189] Despite his overt Toryism, however, the author was ready to celebrate Anne succeeding not only by descent but by the 'universal voice' of the people; and was almost certainly right that many troubled in conscience by the events of 1688 were glad to see the daughter of James II on the throne and ready to express their duty and love.

The sentiments and language of Richard Burridge's *Congratulatory Poem*, dedicated to the queen, similarly disclose Tory hopes and values. Voicing his joy 'to see a STUART (an illustrious family deserving the highest honour of imperial dignity) wield the sceptre again', Burridge provoked the Whigs as much as he praised Anne, 'the most beautiful idea of Royalty and Glory'.[190] Again hoping that Anne would end the 'jars and strifes' that had ruptured the 'distorted *State*', Burridge contrasted the true allegiance subjects owed to her (in implied contrast to William) and praised her devotion to 'your *Mother Church*'.[191] Whigs as well as Tories, however, would have endorsed Burridge's vision of Anne heading William's confederacy to remove oppression and tyranny from Europe, and the establishment of English supremacy 'on either side the Seyne'.[192] It is likely, for example, that the anonymous author of *England's Triumph*, a popular poem on the coronation, had Whig sympathies, since the verse describes William III as 'a good Prince and a Hero of Fame'. Yet, the broadsheet illustrated with a large engraving of Anne enthroned, celebrated 'the second Elizabeth' who would rescue Europe and called on subjects to stand together and behind her 'with a true English heart full of love and good will'.[193]

Along with her Stuart descent and avowed Anglicanism, Anne's Protestantism and commitment to the war and the Hanoverian succession enabled Whig as well as Tory verse panegyric which persistently over the course of her reign represented her as 'The Greatest Hero and the best of Queens'.[194] James Shute's *Pindaric Ode* of 1703 lauds the despatch of Marlborough to command the English forces in Holland but goes to lengths to praise 'glorious Anne' herself as the heir of the mighty Arthur and Alfred, Henry V and Elizabeth. It was, he exulted, 'In mighty Anna's powerful Name' that Marlborough went:

> She speaks, and straight the Hero flies,
> To Battle and to Victories . . .[195]

Victory at Blenheim understandably elicited a wave of celebratory poems which, for all the traces of their partisanship, further praised and represented the queen as a heroine. The leading Whig bards made sure, in lauding Marlborough, also to praise Anne. 'The valiant Sov'reign calls Her General forth,' Matthew Prior wrote in a verse letter celebrating Blenheim; 'The Queen's Commands exalt the Warrior's fires.'[196] For all Marlborough's 'endless Fame', ''Tis ANNA's Glory,' Prior told readers, that she saved the nation and Europe.[197] John Dennis, in his Miltonic *Britannia Triumphans*, similarly heralded a commander whose name 'now fills the breath of fame', but it was, he made clear in a poem dedicated to her:

> Thou too great Queen by whose auspicious Care
> And wisdom these astonishing Events
> Were brought to light . . .[198]

Marlborough may have been *The English Hero* of Clare's 1704 poem, 'Yet, yet to HER', he insisted, we all must attribute the prize; the author of *The Royal Conqueror* made the same point by his title: Marlborough triumphed in the field, but 'Her Majesty hath a signal conquest got.'[199]

Whig poems on the victory at Blenheim promoted Whig values and even attempted to appropriate and represent the queen as *their* champion. Dennis figures her army as that of 'a free born people' and Anne as 'Great Championess of Liberty'; Oldmixon praised 'a queen who makes no other use of her victories than to confirm the liberty of mankind', a monarch who was the synonym of Liberty.[200] Their panegyrics, however, were not merely narrowly partisan and Whig poets praised the queen in strains and terms that rose above party. 'The very best of tender Mothers she', Dennis described her; for Clare she was 'the Best of Queens that ever sate' on the throne; 'Serenely sweet, to all the people kind,' the author of *The Royal Conqueress* described her.[201] Nor was the celebration of Blenheim the preserve of Whig poets. In his hymn to victory, the then client of Robert Harley, Daniel Defoe, lauded 'victorious Marl'bro' ' and a queen the glories of whose happy reign were 'seal'd from Heav'n'.[202] In the spirit of the queen's own wishes and speeches, Defoe explained the hope that, in the wake of victory at Blenheim, '*Faction* and *Parties* die beneath your Fame' and that the queen might lead her subjects to peace and unity.[203] While such hopes were unfulfilled, Blenheim did – at least on the surface – unite the political nation and people in praise of Anne. Whatever the divisions of parties, Blenheim was popularly celebrated and Anne herself heralded as a popular heroine. As *The Royal Conqueress* (incidentally published in Bristol) put it: 'Her Majesty triumphs, her People sing'.[204] A musical interlude to celebrate *Britain's Happiness* was performed at the theatres; in the libretto, the émigré Frenchman, Peter Matthew (who expressed his 'zeal for the best queen . . . in the world') had the performers sing the praises of 'A Queen truly *British*, wise pious and brave':

> The Welfare of All on blest ANNA depends,
> Then honor her most who the World most befriends
> Long-lov'd, like *Eliza*, this Isle may she bless[205]

Though he was a high-church Tory, the popular satirist Edward Ward captured a widely shared mood when in his 1704 poem he wrote of Blenheim:

> The Crown has endless Honour gain'd,
> By the late Victory obtain'd
> And ev'ry Loyal Soul's so glad,
> He tipples off his Cups like Mad,
> And swears we have a Queen, God bless her,
> Worth twenty of her Predecessor [206]

As the repeated comparisons with Elizabeth I indicate, Anne was being widely represented as an heroic queen who restored honour to the nation, as the people's princess. Like Elizabeth, Anne was lauded as another Deborah (a military leader as well as judge); Samuel Wesley believed 'two ELIZAs breathe in ANNE!'; Nahum Tate celebrated 'More than the blessings of *Astraea*'s Reign'; 'Eliza', echoed another poet, 'might have learnt from Her to please', for, in Addison's words, Anne made 'ev'ry Subject Glad, and a whole People blest'.[207]

Like Elizabeth's, Anne's sex presented a problem, especially for a nation fighting an unprecedentedly long war; and in Anne's case there were no stories of her appearing, as the Tudor queen was reported to have done, in armour on the eve of the Armada, defying the limitations of her female body.[208] Perhaps because verse enabled the metaphors that could re-figure the queen as (masculine) warrior and military leader, poets were important agents in overcoming the limitations of gender and representing Anne to have done champion no less than her predecessor, the warrior William III. '*Albion*'s Queen', the author of a Pindaric ode affirmed, 'does all her sex excel'; whatever Marlborough's successes, '*Anna* gave the Hero Power'.[209] In some verses, Anne herself is figured wielding the nation's sword or delivering (as in a poem on the victory at Schellenberg) the 'deciding stroke' that rescued Germany from French oppression.[210] More commonly, however, Anne's role was represented as that of a pious queen whose prayers earned favour with God and secured the victories. Samuel Cobb, for instance, depicted the campaign as a partnership between the queen and her commander Marlborough 'who Fights abroad, while ANNA Prays at home'; a muse tells her that prayers are mightier than the sword.[211] In his poem on the 'glorious successes of the last campaign', John Geree, having praised Marlborough and Admiral Sir George Rooke, similarly added 'But ANNA with *prevailing* Rhet'rick prays'.[212] Through prayer and piety, Anne, as Tate put it in *The Triumph*, made 'HEAV'N, her firm Ally' and the nation's protector.[213] In the Augustan poets' lines, Anne's prayers became the means to represent her as not marginal to the campaigns but decisive in determining the outcome of the battles for the mastery of Europe.

Such a representational strategy was assisted by further, actual victories on the battlefield. In the aftermath of Ramillies, John Chase, in an ode on 'the success of Her Majesty's arms' attributed the victory to 'Godlike ANNE': 'ANNE gave the Word, and Heav'n Success decreed'.[214] The playwright and poet Charles Johnson in his verses on Ramillies told of the French tyrant humbled by a pious woman:

> Such is the moving Form of Piety,
> For sure by that alone great *Anna* broke
> *Europa*'s chains, and bridled haughty *Louis*.[215]

'Mighty *Louis* by a woman fell,' William Wagstaffe agreed, and in his poem on *Ramillies*, the French king laments of the English queen: ' 'tis she that thrusts me on Destruction's brink'.[216] As well as a pious queen, Anne's reputation as formidable virago and 'Britannic Empress' was enhanced by Ramillies.[217] In a birthday entertainment performed before the queen, Europe, Asia and Africa come to England to pay homage and Atlas lays his globe 'at Royal ANNA's Feet', as a sign that 'the whole earth now submits to Her Throne'.[218] Matthew Prior's ode to the queen, written in the style of Spenser, tells 'greatest Anna' that she climbs 'Ascents of Fame/Which nor Augustus nor Eliza knew'.[219] 'Anne o're all the Watry World shall reign,' Oldmixon prophesied in the wake of Sir Cloudesley Shovell's victory at sea; 'We soon might see her *Universal Queen*'.[220] Far from limiting her, Anne's sex was represented as enabling and empowering. Even in a pindaric on Marlborough, it was Anne's 'Illustrious Female Reign' that is the focus of the poem and action ('The Terror of Her Arms will be/An Universal History'); surpassing the glorious heroines of past history, she, the novelist Penelope Aubin proclaimed, was 'The only Princess form'd by Fate/That could retrieve the Glory of our Ancient State'.[221] In these paeans to her *imperium* and glory, contemporaries were presented with another side of the queen and woman who, it was widely said, ruled as a loving mother over all. Ramillies, the Cambridge poet John Paris put it, was the blessing both of 'Great ANNA's *gentle* and *triumphant* Reign'.[222]

In the entertainment staged on the queen's birthday, it was to Anne and Britannia that the continents bowed. In reality the unity of the kingdoms of Britain was held together only by the life of the frail queen who, as we saw, recognized the importance of union to the war effort, the succession and the security of her throne and realm. In her speeches and proclamations Anne publicized union as very much her personal project; poets and panegyrists responded by promoting and celebrating union as a royal blessing and signal triumph no less than those of her arms abroad – or, in the words of Charles Darby's poem, as greater than her military glories.[223] Virtually all the poets make the queen's own points about the union paving the way to victory over France. With union, the author of *The True Born Britain* warned Louis XIV, 'At once the *Britains* will rush on his throne' and the war will soon be over.[224] Union, Elkanah Settle promised in his *Carmen irenicum*, would reinvigorate the nerves of war and render Britain and her queen 'invincible'.[225] The union also facilitated the representation of Anne as truly 'now the Empress of our Isle', as the imperial sovereign of 'Troynovant', the new Troy hymned by Spenser, the British historians and the panegyrists of James VI and I.[226] Perhaps most importantly, the poets presented the union as Anne's own attainment, effected with the aid of providence. The union, Charles Darby complimented her in a poem dedicated to the queen, was 'A work for which by Heav'n You were designed'.[227] 'No doubt,' Settle versed, 'the SOVERAN on th'Immortal Throne/ Reserv'd this Work for ANNE's blest reign alone'.[228] The 'sovereign foundress' of the union, he amplified, 'Great ANNE alone, Resolver and Executer'.[229] Joseph Browne's congratulatory poem praised the peers of England and Scotland, 'the patriots of Great Britain', for their work but the divine work of union had been 'sacred to Anna', had been hers and God's.[230]

To underscore the queen's dominant role and to personalize the achievement of union, poets deployed gendered language and metaphors of birth that also figured the (now) childless Anne as the mother of a truly vigorous offspring. 'And if an off-spring Heav'n should You deny,' Darby wrote of the union, 'Be this your Child, and Royal Progeny.'[231] In Settle's heroic poem, the, union is in several stanzas figured as the product of the queen's 'glorious labour', her 'vast maternal raptures', and is described as 'her filial charge'.[232] Lewis Theobald's pindaric ode hailed union as the 'lovely, long expected Child/On whom our English Queen has smiled' – in another poet's words, the 'happy birth of your Maternal Care'.[233] The representation of Anne as the maker – and the nursing mother – of union not only enabled poets to give her prominence in wartime and figure her as providential empress, the bringing together of the two kingdoms, after all the frustrated efforts and opposition to the scheme, held out some promise too that unity and peace (the queen's oft-reiterated objectives) might be achieved in England and abroad also. Anne, Browne wrote in his congratulatory poem, ending 'dissentions', had 'inspired the people to Unite'.[234] Might the queen's 'Power of healing' (an obvious reference to her touching to cure the king's evil) now pour balm on England's factions and divisions? Anne hoped so and, in the wake of union, a panegyrist who (optimistically foresaw her settling religious divisions) asked rhetorically: 'What has she done? And what shall she not do?'[235]

Despite vatic as well as royal hopes, what Anne could not do was bring peace to the religious and party wars that grew ever more heated over the next two years. What were achieved, however, under 'the most accomplish'd QUEEN on Earth' were more dazzling military victories, notably Marlborough's third triumph, at the Battle of Oudenarde.[236] Though one poet, writing on *The Battle of Audenard*, asserted that 'it must be acknowledged that poetry in the age we live in, is no current coin', the victory elicited several poems which, again, attributed the military successes to the queen.[237] In 1708, even in a poem titled *Marlborough Still Conquers*, one J. Gaynam emphasized Anne's role: 'ANNE's Arms no sooner *see*, but overcome'.[238] 'To HER', Charles Gildon wrote in his poem on Oudenarde, 'we owe this glorious wars success'; and, he added, the promise of peace.[239] A popular song on *Old England's New Triumph*, while giving due credit to Marlborough, has Louis exclaim:

What, vanquish'd by ANNA a-new?
Still beat by a woman!
In forty years no Man
Cou'd, what she has done, ever do.[240]

Nor was Prince George, who had participated in naval battles and victories, forgotten.[241] Congratulating 'ANNA and GEORGE', the victorious 'Royal PAIR', the laureate Nahum Tate informed his fellows that ' 'tis the proper province of poets to present the people with the best memorials they can raise to excite them to a thankful remembrance of such blessings'.[242] Responding to his invocation, Penelope Aubin's pindaric ode to the queen, *The Ecstasy*, encouraged all to 'Dance, Leap, Shout, and Sing for Britain's victory', and 'celebrate our matchless Monarch's Name'.[243] In an ode on *The Female Reign* ('her Majesty is the chief heroine of the ode'), Samuel Cobb figures France lamenting that it does do not have a monarch like 'ANNA, British Heroine'.[244]

The dispelled threat of Franco-Jacobite invasion was the occasion of further triumphal verse that disclosed little of the acute fear the nation must have felt. A verse *Letter to a Friend, upon the Successes of the Year 1708*, disparaging a 'spurious Boy-King' against whom the very winds turned, as a weak figure of 'false courage', asks: 'what can all the Pow'rs of France combin'd effect when oppos'd to *Anna*'s Cause'.[245] Louis, the poem continues, knew that with this last desperate attempt foiled, he had to submit to Britain and her queen. As the allies pressed their victories on into France, poets could truly now present Queen Anne as the arbiter of Europe:

> Great ANNA! Under Heav'n, Her pow'rful Hand
> The Fate of Christian Kingdoms does Command
> . . .
> So *Britain*'s Sov'reign widely does Dispence
> To Europe's States her Mighty Influence;
> Makes at the Nod its Empires High, or Low,
> And bids the Waves of Pow'r or Ebb, or Flow.[246]

With the change of ministry in 1710, and in accordance with the queen's own wishes, victories gave way to negotiations for peace. Even as they celebrated triumphs and victories, poets had been representing Anne as waging war in order to bring about peace and as desirous of people's ease: as Henry Oldmixon put it in his 1706 poem on the victories in Catalonia (*Iberia liberata*), Anne 'Wars for Peace'.[247] After 1709 the poets turned to represent the queen as much a lover of peace as a heroine and re-figured her as the empress to restore a new Augustan age of secure peace in Europe. While at home the furore excited by the impeachment of Sacheverell produced several volumes of verse 'for and against' the minister, poets began to foresee, promote and praise the proposal of peace. George Farquhar's *Barcellona: A Poem or the Spanish Expedition* celebrates the victories of the Earl of Peterborough, Mordaunt and Shovell, but at the same time acknowledges the burdens and charges of war and closes with a pastoral vision of 'Concord and Peace', as 'War was turn'd into a State of Peace.'[248] Similarly in his *Campaign* of the same year, dedicated to Marlborough, Joseph Addison instructs the commander that the objective of the war is 'Britannia's Safety, and the World's Repose':

> . . . the QUEEN demands
> Conquest and Peace from thy Victorious Hands;[249]

As the anonymous author of the *Encomium* intuited, peace was likely to be Marlborough's last victory and the poets' new theme. Accordingly the poet presumes

> . . . to sing the last Campaign;
> Lest if the Peace that's rumour'd, close pursue
> Thy victorys, *Peace*, as a Topick new,
> Divert the Muse's Thanks for late Successes due.[250]

The song composed by the poet laureate for the queen's birthday in 1711 lauded Anne now not in terms of martial glory but as bringing about a new age when

> Winter will create a Spring;
> *Mars* will make his Thunder cease,
> List'ning to the songs of Peace.[251]

Peace preliminaries were signed between Britain and France in June; but a final peace treaty involved long negotiations in Europe and, as the discordant voices in Tate's *Encomium* hinted, party struggles at home. Once settled, the peace, which still divided the parties, became the subject of numerous poems which, while in some cases obviously pursuing party agendas and vendettas, represented Queen Anne as the agent of a glorious settlement. To begin with an example of a high Tory poet, Joseph Trapp (a friend of Sacheverell whose library he inherited) wrote a poem simply entitled *Peace*, and 'inscribed' to Bolingbroke, a Tory regulator of peace terms.[252] Trapp's verses strike out against Whig taxes and ministers and depict Britain as rescued by Sacheverell, Harley, Shrewsbury and other Tory ministers. However, before all, 'Supreme and Eminent Great ANNA stands', and the queen is represented as 'ANNA the Guardian of Mankind's Repose', a queen to whom all Europe pays homage and on whom 'pressing millions passionately gaze'.[253] Marshall Smith dedicated his poem on the peace to the Tories Harley (Earl of Oxford) and Mortimer and, like Trapp, attacked Whig factions that had sought to perpetuate their power until Sacheverell and Harley exposed them. In 1713, however, in his poem it was not primarily the Tories but 'Illustrious ANN' who was 'in Pow'r Great'; Anne who held sway in Europe and whose 'maternal passion' led her to bring peace to her subjects.[254] Also dedicated to Harley, a poem by the Jacobite sympathizer Bevill Higgons castigated factious Whigs who had deliberately prolonged the war for their interest; while he figures Harley as the person who exposed them and made peace possible, he accords to Anne the decisive role:

> *Britannia*'s QUEEN to Tenderness inclin'd,
> Assumes to France a more pacific Mind.[255]

As well as a queen of 'Thunder dread', Anne we see is being represented now in verse again as the tender mother of not only the nation but of Europe and 'distant worlds'.[256]

More moderate Tory poets, such as William Waller who commended the appointment of Harley but was ready also to praise Marlborough, laid even greater emphasis on the dominant role of the queen. Under God, Waller, rector of Walton in Buckinghamshire, attributed the peace entirely to Anne:

To whom must we our Solemn Thanks apply,
As the Chief Agent of the AUTHOR High?
Sure to our Glorious QUEEN, we owe to Her
Our first Acknowledgments without Demur[257]

It was Anne, Waller continued using providential language, who had been predestined to bring peace, out of her Christian antipathy to human loss and her deep concern for the nation's good. Heralding a queen 'God-like as she's Great', Waller figures angels again singing 'Peace on Earth', as representations of Anne as a second redeemer.[258] Religious, indeed apocalyptic, language also characterized Samuel Wesley's *Hymn on Peace*, which effectively presents Anne as restoring a prelapsarian paradise through ending conflict and establishing 'After Consuming War, reviving Peace'.[259]

Beside these celestial flights, some of the celebratory verses that most clearly emerged from official circles appear more muted. Elkanah Settle was the 'city poet' for London and devised mayoral pageants as well as writing commendatory verse. In his *Irene Triumphans* of 1713, Settle prefaced his poem supporting the new ministry and answering objections to the peace, the basis of which the poem assures readers, is 'so firm, and fixt so fast'.[260] Peace, Settle plays out in pastoral metaphors, will bring 'a Train of Blessings'.[261] Against murmurers he asserted that in championing peace, Anne was 'Never so much the HEROINE as now'.[262] The 'poet laureate to her majesty', as Tate described himself on the title page, dedicated his *Triumph of Peace* to the queen. Acknowledging the difficulties the ministry faced, Tate asked in his lines: would envy and opposition destroy the treaty? Some poets had 'with soaring and successful wit', welcomed the return of the celestial dove, peace; and Tate added his voice for 'PEACE and HONOUR' over 'fields of *Blood*' and called for devout offerings to a queen, a 'Royal saint' who had brought 'redoubled blessings' to her realm.[263]

Augustan poetry was undeniably a poetry of party, the poets often clients and agents of ministers, party leaders and factions with their agendas, ambitions and conflicts. From such an observation, however, we should not be led to play down the continuing role of verse as royal panegyric or as the presentation – and representation – of the queen to both literary elites and ordinary subjects. Very few of the poems of Anne's reign are not in the vernacular; many are written in simple rhyme and metre as popular songs or verses. All figure the queen, from her accession in 1702 to her death – significantly not, as some histories have it, as the puppet of party but as the determinant of actions, and fortunes. In large measure such was still the political reality of Augustan England. As importantly, even to the extent that it was not, even (that is) as poets used licence in centring the monarch, their representations of politics, and of Queen Anne, were powerful political influences and forces. Partly because they drew on the literary heritage, traditions and genres of past cultures less rent by party division, and in which the sovereign had ruled personally, poets assisted in sustaining the authority of the monarchy by endowing it with cultural authority They sustained the authority of Anne as well as the institution of monarchy. Despite her sex, Anne was ubiquitously figured as a martial leader as well as tender mother. In some verse, she was sacralized and sanctified in language that must raise questions about a demystification of power or more secular culture in early eighteenth-century England. Almost never critical of the queen herself, poets promoted and celebrated her policies, her power and her person. Each year, on the queen's birthday or New Year's Day, poets competed with anniversary odes that, recalling the language of masques, figured Anne as a sun scattering rays of glory, as divine, 'Heaven's CHOICE', or Astraea.[264] If, at times, the reader of political pamphlets and party polemics comes away with a sense that the monarch was not the principal actor on the stage of state, poetry reminds us how far she was still the focus of representation and panegyric. If the loyalty and love of the people for Anne were a barometer, it may well be true that the hope of an early panegyrist was borne out:

For he that listens to Poetick Songs,
Learns thence the duty which to Crowns belongs.[265]

Support for the crown was by no means confined to poets. In the case of pamphleteers and prose writers, however, party positions and partisan polemics are even more in evidence; in the age of Queen Anne, more than ever, treatises on government, sermons and histories pursued and advanced party agendas more than anything else. While there existed this complicated support for and representation of the government, especially mixed ministries, no regime wanted for committed advocates and advertisers. Moreover, those writers who promoted others for office, as much as those who sought office, needed to demonstrate both their loyalty to the queen and their value as proponents and defenders of her monarchy and of the values dear to her and policies she favoured. Never more so than in this age of frequent elections, party and popular participation in politics, those who formed – and vied to form – governments had also to sell themselves and their programmes to a broad electorate and a yet broader public opinion. The success in representing the queen and her ministries from the pulpit and the press in large measure determined party fortunes as well as support for the monarch. In a political culture in which allegiance to political identities was routine, representation, as Mark Knights has demonstrated, was vital to all political actors and never more so than to the monarch herself.

The first government priority of Anne's reign – and one that, whatever their different tactical preferences, divided parties less than other issues – was the war against France. To obtain regular, heavy taxes and public support for the war, as Anne had discerned and her speeches showed, national morale had to be sustained by what we have learned to call propaganda, or at least by favourable spins on reporting military progress. The official organ of news, the *Gazette*, while reporting the full military details, was surprisingly restrained in celebrating victories: the relation of Blenheim, for example, praised Marlborough's bravery but eschewed triumphalism;[266] the issue for 16 May 1706 ascribed the 'entire and complete victory at Ramillies' to 'the justice of the cause';[267] news of the victory at Oudenarde was, it was reported, 'received . . . with the highest satisfaction imaginable', but otherwise little was said about this crushing defeat of the enemy.[268] Propaganda for the war was conducted rather in new periodicals inaugurated by Robert Harley and the Earl of Godolphin, such as a *Weekly Review of the Affairs of France* which, while promoting a government agenda, posed as a moderate organ of impartiality.[269] Importantly in the early years of the reign, the *Review* was targeted at persuading Tories to support the war by warning of the real dangers presented by France; in this publication, Blenheim was represented as the best outcome 'for their 4s in the pound' taxes the country gentlemen had had.[270] Published three times a week and widely distributed, the *Review* became a vehicle 'for the effective and speedy dissemination of propaganda in the provinces' as well as the capital.[271]

It was by no means the only organ for promoting the war. From the beginning of the reign, a series of authors and publications, with varying (and in some cases unknown) levels of official direction and patronage promoted the war by advertising successes, making the best of setbacks, and promising eventual victory and triumphant peace. To take an early example, *A Relation of the Great and Glorious Success of the Fleet and Forces . . . at Vigo* was 'published by authority'.[272] Passing over the disaster that had followed the allies' attempt to capture Cadiz, the *Relation* made maximum capital out of the capture of the Spanish treasure fleet. 'The attack', it was reported, 'was made with great resolution and bravery'; as well as Spanish vessels, French men-of-war were seized; and few allied ships or men were lost, as all showed 'all the courage and resolution imaginable'. Further naval victories were enthusiastically recounted and celebrated, perhaps by Tory writers who favoured a blue water strategy over the massive military campaign of William's wars. *A Narration of Sir George Rooke's Late Voyage* and his taking of Gibraltar in 1704 opened with the claim that 'in the opinion of candid and disinterested men . . . there has hardly ever been a sea battle better, more fairly and successfully fought than this'.[273] Against circulating (and it was said false) French claims to have had the better of the day, the narrator informed readers that, even though the enemy greatly outnumbered them, their losses were four times those of the allies, on account of 'the superior mettle and behaviour of the confederate fleet'.[274] In true patriotic spirit the author also insisted that 'it was rather the English than the confederate fleet which beat the enemy' and singled out 'English gallantry' as the cause of victory.[275] And that English gallantry and victory he described as 'the essence of this auspicious reign and fortune captivated by the virtues of an excellent queen'.[276] In the same vein, a *Review of the Late Engagement at Sea* dismissed misleading French reporting and quoted letters from the fleet to the effect that they were soundly beaten, and 'stole off in the night'.[277] 'Our fleet fought bravely like true Englishmen,' the *Review* reported, 'and inflicted three times greater casualties on the enemy than they suffered themselves.'[278]

Whatever Tory strategic (and political) preferences, it was land victories that made for spectacular news in 1704 as the allied forces advanced and Marlborough secured the first major victory of the reign. *A Full and Impartial Relation of the Battle*, supposedly by 'an officer who was in the engagement', offered a detailed narrative of a victory in which thirteen thousand persons were taken in a 'visible providence turned to the immortal glory of the arms of the Queen of Great Britain'.[279] A full history of the campaign in Germany related the victory by forces of which 'the greatest part were English and under an English general'.[280] Just as poets sang the praises of Marlborough and the queen, military reports tracked the allied advances – and in particular English successes – to reassure readers that the war was being won. In November 1704 an apparently official despatch related the capture of Landau and Tarabach, the allies 'taking great number of persons without losing above 60 men in the action'.[281] The next summer a long list of officers taken prisoner was appended to *A Full Account of the Duke of Marlborough's Victory over the French* in which, thanks to brilliant tactics, 'the loss on our side was very inconsiderable'.[282] The same month (July), a despatch 'published by authority' from Whitehall reported another victory secured through 'the bravery of our troops', also 'with very small loss on our side'.[283]

Where the great victories, such as Blenheim and Ramillies, were commemorated by thanksgivings, sermons and epic verse, military reports were published to inform readers of steady advances and to reassure them regarding apparent setbacks. Following a first failed siege of Barcelona, an account explained the temporary defeat 'more by our carelessness and rashness than by any vigour of the enemy'.[284] Enemy shells, the relation continued, had been fired to little effect and the prospect of taking the town lay ahead as they withdrew. Fortunately, a second attempt led by Lord Peterborough resulted in the allies capturing the city and enabled the publication of *The History of the Triumphs of Her Majesty's Arms . . . in and about Spain* the next year. Written to show how 'the arms of her sacred majesty Queen Anne' had restored Spain to its lawful sovereign, the detailed account of the campaign manifested 'her majesty's arms having . . . gloriously triumphed everywhere in Catalonia' and the common cause advanced.[285] As well as campaign relations, lives and times of the great admirals Sir George Rooke and Sir Cloudesley Shovell, and of the commander-in-chief Marlborough, told English readers that their recent victories recalled the great days of Crécy and Agincourt and that, along with her generals and admirals, "'tis her majesty's piety ... that prevails ... against the common enemy'.[286]

Marlborough's decisive victory at Oudenarde, officially published from Windsor on 5 July 1708, reported 'the French infantry ... entirely ruined', with no one of note killed on the allied side.[287] Though the claim was exaggerated and allied losses (variously estimated between one and three thousand) understated, this third major defeat opened the allies' advance through Flanders into France itself. From 1707 onwards, annually published histories of the campaign in Flanders related the 'unheard of fervour' of the allied soldiers, the successful siege of Lille, the march on Ghent, and the 'chain of victories with which it pleased God to bless the allies' and 'gave them a happy prospect of a solid peace'.[288] Reporting along with other gains the recapture of Mons, taken by French forces in 1691, the history of the campaign of 1709, 'fruitfully collected by an officer in the English forces', concluded by promising war-weary readers that 'those new conquests ... convinced the French again that no strongholds, superiority of forces nor entrenchments are able to withstand the glorious and victorious arms' of England and her allies, whose people could now confidently expect 'a solid and lasting peace'.[289] Though the officer made the caveat that the failure of Anjou to renounce the crown of Spain might yet disrupt negotiations and necessitate another campaign, it was the last account of the wars as the queen and Tory administration turned government propaganda to a justification and promotion of a policy of peace.[290] That propaganda, notably Swift's bestseller *The Conduct of the Allies*, has enjoyed a greater and more enduring reputation than the many relations of campaigns and victories of the previous decade.[291] Military accounts, however, whether officially published or not, were as vital to the conduct of the allies. In a new culture of nationalism, accountability and public involvement, reports that highlighted acts of bravery and heroism, and advances and victories of the queen's arms, answered or dispelled some of the criticism that the war was fought only for the interest of a party, not the nation. By sustaining English patriotism and morale and by promising eventual victory, war reports also helped to represent the queen as the truly English heroine, ridding her people of a threat to their liberties and founding a mighty new British empire. Less heroic and dramatic than the pindarics and epics published to celebrate triumphs, the war reports undoubtedly helped to bring about what their authors promised and what Queen Anne had desired.

III

From her first days on the throne, Queen Anne had proclaimed her commitment to the Church of England, its discipline, liturgy and clergy. Those who feared that her predecessor had undermined the church looked to her as a nursing mother to nurture and revive it; and Anne added action to her words by charitable endowments and the establishment of a fund to augment the incomes of the poorer clergy.[292] Unlike William III, Anne was unquestionably an Anglican; but, to the disappointment of some high churchmen, she retained a strong belief, as her speeches made clear, in charitable toleration of dissenters. As head of the church, the queen looked for the support of her clergy in an age in which the pulpit was still one of the most effective platforms for persuading the people. In Anne's reign, the sermon – both delivered and published – was probably more influential, and more popular, than it had been for decades.[293] By no means all the clergy, let alone dissenters, shared the queen's brand of piety, Anglicanism and moderation. Every week, however, clergy spoke as members of a church of which she was head and represented her to parishioners. Despite the quarrels and violent clashes occasioned by the fiercest religious disputes since the 1680s, preachers presented to the people a pious queen, favoured by providence and chosen by God. In doing so they revived some of the numinosity of sovereignty which was vital to the authority of the monarchy in a new political age.

We can safely get a gauge of the kind of sermon that Anne favoured as a representation of her in that preached at her coronation by the Archbishop of York, John Sharp, and 'published by her majesty's special command'. Taking as his text Isaiah 49: 23 ('And kings shall be thy nursing fathers'), Sharp told the congregation that God had given them a nursing mother who would vie with the greatest Christian kings.[294] Queen Anne, he informed them quoting her own words, was resolved to uphold the church, punish vice and promote the common cause of Europe and the Protestant succession. Observing that 'no prince ever came to the throne with a more general satisfaction and with more good wishes of the people', Sharp admonished his auditors to avoid divisions and not to obstruct the queen's good intentions but to show duty and gratitude to her.[295] From a clergyman whom Anne described as her intimate 'confessor', this coronation sermon all but reiterated her own speeches from the throne.[296] But there were many preached in a similar vein. In his coronation-day sermon at Gloucester Cathedral, the prebendary Luke Beaulieu, taking the same biblical text, welcomed a native English queen who loved the church and who would lead her people to God by example.[297] Though in praising high churchmen as excellent Christians he hinted at divisions, Beaulieu eschewed passive obedience and called on all to unite behind a monarch under whom they had 'as well grounded an expectation of a happy reign as ever can be'.[298] As an example of a more typical parish sermon, we can take the one by Matthew Hole preached on coronation day at Stokegursy in Somerset. Preaching on Psalm 132, Hole praised an English queen who was 'a hearty defender of the faith' and who came to her throne 'by a direct and lawful succession'.[299] Probably voicing (as well as his own politics) popular joy that the realm would no longer be governed by 'strangers and foreigners', Hole warned his auditors to beware of factions and parties, and enjoined them to offer up prayers for a princess whom God had chosen. 'Let us rejoice for the preservation of monarchy,' he urged, 'the best of all governments'.[300]

While the coronation sermons disclose hints of partisanship and perceptions of discussion, they closely echo the queen's own words and wishes. During Anne's reign, there were many other officially mandated days and services on which the government looked to the pulpit to support the line. The 30 January and 29 May, the anniversary of the Restoration, were already on the calendar as official sermon days and were often in Anne's reign occasions of celebration of monarchy and injunctions to obedience.[301] On 29 May 1707, for example, Willoughby Mynors, with perhaps more zeal than Anne would have applauded, asserted absolute submission to supreme power, as in 1712 Robert Phillips, preaching on *Religion and Loyalty*, reaffirmed the doctrine of nonresistance.[302] Throughout the reign, preachers on the anniversary emphasized the sacredness of monarchy, the Bishop of Hereford (Thomas Bisse) reminding the House of Commons in 1714 that 'there is an awe which majesty itself . . . casts around the persons of princes' whose lustre outshines all.[303]

If such sermons elevated monarchy in general, it was commemoration of Anne herself which was the theme of annual services commanded every 8 March to give thanks on the anniversary of the queen's succession. Preaching to the Commons at the first of these services in 1704, the high church Bishop of Rochester, Francis Atterbury, cited the biblical injunction of duty to kings. More particularly, as he recalled 'that happy day when her majesty began to reign', he recited Anne's virtues of piety, mercy, tenderness and mildness, and called upon all to commemorate annually a monarch who ruled 'with a universal joy and acclamation of her subjects'.[304] On the same day, in his parish church at Epsom, Robert Lloyd lamented the death of William III yet noted that, thanks to God, 'we at the same instant are made happy by the most agreeable succession of the best of queens'.[305] Each year thereafter, loyal preachers rehearsed before all the parishioners of the land the blessings of the queen's reign and the thanks the people owed to her. So in 1705, her prudence and love of her subjects, Benjamin Hoadly told his congregation at St Peter's Poor, 'have made her the delight of her people'; in Dorset, the rector of Stock-Gailord, in a sermon entitled *The Queen as a Nursing Mother*, took delight that 'our sacred queen makes it her care . . . to restore the languishing spirits of religion and banish profaneness' and, rising to the language of masque, saw 'the gentle air-breezes of her royal breath purge . . . the melancholy clouds away'.[306] Four years later, in a sermon delivered to the queen at St James's and published by her command, the Bishop of Exeter emphasized, as his title had it, *The Divine Institution of Magistracy* and the monarch's accountability only to God.[307] All the happiness the people had hoped for at Anne's coronation, Henry Lambe told his parishioners at St Dunstan's, they had enjoyed under a devout, virtuous, bountiful and wise queen under whom all should unite in loyalty.[308] Preaching on Isaiah, in 1711, after the furore over Sacheverell, the royal chaplain John Adams gave thanks for 'the most pious and religious sovereign that ever worshipped God from the British throne' and asked the MPs assembled to hear him to 'contribute to her quiet who takes so much pain for ours'.[309] Deprived of children, Anne, Nathaniel Hough told the congregation at Kensington in 1713, had devoted herself to the church and people. Praising her moderate course between superstition and separation, persecution and confusion, her charity and example, he thanked God 'we yet flourish under her benign influence'.[310] On these festival days, the vicar of Saxthorpe told the flock at Norwich Cathedral on the last anniversary of Anne's succession, the people were assembled to thank God for princes and the blessing of their queen whose reign, Thomas Sherlock preached the same day, had been 'one continued scene of glory and happiness'.[311] Whether they were bishops, royal chaplains or country clergy, whatever their high church of more moderate leanings, those who delivered sermons on the anniversary of the queen's succession led the people in thanks for monarchy and in praise of Queen Anne. That, despite bitter party divisions, to her death she remained a popular monarch may have owed much to these occasions and sermons, which in the main subordinated party politics to urge unity and loyalty to a queen both sacred and 'so tender . . . of the privileges of her people'.[312]

As well as the sermons preached on the anniversary of her succession, sermons delivered to or before the queen were usually given by trusted and loyal clergy, were often printed and published by royal command, and would probably therefore have been read as official representations of the queen and her preferences. Following his coronation sermon, John Sharp's 1703 sermons to the queen on the duty of taking communion frequently and on the need for repentance both advertised Anne's piety and emphasized her own priorities as, no doubt, did Richard Duke's sermon at St James's on the importance of 'the venerable mysteries' of religion – published by her majesty's command.[313] Such events could also turn into occasions when the preacher addressing the queen delivered thanks on behalf of the nation and so implicitly stirred others to display similar gratitude. 'What an auspicious, glorious reign is this?' the archdeacon of Huntingdon, White Kennett, asked rhetorically in his sermon on *The Duties of Rejoycing*, published by royal command.[314] 'We are now entering upon the sixth year of a reign full fraught with glories,' the Bishop of Carlisle concurred in a sermon at St James's; 'our Jerusalem is now most truly built'.[315] After a series of triumphs abroad and at home, in his July 1708 sermon to the queen at Windsor, the royal chaplain Thomas Manningham, told the congregation – and all his readers: 'because her chief delight is to exalt the Lord, therefore the Lord delights to crown her reign with prosperous events'.[316] The queen, the Dean of Canterbury told her majesty as well as his other auditors in 1710, was 'the glory and umpire of all Europe' and 'entire mistress of the hearts of all her own people'.[317] Such sermons in the royal presence would have been attended largely by members of the royal household, ministers and perhaps some MPs, that is, the core of the political nation. Published and read, however – and sermons were among the top-sellers of the Augustan book trade – they advertised the piety and virtues of the queen, as one of her preachers put it, 'in all the several parochial assemblies of the whole island'.[318] Sermons in the royal chapel, at Windsor or St James's, far from private, publicized the queen throughout the land.

Other than those regular anniversaries and sermons before the queen, throughout the reign royal proclamations ordered special services of fasts and thanksgiving with prayers and sermons to seek God's blessing on or give thanks for the success of England's troops and sailors. The majority of the sermons delivered throughout the parishes on these occasions were not published; but a remarkable number were and survive to provide some insight into how sermons promoted the war effort (and eventually the peace) and the queen. In his thanksgiving sermon of November 1702, following Marlborough's victories at Liège and Venlo, Daniel Williams made it clear to his audience that the war England was engaged upon was a just war, indeed, 'one of the wars of the Lord'.[319] Thanking God for the successes which had eluded William III, Williams attributed victories as granted 'in return of solemn national prayers' and, making a virtue of her sex, said: 'God directs these successes at a time when a female sits upon our throne; under *her* conduct, our forces triumph'.[320] On the official thanksgiving day, 3 December, at Oxford the canon of Christchurch dedicated his sermon to the queen, flattering her that no man in so short a time had ever effected such conquests; while the dean of Norwich assured his congregation that the paws of the French lion were pared as 'God hath given us greater victories and successes in this last summer's war than all our foreign expeditions before these last hundred years all put together have been crowned with'.[321] Prideaux, like the rector of Halsham, Holderness, used the thanksgiving to endorse Anne's own admonitions for all to renounce sin and to unite.[322] Celebrating victories while representing the queen as a model and example of piety who won God's favour characterized thanksgiving sermons over the rest of the decade.

The thanksgiving sermons for Blenheim seized the occasion of victory to figure England and her queen as God's own. 'It is now apparent to the world,' William Elstob told the parishes of St Swithin and St Mary Bothaw, 'that God pleads the cause of his anointed'.[323] ''Tis the presence of God,' the minister of the Savoy agreed, that won battles; yet under him it was Anne who was 'the principal contriver of these good events', and for whom he led the people in prayer.[324] Preaching at Chester on the text 'Awake, awake Deborah'

(Judges 5: 12), John Evans compared Anne's victory to that of her biblical predecessor and others, such as Queen Elizabeth, whom God had protected. Noting that for all his brave endeavours, providence had not granted William a victory, he added: 'our queen so evidently manifested herself a mother in our Israel', and now, like Deborah, called her subjects to join in solemn praise and in reformation of their lives'.[325] These biblical and historical parallels were a regular theme of the thanksgiving sermons. In the parish church of St Ethelburg, Luke Milbourne delivered his sermon *Great Britain's Acclamation to Her Deborah*. Preaching on the story (from Judges) of Deborah, 'a mother in Israel', Milbourne paralleled her appointment of Barak as Captain General with Anne's of Marlborough.[326] Deborah, he explained, showed how God 'can raise a weak woman to be as great an instrument of good to his people and can endue her with as many royal qualities such as become the head of a nation as the most heroic and high-born of men'.[327] Deborah also taught that when princes undertook just wars it was the religious duty of subjects to assist them. In Anne, he told them, making the analogy explicit, England had another Deborah, a queen 'whose goodness can never want God's blessing', whose 'piety and goodness have reconciled heaven to us'.[328] 'Our gracious judge and Queen, the mother of our Israel', he proclaimed, 'is coming in triumph'.[329] Joseph Stennett, though sounding a less apocalyptic note, pursued the same theme. Jabin had enslaved the Israelites but under Deborah, 'by the prudent management and good conduct of a woman', they were able to recover their religion and liberty.[330] Now in England God had 'spoken to us by his Providence', and Stennett urged: 'let us pray that a series of victories and triumphs may attend the reign of Queen Anne'.[331] Preaching at York, William Pearson compared Anne also with Hezekiah 'in her pious solitude and constant endeavours to promote virtue and holiness'.[332] When the dissenter Richard Norris preached on the thanksgiving for victory, the parallels that he invoked were of a later Deborah, Queen Elizabeth, whose lustre (he observed) was now somewhat overclouded by that of Anne, the three years of whose reign 'would have been sufficient to have made the longest reigns of her predecessors glorious'.[333] Queen Anne, 'a princess that seems to be the favourite of heaven and the joy and delight of her people', held the fate of Europe in her hands.[334] Even those not her obvious supporters agreed: though, like Stennett, he regretted the disparaging of William III's achievements, Norris acknowledged that it was Anne whom God had made the instrument of victory and Anne for whose auspicious reign all gave thanks. William, Alexander Jephson reminded his parishioners at Camberwell, had saved the English crown and defended it against assault, but it was likely 'our great and glorious Queen Anne' who would 'bring the haughty French king down to sue humbly for mercy at her feet'.[335]

Seeing the benefit of these occasions, the queen and government instituted thanksgivings as regular services at which to celebrate success and promote the war. Though 1705 saw no such spectacular victory as Blenheim, a service was ordered for 23 August to give thanks for the allies' advance in the Spanish Netherlands. Preaching before the queen at St Paul's, the royal chaplain Richard Willis acknowledged that this year had seen no 'signal victory' as last; but he assured auditors and readers that the enemy had been forced from their strongholds.[336] The honour of England was advanced, Francis Atterbury preached at Whitehall, and 'the name of Anne is had in as great or greater veneration as ever that of Elizabeth was'.[337] However, the August sermons identified divisions and quarrels which threatened to advantage the enemy and, as Anne herself, called for united support of the war and queen. The second major triumph, at Ramillies the next May, 1706, at least superficially secured those ends. Within a week of the news, and well before the official service of thanksgiving, John Evans preached and, at the request of his auditory, published a sermon celebrating the victory and 'a spirit of concord and charity . . . revived'.[338] Whatever its costs and difficulties, Evans argued, the war was worth it; then, as well as offering thanks to God who had tilted the scale in England's favour, he delivered a eulogy on Anne:

> we owe all honour, obedience and gratitude to the best of queens by whose admirable management we feel a profound peace at home and are capable of making such a figure abroad whom God delights to place in the first rank of honour in the sight of all Europe. Who can refuse affection to the common mother of her people, or forbear to celebrate the conduct, the application, the temper of her government, or be cool in their prayers for the life, the prosperity, the glory of such a minister of God to us for good?[339]

Sermons on the official thanksgiving day, 27 June, echoed Evans's praise. At St Paul's, the Dean of Canterbury George Stanhope, describing her as the person God most honoured, represented Anne as a sovereign 'never equalled'; 'words cannot express God's peculiar favour of this land', John Whittle told his congregation at Footscray in Kent, and it was for all to give thanks for the queen's glorious victories.[340] At Oxford, John Wilder described his monarch as 'famed for her devotion . . . and much more famed for the glory of her arms than the renowned Elizabeth'.[341] God, he concluded, had given England a second Moses. Preaching at Malton in Yorkshire, the minister William Perse agreed that God had raised another Moses, 'our Moses, as I may without a solecism call our gracious queen . . . whose exemplary piety and devotion is never to be forgotten'.[342]

A thanksgiving appointed for 31 December was probably intended to indulge further celebrations of a successful year of campaigning. 'This marvellous, marvellous year', the veteran Bishop of Salisbury and historian Gilbert Burnet described it in his sermon to parliament.[343] Despite his devotion to

William III and diminished influence under his successor, Burnet could not but express joy at 'a new scene of glory to our renowned queen' and asked: 'what may not yet be expected from a queen that offers up the praise of all the wonders of her reign to that God under whose protection she humbly puts herself?'[344] At Portsmouth, William Ward catalogued miraculous victories in Flanders and Italy, Ramillies and Piedmont, and, again making a parallel with Deborah's defeat of Jabin, reflected: 'such a Deborah, such a mother in our land is our most gracious sovereign'.[345] She was, the curate of Enfield told his parishioners, 'the great nursing mother of the whole confederacy'.[346]

Like her predecessor, Anne, as we saw, regarded the union with Scotland as vital to securing England's safety, the effective prosecution of the war and the Protestant Hanoverian succession. Accordingly she ordered a thanksgiving service on 1 May 1707, which also became a further celebration of England's military victories and a further representation of Anne as blessed by providence to effect what had eluded all her predecessors. Several preachers made it clear in their sermons how the union had been essential to the war: John Bates, for example, preaching at Hackney, explained that Scotland would otherwise have been inclined to support a French invasion; in his sermon at Bartholomew Close, Thomas Freke, declared union a necessary precondition for a Protestant succession.[347] Robert Davidson, the rector of Hayes in Kent, heralded the union as yet another of Anne's successes – and one, he believed, more important than her military victories.[348] The Oxford University fellow Charles Bean concurred: 'though scarce any sovereign was ever blessed with more numerous or more signal successes in war . . . yet [they] come infinitely short of this single triumph without blood'.[349] In uniting the two nations, William Talbot told Anne in a sermon at St Paul's, she had performed 'an undertaking which had baffled all former attempts' and fulfilled Scripture.[350] An opportunity desired for a century, Francis Hutchinson told the congregation at Bury St Edmunds, 'is now happily given us by Providence in our age through the great endeavours of our excellent queen'.[351] 'God has given the Queen her heart's desire,' Giles Dent informed his flock, 'and enabled her to accomplish this great work.'[352] Providence had manifested its favour, Patrick Dujon echoed in Doncaster, 'in the most surprising successes of our arms abroad and now in our happily effected union at home'.[353] Not only another Deborah, Anne, Dent believed, was a second David – who had 'allured the people of Israel to unite with Judah'.[354]

These often-repeated biblical parallels and this insistent on providence were only heightened by the attempted invasion that followed the union and the final crushing victory obtained by the allies at Oudenarde. Preaching on both defeats, Thomas Coulton took as his theme *Nahash's Defeat* as related in the Book of Samuel.[355] For all the recent union, Coulton warned that some might well have aided the Pretender had he landed, and he gave thanks for a double deliverance off the coasts of Scotland and in Flanders. 'Now that God has owned Queen Anne by so many victories and deliverances', he hoped that none would think of supporting Jacobites, for 'who can now be false to her and her government which heaven is so . . . kind to?'³⁵⁶ 'When God has been on our side', Thomas Knaggs posed a rhetorical question in his sermon at St Margaret's Westminster, 'shall we hinder our happiness by divided interests, internal dissentions?' especially when, as another preacher put it, the queen's piety 'hath engaged heaven to fight her battles'.³⁵⁷ God evidently continued to fight her battles, and in 1709 the queen ordered one of the last of the official thanksgivings for military triumphs. In his sermon on 17 February, Joseph Stennett added another biblical sovereign to those to whom Anne had been compared, figuring her as another Abraham whose battles against tyrants (of Canaan) had been fought with God's aid.³⁵⁸ After her crushing victory at Oudenarde, Francis Hare preached to the Commons, Britain and Anne would now 'keep out tyranny . . . from overspreading the earth'.³⁵⁹ All that was required to complete the victory was to love and honour the queen. 'If the main part of our prosperity', Thomas Manningham argued, 'may be reasonably thought to flow in upon us on the account of the exemplary piety on the throne, which God continues to reward . . . then what cheerful obedience ought we to pay to that eminent pattern of goodness?'³⁶⁰

After further advances, at Tournai and Mons and in Spain, the preachers on thanksgiving days, looking back, discerned a clear pattern. 'Every year since this bloody war commenced', Thomas Masters observed on 22 November 1709, 'we have received some special marks of the divine favour'.³⁶¹ The queen's 'undauntedness of spirit', still more her piety, had engaged God's aid.³⁶² Thanks to her, George Stanhope hoped, as he concluded his sermon at St James's, Britain could look to peace.³⁶³ When peace became government policy, loyal preachers promoted it against critics and those who favoured continuing the war. On the day, 16 January 1712, appointed as a fast day to implore God's blessing on a peace, Roger Altham, preaching to the Commons, told MPs that it was their duty to assist their sovereign in supplications for peace.³⁶⁴ In his sermon at St Martin's-in-the-Fields, Joseph Trapp took on the objectors directly before reminding his congregation that a Christian's duty was the pursuit of peace and 'respect and loyalty to our sovereign'.³⁶⁵ William Fleetwood was explicit in his partisanship, entitling his sermon as an address 'against such as delight in war' – though he made clear that it was only an honourable and secure peace he supported.³⁶⁶ Preachers assured their congregations that the best of pious queens, who had secured with God's aid so many victories, could not conclude a dishonourable peace.³⁶⁷ No one, Edmund Chishull argued in his sermon at Hertford, could in conscience disagree with a policy of peace when God's vicegerent assured them that it would crown the glories of war.³⁶⁸

When, despite continuing opposition, peace was signed at Utrecht, the queen and government appointed a thanksgiving day on 7 July to discountenance doubts and to celebrate what was an undoubtedly popular cessation of conflict. Peace, the Bishop of Bath and Wells told both houses of parliament in his sermon that day, was to be more celebrated than their military successes, for 'the triumph now is for an entire, finished victory' secured by a queen who never ceased to care for the public good.[369] The queen was, he closed, newly inaugurated, 'now crown'd with peace' and 'at this her coronation we . . . are likewise to repeat out professions [of] allegiance'.[370] A glorious war, Philip Stubs told the parishioners of St James Garlickhythe in London, had ended in peace that promised 'more glorious consequences' and blessings under 'the most serene and puissant princess which ever swayed the sceptre of these kingdoms'.[371] England's gracious nursing mother, Nicholas Brady preached at Richmond, had revived her grandfather's motto – 'blessed are the peacemakers' – and was herself 'the blessed chief instrument of our quiet and tranquillity'.[372] Anne, a Cambridge University fellow told the flock at Hazelingfield, 'has now called home happy Britain from seas of blood'; it was for subjects to show their gratitude to the queen and her ministers by living peacefully with each other and uniting in her service.[373]

Whatever the divisions of party or within the church, which find expression overtly or between the lines in several sermons, the addresses on days of fast and thanksgiving throughout the war and for the peace most often promoted the ministry's line, and in virtually every case conspicuously praised and gave thanks for the queen herself. These sermons were important in several ways in representing Queen Anne to her people: to the political elites, the electorate and the disenfranchised who talked and gossiped about policy and politics. In the first place (like verse panegyrics) the sermons attributed to a queen who could not actually fight a key role in the support for and victories obtained in the conflict. Those who heard or read these official sermons heard and read of Queen Anne's wars and the queen's peace – not those of a party or interest group. The preachers, that is, helped to keep the monarchy – and Anne – at the centre of policy, politics and public discourse in the new circumstances of powerful parliaments, parties and public opinion. Secondly, as numerous examples we have quoted evidence, preachers persistently described Anne in sacred language and represented her as God's vicegerent and instrument, as the favoured daughter of providence, as another Deborah or Moses leading the new Israel of England to glory. To some historians such language will jar with assumptions about the period as a more secular age. However, as revisionist scholars have argued, eighteenth-century England remained a confessional state; certainly in Anne's reign, religious issues and language were ubiquitous in the culture and discourse, and articulations of divine right were by no means rare.[374] Official sermons and thanksgivings, we might argue, served to re-sacralize the monarchy under a queen who again touched to cure the evil and advertised her commitment to the church.[375] In giving the queen prominence and representing her in providential terms, the preachers also strengthened Anne's claim to embody the nation. The monarch's claim to be, and his or her representation as, the head of the commonweal and embodiment of the nation had been essential to the development and enhancement of sovereignty in Tudor and Stuart England. Regicide and two revolutions, however, not only undermined these claims; they ruptured the connection between the king's two bodies: the person of the ruler and the body of the realm. But in reviving Stuart succession, claiming to be and being presented as the embodiment and mother of the nation – indeed of a British empire – Anne gave new life to political metaphors and languages that had long helped to sustain monarchical authority. The national thanksgiving services and sermons of Queen Anne's reign brought together, at least on those occasions, a people divided by party in shared prayers for a beloved sovereign.

Official thanksgiving sermons may also have set the tone for other locally orchestrated sermons that in Anne's reign placed a greater emphasis on the sacred nature of rule. *A Charge Given at the Triennial Visitation* of the diocese of Salisbury in 1704 addressed the interdependency of monarchy and church and, throughout the reign, churchmen – and not only high churchmen – were leading spokesmen for the crown.[376] The vicar of Elvaston, Anthony Blackwall, titled his sermon at the Nottinghamshire assizes *Duty to God and the Queen* and, glossing Proverbs 24: 21, asserted: the queen 'derives her authority and imperial majesty from God'.[377] Making the traditional argument that the church taught loyalty, Blackwall preached that 'to obey kings and queens is to obey God in his deputies' and that defiance of rulers was a sin.[378] Assize sermons had traditionally been occasions for reflections on order and magistracy; in Anne's reign preachers appeared to have seized the opportunity to extol the monarchy and a queen who (more than her predecessor) was a protector of the church. Loyalty and allegiance were due, John Pierce told those gathered at the Northamptonshire assizes, to God's vicegerent.[379] Though he spoke of reciprocal duties in his sermon on Romans 13 at the Gloucester assizes in 1706, the prebendary Luke Beaulieu reminded his auditors of their duty of subjection to and reverence of monarchy, a sentiment echoed at the Croydon assizes by the Archbishop of Canterbury's chaplain who warned 'against speaking evil of princes and those in authority under them'.[380] As quarrels within the church and state grew hotter, Whig clergy, such as Benjamin Hoadly, took the opportunity of an assize sermon (at Hertford in 1708) to defend limited *iure divino* monarchy.[381] Yet, as he recognized, there were numerous others preaching that whose sermons were published at the request of judges, grand jurymen and leading gentry, and welcomed by congregations. As the rector of Harply put it in his sermon at King's Lynn on *Government and Obedience* and the sanctity of magistracy: 'we love majesty; and monarchy is the interest, and inclination too, of our people'.[382] Albeit often more moderate than their titles might suggest, assize and other sermons with titles like *The Doctrine of Non-resistance Stated* or *Religion and Loyalty* or *The Duties of Subjects to Princes and Magistrates* indicate a tendency for the pulpit in Anne's reign to step back from post-Revolution arguments for the sovereignty of the people.[383] Indeed, the preacher at the Brentwood assizes in August 1712 used the loftiest language when he told the Grand Jury 'a good prince is the representative of the king of heaven, encircled with the rays of majesty which strike with awe and reverence all that approach him'.[384] Lest we think his language outmoded or exceptionally partisan, we should note that the preacher Benjamin Carter delivered his sermon before the Whig Lord Chief Justice Thomas Parker (who was involved in the prosecution of Sacheverell) and the grand jurymen and clergy of Essex – who requested that he publish it. Queen Anne often expressed her preference for moderate clergy and preachers who did not stir controversy; but moderation did not preclude a revived emphasis in the pulpit on the divine right of monarchy and the accountability of princes only to God.

One important subgenre of sermons had elicited sometimes bitter divisions ever since the 30 January was established as a calendrical day of the church to commemorate the martyr Charles I, and was still more contentious after the Revolution of 1688. During Anne's reign, the Tories looked to reclaim the day for their own cause and to appropriate the Stuart Anne to validate Charles I, while his memory was invoked to elevate renewed hereditary monarchy. Accordingly, preaching to the House of Commons on 30 January 1703, the Vice Chancellor of Oxford, emphasizing the importance of observing the day, concluded 'the virtues of our murdered sovereign will securely adorn the crown in the person of his royal granddaughter'.[385] Other high churchmen within the establishment – the Dean of Canterbury, George Stanhope, and the prebendary of Winchester, Robert Eyre, for example – condemned the opponents of Charles I, warned Anne against their successors and extolled monarchy.[386] In a series of sermons, Luke Milbourne, a supporter of Sacheverell, denounced any resistance to a prince even 'though he be a persecutor of the best of men' or a tyrant.[387] One (anonymous) preacher at Putney in 1713 used his sermon to argue that Whigs were no Christians and that all needed to embrace the high church doctrine of passive obedience.[388] Though the preacher implicitly claimed Queen Anne as a friend, it is unlikely that she applauded such sermons, if only because they stirred controversy. It is by no means clear, however, that the queen disapproved of Tory arguments for monarchy: she ordered published the 30 January 1704 sermon by Thomas Sherlock who lavished praise on Charles I as he argued obedience to princes 'the first and highest duty of men acting in society'.[389] Most to the queen's taste were those preachers who, while insisting on honouring the martyr, eschewed extreme statements about royal authority and non-resistance: sermons like the Bishop of St Asaph's, which argued that 30 January instructed rulers not to exceed the law as well as the duty of subjects to obey, or that in 1710 of Bishop William Fleetwood who balanced 'prerogative' and 'liberties'.[390] As a Stuart and champion of the church, Anne derived clear advantages from such sermons and others (like that of Robert Wynne) enjoining 'unity and peace' that most accorded with her own stated wishes, whatever a popular taste for a more Tory political ideology.[391]

The 30 January sermons offer a graphic case study in how the past dominated the political culture of Anne's reign and how history became inextricably entangled in party warfare. Memories of the civil war and the 1688 Revolution were fundamental to the politics of Augustan England, and both the government and image of Queen Anne, the daughter of James II and granddaughter of Charles I, were inseparable from memory and history.[392] Historians and polemicists favourable to Charles I were quick to take advantage of the succession of Anne to link the reputation of the martyr to the Stuart queen. 'The memory of the martyr', the non-juror Charles Leslie instructed the Commons in 1703, was tied to 'the safety and honour of the queen';[393] in 1705 the author of an opera entitled *The Royal Martyr*, in his dedication to the queen, told her 'It is because the blood of this royal martyr yet runs warm in your veins . . . that you, like him, are signalising your zeal for maintenance of the rights of God's church';[394] the epistle dedicating a 1706 edition of the *Eikon Basilike* affirmed 'they can be no good subjects to her majesty and the crown of England that abuse the memory of so excellent a prince'.[395] Throughout Anne's reign, Tories, and some non-partisan conservatives, represented the queen and her reign by frequent comparison to that of Charles I. In his sermon on the anniversary of the Restoration, in 1707, Willoughby Myneors, having lauded Charles I, expressed the view that 'our present sovereign bids fair to be compared with him'.[396] Some high church and Tory apologists, of course, tried to persuade the queen to see the Whigs as no better than the rebels against the martyr.[397] But, as one commentator remarked, it was not only Jacobites and Tories who talked up Charles I: 'I am now confident there are many thousands of loyal and good-natured Englishmen who love his memory'.[398] The memory of Charles I was indeed held dear by the populace; and, whatever the motives of those who wrote, Anne's representation as heir to the martyr and what he stood for only enhanced her popularity.

Some of those who poured praise on Charles I – and on Anne as his heir – had been or were opposed to the 1688 Revolution which had evicted his son and brought in a Dutchman who had not been a champion of the Church of England. A Stuart and a staunch Anglican, Anne had nevertheless supported the Revolution and was committed, as we have seen, to the Protestant succession and the wars to defeat France in order to secure it. Most of all, Anne sought to heal the bitter divisions that were the legacy of 1688 and, while upholding her prerogative, was ready to accept the constitutional consequences of the Revolution and William's reign that produced a partnership with parliaments quite other than that her grandfather would have favoured; while striving for independence from party, she recognized the need to appoint as ministers those who could form a majority and had the support of the people. Augustan histories of the Revolution and the representations of Anne as William's successor were, like histories and memories of Charles I, impossible to detach from party; there were, however, those who followed Anne's preferences in describing her as (both) a Stuart heir by divine right and successor to William by parliamentary statute, and to figure her as much the upholder of Revolution as of royal sovereignty.

However, Anne's succession as a Stuart and daughter of James II was a cue for nonjurors and some Tories to denounce William. A 1703 *Satire* set out 'to prove him as bad as the devil could make him' and hoped that 'his very memory should shrink' and the new queen outshine him, though it acknowledged that her government stood on the same basis.[399] The same year, writing to defend the late king, Bernard Mandeville attacked the many 'villains' who 'daily practice Murder on his Fame' and who 'dare in open streets lampoon his name'.[400] Even, that is, before Sacheverell, there were overt attacks on William III and the Revolution and, on the other side, defences of and paeans to him and it by Whig apologists who represented the late king as 'the glorious instrument of preserving the pure religion, the ancient laws and known liberties of this kingdom'.[401] Given that the effect of the Sacheverell trial was to bring again to the fore the question of whether Anne's title was founded on hereditary right or the Act of Settlement, after 1709 the Revolution became a major issue of party contention which was further embittered by rumours of support for the succession of the Pretender. Rather than either these Whig or Tory histories and polemics, it was those who represented Anne as a continuation of her predecessor and of the Revolution, and smoothed over difficult questions and ambiguities, who most supported and promoted the queen's own preferences. In, for example, his *Hymn to Victory* after Blenheim, Defoe, contrary to those who delighted in contrasting this spectacular success with William's failure, insisted:

The Agency of Sovereign William shines
In all the Parts of your sublime Designs.[402]

Connecting the queen and last king, writers like Alexander Jephson and Benjamin Hoadly argued for not a major shift but a 'glorious continuance' and warned those who vilified William that they implicitly also undermined Anne.[403] In 1709 the independent minister Thomas Bradbury depicted Anne as guided by the same spirit as William in sermons significantly titled *The Divine Right of the Revolution*.[404] Others wrote to reconcile acceptance of the principles of both 1688 and divine right, which were again creating fissures in church and state. In his 30 January sermon for 1710, Luke Milbourne urged all not to 'distort the quiet waters' or to open questions about the justification for the Revolution or the basis of Anne's right, but to 'live peaceably under her government'.[405] In his defence even Sacheverell felt the need to emphasize that he had not spoken against the Revolution.[406]

The evidence suggests that during (especially the later years of) Anne's reign, William was not popular with the general public who, it was said, abstained from the celebrations of his birth and accession days.[407] For her part, not least because she remained committed to a Hanoverian succession, Anne ordered 'yearly commemoration of his mission to this kingdom' and to the end distanced herself from assaults on William's memory.[408] It was those, like Sir John Willes, who wrote in support of 'her Majesty's title', the memory of King William, the legality of the Revolution and the Hanoverian succession, the authority of the queen and parliaments, who most advertised her views and advanced her wishes.[409] The challenge in a fiercely partisan culture was to find writers whose histories promoted more the royal than a party agenda.

It was not only the histories of the civil war and Revolution that were *parti pris*. The reign of Anne saw the publication or republication of some of the great – and distinctly partisan – editions and texts out of which our modern histories have been written: Rymer, Rushworth and Clarendon, to name but three. Histories, however, tended to legitimate monarchy and, in Anne's case, several represented her, through the spectacular victories of her reign, as making history. Very early in her reign, in a popular epitome of the history of England, William Ayloffe, having lauded her piety, prudence and industry, opined that she had 'carried the honour of England even in the first year of her glorious reign to as high a pitch as ever any crown and head had done' and prophesied that she 'seems designed by God and nature for Justice, Empire and Victory'.[410] The epistle dedicatory to Clarendon's *History*, as well as counselling her to champion the church, compared her to Queen Elizabeth 'whose motto you have chosen and whose pattern you seem to have taken for your great example'.[411] The next year saw the publication of the first volume of Rymer's *Foedera*, dedicatory prefaces to which celebrated Anne's 'most auspicious reign' and accomplishments.[412] In 1707 a continuation of Francis Sandford's monumental *Genealogical History of the Kings and Queens of England* praised Anne for all the virtues she had inherited from her ancestors and for effecting a union of England and Scotland that had eluded them.[413] Similarly a history of the lives of the Protestant kings and queens represented her as *Great Britain's Glory* under whom subjects enjoyed as great happiness as ever they had and who would lead the nation to victory and peace.[414]

Not surprisingly, Blenheim and Ramillies were taken up by historians as truly historic victories. Herman Moll's *History of the English Wars* on the continent since 1066 did not hesitate, in the aftermath of Blenheim, to claim that in 'the glorious reign of her present majesty . . . it can be no vanity to say the English have answered the highest character in any age'.[415] And, though a history of 'Charles II's most miraculous preservation', the dedication to the 1709 edition of Thomas Blount's *Boscobel* assured the queen, 'your great and repeated successes will make your illustrious name shine in the accounts of time amongst the princes of greatest fame'.[416] From 1703, Queen Anne even had her own historian, the French émigré Abel Boyer, who that year began, probably under Harley's patronage, *The History of the Reign of Queen Anne, Digested into Annals*.[417] A detailed chronicle of events abroad and at home, published annually to the end of the reign, Boyer's *History* justified the wars, celebrated successes and victories, highlighted 'wonderful and glorious events', and praised the best of queens.[418] Looking back in 1712 to a first volume in which he had promised 'future glories and successes', Boyer felt confidently able to state that never had a monarch achieved so much honour in eight years; listing her fame, wisdom and glory, he concluded: 'I am as sure as history can make me no prince of ours was ever yet so prosperous and successful, so loved, esteemed and honoured.'[419] While he proclaimed his impartiality, in every sense, Boyer's massive 500-page annual histories were a monument to Queen Anne. Though the most important, it was not the only annual history to celebrate her. From 1705, after Blenheim, one David Jones published annually *A Compleat History of Europe*, which (amid its dense detail) singled out English victories 'not to be matched in history'.[420] Such histories, which their multiple volumes, several editions and many sales outlets indicate sold well, served to represent Queen Anne not only as heir to a long line of monarchs, but as a ruler under whom England was entering a glorious new age and establishing supremacy in Europe.[421] They wrote of her, that is, as queen of a new British imperium.

Over the course of the sixteenth and seventeenth centuries, as a succession of kings and queens sought to argue for their authority as divine or unaccountable, they were supported by pamphleteers and prose writers who, in treatises on monarchy, the constitution or the law, endorsed royal rights and refuted those who questioned or contested them. Some advocates for untrammelled sovereignty had exceeded even their monarch's own imperatives and caused difficulties: the civil war lawyer John Cowell in James I's reign, or clerics Sibthorpe and Manwaring under Charles I, for example. But in the main, those who promoted divine right sovereignty, whether they were officially patronized or not, represented the ruler to the political nation and the people. The civil war and Interregnum fundamentally changed this: with the full publication of criticisms of monarchy and apologia for republic, defences of kingship became a partisan rather than (largely) shared discourse. In the country's collective will to put the clock back in 1660, the majority were ready to pretend that constitutional differences had been resolved in favour of the old monarchy. Though this was never other than a fiction, it was arguably not fully exposed as one until the Popish Plot and, most significantly, the 1688 Revolution. Those who enacted the Revolution, as we saw, opted for a fudge: by arguing that James II had abdicated (as opposed to been deposed), they sought to avoid debates about the basis of sovereignty or the rights of resistance. From 1688, however, differences about these constitutional principles were again increasingly publicized, helped to define emerging parties, and were institutionalized by parties. Desirous first and foremost to get support for his continental wars, William III showed little interest in ideological debate or apologia. As a usurper, installed by a coup and a vote of a Convention, he could hardly claim or be represented in the traditional languages and colours of divine, hereditary kingship. His successor, however, was another matter. A Stuart, heir to James II, as well as successor by the Act of Settlement, Queen Anne, a staunch Anglican, could theoretically have revivified and revalorized the discourses of divine, hereditary rule. Her private beliefs on such issues remain unknown to us: Anne was complicit in the removal of her father and in William's rule but (as one who revived touching to cure the evil) had a more sacral view of monarchy than her predecessor.[422] A pragmatist who recognized and accepted the political and constitutional changes effected by 1688 and William's reign, Anne avoided large theoretical statements about her authority – doubtless not least in the hope of not re-stirring the old questions that 1688 had left unanswered: was she, like her father, a divine, hereditary queen or a monarch by parliamentary statute accountable to the legislature and the people?

Insofar as they threatened worse division (which in turn would have jeopardized the war and her rule), those writers who came forward from both parties to debate the basis of her right and the nature and extent of her authority did not always champion the queen's personal wishes. However, those who wrote against contractualism and reasserted royal prerogative – be they independent or moderate Tories – undoubtedly represented monarchy in ways that appealed to the people and may have helped to garner popular support for the queen. And, writing in a variety of genres, pamphleteers and essayists of various political sympathies praised Anne personally and advertised her virtues and blessings to her subjects.

From the beginning of the reign, some apologists for Anne's monarchy were palpably keen to settle old scores and to hijack the queen for their own agendas. William Baron, for example, in defending monarchy and church, lashed out at commonwealthsmen and dissenters who, he maintained, had gained ground since the Revolution and who threatened the crown.[423] In similar vein, the Cambridge professor and devotee of the Stuarts, Joshua Barnes, celebrating what he hoped was the return with Anne of the *Good Old Way*, attacked the

574 REPRESENTING STUART QUEENSHIP

sycophants and dissenters of the previous reign.[424] The author of *The Source of Our Present Fears* chose to remain anonymous. But, while lauding a new queen under whom 'every Englishman may be happy', he pilloried William as a foreign, false king and welcomed his legitimate, hereditary successor who re-established the ancient constitution.[425] Such partisan apologia for monarchy intensified over the reign. In 1705 another anonymous work, *An Essay upon Government*, set out to repudiate the 'republican schemes' of Locke and Blackall so as to (again) argue the patriarchal and divine foundation of monarchy – 'God recognising the power as personating himself'.[426] 'The right of ... hereditary monarchy', the *Essay* asserts, 'was established by God himself'; 'the English government is founded upon the same divine authority and therefore ... hereditary monarchy is unalterably here established'.[427] Others, like the non-juring bishop Henry Gandy, went to print to prove the government of England 'monarchical and hereditary', while an old essay of William Prynne's was republished to make the case for *iure divino* monarchy and to contest arguments that power resided in the people.[428]

These provocations to the Whigs and devotees of what were called 'Revolution principles' increased greatly in number and bitterness in the wake of Sacheverell's sermon and impeachment in 1709.[429] To take one case from hundreds of pamphlets, a (somewhat misleadingly self-described) 'honest Tory', Francis Atterbury, penned a retort to the 'Wh[ig]s' arguments about the limitations to royal prerogative and popular rights', to reiterate the doctrines of divine right and non-resistance.[430] Along similar lines, in 1711, one A. R. maintained *The Rights of the English Monarchy* in a treatise that coupled Whigs with old regicides, denied the sovereign's accountability to the people, and insisted that 'the same absolute power which was in the Conqueror is derived down to her present majesty'.[431] Even after the immediate furore subsided, such treatises continued to be published. The philosopher and fellow of Trinity College Dublin, George Berkeley, delivered a series of discourses advocating unlimited sovereignty and non-resistance which he published in 1712 as *Passive Obedience ... Proved and Vindicated*.[432] In the last year of Anne's reign, Hilkiah Bedford, the non-juring bishop who had helped to print and distribute *The Hereditary Right of the Crown of England Asserted*, published *A Vindication* of the queen's title in which he countered the view that Anne was queen *de facto* rather than *de iure*.[433] As Sacheverell himself returned to the pulpit, William Robertson used the occasion of his sermon to discourse on the sin of resisting princes and the errors of those exponents of it who were 'an exact counterpart of their ancestors ... in King Charles the first's days'.[434]

Though some of these arguments probably echoed her private views, Anne, as her speeches reiterated, did not welcome publications that highlighted and exacerbated divisions. More appealing to her were those who, without displaying party colours or positions, praised and celebrated the Stuart queen. An early example is a history of the royal family, perhaps by the bookseller

John Dunton, and dedicated to Prince George. Opening with a life of Anne, the book praised her piety, modesty, wisdom and valour, and her devotion to her people. Whig in its sympathies for toleration, the text yet heralded Anne as God's representative on earth and as a queen who 'powerfully reigns in the hearts of her subjects'.[435] Denying party affiliation by praising both William III and Charles I, James Gordon, reviewing the first year of Anne's reign, predicted that she would be another Elizabeth, as great as any of her predecessors.[436] The Presbyterian minister and author of a discourse on medals agreed with such an assessment: writing in 1704, James Coningham judged that Anne displayed the virtues of wisdom, charity, piety and resolution, and that 'the steps her Majesty has made towards our future security, to preserve religion and settle her throne in truth and righteousness, give a fair prospect of happiness to future generations'.[437] Victories abroad and the completion of the union at home spurred others, not of obviously partisan position, to celebrate Anne in the loftiest of terms. As well as rehearsing the claims of preachers that Anne's piety was winning the wars on the continent, prose writers singled out her reign as a peculiar blessing. 'In the reign of a queen so good and so gracious,' the author of an *Essay* on the Duke of Marlborough instructed his countrymen, 'how fortunately are men born.'[438] In his *Great Britain's Triumph*, the author, looking ahead to an English resumption of the imperial crown of France, regarded Anne as outflanking Elizabeth in her virtues and attainments.[439] 'We ought to be sensible,' John Edwards told readers, 'how great and rich a treasure we have in her life.'[440] In 1707 *An Oration Sacred to the Imperial Majesty of Anne, Queen of Great Britain*, reviewing the 'miraculous' achievements in a short space of time, lauded female rule and, in particular, 'a real nursing mother' who was 'truly God-like'.[441] Under a princess who was not ambitious for power but bound to her people by cords of love, the author (not unreasonably) believed that 'as factious and divided as we are among ourselves, there is no division or faction against the queen', who was 'universally hailed'.[442]

When we come across a 'satire on her present majesty' entitled *A Cat May Look on a Queen*, we may think that the author of *An Oration* has been proved wrong. On the contrary, John Dunton's work, dedicated to Anne, turns into a paean to the beauty, intelligence and majesty of 'a second Elizabeth', 'an angel incarnate'.[443] 'In a word,' the author sums, 'Queen Anne is a nursing mother to all her subjects and governs 'em with so much spirit and tenderness that she resembles angels who move the heavens.'[444] Though he excuses his title by saying that it was 'satire enough to say that I [can't?] call her infallible', even that caveat was overridden by his failure to find any faults in her. It was, in fine, a 'satire' that 'owns her to be the very best of women'.[445]

Amid the rows over Sacheverell, the historian William Cockburn published an essay 'upon the propitious and glorious reign of our gracious sovereign Anne'. Listing her conquests, virtues and political skills, the author praised a queen who, for all her majesty, worked with parliaments for the common interest and 'square[d] her actions by the golden rule of the law'.[446] A monarch who sought to heal divisions, and be a 'tender mother' to all her people, Anne was content 'to establish her authority in the hearts and affections of her subjects'.[447] Were the crown elective, Cockburn opined, trying to draw together Whigs and Tories, 'all would confer it upon great Anne', 'the best and greatest of princes'.[448] In the preface to his *Essay*, Cockburn referred to 'the many addresses of thanks both from the parliament and the people for the many valuable blessings of the present auspicious reign'.[449] Themselves perhaps a product of the praise of verse panegyrists and prose apologists of the queen, the many civic speeches presented to Anne and published in turn represented her to readers as the virtuous and glorious princess they proclaimed her to be. As Mark Knights has demonstrated, increasingly from James II's reign onwards, public addresses took prominence over public petitions and deployed a language of panegyric, while remaining clear statements of public opinion.[450] After few such discourses in the 1690s, during Anne's reign they became common; over 2,500 were presented to the queen congratulating her on her accession, on military victories, on the union, on her escape from attempted invasions and on concluding peace. Interestingly, the early orations echoed language from Anne's own accession speech and so re-circulated the queen's self-presentation as a popular representation. And reprinted in the *Gazette* these popular panegyrics in turn became 'official' documents of popular support and acclamation in turn republished to readers. Addresses could be – they were – partisan. During the Sacheverell trial, Tories and Whigs used them as weapons in the war over the church and constitution.[451] However, it was the Tories who made most effective use of them then and to sell the peace to a public very ready to embrace it. More importantly from the queen's perspective, such speeches tended to condemn party divisions and were often couched in a language of loyalty and unity – a language, that is, close to the queen's own words and wishes.[452]

There has been no systematic study or close reading of the hundreds of speeches presented to Queen Anne and published; and this cannot be attempted here. A few examples, however, drawn from 1710 (when *A Collection of the Addresses* was also published) will serve to give a flavour of how such texts represented as well as petitioned Anne.[453] As one would expect in that year of the most vicious party war, partisanship was evident in many of them. That from Tory Oxfordshire, for example, condemned 'seditious principles' recently avowed and any doctrine of resistance. The gentry declared their adherence to the lessons of obedience their (and Sacheverell's) university taught and promised to elect to the next parliament those who supported the prerogative, the church and the Protestant succession.[454] The Monmouthshire address similarly criticized – and promised not to elect – those who 'make the defence of their privileges a pretence of invading your majesty's', and vowed to maintain the sacred rights of the queen and the church and to discourage, as Anne desired, profanity and immorality.[455] The address from the corporation of Marlborough was couched in the sharpest language. Vilifying those (Whigs) who revived the rebellious designs that had shed the martyr Charles I's blood, the corporation expressed its abhorrence of 'anti Christian, popish republican ... doctrines' and vowed to support only those who defended the prerogative against such men.[456] On the other side, the gentlemen of Cheshire who accompanied Crew Offley to submit their address and kiss the queen's hand, referring to the many others who had already 'presented their professions of loyalty', praised the success of the queen's arms and her government yet condemned the Sacheverell riots and defended the Revolution and 'Old English Liberty'.[457] With similar sympathies, the Worcestershire address defended the impeachment of Sacheverell as well as announcing a readiness to give their lives 'in defence of your Majesty's sacred person, just faith, and gracious administration of the church of England and of the Protestant succession'.[458] The Norwich address presented by Sir John Holland cleverly echoed Anne's own proscriptions against division and injunctions to union to criticize the Tories for implying that she had not taken adequate care of the church. They (Whigs) by contrast praised her administration and moved to support their 'wise and good princess against any enemies'.[459] As with verse panegyrics and prose pamphlets, partisanship often drove these speeches, which were directed at the electorate as well as the queen. They appropriated her own language (on unity or immorality) to advertise their loyalty to her and to her subjects. Yet, whatever their party objectives, in ventriloquizing and praising Anne, both Tory and Whig addresses positioned her – as she sought to be – above the party fray and as the custodian of the interest of the whole nation. Motivated by party, such loyal discourses yet strengthened the authority and popularity of the queen, assisting her to avoid subordination to party and retain the affection of her people.

During Queen Anne's reign, texts and words were more multiplied, partisan and contested than ever before. Past royal dreams of the monarchy standing as a sovereign signifier, a determinant of meaning and interpretation, had long been scotched; and, following Hobbes's logic, monarchical sovereignty with them. Paradoxically, however, amidst the Babel of contesting voices, Anne's own words continued to resonate – to be echoed, republished and appropriated in and by a multitude of texts: verse and prose, sermons, histories and popular addresses. For all the undoubted diminution of the power of the crown in a new political culture, Queen Anne was represented in words to and *by* public opinion, as much as her governments had necessarily to represent the electorate. Popularity (as we shall further explore) was becoming a new foundation of royal authority; and it was the words of the queen and her protagonists that helped to forge and sustain it.

CHAPTER 14

RE-DEPICTING FEMALE RULE
THE IMAGE OF THE QUEEN

I

The visual representation of William III had presented a political as well as aesthetic challenge. William of Orange was Dutch and not a legitimate successor. Godfrey Kneller rose to the challenge to produce a state portrait which Oliver Millar judged the most successful between Van Dyck's 1636 canvas of Charles I and Allan Ramsey's *George III* of 1762, and which was widely copied, engraved and distributed.[1] The accession of Queen Anne both removed the problems presented by her predecessor and posed new ones. Anne was and insistently represented herself as 'entirely English' and a Stuart heir. But she was also a queen regnant – the first since Elizabeth I whose motto (Semper Eadem) she took as her own, whose style (and dress on occasions) she emulated, and to whom she was often compared. Since Elizabeth's reign, there had been profound changes both in the arts and the nature and perception of monarchy. The image of Elizabeth, especially in later life, was iconic more than realistic; canvases representing her were allegorical, the images of an age in which to describe or depict the queen as a goddess or a vestal virgin reflected the numinosity of monarchy.[2] There were, of course, portraits of queens consort, the wives of Charles II, James II and William; but the question of how to depict female majesty, in a new age of aesthetics, politics and sexual politics, remained.

It was compounded by the prevailing circumstance of Anne's reign – war. William had been well known before his accession as an accomplished military commander, and it is no coincidence that one of Kneller's most memorable images of him was the large canvas at Hampton Court of the king in armour and on horseback, riding along a shore over the emblems of war.[3] While, as we have seen, panegyrists writing in several genres tried to bring Anne to the centre of the wars and attribute to her the victories of her reign, the fact remained that, unlike her predecessor, she was not in arms. And for

whatever reason – possibly changed sensibilities about masculine and feminine identities – she was not often, as was Queen Elizabeth in the Armada
portrait, woodcuts and engravings, figured as a warrior or conqueror.[4] Several
poets and pageant devisers imagined or suggested canvases commemorating
the great victories at Blenheim, Ramillies and Oudenarde: paintings which
might have figured the queen. In his thanksgiving sermon for the victory at
Blenheim, Jean Dubourdieu urged 'let the painters go on with their bold and
noble designs of this battle'.[5] In his 1705 poem, *The Triumph*, Nahum Tate
called for 'another canvas' to represent the victory, while four years later a
poem of *Advice to Mr Vario, the Painter* virtually instructed the Italian Antonio
Verrio, who had painted the great staircases at Hampton Court, to abandon
images of the gods and to represent on canvas

Such Mighty Truths as *German* Plains relate,
Or *Danube*'s Billows to the Ocean told,
When Stain'd with *Gallick* and *Bavarian* Blood, they rowl'd.
Hast, draw a Copy like to ACTION Great![6]

By the time the poem was published, Verrio, who had retired under Anne on
account of near blindness, was dead. There were, however, surprisingly few
artistic depictions of land or sea victories (only the anonymous *Battle of Vigo*
and works by Peter Monamy) and none which in any way represented Anne, as
did the poets, as conqueror and empress.[7]

As new Princess of Denmark, Lady Anne had been painted, probably about
the time of her marriage in 1683, by William Wissing, a pupil of Lely. The
portrait, at St James's Palace, exists in variants which depict Anne three-quarter
length, seated in a landscape with an ermine-trimmed gown over her lap.[8]
Other than the ermine, still a signifier of royalty, there was little to distinguish
the portrait from those of aristocratic women; and one version of Anne's
portrait was for long taken to be an image of Mary II. A slightly later full-length
picture, now in the Scottish National Portrait Gallery, probably a collaboration
between Wissing and Jan van der Vaart, figures Anne more majestically full
length with an architectural background;[9] a 1690 Kneller of the princess, full
length beside an architectural plinth on which is placed a coronet, evokes Van
Dyck, but of the few other portraits only one stands out: Kneller's 1694 canvas
of Anne with her son, the Duke of Gloucester, aged five and her only surviving
child. Likely painted the year of the death of Mary II, the double portrait depicts
Anne as heir and as mother to a son and future dynasty.[10]

When Anne succeeded to the throne, she inherited as principal court painter
Sir Geoffrey Kneller, whom William III had knighted and made a gentleman of
his privy chamber. Kneller, as we saw, painted many portraits of William and
Mary, and the king commissioned from the artist in 1697 the large allegorical

equestrian portrait now at Hampton Court – a monument to a new Hercules inaugurating a golden age. Anne continued Kneller in his post, but he never enjoyed from the queen the favour he had received from her predecessor. It has been suggested that the political and religious differences between monarch and artist may have distanced them: Kneller was a Whig, anticlerical, and lived with a mistress by whom he had a daughter.[11] One should not, however, attribute too much significance to such differences. Van Dyck, after all, was a Catholic who was patronized by the Anglican Charles I, and Kneller painted Tories as well as Whigs, just as his Flemish predecessor had worked for Parliamentarians as much as Royalists. It may be that Anne did not appreciate him as much as did her subjects. In 1703 she made clear that she did 'not care' for the 1701 equestrian portrait of William and evidently did not pay for it.[12] Anne did commission accession portraits from Kneller; it may be significant that he executed no portrait of the queen after 1705, though, it should be noted, there are no other royal commissions we can attribute to the queen's last decade.

Kneller, with his studio, probably painted full-lengths, standing and seated, and a head-and-shoulders of Queen Anne soon after her succession. Examples of the full-length canvas of the queen, in coronation robes and with sceptre and orb, are to be found at the Inner Temple (which probably commissioned a copy of an official state portrait no longer in the royal collection) and at Warwick Castle where Lord Brooke shared Anne's Tory values.[13] The coronation canvas, though of a queen who was already lame and visibly stout, does convey majesty and, indeed, for all the obvious differences, recalls earlier coronation portraits, including that of Queen Elizabeth I. Holding in her left hand the orb and in her right the sceptre, Anne wears, under her ermine robe, a heavy brocaded skirt and a Garter collar with the greater George (fig. 67). The portrait does not flatter the sitter or give her any animation; it conveys dignity and an iconic impression, which may have been designed to gesture to Anne's hereditary descent (unlike her predecessor) from a long line of English monarchs. A second accession type by Kneller was a full-length image of Anne seated in coronation robes with the orb and sceptre.[14] The version now in the royal collection at Windsor is thought to be a studio copy of an early standard portrait, the best examples of which are at Wrest Park (dated 1705) and Drumlanrig, seat of the Duke of Buccleuch.[15] In this last example, the queen is seated on a chair placed on a raised step which leads the viewer to look up at her. Wearing coronation ermine, she holds in her left hand an orb to which she points with her right hand across her lap. On a table to the queen's left, the sceptre lies next to the closed state crown. As with the standing portrait, the composition lays emphasis on the regalia and on the queen rather than the person (fig. 68).

While in the absence of early official portraits in the royal collection we are left with questions about the first state-owned commission, the signed oval

67 Sir Godfrey Kneller, *Queen Anne*, 1703.

Kneller painted in 1702 (now at Kensington) was not only clearly a royal commission; it became the model from which the earliest Queen Anne medals and coins were designed, indicating that the queen was pleased with the picture.[16] The oval depicts Anne in profile to the left, wearing robes of state, a greater George and (uniquely) a crown. Possibly on account of its design as a model for coin, the oval gives Anne a classical, imperial appearance. That accession paintings by other artists seem similarly stiff and formal suggests that it was Anne as much as Kneller who favoured such a representation – though there were some significant differences. It is clear, for example, that Anne early on patronized the Swedish artist, and rival to Kneller, Michael Dahl, who had been patronized by Prince George (Anne's husband) since the 1680s. In 1704, Dahl painted a grand equestrian portrait of Prince George, which alluded to that of William III and which was hung in the queen's Grand Chamber at Windsor.[17] The next year Dahl was commissioned for a canvas of the queen, full length. Dahl's portrait figures Anne, against an architectural background, standing between a rich curtain and a column. Like the column,

68 Sir Godfrey Kneller, *Queen Anne.*

a symbol of rule, the orb and sceptre (on a table next to her) – which she holds with her left hand and to which she gestures, across her body, with her right – highlight the accoutrements of regality (fig. 69).[18] In this case, however, there appears to be some attention to the person, as well as majesty, of the queen. Though she is appareiled in a rich blue, ermined robe of state, Anne wears a gold dress and appears elongated, slimmed and more elegant than in Kneller's coronation portraits. Moreover, in Dahl's portrait, light falls on Anne's bosom, arms and hands, as well as on the ermine, and the rich colours of the robe, (deep red) drapery and (red) tablecloth highlight her delicate ivory skin. Though less accomplished, Dahl's canvas recalls Van Dyck's and Lely's female portraits; importantly, it is the coronation portrait of Anne that represents most successfully the queen's two bodies: her regality and her person.

One other accession portrait commands our attention, though it was not a royal commission. Immediately on Anne's succession, the London Guildhall determined to commission a coronation portrait and decided to hold a competition to select the artist.[19] In May 1702, Godfrey Kneller, Jonathan Richardson, Edmund Lilly, John Closterman and a Mr Lentall submitted *modelli* to the

69 Michael Dahl, *Queen Anne*, 1705.

Court of Aldermen, who appointed Closterman to paint the queen.[20] In contrast with many of his fine and elegant portraits, Closterman's canvas of Anne, now in the National Portrait Gallery, appears stiff and wooden – a 'clumsy composition' in the words of his biographer (fig. 70).[21] The figure of Anne dominates a canvas in which she stands in front of an ascending stair, in state robes, wearing a crown and holding the sceptre and orb. Certainly in contrast to Dahl's picture, she appears stolid and iconic, with a strong emphasis on clothes and objects (she grasps a large orb the colour of her dress) more than on femininity or personality.

It is tempting, therefore, to conclude that Anne's state portraits were prosaic, lifeless and did little to represent the new reign or queen to the people in ways that would have appealed. Tempting, but in need of qualification. For it was not only the Dutch artist Jakob Weyermann who appreciated a portrait in which, he wrote, the viewer could hear the golden fabrics 'crackle'.[22] In 1703 no less a figure than the poet laureate Nahum Tate published a poem, *Portrait-Royal: A*

70 John Closterman, *Queen Anne, c.* 1702.

Poem Upon Her Majesty's Picture Set Up in Guildhall ... Drawn by Mr Closterman, dedicated to Prince George. It was, of course, Tate's duty to write panegyric; however, his views on the painting must be taken seriously as a rare contemporary reading of a royal commission which seems at least to have pleased the queen. Tate praises 'this wonder', 'that Glorious Piece' which, in a visual genre he was ready to admit surpassed words, 'Form to Motion brought'.[23] Finding in the canvas 'Order, Symmetry and Dress', Tate interpreted this portrait as a representation of an empress, an 'Amazonian Terror', a Deborah yet a queen who radiated 'Celestial Calmness, and August Repose'.[24] As the poet reads the symbols – orb, sceptre, crown – he discerns both grandeur and maternal protection in a queen capable of war and peace, a ruler of 'Prideless Pomp'.[25] Tate saw on the canvas another Astraea, a queen of prudence, charity, constancy, mercy and piety – virtues which he urged other artists to paint and 'join to ANNA's Name'.[26] In notes to his verse, he discusses the form of the composition in relation to those of Titian and Van Dyck and 'all the best masters'.[27] The 'Royal Figure', from his view, here commands, 'Rais'd and Embody'd to th'Astonisht Sight': 'O Pow'r, Contemplate here thy own Display'.[28] Even allowing for laureate hyperbole, Tate's reception of the painting is striking.

The large, expensive portrait may have been archaic and iconic. But at least one contemporary saw at the Guildhall another champion and Deborah to lead England to victory and repose.

Tate hoped that artists would go on to advertise Anne's virtues, and to paint her battles and victories – 'the Smother'd Coast and Burning Bay'.[29] His hopes were not fulfilled. Somewhat surprisingly, after the accession portraits, there were no state portraits of Queen Anne and few depictions of the battles and triumphant victories of her reign. There was no want of artists: her favourite Dahl lived until 1743 and Kneller until 1723. Moreover, in 1711 a plan first conceived by William III to establish 'an academy to encourage the art of painting' was realized when sixty members, leading and lesser artists and amateurs, founded the Academy and unanimously elected Kneller to be their first governor – a position to which he was re-elected until 1714.[30] Kneller protested to the Earl of Oxford that the queen, who had always paid him less than other sitters, also omitted to pay his £250 pension.[31] Anne gave Kneller few commissions, though he remained her principal painter. One important commission she did give him was also one of the few examples of a planned poetical commemoration of an English victory. The queen intended to present to Marlborough a canvas to hang in the Long Gallery at Blenheim Palace, which she had gifted him after his monumental victory. Kneller himself informs us that 'In the year 1708 the queen sent her orders to me by the Duke of Shrewsbury (then Lord Chamberlain) to design a large picture twelve foot high and eight foot broad for the upper end of the Long Gallery at Blenheim'.[32] Marlborough, Kneller continues, expressed his personal (and modest) wish that the canvas be allegorical and 'that no person should be represented by the life except the queen's majesty'.[33] As was customary for such large pictures, Kneller prepared a drawing which is all we have of the plan (fig. 71).[34] The composition figures at the centre Queen Anne, in robes of state holding in her left hand a sceptre with 'the eye of Providence on top'.[35] Kneller informs us that she 'is represented by the figure of Generosity' and leans her left arm on the head of a lion (an emblem of power) whose paw rests on a globe, signifying England's and the queen's imperial sway. 'With her right hand [she] presents to a warlike vigorous figure representing Military Merit a model of Blenheim drawn on paper', while on her right stand figures representing Architecture and Prosperity, and above them an eagle, an emblem of the Habsburg emperors, descends with a laurel crown of victory to place on Military Merit's (standing for Marlborough's) head. Further to the viewer's left, by a colonnaded arch festooned with captured standards, stand the figures of Victory and Hercules. On Anne's left, allegorical figures attend representing History (to record fame) and Plenty – which is also figured by a cornucopia poured in front of the queen, symbolizing her beneficence and blessings. Above the royal figure Apollo commands Fame to proclaim the queen and the victory.

71 Sir Godfrey Kneller, *Queen Anne presenting plans of Blenheim to military Merit*, eighteenth century.

The *modello* was a plan for a fittingly large and magnificent tribute to Marlborough and a queen who was destined to rule an empire and who poured out blessings on her people as well as her general: a vast allegorical canvas that recalled in design if not execution Rubens's Whitehall ceiling paintings or Verrio's staircases for Charles II. Yet, though Vertue recalls that Kneller was 'much commended for his skill', the full canvas was not executed, as Marlborough fell out of royal favour.[36] Nor was another equestrian portrait of Marlborough to commemorate the victory at Ramillies – a homage to earlier royal equestrian portraits – completed in large format.[37] Though Kneller was much in demand by aristocratic grandees and Whig patrons, under Anne he enjoyed few royal commissions other than the Blenheim canvas and – probably a commission from Prince George – the portraits (with Dahl) of fourteen admirals, painted in emulation of those portraits done by Lely for James as Duke of York.[38] Of Queen Anne herself we have – even if we count the allegorical Blenheim drawing – no portrait from her principal painter after 1708.

As well as the portraitists working in full and three-quarter length, Anne patronized a miniaturist, the Swedish-born son of a French silk merchant,

Charles Boit, who may have been brought to the queen's attention by his fellow countryman Dahl, whose protégé he was.[39] Boit had been appointed in 1696 court enameller to William III but had left England in 1699, not to return to reside until after Anne's succession. Soon after he came back, Anne commissioned from him an allegorical enamel to commemorate the Battle of Blenheim, but the project met with difficulties and was not complete ten years later when Boit was ordered to repay his £1,000 fee. Despite this setback, or failure, Boit executed at least two miniatures of the queen, one with her consort. A portrait now in the National Portrait Gallery, enamel on copper, has been dated to c.1705.[40] In what may have been intended for Prince George, the miniature depicts Anne, free of any of the trappings of majesty, with a rose complexion highlighted by the deep pink of a gown with only an edge of ermine signifying her regality. Though she appears solid rather than delicate or pretty, Anne is here portrayed very much as a woman rather than a queen. The double-portrait miniature, signed and dated 1706, was very different (fig. 72).[41] Among Boit's largest surviving enamels, the miniature depicts the queen and prince in an

72 Charles Boit, *Queen Anne and Prince George of Denmark*, 1706.

elaborate architectural setting in front of fluted columns. George stands, wearing robes of state, a Garter collar and the greater George, in a pose that recalls Van Dyck's of Charles I, as the prince rests his left hand on a velvet-covered table and has his right hand on his hip. To our right, Anne is seated in a rich gold dress and coronation robe holding the sceptre in her right hand across her lap. While her depiction with the regalia emphasizes her royal state, her seated position on the right (traditionally subordinate) side of the canvas suggests a female obeisance to the husband. It is their love, however, to which the composition also draws attention. The fingers of George's right hand and Anne's left point towards each other and their other hands both rest on the table in front of the orb and crown. The figures are stiff and the faces lack vitality; however, the miniature seems to attempt a portrayal of a royal couple, of a queen devoted to her husband and, as in the great Van Dycks of Charles I and Henrietta Maria, of a relationship between their love and the exercise of rule. We do not know for what purposes the miniature was commissioned; but at 25 × 18 centimetres it was too large to be a jewel or purely personal decoration. Curiously it is the only known depiction of Anne as queen with her beloved husband, George.

Two last canvases we shall consider are representations, but hardly portraits, of Queen Anne. In a painting, attributed to Alexander van Gaelen (who had executed battle scenes), of Queen Anne processing to parliament, she is just visible at the window of a state coach attended by cavalry and yeomen of the guard.[42] Naturally drawn back to the depictions of Charles II's coronation and of Elizabeth I in procession, the viewer is struck by how, though her coach is at the centre, Anne is almost effaced. The same is the case with Peter Tilleman's painting of Queen Anne in the House of Lords, likely executed after the death of Prince George.[43] Enthroned at the back of a long perspective line in the House of Lords, a tiny figure of Anne seems to have been taken from Kneller's coronation portrait. The queen holds the sceptre in her right hand and appears to gesture with her left, making it possible that this was a depiction of a royal speech to the assembled Lords and members of the Commons in the foreground at the bar. Oliver Millar suggested that Tilleman, who executed a pendant piece for the Commons, may have been commissioned by a member of the Upper House, or possibly the Lords as a body, to paint the scene.[44] Whoever commissioned the image, it is a representation not just of a queen in parliament but, with Anne not the prominent figure, of a parliamentary monarch: the representation, that is, of the parliamentary monarchy which England had become.

Queen Anne was not a great patron of the arts, and the portraits we have of her are few and, for the most part, workmanlike. She either did not request that her rather unprepossessing appearance be – as Henrietta Maria's had been for example – depicted in a more flattering light, or no great effort was made to do so. As she advanced in age, Elizabeth I had eschewed realistic portrayals for an iconic mask of youth. In a different era, Anne with her ill-health after many miscarriages and pregnancies seems instead to have retreated from artistic commissions and visual representation. Nor has her painted image been memorable. Today most people who might recognize a Queen Anne style in architecture or furniture would be hard pressed to identify a portrait of Anne herself. Her portrait when Princess of Denmark has been misidentified; in the National Portrait Gallery an oval formerly catalogued as depicting Queen Anne is now listed as an 'unknown woman'.[45] Of all the Stuarts – perhaps of all early modern English monarchs – Anne was the one who has made least visual impression, who failed (if she ever sought) to establish her dynastic pedigree or brand image or advertise her authority on canvas. That may be the accident of personal preference or circumstance. What we must return to consider is that it was to be half a century before another sovereign successfully harnessed the arts of portraiture to support and enhance the exercise of power. In images of Anne, we already see not the portrayal of divine authority, but rather that of parliamentary monarchy, with none of the informality or accessibility on which the popularity and mystique of future monarchs was to be built.

Though portraits of Queen Anne do not seem to have been numerous, copies of canvases from Kneller's studio or after Kneller or Dahl are found in aristocratic houses (such as Melbourne Hall, Hardwick Hall, or Oakly Park) and the Inns of Court. There had been many engraved images published of Anne as Princess of Denmark, both in her father's lifetime (perhaps to advertise dynastic succession) and during William's reign when Anne was regarded by opponents of the king as rightful queen and was accepted by all, especially after her sister Mary's miscarriages and early death, as heir. As princess, Anne's portrait (from Lely, Kneller, Edmund Lilly, Wissing and other artists) was engraved by Abraham Blooteling, Richard Thompson, Peter Vanderbank, Robert Williams (with royal privilege), Isaac Becket and John Smith, a close associate of Kneller and the most accomplished mezzotinter of his age.[46] In addition, to proclaim Stuart dynasty, the princess was figured on a mezzotint (produced after the Revolution) with ovals of William and Mary and Prince George, and in another – probably expressing different political sympathies – with her four Stuart royal predecessors, her sister Queen Mary and her son, the Duke of Gloucester.[47]

On her accession, a few engraved portraits evidently were published with royal privilege and there was obviously a market for mezzotints of the new monarch: Edward Cooper, for example, sold at his shop at the Three Pigeons an engraving of Anne, issued 'cum privilegio regina', after a portrait by Edmund Lilly, depicting the queen in state robes wearing a greater George.[48] There were also several engravings executed after Kneller's coronation portraits. Smith both etched and sold mezzotints of Anne head and shoulders after Kneller at the Lion and Crown in Covent Garden;[49] the prolific mezzotinter John Simon executed plates after portraits by Kneller and Kneller's studio;[50] and Schenck and other (some anonymous) engravers cashed in on the market for a collectable image of the new queen.[51] As well as a full-face bust, Simon engraved the Kneller profile of Anne, his mezzotint declaring that it was 'done from the original picture by which all the medals and coin has been and are now made'.[52] Another profile bust of the queen (after Croker's medal) in antique style in an oval on a plinth, with Anne's motto 'Semper Eadem', was engraved by Robert Spofforth and sold at his shop in Blackfriars.[53] A small depiction of the queen (wearing a greater George) with her motto was also executed by John Sturt who, interestingly, had engraved a double portrait of Queen Mary II with Queen Elizabeth I.[54] The only known engraved double portraits of Anne are that by Edward Cooper, figuring George and Anne in ovals formed of palm branches crowned – an image that predates her accession – and a 1708 double portrait print by Spofforth probably executed to commemorate George.[55]

In the years immediately following her succession, engraved portraits by accomplished mezzotinters of Anne in state robes, with the Garter and in some cases her motto, distributed an image of the new monarch and pronounced her as heir to her female predecessor, Queen Elizabeth. As with portraits, however, there were evidently few new images etched or published after these early types. The Antwerp-born engraver Michael van der Gucht executed variant engravings of Anne after Boit's miniature; whilst these are undated, the compositions suggest that some commemorated military triumphs. In one, for example, the oval portrait of Anne is crowned by Victory and Fame; below a frieze on a plinth depicts a woman in a triumphal chariot and bears the inscription 'Quem velut ad caelum victrice Gloria curru' ('How like to heaven in Glory in her triumphal chariot) (fig. 73).[56] In a second example, Gucht has the crowned oval portrait of Anne supported by an emblematic figure who holds a laurel and who gestures to the inscription between them: 'Vicem gerit illa tonantis' ('Thundering she will bring about change'), a change perhaps explained in the words on each side of the crown at the top of the oval: 'Peace to Us'.[57] In Van der Gucht's engravings, in other words, we have a representation of Anne as she presented herself in words: as a queen who waged war and won victories in order to secure peace. Surprisingly, however, there appear to have been no engravings published to commemorate the great victories of her reign or the Peace of Utrecht. One other striking engraving of Anne by Van der Gucht, however, commands our attention. Of wartime date, but most likely published in the queen's lifetime, it shows Anne kneeling in a private closet at prayer before a book (probably a devotional manual) propped up by other books (fig. 74).[58] In front of the queen, the crown lies on a cushion, symbolizing her abandonment before God of any earthly grandeur. The print bears Anne's title 'Fidei Defensor' and by the books are written 'The Liturgies of the Church of England'. An image that emphasizes Anne's patronage of the

73 Michael van der Gucht, after Charles Boit, *Queen Anne, c.* 1700–25.

Anglican church, the print (with the crown at her feet) recalls the frontispiece to *Eikon Basilike*. But it also recalls the woodcut of Queen Elizabeth at prayer that formed the frontispiece to a volume of her prayers.[59] In this print, Anne is represented as heir to an Anglican tradition which she regards it as her duty to champion: it was the Anne the Tories would have wished to highlight, but we know nothing of the commission or circumstances of its production.

In addition to portraits, there were other popular and satirical prints sold depicting and representing the queen. Since the Restoration, if not before, large engravings or woodcuts had been published as souvenirs of the coronation. That for Anne's was printed and sold by John Overton, an entrepreneurial member of the Overton printing family, who sold maps, topographical views and portraits.[60] His popular print of Anne's coronation depicts, with a key, the procession of drummers, noblemen and women, judges and bishops marching in pairs ahead of Anne under a canopy with her crown carried before her and attended by yeomen of the guard. The figures are quite simple and crude and the features are barely distinguishable, suggesting that this was

74 Michael van der Gucht, *Anna D.G. Angliæ Scotiæ et Hiberniæ Regina Fidei defens &c.*, *c.* 1702–25.

produced to be sold cheaply to a broad audience. A few satirical prints, about which we know little, represented Anne as Europe's champion against Louis XIV. One, for example, titled 'A Bridle for The French King' and evidently modelled on a print published at Vienna, depicts Anne, accompanied by a griffin, approaching a cowering Louis with a bridle, while on his left a woman representing the Dutch republic seizes him.[61] Above the figure of Anne, who is here his protector, the archduke Charles, Austrian claimant to the throne of Spain, sits between Justice and Hope. In cartouches below, inscriptions proclaim that Louis will be made to return what he has taken from Holland and Spain and, in the spirit of some of the panegyrics we have examined, the French king is warned:

> Tyrant if Man Cannot thy pow'r assuage,
> A woman thus shall bridle all thy rage.

If an inscription on an impression in the Library of Congress can be trusted, this print was published in 1706, the year of Ramillies.[62] There is no direct reference to the victory, but it is England and Anne who dominate and terrify a chastened Louis who promises to restore what he has seized. A second example again graphically shows Anne clipping the wings of France (fig. 75). In this anonymous print (which appears also to have been a book illustration) published in London in 1707, Anne is enthroned beneath a canopy with the royal arms and, above, an eclipsed sun.[63] On her lap the queen holds a cock and clips its wings; a thistle, likely symbolizing the union, lies at the foot of her throne. In two small scenes around the central image a naval battle (probably the relief of Barcelona), and a representation of Ramillies are depicted; in a third, Louis sits enthroned with Madame de Maintenon, his unofficial second wife. The meaning is obvious: the defeats at Barcelona and Ramillies have eclipsed Louis and replaced him with a queen who has united her kingdoms into the dominant force in Europe.

Like most cultural texts of the reign, prints figuring Queen Anne could also be overtly partisan. I have suggested that Van der Gucht's representation of her at prayer might have expressed Tory values – as did many prints published during the Sacheverell affair. A 1713 satirical print depicts Anne, enthroned and flanked by Peace and Justice, holding in her left hand a paper which is grasped by a kneeling clergyman, representing the church. Behind him (Whig) figures turn away conspiratorially while one attempts to cut off the kneeling

75 *Queen Anne eclipsing Louis XIV*, satirical print from *Poems on Affairs of State from 1620 to this present year 1707*.

bishop's mitre – that is to say, to emasculate the church.[64] The publisher John Morphew published and sold a number of anti-Whig satirical prints, one a frontispiece to a history of the Calves Head Club, which represented them as fanatics and republicans.[65] A 1710 broadside, with Fame holding an oval of the queen, titled 'The Unfeigned Respect of an English Tory, to the Queen of Great Britain' and sold from shops in Aldersgate Street and Fleet Street compares her to Elizabeth and calls on her to crush 'Oliverian Tyranny' – and its new manifestation in the Whig Party (fig. 76).[66] Another popular Tory print of that year crudely depicts the queen enthroned with sceptre and orb, announcing 'I am resolv'd to Support & Encourage the Church of England', and contrasts the loyalty of the high church party with the greed, ambition and qualified

76 *The Unfeigned Respect of an English Tory, to the Queen of Great Britain*, broadside, 1710.

obedience of their opponents (fig. 77).[67] Whig broadsides also satirized the Jacobites and Sacheverell; but, quite contrary to William's reign, if surviving prints are a reliable guide, it was the Tories who had the better of the competition.[68] More importantly – and again in contrast to William's reign – for all the contemporary perception of 'the Magick Power of Mezzotints', little of that magic was woven into representing Queen Anne as the British heroine and empress celebrated in verse.[69]

The aesthetic refinement of mezzotint has rather cast a shadow over the less accomplished cruder prints and woodcuts of the later seventeenth century. It was, however, these that still reached a broader public and which, by their very form, recalled earlier visual representations of kings and queens and so connected the subject portrayed to tradition and history. It was those less

77 *Wonders Upon Wonders. In Answer to the Age of Wonders. To the Tune of Chivy Chase*, broadside, 1710.

elaborate portraits that also typically formed frontispieces or illustrations to books. In Anne's reign a small number of portrait types formed the frontispieces to a wide range of publications: prayer books and devotional works, histories and sermons. To take an early example, the 1702 edition of Edward Chamberlayne's *Angliae Notitia* carries a frontispiece head and shoulders of Anne, probably after Kneller, in robes of state with a crown beside her right shoulder, and with the inscription 'Anne by the grace of God, Queen of Great Britain, France, and Ireland, Defender of the Faith' (fig. 78). The portrait was repeated in subsequent editions (of 1704 and 1707), in Chamberlayne's *Magnae Britanniae Notitia* of 1710 and, with slight variations, in other works. A second popular portrait type illustrated several editions of the Book of Common Prayer as well as works of piety and reformation.[70] This plain oval depicts Anne wearing robes of state and pearls above a crowned royal arms, with a Latin inscription, and was 'printed and sold at the Bible in Grace Church Street' and

78 *Anne by the Grace of God Queen of Great Brittain, France, & Ireland; Defender of ye Faith*, frontispiece to Edward Chamberlayne's *Angliae Notitia*, 1702.

other venues. A similar portrait, with a crown atop the oval, and without the arms, illustrated Tobias Ellis's *The True Royal English School* and was also sold as a plate, at the Golden Ball in Duck Lane.[71] Several engraved or woodcut images in books represented Anne with her motto: one of the earliest I have found was a frontispiece to William Sherlock's sermon to the queen, presented at St Paul's in September 1704 (fig. 79).[72] On a plinth with a Latin inscription a bust of Anne in profile *à l'antique* is placed beneath a radiant sun, each side of which are scrolls with the motto 'Semper Eadem'. Another image of the queen that illustrated several publications repeated the adage that we have seen on a Van der Gucht engraving. The 1707 *History* of Anne's reign up to the union had an oval portrait of the queen beneath the Latin 'Vicem Gerit Anne Tonantis' (Anne is the vice-regent of the Thunderer); and the same image illustrated *An Oration Sacred to the Imperial Majesty of Anne*, also published that year.[73] As well as these frontispiece engraved images, there were a number of crudely executed portraits reminiscent of older woodcuts that illustrated works such as

79 Anne, frontispiece to W. Sherlock, *A Sermon Preach'd before the Queen, at the Cathedral Church of St. Paul, London, on the Seventh of September, 1704*, 1704.

the *Compendious History of the Monarchs of England* (1712), or popular broadsheets and polemics like *The Truth's Come Out at Last* (1711) and *An Antidote Against the Growth of Popery* (1713) (fig. 80).[74]

Anne's royal arms and her motto frequently appeared on the printed texts of her speeches and proclamations. Occasional cartoons figured her allegorically, for instance as the protector of Religion and Justice to whom Europe made supplication and paid homage.[75] Overall, however, when we consider that the fashion for collecting engravings and the quality of English work practised by artists such as Smith had reached a new height, we cannot but conclude that in number and subject, the prints of Queen Anne were disappointing. Even a casual perusal of the numerous print portraits of nobles, bishops, lawyers and doctors, of exotic figures and freaks of nature (the 104-year-old Henry Evans or the man with a nipple on his stomach) might suggest that the monarch was not, as had earlier been the case, at the centre of the visual culture or the visual imagination of the nation.[76] If that is the case, it must be said that Anne, who

80 Frontispiece to J. P., *An Antidote Against the Growth of Popery, for the Year . . . 1713,* 1713.

showed little interest in art, fostered that development. Unlike her predecessor Elizabeth, Anne, as Toni Bowers has argued, could not make much effective use of symbolic representation.[77] And in a culture in which 'affective represen- tation increasingly came to be understood ... as a matter of faithfulness to [the] materially verifiable', Anne – stout, invalided by illness and miscarriages – was not an especially beautiful or striking female.[78] Changed political circum- stances were unquestionably altering and complicating the representational form of monarchy, perhaps especially female rule; but, as Queen Victoria was to show, the power of visual representation could support and construct new foundations of authority.[79]

While Anne came off worse than her predecessor in the number, quality and sheer propaganda value of the mezzotints and engravings of her, interestingly she far outstripped William in the number of statues commissioned to commemorate her. Since many of these came about through local initiatives, the statues offer further evidence of Anne's popularity (in contrast to William of whom only one public sculpture was erected in his lifetime). London appears to have commissioned a statue of the new queen for the Royal Exchange imme- diately upon her succession – it had not been until 1695 that Nost's of William and Mary had been erected.[80] A decade later, Francis Bird, a protégé of Grinling Gibbons and Caius Cibber, who was awarded the commission to carve figures to be placed over the west portal of St Paul's, was also instructed to design and execute a statue, for the outside, of Queen Anne.[81] The marble statue (which originally stood before the cathedral's western staircase and is now, in a damaged state, near Hastings) represented the queen on a large pedestal with the regalia; at the foot of the pedestal are placed her royal arms and four female figures representing Britain, Ireland, France and America (fig. 81). Anne, that is, is represented as a conqueror and an empress who has not only defeated France but secured a transatlantic empire. A contemporary poem gives us a rare view of how the statue was seen, even before its full unveiling. *A Well Timber'd Poem, on Her Sacred Majesty; Her Marble Statue* takes as its subject the sculpture still hidden behind its wooden enclosure.[82] Even unseen, the poet suggests, the queen's – 'sacred Anna's' – statue draws the crowds like a brilliant sun obscured or eclipsed, soon to burst forth and shine.[83] As the 'unlovely' structure of Noah's Ark contained the 'olive branch and dove' (allusions to Anne's peace), so there was 'here, in glorious Marble, Majesty'.[84] Seeing in the covered statue a moment of majesty itself clouded by rebellion, the author awaits its removal when Whigs will be discredited and 'our Queen will Glorious be agen'.[85] The next year, the year of the Treaty of Utrecht, another poet regarded the now revealed sculpture – 'The Effigie with August, Majestick Mien' – as a monument to the peace.[86] Imagining 'pressing Millions' will gaze at Anne as she goes to St Paul's to give thanks, the poet pauses also to remark how

81 Statue of Anne, nineteenth-century replacement figure, St Paul's Cathedral, London.

Herself, disclos'd, in awful Marble stands;
And all the Temple's awful Front commands[87]

There were plans for many more statues of Queen Anne in London. Shortly after the signing of the peace, the commissioners in charge of a project to build fifty new churches in the city decided that each should be adorned with a statue of the queen.[88] After the succession of the Whig George I, the proposal was reduced to just one statue; but, though the Florentine sculptor Giovanni Battista Foggini was commissioned, no statue was ever erected.[89] Similarly, another project to commemorate the queen came to nought. A drawing in the British Museum by Nicholas Hawksmoor sketches 'A column with the statue of Queen Anne designed to be erected in the Strand against Somerset House Anno 1713'.[90] The design shows a tall fluted column with, atop, a statue of the queen with orb and sceptre standing on a drum – a symbol of her military victory. The 200-feet high monument to a queen who had brought an end to war was never built, perhaps because circumstances changed. As Nicola Smith explains, 'in the years following the accession of the Hanoverian king . . . and the ensuing Jacobite risings, a statue to a Stuart monarch no longer seemed quite such a loyal gesture'.[91]

Loyal gestures to Anne in statuary were not confined to London and many were, unlike some of the projects for the metropolis, completed. As well as statues of the queen at Blenheim and at Oxford University (one given to Christ Church by Robert Harley, one commissioned by University College), there were several civic initiatives for monuments to the queen.[92] At Worcester, for example, Thomas White sculpted a statue of Anne which later stood between statues of Charles I and Charles II on the Guildhall.[93] The city of Chester erected a life-size statue of the queen, in coronation robes and with the regalia at the Old Exchange, probably soon after her accession. Vandalized during eighteenth-century election riots, the statue was moved, and then lost in the 1960s.[94] On the medieval Bargate at Southampton there once stood a wooden statue of Anne that is now in the local museum.[95] In 1708, Robert Rolle gave a statue of the queen to adorn the Exchange at Barnstaple.[96] Some provincial statues appear to have been commissioned to commemorate victories – and, after 1713, peace. It was in 1711 that the city of Gloucester commissioned from John Ricketts a statue of the queen to be erected on Southgate Street.[97] About the same time, Leeds rebuilt its town hall and had a statue of Anne placed on the gable. Now at the centre of the ground floor of the city art gallery, the statue by Andrew Carpenter figures Anne in a niche, in parliament robes wearing a crown and with the orb and sceptre.[98] Another wave of commissioning followed the peace or Anne's illness and death. At Winchester, in 1713, for example, a new Guildhall was built and in the middle of the upper floor was placed a statue of Anne, given to the city following a royal visit.[99] Inspired by the statue he saw at St Paul's, Jacob Bancks, a naval captain and MP for Minehead, and a great admirer of the queen, commissioned for his borough a statue of Anne that has been attributed to Francis Bird. Certainly 'an uncommonly fine piece', completed after Anne's death in 1719 the statue was originally situated in the north aisle of St Michael's church.[100] Other towns set up monuments to the peace.[101]

The number and geographical range of these tributes to Anne in stone are remarkable. The historian of royal statuary discerns a rivalry among some towns to display their loyalty and offers the explanation that these images of Anne reflected, and promoted, the queen as a symbol of national unity, especially after the victories and the union. 'For most people the image of Queen Anne . . . was seen as conciliatory, an emblem promising harmony and national unity.'[102] If the statues did indeed reflect such sentiments, they were truly fitting representations of a Queen Anne who, like her predecessor Elizabeth, presented herself, amid the rancour of party, as a ruler who disliked faction and division and as the mother to all her subjects. Though the histories of these statues became embroiled in the politics of party, at least in her lifetime they represented the queen as she sought to be: as above the fray, as the embodiment of Britain.

II

It was, of course, an accident that Whitehall Palace was largely burned down in 1698; but it is also tempting to see it as a symbol of the political and constitutional alterations brought about by the Revolution and William's reign which, together with social changes, saw a diminished importance of the court in national life as well as affairs of state. William had immediately resolved to 'rebuild [it] much finer than before', but financial exigency and war prevented that hope being realized in stone.[103] In 1702, when Anne succeeded, the author of *The Church of England's Joy on the Happy Accession of Her Most Sacred Majesty* had a personification of Whitehall 'mourn her last estate' and ask:

Will not my Royal Mistress me restore,
To all the Grandeur which I had before?[104]

The parliamentary diarist Narcissus Luttrell reported in October 1702 that the queen intended to rebuild Whitehall; despite 'intermittent public interest', however, nothing came of such intentions, perhaps again on account of costs, perhaps too for related but larger reasons.[105] In 1704 a party poem lamented that Whitehall remained in desolate ruins and wondered:

. . . do not these Ruins most surely presage
That Monarchy's in its decline [106]

Certainly the place of the ruler was changing; and the domestic preference of William and Anne exacerbated as much as reflected this. Though an architectural style bears her name, Queen Anne commissioned very little building and erected no new monument to the Stuart dynasty. Indeed, even more than the Dutch William, her tastes inclined to the small scale and domestic, rather than the grandiose and majestic.[107]

Princess and heir presumptive, Anne and her husband had resided since 1695 at St James's Palace which became the residence of state after Whitehall's destruction. On her accession, a suite of state apartments was planned for her, including a Council Room, Drawing Room and Guard Chamber, with a colonnaded portico leading to the Great Gate.[108] According to Luttrell, Anne herself proposed to 'enlarge her chapel at St James's, turning it into the form of a cathedral'. No major structural alterations took place, but a royal order designated St James's to be the Chapel Royal and Anne provided at her own expense a new altar table and rail in fitting with her Anglican preferences of worship.[109] After these whilst a heavy annual expenditure (of £3,700) was incurred in the maintenance of the palace, there were few changes made other than the provision of apartments for the queen's intimate – and rumoured lover – Sarah Churchill. Despite its 'lack of magnificence', St James's was Anne's (and remained the) official royal residence.[110] Like her predecessor, however, Anne favoured a smaller retreat in London, the Kensington Palace acquired by William in 1689.

Anne took an early interest in Kensington Palace. Within weeks of her accession work began on the gardens, which were greatly increased in size to include a baroque parterre of 30 acres. From 1703 plans were drawn up for new buildings in the gardens and in June 1704 the officers of the works were instructed in 'her Majesty's pleasure' to build an orangery from plans drawn up by Sir John Vanbrugh.[111] The large sum expended (over £6,000) and the nature of the buildings (summerhouses, seats, etcetera) suggest that Anne was planning to live in the palace. Indeed, in 1705 the writing master and topographer John Bowack reported in his *Antiquities of Middlesex* that, just as 'their late Majesties spent [there] the greatest part of their leisure hours and were much pleased with its airy situation', 'Her present Majesty, with her royal consort, are pleased often to spend two or three days here in good weather, and in all probability design to reside here oftener, when 'tis finished.'[112] Inside the palace, a staircase was built at the east end of William III's gallery and plans and costings were drawn up for new rooms for the queen's apartments. Anne also ordered 'substantial quantities' of new furniture for what was her London home in which both her husband and she died.[113]

Before the civil war, and even after the Restoration, the principal palaces outside Whitehall and London had been Hampton Court and Windsor Castle. William and Mary, as we saw, had made Hampton Court their residence and planned to make it the new centre of royal government. Queen Anne did not entirely neglect Hampton Court but evidently did not regard it in the same light and her reign saw a drastic drop in the level of expenditure on the palace and its gardens, on which her predecessor had lavished so much attention.[114] Anne held meetings of her Council at Hampton Court but she and George almost never lodged the night there, though the prince appears to have been fonder of it than was the queen.[115] On her accession, Anne inherited a number of works in progress, notably the mural for the King's Stair that William had commissioned Verrio to paint, to glorify him as another Alexander the Great. The queen licensed the work to be completed and, in late 1703, employed Verrio for the expensive work on her drawing room.[116] Herein, on the west wall, the figure of Britannia (a representation of Anne) was depicted receiving homage from the four corners of the globe; while on the north wall, Prince George was painted reviewing the fleet, the decorations representing the royal couple as victorious admiral and empress. Anne's initial enthusiasm, however, was not long sustained. Verrio complained in June 1705 that he had not been paid and when he enquired regarding the next stage of work, Anne replied 'there was no haste of any more painting'.[117] Any thoughts she had had of making Hampton Court a principal residence had faded: Anne returned to the supplier the statues ordered by William for the gardens and rejected proposals to improve the Fountain Garden.[118] Though she occasionally conducted formal receptions in her bedchamber on visits to Hampton Court, she almost never stayed and her favourite bed was removed.[119] It was after the death of Prince George and her long period of mourning that Anne directed attention and resources towards Hampton Court, though her reasons for doing so remain unclear. In 1710 she gave orders for a new altar piece (designed by Wren), a new pulpit and pews and a new organ for the chapel, and extensive decorative work was executed – by James Thornhill and Grinling Gibbons among others.[120] The same year the queen ordered an overhaul of the park to improve hunting, returned to the project of improving the ornamental waterworks abandoned earlier, and began work on further garden projects for walls and walkways.[121] For the first time from 1710 Anne spent periods of weeks in residence at Hampton Court and revived there something of a court life that had been so lacking; but William's intention for the palace to become the official and ceremonial headquarters of English monarchy was not realized. Anne favoured other locations.

'Queen Anne,' writes the historian of royal building works, 'was the only Stuart monarch who felt that Windsor was her home.'[122] While princess she had purchased there a modest house to which she evidently remained attached throughout her reign. When, on her accession, she inherited the castle, it enjoyed from the outset the favour of her purse. During the first five years of her reign, Anne spent more on Windsor than William had in twice as many years. Indeed, much of the queen's expenditure, rather than on new buildings, went on refurbishing the interior of the palace after her predecessor's neglect. Windsor was the seat of the Garter and a shrine to Stuart kingship which Charles II had carefully restored as a symbol of the continuity and sanctity of his monarchy.[123] Under Anne, a payment for cleaning the equestrian statue of Charles II may give a clue to her sense of attachment to Windsor, where she also expended money on decorations and the chapel organ as well as garden work on the north side.[124] That on her husband's death in 1708 Anne spent more on mourning at her small house outside than she did within the castle suggests that her true home remained what Celia Fiennes described as the 'little retreat out of the palace'.[125] Windsor Castle may for Anne have had not domestic but symbolic importance: as the burial place of Charles I, as the place of St George's Chapel, and as the 'finest palace' after Whitehall burned.[126]

Windsor represented history and antiquity, in ways that were likely to have appealed to Anne. What it appears, however, that some of her contemporaries looked for were new monuments, especially to the nation's and queen's victories over France. In his 1704 thanksgiving sermon for the victory at Blenheim, the preacher Jean Dubourdieu, who would have witnessed in his native France the power of royal architectural monuments, urged the English 'architects and engravers' to 'erect monuments and triumphal arches' to commemorate the 'names and exploits' of the victors.[127] The only monument built, however, was (albeit paid for from the public purse) not a royal or national one but Blenheim Palace, a seat for the hero Marlborough. In the absence of a royal or national building, contemporaries tried to make Blenheim the monument to Anne that it was not. In his 1707 ode, Elijah Fenton praised the Woodstock palace as a royal site:

> High on thy Pow'r the grateful Flag display,
> Due to thy QUEEN's Reward, and Blenheim's Glorious Day.[128]

The same year, the author of *The Country Vicar's Address to Her Majesty* described Blenheim as a monument to the queen as well as to Marlborough:

> Fam'd *Woodstock* too, with its rich Manor,
> Will show the Grandeur of the Donor;[129]

'These things,' he assured Anne, 'will speak your Majesty/Most Great to all Posterity.'[130]

Blenheim, however, was not in fact a monument to the queen. Nor, as one contemporary slightingly put it, did the monarchy have anything to match it in its sheer architectural bravura and modernity. A 1708 poem consisted of a fictional dialogue between Windsor Castle, Anne's favoured palace, and 'Blenheim House, the seat of the Duke of Marlborough', in which each building makes claim to supremacy.[131] Windsor argues its antiquity, its relationship to the Garter, its long existence as a home of English monarchs – and especially the visits paid to it by Anne, 'the chiefest glory of a Crowned Head'.[132] Blenheim counters that the claim to antiquity is no longer enough:

> Those Days are alter'd now; for Queens or Kings
> And Peers delight in fashionable Things;
> Tho' formerly they antient Mansions chose,
> Yet now their Humour alters like their Cloaths.[133]

More audaciously, Blenheim matches Windsor's boast of monarchs and Queen Anne by trumpeting Marlborough and his 'immortal Fame'.[134] Freely confessing that he has not hosted 'So many Kings and Queens', Blenheim asserts:

Yet what I want in that respect to you,
Marl'brough, by all extolled to the Skies,
Makes up in many Fights and Victories.
Who hears of *Ramillies*, but must confess
All that he heard or read before was less.[135]

Blenheim concludes:

I'll grant you Honour for your antient Fame,
And I'll rest pleased with my Modern Name.[136]

In this playful dialogue, I would suggest we may discern several important and interrelated points. 'Blenheim' speaks for a transformed Britain in which the new challenges the old, in which taste is set as much by peers as by monarchs, in which a military hero and a politician can boast a fame that vies with, if it does not outstrip, that of monarchs. As Blenheim has the last word, we are led to recall the observation that the ruined Whitehall symbolized 'That Monarchy's in its decline'. Anne's retreat from the grand old palaces of majesty to a more domestic setting and style contrasted with the grandeur of her subject whose own palace – the only non-royal and non-episcopal palace in England – was also intended as a national monument built with clear echoes of Louis XIV's Versailles. At Blenheim it was a subject represented as an omnipotent being as well as conqueror. Power – and the power of image – as well as patronage were transferring from the crown to the aristocracy.

III

It is not surprising that in a reign which saw spectacular military victories, medals were frequent and important representations of Queen Anne and her government. However, it was almost certainly before the Battle of Blenheim that the Presbyterian minister James Coningham advocated the importance of medals which 'have the stamp of authority and the prince's person upon them' for their representation of regality.[137] In his 100-page *Critical Essay on the Modern Medals*, Coningham observed – not entirely accurately – that medals had not been sufficiently supported and lamented that there had been too many satirical or 'mock medals' which he regarded as 'an abuse of liberty and an encroachment upon the sovereignty itself'.[138] In Queen Anne's reign, Coningham saw new possibilities and new hope. Reflecting on the queen and her ministers, the essayist could not but conclude: 'what a great subject our medallists have here to employ themselves'.[139] The medal of Anne issued the previous year, which Coningham judged close in quality to those of the ancients, promised a revival of the medallic representation of the sovereign.

Stressing the importance of publicizing and recording for posterity Anne's magnanimity, charity, clemency, piety and protection of the church and faith, Coningham urged that 'neither her reign nor person can be better represented ... than in a medallic history'.[140] Though he recognized the new political reality which meant that such medals 'cannot be complete without adding that of them that serve her', Coningham made clear that it was on the obverse of medals that 'the Queen would appear everywhere in her greatness' and that the reverse would figure her ministers in (as he hoped) 'their due subordination'.[141]

Anne wasted no time in commissioning her first medal, issued before the usual coronation medal, to mark her accession on 8 March 1702. Her own direction of the design is strongly suggested by the image and legend, which both echoed the queen's address to parliament wherein she informed them that 'I know my own heart to be entirely English' and that she was devoted to 'the happiness and prosperity of England'.[142] The medal, with an obverse bust of Anne crowned and draped and facing left, figures on the reverse, on a pedestal, within branches of oak (the emblem of England) and laurel, a heart (the queen's) with a crown above. The inscription on the pedestal advertises Anne's legitimate – and Stuart – descent, 'atavis regibus' ('From royal ancestors'), and the legend ('Entirely English', significantly in English) summarizes the famous first speech in an axiom. As well as in gold and silver, John Croker executed the medal in copper which, together with the English inscription, suggests that it was intended for wide distribution (fig. 82).[143] From her very first day, Anne was using familiar symbols as well as words to represent herself as a popular and national queen who might reunite her people and kingdom. Indeed, a variant accession medal depicts on the reverse a chain of roses (the national flower of England), each containing a heart, linked by a crown and radiant heart and

82 Hawkins, *Medallic Illustrations*, plate CXV, 1.

above an inscription – 'Quis separabit' ('Who shall [dare to] separate them?'). The legend 'United by God in Love and Interest' conjoins old and new political values and forms to assert the tie between the new queen and her subjects.[144]

If, in its dynamic and national proclamations, Anne's accession medal marked some distance from the illegitimate, and Dutch, William, her coronation medal reassured Whigs that there would be no deviation from the course of war against France.[145] On the reverse of this medal, which was distributed at the coronation, the queen is represented as Pallas hurling thunderbolts against a monster with four arms and snakes as lower limbs. The legend reads: 'She is the vice-gerent of the Thunderer'. Clearly, in this design by her artist Godfrey Kneller, Anne is deftly represented as a warrior, the agent of God against his, as well as her and England's, enemy. However, as Abel Boyer observed, the hydra against which he hurls her thunderbolts was a traditional emblem of 'rebellion, sedition, schism, heresy, etc.'[146] Together with assurances, which she had given to her Privy Council on the day after William's death, that she would support the common cause, Anne was asserting, along with the power of her sex, her authority at home, and perhaps warning any who might have sought to take advantage of her succession to foment trouble or division. As well as the gold, silver and copper medals given and distributed at the coronation, medalets or jetons were issued for sale in the streets.[147] Having advertised her own authority and capacity to lead the country in war, the next month Anne issued a medal with on the reverse of her (uncrowned) bust, an armoured figure of her husband, Prince George, to mark her investing him with the title of generalissimo of her forces and Lord High Admiral.[148] With her husband as commander, the medal announced, the queen was indeed prepared for war.

One of England's earliest victories in Anne's reign was the battle at Vigo Bay and the capture of a Spanish bullion ship. As well as medals issued by the allies, the victory, perhaps to boost morale at the beginning of the new reign, was commemorated on English medals and coins. On the reverse of the accession-type bust of Anne, Vigo harbour is depicted with vessels burning, inside a Latin legend announcing the French and Spanish fleets captured and burned.[149] Like the Vigo medal, others by Croker marking Marlborough's successes on the first campaign on the Meuse issued in copper were probably commissioned to rally public support for the costly war, which had become increasingly unpopular under William, and to hint at a new promise of victories.[150] Those victories, of course, were not won by Anne personally; and Toni Bowers has suggested that the queen's portrait bust on the obverse of medals was subordinated to scenes of others' triumphs on the reverse, such as that of 1703 showing Marlborough on horseback receiving the surrender of Bonn, Huy and Limbourg.[151] As we have seen with panegyrics, the representation of a queen who could not, as her predecessor, lead armies as a warrior involved some deft rhetorical moves; but on medals the obverse bust reminded all of the queen whom Marlborough served and in whose name victories were won. In the case of the first decisive victory of the reign, variants of the commemoration medal may suggest English medallists' determination to advertise a royal triumph, rather than that of a brilliant commander. For whereas a Dutch medal figured on the reverse Marlborough on a rearing horse with the battlefield behind him, Croker's Blenheim medal depicts Britannia seated on a globe with an emblem of victory and with a captive bound on piles of French arms and standards.[152] As well as alluding to her features, Britannia symbolized Anne and here the triumph is undoubtedly rendered as hers.

Just as the Duke of Marlborough was absent from the English medallic commemoration of Blenheim, so Queen Anne's admirals were missing from the medal issued the same year to mark the capture of Gibraltar by Sir George Rooke and Sir Cloudesley Shovell. The medal itself put the best spin on what was at the most a half-victory after the failure to take Barcelona. On the reverse, again, rather than the images of the admirals, Neptune in his sea chariot presents his trident and a crown to Britannia who stands on the shore.[153] Along with the legend 'Naval Victories', the image gestures to the old Stuart claim of English sovereignty of the seas, secured now by a queen who presided over, even if she was not engaged in, such victories.

Over the course of the following campaigns, numerous medals were struck on the continent to commemorate English as well as allied successes; and in England, Croker was commissioned for one, issued in copper as well as gold and silver, to celebrate the taking of Barcelona which Rooke had attempted two years earlier.[154] On the reverse of Anne's bust a scene of the city depicted an eclipsed sun – almost certainly a symbolic claim to Anne eclipsing the Sun King, Louis XIV of France. If such a claim may have appeared premature on 12 May, the victory of Ramillies less than two weeks later underpinned it, the battle inflicting on France the greatest defeat it had suffered. On the reverse of the official medal commemorating the victory, the legend and inscription simply announced: 'The French defeated at Ramillies ...', 'Flanders and Brabant recovered'.[155] To display graphically the scope of this victory, however, two figures of Fame, with trumpets, hold a map of the conquered provinces, showing just how extensive and how important were the territorial gains. Interestingly again, while he was celebrated on continental plaques and medals, Marlborough was not figured on the medal. Similarly, the only medal struck to commemorate the repulse of the French invasion fleet in March 1708 depicted Britannia (an emblem of the queen as well as kingdom) armed with spear and shield, protecting Scotia from the French fleet.[156] Not only the portrayal of a female protector and victor, and the greater strength that came from the union, the medal evoked, as it must have been intended to, Elizabeth's repulse of the Armada fleet. As Britannia's second Elizabeth, the message was that Anne had repelled her kingdom's enemies.

As successive victories were won, the image of Anne on medals became increasingly triumphant and imperial. The medal celebrating the Battle of Oudenarde in July 1708 has a new (post-union) crowned bust of the queen, in classical dress and wearing the collar and George, with on the reverse two captives bound to a column or pillar (an emblem of empire) decorated with French standards and surmounted by the (female) figure of Victory (fig. 83).[157] As William III had done on the engraved image of him between two columns, Anne was appropriating imperial conceits and even claiming to replace French with British suzerainty.[158] In June 1710 the obverse of the medal marking the taking of Douai now bore the legend that publicized Anne as Augusta – named after the first emperor of Rome; while on the reverse Victory fixes a shield to a classical column and (on the right) the figure of Bellona, the ancient Roman war goddess, pursues a French soldier.[159]

In all these cases, war medals, issued to celebrate victories secured by men, repeat images of mythological and emblematic female figures: Pallas, Bellona, in general Victory, and by allusion Elizabeth I. Croker's medals, that is, did much to represent the war as the queen's and so to counter the accusations of some that it was a war favoured by only a party. Where on countless continental medals, the figure of Marlborough appears, with foreign princes such as Eugene of Savoy, the queen's brilliant commander was not depicted on any official English medal: other than allegorical figures, only Anne's husband George was represented – and then on the reverse of the queen's bust. Though there is no direct evidence, it seems likely that these commissions were the queen's own; and that Anne took from medals that were widely distributed (most were issued in copper) the opportunity to advertise the war, victories and triumphs as hers

83 Hawkins, *Medallic Illustrations*, plate CXXVII, 6.

and the nation's. The same must be said of the official medals issued to celebrate the much longed for Peace of Utrecht. In one variant, the reverse figures, seated, a sturdy (like the queen) Britannia holding an olive branch and a spear between (on her right) a ship and (left) a peaceful bucolic scene of ploughing and sowing, inside a legend from Horace: 'They know peace by laying aside their arms'; in another Britannia stands, dominating the scene.[160] Just as the coronation medals at the beginning of the reign, Anne's peace medals were given to Members of Parliament, presumably in gold and silver, and distributed more broadly in copper. For all the pastoral imagery of harmony and the representation of England as victorious in peace as in war, the Peace of Utrecht (as we saw) divided the nation and led to charges that the ministry abandoned the allies and accepted an inglorious conclusion after glorious victories. Indeed, the emperor refused to be part of it and Louis XIV seemed as ready to commemorate peace as his enemies.[161] But in England, Utrecht medals helped to sell the peace to the nation which would, as their queen had always assured them she desired, advance the people's wealth and happiness. At the start of Horace's Ode 4, 14, from which the legend of the Utrecht medal is taken, the poet asks what honours could suffice to eternize the virtues of Augustus. In peace as they had in war, medals representing Anne as Amazon, protectress and empress had sought similarly to present England's Augusta as the 'mightiest of chieftains' whom 'The sun beholds from heaven on high'.[162]

The battles and victories of the wars of the Spanish Succession were naturally the principal events commemorated on medals; but they were not the only ones. Indeed, what supports a suggestion that Queen Anne herself may have been involved in the commissions to Croker are the medals issued to celebrate enactments dear to her personally. At home perhaps nothing was of more concern to Anne than the state and status of the Anglican church and clergy. On 3 April 1704, in an act of munificence quite out of character with a history of monarchs raiding the church, Anne returned to the church the revenue of first fruits and tenths which Henry VIII had taken from the papacy at the Reformation. A statute established a corporation to administer the fund, which has become known as Queen Anne's Bounty; and a medal was struck to mark it and to publicize this more than symbolic demonstration of Anne's making good her promise to protect and preserve the church. The medal, issued in gold, silver and copper, is interesting (fig. 84).[163] Two variants of the obverse feature the same portrait bust of the queen, laureate rather than crowned; one has the legend 'Anne Augusta'. On the reverse (of both) Anne, seated on a throne, presents the charter (of incorporation of the fund) to kneeling clergy inside the legend 'Pietas Augustae'. The image recalls, as it was surely meant to, images of Henry VIII – presenting a charter to the Barber Surgeons or the Bible to his bishops.[164] Whilst Anne's gesture reverses the Henrician act of taking church revenues, like her Tudor forebear, she is publicizing her royal supremacy:

84 Hawkins, *Medallic Illustrations*, plate CXIX, 1.

as a beneficence. A proclamation of (imperial) authority, as well as of patronage of the Church of England, and a reminder to the bishops and clergy that they owed obedience to her, the medal conveyed to a broad public values that were central to Anne's rule.

Next to the church, the royal project closest to Anne's heart was the union, which she had described in her speech of 11 March 1702 as very necessary for the peace and security of her kingdoms and which she continued to press in speeches over the next five years.[165] Enacted on 1 May 1707, the union, as well as necessitating a new coinage, was commemorated by various official medals and by medalets and counters. Most varieties display on the reverse of the queen's bust the British shield (with English and Scottish arms) within the Garter, crowned and between branches of palm and laurel.[166] On one side the heraldic lion holds a shield bearing the rose and thistle (the emblems of England and Scotland) united; on the other a unicorn has a union shield. A pedestal supporting the shield is inscribed with the entwined letters AR – Anna Regina. On this medal, which figures the union by means of several heraldic devices (the conjunction of the St George and St Andrew crosses, for example), Anne's personal cipher is placed prominently beneath the crowned arms, representing the union as very much her personal blazon and achievement.[167] In a variant of these reverses, designed by Samuel Bull, an engraver at the Mint, the heraldic beasts do not appear. Instead the arms of Britain on a shield crowned are supported by two putti.[168] In this version, the plinth is inscribed with Anne's personal motto – 'Semper Eadem'. Finally, a third variant, uncertainly dated and assigned to Croker, carries a statue of Pallas inside an inscription intimating that Anne will be the defender and champion of a new Troy – a reference back to the old myths about Brutus, who founded a city (London) he called Troia Nova on the banks of the Thames.[169] Where by her cipher and motto other medals represented the union as Anne's accomplishment, on this version Pallas (who appeared on other of her medals) and the reference to Troy gesture towards the queen as fulfilling an ancient prophecy and destiny and founding a new British empire. Like Pallas, too, Anne, though a warrior, disliked war and preferred to use her wisdom as the queen had done to complete the union.[170]

Medals to mark Queen Anne's Bounty and celebrate the union publicized major personal initiatives and achievements. In November 1708 the queen suffered the greatest personal blow of her reign and life: the death of her husband Prince George of Denmark. Interestingly, while Anne went into months of mourning and though the Copenhagen medallist Michael Roeg was commissioned by Frederick IV of Denmark to strike commemorative medals, no medal was issued in England.[171] Whether or not grief explained this, the absence of any official medal figuring Prince George (after the early reverse portrait) emphasizes the medallic representation of Anne as a singular figure of authority. Far from executing Coningham's project of a series of medals on which her officers and ministers would be depicted 'in their due subordina-tion', on reverses it was only Anne who was represented 'in her greatness', with mythological and allegorical supporters and inscriptions making claims for her authority greater, perhaps, than was the political reality in the age of party.[172] Party politics were not absent from medallic representation. In what amounts to a testament to their importance in distributing a message, medals and badges in support, and mockery, of Dr Sacheverell were cast, given and worn as tokens of allegiance.[173] And Jacobite medals (as we shall see) were imported from France and some possibly cast in England across the reign. In the main, however, medals represented Anne as she would have wished to be: above the factious politics of party ministry and manoeuvre, as head of a revered church and united people. Anne's medals, we might suggest, represented a fading ideal, even a fiction. But insofar as they reflected and may have sustained and strengthened her popularity to the end of her reign, they helped the queen to exercise such independence as she had and enabled her still, in a powerful symbolic sense, to embody as well as represent Britain.

IV

Following the great recoinage of 1696–7 and the final withdrawal of the old hammered coins in 1695, in coin Anne's reign may at first sight appear less significant in numismatic history than that of her predecessor, William III. However, both the queen's gender and taste and particular events in her reign effected important changes in the representation of the sovereign and the nation, especially on gold and silver coins. Soon after her accession, Anne replaced the shield of Nassau that had adorned the reverse of William's coins with a (Tudor) rose or the star of the Order of the Garter.[174] More revealing of her self-image and concern with her visual representation, Anne ordered an alteration to the bare bust of the monarch that had appeared on the obverse of gold coins. 'The portly queen put in an objection to her corpulent contours being represented without a covering and in consequence she is portrayed on gold coins amply clothed.'[175] On her gold five, two and one guinea and half-guinea coins, Anne's bust, unlike her predecessor facing left, is figured in classical drapery inside an inscription 'Anne Dei Gratia', with on the reverse, the four shields of England, Scotland, Ireland and France crossed by sceptres. This basic pattern was repeated during the first half of the reign on silver crowns and half-crowns as well as on gold coins. Early in the reign, however, events led to the minting of other special coins, known as Vigo coins because they add that name to the legend around the queen's bust.[176] These coins were struck from bullion captured by an Anglo-Dutch expedition under Vice-Admiral Sir George Rooke, which had seized a Spanish silver fleet in the port of Vigo. The guinea, crown, shilling and sixpenny coins commemorated what Robert Harley described as 'a most glorious expedition' and one of the early military successes of the reign.[177] On these coins, as well as the figure of Anne above the place of triumph on the obverse, on the reverse a Tudor rose is centred between the four shields.

While the great victories of Blenheim and Ramillies were not similarly commemorated on coin, Anne, necessarily as well as willingly, ordered new coinage to mark the union with Scotland in 1707. After 1707, gold and silver coins, to represent the union, the English and Scottish arms on the reverse were placed side by side in one shield and repeated in the first and fourth quarters, with the shield of France now in the second quarter.[178] Some of the silver post-union coins were struck at the Edinburgh mint with a small E placed below the queen's bust to denote the place; and all post-union reverses feature the Garter star and not a rose, a symbol perhaps too identified with England rather than Britain.[179] Coins, that is, publicized what Anne regarded as her greatest achievement: the unity of her kingdoms and peoples into one Great Britain.

For most of the reign that advertisement appears to have been confined to gold and silver coins – and hence the audience of these images to wealthier subjects. The great recoinage of 1696 had produced plenty of low-denomination coinage and Anne had no copper coins struck to commemorate the union. Later in the reign, pattern pieces were made for halfpennies and farthings. On the reverse of the draped bust of Anne, these figure Britannia, with the features of the queen, seated with her spear and shield and an olive branch, a symbol of peace and victory. (On some patterns the inscription 'Bello et Pace' is added; in

1713 to celebrate Utrecht, 'Pax Missa per Urbem'.)[180] What is – appropriately – different about the figure, when compared with the Britannia introduced by Charles II, is the covering of her legs to the ankles. Where Charles's first Britannia coins issued in 1672 were (infamously) modelled by the woman he yearned to be his mistress, the Duchess of Richmond, on Anne's coins a more modest representation, especially since Britannia bore attributes of the queen, was more in keeping with Anne's reputation for piety and moral reformation.[181] There is some dispute whether these copper pattern pieces – the first to be made by the Royal Mint rather than under licence – ever became current coin.[182] But Isaac Newton, Master of the Mint, attributed importance to them and it seems that the farthings were put into circulation, though only in 1714 about the time of Anne's death. If that is the case, the lowest denomination coins served more to memorialize than represent the first true queen of Britain, a Britannia indeed triumphant by 1713 in war and peace.

I began by observing that Queen Anne's image is perhaps the least recognized of the Stuarts. And scholars have accurately described her portraits as lacking in majesty to the point of being almost bourgeois. That her image is not striking may evidence no more than the queen's lack of interest, or her taste. It may be, however, that, just as she pursued a careful moderation in both asserting her authority and accepting the constitutional limitations on monarchy that 1688 and its consequences had brought, so Anne sought also to represent herself visually as both a queen and yet not – or at least less – an object of mystery and veneration. The image of Queen Anne lacks numinosity. But it did not lack popularity. As the statues erected by private initiative, still more the vast numbers of engravings testify, the image of the queen circulated broadly and was bought, in various forms (ceramics as well as prints), by collectors and ordinary subjects. And Anne herself appears to have recognized the importance of reaching out to her people in visual forms as she did in speeches. Anne did not determine or control all the images of her that reached her subjects. But many engravings and medals, as we have seen, represent policies, values and commitments close to Anne's personal wishes: her support for the war, her love of the church, and her desire for peace and unity. Though her portraits aesthetically disappoint us today, we are left with the suggestion that in various visual media, especially in those (neglected) forms like medals and coins over which the monarch still exercised some control, Queen Anne may have tried to represent her own wishes in an age of party conflict and of the increasing dependence of the sovereign on party ministries. At least the image of the queen that circulated was far removed from the reality of the sick, aged woman who had to perform in person on the stage of majesty.

CHAPTER 15

STUART RITUALS

QUEEN ANNE AND THE PERFORMANCE OF MONARCHY

I

A Stuart, daughter of James II who had maintained her as princess a court, Queen Anne was fully schooled in her youth in the performative aspects of the monarchy. During her lifetime, Anne would also have seen important changes in royal rituals, in the nature of the court and in the representation of regality. After the vitality and gaiety of her uncle Charles II's court, her father had retrenched spending and reformed moral laxity. Under William and Mary, the importance of ritual, festival and court life had declined as the king was often absent at war, the queen was temperamentally disinclined to gay sociability, and many of the old Stuart courtier families were replaced by Dutchmen and Whigs with little experience of court life or pageantry. There can be little doubt that by the death of William III, both the performance of majesty and the court had become less significant in the political and social life of the nation.

However, just as Anne's succession as legitimate Stuart heir presented an opportunity to heal the wounds of 1688, it also signalled an occasion to revitalize ritual forms that would recall former Stuart rule and reunite a divided nation behind the dynasty and monarchy. Anne, after all, was not only the daughter of James II, she had supported the Revolution and stepped aside to facilitate William's assumption of the throne and to enable his continued rule after the death of her sister Queen Mary in 1694. As many reminded her, and as she was quite ready to acknowledge, Anne owed her title in 1702 both to her birth and to the Revolution. As queen she hoped – and never ceased to hope – that she might temper the heat of party and reign as the acknowledged and loved nursing mother of all her people. Faced with bitter religious divisions as intense as those of party, earlier Tudor monarchs, notably Queen Elizabeth I, had, with some success, deployed display, ceremony and ritual to unite and embody the whole nation. Significantly, as we shall have further cause to discuss, Queen Anne early on adopted Queen Elizabeth's motto ('Semper

Eadem') and emulated her dress – perhaps to connect with an (idealized) golden age in the past as well as with the last queen consort.[1] Though shy, awkward and already in poor health on her accession, and while she never came close to Elizabeth's sense of occasion, Anne certainly did not neglect, at least early on, the performative aspects of majesty. Her reign, however, did not see the revitalization of royal ritual or the revival of the court. A perhaps irreversible decline under William, and other social and political changes as well as her own disposition, rather stressed further decline that both reflected – and in turn had large consequences for – changes in the status of the monarchy itself. Within her limitations of resources, circumstances and character, Anne staged her queenship and earned (and retained) a high level of popularity. But, whatever her hopes had been, she failed to restore the monarch and court as the focus of the social life, or as the symbolic centre, of the nation. Despite her adoption of the motto 'Semper Eadem', the court and ritual life of Queen Anne were far removed from that of Gloriana and the queen herself a dim light when compared with the dazzle of her predecessor.

II

In the weeks after her accession, Queen Anne received numerous addresses of condolences for the death of William III, 'Protector of our religion and liberties'.[2] Obsequies for the deceased predecessor were the first ritual obligations of a new monarch, and in Anne's case, whatever the past tensions between them, a public display of respect for William presented an opportunity to manifest in ritual continuity with her predecessor as well as restored Stuart rule. Evidently it was 'several times debated in Council whether the late king should be publicly or privately buried'.[3] Though 'it was at the last carried for the latter', the funeral on Sunday, 12 April, involved a procession behind the corpse in an open chariot, 'attended with a very large chain of coaches' from Kensington to Westminster Abbey where William's body was interred with that of his consort and in the same vault as Charles II.[4] While, in keeping with royal traditions, Anne did not participate, she was symbolically present via her husband, Prince George, who was Chief Mourner. Though the privacy of the occasion contrasted (perhaps deliberately) with the extraordinary full state pomp of Mary's funeral in 1695, which had revived Tudor ceremonial, Anne had buried the figure high Tories saw as an illegitimate usurper in the mausoleum of kings – and of Stuarts.[5] It was a signal that the new, Anglican queen would not overturn the government of her predecessor nor permit a vengeful purge of his (Whig) supporters.

A gesture to those with different sympathies, as well as to the Stuart past, was surely intended in the decision to stage Anne's coronation on 23 April, St George's Day and the coronation day of both James II and Charles II. Commissioners met regularly to make preparations, including for coronation medals to be distributed on the day, and for new suits for the foot guards 'that they might appear with more splendour'.[6] Evidently 'vast numbers of people' from outside the metropolis, as well as Londoners, came to see the ceremony, which was planned to be of 'great splendour'.[7] Given the divisions within the realm, and the hopes and fears of various parties, it was vital that the ceremony legitimated the queen and bound her to her subjects.[8] About mid-morning, the nobility having pressed into Westminster Hall, the sword and spurs were presented to the queen, who was seated under the canopy of state.[9] After the dean and prebendaries of Westminster brought the crown, regalia and Bible, the procession began to Westminster Abbey. Behind drums, trumpets, Gentlemen of the Privy Chamber, Councillors, judges and nobles, Prince George led the nobles who bore the regalia. Attended by her Captains of the Guard and Gentlemen Pensioners and her bedchamber ladies, the queen was carried 'in a low open chair' so as to be seen, 'in her royal robes of crimson velvet, wearing the collar of the Order of the Garter . . . and on her head a rich circlet of gold and diamonds'. As the cavalcade passed, 'the houses on each side being crowded with spectators', they expressed 'their great joy and satisfaction by loud and repeated acclamations'.[10]

In the abbey the regalia were presented at the altar in a full Anglican service that itself represented the new ruler. After a litany was sung and the Creed recited, the Archbishop of York preached on Isaiah 49: 23: 'Kings shall be thy nursing fathers and their queens thy nursing mothers'.[11] After the sermon, the queen – in a gesture that distanced her from her Stuart forebears – took the Test (established by parliament) as well as the coronation oath, before being anointed and crowned. When the Bible was presented to her, Anne, in another public manifestation of her devotion to the church, 'vouchsafed to kiss the bishops', as the treasurer of her household 'threw about' coronation medals to the assembled. After the queen had received Holy Communion and final prayers, the procession returned in order to Westminster Hall, Anne wearing her crown.[12]

In Westminster Hall the queen sat down to dinner with her newly appointed household officers and the nobility; because a parliament was in session, all the MPs were in attendance at the coronation and were entertained at dinner in the Exchequer Chamber. As well as a union of crown and church, the coronation ceremonies, the homage and not least the dining represented the monarch in loving union with her peers and, on this occasion, her Commons. As for the people who had expressed their joy and shouted their affirmation of the queen's right, they too had their reward. About half-past eight, as at the conclusion of a ritual day that had commenced before eleven, the queen returned to St James's, for the delectation of the populace, 'the day concluded with bonfires, illuminations [and] ringing of bells'. Along with the 'splendour and magnificence', Anne would have taken particular comfort in the 'demonstration of a general . . . joy' by her people whom, as she said in her first speech and repeated in several others from the throne, she sought to unite behind their new 'English' queen.

To mark the event, and to involve those who had not been able to attend, the form of the procession to the coronation was officially published by the Earl Marshal and reported in the *London Gazette* and a host of other newspapers.[13] Interestingly, there is evidence that the coronation was indeed a day of national ritual and rejoicing. On the 23rd at Lincoln, for example, Colonel Pownal entertained all the gentry, clergy and army officers to dinner, while the people in their respective parishes, having erected marquees, 'dined publicly in the streets', the city conduits flowing with free wine.[14] At Ludlow and Wootton Bassett the mayor and aldermen 'drank plentifully' the queen's health, providing wine and a fireworks display for the citizenry; at Exeter, Sir Thomas Jefford ordered a five-gun salute to the queen as well as providing a ten-gallon barrel of punch, a day of music and an evening bonfire.[15] The High Sherriff of Penrith in Cumberland led the party to church on the coronation morning before a public toast to the queen and Prince George in the market square.[16] In Nottingham 'the solemnity of her Majesty's coronation was celebrated . . . with great magnificence' as, in a ritual complementary to those in London, the mayor and corporation assembled at the Guildhall and then processed in a cavalcade, with pageant figures 'through all the principal streets of the town'. Along with local inhabitants, visitors from across the county were 'generously' entertained: 'a universal cheerfulness appeared in all faces and all mouths were filled with expressions of dutiful affection and loyalty to her majesty and hearty wishes for her long and prosperous reign'.[17] At Chichester it was (at least according to the account in the *Post Man*) the young gentlemen and tradesmen who organized themselves into a band to march to the market cross. After prayers at the cathedral, attended by young virgins dressed in white, they returned to the cross to drink the queen's health before an afternoon of sports and games (bull baiting, dancing), lubricated by 'large spouts of good wine'. As night fell, 'every house in the town was illuminated from top to bottom, [and] bonfires in every street'. 'Plenty of liquor was allowed to all sorts of people', who all enthusiastically 'repeated huzzas of long live the queen'.[18]

Even if not all such celebrations fitted with Queen Anne's sobriety, they were a promising sign that the magistracy, political classes and the people could come together in and through ritual celebration, and that the bitter divisions of William's reign might be allayed, as Anne so much hoped. For even the minister of the German Lutheran congregation in Trinity Lane, who might not have had most to celebrate in the succession of a staunchly Anglican queen, recalled to his flock who had just witnessed the coronation: 'did you not flock to the place of coronation with great trouble and expense, not caring for the inconvenience you sustained by the multitude of people?' 'Was not,' he added, 'your very heart taken with the lustre of that glorious theatre?'[19] All eyes had been fixed on the queen, and on the 'lustre' of her birth, her virtue and her majesty.[20] As it was meant to, the coronation had brought the nation together.

Queen Anne was to be frustrated in her hopes of ending the party rivalries that divided her people. But she continued – often against the obstacles of ill-health and temperamental disinclination – to sustain and lead state rituals that served at least to ameliorate bitter partisanship. We have reviewed the regular services of thanksgiving that the queen mandated on occasions of victory.[21] It is important to note that Anne turned these into royal performances. The first monarch since Elizabeth to attend the services at St Paul's in person, Anne on thanksgiving days received the compliments of the nobility at St James's before the procession to the cathedral.[22] Boyer's *History* recounts the first of these thanksgivings solemnized on 12 November 1702.[23] At eight in the morning, MPs and Lords in their coaches led a procession of Members in Chancery and judges before the queen, attended by her Knight Marshal and Gentlemen Ushers, her principal household officers, her Maids of Honour and yeomen of the guard. 'Habited in purple, wearing her collar and George' in a coach followed by her Horse Guards, Anne passed from St James to Temple Bar, thence to Ludgate and St Paul's. Met at the cathedral door by the officers of arms, the queen walked, with the sword of state carried before her and escorted by her Master of the Horse and Lord Chamberlain, into the choir. At the west end of the choir, opposite the altar, Anne was seated on a throne of state with her peers, Commons and servants, the mayor and aldermen in galleries and stalls around her. As the prayers were said and the litany was sung, the service became not only a thanksgiving to God but an act of worship of the queen. As, after the service, she made her return 'in the same state' or pomp, at Ludgate a 'pyramidical illumination' (presumably some kind of firework) and inscription heralded her as a conqueror.

The 1702 ceremonies established the pattern for the rituals of thanksgiving for victories at Blenheim and Ramillies, the defeat of the Pretender, the union and – finally – the Peace of Utrecht. On 7 September 1704, the day of thanksgiving for the decisive triumph at Blenheim, the streets from St James's (to St Paul's) were hung with blue cloth and the balconies and windows along the way 'hung with carpets and rich tapestry'.[24] In an even more elaborate ceremony, Anne, and this time Prince George, were conducted to two thrones at the west end. Envoys from foreign states were on this occasion seated in the Middle Gallery (next to the peers) to have a prime view of a service of triumph as well as thanks.[25] Before, during and after the service a gun salute underscored 'this victory . . . the most glorious and considerable that has been gained in many years'.[26] The procession to St Paul's for the thanksgiving for the victory at Ramillies, on 27 June, appears, if anything, to have been even larger and more elaborate. And, as well as large numbers of royal officials and peers named in Boyer's account, the ambassador from Prussia formed part of the cavalcade,

'attended with a fine equipage and his . . . daughter, in a coach and six horses'.[27]
Along with an even more ceremonial conduct of the queen to the choir, even
more guns (on the river and at St James's, as well as from the Tower) were
fired to mark the victory. The thanksgiving for the success at Oudenarde on
19 August 1708 was the last at St Paul's that Anne attended before the peace.[28]
A few weeks later, the death of her husband Prince George, and exacerbated
illness, commenced a period when Anne withdrew from these public thanksgivings (as, we shall see, other rituals), instead attending a service in her Chapel
Royal at St James's. Though the queen went to her chapel 'with the usual solemnity', the grand public procession was suspended until the end of the reign.[29]

Whilst they ceased in the latter half of the reign, it is important to stress the
very public ritual that these services of thanksgiving had constituted during
Anne's first seven years. As well as all the attending officers, city companies,
militia and servants, the accounts of each occasion emphasize the large
numbers of spectators. In 1702 the 'public demonstrations' and 'acclamations'
by 'the inhabitants of this great and populous city' were deemed fitting to the
occasion; in 1706 it was reported that the balconies were 'crowded with spectators' who, doubtless encouraged by the evening fireworks and bonfires,
expressed 'public joy' and 'demonstrations of loyalty and affection to her
majesty's sacred person'.[30] Indeed, so great was the competition for viewing
space that enterprising innkeepers advertised for rent rooms or balconies over-
looking the route; for the thanksgiving for Ramillies, for example, a hosier near
Middle Temple Gate advertised 'a balcony with a handsome wainscot dining
room', for a party of sixteen to eighteen persons.[31] Though in the end ill-health
prevented her attending, a 1713 advertisement offered an empty house 'to see
the queen go to St Paul's'.[32]

Nor, as with the coronation, were the rituals of thanksgiving confined to the
capital. In 1704, for instance, as well as the thanksgiving at St Paul's, 'this festival
was observed in all the other parts of her Majesty's dominions' – 'if not with the
same solemnity, yet with as great affection and loyalty'.[33] Evidently, whatever
the burdens of war, these thanksgivings for victory were popular national occasions and served to make Anne a popular queen and national figurehead. The
thanksgivings, of course, also represented Queen Anne as she sought to be: as
pious heroine of a church, and as devoted to its rituals and liturgy. In St Paul's,
and in the procession to and from it, Anne was surrounded by her bishops and
royal chaplains, who sat close to her in the cathedral. The service, with sung
litanies, Te Deums, a full choir and organ music, manifested Anglican worship
revived and royally favoured, in contrast to William III's religious taste and
preferences. Anne may have reassured nonconformists that she had no desire
to persecute dissent; but the public thanksgivings were those of an avowed
Anglican monarch and probably explain the rising popularity of the church as
well as monarchy during her reign. Some evidence to support this suggestion

comes from a fictional dialogue published in the *View of the Times*, shortly after the thanksgiving for Blenheim.[34] In the discussion between 'Observator' and 'Countryman', the former asks the latter what he thought of the Thanksgiving Day, or (as he put it revealingly) 'the show day'. ''Twas a sad day for us,' Observator opines before getting his answer, 'to see the queen . . . ride so triumphantly to St Paul's . . . for a church victory. We had no such superstitious doings in the last reign. Our glorious K. William never set his foot within that cathedral . . . is this not rash popery?' Agreeing, the Countryman expresses his loathing of the prayers and singing; the Observator similarly laments 'that ever I should see my queen go to St Paul's to sing Te Deum'. The passage reminds us that, for all the appearance of unity, not all took joy from the thanksgivings. But, as this satire of silly 'dunces', low churchmen and nonconformists itself suggests, most of the populace were in favour of the services on these 'solemn occasions' and supporters of the church as well as queen.

An established and popular event on the royal ritual calendar was the Festival of the Garter, often involving, as well as the services, a magnificent public procession to Windsor. William III, as we have seen, was absent abroad from some of the most notable Garter festivals, and the then Princess Anne evidently considered the king was little interested in the Garter ceremonies.[35] As her letter as princess suggests, Anne took a greater interest in the Order and its ceremonies which had been important to her predecessor Queen Elizabeth and her Stuart forebears, especially Charles I. Within days of succeeding to the throne, she held a chapter of the Garter to fill the vacant stalls and appointed St George's Day for her coronation.[36] In October of her first year, it was from 'her seat of Sovereign of the most noble order of the Garter' that the queen touched several to cure the king's evil.[37] Anne held regular chapters of the Order at Hampton Court and St James's, as well as Windsor, at which newly elected knights were installed with 'the usual ceremonies'.[38] Such occasions evoked poems published in the newspaper press, such as that on the instalment of Treasurer Godolphin, in 1704.[39] In his case, an account of the installation reports a procession from the chapel to the castle at Windsor, with trumpets and drums, though the queen was evidently not present.[40]

During Anne's reign the *Gazette* and most of the newspapers regularly reported gossip about who was to be elected a knight, about chapters and installations; but the brief notices seldom offer details of the ceremonies either because they were familiar or of lesser import.[41] Popular and more learned publications indicate an interest in St George and the Garter during Anne's reign; and towards the end of it poets judged that the Order had grown in dignity' under the Queen.[42] 'How do's thy Order in Succession rise,' wrote the author of *The Garter*, a poem in honour of those made knights companion in 1712.[43] The next year another poet, while lamenting the past decline of the Order, praised the queen for its revitalization:

... ANNA does its antient Worth restore,
Exalt it too 'bove what it was before;
Nev'r was it by mor Worthy *Patriots* worn,
Nor ev'r did braver *Englishmen* adorn;[44]

The poet's praise of Beaufort, Oxford and (by 1713) the pro-Tory Strafford may suggest that the Garter had not escaped the struggles of party. But at the end of the reign of a queen who never failed to wear her Garter badge and ribbon, the prestige of the Garter remained high. During the next reign, the artist commemorated Queen Anne with the Knights of the Garter by a canvas that captured the splendour of a chapter (fig. 85).[45]

While they were commemorated annually by sermons and church services, Anne participated in no rituals or celebrations of either 30 January or 29 May, the anniversaries of the regicide and Restoration, nor (perhaps more surprisingly) of 17 November, Queen Elizabeth's accession day. 'Rather, Anne chose to emphasise those anniversaries personal to her and her rule, in particular that of the royal birth on 6th February.'[46] Each year Anne's birthday was celebrated

85 Peter Angelis, *Queen Anne and the Knights of the Garter*, 1720s.

by visits from her nobles, by a service at chapel, an ode written in her honour and praise, and an evening 'drawing room', or assembly, with entertainment. On the first day of her reign, according to her annalist, 'there had not been such a magnificent appearance at court for twenty years', and until the death of Prince George there were yearly references to a 'splendid' or 'extremely magnificent' court, and to the 'magnificence of [the] habits' – that is, clothes – of the nobility and gentry.[47] Nor were the celebrations confined to the court: in 1703 the royal birthday was solemnized by 'extraordinary rejoicings throughout the whole kingdom'.[48] The court festivities, which included 'a very great crowd', often ended with public fireworks; and her last birthday was 'observed in the cities of London and Westminster' with what the *British Mercury* described as 'the usual solemnity as ringing of bells, bonfires, illuminations and other demonstrations of joy'.[49] As well as extending to concerts of music in the suburbs, such as Southwark, the celebrations spread beyond London.[50] At Rochester in 1704, along with barrels of beer to drink the queen's health, there were bells, bonfires and fireworks to mark her birthday; in Devon in 1713, in Axminster, Honiton and Colyton, the queen's birthday was celebrated by 'a vast concourse of people from the country', with bonfires, music, fireworks and plentiful drink, even though the benefactor was too ill to be present.[51] As such newspaper accounts imply, far from being remote, in an age of publicity the entertainments at court were widely reported and 'the common people are very much pleased that so much respect is shown to the queen' and sought to emulate it.[52] It may be that, in this at least, Anne's birthday celebrations reflected and enhanced her popularity, as had the commemoration of Elizabeth's accession day a century earlier.[53] Moreover, reported and often printed, the odes and entertainments presented to her on her birthday represented and published Anne as the conquering empress of a new British imperium. *England's Glory* was the title of a verse that formed part of the musical entertainment for the queen in 1706, in which Europe and Asia lay themselves at Britannia's and 'Royal ANNA's feet'.[54] 'In Dances and Songs,' the Chorus sang, 'let obedience be shown' to her who extended 'o'er the Globe' Britain's 'Dominion'.[55] The masques that had represented King Charles I as a god may have passed in the new age and politics of Augustan England, yet Anne's birthday entertainments continued to praise 'the sacred Majesty' of Britain's 'incomparable Queen'.[56]

In addition to these personal birthday celebrations, Queen Anne was formally entertained on occasions by the City and, as with earlier monarchs, was lauded in mayoral pageants. The first October of her reign, for example, Anne accepted an invitation from the mayor and aldermen to dine on Lord Mayor's Day.[57] On the 25th, attended by court officers, nobles and gentry, and the City companies, the queen was conducted to the Guildhall, being greeted as she processed 'with loud acclamations of the people and as great demonstrations of joy as have been known in the memory of man upon the like occasion'.[58] In 1708 the entertainment for the newly installed mayor Sir Charles Duncombe, as well as celebrating her 'Praetor' lauded England's 'Augusta' and 'Great ANNA's Reign'.[59] Still, in early eighteenth-century England civic ritual hymned sacred monarchy.

The most obvious ritual statement of sacred monarchy, of course, had been the ceremony of touching to cure the king's evil, which had survived the regicide, becoming even more popular at the Restoration.[60] After the 1688 Revolution, Jacobites denied that a usurper had inherited the mystical power of healing, while for his part William III discountenanced it, going so far as to advise petitioners that they had better seek out the Pretender![61] On this matter, as others, Augustan England was torn not only between Williamites and Jacobites but between believers in such mystical powers and sceptics. 'Where ANNA's *Physician*,' wrote one panegyrist on the union in 1708, 'who can doubt the *Cure*?'[62] On the other hand, a surgeon, Thomas Fern, the next year argued forcefully that the royal touch had no curative efficacy for scrofula: 'several persons have never been the better for being touched nor ever received any greater benefit by this means than the gold that was given them'.[63] It was, he asserted, medicines that cured them. Because he was promoting his own miraculous potions for profit, Fern had a vested interest in his case. However, that he expected to persuade punters that scrofula was a physician's rather than a sovereign's business indicates that some – though by no means all – had come to doubt the royal thaumaturgical power.[64] Evidently Queen Anne was not one of them. She resumed the practice abandoned in England for fifteen years and in 1704 resolved 'to touch as many poor people as I can before hot weather comes'.[65] And there was clearly pent-up demand. 'Several thousands of people' came to London 'out of the country waiting for her healing' and the Lord Almoner was forced to turn many away.[66] Ever ready to seek popularity and to connect with her people, Anne regularly touched. The numbers were such that tickets were issued and notices posted in the *Gazette*, informing the sick when to come to court, continued to the end of the reign.[67] The historian of Augustan ritual estimates that between one and two hundred sufferers were touched twice weekly during the court season, meaning that scores of thousands of largely ordinary subjects came into Anne's presence for this purpose alone.[68] At the ceremonies of healing, Anne (as had been traditional) presented those touched with a 'touch piece', which figured on the reverse St Michael slaying the dragon – a familiar image of the triumph of Christian virtue over evil – with the legend 'To God alone the Glory'. The religious significance of the occasion clearly meant much to the queen, who fasted before the ceremonies and prepared herself spiritually.[69] As well as a re-assumption of Stuart custom and power, the ceremonies of healing were another powerful performance of the Supreme Headship and, of course, a concrete manifestation of the care of England's nursing mother for all, especially her afflicted, subjects. Modernist histories and prejudices should not lead us to discount its importance. Dr Johnson famously recalled the solemnity of the occasion when he was touched and cherished his touch piece which is now in the British Museum.[70] The evidence that others preserved and handed down these tokens, along with the large numbers who sought to be cured, suggests that this (last) vestige of the numinosity of monarchy still had currency.[71] Though, like William III, King George I suspended the practice, he continued to be importuned by those who continued to believe in this royal power.[72] Well into the eighteenth century, we find evidence of popular belief in the power of the royal touch and touch pieces and memorabilia.[73] Rather than the mass of their subjects, it was the Hanoverians themselves, perhaps because they were not descended of the royal blood, who ended the practice – and with it surrendered much of the mystical power of early modern monarchy.

III

From at least the reign of Henry VIII, the showcase of majesty – of the magnificence and splendour of monarchy – had been the court. Over the course of the sixteenth century, the court had increasingly drawn nobles and gentry from the provinces to what became the centre of patronage and power as well as of display. For all his very different style, Charles II had seen the importance of reviving the court at the Restoration and re-established court ritual and social life as the manifestations – and supports – of restored kingship. In 1660, Charles II's court was large and still a vital potential source of patronage and power as well as prestige: the centre of fashion and influence.[74] It was, however, Charles II's reign that also saw the decline of the court as financial exigencies forced economies and political crisis narrowed the circle of attenders. James II, as we have seen, initiated stringent savings and cuts, reducing the size – and hence influence – of his household, while his policies alienated many Protestant courtiers and his puritanism deterred the pleasure-seekers of his brother's entourage.[75] 'If the royal state began to sink under Charles II and James II, it was to decline even more rapidly under William and Mary.'[76] This was not primarily due to financial hardship: their household was larger than their predecessor's. It was more a consequence of the promotion of a new sober courtier class, Whigs as well as foreigners, and of the dour personality of the king which was only partially enlivened by that of his wife.[77] The court of William, whatever the king's desire for political independence, was the court of a party more than the nation. The destruction of Whitehall in the fire of 1698 symbolized – as well as exacerbated – the decline of the early modern court as the social, cultural and political centre of the realm.

There was the prospect of a revival under Queen Anne. English and a Stuart, she was more than willing to bring back some of the old political families.

Anne removed William's Dutch retainers and some of the extreme Whigs and republicans and brought in her old servants as princess; but, leaving about half of her predecessor's appointees in their places, she signalled her intention to constitute her court as she would have liked her kingdom to be: not a party but a 'family' (a term often used at the time to describe the court) presided over by a maternal queen.[78] Moreover, Anne announced that she attributed importance to the court as a representation of monarchy. In her first speech to parliament of March 1702, while promising in a time of war to 'straighten myself in my own expenses', the queen asserted her determination to have 'a just regard to the support of the honour and dignity of the crown'.[79] Early commentators certainly did not anticipate the further decline in the court that was to be the legacy of Anne's reign. In his description of England, published in 1703, Guy Miege described 'the present Queen's court'. Having listed the 500 dishes and 86 tables of the pre-civil war court, Miege acknowledged the 'truth' that 'our court ever since is fallen much short of what it has been formerly both in the greatness of the household and the prodigious plenty it lived in'.[80] 'However,' he continued, 'it makes still a very good figure, such as exceeds most courts of Europe'; and to demonstrate that, he outlined all the principal departments and officers, functional and ceremonial, that constituted the court.[81] Reporting on the celebration of the queen's first birthday since her accession, on 6 February 1703, the annalist Abel Boyer noted that 'it was remarked that there had not been such a magnificent appearance at court for twenty years past'.[82] Together with Nahum Tate's description of 'ANNA's exemplary Court' that he expected would 'Cherish all', the prospect in 1703 must have seemed to be that of the revival of the royal court as a centre of majesty.[83]

It was not to be. Contemporaries did continue to praise Anne's court, on a number of counts: in his 1707 poem *The British Court*, Joseph Browne expresses his appreciation of the beautiful women and 'charming throng' who attended on the queen.[84] But rather than the gaiety, it was the sobriety and piety of the court that drew admirers. 'The bold licentiousness of former courts,' the preacher John Evans lauded in his 1706 thanksgiving sermon, 'is remarkably discountenanced by the royal precept and example.'[85] Her court, the historian William Cockburn agreed in 1710, 'is adorned with virtue and sanctified with piety', and had a great and beneficial influence on the nation.[86] Like a good frugal housewife, Anne was also praised for her hatred of luxury. Cockburn thought it laudable that in wartime she had abridged her household and curtailed expenses at court, while a panegyric oration of 1707 expressed admiration for a parsimonious mistress who by 'a prudent dispensation of her reserve' had maintained order, decorum and elegance in her household, and kept up the honour and dignity of the crown.[87]

Anne did indeed turn her attention to administrative reform and the elimination of waste and corruption. She prohibited the sale of offices and reduced perquisites.[88] But, faced with a Civil List revenue that yielded less than had been anticipated, the queen was forced to make substantial cuts in the household, leaving her with a court smaller than that of any except her father.[89] Shortage of money compromised administrative reform, left salaries unpaid and reduced the court as a centre of patronage; but it was not Anne's only problem, or failing. Whatever her hopes, she failed to preside over a court or country that was not divided by party. Some party advocates clearly dismissed her intentions, arguing that 'Two Parties should not in one Court abide'.[90] After 1710, Anne herself purged some of the Whig office holders and, at many points in her reign, Whigs and Tories virtually boycotted the court and even 'did their best to spoil its various ceremonial and social activities'.[91]

Nor, it must be said, was Anne herself best suited to reconstituting the court as the centre of entertainment, fashion and social life. While less dour and puritanical than her Dutch predecessor, Anne was shy, deeply pious (in ways that many of the aristocratic *beau monde* were not) and – most important – ill for most of her reign. Temperament and ill health did not preclude all gaiety and entertainment. At court, as well as her daily attendance at chapel, which was a social as well as religious ritual, Anne held thrice-weekly public drawing rooms at which, at least according to Jonathan Swift, attended 'all her ministers, foreigners and persons of quality', for the conduct of business and politics as well as the pursuit of pleasure.[92] In addition, during the early years of her reign when Anne kept court during the summer at Windsor, there were fortnightly balls held for the 'beaus & belles' who requested them.[93] As we have seen, the queen's birthdays were celebrated by odes, musical and dramatic entertainments, as were Prince George's birthday, New Year's Day, the anniversary of the queen's succession and other special occasions, such as Union Day, when a concert and dance were staged to commemorate the union of England and Scotland.[94] On occasions, planned entertainments were abandoned; doubtless many more were spoiled by the queen's indisposition.[95] With the death of Prince George in October 1708, however, Anne withdrew from virtually all festivities and entertainments, both out of respect and on account of the large blow the loss of her husband inflicted on her emotional health. After 1708 it seems that plans for twice-weekly summer courts at Windsor were aborted and for the next two years there were at best low-key celebrations of the queen's birthday and New Year's Day, no odes or entertainments being reported. From the time of her birthday in February 1711, Anne did resume court social life with odes, a concert, a play and a ball.[96] Thenceforth she celebrated her birthdays until the end of her reign and in September 1711 revived 'cards and dancing' at her court at Windsor.[97] But what may always have been something of an effort for Anne – we recall it was the beaus and belles who had requested a ball – did not secure what she intended.

After Boyer's early report of a greater appearance at court in 1703 than had been seen since the reign of Charles II, contemporaries rather remarked a falling off of attendants at court. The author of *Occasional Thoughts Concerning Our Present Divisions* noted how, under William III, Anne with the Prince of Denmark 'happy in each others company, had delighted themselves with a sort of retirement, their court not being so crowded with those in authority', and may (since he said nothing otherwise) have thought the same of her court as queen.[98] Certainly there were now many rival attractions to a royal court that was downsizing and where, for much of the reign, the queen was not disposed to gaiety. As the royal household was cut back, those aspiring to place or pension would have looked to an expanding wartime administration as much as to the court itself. And as the key to influence and patronage increasingly lay with party managers and brokers rather than dedicated courtiers, aspirants for place doubtless spent less time at court meeting, manoeuvring and networking. Political change, that is, exacerbated, as it reflected, the decline of court life. With less going on, nobles, gentry and clients stayed away; the more they stayed away, the less important the court became. Where the Tudors had endeavoured to create a court that would outshine the greatest noble household, by Anne's reign other households and venues were attracting the political classes. A 1709 poem on the victory at Oudenarde described Blenheim Palace, the greatest architectural statement of the reign, as 'this Rural Court' and described Marlborough's 'palace' in traditionally regal terms, and as a place 'of State, of Politicks, of Peace and War'.[99] While, in the shires, the courts of the nobility had always been centres of social life and influence, Blenheim seemed to stand, more than a ruined Whitehall, for the nation.[100] In the metropolis too there were (relatively) new centres of influence as well as entertainment, and of politicking as well as partying. By Anne's reign, clubs and coffee houses had taken on distinct political, indeed party identities and had begun to ape some of the characteristics of a court: the Whig Kit Kat Club had forty-eight of its members painted by Kneller, artist to the court. In the words of the leading historian of the Augustan court, 'political clubs, the Kit-Cat in particular, operated like small kingless courts' where plots were laid and patronage was dispensed.[101] Significantly, Swift made a similar comparison between the court and a coffee house. In his *Journal to Stella*, in March 1712, in a significant ordering of spaces, Swift told her 'The Court serves me for a Coffee house, once a week I meet acquaintances there'.[102] Though he obviously still regarded the court as a centre of gossip and sociability, Swift's comparison is startling in its implication that the court is now but one place of resort and by no means his only source of news or entertainment. The political reality was that frequent parliaments and parties had shifted influence and power from the court to parties and politicians who gathered to socialize and intrigue in a London which provided innumerable venues – theatres and taverns as well as clubs and coffee houses – that in their sheer entertainment value rivalled a sober court. The court that had once been the centre of national life was now but one of several spheres of influence and no longer the place where the ruling class congregated and was 'overawed with majesty'.[103]

On the occasion of the queen's birthday in 1711 when once again the court was full, Edward Harley reported how 'the common people are very much pleased that so much respect is shown to the queen'.[104] From her accession to the end of her reign, through speeches, addresses and birthday entertainments, Anne remained very popular with her common subjects, who were less embroiled in party politicking than the elites. In representing herself as their mother, Anne self-consciously emulated Queen Elizabeth's careful cultivation of her ordinary subjects. What she did not copy was a principal means by which her predecessor had represented herself to a public beyond the metropolis: the progresses through the counties and towns of England in which, as well as lodging at noble households, the queen and court were on display to the nation, their passage with hundreds of carts drawing spectators in large numbers. Royal progresses had declined since the early seventeenth century and still more since the reign of Charles II. James II belatedly planned an extensive tour of his realm in 1687, to promote his Indulgence; William III undertook only one, following his triumph at Namur in 1695.

Anne's accession looked to revive the progresses of a monarch who, unlike her predecessor, was not going to spend long absences fighting abroad and who enjoyed immediate popularity as English and a legitimate successor to her father. On 18 August 1702, Lord Godolphin informed Robert Harley that the queen had resolved to go on progress to Bath and that he was expecting to spend a month there.[105] The royal train in fact set out on the 26th from Windsor, to visit, as was traditional on earlier royal progresses, Oxford University.[106] As she approached the city, the vice-chancellor and dons rode out to receive the queen 'with the greatest splendour'.[107] Having welcomed her with a speech, they escorted her to her 'court' or lodgings at Christ Church, Henry VIII's foundation on land taken from Wolsey. During supper, Mr Finch praised Anne who had allayed the people's fears and who, he predicted, would lead England to triumphs.[108] On her conduct to and from the Sheldonian Theatre, where she was entertained with vocal and instrumental music, 'great numbers of persons of all . . . ages, degrees and qualities crowd[ed] from all parts of that famous university and parts adjacent to behold her majesty's royal person'.[109] The next morning, having been presented with the gifts dear to her of a Bible and prayer book, the queen and Prince George left Oxford, escorted by the Lord Lieutenant and leading gentlemen of the county. Having rested at Gloucester and Cirencester, Anne entered Bath at 8 o'clock, accompanied by a 'splendid train' of citizens in their finery, two hundred virgins – some dressed as Amazons as a compliment to a warrior queen – and dancers.[110] At the city's west gate, the mayor and corporation welcomed her with music, and along streets illuminated by 'a great number of flambeaux' or torches, which were also carried each side of her coach, she was led to her lodgings. All along the way, bells rang and crowds from the city and surrounding country joyfully shouted 'long live Queen Anne'.[111]

While she sojourned in Bath, Anne touched to cure the evil and gave charitable gifts to the poor.[112] Even longer than Godolphin had predicted, the royal party remained for six weeks. During her stay, Anne also made a visit to neighbouring Bristol. On 3 September the queen and prince 'with the whole court', coming towards the port, were met by a large number of citizens and two hundred ships' captains who conducted the royal party to the city gates.[113] Thence the mayor and aldermen led the royal train along Old Market, where scaffolds and balconies on both sides were full of joyful spectators. At St Nicholas Gate a triumphal arch had been erected and cannon were fired from ships on the quay. Having knighted the mayor and invited the aldermen, councillors and eminent citizens to kiss her hand, Anne returned on the evening of 6 September, to spend a further month taking the waters in Bath. On 8 October, after the traditional gift, attended by the mayor, aldermen and Common Councillors, Anne was escorted to the city boundaries, thence by the sheriff to the border of Somerset. As they travelled over the Wiltshire Downs, the party was met by 'a great number of shepherds', playing country songs and music on reed pipes and by a group of spinners with their wheels, both symbols of pastoral simplicity and loyalty.[114] Anne rewarded them all, giving the shepherds 30 guineas which they (understandably) received with 'loud and repeated prayers and acclamations for her majesty's long life'.[115] En route home, at Marlborough, a group of scholars from the school in shepherd's garb presented the queen with verses that flattered her 'great family', after which the mayor and aldermen entertained her in the town hall before she retired for the night to the Duke of Somerset's house. Having left Marlborough under 'a canopy of garlands', Anne and George were welcomed back into London on the 13th, as preparations were made for a formal reception with pageants.[116]

On this progress, Boyer reports that everywhere the queen met with 'the greatest popular demonstration of joy', and expressions of loyalty and affection.[117] For her part, Anne reciprocated with grace and manifested that 'tender and motherly regard ... for her subjects' that she often spoke of.[118] For when she learned that several citizens had been temporarily evicted from their lodgings to accommodate the royal party, the queen declared that 'she and the prince came there only to enjoy the common benefit of the waters and not to hinder anybody from the same privilege', and that she had not wanted to turn any out of their homes.[119] The progress was clearly a great success and, in a return to Elizabethan practice, an account of it, with the queen's speech to the university and all the poems offered to her, was published for sale.[120] As an Oxford verse reminded her:

When haughty Monarchs their proud state expose,
And Majesty an awful Greatness shows
Their Subjects, Madam with amazement seized,
Gaze at the Pomp, rather surprised than pleas'd.
But your more gentle Influence imparts
Wonder at once, and Pleasure to our Hearts.
Where e'yre you come Joy shines in ev'ry Face.[121]

One might have expected – and many hoped – that a progress which revived Tudor pageantry and cemented Anne's popularity would have been repeated, perhaps especially during long campaigns when subjects were being asked for high taxes and when the queen's presence appeared to moderate the divisions of party. It seems almost certain that Anne herself, having experienced the love of her subjects, intended further progresses, but no other was undertaken. In 1703, for example, the MP Narcissus Luttrell reported in his *Brief Historical Relation* that 'the queen designs for Newmarket in Easter week, to see the horses racing', only to note a few days later that, while the nobles were heading off, 'her majesty and the prince will not be there, as once intended'.[122] Evidently, as it was to do often, ill-health prevented an always sickly Anne from making the journey. It may have been for that reason it was reported in June that 'her majesty and the prince design for the Bath in August', intending to stay again for six weeks.[123] After some uncertainty about the progress, the queen and prince made it in late August.[124] The *Gazette* for 19 August ran a brief report of the queen's reception into the city which was again attended by 'vast numbers of people'; but our sense is that, on account of Anne's health (sedans were prepared to carry her), this may have been a lower-key event.[125] Thereafter a whole series of planned progresses – health visits to Bath in May, a journey to Winchester in September 1704 – was cancelled.[126] In April of the next year the queen was well enough to plan a visit to Newmarket for the racing and to Cambridge, to make the compliment she had paid to Oxford in her first year.[127] When she duly arrived at Newmarket on the 10th, 'all the nobility and gentry of that and the neighbouring counties came in great numbers' to salute her.[128] The following Monday (the 16th), the queen and prince made a formal entry into Cambridge, having been met a mile outside the town by the mayor, aldermen and corporation. 'Amidst the acclamation of an infinite number of people' and university scholars who shouted 'Vivat regina', the royal party processed through streets strewn with flowers while bells were rung and the conduits flowed with wine.[129] Welcomed by the Duke of Somerset in his capacity as chancellor of the university, she proceeded to the Regent House to confer degrees on nobles and her royal chaplain. At Trinity College (the sister college to Christ Church), Anne knighted the vice-chancellor and others (including Isaac Newton) before receiving three hundred ladies to kiss her hand.[130] The queen dined at Trinity with over two hundred nobles and gentlemen 'with the greatest order and magnificence'.[131] In the afternoon she took in other colleges – St John's, King's (for prayers), Queen's – before returning to Newmarket for sport.

During the summer, Anne made a journey to Winchester with the intention, Luttrell reports, of completing the palace commenced by Charles II.[132] Though she stayed for less time than had been intended, the queen made a formal entry into the city and visited the deanery, where in speeches she was congratulated on her military victories and praised for her piety.[133] Thereafter, most of her progresses were cancelled. She returned to Newmarket in October 1706 and 1707 for days of horse-racing but cancelled her annual trip the next year (probably on account of Prince George's poor health) and evidently entertained no other during the two years she was into mourning.[134] As with her resumption of court entertainments, Anne planned another visit to Bath in the summer of 1711 but was not well enough to travel, and there is no record of any further progresses being decided upon (let alone undertaken) before the end of the reign.

For all her shyness, Anne evidently felt comfortable before her ordinary subjects and, as we saw at Bath, was able to combine majesty with a common touch and to foster the affection for monarchy that had not dimmed with the declining power of the crown. As the historian William Cockburn wrote of her in 1710, she was 'both majestic and pleasant', was accessible and capable of 'conversing familiarly with her subjects'.[135] Such was sufficient perhaps to ensure her popularity, even as one historian claimed, for subjects to regard her as a 'common parent'.[136] However, these occasions, through no fault of her own, were few and far between, and progresses were confined to a restricted corner of her kingdoms. Not seeing her in person, most of Anne's subjects read and heard of her, sometimes in her own words, but more often through media which were increasingly dominated by division and party. One cannot help wondering whether, had Anne been more visible, she might have exercised greater independence, influence (not least on elections) and authority; but such a reflection must be left to the 'what ifs' of history.

IV

Traditionally the image and reputation of an early modern monarch were inseparable from his or her roles as custodian of justice and Supreme Head of the Church. Since the Restoration – or more accurately the Popish Plot – both religion and justice had been as much tied in with the politics of parties and, of course, the 1688 Revolution had raised the most fundamental questions about both the law and the church and the king's responsibilities and rights in connection with each. James II had lost his throne not least on account of what was widely perceived as a miscarriage of justice in the prosecution of the seven bishops; William III (whom many regarded as an unlawful king) found for much of his reign that the processes that should have represented him as the preserver of justice and the laws proved contentious and contested. As in other respects, there appears to have been a sense with Anne's succession that things would be better and that justice might shine again after being tarnished. In 1702, for example, the prominent London bookseller John Dunton, in his *History* of characters of the royal family wrote of the new queen Anne: 'As for her Justice (the third perfection of a good monarch), if we enter her courts of judicature, there shall we behold Justice with her sword and balance, equally dividing and impartially weighing out the rewards of virtue and punishments of vice; poverty never excluding the innocent, nor power absolving the guilty.'[137] Her justice, he added, 'is blind' (impartial) to all offenders. Other than Anne's speech of 11 March, in which she recommended justice to her MPs, it is not clear on what evidence in these early months of the reign Dunton based his praise.[138] But his was not a lone voice. In 1704, Elkanah Settle figured Astraea, goddess of Justice, returned to England from exile and now

> By ANNE rais'd higher yet, it safely stands,
> Deckt with new Gemms, new Luster, from Her Hands.
> To fix for ever her unshaken Throne[139]

Congreve was one of many other panegyrists who singled out this royal virtue. In his pindaric ode offered to the queen in 1706, he wrote:

> For now is come the promis'd Hour,
> When Justice shall have Pow'r;
> Justice to Earth restor'd!
> Again Astraea reigns!
> ANNA Her equal scale maintains[140]

Looking back over the years in his 1710 *Essay* on the reign of Queen Anne, the historian William Cockburn, observing that under her 'Justice is dispensed with an equal and impartial hand' and none were oppressed, was certain that it was her exercise of justice that gained 'the esteem and reverence of her subjects'.[141] In a realm in which the administration of justice, as the preacher Henry Coleman put it, was 'of the most tender and important concern', Anne was represented as another Elizabeth, as Astraea herself, as a just ruler.[142]

And the reality was that, apart from the infamous trial of Dr Henry Sacheverell (to which we will return), there were no major judicial causes célèbres or show trials in Anne's reign, no party witch hunts or highly contentious treason trials of the sort that had sullied her predecessors' reputations as just monarchs. That is not to say there were no trials that involved the queen. In 1704 one Scotsman, David Lindsay, was tried for returning from France (an enemy realm) without the licence of the Privy Council.[143] Lindsay admitted to the facts but pleaded not guilty on the ground that he had presented himself to the government in Scotland and so claimed the indemnity the queen had offered in her proclamation of March. The prosecution argued that a pardon in Scotland did not discharge a crime committed in England and Lindsay was found guilty by the jury and sentenced to death. There is no evidence, however, that the trial attracted public interest. What did draw some attention was the trial of Thomas Green and the crew of the *Worcester* who were tried in Scotland and condemned to death for piracy.[144] With the evidence uncertain (testimony was given by unreliable 'blacks', or Indians), Queen Anne herself ordered the postponement of his execution. The case became embroiled in Anglo-Scottish politics, with nationalists proclaiming Green's innocence; and papers were published pro and con, along with Green's own last speech protesting his innocence and accusing the government of denying him a proper legal defence.[145] It was said there were eighty thousand armed men at the execution at Leith and, according to Defoe, 'these things left a corroded mass of ill blood in the minds of people on either side'.[146] If so, the ill blood spread more in Scotland than England and there is no clear evidence that the proceedings tainted Anne's reputation.

Closer to home and Anne herself was the case of William Gregg. Gregg was employed by Robert Harley, one of Anne's Secretaries of State, in 1704.[147] Sent to Scotland by his patron to report on the parliament there, Gregg instead opened a treasonous correspondence with a French minister of war, and forwarded him government papers. Detected, Gregg was tried and executed for treason in April 1708. He denied 'any zeal for the Pretender', whom he disowned, but admitted his crimes which he said, probably truthfully, were motivated by money.[148] Enemies of Harley, however, especially the Whig Sunderland tried to implicate the minister and there was talk of a possible attainder.[149] But Gregg categorically refused to incriminate Harley who, he asserted, had not been privy to his correspondence with France, and asked forgiveness of the queen. Despite his careless office organization exposed by the case, Harley survived impeachment; what might have been a damaging public party clash over royal justice was avoided – not least by Gregg's guilty plea; and public opinion condemned Gregg rather than the queen's minister. Though the *Observator* and other Whig organs did try to use the case to tar the Tories with Jacobitism, Gregg's execution aroused no major public controversy, leaving the reputation of royal justice intact.[150] It was as 'Astraea' that Anne was remembered on her death.

No early modern monarchs so identified themselves and their rule with the Church of England as Charles I and Queen Anne. As princess, Anne had shown her devotion to the Anglican faith and rites and had, not least for that reason, deserted her Catholic father in 1688. From even before her accession, the bishops and clergy looked to Anne to be what the Dutch Calvinist William III had not been: a champion of the church, an active Supreme Head who would restore and preserve it. In one of her earliest speeches to parliament, only weeks after her succession, Anne, while announcing that she would honour the Act of Toleration, declared 'my own principles must always keep me entirely firm to the interests and religion of the Church of England and will incline me to countenance those who have the truest zeal to support it'.[151] In November the archbishops and bishops assembled in Convocation addressed the queen, thanking God for her and her resolution to protect the church.[152] As they anticipated the renewal of the old partnership of mitre and crown, they promised to do all to sustain her government and, they told her, half in praise, half in admonishment, 'we are encouraged to promise ourselves that whatever may be wanting to restore our church to its due rights and privileges, your Majesty will have the glory of doing it'.[153] Anne responded, assuring them of her endeavours to preserve the doctrine and discipline, rights and privileges of the church, and exhorting them to union which she believed was essential to it.[154] In her first months on the throne, then, Anne represented herself as an Anglican queen who regarded the church as inseparable from the state and her majesty.

Even, however, as she so represented herself, Anne's desire to stand as a champion of the church and of religious unity was an unrealistic ideal. The experience of Charles II's reign had shown that an alliance between the Church of England and the crown could not accommodate a policy of toleration and so could not, as it once (at least in some measure) had, unite the people. It is significant that in their address to Anne praising her speech to parliament, the bishops in Convocation made no reference to the queen's promise to maintain toleration – a promise she repeated in her speech to parliament in February the next year.[155] The reality was that the bishops and clergy were divided, but that there were many who did not believe toleration was compatible with the 'rights and privileges' of the church and who were hoping Anne would reverse, or at least reduce, the protection nonconformists had been given. Already in 1702, the figure who was more than any other to divide the church and nation was expressing doubts about royal policy. The then fellow of Magdalen College Oxford, Dr Henry Sacheverell, that year published, along with *The Character of a Low Churchman*, *The Political Union*, a discourse on the interdependence of religion and government, in which he denounced the 'confused swarm of sectarists' who threatened both.[156] He was not an isolated figure. The author of *The Case of the Church of England*, defending every ceremony and liturgy, insisted that dissenters needed to obey; William Baron denounced all separatists as seditious; and Thomas Bennet condemned them as 'arrant schismatics'.[157] There were, of course, more moderate voices: on thanksgiving day

1703, Richard Fiddes preached on the desirability of mutual peace and charity, albeit on the church's terms; and Bishop Hoadly argued for persuading rather than persecuting nonconformists.[158] But the divisions could not be denied and were compounded by the identification of high and low churchmen respectively with Tories and Whigs. As Daniel Defoe wrote in his aptly titled *A Challenge of Peace*, 'we should not have a tenth part of the differences in state affairs did not church matters and state matters mingle so much together'.[159] Anne's representation as ruler and Supreme Head was premised on an integration of church and crown that would foster unity. In fact, the divisions over religion exacerbated party differences (and vice versa), frustrating the image of queenship as well as her desired ends.

Indeed, both party and religious differences were escalated by the high church and Tory campaign to end occasional conformity, by which dissenters who made token appearances at Anglican communion were qualified for office and place. In the polemical exchanges of a bitter pamphlet war, as well as manoeuvres in both houses of parliament, Tories and Whigs fought to promote and block bills against occasional conformity.[160] In the preface to his tract on *Peace at Home*, Sir Humphrey Mackworth told Queen Anne that her policy of preserving the church and tolerating dissenters could only work if the latter were not allowed into office. Toleration, he added, was one thing; an entrée into places for which a qualification was adherence to the Anglican church was another.[161] On the opposite side, the Whig champion Bishop Burnet, the leader of the opposition to the bills against occasional conformity in the Lords, argued that those who promoted the measures were enemies to the queen's very position and title.[162] Nor did the collapse of the bill (in the Lords) end the controversy. In a sermon preached at the Hertford assizes in August 1704 (the perhaps appropriately named) John Savage denounced occasional conformity as 'but the mental reservation of a Jesuit' and asserted that with such toleration 'a deluge of atheism and profaneness, of faction and sedition has flown in', perverting the state as well as the church.[163] This, Defoe opined, was the fundamental issue that divided the parties; 'our soldiers fight abroad,' he not inaccurately put it, 'our Priests at home'.[164]

The religious party wars over occasional conformity did not, however, entirely swamp Anne's ideal or image as both preserver of the church and charitable to dissenters. For one, some of her royal chaplains endeavoured to support and promote her injunctions to brotherly love and charity among all her subjects. At St Paul's, on the thanksgiving day, Richard Willis, preaching on Isaiah 11: 13–14, urged that Ephraim and Judah should join in worshipping God together; bringing his lesson to his own times, he insisted 'neither side must vex or oppress the other' and praised his sovereign 'who loves Judah, is against vexing Ephraim, and is zealous and hearty against the Philistines'.[165] In the wake of England's decisive victory over the French, other clergy supported

Anne's plea for charity and unity. In a sermon preached on Anne's anniversary day in 1705 and published as *The Queen a Nursing Mother*, Richard Stephens, rector of Stock Gaylard in Dorset, told his auditors (in notably gendered language) they had a queen 'who takes the church like a darling favourite into her closest embraces, and throws the arms of her clemency round the necks of her dissenting children'.[166] The church, he assured them, had nothing to fear under an English queen who, unlike her predecessor, had been 'nourished up in her bosom': 'the head of the Church is now the head of the Church indeed'.[167]

While the divisions did not go away, for some years after the failure of the bills against occasional conformity, there was a measure of quiet in the church and at least some approximation to Queen Anne's ideal. In 1707 the pseudonymous author Philometrius published on the title page of his *The Country Vicar's Address To Her Majesty*, a Latin epigraph announcing that violent conflict had ceased and moderate courses were flourishing.[168] The dedicatory preface to this treatise that pleaded for moderation and argued that most desired it praised the queen as 'The world's Moderate Governess', who had resisted the calls of extremists while defending the church.[169] In a sermon preached at Bishop Stortford the next year, John Waller (a fellow of Corpus Christi Cambridge), echoing what Anne herself had expressed, conjoined *Religion and Loyalty* and described a church and queen which and who 'sought to be inseparable in our affections'.[170] If such celebrations of moderation and harmony were the view of the typical provincial vicar or congregation in 1708, they were soon to be shattered by events that not only undermined royal policy but split the nation as well as the church.

Henry Sacheverell had, ever since his 1702 *Character of a Low Church-Man*, preached controversial sermons attacking dissenters but had mainly confined himself to addresses to the dons of high-Tory Oxford. In 1709, however, he secured a chaplaincy in Southwark and on 5 November delivered at St Paul's a sermon which railed against nonconformists. Entitled *The Perils of False Brethren Both in Church and State*, the address departed in every way from moderation and harmony.[171] Using language such as 'mongrels' about noncon-formists, Sacheverell reopened old divisions by comparing dissenters to those who had perpetrated the Powder Plot and the regicide.[172] Talk from such men of 'moderation', he declaimed, was but 'canting [a word used of the civil war sects] expressions'; and he argued that toleration should never be extended to fanatics intent on destroying the church.[173] Even more divisively, Sacheverell reopened an issue that under Anne had lain dormant: that of the powers of and obedience due to the crown. Charting, as had Royalist polemicists, a puritan conspiracy against the monarchy since the days of Elizabeth I, Sacheverell – in terms that revived a recent bitter controversy – characterized nonconformists 'as much occasional loyalists to the state as they are occasional conformists to the church'.[174] The church, he repeated a familiar conceit, and the state sustained each other; but, radically in 1709, he asserted that both rested on the doctrine of unconditional obedience to the supreme governor, on the illegality of any resistance to either monarch or bishop. Because they did not subscribe to such principles, nonconformists could not be tolerated. For, he closed, not only had they published 'treasonable reflections' on the queen, they had impugned her right to the throne and sought 'to make her a creature of their own power', claiming that she owed her crown to them.[175] In a sermon which may have had a publication run of 100,000 copies, Sacheverell reopened and salted the wounds of division that had caused, and were the legacy of, 1649 and 1688. When the Whig government impeached him, all these rents were made worse by party and tainted the government and even the queen.

As literally many hundreds of polemical pamphlets and scores of thousands of pages argued pro and con, the trial of Sacheverell proceeded.[176] Found guilty but given the mild sentence of a ban on preaching for three years, Sacheverell emerged as something of a popular hero, multitudes gathering everywhere as he undertook what was virtually a triumphant progress from London to Shropshire. The rich story of the Sacheverell affair cannot be our subject here.[177] What concerns us is how the 'disputes and controversies' he engendered, which one preacher feared would last 'to the end of the world', damaged the church and Queen Anne's image as head of a church that might include all her subjects.[178] Anne may even have tried to play a double game; while she supported her Whig ministry's impeachment of Sacheverell, she almost certainly exerted some influence to ensure that he was not severely punished.[179] Though on religious issues more a (moderate) Tory than a Whig, Anne still most of all desired quiet. In her speech of 5 April, she told her MPs that she regretted, without itemizing them, the revival of 'questions and disputes of a very high nature' which threatened, along with division, her supremacy and rule.[180]

The 'great controversy', the public clamour which Sacheverell excited, did not quickly die down.[181] Both high and low churchmen claimed the real victory – and the queen's support. However, in his sermon to the lower House of Convocation on 8 March 1711, just a year after Sacheverell's impeachment, the proctor of Canterbury, Ralph Blomer, praising Anne for restoring the decayed spirit of Christianity, reminded them how much it mattered to the queen that 'breaches' in that 'common Christianity' and in the church be repaired.[182] In her letter to the Archbishop of Canterbury that August, Queen Anne, exercising her supremacy, and passing over the controversies, called for attention to morality, discipline and charity in the church.[183] Others supported her quest for accommodation. In 1711 the moderate nonconformist John Humfrey proposed the *Seasonable Suggestion* that anyone who owned the creed and swore fidelity to the queen 'is to be held for a member of that church whereof she is head'.[184] For all the reopening of the fundamental issues and divisions of 1688, the clergy supported the Hanoverian succession and so, in that, also Anne's desire.[185]

In his 1713 sermon on the anniversary of the queen's succession, Nathaniel Hough, remarking that Anne had had no children who had survived, observed that 'her Majesty seems to have translated that care and affection wholly upon the Church of England'.[186] Whatever the bitter controversy and divisions generated by the debates over occasional uniformity or Sacheverell, Anne's image as nursing mother of the church survived. In part this was due to her own intense personal piety which rose above doctrinal disputes. The queen was famously devout, and sought to promote devotion and morality and to discountenance profanity, as she encouraged the observation of fasts. 'If all her subjects were like the queen,' John Dunton wrote in 1708, 'we then should have a kingdom of saints.'[187] Anne continued William and Mary's drive to counter atheism and profanity, but as an Anglican queen did so by personal example and as leader of a national church to which she was devoted. Not since Charles I had the Church of England had such a sovereign so identified with the Anglican faith and church.

Nor since Charles I had any ruler done so much to sustain the church and clergy. Anne was well known for her personal charity. In 1704, however, she made the extraordinary gesture (as we saw) of sacrificing – for the first time since the Henrician Reformation – the royal revenues from first fruits and tenths and granting them to the church for the augmentation of the maintenance of the poorer clergy. Her reign also saw a new wave of church building, especially during the Tory administration. Anne delivered speeches to parliament encouraging the practice, and in 1711 Harley (now Earl of Oxford) was praised for legislation aimed at building fifty new churches in London, which, though it did not reach its target, did add what became known as Queen Anne churches to the landscape and religious life of the capital.[188]

In his 1713 sermon on the queen's anniversary, Nathaniel Hough preached on the coronation text from Isaiah: 'Kings shall be thy Nursing Fathers and their Queens thy Nursing Mothers'.[189] Hough began by recalling the nursing father of the church, Charles I, before proceeding to its new mother, Queen Anne, whose tender regard and moderation had set an example for all to follow if they would.[190] Hough itemized Anne's laws and proclamations regarding the church, her bounty and her appointments, as well as her personal piety.[191] Considering all, Hough did not doubt that not only his own generation but their children's children would 'call her with the same reason and experience, with the same duty and loyalty, with the same gratitude and great affection that we do, the nursing mother of the church'.[192]

V

Second only to her commitment to preserving and strengthening the church, there was one project with which, even more than her ministers, Anne was personally identified: the union of England and Scotland. For the queen this was not an end in itself, desirable though it was to unify the people of her king-doms. As a queen who often invoked Elizabeth I, she was always aware that Scotland rendered England only half an island and vulnerable to invasion from the northern kingdom. More immediately, Scotland presented a potential and serious threat to what Anne was determined to secure: a Protestant, Hanoverian succession. Scotland had shown loyalty to the Stuarts; planned Jacobite inva-sions were encouraged by (not unrealistic) hopes of Scottish support. Most seriously, when Anne died without issue, it was a real possibility that Scotland would reject a Hanoverian successor and recall the Pretender to the throne as James VIII. As the author of a pamphlet on the union and the Hanoverian succession warned in 1704, England's security and welfare 'hang upon the single thread of her Majesty's valuable life'.[193] William III, especially after the death of Anne's son the Duke of Gloucester in 1700, had recommended moves to unite the two kingdoms. But it was Anne who quickened the pace, immedi-ately appointing commissioners from both countries to meet in 1702. The initial moves floundered as the Edinburgh parliament asserted Scottish national independence; but the queen and her ministers persisted and threat-ened the Scots with economic sanctions.[194] Anne made the union a personal matter. In her speech of 6 March to an English parliament in which there was high Tory opposition to the policy, she announced the passing of the Act as having given her 'the greatest satisfaction'.[195] The union, she told MPs, she considered a 'matter of the greatest importance to the wealth, strength and safety of the whole island' and she felt sure that it would be 'spoke of hereafter to the honour of those who have been instrumental in bringing it to a happy conclusion'.

Many contemporaries, and not only panegyrists, were ready to accord that honour to Anne herself. It was Anne who 'passionately' recommended union, the Coffee Master in a pamphlet dialogue agreed with the poet John Dennis.[196] On the passing of the Act, Anne was congratulated in numerous addresses, sermons, panegyrical poems and treatises.[197] 'God has given the queen her heart's desire,' Giles Dent preached in his thanksgiving sermon, 'and enabled her to accomplish this great work, which so many of her predecessors attempted in vain.'[198] It was the queen, Richard Allen told his congregation, who had 'animated' union – not least by her speeches.[199] 'This opportunity hath been wished for these hundred years,' Francis Hutchinson told those assembled in St Edmondsbury, 'and is now happily given us by Providence . . . through the great endeavours of our excellent queen.'[200] It was Anne, John Bates preached at Hackney, who had designed and prosecuted union for 'the common good' and defence: 'Britain will be a brazen wall.'[201] Poets extolled the achievement to even greater heights – 'This union looks so like a Work *Divine*' – but joined the clergy in presenting it as very much the queen's own.[202] Charles Darby and Lewis Theobald, in odes on the union, described it as a 'birth', the now childless

Anne's 'child' and 'Royal Progeny'.[203] 'Heavens commissioned' Anne, Elkanah Settle claimed in his *Carmen irenicum*, or heroic song, as the 'sovereign foundress' of union.[204] Having drawn the scheme for union from heaven, the poet laureate similarly declared, Anne 'Finish'd the Glorious Work that Providence begun'.[205]

It was the union as much as the great victories of English arms on the continent that prompted contemporaries to re-imagine a British empire arising to dominate the world. 'The empire of Great Britain', Richard Enock was sure, 'is safe and happy' under Queen Anne and union; 'British Glory shall immortal be', the anonymous author of *The True-Born Britain* proclaimed.[206] 'Great ANNA' is 'now the Empress of our Isle' and Britain would hold sway in Europe, a broadside poem predicted.[207] Settle celebrated the queen's 'imperial sovereignty', which recalled 'Troynovant' and the union that shall render Britain 'invincible'.[208] As victories reduced France, predictions of British imperial sway appeared anything but fanciful; as Jacobite invasions were repelled, with the Scots remaining loyal, the objective of peaceful Hanoverian succession – a 'sweet calm' – looked closer.[209] In a speech of April 1710, Queen Anne described the union as 'one of the greatest blessings of my reign'.[210] It was not hyperbole: others judged it 'the greatest glory of her reign' – 'a greater glory than either of the two great battles which we glory in'.[211] And more than Blenheim or Ramillies, the glory was hers.

VI

What then of Anne herself? In a personal monarchy, we have observed, the person, and personality, of the ruler were the most important representation of rule. Various developments since the reign of Charles II had made that less true – but by no means untrue. The politics of the reign of William III were shaped by the war, the king's long absences, the emergence of ministries dominated by parties, and a shift in the balance of power from crown to parliament and from the court to the capital; yet it would be wrong to underplay the extent to which those very developments were influenced also by the character and image of first William and Mary, then William alone. The genuine and widespread joy at Anne's succession was not merely the ugly face of English xenophobia (against a Dutchman); from what they knew of her, the people expected to be delighted by their queen, the first queen regnant in a century. Indeed, expectations were very high, perhaps dangerously high if Nicholas Brady's sermon on the death of King William was typical. In overtly gendered language, Brady praised the princess now become queen for being a good wife and mother and for her piety. Perhaps on account of her sex as well as her own willingness (in 1688) to put her country and church before the tie of blood, he felt that under her 'we may hope to experience an amicable composure of those differing opinions which . . . served to rend and divide us into parties and factions'.[212] As well as being descended from a race of kings (being a Stuart), Anne was assessed by Brady as having 'the true art of governing' which lay, he believed, in arguing 'reverence and love'.[213] What Brady hoped was that Anne at thirty-seven (he was optimistic) would give birth to a prince, bred up in her virtues, to succeed her.[214] Other preachers concurred that Anne's ancestry and qualities promised much: Francis Hext looked forward to her 'pulling down French tyranny'; Richard Allen anticipated not merely another Elizabeth but an 'illustrious queen' who 'may lead us (as Joshua did the Israelites) into . . . Canaan'.[215]

The preachers who delivered sermons on William's death sketched some of the qualities of the new queen: her piety, wisdom, magnanimity, frugality and mercy. However, it was the bookseller John Dunton who first published a 'character' of Anne for her new subjects. Dunton sketched the life and character of Anne as princess, highlighting her piety, temperance, modesty and humility, and her virtues as a good wife and housewife.[216] Succession to the crown, Dunton assured readers, had not fostered pride or aloofness in Anne but sharpened her humility and sense of responsibility. She remained plain in her dress, and approachable without being over-familiar; she resolved to promote piety and virtue; she was wise at Council and in government, and dedicated to the welfare of her subjects. Anne, Dunton observed, ruled by example rather than decree: her personal qualities were her mode of government and she valued no prerogative that did not promote virtue and the public good. Under Queen Anne, he reassured readers with unfavourable memories of the last Stuarts, there would be no 'arbitrary proceedings'.[217] While formidable against enemies abroad, at home 'she powerfully reigns in the hearts of her subjects', thanks to 'a steady course of just and gentle government'.[218] Dunton closed his biography by prophesying that Anne would 'render herself truly glorious' and be 'esteemed and honoured'.[219]

Even allowing for the exaggeration of panegyric, Dunton described a queen who did indeed gain a greater reputation with her subjects than she has been accorded by history. Five years after her accession, an *Oration* praised her in terms recognizable from accession panegyrics: as a good woman and submissive wife, as pious, discerning, frugal in her household, yet as victorious over England's enemies and sagacious in government at home.[220] During her reign, none ever charged her with overstretching her prerogative. As we have seen, she was often favourably compared to Elizabeth, some going so far as to suggest that the earlier queen might have learned from Anne the (now even more indispensable) art of 'pleasing' her people.[221]

In one important respect, Anne – and her public representation – differed markedly from Elizabeth. Anne was married and publicized her happy marriage: 'she is the greatest pattern of conjugal love,' Dunton had written of the queen and prince in 1702.[222] George indeed was more than a personal support to the queen. As admiral he involved the throne, in ways that Anne could not, directly in the war and was congratulated on his role in the victory at Vigo.[223] Ill-health and ineptitude prevented George taking the larger role in affairs that Anne always certainly desired for him, yet he at times attended Council, as well as the Lords, and Anne appointed him to head up her cherished commission for Queen Anne's Bounty.[224] Still his most important place in the reign and image of the reign was in highlighting the domestic aspects at a time when the affinities between a good household and kingdom were still often assumed. Anne and George were, observers reported, 'like two turtles, happy only in each other's company'; none could, the poet Charles Johnson averred, 'A more endearing Couple show'.[225] As an ode to the queen on the prince's death described him:

> He half in all thy grand Affairs
> Doubled The Joys and shar'd Thy Cares.[226]

The royal couple had, like – and for the first time since – Charles I and Henrietta Maria, presented to subjects 'the brightest Patterns of Connubial Love'.[227] Anne was literally but half herself for some years after his death, and her subjects were urged 'to soften and mitigate her sorrow'.[228] Prince George helped resolve what were still anxieties about female rule, especially in time of war; Anne's happy marriage shored her up and may have protected her from more intrusive public speculations about her relations with female favourites such as Sarah Churchill and Abigail Masham, who may have been her lovers. A Lutheran with leanings to the Whigs, George also complemented Anne's Anglicanism and inclination to Toryism. A man of 'extensive goodness' (even if not exceptional talent), George himself, it was said, won the affection of the people, as the loving consort of a popular queen.[229]

Charles II, according to Burnet, had memorably said of Prince George that 'he had tried him, drunk and sober, but . . . there was nothing in him'.[230] Like her husband, Anne has been described as colourless and dull. It is something of an irony that Anne so consciously took as her model a Queen Elizabeth who had awed and dazzled her councillors and subjects. Unlike Elizabeth, who until late in life enjoyed vigorous health and energy, poor Anne ascended the throne obese, gout-ridden and scarcely able to walk – broken by seventeen pregnancies in as many years, only five resulting in live births. Within the limitations of her health and character, she endeavoured some revival of a court and ritual monarchy. But, along with her personal disabilities, circumstances had much altered since the reign of Elizabeth, and Anne could not reconstitute a court or monarchy that was a beacon of majesty, the centre of aristocratic social life, and of patronage and influence. Like her female predecessor, however, she did succeed – even in an age when bitterly fought elections divided the people – in securing the affections of the populace and advancing that process by which the monarch came to embody the nations of Britain and a nationalist spirit.[231] Hundreds of (many evidently spontaneous) addresses to Anne attributed to her personally (and expressed gratitude to her for) military victories, the union, the repulsion of Jacobite invasion and the peace.[232] Even in this era of the height of party conflict, Anne in some measure fulfilled her desire to be a *symbol* of the nation, a symbol of unity: if not a queen independent of parties, still herself largely immune from the bitter vitriol of party warfare. For all the political developments that were to make older discourses and practices redundant, in the eyes of her subjects 'She *Reign'd* a *Mother*, and she *Liv'd* a *Queen*'.[233]

CHAPTER 16

PARTY CONTEST AND THE QUEEN

I

The images and representation of the monarch in early modern England had always been appropriated and contested, even when opposition was considered illegitimate or treasonable. For long, attacks on the monarch's 'evil counsellors' enabled opposition, while sustaining the fiction that all were dutifully loyal to the king or queen. Under the early Stuarts, however, that subterfuge was exposed: by rulers who refused to distance themselves from their supposed 'evil counsellors', and by critics who in parliament and in pamphlets did not step back from direct attacks on the king. When those who fought on the parliamentary side in the civil war claimed they were fighting for, not against, the king, they evidenced the prevailing hold of long-held tenets that the king could do no wrong and could not be opposed; but they also graphically demonstrated the reality that sovereignty was not immune from even violent opposition. Though in 1660, almost all were invested in not drawing attention to that reality, indeed were anxious to reconstitute the old order, the political nation – and the king himself – were even more determined that political conflicts should henceforth be resolved without another recourse to civil war. During Charles II's reign, in the crisis of the Popish Plot, opposition to the king was – if not quite legitimized – acknowledged, organized and publicized. The emergence of the Whigs and Tories, albeit their very names expressed a continuing contempt for factions, began to institutionalize and socialize political differences into not armies but parties.[1] Towards the end of his reign, Charles II, for all his reluctance to do so, felt the need to align himself with a party and to depend on its support for the maintenance of his authority.

Because he threatened the interests of both Whigs and Tories, James II had the temporary effect of ameliorating the politics of party: 1688, as they had often painfully to reflect, saw Tories as much as Whigs in opposition to the king. The principles which divided them, however, had not gone away and divisions were bitterly sharpened by the decision to offer the throne to

William III, by the so-called Revolution settlement, and by noisily contesting interpretations of what it was that had – or had not – been settled. While he may have entered England (to pressure James to negotiate) with the Tories' approval, William was regarded as a Whig king. To secure support for his wars, William, as we have seen, endeavoured to court both parties and form administrations that preserved him from dependence on any one party. In consequence he never fully enjoyed the loyalty of either. Moreover, the unprecedentedly long wars of his reign revived old Country opposition and suspicion of executive royal power, now massively enhanced by the patronage of hundreds of new places and by a large army. The party history of William's reign is complicated by 'country' and 'court' factions within both parties, which at times meant William faced opposition from those who might have been expected to be his natural supporters. Overall, however, his reign furthered the legitimation of opposition (not least to a foreign king) and saw parties, whatever their internal dissensions, emerge as an established feature of social and political life.

The events of 1688 and William's wars and reign also changed the political culture of England in ways that influenced how contemporaries thought – and how we must think – about the nature of authority and opposition to his successor. As in William's reign, under Anne different attitudes to the nature and extent of royal sovereignty followed, as notoriously during the Sacheverell trial, party affiliations: the Tories (especially under a queen more sympathetic to them) were more inclined to emphasize unbridled sovereign authority, the Whigs to argue for limited rule. Whatever the differences, however – and perhaps not least because they were the public disagreements of now-established parties – by Anne's succession there appears to have been a move towards far less emphasis on the numinosity, the divine mystery, of regality. In 1704, for example, the poet and playwright Elkanah Settle, who hovered between Whig, Tory and no party allegiance, described royal authority as divine yet granted by subjects: "'Tis thus the bending knees and devoted hearts erect the throne of majesty . . . 'tis from hence the crowned head is installed the anointed and vicegerent of God'.[2] 'The universal vox populi,' he continued, 'is the true vox dei that calls him the rightful successor to the throne.' Many expressed similar sentiments. In his treatise on *Iure Divino*, Daniel Defoe, at the time one of Harley's agents, distanced himself from any 'opinion that kings came down from heaven with crowns upon their heads'.[3] The (partisan) author of *A General View of Our Present Discontents* believed 'the notion of the divine right of monarchy is such an absurdity' as not to warrant contesting.[4] By the end of the reign, a preacher on the thanksgiving day considered the English 'strangers to those impressions of awe and veneration' which had been central to the 'humble deference' to sovereigns.[5] Some, predominantly Whigs, of course applauded these changes, and celebrated what they described as a balanced or moderate constitution, in which the people enjoyed not only freedom but agency. The Whig Bishop Hoadly, for example, spoke of the 'happy balance' of the constitution which preserved the 'greatness of the prince' and the liberty of the subject.[6] Many commentators described the crown as a trust on behalf of the people; Simon Clement praised what he called England's 'regal commonwealth' as the greatest happiness of its people.[7] There were others less inclined to celebrate a balanced constitution: the satirist Joseph Browne, deriding the 'usurping Pow'r of *Liberty*', lamented that many now felt they 'may safely approach the Throne' and warned that, with political changes, 'The Mob are then our Sov'reign Lords that rule'.[8] But whether supporters or detractors, contemporaries appear to have agreed that things had changed.

Indeed, on all sides we detect a new language about monarchy. The author of *Liberty*, who described a kind of bargain – 'this Compact' Settle called it – between the monarch and the people also characterized the relations between ruler and subjects as a 'mutual Friendship'.[9] Henry Lambe, chaplain to the Duke of Marlborough, used the same idiom: Anne, he told his congregation, 'appears at once both Queen, and Friend'.[10] As such language suggests, Anne was more regarded as a person, a woman than a mystical being; and it was her (all too frail) personal body that contemporaries debated, rather than the mystical body politic of the realm. When he visited Kensington Palace in 1707, Sir John Clerk, seeing the queen in extreme agony with gout, reflected 'what are you poor mean like mortal, thought I, who talks in the style of a sovereign'.[11] Clerk kept his thoughts to himself, but others went more public. Defoe felt sure that

> . . . all the people will be happy when,
> They're but content to let their Kings be Men.[12]

Increasingly, it seems, the people were happy to let kings be but men. Even in his panegyric on Anne, John Dunton made clear that he viewed princes as 'men'. 'I look on the Queen,' he announced in print, 'as a mortal woman', adding 'the queen's royal body is no better than . . . a house of moving clay'.[13] Together with those who rejected the royal touch for more 'rational' explanations of curing scrofula, such graphic comments indicate perceptions of Queen Anne as human and frail more than mystical or divine.[14]

It may be that the queen herself contributed to such perceptions. Though she touched to cure the evil and was devoted to ceremonies, Anne – whatever her private beliefs – never promulgated theories of her divine right; nor (in this the opposite of her beloved predecessor Elizabeth) did she cultivate mystery or a sense of awe. Anne's portraits, as we saw, represent her not only as very human but as ordinary and plain, almost bourgeois and domestic. Moreover, while endeavouring to retain some independence from party, she acted as though she fully accepted, and so further legitimated, the constitutional monarchy that had – piecemeal and awkwardly, rather than inevitably – emerged during William's reign. Accordingly by the end of her reign, for all the affection she had engendered in her people, they no longer looked upon the throne with awe. 'The Monarch,' Defoe put it, with only slight exaggeration, 'rules their hearts by their own choice.'[15] Preaching on 7 July 1713, the day of thanksgiving for the peace, William Law bemoaned the fact that men questioned their governors and even argued that authority came from the people. Such, he feared, 'deride the name of majesty and laugh at the empty title of Supreme', which had become but 'pageantry and mock honour'.[16] Law was a non-juror; but his views were echoed by the moderate Philip Bisse, a supporter and client of Harley. In his sermon for 29 May 1711, commemorating the Restoration, Bisse, looking back the half-century to 1660, felt that, despite all that was restored, 'the minds of men have never yet recovered their ancient settlement'.[17] He explained: 'The crown was indeed restored to its outward dignity, the church to its discipline and worship, but when will the dishonourable notions that crept into the thoughts of men during those confusions suffer either of them to recover their ancient reverence.'[18]

Conservative commentators had for long attributed that loss of 'reverence' to a world of unregulated print and publicity. From the Restoration, attempts had been made (as before the civil war) to establish a state licensing of all publications.[19] Never very effective, the licensing system lapsed in 1679; and though the law was reimposed in 1685 and renewed in 1693, the Licensing Act ceased to operate after 1695. This was months after the passing of the Triennial Act of 1694, which mandated that parliament meet annually and that elections be held every three years. In Alan Downie's words, the feverish electoral activity contributed to 'the rise of a virulent political press' and Queen Anne was the first to inherit the legacy of both measures, which were to change fundamentally the political culture and the nature of opposition to the government.[20] Though the legislation regulating the press lapsed, the debate about print and censorship remained heated. During Anne's twelve years on the throne there were more than that number of works whose titles were concerned with 'regulating' or 'restraining' the press, and hundreds more pamphlets and sermons that agonized over the issue. What was obvious to all is how the lapse of licensing had greatly increased the amount – and the distribution and readership – of printed works. In 1703, the non-juring churchman Charles Leslie described how those who sought to denigrate 30 January and the memory of Charles I gave away books or simply left 'inspection copies' at houses, returning to collect the money (or book) later.[21] The next year an author decried 'the multitude of pamphlets that swarmed about the streets and covered the tables of most coffee houses'.[22] It was estimated in 1712 that between thirty and forty thousand books were published on the religious controversy stirred by Sacheverell.[23] And authors of all political sympathies doubtless regretted, along with John How the printer, that news 'and all other sorts of papers are suffered to be pirated and cried about the streets by a parcel of vagabond hawkers'.[24] 'Even those that can neither write not read', another argument for licensing claimed, 'are become authors by carrying some malicious tales to the next office of intelligence'.[25]

Such a broad distribution and unrestrained production of pamphlets were perceived by many contemporary observers as undermining authority, even the monarchy. In 1703 one adviser counselled parliament to outlaw plays (performed and printed) 'because they render the high dignity and office of a king or queen very little and familiar to the crowd'.[26] They 'make the noble dignity of a monarch', he asserted, 'seem a trifle in the eyes of the populace'.[27] An interpreter of Aesop's fables drew from one the 'moral' that

> Unhappy the Nation where Factions are in't,
> And Libels and Lies are encourag'd in Print
> Where each Scribbling – Fool, in a fit of the Spleen,
> Dairs Rail at our States-men, or Tutor the Queen.[28]

The only solution, the author concluded, was to 'put down your Mercuries, Courants, and Reviews'.[29] Throughout the reign, there were frequent laments that sacred authorities and subjects were being 'irreverently' handled and that the most common folk were being tutored by print polemicists to intrude into matters of government.[30] 'Every private person sets up for a judge of matters of state', warned a treatise entitled *An Antidote Against Rebellion*, and 'what begins in folly ends in madness'.[31] A satirist versed the same early warning:

> Drapers and Butchers, Footmen and Physicians,
> With one Concert set up for Politicians:
> Of Things above them impudently prate,
> Censure out *States-Men*, and bely the *State*.[32]

They went so far, he noted, to 'grieve the *Best of Sovereigns* to her Face'.[33] Such concerns only mounted with the vast increase in polemical print in 1710. 'Everyone would tell a Queen what she must do, govern a kingdom, advise a judge, instruct a General,' the preacher Thomas Knaggs regretted in his sermon, as he called on subjects to leave such matters to their rulers.[34] The debates over Sacheverell, however, reopened the very fundamentals of the rights of rulers and subjects, and even in the provinces it was reported that 'the measures of obedience are the present subject of all debates in our country'.[35] Two years later the issue of peace excited a public debate that some still felt 'intruded' into affairs of state and encroached upon 'that great indisputable prerogative' (of making war and peace) of the crown.[36] In his thanksgiving sermon in Cambridgeshire on the conclusion of the Treaty of Utrecht, Law mocked 'the meanest mechanic [who] dares to pretend to be wiser than his governors and censure the proceedings of crowned heads'.[37] Though no such politic-would-be had a qualification in judgement, he lamented, ''tis no purpose to tell them the difference between prince and people, that there is a reverence due for all the royal administrations'. 'For Alas! . . . they have been so long accustomed to be free with the regal power, that they look upon it to be as much their business as to settle their private accounts'.[38]

The problem with print of course was that it was, as it had been since its inception, a medium assiduously used by kings, queens and governments as well as by their critics and defenders. Anne herself benefited from the publication of her speeches; and her ministries and servants, as we have seen, wrote to promote and defend government policies, Harley orchestrating propaganda campaigns from the earliest years of Anne's reign.[39] Accordingly there were voices in Augustan England opposing the restraint of the press that even the queen, in her early proclamation, seemed to wish to reimpose. In outlining in 1704 his *Reasons Against Restraining the Press*, along with arguments against placing a 'padlock' on anyone's lips, Matthew Tindal judged that 'no ministry can be hurt by the liberty of the press, since they have a number of dependents ready upon all occasions to write in justification of their conduct, nay to gild over the worst of their actions'.[40] In 1712 it was a self-proclaimed 'Tory Author' who wrote a treatise defending a free press. Reminding his readers (and historians today) that manuscript libels had caused as much damage as printed squibs, he announced his love of a free press and advised ministers to 'give as good an account of their words and actions as they can' to silence their critics and opponents.[41] In 1712, after all, it was the Whigs who were getting the worse of the press and, as another advocate of freedom put it, though schismatics had expected the press would give them the advantage in religious controversy, 'they are now in a much lower condition' and the church had 'gained . . . considerable advantages by the freedom of the press'.[42] While it was recognized on all sides that the press could misinform and mislead, that only pointed up the need for all to use it to counter misinformation and lies and so to legitimate it.[43] More than any of her predecessors, Queen Anne's successive and different ministries faced the onslaught of a whole cohort of journalistic organs and pamphlets, which made up a new, avowedly political press. That was largely a consequence of the full development, in the wake of the Triennial Act, of parties with organizations, machinery and polemical campaigns geared to winning seats in elections.[44] The press was, in Mark Knights' words, 'intrinsic to partisan politics'.[45]

That very organization, indeed the existence of parties, was in some ways itself an opposition to Queen Anne. The queen, as we have seen, represented herself, especially in speeches from the throne, as desirous of ruling a united country and as a sovereign who hated faction and division.[46] Contemporaries of all persuasions recognized the importance of this to their new sovereign. In 1704 the preface to a treatise on *The Interest of England* recalled her own promise to employ equally all those well affected to her service and her words decrying 'heats and animosities' which she sought to end.[47] The author of *Occasional Thoughts* on the country's divisions not only cited her but foresaw the real possibility that she might succeed: 'by graciously showering down her favours where virtue (not party) recommends', he felt that 'both parties appear ready to serve her . . . and supply her with their purses'.[48] Under the new queen, a late chaplain for William III agreed, 'we may hope to experience an amicable composure of . . . differing opinions'.[49] Such hopes continued to be reiterated throughout the reign, but were not fulfilled. Parties had developed during William III's reign, competed for place and contended over religious and constitutional principles. Anne as a legitimate Stuart successor might have tempered some of the bitter divisions that were the legacy of 1688 but, as much as her predecessor, she was compelled to live with and rule with parties, whatever her preference for independent servants and mixed ministries. During William's reign, as Simon Clement was to reflect, the Whigs had fragmented into Court and Country wings, and in some measure principles had been overtaken by interests, the pursuit of pensions and places.[50] With the people growing more 'indifferent in their affections for parties', and a 'moderate temper' prevailing on the accession of Queen Anne, at first it seemed as though the queen might rule a realm less divided.[51] But party animosities were soon again stirred: by the Tories' attempts to secure a bill against occasional conformity and by attacks on the Whigs and dissenters. Thereafter, issues as well as a competition for places divided the parties, thus compromising Anne's wishes and ideals; and successive ministries both moved to weaken their rivals and immediately created opponents of the (queen's) government they formed.

After their election victory in 1702, the Tories began a campaign to pass a bill against occasional conformity and proceeded to accuse the Whig chancellor, Lord Halifax, of breaches of trust in his office; both moves were defeated in what was a Whig-dominated House of Lords.[52] Having resisted Tory pressure, Anne attempted to form a moderate ministry led by Robert Harley, in the spring of 1704. The summer elections gave the Whigs large gains and made the rival parties roughly equal in the Commons. The queen determined to hold on to a mixed-party ministry but contemporaries had no doubt that, even as the whole nation celebrated the victories at Blenheim and Ramillies, the divisions were as sharp as ever. As the preface to a sermon on Romans 13 put it in 1706, 'in our unhappy state of division whatever side of the question we take we please but one party'.[53] In his satire on Tory *Iure Divino* the same year,

Defoe promised the queen that warring parties unwittingly enhanced her independence:

> The public Struggles of our Party – Powers,
> Break their own Int'rests, and establish yours.[54]

Though not entirely without point, his assessment was over-optimistic, for warring parties and contending ideologies frustrated governments. As a Whig panegyrist on England's victories acknowledged, 'Faction's still as rampant as before' and the parties 'different principles profess'.[55] The Tories opposed the union and criticized the conduct of the war, while the Whigs pressured the queen for more influence in return for their support of the ministry. The passing of the union, Anne's personal project, led some to argue that 'neither of [the] parties have the game in their hands as they have formerly . . . fancied to themselves' and that 'as factious and divided as we are, there is no division or faction againt the queen'.[56] Yet Harley was forced out of office and the Whigs stormed the Commons in 1708 after securing a clear majority at the election.[57] The next year Anne lost the last Tory of her cabinet when Pembroke was removed as First Lord of the Admiralty and the queen, weakened by Prince George's death, surrendered to total Whig dominance. The moderate minorities she had favoured had collapsed; and perhaps the principle of moderation had itself been discredited. In that spirit, a 1708 treatise argued *The Danger of Moderation*. Parties were now, the author observed, a fact of life in the country as well as in the capital: 'the names of Whig and Tory . . . are now so thoroughly known and established that they serve as well as the Tower mark to warrant the value and weight of all the current men in the kingdom, so that every man now passes or is cried down in the country, is received or rejected . . . according as he is tendered under one of these names'.[58] Indeed, Anne was rescued from a complete Whig dominance of her government not by a revival of moderation but by the resurgence of the Tories in the fallout from the trial of Sacheverell. Queen Anne did not escape the party politics or the permanent oppositions to her successive ministries that it involved.

The Whigs and Tories had always been characterized and divided by principles as well as interests or the pursuit of office. Traditionally the Tories stood for the royal prerogative, divine right, the church, the landed interest and a preference for naval over land campaigns; the Whigs for limited monarchy, the liberties of the subject, toleration of dissent, the monied interest and continental campaigns. The events of 1688 had temporarily disrupted such a characterization as the Tories became a party of opposition and country Whigs alike resisted the attempts of William's court Whigs to enhance the executive and build a standing army. As we have seen, Anne's succession soon rekindled the party religious wars over nonconformity, and Defoe and others linked such quarrels to Tory plans to re-establish *iure divino* monarchy, repeal the Act of Settlement and renounce the succession of Hanover.[59] Party polemicists continued to caricature each other – as Jacobites or republicans respectively. However, perhaps on account of the war effort, Anne's silence on matters of her title and authority, and (possibly early in the reign) the indulgence of a hope that she might yet produce a successor, such issues did not come to the fore. Sacheverell drew attention to all those issues and opposed principles, and to the connections between them. In his sermon of 1709, Sacheverell had not only attacked dissenters as enemies of the church, he had compared them to civil war regicides and so branded them as republican enemies of monarchy; he had also reopened the big questions about 1688: whether subjects had the right to resist sovereign monarchy, hence the legitimacy of the Revolution itself.[60] As the thousands of pamphlets prompted by his sermon and trial generated heat, churchmen branded Whigs as commonwealthsmen and Whigs like Hoadly accused the Tories of being Jacobites who sought to lure the people into slavery.[61] In the midst of such clashes, the subtleties of the analysis of *Faults on Both Sides*, which reminded readers that many Tories were pro-Revolution and pro-Hanover, and that the honest on both sides opposed absolutism and republic, were drowned out. The passions and principles of 1688, 1649 and 1642 were all paraded, leading not a few to predict renewed civil conflict. 'We have had now', William Bisset noted in 1710, 'a year of extreme violence and conflict such as cannot be matched without a civil war.'[62] The fallout from the Sacheverell affair shattered Anne's hope of rebuilding a mixed ministry of loyal servants. In 1710 moderation was hard to sustain in an atmosphere of 'Modern Raging Zeal' and the summer elections produced the most decisive of all party victories of Anne's reign to date, making it more difficult for the queen to check vengeful Tory measures or to deny them office.[63] The creation of twelve new Tory peers gave them a majority in the upper house as well as dominance in the lower.[64]

Anne may have been opposed to Tory attacks on Marlborough and Walpole but she, and her minister Harley, were at one with them on a policy of peace. Contrary to Anne's hopes, however, that all would unite behind a peace which would ease the burdens on her subjects, the peace negotiations themselves exacerbated party divisions: Tory advocates accused the Whigs and Dutch of trying to disrupt the peace so as to sustain a war from which they and the monied interest had profited; opponents charged that the Tories pursued dishonourable terms, betrayed the allies, abandoned the principles on which the wars had been fought, and secretly plotted to bring in the Pretender.[65] There were real debates to be had about the timing and terms of peace; but as the author of a treatise on *The Interest of Europe* (an opponent of peace) admitted, any arguments pro and con were 'variously received according to the different interests and inclinations of men and parties'.[66] Queen Anne herself – in this consistent to the end – hoped 'that neither they who envy the making of a good peace, nor who think it their interest to continue the war' would obstruct her endeavours for the good of Britain; and at least one supporter advocated a 'new scheme of government' in which all affairs would be handled by a Privy Council of independents with a non-partisan president.[67] Anne got the peace in Europe she wanted but not the end of party wars – or opposition – at home. Tories attacking Whigs as descendants of republicans appropriated Anne's speech to denounce their enemies while one bold Whig apologist tried to claim Sacheverell for his party![68]

Party divisions dogged Anne's reign to the end. In her last parliament, Whigs and Tories fought again over the union and a commercial treaty with France, and the issue of the succession (though it divided the Tories) became the subject of rumours and accusations.[69] Some again thought that the nation was heading towards civil war. As events turned out, one of Anne's greatest wishes was fulfilled when George I was proclaimed on her death and succeeded peacefully. Yet, though he was supported by Hanoverian Tories as well as the ministry and the Whigs, George's succession did not see a return to moderation: '"moderation" was as dead as Queen Anne'.[70] Eschewing his predecessor's efforts at a mixed ministry, George dismissed her ministers and formed a ministry entirely of Whigs, consigning Tories to decades of opposition. During the early eighteenth century, opposition to the government was valorized and legitimated in the phrase 'loyal opposition'. Anne, who would have been appalled by the development, had attempted to resist the dominance of party, but had enjoyed only brief and partial successes before the personal clashes, ideological differences, organization and orchestrated polemics of parties defeated her ideal of a British people all united under her beneficent rule; and effectively made opposition a permanent feature of politics – and monarchy.

The existence, development and triumph of parties defeated her desire for unity and meant all her ministries dealt with rivals and opponents; but what of opposition to the queen's person? The circumstances of the accession, and events during the reign, of William III had complicated the nature of opposition. Many who had welcomed William's intervention as a means of putting pressure on James II were opposed to his taking the throne. As we saw, the Tories, the natural supporters of prerogative, became a party of opposition. During the course of William's reign, as war expanded the bureaucracy and the patronage of the crown, anti-court Whigs opposed what they saw as a growth in corruption and opposed the king's attempts to build a standing army. Opposition to William was partisan and ideological; but it was also personal and popular. As we have seen, there was widespread xenophobia against a Dutchman who did little to accommodate his style to English ways, and that hostility mounted with the perception that his long and costly wars were fought more for Dutch than English interests. As well as their dislike of a foreigner, many ordinary subjects, not fiercely partisan, doubted William's right to the throne (especially after the death of his wife in 1694). The king suffered direct personal attacks: on his appearance and sexuality as well as his legitimacy and policies; Defoe claimed that even on his death his very ashes were insulted.[71] However, alongside this catalogue of criticism and insult, we must remind ourselves that much of what William wanted to achieve he secured, notably resources for a confederate war against Louis XIV that checked, and was to break, French power in Europe. In exchange for support for his wars and a Protestant Hanoverian succession, William had appeared willing to sacrifice English royal prerogatives and powers, particularly in the Act of Settlement (1701), though its provisos did not come into force until after Anne's death. Should we then take such limitations on the crown, from the Bill of Rights to the Act of Settlement, as opposition? Certainly they were a form of opposition to the monarchy even if the particular monarch, as the price of greater objectives, was willing to accept them. By 1702, as a consequence of political change and personal circumstances, opposition was no straightforward matter, though it is pretty clear that William was not much venerated by his subjects.

Queen Anne, at least on her accession, met with a far more positive reception. That was due both to what she was and to what she was not. Anne was not foreign – and was therefore less likely to be perceived as promoting foreign interests or placing foreigners in the English court and civil service. She was also not a man which, while in traditional patriarchal prejudices placed her at a disadvantage, meant that, unlike William, she was not absent for most of her reign and could therefore stand as the visible symbol of the nation. What Anne was, as we need here yet again to remark, was legitimate and a Stuart. In both regards, she was welcome and popular to a generation that had been traumatized by 1688 and had never quite come to terms with what they had done. As with that of Charles II in 1660, the succession of Anne permitted the indulgence of a fiction that legitimate succession had not been disrupted and may have helped salve many troubled consciences. As a Stuart, Anne's accession may even have helped to atone for what had been done to her father. With more skill than her predecessor, the queen immediately crafted her representation from these very strengths. As we saw, in loud terms she proclaimed her Englishness and descent; she appropriated the tropes and memory of that last emblem of Englishness, Queen Elizabeth; and she spoke of her personal desire for healing and settling. What was also popular with the nation at large was Anne's avowed devotion to the church and her determination as queen to prosecute the war to victory. Anne represented herself as the symbol and hope of England, of a united Britain (she recommended union in her first speech), of triumph after military setbacks and of harmony in church and state. It was this image and this representation which, we have seen, were defeated by old ideological differences that Anne's succession did not end and, in some areas, worsened.

Like William, Queen Anne achieved many goals that were hers as much as her ministers': spectacular victories that checked France, union with Scotland, the creation of a Britain that emerged as the dominant power in Europe, some strengthening of the church, and a Protestant succession. To each, however, there was a powerful current of opposition and, though more popular than her predecessor, criticism did not spare the crown or the queen herself. One strand of the opposition that was not (directly) a facet of party was a Country critique of the court and government.[72] Not least on account of the hardening of parties during her reign, the Country opposition to Anne may have been less marked than that to William. Yet, as Geoffrey Holmes reminds us, in every session of parliament from 1702 to 1714 place bills were proposed to prevent any holding government office from sitting as an MP and to weaken the capacity of the crown to control the House of Commons. Country opposition was also an ideology publicized in print as well as a campaign in parliament. In 1703 the self-styled 'Lover of his Country' published a classic Country treatise in *A Vindication of the Constitution of the English Monarchy, and the Just Rights of the People*. Observing that it was not until the Restoration that MPs were in public employment, the author traced thence the development of a practice that had become an 'epidemical disease'.[73] Asking 'who is able to withstand such a general corruption?', the author praised the new queen for her tender regard for her people but criticized her for not having tackled this canker, 'the nation remaining still in the same bleeding condition it was before her Majesty came to the throne'.[74] Without reform of such abuse, the pamphlet warned, there was little prospect of success abroad.[75] The next year, one Robert Crosfeild (who had been prosecuted the previous year for accusations against the government) made the explicit criticism that since Anne's succession corruption was worse not better and, in a direct insult to the queen's self-representation as parsimonious, reminded readers that Queen Elizabeth, devoted to the public good, had carried on great wars with little money.[76] God had chosen Anne, the author admonished, to restore government to the strength of Elizabeth's days and it was now incumbent upon her to act against peculation by legislating against MPs holding office or pension. 'Sycophantry is the Court disease', a published letter from the country warned; 'And Vertue has few Friends at Court'.[77] As under William, increasingly during Anne's reign the expense of the wars exacerbated criticisms that bloated bureaucrats continued them for their own not the national interest. The 'Man of Honour', a poem reiterated in 1706, was 'a true country man' who sought no 'public places' but loved his queen and nation.[78] As 'Taxes increase', a simple ballad put it in 1711, '*Honesty* do's cease' and 'New offices your money draws'.[79] Through changes of ministry, similar sentiments were echoed throughout the reign. Along with its opposition to peace in 1713, the *Dialogue Between a New Courtier and a Country Gentleman* continued the attack on office-holding MPs and all who sought place or election merely for self.[80] That this, as other pamphlets, was also driven by party agenda underlines the point: a Country critique of the government and queen remained a powerful ideology, at times appropriated by parties but independent of them.

Traditionally, Country opposition had stressed a regard for the liberties and properties of the people and the need for limitations to the power of the monarch. Under Charles II and James II this strand of opposition had been championed by (though never entirely subsumed under) the Whig Party; but after 1688 it was the discourse of Tories, new Country or old Whigs and, as before the civil war, of independents. Too much has been made of the assertion that Anne did not believe in divine right and was more than content to accept her role as a constitutional monarch.[81] Whatever the truth of that – and her resistance to appointing minorities simply according to the outcome of elections questions it – Anne was not spared a discourse that emphasized the need to limit the powers of the crown. Soon after her succession, for instance, a pamphlet asserted that Anne owed her title and crown to the Revolution and to parliament (rather than hereditary right), and argued that monarchs entered into a contract with their subjects which bound them to the laws. Anne, the author repeated, exercised her authority as 'settled by the Convention of Estates'.[82] The publication of an enlarged 1703 edition of the old Whig polemicist Henry Care's *English Liberties*, though polite to the new queen, tutored her in the limits to royal power inscribed in Magna Carta, a horde of statutes and the Petition of Right, as well as parliaments.[83] John Dennis's play, *Liberty Asserted*, similarly praised 'the government of the best of queens' while also warning against any arbitrary power.[84] The limitations to royal authority and the accountability of monarchs were a refrain of Anne's reign, perhaps because it was known that the Tories were keen to re-emphasize divine right, possibly because it was believed in some circles that Anne herself was more sympathetic to this than her biographer has concluded. A popular satire ridiculing *iure divino* as 'the Blockheads' *Plea*' retorted:

. . . Kings, so Jove-like, we could never see,
That they account to none but the Almighty HE.[85]

This, he argued, was a Turkish model unsuited to the England of Queen Anne. Defoe's 1706 satire on *iure divino* monarchy extended to twelve books in which he countered at length what he saw as resurgent efforts to represent sovereignty as sacred and resistance as sinful. While denying that he intended any criticism of the queen, Defoe made plain his view that 'monarchy . . . limited by parliament and dependent upon law' was 'best for this nation'.[86] Against those (high churchmen) who sought to delude her (or 'Press her to Powers *illegal Exercise*'), Defoe instructed the queen that her true authority lay in the love and approbation of her people.[87]

Whatever the queen's reaction to such views, there can be no doubting that she would have regarded rearticulations of the Good Old Cause or of Commonwealth sentiments as an affront. Clergy complained that works by John Toland and other 'republican antimonarchical' treatises circulated, and Edward Ward 'unmasked' the continuing activities of the Calves Head Club which celebrated the regicide and continued to meet throughout Anne's reign.[88] In 1709 the pamphlet *Vox Populi, Vox Dei*, if it did not directly recommend a republic, supported resistance to princes and argued the ultimate sovereignty of the people: 'all government, authority and magistracy proceeds from the people'.[89] Radically inverting old paradigms to assert that preaching absolutism was worse than rebellion, the author claimed that acts of resistance to princes often had God's approval and were a subject's natural right. As rage over the Sacheverell trial raised the stakes along with the temperature, such near-republican apologia were heard more frequently. Accordingly, a 1710 pamphlet on the rights and preroga-tives of kings argued that royal authority had always been conditional and at the will of the people who retained the right to deprive rulers and alter the succes-sion.[90] The next year (or so it was claimed), in a direct affront to 'the best of all Queens', a procession of Kit Kat men and others from St James's Palace to the Royal Exchange was planned in support of the Good Old Cause.[91] Right to the end of the reign we find old Commonwealth ideas reiterated. In what one anony-mous pamphlet described as a reassertion of Whig principles, the execution of Charles I was applauded, Charles II's restoration was presented as against the sovereignty of the people, and Cromwell was praised as a model ruler.[92]

As well as continuing apologia for republics, there were many references to murmur, discontent and criticism of government. Immediately on succeeding to the throne, we recall, Anne had denounced libels against the government; but it is apparent that her prescriptions had little if any effect.[93] Luke Milbourne lamented in a sermon of 1704 that 'we have indeed a sullen generation in these kingdoms', prone to 'grunting discord'.[94] William Elstob similarly decried the 'complaints and murmurings' of those who did not fear 'to arraign our most gracious sovereign herself in the persons of her ministry'; while the author of *King William's Ghost* claimed that 'any country man that is not, perhaps, master of an acre of land, shall undertake you to demonstrate his sovereign off the throne'.[95] Even victories did not quell such discontent. In 1706 a chaplain of the Archbishop of Canterbury, preaching at the assizes in Surrey and taking as his theme 'against speaking evil of princes', identified the 'great evil of a freedom and licence in censuring the persons and administration of princes'.[96] Three years later two preachers contemned the 'monstrous ingratitude' of those who murmured and grumbled even in time of victory or who 'dispar-aged' the administration.[97] 'Too general a sullenness attends our triumphs,' the author of *A General View of Present Discontents* opined in 1710, 'and the nation is misrepresented as labouring under the most dreadful mismanagement'.[98]

While most of these expressions of discontents were vaguely directed against successive ministries, as Elstob had put it, in the person of her ministers, the queen herself was also arraigned. And Anne was directly as well as allusively criticized in pamphlet polemics. The 'Well Wisher to the Peace of Britain' in his 1707 vindication of the ministry noted that 'even the royal authority cannot shelter the queen herself from the virulency of some pens' – though he was coy about specifying the 'odious' aspersions he had in mind.[99] In my (limited) reading of the pamphlet literature, I have not found 'virulent' attacks on the queen. However, as we have seen, Anne was not spared criticism of the continuing corruption that some perceived, and the riot planned (on Queen Elizabeth's anniversary in 1712) against the peace was a direct personal affront to Queen Anne who some also rumoured was dead.[100] The opposition that struck right into the queen's bedchamber was the criticism of her penchant for, and feared dependence on, her favourites, Sarah Churchill and Abigail Masham. There was a long tradition in early modern England of an opposition literature directed against favourites, and rulers who had them; and, as the case of James I reminds us, that opposition was never so virulent as when favouritism was linked to homosexuality. The exact nature of Queen Anne's relations with her favourites remains unclear: Sarah Churchill's biographer describes Anne as 'romantically, but platonically, in love with Sarah', with whom she conducted an intimate and equal correspondence as Mrs Morley and Mrs Freeman; the *ODNB* entry on Abigail Masham describes 'a degree of emotionalism in her relations with the queen'.[101] Whether rightly or not, contemporaries were less coy about the relationships than modern biographers. In a 1708 pamphlet 'dialogue' between Madam de Maintenon (wife of Louis XIV) and Abigail Masham, Masham tells her French counterpart that 'at court I was taken for a more modish lady, was rather addicted to another sort of passion of having too great a regard for my own sex, in so much that few people thought I would ever have married'.[102] To free herself from the aspersion, Masham tells Maintenon she resolved to marry quickly; but the two go on to discuss lesbianism in convents and at court, as well as men. The dialogue was of course fictitious; however, the introduction of lesbian relations into a discussion of Masham's deeply 'Machiavellian' plot to supplant Churchill and dominate the queen evidences a profound contemporary concern about inappropriate influence.[103]

In fact 1708 saw the publication of several treatises on the inappropriate influence of favourites which it is hard not to read as personal criticism of Queen Anne. Two such treatises were concerned directly with the illicit favourite of Elizabeth, the queen to whom Anne so often compared herself. *The Perfect Picture of a Favourite* was subtitled 'Secret Memoirs of Robert Dudley', that is, of Elizabeth's favourite the Earl of Leicester, with whom it was bruited she had had a love affair and illegitimate offspring.[104] The prefatory epistle was written by

James Drake who, bitter at the rejection of the Occasional Conformity bill, had in 1704 insulted the queen and was later prosecuted for remarks in his *Mercurius Politicus*.[105] In the epistle Drake criticized the excessive influence Dudley had been granted and the dangers of a favourite controlling access to the queen, 'of which', he observed, 'parallel instances might be given from the history and observation of all times and nations'.[106] This invitation to make 'parallels', the common mode of reading histories as coded political commentary, was probably present too in *The Secret History of the Most Renowned Queen Elizabeth and the Earl of Essex*, an account of the 'amours' that promoted Essex above his talents and of a queen strong yet 'too weak to be proof against the impression of love'.[107] Two other works made more explicit and topical reference to female favourites. *the Character of an Ill-Court-Favourite* was, the title page announced, translated out of French (translation was another way of denying and inviting contemporary application) and first published in England in 1681 at the height of the Popish Plot crisis.[108] A critique of the pernicious advice and artifices of favourites, the treatise warned that 'there are she favourites as well as bearded ones' and that 'their passions and enchantments are the stronger' of the two sexes.[109] Finally, *The Picture of a Female Favourite* told briefly in verse the life of a female favourite – again of Queen Elizabeth – who plotted the death of Essex and worked on the queen to bring it about.[110] Anne's favourites were, of course, embroiled in the politics of party and so attracted odium on partisan grounds.

The greatest opposition – indeed direct threat – to Anne came from the Jacobites. Some historians (and some contemporaries) have questioned the assumption behind that sentence and suggested (or feared) that at certain points Queen Anne herself inclined towards the restoration of her half-brother, the son of James II. While there is evidence that Anne and her ministers kept open lines of communication with St Germain, and even held out hopes or offered noncommittal promises of support, it has been persuasively concluded that Anne had no stomach for a Jacobite successor.[111] From the moment she acceded to the throne, Queen Anne avowed her commitment to a Protestant, Hanoverian succession and repeated it on several occasions. Moreover, she vigorously pursued the union and supported the Regency Act to secure and facilitate the succession of Hanover.[112] Admittedly Anne rejected proposals to have her successor reside in England; but this stemmed more from a concern that opposition might coalesce around a rival power base than antipathy to the Hanoverian succession itself.[113] If Anne was not a Jacobite, the Jacobites were her opponents dedicated to preventing what she announced as of central importance to her.

Much of that opposition – and the resources and organization for any planned uprising – came from abroad. As Edward Corp, Evelyn Cruickshanks, Paul Monod, Daniel Szechi, Richard Sharp and others have shown, there was a

concerted campaign of planning and propaganda in France to restore James III
(as he was to them) to the throne, involving not least the production and distribution of engraved portraits of the Pretender and medals, the inscriptions to
which often described him as 'the heir'.[114] That 'images of this kind circulated
widely' and were advertised for sale in England suggests there was an English
market for them and at least an interest in, if not commitment to, the Stuarts in
exile.[115] Indeed, the succession of Queen Anne the year after the death of her
father James II appears to have stimulated that interest. With a Stuart again on
the throne, it was easier to look back more sympathetically to the reign of James,
and a Stuart queen cannot but have led many to reflect on the Pretender, the
heir to James branded as an imposter in 1688. The early years of Anne's reign
saw the publication of several sympathetic accounts of James II. In 1704, for
example, *An Abridgment of the Life of King James II*, based on the papers of the
Jesuit Francis Sanders, was translated into English and published at Maidstone,
for sale at two shillings.[116] Consisting of long quotations from James's own
memoirs, the life described a pious, devout and good king who had schooled
his son in virtue. A Pindaric ode of 1708 described the transubstantiation of
James II to grace and threatened hell to all who usurped a crown or 'lawful king
depose'.[117] Verses on all the Stuarts (though praising William III as a hero)
singled out James as 'a mighty saint', while a poem of 1706 described the 'dove
like innocence' of a king who had risked his life for England and who had truly
loved his people.[118] 'With him', the author claimed, 'the Genius of our Isle withdrew'.[119] As the tract praising William already suggests, not all those accounts
emanated from ardently Jacobite circles; and in 1706 the former radical Whig
Robert Ferguson, in his *History of the Revolution*, depicted James II as a king of
'gentle persuasions', averse to force and genuinely in favour of toleration: 'how
remote it was from his thoughts to injur us in the possession of our religion'.[120]
James, others concurred with hindsight, had been no major threat to the religion or laws of England.[121]

   This painful rehabilitation of the king and father whom Queen Anne had
deserted in 1688 was a form of opposition in itself. It was also part of a move to
present James's son, James Francis Edward, as legitimate and as qualified to be
king and successor. In 1703 there was printed in London and sold for three
pence King James's advice to his son, instructing him to be a tender parent to
his subjects, to establish freedom of conscience for all and 'not to give them any
disturbance in the quiet possession of their estates or religion'.[122] More pointedly, with the unpopularity of William's reign in mind, the advice counselled
the Pretender to avoid wars and keep costly expenses in check and to understand English ways: to be, in other words, the opposite of Dutch William.[123] On
the eve of the planned invasion of Scotland in 1708, there was also a pamphlet
campaign to demonstrate James Francis Edward's legitimacy. The *Apotheosis
Basilike* (an echo back to Charles I) described Mary of Modena, James II's

second queen, as 'true mother of our only son'; and the concern to counter revived arguments of the prince's legitimacy suggests that they were circulating freely.[124] In his sermon of March 1708, for example, published as *The Case of the Pretender Stated*, Joseph Cannell laid out (old) evidence that the birth was forged and damned the Pretender as noxious.[125] The invasion failed; however, in 1710 depositions were published from 1688 attesting to the legitimacy of the prince and it was thought that they might incline the people to 'cast their eyes on that Prince'.[126] The author's suggestion that the depositions were leading the people to think again about the charge of legitimacy is supported by two lengthy retorts to them which went laboriously through all the old points about the queen's belly, her breasts, her lying in, her lactation, besmirched smocks and bloody sheets.[127] The 'evidence' (always open to more than one interpretation) had not changed since 1688; the popular mood and electoral fortunes had.

The Tory landslide that followed the trial of Sacheverell and the Tory riots in London unquestionably raised the spirits and hopes of the Jacobites.[128] It was reported in 1712 that there were plans for a Jacobite Club to be established as a counter to the Calves Head, where boars' heads were to be roasted as an insult to the Dutch.[129] Prospective members, it was said, were looking to peace negotiations with France as an opportunity to bring in the Pretender and even hoping that some in the ministry favoured it.[130] To advance the prospects of a Jacobite succession, the people were being told that James Francis Edward was a man of consummate virtues and ready to convert to Protestantism. Such a conversion, had it been a serious prospect, might indeed have converted more Tories, and many of the people, to a Stuart succession; and with 'the poor credulous multitude ... set a madding', and Jacobite toasts being drunk all over town, some feared *Hannibal at the Gate*, that is, the menace from France on the doorstep.[131] As from 1712, talk of the Pretender as a possible candidate for the succession grew louder, opponents felt the need to make the case against him. Defoe, probably working for Harley, wrote several treatises on the subject, which he regarded as 'the main thing which agitates the minds of men'.[132] Defoe asked in 1713 what the people were asking: what would happen if the queen should die? While he had no doubt that Anne was set on a Hanoverian succession, the fate of that and the union were she to die was, he felt, uncertain. As it was 'evident that the divine hereditary right of the crown is the great article now in debate', Defoe penned moderate and measured consideration of the Hanoverian and Jacobite cases, before concluding for Protestant succession.[133]

The Peace of Utrecht excluded James from France, leading the Pretender to issue a formal protest asserting his right and warning his English subjects that they 'must necessarily become a prey to foreigners'.[134] Despite (or perhaps because of) the treaty, the Electress Sophia of Hanover feared the Tories intended to repeal the Act of Settlement to make way for the Stuart and, with what degree of seriousness remains uncertain, Harley and Bolingbroke urged James to convert to Protestantism.[135] Some MPs, seeing his near presence even after Utrecht as a sign of his planned succession, addressed Queen Anne, asking her to insist that James not be permitted to reside in Lorraine.[136] During the last months of the reign, the atmosphere reached fever pitch as the succession remained uncertain and Anne's health began to fail. Hanoverian supporters republished proofs against the Pretender's legitimacy, mocked his (supposed) Protestantism and declarations, and accused him of desiring absolutist rule.[137] The Pretender, Viscount Barrington argued in his *A Dissuasive from Jacobitism*, was educated in bigotry and tyranny, and would certainly seek revenge against those who had denied him in 1688.[138] Barrington even warned the gentry that their church lands (obtained at the Reformation) might be seized.[139] Clearly he felt he needed to throw every available bit of dirt at the Pretender because, as he put it, 'the increase of Jacobitism ... has spread so much within this last three years among all sorts of people that a stranger should be apt to think that the Elector of Hanover was... the Pretender'.[140] Those 'spreading the Pretender's picture with a load of commendations of his parts and person' were obviously gaining levels of support that made it an open question, right up to Anne's death, as to who would succeed her.[141]

So how great was the Jacobite threat and how near did Jacobites come to overturning Anne's wish for a Protestant succession? More recent scholarship has rightly rejected the condescension of earlier (Whig) historians who dismissed Jacobites as a tiny and hopeless minority flying in the face of history.[142] The numbers of Catholics, though contemporaries claimed they 'swarmed', were small.[143] But there were Jacobites in the government and in parliament who swore allegiance to Queen Anne yet were opposed to a Hanoverian succession; and, though their enemies exaggerated their number for polemical purposes, there were, as well as outright non-jurors, high church clergy who favoured a Stuart succession – if the Pretender was willing to renounce Rome.[144] Not least because he fell out with Hanover, Harley appears to have been willing to support the succession of an Anglican Stuart, though how likely he believed James's conversion to be remains unknown.

The real strength of Jacobitism – and its importance as an opposition to one of Anne's cherished policies – lay in its popular support. Many had been uncomfortable with the eviction of James II; the foreign William III had been very unpopular; and when it came to church and crown, the instincts of the people were usually Tory, as election results confirmed. The costs and burdens of war made them more so. Toryism was not Jacobitism but, as circumstances in the 1690s had shown, it could become so – and Sacheverell recreated those circumstances.[145] Even on the eve of his notorious sermon, in the wake of the failed Jacobite invasion, a preacher had asked: 'Had the late invaders landed, and raised an intestine war, who would have stood neuter, who would have basely complied, and who would have basely confederated with them and fought on their side'; ' 'tis well,' he concluded, 'we know not'.[146] During the Tory and high church riots that swept through London after Sacheverell's trial, Jacobites infiltrated and sought to turn the crowd to support of a Pretender who, they assumed, would (unlike Hanover) protect the church. Jacobites contributed 'significantly' to the Tory landslide of 1710, giving the campaign its 'energy and enthusiasm'; and a caucus (sixteen of the forty-five Scots MPs, for instance) of Jacobites was returned to the Commons.[147] The uncertainties about the succession and popular allegiance were therefore real. The Jacobites had influence in the Tory-dominated parliaments of the rest of the reign and *might* have won more of their Tory friends to St Germain.[148] As it was, Queen Anne died not completely certain that George of Hanover would succeed her.[149]

<h2 style="text-align:center">II</h2>

Queen Anne died on 1 August 1714, aged forty-nine. That very morning, a meeting of the Privy Council, composed of leading Tories and Whigs, sent a message to the Elector of Hanover to embark for England with all speed. 'In the hour of her extremity,' wrote Anne's biographer, 'the queen's subjects were unified as never before during her reign.'[150] Or apparently so.

Immediately and traditionally, sermons and panegyrics praised the queen, often in the very terms in which she had represented herself. Lewis Theobald, for example, gesturing to Anne's self-representation as a second Elizabeth, opened his verse mausoleum to the queen with the words 'Astraea's now/no more'.[151] England, the author of a funeral oration on the death of Anne concurred, had 'more than one Elizabeth'.[152] In death Anne was remembered, as she had represented herself, as a nursing mother of her people: 'she Reign'd a *Mother*,' Theobald preached; a good 'mother', an oration put it, who sorrowed over 'the discord in her family'.[153] Anne was represented at her death as a queen who had cared for her people and ruled with love. She was 'tender', Smith recalled; her people's happiness, another funeral oration put it, was the daily care of a queen who loved her subjects; she had, Nathaniel Marshall told his congregation at Finchley, 'a tender regard to the people's welfare' and would 'live long in the hearts of her people'.[154] Even on her deathbed, an elegy figured her concerned most for her sorrowing people.[155]

Anne was remembered by her contemporaries in death as in life, for her speeches. 'Remember,' a preacher urged, those 'so moving declarations wherein she assured her beloved subjects that their quiet, their happiness, their prosperity, is her only concern.'[156] An elegy on Anne's death lamented that she whose speeches had conveyed such 'princely care and love' was now speechless.[157] Immediately on her death, a collection of all her speeches was published (and sold for 6d) as a memorial of the queen.[158] Mostly, Anne was celebrated for her devotion and piety – again personal qualities to which she had drawn attention in life. She was, a sermon put it, 'a religious honourer of God and his word'; her regular demonstrations of piety in attending thanksgiving services were recalled, her long hours in devotion lauded.[159] Queen Anne, William Reeves preached in his sermon the day after her death, had been conspicuous for works of mercy and charity, for building churches and propagating the gospel: she made, he said, 'our religion lovely at home by her own example'.[160] The queen's bequest, John Rowden concurred, was 'religion in its primitive purity'.[161] Elegists and panegyrists alike explained that from this piety flowed other virtues. 'She was,' a sermon preached in Gloucestershire summed, 'a princess of transcendent virtues.'[162] Theobald listed her mercy and compassion, others her uxoriousness, her parsimony, her justice and respect for laws, and her humility and wisdom that made her what Marshall called a 'Royal Pattern'.[163] 'Her gracious influence,' Reeves wrote in poetic strains, 'descended upon all her subjects like the drops of dew that water the earth.'[164]

As well as a pattern of personal virtues, Anne was also immediately commemorated as a champion of the nation and as a queen who had led her kingdoms towards a glorious future. 'Oh! She was all a Nation could require,' Lewis Theobald's memorial to her stated; 'Anna has been,' a funeral address claimed, 'the most glorious, the most renowned princess that ever heaven bestowed on earth.'[165] Under her, great victories had delivered enslaved nations and Britain had become the arbiter of Europe. During her reign, 'the glory of the British name went further than it ever had before'.[166] In his *Funeral Pindaric Ode*, Joseph Harris wrote of his late queen and his country in apocalyptic language:

Like *Moses*, she had led the Murmuring Crowd
Beneath the Rule of Her most Sacred Wand
. . .
And left 'em Safe, ent'ring the Promis'd Land[167]

This was a land that, he envisaged, could rule the oceans.[168]

Such elegies and eulogies imagined an entire nation united in sad mourning for their lost 'saint' — 'the national loss,' as Rowden described it, 'which we now lament'.[169] The reality was somewhat different. Even in death, Anne did not secure the unity she had so passionately desired; in some cases her memory was (as her authority had been) blatantly used for party purposes. The title of *Britannia's Tears*, a lamentation on the death of Anne, for example, opens with the apparent unity of 'The Nation's Loss . . . writ on ev'ry Cheek'.[170] But the poem proceeds to attack the Whigs whose 'daily Cant was how to Thwart the Throne' and the church and who, it was claimed, sullied her memory:

With Pride, they Vaunt it o're Great ANNA's Hearse,
Lampoon her Reign . . .[171]

The high church clergyman Nathaniel Collier, who compared rulers to gods and argued unconditional obedience, similarly condemned (he hardly needed to name them) the 'barbarous wretches' who dared to 'pursue her to grave and trample upon her ashes'.[172] On the other part, on the eve of what was to be their triumph with the arrival of George I, the Whigs similarly used Anne's death to make party points and settle scores after years of Tory rule. There had been, Elisha Smith told his congregation at Wisbech, a real threat that the Pretender could have been brought in by the last administration and there remained, he believed, too many not attached to Revolution principles.[173] While praising Anne's memory, he contemned ideas of hereditary succession, passive obedience and divine right, which needed to be rejected so as to unite the nation behind King George. Ferdinando Shaw, preaching at Hackney, observed that the only blemish on Anne's reign had been the 'furious clergymen and intriguing ministers' who had supported them – that is, the Tories.[174] Now they were defeated in their design of bringing in the Pretender and fomenting civil war, he also heralded George as the hope of all. A historian, reviewing 'the Life and reign of Queen Anne', exhibited similarly Whiggish sympathies. The glorious wars of her reign, he posited, had not been supported by the Tories; Harley had plotted against the national interest; with his support Sacheverell had created fury and division; 'after the peace', during the Tory dominated ministry, 'there was nothing but quarrels and contentions among the ministers'.[175] The anonymous author did not stop short of criticizing Queen Anne herself: the queen, he feared, while 'having no ill designs herself was easily led by favourites' – the last, Abigail Masham, was a Tory friend of Harley's; and though 'Queen Anne was doubtless a good and well meaning princess . . . [she] had high notions of the church'.[176] It would seem that, despite Edward Gregg's claim, Anne's subjects were not quite as united even in – or over – her death.

III

'Anne. A Dead Queen.' In *1066 and All That*, the chapter on Queen Anne has little to say about her other than that she 'had many favourites (all female)' and 'besides being dead she was extremely kind hearted'.[177] In a throwaway line that (typically of Sellar and Yeatman) is revealing as well as humorous, the entry ends: 'the Whigs being the first to realise that the Queen had been dead all the time chose George I as king'.[178]

Academic history and memory have not been much kinder or paid the queen much attention. Anne has been the subject of far fewer biographies than most monarchs and a fraction of the number of studies of her heroine Queen

Elizabeth – or her next female successor Queen Victoria. The biographies that we have and the general histories of the period tend to narrate her reign as a series of events and campaigns determined and conducted by others. Insofar as they focus on the queen, it is as a weak invalid (which she was), a mother whose children all died and so who failed in her duty to produce an heir, and as a woman dominated by the party leaders or worse by other women on whom she was emotionally dependent. The historical monument to the reign remains G. M. Trevelyan's three-volume history, completed in 1934.[179] Trevelyan's detailed narrative focuses more on events than on Queen Anne, though he does describe her as 'wisest and most triumphant of her race' – albeit a race of Stuarts for whom he had little regard.[180] Written in the 1930s, the titles of Trevelyan's volumes understandably highlighted the great battles (of Blenheim and Ramillies) which England had won. Most of all, Trevelyan's Whig bias leads him to close with an epilogue on the Whig hegemony under the Hanoverians, as if to see Anne as something of a byway in the inexorable path of English history.[181] The year in which Trevelyan completed his massive trilogy, 1934, Sir George Clark published his volume in the *Oxford History of England* as *The Later Stuarts*.[182] Though he attributed great importance to her reign, Clark concluded with a low estimation of the queen. 'Queen Anne was neither a very intelligent nor a commanding woman.'[183] 'Homely' (as we will see, a term often repeated), 'cold and formal', emotional, and with a good speaking voice 'her only personal attraction', Anne was not the person who really mattered in the reign. 'The man of the moment was Marlborough.'[184]

Queen Anne was not the only figure to suffer from the nationalism, chauvinism and misogyny of inter-war and post-war historical writing; but she suffered more than most – and certainly in terms of neglect as well as condescension. From when Trevelyan wrote in the 1930s to 1979, there were only two biographies of Anne published. In 1970, David Bronte Green published a popular biography which was not very complimentary about Anne and which received even less complimentary reviews from historians.[185] Poorly researched, leaning on biased accounts, 'Whig with a vengeance' and lacking in analysis, this 'disappointing' book did not provide the biography that was needed for post-war times.[186] A female popular biographer served her little better. In her *Life and Times of Queen Anne* the amateur historian Gila Curtis described her as 'passive', 'homely', 'small-minded', one whose character, as the introduction put it, 'contrasted with the heroic period to which she gave her name'.[187] And it was this rather disparaging portrait that passed into most student textbooks. In his bestselling Penguin history of *The Stuarts*, J. P. Kenyon trenchantly summed up the last Stuart: 'Queen Anne was the quintessence of ordinariness; she also had more than her fair share of small mindedness, vulgarity and downright meanness'; 'corpulent and prematurely middle aged', 'plain and predatory' with a body 'battered into shapelessness by a . . . succession of pregnancies',

Anne ('ignorant') bowed to the will of others; her death, when it came, was an 'anticlimax'.[188]

Scholarly neglect and condescension were finally reversed with the only serious biography of Anne published to date, Edward Gregg's *Queen Anne*, now in its second edition in the Yale English Monarchs Series.[189] After extensive research in continental as well as English archives, Gregg presented a careful new narrative of the domestic events and foreign policy of the reign. From it emerges a Queen Anne who, albeit unwell and of limited intelligence, could be shrewd and influential, a queen who pursued her own policies and was determined to rule as well as reign, avoiding dependence on party leaders and even favourites. Gregg's Anne, together with Geoffrey Holmes's study of the politics of the reign, restored the queen to the place of a prominent player in the manoeuvres of ministries and parties. This revised character of the queen has in some measure informed the textbooks of the period since 1980. In his spirited Penguin history of the seventeenth century, Mark Kishlansky, though still describing her as 'dull, taciturn', fat, stupid, of 'pillow face [and] bulging watery eyes', credited her with sustaining ministerial coalitions, resisting the dominance of parties and winning popular affection.[190] The relevant volume in the New Oxford History similarly figures her as one not easily 'flattered into a compliance', while concluding that overall she was 'earnestly feted, gently mocked . . . or silently ignored'.[191]

It is the last fate that remains striking. In thirty years, there has been no major new study of Anne, though late seventeenth-century history has undergone rich revisions and controversies. Nor have our own changing circumstances and values, including our own refigured politics (of image and gender, for example) led historians back to her reign. Curiously, neither female nor feminist historians have been drawn to her – Linda Colley described her as 'poor dumpy Queen Anne'; she does not appear in the online Biographies of British Women, though under her initial letter, Anne of Cleves and Anne of Hanover (daughter of George II) do.[192] Today Queen Anne is little known to students of history or to an intelligent lay public that voraciously consumes histories of Tudor consorts and queens. She has not been the subject of a film or TV programme since 1989, when in *Yellowbeard* she was played – as fat, senile and ruled by Sarah Churchill – by a man! Anne appears nowhere on the BBC's list of famous Britons which ranked Elizabeth I as seventh.[193] Unlike her predecessor's, her speeches are never quoted, nor is her image recognized. Popular website biographies dwell on the unattractive: she was so fat she had to be buried in a square coffin; she was 'stout, gouty, short sighted and very small'; she was a 'homely' (again) woman in a milieu of brilliant men; her fondness for booze led to her being nicknamed 'Brandy Nan'; she was described by Churchill, her own intimate, as 'that thing'.[194]

There may be something here of the Hollywood factor. As a woman, Anne is (and was) judged on her appearance and on the traditional feminine virtues – of maternity, not least. She was not attractive, and unlike Elizabeth she had neither the opportunity nor perhaps the inclination to be portrayed in overtly flattering ways or as a timeless mask. Chivalry had passed and the frailties of the royal – and female – body were now public and publicized. Like the Virgin Queen, Anne had some success in representing herself as the metaphorical mother of the nation; but her childlessness, all the more tragic because the consequence of biological failure – 'a series of maternal disappointments' rather than choice – led to great political anxieties, and potentially to civil war.[195] Anne's reign is remembered today for the union of England and Scotland into Great Britain, for the establishment of Britain as a world power, as an age of literary brilliance and refined architecture and decorative taste. The queen herself is remembered for what she did not produce (a living heir) and what she was not – the heir to England's last queen. At the end of her reign, Britain was embarking on a new era. Anne, however, is often described as a 'last of an era' queen: the last sovereign to touch for the king's evil, the final Stuart monarch, the last to rule with mixed ministries, the last to veto an act of parliament.[196]

These contrasts between the spectacular achievements of the reign and the low estimation of the ruler may be unparalleled in our early modern history. The contrasts in part signify a changed political landscape in which the monarch had become less central as actual ruler and symbol of the nation. Yet we should recall how contemporary panegyrists, in hundreds of verses, songs and sermons figured Anne as that symbolic centre, as the effective 'cause' of Britain's victories and aggrandizement. To return to *1066 and All That*, she was not 'dead' during her reign. She became dead – to history and memory – afterwards, as many of the ideals and principles she had stood for were overtaken by a half-century of one-party rule. And, as any modern politicians would instinctively know, she has faded from history and memory, not only as a consequence of events, but on account of her own very limited success in writing, depicting and staging her majesty. One assessment may stand as an elegy on Anne and an epitaph to my study of images of monarchy:

> Poor Queen Anne, her name is not as revered as other Queens of England. She seemed to lack the charisma of Elizabeth I, Mary I [sic], and Victoria . . . and yet in her reign great deeds were done.[197]

EPILOGUE

I

Queen Anne's motto was 'Semper Eadem' – 'Always the same'. It was also Elizabeth I's motto and, as we have seen, Anne (and contemporaries) often invoked Elizabeth and wore an Elizabethan-style dress on the occasion of a speech to parliament. And yet the distance between Elizabeth I and Anne was even greater than the century that separated them. Things in 1702 were very far from being the same as 1603. Elizabeth had had to deal with contending ministers and factions, favourites and recalcitrant parliaments; but she had ruled England as a personal monarch on whose wishes the fortunes of all ulti- mately depended. More importantly from the perspective of this study, Elizabeth had made herself the focus and centre of the imagination of her subjects, as well as her ministers, MPs and foreign ambassadors For all her old age and physical decay, she had continued to weave a magic and certainly retained a sanctity in her person as well as in the monarchy. At the end of the sixteenth century, the divinity of kings was a given and many worshipped Elizabeth as a goddess. Queen Anne did not, apparently did not desire to make such claims, and could not in the same way have made them. She believed that she ruled by God's will; her touching to cure the king's evil suggests she believed in some sacred powers inherent in royalty. But she had put her religion before hereditary succession; she acceded to a monarchy she knew and accepted had changed; and she embraced, if not the full logic of party, what we would call constitutional, parliamentary monarchy, as a development that could not be reversed. As importantly, Anne, for all her gestures to Elizabeth, presented herself as a mortal rather than a goddess. Whatever the extravagant conceits of panegyrical verse lauding her as Pallas or Astraea, Anne's self-presentation was as an all-too-frail human. Her invalidity, gout and pain-wracked body did not help. Others, however, including Elizabeth, had encouraged and enjoyed flat- tering and elevating portrayals that overrode physical imperfections – or had emphasized their mystical body over their personal body. Anne, by contrast, was depicted and represented as what countless historians have described her: 'homely'. Her image radiates nothing of the numinous; she appears, on canvases far removed from the allegorical representations of her female predecessor, as domestic, even bourgeois.[1] And that, outside the (sometimes now arch) conventions of verse panegyric, was how others appear to have seen her – as a 'poor', 'sick' mortal woman as much as a queen.

'Poor dumpy Queen Anne,' wrote Linda Colley, 'has always seemed more of a Brunswick than Britain's last legitimate Stuart sovereign.'[2] Historians of politics describe her reign as advancing the sort of constitutional monarchy of the eighteenth century that would have been unrecognizable and anathema to her Stuart predecessors of the seventeenth century. In truth, like many of her contemporaries, Anne looked backwards as well as forwards. But, as we have seen, the past was itself a complicated and contested legacy. The 1688 Revolution, in which Anne had deserted her Stuart father, had profoundly shaken the still-prevailing (or, rather, reconstructed) ideology of divine-right monarchy and succession. William of Orange had succeeded without a legitimate claim to the throne and had accepted restrictions on his prerogative imposed by a Convention and by parliament. During his reign, to secure resources for war and a Protestant succession, he had surrendered further prerogatives. Less remarked but of no less importance, he had also effected a revolution in the *image and style* of monarchy. Unlike James II who, while pursuing popularity, extolled to the greatest heights the mystery and divinity of kingship, William declined to touch to cure the king's evil and reduced royal ceremonial. Certainly William, and his promoters, invoked providence as a foundation of his right and rule; and his portrayal as a Christian knight appropriated scriptural iconographies of kingship. In his person, however, William did not emphasize the mysteries of majesty nor the mystical body of sovereignty. In 1688, still more by 1702, the image as well as the nature of monarchy had changed, and the changed image, as well as reflecting other changes, enabled and hastened them. When Anne donned Elizabethan dress, it was more about an invocation and appropriation of the last female ruler rather than a reassumption of a style (still less a reality) of majesty. Things had changed beyond the possibility of such a resumption.

In 1660, where the story of this volume began, it is fair to say that no one could have foreseen the changes that had transformed majesty and monarchy by the first decade of the eighteenth century. At the Restoration – a term ubiquitously used by contemporaries – the rhetoric was of a seamless return to the situation before the civil war and regicide. Charles II dated his accession from 1649, and invoked and appropriated the words and images of his father. Along with panegyrists, a nation traumatized by civil conflict, regicide and republic greeted Charles as the father of the commonweal, as the sun in the firmament or pilot of the ship of state, as a sacred successor and king. He performed the role of sacred sovereign by touching to cure more subjects than any predecessor, as well as by patronizing baroque canvases that depicted (and argued for) the sanctity of majesty. Yet, while he inherited his father's concern for ceremonies and proprieties, Charles II was much more informal, accessible and approachable – even to those who encountered him strolling in St James's Park. Nor was this simply a matter of character. Charles's interregnum experience (of flight, hardship and the need to win – not assume – support) had schooled him to a different self-presentation and image. From the Declaration of Breda onwards, Charles courted his people as a man, as well as a divine monarch. While he mystified his kingship in the royal touch or on canvases by Verrio, he publicized his human, masculine body, sporting with mistresses or manning a fire hose on the streets of London. Charles had an elevated sense of his authority, but experience had taught him that it could not just be taken as read. Whether by building a following in the Commons or pursuing popularity in the nation, Charles acted as though he knew that things had changed, that support needed to be constructed; and that a new style, a new image of kingship was requisite for changed times. While skilfully invoking old tropes and conceits yet acknowledging the need for new discourses and modes, Charles II (as sacred king and whoremonger) embodied the ambiguities and contradictions of the Restoration. He seemed to make the (partly fictional) stories the people told themselves – and we recall his own story of hiding in the oak tree – a form of truth that enabled those contradictions to be contained, at least for a time. And when crisis threatened him, in the Popish Plot, though he re-emphasized the sanctity of divine monarchy, Charles made the most pragmatic of moves, the consequence of which was ultimately to effect a bloodless constitutional revolution: he relied on the support of a party, the Tories. In doing so, the king not only made his kingship dependent, conditional on that support; he gave emerging parties a touch of legitimacy that helped remove the taint of 'factionalism' and emboldened them as political agents.

Charles II survived – and indeed had his authority extolled – because he made shrewd calculations about the changed political relations of post-Restoration England and appealed (in every sense of that word) to ordinary people as king and as 'old Rowley', the rake nicknamed after his favourite racing stallion. During the last years of his reign, after facing bitter opposition that led England again to the brink of civil war, Charles was able to enjoy enhanced, even sacred authority not (or not just) because he claimed it but because the people supported the Tories in *granting it to him* – if only because they desired peace and the old order rather than Whig rebellion. During those last years Charles reconstituted his image in line with his experience of recent events but also in accordance with popular expectation and desire. He now represented a more removed majesty, a more sacred kingship, a more mystical royal body.

Just as he had come to depend upon one party, so he renounced the ambiguous self-representation which had been successful in 1660 but had drawn criticism later. He appreciated, that is, more than ever, that royal representations needed in a new sense to represent: now to *reflect popular opinion* as well as represent authority to the people.

Far more than his brother, it was James II who represented and re-embodied the values and image of his father and of pre-civil war monarchy. What one senses at times Charles II performed and only half believed, James wholeheartedly believed and embraced as natural. That is not to say, as some historians have, that James lacked a political sense or skill. As Duke of York he had won the people's affection and been a popular Admiral and Viceroy of Scotland. As his memoirs evidence, he also had, whether one agrees with them or not, a sense of political tactics and was keen to advise his brother that in 1660 the old order had been restored; and the last years of his brother's reign (after the defeat of the Whigs) confirmed him in that belief. Accordingly as king, James adopted a style more akin to that of Charles I (the Charles I of the 1630s rather than the 1640s) than Charles II. He took his divine authority and succession – and this, he felt, was confirmed by his crushing defeat of the challenge by his half-nephew Monmouth – as a given, not as an argument that had to be made. Where Charles II spoke and performed to become and remain king, James felt that he simply *was* a sacred ruler. Far less than when he was Duke of York did he court support – until at least the final moments of his reign, and then later from exile. Like Charles I, James II represented himself as what he was certain he was, whereas Charles II had fashioned his image(s) in order to be what he wanted to be.

That the 1688 Revolution caused such anxiety and that the Stuarts remained popular throughout William's reign cautions us not to dismiss James II's beliefs as outmoded or simply wrong. James may have miscalculated in not fully appreciating the conditional nature of divine right or understanding the semi-fictional narratives and discourses of state, but those half-truths or willed truths continued (as they still often do in advanced polities) to have and exercise authority. Scholars have been deeply divided about whether 1688 brought about fundamental revolution or was largely a palace coup that left the fundamentals of monarchy unaltered. What we need to appreciate is that, as well as reflecting contrary ideological (and party) positions at the time, those two positions could be held by the same people – and were by many Tories, at least initially – leading them to accept the fact and not the full implications of the events of 1688.

Still after the Revolution, the discourse, images and performances that had validated a succession of early modern kings and queens were deployed not just *to* but *by* the people, to sustain a sense of continuity and order. It was hard after 1688, however, not to acknowledge that the fictions which had enabled Restoration were indeed fictions: that revolution was being written, disguised, as continuity. Far more than in 1660, during the 1690s men and women with ideological agendas greater than their loyalty to a foreign prince were willing to lift the veil and expose what had happened: were ready to state, either approvingly or disapprovingly, that things had changed and that the king owed his title and authority to parliament and people, not to divine succession. The rehearsal of such differences was not new in the 1690s. What was new was a king who, unlike Charles II, showed little interest in resisting the exposure of fundamental differences or in battling to defend conceits, about some of which he was himself sceptical. Even less than James II did William represent or embody his people. He remained Dutch; he devoted little time to the perform-ance of majesty; he diminished the court as a focus of the nation; he ceased to touch to cure the king's evil. Just as important as the constitutional changes that his reign witnessed in relations between crown and parliament were the vital cultural changes in the style, representation and perception of monarchy, and what we must term the socio-psychological changes in the affective relation-ships between monarch and subjects. If as Paul Korshin (rightly) argued decades ago, there were profound figurative and typological changes in the seventeenth century, I would suggest that in terms of the figures and typologies of monarchy, the greatest changes came in the reign of the Dutch Calvinist William III.[3] Change, as Korshin warned, does not discount all continuity: many of those who presented and represented William, as we saw, appropri-ated old valorizing languages and tropes *for* him. Yet they were not much deployed or valorized *by* him and as a consequence lost much of the authority they had carried. Even more than the constitution, it was changes in the discourses, portrayals and performances, the images and representations of monarchy, that transformed the institution and the state.

While it is often argued that war brought about the greatest changes, in some measure the long wars for a time concealed these cultural and representational changes. For, though demystified by a king who showed little interest in the numinous, the monarch – especially a warrior prince such as William – was figured as the champion of the realm, indeed head of a new empire. The reality was that war distracted William from the performance of kingship and exacer-bated the party divisions which undermined the traditional tropes of monarchy and began to dominate the public discourse of state.

Queen Anne inherited a monarchy that in *representational* terms, as well as in constitutional authority, was greatly transformed. Like her uncle Charles II, in some ways she spoke and acted as though it were not: as well as invoking Elizabeth, she presented herself as a Stuart, as English and an Anglican, as the mother of a nation not the patron of a party. From the outset, however, Anne accepted the parliamentary limitations to her authority enacted in her prede-cessor's reign. Moreover, she acknowledged – and furthered – the reduced place and importance of the court and monarchy in the lives and imaginations of her subjects. Anne touched to cure the king's evil but probably as much out of duty (and popular demand) as a public proclamation of divine right monarchy. Though popular, she neither exhibited any natural charisma nor endeavoured to acquire it. The most extravagant extollation of her authority and person came not *from* the queen but (as well as from high churchmen) from the many popular addresses presented *to* her by people who, as the Sacheverell affair made evident, still longed for some mysterious authority in state and church. Revealingly, Anne did not even capitalize, as Charles II would surely have done, on the Sacheverell case and its fallout. As well as being displeased with the bitter divisions he had opened, she showed little sympathy with Sacheverell's efforts to free her title from the Act of Settlement, or to take up the (still powerful and popular) memory of the martyr Charles I for a representation of sacred kingship. Anne was popular for what she was and the Stuart past (and perhaps potential future) she embodied as much as for any image of herself (beyond her Englishness) that she publicized. For all the rhetoric of motherhood, she was not a mother; nor as a woman could she, as William had, embody or figure the realm (despite the valiant attempts of poets) as a warrior. As a powerful influence and force in politics, monarchy was very much alive in 1714 as in 1702. But in terms of a powerful *image*, or representation, the monarchy as the affective centre of the nation was – well, if not 'dead', moribund.

II

George I, whose succession Anne had laboured to secure, was welcomed in many of the normal, traditional discourses of panegyric. Efforts were made to represent him as a true English successor, though he was not. So Joseph Harris greeted him as the heir of James I and the Plantagenets; a poem on George's arrival saw in him the revival of 'Third Edward's Son . . . the Black Prince'; and Ralph Erskine congratulated the king on acceding to a throne 'which is by Birth, by Worth, by Law your own'.[4] Several figured George as the successor to William III. However, perhaps recalling the hostility to foreign kingship, poets and panegyrists made efforts to depict George, whose sharing a name with the national saint helped, as all but English. Though in reality he spoke English quite poorly when he arrived, George was described as speaking the language 'pretty readily' as well as being a prince who understood the English constitution and English manners and ways.[5] 'St George our Champion is, and King', a welcome verse proclaimed, and the new king who was, to the relief of subjects, an actual father, was heralded as father of the Protestant family of the realm.[6] George's peaceful accession after the deep uncertainties, divisions and plots over the succession also gave some credibility to the revival of hopes that he could be a true father to *all* his people, to a united nation. Where Anne had been unable to allay the disputes between parties, a poet, claiming that 'No symptom now of discontent is found' and 'all with zeal express their loyalty', predicted that George could heal divisions.[7] 'The name of party is no more heard of,' the author of *The State of the Nation* asserted. John Dennis agreed: James I had united the crowns, Anne the kingdoms, but for George I a 'happier union is reserv'd': 'The Union of Affections and Hearts'.[8] Under such a king, all prophesied as they hoped, that Britain would go on to greater glory: to empire in Europe, over the Indies, over the globe.[9]

Even amid the relief and euphoria of a peaceful succession, supported by leading Tories as well as Whigs, discordant and bitterly partisan voices were heard. The Whig Charles Povey gave a taste of the coup that was to remove all Tories from office when he (perhaps counselling George) argued that 'no nation was ever so much abused . . . as the Britains [*sic*] were by the last managers of the state'.[10] On the other side, the high church Tory satirist Edward Ward scoffed at the 'republican procession' of George's coronation:

Huzza'd by all their factious Brothers,
But pelted, hiss'd, and scoff'd by others[11]

But the prevailing mood in 1714 was of new possibilities for co-operation even if not the removal of all differences: as the preacher Samuel Wright phrased it, 'the reconciling men's tempers to one another while their thoughts are allowed to vary'.[12] One clergyman, in a sermon on the king's accession, tried to help the process of 'reconciling'. Though, he noted, George was placed on the throne by virtue of a parliamentary statute, 'he must be acknowledged to sit there by a divine right'. And 'he is to be owned as one sent of God through the power to be conveyed into his hands by the mediation of men'.[13] It was those who secured the rights of the people and who were chosen by them, the author of *The People's Choice, the Lord's Anointed*, concurred, who had God's approbation.[14] Popular consent was now divine right. Already we are in a new world in which, as the author of *The Kingdom Turned About* put it, 'old things are passing away and all things are becoming new'.[15]

For all the familiar tropes of succession rhetoric, under George I things did become new – or, we should say, changes were accelerated. And not least in the style of monarchy, what changed were the nature of the court and the image and representation of the new dynasty and king.

The first Hanoverian was once caricatured as foreign, philistine and boorish, the German who was found hoeing turnips when news arrived of his succession to the British throne.[16] Virtually unable to speak English, rude, remote and awkward, George was described as deeply unpopular with his new subjects. Recently an excellent study has challenged many of these long-standing stereotypes. Hannah Smith persuasively argued that George I was successfully represented as heir to William III, as a Protestant military leader; and she provided plentiful documentation of loyal support for him in the localities. Yet Smith herself is rightly cautious about a revisionism too far. She concedes that there was little obviously to admire in the person of George, whose recent biographer describes him as 'stiff, withdrawn and . . . sullen'.[17] Most significantly in terms of image, George made almost no impression. Unable to speak English and uncomfortable with ceremony and splendour, he paid little attention to his life at court, which has been described as 'mundane', a place of 'residual tedium'.[18] Frugal and diligent, George showed no interest in commissioning a new royal image or building for the Hanoverian dynasty. 'He spent considerably more in the upkeep of his horses . . . than he did on the theatre, music and payments to writers combined'.[19] Even more than under his predecessor, the focus of aristocratic social life shifted from the court to the metropolis. And though, as Jonathan Clark has demonstrated, there was still a powerful belief in the divinity of kings, George did all he could to undermine it.[20] Not only did he end the touching for the king's evil which Anne had revived, he put a stop to the Maundy services, ceremonies on the Thursday before Easter when the monarch (in imitation of Christ) had washed the feet of selected poor people, and did not even attend the service.[21] George 'firmly spurned the mantle of sacred kingship' – out of distaste for ceremony but also perhaps on account of his interest in Enlightenment philosophy and experimental science which, in seeking explanations for all phenomena, were eroding what had been (and to most still were) mysteries.[22]

Linda Colley has suggested that the appeal of Jacobitism to many in the early eighteenth century lay in the failure of the Hanoverians to fulfil the expectations of subjects in terms of the image and symbolism, the 'magic' of monarchy: 'Jacobitism . . . was at base a far more neutral hunger for a sentimental, highly coloured royalism that the early Hanoverians left unsatisfied'.[23] While there may be something in this, that hunger was no less manifest in the local celebrations of the Hanoverians and the commissioning of loyalist art (including cheap portraits in wax, 'sold all over the town and county') and artefacts (drinking glasses, pottery and the like) that expressed civic and popular support for the dynasty.[24] Whether or not 'the idea of the monarch as "demi-god" had been abandoned' – and Clark's work cautioned against too easily concluding that – there was still among subjects a craving for an affective bond with their ruler, a craving which in their different ways both George III and Queen Victoria sought, and were able, to satisfy.[25]

III

This language of 'sentimentality' and 'affect' returns me to the beginning of the large project, a history of royal representation from Henry VIII, that this volume brings to a close. I have argued that, under the pressure of the crisis of breaking from Rome and preserving his authority, Henry embarked on a campaign to represent (and so constitute) himself as the embodiment of the nation and sacred sovereign. As part of that he sought to form what one of his spin doctors called a 'lovely bond', an affective relationship with subjects. Henry and his successors, most notably Queen Elizabeth, despite criticism and opposition, succeeded in forming affective bonds with their people who by the end of the sixteenth century were avidly purchasing souvenirs of their monarchs. While he was by no means the first to use words, images or display to advertise his authority, Henry VIII, in a new world of print and publicity, founded a representative monarchy: indeed, a monarchy that depended in large measure on its representations for effective rule.[26]

The success or failure of subsequent reigns to a great extent came down to the success or failure of an individual ruler in the arts of representation. James I, so astute at times in political manoeuvre, lacked the kind of charisma or image which Henry and Elizabeth had schooled subjects to expect. Neither James nor Charles I (at least until near death) won the widespread devotion of their people. Undoubtedly, the problems they inherited, of financial difficulty, religious divisions, recalcitrant parliaments and a public culture of libel and contest, made the exercise of rule more difficult. However, Elizabeth had faced some of the same problems without the same consequences; and, as Charles's early and last years on the throne remind us, a fund of loyalty was there to be nurtured by carefully pitched messages and symbols as well as actions. Mounting political divisions made it harder but more necessary for the monarch to present himself as the father, and the body, of the realm. At a key point in his reign, during the 1630s, Charles did not pay sufficient attention to this and allowed others (dramatically Prynne, Burton and Bastwick, later the Scots) to better the king in representing themselves. A developing contest over image was one of the causes of the civil war, but it was yet more a consequence of civil conflict. During the 1640s parliament and king struggled for support and mastery not over (at least not over publicly proclaimed) different ideologies; they contested to claim the same discourses and signs that had validated authority for a century or more.

In 1649, through death, Charles I brilliantly reclaimed such discourses and signs for monarchy. After 1649 successive republican regimes failed either to reappropriate them or to devise new representations that would enable a regime founded on force to acquire legitimacy or popular acceptance. As the myriad circulating mementos of the martyr testified, there remained during the 1650s a powerful affective tie between the people and monarchy, a bond which even the respected Oliver Cromwell was never able to forge.[27] More assiduously than his Stuart predecessors, Charles II sought to renew the bond. To do so, he deployed traditional tropes and conceits, evoking national fervour, invoking his father, appealing to old customs and ceremonies. Yet, fully aware of the profound changes that civil war, regicide and republic had effected, more than any predecessor he courted popularity, by means of easy familiarity, wit, charm and what we might now describe as 'blokeishness' – as everyday masculinity that spoke to the people.[28] Like Henry and Elizabeth, Charles II combined the mystical with the ordinary; in his case, the sacred with the debauched. He did so, I suspect, because he calculated (rightly during the Popish Plot) that a monarch could draw on popular loyalty and affection to sustain and enhance his authority. In 1660 Charles, while never doubting his divine right, had preferred to emphasize his moderation, openness to counsel, and readiness to please. During the 1680s, he permitted the Tories, the church and a willing populace to proclaim his sovereignty in lofty and sacral strains. Charles's so-called absolutist rule in the five years after the Plot rested on popular support. He reconstituted an affective bond with his people not least because he crafted his image and representation with one eye on what the people needed and desired him to be. In fashioning their image, the Tudor rulers (who faced rebellion and riots as the price of religious change) could never afford to ignore their subjects: I have argued that a burgeoning public sphere from the time of the Reformation made them more accountable as well as more public.[29] Civil war and the Commonwealth, however, had educated subjects in the language of their ancient and natural rights, had taught them to be political agents and citizens. Acutely aware of that, Charles ruled, for all the invocation of the past, as a different kind of monarch to his father: he re-established a representational monarchy but one that *drew from* as well as *appealed to* subjects enfranchised by recent experience.

After James II's brief attempt at reviving his father's style of rule, neither William nor Anne made the same effort to make themselves the focus of the cultural and social life of the realm, of the 'social imaginary' of the people.[30] Political historians, especially of a Whig persuasion, might observe that they had no choice. As a consequence of the constitutional changes that accompanied the 1688 Revolution, William's wars, frequent parliaments and elections, and the rise of party, they would say, the conditions for a representational monarchy no longer existed. Or as Habermas observed, the representational monarchy perforce gave way to a fully developed rational public sphere in which ultimately it was voters, not kings, who were represented – and now in both senses. What, however, constitutional history risks losing a sense of is the psychology of subjectivity and citizenship. Hannah Smith's rich evidence of a popular yearning for some of the old 'magic' of kingship, Colley's discussion of a void left by the early Georges, suggest that there was yet still the potential in the eighteenth century to build on Charles II's new reconstruction of the affective relations with his people.

George III (at a time of vulnerability to illness and Revolution) and Queen Victoria (a pattern of domestic family happiness) were to show how royal authority, as well as a royal image, could be fabricated out of subjects' anxieties and hopes. Some of the most brilliant, charismatic leaders of our own times – Reagan and Clinton, Thatcher and Blair – have, through intuiting and subsuming popular concerns and dreams, represented themselves in ways that enabled them to pursue what seemed quite unpopular political courses. More than institutions, party organization or policies, the fortunes of modern politicians depend upon their image, their bond with the electorate, and their capacity to be both authoritative and responsive, removed and familiar. Modern democratic politics in the age of the Internet makes the arts of image and representation different to those prevailing in sixteenth- and seventeenth-century England. I hope, however, to have shown that, as well as important constitutional and political changes, it was the culture of authority and particularly rulers' skills in representing themselves in changing circumstances that determined not only their own fortunes but, at times, the course of history. With the accession of George III, the English were again ready to adopt the new king 'as the beginning of a sacred line'.[31] Far from obstructing the development of the representative state, representational monarchy from the beginning – and still more from 1649 – facilitated the emergence of such a state whose citizens are enfranchised yet still *desire* pleasing words, images and performances from authority: representations.

NOTES

Abbreviations

BL   British Library
BM   British Museum
Bodleian Nich. Newspapers   John Nichols Collection of Newspapers, Bodleian Library, Oxford
ESTC   English Short Title Catalogue
GAC   Government Art Collection
NPG   National Portrait Gallery
Thomason   The Thomason Collection of Civil War Tracts, British Library, London
Wing   Donald G. Wing, *Short-title Catalogue of Books Printed in England, Scotland, Ireland, Wales, and British America, 1641–1700* (2nd edn, 4 vols, 1972–98)
Anthony Wood   Wood Collection, Bodleian Library, Oxford

Preface

1. See, for some of the best examples, T. Harris, *Restoration: Charles II and His Kingdoms, 1660–1685* (London; New York, 2005); T. Harris, *Revolution: The Great Crisis of the British Monarchy, 1685–1725* (London; New York, 2006); A Houston and S. Pincus eds, *A Nation Transformed: England After the Restoration* (Cambridge, 2001); T. Harris, *London Crowds in the Reign of Charles II: Propaganda and Politics from the Restoration until the Exclusion Crisis* (Cambridge, 1987); M. Knights, *Representation and Misrepresentation in Later Stuart Britain: Partisanship and Political Culture* (Oxford, 2004); M. Knights, *Politics and Opinion in Crisis, 1678–1681* (Cambridge, 1994); P. Seaward, *The Cavalier Parliament and the Reconstruction of the Old Regime, 1661–1667* (Cambridge, 1989); P. Lake and S. Pincus eds, *The Politics of the Public Sphere in Early Modern England* (Manchester, 2007).
2. See Anna Keay, *The Magnificent Monarch: Charles II and the Ceremonies of Power* (London, 2008).
3. For example, R. Bucholz, *The Augustan Court: Queen Anne and the Decline of Court Culture* (Stanford, 1993); John Brewer, *The Pleasures of the Imagination: The Emergence of English Culture in the Eighteenth Century* (London, 1997); T. Blanning, *The Culture of Power and the Power of Culture: Old Regime Europe 1660–1789* (Oxford, 2002).
4. For the latter view, see especially Jonathan Scott, *England's Troubles: Seventeenth-Century English Political Instability in European Context* (Cambridge, 2000).
5. See S. Pincus, *1688: The First Modern Revolution* (New Haven, CT, and London, 2009); I am grateful to Steve Pincus for stimulating discussions. T. Blanning, J. Clark et al., 'Round Table: Steven Pincus, *1688: The First Modern Revolution*', *British Scholar*, 2 (2010).
6. See, for example, J. C. D. Clark, *English Society 1688–1832: Ideology, Social Structure and Political Practice during the Ancien Regime* (Cambridge, 1995; 2nd revised edn, 2000); Clark, '1688: Glorious Revolution or Glorious Reaction?' in C. Barfoot and P. Hoftijzer eds, *Fabrics and Fabrications: The Myth and Making of William and Mary* (Amsterdam, 1990), pp. 7–15.

Introduction

1. See K. Sharpe, *Selling the Tudor Monarchy: Authority and Image in Sixteenth-Century England* (New Haven, CT, and London, 2009).
2. See K. Sharpe, *Image Wars: Promoting Kings and Commonwealths in England, 1603–1660* (New Haven, CT, and London, 2010).
3. Ibid., *passim*.
4. *The Form and Order of the Coronation of Charles the II, King of Scotland Together with the Sermon Then Preached by Mr. Robert Dowglas &c, and The Oath Then Taken with Several Speeches Made: As It Was Acted at Scoone, the First Day of January, 1651* (Wing D2030A, 1660), p. 15, and see *passim*; R. Hutton, *Charles the Second* (Oxford, 1989), ch. 4.
5. See, for example, *The King of Scotland's Negotiations at Rome, for Assistance Against the Common-Wealth of England* (Thomason E612/6, 1650); W. C. Abbott ed., *The Writings and Speeches of Oliver Cromwell* (4 vols, Cambridge, MA, 1937–47), IV, pp. 731–2.
6. D. Underdown, *Royalist Conspiracy in England, 1649–1660* (New Haven, CT, 1971); Hutton, *Charles the Second*, ch. 5.
7. A. Bryant ed., *The Letters, Speeches and Declarations of King Charles II* (London, 1935), pp. 33, 65.
8. Ibid., pp. 34, 36. Charles often expressed his 'great hopes', ibid., pp. 42, 44, 45, 46, 66, 78.
9. Ibid., p. 34.
10. Ibid., p. 81.
11. Ibid., p. 71.
12. See F. F. Madan, *A New Bibliography of the Eikon Basilike of King Charles I* (Oxford, 1950), no. 8. See the text in P. Knachel ed., *Eikon Basilike* (Ithaca, NY, 1966), pp. 158–71.
13. *The Declaration and Resolution of His Highnesse the Prince of Wales, Upon the Death of his Royall Father* (C 2956, Edinburgh, 1649).
14. Ibid., p. 1.
15. Ibid.
16. Ibid., p. 4.
17. *A Fountain of Loyal Tears Poured Forth by a Sorrowful Son for the Untimely Death of His Royal Father Being a Form of Prayer to be Used by all Those That Yet Retain a Spark of Religion to God, or Loyalty to Their Prince: Recommended by King Charles the II, to be Used by all His Faithful Subjects Throughout His Dominions* (Wing C3008, Paris, 1649).
18. Ibid., p. 2.
19. Ibid., p. 4
20. Ibid., p. 8.
21. Ibid., p. 14.
22. *A Declaration by the Kings Majesty, to His Subjects of the Kingdoms of Scotland, England, and Ireland* (Wing C2960aA, Edinburgh 1650), p. 1 and *passim*. See also *By the King, Charles by the Grace of God, King of Great Brittain, France and Ireland, Defender of the Faith, to All and Sundry His Lieges and Subjects* (C3638, Edinburgh, 1650).
23. *King Charles II. His Declaration to All His Loving Subjects of the Kingdom of England. Dated from his Court at Breda in Holland, the 4/14 of April 1660* (C2985, 1660), one page.
24. There has been little attention paid to the rhetorics of this famous declaration. In his authoritative recent history, Tim Harris hardly mentions it in his account of the Restoration; Tim Harris, *Restoration: Charles II and His Kingdoms* (London; New York, 2005); cf. Hutton, *Charles the Second*, pp. 129–30.
25. *A Letter from His Majesty to the Speaker of the Commons Assembled in Parliament with His Majesties Declaration Enclosed* (Wing C3096, 1660).
26. Ibid., p. 4.
27. Ibid., p. 5.
28. Ibid., p. 7.
29. J. Milton, *The Readie and Easie Way to Establish a Free Commonwealth and the Excellence Therof Compar'd with the Inconveniences and Dangers of Readmitting Kingship in this Nation* (Wing M2174, 1660).
30. Bryant, *Letters, Speeches and Declarations of King Charles II*, p. 92.
31. Ibid., p. 90.
32. Ibid.
33. See Thomas Blount, *Boscobel, Or, The History of His Sacred Majesties Most Miraculous Preservation After the Battle of Worcester, 3 Sept. 1651* (Wing B3329, 1660), p. 54; and A. M. Broadley ed., *The

Royal Miracle: A Collection of Rare Broadsides (London, 1912), p. 58. Cf. below, ch. 2, pp. 111–14 for the humble clothes Charles wore. It was said that some wept when they saw the king's bedraggled condition.

34. Below, ch. 3, pp. 186–9 & 192–3 and for letters to Lane, Bryant, *Letters, Speeches*, pp. 25, 38.
35. See M. Knights, *Politics and Opinion in Crisis, 1678–81* (Cambridge, 1994); P. Lake and S. Pincus eds, *The Politics of the Public Sphere in Early Modern England* (Manchester, 2007); See below, ch. 4, pp. 202–11.

1 Rewriting Royalty

1. Thomas Forde, *Theatre of Wits Ancient and Modern Attended with Severall Other Ingenious Pieces from the Same Pen* (Wing F1548A, 1661), containing *Fragmenta Poetica or Poetical Diversions With a Panegyrick Upon His Sacrd Majestie's Most Happy Return, on the 29th May 1660*, p. 23.
2. R. Atkyns, *The Original and Growth of Printing Collected Out of History, and the Records of this Kingdome: Wherein Is Also Demonstrated, that Printing Appertaineth to the Prerogative Royal, and Is a Flower of the Crown of England* (Wing A4135, 1660), sig. B1^v.
3. Kevin Sharpe, *Image Wars* (New Haven, CT, and London, 2010), ch.5
4. A. Bryant, *The Letters, Speeches, and Declarations of King Charles II* (1935), pp. xi–xii; Géraud de Cordemoy, *A Philosophicall Discourse Concerning Speech* (C6282, 1668), sig. A2^v.
5. I commenced my study of these (then unstudied) speeches in 2004, but Annabel Patterson has been the first to address them in publication. See A. Patterson, *The Long Parliament of Charles II* (New Haven, CT and London, 2008), ch. 3. Patterson, I think rightly, concludes that Charles wrote most of these speeches. While one must sympathize with her judgement that it may be 'tedious' to close-read each speech in its context, she makes a powerful argument for why we need to do so – 'their every word was taken to be weight bearing' (p. 63) – and so I extend her valuable discussion.
6. *His Majesties Gracious Speech to the House of Peers, the 27th of July, 1660. Concerning the Speedy Passing of the Bill of Indempnity & Oblivion* (C3070, 1660).
7. Ibid., p. 2. The king added that 'I owe my being here to God's blessing upon the intentions and resolutions I then expressed'.
8. Ibid., p. 4.
9. Ibid., p. 5.
10. Ibid.
11. Bryant, *Letters, Speeches, Declarations*, pp. 102–3.
12. Ibid., p. 103.
13. Ibid.
14. *His Majesties Most Gracious Speech, Together with the Lord Chancellors, to the Two Houses of Parliament, on Thursday the 13 of September, 1660* (C3073, 1660), p. 4.
15. Ibid., p. 5.
16. Ibid., pp. 11–15, quotation, p. 12.
17. Ibid., p. 11, my italics.
18. Ibid., p. 18.
19. Ibid., p. 19.
20. *Journal of the House of Lords: volume 11: 1660–1666*, p. 236.
21. Ibid. Clarendon followed the king, underlining the great things they had achieved and the affection Charles felt for his Parliamentarians, ibid., pp. 236–9.
22. *His Majesties Gracious Speech to the Lords and Commons, Together with the Lord Chancellors at the Opening of the Parliament on the 8th day of May, 1661* (C3071, 1661), p. 1.
23. Ibid., p. 2.
24. Ibid.
25. Ibid.
26. Ibid., pp. 5–6.
27. Ibid., p. 6.
28. Ibid., p. 9.
29. Ibid., p. 13.
30. Ibid., pp. 15–17. On Venner's rising, see R. Hutton, *The Restoration: A Political and Religious History of England and Wales* (Oxford, 1985), pp. 150–1; J. Miller, *Charles II* (London, 1991), pp. 70–1.
31. *His Majesties Gracious Speech . . . 8th day of May, 1661*, p. 20.
32. As Annabel Patterson recently argued, it is a parliament that has received surprisingly little attention; see A. Patterson, *The Long Parliament of Charles II* (New Haven, CT, and London, 2008).

33. 8 July 1661, *Journal of the House of Lords, II*, p. 303.
34. 30 July 1661, ibid., pp. 331–2; *His Majesties Gracious Speech to both Houses of Parliament, on Tuesday, July 30. 1661 the Day of their Adjournment* (C0344, 1661).
35. 20 November 1661, ibid., p. 332.
36. Ibid.
37. Ibid., p. 333.
38. To Commons, 10 January 1662, *The History and Proceedings of the House of Commons* (3 vols, 1742), p. 51.
39. Ibid., p. 52.
40. Ibid.
41. Ibid., p. 53.
42. *His Majesties Declaration to All His Loving Subjects, December 26, 1662* (Wing C2988, 1662).
43. *History and Proceedings of the House of Commons, I*, p. 60.
44. Ibid.
45. Ibid., p. 61.
46. Ibid.
47. Ibid.
48. See Charles's letter in Bryant, *Letters, Speeches, Declarations*, p. 142.
49. Speech of 12 June 1663, *History and Proceedings of the Commons, I*, p. 66.
50. Ibid., p. 67.
51. Ibid.
52. Ibid.
53. Bryant, *Letters, Speeches, Declarations*, p. 145; *His Majesties Most Gracious Speech to Both Houses of Parliament at their Prorogation on Monday the Seven and Twentieth of July, 1663* (Wing C3136, 1663).
54. *His Majesties Most Gracious Speech to Both Houses of Parliament, on Monday the One and Twentieth of March, 1663/4* (Wing C3137, 1664), p. 3; *Journal of the House of Lords, II*, p. 478.
55. Ibid., p. 4. See Hutton, *Charles II*, ch. 9.
56. *Speech . . . One and Twentieth of March*, p. 4.
57. Ibid., p. 6.
58. Ibid., pp. 6–7.
59. Ibid., p. 8.
60. Ibid.
61. *His Majesties Gracious Speech to Both Houses of Parliament, on Tuesday April 5. 1664. at the Passing of Two Bills the One Entituled, An Act for the Assembling and Holding of Parliaments Once in Three Years, at the Least, and for the Repeal of an Act Entituled, An Act for the Preventing of Inconveniences Happening by the Long Intermission of Parliament* (Wing C3049, 1664), p. 3.
62. *His Majesties Gracious Speech to Both Houses of Parliament on Thursday, November 24, 1664* (Wing C3051, 1664), pp. 4–5.
63. Ibid., p. 6.
64. Ibid., pp. 6–7.
65. Ibid., p. 7.
66. *His Majesties Gracious Speech to both Houses of Parliament Together with the Lord Chancellor's, Delivered in Christ Church Hall in Oxford, the 10th of October, 1665* (Wing C3052, 1665), p. 2.
67. Ibid., pp. 4–19.
68. Ibid., pp. 9, 15; L. Colley, *Britons: Forging the Nation, 1707–1837* (New Haven, CT, and London, 1992).
69. *His Majesties Gracious Speech . . . the 10th of October, 1665*, p. 16.
70. See below, ch. 2.
71. *His Majestie's Most Gracious Speech to Both Houses of Parliament, the One and Twentieth day of September, 1666* (Wing C3139, 1666), p. 3.
72. Ibid.
73. Ibid., p. 4.
74. *His Majesties Most Gracious Speech to Both houses of Parliament, on Friday the 8th of February, 1666 at their Prorogation* (Wing C3142, 1667), p. 5.
75. N. Smith ed., *Marvell: The Poems of Andrew Marvell* (London, 2003), pp. 360–94.
76. Hutton, *Charles II*, pp. 250–2; C. Roberts, 'The Impeachment of the Earl of Clarendon', *Historical Journal*, 13 (1957), pp. 1–18.
77. *His Majesties Most Gracious Speech to both Houses of Parliament on Monday the 10th of February, 1667* (Wing C3147, 1668). Charles announced his league with the Dutch and efforts to unite Protestants.

78. *His Majesties Most Gracious Speech to Both Houses of Parliament, with the Lord Keepers, on Tuesday, October 19. 1669* (Wing C3148, 1669), p. 1.
79. Ibid., pp. 5–8.
80. *His Majesties Most Gracious Speech to Both Houses of Parliament, with the Lord Keepers, on Monday February 14, 1669/70* (Wing C3151, 1670), p. 4.
81. Ibid.
82. Hutton, *Charles II*, ch. 10.
83. *His Majesties Most Gracious Speech, Together with the Lord Chancellors, to Both Houses of Parliament Delivered at the Opening of the Parliament on Tuesday, February 4. and Wednesday February 5. 1672/3* (Wing C3172, 1673), p. 4.
84. Ibid.
85. Ibid., p. 5.
86. King's answer to address of Commons, 24 February 1673, *Journals of House of Lords*, XII, p. 540. See Harris, *Restoration*, pp. 63–4.
87. *His Majesties Most Gracious Speech to Both Houses of Parliament, Saturday March 8. 1672/3 in Answer to their Humble Petition and Address* (Wing C3153A, 1673), p. 4.
88. *His Majesties Most Gracious Speech, Together with the Lord Chancellors, to Both Houses of Parliament, on Monday, October 27, 1673* (Wing C3177, 1673), p. 4.
89. Bryant, *Letters, Speeches, Declarations*, p. 270.
90. *His Majesties Gracious Speech, Together with the Lord Keepers, to Both Houses of Parliament, January 7. 1673/4: Published by His Majesties Special Command* (Wing C3075, 1674), p. 4.
91. Ibid., pp. 5–6: 'I know you have heard much of my alliance with France, and I believe it hath been very strangely misrepresented to you as if there were certain secret articles of dangerous consequence. . . . I assure you there is no other treaty with France . . . not already printed, which shall not be made known.'
92. For a recent narrative of the Plot, see Harris, *Restoration*, ch. 3; see also J. Miller, *Popery and Politics in England, 1660–1688* (Cambridge, 1973). For a study of government attempts to counter and control accounts and narratives of the Plot, see P. Hinds, 'The Horrid Popish Plot': Roger L'Estrange and the Circulation of Political Discourse in Late Seventeenth-Century London (Oxford, 2010).
93. See M. Knights, *Politics and Public Opinion in Crisis, 1678–1681* (Cambridge, 1994); S. Randall, 'Newspapers and their Publishers during the Popish Plot and Exclusion Crisis', in J. Hinks and C. Armstrong eds, *Book Trade Connections from the Seventeenth to the Twentieth Centuries* (New Castle, Delaware, 2008), pp. 45–70.
94. *His Majesties Gracious Speech, Together with the Lord Keepers, to Both Houses of Parliament, April 13, 1675* (Wing C3078, 1675), p. 3.
95. Ibid., pp. 3–4.
96. Ibid., p. 4.
97. Patterson, *Long Parliament*, p. 83. As Patterson shows, Marvell paid close attention to, and on occasions forwarded to his constituents, royal speeches.
98. On Finch, see *ODNB*; A. Chalmers, *General Biographical Dictionary* (32 vols, 1812–17) XIV, p. 304.
99. *His Majesties Gracious Speech, Together with the Lord Keepers, to Both Houses of Parliament, April 13, 1675*, p. 7.
100. Ibid., p. 9.
101. Ibid., p. 22.
102. D. Ogg, *England in the Reign of Charles II* (2 vols, Oxford, 1956), II, pp. 530–4.
103. Ibid., pp. 535–49.
104. *His Majesties Gracious Speech to Both Houses of Parliament, on Munday the 28th of January, 1677/8* (Wing C3060, 1678), p. 3.
105. Ibid., p. 7.
106. Ogg, *England in the Reign of Charles II*, II, pp. 550–2. See too *His Majesties Gracious Speech, Together with the Lord Chancellors, to both Houses of Parliament, on Thursday the 23d of May, 1678* (Wing C3086, 1678).
107. This speech was evidently not published, *Journals of House of Lords*, XIII, p. 252.
108. Ibid.
109. *His Majesties Most Gracious Speech Together with the Lord Chancellors to Both Houses of Parliament, on Munday the 21st of October, 1678* (Wing C3182, 1678), p. 4. The speech was published by his majesty's special command.
110. Ibid.

111. Ibid., pp. 4–5.
112. Ibid., p. 14 and see pp. 6–16 *passim*.
113. Ibid., p. 19.
114. Ibid., p. 20.
115. *His Majesties Most Gracious Speech to Both Houses of Parliament, on Saturday the 9th of November, 1678* (Wing C3156, 1678), p. 3.
116. Ibid., p. 4.
117. Ibid.
118. Ogg, *England in the Reign of Charles II*, pp. 576–9.
119. Bryant, *Letters, Speeches, Declarations*, p. 305.
120. *His Majesties Most Gracious Speech, Together with the Lord Chancellors, to Both Houses of Parliament, on Thursday the 6th of March, 1678/9* (Wing C3184A, 1679), pp. 3–4.
121. Ibid., p. 5.
122. Ibid., p. 7.
123. Ibid.
124. Ibid., p. 18.
125. Ibid., pp. 5, 17.
126. *His Majesties Most Gracious Speech Together with the Lord Chancellors to Both Houses of Parliament, on Wednesday the 30th of April, 1679* (Wing C3186, 1679).
127. See below (James's memoirs).
128. See below pp. 34–5.
129. Ogg, *England in the Reign of Charles II*, II, pp. 548–606 *passim*. See also *His Majesties most Gracious Speech to Both Houses of Parliament on Wednesday the 15th of December, 1680* (Wing C3159, 1680).
130. *His Majesties Most Gracious Speech to Both Houses of Parliament, at the Opening of the Parliament at Oxford, Monday the 21st of March, 1680/81* (Wing C3162, 1681), p. 3 and *passim*.
131. Bryant, *Letters, Speeches, Declarations*, p. 317.
132. E. Cooke, *Memorabilia, or, The Most Remarkable Passages and Counsels Collected out of the Several Declarations and Speeches That have been made by the King, His L[ord]. Chancellors and Keepers, and the Speakers of the Honourable House of Commons in Parliament since His Majesty's Happy Restauration, Anno 1660 till the End of the Last Parliament, 1680 . . . by Edward Cooke* (Wing C5998, 1681). Patterson, in stating that no collection of Charles's speeches was printed until 1772, appears to pass over this work.
133. Ibid., pp. 1–3.
134. Ibid., p. 3; my italics.
135. Ibid.
136. Ibid.
137. Ibid., Addenda (after p. 108).
138. *His Majesties Declaration Whereas Upon Complaint of the Several Injuries, Affronts and Spoils Done by the East and West-India Companies, and Other the Subjects of the United Provinces* (Wing C2950, 1665).
139. *A Letter from His Majesty to the Speaker of the Commons Assembled in Parliament with His Majesties Declaration Enclosed* (Wing C3096, 1660), p. 3.
140. Ibid. (repaginated for Declaration), p. 1; cf. *King Charles II. His Declaration to All His Loving Subjects of the Kingdome of England. Dated from his Court at Breda in Holland the 4/14 of Aprill 1660. And Read in Parliament, May 1. 1660* (Thomason E.765/11, 1660).
141. *A Letter from His Majesty*, p. 1.
142. Ibid., pp. 1–2.
143. Ibid., p. 2.
144. Ibid., p. 3.
145. Ibid., pp. 1, 2.
146. *His Majesties Declaration to All His Loving Subjects of His Kingdom of England and Dominion of Wales Concerning Ecclesiastical Affairs* (Wing C2997, 1660).
147. Ibid., pp. 5, 7.
148. Ibid., p. 8.
149. Ibid., p. 9.
150. G. W. Bernard, 'The Church of England, c.1529–c.1642', *History*, 75 (1990), pp. 183–206. I am grateful to George Bernard for many stimulating discussions of this essay and subject.
151. Hutton, *Restoration*, pp. 150–1; *His Majesties Declaration to All His Loving Subjects, December 26, 1662* (Wing C2988, 1662).

152. *His Majesties Declaration*, p. 2.
153. Ibid., p. 4.
154. Ibid., p. 5.
155. Ibid.
156. Ibid., p. 6.
157. Ibid., p. 12.
158. *His Majesties Declaration to His City of London, Upon Occasion of the Calamity by the Lamentable Fire* (Wing C3004, 1666), quotation, p. 3.
159. Ibid., p. 10.
160. *His Majesties Declaration. Charles R. His Majesty in His Princely Compassion and Very Tender Care, Taking into Consideration the Distressed Condition of Many His Good Subjects* (Wing C2951, 1666).
161. *His Majesties Declaration to All His Loving Subjects, March 15th 1671/2* (Wing C2990, 1672).
162. For example, ibid., pp. 5–7.
163. *His Majesties Declaration for Enforcing a Late Order Made in Council* (Wing C2965, 1675).
164. See Tim Harris, *London Crowds in the Reign of Charles II: Propaganda and Politics from the Restoration until the Exclusion Crisis* (Cambridge, 1987).
165. *His Majesties Declaration for the Dissolution of His Late Privy-Council, and for Constituting a New One, Made in the Council-Chamber at Whitehall, April the Twentieth, 1679* (Wing C2967, 1679).
166. Ibid., p. 2.
167. Ibid.
168. Ibid., p. 3.
169. Ibid.
170. *His Majesties Declaration to All His Loving Subjects, June the Second, 1680* (Wing C2994, 1680). On Walter see Hutton, *Charles II*, pp. 25–6, 125–6, 390 and *ODNB*.
171. *His Majesties Declaration to All His Loving Subjects, Touching the Causes & Reasons that Moved Him to Dissolve the Two Last Parliaments* (Wing C3000, 1681). See P. Harth, *Pen for a Party: Dryden's Tory Propaganda in its Contexts* (Princeton, NJ, 1993), pp. 68–72.
172. Ibid., p. 4.
173. Ibid., p. 6.
174. Ibid.
175. Ibid., p. 7.
176. Ibid.
177. Ibid., pp. 8–9.
178. Did Charles II recall the civil war parliamentary tactic of claiming, while fighting the king, to be preserving his authority?
179. *His Majesties Declaration*, p. 9.
180. Ibid., p. 10.
181. *A Letter from a Person of Quality to his friend concerning His Majesties late Declaration touching the Reasons which moved him to dissolve the Two last Parliaments at Westminster and Oxford* (Wing L1428, 1680). See also Harth, *Pen for a Party*, pp. 72–3.
182. See K. Sharpe, *Image Wars: Promoting Kings and Commonwealths in England, 1603–1660* (New Haven, CT, and London, 2010), pp. 400–3.
183. *Letter from a Person of Quality*, pp. 1, 8.
184. J. Dryden, *His Majesties Declaration Defended in a Letter to a Friend Being an Answer to a Seditious Pamphlet, Called A letter from a Person of Quality to His Friend: Concerning the Kings Late Declaration Touching the Reasons Which Moved Him to Dissolve the Two Last Parliaments at Westminster and Oxford* (Wing D2286), p. 1.
185. M. Knights, *Representation and Misrepresentation in later Stuart Britain: Partisanship and Political Culture* (Oxford, 2005), p. 122. The addresses were published in the *Gazette*. See, for example, *London Gazette*, 6 June, 9 June, 20 June, 23 June, 27 June. Knights estimates that at least forty thousand signed the addresses; Knights, *Politics and Opinion in 1678–81* (Cambridge, 1994), p. 336 and see pp. 316–45 *passim*. Opinion, of course, remained divided but, on this occasion, Charles upstaged the Whigs.
186. On the last years of Charles II, see Grant Tapsell, *The Personal Rule of Charles II, 1681–85* (Woodbridge, 2007). Tapsell, while recognizing the turning of popular opinion, emphasizes the partisanship and divisions of the period 1681–5.
187. *His Majesties Declaration to All His Loving Subjects, Concerning the Treasonable Conspiracy Against His Sacred Person and Government, Lately Discovered Appointed to be Read in All Churches and*

Chappels Within this Kingdom (Wing C2998, 1683); Harth, *Pen for a Party*, pp. 222–4. On the Rye House plot, see Hutton, *Charles II*, pp. 420–4; Harris, *Restoration*, pp. 311–17; Tapsell, *Personal Rule*, pp. 27–8, 47–8, 102–6.

188. *His Majesties Declaration*, p. 5.
189. Ibid., p. 7.
190. Ibid.
191. *His Majesties Declaration*, p. 15.
192. Ibid., p. 19.
193. See *London Gazette*, 5 July, 9 July, 12 July (quotation), 16 July, 19 July, 23 July, 26 July, 30 July; see also Tapsell, *Personal Rule*, pp. 102–6, for government efforts to counter dissident publishing.
194. See K. Sharpe, *Selling the Tudor Monarchy: Authority and Image in Sixteenth-Century England* (New Haven, CT, and London, 2009), pp. 97–101, 208–12, 254–6, 344–7; Sharpe, *Image Wars*, pp. 35–40, 150–9, 317–19.
195. See, for example, R. Clavel, *The General Catalogue of Books Printed in England Since the Dreadful Fire of London, 1666, to the End of Trinity Term, 1674 Together with the Titles of All Publick and Private Acts of Parliament: Proclamations* ... (Wing C4600, 1675), pp. 76ff.; Bodleian Library, Oxford, Ashmole H.23.
196. *By the King. A Proclamation for the Suppression of Coffee-houses* (Wing C3515, 1675).
197. *By the King. A Proclamation, for the Due Observation of Certain Statutes Made for the Suppressing of Rogues, Vagabonds, Beggers, and Other Idle Disorderly Persons, and for Relief of the Poore* (Wing C3476, 1661); *By the King. A Proclamation for the Observation of the Lords Day, and for Renewing a Former Proclamation Against Vitious, Debauched and Profane Persons* (Wing C3497, 1663); *By the King, a Proclamation* (Wing C3598A, 1675).
198. *A Proclamation for the Observation of the Nine and Twentieth Day of May Instant, as a Day of Publick Thanksgiving* (Wing C3498, 1661); *By the King. A Proclamation for the Better Ordering of Those Who Repair to the Court for their Cure of the Disease Called the Kings-evil* (Wing C3452, 1662).
199. Sharpe, *Selling the Tudor Monarchy*, pp. 330–3; Sharpe, *Image Wars*, pp. 35–8, 299–303.
200. For example, *By the King. A Proclamation, for a General Fast Throughout the Realm of England* (Wing C3298, 1661); *By the King. A Proclamation Appointing the General Fast* (Wing C3232, 1665); *By the King. A Proclamation for a Generall Fast* (Wing C3307, 1678); *By the King. A Proclamation for a General Fast* (Wing C3309, 1679); *By the King, a Proclamation for a General Fast* (Wing C3310, 1680). There were no fasts appointed after 1680.
201. *A Form of Prayer with Thanksgiving To Be Used of All the King's Majesties Loving Subjects the 29th of May Yearly for His Majestie's Happy Return to his Kingdoms, it Being Also the Day of His Birth* (Wing C4171, 1661).
202. Ibid., sigs B1^v–B2.
203. Ibid., sigs B3^v–B4.
204. Ibid., sig. C2.
205. Ibid., sig. C2^v.
206. Ibid., sig. C4.
207. Ibid., sig. C4^v.
208. Ibid., sigs D4, E2^v.
209. Ibid., sig. E3^v.
210. *A Form of Prayer, with Thanksgiving, to be Used of all the Kings Majesties Loving Subjects. The 28th. of June, 1660. For His Majesties Happy Return to His Kingdoms* (Thomason E.1030/9, 1660).
211. *A Form of Common Prayer, to be Used Upon the Thirtieth of January* (Wing C4114, 1661), title page. The text was published 'cum privilegio' and carries the king's order that it be used throughout the realm.
212. Ibid., sigs C1^v–C2^v, C3^v–D1^v; James I, *A Meditation Upon the 27, 28, 29, Verses of the XXVII. Chapter of St. Matthew. Or A Paterne for a Kings Inauguration. Written by the Kings Maiestie* (STC 14382, 1620); see Sharpe, *Image Wars*, pp. 33–4.
213. *Form of Common Prayer the Thirtieth of January*, sig. F1^v.
214. Ibid., sig. F2.
215. Ibid. sigs F2–F2^v.
216. Ibid., sig. F3^v.
217. Ibid., sig. F4.
218. See below p. 196.
219. *The King's Psalter* (Wing K606, 1670).
220. Ibid., sigs E4^v, G3^v.

221. Ibid., sigs [H2^v], ch. 47, sig. L7^v.
222. Ibid., sigs M1^v–M2.
223. Ibid., sig. M1.
224. Ibid., sig. A3^v: 'This treatise . . . is composed on purpose to succeed *The King's Primer*.
225. *A Form of Prayer, to be Used Upon the twelfth of June in All Churches and Chappels within the Cities of London and Westminster . . . upon the Nineteenth of the Said Moneth, in All Other Churches and Chappels within the Rest of His Majesties Dominions . . . : Being the Several Days Appointed for a General Fast, to Be Kept in the Respective Places, for the Averting Those Sicknesses and Diseases* (Wing C4143, 1661). The title page also refers to the 'dearth and scarcity' caused by immoderate rain.
226. *A Form of Common Prayer to be Used on Wednesday the 5th of April, Being the Day of the General Fast Appointed by His Majesties Proclimation of Imploring Gods Blessing on His Majesties Naval Forces* (Wing C4115, 1665); *A Form of Common Prayer to be Used on Wednesday the 27th of March, 1672 . . . Being the Days of the General Fast Appointed by His Majesties Proclamation, for Imploring Gods Blessing on His Majesties Naval Forces* (Wing C4117, 1672); *A Form of Common Prayer with Thanksgiving for the Late Victory by His Majesties Naval Forces Appointed to be Used in and about London, on Tuesday the Twentieth of June, and through all England on Tuesday the Fourth of July* (Wing C4120, 1665); *A Form of Common Prayer, with Thanksgiving, for the Late Victory by His Majesties Naval Forces Appointed to be Used in and about London on Tuesday the 14th of August, and through All England, on Thursday the 23d of August* (Wing C4121, 1666).
227. Wing C4120, sigs C2^v, H2^v.
228. *A Form of Common Prayer to be Used on Wednesday the Tenth Day of October Next, throughout the Whole Kingdom of England and Dominion of Wales Being Appointed by His Majesty a Day of Fasting and Humiliation in Consideration of the Late Dreadful Fire* (Wing C3303, 1666), sig. D1^v.
229. *A Form of Prayer, to be Used upon the Fifteenth of January . . . for a General Fast, to be Kept . . . for the Averting those Sicknesses and Diseases, that Dearth and Scarcity, which Justly May be Feared from the Unseasonableness of the Weather* (Wing C4142, 1661), D3^v.
230. *A Form of Common Prayer, to be Used on Wednesday the 4th of February, 1673/4, within the Cities of London and Westminster . . . : and on Wednesday the 11th of Febr. Next through the Rest of the Whole Kingdom of England, Dominion of Wales, and Town of Berwick upon Tweed: Being the Days of the General Fast Appointed by His Majesties Proclamation, for Imploring Gods Blessing on His Majesty, and the Present Parliament* (Wing C4118, 1674).
231. Ibid., sig. C4^v.
232. *A Form of Prayer, to be Used on Wednesday November the Thirteenth, Being the Fast-day Appointed by the King to Implore the Mercies of Almighty God in the Protection of His Majesties Sacred Person, and in Him of All His Loyal Subjects, and the Bringing to Light More and More All Secret Machinations Against His Majesty, and the Whole Kingdom* (Wing C4145, 1678).
233. Ibid., sig. A1^v.
234. Ibid., sig. B3.
235. Ibid., sig. F3^v.
236. Ibid.
237. Ibid., sigs F3^v–F4.
238. J. Dryden, *Absalom and Achitophel: A Poem* (Wing D2215, 1681).
239. *A Form of Prayer and Thanksgiving to be Used on Friday the Eleventh of April Being the Fast-day Appointed by the Kings Proclamation, to Seek Reconciliation with Almighty God* (Wing C4146, 1679).
240. Ibid., sig. A3.
241. Ibid., sig. A4^v.
242. *A Form of Prayer, to be Used on Wednesday the 22nd of December Being the Fast-day Appointed by the Kings Proclamation: To Seek Reconciliation with Almighty God, and to Beseech Him, That He Would Avert His Hearts of All Loyal Protestants* (Wing C4148, 1680), text on title page.
243. Ibid., sigs A2, B3, B4, my italics.
244. Ibid. sig. C4.
245. Ibid., sigs F3–F4^v.
246. *A Form of Prayer with Thanksgiving, to be Used on Sunday, September the 9th Being the Day of Thanksgiving Appointed by the Kings Declaration: To Be Solemnly Observ'd in All Churches, and Chappels within this Kingdom, and in Due Acknowledgment of God's Wonderful Providence, and Mercy, in Discovering, and Defeating the Late Treasonable Conspiracy Against His Sacred Majesties Person, and Government* (Wing C4172, 1683).
247. Ibid., sigs B2^v–B3.

248. Ibid., sig. C3.
249. Ibid., sig. C3, my italics.
250. Ibid., sigs C3–C3ᵛ.
251. Ibid., sigs F3–F3ᵛ.
252. See below pp. 91–3 on printing press and publicity.
253. *Theatre of Wits Ancient and Modern Attended with Severall Other Ingenious Pieces from the Same Pen viz. I. Faenestra in pectore, or, A century of familiar letters, II. Loves labyrinth: A tragi-comedy, III. Fragmenta poetica, or, Poetical diversions, IV. Virtus redivivi, a Panegyrick on our late king Charles of ever blessed memory concluding with A Panegyrick on His Sacred Majesties Most Happy Return* (Wing F1548A), IV, p. 21.
254. Henry Oxinden, *Charles Triumphant* (Wing O840, 1660), sig. A6.
255. Arthur Brett, *The Restauration Or, A poem on the Return of the Most Mighty and Ever Glorious Prince, Charles the II. to His Kingdoms* (Wing B4397, 1660), p. 3; on Brett, see *ODNB*.
256. As well as being largely ignored by historians of Restoration politics, many of these writers await critical study. See N. Jose, *Ideas of the Restoration in English Literature, 1660–1671* (Cambridge, MA, 1984), especially ch. 3; D. Mermin, 'Women Becoming Poets: Katherine Philips, Aphra Behn, Anne Finch', *English Literary History*, 57 (1990), pp. 335–55; E. Hobby, *Virtue of Necessity: English Women's Writing, 1649–1688* (London, 1988).
257. Rachel Jevon, *Exultationis Carmen to the Kings Most Excellent Majesty Upon His Most Desired Return by Rachel Jevon; Presented with Her Own Hand, Aug. 16th* (Wing J730, 1660); J. Dryden, *To His Sacred Maiesty a Panegyrick on His Coronation* (Wing D2386, 1661); John Evelyn, *A Panegyric to Charles the Second Presented to His Majestie the xxxiii. [sic] of April, Being the Day of His Coronation, MDCLXI* (Wing E3506, 1661); Bernard James, *A Poem upon His Sacred Majesties Distresses, and Late Happy Restauration* (Wing B1995, 1660). See Carver, 'The Restoration Poets and Their Father King', *Huntington Library Quarterly*, 40 (1977), pp. 332–51.
258. Brett, *Restauration*, p. 21; Jevon, *Exultationis Carmen*, p. 5.
259. *Votivum Carolo, or, A Welcome to His Sacred Majesty Charles the II from the Masters and Scholars of Woodstock-School in the County of Oxford* (Wing W 3475, 1660), p. 5; *Domiduca Oxoniensis, sive, Musae Academicae Gratulatio ob Auspicatissimum Serenissimae Principis Catharinae Lusitanae, Regi Suo Desponsatae, in Angliam Appulsum, Oxoniae* (Wing O875, Oxford, 1662), sig. A2ᵛ; J. Dryden, *Astraea redux. A poem on the happy restoration & return of His sacred Majesty Charles the Second* (Wing D2244, 1660).
260. Charles Cotton, *A Panegyrick to the King's Most Excellent Majesty by Charles Cotton* (Wing C6387, 1660), p. 4; Edmund Waller, *To the King, Upon His Majesties Happy Return* (Wing W529, 1660), p. 8.
261. *A Mixt Poem, Partly Historicall, Partly Panegyricall, Upon the Happy Return of His Sacred Majesty Charles the Second and His Illustrious Brothers, the Dukes of York and Gloucester* (Wing C7300, 1660), p. 15.
262. For example, Oxinden, *Charles Triumphant*, p. 19.
263. Martin Lluelyn, *To the Kings Most Excellent Majesty* (Wing L2628, 1660), p. 5; Brett, *The Restauration*, p. 7.
264. *Anglia Rediviva: A Poem on His Majesties Most Joyfull Reception into Enland* [sic] (Thomason E.1029/3, 1660), p. 6.
265. *Votivum Carolo*, pp. 7, 10, 16.
266. Ibid., pp. 1–2. On Gregory, see *ODNB*.
267. Ibid., p. 2.
268. James, *Poem upon His Sacred Majesties Distresses*, p. 5.
269. Cf. Jose, *Ideas of the Restoration*, ch. 2.
270. John Evelyn, *A poem upon His Majesties coronation the 23. of April 1661* (Wing P2711, 1661), p. 9; Waller, *To the King*, p. 8.
271. Dryden, *Astraea Redux*, p. 14.
272. For example, William Pestell, *A Congratulation to His Sacred Majesty, Upon His Safe Arrival and Happy Restauration to His Three kingdoms, May 29th* (Wing P1676A, 1660), p. 7; Thomas Southland, *To the King, upon His Majesties happy return. By a Person of Honour* (Wing T1496aA, 1660), p. 3.
273. Arion on a Dolphin, in K. Philips, *Poems by the Incomparable Mrs. K.P* (Wing P2032, 1664), p. 9.
274. Jevon, *Exultationis Carmen*, p. 2; Charles Cotton, *A Panegyrick to the King's Most Excellent Majesty by Charles Cotton* (Wing C6387, 1660), p. 7.
275. 'A Satyr', in H. Love ed., *The Works of John Wilmot, Earl of Rochester* (Oxford, 1999), pp. 86–7.
276. 'At home the hateful names of Parties cease', Dryden, *Astraea Redux*, p. 15.

277. Edmund Waller, *Instructions to a Painter for the Drawing of a Picture of the State and Posture of the English Forces at Sea, Under the Command of His Royal Highness in the Conclusion of the Year 1664* (Wing W499, 1665), a broadside.

278. *Instructions to a Painter for the Drawing of the Posture & Progress of His Ma[jes]ties Forces at Sea, Under the Command of His Highness Royal Together with the Battel & Victory Obtained Over the Dutch, June 3, 1665* (Wing W500, 1666).

279. Ibid., p. 16.

280. Ibid., pp. 16, 17.

281. Below, ch. 4, p. 215.

282. *ODNB*. Richard L. Greaves, 'Wild, Robert (1615/66–1679)', *Oxford Dictionary of National Biography*, 2004, online Jan. 2008.

283. R.[obert] W.[ild], *A Panegyrique Humbly Addrest to the Kings Most Excellent Majesty on His Auspicious Meeting His Two Houses of Parliament, February the 4th, 5th 1672/3: and His Most Gratious Speech There Delivered on that Occasion* (Wing W2144B, 1673). A nonconformist minister, Wild expressed his gratitude for the king's Declaration of Indulgence, *ODNB*.

284. Ibid., sig. A2, p. 1.

285. Ibid., pp. 2–3.

286. Ibid., pp. 5–6.

287. Ibid., p. 6.

288. Ibid.

289. Robert Wild, *Iter Boreale. Attempting Something Upon the Successful and Matchless March of the Lord General George Monck, from Scotland, to London, the Last Winter* (Wing W2133A, 1660).

290. R. Wild, *Dr. Wild's Humble Thanks for His Majesties Gracious Declaration for Liberty of Conscience, March 15, 1672* (Wing W2129A, 1672); *ODNB*.

291. *The Second Advice to the Painter* (Wing S2255A, 1679).

292. Ibid., p. 3.

293. Ibid., p. 4.

294. Ephelia, *A Poem as it Was Presented to His Sacred Majesty on the Discovery of the Plott, Written by a Lady of Quality* (Wing P2668, 1679). Ephelia has been identified as Lady Mary Villiers, Huntington Library catalogue entry 471489.

295. See also *Female Poems on Several Occasions Written by Ephelia* (Wing P2030, 1679).

296. *A Worthy Panegyrick Upon Monarchy; Written Anno MDCLVIII* (Wing W3633, 1680), a broadside.

297. *A Panegyrick to the King* (Wing P267, 1681).

298. *The Glory of the English Nation, or An Essay on the Birth-day of King Charles the Second* (Wing G877, 1681), one page.

299. On opposition satires, see H. Love, *English Clandestine Satire, 1660–1702* (Oxford, 2004) and below, ch.4.

300. *An Heroic Poem on Her Highness the Lady Ann's Voyage into Scotland with a Little Digression Upon the Times* (Wing H1587, 1681); *The Present State of England: A Pleasant New True Ballad* (Wing P3261, 1681).

301. Dryden, *Absalom and Achitophel*, 'To the Reader'. See S. Zwicker, *Dryden's Political Poetry* (Providence, RI, 1972), pp. 83–101; Zwicker, *Politics and Language in Dryden's Poetry* (Princeton, NJ, 1984), pp. 85–103.

302. 'But now the Tide is come about', *Murder Out at Last*, Bodleian Firth c.15 (17), no. 26.

303. *The Recovery* (Wing R654; Wing gives this as ?1682 but the copy in Bodleian Wood 417 is dated, more convincingly, 1681).

304. *The Poets Address to His Most Sacred Majesty* (Wing P2737, 1682).

305. M. Taubman, *An Heroick Poem to His Royal Highness the Duke of York on His Return from Scotland with Some Choice Songs and Medleyes on the Times* (Wing T239, 1682); see also Bodleian Firth c.15 (17), a volume of political ballads from 1682.

306. *A Congratulatory Poem on His Royal Highness, James, Duke of York* (Wing C5823, 1682), p. 2.

307. *Congratulatory Poem on His R. H's Entertainment in the City* (Wing C5822, 1682).

308. *An elegie on the Earl of Essex Who Cut His Own Throat in the Tower. July 13. 1683* (Wing E416, 1683); *An Elegy on the Death of Algernon Sidney, Esq. Who Was Found Guilty of High-Treason, and Beheaded at Tower-Hill on Friday the 7th of December, 1683* (Wing E369, 1683); *Collonel Sidney's Overthrow; or, An account of His Execution Upon Tower-Hill, on Friday the 7th. of December, 1683. Who Was Condemned for High Treason Against His Sacred Majesty, for Endeavouring the Subversion of the Government* (Wing C5413, 1683). See also N. Thompson, *A Collection of 86 Loyal Poems All of them Written Upon the Two Late Plots* (Wing T1005, 1685), *passim*.

309. J. Dryden, *The Medall, a Satyre Against Sedition* (Wing D2311, 1682), sig. A3ᵛ.

310. Ibid., sig. A4ᵛ.
311. Ibid., p. 10; Thompson, *Collection*, p. 149.
312. See note 336.
313. 'Y'insinuate loyalty', *The Medall*, sig. B1.
314. Nathaniel Thompson, *A Choice Collection of 180 Loyal Songs All of Them Written Since the Two Late Plots* (Wing T1003, 1685).
315. Ibid., sig. A2.
316. J. Evelyn, *A Panegyric to Charles the Second Presented to His Majestie the xxxiii. [sic] of April, Being the Day of His Coronation, MDCLXI* (Wing E3506, 1661), p. 4; J. Heath, *The Glories and Magnificent Triumphs of the Blessed Restitution of His Sacred Majesty K. Charles II from His Arrival in Holland 1659/60 Till this Present* (Wing H1335, 1662), 'To the Reader'.
317. W. Charleton, *An Imperfect Portraiture of His Sacred Majesty Charles the II. By the Grace of God King of Great Britain, France, and Ireland, Defender of the Faith* (Wing C3677, 1661), pp. 4 and 1–4 *passim*.
318. Ibid., pp. 6, 19.
319. J. Bird, *Ostenta Carolina, or, The Late Calamities of England with the Authors of them the Great Happiness and Happy Government of K. Charles II Ensuing* (Wing B2954, 1661), p. 21.
320. William Douglas, *Oratio panegyrica ad Eisodia potentissimi monarchae, Caroli II* (D2043, 1660), p. 21.
321. Jose, *Idea of The Restoration*, chs 1, 2.
322. We await a full study of the contested polemics of Restoration historical writing. Meanwhile see R. MacGillivray, *Restoration Historians and the English Civil War* (The Hague, 1974); B. Worden, *Roundhead Reputations: The English Civil War and the Passions of Posterity* (London and New York 2001); L. Okie, *Augustan Historical Writing: Histories of England in the English Enlightenment* (Lanham, MD, 1991); P. Hicks, *Neoclassical History and English Culture: From Clarendon to Hume* (Basingstoke, 1996); M. Zook, 'The Restoration Remembered: The First Whigs and the Making of their History', *Seventeenth Century*, 17 (2002), pp. 213–34; M. Knights, 'The Tory Interpretation of History in the Rage of Parties', *Huntington Library Quarterly*, 68(2005), pp. 353–73; R. C. Richardson, 'Re-Fighting the English Revolution: John Nalson (1637–1686) and the Frustrations of Late Seventeenth-Century English Historiography', *European Review of History*, 14 (2007), pp. 1–20.
323. Richard Baker, *A Chronicle of the Kings of England From the Time of the Romans Government Unto the Death of King James* (Wing B505, 1660). See M. Brownley, 'Sir Richard Baker's Chronicle and Later Seventeenth-Century English Historiography', *Huntington Library Quarterly*, 52 (1989), pp. 482–500.
324. Ibid., pp. 507ff.
325. E. Leigh, *Choice Observations of All the Kings of England from the Saxons to the Death of King Charles the First Collected out of the Best Latine and English Writers* (Wing L987, 1661), sigs A2–A6, p. 221.
326. P. Enderbie, *Cambria Triumphans, or, Britain in its Perfect Lustre Shewing the Origen and Antiquity of that Illustrious Nation, the Succession of their Kings and Princes* (Wing P728, 1661), sig. A2.
327. Ibid., sigs A2–A2ᵛ.
328. Walter Charleton, *Chorea Gigantum, or, The Most Famous Antiquity of Great-Britan [sic], Vulgarly Called Stone-Heng [sic], Standing on Salisbury Plain, Restored to the Danes by Walter Charleton* (Wing C3666, 1663).
329. Ibid., sigs A3–A3ᵛ.
330. Ibid., sig. A4ᵛ.
331. R. Baker, *A Chronicle of the Kings of England from the Time of the Roman's Government unto the death of King James Whereunto Is Added, the Reign of King Charles the First, with a Continuation of the Chronicle, in This Fourth Edition, to the Coronation of His Sacred Majesty King Charles the Second that Now Reigneth* (Wing B505A, 1665), sigs A4–A4ᵛ.
332. *The First Part of the History of England Extending to the Conquest of so Much of Britain as Was Subjected by the Romans* (Wing F978, 1668).
333. Ibid., pp. 31–4.
334. Ibid., pp. 31, 35.
335. Ibid., pp. 20–2.
336. W. Churchill, *Divi Britannici Being a Remark Upon the Lives of All the Kings of this Isle from the Year of the World 2855, unto the Year of Grace 1660* (Wing C4275, 1675), sigs A1–A2ᵛ. Horace, *Odes*, III, 5.
337. See also *Divi Britannici*, pp. 39–40, 361–2.
338. Ibid., pp. 6, 18.
339. Ibid., pp. 20–1.
340. P. Heylyn, *A Help to English History Containing a Succession of All the Kings of England, the English Saxons, and the Britains* (Wing H1719, 1675). See A. Milton, *Laudian and Royalist Polemic in Seventeenth-Century England: The Career and Writings of Peter Heylyn* (Manchester, 2007), pp. 116–17.
341. Ibid., pp. 5–6.

342. Heylyn, *A Help to English History* (Wing H1720, 1680), p. 43.

343. *History of the Life and Death of Pomponius Atticus Written by His Contemporary and Acquaintance Cornelius Nepos; Translated out of His Fragments, Together with Observations, Political and Moral, thereupon* (Wing N427, 1677), sig. A5.

344. Ibid., p. 94.

345. Ibid.

346. Ibid., pp. 223, 231.

347. F. Sandford, *A Genealogical History of the Kings of England, and Monarchs of Great Britain, &c. from the Conquest, anno 1066 to the Year 1677* (Wing S651, 1677), sigs A–A2ᵛ.

348. Ibid., sig. A1ᵛ.

349. Ibid., sig. A2ᵛ.

350. Ibid., p. 578.

351. The first volume of J. Rushworth, *Historical Collections of Private Passages of State* (Wing R2317) was published in 1680, J. Nalson's *An Impartial Collection of the Great Affairs of State, from the Beginning of the Scotch Rebellion in the Year MDCXXXIX. To the Murther of King Charles I* (Wing N1060A), in 1682. See F. Henderson, '"Posterity to judge": John Rushworth and his Historical Collections', *Bodleian Library Record*, 15 (1996), pp. 247–59; Richardson, 'Refighting the English Revolution'.

352. Baker, *A Chronicle of the Kings of England* (Wing B508A, 1679). The portrait had not appeared in earlier editions.

353. H. C., *The Plain Englishman's Historian, or, A Compendious Chronicle of England from its First Being Inhabited to this Present Year 1679* (Wing C45, 1679). The whole of English history was covered in 140 pages. See 'To the Reader'.

354. Ibid., pp. 123, 135.

355. Ibid., p. 141.

356. R. Filmer, *Patriarcha* (Wing F922, 1680).

357. *The Imperfection of Most Governments Taken Out of the Epitomy of the Roman History Written by Lucius Annaeus Florus* (Wing F1381A, 1680), title page.

358. Ibid., p. 3.

359. Ibid.

360. T. Yalden, *Compendium Politicum, or, The Distempers of Government Under these Two Heads, the Nobilities Desire of Rule, the Commons Desire of Liberty: With their Proper Remedies, in a Brief Essay on The Long Reign of King Henry III* (Wing Y6, 1680), sigs A6–A7, p. 76. Cotton's original purpose in writing had been rather different.

361. Ibid., p. 77.

362. W. B., *The White Rose, or, A Word for the House of York, Vindicating the Right of Succession in a Letter* (Wing B5268, 1680), p. 9.

363. Ezerel Tonge, *The Northern Star, The British Monarchy, or, The Northern the Fourth Universal Monarchy Charles II, and His Successors, the Founders of the Northern, Last, Fourth and Most Happy Monarchy* (Wing T1879, 1680); *Boscobel, or, The Compleat History of His Sacred Majesties Most Miraculous Preservation after the Battle of Worcester* (Wing B3331, 1680); J. Price, *The Mystery and Method of His Majesty's Happy Restauration Laid Open to Publick View by John Price* (Wing P3335, 1680).

364. R. Brady, *A Complete History of England from the First Entrance of the Romans under the Conduct of Julius Caesar unto the End of the Reign of King Henry III* (Wing B4186, 1685). On Brady see *ODNB* and J. G. A. Pocock, 'Robert Brady, 1627–1700: A Cambridge Historian of the Restoration', *Cambridge Historical Journal*, 10 (1950–2), pp. 186–204.

365. R. Brady, *A True and Exact History of the Succession of the Crown of England: Collected out of Records, and the Best Historians* (Wing B4195, 1681), p. 35.

366. Ibid., p. 44.

367. E. Cooke, *The History of the Successions of the Kings of England from Canutus, the First Monarch* (Wing C6000, 1682), p. 51.

368. J. Watson, *Memoirs of the Family of the Stuarts and the Remarkable Providences of God Towards them in an Historical Account of the Lives of those His Majesty's Progenitors of that Name That Were Kings of Scotland* (Wing W1081, 1683), sigs A4, B3.

369. Ibid., sigs B3ᵛ–B4.

370. Jean Baptiste de Rocoles, *The History of Infamous Impostors* (Wing R1766, 1683).

371. *The Rebels Doom, or, An Historical Account of the Most Remarkable Rebellions from Edward the Confessor's Reign to His Present Majesties Happy Restauration: With the Fatal Consequences That Have Always Attended Such Disloyal Violations of Allegiance* (Wing R599, 1684), sig. A2.

372. See H. R. Trevor Roper, *Queen Elizabeth's First Historian: William Camden and the Beginnings of English 'Civil History'* (Neal Lecture, 1971).

373. Gilbert Sheldon, *The Dignity of Kingship Asserted: in Answer to Mr. Milton's Ready and Easie Way to Establish a Free Common-wealth* (Wing S3069, 1660).

374. Ibid., sig. A6ᵛ.

375. Ibid., p. 80.

376. Ibid., sig. A6.

377. R. Mocket, *God and the King* (STC 14419, 1615); ibid. (Wing M2302, 1663); G. Williams, *Jura Majestatis, the Rights of Kings both in Church and State* (Wing W2669, Oxford 1644); ibid., Bodleian Bliss A 318 (2).

378. E. Chamberlayne, *Angliae notitia, or The Present State of England Together with Divers Reflections upon the Antient State Thereof* (3rd edn, 1669, Bodleian Wood 566), pp. 46, 104.

379. Ibid., pp. 58, 524.

380. Philipps, *Regale Necessarium, or, The Legality, Reason, and Necessity of the Rights and Priviledges Justly Claimed by the Kings Servants* (Wing P2016, 1671); quotation, p. 633; S. Bethel, *The Present Interest of England Stated by a Lover of His King and Country* (Wing B2072A, 1671), sig. A2ᵛ. Bethel was the author of *The World's Mistake in Oliver Cromwell*, see *ODNB*.

381. Philipps, *Regale Necessarium*, sig.A2.

382. See S. Mintz, *The Hunting of Leviathan* (Cambridge, 1962), appendix.

383. Thomas Tenison, *The Creed of Mr. Hobbes Examined in a Feigned Conference Between Him and a Student in Divinity* (Wing T691, 1670), sig. A3ᵛ, p. 188.

384. J. Shafte, *The Great Law of Nature, or, Self-preservation Examined, Asserted and Vindicated from Mr. Hobbes His Abuses in a Small Discourse, Part Moral, Part Political and Part Religious* (Wing S2888, 1673), sig. A3ᵛ.

385. Ibid., sig. A2ᵛ.

386. Ibid., p. 85.

387. E. Hyde, *A Brief View and Survey of the Dangerous and Pernicious Errors to Church and State, in Mr. Hobbes's Book, Entitled Leviathan by Edward Earl of Clarendon* (Wing C4421, Oxford, 1676), sig. *3.

388. Ibid., sig. *4, pp. 73–5.

389. See below, pp. 67–8.

390. J. Nalson, *The Common Interest of King and People Shewing the Original, Antiquity and Excellency of Monarchy, Compared with Aristocracy and Democracy, and Particularly of Our English Monarchy* (Wing M93, 1678).

391. Ibid., pp. 29, 64.

392. Ibid., p. 64.

393. Ibid., p. 129.

394. Ibid., pp. 164, 200.

395. Ibid., p. 266.

396. See G. Schochet, *Patriarchalism in Political Thought: The Authoritarian Family and Political Speculation and Attitudes Especially in Seventeenth-Century England* (Oxford, 1975); H. Nenner, *The Right to be King: Succession to the Crown of England, 1603–1714* (Basingstoke, 1995). Gaby Mahlberg summarizes the arguments from patriarchy and attempts by republican sympathizers to counter them in G. Mahlberg, *Henry Neville and English Republican Culture in the Seventeenth Century* (Manchester, 2009), ch. 3.

397. W. P. [?William Prynne], *The Divine Right of Kings Asserted in General: Ours in Particular; Both by the Laws of God, and this Land* (Wing P128, 1679).

398. See ibid., p. 3.

399. R. Constable, *God and The King, or, Monarchy Proved from Holy Writ to be the Onely Legitimate Species of Politick Government, and the Onely Polity Constituted and Appointed by God wherein the Phantasied Principles of Supereminencing the Peoples Welfare above the Kings Honour, and Popular Election of Kings Are Manifested to be Groundless and Unseasonable* (Wing C5935, 1680).

400. J. Brydall, *Jura Coronae His Majesties Royal Rights and Prerogatives Asserted, Against Papal Usurpations, and all Other Anti-monarchical Attempts and Practices* (Wing B5260, 1680).

401. Ibid., p. 123.

402. H. Neville, *Plato Redivivus, Or, A Dialogue Concerning Government* (Wing N515, 1681). See Mahlberg, *Henry Neville*, pp. 163–82 and *passim*.

403. W. W., *Antidotum Britannicum, or, A Counter-pest Against the Destructive Principles of Plato Redivivus wherein His Majesties's Royal Prerogatives Are Asserted* (Wing W140, 1681).

404. Ibid., p. 15.

405. Ibid., sig. (a) 4, p. 121.

406. Ibid., sigs A2ᵛ–A3.

407. *Britanniae speculum, or, A Short View of the Ancient and Modern State of Great Britain* (Wing B4819, 1683). The text mentions Neville on p. 200; on Neville, see *ODNB*.

408. G. MacKenzie, *Jus Regium, or, The Just and Solid Foundations of Monarchy in General: and More Especially of the Monarchy of Scotland, Maintain'd against Buchannan, Naphtali, Dolman, Milton &c.* (Wing M163, 1684).

409. J. Wilson, *A Discourse of Monarchy More Particularly of the Imperial Crowns of England, Scotland, and Ireland According to the Ancient, Common, and Statute-laws of the Same: with a Close from the Whole as it Relates to the Succession of His Royal Highness James Duke of York* (Wing W2921, 1684). See pp. 79–82 and section V *passim*. Wilson was 'semi-official royalist propagandist for James II', *ODNB*.

410. R. Cust, *The Forced Loan and English Politics, 1626–1628* (Oxford, 1987), pp. 62–5; K. Sharpe, *The Personal Rule of Charles I* (New Haven, CT, and London, 1992), p. 282.

411. See S. Letsome, 'An Index to the Sermons Published since the Restoration (2 Parts, 1734–8)'; C. Edie, 'Right Rejoicing: Sermons on the Occasion of the Stuart Restoration 1660', *Bulletin of the John Rylands Library*, 62 (1979), pp. 61–86: T. Claydon, 'The Sermon, the "Public Sphere" and the Political Culture of late Seventeenth-Century England' in L. A. Ferrell and P. McCullough eds, *The English Sermon Revised: Religion, Literature and History, 1600–1750* (Manchester, 2001), pp. 208–34; D. Appleby, 'Issues of Audience and Reception in Restoration Sermons', in G. Baker and A. McGruer eds, *Readers, Audiences and Coteries in Early Modern England* (Newcastle, 2006), pp. 10–27.

412. R. Mossom, *England's Gratulation for the King and His Subjects Happy Union. First Preach't on the Day of Publique Thanksgiving, Appointed by the Parliament, May the 10th. 1660. Since Publish't as a Common Tribute to Caesar* (Wing M2860, 1660).

413. F. Gregory, *David's Returne from his Banishment Set Forth in a Thanks-giving Sermon for the Returne of His Sacred Majesty Charles the II, and Preached at St. Maries in Oxon, May 27, 1660* (Wing G1888, 1660).

414. S. Ford, *Parallela; or The Loyall Subjects Exultation for the Royall Exiles Restauration. In the Parallel of K. David and Mephibosheth on the one Side; and Our Gracious Sovereign K. Charls, and His Loving Subjects, on the other. Set Forth in a Sermon Preached at All-Saints Church in Northampton, Jun. 28. 1660* (Wing F1492, 1660), p. 4. On Ford, see *ODNB*.

415. Ford, *Parallela*, p. 39.

416. J. Paterson, *Post Nubila Phoebus, or, A Sermon of Thanksgiving for the Safe and Happy Returne of Our Gracious Sovereign* (Wing P687, 1660).

417. Ford, *Parallela*, p. 45; Paterson, *Post Nubila Phoebus*, p. 20.

418. G. Morley, *A Sermon Preached at the Magnificent Coronation of the Most High and Mighty King Charles the IId* (Wing M2794, 1661), sigsA2–A4ᵛ.

419. Ibid., p. 33.

420. *By the King. A Proclamation, for the Observation of the Nine and Twentieth Day of May instant, as a Day of Publick Thanksgiving, According to the Late Act of Parliament for that Purpose* (Wing C3498, 1661).

421. P. Heylyn, *A Sermon Preached in the Collegiate Church of St. Peter in Westminster, on Wednesday May 29th, 1661 Being the Anniversary of His Majesties Most Joyful Restitution to the Crown of England* (Wing H1734, 1661).

422. H. King, *A Sermon Preached at White-Hall on the 29th of May* (Wing K504, 1661), quotations on pp. 17 and 31.

423. A. Walker, *God Save the King: or Pious and Loyal Joy, the Subjects Duty, for their Soveraign's Safety. Opened in a Sermon at Aldermanbury, upon the 30 of May* (Wing W303, 1660), sigs A2, A3.

424. J. Lynge, *David's Deliverance, or, A Sermon Preached at the Sessions Holden at Maidstone in Kent, upon April 23, 1661 Being the Day of the Coronation of King Charles the II / by John Lyngue* (Wing L3571, 1661), p. 20.

425. E. Willan, *Beatitas Britanniae, or, King Charles the Second, Englands beatituded as preached to the incorporation of the honour of Eay* [sic], *in the county of Suffolk, March 31, 1661* (Wing W2260, 1661), pp. 12, 18.

426. H. White, '*Thysia 'aineseōs, or A Thank-offering to the Lord for the Happy Recal of Our Dread Soveraign Charles* (Wing W1771A, 1660), p. 16.

427. T. Reeve, *England's Beauty in Seeing King Charles the Second Restored to Majesty Preached by Tho. Reeve in the Parish Church of Waltham Abbey in the County of Essex* (Wing R688, 1661), sig. A2ᵛ.

428. Ibid., p. 27.

429. Ibid., pp. 56–7.
430. Willan, *Beatitas Britanniae*, p. 37; Lynge, *David's Deliverance*, p. 20.
431. John Riland, *Elias the Second, his coming to restore all things* (Wing R1519, Oxford 1662), p. 17.
432. See G. Hall, *A Fast-sermon, Preached to the Lords in the High-Court of Parliament Assembled on the Day of Solemn Humiliation for the Continuing Pestilence* (Wing H335, 1666); E. Stillingfleet, *A Sermon Preached before the Honourable House of Commons at St. Margarets Westminster, Octob. 10, 1666 Being the Fast-day Appointed for the Late Dreadfull Fire in the City of London* (Wing S5639, 1666); R. Perrinchief, *A Sermon Preached before the Honourable House of Commons, at St. Margarets Westminster, Nov. 7 Being the Fast-day Appointed for the Plague of Pestilence* (Wing P1606, 1666). See also R. Allestree, *A Sermon Preach'd before the King, Decemb. 31, 1665, at Christ-Church in Oxford* (Wing A1166, 1666).
433. B. Laney, *A Sermon Preached before His Majesty at Whitehall, March 12, 1664/5 by B. Lord Bishop of Lincoln* (Wing L347, 1665), pp. 25–7.
434. Ibid., p. 3.
435. N. Hardy, *Lamentation, mourning, and woe sighed forth in a sermon preached in the parish-church of St. Martin in the Fields, on the 9th day of September: being the next Lords-day after the dismal fire in the city of London* (Wing H728, 1666), p. 29.
436. W. Sancroft, *Lex Ignea, or, The school of Righteousness, a Sermon Preach'd before the King, Octob. 10. 1666 at the Solemn Fast Appointed for the Late Fire in London* (Wing S554, 1666), p. 50.
437. Perrinchief, *Sermon*, p. 56.
438. J. Dolben, *A Sermon Preached before the King, Aug. 14, 1666 Being the Day of Thanksgiving for the Late Victory at Sea* (Wing J1833, 1666), pp. x–xii.
439. S. Ford, *Thaumasia Kyriou en Bythō. Or the Lords Wonders in the Deep: Being a Sermon* (Oxford, 1665).
440. Ibid., p. 27.
441. See, for example, J. Wilkins, *A Sermon Preached Before the King upon the Twenty Seventh of February, 1669/70 by John Lord Bishop of Chester* (Wing W2210, 1670), p. 21; "tis this fear of a deity and the sense of our obligation to him that is the only effectual means to restrain men within the bounds of duty".
442. See J. Spurr, *The Restoration Church of England, 1646–1689* (New Haven, CT, and London, 1991), ch. 2.
443. J. North, *A Sermon Preached before the King at New Market, October 8, 1671* (Wing N1289, 1671), p. 15 and *passim*.
444. William Lloyd, *A Sermon Preached before the King at White-Hall, March 6, 1673/4* (Wing L2708, 1674), pp. 14, 18.
445. Ibid., p. 11.
446. W. Cave, *A Sermon Preached before the King at White-Hall, January xxiii. 1675/6* (Wing W1605, 1676), p. 10.
447. H. Killigrew, *A Sermon Preach'd before His Majesty at White-Hall, May 29th, 1668* (Wing K447, 1668), p. 34.
448. J. Lake, *A Sermon Preached at Whitehal upon the 29th day of May, 1670* (Wing L197, 1670), p. 29. The sermon was published by royal command.
449. S. Gardner, *A Sermon Preached at the Visitation Held at High Wickham in the County of Bucks. May 16. 1671* (Wing G248A, 1672), p. 34.
450. E. Stillingfleet, *A Sermon Preached November V, 1673, at St. Margarets Westminster* (Wing S5645, 1674), p. 39.
451. R. Meggott, *A Sermon Preached before the Right Honourable the Lord Major and Aldermen, &c. at Guild-Hall Chappel, January the 30th 1673/4* (Wing M1621, 1674), sig. A2.
452. Ibid., p. 33.
453. J. Meriton, *A Sermon Preached before the King at White-hall July 30, 1676* (Wing M1821, 1677), p. 31.
454. J. Duport, *Three Sermons Preached in St. Maries Church in Cambridge* (Wing D2655, 1676), p. 47.
455. Thomas Cartwright, *A Sermon Preached July 17, 1676, in the Cathedral Church of St. Peter in York* (Wing C703, 1676), pp. 2, 7.
456. Ibid., p. 33.
457. Ibid., p. 34.
458. Thomas Sprat, *A Sermon Preached before the King at White-Hall, Decemb. the 24th. 1676* (Wing S5052, 1677), p. 35; W. Pindar, *A Sermon Preached before the Right Honourable the Lord Mayor, and Aldermen of London, at Guild-Hall Chappel* (Wing P2251, 1677), p. 15.

459. T. Lamplugh, *A Sermon Preached before the House of Lords on the Fifth of November, in the Abby-church at Westminster by . . . Thomas, Lord Bishop of Exeter* (Wing L306, 1678), pp. 22, 38, 41.

460. W. Lloyd, *A Sermon at the Funeral of Sir Edmund-Bury Godfrey* (Wing L2699, 1678). On the death of Sir Edmund Bury Godfrey, see Harris, *Restoration*, p. 137.

461. B. Camfield, *A Sermon Preached on the Fast-day, November the xiiith, 1678* (Wing I 340, 1678), quotation, p. 8.

462. J. Sharp, *A Sermon Preached on the Day of the Public Fast, April the 11th, 1679, at St. Margarets Westminster, before the Honourable House of Commons* (Wing S2984, 1679), pp. 34–5 (my italics); see Harris, *Restoration*, pp. 241–3.

463. J. Bedle, *A Sermon Preached in S. Lawrence-Jewry Church on the Fifth of November, Anno Dom. 1678* (Wing B2675, 1679), p. 28. Bedle was a royal chaplain.

464. S. Patrick, *A Sermon Preached before the King, on the Second Sunday in Advent, Decemb. viii, 1678* (Wing P841, 1679), p. 39.

465. J. Goodman, *A Sermon Preached before the Right Honourable Lord Mayor and Aldermen of London at the Guild-Hall Chappel on Decemb. 18th 1681* (Wing G1126, 1681), sig. A4. Goodman was a royal chaplain.

466. Ibid., p. 32.

467. C. Hickman, *A Sermon Preach'd before the Lord Mayor and Court of Aldermen, June 27, 1680* (Wing H1895, 1680), p. 20.

468. R. Hancock, *A Sermon Preached before the Right Honourable the Lord Mayor, and the Court of Aldermen, at Guildhall-Chappel, Septemb. 19, 1680* (Wing H645, 1680), p. 14.

469. Ibid., p. 15.

470. Ibid.

471. E. Sclater, *A Sermon Preached in the Church of Putney in the County of Surrey upon the 24th of April, 1681, His Majesty's Declaration Being Read that Day* (Wing S912, 1681), quotation, p. 26.

472. J. Byrom, *The Necessity of Subjection Asserted in an Assise-sermon Preached in the Cathedral Church at Sarum, July 17, 1681* (Wing B640–8, 1681), p. 25.

473. J. Okes, *A Sermon Preached at the Assizes Held at Reading, in the County of Berks, July 12th, 1681* (Wing O194, 1681), p. 4.

474. S. Freeman, *A Sermon Preach'd at the Funeral of Sir Tho. Bludworth, Kt., Late Alderman of the City of London, on Wednesday, May 24th, 1682* (Wing S2143, 1682), p. 27.

475. W. Clifford, *The Power of Kings, Particularly the British Monarchy Asserted and Vindicated, in a Sermon Preached at Wakefield in the County of York, Sunday, October the 30th, 1681* (Wing C4715, 1682), sig. A1, p. 30.

476. E. Calamy, *A Sermon Preached before the Lord Mayor, Aldermen, and Citizens of London at Bow-Church on the 29th of May 1682* (Wing C216, 1682), p. 3.

477. Ibid., p. 4.

478. Ibid., pp. 11–12.

479. Ibid., pp. 34–5.

480. Ibid., p. 35.

481. B. Calamy, *A Sermon Preached before the Right Honourable the Lord Mayor, and the Court of Aldermen, at Guild-Hall Chappel upon the 30th of September, 1683* (Wing C218, 1683), p. 8.

482. Okes, *A Sermon*, epistle dedicatory; Byrom, *Necessity of Subjection*, sigs A2–A2ᵛ; J. Bennion, *Moses's charge to Israel's judges opened in an assise sermon preached at Salisbury, Feb. 27, 1680* (Wing B1890, Oxford, 1681), sig. A3ᵛ.

483. Scroggs, *DNB*.

484. W. Cave, *A Sermon Preached before the Right Honourable, the Lord Mayor, Alderman and Citizens of London, at S. Mary-le-Bow on the Fifth of November, 1680* (Wing C1606, 1680), sig. A3ᵛ.

485. The argument of, among others, J. C. D. Clark in *English Society, 1688–1832: Ideology, Social Structure and Political Practice during the Ancien Regime* (Cambridge, 1985).

486. Francis Turner, *A Sermon Preach'd before the King in the Cathedral Church of Winchester upon Sunday, Septemb. 9, 1683 Being the Day of Publick Thanksgiving for the Deliverance of His Sacred Majesties Person and Government from the Late Treasonable Conspiracy* (Wing T3282, 1683).

487. Ibid., pp. 21–2.

488. J. Price, *A Sermon Preached at Petworth in Sussex, September 9, 1683 Being a Day of Solemn Thanksgiving for the Gracious and Wonderful Deliverance of the King, His Royal Brother, and the Government from the Late Barbarous Conspiracy* (Wing P3337, 1683), pp. 11–13 and *passim*.

489. S. Scattergood, *A Sermon Preached at Blockley in Worcestershire upon the Thanksgiving-day, Sept. 9, 1683* (Wing S844, 1683), p. 22 and *passim*.

490. J. Harrison, *A Thanksgiving Sermon for Discovery of the Late Phanatick Plot, September 9, 1683* (Wing H895, 1683).
491. C. Powell, *The Religious Rebel, a Sermon Preach'd at South-Marston near Hyworth in Wiltshire, on the Ninth of September, Being the Day of Publick Thanksgiving for the Deliverance of His Majesty's Sacred Person, His Royal Brother, and the Government from the Late Hellish Fanatick Conspiracy* (Wing P3046, 1683), pp. 3, 9.
492. J. Fitzwilliam, *A Sermon Preach'd at Cotenham, Near Cambridge, on the 9th. of September, 1683* (Wing F1106, 1683), p. 29.
493. Ibid., sig. A2, p. 33.
494. G. Hickes, *The Harmony of Divinity and Law, in a Discourse about Not Resisting of Soveraign Princes* (Wing H1850, 1684), sig. A3.
495. J. Turner, *A Sermon Preached at Epsom upon the 9th of September* (Wing T3317, 1683), p. 39.
496. G. Hickes, *A Sermon Preached at the Church of St. Bridget, on Easter-Tuesday, Being the First of April, 1684* (Wing H1866, 1684), p. 4.
497. R. Pearson, *The Study of Quietness Explained, Recommended, and Directed in a Sermon Preached Before the Right Honourable the Lord Mayor and Court of Aldermen, at the Guild-Hall chappel, March 16, 1683/4* (Wing P1017, 1684), p. 29 and *passim*.
498. *By the King. A Proclamation, for Observation of the Thirtieth day of January* (Wing C3349, 1661); see Andrew Lacey, *The Cult of King Charles the Martyr* (Woodbridge, 2003), ch. 5.
499. H. King, *A Sermon Preached the 30th of January at White-Hall, 1664* (Wing K507, 1665), quotation, p. 49.
500. J. Glanvill, *A Loyal Tear Dropt on the Vault of Our Late Martyred Sovereign in an Anniversary Sermon on the Day of his Murther* (Wing G813A, 1667), p. 2.
501. Ibid., pp. 6, 23.
502. T. Lambert, *Sad Memorials of the Royal Martyr, or, A Parallel betwixt the Jewes Murder of Christ and the English Murder of King Charls the First Being a Sermon Preached on the Solemnity of His Majestie's Martyrdom in the Cathedral-Church of Sarum, An. Dom. 1669* (Wing L244, 1670), sig. A3.
503. J. Duport, *Three sermons preached in St. Maries Church in Cambridge* (Wing D2655, 1676), p. 26 and *passim*.
504. E. Pelling, *A Sermon Preached on the Thirtieth of January, 1678/9* (Wing P1091, 1679).
505. J. Cave, *A Sermon Preached in a Country-audience on the Late Day of Fasting and Prayer, January 30 by a Priest of the Church of England* (Wing C1585, 1679), pp. 12, 17, 26.
506. S. Crossman, *Two Sermons Preached in the Cathedral-church of Bristol, January the 30th 1679/80 and January the 31th 1680/81* (Wing S7271, 1681); F. Turner, *A Sermon Preached Before the King on the 30/1 of January 1680/1* (Wing T3280, 1681).
507. E. Pelling, *A sermon preached on the anniversary of that most execrable murder of K. Charles the first royal martyr* (Wing P 1090, 1682), sig. A2ᵛ. Pelling was a high churchman and chaplain to the Duke of Somerset, *ODNB*.
508. See below, pp. 392–5.
509. J. Ellesby, *The Doctrine of Passive Obedience Asserted in a Sermon Preach'd on January 30, 1684* (Wing E537, 1684), sigs A2–A2ᵛ, p. 20. Ellesby was vicar of Chiswick.
510. Ibid., sig. A2ᵛ.
511. Since I drafted these words, Mark Knights has published the brilliant *Representation and Misrepresentation in Later Stuart Britain: Partisanship and Political Culture* (Oxford, 2005).
512. See Marjorie Huntley, 'The Politics of Honour in Restoration Theatre: Moments of Crisis, 1660–88' (Southampton PhD, 2007). I am grateful to Marjorie Huntley for many stimulating discussions.
513. M. Carter, *Honor Redivivus or An Analysis of Honor and Armory* (Wing C659, 1660), p. 61.
514. Ibid. (Wing C661, 1673).
515. William Ramsay, *The Gentlemans Companion, or, A Character of True Nobility and Gentility in the Way of Essay* (Wing R207, 1676 edn), p. 24.
516. Ibid., p. 67.
517. J. Logan, *Analogia Honorum, or, A Treatise of Honour and Nobility, According to the Laws and Customes of England Collected out of the Most Authentick authors* (Wing L2834, 1677).
518. Ibid., p. 19.
519. Ibid., p. 23.
520. F. Sandford, *A Genealogical History of the Kings of England, and Monarchs of Great Britain, &c. from the Conquest, anno 1066 to the Year, 1677* (Wing S651, 1677), sig. A.
521. Ibid., sig. Aᵛ.
522. Ibid., sigs Aᵛ–A2.

523. Ibid., sigs A1^v–A2.
524. H. K., *The Genealogies of the High-born Prince & Princess, George and Anne of Denmark* (Wing K124A, 1684), preface.
525. Ibid., p. 100.
526. Ibid., A1^v.
527. See, for example, Andrew McRae, *Literature and Domestic Travel in Early Modern England* (Cambridge, 2009); G. Maclean, *The Rise of Oriental Travel: English Visitors to the Ottoman Empire, 1580–1720* (Basingstoke, 2006); Claire Jowiit, *Voyage Drama and Gender Politics 1589–1642: Real and Imagined Worlds* (Manchester, 2003); Anna Suranyi, *The Genius of the English Nation: Travel Writing and National Identity in Early Modern England* (Newark, DE, 2008); Ivo Kamps and Jyotsna Singh, eds, *Travel Knowledge: European 'Discoveries' in the Early Modern Period* (Basingstoke, 2001); Stuart Schwartz, *Implicit Understandings: Observing, Reporting and Reflecting on the Encounters between Europeans and Other Peoples in the Early Modern Era* (Cambridge, 1994).
528. Anon., *Europae Modernae Speculum, or, A View of the Empires, Kingdoms, Principalities, Seignieuries, and Common-wealths of Europe* (Wing E3417, 1665), p. 252.
529. Ibid., p. 253.
530. J. Ogilby, *Africa being an Accurate Description of the Regions of AEgypt, Barbary, Lybia, and Billedulgerid, the Land of Negroes, Guinee, AEthiopia and the Abyssines* (Wing O163, 1670), sigs B1–B1^v.
531. P. Rycaut, *The Present State of the Ottoman Empire* (Wing R2414, 1670), sigs A3, A4^v.
532. Ibid., sig. A4^v. Rycaut may have been answering the charge that absolute monarchy was a form of Turkish slavery.
533. Samuel Collins, *The Present State of Russia* (Wing S5385, 1671); Lancelot Addison, *West Barbary, or, A Short Narrative of the Revolutions of the Kingdoms of Fez and Morocco with an Account of the Present Customs, Sacred, Civil, and Domestick* (Wing A532, 1671); F. Caron, *A True Description of the Mighty Kingdoms of Japan and Siam* (Wing C608, 1671).
534. Robert Fage, *Cosmographie, or, A Description of the Whole World* (Wing F82B, 1671), see pp. 45–9.
535. Sir Roger Manley, *The Russian Imposter, or, The History of Muskovie, under the Usurpation of Boris and the Imposture of Demetrius, Late Emperors of Muskovy* (Wing M440A, 1674). 'I found so much parallel betwixt these troubles and those of my native country', sig. A2.
536. William Hubbard, *The Present State of New-England Being a Narrative of the Troubles with the Indians in New-England, from the First Planting thereof in the Year 1607, to this Present Year 1677, but Chiefly of the Late Troubles in the Two Last Years 1675, and 1676* (Wing H3212, 1677). See epistle dedicatory.
537. Nathaniel Crouch, *The Wars in England, Scotland and Ireland* (Wing C7357, 1681), sigs A3–A4.
538. R. Blome, *Britannia, or, A geographical description of the kingdoms of England, Scotland, and Ireland* (Wing B3207, 1673), p. 12.
539. Ibid., p. 29.
540. See S. Zwicker, *Lines of Authority: Politics and English Literary Culture, 1649–1689* (Ithaca, NY, 1993). I am grateful to Steven Zwicker for many hours of discussion of literature and politics in Restoration England.
541. See S. Zwicker, 'The Constitution of Opinion and the Pacification of Reading', in K. Sharpe and S. Zwicker eds, *Reading, Society and Politics in Early Modern England* (Cambridge, 2003), pp. 295–316.
542. *Poems, Songs, and Sonnets, Together with a Masque by Thomas Carew* (Wing C 566, 1670); *The Works of Sr. William Davenant, Kt. Consisting of those which Were Formerly Printed and those which He Design'd for the Press* (Wing D320, 1673); *The Temple. Sacred Poems, and Private Ejaculations./by Mr. George Herbert* (Wing H1520A, 1667).
543. M. Kishlansky, 'Turning Frogs into Princes: Aesop's *Fables* and the Political Culture of Early Modern England', in M. Kishlansky and S. Amussen eds, *Political Culture and Cultural Politics in Early Modern England* (Manchester, 1995), pp. 338–60; J. Ogilby, *The Fables of Aesop Paraphras'd in Verse Adorn'd with Sculpture, and Illustrated with Annotations* (Wing A693, 1665); A. Patterson, *Fables of Power: Aesopian Writing and Political History* (Durham, NC, and London, 1991), especially pp. 85–94.
544. J. Ogilby, *The Works of Publius Virgilius Maro* (Wing V612, 1665); pp. 25, 79 and *passim*.
545. Ibid., sig. A3.
546. *The Princesse Cloria, or, The Royal Romance in Five Parts, Imbellished with Divers Political Notions, and Singular Remarks of Modern Transactions* (Wing P3493, 1665).

547. George MacKenzie, *Aretina; or, The Serious Romance* (Wing M151, 1660); C. Cotterell, *Cassandra the Fam'd Romance: the Whole Work, in Five Parts Written Originally in French, and Now Elegantly Rendred into English by Sir Charles Cotterell* (Wing L101, 1661). For the earlier Romance tradition see P. Salzman, *English Prose Fiction 1558–1700: a Critical History* (Oxford, 1985); S. Mentz, *Romance for Sale in Early Modern England: The Rise of Prose Fiction* (Aldershot, 2006). See also M. McKeon, *The Origins of the English Novel, 1600–1740* (2nd edn, Baltimore, MD, 2002).

548. *Cassandra*, sigs A4–A4ᵛ.

549. Charles Blount, *Boscobel, or, The Compleat History of His Sacred Majesties Most Miraculous Preservation after the Battle of Worcester* (Wing B3331, 1680), 2nd part, preface (n.p.).

550. A. M. Broadley, *The Royal Miracle: a Collection of Rare Tracts, Broadsides, Letters, Prints, & Ballads Concerning the Wanderings of Charles II after the Battle of Worcester* (1912), p. 257.

551. Ibid.; R. Ollard, *The Escape of Charles II after the Battle of Worcester* (London, 1966); B. Weiser, 'Owning the King's Story: The Escape from Worcester', *Seventeenth Century*, 14 (1999), pp. 43–62. I am preparing my own analysis of these narratives as political polemic.

552. J. Danvers, *The Royal Oake, or, An Historical Description of the Royal Progress, Wonderful Travels, Miraculous Escapes, and Strange Accidents of His Sacred Majesty* (Wing D237, 1660); *White-ladies: or His sacred Majesties Most Miraculous Preservation, after the Battle at Worcester* (Wing W1861, 1660); Thomas Blount, *Boscobel, or, The Compleat History of His Sacred Majesties Most Miraculous Preservation after the Battle of Worcester* (Wing B3328, 1662).

553. For a discussion of a set of pictures that exactly performs that negotiation, see below, ch. 2, pp. 111–14.

554. Weiser, 'Owning the King's Story', pp. 45, 51.

555. Blount, *Boscobel*, p. 77: 'the Royal Oak has . . . been deprived of all its young boughs by the numerous visitors of it to keep them in memory of his majesty's happy preservation; in so much that Mr Fitzherbert the proprietor has been forced to . . . fence it about with a high pale'.

556. Weiser, 'Owning the King's Story', p. 54.

557. Blount, *Boscobel*, sig. A3ᵛ.

558. Ibid., second part, pp. 33–4.

559. Ibid., second part, preface.

560. *Grimalkin, or, The Rebel-cat a Novel Representing the Unwearied Attempts of the Beasts of His Faction against Sovereignty and Succession since the Death of the Lyons in the Tower* (Wing G2026, 1681).

561. Ibid., p. 3.

562. Weiser, 'Owning the King's Story', pp. 53–5.

563. J. Raymond, *Pamphlets and Pamphleteering in Early Modern Britain* (Cambridge, 2003), p. 138. I am grateful to Joad Raymond for many helpful discussions.

564. J. G. Muddiman, *The King's Journalist, 1659–1689: Studies in the Reign of Charles II* (London, 1923).

565. *Current Intelligence*, 28 June 1666.

566. *Current Intelligence*, 2 July 1666.

567. *An Exact Relation of the Several Engagements and Actions of His Majesties Fleet, under the Command of His Highness Prince Rupert and of all Circumstances Concerning this Summers Expedition, anno 1673* (Wing E3696, 1673), p. 21 and *passim*; *A True Relation of the Engagement of His Majesties Fleet under the Command of His Royal Highness with the Dutch fleet, May 28, 1672* (Wing S775, 1672), p. 7 and *passim*.

568. K. Sharpe, 'Restoration and Reconstitution: Politics, Society and Culture in the England of Charles II', in C. MacLeod and J. M. Alexander eds, *Painted Ladies: Women at the Court of Charles II* (New Haven, CT, and London, 2001), p. 22.

569. J. Paterson, *Post Nubila Phoebus*, p. 6; F. Gregory, *David's Returne from His Banishment*, p. 28.

570. T. Sprat, *The History of the Royal-Society of London* (Wing S5032, 1667), p. 362.

571. See, for example, *An Impartial Enquiry into the Administration of Affair's in England with Some Reflections on the Kings Declaration of July 27, 1683* (Wing I83, 1683), p. 84.

2 Redrawing Regality

1. *Painted Ladies: Women at the Court of Charles II* was held at the National Portrait Gallery, London from October 2001 to January 2002. See C. MacLeod and J. Alexander eds, *Painted Ladies: Women at the Court of Charles II* (Exhibition catalogue, New Haven, CT, and London, 2001).

2. O. Millar, *Sir Peter Lely, 1618–80* (London, 1978); R. B. Beckett, *Lely* (London, 1951). See also C. H. Collins Baker, *Lely and the Stuart Portrait Painters* (2 vols, London, 1912).
3. Though see S. Stevenson and D. Thomson, *John Michael Wright: The King's Painter* (Edinburgh, 1982).
4. Most recently in Tim Harris, *Restoration: Charles II and His Kingdoms, 1660–1685* (London and New York, 2005).
5. MacLeod and Alexander eds, *Painted Ladies*, p. 50.
6. O. Millar, *The Tudor, Stuart and Early Georgian Pictures in the Collection of Her Majesty the Queen* (London, 1963), p. 119.
7. Ibid., p. 120.
8. Below, pp. 114–15.
9. *Burlington Magazine*, 103 (February 1961), p. 43.
10. In particular, the New Historicism led by Stephen Greenblatt.
11. See, most obviously, the work of Michael Baxandall, *The Limewood Sculptors of Renaissance Germany* (New Haven, CT, and London, 1980); *Painting and Experience in Fifteenth-Century Italy: A Primer in the Social History of Pictorial Style* (Oxford, 1972). See also Baxandall, *Patterns of Intention: On the Historical Explanation of Pictures* (New Haven, CT, and London, 1985). For eighteenth-century England, see John Barrell, *The Dark Side of the Landscape: The Rural Poor in English Painting, 1730–1840* (Cambridge, 1980); *Painting and the Politics of Culture: New Essays on British Art, 1700–1850* (Oxford, 1992).
12. K. Sharpe, *Selling the Tudor Monarchy: Authority and Image in Sixteenth-Century England* (New Haven, CT, and London, 2009), chs 4, 10.
13. K. Sharpe, 'Van Dyck, the Royal Image and the Caroline Court', in K. Hearn ed., *Van Dyck and Britain* (London, 2009), pp. 14–23; Kevin Sharpe, *Image Wars:Promoting Kings and Commonwealths in England, 1603–1660* (New Haven, CT, and London, 2010), pp. 454–5.
14. See, for example, Millar, *Tudor, Stuart and Early Georgian Pictures*, p. 113, National Portrait Gallery, NPG 1499, 6276.
15. Ibid., p. 117.
16. See Sharpe, *Selling the Tudor Monarchy*, pp. 135–7.
17. Millar, *Tudor, Stuart and Early Georgian Pictures*, p. 117.
18. Leemput painted a variant probably for Sir Edward Seymour, in ibid.
19. Below, pp. 104–6.
20. See NPG D26416, D26419, D18490, D18444, D18475, D18530, D32294, D22681; British Printed Images no. 1843.
21. Millar, *Tudor, Stuart and Early Georgian Pictures*, p. 120; Millar, *Lely*, pp. 11–12; Government Art Collection 5592.
22. Government Art Collection 8306; see Sharpe, *Image Wars*, pp. 199–200.
23. Diana De Marly, 'The Establishment of Roman Dress in Seventeenth-Century Portraiture', *Burlington Magazine*, 117 (1975), pp. 443–51.
24. Kevin Sharpe, *The Personal Rule of Charles I* (New Haven, CT, and London, 1992), p. 219; Susan J. Barnes, Nora De Poorter, Oliver Millar and Horst Vey, *Van Dyck: A Complete Catalogue of the Paintings* (New Haven, CT, and London, 2004), IV, 58, p. 475.
25. See below, p. 216.
26. Sonia Wynne, ' "The Brightest Glories of the British Sphere": Women at the Court of Charles II', in MacLeod and Alexander eds, *Painted Ladies*, p. 47.
27. There were more engraved images of Charles with Catherine of Braganza, see below, p. 103.
28. Millar, *Tudor, Stuart and Early Georgian Pictures*, pp. 130–1.
29. Sharpe, *Personal Rule*, pp. 219–21, plate 21.
30. Diana Dethloff, 'Portraiture and Concepts of Beauty in Restoration Painting', in MacLeod and Alexander eds, *Painted Ladies*, pp. 24–35, especially p. 34. I am grateful to Diana Dethloff for many helpful discussions.
31. MacLeod and Alexander eds, *Painted Ladies*, no. 37, pp. 124–5. I am very grateful to Julia Alexander for discussions of this portrait and much else. Cf. the image of Barbara Villiers as Mary Magdalen, in ibid., no. 35, pp. 122–3.
32. Ibid., no. 45, p. 134.
33. Ibid., no. 12, pp. 88–9; cf. Barbara Villiers as St Catherine, in ibid., no. 41, pp. 129–30.
34. See, for example, the portrait of the Duchess of Portsmouth, in ibid., no. 52, p. 147.
35. George de F. Lord, *Poems on Affairs of State: Augustan Satirical Verse, 1660–1714. Vol. 1, 1660–1678* (New Haven, CT, and London, 1963), p. 152; see C. MacLeod, ' "Good, but not Like": Peter Lely, Portrait Practice and the Creation of a Court Look', in MacLeod and Alexander eds, *Painted Ladies*, pp. 50–61, especially p. 54.

36. See K. Sharpe, *Criticism and Compliment: The Politics of Literature in the England of Charles I* (Cambridge, 1987), chs 5, 6.
37. MacLeod and Alexander eds, *Painted Ladies*, p. 125.
38. De Marly, 'Establishment of Roman Dress'.
39. Above, ch. 1, p. 50.
40. Millar, *Tudor, Stuart and Georgian Pictures*, p. 153. On Hendrik Danckerts, see *ODNB*.
41. Millar, *Tudor, Stuart and Georgian Pictures*, pp. 153–4, nos 398–401.
42. Ibid., p. 137, no. 317.
43. Below, ch. 2, pp. 111–14.
44. Above, ch. 1 pp. 50–1.
45. MacLeod and Alexander, *Painted Ladies*, no. 19, pp. 98–9; On Marvell's *Last Instructions*, see below, ch. 2, p. 144.
46. Millar, *Tudor, Stuart and Georgian Pictures*, pp. 21, 252–4. The portraits are listed as 'Flagmen of Lowestoft'.
47. NPG 1101. The portrait was once attributed to Edward Lutterell [C.H. Collins Baker, *The Stuart Portrait Painters*, vol. 2 (1912), p. 208] but disputed [David Piper, *Catalogue of Seventeenth-Century Portraits in the National Portrait Gallery, 1625–1714* (1963), p. 141].
48. The canvas is in the Museum of London, no. 79.18.
49. Macleod and Alexander eds, *Painted Ladies*, p. 83.
50. D. Solkin, 'Isaac Fuller's Escape of Charles II; A Restoration Tragicomedy', *Journal of the Warburg and Courtauld Institutes*, vol. 62 (1999), pp. 199–240, especially pp. 204–5.
51. J. Ogilby, *The Entertainment of His Most Excellent Majestie Charles II, in His Passage through the City of London to His Coronation Containing an Exact Accompt of the Whole Solemnity, the Triumphal Arches, and Cavalcade* (Wing O 171, 1662).
52. Below, ch. 3, p. 159.
53. See Millar, *Tudor, Stuart and Georgian Pictures*, no. 285, p. 129; S. Stevenson and D. Thomson, *John Michael Wright: The King's Painter* (Edinburgh, 1982), no. 28, pp. 80–2.
54. Millar, *Tudor, Stuart and Georgian Pictures*, p. 129.
55. See S. Foister, *Holbein and England* (New Haven, CT, and London, 2004), pp. 152–6.
56. Millar, *Tudor, Stuart and Georgian Pictures*, p. 129. The image appears to have been the model for the miniatures on plea rolls during the 1670s. I owe this information to the kindness of Molly McClain.
57. Millar, *Tudor, Stuart and Georgian Pictures*, p. 120, no. 237.
58. Ibid., no. 316, p. 136; NPG 531.
59. H. Levins, 'Social History of the Pineapple', http://www.levins.com/pineapple.html
60. 'Il est le meilleur et le plus beau de tous les fruits qui soient sur cette terre. C'est sans doute pour cette raison que le roi des rois lui a mis une couronne sur la tête qui est une marque essentielle de sa royauté', R. P. Duterte, *Histoire Generale des Antilles Habitees par les Francais* (1667), quoted in C. Py and M. Tisseau, *L'Ananas* (Paris, 1965), p. 3.
61. Millar, *Tudor, Stuart and Georgian Pictures*, no. 296, pp. 132–3.
62. Ibid., no. 207, p. 297.
63. Sharpe, *Personal Rule*, pp. 102–4; Sharpe, *Image Wars*, pp. 235–6.
64. Millar, *Tudor, Stuart and Georgian Pictures*, p. 133.
65. David Ogg, *England in the Reign of Charles II* (2 vols, 1956), I, pp. 386–8.
66. Millar, *Tudor, Stuart and Georgian Pictures*, p. 22; see also fig. 12; J. Douglas Stewart, *Sir Godfrey Kneller and the English Baroque Portrait* (Oxford, 1983), ch. 2.
67. Government Art Collection, no. 12789. I am grateful to the GAC for permission to view this double portrait.
68. Millar, *Tudor, Stuart and Georgian Pictures*, no. 269, p. 127.
69. Ibid., no. 319, p. 138. Millar puts the date as c.1683; it may be earlier.
70. NPG 4691.
71. Walker Art Gallery, Liverpool, WAG3023.
72. NPG 137.
73. Millar, *Tudor, Stuart and Georgian Pictures*, p. 133, no. 298.
74. See below, ch. 3, p. 170.
75. NPG 4691.
76. Solkin, 'Isaac Fuller's Escape', p. 211.
77. The paintings are in the NPG, nos 5247–5251.
78. Sokin, 'Isaac Fuller's Escape', p. 211.

79. See, for example, the title page to Francis Quarles, *The Shepherd's Oracle* (1646) which was also a separate print, British Printed Images, no. 7300, and C. Walker, *Anarchia Anglicana, or, The History of Independency. Being a Continuation of Relations and Observations Historical and Politique Upon This Present Parliament* (Wing W316, 1649), p. 112.
80. Solkin, 'Isaac Fuller's Escape', p. 227.
81. Ibid., pp. 211, 237; N. K. Maguire, *Regicide and Restoration: English Tragicomedy, 1660–1671* (Cambridge, 1992).
82. One recalls also Pepys's observing, on seeing a dog shitting in Charles barge, 'me think that a King and all that belong to him are but just as others are', 25 May 1660, in R. Latham and W. Matthews eds, *The Diary of Samuel Pepys* (11 vols London, 1970–83), I, p. 158.
83. Above, ch. 1, pp. 88–90.
84. Solkin, 'Isaac Fuller's Escape', p. 234. The ceiling canvas in now in Nottingham Castle museum; see Millar, *Tudor, Stuart and Georgian Pictures*, p. 129.
85. The early seventeenth century saw the beginnings of a transition, see E. Chaney ed., *The Evolution of English Collecting: Receptions of Italian Art in the Tudor and Stuart Periods* (New Haven, CT, and London, 2003).
86. For a catalogue, see R. Loborsky and E. M. Ingram, *A Guide to English Illustrated Books, 1536–1603* (2 vols, Tempe, AZ, 1998); for a study, see T. Watt, *Cheap Print and Popular Piety, 1550–1640* (Cambridge, 1991).
87. T. T., *A Booke, Containing the True Portraiture of the Countenances and Attires of the Kings of England, from William Conqueror, Unto Our Soueraigne Lady Queene Elizabeth Now Raigning Together With a Briefe Report of Some of the Principall Acts of the Same Kings* (STC 23626, 1597). Peter Stent ran the first shop dedicated to prints, see A. Globe ed., *Peter Stent, London Printseller, circa 1642–1665* (Vancouver, 1985).
88. See Sharpe, *Image Wars*, p. 430; Sharpe, *Selling the Tudor Monarchy*, pp. 365–6.
89. See Thomas Hobbes, *Leviatuam* (1651)
90. J. Evelyn, *Sculptura, or, The History, and Art of Chalcography and Engraving in Copper with an Ample Enumeration of the Most Renowned Masters and their Works* (Wing E3513, 1662), p. 26.
91. H. King, *A Sermon Preached the 30th of January at White-Hall, 1664* (Wing K507, 1665), p. 31.
92. *Troia Rediviva, or, The Glories of London Surveyed in an Heroick Poem* (Wing T2302, 1674), pp. 23–4.
93. Roland Fréart, Sieur de Chambray, *An Idea of the Perfection of Painting Demonstrated from the Principles of Art . . . Rendred English by J. E., Esquire, Fellow of the Royal Society* (Wing C1922, 1668), sig. A2.
94. Beginning the process skilfully charted by David Solkin in *Painting for Money: The Visual Arts and the Public Sphere in Eighteenth-Century England* (New Haven, CT and London, 1993).
95. T. Flatman, *Poems and Songs by Thomas Flatman* (Wing F1151, 1674), p. 91.
96. R. F. Sieur de Chambray, *An Idea of the Perfection of Painting* (1668), preface.
97. *The Excellency of the Pen and Pencil Exemplifying the Uses of them in the Most Exquisite and Mysterious Arts of Drawing, Etching, Engraving, Limning, Painting* (Wing E3779, 1668).
98. Ibid., p. 63.
99. W. Salmon, *Polygraphice, or, The Art of Drawing, Engraving, Etching, Limning, Painting, Washing, Varnishing, Colouring, and Dying in Three Books* (Wing S444, 1672).
100. Ibid., p. 187.
101. A. Browne, *Ars Pictoria, or, An Academy Treating of Drawing, Painting, Limning, Etching* (Wing B5088, 1675), p. 19.
102. *Westminster-Drollery, or A choice collecion of the newest songs & Poems both at Court and theaters by a person of quality* (Wing W1458, 1671), p. 123.
103. Ibid., p. 124.
104. W. Aglionby, *Painting Illustrated in Three Dialogues; Containing Some Choice Observations upon the Art, Together with the Lives of the Most Eminent Painters* (Wing A765, 1685), sig. B3.
105. Ibid., sig. B4^v.
106. Ibid., p. 31.
107. Browne, *Ars Pictoria*, p. 39.
108. Bodleian Wood 276a.
109. M. Wren, *Monarchy Asserted, or The State of Monarchicall and Popular Government* (Wing W3678, 1660), sig. A1.
110. MacLeod and Alexander eds, *Painted Ladies*, p. 58.
111. Chambray, *Idea of the Perfection of Painting*, sig. A4. See M. Lee Jr, *The Cabal 1667–74* (Urbana, IL, 1965).

112. Millar, *Tudor, Stuart and Georgian Pictures*, p. 23.
113. See Sharpe, *Image Wars*, pp. 510–11.
114. H. Colvin ed., *The History of the King's Works, Vol. 5, 1660–1782* (London, 1976), p. 3.
115. S. Thurley, 'A Country Seat Fit for a King: Charles II, Greenwich and Winchester', in E. Cruickshanks ed., *The Stuart Courts* (Stroud, 2000), pp. 214–39, quotation, p. 218; Colvin, *King's Works*, pp. 140–52.
116. Ibid., p. 226.
117. Ibid., p. 233.
118. R. Freart de Chambray, *A Parallel of the Antient Architecture with the Modern* (Wing C1923, 1664), sigs A2–A4ᵛ.
119. Ibid., sig. A3.
120. Ibid., sig. A4.
121. E. Waller, *Upon Her Maiesties New Buildings at Somerset-House* (Wing W531, 1665); J. Webb, *A Vindication of Stone-Heng Restored* (Wing W1203, 1665), epistle dedicatory to Charles II.
122. Colvin, *King's Works*, p. 129.
123. S. Thurley, *Whitehall Palace: An Architectural History of the Royal Apartments, 1240–1698* (New Haven, CT, and London, 1999), pp. 106–11.
124. Colvin, *King's Works*, pp. 313–29.
125. Ibid., pp. 316–17.
126. Colvin, *King's Works*, p. 322.
127. Ibid.
128. Ibid., p. 324.
129. Ibid., p. 326; Millar, *Tudor, Stuart and Georgian Pictures*, no. 298, p. 133.
130. Colvin, *King's Works*, p. 326; see, for example, *The Princely Pellican. Royall Resolves Presented in Sundry Choice Observations, Extracted from His Majesties Divine Meditations* (Wing P3491, 1649).
131. Colvin, *King's Works*, pp. 327–8.
132. Ibid., pp. 269–70; see E. Waller, *A Poem on St. James's Park as Lately Improved by His Majesty. Written by Edmund Waller, Esq* (Wing W508, 1661); A de Gooyer, 'Edmund Waller on St. James's Park', *Restoration: Studies in English Literary Culture, 1660–1700*, 31 (2007), pp. 46–72.
133. Above, ch. 1, p. 32.
134. Colvin, *King's Works*, p. 347.
135. 'On the Rebuilding of London', in J. Wells, *Poems upon Divers Occasions* (Wing W1290, 1667), p. 120.
136. J. Heath, *A Chronicle of the Late Intestine War in the Three Kingdoms of England, Scotland and Ireland* (Wing H1321, 1676), p. 565. See J. Summerson, *Architecture in Britain, 1530–1830* (New Haven, CT, and London, 1993), pp. 188–9.
137. P. Backscheider, *Spectacular Politics: Theatrical Power and Mass Culture in Early Modern England* (Baltimore, MD, 1993), pp. 50–1; on Pratt, see R. T. Gunther, *The Architecture of Sir Roger Pratt* (London, 1928); Colvin, *King's Works*, p. 16. On Charles I and St Paul's, see Sharpe, *Personal Rule*, pp. 322–7.
138. Summerson, *Architecture*, pp. 221–3.
139. B. Cherry and N. Pevsner, *London 3: North West* (London and New York, 1991), p. 562.
140. N. Smith, *The Royal Image and the English People* (Aldershot, 2001), p. 68.
141. J. Heath, *The Glories and Magnificent Triumphs of the Blessed Restitution of His Sacred Majesty King Charles II from his Arrival in Holland 1659/60 till this Present* (Wing H1335, 1662), pp. 165–6.
142. Latham and Matthews eds, *Diary of Samuel Pepys*, I, p. 99.
143. Smith, *Royal Image*, p. 124, plate 5:3; Backscheider, *Spectacular Politics*, p. 12.
144. M. Whinney, *Sculpture in Britain, 1530–1830* (London, 1988), p. 96.
145. See Smith, *Royal Image*, pp. 119–20, plate 5:1. The statue is now at the Old Bailey.
146. Ibid., p. 109.
147. See S. Williams 'The Pope-Burning Processions of 1679, 1680 and 1681', *Journal of Warburg and Courtauld Institutes*, 21 (1958), pp. 104–18.
148. Smith, *Royal Image*, p. 121.
149. Whinney, *Sculpture*, p. 112.
150. BM 1880, 1113.3869. There are apparently several states of this engraving.
151. Smith, *Royal Image*, p. 121.
152. Whinney, *Sculpture*, p. 112. In 1681 the Aldermen authorized an addition to the inscription on the Monument, blaming papists for the Fire; city opponents of the king and duke added words warning of 'popish frenzy' (http://www.themonument.info/history/north_panel_inscription.asp); Smith, *Royal Image*, pp. 121–2.

153. Whinney, *Sculpture*, p. 118; Smith, *Royal Image*, pp. 83–5 (see plate 3:9); Aglionby, *Painting Illustrated in Three Dialogues*, sig. B3ᵛ.
154. Whinney, *Sculpture*, p. 119.
155. S. Philipps, *To the Learned and Worthy Artist Mr. Grinsted [sic] Gibbons* (Wing P2024, 1684), sig. A1.
156. Ibid., p. 2.
157. Ibid., p. 3.
158. Whinney, *Sculpture*, pp. 116, 121.
159. Smith, *Royal Image*, p. 128.
160. Ibid., p. 126.
161. Ibid., p. 2.
162. Fitzwilliam Museum, Cambridge, M.1–1948.
163. There has been relatively little work on Restoration medals, but see J. Whiting, *Commemorative Medals: A Medallic History of Britain from Tudor Times to the Present Day* (Newton Abbot, 1972).
164. Sharpe, *Image Wars*, pp. 430, 438.
165. A. W. Franks and H. A. Grueber, *Medallic Illustrations of the History of Great Britain* (2 vols, 1885), I, p. 394, no. 18; E. Hawkins, *Medallic Illustrations of the History of Great Britain and Ireland to the Death of George II* (1904–11), plate XXXV, no. 8.
166. Franks and Grueber, *Medallic Illustrations*, I, pp. 437–44, nos 6–22; Hawkins, *Medallic Illustrations*, plate XL, nos 6–22.
167. Franks and Grueber, *Medallic Illustrations*, I, p. 450, no. 34; Hawkins, *Medallic Illustrations*, plate XLI, no. 16.
168. Franks and Grueber, *Medallic Illustrations*, I, pp. 455–6, nos 44–5; Hawkins, *Medallic Illustrations*, plate XLII, nos 10–11.
169. Franks and Grueber, *Medallic Illustrations*, I, p. 457, no. 48; Hawkins, *Medallic Illustrations*, plate XLIII, no. 3.
170. Franks and Grueber, *Medallic Illustrations*, I, p. 460, no. 53; Hawkins, *Medallic Illustrations*, plate XLIII, no. 8.
171. Franks and Grueber, *Medallic Illustrations*, I, pp. 458–9, nos 50, 52.; Hawkins, *Medallic Illustrations*, plate XLIII, nos 5, 7.
172. Franks and Grueber, *Medallic Illustrations*, I, p. 460, no. 54; Hawkins, *Medallic Illustrations*, plate XLIV, no. 1, by John Roettier.
173. Franks and Grueber, *Medallic Illustrations*, I, p. 462, no. 56; Hawkins, *Medallic Illustrations*, plate XLIV, no. 3.
174. Franks and Grueber, *Medallic Illustrations*, I, p. 462, nos 56–7; Hawkins, *Medallic Illustrations*, plate XLIV, nos 3–4.
175. Franks and Grueber, *Medallic Illustrations*, I, pp. 472–3, nos 76–7; Hawkins, *Medallic Illustrations*, plate XLV, nos 7–8.
176. Franks and Grueber, *Medallic Illustrations*, I, pp. 473–5, nos 78–81; Hawkins, *Medallic Illustrations*, plate XLV, nos 9–12.
177. Franks and Grueber, *Medallic Illustrations*, I, pp. 480–6, nos 90–103; Hawkins, *Medallic Illustrations*, plate XLVI, *passim*; for quotation, no. 6.
178. Franks and Grueber, *Medallic Illustrations*, I, pp. 483–4, no. 96; Hawkins, *Medallic Illustrations*, plate XLVI, no. 8.
179. Franks and Grueber, *Medallic Illustrations*, I, p. 503, no. 139; Hawkins, *Medallic Illustrations*, plate XLVIII, no. 10.
180. Franks and Grueber, *Medallic Illustrations*, I, pp. 533, 535, nos 182, 185; Hawkins, *Medallic Illustrations*, plate LIII, no. 4, LIV, no. 3.
181. Franks and Grueber, *Medallic Illustrations*, I, p. 553, no. 214; Hawkins, *Medallic Illustrations*, plate LVI, no. 6.
182. Franks and Grueber, *Medallic Illustrations*, I, pp. 573, 577, 580, nos 245, 247–53; Hawkins, *Medallic Illustrations*, plate LIX, nos 6–12.
183. Antony Griffiths, 'Advertisements for medals in *The London Gazette*', *The Medal*, 15 (1989), p. 4.
184. Franks and Grueber, *Medallic Illustrations*, I, p. 583, no. 259; Hawkins, *Medallic Illustrations*, plate LX, no. 8.
185. Franks and Grueber, *Medallic Illustrations*, I, pp. 581, 589, nos 255, 266; Hawkins, *Medallic Illustrations*, plate LX, nos 4–5; LX, no. 2.
186. Franks and Grueber, *Medallic Illustrations*, I, p. 593, no. 274; Hawkins, *Medallic Illustrations*, plate LXI, no. 8.

187. Franks and Grueber, *Medallic Illustrations*, I, p. 595, no. 278; Hawkins, *Medallic Illustrations*, plate LXII, no. 2.
188. Franks and Grueber, *Medallic Illustrations*, I, p. 601, no. 289; Hawkins, *Medallic Illustrations*, plate LXII, no. 12.
189. See the coin engraved in Huntington Library, Richard Bull Granger, nos 12, 33; H. N. Humphreys, *The Coins of England* (1846), p. 84; see also E. Besly, *Coins and Medals of the English Civil War* (London, 1990).
190. T. Saunderson, *A Royall Loyall Poem* (Wing S758, 1660), p. 7.
191. J. Tatham, *Londons Glory Represented by Time, Truth and Fame: at the Magnificent Triumphs and Entertainment of His Most Sacred Majesty Charls the II* (Wing T222, 1660), p. 3.
192. Amelot de La Houssiae, Abraham-Nicolas, Sieur, *The History of the Government of Venice* (Wing A2974, 1677), p. 118.
193. T. Bayly, *The Royal Charter Granted unto Kings by God Himself* (Wing B1515, 1682), p. 9.
194. *A Proclamation for Making Currant His Majesties Farthings & Half-pence of Copper, and Forbidding All Others to be Used* (Wing C3348, 1672); Huntington Library, Bull Granger, 12, 34; Fitzwilliam Museum website http://www.Fitzwilliam.cam.ac.uk; G. Brooke, *English Coins* (London 1932), p. 227.
195. Huntington Library, Bull Granger 12, 34ᵛ; http://www.fitzmuseum.cam.ac.uk/dept/coins/exhibitions/CoinOfTheMoment/token/
196. Huntington Library, Bull Granger, 12, 34; E. Hawkins, *The Silver Coins of England* (1841), pp. 214–15; P. Rayner, *English Silver Coinage from 1649* (London 1992), p. 9.
197. Huntington Library, Bull Granger 12, 33; Hawkins, *Silver Coins*, p. 211; Rayner, *English Silver Coinage*, pp. 109, 145.
198. Huntington Library, Bull Granger, 12, 33ᵛ; Hawkins, *Silver Coins*, pp. 216–19; Rayner, *English Silver Coinage*, p. 145.
199. Huntington Library, Bull Granger, 12, 33ᵛ; R. Kenyon, *The Gold Coins of England* (1884), p. 170.
200. Huntington Library, Bull Granger, 12, 34; H. Montagu, *The Copper, Tin and Bronze Coinage and Patterns for Coins of England* (1885), p. 26.
201. Huntington Library, Bull Granger, 12, 34; Montagu, *The Copper, Tin and Bronze Coinage*, pp. 25–35.
202. Huntington Library Bull Granger, 12, 34; Montagu, *The Copper, Tin and Bronze Coinage*, pp. 28–31.
203. http://www.coinoftheyear.com/1672.php; Montagu, *The Copper, Tin and Bronze Coinage*, p. 29.
204. O. Pissarro, 'Prince Rupert and the Invention of Mezzotint', *Walpole Society*, XXXVI (1956–8), pp. 1–9; C. Wax, *The Mezzotint: History and Technique* (London and New York, 1990), pp. 16–23.
205. A. Griffiths, 'Early Mezzotint Publishing in England – II: Peter Lely, Tompson and Browne', *Print Quarterly*, VII (1990), pp. 130–45; see also the National Portrait Gallery Research programme on 'The Early History of Mezzotint', http://www.npg.org.uk/research/programmes/early-history-of-mezzotint.php
206. For Pepys, see MacLeod and Alexander eds, *Painted Ladies*, p. 56. For standardization, see, for example, David Loggan's engraved portraits of Restoration bishops, eg. NPG nos 632, 633, 635–7, 639, 644, NPG D5802.
207. Huntington Library, Bull Granger, 12/24, 25, 28, 45, 54, 60.
208. Ibid., 12/61, 81ᵛ, 103; Browne *ODNB*.
209. Aglionby, *Painting Illustrated in Three Dialogues*, sigs A1–C2ᵛ; Evelyn, *Sculptura*, p. 100.
210. NPG D26416; Huntington Library, Bull Granger, 12/5ᵛ–6; British Museum P, 5.5.
211. BM 1868,0822.1136.
212. For example, NPG D22818, D22676, D26444, D22674.
213. See, for examples, NPG D22681, D22684, D22686–8, D18472–4, D18509, D18516, D18511; Huntington Library, Bull Granger, 12/11, 16, 18, 24.
214. NPG D18534; cf. Marshall BM 1861,0413.539.
215. Huntington Library, Bull Granger, 12, 7ᵛ.
216. Huntington Library, Bull Granger, 12/13.
217. Huntington Library, Bull Granger, 12/15; BM 1861,0413.539. The engraving was the frontispiece to John Browne, *Adenochoiradelogia, or, An Anatomick-chirurgical Treatise of Glandules & Strumaes, or Kings-Evil-swellings together with the Royal Gift of Healing* (Wing B5123, 1684), but may also have existed as a separate engraving.

218. NPG D2945; T. Sprat, *The History of the Royal-Society of London for the Improving of Natural Knowledge by Tho. Sprat* (Wing S5032, 1667). See M. Hunter, *Science and Society in Restoration England* (Cambridge 1981), pp. 194–7, for the argument that the plate was originally etched for a different book.
219. Huntington Library, Bull Granger, 12/25.
220. Huntington Library, Bull Granger, 12/26. Charles made his entry on his birthday, 29 May.
221. Huntington Library, Bull Granger, 12/30; BM 1883,0414.135. See A. Griffiths, *The Print in Stuart Britain, 1603–1689* (London, 1998), no. 129, pp. 194–5.
222. Though see John Overton, *A Catalogue of Books, Pictures, and Maps. Neately Cut in Copper* (Wing O616A, 1675).
223. Huntington Library, Bull Granger, 12/43–5; NPG D2942, D11128, D11129; BM 1868,0328.655; Y,1.8; 1890,0521.7; 1870,0709.764; 1871,0610.790; 1850,1109.21; 1861,1214.424.
224. Huntington Library, Bull Granger, 12/45; see L. Knoppers, 'The Politics of Portraiture: Oliver Cromwell and the Plain Style', *Renaissance Quarterly*, 51 (1998), pp. 1,314–15. I am grateful to Laura Knoppers for many stimulating discussions.
225. Huntington Library, Bull Granger, 12/31.
226. Ibid., 12/32. Both engravings illustrated Ashmole's *The Institution, Laws & Ceremonies of the Most Noble Order of the* Garter (Wing A3983, 1672) but were probably also sold as separates.
227. Huntington Library, Bull Granger 12/46–7; NPG D22773, D20014, D22777–9; see also BM 1902,1011.6885.
228. Huntington Library, Bull Granger, 12/55–6; NPG D18573, BM 1864,0813.167, 1858,0213.226, 1864,0813.108, P,5.45, P,5.46, P,2.97, 1902,1011.118, 1902,1011.5319. Significantly many of the engravings are early and late in Charles's reign.
229. Examples are (Mary) Huntington Library, Bull Granger 12/59ᵛ; NPG D32751, D8439, D19676, D32754, D11411; BM P,5.54, 1874,0808.1129; (Rupert), NPG D13175; BM 1902,1011.243, 1902,1011.5307.
230. Huntington Library, Bull Granger 12/87, 105, 13/1v, 2v, 4, 7, 13, 23.
231. Huntington Library, Bull Granger 17/7–11, 13–16.
232. See K. Sharpe, '"Thy Longing Country's Darling and Desire": Aesthetics, Sex and Politics in the England of Charles II', in C. MacLeod and J. Alexander eds, *Politics, Sex and Representation at the Court of Charles II* (New Haven, CT, and London, 2007), pp. 1–32.
233. See M. Jones, *The Print in Early Modern England: An Historical Oversight* (New Haven, CT, and London, 2010), chs 5–7, and Sheila O'Connell, *The Popular Print in England* (London, 1999).
234. See, for example, Huntington Library, Bull Granger, 14/31–2.
235. Huntington Library, Bull Granger 14/44ᵛ.
236. Ibid., 15/13–15.
237. Ibid., 14/62; see NPG D11017.
238. Huntington Library, Bull Granger, 13/27ᵛ, 14/29. On the advertising of topical prints see Claire George, 'Early Modern Rambler', http://newspaperadvertisements.wordpress.com.
239. Engraved images of Charles II appeared in John Nalson's *The Common Interest of King and People Shewing the Original, Antiquity and Excellency of Monarchy* (Wing N93, 1678), and in the 1681 edition of *Eikon Basilike The Pourtraicture of His Sacred Majesty in His Solitudes and Sufferings* (Wing E311A).
240. NPG D11401.
241. NPG D11408; D11399–11400; A. Griffiths, 'The Print in Stuart Britain Revisited', *Print Quarterly*, 17 (2000), pp. 115–23, especially pp. 121–2.
242. Huntington Library, Bull Granger, 12/20.
243. NPG D18535.
244. R. B., *The Wars in England, Scotland and Ireland, or, An Impartial Account of all the Battels, Sieges, and Other Remarkable Transactions, Revolutions and Accidents, which Have Happened from the Beginning of the Reign of King Charles I, in 1625, to His Majesties Happy Restauration, 1660* (Wing C7357, 1681).
245. For a study of printed images produced by the Popish Plot, including popular images on playing cards, see M. Knights, 'Possessing the Visual: The Materiality of Visual Print Culture in Later Stuart Britain', in J. Daybell and P. Hinds eds, *Material Readings of Early Modern Culture: Texts and Social Practices, 1580–1730* (Basingstoke, 2010), pp. 85–122.
246. L. Madway, '"The Most Conspicuous Solemnity": The Coronation of Charles II', in E. Cruickshanks ed., *The Stuart Courts* (Stroud, 2000), pp. 141–57, especially p. 152.

3   Rituals of Restored Majesty

1. See K. Sharpe, 'The Image of Virtue: The Court and Household of Charles I 1625–1642', in
D. Starkey ed., *The English Court from the Wars of the Roses to the Civil War* (London, 1987),
pp. 226–60; K. Sharpe, *The Personal Rule of Charles I* (New Haven, CT, and London, 1992),
pp. 209–22.
2. T. P. Slaughter ed., *Ideology and Politics on the Eve of the Restoration: Newcastle's Advice to Charles II*
(Philadelphia, PA, 1984), pp. xxvi, 44–5. Cf. p. xxvi: 'for what preserves you kings more than cere-
mony? The cloth of estates . . . great officers, heralds, drums, trumpeters, rich coaches . . .'
3. On Charles II, see A. Keay, *The Magnificent Monarch: Charles II and the Ceremonies of Power*
(London, 2008). See K. Sharpe, *Image Wars: Promoting Kings and Commonwealths in England* (New
Haven, CT, and London, 2010); S. Kelsey, *Inventing a Republic: The Political Culture of the English
Commonwealth 1649–1653* (Manchester, 1997); R. Sherwood, *The Court of Oliver Cromwell*
(London, 1977); R. Sherwood, *Oliver Cromwell: King in All But Name, 1653–1658* (Stroud, 1997).
4. J. Heath, *The Glories and Magnificent Triumphs of the Blessed Restitution of His Sacred Majesty
K. Charles II* (Wing H1335, 1662), 'To the Reader'.
5. T. Reeve, *England's Beauty in Seeing King Charles the Second Restored to Majesty* (Wing R688, 1661),
sigs A2–A2^v.
6. Heath, *Glories and Magnificent Triumphs*, pp. 10–13, 62.
7. Ibid., p. 14.
8. Ibid., pp. 26–7.
9. Ibid., p. 30.
10. Ibid., pp. 30–1.
11. Ibid., p. 31.
12. Ibid.
13. Ibid.
14. See, for example, *Gloucester's Triumph at the Solemn Proclamation of King Charles the Second* (Wing
G884B, 1660), especially p. 5.
15. Heath, *Glories and Magnificent Triumphs*, pp. 48, 61–2.
16. Ibid., p. 82.
17. Ibid., p. 52.
18. Ibid., p. 75.
19. Ibid., p. 67.
20. Ibid., pp. 76–7. Charles suggested that Downing had been loyal to him but concealed his loyalty!
21. Ibid., pp. 79–80.
22. Ibid., p. 87.
23. Ibid., p. 107.
24. Ibid., p. 114.
25. Ibid., p. 121.
26. Sir Edward Walker, *A Circumstantial Account of the Preparations for the Coronation of His Majesty
King Charles the Second and a Minute Detail of that Splendid Ceremony . . . to which Is Prefixed, an
Account of the Landing, Reception, and Journey of His Majesty from Dover to London* (1820), p. 18.
27. Ibid., p. 19. Charles would almost certainly have been aware of the precedent occasion.
28. E. Leigh, *Choice Observations of All the Kings of England* (Wing L987, 1661), sig. A4^v: 'I have not
found a fitter parallel in every respect for your Majesty than Queen *Elizabeth*. . . . After her
Coronation, being presented with a Bible, as she passed by the little Conduit in *Cheapside*, she
received the same with both her hands, and kissing it said; That it had ever been her chief delight,
and should be the rule by which she meant to frame her Government. Your Majesty in your entering
into the City, at the presentment of the Bible to you by the Reverend *London* Ministers, used
this speech, worthy to be written in Gold: I thank you for this Book above all other gifts, and assure
you, I shall make it my first care to set up Gods Worship and service; this is the Book must guide us
all.'
29. See M. Jenner, 'The Roasting of the Rump: Scatology and the Body Politic in Restoration England',
Past and Present, 177 (2002), pp. 84–120.
30. Heath, *Glories and Magnificent Triumphs*, p. 138.
31. Ibid.
32. Ibid., p. 149.
33. Ibid., pp. 151–2.
34. Ibid., p. 164.
35. Ibid., pp. 174–82.

36. R. Knowles ed., *The Entertainment of His Most Excellent Majestie Charles II in His Passage through the city of London to His Coronation by John Ogilby* (Binghamton, NY, 1988), p. 9. See G. Reedy, 'Mystical Politics: The Imagery of Charles II's Coronation', in P. Korshin ed., *Studies in Change and Revolution* (Menston, UK, 1972), pp. 19–422.
37. Walker, *Circumstantial Account*, p. 66.
38. Heath, *Glories and Magnificent Triumphs*, p. 194.
39. Walker, *Circumstantial Account*, p. 78.
40. J. Ogilby, *The Relation of His Majestie's Entertainment passing through the city of London to his Coronation: With a Description of the Triumphal Arches and Solemnity, by John Ogilby* (Wing 0181, 1661), sigs. a*.
41. Lorraine Madway describes the king as the dominant figure in the decisions and preparations, L. Madway, '"The Most Conspicuous Solemnity": The Coronation of Charles II', in E. Cruickshanks ed., *The Stuart Courts* (Stroud, 2000), pp. 141–57.
42. Walker, *Circumstantial Account*, p. 28.
43. Ibid., pp. 29–34.
44. Ibid., p. 35.
45. Quoted in Knowles, *Entertainment*, p. 14.
46. Ogilby, *Relation*, p. 1.
47. See above, ch.2, p. 103.
48. Knowles, *Entertainment*, pp. 10–12.
49. See Ogilby, *ODNB*.
50. J. Ogilby, *The Kings Coronation Being an Exact Account of the Cavalcade* (Wing O 0175, 1685), pp. 2–3; Ogilby, *Relation*, pp. 2–10; see Virgil, *Aeneid*, XI. I can offer here only a brief description of the pageants and arches, which is no substitute for reading Ogilby's or Knowles's modern facsimile edition.
51. Ogilby, *Relation*, p. 5.
52. Ibid., p. 6.
53. Ibid., p. 8.
54. Ibid., p. 9.
55. Ibid., pp. 9–10.
56. Ibid., pp. 11–14. (The theme predates Verrio's canvas of *The Sea Triumph of Charles II*, above ch. 2, p. 106).
57. Ibid., p. 17.
58. Ibid., pp. 18–19.
59. Ibid., pp. 21–5.
60. Ibid., p. 25.
61. Ibid., p. 27.
62. Ibid., pp. 29–32.
63. Ibid., p. 32.
64. Walker, *Circumstantial Account*, p. 78.
65. Ogilby, *Relation* (Wing O181, 1661); Ogilby, *Relation* (Wing O171, 1662); Knowles, *Entertainment*, p. 16.
66. Knowles, *Entertainment*, pp. 16–17.
67. Ibid., p. 24.
68. Ibid., p. 17.
69. Heath, *Glories and Magnificent Triumphs*, 'To the Reader'.
70. P. Heylyn, *A Sermon Preached in the Collegiate Church of St. Peter in Westminster, on Wednesday May 29th, 1661 Being the Anniversary of His Majesties Most Joyful Restitution to the Crown of England* (Wing H 1734, 1661), p. 44; cf. Heath, *Glories and Magnificent Triumphs*, p. 207.
71. Walker, *Circumstantial Account*, p. 68.
72. J. Heath, *A Brief Chronicle of all the Chief Actions so Fatally Falling Out in These Three Kingdoms* (Wing 1318A, 1662), p. 49.
73. See, for example, S. Anglo, *Images of Tudor Kingship* (London, 1992); T. K. Rabb, 'Play not Politics: Who Really Understood the Symbolism of Renaissance Art?', *Times Literary Supplement* (10 November 1995), pp. 18–20. See K. Sharpe, *Selling the Tudor Monarchy: Authority and Image in Sixteenth-Century England* (New Haven, CT, and London, 2009), pp. 48–9.
74. Heath, *Glories and Magnificent Triumphs*, p. 206.
75. http://www.christies.com/LotFinder/lot_details.aspx?intObjectID=5286579. There is a Restoration commemorative caudle cup figuring Charles II in the Museum of London (see image 001891).
76. See below, ch.3, pp. 164–7.

77. J. Ogilby, *The Kings Coronation Being an Exact Account of the Cavalcade, with a Description of the Triumphal Arches, and Speeches Prepared by the City of London for His late Majesty Charles the Second, in His Passage from the Tower to Whitehall: Also the Narrative of His Majesties Coronation, with His Magnificent Proceeding and Feast in Westminster-Hall, April the 23th* (Wing O 176, 1685); E. Ashmole and F. Sandford, *The Entire Ceremonies of the Coronations of His Majesty King Charles II. and of Her Majesty Queen Mary, Consort to James II* (1761).
78. Ogilby, *Coronation*, pp. 9–11; Ashmole and Sandford, *Entire Ceremonies*, pp. 1–5.
79. Ogilby, *Coronation*, p. 12.
80. Ibid., p. 12; Ashmole and Sandford, *Entire Ceremonies*, p. 8.
81. Ogilby, *Coronation*, p. 12.
82. Ibid., p. 13; Ashmole and Sandford, *Entire Ceremonies*, p. 12.
83. Ashmole and Sandford, *Entire Ceremonies*, pp. 14–15; Ogilby, *Coronation*, p. 13.
84. Ogilby, *Coronation*, p. 13; Ashmole and Sandford, *Entire Ceremonies*, pp. 18–22.
85. Ashmole and Sandford, *Entire Ceremonies*, p. 23; Ogilby, *Coronation*, p. 14.
86. Ashmole and Sandford, *Entire Ceremonies*, pp. 19, 21.
87. E. Walker, *A Circumstantial Account of the Preparations for the Coronation of His Majesty King Charles the Second and a Minute Detail of that Splendid Ceremony* (1820), p. 82, my italics.
88. Heath, *Glories and Magnificent Triumphs*, p. 199.
89. Walker, *Circumstantial Account*, p. 114.
90. Ibid., p. 122.
91. Ashmole and Sandford, *Entire Ceremonies*, p. 31.
92. Heath, *Glories and Magnificent Triumphs*, pp. 252ff.
93. Ibid., p. 254.
94. Ibid., p. 256.
95. Ibid.
96. J. Tatham, *Aqua Triumphalis, Being a True Relation of the Honourable the City of Londons Entertaining Their Sacred Majesties upon the River of Thames and Wellcoming Them from Hampton-Court to White-Hall Expressed and Set Forth in Severall Shews and Pageants the 23. day of August, 1662*, see imprimatur; *Neptunes Address to His most Sacred Majesty Charls the Second: King of England, Scotland, France and Ireland, &c. Congratulating His Happy Coronation Celebrated the 22th. day of Aprill, 1661* (Wing T230, 1661); E. Halfpenny, ' "The Citie's Loyaltie Display'd": A Literary and Documentary Causerie of Charles II's Coronation Entertainment', *Guildhall Miscellany*, 10 (1959), pp. 19–35, especially pp. 28–35.
97. J. Tatham, *Londons Glory Represented by Time, Truth and Fame: at the Magnificent Triumphs and Entertainment of His most Sacred Majesty Charls the II* (Wing T222, 1660); on Tatham, see *ODNB*.
98. Tatham, *Aqua Triumphalis*, sig. B3ᵛ.
99. As well as Tatham's text, Heath summarizes the pageants in *Glories and Magnificent Triumphs*, pp. 257–67.
100. Tatham, *Aqua Triumphalis*, pp.10–11.
101. Ibid., pp. 7–8, 10–11. Thetis mentions 'murmurs', 'quarrels'.
102. Ibid., pp. 10–11.
103. Ibid., p. 11.
104. 'Not to inform the knowing person but to help such as are unacquainted with poetical authors and history, I set down the explanations', ibid., p. 2.
105. Ibid., pp. 5–6.
106. Ibid., p. 11.
107. J. Grantham Turner, 'Pepys and the Private Parts of Monarchy', in G. Maclean ed., *Culture and Society in the Stuart Restoration* (Cambridge, 1995), pp. 102–5; R. C. Latham and W. Matthews eds, *The Diary of Samuel Pepys* (11 vols, 1970–83), II, p. 302; IV, p. 371; V, pp. 20–1. I am grateful to Dr Alexandra Lumbers for the last reference.
108. See Anna Keay, *Magnificent Monarch*, and R. Ollard, *The Image of the King: Charles I and Charles II* (London, 1979).
109. K. Sharpe, *The Personal Rule of Charles I* (New Haven, CT, and London, 1992), pp. 219–22.
110. Heath, *Glories and Magnificent Triumphs*, p. 210.
111. Knowles, *Entertainment*, pp. 14–15; *The Pedegree and Descent of His Excellency, General George Monck. Setting Forth How He is Descended from King Edvvard the Third, by a Branch and Slip of the White Rose, the House of York* (Wing P1048, 1660); *The Rump, or A Collection of Songs and Ballads* (Wing B4850B, 1660).

112. William Pestell, *A Congratulation to His Sacred Majesty, upon His Safe Arrival and Happy Restauration to His Three Kingdoms, May 29th, Being His Birth-day, and Our Year of Jubile, 1660* (Wing P1676A, 1660), p. 4.
113. *The History of that Most Famous Saint & Souldier St. George of Cappadocia. The Institution of that Most Noble Order of St. George, Commonly Called the Garter* (Wing H2142, 1661), sigsA2–A2ᵛ.
114. Walker, *Circumstantial Account*, pp. 42–4; Madway, 'Most Conspicuous Solemnity', pp. 142–3.
115. Ibid., pp. 44–9.
116. *A Perfect Catalogue of All the Knights of the Most Noble Order of the Garter. From the First Institution of it, untill this Present April, Auno [sic] 1661* (Thomason E1087/13, 1661).
117. Knowles, *Entertainment*, p. 15.
118. Ibid., p. 15; R. Johnson, *The Famous History of the Seven Champions of Christendom. St. George of England, St. Denis of France, St. James of Spain, St. Anthony of Italy, St. Andrew of Scotland, St. Patrick of Ireland, and St. David of Wales* (Wing J796, 1660); *St. George for England. To the Tune of Cook Laurell* (Wing S310A, 1660). Cf. *The Life and Death of the Famous Champion of England, S. George* (Wing L2015, 1660).
119. T. Lowick, *The History of the Life & Martyrdom of St. George, the Titular Patron of England* (Wing L3320, 1664), sig. A2.
120. Ibid., sig. A2ᵛ.
121. *Merry Drollery, Complete, or, A Collection of Jovial Poems, Merry Songs, Witty Drolleries* (Wing M1861, 1670), pp. 309–12.
122. E. Ashmole, *The Institution, Laws & Ceremonies of the Most Noble Order of the Garter Collected and Digested into one Body by Elias Ashmole* (Wing A3983, 1672).
123. Ibid., pp. 196, 207; above, ch. 2, p. 116.
124. Ashmole, *Institution*, p. 230.
125. Ibid., pp. 567–9.
126. Ibid., p. 421. Anna Keay, I think, understates Charles's interest in the Garter: *Magnificent Monarch*, pp. 180–2.
127. Ashmole, *Institution*, pp. 592–3, and also Huntington Library, Bull Granger, 12/32.
128. *The Order of the Ceremonies Used at the Celebration of St. Georges Feast at Windsor, When the Sovereign of the Most Noble Order of the Garter Is Present* (Wing O384, 1671; 0385, 1674).
129. F. Sandford, *A Genealogical History of the Kings of England, and Monarchs of Great Britain, &c. from the Conquest, anno 1066 to the year, 1677* (Wing S651, 1677), pp. 532, 564–5, 569, 573.
130. *True Account of the Invitation and Entertainment of the D. of Y. at Merchant-Taylors-Hall by the Artillery-men on Tuesday, October 21th, 1679* (Wing T2376, 1679).
131. Ibid., p. 2.
132. Ibid., p. 1.
133. Ibid., p. 2.
134. A. Barclay, 'Charles II's Failed Restoration: Administrative Reform Below Stairs, 1660–4', in Cruickshanks, *Stuart Courts*, p. 158.
135. Quoted in ibid., p. 160.
136. G. E. Aylmer, *The Crown's Servants: Government and the Civil Service under Charles II, 1660–1685* (Oxford, 2002), p. 70.
137. Ibid., p. 72.
138. Ibid., p. 152.
139. C. Firth and R. Rait eds, *Acts and Ordinances of the Interregnum, 1642–1660* (3 vols, 1911), I, p. 833; 12, Ch. II, cap. 24; W. C. Costin and J. S. Watson, *The Law & Working of the Constitution: Documents 1660–1914* (2 vols, 1952) I, pp. 2–4.
140. Barclay, 'Charles II's Failed Restoration', p. 164 and pp. 158–70 *passim*.
141. E. Chamberlayne, *Angliae Notitia, or, The Present State of England* (Wing C1820, 1669), pp. 271, 290.
142. Keay, *Magnificent Monarch*, pp. 154–5, 137–41.
143. F. Philipps, *Regale Necessarium, or, The Legality, Reason, and Necessity of the Rights and Priviledges Justly Claimed by the Kings Servants and Which Ought to be Allowed unto Them* (Wing P2106, 1671), pp. 24–5; Henry Pierrepoint, *ODNB*; Latham and Matthews eds, *Diary of Samuel Pepys*, VII, pp. 414–5. For a similar treatment of Rochester for impropriety at court, see Hutton, *Charles II*, p. 278.
144. Hutton, *Charles II*, p. 453.
145. Ibid.
146. Ibid.
147. Above, ch. 2, p. 120.

148. Aylmer, *Crown's Servants*, p. 248. The king touched seven thousand in 1660 alone, see Keay, *Magnificent Monarch*, pp. 112–8 and appendix 1.

149. See, for example, *A Proclamation for the Better Ordering of Those Who Repair to the Court for their Cure of the Disease Called the Kings-evil* (Wing C3452, 1662).

150. Aylmer, *Crown's Servants*, fig. 6A; Ashmolean Museum, Oxford WA.C.IV.229; British Museum 1872,1012.5141.

151. S. Zwicker, *Politics and Language in Dryden's Poetry: The Arts of Disguise* (Princeton, NJ, 1984).

152. J. Evelyn, *Publick Employment and an Active Life Prefer'd to Solitude and all its Appanages* (Wing E3510, 1667), pp. 39–40.

153. See, for example, K. Sharpe, *Criticism and Compliment: The Politics of Literature in the England of Charles I* (Cambridge, 1987), ch. 6.

154. Hutton, *Charles II*, pp. 186–8.

155. Ibid., pp. 279–80, 334–5; Macelod and Alexander eds, *Painted Ladies*, p. 136; Keay, *Magnificent Monarch*, pp. 130–1.

156. Hutton, *Charles II*, p. 336.

157. See R. Latham and W. Matthews, *The Diary of Samuel Pepys*, 11 vols (London, 1970–83), III, p. 302: IV, p. 371; V, p. 20; VI, p. 267; O. Airy ed., *Burnet's History of His Own Time* (2 vols), II, p. 455.

158. H. Love ed., *The Works of John Wilmot, Earl of Rochester* (Oxford, 1999), pp. 86–7.

159. See S. Wiseman, '"Adam, the Father of all Flesh," Porno-political Rhetoric and Political Theory in and after the English Civil War', *Prose Studies*, 14 (1991), pp. 134–57; for, a similar denunciation of an allegedly debauched Hugh Peters, see also W. Yonge, *England's Shame, or, The Unmasking of a Politick Atheist Being a Full and Faithful Relation of the Life and Death of that Grand Impostor, Hugh Peters* (Wing Y44, 1663).

160. See, for example, R. Graham, Viscount Preston, *Angliae Speculum Morale. The Moral State of England, with the Several Aspects it Beareth to Virtue and Vice* (Wing P3310, 1670).

161. Below, ch. 4, pp. 214–15.

162. See *Astraea Redux* and *Absalom and Achitophel*; see S. Zwicker, *Lines of Authority: Politics and English Literary Culture, 1649–1689* (Ithaca, NY, 1993), ch. 5.

163. I argue this case in K. Sharpe, '"Thy Longing Country's Darling and Desire": Aesthetics, Sex, and Politics in the England of Charles II', in C. MacLeod and J. Alexander eds, *Politics, Transgression, and Representation at the Court of Charles II* (New Haven, CT, and London, 2008), pp. 1–32.

164. See M. Jenner, 'The Roasting of the Rump: Scatology and the Body Politic in Restoration England', *Past and Present*, 177 (2002), pp. 84–120.

165. See R. Hutton, *The Rise and Fall of Merry England: The Ritual Year, 1400–1700* (Oxford, 1994), ch. 6.

166. See J. Grantham Turner, 'Pepys and the Private Parts of Monarchy', in G. Maclean ed., *Culture and Society in the Stuart Restoration* (Cambridge, 1995), pp. 95–110; cf. Turner, *Libertines and Radicals in Early Modern London: Sexuality, Politics and Literary Culture, 1630–1680* (Cambridge, 2002) and W. Chernaik, *Sexual Freedom in Restoration Literature* (Cambridge, 1995).

167. See T. Harris, 'The Bawdy House Riots of 1668', *Historical Journal*, 27 (1986), pp. 537–56. Ronald Hutton emphasizes the popularity of Charles II in *Debates in Stuart History* (Basingstoke, 2004), ch. 5.

168. J. Grantham Turner, *One Flesh: Paradisal Marriage and Sexual Relations in the Age of Milton* (Oxford, 1987); cf. Zwicker, *Lines of Authority*, ch. 4.

169. For a general study of the political culture of the law, see H. Nenner, *By Colour of Law: Legal Culture and Constitutional Politics, 1660–1689* (Chicago, IL, 1977).

170. Hutton, *Charles II*, p. 139.

171. Ibid., pp. 258, 433.

172. Heath, *Glories and Magnificent Triumphs*, pp. 172–5.

173. J. Heath, *A Brief Chronicle of the Late Intestine War* (Wing H1319, 1663), pp. 842, 852–3.

174. G. Bate, *The Lives, Actions, and Execution of the Prime Actors, and Principall Contrivers of that Horrid Murder of Our Late Pious and Sacred Soveraigne, King Charles the First* (Wing B1084, 1661), p. 20.

175. *The Tryal of Sir Henry Vane, Kt. at the Kings Bench, Westminster, June the 2d. and 6th, 1662* (Wing T2216, 1662); Heath, *Brief Chronicle*, p. 782.

176. *Tryal of Sir Henry Vane*, p. 85.

177. Ibid., p. 88.

178. Heath, *Brief Chronicle*, p. 782.

179. R. L'Estrange, *Considerations and Proposals in Order to the Regulation of the Press Together with Diverse Instances of Treasonous, and Seditious Pamphlets, Proving the Necessity Thereof* (Wing L1229, 1663), sig. A3.
180. See on these trials, K. Sharpe, *The Personal Rule of Charles I* (New Haven, CT, and London, 1992), pp. 758–65; C. Herrup, *A House in Gross Disorder: Sex, Law, and the 2nd earl of Castlehaven* (Oxford, 1999); A. Bellany, *The Politics of Court Scandal in Early Modern England: News Culture and the Overbury Affair, 1603–1660* (Cambridge, 2002).
181. *An Exact Account of the Trials of the Several Persons Arraigned at the Sessions-house in the Old-Bailey* (Wing E3590, 1678). Judging by the number of such tracts, there appears to have been a growing public interest in the processes of justice.
182. *The Execution of Henry Bury* (Wing E3851A, 1679); *The Tryals of Robert Green, Henry Berry, & Lawrence Hill, for the Murder of Sir Edmond-Bury Godfrey* (Wing T2257, 1678).
183. For a good account see T. Harris, *Restoration: Charles II and His Kingdoms, 1660–1685* (London and New York, 2005), ch. 3; J. P. Kenyon, *The Popish Plot* (London, 1972).
184. *A True Relation of the Execution of Mr. William Staley at Tyburn* (Wing T2949, 1678), p. 3.
185. http://www.catholic.org/saints/saint.php?saint_id=3987
186. *The Tryal of Edward Coleman, Gent. for Conspiring the Death of the King* (Wing T2185, 1678), pp. 15–16 and *passim*; *The Lord Chief Justice Scroggs His Speech in the King-Bench, the First Day of This Present Michaelmas Term 1679* (Wing S2122, 1679), p. 6. J. Pollock assesses that Scroggs treated evidence fairly and followed 'rules of procedure', J. Pollock, *The Popish Plot* (London, 1903), pp. 355–6.
187. Pocock, *Popish Plot*, p. 355.
188. J. Corker, *Stafford's Memoires, or, A Brief and Impartial Account of the Birth and Quality, Imprisonment, Tryal, Principles, Declaration, Comportment, Devotion, Last Speech, and Final End, of William, Late Lord Viscount Stafford* (Wing C6306, 1681); *The Relation of the Tryal and Condemnation of Edward FitzHarris* (Wing R881A, 1681); *The Arraignment, Tryal and Condemnation of Stephen Colledge* (Wing A3762, 1681); *The Triall of Henry Carr . . . also the Tryal of Elizabeth Cellier, at Kings Bench Bar, July the 11th, 1680* (Wing T2190, 1681); *An Account of the Tryals of William Ld. Russell, William Hone, John Rouse, and William Blake* (Wing A419, 1683). All these trials were the subject of contesting accounts, elegies, poems, etc.
189. *Arraignment, Tryal and Condemnation of Stephen Colledge*, p. 97.
190. Harris, *Restoration*, pp. 191–2; A. Havighurst, 'The Judiciary and Politics in the Reign of Charles II', *Law Quarterly Review*, 66 (1950), part II, pp. 250–2 and 229–52 *passim*.
191. Ibid., pp. 242, 247.
192. Ibid., p. 250.
193. Of course, the resurgence of the Tories reversed the Whig-packed juries of 1680–1. See G. de Krey, *London and the Restoration, 1659–1683* (Cambridge, 2005), pp. 231–8, 370–82 and *passim*.
194. Havighurst, 'The Judiciary and Politics in the Reign of Charles II', pp. 245–6. For a different emphasis, however, see Lois Schwoerer, 'The Trial of Lord William Russell (1683): Judicial Murder?', *Journal of Legal History*, 9 (1988), pp. 142–68.
195. Havighurst, 'The Judiciary', pp. 232, 247; Pollock, *Popish Plot*, pp. 355–6, 371.
196. See K. Sharpe, *Image Wars: Promoting Kings and Commonwealths in England* (New Haven, CT, and London, 2010), pp. 115–18, 250–4.
197. See J. Morrill, 'The Religious Context of the English Civil War', *Transactions of the Royal Historical Society*, 34 (1984), pp. 155–78; Morrill, 'Introduction: England's Wars of Religion', in *The Nature of the English Revolution* (London; New York, 1993), pp. 33–44.
198. Below, ch. 3, pp. 177–8.
199. A. Bryant ed., *The Letters, Speeches and Declarations of King Charles II* (London, 1935), p. 85.
200. See J. Spurr, *The Restoration Church of England, 1646–1689* (New Haven, CT, and London, 1991); I. Green, *The Re-establishment of the Church of England, 1660–1663* (Oxford, 1978). On the inherent ambiguities of the Restoration supremacy, see J. Rose, 'Royal Ecclesiastical Supremacy and the Restoration Church', *Historical Research*, 80 (2007), pp. 324–45.
201. R. Hutton, 'The Religion of Charles II', in R. M. Smuts ed., *The Stuart Court and Europe: Essays in Politics and Political Culture* (Cambridge, 1996). pp. 228–46.
202. Ibid., pp. 237–8.
203. Ibid., p. 238 and *passim*.
204. Spurr, *Restoration Church*.
205. Ibid., pp. 42–60; J. Glanvill, *A Loyal Tear Dropt on the Vault of Our Late Martyred Sovereign* (Wing G813, 1667), p. 27.
206. Spurr, *Restoration Church*, p. 51.

207. Ibid., pp. 51–2.

208. P. Seawead, *The Cavalier Parliament and the Reconstruction of the Old Regime, 1661–1667* (Cambridge, 1989), pp. 189–91.

209. W. Assheton, *Toleration Disapprov'd and Condemn'd by the Authority and Convincing Reasons* (Wing A4047, 1670); cf. J. Shafte, *The Great Law of Nature, or, Self-preservation Examined, Asserted and Vindicated from Mr. Hobbes his Abuses* (Wing S2888, 1673), p. 78; S. Bethel, *The Present Interest of England Stated by a Lover of his King and Country* (Wing B2072, 1671), pp. 13–15.

210. Spurr, *Restoration Church*, pp. 61–7; above, ch. 1, p. 74.

211. *Interrogatories, or, A dialogue between Whig and Tory* (Wing I272, 1681), broadside.

212. A phrase and idea I take from G. Bernard, 'The Church of England, c.1529–c.1642', *History*, 75 (1990), pp. 183–206. I am grateful to George Bernard for many fruitful discussions of this subject.

213. *The Works of that Learned and Judicious Divine, Mr. Richard Hooker* (Wing H2633, 1682), sigs A2–A3ᵛ. The reiteration reminds us, of course, that this was more a polemical stance than innocent description.

214. B. Calamy, *A Sermon Preached Before the Lord Mayor, Aldermen, and Citizens of London at Bow-Church on the 29th of May 1682* (Wing C216, 1682), especially p. 28.

215. C. Powell, *The Religious Rebel a Sermon Preach'd at South-Marston near Hyworth in Wiltshire* (Wing P3046, 1683), pp. 15, 23–4.

216. F. Turner, *A Sermon Preach'd Before the King in the Cathedral Church of Winchester* (Wing T2382, 1683), p. 2 and *passim*; S. Scattergood, *A Sermon Preached at Blockley in Worcestershire* (Wing S844, 1683), p. 30 and *passim*.

217. J. Scott, *A Sermon Preached Before the Right Honourable the Lord Mayor, and Court of Aldermen, at the Guild-Hall Chappel, the 16th of December, 1683* (Wing S2067, 1684), pp. 29, 34.

218. W. Prynne, *The First Tome of an Exact Chronological Vindication and Historical Demonstration of our British, Roman, Saxon, Danish, Norman, English Kings Supream Ecclesiastical Jurisdiction* (Wing P3950A, 1666), sigs B1–B1ᵛ and epistle dedicatory *passim*. See Prynne, *ODNB*.

219. T. Tenison, *The Creed of Mr. Hobbes Examined in a Feigned Conference Between Him and a Student in Divinity* (Wing T691, 1670).

220. S. Parker, *A Discourse of Ecclesiastical Politie Wherein the Authority of the Civil Magistrate over the Consciences of Subjects in Matters of Religion Is Asserted* (Wing P459, 2670), pp. xliv.

221. E. Stillingfleet, *A Sermon Preached November V, 1673 at St. Margarets Westminst.* (Wing S 5643, 1674), p. 39; cf. W. Penn, *England's Present Interest Discover'd* (Wing P1279, 1675).

222. Spurr, *Restoration Church*, p. xii. See also Spurr, 'Perjury, Profanity and Politics', *Seventeenth Century*, 8 (1993), pp. 29–50.

223. Hutton, 'Religion of Charles II', pp. 237, 240; cf. Keay, *Magnificent Monarch*, ch. 8.

224. Spurr, *Restoration Church*, p. 29.

225. J. Dolben, *A Sermon Preached before His Majesty on Good-Friday at Whitehall, March 24, 1664/5* (Wing D1831, 1665), p. 36.

226. E. Stillingfleet, *A Sermon Preached before the King, March 13, 1666/7* (Wing S5641, 1667), p. 27.

227. M. Barne, *A Sermon Preached before the King at Newmarket April 24, 1670* (Wing B860, 1670), p. 8.

228. Parker, *Discourse*, p. xlv.

229. B. Calamy, *A Sermon Preached before the Lord Mayor, Aldermen, and Citizens of London at Bow-Church on the 29th of May 1682* (Wing C216, 1682), p. 31.

230. Spurr, *Restoration Church*, pp. 228–9; G. Burnet, *Some Passages of the Life and Death of the Right Honourable John, Earl of Rochester Who Died the 26th of July, 1680* (Wing B5922, 1680).

231. Spurr, *Restoration Church*, p. 373.

232. Hutton, *Charles II*, p. 450.

233. J. Clare, *Drama of the English Republic, 1649–1660* (Manchester, 2002), pp. 181–91. Andrew Walkling is making a systematic study of the court entertainments of Charles II. See Walkling, 'Politics and the Restoration Masque: The Case of *Dido and Aeneas*', in Maclean, *Culture and Society*, pp. 52–69; Walkling, 'Masque and Politics at the Restoration Court: John Crowne's *Callisto*', *Early Music*, 24 (1996), pp. 27–62; 'The Apotheosis of Absolutism and the Interrupted Masque: Theater, Music, and Monarchy in Restoration England', in C. MacLeod and J. Alexander eds, *Politics, Transgression, and Representation at the Court of Charles II* (New Haven, CT, and London, 2007), pp. 193–231.

234. P. Holman, *Henry Purcell* (Oxford, 1984), p. 2.

235. See Keay, *Magnificent Monarch*, pp. 148–9; Holman, *Purcell*, pp. 13–15 and *passim*; M. Campbell, *Henry Purcell, Glory of His Age* (London, 1993), pp. 20–1, 26–7, 31–2, ch. 5, *passim*.

236. Holman, *Purcell*, p. 125.

237. Ibid., p. 198.
238. Hutton, *Charles II*, p. 450.
239. Ibid., p. 448.
240. J. Evelyn, *A Panegyric to Charles the Second* (Wing E3506, 1661), p. 14.
241. Ibid.
242. T. Sprat, *The History of the Royal-Society of London for the Improving of Natural Knowledge* (Wing S5032, 1667), epistle dedicatory to king.
243. Ibid., p. 62.
244. Ibid., p. 56.
245. Ibid., pp. 113, 426.
246. Ibid., p. 427.
247. Ibid., p. 133.
248. J. Wilkins, *An Essay Towards a Real Character, and a Philosophical Language* (Wing W2196, 1668), sig. B.
249. J. Webb, *An Historical Essay Endeavoring a Probability that the Language of the Empire of China is the Primitive Language* (Wing W1202, 1669), sig. A2.
250. Above, ch. 1, p. 11.
251. S. Owen, *Restoration Theatre and Crisis* (Oxford, 1996), p. 16.
252. Ibid., p. 11.
253. Ibid., p. 14. See D. Hughes, *English Drama, 1660–1700* (Oxford, 1996). And D. Hume, *The Development of English Drama in the Late Seventeenth Century* (Oxford, 1976).
254. N. Maguire, *Regicide and Restoration: English Tragicomedy, 1660–1671* (Cambridge, 1992).
255. Owen, *Restoration Theatre*, p. 19; cf. D. Hughes, 'Restoration and Settlement: 1660 and 1688', in D. Fisk ed., *The Cambridge Companion to English Restoration Theatre* (Cambridge, 2000), ch. 8.
256. This remains a vast subject which I can only gesture to in this study of royal representations.
257. J. Tatham, *The Rump: or The Mirrour of the Late Times A New Comedy* (Wing T234A, 1661); Hughes, *English Drama*, pp. 30–1.
258. E. Howard, *The Usurper, a Tragedy as it Was Acted at the Theatre Royal by His Majesties Servants* (Wing H2975, 1668); Hughes, *English Drama*, p. 35.
259. *The Unfortunate Usurper a Tragedy* (Wing U59, 1663), quotations pp. 53, 71; see Hughes, *English Drama*, p. 56 n.
260. J. Caryll, *The English Princess, or, The Death of Richard III. A Tragedy* (Wing C744, 1667), p. 43.
261. E. Avery, 'The Restoration Audience', *Philological Quarterly*, 45 (1966), pp. 54–61; H. Love, 'Who Were the Restoration Audience?', *Yearbook of English Studies*, 10 (1980), pp. 21–44; see *A True, Perfect, and Exact Catalogue of all the Comedies, Tragedies, Tragi-comedies, Pastorals, Masques and Interludes, that Were Ever Yet Printed and Published, Till this Present Year 1671 All which You May Either Buy or Sell, at the Shop of Francis Kirkman, in Thames-Street, Over Against the Custom House* (Wing K637A, 1671).
262. R. Baker, *Theatrum Triumphans, or, A Discourse of Plays* (Wing B514, 1670), pp. 128, 141 and 128–41 *passim*.
263. W. M., *Huntington Divertisement, or, An Enterlude for the Generall Entertainment at the County-feast, Held at Merchant-Taylors Hall, June 20, 1678* (Wing M95, 1678), sig. B.
264. Ibid., p. 26.
265. Ibid., p. 48.
266. J. D., *The Coronation of Queen Elizabeth, with the Restauration of the Protestant Religion, or, The Downfal of the Pope Being a Most Excellent Play, as it was Acted Both at Bartholomew and Southwark Fairs, this Present Year, 1680* (Wing D31, 1680).
267. N. Lee, *Lucius Junius Brutus, Father of His Country a Tragedy* (Wing L852, 1681); Owen, *Theatre and Crisis*, ch. 8, pp. 253–4.
268. Owen, *Theatre and Crisis*, pp. 220–5; Hughes, *English Drama*, p. 278.
269. N. Tate, *The Ingratitude of a Common-wealth, or, The Fall of Caius Martius Coriolanus as it is Acted at the Theatre-Royal* (Wing T190, 1682), epistle dedicatory.
270. Ibid., Prologue, sig. A4.
271. Ibid., Epilogue, p. 64.
272. Owen, *Theatre and Crisis*, pp. 267–9; J. Banks, *The Unhappy Favourite, or, The Earl of Essex a Tragedy: Acted at the Theatre Royal by Their Majesty's Servants* (Wing B663, 1682), prologue to king and queen (not paginated).
273. For example, J. Dryden, *Prologue to His Royal Highness Upon His First Appearance at the Duke's Theatre Since his Return from Scotland Written by Mr. Dryden* (Wing D2336, 1682); Dryden,

Prologue to the King and Queen at the Opening of their Theatre (Wing D 2339A, 1683); A. Behn, *Prologue to Romulus Spoken by Mrs. Butler* (Wing B1760, 1682).

274. J. Fitzwilliam, *A Sermon Preach'd at Cotenham, Near Cambridge, on the 9th. of September, 1683* (Wing F1106, 1683), p. 31.
275. There are many popular biographies of Charles II. The authoritative scholarly studies are Hutton, *Charles II*, and J. Miller, *Charles II* (London, 1991).
276. R. Kingston, *Vivat Rex a Sermon Preached Before the Right Worshipful the Mayor, Aldermen, Council and Citizens of Bristol* (Wing K617, 1683), p. 10.
277. Miller, *Charles II*, p. xiii.
278. R. Ollard, *The Image of the King: Charles I and Charles II* (London, 1979).
279. Hutton, *Charles II*, Conclusion, pp. 446–58 and *passim*.
280. Ollard, *Image of the King*, p. 147.
281. Heath, *Glories and Magnificent Triumphs*, pp. 76–7.
282. W. Charleton, *A Character of His Most Sacred Majesty, Charles the Second* (Wing C3665, 1661), p. 10.
283. Hutton, *Charles II*, p. 447.
284. Samuel Tuke, *A Character of Charles the Second, Written by an Impartial Hand and Exposed to Publick View for Information of the People* (Wing T3232, 1660), p. 4.
285. Ibid., p. 6.
286. Arthur Brett, *The Restauration Or, A Poem on the Return of the Most Mighty and Ever Glorious Prince, Charles the II. to His Kingdoms* (Wing B4397, 1660), p. 9.
287. See, for example, Francis Gregory, *David's Returne from his Banishment Set Forth in a Thanks-giving Sermon for the Returne of His Sacred Majesty Charles the II* (Wing G1888, 1660), pp. 20–2; Charleton, *Character*.
288. Amelot de La Houssiae, *The History of the Government of Venice* (Wing A2974, 1677), p. 42.
289. They included greyhound racing, fishing, tennis, swimming, falconry, horse racing, gambling, bowling, hawking, dancing, sailing and the theatre; see Hutton, *Charles II*, pp. 378–9, 448–9.
290. Fabian Philipps, *Ursa Major & Minor* (Wing P2019A, 1681), p. 46.
291. Aurelian Cook, *Titus Britannicus an Essay of History Royal, in the Life & Reign of His Late Sacred Majesty, Charles II* (Wing C5996, 1685), pp. 505–6; Hutton, *Charles II*, pp. 133–4.
292. Sharpe, 'His Longing Country's Darling'; *Eikon Basilike Deutera, The Pourtraicture of His Sacred Majesty King Charles II* (Wing E312, 1694), p. 80.
293. Keay, *Magnificent Monarch*, p. 111.
294. Cook, *Titus Britannicus*, epistle dedicatory (unpaginated).
295. Ibid., p. 380.
296. See Brian Weiser, *Charles II and the Politics of Access* (Woodbridge, 2003), ch. 3.
297. Hutton, *Charles II*, p. 458.
298. Ibid., p. 156.
299. See James's own war memoirs, A. Lytton Sells ed., *The Memoirs of James II: His Campaigns as Duke of York, 1652–1660* (Bloomington, IN, 1962); Ogilby, *Relation of His Majestie's entertainment*, p. 19.
300. See James II, *ODNB*.
301. Above, ch. 2, p. 102.
302. J. Callow, *The Making of James II* (Stroud, 2000), pp. 218–21; J. Miller, *James II: A Study in Kingship* (London, 1991), p. 50.
303. E. Waller, *Instructions to a Painter for the Drawing of the Posture & Progress of His Ma[jes]ties Forces at Sea* (Wing W500, 1666), p. 15.
304. J. Logan, *Analogia Honorum, or, A Treatise of Honour and Nobility* (Wing L2834, 1677), p. 8.
305. Hutton, *Charles II*, p. 387.
306. W. B., *The White Rose, or, A Word for the House of York* (Wing B5268, 1680), p. 1.
307. *A True Narrative of the Reception of Their Royal Highnesses at Their Arrival in Scotland* (Wing T2837, 1680), p. 2 and *passim*.
308. Ibid., pp. 2–3.
309. *A True and Exact Relation of His Royal Highness, James, Duke of Albany and York His Progress from Edinburgh to Linlithgow, from thence to Stirling, and Back Again to Edinburgh* (Wing T2443, 1681), p. 3.
310. Hutton, *Charles II*, p. 412.
311. M. Taubman, *An Heroick Poem to His Royal Highness the Duke of York on His Return from Scotland with Some Choice Songs and Medleyes on the Times* (Wing T239, 1682); on Taubman, see *ODNB*. See also C. Calle, *On His Royal Highness's Miraculous Delivery, and Happy Return* (Wing C299, 1682); *A*

Congratulatory Poem on His Royal Highness, James, Duke of York (Wing C5823, 1682); *Great York and Albany, or, The Loyal Welcome to His Royal Highness on His Return from Scotland to the Tune of, 'Hey boys up Go We.'* (Wing G1788, 1682); *His Royal Highness the Duke of York's Welcom to London a Congratulatory Poem*, London (Wing H2089, 1682); *London's Joy and Loyalty on His Royal Highness the Duke of York's Return out of Scotland to the Tune of London's Loyalty* (Wing L2933, 1682).

312. Taubman, *Heroic Poem.*
313. T. Otway, *Epilogue to Her Royal Highness, on Her Return from Scotland* (Wing 546, 1682).
314. *Great York and Albany*, n.p.
315. Calle, *On His Royal Highness's Miraculous Delivery*, n.p.
316. *A Congratulatory Poem to Her Royal Highness upon the Arrival of Their Royal Highness's in England, May the 27th, 1682* (Wing C5833, 1682).
317. *London's Joy and Loyalty on His Royal Highness the Duke of York's Return out of Scotland to the Tune of London's Loyalty* (Wing L2933, 1682).
318. Sharpe, *Image Wars*, pp. 104–7, 234–5, 244–7.
319. *Calendars of State Papers Domestic, 1663–4*, pp. 122, 247, 264–5, 287.
320. *Calendars of State Papers Domestic, 1664–5*, pp. 414, 512, 538, 555, 568.
321. *Calendars of State Papers Domestic 1671*, pp. 391–2, 437, 489–91.
322. *Calendars of State Papers Domestic 1677–8*, p. 313; see also pp. 95, 232, 295–6, 318.
323. *Calendars of State Papers Domestic 1663–4*, p. 594; *1664–5*, pp. 71, 244, 247, 480, 488, 493, 499; *1671–2*, pp. 429, 475; *1673*, pp. 164–5, 254–5, 411; *1675–6*, p. 183; *1676–7*, p. 510; *1677–8*, pp. 232, 295, 296, 318.
324. *Calendars of State Papers Domestic 1676–7*, p. 62; *1682*, pp. 111–55; and again in September, pp. 454–84.
325. Hutton writes of the king's 'restless energy', *Charles II*, p. 278.
326. Latham and Matthew eds, *Diary of Pepys*, I, p. 158.
327. Cook, *Titus*, p. 505; Rochester, 'A Ramble in St James's Park', in Love, *Works of Rochester*, pp. 76–81.
328. A. Browning ed., *Memoirs of Sir John Reresby* (Glasgow, 1936), p. 259.
329. See Weiser, *Charles II and the Politics of Access.*

4 A Changed Culture, Divided Kingdom and Contested Kingship

1. Above, ch. 1, pp. 88–9.
2. J. Dryden, *To His sacred Maiesty, A Panegyrick on His Coronation* (Wing D2386, 1661), p. 7; *His Majesties Most Gracious Speech, together with the Lord Chancellors, to the Two Houses of Parliament, on Thursday the 13 of September, 1660* (Wing C3073, 1660), p. 12. See also E. Willan, *Beatitas Britanniae, or, King Charles the Second, Englands Beatitude as Preached to the Incorporation of the Honour of Eay, in the County of Suffolk, March 31, 1661* (Wing W2260, 1661), p. 36.
3. The term 'Whig' was applied to Presbyterian Covenanters in the west of Scotland and 'Tory' to outlaw Irish papists or Royalists, *OED*. My emphasis in this chapter is on contested memory.
4. G. Morley, *A Sermon Preached at the Magnificent Coronation of the Most High and Mighty King Charles the IId King of Great Britain* (Wing M2794, 1661), sig. A2.
5. Ibid., sig. A2ᵛ.
6. Ibid., sig. A4.
7. Willan, *Beatitas Britanniae*, pp. 12, 19–20, 34, 36.
8. A. Brett, *The Restauration Or, A Poem on the Return of the Most Mighty and Ever Glorious Prince, Charles the II. to His kingdoms* (Wing B3497, 1660), p. 8.
9. J. Davies, *The Civil Warres of Great Britain and Ireland Containing an Exact History of their Occasion, Originall, Progress, and Happy End / by an Impartiall Pen* (Wing D393, 1661), sigs *2–*2ᵛ.
10. W. C., *The History of the Commons Warre of England throughout These Three Nations Begun from 1640 and Continued till this Present Year 1662* (Wing C154, 1662); J. Heath, *A Brief Chronicle of the Late Intestine War in the Three Kingdoms of England, Scotland and Ireland* (Wing H1319, 1663); Heath, *A Brief Chronicle of all the Chief Actions So Fatally Falling Out in These Three Kingdoms, viz. England, Scotland & Ireland from the Year, 1640, to This Present Twentieth of November, 1661* (Wing H1318A, 1662); R. Baker, *A Chronicle of the Kings of England* (Wing B504, 1660). On Restoration histories of the civil war, see R. Macgillivray, *Restoration Historians and the English Civil War* (The Hague, 1964).
11. T. Sprat, *The History of the Royal-Society of London* (Wing S5032, 1667), p. 44. This vitally important treatise of Restoration politics is too often confined to studies of science.

12. R. Meggott, *A Sermon Preached Before the Right Honourable the Lord Major and Aldermen, &c. at Guild-Hall Chappel, January the 30th 1673/4* (Wing M1621, 1674), pp. 37, 47.

13. T. Cartwright, *A Sermon Preached July 17, 1676, in the Cathedral Church of St. Peter in York* (Wing C703, 1676), p. 33.

14. Heath, *Chronicle of the Late Intestine War* (Bodleian K1 18 Art, 1676).

15. G. Bate, *The Lives, Actions, and Execution of the Prime Actors, and Principall Contrivers of that Horrid Murder of Our Late Pious and Sacred Soveraigne, King Charles the First* (Wing B1084, 1661); Bate was first physician to the king, *ODNB*; W. Winstanley, *The Loyall Martyrology, or, Brief Catalogues and Characters of the Most Eminent Persons Who Suffered for their Conscience During the Late Times of Rebellion* (Wing W3066, 1665), quotation, p. 75; on the royalist biographer and poet Winstanley, see *ODNB*.

16. A. Lacey, *The Cult of King Charles the Martyr* (Woodbridge, 2003), p. 164 and ch. 5 *passim*.

17. *Cromwell's Conspiracy. A Tragy-comedy, Relating to Our Latter Times* (Wing C7193, 1660); Baker, *Chronicle*, pp. 543–5.

18. R. Flecknoe, *Heroick Portraits* (Wing F1225, 1660), sigs H–H2; Flecknoe, *The Idea of His Highness Oliver, Late Lord Protector* (Wing F1226, 1659); Flecknoe, *ODNB*.

19. A. Cowley, *A Vision, Concerning His Late Pretended Highnesse, Cromwell* (Wing C6695, 1661), p. 3.

20. S. Bethel, *The World's Mistake in Oliver Cromwell* (Wing B2079B, 1668), pp. 1–2.

21. See, for example, R. Wild, *Oliver Cromwells Ghost, or, Old Noll Newly Revived* (Wing W2143, 1678).

22. J. Riland, *Elias the Second His Coming to Restore All Things, or, God's Way of Reforming by Restoring; and, Moses the Peace-maker His Offers to Make One of Two Contending Brethren in Two Sermons: the Former Preacht in Warwick at the Generall Assize There Held August 19, 1661: the other in Coventry at the Annuall Solemnity of the Maior's Feast on All-Saints Day* (Wing R1519, 1662), sermon II, p. 41.

23. Cf. A. Houston and S. Pincus, 'Introduction: modernity and later seventeenth-century England', in Houston and Pincus eds, *A Nation Transformed: England after the Restoration* (Cambridge, 2001), pp. 1–19.

24. W. C., *History of the Commons Warre*, sig. A3ᵛ.

25. Ibid.

26. Heath, *A Brief Chronicle of the Late Intestine War* (Wing H1319, 1663), preface to reader.

27. J. Nalson, *The Common Interest of King and People* (Wing N93, 1678), p. 99.

28. R. L'Estrange, *An Account of the Growth of Knavery under the Pretended Fears of Arbitrary Government and Popery with a Parallel Betwixt the Reformers of 1677 and Those of 1641 in their Methods and Designs* (Wing L1193, 1678).

29. Wild, *Oliver Cromwell's Ghost*.

30. C. Blount, *An appeal from the country to the city* (Wing B3300, 1679); on Blount, see *ODNB*.

31. J. Rushworth, *Historical Collections of Private Passages of State* (Wing R2317–19, 1680); J. Nalson, *An Impartial Collection of the Great Affairs of State, from the Beginning of the Scotch Rebellion in the Year MDCXXXIX. To the Murther of King Charles I* (Wing N106A, 1682).

32. *Eikon Basilike* (Wing E311A, 1681); see, for example, T. May, *A Breviary of the History of the Parliament of England* (Wing M1397, 1680). On May, see *ODNB*.

33. *Arbitrary Government Displayed to the Life* (Bodleian Libraries. 8° C504, 1682).

34. E. Hickeringill, *The History of Whiggism* (Wing H1809, 1682). On Hickeringill, see *ODNB*.

35. G. Aylmer, *The Crown's Servants: Government and the Civil Service under Charles II, 1660–1685* (Oxford, 2002), ch. 4.

36. Houston and Pincus eds, *A Nation Transformed, passim*.

37. See N. Cuddy, 'The Real, Attempted "Tudor Revolution in Government": Salisbury's 1610 Great Contract', in G. Bernard and S. Gunn eds, *Authority and Consent in Tudor England* (Aldershot, 2002), pp. 249–70.

38. Ibid.; E. Lindquist, 'The Failure of the Great Contract', *Journal of Modern History*, 57 (1985), pp. 617–51.

39. F. Philipps, *Tenenda non Tollenda, or, The Necessity of Preserving Tenures in Capite and by Knight-service* (Wing P2019, 1660), sig. A2. This is an important but neglected work, one of three by Philipps against the abolition of feudal tenures, *ODNB*.

40. Philipps, *Tenenda non Tollenda*, sig. A4.

41. F. Philipps, *The Antiquity, Legality, Reason, Duty and Necessity of Prae-emption and Pourveyance, for the King* (Wing P2004, 1663), p. 268.

42. Ibid., p. 275.

43. Ibid., p. 307.

44. *His Majestie's Gracious Speech, Together with the Lord Chancellor's, to Both Houses of Parliament; on Saturday the 29th day of December, 1660* (Wing C3074, 1660), p. 31; T. Fuller, *A Panegyrick to His Majesty on His Happy Return* (Wing F2452, 1660), p. 11.

45. S. Bethel, *The Present Interest of England* (B2072, 1671). See S. Pincus, 'From Holy Cause to Economic Interest: The Study of Population and the Intervention of the State', in A. Houston and S. Pincus eds, *A Nation Transformed: England after the Restoration* (Cambridge, 2002), pp. 272–98; see also ibid., introduction, pp. 1–19.

46. On the language of interest, see J. Gunn, *Politics and the Public Interest in the Seventeenth Century* (London, 1969); E. Vallance, 'The Decline of Conscience as a Political Guide: William Higden's *View of the English Constitution* (1709)', in H. Braun and E. Vallance, *Contexts of Conscience in Early Modern Europe, 1500–1700* (Basingstoke, 2004), pp. 67–81.

47. G. S., *The Dignity of Kingship Asserted: In Answer to Mr. Milton's Ready and Easie Way to Establish a Free Common-wealth* (Wing S3069, 1660), sig. A6.

48. M. Wren, *Monarchy Asserted, or The State of Monarchicall and Popular Government; in Vindication of the Considerations upon Mr. Harringtons Oceana* (Wing W3677, 3678; 1659, 1660).

49. T. Reeve, *England's Beauty in Seeing King Charles the Second Restored to Majesty* (Wing R688, 1661), p. 35.

50. R. Latham and W. Matthews eds, *Diary of Samuel Pepys* (11 vols, 1970–83), I, p. 158; *Votivum Carolo, or, A Welcome to His Sacred Majesty Charles the II from the Masters and Scholars of Woodstock-School in the County of Oxford* (Wing W3475, 1660), p. 3.

51. T. Hobbes, *Leviathan, or, The Matter, Form, and Power of a Common-wealth* (Wing H2248, 1651).

52. Hobbes, *Leviathan* (Wing H2248A, 1676). See J. Parkin, *Taming the Leviathan: The Reception of the Political and Religious Ideas of Thomas Hobbes in England, 1640–1700* (Cambridge, 2007), chs 4–6.

53. *An Elegie upon Mr. Thomas Hobbes of Malmesbury Lately Deceased* (Wing E458, 1679), one page.

54. *The Solemn Mock-procession, or, The Tryal & Execution of the Pope and His Ministers on the 17 of Nov.* (Wing S4452D, 1680), p. 5.

55. T. Rymer, *A General Draught and Prospect of Government in Europe, and Civil Policy Shewing the Antiquity, Power, Decay, of Parliaments* (Wing R2426, 1681), p. 77.

56. Ibid., p. 78.

57. Hickeringill, *History of Whiggism* (Bodleian Ashmole 1679/22, 1682), p. 6.

58. Rymer, *A General Draught*, p. 70.

59. J. Dryden, *His Majesties Declaration Defended in a Letter to a Friend Being an Answer to a Seditious Pamphlet* (Wing D2286, 1681), p. 16.

60. J. Evelyn, *Publick Employment and an Active Life Prefer'd to Solitude* (Wing E3510, 1667), pp. 115–16.

61. Hickeringill, *History of Whiggism*, see K. Sharpe and S. Zwicker, *Refiguring Revolutions: Aesthetics and Politics from the English Revolution to the Romantic Revolution* (Berkeley, CA, and London, 1998), introduction, pp. 1–24.

62. E. Chamberlayne, *Angliae Notitia, or The Present State of England Together with Divers Reflections upon the Antient State Thereof* (Wing C1819, 1667), p. 32.

63. F. Philipps, *Regale Necessarium, or, The Legality, Reason, and Necessity of the Rights and Priviledges Justly Claimed by the Kings Servants* (Wing P2016, 1671), sigs A2–A2ᵛ; J. Nalson, *The Common Interest of King and People* (Wing N93, 1678), p. 126.

64. W. Dugdale, *The Antient Usage in Bearing of Such Ensigns of Honour as Are Commonly Call'd Arms* (Wing D2477C, 1682), sig. A1.

65. *Elegie upon Mr. Thomas Hobbes*; see K. Sharpe, 'Restoration and Reconstitution: Politics, Society and Culture in the England of Charles II', in C. McLeod and J. Alexander eds, *Painted Ladies* (London, 2001), pp. 7–21.

66. K. Sharpe, *Image Wars: Promoting Kings and Commonwealths in England, 1603–1660* (New Haven, CT, and London, 2010), ch. 9.

67. D. Kastan, 'Print, Literary Culture and the Book Trade', in D. Loewenstein and J. Mueller eds, *The Cambridge History of Early Modern English Literature* (Cambridge, 2002), ch. 3, especially p. 107.

68. See H. Webber, *Paper Bullets: Print and Kingship under Charles II* (Lexington, KY, 1996).

69. J. Heath, *The Glories and Magnificent Triumphs of the Blessed Restitution of His Sacred Majesty K. Charles II* (Wing H1335, 1662), pp. 271–2.

70. R. Brathwaite, *To His Majesty Upon His Happy Arrivall in Our Late Discomposed Albion* (Wing B4277, 1660), p. 10.

71. *Speculum Politiae, or, Englands Mirrour Being a Looking-glass for the Body Politick of this Nation* (Wing S4852, 1660), sig. A2.

72. G. S., *The Dignity of Kingship Asserted*, sig. A6ᵛ.

73. 14 Ch. II cap. 33; Kastan, 'Print, Literary Culture', p. 108.
74. See J. Walker, 'The Censorship of the Press during the Reign of Charles II', *History*, 35 (1950), pp. 219–38; G. Kemp, 'L'Estrange and the Publishing Sphere', in J. McGelligott ed., *Fear, Exclusion and Revolution: Roger Morrice and Britain in the 1680s* (Aldershot, 2006), pp. 67–90.
75. See A. Duncan-Page and B. Lynch eds, *Roger L'Estrange and the Making of Restoration Culture* (Aldershot, 2008); P. Hinds, 'Roger L'Estrange, the Rye House Plot, and the Regulation of Political Discourse in Late Seventeenth-Century London', *The Library*, 3 (2002), pp. 3–31; *The Horrid Popish Plot: Roger L'Estrange and the Circulation of Political Discourse in Late Seventeenth-Century London* (Oxford, 2009).
76. R. L'Estrange, *Considerations and Proposals in Order to the Regulation of the Press Together with Diverse Instances of Treasonous, and Seditious Pamphlets, Proving the Necessity Thereof* (Wing L1229, 1663), sig. A3v and epistle dedicatory, *passim*.
77. Ibid., p. 26.
78. G. Kitchin, *Sir Roger L'Estrange: A Contribution to the History of the Press in the Seventeenth Century* (London, 1913).
79. R. Atkyns, *The Original and Growth of Printing Collected out of History, and the Records of this Kingdome: Wherein Is also Demonstrated, That printing Appertaineth to the Prerogative Royal, and Is a Flower of the Crown of England* (Wing A4135, 1664); Atkyns, *The Original and Growth of Printing* (Wing A4134, 1660). 'Texts and laws are the foundations of monarchy.'
80. Atkyns, *Original and Growth of Printing Collected out of History*, sig. B2, pp. 3, 6–7.
81. Ibid., sig. B1ᵛ.
82. Ibid., p. 2; above, ch. 1, pp. 91–2.
83. E. Howard, *The Usurper, A Tragedy as It Was Acted at the Theatre Royal by His Majesties Servants* (Wing H2975, 1668), sig. A2.
84. *Troia Rediviva, or, The Glories of London Surveyed in an Heroick Poem* (Wing T2301, 1674); N. Hardy, *Lamentation, Mourning, and Woe Sighed Forth in a Sermon Preached in the Parish-church of St. Martin in the Fields, on the 9th day of September: Being the Next Lords-day after the Dismal Fire in the City of London* (Wing H728, 1666), p. 21.
85. J. Ogilby, *Africa: Being an Accurate Description of the Regions of Aegypt, Barbary, Lybia, and Billedulgerid* (Wing O163, 1670), sigs C–C2ᵛ.
86. This is at last receiving full attention, see Mark Knights, *Politics and Opinion in Crisis, 1678–1681* (Cambridge, 1994); H. Love, 'The Look of News: Popish Plot Narratives 1678–1680', in J. Barnard and D. Mckenzie eds, *The Cambridge History of the Book in Britain, vol. 4: 1557–1695* (Cambridge, 2002), pp. 652–6; S. Randall, 'Newspapers and Their Publishers During the Popish Plot and Exclusion Crisis', in J. Hinks and C. Armstrong eds, *Book Trade Connections from the Seventeenth to the Twentieth Centuries* (New Castle, DE, 2008), pp. 45–70.
87. See R. Weil, ' "If I did say so, I lyed" ': Elizabeth Cellier and the Construction of Credibility in the Popish Plot Crisis', in S. Amussen and M. Kishlansky eds, *Political Culture and Cultural Politics in Early Modern England* (Manchester, 1995), pp. 189–209; M. Knights, *Representation and Misrepresentation in Later Stuart Britain: Partisanship and Political Culture* (Oxford, 2004), especially part II.
88. J. Nalson, *The Countermine, or, A Short But True Discovery of the Dangerous Principles and Secret Practices of the Dissenting Party* (Wing N96, 1677), p. 3 and *passim*.
89. Nalson, *Common Interest*, p. 265.
90. In the Bodleian we have bound volumes of pamphlets arguing for various points of view collected by Anthony Wood.
91. W. Scroggs, *The Lord Chief Justice Scroggs His Speech in the King-Bench, the First Day of this Present Michaelmas Term 1679 Occasioned by the Many Libellous Pamphlets Which Are Publisht Against Law* (Wing S2122, 1679), p. 7 and *passim*; see, for example, the collection of newspapers for 1679 in Bodleian Nich. Newpapers 1B.
92. Bodleian Nich. Newpapers 1B. See M. Knights, *Representation and Misrepresentation in Later Stuart Britain: Partisanship and Political Culture* (Oxford, 2005), part II.
93. Bodleian Wood 424.
94. J. Rushworth, *The Tryal of Thomas, Earl of Strafford* (Wing R2333, 1680), sig. C1; *The Disloyal Forty and Forty One and the Loyal Eighty Presented to Publick View in a Prospect & Scheme, Shewing the Difference of the Years Forty and Forty One from the Year Eighty: Drawn Up and Published to Answer the Clamours of the Malicious and to Inform the Ignorant* (Wing D1670, 1680), p. 2.
95. *Whig and Tory, or, The Scribling Duellists* (Wing W1646, 1681).
96. *Britanniae Speculum* (Wing B4819, 1683), p. 185.

97. J. Dryden, *A Defence of the Papers Written by the Late King of Blessed Memory* (Wing D2261, 1686), sig. A2.
98. A. Cook, *Titus Britannicus An Essay of History Royal, in the Life & Reign of His late Sacred Majesty, Charles II* (Wing C5996, 1785), pp. 424–5.
99. J. Habermas, *Strukturwandel der Öffentlichkeit. Untersuchungen zu einer Kategorie der Bürgerlichen Gesellschaft* (Berlin, 1962), translated as *The Structural Transformation of the Public Sphere: An Inquiry into a Category of Bourgeois Society* (Cambridge, 1989). For a revision of this thesis more applicable to early modern England, see P. Lake and S. Pincus eds, *Rethinking the Public Sphere in Early Modern England* (Manchester 2007); Lake and Pincus, 'Rethinking the Public Sphere in Early Modern England', *Journal of British Studies*, 45 (2006), pp. 270–92.
100. K. Sharpe, *Selling the Tudor Monarchy: Authority and Image in Sixteenth-Century England* (New Haven, CT, and London, 2009).
101. S. Pincus, '"Coffee Politicions Does Create": Coffeehouses and Restoration Political Culture', *Journal of Modern History*, 67 (1995), pp. 807–34; see also B. Cowan, *The Social Life of Coffee: The Emergence of the British Coffeehouse* (New Haven, CT, and London, 2005). On the Restoration public sphere, see Knights, *Representation, passim*, and S. Pincus, 'The State and Civil Society in Early Modern England: Capitalism, Causation and Habermas's Bourgeois Public Sphere', in Lake and Pincus, *The Politics of the Public Sphere*, pp. 213–31 and *passim*.
102. W. Charleton, *An Imperfect Pourtraicture of His Sacred Majesty Charls the II* (Wing C3677, 1661), p. 3.
103. Pincus, '"Coffee Politicions Does Create"', p. 812.
104. Ibid., pp. 813–14.
105. E. Chamberlayne, *Angliae Notitia, or The Present State of England* (Wing C1819, 1669), p. 39. On public opinion in the localities, see Knights, *Politics and Opinion*, part II; Knights, *Representation and Misrepresentation*, ch. 2.
106. J. Dolben, *A Sermon Preached Before the King on Tuesday, June 20th. 1665 Being the Day of Solemn Thanksgiving for the Late Victory at Sea* (Wing D1832, 1665), p. 20.
107. T. Jordan, *The triumphs of London performed on Friday, Octob. 29, 1675* (Wing J1068, 1675), p. 22.
108. Ibid., p. 23.
109. Ibid.
110. Pincus, '"Coffee Politicions Does Create"', pp. 822–3.
111. Ibid., pp. 827–9.
112. Ibid., p. 831.
113. Ibid., p. 832.
114. W. M., *Huntington Divertisement, or, An Enterlude for the Generall Entertainment at the County-feast, Held at Merchant-Taylors Hall, June 20, 1678* (Wing M95, 1678), p. 17.
115. Ibid., p. 22. Note that the entertainment was licensed by L'Estrange.
116. Ibid., p. 25.
117. Ibid., p. 26.
118. Cowan, *Social Life of Coffee*, pp. 199–209.
119. Ibid., pp. 225–9 and p. 227, fig. 37.
120. H. Clark, *His Grace the Duke of Monmouth Honoured in His Progress in the West of England* (Wing C4456, 1680).
121. J. Nalson, *The Complaint of Liberty and Property Against Arbitrary Government* (Wing N95, 1681), pp. 3–4; 'A Letter to the Earl of Shaftesbury' (Bodleian Ashm. G 5 [112], 1680), p. 2.
122. F. Philipps, *Ursa Major & Minor, or, A Sober and Impartial Enquiry into those Bugbear Pretended Fears and Jealousies of Popery and Arbitrary Power* (Wing P2019A, 1681), pp. 47–8.
123. J. Dryden, *His Majesties declaration defended in a letter to a friend being an answer to a seditious pamphlet* (Wing D2286, 1681), p. 5.
124. *Heraclitus Ridens* (January 1681, Bodleian Nicholas Newspapers 3A/40).
125. *A Dialogue between Tom and Dick over a Dish of Coffee Concerning Matters of Religion and Government* (Wing D1337, 1680).
126. T. Rymer, *A General Draught and Prospect of Government in Europe, and Civil Policy* (Wing R2426, 1681), p. 88.
127. *The Deliquium: or, The Grievances of the Nation Discovered in a Dream* (Wing D908, 1681), broadside.
128. J. Brydall, *A New-Years-gift for the Anti-prerogative-men* (Wing B5264, 1682), p. 26.
129. B. Calamy, *A Sermon Preached Before the Lord Mayor, Aldermen, and Citizens of London at Bow-Church on the 29th of May 1682* (Wing C216, 1682), p. 18.
130. Ibid., pp. 18–19.

131. T. Long, *King David's Danger and Deliverance, or, The Conspiracy of Absolon and Achitophel Defeated in a Sermon Preached in the Cathedral Church of Exon, on the Ninth of September, 1683* (Wing L2972, 1683), p. 23. Long was a prebendary of the cathedral and a long-time polemicist against dissenters, *ODNB*.

132. *A Thanksgiving Sermon for Discovery of the Late Phanatick Plot, September 9, 1683* (Wing H895, 1683), p. 16; Cf. J. Price, *A sermon Preached at Petworth in Sussex, September 9, 1683 Being a Day of Solemn Thanksgiving for the Gracious and Wonderful Deliverance of the King, His Royal Brother, and the Government from the Late Barbarous Conspiracy* (Wing P3337, 1683), p. 12.

133. P. Lathom, *The Power of Kings from God A Sermon Preached in the Cathedral Church of Sarum the XXIX Day of June, 1683* (Wing L574, 1683), pp. 16–17, 38.

134. J. Scott, *A Sermon Preached Before the Right Honourable the Lord Mayor, and Court of Aldermen, at the Guild-Hall Chappel, the 16th of December, 1683* (Wing S2067, 1684), p. 13 and *passim*.

135. *The Last Speech & Behaviour of William, Late Lord Russel, upon the Scaffold in Lincolns-Inne-Fields, a Little Before His Execution, on Saturday, July 21, 1683 Being Condemned for High-treason in Conspiring the Death of the King and the Subversion of the Government, &c. also the Last Speeches, Behaviour, and Prayers of Capt. Thomas Walcot, John Rouse, Gent., and William Hone, Joyner, a Little before Their Execution at Tyburn, on Friday the 20th of July 1683* (Wing L504, 1683), p. 10.

136. *The Rebels Doom, or, An Historical Account of the Most Remarkable Rebellions from Edward the Confessor's Reign to His Present Majesties Happy Restauration: with the Fatal Consequences that Have Always Attended Such Disloyal Violations of Allegiance* (Wing R599, 1684). See Isocrates, *Cyprian Orations*, 54.

137. R. Pearson, *The Study of Quietness Explained, Recommended, and Directed in a Sermon Preached Before the Right Honourable the Lord Mayor and Court of Aldermen, at the Guild-Hall Chappel, March 16, 1683/4* (Wing P1017, 1684).

138. *A Character of London-village, by a Countrey-poet* (Wing C2019, 1684).

139. J. Miller, *Charles II* (London, 1991), p. 70.

140. R. Hutton, *Charles the Second* (Oxford, 1989), p. 183.

141. Ibid., p. 210; cf. T. Wilson, *A Sermon on the Martyrdom of King Charles I Preached January 30, 1681* (Wing 2937, 1682), pp. 21–3.

142. Wilson, *Sermon*, pp. 22–3; *Cal. Stat Pap. Dom 1666*, pp. 366–7.

143. Hutton, *Charles the Second*, p. 244.

144. Ibid., pp. 374–6.

145. The use of history as polemic during the Exclusion Crisis and Popish Plot awaits full study.

146. H. Elsynge, *The Ancient Method and Manner of Holding Parliaments in England by Henry Elsynge* (Wing E646, 1679); R. Cotton, *The Antiquity and Dignity of Parliaments* (Wing C6482, 1680).

147. *Memoirs of Queen Mary's Days Wherein the Church of England, and All the Inhabitants May Plainly See As in a Glass, the Sad Effects Which Follow a Popish Successor Enjoying the Crown of England* (Wing M1669, 1679); M. D., *A Brief History of the Life of Mary, Queen of Scots* (Wing D57, 1681).

148. R. Howard, *The Life and Reign of King Richard the Second by a Person of Quality* (Wing H3001, 1681).

149. S. Clarke, *The History of the Glorious Life, Reign, and Death of the Illustrious Queen Elizabeth* (Wing C4523, 1682).

150. On Reformation prophecy as opposition, see S. Jansen, *Political Protest and Prophecy under Henry VIII* (Woodbridge, 1991).

151. R. Wilkison, *Strange News from Bishop-Hatfield in Hertford-shire, January the 25 1680. Being a Relation of Elizabeth Freeman* (Wing W2247A, 1681).

152. W. Sanders, *The True and Wonderful Relation of the Dreadful Fighting and Groans That Were Heard and Seen in the Ayr on the Fifteenth of this Instant January, in Carmarthen, in South-Wales* (Wing T2588, 1681).

153. R. L'Estrange, *Considerations and Proposals in Order to the Regulation of the Press* (Wing L1229, 1663), sig. A2ᵛ.

154. Nalson, *Common Interest*, p. 25. On the survival of republican ideology, see J. Champion, *The Pillars of Priestcraft Shaken: The Church of England and its Enemies, 1660–1730* (Cambridge, 1992), pp. 179–95; D. Wotton ed., *Republicanism, Liberty, and Commercial Society, 1649–1776* (Stanford, CA, 1994).

155. H. Neville, *Plato Redivivus, or, A Dialogue Concerning Government Wherein by Observations Drawn from Other Kingdoms and States Both Ancient and Modern an Endeavour Is Used to Discover the Present Politick Distemper of Our Own with the Causes and Remedies* (Wing N513, 1681); H. Care, *English Liberties, or, The Free-born Subject's Inheritance* (Wing C516, 1680); quotation, p. 80. On

Neville, see *ODNB*; on Care, see L. Schwoerer, *The Ingenious Mr. Henry Care, Restoration Publicist* (Baltimore, MD, 2001).

156. Above ch. 1, pp. 22–3.

157. C. Hammond, *Truth's Discovery, or, The Cavaliers Case Clearly Stated by Conscience and Plain-dealing* (Wing H498, 1664), p. 11.

158. See W. Lamont, *Marginal Prynne 1600–69* (London, 1963).

159. See A. McRae, *Literature, Satire, and the Early Stuart State* (Cambridge, 2004); A. Bellany, '"Raylinge Rymes and Vaunting Verse": Libellous Politics in Early Stuart England, 1603–1628', in K. Sharpe and P. Lake eds, *Culture and Politics in Early Stuart England* (Basingstoke, 1994), pp. 285–310; A. Bellany, 'The Embarrassment of Libels: Perceptions and Representations of Verse Libeling in Early Stuart England', in Lake and Pincus eds, *Politics of Public Sphere*, pp. 144–67; A. Bellany, *The Politics of Court Scandal in Early Modern England: News Culture and the Overbury Affair, 1603–1660* (Cambridge, 2002). I am grateful to both Andrew McRae and Alastair Bellany for many fruitful discussions of this subject.

160. See 'A Satyr' (on Charles II) in H. Love ed., *The Works of John Wilmot, Earl of Rochester* (Oxford, 1999), pp. 86–7.

161. Above, ch.1, pp. 50–1.

162. J. Denham, *Directions to a Painter for Describing Our Naval Business in Imitation of Mr. Waller* (Wing D998, 1667).

163. Ibid., p. 39.

164. Ibid., p. 19.

165. See Marvell's 'Last Instructions to a Painter', written in 1667. Though not published until 1689, the poem was widely circulated. See N. Smith ed., *The Poems of Andrew Marvell* (London, 2003), pp. 360–94. See also S. Zwicker, *Lines of Authority: Politics and English Literary Culture, 1649–1689* (Ithaca, NY, 1993), ch. 4.

166. J. Turner, 'From Revolution to Restoration in English Literary Culture', in D. Loewenstein and J. Mueller eds, *The Cambridge History of Early Modern English Literature* (Cambridge, 2002), pp. 810–11.

167. J. Nalson, *The Countermine, or, A Short But True Discovery of the Dangerous Principles and Secret Practices of the Dissenting Party* (Wing N96, 1677), p. 285.

168. See above, p. 721, n. 80

169. *An Account of Their Royal Highnesses the Duke and Dutchess of York, Their Arrival and Reception in Scotland, the 26. of Octob. 1680* (Wing A424C, 1680), one page.

170. E. Settle, *Londons Defiance to Rome, a Perfect Narrative of the Magnificent Procession, and Solemn Burning of the Pope at Temple-Barr, Nov. 17th, 1679* (L2923, 1679).

171. Ibid., p. 3.

172. Ibid.

173. *The Solemn Mock-procession, or, The Tryal & Execution of the Pope and His Ministers on the 17 of Nov. at Temple-bar* (Wing S4452D, 1680), pp. 5–6 and *passim*.

174. Ibid., p. 6.

175. T. Hunt, *The Great and Weighty Considerations, Relating to the Duke of York, or, Successor of the Crown* (Wing H3753, 1680), pp. 13, 20, 32. On the lawyer and Whig polemicist Hunt, see *ODNB*.

176. Ibid., p. 24.

177. J. Tyrell, *Patriarcha non Monarcha, The Patriarch Unmonarch'd* (Wing T3591, 1681), p. 227 and *passim*. Tyrell was a Whig theorist and friend of John Locke. On Catholic conspiracy see, for example, W. Denton, *The Ungrateful Behaviour of the Papists, Priests, and Jesuits, towards the Imperial and Indulgent crown of England towards Them, from the Days of Queen Mary unto This Present Age* (Wing D1068A, 1679); *A Catalogue of the Names of those Holy Martyrs who Were Burned in Queen Maries Reign* (Wing C1404, 1679); *The Muses Fire-works upon the Fifth of November: or, The Protestants Remembrancer of the Bloody Designs of the Papists in the Never-to-be-forgotten Powder-Plot* (Wing M3142, 1680); J. Williams, *The History of the Powder Treason, to which Is Added a Parallel betwixt the Present Popish Plot* (Wing W2707, 1681).

178. A. Bryant ed., *The Letters, Speeches and Declarations of King Charles II* (London, 1935), pp. 311–12. On Monmouth's part in the Exclusion Crisis, see T. Harris, *Restoration: Charles II and His Kingdoms 1660–1685* (London and New York, 2005), pp. 146–7, 161–3.

179. *An Account of the Noble Reception of His Grace the D. of Monmouth, by the Citizens of the Cit[y] of Chichester on the 15 of this Instant February* (Wing A335, 1682).

180. *A True and Wonderful Account of a Cure of the Kings-evil by Mrs. Fanshaw, Sister to His Grace the Duke of Monmouth* (Wing T2584, 1681).

181. *An Impartial Enquiry into the Administration of Affairs in England with Some Reflections on the Kings Declaration of July 27, 1683* (Wing I83, 1683).
182. Bryant, *Letters, Speeches*, pp. 324–5.
183. *Impartial Enquiry*, pp. 73–4.
184. Ibid., p. 73.
185. Ibid., pp. 82–3.
186. Ibid., p. 83.
187. Though, after 1681, he was at least able again to pose as a king above party, see J. R. Jones, *Charles II: Royal Politician* (London, 1987), ch. 8.
188. R. Hutton, *Debates in Stuart History* (Basingstoke, 2004), ch. 5.
189. Ibid., p. 170.
190. Hutton sums up these contradictions well in the conclusion to his *Charles the Second*, pp. 446–58. I am more sympathetic to the need for them in the circumstances in which Charles ruled.
191. Cf. R. Hutton, 'The Making of the Secret Treaty of Dover 1668–70', *Historical Journal*, 29 (1986), pp. 297–318.
192. Above ch. 3, p. 713 n. 157.
193. Hutton, *Debates*, pp. 135–52.
194. *A True Relation of the Late King's Death* (Wing T2986, 1685), one page.
195. See also R. Hudelston, *A Short and Plain Way to the Faith and Church Composed Many Years Since by . . . Mr. Richard Hudelston* (Wing H3257, 1688).
196. *Eikon Basilike Deutera, The Pourtraicture of His Sacred Majesty King Charles II with his Reasons for Turning Roman Catholick* (Wing E312, 1694).
197. Ibid., p. 81.
198. Ibid., pp. 154–62, 173 and *passim*.
199. *Suspiria, or, Sighs on the Death of the Late Most Illustrious Monarch Charles the II* (Wing S6203, 1685), broadside.
200. T. Flatman, *On the Death of Our Late Sovereign Lord King Charles II of Blessed Memory a Pindarique Ode* (Wing F1141, 1685), p. 4; N. Tate, *On the Sacred Memory of Our Late Sovereign, with a Congratulation to His Present Majesty Written by N. Tate* (Wing T200, 1685), p. 5.
201. T. Wood, *A Pindarick Ode, Upon the Death of His Late Sacred Majesty King Charles the Second* (Wing W3410A, 1685), p. 4; F. Fane, *A Pindarick Ode on the Sacred Memory of Our Late Gracious Sovereign King Charles II* (Wing F410, 1685), p. 3.
202. A. Cook, *Titus Britannicus an Essay of History Royal, in the Life & Reign of His Late Sacred Majesty, Charles II* (Wing C5996, 1685), sig. A7; T. Otway, *Windsor Castle, in a Monument to Our Late-sovereign K. Charles II of Ever Blessed Memory a Poem* (Wing O570, 1685), p. 17.
203. F. Wood, *On the Death of His Late Sacred Majesty King Charles II, of Ever Blessed Memory a Pindarique Ode* (Wing W3389, 1685), p. 5; A. Behn, *A Poem Humbly Dedicated to the Great Patern of Piety and Virtue Catherine, Queen Dowager on the Death of Her Dear Lord and Husband, King Charles II/by Mrs. Behn* (Wing B1755, 1685), p. 1.
204. E. Phillips, *An Humble Offering to the Sacred Memory of the Late Most Serene and Potent Monarch Charles II* (Wing P2085, 1685), p. 2. Phillips was Milton's nephew, see *ODNB*.
205. A. Behn, *A Pindarick on the Death of Our Late Sovereign with an Ancient Prophecy on His Present Majesty* (Wing B1750, 1685), pp. 2, 6 and *passim*. On Behn, see J. Todd, *The Secret Life of Aphra Behn* (London, 1996), and D. Hughes, *The Theatre of Aphra Behn* (Basingstoke, 2001).
206. J. Dryden, *Threnodia Augustalis a Funeral-Pindarique Poem, Sacred to the Happy Memory of King Charles II* (Wing D2383, 1685), pp. 13, 15, 19.
207. Ibid., p. 18.
208. T. D'Urfey, *An Elegy Upon the Late Blessed Monarch King Charles II and Two Panegyricks Upon Their Present Sacred Majesties, King James and Queen Mary Written by Mr. Durfey* (Wing D2720, 1685).
209. Fane, *Pindarick Ode*, p. 6.
210. E. Arwaker, *The Vision: a Pindarick Ode: Occasion'd by the Death of Our Late Gracious Sovereign King Charles II* (Wing A3913, 1685).
211. Flatman, *On the Death of Our Late Sovereign*, p. 7.
212. *Musa Praesica the London Poem, or, An Humble Oblation on the Sacred Tomb of Our Late Gracious Monarch King Charles the II* (Wing M3129, 1685).
213. Ibid., pp. 2–3.
214. Ibid., p. 4.
215. Ibid., pp. 3, 10–12.
216. Ibid., p. 15.

217. H. Anderson, *A Loyal Tear Dropt on the Vault of the High and Mighty Prince, Charles II, of Glorious and Happy Memory by Henry Anderson* (Wing A3091, 1685). Anderson was vicar of King's Somborne, Hampshire; cf. Charles II, *A Fountain of Loyal Tears Poured Forth by a Sorrowful Son, for the Untimely Death of His Royal Father* (Wing C3008, 1649).
218. Anderson, *Loyal Tear*, p. 17 and *passim*.
219. Ibid., p. 10.
220. Ibid., p. 13.
221. Ibid., p. 17. Cf. 'Pomp rather shews a Monarch weak, then great', Mr Crown, *A Poem, on the Lamented Death of Our Late Gratious Soveraign, King Charles the II, of Ever Blessed Memory with a Congratulation to the Happy Succession of King James the II* (Wing C7397, 1685), p. 8.
222. *Eikon Basilike*, p. 155.
223. Cook, *Titus Britannicus*, sig. C1.
224. *A Poem on the Most Deplorable Death of the Mighty Monarch, Charles II, King of England, Scotland, France, and Ireland* (Wing P2701, 1685), p. 2.

Part II Prologue: A King Represented and Misrepresented

1. See K. Sharpe, *Image Wars: Promoting English Kings and Commonwealths, 1603–1660* (New Haven, CT, and London, 2010), pp. 391–403.
2. Below, ch. 8, pp. 310–29.
3. See, for example, P. Monod, *Jacobitism and the English People, 1688–1788* (Cambridge, 1999); E. Corp, *A Court in Exile: The Stuarts in France, 1689–1718* (Cambridge, 2004); D. Szechi, *The Jacobites: Britain and Europe, 1688–1788*; R. Sharp, *The Engraved Record of the Jacobite Movement* (Aldershot, 1999).

5 A King of Many Words

1. J. Callow, *The Making of King James II: The Formative Years of a Fallen King* (Stroud, 2000), p. 2.
2. Ibid.
3. For a brief attempt to draw attention to them, see K. Sharpe, 'Whose Life Is It Anyway? Writing Early Modern Monarchs and the "Life" of James II', in K. Sharpe and S. Zwicker, *Writing Lives: Biography and Textuality, Identity and Representation in Early Modern England* (Oxford, 2008), pp. 233–52.
4. Sharpe, 'Whose Life'; Callow, *Making of James II*, p. 3.
5. Sharpe, 'Whose Life'; Callow, *Making of James II*, p. 306, n. 9.
6. Sharpe, 'Whose Life'; Callow, *Making of James II*, pp. 4–6; E. Gregg, 'New Light on the Authorship of the *Life of James II*', *English Historical Review*, 108 (1993), pp. 947–65; A. Lytton Sells, *The Memoirs of James II: His Campaigns as Duke of York* (Bloomington, IN, 1962), p. 19; J. Miller, *James II: A Study in Kingship* (Hove, 1977), pp. 243–5. See Charles James Fox, *History of the Early Part of the Reign of James the Second* (Philadelphia, PA, 1808). Carte was likely an agent for the Jacobites, see *ODNB*. See his notes in Bodleian Carte MSS, pp. 180–1, 198.
7. J. Macpherson, *Original Papers Containing The Secret History of Great Britain, from the Restoration to the Accession of the House of Hanover to which Are Prefixed Extracts from the Life of James II As Written by Himself* (2 vols, 1775).
8. Macpherson, *ODNB*; H. R. Trevor Roper, *The Invention of Scotland: Myth and History* (New Haven, CT, and London, 2009), chs 4–6.
9. Miller, *James II*, p. 244.
10. Ibid. There is a distinction between the use of first- and third-person pronouns, though it is not entirely reliable, see Lytton Sells, *Memoirs of James II*, p. 19; Sharpe, 'Whose Life', p. 243.
11. Sharpe, 'Whose Life', p. 244; Callow, *Making of James II*, p. 6; J. Clarke, *The Life of James the Second, King of England, Memoirs Collected out of Writ of His Own Hand* (2 vols, 1816), I, pp. xxvi–xxvii. This second copy of Dicconson, once owned and annotated by James III, is now at Windsor.
12. For example, Clarke, *Life of James II*, I, pp. 159, 267, 515–17, 565, 591; II, pp. 9, 328, 501, 582, 585.
13. Lytton Sells, *Memoirs*, pp. 15–16.
14. Ibid., p. 16.
15. Ibid., pp. 30–1.

16. Callow, *Making of King James II*, p. 311, n. 57; G. Davies ed., *Papers of Devotion of James II, Being a Reproduction of the Ms. in the Handwriting of James the Second* (Roxburgh Club, Oxford, 1925), pp. xi–xii and *passim*.
17. Callow, *Making of King James II*, p. 24.
18. Miller, *James II*, pp. 243–5.
19. Lytton Sells, *Memoirs*, p. 19.
20. Clarke, *Life of James the Second*, II, p. 242.
21. Ibid., pp. 242–3.
22. Callow, *Making of King James II*, p. 2. Callow does not comment on the significance of the binding, but we have learned how the materiality of books often indicates their significance for owners and readers.
23. Lytton Sells, *Memoirs*, p. 15.
24. G. Burnet, *History of His Own Time*, ed. M. Routh (6 vols, Oxford, 1833), I, p. 304.
25. Sharpe, 'Whose Life', p. 247.
26. Lytton Sells, *Memoirs*, p. 19.
27. Ibid., p. 19.
28. Callow, *Making of King James II*, p. 4.
29. The first copyright act was 1709, 8 Anne c. 19.
30. Clarke, *Life of James II*, pp. 243–4.
31. Ibid., I, pp. 2–4. On the episode, see S. R. Gardiner, *History of England, 1603–1642* (10 vols, 1905), X, pp. 191–3.
32. Clarke, *Life of James II*, I, p. 9.
33. Ibid., pp. 12, 15–16, 19.
34. Ibid., pp. 18–19.
35. Ibid., pp. 32, 34–5.
36. Ibid., p. 46.
37. On Edward VI's chronicle, see K. Sharpe, *Selling the Tudor Monarchy: Authority and Image in Sixteenth-Century England* (New Haven, CT, and London, 2009), pp. 195–7.
38. Clarke, *Life of James II*, pp. 29–30, 46.
39. See, for example, ibid., pp. 50–1.
40. Ibid., p. 50.
41. Ibid., pp. 51–2.
42. Lytton Sells, *Memoirs*, p. 6.
43. Ibid., pp. 59, 96, 105.
44. Ibid., pp. 110–12.
45. Ibid., p. 127.
46. Ibid., pp. 140, 151.
47. Ibid., pp. 70, 100.
48. Ibid., pp. 142, 168, 171.
49. Ibid., p. 171.
50. Ibid., pp. 150, 157.
51. Ibid., pp. 148, 239–40.
52. Ibid., pp. 138, 271.
53. Ibid., p. 219.
54. Clarke, *Life of James II*, I, pp. 391, 393.
55. Ibid., p. 391.
56. Ibid., pp. 395–6.
57. Ibid., p. 396: 'the restless party of the republicans were secretly working to destroy the government and for that end the chief of them had private meetings and consultations.'
58. Ibid., pp. 405–18. James also commissioned portraits of his flag officers from this campaign. See J. Jones, *The Anglo-Dutch Wars of the Seventeenth Century* (London and New York, 1996), ch. 7.
59. Clarke, *Life of James II*, p. 420.
60. Ibid., p. 424.
61. Ibid., pp. 425–8, 430.
62. Ibid., pp. 431–7 *passim*.
63. Ibid., pp. 439–40.
64. Ibid., pp. 445, 449.
65. Ibid., pp. 452–3.
66. Ibid., pp. 455–72.

67. Ibid., pp. 399, 455.
68. Ibid., p. 455.
69. Ibid., pp. 482-3.
70. Ibid., p. 487.
71. Ibid., p. 485.
72. Ibid., pp. 490-18, 504.
73. Ibid., p. 515.
74. Miller suggests that the memoirs for the period after 1678 were written up separately, and marginal references to original memoirs resume, *James II*, p. 245; cf. Callow, *Making of King James II*, p. 24.
75. Clarke, *Life of James II*, I, pp. 524-5.
76. Ibid., p. 541.
77. Ibid., p. 542.
78. Ibid., pp. 551, 554-5.
79. Ibid., p. 557. It is worth noting James's trust in the people at this critical juncture.
80. Ibid., p. 558. Doubtless James was recalling his father's aborted attempt to bring his opponents onto the Privy Council on the eve of civil war, see C. Roberts, *Schemes and Undertakings: A Study of English Politics in the Seventeenth Century* (Columbus, OH, 1985), ch. 2.
81. Clarke, *Life of James II*, I, pp. 560-23.
82. Ibid., p. 566.
83. Ibid., p. 614. It is interesting how differently James and Charles drew on the memories of civil war.
84. Ibid., p. 633.
85. Ibid., pp. 644-5, 646, 662. James was pressured by Charles II and Danby to agree his daughter Mary's marriage with William of Orange, in the hope that a Protestant match might improve his popularity and defuse moves to exclude him.
86. Ibid., p. 673.
87. Ibid., pp. 678, 680.
88. Ibid., pp. 683, 695.
89. Ibid., pp. 723-4.
90. Ibid., pp. 733-4.
91. T. Harris, *Restoration: Charles II and His Kingdoms, 1660-1685* (London and New York, 2005), pp. 310-12.
92. Clarke, *Life of James II*, I, pp. 746-7.
93. Ibid., pp. 702, 735.
94. Ibid., p. 2.
95. Ibid., p. 157.
96. Ibid., p. 156.
97. Ibid., pp. 2-3, 8.
98. Ibid., pp. 43, 46.
99. Ibid., p. 44.
100. Ibid., pp. 18, 94, 181.
101. Ibid., pp. 102-3, 106.
102. Ibid., pp. 111-14.
103. Ibid., p. 116: 'One would have thought the king's sincerity in telling so plainly what he would do should have made his word be taken for what he promised what he would not do, and have reassured the Church of England he had no further aims than a bare liberty of conscience.'
104. Ibid., pp. 24-5, 27, 71, 114, 131, 140-1, 151, 177.
105. Below, ch. 7, pp. 300-2.
106. Callow, *Making of King James II*, p. 306, n. 5; W. Matthews ed., *Charles II's Escape from Worcester: A Collection of Narratives Assembled by Samuel Pepys* (Berkeley and Los Angeles, CA, 1966), p. 98.
107. Clarke, *Life of James II*, I, p. 36, II, p. 278. The latter episode closely follows the story of Charles II in disguise helping with cooking in an inn.
108. Ibid., I, pp. 4-5.
109. Ibid., p. 632; J. Daems and H. Nelson eds, *Eikon Basilike* (Peterborough, Ontario, 2005), p. 194. Clarke, *Life of James II*, p. 239; K. Sharpe, *The Personal Rule of Charles I* (New Haven, CT, and London, 1992), pp. 914-19.
110. Below, ch. 8, pp. 336-40.
111. Clarke, *Life of James II*, II, p. 229.
112. On Edward VI's Diary, see Sharpe, *Selling the Tudor Monarchy*, pp. 195-7.

113. J. Ogilby, *The Relation of His Majestie's Entertainment* (Wing O181, 1661), p. 19.
114. See Clarke, *Life of James II*, I, pp. 487; Davies, *Papers of Devotion*, pp. xvii, xxiv, 4, 61, 67, 92–3, 96–9, 108, 137–8, 162; Callow, *Making of King James*, pp. 91–2, 114, 148; *ODNB*. In the *Memoirs* of Count Grammont, James appears as a leading libertine with many mistresses but they were not published in English (with a key) until 1719.
115. Bodleian Firth b.20.
116. Above, ch. 2, p. 122.
117. *An Account of What His Majesty Said at His First Coming to Council* (Wing J150, 1685), one page.
118. 'The Lords of the Council were humble suitors to his majesty that these his gracious expressions might be made public.' The speech was printed by the royal printers Henry Hills and Thomas Newcomb. On its popular reception, see S. Pincus, *1688: The First Modern Revolution* (New Haven, CT, and London, 2009), pp. 96–9.
119. *His Majesties Most Gracious Speech to Both Houses of Parliament, on Friday the 22th of May, 1685. Published by His Majesties Command* (Wing J225, 1685), p. 3.
120. Ibid.
121. Ibid., p. 4.
122. Ibid.
123. Ibid., p. 5.
124. 'I cannot doubt that I shall fail of suitable returns from you', ibid.
125. Ibid.
126. Ibid., p. 7.
127. Miller, *James II*, p. 136.
128. *His Majesties Most Gracious Speech to Both Houses of Parliament, on Saturday the 30th of May, 1685* (Wing J228, 1685), p. 3.
129. Ibid., p. 4.
130. Ibid.
131. *The Manner of Procession to the Parliament-house in Scotland with His Majesties Letter to the Parliament, the Lord High Commissioners Speech, the Lord High Chancellors Speech, and the Parliaments Answer* (Wing M460, Dublin, 1685), p. 4.
132. Ibid., p. 5.
133. Ibid., pp. 5–6.
134. Ibid., pp. 6–8.
135. Ibid., p. 8.
136. See R. Clifton, *The Last Popular Rebellion: The Western Rising of 1685* (London, 1984); T. Harris, *Revolution: The Great Crisis of the British Monarchy, 1685–1720* (London and New York, 2006), ch. 2.
137. *His Majesties Most Gracious Speech to Both Houses of Parliament, on Munday the 9th of November, 1685* (Wing J229, 1685), p. 3.
138. Ibid., pp. 3–4.
139. See L. Schwoerer, *No Standing Armies! The Anti-army Ideology in 17th-Century England* (Baltimore, MD, 1974).
140. *His Majesties Speech . . . 9th of November, 1685*, p. 4.
141. In the Edict of Fontainebleau the following January, Louis XIV expelled the Huguenots from France.
142. Miller, *James II*, p. 146.
143. *By the King a Declaration* (Wing J156, 1685).
144. *His Majesties Gracious Declaration to All His Loving Subjects for Liberty of Conscience* (Wing J186, 1687). The declaration was written with the help of the Quaker William Penn whom James appointed as an envoy to win William of Orange's support. See Penn, *ODNB*; R. Boyer, 'English Declarations of Indulgence of 1687 and 1688', *Catholic Historical Review*, 50 (1964), pp. 332–71; W. Speck, 'James II's Revolution: Royal Policies, 1686–92', in J. Israel ed., *The Anglo-Dutch Moment* (Cambridge, 1991), pp. 47–72.
145. *His Majesties Gracious Declaration*, ibid., p. 1.
146. Ibid.
147. Ibid.
148. Ibid., p. 4.
149. Clarke, *Life of James II*, II, pp. 71, 89, 140–1.
150. *His Majesties Gracious Declaration to All His Loving Subjects for Liberty of Conscience* (Wing J190, 1688), p. 1. This declaration includes the King in Council's order, dated 4 May 1688, to have the 27 April 1687 declaration read 'at the usual time of divine Service'.
151. Ibid., p. 3.

152. Ibid., p. 4.
153. Ibid.
154. Ibid.,
155. *A True Representation of His Majesties Declaration for Prevention of Those Prejudices which Are Rais'd Against Reading of It, by Misguided Men* (Wing J396, 1688), quotation, p. 2.
156. Miller, *James II*, ch. 12, *passim*.
157. *By the King, A Declaration. James R. Whereas We Have Been Informed that Divers Abuses Have Been Committed in the Quartering of Officers and Soldiers Contrary to Our Declaration* (Wing J157, 1688).
158. *By the King, A Declaration Having Already Signified Our Pleasure to Call a Parliament . . . It Is Our Royal Purpose to Endeavour a Legal Establishment of an Universal Liberty of Conscience for All Our Subjects* (Wing J158, 1688).
159. Ibid.; Miller, *James II*, pp. 197–8.
160. See below, ch. 8, pp. 318–22.
161. *The Declaration of His Highnes William Henry, by the Grace of God Prince of Orange, &c. of the Reasons Inducing Him, to Appear in Armes in the Kingdome of England, for Preserving of the Protestant Religion, and for Restoring the Lawes and Liberties of England, Scotland and Ireland* (Wing W2328C, 1688).
162. *By the King, A Declaration* (Wing J161, 1688), broadside; Miller, *James II*, p. 199.
163. *Declaration*, my italics.
164. This claim was at odds with James's recent efforts to manage elections, see W. Speck, *Reluctant Revolutionaries: Englishmen and the Revolution of 1688* (Oxford, 1988), pp. 216–17; J. R. Jones, *The Revolution of 1688 in England* (New York, 1972), ch. 6 *passim*.
165. Miller, *James II*, p. 207.
166. Harris, *Revolution*, pp. 276–90.
167. *His Majesties Reasons for Withdrawing Himself from Rochester Writ with His Own Hand and Ordered by Him to be Published* (Wing J376, 1688).
168. Ibid., my italics.
169. Below, ch. 8, pp. 326–31.
170. *By the King, a Proclamation for Prohibiting the Transportation of Frames for Knitting and Making of Silk-stockings, and Other Wearing Necessaries* (Wing J337, 1686); *By the King a Proclamation Prohibiting the Importation of Foreign Needles* (Wing J367, 1687); *By the King, a Proclamation for Putting in Execution the Law Against Importation and Selling of Foreign Buttons, and Prohibiting All Foreign Buttons Whatsoever* (Wing J341, 1687). Quotation from *A Proclamation Anent Linencloth* (Wing S1019J, 1688).
171. *By the King, a Proclamation for Restraining the Number and Abuses of Hackney Coaches in and about the Cities of London and Westminster* (Wing J347, 1687); *By the King, a Proclamation for the Better Execution of the Office of Making and Registring Policys of Assurances in London* (Wing J349, 1687).
172. *By the King, a Proclamation. James R. Whereas Our Dearest Brother of Blessed Memory, by His Royal Proclamation Bearing Date the Fifteenth Day of September, in the Twelfth Year of His Reign, for Preventing the Exportation of Wooll* (Wing J254, 1687); *By the King, a Proclamation for Putting in Execution the Additional Act for Improvement of Tillage* (Wing J340, 1687).
173. *By the King a Proclamation Containing His Majesties Gracious Indemnity* (Wing J322, 1685).
174. *A Proclamation of the Kings Majesties Most Gracious and General Pardon* (Wing J363, 1685).
175. *By the King, a Proclamation Containing His Majesties Gracious and Ample Indemnity* (Wing J320, Edinburgh, 1688).
176. *By the King, a Proclamation Appointing a Time of Publick Thanksgiving and Prayer Throughout the Kingdom* (Wing J313, 1687); see Sharpe, *Image Wars*, pp. 148–9.
177. *By the King, a Proclamation. James R. We Have Received Undoubted Advice, that a Great and Sudden Invasion from Holland, with an Armed Force of Foreigners and Strangers, Will Speedily Be Made in a Hostile Manner upon This Our Kingdom* (Wing J260, 1688).
178. *By the King, A Proclamation* (Wing J262, 1688).
179. *A Proclamation for the Speedy Calling of a Parliament* (Wing J360, 1688).
180. For example, *A Proclamation, for an Anniversary Thanksgiving, in Commemoration of His Majesties Happy Birth-day* (Wing J327B, 1685); *By the King, a Proclamation Appointing a Time of Publick Thanksgiving and Prayer Throughout the Kingdom* (Wing J313, 1687).
181. Sharpe, *Image Wars*, pp. 35–8, 145–50.
182. *A Form of Prayer with Thanksgiving to Almighty God for Having Put an End to the Great Rebellion by the Restitution of the King and Royal Family and the Restauration of the Government after Many*

Years Interruption which Unspeakable Mercies Were Wonderfully Compleated upon the 29th of May in the Year 1660, and in Memory thereof that Day in Every Year is by Act of Parliament to be for ever Kept Holy/by His Majesties special command (Wing C4176, 1685), sig. A2ᵛ.

183. Ibid., sigs B1ᵛ–B2.

184. *A Form of Prayer and Thanksgiving to Almighty God for His Majesties Late Victories Over the Rebels* (Wing C4122, 1685), sigs A2, A4ᵛ.

185. *A Form of Prayer with Thanksgiving to be Used Yearly upon the Fifth Day of November* (Wing C4175, 1685).

186. *A Form of Prayer with Thanksgiving to Almighty God to be Used in all Churches and Chapels within This Realm Every Year, upon the Sixth Day of February, Being the Day on which His Majesty Began His Happy Reign* (Wing C4174, Dublin 1685), sig. B3.

187. See *A Form of Prayer with Fasting, to be Us'd Yearly Upon the 30th of January* (Wing C4167, 1685).

188. *A Form of Prayer and Thanksgiving to Almighty God for the Prosperity of the Christian Arms Against the Turks and especially for Taking the City of Buda* (Wing C4124, 1686).

189. *A Form of Prayer and Thanksgiving for the Safe Delivery of the Queen and Happy Birth of the Young Prince to be Used . . . in all Churches and Chapels* (Wing C4168, 1688), sig. A3.

190. Ibid., sigs A4–A4ᵛ.

191. See Clarke, *Life of James II*, II, p. 170. There has been a historiographical as there was a contemporary disagreement about James's sincerity. Mark Knights is inclined to doubt it ('"Mere religion" and the "Church- State" of Restoration England: The Impact and Ideology of James II's Declarations of Indulgence', in A. Houston and S Pincus eds, *A Nation Transformed: England After the Restoration* (Cambridge, 2001), pp. 41–70). I am more persuaded by John Miller who observes that James was disinclined to duplicity and at least believed in the sincerity of his advocacy of toleration (J. Miller, 'James II and Toleration', in E. Cruickshanks ed., *By Force or Default? The Revolution of 1688–1689* Edinburgh, 1989), pp. 8–27, especially, p. 17). On James and the Huguenots, see R. Gwynn, 'James II in the Light of his Treatment of Huguenot Refugees in England, 1685–1686', *English Historical Review*, 92 (1977), pp. 820–33.

192. J. Wilson, *A Pindarique to Their Sacred Majesties, James II and His Royal Consort Queen Mary, on their Joynt Coronations at Westminster, April 23, 1685*, p. 7. *ODNB* describes Wilson as a 'semi-official royalist propagandist for James II'.

193. A. Behn, *Pindarick Poem on the Happy Coronation of His Most Sacred Majesty James II and His Illustrious Consort Queen Mary by Mrs. Behn* (Wing B1751, 1685), p. 18; E. Settle, *An Heroick Poem on the Coronation of the High and Mighty Monarch, James II. King of England* (Wing S2692, 1685), p. 8.

194. T. Otway, *Windsor Castle, in a Monument to Our Late-sovereign K. Charles II of Ever Blessed Memory, A Poem* (Wing, 1685), pp. 22–3, 28 and *passim*.

195. *An Elegy on James Scot, Late Duke of Monmouth* (Wing E419, 1685).

196. *An Elegy on James Scot, Late Duke of Monmouth* (Bodleian Ash. G15/27, 1685).

197. H. Anderson, *A Loyal Tear Dropt on the Vault of the High and Mighty Prince, Charles II, of Glorious and Happy Memory by Henry Anderson* (Wing A3091, 1685), p. 25.

198. Wilson, *Pindarique*, p. 5.

199. J. Crowne, *A Poem, on the Lamented Death of Our Late Gratious Soveraign, King Charles the II, of Ever Blessed Memory with a Congratulations to the Happy Succession of King James the II* (Wing C7397, 1685), pp. 15–16. On Crowne, see S. Owen, *Restoration Theatre and Crisis* (Oxford, 1996), pp. 62–109.

200. F. Fane, *A Pindarick Ode on the Sacred Memory of Our Late Gracious Sovereign King Charles II* (Wing F410, 1685), p. 8; R. Mansell, *A Poem Upon the Coronation of His Most Sacred Majesty King James II* (Wing M515, 1685), p. 3.

201. P. Kerr, *In Illustrissimum, ac Serenissimum, Jacobum II, Regem Magnae Britaniae, Franciae, & Hiberniae, &c. cum publice coronam regalem indueret carmen epiphonetikon. A Panegyrick Poem on the Coronation of the Illustrious and Serene, James II, King of Great Britain, France, and Ireland* (Wing K344, 1685).

202. J. Pike, *A Loyal Subject's Loveing Advice* (Wing P2223A, 1685), p. 2.

203. Above, ch. 4, p. 221.

204. J. Phillips, *An Humble Offering to the Sacred Memory of the Late Most Serene and Potent Monarch Charles II* (Wing P2085, 1685), p. 2; E. Arwaker, *The Second Part of The Vision, a Pindarick Ode Occasioned by Their Majesties Happy Coronation* (Wing A3912, 1685), p. 3; A. Behn, *Pindarick Poem on the Happy Coronation*, p. 17.

205. *Musa Praesica the London Poem* (Wing M3129), p. 15; N. Thompson, *A Collection of 86 Loyal Poems* (Wing T1007, 1685), pp. 128, 349.

206. Arwaker, *Second Part*, p. 5.

207. See, for example, Mansell, *Poem on Coronation*.
208. *A Poem on the Coronation of Our Most Illustrious King James* (Bodleian, Ashmole Manuscripts 1096/10), p. 1; Cf. Thompson, *Collection of 86 Loyal Poems*, p. 381.
209. *A Poem on the Coronation*, p. 5. See P. Burke, *The Fabrication of Louis XIV* (New Haven, CT, and London, 1994).
210. Thompson, *Collection of 86 Loyal Poems*, p. 387.
211. Ibid., p. 388; Cf. J. Dryden, *Threnodia Augustalis, a Funeral-pindarique Sacred to the Happy Memory of King Charles II/by John Dryden* (Wing D2383, 1685), p. 23.
212. For example, W. P., *Tears Wip'd Off, or, The Second Essay of the Quakers by Way of Poetry Occasioned by the Coronation of James and Mary* (Wing P138, 1685); W. Penn, *The Quakers Elegy on the Death of Charles Late King of England Written by W.P., a Sincere Lover of Charles and James* (Wing P1349, 1685).
213. Anderson, *A Loyal Tear*, p. 26; *Suspiria, or, Sighs on the Death of the Late Most Illustrious Monarch Charles the II* (Wing S6203, 1685), broadside.
214. T. R. de L., *The All-conquering Genius of the Most Potent, and Most Serene Prince James II. King of England, Scotland, France and Ireland* (Wing L83B, 1685), p. 3.
215. *A Panegyric to the King* (Bodleian Ashmole G15/89, 1685); *A Loyal New-Years gift, or, An Acrostick on the Prayer of Every True Subject God Bless King James the Second and Let Him Live Long and Happily* (Wing L3355, 1685), broadside.
216. A Behn, *A Pindarick on the Death of Our Late Sovereign with an Ancient Prophecy on His Present Majesty* (Wing B1752, 1685), p. 7.
217. Wilson, *A Pindarique*, p. 5; *To the King: A Congratulatory Poem* (Wing T1488, 1685), p. 3; J. Baber, *A Poem Upon the Coronation* (Wing B245, 1685), p. 4.
218. Fane, *Pindarick Ode*, p. 8.
219. Dryden, *Threnodia Augustalis*, p. 25; Thompson, *86 Loyal Songs*, p. 259; Behn, *Pindarick on the Death of Our Late Sovereign*, p. 8; T. R. de L., *The All-conquering Genius of the Most Potent, and Most Serene Prince James II*.
220. *Suspiria*.
221. *The Poets Address to King James II. Surnamed the Just* (Wing P2738, 1685).
222. Baber, *A Poem Upon the Coronation*, pp. 2–3.
223. Ibid., p. 5.
224. Thompson, *Collection of 86 Loyal Poems*, p. 382.
225. Settle, *An Heroic Poem*, p. 1.
226. Baber, *Poem on Coronation*, p. 5.
227. W. P., *Tears Wip'd Off*, p. 4.
228. A. Behn, *Aesop's Fables with His Life in English, French and Latin* (Wing A703, 1687).
229. *A Pindarick-poem Upon His Most Sacred Majestie's Late Gracious Indulgence, in Granting a Toleration, and Liberty of Conscience in Matters of Religion* (Wing P2260, 1687); J. Dryden, *The Hind and the Panther. A Poem, in Three Parts* (Wing D2284, 1687).
230. *A Pindarick-poem*, sig. A2.
231. Ibid., p. 1.
232. Ibid.
233. Ibid., p. 3.
234. Ibid.
235. Ibid., p. 6.
236. Ibid., p. 8.
237. Ibid., p. 3.
238. Ibid., p. 5.
239. Ibid., p. 7.
240. Ibid., p. 8.
241. P. Hammond and D. Hopkins eds, *The Poems of John Dryden, Vol.3, 1686–1693* (Harlow, 2000), p. 33; cf. Dryden, *Hind and Panther*, Part III, ll. 221–4, in ibid., p. 131.
242. Ibid., pp. 32–3.
243. Dryden, *Hind and Panther*, Part III, ll. 33, 1,296; ibid., pp. 122, 180.
244. *Hind and Panther*, Epistle to Reader in ibid., p. 39.
245. *Hind and Panther*, Part III, ll. 1,130–4, p. 173.
246. Epistle to Reader in ibid., p. 39.
247. See in ibid., l.28, p. 40.
248. Ibid., l.42. p. 41.
249. Ibid., l.51, p. 41.

250. Above ch. 3, p. 179.
251. *Some Historical Memoires of the Life and Actions of His Royal Highness, the Renowned and Most Illustrious Prince James Duke of York and Albany, &c. Only Brother to His Most Sacred Majesty King Charles II* (Wing S4513, 1683), sig. A3.
252. Ibid., sigs A3–A3ᵛ, pp. 71, 134–6.
253. *The Excellency of Monarchy a Panegyrick Written anno 1658 by a Learned and Truly Loyal Gentleman for Information of the Miserably Misled Commonwealths-men . . . of that Deceitful Age and Now Reviv'd by a Friend to the Author and an Honourer of the Establish'd Government of These Nations* (Wing E3777, 1685).
254. N. Johnston, *The Excellency of Monarchical Government, Especially of the English Monarchy* (Wing J877, 1686), quotation part of full title. Mark Goldie describes the tract as 'the last major statement of absolutism prior to the fall of the house of Stuart', *ODNB*.
255. Ibid., sigs (a)2ᵛ–(a)3.
256. Ibid., sig (a)3ᵛ.
257. E. Pettit, *The Visions of Government, &c. wherein the Antimonarchial Principles and Practices of All Phanatical Commonwealths-men, and Jesuitical Politicians Are Discovered, Confuted, and Exposed, As It Was Published in the Last Year of His late Majesty's Happy Reign* (Wing P1893, 1686).
258. Ibid., sigs (a)1–(b)8ᵛ.
259. Ibid., sig. (a)2.
260. J. Barnes, *The History of that Most Victorious Monarch Edward III, King of England and France, and Lord of Ireland, and First Founder of the Most Noble Order of the Garter* (Wing B871, 1688), sig. A2.
261. J. Gibbon, *Edovardus Confessor Redivivus. The Piety and Vertues of Holy Edward the Confessor, Reviv'd in the Sacred Majesty of King James the II* (Wing G649, 1688).
262. T. Manningham, *A Solemn Humiliation for the Murder of K. Charles I* (Wing M509, 1686); *Basiliká the Works of King Charles the Martyr* (Wing C2076, 1687).
263. T. Sprat, *A True Account and Declaration of the Horrid Conspiracy Against the Late King, His Present Majesty, and the Government As It was Order'd to be Published by His late Majesty* (Wing S5065, 1685), pp. 15, 136.
264. F. Sandford, *The History of the Coronation of the Most High, Most Mighty, and Most Excellent Monarch, James II* (Wing S652, 1687). See title page.
265. Ibid., sigs B1–1ᵛ.
266. S. Clarke, *The Historian's Guide: or, Britains Remembrancer Being a Summary of all the Actions, Exploits, Sieges, Battels, Designs, Attempts, Preferments, Honours, Changes, &c. and Whatever Else Is Worthy Notice that Hath Happened in His Majesty's Dominions, from 1600 to 1688* (Wing C4521, 1688). Wing attributes the work to Samuel Clarke, a former pastor of St Bennet-Fink.
267. Ibid., pp. 167, 183–4.
268. Ibid., p. 188.
269. E. Warren, *Religious Loyalty, or, Old Allegiance to the New King a Sermon, Preached on the Eighth of February 1684* (Wing W968, 1685).
270. Ibid., p. 5.
271. Ibid., pp. 19–20.
272. E. Wettenhall, *Hexapla Jacobaea, a Specimen of Loyalty Towards His Present Majesty James the II, of Great Britain, France and Ireland King* (Wing W1501, 1686).
273. B. Camfield, *A Sermon Preach'd upon the First Sunday after the Proclamation of the High and Mighty Prince, James the II, by the Grace of God, King of England, Scotland, France, and Ireland, &c., Which Was Made at Leicester, February the 10th, 1684/5* (Wing C386, 1685), p. 10.
274. T. Heyrick, *A Sermon Preached at Market Harborow in the County of Leicester, on the 17th Day of February, 1684/85 Being the Day on which Our Sovereign Lord James II Was There Proclaimed King* (Wing H1755, 1685), p. 10.
275. Ibid., p. 26.
276. Ibid.
277. J. Curtois, *A Discourse Shewing that Kings Have their Being and Authority from God* (Wing C7700, 1685).
278. Ibid., p. 23.
279. Ibid.
280. See, for example, J. Ellesby, *The Doctrine of Passive Obedience Asserted in a Sermon Preach'd on January 30, 1684* (Wing E537, 1685).
281. B Woodroffe, *A Sermon Preach'd January XXX. 1684/5 Being the Fast for the Martyrdom of King Charles I of Blessed Memory* (Wing W3469, 1685), dedication to James II (n.p.).

282 F. Turner, *A Sermon Preached Before Their Majesties K James II. and Q. Mary at Their Coronation in Westminster-Abby April 23. 1685. By Francis Lord Bishop of Ely, Lord Almoner to His Majesty. Published by His Majesties Special Command* (Wing T3290, Dublin 1685), p. 14.

283. Ibid., p. 13.

284. Ibid., p. 14.

285. Ibid., p. 15.

286. W. Jegon, *The Damning Nature of Rebellion, or, The Universal Unlawfulness of Resistance under Pain of Damnation, in the Saddest Sense Asserted in a Sermon Preached at the Cathedral of Norwich, May 29, 1685, Being the Anniversary-day of the Birth of His Late Majesty Charles II, and of the Happy Restauration Both of Him and of the Government from the Great Rebellion* (Wing J530, 1685). Jegon, a fellow of King's Cambridge, was rector of Swanton Morley in Norfolk.

287. E. Pelling, *A Sermon Preached at Westminster-Abbey on the 26th of July, 1685 Being the Thanksgiving-day for His Majesties Victory Over the Rebels* (Wing P1098, 1685), p. 17. Pelling, a high churchman, was chaplain to the Duke of Somerset.

288. Ibid., pp. 27–8.

289. C. Allestree, *A Sermon Preach'd at Oxford, before Sir. Will. Walker, Mayor of the Said City, upon the 26th of July 1685 Being the Day of Thanksgiving for the Defeat of the Rebels in Monmouth's Rebellion* (Wing A1081, 1685); J. Hinton, *A Sermon Preached in the Parish Church of Newbury, Berks, on the 26th of July, 1685 Being the day of Thanksgiving for His Majesty's Late Victory over the Rebels* (Wing H2068, 1685).

290. T. Wagstaffe, *A Sermon Preached on the 26th day of July, 1685 Being the Day of Thanks-giving Appointed for His Majesty's Victory over the Rebels: in the United Parishes of St. Margaret Pattons, and St. Gabriell Fenchurch, London* (Wing W214, 1685), pp. 17, 19, 32.

291. C. Hutton, *The Rebels Text Opened, and their Solemn Appeal Answered Being a Sermon Preach'd in the Parish Church of Up-Lime, on the Thanksgiving-day for Our Wonderful Deliverance from the Late Horrid Rebellion, Being Sunday, July 26. 1685* (Wing H3840, 1686), quotation p. 28.

292. T. Long, *The Unreasonableness of Rebellion in a Sermon Preached at St. Peters, Exon. On the 26th of July, 1685* (Wing L2983, 1685), p. 25.

293. W. Stainforth, *A Sermon Preach'd in the Cathedral Church of St. Peter in York, on the 6th of February 1685/6 Being the Day on which His Majesty Began His Happy Reign* (Wing S5171, 1686); C. Wyvill, *The Duty of Honouring the King and the Obligations We Have Thereto Delivered in a Sermon Preached at Richmond in York-shire, on the 6th of February, 1685/6 Being the Day on which His Majesty Began His Happy Reign* (Wing W3786, 1686), quotation, p. 28.

294. T. Staynoe, *Subjection for Conscience Sake in a Sermon Preached Before the Right Honourable the Lord Mayor, the Court of Aldermen, and the Several Companies at Bow-Church on the Sixth of February, Being the King's Day* (Wing S5356, 1686).

295. T. Cartwright, *A Sermon Preached upon the Anniversary Solemnity of the Happy Inauguration of Our Dread Soveraign Lord King James II in the Collegiate Church of Ripon, February the 6th. 1685/6* (Wing C706, 1686), sig. A2^v.

296. Ibid., p. 3.

297. Ibid., p. 11.

298. Ibid., p. 15.

299. Ibid., p. 14.

300. Ibid., p. 13.

301. T. Codrington, *A Sermon Preached before the Queen Dowager in Her Majesties Chappel at Somerset-house on Quinquagesima Sunday February the 6th. 1686/7: Being Also the Anniversary Day of His Late Majesty King Charles the II. of Blessed Memory* (Wing C4880, 1687).

302. Codrington, *ODNB*.

303. J. Mackqueen, *Gods Interest in the King Set Forth in a Sermon Preached in the Cathedral of Edinburgh October the 14th at the Anniversary Commemoration of His Majesties Birth* (Wing M226, 1687); W. Wall, *A Sermon Preach'd Before the King and Queen in Their Majesties Chappel at St. James's on Sunday, October 24, 1686 by the Reverend Father Dom. W. M. Monk of the Holy Order of St. Benedict* (Wing M108, 1687).

304. Ibid., p. 29.

6 A Popish Face? Images of James II

1. O. Millar, *The Tudor, Stuart and Early Georgian Pictures in the Collection of Her Majesty The Queen* (2 vols, London, 1963), I, p. 124.

2. The Flagmen of Lowestoft are now in the National Maritime Museum.
3. Millar, *Tudor, Stuart and Early Georgian Pictures*, I, p. 120.
4. Ibid., p. 21.
5. Ibid., p. 37; BL Harleian MS. 1890.
6. Above, ch. 2.
7. Millar, *Tudor, Stuart and Early Georgian Pictures*, I, pp. 120-1, nos 239-41.
8. Ibid., p. 120, no. 240; II, plate 100. See also National Portrait Gallery [NPG] D11410. See S. Barnes, N. De Porter, O. Millar and H. Vey eds, *Van Dyck: A Complete Catalogue of the Paintings* (New Haven, CT, and London, 2004), *IV*, 177, p. 567; IV, 214, p. 597. There are also gestures in the portraits of Charles I, notably *Le Roi à la chasse*, ibid., IV, 50, p. 467.
9. National Maritime Museum BHC 2797.
10. NPG 666. See J. Douglas Stewart, *Sir Godfrey Kneller and the English Baroque Portrait* (Oxford, 1983), p. 112, no. 385 and plate 18a.
11. Fitzwilliam Museum, Cambridge, PD.815-1963; on Van de Velde the Elder, see *ODNB*. There are several of his marine canvases, including *The Battle of Lowestoft*, in the National Maritime Museum.
12. Millar, *Tudor, Stuart and Early Georgian Pictures*, I, p. 141, no. 333; L. Cust and C. H. C. Baker, 'Notes', *Burlington Magazine*, 28 (1915), pp. 112-13, 116, plate 1A.
13. Quoted in Millar, *Tudor, Stuart and Early Georgian Pictures*, I, p. 141; P. Hammond and D. Hopkins eds, *The Poems of John Dryden Vol. III, 1686-1693* (Harlow, Essex, 2000), p. 15, ll. 127-32; and pp. 3-18 *passim*; M. Reynolds, *The Learned Lady in England 1650-1760* (Boston, MA, 1920), pp. 85-6, 139-41.
14. Millar, *Tudor, Stuart and Early Georgian Pictures*, I, p. 22.
15. Stewart, *Sir Godfrey Kneller*, p. 38.
16. Ibid., p. 112, no. 386.
17. Ibid., p. 112, no. 387; cf. p. 34.
18. Ibid., p. 122, no. 388, plate 29c.
19. Barnes et al., *Van Dyck*, IV, 54, 58, pp. 471-5.
20. Stewart, *Sir Godfrey Kneller*, p. 112, no. 389, plate 83a.
21. For the Largillière, see National Maritime Museum BHC2798; Millar, *Tudor, Stuart and Early Georgian Pictures*, I, p. 22.
22. See below, ch. 6, pp. 272-6.
23. Millar, *Tudor, Stuart and Early Georgian Pictures*, I, pp. 121, 123, 127, 138-9, nos 244, 245, 269, 321, 322, 323, 325.
24. Stewart, *Sir Godfrey Kneller*, p. 38.
25. Millar, *Tudor, Stuart and Early Georgian Pictures*, I, pp. 155-6, nos. 413, 415; Stewart, *Sir Godfrey Kneller*, p. 28.
26. Stewart, *Sir Godfrey Kneller*, p. 28.
27. See *A Catalogue of the Collection of Pictures &c Belonging to King James the Second* (ESTC T070978, 1758), for example nos 688, 694, 804, pp. 61-2 and *passim*.
28. Stewart, *Sir Godfrey Kneller*, p. 30.
29. Ibid., no. 674, p. 129, plate 19c.
30. Ibid., p. 29.
31. Ibid., pp. 113, 136, nos 412, 779, plates 19a, 20a.
32. Millar, *Tudor, Stuart and Early Georgian Pictures*, I, p. 146, no. 348.
33. Stewart, *Sir Godfrey Kneller*, p. 30.
34. A. Clark ed., *The Life and Times of Anthony Wood*, vol. 3, 1682-1695 (Oxford, 1894), pp. 236-7.
35. J. Gother, *A Discourse of the Use of Images in Relation to the Church of England and the Church of Rome* (Wing G1328, 1687). Gother had been sent to England as a missionary in 1681 and wrote Catholic polemic, *ODNB*.
36. Gother, *Discourse*, p. 5, for a citation of Montagu.
37. Ibid., pp. 20-1.
38. R. Montagu, *Appello Caesarem A Just Appeale from Two Uniust Informers. By Richard Mountagu* (STC 18030, 1625). On Montagu, see *ODNB*.
39. For the thirty-six sittings, see Stewart, *Sir Godfrey Kneller*, p. 38, n. 57.
40. Millar, *Tudor, Stuart and Early Georgian Pictures*, p. 25.
41. NPG D10653.
42. NPG D11959.
43. Huntington Library, San Marino, Richard Bull Granger, 18/6.
44. Ibid., 18/8.

45. BM Registration no. 1884,1011.157. See A. Griffiths, *The Print in Stuart Britain 1603–1689* (London, 1998), p. 220, and plate 205, p. 295.
46. Stewart, *Sir Godfrey Kneller*, p. 21. Becket was the first major English mezzotint engraver.
47. Huntington Library, Bull Granger, 18/4.
48. Ibid., 18/23; NPG D10649.
49. See, for example, Huntington Library, Bull Granger 18/2ᵛ, 17, 19.
50. Ibid., 18/17ᵛ.
51. Ibid.; see G. Finger, *Sonatae XII pro diversis instrumentis quarum tres priores pro violinos & viola di gamba* (Wing F949, 1688).
52. M. Campbell, *Henry Purcell: Glory of His Age* (Oxford, 1995), p. 249.
53. Huntington Library Bull Granger, 18/58ᵛ; J. Michael Wright, *An Account of His Excellence, Roger Earl of Castlemaine's Embassy from His Sacred Majesty James IId, King of England, Scotland, France, and Ireland, &c. to His Holiness Innocent XI Published Formerly in the Italian Tongue by Mr. Michael Wright . . . and Now Made English* (Wing W3702, 1688).
54. Huntington Library, Bull Granger, 18/33, 33ᵛ, 34, 35.
55. R. Sharpe, *The Engraved Record of the Jacobite Movement* (Aldershot, 1996), p. 2.
56. On the Magdalen College affair, see T. Harris, *Revolution: The Great Crisis of the British Monarchy, 1685–1720* (London and New York, 2006), pp. 226–9.
57. NPG D10697; see Sharpe, *Engraved Record*, no. 71, p. 81, plate 71.1, p. 41; cf. NPG D34714. Kneller painted the original portrait when James Francis Edward was just a week old, F. Verney and M. Verney eds, *Memoirs of the Verney Family* (2 vols, London and New York, 1904), II, p. 459.
58. Sharp, *Engraved Record*, no. 75; see plate 75.11, p. 3.
59. Ibid., no. 67, p. 81; cf. an anonymous version, ibid., no. 69, p. 81; ibid., no. 76, p. 83.
60. See below ch. 8, p. 313.
61. Sharpe, *Engraved Record*, p. 43.
62. See Huntington Library, Bull Granger, 18/11ᵛ; Sharpe, *Engraved Record*, no. 70, pp. 81–2; BM Sat 166, Griffiths, *Print in Stuart Britain*, no. 209, p. 300.
63. Below ch. 8, pp. 313–22.
64. Below ch. 7, pp. 287–8.
65. See T. Ramsay, *Discors concordia or Unanimity in Variance. Representing Such As, Upon His Maiesties Late Declaration for Liberty of Conscience, Did Express, by Their Addresses, Their Gratitude and Loyalty* (Bodleian, Ashm. H 24 [2], 1687). The engraving is signed by Ramsay.
66. Engraved in Huntington Library, Bull Granger, 18/15ᵛ; F. Sandford, *A Genealogical History of the Kings and Queens of England, and Monarchs of Great Britain, &c. From the Conquest, Anno 1066. to the Year 1707* (ESTC, T147652, 1707), p. 548c.
67. Harris, *Revolution*, p. 296.
68. Above, ch. 2, pp. 131–3.
69. A. W. Franks and H. A. Grueber, *Medallic Illustrations of the History of Great Britain* (2 vols, 1885), I, pp. 586, 589, nos 263, 266: E. Hawkins, *Medallic Illustrations of the History of Great Britain and Ireland to the Death of George II* (1904–11), plates LX, 12, LXI, 2.
70. Franks and Grueber, *Medallic Illustrations*, I, p. 603, no. 1; Hawkins, *Medallic Illustrations*, LXIII, 1; cf. LXIV, 3.
71. Franks and Grueber, *Medallic Illustrations*, I, pp. 603–4, nos 2–3; Hawkins, *Medallic Illustrations*, plate LXIII, 2–4. Medals were given away at coronations.
72. Franks and Grueber, *Medallic Illustrations*, I, p. 604, no. 4; Hawkins, *Medallic Illustrations*, plate LXIII, 4.
73. Franks and Grueber, *Medallic Illustrations*, I, p. 605, no. 5; Hawkins, *Medallic Illustrations*, plate LXIII, 5.
74. Franks and Grueber, *Medallic Illustrations*, I, p. 606, no. 7; Hawkins, *Medallic Illustrations*, plate LXIII, 7.
75. Franks and Grueber, *Medallic Illustrations*, I, p. 607, no. 10; Hawkins, *Medallic Illustrations*, plate LXIII, 9.
76. Hawkins, *Medallic Illustrations*, plate LXIII, 15.
77. Pliny, *Natural History*, Book 10, 3–6; H. Rackham ed., *Pliny, Natural History*, III (Cambridge, MA, 1940), p. 299.
78. Franks and Grueber, *Medallic Illustrations*, I, p. 613, no. 22; Hawkins, *Medallic Illustrations*, plate LXIV, 7.
79. Franks and Grueber, *Medallic Illustrations* I, p. 613, no. 23; Hawkins, *Medallic Illustrations*, plate LXIV, 8.

80. Franks and Grueber, *Medallic Illustrations* I, p. 614, no. 24; Hawkins, *Medallic Illustrations*, plate LXIV, 9.
81. J. Clarke, *The Life of James II* (2 vols, 1816), I, p. 731.
82. Franks and Grueber, *Medallic Illustrations*, I, p. 614, no. 25; Hawkins, *Medallic Illustrations*, plate LXIV, 10.
83. Franks and Grueber, *Medallic Illustrations*, I, p. 614, no. 25; Hawkins, *Medallic Illustrations*, plate LXIV, 12.
84. Franks and Grueber, *Medallic Illustrations*, I, pp. 616–17 nos 28–9; Hawkins, *Medallic Illustrations*, plate LXV, 1–2.
85. Franks and Grueber, *Medallic Illustrations*, I, p. 615, no. 26; Hawkins, *Medallic Illustrations*, plate LXIV, 11.
86. Franks and Grueber, *Medallic Illustrations*, I, pp. 621, 622–3, 36–9; Hawkins, *Medallic Illustrations*, plate LXV, 9; LXVI, 1–3.
87. Franks and Grueber, *Medallic Illustrations*, I, pp. 627–9, nos 46–50; Hawkins, *Medallic Illustrations*, plate LXVI, 9–13.
88. Franks and Grueber, *Medallic Illustrations*, I, p. 627, no. 46; Hawkins, *Medallic Illustrations*, plate LXVI, 9.
89. Franks and Grueber, *Medallic Illustrations*, I, p. 628, no. 48; Hawkins, *Medallic Illustrations*, plate LXVI, 11.
90. Franks and Grueber, *Medallic Illustrations*, I, pp. 629–30, nos 49–51; Hawkins, *Medallic Illustrations*, plate LXVI, 12–13, LXVII, 1.
91. Franks and Grueber, *Medallic Illustrations*, I, p. 630, no. 51; Hawkins, *Medallic Illustrations*, plate LXVII, 1.
92. See Franks and Grueber, *Medallic Illustrations*, I, pp. 630–1, nos 52–3; Hawkins, *Medallic Illustrations*, plate LXVII, 2–3, below p. 435.
93. Though 1696, when the nation signed the Association, marked a turning point in the recognition of William, the uncertainties about the succession dogged his – and Anne's – reign and were perhaps only finally resolved with the defeats of the Jacobites in 1715 and 1745.
94. See above, ch. 2, pp. 133–5.
95. http://www.coins.nd.edu/ColCoin/ColCoinIntros/Br-Copper.intro.html; H. Montagu, *The Copper, Tin and Bronze Coinage and Patterns for Coins of England* (1885), pp. 36–7.
96. See H. Seaby and P. Rayner, *The English Silver Coinage from 1649* (London, 1968), p. 35; Guy de la Bedoyère, 'English Milled Coinage of the 17th Century' (www.romanbritain.freeserve.co.uk/milledcoinage.htm); http://www.ukcoinpics.co.uk/j2/index.html; P. Rayner, *English Silver Coinage from 1649* (London, 1992), p. 11.
97. http://www.24carat.co.uk/frame.php?url=britannia3.html.
98. See above ch. 2, p. 100.
99. N. Smith, *The Royal Image and the English People* (Aldershot, 2001), p. 126.
100. Ibid., p. 140, n. 26.
101. Ibid., plate 5.4, p. 127.
102. Ibid., p. 133.
103. Ibid., pp. 131–2.
104. Ibid., p. 128.
105. Ibid., p. 130.
106. Ibid., plate 5.6, p. 132; cf. plate 5.7, p. 133.
107. Ibid., p. 128. See P. Burke, *The Fabrication of Louis XIV* (New Haven, CT, and London, 1992), p. 93.
108. Smith, *Royal Image*, p. 128.
109. Ibid., p. 130.
110. For example, at University College, ibid., plate 5.9, p. 138.
111. Above ch. 2, pp. 231–6.
112. S. Thurley, *Whitehall Palace: An Architectural History of the Royal Apartments, 1240–1698* (New Haven, CT, and London, 1999), p. 127.
113. H. Colvin, *The History of the King's Works Vol. 5, 1660–1782* (London, 1976), p. 311.
114. Ibid., p. 151.
115. Ibid., p. 153; S. Thurley, *Hampton Court: A Social and Architectural History* (New Haven, CT, and London, 2003), pp. 143–5.
116. Ibid., pp. 155, 328–30.
117. Ibid., p. 236.
118. Ibid.
119. Ibid., 126.

120. G. Parnell, 'The King's Guard Chamber: A Vision of Power', *Apollo*, 140 (1994), pp. 60–4; Thurley, *Whitehall*, p. 135.
121. Thurley, *Whitehall*, p. 127.
122. Ibid., pp. 127–30.
123. Colvin, *King's Works*, V, p. 286.
124. Ibid., pp. 286–7; K. Sharpe, *Image Wars: Promoting Kings and Commonwealths in England, 1603–1660* (New Haven, CT, and London, 2010), p. 223.
125. Thurley, *Whitehall*, pp. 132–3.
126. Ibid., p. 136; Colvin, *King's Works*, V, p. 300.
127. Thurley, *Whitehall*, p. 135.
128. E. de Beer ed., *The Diary of John Evelyn, IV, 1673–89* (Oxford, 1955), p. 416, 14 February.
129. Thurley, *Whitehall*, p. 133.
130. Ibid., pp. 133–5; Colvin, *King's Works*, V, pp. 290–1.
131. De Beer, *Diary of John Evelyn*, IV, p. 534; Thurley, *Whitehall*, p. 134; Colvin, *King's Works*, V, p. 290.
132. Thurley, *Whitehall*, p. 134.
133. Colvin, *King's Works*, V, pp. 291–3.
134. Gother, *A Discourse of the Use of Images*, p. 6.
135. Thurley, *Whitehall*, p. 135.

7 Staging Catholic Kingship

1. K. Sharpe, *Image Wars: Promoting English Kings and Commonwealths, 1603–1660* (New Haven, CT, and London, 2010), pp. 92–3, 233–4.
2. L. Madway, '"The Most Conspicuous Solemnity": The Coronation of Charles II', in E. Cruickshanks ed., *The Stuart Courts* (Stroud, 2000), p. 153.
3. F. Sandford, *The History of the Coronation of the Most High, Most Mighty, and Most Excellent Monarch, James II* (Bodleian Ashmole 1745, 1687), pp. 1–2.
4. *The Ceremonies, Form of Prayer, and Services Used in Westminster-Abby at the Coronation of King James the First and Queen Ann, His Consort Performed by Dr. Whitgift . . .; with an Account of the Procession from the Palace to the Abby . . .: with the Coronation of King Charles the First in Scotland* (Wing C1676, 1685).
5. Sandford, *History of the Coronation*, pp. 2–4, 7, 213.
6. Ibid., p. 4.
7. Ibid., p. 19. The suggestion that a communion had been planned is supported by Archbishop Sancroft's notes for preparation on 'the communion service as it stood in King Charles I's time', G. Wickham Legg, *English Coronation Records* (London 1901), p. 313. Sancroft noted the alterations to the normal service for the coronation, see Bodleian Tanner MS 31, f. 74, and L.G. Wickham Legg, *English Coronation Records* (London, 1901), p. 287.
8. Sandford, *History of the Coronation*, p. 22.
9. Ibid., p. 27.
10. Ibid., pp. 28, 31, 33.
11. On Charles I's decision not to stage a civic entry, see Sharpe, *Image Wars*, pp. 233–5.
12. Sandford, *History of the Coronation*, p. 45.
13. Ibid., pp. 45–56.
14. Ibid., p. 57.
15. Ibid., pp. 57–8.
16. Ibid., pp. 60, 61–4.
17. Ibid., p. 65.
18. Ibid., pp. 65–80; M. Campbell, *Henry Purcell: Glory of His Age* (London 1993), p. 83.
19. Sandford, *History of the Coronation*, pp. 81–2.
20. Ibid., p. 83.
21. Ibid., pp. 85–6.
22. Ibid., pp. 87–8.
23. Ibid., p. 89.
24. Ibid., pp. 92–4.
25. Ibid., p. 4.
26. Wickham Legg, *Coronation Records*, pp. xxxiii, 287.
27. Sandford, *History of the Coronation*, p. 96.
28. Ibid., p. 102.

29. Ibid.
30. Ibid., p. 107.
31. Ibid., title page and sigs B1–B1ᵛ.
32. Ibid., sigs B1–B1ᵛ.
33. Ibid., sig B2.
34. Sandford, *ODNB*.
35. *An Account of the Ceremonial at the Coronation of Their Most Excellent Majesties, King James II and Queen Mary, at Westminster the 23 of April 1685* (Wing A260, 1685).
36. *Whitehall, April 23 This Day Being the Festival of St. George, the Coronation of Their Sacred Majesties King James the Second and Queen Mary Was Performed at Westminster in Manner Following* (Wing T925, 1685); *The Description of the Coronation of His Sacred Majesty K. James II. and His Illustrious Consort Queen Mary Celebrated on the 23th day of April, 1685* (Wing D1156, 1685); *A Description of the Ceremonial Proceedings at the Coronation of Their Most Illustrious, Serene, and Sacred Majesties, King James II and His Royal Consort Queen Mary Who Were Crowned at Westminster-Abby, on Thursday the 23th. of April, 1685* (Wing D1154, 1685).
37. *Description of the Ceremonial Proceedings.*
38. P. Ker, *In Illustrissimum, ac Serenissimum, Jacobum II, Regem Magnae Britaniae, Franciae, & Hiberniae, &c. cum publice coronam regalem indueret carmen epiphonetikon A panegyrick poem on the Coronation of the Illustrious and Serene, James II, King of Great Britain, France, and Ireland* (Wing K344, 1685); A. Behn, *A Pindarick Poem on the Happy Coronation of His Most Sacred Majesty James II and His Illustrious Consort Queen Mary by Mrs. Behn* (Wing B1751).
39. *A Poem on the Coronation of Our Most Illustrious Sovereign K. James II. and His Gracious Consort Queen Mary, Who Were Crown'd at Westminster, on St. George's-Day, Being the 23th. this Instant April 1685/Written by a Person of Quality* (Wing P2689A, 1685), pp. 1, 3 and *passim*; *A New Song Upon the Coronation of King James II to the Tune of King James's Jig* (Wing N776, 1685).
40. *Englands Royal Renown, in the Coronation of Our Gracious Soveraign King James the 2d. and His Royal Consort Queen Mary, Who Were Both Crowned at Westminster, the Twenty Third of April, 1685. To the Tune of, The Cannons Roar* (Wing E3042, 1685), broadside.
41. Fitzwilliam Museum Cambridge, C.1644–1928.
42. Though most cards were dominated by negative images of the king, see J. R. S. Whiting, *A Handful of History* (Dursley, 1978), pp. 106, 109, 111.
43. R. Lowman, *An Exact Narrative and Description of the Wonderfull and Stupendious Fireworks in Honour of Their Majesties Coronations, and for the High Entertainment of Their Majesties, the Nobility, and City of London; Made on the Thames, and Perform'd to the Admiration and Amazement of the Spectators, on April the 24, 1685.*
44. Ibid.; Sandford, *History of the Coronation*, p. 125.
45. Sandford, *History of the Coronation*, p. 125; Lowman, *An Exact Narrative.*
46. The quotation is from Robert Burton, *The Anatomy of Melancholy* (Wing B6182, 1652), art. 1, section 2, memb. 3, sub. 15, p. 140.
47. Lowman, *An Exact Narrative*, p. 2.
48. *Augustus Anglicanus a Compendious View of the Life and Reign of that Immortal and Glorious Monarch Charles II* (Wing A4215, 1686), p. 191.
49. Above, ch. 3.
50. See Taubman, *ODNB*.
51. M. Taubman, *London's Annual Triumph Performed on Thursday, Octob. 29, 1685, for the Entertainment of the Right Honourable Sir Robert Jeffreys, Kt* (Wing T241, 1685), sigs A2–A2ᵛ.
52. Ibid., pp. 4–6.
53. Ibid., pp. 7–9.
54. Ibid., p. 12.
55. M. Taubman, *London's Yearly Jubilee Perform'd on Friday, October XXIX, 1686 for the Entertainment of the Right Honourable Sir John Peake, Knight, Lord Mayor of the City of London* (Wing T244, 1686).
56. Ibid., p. 6.
57. Ibid., pp. 6–9.
58. Ibid., p. 9.
59. Ibid., pp. 9–13.
60. M. Taubman, *London's Triumph, or, The Goldsmiths Jubilee Containing a Description of the Several Pageants and Speeches, Made Proper for the Occasion, Together with a Song, for the Entertainment of His Majesty, who, with His Royal Consort, the Queen Dowager, Their Royal Highnesses the Prince and Princess of Denmark, and the Whole Court, Honour His Lordship This Year with their Presence* (Wing T243, 1687), epistle dedicatory; cf. p. 9.

61. Ibid., pp. 4-5.
62. Ibid., p. 7.
63. Ibid., p. 10.
64. Ibid., pp. 11-12.
65. Ibid., p. 12.
66. M. Taubman, *London's Anniversary Festival, Performed on Monday, October the 29th. 1688 For the Entertainment of the Right Honourable, Sr. John Chapman, Kt. Lord Mayor of the City of London; Being Their Great Year of Jubilee* (Wing T240, 1688).
67. From *Aeneid*, VI, 2, 75; Taubman, *London's Anniversary*, sig. A2.
68. Taubman, *London's Anniversary*, p. 8. On the surrender and restoration of the City's charter, see G. de Krey, *London and the Restoration, 1659-1683* (Cambridge, 2005), pp. 382-5; de Krey, *A Fractured Society: The Politics of London in the First Age of Party, 1688-1715* (Oxford, 1985), pp. 47-8.
69. Ibid., p. 7.
70. Ibid., p. 12.
71. K. Sharpe, *The Personal Rule of Charles I* (New Haven, CT, and London, 1992), p. 210.
72. It is very regrettable that Andrew Barclay has not published his important thesis on 'The Impact of King James II on the Departments of the Royal Household' (Cambridge PhD, 1993), on which I draw here.
73. See J. Callow, *The Making of King James II* (Stroud, 2000), ch. 3.
74. J. Miller, *James II: A Study in Kingship* (Hove, 1978), p. 42.
75. Ibid.
76. Barclay, 'Impact of James II', p. 135.
77. Ibid., p. 136.
78. For the court as a 'point of contact', see G. R. Elton, 'Tudor Government: The Points of Contact 3: The Court', *Transactions of the Royal Historical Society*, 26 (1976), pp. 211-28.
79. Barclay, 'Impact of King James II', pp. 29, 136.
80. Ibid., p. 58.
81. Ibid., p. 62.
82. Ibid., pp. 63-5, 69.
83. Ibid., p. 76; R. C. Chandaman, *The English Public Revenue, 1660-1688* (Oxford, 1975), pp. 256-61, appendix 3.
84. Barclay, 'Impact of James II', p. 65.
85. Ibid., pp. 79, 90.
86. Callow, *Making of King James II*, pp. 112-15, 173; Miller, *James II*, pp. 120-2.
87. Miller, *James II*, pp. 121-2.
88. Ibid., p. 122.
89. Ibid., pp. 121-2. Above, I argued that Charles II may have benefited from his reputation as a womanizer – not least on account of a reaction to Commonwealth puritanism. By the 1670s, however, the moral tide had turned against debauchery – and James may have sought to represent himself accordingly. I owe this point to a discussion with Mark Knights.
90. Barclay, 'Impact of James II', ch. 4.
91. Ibid., pp. 120-3.
92. Ibid., p. 124.
93. Ibid., p. 125.
94. Ibid., p. 130.
95. Ibid., pp. 131, 142-3; Miller, *James II*, pp. 142-3, 146-7; J. Clarke, *The Life of James II* (2 vols, 1816), II, p. 621.
96. Barclay, 'Impact of James II', p. 159.
97. Ibid., pp. 105-10.
98. Ibid., pp. 111-12.
99. Ibid., p. 114.
100. Ibid., p. 110.
101. See E. Corp, *A Court in Exile: The Stuarts in France, 1689-1714* (Cambridge, 2004), pp. 155-6.
102. Clarke, *Life of James II*, II, pp. 620-1.
103. Corp, *Court in Exile*, p. 263 and see n. 40.
104. J. Spurr, *The Restoration Church of England, 1646-1689* (New Haven, CT, and London, 1991), p. 92.
105. Ibid., p. 93.
106. Ibid., p. 95.

107. Barclay, 'Impact of James II', p. 38.
108. S. Clarke, *The Historian's Guide, or, Britains Remembrancer Being a Summary of all the Actions, Exploits, Sieges, Battels, Designs, Attempts, Preferments, Honours, Changes, &c. and Whatever Else is Worthy Notice that Hath Happened in His Majesty's Dominions, from 1600 to 1688* (Wing C4521, 1688), p. 187.
109. *Calendar of State Papers Domestic, 1687–9*, pp. 48, 51, nos 230, 255.
110. Ibid., p. 66, no. 320.
111. Ibid., p. 67, no. 330.
112. Ibid., pp. 67–8, no. 332; Clarke, *Historian's Guide*, p. 188.
113. *Cal. Stat. Pap. Dom., 1687–9*, p. 66, no. 320.
114. Clarke, *Life of James II*, II, pp. 43–6.
115. *Cal. Stat. Pap. Dom., 1685*, p. 204, no. 906.
116. Miller, *James II*, p. 141. On Monmouth's rebellion, see P. Earle, *Monmouth's Rebels: The Road to Sedgemoor, 1685* (London, 1977).
117. Clarke, *Life of James II*, II, p. 29.
118. Miller, *James II*, p. 141.
119. Clarke, *Life of James II*, II, p. 37; on Walters, see above, ch. 4, pp. 216–17.
120. As James himself acknowledged with hindsight, Clarke, *Life of James II*, II, p. 36.
121. *Cal. Stat. Pap. Dom., 1685*, p. 329, no. 1629.
122. Miller, *James II*, p. 142.
123. See J. Tutchin, *The Protestant Martyrs: or, The Bloody Assizes Giving an Account of the Lives, Tryals, and Dying Speeches, of All those Eminent Protestants that Suffered in the West of England, by the Sentence of that Bloody and Cruel Judge Jefferies* (Wing T3382aA, 1688).
124. *An Account of the Proceedings Against the Rebels, at Dorchester; at an Assize Holden there 4th and 5th September, 1685.* (Bodleian Ashmole F 5 [141], 1685); *An Account of the Proceedings Against the Rebels at an Assize Holden at Exeter, on the 14th. of this Instant September, 1685* (Bodleian Ashmole F 5 [143], 1685); *A Further Account of the Proceedings Against the Rebels in the West of England, who on the 10th of September, 1685, to the Number of Two-hundred fifty One, Received Sentence of Death at Dorchester for High-Treason* (Wing F2545, 1685).
125. Clarke, *Life of James II*, II, p. 45.
126. Ibid., p. 43.
127. Ibid., p. 46.
128. *Cal. Stat. Pap. Dom., 1685*, p. 329, no. 1629.
129. Ibid., p. 336, no. 1663.
130. James regretted this, Clarke, *Life of James II*, II, p. 44.
131. W. Gibson, *James II and the Trial of the Seven Bishops* (Basingstoke, 2009). This study, though useful, is throughout decidedly antagonistic to James and, while claiming to restore a historiographical balance, comes close in places to rehearsing Whig polemics.
132. Miller, *James II*, p. 186.
133. Ibid., p. 187; Gibson, *James II and Trial*, ch. 5.
134. Below, ch. 8.
135. See *Quadriennium Jacobi, or, The History of the Reign of King James II from His First Coming to the Crown to His Desertion* (Wing Q6, 1689), pp. 166–76, quotation, p. 166.
136. Miller, *James II*, p. 186.
137. See G. Bennett, 'The Seven Bishops: A Reconsideration', in D. Baker ed., *Religious Motivation: Biographical and Sociological Problems for the Church Historian* (Oxford, 1978), pp. 267–87, especially pp. 283–4.
138. See K. Sharpe, *The Personal Rule of Charles I* (New Haven, CT, and London, 1992), pp. 758–66.
139. James did admit Huguenot refugees from France, Clarke, *Life of James II*, II, p. 170.
140. J. Baber, *A Poem Upon the Coronation by J. Baber* (Wing B245, 1685), p. 2. It is not certain that he was the John Baber listed in *ODNB*.
141. H. Anderson, *A Loyal Tear Dropt on the Vault of the High and Mighty Prince, Charles II, of Glorious and Happy Memory by Henry Anderson* (Wing A3091, 1685), p. 25; T. Long, *The Unreasonableness of Rebellion in a Sermon Preached at St. Peters, Exon. On the 26th of July, 1685* (Wing L2983, 1685), p. 25. Long was a prebendary of Exeter Cathedral.
142. J. Goodman, *A Sermon Preached before the Right Honourable the Lord Mayor and the Court of Aldermen at Guild-hall Chappel on the XXV of January, 1684* (Wing G1127, 1685), p. 22.
143. For example, J. Usher, *Britannicarum ecclesiarum antiquitates* (Wing U160, 1687); J. Usher, *A Discourse of the Religion Anciently Professed by the Irish and Brittish by the Most Reverend and Learned James Usher* (Wing U170, 1687); R. Parr, *The Life of the Most Reverend Father in God,*

James Usher, Late Lord Arch-Bishop of Armagh, Primate and Metropolitan of all Ireland (Wing P548, 1686).

144. W. P., *Tears Wip'd Off, or, The Second Essay of the Quakers by Way of Poetry Occasioned by the Coronation of James and Mary* (Wing P138, 1685); Miller, *James II*, p. 156.

145. *The Dissenter's Discription of True Loyalty* (Wing D1687, 1687), broadside.

146. T. Cartwright, *A Sermon Preached upon the Anniversary Solemnity of the Happy Inauguration of Our Dread Soveraign Lord King James II in the Collegiate Church of Ripon, February the 6th. 1685/6* (Wing C706, 1686), p. 11. Cartwright was Dean of Ripon and a royal chaplain.

147. *A Poem Occasioned by His Majesties Most Gracious Resolution Declar'd in His Most Honourable Privy Council, March 18, 1686/7. For Liberty of Conscience* (Wing P2678, 1687). See also for a full defence of toleration, *A Pindarick-poem upon His Most Sacred Majestie's Late Gracious Indulgence, in Granting a Toleration, and Liberty of Conscience in Matters of Religion* (Wing P2260, 1687), passim.

148. C. Trinder, *The Speech of Charles Trinder, Recorder of Gloucester at His Entrance upon that Office, January the 8th, 1687/8* (Wing T2283, 1688), p. 15.

149. R. L'Estrange, *An Answer to A Letter to a Dissenter, upon Occasion of His Majesties Late Gracious Declaration of Indulgence* (Wing A 3319, 1687), p. 2 and passim. L'Estrange had some doubts about toleration, however; see *ODNB*.

150. *A Collection of the Several Addresses in the Late King James' Time Concerning the Conception and Birth of the Pretended Prince of Wales* (Bodleian Pamph. B 179/46, date uncertain), p. 3.

151. G. Davies ed., *Papers of Devotion of James II* (Roxburgh Club, Oxford, 1925), p. 23. See above, ch. 5, n. 191.

152. *Articles Agreed Upon by the Archbishops and Bishops of Both Provinces and the Whole Clergy in the Convocation Holden at London in the year 1562 for the Avoiding of Diversities of Opinions and for the Stablishing of Content Touching True Religion: Reprinted by His Majesties Commandment with His Royal Declaration Prefixed Thereunto* (Wing C4006, 1686).

153. *His Majesties Commission for the Rebuilding of the Cathedral Church of S. Paul in London* (Wing J155, 1685); *Cal. Stat. Pap. Dom., 1686–7*, p. 4, no. 20.

154. J. Betham, *A Sermon Preach'd Before the King and Queen in Their Majesties Chappel at St. James, Upon the Annunciation of Our Blessed Lady, March 25, 1686* (Wing B2060, 1686), pp. 31–2.

155. P. Ellis, *A Sermon preach'd Before the King on November the 13, 1686 Being the Feast of all the Saints of the H. Order of St. Benedict* (Wing E598, 1686), p. 28 and passim.

156. See, for example, W. Hall, *A Sermon Preach'd before Her Majesty the Queen Dowager in Her Chappel at Somerset-House, upon the Fifth Sunday after Easter, May 9, 1686/by William Hall* (Wing H447, 1686).

157. J. Ayray, *A Sermon Preached before Her Majesty the Queen Dowager in Her Chappel at Sommerset House, upon the Second Sunday after Easter, April 10, 1687/by F. James Ayray . . . Chaplain and Preacher in Ordinary to His Excellency the Spanish Ambassador* (Wing A4297B, 1687), pp. 22–3, 25–6.

158. L. Sabran, *A Sermon Preached Before the King at Chester, on August xxviii, 1687, Being the Feast of S. Augustin* (Wing S221, 1687).

159. J. Bossuet, *An Exposition of the Doctrine of the Catholic Church in Matters of Controversie by James Bénigne Bossuet* (Wing B3784, 1686); *Kalendarium Catholicum for the Year 1686* (Wing A1854, 1686).

160. See the collection of Catholic books advertised and sold by T. Basset at the end of W. Claggett, *A Discourse Concerning the Worship of the Blessed Virgin and the Saints* (Wing C4384, 1686), after p. 144.

161. *Assertio septem sacramentorum, or, An Assertion of the Seven Sacraments Against Martin Luther by Henry the VIII* (Wing H1468, 1687); T. Bridoul, *The School of the Eucharist Established upon the Miraculous Respects* (Wing B4496, 1687).

162. C. Milton, *The State of Church-affairs in this Island of Great Britain under the Government of the Romans and British Kings* (Wing M2085, 1687). On Christopher Milton, see *ODNB*.

163. Their fears would not have been allayed by M. Altham's, *Some Queries to Protestants Answered and an Explanation of the Roman Catholick's Belief in Four Great Points Considered* (Wing A2934, 1686).

164. E. Sclater, *Consensus Veterum, or, The Reasons of Edward Sclater, Minister of Putney, for His Conversion to the Catholic Faith and Communion* (Wing S910, 1686); cf. P. Manby, *The Considerations which Oblig'd Peter Manby Dean of London-dery, to Embrace the Roman Catholic Religion* (M384, 1687).

165. *Copies of Two Papers Written by the Late King Charles II of Blessed Memory* (Wing C2942, 1685; C2944, 1686). See C2942, p. 2. Dryden argued that they were Charles II's; see his *A Defence of the Papers Written by the Late King of Blessed Memory, and Duchess of York, Against the Answer Made to Them* (Wing D2261, 1686). Cf. R. Hudleston, *A Short and Plain Way to the Faith and Church Composed Many Years Since by . . . Mr. Richard Hudleston . . . of the Order of St. Benedict; and Now Published . . . by His Nephew, Mr. Jo. Hudleston . . .; to which Is Annexed His late Majesty King Charles the Second His Papers Found in His Closet after His Decease* (Wing H3257, 1688). Charles II's biographer doubts their authenticity, see R. Hutton, 'The Religion of Charles II', in R. Smuts ed., *The Stuart Court and Europe* (Cambridge, 1996), p. 235.
166. Huntington Library, San Marino, RB 133456, facing p. 3.

8   Countering 'Catholic Kingship' and Contesting Revolution

1. A sample collection of this literature is in T. Jones ed., *A Catalogue of the Collection of Tracts for and against Popery Published In or About the Reign of James II* (Chetham Society, 58, Manchester, 1859). I owe this reference to the kindness of Mark Knights.
2. J. Canaries, *Rome's Additions to Christianity Shewn to Be Inconsistent with the True Design of So Spiritual a Religion in a Sermon Preached at Edinburgh* (Wing C421, 1686).
3. W. Clagett, *A Discourse Concerning the Worship of the Blessed Virgin and the Saints* (Wing C4384, 1686), p. 1.
4. H. More, *A Brief Discourse of the Real Presence of the Body and Blood of Christ in the Celebration of the Holy Eucharist* (Wing M2643, 1686); Canaries, *Rome's Additions*, p. 12.
5. W. Wake, *A Defence of the Exposition of the Doctrine of the Church of England Against the Exceptions of Monsieur de Meaux, Late Bishop of Condom, and His Vindicator* (Wing W236, 1686). Stratford became Bishop of Chester under William and Mary, and Wake a royal chaplain, *ODNB*.
6. W. Sherlock, *The Protestant Resolution of Faith* (Wing S3334A, 1686), sig. A3. 'Sherlock was a prolific author of anti-Catholic publications in James's reign', *ODNB*.
7. W. Sherlock, *An Answer to a Late Dialogue between a New Catholick Convert and a Protestant to Prove the Mystery of the Trinity to be as Absurd a Doctrine as Transubstantiation* (Wing S3261, 1687); P. Allix, *A Discourse Concerning Penance* (Bodleian 4° Z 16[5] Jur., 1688).
8. S. Freeman, *A Plain and Familiar Discourse by Way of Dialogue Betwixt a Minister and His Parishioner, Concerning the Catholick Church in Three Parts* (Wing F2142, 1687). Freeman described himself as 'a divine of the Church of England'.
9. Ibid., 'To the Reader'.
10. W. Payne, *A Discourse of the Communion in One Kind in Answer to a Treatise of the Bishop of Meaux's, of Communion Under Both Species, Lately Translated into English* (Wing P900, 1687), 'An Answer to the Preface of the Publisher' not paginated.
11. W. Sherlock, *A Discourse Concerning a Judge of Controversies in Matters of Religion* (Wing S285, 1686), preface.
12. W. Chillingworth, *Mr. Chillingworth's Book Called The Religion of Protestants, a Safe Way to Salvation Made More Generally Useful by Omitting Personal Contests, but Inserting Whatsoever Concerns the Common Cause of Protestants, or Defends the Church of England* (Wing C3885, 1687), sig. A2. The book was first published in 1638.
13. Ibid.
14. *Copies of Two Papers Written by the Late King Charles II of Blessed Memory* (Wing C2942, 1685); see above, ch. 7, p. 307.
15. *An Answer to Some Papers Lately Printed Concerning the Authority of the Catholick Church in Matters of Faith, and the Reformation of the Church of England* (Wing S5562, 1686), sig. A3. The treatise has been attributed to Edward Stillingfleet, Dean of St Paul's.
16. J. Tillotson, *A Discourse Against Transubstantiation* (Wing T1196, 1687); Tillotson, *The Indispensable Necessity of the Knowledge of the Holy Scripture in Order to Man's Eternal Salvation and Ignorance therein, the Mother of Idolatry and Superstition Asserted in a Sermon* (Wing T1198, 1687); Tillotson, *A Seasonable New-years-gift a Sermon Preached at White-Hall before His Late Majesty by John Tillotson* (Wing T1120, 1687), p. 4 and *passim*; *The Works of the Learned Isaac Barrow, D.D., Late Master of Trinity-College in Cambridge Published by the Reverend Dr. Tillotson* (Wing B926, 1687).
17. G. V. Bennett, 'The Seven Bishops: A Reconsideration', in D. Baker ed., *Religious Motivation: Biographical and Sociological Problems for the Church Historian* (Oxford, 1978), pp. 267–87; cf. Bennett, *The Tory Crisis in Church and State, 1688–1730* (Oxford, 1975), chs 1–2.

18. Bodleian Firth b.20 (6), no. 135.
19. J. Dryden, *A Defence of the Papers Written by the Late King of Blessed Memory, and Duchess of York, Against the Answer Made to Them* (Wing D2261, 1686), p. 126.
20. *The Explanation* (Bodleian Pamph. B. 179 [72], ? 1688).
21. E. Warren, *Religious Loyalty, or, Old Allegiance to the New King a Sermon, Preached on the Eighth of February 1684* (Wing W968, 1685), p. 12.
22. W. Wall, *A Sermon Preach'd before the King and Queen in Their Majesties Chappel at St. James's on Sunday, October 24, 1686 by the Reverend Father Dom. W. M. Monk of the Holy Order of St. Benedict* (Wing M108, 1687), p. 17.
23. Ibid., p. 44.
24. See G. Burnet, *An Enquiry into the Measures of Submission* (Wing B5808, 1688), p. 4.
25. See Mark Knights, 'Possessing the Visual: The Materiality of Visual Print Culture in Later Stuart Britain', in J. Daybel and P. Hinds eds, *Material Readings of Early Modern Culture* (Basingstoke, 2011), pp. 85–122.
26. Above ch 6, pp. 277–80.
27. A. W. Franks and H. A. Grueber, *Medallic Illustrations of the History of Great Britain* (2 vols, 1885), I, p. 620, no. 35; E. Hawkins, *Medallic Illustrations of the History of Great Britain and Ireland to the Death of George II* (1904–11), plate LXV, 8.
28. Franks and Grueber, *Medallic Illustrations*, I, p. 621, no. 36; Hawkins, *Medallic Illustrations*, plate LXV, 9.
29. Franks and Grueber, *Medallic Illustrations*, I, pp. 622–3, 626, nos 37–40, 43; Hawkins, *Medallic Illustrations*, plate LXVI, 1–4, 7.
30. Franks and Grueber, *Medallic Illustrations*, I, pp. 622–3, nos 37–9; Hawkins, *Medallic Illustrations*, plate LXVI, 1–3.
31. Huntington Library, Richard Bull Granger 18/55.
32. Ibid., 18/76^v.
33. Ibid, 18/77, 77^v. The unmoveable rock also evokes Marshall's frontispiece to the *Eikon Basilike*.
34. Ibid., 18/79.
35. Ibid., 19/6.
36. Ibid., 18/92.
37. See R. Weil, 'The Politics of Legitimacy: Women and the Warming-pan Scandal', in L. Schwoerer ed., *The Revolution of 1688–89: Changing Perspectives* (Cambridge, 1992), pp. 65–82.
38. *A Form of Prayer with Thanksgiving for the Safe Delivery of the Queen; and Happy Birth of the Young Prince* (Wing C4169, 1688). The prayer was printed at royal command.
39. Ibid., sig. A4.
40. Ibid., sig. A2^v.
41. Ibid., sig. A3.
42. Ibid.
43. *Englands Triumph for the Prince of Wales, or, A Short Description of the Fireworks, Machines &c Which Were Represented on the Thames . . . on Tuesday July 17* (Wing E3066A, 1688).
44. Ibid.
45. *Strenae natalitiae Academiae Oxoniensis in celsissimum principem* (Wing O969, Oxford, 1688), sig. S1.
46. Ibid., sig. T2.
47. Ibid., sigs T1–T1^v.
48. T. D'Urfey, *A Poem Congratulatory on the Birth of the Young Prince Most Humbly Dedicated to Their August Majesties King James, and Queen Mary* (Wing D2762, 1688), p. 11.
49. Ibid., p. 4.
50. A. Behn, *A Congratulatory Poem to Her Most Sacred Majesty, on the Universal Hopes of all Loyal Persons for a Prince of Wales by Mrs. A. Behn* (Wing B1721, 1688), pp. 2, 5, 7. See also Behn, *A Congratulatory Poem to His Most Sacred Majesty on the Happy Birth of the Prince of Wales by Mrs A. Behn* (Wing B1725, 1688).
51. Franks and Grueber, *Medallic Illustrations*, I, p. 628, no. 48; Hawkins, *Medallic Illustrations*, plate LXVI, 11.
52. R. Sharp, *The Engraved Record of the Jacobite Movement* (Aldershot, 1996), p. 2, plate 75, 11.
53. J. Miller, *James II: A Study in Kingship* (Hove, 1977), p. 186.
54. Ibid., pp. 133–4.
55. Ibid., p. 134.
56. An argument widely used; see, for example, *An Account of the Reasons of the Nobility and Gentry's Invitation of His Highness the Prince of Orange into England being a Memorial from the*

English Protestants Concerning their Grievances: with a Large Account of the Birth of the Prince of Wales, Presented to Their Highnesses the Prince and Princess of Orange (Wing A379, 1688), p. 9. Cf. *A Defence of Their Majesties King William and Queen Mary, Against an Infamous and Jesuitical Libel Entituled, A True Portraicture of William Henry, Prince of Nassau* (Wing J1200A, 1689), p. 22.

57. *An Account of the Reason's of the Nobility and Gentry's Invitation of His Highness the Prince of Orange*, p. 9.
58. *A Collection of the Several Addresses in the Late King James's Time Concerning the Conception and Birth of the Pretended Prince of Wales* (Bodleian Pamph. B 179/46, ?1700).
59. Ibid., pp. 7, 9, 15.
60. Ibid., p. 13.
61. *An Account of the Reasons of the Nobility and Gentry's Invitation of His Highness the Prince of Orange*, p. 24.
62. *An Account of the Pretended Prince of Wales, and Other Grievances* (Wing A340, 1688).
63. Ibid., especially pp. 10–18.
64. Ibid., pp. 19ff.
65. Franks and Grueber, *Medallic Illustrations*, I, p. 630, no. 52; Hawkins, *Medallic Illustrations*, plate LXVII, 2.
66. Franks and Grueber, *Medallic Illustrations*, I, p. 631, no. 53; Hawkins, *Medallic Illustrations*, plate LXVII, 3.
67. Huntington Library, Bull Granger, 18/29; Sharp, *Engraved Record*, p. 82, plate 70.
68. Miller, *James II*, pp. 198–9.
69. *At the Council-chambers in Whitehall Monday the 22 of October, 1688* (Wing D1079, 1688).
70. Ibid., pp. 15–19.
71. Ibid., pp. 25, 31.
72. Ibid., p. 40; J. Dryden, *Britannia Rediviva, A Poem on the Birth of the Prince* (Wing D2251, 1688), p. 5.
73. *The Several Declarations Together with the Several Depositions Made in Council on Monday the 22d of October 1688 Concerning the Birth of the Prince of Wales* (Wing E2916, 1688), title page.
74. *The Confession of Mrs. Judith Wilks, the Queens Midwife with the Full Account of Her Runing Away by Night, and Going into France* (Wing W2257, 1688).
75. *Idem iterum: or, The History of Q. Mary's Big-belly from Mr. Fox's Acts and Monuments* (Wing I33, 1688). Queen Mary Tudor had believed she was pregnant.
76. *A Defence of Their Majesties*, p. 22. See also *A Second Collection of the Newest and Most Ingenious Poems, Satyrs, Songs, &c. Against Popery and Tyranny Relating to the Times* (Wing S2266, 1689), p. 27.
77. *A Second Collection*, p. 29.
78. Miller, *James II*, pp. 195–9.
79. For the narrative, see T. Harris, *Revolution: The Great Crisis of British Monarchy, 1685–1720* (London and New York, 2006), ch. 7; J. Carswell, *The Descent on England: A Study of the English Revolution of 1688 and its European Background* (London, 1969); W. Speck, *Reluctant Revolutionaries: Englishmen and the Revolution of 1688* (Oxford, 1988), ch. 4; for an excellent controversial modern analysis, see Steve Pincus, *1688: The First Modern Revolution* (New Haven, CT, and London, 2009).
80. See J. Childs, *The Army, James II and the Glorious Revolution* (Manchester, 1980).
81. Speck, *Reluctant Revolutionaries*, pp. 81–3.
82. On the political struggles in the Netherlands, see P. Geyl, *Orange and Stuart, 1641–1672* (London, 1969).
83. Speck, *Reluctant Revolutionaries*, pp. 219–20; cf. J. Israel ed., *The Anglo-Dutch Moment: Essays on the Glorious Revolution and its World Impact* (Cambridge, 1991), pp. 12–13.
84. *The Declaration of His Highnes William Henry, by the Grace of God Prince of Orange, &c. of the Reasons Inducing Him, to Appear in Armes in the Kingdome of England, for Preserving of the Protestant Religion, and for Restoring the Lawes and Liberties of England, Scotland and Ireland* (Wing W2328C, 1688). This is the Declaration that James answered. William's Declaration is discussed here as a text of opposition. See T. Claydon, 'William III's "Declaration of Reasons" and the Glorious Revolution', *Historical Journal*, 39 (1996), pp. 87–108. This rightly questions the effectiveness of William's declaration and emphasizes the success of James and his supporters in countering it.
85. Ibid., sig. A2.
86. Ibid., p. 7.

87. Ibid., p. 8.
88. Ibid.
89. Ibid., p. 9.
90. See Speck, *Reluctant Revolutionaries*, p. 83.
91. G. Burnet, *The Expedition of His Highness, the Prince of Orange, for England Giving an Account of the Most Remarkable Passages Thereof* (Wing B5790, 1688), p. 3.
92. *By the King, a Proclamation* (Wing J260, 1688), one page.
93. Claydon, 'William III's "Declaration of Reasons"', especially pp. 91–2.
94. *By the King, a Proclamation. For Restoring Corporations to their Ancient Charters, Liberties, Rights and Franchises* (Wing J344, 1688).
95. *The Declaration of His Highnes William Henry*, pp. 9–10.
96. *By the King, a Proclamation* (Wing J263, 1688).
97. Israel ed., *Anglo-Dutch Moment*, pp. 15–16.
98. *A True and Exact Relation of the Prince of Orange His Publick Entrance into Exeter* (Wing T2458, 1688), broadside.
99. *The Copy of the Association Signed at Exeter by the Lords and Gentlemen that Went to the Prince of Orange*; Speck, *Reluctant Revolutionaries*, pp. 225, 230–1.
100. Miller, *James II*, pp. 201–2.
101. *By the King, a Declaration* (Wing J161, 1688).
102. Speck, *Reluctant Revolutionaries*, p. 88.
103. *The Prince of Orange's Third Declaration* (Wing S4914G, 1688).
104. *The Common Interest of King & Kingdom in this Confus'd Conjuncture, Truly Stated, and to Consist in the Speedy Calling of a Free Parliament* (Wing C5569, 1688), p. 8.
105. Ibid., pp. 4–5.
106. *The Declaration of the Nobility, Gentry, and Commonalty at the Rendezvous at Nottingham, Nov. 22. 1688* (Wing D717, 1688); Miller, *James II*, pp. 202–3.
107. Speck, *Reluctant Revolutionaries*, p. 229.
108. Miller, *James II*, p. 205.
109. Speck, *Reluctant Revolutionaries*, p. 89; Claydon, 'William III's "Declaration of Reasons"', p. 96.
110. M. Routh ed., *Bishop Burnet's History of His Own Time* (6 vols, Oxford, 1833), III, p. 353.
111. Speck, *Reluctant Revolutionaries*, p. 88.
112. R. A. Beddard ed., *The Revolutions of 1688* (Oxford, 1991), p. 14.
113. See *To His Highness the Prince of Orange, the Humble Address of the Lord Mayor, Aldermen and Commons of the City of London, in Common Council Assembled* (Wing T1371, 1688).
114. Harris, *Revolution*, ch. 7; See also R. Beddard, 'The Loyalist Opposition in the Interregnum: A Letter of Dr Francis Turner, Bishop of Ely, on the Revolution of 1688', *Bulletin of the Institute of Historical Research*, 40 (1967), pp. 101–9; Speck, *Reluctant Revolutionaries*, pp. 236–7.
115. *The Prince of Orange His Declaration: Shewing the Reasons Why He Invades England. With a Short Preface, and Some Modest Remarks on it. Animadversions upon the Declaration of his Highness the Prince of Orange* (Wing W2331, 1688); Claydon, 'William III's "Declaration of Reasons"'.
116. *The Prince of Orange His Declaration*, pp. 27–8.
117. *His Majesties Reasons for With-drawing Himself from Rochester Writ with His Own Hand and Ordered by Him to be Published* (Wing J376, 1688); G. Burnet, *Reflections on a Paper, Intituled, His Majesty's Reasons for Withdrawing Himself from Rochester* (Wing B5850, 1689).
118. For example, *A Review of the Reflections on the Prince of Orange's Declaration* (Wing R1199, 1688); *An Answer to a Paper Intitled, Reflections on the Prince of Orange's Declaration* (Wing A3331, 1688); *A Short Answer to a Large Paper, Intituled, A Continuation of Brief and Modest Reflections* (Wing S3558, 1688).
119. See Israel ed., *Anglo-Dutch Moment*, p. 1; for Stoop, see above, ch. 2, p. 103.
120. Israel ed., *Anglo-Dutch Moment*, p. 1; see *News from White-Hall, Being an Account of the Arrival of the High and Mighty Prince William Henry of Orange and Nassaw, at St. James's* (Wing N1026B, 1688).
121. Israel ed., *Anglo-Dutch Moment*, pp. 2–3.
122. R. Beddard ed., *A Kingdom without a King: The Journal of the Provisional Government in the Revolution of 1688* (Oxford, 1988).
123. Israel ed., *Anglo-Dutch Moment*, p. 6.
124. Ibid. See M. Goldie, 'The Revolution of 1689 and the Structure of Political Argument: An Essay and an Annotated Bibliography of Pamphlets on the Allegiance Controversy', *Bulletin of Research in the Humanities*, 83 (1980), pp. 473–564.

125. As well as Beddard, Harris, Israel, Pincus, Speck cited, see J. P. Kenyon, *Revolution Principles: The Politics of Party, 1689-1720* (Cambridge, 1977); D. Hoak and M. Feingold eds, *The World of William and Mary: Anglo-Dutch Perspectives on the Revolution of 1688* (Stanford, CA, 1996); L. Schwoerer ed., *The Revolution of 1688: Changing Perspectives* (Cambridge, 1992); E. Cruickshanks ed., *By Force or by Default? The Revolution of 1688* (Edinburgh, 1989); J. Clark, *English Society, 1660-1832: Religion, Ideology and Politics during the Ancien Regime* (Cambridge, 2000); C. Wilson, '1688 and the Historians', *History Today*, 38 (1988), pp. 3-7.
126. Claydon, 'William III's "Declaration of Reasons".
127. *The History of the Most Illustrious William, Prince of Orange Deduc'd from the First Founders of the Ancient House of Nassau: Together with the Most Considerable Actions of the Present Prince* (Wing H2170, 1688), pp. 1, 33.
128. Ibid., p. 190.
129. T. Rymer, *A Poem on the Prince of Orange His Expedition and Success in England Written by Mr. Rymer* (Wing R2428, 1688), quotation, p. 3.
130. T. Claydon, *William III and the Godly Revolution* (Cambridge, 1996); Claydon, *William III* (Harlow 2002).
131. Below, chs 9-12.
132. J. R. Jones, 'James II's Revolution: Royal Policies, 1686-92', in Israel ed., *Anglo-Dutch Moment*, pp. 47-71, quotation, p. 47.
133. G. Burnet, *An Enquiry into the Present State of Affairs, and in Particular, Whether We Owe Allegiance to the King in these Circumstances? and Whether We Are Bound to Treat with Him, and to Call Him Back Again, or Not?* (Wing B5811, 1688), p. 7. The quotation echoes Milton's *Eikonoklastes*.
134. Ibid., p. 3.
135. *The Advantages of the Present Settlement, and the Great Danger of a Relapse* (Wing A601, 1689), quotation, p. 29.
136. For examples, see *A Defence of Their Majesties King William and Queen Mary* (Wing J1200A, 1689), p. 13; C. Caesar, *Numerus Infaustus A Short View of the Unfortunate Reigns of William the Second, Henry the Second, Edward the Second, Richard the Second, Charles the Second, James the Second* (Wing C203, 1689), p. 80; *The Advantages of the Present Settlement*, p. 22; E. Bohun, *The History of the Desertion, or, An Account of all the Publick Affairs in England, from the Beginning of September 1688 to the Twelfth of February Following* (Wing B3456, 1689); J. Heath, *Englands Chronicle, or, The Lives & Reigns of the Kings and Queens from the Time of Julius Caesar to the Present Reign of K. William and Q. Mary* (Wing H1325, 1689), p. 230; *The Abdicated Prince* (Wing A71, 1690). R. Ferguson, *A Brief Justification of the Prince of Orange's Descent into England, and of the Kingdoms Late Recourse to Arms* (Wing F733, 1689), quotation, p. 22.
137. *A Defence of Their Majesties*, p. 14.
138. *The Bloody Duke, or, The Adventures for a Crown A Tragi-comedy* (Wing B3233, 1690); *An Account of the Transactions of the Late King James in Ireland* (Wing A409, 1690), p. 58.
139. *The Anatomy of an Arbitrary Prince, or, King James the II Set Forth in His Proper Colours* (Wing A3054, 1689); *The History of the Late Revolution in England with the Causes & Means by which It Was Accomplish'd* (Wing H2166, 1689).
140. *Quadriennium Jacobi, or, The History of the Reign of King James II from His First Coming to the Crown to His Desertion* (Wing Q6, 1689).
141. *History of the Late Revolution*; J. Phillips, *The Secret History of the Reigns of K. Charles II and K. James II* (Wing S2347, 1690); R. B., *The Secret History of the Four Last Monarchs of Great Britain, viz., James I, Charles I, Charles II, James II to which Is Added, an Appendix Containing the Later Reign of James the Second, from the Time of His Abdication of England to this Present January, 1691* (Wing C7346, 1691).
142. Caesar, *Numerus Infaustus*, p. 99 and *passim*.
143. *An Order of the Lords Spiritual and Temporal Assembled at Westminster, for the Not Observing the Sixth Day of February* (Bodleian Ashmole H23 [424], 1690).
144. *A Full and True Relation of the Death of K. James who Departed this Life, the 27th of March* (Wing F2320, 1689).
145. Burnet, *An Enquiry into the Present State of Affairs*, p. 16; Kenyon, *Revolution Principles*, ch. 1.
146. D. Whitby, *Obedience Due to the Present King, Notwithstanding Our Oaths to the Former Written by a Divine of the Church of England* (Wing F2512, 1689).
147. On the non-jurors, see J. Overton, *The Non-Jurors: Their Lives, Principles and Writings* (London, 1902); G. Bennett, *The Tory Crisis in Church and State, 1688-1730* (Oxford, 1975), p. 10.

148. See, for example, H. Maurice, *The Lawfulness of Taking the New Oaths Asserted* (Wing M1364, 1689).
149. *A Justification of the Whole Proceedings of Their Majesties King William and Queen Mary* (Wing J1264, 1689).
150. Above, n. 102.
151. Beddard ed., *A Kingdom without a King*, p. 29.
152. Ibid., p. 34.
153. *His Majesties Late Letter in Vindication of Himself Dated at St. Germans en Laye, the Fourteenth of this Instant January, 1688/9* (Bodleian Gough Lond. 3 [18] 1689), p. 3 and *passim*.
154. Ibid., p. 1.
155. Ibid., p. 2.
156. Ibid.
157. Ibid., p. 3.
158. Ibid.
159. The metaphor of politics as a card game had a long history in early modern England but was given greater force by the rival party packs of cards issued during the Popish Plot and to commemorate the Revolution; see J. Whiting, *A Handful of History* (Dursley, 1978), chs 4, 9.
160. Ibid., pp. 3-4.
161. *His Majesties Letter from St. Germans to the Convention, in Order to Settle these Kingdoms: That Was Refused to be Open'd* (Wing J199, 1689). The author of the remarks on James's letter also refused to respond to the declaration.
162. *His Majesties Letter to the House of Lords and Commons, Writ from St. Germains the 3d of February 1688* (Wing J207, 1689).
163. Ibid., p. 2.
164. *His Majesties Letter to the Lords Spiritual and Temporal Commissioners of Shires and Burroughs Assembled, or to be Assembled at Edenborough* (Wing J209, Edinburgh, 1689). The Scottish parliament permitted the letter to be read but resolved that James had forfeited his throne; see Harris, *Revolution*, pp. 389-91.
165. Speck, *Reluctant Revolutionaries*, ch. 5; R. Beddard, 'The Unexpected Whig Revolution of 1688', in Beddard, *Revolutions of 1688*, pp. 11-101, especially 86-94; Beddard ed., *Kingdom without a King*, *passim*.
166. Speck, *Reluctant Revolutionaries*, p. 100; Harris, *Revolution*, ch. 8.
167. See, for a few examples, Ferguson, *Brief Justification*; *An Answer to the Desertion Discussed* (Wing B3446, 1689); *A Vindication of those who Have Taken the New Oath of Allegiance to King William and Queen Mary* (Wing V535, 1689); *A Justification of the Whole Proceedings*; *The Absolute Necessity of Standing by the Present Government* (Wing A112, 1689); *A Full Answer to the Depositions and to all Other the Pretences and Arguments whatsoever Concerning the Birth of the Prince of Wales* (Wing F2342, 1689).
168. *A Modest Attempt for Healing the Present Animosities in England* (Wing M2359, 1690).
169. J. Spurr, *The Restoration Church of England, 1646-1689* (New Haven, CT, and London, 1991), pp. 101-4. Four hundred clergy were ejected for not swearing allegiance to the new regime.
170. Beddard, 'Unexpected Whig Revolution', p. 93; cf. pp. 94-6.
171. See E. Gregg, 'France, Rome and the Exiled Stuarts', in E. Corp ed., *A Court in Exile: The Stuarts in France, 1689-1718* (Cambridge, 2004), especially p. 22.
172. *A Declaration of His Most Sacred Majesty, King James II. To All His Loving Subjects in the Kingdom of England* (Wing J165, 1689).
173. *The Declaration of His Highness William Henry, by the Grace of God, Prince of Orange, &c. of the Reasons Inducing Him, to Appear in Arms for Preserving of the Protestant Religion* (Wing W2330, 1689); M. Sheane, *King William's Victory: The Battle of the Boyne* (Ilfracombe, 2006).
174. Gregg, 'France, Rome and the Exiled Stuarts', p. 34.
175. *His Majesties Most Gracious Declaration to All His Loving Subjects Commanding their Assistance against the Prince of Orange, and His Adherents* (Wing J216, 1692).
176. Gregg, 'France, Rome and the Exiled Stuarts', pp. 34-44.
177. W. Sherlock, *A Second Letter to a Friend, Concerning the French Invasion in which the Declaration Lately Dispersed under the Title of His Majesty's Most Gracious Declaration, to All His Loving Subjects Commanding their Assistance Against the P. of Orange and His Adherents, Is Entirely and Exactly Published, According to the Dispersed Copies: With Some Short Observations Upon It* (Wing S3340, 1692). Sherlock initially opposed the oaths to William but became an ardent convert to the Williamite cause after the Battle of the Boyne, *ODNB*.

178. *The Jacobites Hudibras Containing the Late King's Declaration in Travesty* (Wing J104, 1692).
179. *Reflections Upon the Late King James's Declaration, Lately Dispersed by the Jacobites* (Wing R730, 1692).
180. Ibid., quotation p. 28 and *passim*; on the controversy over the authorship of *Eikon Basilike*, see A. Lacey, *The Cult of King Charles the Martyr* (Woodbridge, 2003), ch. 6.
181. *His Majesties Most Gracious Declaration to All His Loving Subjects* (Wing J217A, 1693); J. Welwood, *An Answer to the Late K. James's Last Declaration Dated at St. Germains* (W1301, 1693), p. 40. On Welwood, see *ODNB*. See also *Some Short Reflections Upon K. James's Late Declarations, Dated at S. Germains, April 17, 1693* (Wing S4615B, 1693).
182. Welwood, *An Answer*, p. 1.
183. Ibid., p. 2.
184. Our understanding and knowledge have been hugely advanced by Edward Corp, see *A Court in Exile: The Stuarts in France, 1689–1718* (Cambridge, 2004) and E. Corp ed., *The Stuart Court in Rome: The Legacy of Exile* (Aldershot, 2003).
185. See, for examples of a vast revisionist literature, E. Cruickshanks and J. Black eds, *The Jacobite Challenge* (Edinburgh, 1988); P. Monod, *Jacobitism and the English People, 1688–1788* (Cambridge, 1989); M. Pittock, *Jacobitism* (Basingstoke, 2003).
186. I here draw entirely on Corp, *A Court in Exile*.
187. Ibid., chs 2–3 *passim*.
188. Ibid., pp. 171–5.
189. Ibid., ch. 5.
190. Ibid., p. 110; D. Szechi, 'The Image of the Court: Idealism, Politics and the Evolution of the Stuart Court, 1689–1730', in Corp ed., *The Stuart Court in Rome*, p. 51.
191. Corp, *A Court in Exile*, pp. 155–6, 235–6; E. Corp, *James II and Toleration: The Years in Exile at Saint-Germain-en-Laye* (1997).
192. H. Erskine Hill, 'Poetry at the Exiled Court', in Corp, *A Court in Exile*, pp. 215–34.
193. Corp, *A Court in Exile*, ch. 7; E. Corp, *The King Over The Water: Portraits of the Stuarts in Exile after 1689* (Scottish National Portrait Gallery, Edinburgh, 2001), p. 33.
194. Above, ch. 6, p. 268.
195. Corp, *A Court in Exile*, pp. 183–4 and ch. 7 *passim*.
196. Corp, *King Over the Water*, p. 34.
197. See above ch. 6, p. 275.
198. Corp, *King Over the Water*, p. 32, fig. 3. Interestingly, with the expulsion of the Stuarts these dogs fell out of favour (until Queen Victoria's reign), so a sense of their symbolic association may have been shared by the enemies of the Stuarts as well as their supporters (http://www.maynorth.com/history.html).
199. O. Millar, *Tudor, Stuart and Early Georgian Pictures in the Collection of Her Majesty The Queen* (London, 1963), pp. 88–9, no. 151.
200. Corp, *King Over The Water*, fig. 6 and pp. 36–7.
201. Millar, *Tudor, Stuart and Early Georgian Pictures*, no. 150, p. 98; see K. Sharpe, *Image Wars: Promoting Kings and Commonwealths in England, 1603–1660* (New Haven, CT, and London, 2010), pp. 206–7.
202. Corp, *King Over The Water*, pp. 37–8, fig. 11.
203. Millar, *Tudor, Stuart and Early Georgian Pictures*, no. 152, p. 99; Sharpe, *Image Wars*, pp. 207–8.
204. Corp, *King Over The Water*, pp. 40–2.
205. Ibid., p. 40.
206. Corp, *A Court in Exile*, p. 185; A. W. Franks and H. A. Grueber, *Medallic Illustrations of the History of Great Britain* (2 vols, 1885), II, pp. 193–6, nos 503–7; Hawkins, *Medallic Illustrations of the History of Great Britain and Ireland to the Death of George II* (London, 1904–11), plate CX, 1–8. See N. Woolf, *The Medallic Record of the Jacobite Movement* (London, 1988), pp. 45–6, and fig. no. 14.2a.
207. Franks and Grueber, *Medallic Illustrations*, II, p. 192, no. 500; Hawkins, *Medallic Illustrations*, plate CIX, 6.
208. Corp, *King Over The Water*, p. 15.
209. Corp, *A Court in Exile*, p. 182.
210. Ibid., pp. 183–4; R. Sharp, *The Engraved Record of the Jacobite Movement* (Aldershot, 1996), p. 2.
211. Sharp, *Engraved Record of the Jacobite Movement*, p. 2.
212. Ibid., p. 7.
213. Ibid., p. 8, plate 684, 'King James and His Family'; see K. Sharpe, *Remapping Early Modern England* (Cambridge, 2000), p. 32.

214. Corp, *A Court in Exile*, p. 183, n. 17.
215. Ibid., p. 184, n. 23.
216. Corp, *King Over The Water*, p. 37, fig. 7.
217. G. Scott, 'The Court as a Centre of Catholicism', in Corp ed., *A Court in Exile*, pp. 235–56; quotation, p. 237.
218. See K. Sharpe, 'Whose Life Is It Anyway? Writing Early Modern Monarchs and the "Life" of James II', in K. Sharpe and S. Zwicker eds, *Writing Lives: Biography and Textuality, Identity and Representation in Early Modern England* (Oxford, 2008), pp. 233–54.
219. Corp, *A Court in Exile*, p. 262.
220. G. Davies ed., *Papers of Devotion of James II: Being a Reproduction of the Ms. in the Handwriting of James the Second Now in the Possession of Mr. B. R. Townley Balfour* (Roxburgh Club, Oxford 1925).
221. Ibid., pp. xxix–xxx; and appendix II.
222. Ibid., p. 27.
223. Ibid., p. 53.
224. Ibid.
225. Ibid., pp. 56–7.
226. Ibid., pp. 14, 62.
227. Ibid., p. 62.
228. Ibid., p. 103.
229. Ibid., pp. 23–6.
230. For example, ibid., pp. 49, 85.
231. Ibid., pp. 63, 164.
232. Ibid., pp. 70–3, 106.
233. Ibid., pp. 63, 67–8.
234. Ibid., pp. 83, 96.
235. Ibid., p. 3.
236. Ibid., p. 14 and *passim*; on James I, see Sharpe, *Image Wars*, pp. 26–8, 33–4.
237. Davies, *Papers of Devotion*, pp. 99, 143.
238. Ibid., p. 80.
239. Ibid., pp. 137, 158–9.
240. Ibid., p. 158.
241. See J. Clarke, *The Life of James II* (2 vols, 1816), II, pp. 617–42.
242. Davies, *Papers of Devotion*, p. 92.
243. Ibid., p. 111.
244. Ibid., p. 83.
245. *The Pious Sentiments of the Late King James II of Blessed Memory. Upon Divers Subjects of Piety. Written with His Own Hand, and Found in His Cabinet After His Death* (1704); Corp, *A Court in Exile*, p. 235.
246. See Sharpe, *Image Wars*, pp. 391–400.
247. Davies, *Papers of Devotion*, p. 128.
248. A. Lacey, *The Cult of King Charles the Martyr* (Woodbridge, 2003), ch. 6.
249. *Royal Tracts in Two Parts: The First, Containing all the Select Speeches, Orders, Messages, Letters, &c. of His Sacred Majesty, Upon Extraordinary Occasions, Both Before, and Since His Retiring out of England: The Second, Containing Imago Regis, or, The Sacred Image of His Majesty, in His Solitudes and Sufferings, Written During His Retirements in France* (Wing J384, 1692). See L. Knoppers, 'Reviving the Martyr: Charles I as a Jacobite Icon', in T. Corns ed., *The Royal Image: Representations of Charles I* (Cambridge, 1999), pp. 263–87.
250. Davies, *Papers of Devotion*, p. 30.
251. Henri-Emmanuelle de Roquette, *A Funeral Oration Upon the Death of the Most High, Most Mighty, Most Excellent, and Most Religious Prince, James the Second . . . Spoken the 19th day of September, 1702. in the Church of St. Mary de Chaillot* (ESTC T 071027, 1703), quotation, p. 2.
252. *The Generous Muse. A Funeral Poem, in Memory of His Late Majesty K. James the II* (ESTC N000609, 1701), pp. 6, 8 and *passim*.
253. J. Tutchin, *The British Muse: or Tyranny Expos'd: A Satyr, Occasion'd by All the Fulsom and Lying Poems and Elegies, That Have Been Written on the Death of the Late King James* (ESTC T099193,? Dublin, 1702).
254. *An Exact Account of the Sickness and Death of the Late King James II. As Also of the Proceedings at St. Germains Thereupon. In a Letter from an English Gentleman in France, to His Friend in London* (ESTC T07460, 1701).

255. *A Funeral Oration Upon the Late King James. Composed from Memoirs Furnished by Mr. Porter, his Great Chamberlain ... Dedicated to the French King, and Published by his Authority* (ESTC T144376, 1702), p. 14.
256. *The Generous Muse*, p. 2.
257. *A Funeral Oration*, pp. 18–27.
258. Ibid., p. 25.
259. Ibid., p. 26.
260. *An Exact Account of the Sickness and Death of the Late King James II*, p. 2.

Prologue to Part III

1. For a general account, see H. Butterfield, *The Whig Interpretation of History* (London, 1931). See also M. Bentley, *Modernizing England's Past: English Historiography in the Age of Modernism, 1870–1970* (Cambridge, 2005), especially part 1.
2. For recent formulations of the modernizing argument, see J. Brewer, *The Sinews of Power: War, Money and the English State, 1688–1783* (London, 1989); S. Pincus, *1688: The First Modern Revolution* (New Haven, CT, and London, 2009).
3. This term, which dates back to at least the late 1980s, is now a textbook commonplace; see P. Baines, *The Long 18th Century* (London, 2004).
4. This is a subject that awaits full investigation. See A. Williams, *Poetry and the Creation of a Whig Literary Culture, 1681–1714* (Oxford, 2005).
5. L. G. Shwoerer, 'Propaganda in the Revolution of 1688–89', *American Historical Review*, 82 (1977), pp. 843–74; Schwoerer ed., *The Revolution of 1688: Changing Perspectives* (Cambridge, 1992), introduction.
6. For the failure of the republic, see K. Sharpe, '"An Image Doting Rabble": The Failure of Republican Culture in Seventeenth-Century England', in K. Sharpe and S. Zwicker eds, *Refiguring Revolutions: Aesthetics and Politics from the English Revolution to the Romantic Revolution* (Berkeley, CA, and London, 1998), pp. 25–56, 302–11.
7. See P. Monod, *Jacobitism and the English People, 1688–1788* (Cambridge, 1989).
8. E. Corp, *A Court in Exile: The Stuarts in France, 1689–1718* (Cambridge, 2004).
9. Above, ch. 8, pp. 674–87; R. Sharp, *The Engraved Record of the Jacobite Movement* (Aldershot, 1996); N. Woolf, *The Medallic Record of the Jacobite Movement* (London, 1988).
10. Below, ch. 12, pp. 485–8.
11. Below, ch. 12.
12. T. Claydon, *William III and the Godly Revolution* (Cambridge, 1996).
13. Below, ch. 9, pp. 373–82.
14. Below, ch. 9, pp. 395–7.
15. Below, ch. 9, pp. 397–407.
16. Above, ch. 8, pp. 312–13.
17. Above, ch. 8, pp. 329–30; below ch. 12, p. 485.
18. Below, ch. 11, pp. 468–9.
19. Below, ch. 12, pp. 484–9.
20. Queen Anne, *ODNB*.
21. Below, ch. 9, pp. 377–8.
22. See J. Garrett, *The Triumphs of Providence: The Assassination Plot, 1696* (Cambridge, 1980).
23. S. Baxter, *William III* (London 1966), p. 337.
24. Below, ch. 12, pp. 492–4.
25. Below, ch. 12, pp. 493–4. While recent work on post-Restoration republicanism has argued that a Commonwealth discourse was not incompatible with limited monarchy, the commonwealthsmen must be discussed as critics and opponents of the regime. See, for example, B. Worden, 'Republicanism and the Restoration 1660–1683', in D. Wootton ed., *Republicanism, Liberty and Commercial Society, 1649–1776* (Stanford, CA, 1994), pp. 175–93.
26. Above, ch 1, pp. 81–2; below, ch. 9, pp. 393–5.
27. Below, ch. 12, pp. 484–8.
28. Baxter, *William III*, pp. 384–5.
29. Below, ch. 13, pp. 521–2.
30. Sharpe, '"An Image-Doting Rabble" : The Failure of Republican Culture in Seventeenth-Century England', in Sharpe, *Remapping Early Modern England* (Cambridge, 2000), pp. 223–66.

9 Scripting the Revolution

1. See T. Claydon, *William III* (2002), p. 16 and ch. 1 *passim*.
2. L. Schwoerer, *The Declaration of Rights, 1689* (Baltimore, MD, 1981), ch. 5; T. Claydon, *William III and the Godly Revolution* (Cambridge, 1996), pp. 24–5.
3. Claydon, *William III and the Godly Revolution*, p. 64.
4. Lord Somers wrote that of 1698, for example, below, ch. 9, p. 361.
5. Baxter, *William III*, ch. 18.
6. *His Majesty's Most Gracious Speech in the House of Lords, to the Lords and Commons Assembled at Westminster the Eighteenth Day of February, 1688/9* (Wing W2372F, 1689), two pages.
7. *His Majesties Most Gracious Speech to Both Houses of Parliament, on Saturday the Sixteenth of March, 1688* (Wing W 2372H, 1689), p. 3.
8. Ibid., p. 4, my italics.
9. Ibid.
10. Though see Claydon, *William III*, pp. 103–5.
11. Baxter, *William III*, pp. 248–51.
12. *His Majesties Most Gracious Speech to Both Houses of Parliament, on Friday the 28th of June, 1689* (Wing W2374, 1689), p. 3. Being sensible meant having a strong feeling. For the political contexts of William's speeches, see H. Horwitz, *Parliament, Policy and Politics in the Reign of William III* (Manchester, 1977).
13. *His Majesties Most Gracious Speech*, p. 3.
14. Ibid., p. 4.
15. Ibid.
16. Ibid.
17. *His Majesties Most Gracious Speech to Both Houses of Parliament, on Saturday the 19th. of October, 1689* (Wing W2376, 1689), p. 3.
18. Ibid., p. 4.
19. Cobbett, *Parliamentary History*, V, pp. 404–5.
20. For example, *His Majesties Most Gracious Speech to Both Houses of Parliament, on Tuesday the Twenty Fifth of November, 1690* (Wing W2385A, 1690), p. 3; *His Majesties Most Gracious Speech to Both Houses of Parliament, on Munday the Fifth Day of January, 1690* (Wing W2386, 16910, p. 3.
21. *His Majesties Speech* (Wing W2386), p. 4.
22. *His Majesties Most Gracious Speech to Both Houses of Parliament, on Thursday the Second of October, 1690* (Wing W2383, 1690), p. 3.
23. Ibid., p. 4.
24. Ibid., p. 3.
25. Ibid.
26. Ibid.; *His Majesties Most Gracious Speech to Both Houses of Parliament, on Tuesday the Fourteenth Day of March, 1692/3* (Wing W2395, 1693), p. 3. For the non-juror Thomas Wagstaffe's response to this speech, see below, ch. 12, p. 489.
27. Ibid., p. 313.
28. *His Majesties Most Gracious Speech to Both Houses of Parliament, on Tuesday the Seventh Day of November, 1693* (Wing W2396, 1693), p. 3.
29. Ibid.
30. Baxter, *William III*, p. 318.
31. *His Majesties Most Gracious Speech to Both Houses of Parliament, on Munday the Twelfth Day of November, 1694* (Wing W2400, 1694), p. 3.
32. Ibid., p. 4.
33. Cobbett, *Parliamentary History*, V, p. 861.
34. Ibid., p. 333.
35. On the progress, see below, ch. 11, pp. 969–73.
36. *His Majesties Most Gracious Speech to Both Houses of Parliament, on Saturday the Twenty Third Day of November, 1695* (Wing W2403, 1695), p. 3.
37. Ibid., p. 3; below, ch. 9, pp. 377–8.
38. Ibid., p. 3.
39. Cobbett, *Parliamentary History*, V, p. 965; Baxter, *William III*, p. 334.
40. *His Majesties Most Gracious Speech to Both Houses of Parliament, on Munday the Twenty Fourth Day of February, 1695* (Wing W2406, 1696), p. 3.
41. Cobbett, *Parliamentary History*, V, pp. 990–1; Baxter, *William III*, p. 337.

42. *His Majesties Most Gracious Speech to Both Houses of Parliament, on Monday the Twenty Seventh Day of April, 1696* (Wing W2407, 1696).
43. Baxter, *William III*, p. 340.
44. *His Majesties Most Gracious Speech to Both Houses of Parliament, on Tuesday the Twentieth Day of October, 1696* (Wing W2408, 1696).
45. Ibid., p. 4.
46. Ibid.
47. Ibid.
48. Cobbett, *Parliamentary History*, V, p. 996.
49. *His Majesties Most Gracious Speech to Both Houses of Parliament, on Friday the Sixteenth Day of April, 1697* (Wing W2410, 1697), p. 3.
50. Ibid., pp. 3–4.
51. Ibid., p. 359.
52. *His Majesties Most Gracious Speech to Both Houses of Parliament, on Friday the Third Day of December, 1697* (Wing W2413, 1697), one page.
53. Cobbett, *Parliamentary History*, V, pp. 166–7.
54. Baxter, *William III*, pp. 360–2.
55. Ibid., pp. 363–4.
56. *His Majesties Most Gracious Speech to Both Houses of Parliament, on Tuesday the Fifth Day of July, 1698* (Wing W2416, 1698), one page.
57. Baxter, *William III*, pp. 366–7.
58. H. Horwitz, *Parliament, Policy and Politics in the Reign of William III* (Manchester, 1977), pp. 239–42.
59. John Somers, *ODNB*.
60. *His Majesties Most Gracious Speech to Both Houses of Parliament, on Friday the Ninth Day of December, 1698* (Wing W2417, 1699), p. 3.
61. Ibid., p. 4.
62. Cobbett, *Parliamentary History*, V, pp. 1,191–2.
63. Horwitz, *Parliament, Policy and Politics*, pp. 249–50; Baxter, *William III*, p. 370.
64. *His Majesties Most Gracious Speech to Both Houses of Parliament, on February first, 1699* (Wing W2418, 1699), one page.
65. Cobbett, *Parliamentary History*, V, p. 1,193.
66. Horwitz, *Parliament, Policy and Politics*, pp. 252–3.
67. *His Majesties Most Gracious Speech to Both Houses of Parliament, on Thursday the Fourth Day of May, 1699* (Wing W2420, 1699).
68. Ibid., p. 4.
69. Horwitz, *Parliament, Policy and Politics*, p. 261; Baxter, *William III*, p. 374.
70. Baxter, *William III*, p. 382.
71. *His Majesties Most Gracious Speech to Both Houses of Parliament, on Tuesday the Eleventh Day of February, 1700* (Wing W2423, 1700), p. 3.
72. Horwitz, *Parliament, Policy and Politics*, p. 283.
73. *His Majesties Most Gracious Speech to Both Houses of Parliament, on Thursday the Twelfth Day of June, 1701* (ESTC N017561, 1701), p. 3.
74. Ibid., my italics.
75. *His Majesties Most Gracious Speech to Both Houses of Parliament: on Wednesday the One and Thirtieth Day of December, 1701* (ESTC N032988, 1702), two pages, not paginated.
76. Horwitz, *Parliament, Policy and Politics*, pp. 300–1.
77. Ibid., p. 300.
78. Cobbett, *Parliamentary History*, V, p. 1,329.
79. Baxter, *William III*, p. 382.
80. See, for example, Horwitz, *Parliament, Policy and Politics*, pp. 36, 38, 53, 62, 104, 162, 184, 226, 252, 300; above, notes 19, 33, 39, 48, 65, 78.
81. See *The Declaration of His Highnes William Henry, by the Grace of God Prince of Orange, &c. of the Reasons Inducing Him, to Appear in Armes in the Kingdome of England, for Preserving of the Protestant Religion, and for Restoring the Lawes and Liberties of England, Scotland and Ireland* (Wing W2328, 1688); *By His Highness William Henry, Prince of Orange, a Third Declaration* (Wing W2486, 1688); above, ch. 8, pp. 320–60.
82. *Their Majesties Declaration Against the French King* (Wing W2502, 1689); see *By the King and Queen, A Declaration* (Wing W2500, 1689); *By the Prince of Orange, a Declaration for the Better Quartering of the Forces* (Wing W2317, 1689).

83. Above ch. 8, pp. 329–30.
84. Claydon, *William III and the Godly Revolution*, pp. 82–3. Claydon does not discuss the proclamations.
85. Ibid., p. 82.
86. See, for example, Wing W 2547, 2561, 2565, 2586–7, 2592, 2597, 2602–3, 2631, 2636.
87. *By the King and Queen, a Proclamation for Recalling and Prohibiting Seamen from Serving of Foreign Princes and States* (Wing W2602, 1689); *By the King and Queen, a Proclamation* (Wing W2527, 1689); *By the King and Queen, a Proclamation for Dissolving this Present Parliament* (Wing W2530, 1689).
88. *By the King and Queen, a Proclamation for the Discovery and Apprehending of High-way-men and Robbers* (Wing W2608, 1689); *By the King, a Proclamation, for the Speedy and Effectual Putting in Execution the Act of Parliament for Regulating the Measures and Prices of Coals* (Wing W2475, 1695).
89. *By the King and Queen, a Proclamation for Collecting and Levying the Arrears of Hearth-Money* (Wing W2587, 1689).
90. *By the King and Queen, a Proclamation for Prohibiting the Importation, or Retailing of Any Commodities of the Growth or Manufacture of France* (Wing W2598, 1689).
91. *By the King and Queen, a Proclamation Concerning Papists, and Other Disaffected Persons* (Wing W2559, 1691).
92. See *By the King and Queen a Proclamation for Discovering and Apprehending the Late Bishop of Ely, William Penn, and James Grahme* (Wing W2588, 1691).
93. *By the King and Queen, a Proclamation* (Wing W2525, 1689).
94. *By the King and Queen, a Proclamation Commanding all Papists, and Reputed Papists, forthwith to Depart from the Cities of London and Westminster* (Wing 2555, 1690); *By the King and Queen, a Proclamation for the Confinement of Popish Recusants within Five Miles of their Respective Dwellings* (Wing W2607, 1690).
95. *By the King and Queen, a Proclamation for a General Fast* (Wing W2569, 1689).
96. *By the King and Queen, a Proclamation for a General Fast* (Wing W2573, 1691).
97. *By the King and Queen, a Proclamation. William R. Whereas it Hath Pleased Almighty God, in his Providence Towards Us and Our People, to Manifest His Power and Mercy in Giving Us Success and Victory over Our Enemies and Rebellious Subjects in Ireland* (Wing W2545, 1690).
98. *By the King and Queen, a Proclamation, for a Publick Thanksgiving* (Wing W2579, 1692); Baxter, *William III*, p. 296.
99. *By the King and Queen, a Proclamation for a Publick Thanksgiving* (Wing W2581, 1694).
100. *By the Lords Justices, a Proclamation for a Publick Thanksgiving* (Wing E950, 1695).
101. E. Turner, 'The Lords Justices of England', *English Historical Review*, 29 (1914), pp. 453–76.
102. *By the King, a Proclamation for Dissolving this Present Parliament, and Declaring the Speedy Calling Another* (Wing W2466, 1695); *By the King, a Proclamation for a General Fast and Humiliation Throughout the Whole Kingdom* (Wing W2454, 1695).
103. *By the King, a Proclamation for a Publick Thanksgiving* (Wing W2458, 1697).
104. Below ch. 11, pp. 475–6.
105. *By the King, a Proclamation for a General Fast and Humiliation Throughout the Whole Kingdom* (Wing W2454, 1695); *By the King, a Proclamation, for a Publick Thanksgiving* (Wing W2457, 1696); *By the King, a Proclamation for a General Fast* (Wing W2455, 1697).
106. Claydon, *William III and the Godly Revolution*, p. 115; D. Hayton, 'Moral Reform and Country Politics in the Late Seventeenth-Century House of Commons', *Past and Present*, 128 (1990), pp. 48–91; R. Craig, 'Providence, Protestant Union and Godly Reformation in the 1690s', *Transactions of the Royal Historical Society*, 3 (1993), pp. 151–69.
107. *A Proclamation Against Vitious, Debauched, and Profane Persons* (Wing W2553, 1692).
108. *By the King, a Proclamation, for Preventing and Punishing Immorality and Prophaneness* (Wing W2473, 1698).
109. *By the King, a Proclamation, for Preventing and Punishing Immorality and Prophaneness* (Wing W2474, 1699); Claydon, *William III and the Godly Revolution*, pp. 116–18.
110. Claydon, *William III and the Godly Revolution*, p. 120.
111. See Nottingham's imprimatur announcing that a service was published at the king's and queen's pleasure and at royal command, *A Form of Prayer and Solemn Thanksgiving to Almighty God for the Wonderful Preservation of His Majesties Person* (Wing C4123, 1690).
112. Cf. Claydon, *William III and the Godly Revolution*, p. 115.
113. *A Form of Prayer and Thanksgiving to Almighty God for Having Made His Highness the Prince of Orange the Glorious Instrument of the Great Deliverance of this Kingdom from Popery and Arbitrary Power* (Wing C4125, 1689).

114. Ibid., sigs A2^v, A3^v.
115. *A Prayer for His Highness the Prince of Orange, to be Used Immediately after the Prayer for the Royal Family* (Wing C4188EC, 1688).
116. *A Form of Prayer to be Used on Wednesday the Twelfth Day of March Next Ensuing* (Wing C4150, 1689), quotation sig. B2.
117. Ibid., sigs B3^v, C4^v.
118. Claydon, *William III and the Godly Revolution*, p. 109.
119. T. Wilson, *God, the King, and the Countrey, United in the Justification of this Present Revolution* (Wing W2950, 1691), p. 37.
120. For example, *A Form of Prayer and Solemn Thanksgiving to Almighty God for the Wonderful Preservation of His Majesties Person, and His Good Success towards the Reducing of Ireland together with His Safe and Happy Return into this Kingdom* (Wing C4123, 1690); *A Form of Prayer and Thanksgiving to Almighty God for the Preservation of Their Majesties, the Success of their Forces in the Reducing of Ireland* (Wing C4126, 1691).
121. See forms of prayers 1692–4, Wing C 4131, 4139–40, 4156–7.
122. *A Form of Prayer to be Used Next After the Prayer in the Time of War and Tumults throughout the Kingdom of England, Dominion of Wales and Town of Berwick upon Tweed, in all Churches and Chappels at Morning and Evening Prayer as Often as there is Divine Service During the Time of Their Majesties Fleets Being at Sea* (Wing C4140, 1693).
123. *A Form of Prayer to be Used on Wednesday the Tenth of May Next* (Wing C4156, 1693), quotation sig. B2.
124. *A Form of Prayer to be Used on Wednesday the Three and Twentieth Day of this Instant May* (Wing C4157, 1694), quotation sig. B2.
125. *A Form of Prayer and Thanksgiving to Almighty God to be Used on Thursday the Sixteenth of April Next throughout the Kingdom of England . . . for Discovering and Disappointing a Horrid and Barbarous Conspiracy of Papists and other Trayterous Persons to Assassinate and Murder His Most Gracious Majesties Royal Person* (Wing C4132, 1695), sig. C3^v.
126. Ibid., sig. C1.
127. Ibid., sig. D2^v.
128. *A Form of Prayer and Thanksgiving to Almighty God, to be Used throughout the Cities of London and Westminster, and Elsewhere . . . for Granting to the Forces of His Majesty, and His Allies, so Great Success in Taking the Town and Castle of Namur* (Wing C4133, 1695).
129. Ibid., sig. A2.
130. Ibid., sig. A3^v.
131. Ibid., sig. B3.
132. Ibid., sig. B4.
133. Baxter, *William III*, pp. 336–7; J. F. Mansergh, 'The Assassination Plot Against William III, 1696', *Notes and Queries* (1892), pp. 131–2.
134. *A Form of Prayer to be Used in all Churches and Chapels throughout the Kingdom of England, Dominion of Wales, and Town of Berwick upon Tweed, on Friday the Twenty Sixth Day of June Next* (Wing C4160, 1696).
135. *A Form of Prayer and Thanksgiving, to be Used [n]ext after the General Thanksgiving; in all Churches and Chapels within the Cities of London and Westminster, till the Sunday Month after His Majesties Return* (Wing C4134B, 1696), p. 4.
136. *A Form of Prayer to be Used Next after the Prayer in the Time of War and Tumults, throughout the Kingdom of England* (Wing C4141, 1696).
137. *A Form of Prayer and Thanksgiving to Almighty God for His Majesties Safe Return, and for the Happy and Honourable Peace, of which God Has Made Him the Glorious Instrument* (Wing C4135, 1697), sig. B3^v.
138. Ibid., sigs C3–C3^v.
139. Ibid., sig. C4^v.
140. *A Form of Prayer to be Used Next after the Prayer in Time of War and Tumults; throughout the Kingdom of England . . . as Often As There Is Divine Service, During the Time of His Majesties Absence* (Wing C4141A, 1697).
141. *A Form of Prayer to be Used in All Churches and Chapels . . . for the Imploring a Blessing from Almighty God upon His Majesty and All His Dominions, and for Averting of those Judgments which Our Manifold Sins and Provocations Have Most Justly Deserv'd, and that God Would, in His Great Mercy and Goodness, Relieve and Comfort Such As Suffer Abroad for the Protestant Religion* (Wing C4163, 1699).
142. Ibid., sigs C1^v–C2.

143. Ibid., sig. C2ᵛ.
144. *A Form of Prayer . . . for the Imploring a Blessing from Almighty God, Upon the Consultations of this Present Parliament, and for the Preservation of the Protestant Religion, and the Publick Peace* (Wing C4164), sig. C2.
145. Ibid., sig. C4ᵛ.
146. This revisionism was pioneered by J. C. D. Clark, *English Society, 1688–1832: Ideology, Social Structure and Political Practice during the Ancien Regime* (Cambridge, 1985).
147. Cf. Claydon, *William III and the Godly Revolution*, p. 83.
148. J. Strype, *David and Saul a Sermon Preached on the Day of National Thanksgiving for God's Gracious Deliverance of the King's Majesty from an Assassination and the Kingdom from a French Invasion* (Wing S6021, 1696), p. 21.
149. A. Williams, *Poetry and the Creation of Whig Literary Culture, 1681–1714* (Oxford, 2005).
150. Ibid., pp. 7, 30–1, 49–55.
151. Ibid., p. 173.
152. Ibid., p. 205.
153. *Vota Oxoniensia pro serenissimis Guilhelmo rege et Maria regina M. Britanniae &c. nuncupata quibus accesserunt Panegyrica oratio & carmina gratulatoria, comitiis in Theatro Sheldoniano habitis, ipso inaugurationis die XI april, MDCLXXXIX* (Wing O992A, Oxford 1689).
154. Ibid., sig. Z1ᵛ.
155. Ibid., sigs X1ᵛ, Y, Z2.
156. Ibid., sigs Y2ᵛ, Bb1.
157. *Musae cantabrigienses, serenissimis principibus Wilhelmo et Mariae Angliae Franciae & Hiberniae regi ac reginae publicae salutis ac libertatis vindicibus, haec officii & pietatis ergo d.d.* (Wing C344, Cambridge, 1689), sig. A1.
158. Ibid., sigs A3ᵛ, A4, B1v, D2v, D4.
159. Sig. A4ᵛ.
160. Ibid., sigs A3, B2, D4.
161. Ibid., sigs C4ᵛ, E1.
162. J. Dennis, *An Ode Upon the Glorious and Successful Expedition of His Highness the Prince of Orange, now King of England* (Wing O136, 1689); on Dennis see Williams, *Poetry and the Creation of a Whig Literary Culture*, via index and *ODNB*.
163. Dennis, *An Ode Upon the Glorious and Successful Expedition*, pp. 1–2, 7.
164. *Britain Reviv'd in a Panegyrick to Their Most August Majesties, William and Mary: a Pindarick Poem* (Wing B4803A, 1689), two pages.
165. *A Congratulatory Poem to His Royal Highness, the Prince of Orange* (Bodleian Pamph. B 189 (48), 1689), pp. 5–7 and *passim*.
166. *A Second Collection of the Newest and Most Ingenious Poems, Satyrs, Songs, &c. Against Popery and Tyranny Relating to the Times* (Wing S2266, 1689); J. Tutchin, *An Heroick Poem upon the Late Expedition of His Majesty, to Rescue England from Popery, Tyranny, and Arbitrary Government by John Tutchin, Gent* (Wing T3377, 1689), pp. 8, 12 and *passim*; *The Double Deliverance on the Never to be Forgotten Fifth of November: A Poem* (Wing D1955A, 1690), p. 4.
167. *A Poem on the Accession of . . . the Prince and Princess of Orange to the Imperial Crown of England; Being a Paraphrase on the 45th Psalm* (Bodleian C 6.16 [7] Th., 1689), p. 4 and *passim*.
168. *A Poem in Vindication of the Late Publick Proceedings by Way of Dialogue Between a High Tory and a Trimmer to which Is Added the high Tory's Catechism* (Wing P2677, 1689).
169. Below, ch. 9, pp. 400–7.
170. For example, T. Shadwell, *Poem on the Anniversary of the King's Birth by Tho. Shadwell* (Wing S2864A, 1690); *The Double Deliverance*.
171. E. Miner, *Poems on the Reign of William III* (Augustan Reprint Society, Los Angeles, CA, 1974), p. 1.
172. G. Stepney, *An Epistle to Charles Montague Esq., on His Majesty's Voyage to Holland by Mr. George Stepney* (Wing S5467, 1691). On the Williamite career diplomat and verse writer Stepney, see *ODNB*.
173. Stepney, *An Epistle*, p. 2.
174. Ibid., pp. 4, 10.
175. A. Danvers, *A Poem Upon His Sacred Majesty, His Voyage for Holland by Way of Dialogue between Belgia and Britannia* (Wing D221, 1691).
176. T. D'Urfey, *A Pindarick Poem on the Royal Navy Most Humbly Dedicated to Their August Majesties, K. William, and Q. Mary* (Wing 2760, 1691), pp. 7–8. D'Urfey wrote many birthday odes for William and Mary, *ODNB*.

177. D'Urfey, *Pindarick Poem*, p. 14.
178. T. Brown, *A Congratulatory Poem on His Majesty's Happy Return from Holland Written by Mr. Browne* (Wing B5055, 1691), pp. 4, 9.
179. Ibid., p. 9.
180. *Britannia Victrix, or, The Triumphs of the Royal Navy in the Late Victorious Ingagement with the French fleet May, 1692 a Pindarick Poem* (Wing B4818, 1692); M. Morgan, *A Poem Upon the Late Victory over the French Fleet at Sea* (Wing M2737, 1692).
181. R. Ames, *The Jacobite Conventicle a Poem* (Wing A2984, 1692), p. 20.
182. *The True and Genuine Explanation of One K. James's Declaration* (Wing T2495, 1693); N. Tate, *An Ode upon His Majesty's Birth-day Set to Musick by Dr. Staggins; Performed at Whitehall, November, 1694* (Wing T197A, 1694), p. 2.
183. R. Bovet, *A Congratulatory Poem, to the Honourable Admiral Russell, on His Glorious Victory over the French Fleet* (Wing B3863, 1693), pp. 5, 8 and *passim*.
184. *An Excellent New Poem Upon the Happy Proceedings of Their Majesties Royal Army by Sea and Land with a Reflection Upon the Insulting Jacobites* (Wing E3813, 1693).
185. M. Prior, *To the King, an Ode on His Majesty's Arrival in Holland, 1695 by Mr. Prior* (Wing P3516, 1695), p. 4. On Prior, see C. Barfoot, ' "Hey for praise and panegyric": William III and the Political Poetry of Matthew Prior', in C. Barfoot and P. Hoftijzer, *Fabrics and Fabrications: The Myth and Making of William and Mary* (Amsterdam, 1990), pp. 135-88. His poetry has been described as displaying a 'laureate bent', *ODNB*.
186. W. Partridge, *A Consolatory Poem Address'd to His Most Sacred Majesty by W. Partridge* (Wing P635, 1695), p. 6.
187. T. Yalden, *On the Conquest of Namur a Pindarique Ode Humbly Inscrib'd to His Most Sacred and Victorious Majesty by Mr. Tho. Yalden* (Wing Y7, 1695), pp. 9-11; Yalden was a poet and clergyman who became high church under Anne, *ODNB*.
188. W. Congreve, *A Pindarique Ode Humbly Offer'd to the King on His Taking Namure by Mr. Congreve* (Wing C5871, 1695), p. 5.
189. J. Addison, *A Poem to His Majesty, Presented to the Lord Keeper by Mr. Addison* (Wing A511, 1695), p. 4. On the Kit Kat Club, see O. Field, *The Kit-Cat Club* (London, 2008).
190. Mr Denne, *A Poem on the Taking of Namur, by His Majesty. By Mr. Denne* (Wing 1024B, 1695), p. 3.
191. C. Cole, *Triumphant Augustus a Congratulate Poem on His Majesty's Safe Return* (Wing C5020, 1695), p. 6.
192. Ibid., p. 4.
193. R. Bovet, *A Poem Humbly Presented to His Most Excellent Majesty King William the Third Upon His Most Miraculous and Happy Preservation from that Barbarous Jacobitish Conspiracy to Assassinate His Royal Person* (Wing B3865, 1696), pp. 3, 5 and *passim*.
194. Ibid., p. 10.
195. Ibid., p. 8; Suffolk, *An Essay Upon Pastoral as also an Elegy Dedicated to the Ever Blessed Memory of Her Most Serene Majesty Mary the Second, Queen of England* (Wing S6159, 1695), p. 12 and *passim*.
196. *A Poem Upon Occasion of the Happy Discovery of the Late Horrid Plot Against the Life of His Most Sacred Majesty* (Wing P2713, 1696), pp. 2, 7 and *passim*.
197. M. Prior, *Verses Humbly Presented to the King at His Arrival in Holland after the Discovery of the Late Horrid Conspiracy Against His Most Sacred Person* (Wing P3517, 1696), sig. A1ᵛ.
198. J. W., *A Poem Occasion'd by the General Peace by J. W. Gent* (Wing W63, 1697), p. 7.
199. For example, G. B., *A Panegyrick on His Most Excellent Majesty King William IIId Occasioned by the Happy Conclusion of the General Peace, September the 20th, 1697* (Wing B68,1697); *A Poem on the Peace Happily Concluded Between England, Spain, Holland and France at Reswick, 1697* (Wing P2703, 1697).
200. J. Glanvill, *A Panegyrick to the King by John Glanvill* (Wing G795, 1697), pp. 10-11; on Glanvill, a translator and poet, see *ODNB*.
201. J. Browne, *A Panegyrick Upon His Majesties Glorious Return from the Wars, after the Conclusion of a General Peace* (Wing B5044, 1697), p. 10. Browne was a doctor.
202. G. B., *A panegyrick on His Most Excellent Majesty*, p. 12.
203. Ibid., p. 11; Glanvill, *A Panegyrick*, p. 10.
204. Glanvill, *A Panegyrick*, p. 10. On moral reformation, see D. Bahlman, *The Moral Revolution of 1688* (New Haven, CT, and London, 1957); Claydon, *William III and the Godly Revolution*, pp. 111-21, 161-4 and *passim*; S. Burt, 'The Societies for the Reformation of Manners: Between John Locke and the Devil in Augustan England', in R. Lund ed., *The Margins*

of Orthodoxy: Heterodox Writing and Cultural Response, 1660–1750 (Cambridge, 1995), pp. 149–69.

205. N. Tate, *The Anniversary Ode for the Fourth of December, 1697 His Majesty's Birth-day* (Wing T176, 1698), p. 3.

206. M. Morgan, *A Poem to the King Upon the Conclusion of Peace by Matt. Morgan* (Wing M2736, 1698), p. 10; T. D'Urfey, *Albion's Blessing a Poem Panegyrical on His Sacred Majesty, King William the III, and on His Happy Return, and the Publishing the Late Glourious Peace* (Wing D2699, 1698), pp. 1, 10.

207. *A Congratulatory Poem on the Safe Arrival of King William to England in this Present Year 1699* (Wing C5829, 1699), broadside.

208. Ibid.; J. Guy, *On the Happy Accession of Their Majesties King William and Queen Mary to the Throne of England &c. a Pindarique Ode: with a Preface Shewing the Occasion of the Publication at this Time* (Wing G2277, 1699), sig. A2.

209. M. Prior, *Carmen Saeculare for the Year 1700 to the King* (Wing P3507, 1700).

210. Ibid., p. 20. The phrase offers an interesting perspective on the idea of the king's two bodies.

211. J. Hopkins, *Gloria, A Poem, in Honour of Pious Majesty, Occasioned by the Safe, Happy, and Much-wish'd for Return of our Dread Soveraign lord King William* (Wing H2746, 1700), p. 7.

212. W. B., *An Ode on the Death of William, Duke of Gloucester by W. B. of St. John's, Oxon* (Wing B5187, 1700), p. 12.

213. J. Gibbs, *A Consolatory Poem Humbly Addressed to Her Royal Highness upon the Much Lamented Death of His Most Illustrious Highness, William, Duke of Gloucester* (Wing G662, 1700), p. 6.

214. J. Tutchin, *The British Muse: or Tyranny Expos'd. A Satyr Occasioned by all the Fulsom and Lying Poems and Elegies, that have Been Written in on the Occasion of the Death of the Late King James* (ESTC N033451, 1702).

215. *The Poet's Address to his Majesty King William. Occasion'd by the Insolence of the French King, in Proclaiming the Sham Prince of Wales, King of England, Scotland, and Ireland* (ESTC N046575, 1702).

216. Ibid., p. 9.

217. Dennis, *An Ode Upon the Glorious and Successful Expedition*, p. 5; *An Historical Poem upon His Late Majesty King James II* (ESTC T036325, 1701), p. 2.

218. For example, Browne, *Panegyric*, p. 6; Tate, *Ode*, p. 1; Partridge, *Consolatory Poem*, p. 5.

219. Bovet, *Poem*, p. 12; Prior, *Verses*, sig. A2.

220. Brown, *A Congratulatory Poem*, p. 8; N. Tate, *A Poem, Occasioned by His Majesty's Voyage to Holland, the Congress at the Hague, and Present Siege of Mons written by N. Tate* (Wing T205, 1691), p. 13.

221. *Musae Cantabrigienses*, sig. B2; Dennis, *An Ode Upon the Glorious and Successful Expedition*, p. 4; R. Blackmore, *Prince Arthur an Heroick Poem in Ten Books* (Wing B3080, 1695); for Blackmore, see *ODNB*.

222. Glanvill, *Panegyrick to the King*, p. 7.

223. T. Shadwell, *A Congratulatory Poem on His Highness the Prince of Orange His Coming into England* (Wing S2839, 1689), p. 2.

224. Tate, *Ode*, p. 2.

225. W. Colepeper, *An Heroick Poem upon the King Humbly Presented to the Queen* (Wing C7564, 1694), p. 9.

226. Suffolk, *Pastoral Poem*, p. 6. The literary contribution to the Whig interpretation of history awaits its historian.

227. Addison, *A Poem to His Majesty*, p. 10; Browne, *Panegyrick*, p. 10.

228. Miner, *Poems on the Reign of William III*, p. iii.

229. C. Montagu, Earl of Halifax, *An Epistle to the Right Honorable Charles, Earl of Dorset and Middlesex, Lord Chamberlain of His Majesties Household* (Wing H288, 1690), p. 9.

230. Addison, *Poem*, p. 3; R. Howard, *Poems on several occasions. Written by the honourable Sir Robert Howard* (Wing H3004, 1696), sig. A3.

231. *A New-years Offering to His Most Victorious Majesty King William III* (Wing N820B, 1697), p. 1; G. B., *A Panegyrick*, p. 12.

232. Many are collected in W. Cameron ed., *Poems on Affairs of State: Augustan Satirical Verse, 1660–1714. Vol. 5* (New Haven, CT, and London, 1971) and F. Ellis ed., *Poems on Affairs of State: Augustan Satirical Verse, 1660–1714. Vol. 6, 1697–1704* (New Haven, CT, and London, 1970); cf. below ch. 12.

233. Cf. Williams, *Poetry and the Creation of a Whig Literary Culture*, p. 192.

234. L. Schwoerer, 'Images of Queen Mary II 1689–1694', *Renaissance Quarterly*, 42 (1989), pp. 717–48.

235. *Vota Oxoniensia*, sig. Z2ᵛ.
236. M. Morgan, *A Poem to the Queen, Upon the King's Victory in Ireland, and His Voyage to Holland* (Wing M2735, 1691), p. 29.
237. *Musae Cantabrigienses*, sig. B3ᵛ.
238. Dennis, *An Ode Upon the Glorious and Successful Expedition*, p. 6.
239. A. Behn, *A Congratulatory Poem to Her Sacred Majesty, Queen Mary Upon Her Arrival in England by Mrs. A. Behn* (Wing B1723, 1689), p. 4.
240. Ibid., p. 5.
241. T. Rymer, *A Poem on the Arrival of Queen Mary, February the 12th, 1689* (Wing R2427, 1689), p. 4; Williams, *Poetry and the Creation of a Whig Literary Culture*, pp. 122–3.
242. See A. Garganigo, 'William without Mary: Mourning Sensibly in the Public Sphere', *Seventeenth Century*, 23 (2008) pp. 105–41.
243. *An Elegy Upon the Most Pious and Incomparable Princess, Mary Queen of England* (Wing E484A, 1694), broadside.
244. G. Stepney, *A Poem Dedicated to the Blessed Memory of Her Late Gracious Majesty Queen Mary by Mr. Stepney* (Wing S5468, 1695), p. 1; P. Gleane, *An Elegy on the Death of the Queen Written by Peter Gleane* (Wing G848, 1695), p. 1; W. Walsh, *A Funeral Elegy Upon the Death of the Queen Addrest to the Marquess of Normanby* (Wing W646, 1695), p. 7.
245. D. Defoe, *The Life of that Incomparable Princess, Mary, Our Late Sovereign Lady, of Ever Blessed Memory* (Wing L2036, 1695), p. 59.
246. Ibid., pp. 64–5; J. Abbadie, *A Panegyric on our Late Sovereign Lady Mary Queen of England, Scotland, France, and Ireland* (Wing A56, 1694), pp. 3–4; H. Park, *Lachryme sacerdotis a Pindarick Poem Occasion'd by the Death of that Most Excellent Princess, our Late Gracious Sovereign Lady, Mary the Second of Glorious Memory* (Wing P362, 1695), p. 4.
247. G. Burnet, *An Essay on the Memory of the Late Queen* (Wing B5783, 1695), p. 23; Abbadie, *A Panegyric*, p. 22.
248. N. Tate, *Mausolaeum, a Funeral Poem on our Late Gracious Sovereign Queen Mary* (Wing T194, 1695), p. 7.
249. *A Pindarique Ode, Humbly Offer'd to the Ever-blessed Memory of Our Late Gracious Sovereign Lady, Queen Mary Written by J. D., Gent* (Wing C4772, 1694). Wing assigns this to the schoolmaster and author Samuel Cobb, on whom see *ODNB*.
250. Abbadie *Panegyric*, p. 1; *A Funeral Eclogue Sacred to the Memory of Her Most Serene Majesty, Our Late Gracious Queen Mary* (Wing F2531, 1695), p. 5.
251. S. Wesley, *Elegies on the Queen and Archbishop by Samuel Wesley* (Wing W1368, 1695), p. 8.
252. *Great-Britain's Lamentation for Her Deceased Princess, or, An Elegy Upon the Death of that Most Illustrious Mary, Queen of England, Scotland, France and Ireland* (Wing G1667A, 1695); Burnet, *Essay*, p. 60.
253. Gleane, *Elegy*, p. 4.
254. *To the Pious and Sacred Memory of our Late Dread Soveraign, Mary, Queen of England* (Wing T1595, 1695), broadside; P. Hume, *A Poem Dedicated to the Immortal Memory of Her Late Majesty the Most Incomparable Q. Mary by Mr. Hume* (Wing H3663A, 1695), p. 5.
255. J. Talbot, *Instructions to a Painter Upon the Death and Funeral of Her Late Majesty, Q. Mary, of Blessed Memory by J. Talbot* (Wing T13, 1695), p. 7; *The Mourning Poets, or, An Account of the Poems on the Death of the Queen in a Letter to a Friend* (Wing M2993, 1695), pp. 4, 11.
256. See R. Steele, *The Procession a Poem on Her Majesties Funeral* (Wing S5381, 1695), p. 7; Park, *Pindaric*, p. 4.
257. Stepney, *Poem*, p. 3; *To the Pious and Sacred Memory of our Late Dread Soveraign*.
258. Abbadie, *A Panegyric*, p. 21.
259. W. Speck's long biography of Mary in *ODNB*.
260. Claydon, *William III and the Godly Revolution*.
261. Ibid., p. 83.
262. Ibid., p. 87. I am also grateful for this information about the prominence of sermons to a hitherto unpublished study by Steven Zwicker.
263. Claydon, *William III and the Godly Revolution*, pp. 83, 96, 116–17.
264. G. Burnet, *A Sermon Preached in the Chappel of St. James's, Before His Highness the Prince of Orange, the 23d of December, 1688* (Wing B5884, 1689), p. 1.
265. Ibid., p. 20.
266. G. Burnet, *A Sermon Preached at the Coronation of William III and Mary II, King and Queen of England, France, and Ireland, Defenders of the Faith in the Abby-Church of Westminster, April 11, 1689* (Wing B5888, 1689), pp. 5, 20, 29.

267. J. Tillotson, *Sermon Preached at Lincolns-Inn-Chappel, on the 31th [sic] January, 1688 Being the Day Appointed for a Publick Thanksgiving to Almighty God for Having Made His Highness the Prince of Orange the Glorious Instrument of the Great Deliverance of this Kingdom from Popery & Arbitrary Power* (Wing T1236, 1689), pp. 26, 37.

268. S. Patrick, *A Sermon Preached at St. Paul's Covent Garden on the Day of Thanksgiving Jan. XXXI, 1688 for the Great Deliverance of this Kingdom by the Means of His Highness the Prince of Orange from Popery and Arbitrary Power* (Wing P847, 1689), pp. 24, 27.

269. J. Strype, *A Sermon Preached at the Assizes at Hertford, July viii, 1689* (Wing S6025, 1689), p. 15.

270. W. Wilson, *A Sermon Preached Before the Judges at the Assizes Held at Nottingham, on the 19th of July, 1689 by W. Wilson* (Wing W2957, 1689), quotation p. 14; Wilson, *A Sermon Preached Before the Mayor, Aldermen, and Common-Council of Nottingham in St. Peter's Church, on the 14th of Febr. 1688/9 Being the Thanksgiving Day for Our Deliverance from Popery and Arbitrary Power* (Wing W2956, 1689).

271. W. Perse, *A Sermon Preached in the Cathedral of St. Peters in York on the Fifth Day of Novemb. 1689 by William Perse* (Wing P1654, 1689).

272. Wilson, *A Sermon Preached Before the Judges at the Assizes*, p. 28.

273. *A Discourse, Shewing that It Is Lawfull, and Our Duty to Swear Obedience to King William, Notwithstanding the Oath of Allegiance Taken to the Late King. By a Divine in the North* (Wing D1618AB, 1689), p. 28; see title pages of Perse and Wilson and on Churchill, *ODNB*.

274. Claydon, *William III and the Godly Revolution*, p. 51 and ch. 1.

275. G. Burnet, *A Sermon Preached before the King and Queen at White-Hall on the 19th Day of October, 1690* (Wing B5893, 1690), p. 35.

276. J. Tillotson, *A Sermon Preach'd Before the Honourable House of Commons* (Wing T1241, 1690), p. 33; see G. Hickman, *A Sermon Preached Before the Honourable House of Commons, at St Margaret's Westminster, on Sunday the 19th of October, 1690 Being the Thanksgiving-day for the Wonderful Preservation of His Majesties Person* (Wing H1898, 1690).

277. G. Burnet, *A Sermon Preached at White-hall, on the 26th of Novemb. 1691 Being the Thanksgiving-day for the Preservation of the King, and the Reduction of Ireland* (Wing B5897, 1691).

278. G. Tullie, *A Sermon Preached October the 19, 1690, Before the Right Worshipful the Mayor, Aldermen, and Sheriff, &c. of the Town and County of New-Castle upon Tyne Being the Day Appointed for a General Thanks giving for His Majesties's Safe Return and Happy Success in Ireland* (Wing G3242, 1691).

279. W. Fleetwood, *A Sermon Preach'd before the Honourable the Lord Mayor and Court of Aldermen, at St. Mary le Bow, on Friday the 11th of April, 1692* (Wing F1253, 1692), quotation p. 12.

280. Ibid., pp. 28–9.

281. S. Slater, *A Sermon Preached on the Thanksgiving Day the 27th day of October, 1692* (Wing S3974, 1693), pp. 2, 9, 12; on Slater, see *ODNB*.

282. Slater, *Sermon*, pp. 31–2.

283. J. Sharp, *A Sermon Preach'd Before the King & Queen, at White-hall the 12th of November, 1693: Being the Day Appointed for a Publick Thanksgiving to Almighty God, for the Gracious Preservation of His Majesty, and His Safe Return* (Wing S2998, 1693), pp. 26–7.

284. See, for example, S. Peck, *A Sermon Preached at St. Edmonds-Bury, in Suffolk, at the Assizes, March 18th, 1692/3* (Wing P1037, 1693); J. Lambe, *A Sermon Preached before the Queen at White-Hall, on Wednesday, March 22. 1692* (Wing L225, 1693).

285. J. Howard, *The True Interest of a Nation, or, The Duty of Magistrates, Ministers, and People, in Order to the Further Settlement and Prosperity of these Kingdoms a Sermon Preached at the Assizes Held at Buckingham, July the 5th, 1692* (Wing H2984, 1693), p. 26.

286. G. Burnet, *A Sermon Preached Before the Queen at White-Hall on the 29th of May, 1694, Being the Anniversary of King Charles II, His Birth and Restauration* (Wing B5901, 1694), p. 27.

287. J. Petter, *A Sermon Preached Before Their Majesties, K. William and Q. Mary's Forces, at Gant in Flanders the Sunday Before they Marched into the Camp, 1694* (Wing P1890, 1694), pp. 23, 28.

288. R. Kidder, *Of Fasting a Sermon Preached before the Queen at White-hall, on May 23, MDCXCIV, Being a Day of Publick Humiliation* (Wing K408, 1694), p. 27. Kidder was Bishop of Bath and Wells.

289. L. Blackburne, *The Unreasonableness of Anger A Sermon Preach'd Before the Queen at White-hall, July 29, 1694* (Wing B3068, 1694), pp. 22–3 and *passim*. As many others, the sermon was published at royal command.

290. S. Carte, *A Dissuasive from Murmuring Being a Sermon on 1 Cor. X. 10. Preached by Sam. Carte, M.A. Imprimatur, May 14. 1694* (Wing C651C, 1694).

291. Ibid.
292. J. Smalwood, *A Sermon Preachel Before the King at Mont-St: Andre-Camp, June 29, 1694* (Wing S4007, 1695)
293. J. Adams, *A Sermon Preach'd at White-Hall on Sunday, September 8, 1695 Being the Day of Thanksgiving for the Taking of Namur, and the Safety of His Majesty's Person* (Wing A485, 1695), pp. 16, 22.
294. V. Alsop, *Duty and Interest United in Prayer and Praise for Kings and All That Are in Authority from I Tim. II. 1,2: Being a Sermon Preach'd at Westminster Upon the Late Day of Thanksgiving, Sept. 8, 1695* (Wing A2908, 1695), p. 12.
295. Ibid., pp. 22, 31.
296. T. Knaggs, *A Sermon Preach'd at All-Hallows in New Castle upon Tyne, on the 22d. of September, 1695. Being the Day of Thanksgiving to Almighty God for the Taking the Town and Castle of Namur* (Wing K663E, 1695), p. 15.
297. W. Wake, *A Sermon Preached in the Parish Church of St. James, Westminster, April xvith, 1696 Being the Day of the Publick Thanksgiving for the Preservation of His Majesty's Person from the Late Horrid and Barbarous Conspiracy* (Wing W270, 1696), p. 222 and *passim.*
298. J. Strype, *David and Saul a Sermon Preached on the Day of National Thanksgiving for God's Gracious Deliverance of the King's Majesty from an Assassination and the Kingdom from a French Invasion* (Wing S6021, 1696), 'To my beloved auditors . . .'.
299. W. Stephens, *A Thanksgiving Sermon Preach'd Before the Right Honourable the Lord Mayor, Court of Aldermen, Sheriffs, and Companies of the City of London at St. Mary-le-bow, April 16, 1696, upon Occasion of His Majesty's Deliverence from a Villanous Assassination in Order to a French Invasion* (Wing S5465, 1696), pp. 17-18.
300. J. Shower, *A Thanksgiving Sermon Upon Thursday the Sixteenth of April, 1696* (Wing S3694, 1696), pp. 11, 15; on Shower, see *ODNB.*
301. F. Gregory, *A Thanksgiving Sermon for the Deliverance of our King from the Late Intended Assassination of His Sacred Person and of the Kingdom from the French invasion* (Wing G1906, 1696), pp. 9-10.
302. T. Dorrington, *The Honour Due to the Civil Magistrate Stated and Urg'd in a Sermon Compos'd for the Day of Thanksgiving for the Happy Discovery of the Late Horrid and Execrable Conspiracy Against His Majesties Sacred Person and Government* (Wing D1942, 1696), pp. 7-8.
303. G. Burnet, *A Sermon Preached before the King, at Whitehall, on the Second of December, 1697. Being the Day of Thanksgiving for the Peace* (Wing B5907, 1698).
304. Ibid., p. 4.
305. Ibid., pp. 4,7.
306. Ibid., p. 11.
307. Ibid., p. 20.
308. Ibid., p. 31.
309. T. Comber, *A Sermon Preached in the Cathedral Church of Durham on the Second of December Being the Day of Thanksgiving for the Peace* (Wing C5493, 1697), p. 9.
310. Ibid., p. 10; cf. p. 26.
311. R. L., *A Thanksgiving Sermon for His Majesty's Safe Return and for the Happy and Honourable Peace, of which God Has Made Him the Glorious Instrument, Preached in Highgate Chapel, on Thursday the 2d of December, 1697* (Wing L56C, 1697), pp. 7,18.
312. Ibid., p. 11.
313. J. Gardiner, *A Thanksgiving-sermon for the Peace: Preach'd at St Michael Crookedlane, December the 2d, 1697* (Wing G228A, 1697), pp. 2, 18, 27, 28 and *passim.*
314. J. Leng, *A Sermon Preach'd before the King at Newmarket, on Sunday the 16th day of April, 1699 by John Leng* (Wing L1050, 1699); T. Knaggs, *A Sermon Against Profaneness & Immorality. Preach'd at the Assizes at Kingston Upon Thames, April 9. 1701* (ESTC T089633, 1701).
315. Knaggs, *Sermon*, p. 10.
316. R. Eyre, *The Sinner a Traitor to His King and Country in a Sermon Preach'd in the Cathedral-Church of Winchester, at the Assizes Held There, July 24, 1700* (Wing E3943, 1700), pp. 19; Eyre was a fellow of the College.
317. M. Heynes, *A Sermon for Reformation of Manners, Preach'd at St. Paul's church in Bedford, at the Assizes there Held, March the 15th, 1700* (ESTC T008428, 1701), p. 22.
318. Ibid., p. 3.
319. F. Atterbury, *A Sermon Preach'd before the Honourable House of Commons, at St. Margaret's Westminster, May the 29th. 1701* (ESTC T055994, 1701).

320. T. May, *An Epitomy of English History wherein Arbitrary Government is Display'd to the Life* (Wing M1416D, 1690), p. 36. On the sermons, see A. Lacey, *The Cult of King Charles the Martyr* (Woodbridge, 2003).

321. G. Burnet, *The Royal Martyr Lamented in a Sermon Preached at the Savoy on King Charles the Martyr's day, 1674/5 by Gilbert Burnet* (Wing B5870, 1689); G. Burnet, *The Royal Martyr, and the Dutiful Subject, in Two Sermons* (Huntington Library 227452, 1675). This was reissued under the same title in 1689 (Bodleian Firth e.110 [2]) but lacks the second sermon.

322. On Royston, see *ODNB*.

323. W. Stainforth, *A Sermon Preached in the Cathedral and Metropolitan Church of St. Peter in York, January 30th, 1688/9* (Wing S5173, 1689).

324. W. Sherlock, *A Sermon Preach'd before the Honourable House of Commons, at St. Margaret's Westminster, January the xxxth, 1691/2* (Wing S3350, 1692), quotation, p. 22.

325. C. Blount, *King William and Queen Mary, Conquerors* (Wing B3309, 1693), sig. A2ᵛ. See M. Goldie, 'Charles Blount's Intention in Writing "King William and Queen Mary Conquerors" (1693)' *Notes and Queries*, 223 (1978), pp. 527–32.

326. Lacey, *Cult of the Martyr*, pp. 177–8.

327. J. Gailhard, *Some Observations Upon the Keeping the Thirtieth of January, and Twenty Ninth of May* (Wing G129, 1694), quotation, p. 1; Gailhard, *A Just and Sober Vindication of the Observations Upon the Thirtieth of January, and Twenty Ninth of May* (Wing G122, 1694); see also *A Birchen Rod for Dr. Birch, or, Some Animadversions Upon His Sermon Preached Before the Honourable the House of Commons, at St. Margaret's Westminster, January 30, 1694 in a Letter to Sir T. D. and Mr. H.* (Wing B2941, 1694).

328. Lacey, *Cult of the Martyr*, pp. 181–3.

329. R. Newman, *A Sermon Preached in the Parish-church of St. Sepulchres, on Monday the 30th of January, 1693/4* (Wing N924, 1694), pp. 6, 16, 18, 21 and *passim*.

330. J. Hartcliffe, *A sermon preached before the honourable House of Commons, at St. Margaret Westminster, on the thirtieth of January, 1694/5* (Wing H970, 1695), p. 15.

331. Ibid.

332. J. Humphreys, *A Sermon Preach'd Before the House of Lords, at the Abbey-church of St. Peter's Westminster, on Thursday, the 30th of January, 1695/6 Being the Martyrdom of K. Charles I* (Wing H3721, 1696), p. 2 and *passim*.

333. Ibid., p. 30.

334. J. Williams, *A Sermon Preach'd Before the King at Whitehall, on January 30, 1696 by John Lord Bishop of Chichester* (Wing W2729, 1697), p. 31.

335. J. Toland, *Amyntor, or, A Defence of Milton's Life Containing I. a General Apology for all Writings of that Kind . . . III. A Complete History of the Book Entitul'd Icon Basilike, Proving Dr. Gauden and not King Charles the First to be the Author of It* (Wing T1760, 1699); cf. D. J., *King Charles I, No Such Saint, Martyr or Good Protestant as Commonly Reputed, but a Favourer of Papists and a Cruel and Oppressive Tyrant all Plainly Proved from Undeniable Matters of Fact: To which Are Added Dr. Burnet's, now Bishop of Salisbury, and Other Reasons, against the Keeping up Any Longer the Observation of a Fast on the 30th of January* (Wing J7, 1698).

336. S. Bradford, *A Sermon Preached Before the King, in St. James's Chappel, January 30th, 1698/9* (Wing B4121, 1699), pp. 7–8 and *passim*; Bradford, *ODNB*.

337. J. Sharp, *A Sermon Preached Before the Lords Spiritual and Temporal in Parliament Assembled in the Abbey-church at Westminster, on the Thirtieth of January, 1699/1700 by the Most Reverend Father in God, John, Lord Arch-bishop of York* (Wing S2999, 1700), p. 1 and *passim*.

338. E. Hickeringill, *A Sermon Preach'd on the 30th of January Vindicating King Charles the Martyr, and the Keeping of the Day by E. H* (Wing H1826, 1700), p. 21; Hickeringill, *ODNB*.

339. *Animadversions on the Two Last 30th of January Sermons, the One Preached to the Honourable House of Commons, the Other to the Lower House of Convocation. In a Letter* (ESTC T010584, 1702).

340. See Lacey, *Cult of the Martyr*, chs 6–7.

341. R. B. Walker, 'The Newspaper Press in the Reign of William III', *Historical Journal*, 17 (1974), pp. 691–709.

342. P. W., *A Full and True Account of the Two Great Victories, Lately Obtained before Lymerick, by K. William's Forces, over the French and Irish Rebels* (Wing W88, 1690).

343. Ibid., two pages.

344. *An Account of the Victory Obtain'd by the King in Ireland, on the First Day of this Instant July, 1690* (Wing A421, 1690).

345. *An Exact Journal of the Victorious Progress of their Majesties Forces under the Command of Gen. Ginckle, this Summer in Ireland Giving a Particular Account of the Several Skirmishes, Battles, Sieges*

and Surrenders of Athlone, Galloway, Slego, &c. (Wing E3651, 1691), pp. 12, 19, 21, 31–2 and *passim*.

346. J. Beek, *The Triumph-royal Containing a Short Account of the Most Remarkable Battels, Sieges, Sea-fights, Treaties, and Famous Atchievements [sic] of the Princes of the House of Nassau* (Wing B1686, 1691), epistle dedicatory, sig. A2ᵛ, and *passim*.

347. T. Spencer, *A True and Faithful Relation of the Proceedings of the Forces of Their Majesties K. William and Q. Mary in their Expedition against the French in the Caribby Islands in the West Indies* (Wing S4963, 1691).

348. J. Ashby, *The Account Given by Sir John Ashby Vice-Admiral, and Reere-Admiral Rooke to the Lords Commissioners. Of the Engagement at Sea, between the English, Dutch, and French Fleets, June the 30th. 1690* (Wing A3938, 1690); *An Account of a Late Engagement at Sea near Rye on the Coast of Sussex with the Particulars of Taking a French Man of War, and Bringing Her into the Said Port* (Wing A184, 1691); *An Account of the Late Actions at Sea, between the Saint Alban's and the Happy Return, Two of Their Majesties Men of War, and Twenty Four Sail of French Ships with their Convoy of 36 Guns, near the Port of Cherbourg: with an Account of the Sinking the Convoy* (Wing A306AB, 1691); *An Account of the Late Engagement at Sea, on the Coast of Spain, between Two of Their Majesties' Fifth Rate Frigates with Two French Men of War* (Wing A309aA, 1691); *An Account of the Late Great Victory, Obtained at Sea, against the French by Their Majesties Fleet, Commanded in Chief by Admiral Russell* (Wing A310, 1692).

349. *Account of the Late Great Victory, Obtained at Sea*, sig. A2.

350. Ibid., sigs A2–A2ᵛ.

351. For a narrative, see B. Cox, *King William's European Joint Venture* (Assen, 1995).

352. *The Paris Relation of the Battel of Landen, July 29th, 1693 ... Publish'd by the French King's Authority, with His Letter: ... as Also Reflexions upon the King's Letter, by a Very Learned French Pen and Observations by Another Hand Here, Proving the French King and His Gazeteers Account to be Inconsistent with Themselves, and One Another, as well as Contrary to Truth, and that though the French Kept the Field, yet They Were really Loosers by the Action* (Wing P360, 1693).

353. *A Particular Relation of the Battel, Fought on the 29th of July, 1693, Between the Confederate Army, Commanded by His Majesty of Great Britain and the Elector of Bavaria, &c. and that of France* (Wing P597A, 1693), p. 6; *A Relation of the Battel of Landen* (Wing R815A, 1693), one page.

354. J. Welwood, *A Reply to the Answer Doctor Welwood Has Made to King James's Declaration which Declaration Was Dated at St. Germaines, April 17th, S.N., 1693* (Wing R1066, 1694), p. 5.

355. *Whitehall, August 29. 1695. This Morning Arrived Here an Express from His Majesties Camp with the Good News of the Surrender of the Castle of Namur* (Wing T937, 1695).

356. *An Exact Account of the Siege of Namur with a Perfect Diary of the Campagne in Flanders* (Wing E3582A, 1695), pp. 16, 46 and *passim*.

357. Ibid., sigs A4–A4ᵛ.

358. Ibid., sig. A4ᵛ.

359. Though for a fine brief guide, see K. O'Brien, 'History and Literature, 1660–1780', in J. Richetti ed., *The Cambridge History of English Literature, 1660–1780* (Cambridge, 2005), pp. 365–90. See M. Knights, 'The Tory Interpretation of History in the Rage of Parties', in P. Kewes ed., *The Uses of History in Early Modern England* (San Marino, CA, 2006), pp. 347–66; cf. above, ch. 8, p. 325, n. 136.

360. J. Somers, *A Brief History of the Succession of the Crown of England* (Wing S4639, 1689).

361. Ibid., pp. 13, 15 and *passim*.

362. *A Short Historical Account Touching the Succession of the Crown* (Wing S3595, 1689); *A New History of the Succession of the Crown of England* (Wing N646, 1689), p. 15.

363. *A True Relation of the Manner of the Deposing of King Edward II* (Wing T3002, 1689); C. Caesar, *Numerus infaustus a Short View of the Unfortunate Reigns of William the Second, Henry the Second, Edward the Second, Richard the Second, Charles the Second, James the Second* (Wing C203, 1689); J. Heath, *Englands Chronicle, or, The Lives & Reigns of the Kings and Queens from the Time of Julius Caesar to the Present Reign of K. William and Q. Mary* (Wing H1325, 1689). The chronicle title itself lends continuity to the usurpers. Heath had died in 1664.

364. Caesar, *Numerus infaustus*, p. 77.

365. *Quadriennium Jacobi, or, The History of the Reign of King James II from his First Coming to the Crown to His Desertion* (Wing Q6, 1689), preface, sigs A3–A4ᵛ and p. 258.

366. *The Secret History of the Reigns of K. Charles II and K. James II* (Wing S2347, 1690, assigned to Phillips by Wing), sig. A2ᵛ. See also Phillips, *The Secret History of K. James I and K. Charles I Compleating the Reigns of the Four Last Monarchs by the author of The Secret History of*

K. Charles II and K. James II (Wing S2339, 1690). On secret histories, see M. McKeon, *The Secret History of Domesticity: Public, Private, and the Division of Knowledge* (Baltimore, MD, 2005), chs 13, 14.

367.   *The History of the Late Revolution in England with the Causes & Means by which It Was Accomplish'd* (Wing H2166aA, 1689), sig. A2ᵛ, p. 1 and *passim*.

368.   G. Miege, *A Complete History of the Late Revolution from the First Rise of it to this Present Time in Three Parts* (Wing M2007, 1691), quotation, p. 31.

369.   R. B., *The History of the House of Orange, or, A Brief Relation of the Glorious and Magnanimous Achievements of His Majesties Renowned Predecessors and Likewise of His Own Heroick Actions* (Wing C7734, 1693); J. S., *An Historical Account of the Memorable Actions of the Most Glorious Monarch William III, King of England, Scotland, France and Ireland, Prince of Orange &c* (Wing J33, 1690).

370.   R. B., *The History of the Two Late Kings, Charles the Second and James the Second* (Wing C7340, 1693); R. B., *England's Monarchs* (Wing C7317, 1694), pp. 203–7; R. Coke, *A Detection of the Court and State of England During the Four Last Reigns* (Wing C4973, 1694); T. Oates, *Eikon Basilike, or, The Picture of the Late King James, Drawn to the Life in which Is Made Manifest, that the Whole Course of His Life Hath to this Day Been a Continued Conspiracy against the Protestant Religion, Laws and Liberties of the Three Kingdoms* (Wing O36, 1696); Oates, *Eikon Vasilike Tetarte, or, The Picture of the Late King James Further Drawn to the Life* (Wing O40, 1696); D. Jones, *The Secret History of White-Hall, from the Restoration of Charles II down to the Abdication of the Late K. James* (Wing J934, 1697); Jones, *A Continuation of the Secret History of White-hall from the Abdication of the Late K. James in 1688 to the Year 1696* (Wing J929, 1697); Jones, *The Tragical History of the Stuarts* (Wing J934B, 1697); On Jones, see *ODNB* and H. Snyder, 'David Jones, Augustan Historian and Pioneer English Annalist', *Huntington Library Quarterly*, 44 (1980), pp. 11–26.

371.   T. Rymer, *Edgar, or the English Monarch an Heroick Tragedy* (Wing R2424A, 1693); J. S., *Great Britain's Glory: Being the History of King Arthur with the Adventures of the Knights of the Round Table* (Wing S65, 1700).

372.   J. Sellers, *The History of England Giving a True and Impartial Account of the Most Considerable Transactions in Church and State, in Peace and War, During the Reigns of all the Kings and Queens, from the Coming of Julius Caesar* (Wing S2474A, 1697); W. Pudsey, *A Political Essay, or, Summary Review of the Kings and Government of England since the Norman Conquest* (Wing P4172, 1698), quotation, p. 161.

373.   J. Somers, *The True Secret History of the Lives and Reigns of all the Kings and Queens of England, from King William the First, Called the Conquerour* (ESTC T147699, 1702).

374.   J. Welwood, *Memoirs of the Most Material Transactions in England, for the Last Hundred Years, Preceding the Revolution in 1688* (ESTC T108395, 1702). The fourth part of Rushworth's *Historical Collections* was published in 1701; see *Historical Collections the Fourth and Last Part. In Two Volumes* (N033540, 1701), quotation, p. i.

375.   Below, ch. 12.

376.   See M. Knights, *Representation and Misrepresentation in Later Stuart Britain: Partisanship and Political Culture* (Oxford, 2004); C. Rose, *England in the 1690s: Revolution, Religion and War* (Oxford, 1999), ch. 3.

377.   For an excellent overview, see M. Goldie, 'The Revolution of 1689 and the Structure of Political Argument: An Essay and an Annotated Bibliography of Pamphlets on the Allegiance Controversy', *Bulletin of Research in the Humanities*, 83 (1980), pp. 473–564.

378.   See R. Beddard ed., *A Kingdom without a King: The Journal of the Provisional Government in the Revolution of 1688* (Oxford, 1988).

379.   G. Burnet, *An Enquiry into the Present State of Affairs, and in Particular, whether We Owe Allegiance to the King in these Circumstances? and whether We Are Bound to Treat with Him, and to Call Him Back Again, or Not?* (Wing B5811, 1689).

380.   T. Long, *A Resolution of Certain Queries Concerning Submission to the Present Government . . . by a Divine of the Church of England* (Wing L2980, 1689), quotation, p. 54.

381.   For example, Robert Ferguson, *A Brief Justification of the Prince of Orange's Descent into England* (Wing F733, 1689).

382.   Burnet, *Enquiry*, p. 3; e.g. D. Defoe, *The Advantages of the Present Settlement, and the Great Danger of a Relapse* (Wing A601, 1689); *A Justification of the Whole Proceedings of Their Majesties King William and Queen Mary* (Wing J1264, 1689).

383.   E. Bohun, *The History of the Desertion, or, An Account of all the Publick Affairs in England, from the Beginning of September 1688 to the Twelfth of February Following* (Wing B3456, 1689); [Bohun], *An Answer to the Desertion Discuss'd* (Wing B3446, 1689). On Bohun, see *ODNB*.

384. F. Fulwood, *Agreement Betwixt the Present and the Former Government, or, A Discourse of this Monarchy, whether Elective or Hereditary?* (Wing F2495, 1689), p. 42; Fullwood, *ODNB*.
385. For example, P. Jurieu, *A Defence of Their Majesties King William and Queen Mary, against an Infamous and Jesuitical Libel* (Wing J1200A, 1689).
386. Ferguson, *A Brief Justification*, p. 34.
387. D. Defoe, *Reflections Upon the Late Great Revolution Written by a Lay-hand in the Country for the Satisfaction of Some Neighbours* (Wing D844, 1689); A. B., *Allegiance Vindicated, or, The Takers of the New Oath of Allegiance to K. William & Q. Mary Justified and the Lawfulness of Taking It Asserted* (Wing A597, 1690), p. 28.
388. C. Blount, *King William and Queen Mary, Conquerors, or, A Discourse Endeavouring to Prove that Their Majesties Have on their Side, Against the Late King, the Principal Reasons that Make Conquest a Good Title* (Wing B3309, 1693).
389. D. Whitby, *Obedience Due to the Present King, notwithstanding Our Oaths to the Former Written by a Divine of the Church of England* (Wing F2512, 1689), quotation, p. 4; *A Discourse, Shewing that It Is Lawfull, and Our Duty to Swear Obedience to King William, notwithstanding the Oath of Allegiance Taken to the Late King. By a Divine in the North* (Wing D1618A, 1689), quotation, p. 5; *Advantages of the Present Settlement*.
390. *A Discourse, Shewing that It Is Lawfull, and Our Duty to Swear Obedience to King William*, p. 2; R. Claridge, *A Defence of the Present Government under King William and Queen Mary Shewing the Miseries of England under the Arbitrary Reign of the Late King James II, the Reasonableness of the Proceedings against Him* (Wing C4432, 1689), quotation, p. 1.
391. *A Vindication of Those Who Have Taken the New Oath of Allegiance to King William and Queen Mary, upon Principles Agreeable to the Doctrines of the Church of England in a Letter to a Noble Lord* (Wing V535, 1689), p. 11.
392. Jurieu, *A Defence of Their Majesties King William and Queen Mary*, p. 14; Defoe, *The Advantages of the Present Settlement; The Anatomy of an Arbitrary Prince, or, King James the II Set Forth in his Proper Colours, and What England May Expect from such a One* (Wing A3054, 1689), broadside.
393. Claridge, *Defence of Present Government*, p. 9; Jurieu, *A Defence of Their Majesties*.
394. Whitby, *Obedience Due to the Present King*, p. 8.
395. See, for example, T. Mariott, *The Danger of Division, and Necessity of Unity Opened in a Sermon Preached at St. Lawrence's Church* (Wing M716, 1689); J. Collinges, *The Happiness of Brethrens Dwelling Together in Unity* (Wing C5318, 1690).
396. *A Modest Attempt for Healing the Present Animosities in England Occasion'd by a Late Book, Entituled, A Modest Enquiry, &c., in a Dialogue between Testimony, a Zealous Dissenter, and Hot-head, a Chollerick Bigot: Trimmer, Moderator* (Wing M2359, 1690).
397. *A Letter to a Dissenting Clergyman of the Church of England, Concerning the Oath of Allegiance and Obedience to the Present Government* (Wing L1634, 1690), p. 4.
398. W. Sherlock, *The Case of Allegiance Due to Soveraign Powers Stated and Resolved, According to Scripture and Reason, and the Principles of the Church of England, with a More Particular Respect to the Oath, Lately Enjoyned, of Allegiance to Their Present Majesties, K. William and Q. Mary* (Wing S3276, 1691), pp. 13, 21 and *passim*.
399. *His Majesties Most Gracious Declaration to All His Loving Subjects* (Wing J217A, 1693).
400. [Attributed to D. Defoe and/or J. Welwood], *An Answer to the Late K. James's Last Declaration, Dated at St. Germains, April 17. s.n. 1693* (Wing W1302, 1693); cf. *Some Short Reflections Upon K. James's Late Declarations, Dated at S. Germains, April 17, 1693* (Wing S4615, 1693).
401. P. Allix, *A Letter to a Friend Concerning the Behaviour of Christians under the Various Revolutions of State-governments* (Wing A1225, 1693); on Allix, see *ODNB*.
402. *An Enquiry into the Nature and Obligation of Legal Rights with Respect to the Popular Pleas of the Late K. James's Remaining Right to the Crown* (Wing I218, 1693), p. 2.
403. *An Account of Mr. Blunts Late Book Entituled, King William and Queen Mary Conquerors Now Under the Censure of the Parliament* (Wing A213, 1693), pp. 9, 18 and *passim*; Samuel Johnson, *An Argument Proving, that the Abrogation of King James by the People of England from the Regal Throne, and the Promotion of the Prince of Orange, One of the Royal Family, to the Throne in Opposition to all the False and Treacherous Hypotheses of Usurpation, Conquest, Desertion, and of Taking the Powers That Are upon Content* (Wing J823A, 1693); see also G. Miege, *The New State of England under Their Majesties K. William and Q. Mary in Three Parts* (Wing M2021, 1693), p. 101.
404. Miege, *The New State of England*, part II, pp. 122–3.
405. Blount, *King William and Queen Mary Conquerors*, sig. A3.

406. M. Tindal, *An Essay Concerning Obedience to the Supreme Powers, and the Duty of Subjects in all Revolutions with Some Considerations Touching the Present Juncture of Affairs* (Wing T1299, 1694); on Tindal, see *ODNB*; R. Fleming, *The Present Aspect of Our Times and of the Extraordinary Conjunction of Things Therein in a Rational View and Prospect of the Same* (Wing F1270, 1694), quotations, pp. 10, 13.

407. D. Defoe, *The Englishman's Choice, and True Interest in a Vigorous Prosecution of the War Against France, and Serving K. William and Q. Mary, and Acknowledging their Right* (Wing D831, 1694), pp. 4–5, 9, 23.

408. *A Dialogue Between the King of France and the Late King James, Occasion'd by the Death of the Queen* (Wing D1332A, 1695).

409. *The Court of St. Germain's: or, The Secret History of the Late King James and Queen Mary From their First Arrival in France, to this Time* (Wing C6591A, 1695). Here, as so often in the seventeenth century, the undermining of masculinity was a device for undermining authority.

410. *England's Deliverance from Popery and Slavery and the Piety and Justice of King William and Queen Mary of Ever Blessed Memory, in Ascending the Throne of these Dominions, Asserted* (Wing E2957A, 1695); see also W. Fuller, *A Brief Discovery of the True Mother of the Pretended Prince of Wales, Known by the Name of Mary Grey* (Wing F2479, 1696).

411. *Anglia Grata: or, A Hearty-English-welcome to King William after a Successful Campaign* (Wing A3177A, 1695).

412. Ibid., pp. 2, 9.

413. *Simeon and Levi, or, Jacobite Villany and French-treachery Hand in Hand Being Remarks upon the Horrid and Barbarous Conspiracy to Assassinate the Person of His Most-Sacred Majesty King William, as also on the Intended-Invasion from France: Published for the Edification of the Jacks, and their Brethren the Papists, and the Whole Tribe of Non-jurors* (Wing S3789, 1696), pp. 22, 28 and *passim*.

414. T. Percival, *The Rye-house Travestie, or, A True Account and Declaration of the Horrid and Execrable Conspiracy against His Majesty King William and the Government* (Wing P1454A, 1696); J. Macky, *A View of the Court of St. Germain from the Year 1690, to 95*, pp. 1, 17–18; J. Bundy, *Great Britain's glory: properly call'd, King William proclaim'd the second time* (Wing B5473, 1696).

415. *An Impartial Account of the Horrid and Detestable Conspiracy to Assassinate His Sacred Majesty King William* (Wing I70, 1696); *The Art of Assassinating Kings Taught Lewis XIV and James II by the Jesuites: wherein Is Discovered the Secret of the Last Conspiracy Form'd at Versailles in Sep. 1695, against the life of William III* (Wing A3785, 1696), quotation, p. 119.

416. J. Abbadie, *The History of the Late Conspiracy against the King and the Nation* (Wing A52, 1696), pp. 3, 192.

417. Ibid., p. 64.

418. A. Borfet, *The Minister of Richmond's Reasons for Refusing to Subscribe the Association but under the Following Sense with Reflections Thereupon* (Wing B3763, 1696), quotation, p. 6.

419. Ibid., pp. 3–7; W. Atwood, *Reflections Upon a Treasonable Opinion, Industriously Promoted, Against Signing the National Association and the Entring into it Prov'd to be the Duty of all Subjects of this Kingdom* (Wing A4179, 1696).

420. *A Free Discourse wherein the Doctrines which Make for Tyranny Are Display'd the Title of Our Rightful and Lawful King William Vindicated, and the Unreasonableness and Mischievous Tendency of the Odious Distinction of a King de facto, and de jure, Discover'd* (Wing H2995A, 1697), p. 66. In the end the number who refused to sign was small. I am grateful to Mark Knights for this information.

421. Ibid., pp. 99–100.

422. *Jacobus Secundus, Dei gratia, magnae Britanniae, Franciae & Hiberniae Rex, defensor fidei, omnibus regibus principibus, rebuspublicis &c. postqàm diuturno tamque funesto toti Christianae reipublicae bello Europa conflagravit* (Wing J152, 1697).

423. *The Late King James's Second Manifesto Directed to the Protestant Princes Answered Paragraph by Paragraph* (Wing L552, 1697); *The Late King James's Manifesto Answer'd, Paragraph by Paragraph wherein the Weakness of His Reasons Is Plainly Demonstrated* (Wing L550, 1697).

424. *A Dialogue Between the French King, and the Late King James at St. Germains en Laye: Occasion'd by the Signing of the Peace* (Wing D1331A, 1697).

425. *The Revolution Justified from Principles of Reason and Scripture* (Wing R1208, 1697), pp. 37–8.

426. *Ratio Ultima for a Full Compliance with the Present Government: Argued in a Letter to a Person of Honour in the Country* (Wing R301, 1697), pp. 2, 18 and *passim*.

427. Ibid., p. 18.

428. R. Kingston, *Tyranny Detected and the Late Revolution Justify'd by the Law of God* (Wing K616, 1699), p. 57; Richard Kingston, *ODNB*.

429. Ibid., pp. 149, 273.

430. T. White, *The Grounds of Obedience and Government. Being the Best Answer to All that Has Been Lately Written in Defence of Passive Obedience and Non Resistance* (Wing W2818, 1700).

431. W. Fuller, *A Plain Proof of the True Father and Mother of the Pretended Prince of Wales* (Wing F2485, 1700); Fuller, *Mr. Fuller's Answer to the Jacobites* (Wing F2477, 1700). On Fuller, see R. Weil, *Political Passions: Gender, the Family and Political Argument in England 1680–1714* (Manchester, 1999), pp. 92, 102.

432. *A Letter to a Minister of State, Concerning the Pretended Prince of Wales's Being Proclaim'd King of England* (ESTC T038069, 1701).

433. J. Toland, *Anglia libera: or the Limitation and Succession of the Crown of England Explain'd and Asserted* (ESTC N021896, 1701).

434. D. Defoe, *The Succession to the Crown of England, Considered* (ESTC N024531, 1701), pp. 4, 21; Defoe, *An Argument, Shewing, that the Prince of Wales, tho' a Protestant, Has No Just Pretensions to the Crown of England* (ESTC T121325, 1701).

435. G. Stepney, *An Essay upon the Present Interest of England* (ESTC T033478, 1701); *The Present Disposition of England Considered* (ESTC T044212, 1701), p. 21.

436. D. Defoe, *The True-Born Englishman. A Satyr* (ESTC N000306, 1701), p. 16.

437. Baxter, *William III*, pp. 255, 399–400; T. Claydon, *William III* (Harlow, 2002); 'important explanations for William's unpopularity centre on his personality', William III, *ODNB*.

10 Figuring Revolution

1. L. Jardine, *Going Dutch: How England Plundered Holland's Glory* (London, 2008); see also P. Sellin ed., *Anglo-Dutch Cross Currents in the Seventeenth and Eighteenth Centuries* (Los Angeles, CA, 1976).

2. See W. Honey, 'Royal Portraits in Pottery and Porcelain', *Burlington Magazine*, 70 (1937), pp. 218–29; below, ch. 10, pp. 445–6.

3. Above ch. 8, pp. 312–13; ch. 9, pp. 379–80.

4. See P. Burke, *The Fabrication of Louis XIV* (New Haven, CT, and London, 1992).

5. See T. Blanning, *Culture of Power and the Power of Culture: Old Regime Europe 1660–1789* (Oxford, 2002), pp. 46–7.

6. R. Wilkinson, *Louis XIV* (London, 2007), ch. 5.

7. Burke, *The Fabrication of Louis XIV*, ch. 6.

8. See E. Chaney ed., *The Evolution of English Collecting: Receptions of Italian Art in the Tudor and Stuart Periods* (New Haven, CT, and London, 2003); K. Sharpe, *Image Wars: Promoting Kings and Commonwealths in England* (New Haven, CT, and London, 2010), chs 2, 6.

9. P. MacCubbin and M. Hamilton-Phillips eds, *The Age of William III & Mary II: Power, Politics, and Patronage, 1688–1702* (Williamsburg, VA, 1989), p. 252; B. Cowan, 'Art and Connoisseurship in the Auction Market of Later Seventeenth-Century London', in N. Demarchi and H. van Miegroet eds, *Mapping Markets for Paintings in Europe 1450–1750* (Tournhout, 2006), pp. 263–84.

10. See I. Pears, *The Discovery of Painting: The Growth of Interest in the Arts in England 1680–1768* (New Haven, CT, and London, 1988).

11. C. Dufresnoy, *De Arte Graphica, The Art of Painting by C.A. Du Fresnoy; with Remarks; Translated into English, together with an Original Preface Containing a Parallel betwixt Painting and Poetry, by Mr. Dryden* (Wing D2458, 1695); M. Smith, *The Art of Painting According to the Theory and Practice of the Best Italian, French, and German Masters* (Wing S4129A, 1693); C. K., *Art's Master-piece* (Wing K2, 1697, K3, 1700); J. Smith, *The Art of Painting in Oyl* (ESTC T098429, 1701).

12. P. Monier, *The History of Painting, Sculpture, Architecture, Graving, and of those Who Have Excell'd in them in Three Books* (Wing M2419, 1699), quotation, p. 4; J. Elsum, *Epigrams upon the Paintings of the Most Eminent Masters, Antient and Modern with Reflexions upon the Several Schools of Painting* (Wing E643, 1700).

13. *An Essay upon Sublime Translated from the Greek of Dionysius Longinus Cassius* (Wing L2998, 1698); J. Wright, *Country Conversations Being an Account of Some Discourses that Happen'd in a Visit to the Country Last Summer, on Divers Subjects: Chiefly of the Modern Comedies, of Drinking, of Translated Verse, of Painting and Painters, of Poets and Poetry* (Wing W3693, 1694).

14. A. Boyer, *The History of King William the Third. In III parts* (ESTC T091241, 1702–3), III, p. 517.

15. H. Walpole, *Anecdotes of Painting in England* (4 vols, 1782), III, pp. 193–6.
16. Especially, MacCubbin and Hamilton-Phillips, *The Age of William III & Mary II*.
17. Ibid., p. 249.
18. Ibid., p. 250.
19. T. Scheurleer, 'Documents on the Furnishing of Kensington House', *Walpole Society*, 38 (1960–2), p. 19, and pp. 15–58 *passim*.
20. J. Rosenberg, *Dutch Art and Architecture 1600–1800* (New Haven, CT, and London, 1993), pp. 351–2.
21. J. Stewart, *Sir Godfrey Kneller and the English Baroque Portrait* (Oxford, 1983), p. 39.
22. John Riley, *ODNB*.
23. O. Millar, *Tudor, Stuart and Early Georgian Pictures in the Collection of Her Majesty the Queen* (London, 1963), p. 141.
24. Stewart, *Sir Godfrey Kneller*, p. 40; Kneller, *ODNB*.
25. Millar, *Tudor, Stuart and Early Georgian Pictures*, p. 142.
26. Ibid., p. 142, no. 335, plate 149; cf. ibid., p. 129, no. 285, plate 123. See S. Barnes, N. de Poorter, O. Millar and H. Vey eds, *Van Dyck: A Complete Catalogue of the Paintings* (New Haven, CT, and London, 2003), p. 471, plate IV, 53.
27. Ibid., p. 143, no. 338, plate 150; Barnes et al., *Van Dyck*, p. 520, plate IV, 114.
28. Stewart, *Sir Godfrey Kneller*, p. 40.
29. Ibid.; Millar, *Tudor, Stuart and Early Georgian Pictures*, p. 142.
30. Stewart, *Sir Godfrey Kneller*, p. 41.
31. Ibid., pp. 43–4.
32. See C. Macleod and J. Alexander eds, *Painted Ladies: Women at the Court of Charles II* (New Haven, CT, and London, 2001); above, ch. 2, pp. 99–100.
33. Stewart, *Sir Godfrey Kneller*, nos 313, 312, plate 38a.
34. See K. Sharpe, 'Van Dyck, the Royal Image and the Caroline Court', in K. Hearn ed., *Van Dyck and Britain* (London, 2009), pp. 14–23.
35. Stewart, *Sir Godfrey Kneller*, p. 45.
36. Ibid., p. 44; K. Sharpe, *The Personal Rule of Charles I* (New Haven, CT, and London, 1992), p. 212.
37. Ibid., p. 41; see also J. Stewart, 'William III and Sir Godfrey Kneller', *Journal of the Warburg and Courtauld Institutes*, 33 (1970), pp. 330–6.
38. Millar, *Tudor, Stuart and Early Georgian Pictures*, pp. 142–3, no. 336, plate 165; Stewart, *Sir Godfrey Kneller*, p. 139, no. 842.
39. Millar, *Tudor, Stuart and Early Georgian Pictures*, p. 143.
40. Stewart, *Sir Godfrey Kneller*, p. 140, no. 844. See National Portrait Gallery [NPG], D 11922.
41. Stewart, *Sir Godfrey Kneller*, p. 139, no. 843.
42. Millar, *Tudor, Stuart and Early Georgian Pictures*, p. 143, no. 337, plate 146; Stewart, *Sir Godfrey Kneller*, p. 140, no. 846. There is a 1700 variant now in New York, ibid., p. 140, no. 845.
43. A. de Vries, *Dictionary of Symbols and Imagery* (Amsterdam, 1981), pp. 356–7.
44. Virgil, *Eclogues*, IV, poem 4; translation from Perseus using J. B. Greenough ed., *Virgil Eclogues* (Boston, MA, 1900).
45. Stewart, *Sir Godfrey Kneller*, p. 54; Millar, *Tudor, Stuart and Early Georgian Pictures*, p. 133; F. Yates, 'Queen Elizabeth as Astraea', *Journal of the Warburg and Courtauld Institutes*, 10 (1947), pp. 27–82.
46. Stewart, *Sir Godfrey Kneller*, p. 54.
47. *The Works of Virgil Containing His Pastorals, Georgics and Aeneis: Adorn'd with a Hundred Sculptures Translated into English Verse by Mr. Dryden* (Wing V616, 1697).
48. Cf. S. Baxter, 'William III as Hercules: The Political Implications of Court Culture', in L. Schwoerer ed., *The Revolution of 1688–1689: Changing Perspectives* (Cambridge, 1992), pp. 95–106, especially p. 97.
49. H. Dunthorne, 'William in Contemporary Portraits and Prints', in E. Mijers and D. Onnekink eds, *Redefining William III: The Impact of the King-Stadholder in International Context* (Aldershot, 2007), pp. 263–76, especially p. 270.
50. Millar, *Tudor, Stuart and Early Georgian Pictures*, p. 143; see below, ch. 10, pp. 437–42.
51. N. Lutrell, *A Brief Historical Relation of State Affairs, 1678–1714* (6 vols, 1857), IV, pp. 343–4; MacCubbin and Hamilton-Phillips, *The Age of William III & Mary II*, p. 255.
52. Stewart, *Sir Godfrey Kneller*, p. 52.
53. Verrio, *ODNB*.
54. The Schalken is now in the Rijksmuseum, Amsterdam; the Jan Wycks of the Boyne and Namur are both in the National Army Museum. There are versions of the Boyne also at Petworth and

Blenheim. In addition to these, the miniaturist Charles Boit executed an enamel on copper, NPG 1737.

55. Stewart, *Sir Godfrey Kneller*, p. 34; Smith, *ODNB*.
56. A. Griffiths, 'Early Mezzotint Publishing in England: John Smith, 1652–1743', *Print Quarterly*, 6 (1989), pp. 243–57.
57. Huntington Library, Richard Bull Granger, 20/12ᵛ.
58. See, for example, NPG D7745, D11944.
59. Huntington Library, Bull Granger, 20/11; Stewart, *Sir Godfrey Kneller*, p. 140, no. 844.
60. Huntington Library, Bull Granger, 20/15; NPG D11957; see also NPG D11525.
61. NPG D32764; Huntington Library, Bull Granger, 20/15ᵛ.
62. See NPG D17035, D17036, D21577, D7744, D21576, D7743; Huntington Library, Bull Granger, 20/8ᵛ, 15.
63. NPG D11530.
64. Huntington Library, Bull Granger, 20/20, 21ᵛ, 13; NPG D31079.
65. NPG D17048, D10674; see also Huntington Library, Bull Granger, 20/38ᵛ.
66. Huntington Library, Bull Granger, 20/9–9ᵛ, 10–21 *passim*.
67. NPG D10884, Huntington Library, Bull Granger, 20/7ᵛ.
68. Huntington Library, Bull Granger, 20/9, 10, 21ᵛ, 23ᵛ.
69. Huntington Library, Bull Granger, 20/22; on De Hooghe, see J. Landwehr, *Romeyn de Hooghe, the Etcher: Contemporary Portrayal of Europe, 1662–1707* (Leiden, 1973).
70. NPG D21650.
71. A. Griffiths, *The Print in Stuart Britain, 1603–1689* (London, 1998), pp. 303–4, no. 212; MacCubbin and Hamilton-Phillips, *The Age of William III & Mary II*, p. 289.
72. Lens, *ODNB*; Griffiths, *Print in Stuart Britain*, pp. 263–4.
73. Griffiths, *Print in Stuart Britain*, pp. 304–5, no. 213.
74. Ibid., pp. 176–8, no. 115; see K. Sharpe, *Image Wars*, pp. 503–5; British Museum 1898, 0911.292, AN159417001. See this print on British Printed Images (http://www.bpi1700.org.uk/research/printOfTheMonth/august2006.html), an invaluable database of print images to 1700. See also C. Rose, *England in the 1690s: Revolution, Religion and War* (Oxford, 1999), pp. 258–9; M. Jones, *The Print in Early Modern England* (New Haven, CT, and London, 2010), p. 106.
75. Griffiths, *Print in Stuart Britain*, pp. 305–6, no. 214.
76. Ibid., p. 264.
77. See versions in NPG D7754, D9250; BM AN397387001.
78. Anne, *ODNB*.
79. Yale University Beinecke Library, BrSides 1988 80; MacCubbin and Hamilton-Phillips, *The Age of William III & Mary II*, p. 7.
80. A. F. Johnson, *A Catalogue of Engraved and Etched English Title Pages* (Oxford Bibliographical Society, 1934).
81. S. J., *An Historical Account of the Memorable Actions of the Most Illustrious William Henry, Prince of Orange and More Particularly His Last Generous and Glorious Expedition to England to Deliver the Three Kingdoms from Slavery and Arbitrary Power, and to Secure the Protestant Religion Against Popery* (Wing J32A, 1689).
82. T. S., *Englands Great Deliverance, or Great Britains Fears and Tears in Joy Completed* (Wing S159, 1689); *The Court of England, or, The Preparation for the Happy Coronation of King William and Queen Mary* (Wing C6589, 1689).
83. *The History of the Wars in Ireland* (Wing H2190, 1690); *A Congratulatory Poem on King William's Victories in Ireland* (Wing C5824A, 1690).
84. C. la Fin, *Sermo Mirabilis: or The Silent Language* (Wing L176B, 1693).
85. *A Short History of the Succession of the Kings and Queens of England, from William the Conqueror, to His Present Majesty King William, the III* (Wing S3602, 1694).
86. *England's Deliverance from Popery and Slavery and the Piety and Justice of King William and Queen Mary of Ever Blessed Memory, in Ascending the Throne of these Dominions, Asserted* (Wing E2957A, 1695); see also *A Brief History of the Pious and Glorious Life and Actions of the Most Illustrious Princess, Mary Queen of England, Scotland, France and Ireland* (Wing S46, 1695).
87. J. Seller, *The History of England Giving a True and Impartial Account of the Most Considerable Transactions in Church and State* (Wing S2474, 1696).
88. G. Walker, *The Protestant's Crums of Comfort* (Wing W343, 1697), facing title page.
89. J. Woodward, *An Account of the Societies for Reformation of Manners* (Wing W3512, 1699); see fifth edition, 1701 (ESTC T074628).

90. E. Dering, *The Most Excellent Maria, in a Brief Character of Her Incomparable Virtues and Goodness* (ESTC T135759, 1701).
91. J. A., *Princely Excellency: or, Regal Glory* (ESTC T1044327, 1702); E. Chamberlayne, *Angliae Notitia, or, The Present State of England* (Wing C1836, 1700); on Chamberlayne, see *ODNB*.
92. N. Smith, *The Royal Image and the English People* (Aldershot, 2001), pp. 143–4, fig. 6.1.
93. Ibid., p. 163, n.72.
94. Ibid., p. 134.
95. Ibid.; see also P. Gleane, *A Poem, Occasioned by the Magnificent Proceeding to the Funeral of Her Late Majesty Queen Mary II* (Wing G848A, 1695), p. 15; D. Defoe, *The Life of that Incomparable Princess, Mary* (Wing L2026, 1695), p. 77.
96. See John Nost, *ODNB*.
97. We should perhaps be cautious about taking this as a sign of William's popularity when there were sales of porcelain figuring the king and queen.
98. M. Morgan, *A Poem to the King Upon the Conclusion of Peace by Matt. Morgan* (Wing M2736, 1698), p. 10.
99. J. Harris, 'The Architecture of the Williamite Court', in MacCubbin and Hamilton-Phillips, *The Age of William III & Mary II*, pp. 225–33, quotation, p. 233.
100. S. Thurley, *Whitehall Palace: An Architectural History of the Royal Apartments, 1240–1698* (New Haven, CT, and London, 1999), p. 127.
101. Ibid., pp. 137–40.
102. See T. Tenison, *A Sermon Preached at the Funeral of Her Late Majesty Queen Mary of Ever Blessed Memory* (Wing T721, 1695), p. 18.
103. Thurley, *Whitehall*, p. 143.
104. Ibid.; Luttrell, *A Brief Historical Relation of State Affairs*, IV, p. 351.
105. Thurley, *Whitehall*, pp. 144–5.
106. S. Thurley, *Hampton Court: A Social and Architectural History* (New Haven, CT, and London, 2003), pp. 151–2.
107. Ibid., p. 153; M. Ede, *Arts and Society in England under William and Mary* (London, 1979), p. 122.
108. Thurley, *Hampton Court*, pp. 153, 163, 168.
109. Ibid., p. 182.
110. Ibid., p. 183.
111. Ibid., p. 194.
112. Ibid., p. 205.
113. Above, ch. 11, pp. 457–9.
114. Thurley, *Hampton Court*, pp. 195–9.
115. Ibid., p. 212.
116. E. Wind, 'Julian the Apostate at Hampton Court', *Journal of the Warburg and Courtauld Institutes*, 3 (1939–40), pp. 127–37.
117. Thurley, *Hampton Court*, p. 212.
118. Ibid., p. 152.
119. H. Colvin ed., *The History of the King's Works, V, 1660–1782* (London, 1976), p. 127; see also J. Hayes, *Kensington Palace: A History and Guide* (London, 1983).
120. Colvin, *The History of the King's Works*, p. 127; though William did entertain there in 1699, p. 194.
121. See J. Dixon Hunt, 'The Anglo-Dutch Garden', in MacCubbin and Hamilton-Phillips eds, *The Age of William III and Mary II*, pp. 234–43; J. Dixon Hunt and E. de Jong, 'The Anglo-Dutch Garden in the Age of William and Mary', *Journal of Garden History*, 8 (1988), pp. 3, 10. See also D. Jacques and A. J. van Der Horst, *The Gardens of William and Mary* (London, 1988).
122. W. Harris, *A Description of the King's Royal Palace and Gardens at Loo* (Wing H882, 1699), sig. A2.
123. Ibid., pp. 2–3.
124. Ibid., pp. 24–5.
125. Ibid., pp. 30, 39.
126. Ibid., p. 40.
127. Ibid.
128. Ibid., pp. 2–3.
129. Thurley, *Hampton Court*, p. 229.
130. Ibid.
131. Ibid., p. 230; E. de Jong, ' "Netherlandish Hesperides": Garden Art in the Period of William and Mary 1650–1702', in Dixon Hunt and De Jong, 'Anglo–Dutch Garden', pp. 15–40.

132. D. O. Wijnands, 'Hortus Auriaci: The Gardens of Orange and their Place in Late Seventeenth-Century Botany and Horticulture', in Dixon Hunt and De Jong eds, 'Anglo–Dutch Garden', pp. 61–86.

133. S. Switzer, *Ichnographia Rustica* (ESTC T061261, 3 vols, 1742), I, p. 79; Thurley, *Hampton Court*, pp. 229, 235; J. R. Jones, 'The Building Works and Court Style of William and Mary', in Dixon Hunt and De Jong, 'Anglo–Dutch Garden', pp. 1–13, especially p. 7.

134. Thurley, *Hampton Court*, pp. 233–7; Dixon Hunt and De Jong, eds 'Anglo-Dutch Garden', pp. 215–16.

135. Thurley, *Hampton Court*, p. 237.

136. Dixon Hunt and De Jong, 'Anglo-Dutch Garden', pp. 31, 57–8.

137. Switzer, *Ichnographia Rustica*, I, pp. 55–6.

138. J. Bloom, *English Seals* (London, 1906), p. 50.

139. J. Campbell, *Lives of the Lord Chancellors and Keepers of the Great Seal* (10 vols, 1857), IV, p. 405.

140. Ibid., p. 412.

141. Bloom, *English Seals*, pp. 90–1.

142. See J. Wyon, *The Great Seals of England* (1887), pp. 109–11.

143. The seals are illustrated in W. Sandford, *A Genealogical History of the Kings and Queens of England, and Monarchs of Great Britain* (ESTC T147652, 1707), p. 548 c, d. Wyon regretted the unoriginality of the seal; but this may have been the point, *Great Seals*, p. 113.

144. Wyon, *Great Seals*, p. 113.

145. A. W. Franks and H. A. Grueber, *Medallic Illustrations of the History of Great Britain* (2 vols, 1885), I, pp. 634–5, no. 58; E. Hawkins, *Medallic Illustrations of the History of Great Britain and Ireland to the Death of George II* (1904–11), plate LXVII, 7.

146. Franks and Grueber, *Medallic Illustrations*, I, pp. 635–6, no. 59; Hawkins, *Medallic Illustrations*, plate LXVII, 8.

147. Franks and Grueber, *Medallic Illustrations*, I, pp. 637–41, nos 61–7; Hawkins, *Medallic Illustrations*, plate LXVIII, 1–7.

148. Franks and Grueber, *Medallic Illustrations*, I, p. 638, no. 63; Hawkins, *Medallic Illustrations*, plate LXVIII, 2.

149. Franks and Grueber, *Medallic Illustrations*, II, p. 639, no. 64; Hawkins, *Medallic Illustrations*, plate LXVIII, 3.

150. Franks and Grueber, *Medallic Illustrations*, I, p. 640, nos 65–6; Hawkins, *Medallic Illustrations*, plate LXVIII, 5.

151. Franks and Grueber, *Medallic Illustrations*, I, p. 641, no. 67; Hawkins, *Medallic Illustrations*, plate LXVIII, 6.

152. Franks and Grueber, *Medallic Illustrations*, I, p. 645, no. 74; cf. pp. 650–1, nos 3, 4, 6; Hawkins, *Medallic Illustrations*, plate LXIX, 1–5.

153. Franks and Grueber, *Medallic Illustrations*, I, p. 651, no. 6; Hawkins, *Medallic Illustrations*, plate LXIX, 5.

154. Franks and Grueber, *Medallic Illustrations*, I, p. 657, no. 17; Hawkins, *Medallic Illustrations*, plate LXX, 4.

155. Franks and Grueber, *Medallic Illustrations*, I, p. 658, no. 18; Hawkins, *Medallic Illustrations*, plate LXX, 5.

156. Franks and Grueber, *Medallic Illustrations*, I, p. 660, no. 20; Hawkins, *Medallic Illustrations*, plate LXX, 17.

157. Franks and Grueber, *Medallic Illustrations*, I, pp. 652–3, no. 25; Hawkins, *Medallic Illustrations*, plate LXX, 10.

158. K. Sharpe, *Selling the Tudor Monarchy*, p. 26.

159. Franks and Grueber, *Medallic Illustrations*, I, p. 663, no. 26; Hawkins, *Medallic Illustrations*, plate LXX, 11.

160. Franks and Grueber, *Medallic Illustrations*, I, pp. 664–5, nos 29–30; Hawkins, *Medallic Illustrations*, plate LXXI, 3, 4.

161. Franks and Grueber, *Medallic Illustrations*, I, p. 668, no. 38; Hawkins, *Medallic Illustrations*, plate LXXI, 10.

162. For example, Franks and Grueber, *Medallic Illustrations*, I, pp. 668–9, no. 39; Hawkins, *Medallic Illustrations*, plate LXXI, 11.

163. Franks and Grueber, *Medallic Illustrations*, I, pp. 672–3, no. 45; Hawkins, *Medallic Illustrations*, plate LXXII, 5.

164. For examples, Franks and Grueber, *Medallic Illustrations*, I, pp. 668, 671, nos 39, 42; Hawkins, *Medallic Illustrations*, plates LXXI, 11; LXXII, 2–3.

165. Above ch. 2, pp. 129–33.

166. Franks and Grueber, *Medallic Illustrations*, I, p. 680, no. 59; Hawkins, *Medallic Illustrations*, plate LXXIII, 10.
167. Though some were struck in Holland, inscriptions evidence they were made for English circulation.
168. Franks and Grueber, *Medallic Illustrations*, I, pp. 682–3, no. 63; Hawkins, *Medallic Illustrations*, plate LXXIII, 12; above, pp. 904–7.
169. Franks and Grueber, *Medallic Illustrations*, I, p. 686, nos 69–70, pp. 687–92, nos 73–85; Hawkins, *Medallic Illustrations*, plates LXXIV, 5–6; LXXV, 1–13.
170. For medals in cheap copper and lead, see Franks and Grueber, *Medallic Illustrations*, I, pp. 692–6, nos 86–95; Hawkins, *Medallic Illustrations*, plate LXXVI, 1–9.
171. See L. Schwoerer, 'Images of Queen Mary II, 1689–1694', *Renaissance Quarterly*, 42 (1989), pp. 717–48.
172. Franks and Grueber, *Medallic Illustrations*, II, pp. 1–2, nos 152, 154; Hawkins, *Medallic Illustrations*, plate LXXXII, 1–3.
173. Franks and Grueber, *Medallic Illustrations*, I, p. 713, nos 128–9; Hawkins, *Medallic Illustrations*, plate LXXIX, 6–7.
174. Franks and Grueber, *Medallic Illustrations*, II, p. 81, no. 294; Hawkins, *Medallic Illustrations*, plate XCIII, 4.
175. Franks and Grueber, *Medallic Illustrations*, II, pp. 106–24, nos 334–70; Hawkins, *Medallic Illustrations*, plates XCVII–C.
176. Franks and Grueber, *Medallic Illustrations*, II, pp. 123–4, nos 369–70; Hawkins, *Medallic Illustrations*, plate C, 9–10.
177. Franks and Grueber, *Medallic Illustrations*, I, p. 707, no. 117; Hawkins, *Medallic Illustrations*, plate LXXVIII, 8.
178. Franks and Grueber, *Medallic Illustrations*, I, pp. 714, 717, nos 132, 138; Hawkins, *Medallic Illustrations*, plates LXXIX, 9; LXXX, 3–4.
179. Franks and Grueber, *Medallic Illustrations*, I, p. 720, nos. 143–4; Hawkins, *Medallic Illustrations*, plate LXXXI, 1–2.
180. Franks and Grueber, *Medallic Illustrations*, I, p. 717, no. 137; Hawkins, *Medallic Illustrations*, plate LXXX, 4.
181. Franks and Grueber, *Medallic Illustrations*, II, pp. 12–13, nos 174, 176; Hawkins, *Medallic Illustrations*, plate LXXXIII, 5–6.
182. Franks and Grueber, *Medallic Illustrations*, II, p. 23, nos 191–2; Hawkins, *Medallic Illustrations*, plate LXXXV, 2.
183. Franks and Grueber, *Medallic Illustrations*, II, pp. 28–43, nos 200–28; Hawkins, *Medallic Illustrations*, plates LXXXV, LXXXVI.
184. Franks and Grueber, *Medallic Illustrations* II, pp. 38–43, nos 219–26; Hawkins, *Medallic Illustrations*, plate LXXVII, 3–9.
185. For examples, Franks and Grueber, *Medallic Illustrations*, II, pp. 52–4, nos 244–9; Hawkins, *Medallic Illustrations*, plate LXXXVIII, 11–15.
186. For examples, Franks and Grueber, *Medallic Illustrations*, II, pp. 55–62, 64–5, nos 250–63, 287–9; Hawkins, *Medallic Illustrations*, plate XC, 1–10.
187. The medal depicting the French cock is Franks and Grueber, *Medallic Illustrations*, II, p. 54, no. 249; Hawkins, *Medallic Illustrations*, plate LXXXVIII, 14–15.
188. See Franks and Grueber, *Medallic Illustrations*, II, p. 74, no. 285; Hawkins, *Medallic Illustrations*, plate XCII, 4.
189. Franks and Grueber, *Medallic Illustrations*, II, pp. 84–5, nos 301–2; Hawkins, *Medallic Illustrations*, plate XCIII, 10–11.
190. Franks and Grueber, *Medallic Illustrations*, II, pp. 96–100, nos 319–24; Hawkins, *Medallic Illustrations*, plates XCV, 7–9; XCVI, 1–3.
191. Franks and Grueber, *Medallic Illustrations*, II, p. 102, no. 327; Hawkins, *Medallic Illustrations*, plate XCVI, 7.
192. Franks and Grueber, *Medallic Illustrations*, II, pp. 128–43, nos 378–402; Hawkins, *Medallic Illustrations*, plates CI–CIII.
193. Franks and Grueber, *Medallic Illustrations*, II, p. 137, no. 392; Hawkins, *Medallic Illustrations*, plate CII, 6.
194. Franks and Grueber, *Medallic Illustrations*, II, pp. 150–5, nos 413–20; Hawkins, *Medallic Illustrations*, plate CIV, 1–6.
195. Franks and Grueber, *Medallic Illustrations*, II, p. 150, no. 413; Hawkins, *Medallic Illustrations*, plate CIV, 1.

196. Franks and Grueber, *Medallic Illustrations*, II, p. 152, no. 415; Hawkins, *Medallic Illustrations*, plate CIV, 3.
197. Franks and Grueber, *Medallic Illustrations*, II, p. 153, no. 417; cf. pp. 153–4, nos 418–19; Hawkins, *Medallic Illustrations*, plate CIV, 5–6.
198. For example, Franks and Grueber, *Medallic Illustrations*, II, p. 163, no. 435; Hawkins, *Medallic Illustrations*, plate CV, 6.
199. Franks and Grueber, *Medallic Illustrations*, II, p. 166, no. 443; Hawkins, *Medallic Illustrations*, plate CV, 12.
200. Franks and Grueber, *Medallic Illustrations*, II, p. 177, no. 468; Hawkins, *Medallic Illustrations*, plate CVII, 4–5.
201. See below, ch. 11, p. 459.
202. Franks and Grueber, *Medallic Illustrations*, II, pp. 190–1, nos 496–7; Hawkins, *Medallic Illustrations*, plate CIX, 2–3.
203. Franks and Grueber, *Medallic Illustrations*, II, p. 192, no. 499; Hawkins, *Medallic Illustrations*, plate CIX, 5.
204. See above, ch. 9, p. 406. One medal of James II with Prince James imitates the double portrait of William and Mary; Franks and Grueber, *Medallic Illustrations*, II, p. 203, no. 518; Hawkins, *Medallic Illustrations*, plate CXI, 6.
205. See Franks and Grueber, *Medallic Illustrations*, II, pp. 193–4, nos 500–6; Hawkins, *Medallic Illustrations*, plates CIX, 6; CX, 1–7.
206. Franks and Grueber, *Medallic Illustrations*, II, pp. 199–200, no. 512; Hawkins, *Medallic Illustrations*, plate CX, 14.
207. In contrast to the Dutch medal, Franks and Grueber, *Medallic Illustrations*, II, pp. 198–9, no. 511; Hawkins, *Medallic Illustrations*, plate CX, 13.
208. R. Ruding, *Annals of the Coinage of Great Britain* (3 vols, 1840), II, pp. 30–1.
209. Ibid., p. 31.
210. Ibid., p. 47.
211. Ibid., p. 48.
212. *His Majesties Most Gracious Speech to Both Houses of Parliament, on Tuesday the Twentieth day of October, 1696* (Wing W2408, 1696), p. 3.
213. G. Brooke, *English Coins: From the Seventh Century to the Present day* (London, 1950), p. 223. See Ming-Hsun Li, *The Great Recoinage of 1696 to 1699* (London, 1963).
214. H. Seaby and P. Rayner, *The English Silver Coinage from 1649* (London, 1968), p. 14.
215. Ruding, *Annals of the Coinage*, II, p. 57.
216. W. Fleetwood, *A Sermon against Clipping, Preach'd before the Right Honourable the Lord Mayor and Court of Aldermen, at Guild-Hall Chappel, on Decemb. 16. 1694* (Wing F1248, 1694), pp. 5–6.
217. *A Sermon on the Restoring of the Coyn with Reference to the State of the Nation, and of the Church therein by a Minister of the Church of England* (Wing S2629, 1697), pp. 3, 14, 21 and *passim*.
218. P. Seaby, *The Story of British Coinage* (London, 1985), pp. 127–8.
219. Seaby and Rayner, *The English Silver Coinage*, p. 13.
220. For illustrations, see http://ukcoinpics.co.uk/w3/index.html.
221. Seaby and Rayner, *The English Silver Coinage*, pp. 15–16.
222. Ruding, *Annals of the Coinage*, II, p. 58; www.coins.nd.edu/ColCoin/ColCoinIntros/Br-Copper.intro.html.
223. See K. Sharpe, *Selling the Tudor Monarchy: Authority and Image in Sixteenth-Century England* (New Haven, CT, and London, 2009), p. 390.
224. Victoria and Albert Museum, nos C.201–1938, 414:823/1–1885.
225. See A. Ray, 'Delftware in England', in MacCubbin and Hamilton-Phillips, *The Age of William III and Mary II*, pp. 310–17. On Mary's collection, see Defoe, quoted in S. van Raaij ed., *The Royal Progess of William & Mary* (Amsterdam, 1988), pp. 103–4.
226. Ray, 'Delftware', p. 305. Many mugs and plates survive in museums and come up at auctions; see, for example, Fitzwilliam Museum Cambridge, C.1634–1928.
227. Ibid., p. 306; R. Warren, 'Lambeth Earthenware (Lambeth Delft)', *Transactions of the English Ceramic Circle*, 4 (1937), pp. 12–22. See, for an example, Victoria and Albert Museum, no. 310:4–1889.
228. Ray, 'Delftware', p. 306.
229. The history of consumption (recently an industry in studies of the eighteenth century) has largely ignored the seventeenth century.
230. Along with his biographers, I also argue William's lack of popularity; but, despite the absence of statues in his honour, the evidence of everyday material objects, which awaits a full

investigation, raises large questions about the relationship between consumption and perceptions of monarchy.

231. D. Piper, *The English Face* (London, 1978), ch. VI; see H. Dunthorne, 'William in Contemporary Portraits and Prints', in E. Myjers and D. Onnekirk eds, *Refiguring William III: The Impact of the King-Stadtholder in International Context* (Aldershot, 2003), pp. 263–76; S. Schama, 'The Domestication of Majesty: Royal Family Portraiture, 1500–1850', *Journal of Interdisciplinary History*, 17 (1986), pp. 155–83.
232. Dunthorne, 'William in Contemporary Portraits', p. 276.

11 A King off the Stage

1. See K. Sharpe, *Selling the Tudor Monarchy: Authority and Image in Sixteenth-Century England* (New Haven, CT, and London, 2009), pp. 63–4.
2. K. Sharpe, *Image Wars: Promoting Kings and Commonwealths in England 1603–1660* (New Haven, CT, and London, 2010), pp. 93–9.
3. Above, ch. 7, pp. 287–95; T. Harris, *Revolution: The Great Crisis of the British Monarchy, 1685–1725* (London, 2005), pp. 48–9.
4. *A True and Exact Relation of the Prince of Orange His Publick Entrance into Exeter* (Wing T2458, 1688).
5. *Great News from Salisbury, the Sixth of December 1688* (Wing G1729A, 1688), broadside.
6. *News from White-Hall, Being an Account of the Arrival of the High and Mighty Prince William Henry of Orange and Naffaw, at St. James's. With the King's Retirement down the River* (Wing N1026B, 1688).
7. *A True Account of His Highness the Prince of Orange's Coming to St. James's, on Tuesday the 18th of December 1688* (Wing T2335C, 1688), one page.
8. *A Proclamation. Whereas It Hath Pleased Almighty God in His Great Mercy to this Kingdom, to Vouchsafe Us a Miraculous Deliverance from Popery and Arbitrary Power* (Wing E2200C, 1689).
9. *The Manner of the Proclaiming of King William, and Queen Mary, at White-Hall, and in the City of London, Feb. 13, 1688/9* (Wing M476A, 1689), one page.
10. *By the King and Queen, a Proclamation in Order to Their Majesties Intended Coronation* (Wing W2613, 1689).
11. L. Schwoerer, 'The Coronation of William and Mary, April 11, 1689', in Schwoerer ed., *The Revolution of 1688: Changing Perspectives* (Cambridge, 1992), pp. 107–30, quotation, p. 109.
12. Schwoerer, 'The Coronation of William and Mary'; Sharpe, *Selling the Tudor Monarchy*, p. 419–23.
13. Schwoerer, 'The Coronation of William and Mary', p. 117.
14. Ibid., p. 123.
15. *The Form of Prayers and Services Used in Westminster-Abby at the Coronation of the Kings and Queens of England with an Account of the Procession from the Palace to the Abby* (Wing C4179, 1689).
16. J. Ogilby, *The King's Coronation Truly Described in the Exact Narrative of the Coronation of King Charles II* (Wing O176A, 1689).
17. *The Form of the Proceeding to the Coronation of Their Majesties King William and Queen Mary, the Eleventh Day of this Instant April, 1689* (Wing F1580, 1689).
18. Ibid.; see also *An Exact Account of the Ceremonial at the Coronation of Their Most Excellent Majesties King William and Queen Mary, the Eleventh Day of this Instant April, 1689* (Wing E3565, 1689), p. 2 and *passim*.
19. Ibid., p. 3; see also State Papers William and Mary, I, 18.
20. *An Exact Account*, p. 3; G. Burnet, *A Sermon Preached at the Coronation of William III and Mary II* (Wing B5888, 1689).
21. *An Exact Account*, p. 3.
22. *A Description of the Ceremonial Proceedings at the Coronation of Their Most Sacred Majesties, King William III. and Queen Mary II. Who Were Crowned at Westminster-Abby, on Thursday the 11th. of April, 1689* (Wing D1154A, 1689).
23. Schwoerer, 'The Coronation of William and Mary', pp. 107, 126–7.
24. *News from Bath Being a True and Perfect Relation of the Great and Splendid Procession, and Joyful Transactions there, on the 11th day of April, Being the Coronation-day of Their Most Sacred Majesties William and Mary* (Wing N948, 1689), one sheet.
25. Harris, *Revolution*, p. 355.
26. S. Baxter, *William III* (London, 1966), p. 248.

27. P. MacCubbin and M. Hamilton-Phillips eds, *The Age of William III & Mary II: Power, Politics, and Patronage, 1688–1702* (Williamsburg, VA, 1989), p. 39.
28. Above, ch. 10, pp. 442–3.
29. *An Exact Relation of the Entertainment of His Most Sacred Majesty William III. King of England, Scotland, France and Ireland; Hereditary Stadtholder of the United Netherlands, &c. At the Hague. Giving a Particular Description of His Majesty's Entry There, Jan. 26. 1690/1 and of the Several Triumphant Arches, Pyramids, Pictures, &c. with the Inscriptions and Devices* (Wing E3688, 1691).
30. Ibid., pp. 22–5.
31. J. Beek, *The Triumph-royal Containing a Short Account of the Most Remarkable Battels, Sieges, Sea-fights, Treaties, and Famous Atchievements of the Princes of the House of Nassau &c. Describ'd in the Triumphal Arches, Piramids, Pictures, Inscriptions, and Devices Erected at the Hague in Honour of William III* (Wing B1686, 1691).
32. Ibid., sig. A2.
33. Ibid., sig. A2^v.
34. Ibid., sigs A4–A4^v.
35. *A Description of the Most Glorious and Most Magnificent Arches Erected at The Hague for the Reception of William III, King of Great Britain with all the Motto's and Latin Inscriptions that Were Written upon Every One of the Said Arches/Translated into English from the Dutch* (Wing D1163, 1691).
36. Beek, *The Triumph-royal*, p. 28.
37. Ibid., pp. 43, 61, 77.
38. Ibid., fig. LVIII, pp. 78–9.
39. Ibid., p. 39.
40. Ibid., sig. A4.
41. There appears to be an allusion to the contrast between Dutch celebrations and the absence of them in England, ibid., p. 44.
42. R. Steele, *The Procession A Poem on Her Majesties Funeral* (Wing S5381, 1695), p. 8; cf. P. Gleane, *A Poem, Occasioned by the Magnificent Proceeding to the Funeral of Her Late Majesty Queen Mary II of Blessed Memory* (Wing G848A, 1695), p. 10.
43. *The Form of the Proceeding to the Funeral of Her late Majesty Queen Mary II. Of Blessed Memory, from the Royal Palace of Whitehall to the Collegiate Church at Westminster* (Wing F1582B, 1695).
44. Gleane, *A Poem*, sig. A2^v, pp. 7, 11, 15; D. Defoe, *The Life of that Incomparable Princess, Mary, Our Late Sovereign Lady, of Ever Blessed Memory Who Departed this Life, at Her Royal Pallace at Kensington, the 28th of December, 1694* (Wing L2036, 1695), pp. 78–9.
45. N. Tate, *Mausolaeum, a Funeral Poem on Our Late Gracious Sovereign Queen Mary of Blessed Memory by N. Tate* (Wing T194, 1695).
46. J. Howe, *A Discourse Relating to the Much-lamented Death and Solemn Funeral of Our Incomparable and Most Gracious Queen Mary* (Wing H3023, 1695), pp. 1–2.
47. *The Queene Leying in State Who Departed this Life the 28 day of December 1694 to the Great Greefe of all Good Subiects* (Wing Q153, 1695).
48. *The Mourning Court, or, The Solemn Representation of the Royal Funeral of that Most Illustrious Princess Mar[y], Late Queen of England, Scotland, France, and Ireland, &c. Who Changed this Earthly Crown for a More Glorious and Celestial Diadem on the 28th of December, 1694, and Was Interred in King Hen[ry's] chappel at Westminster, on the 5th of March 1695* (Wing M2991A, 1695), broadside.
49. *The Royal Funeral, or, The Mourning State and Solemnity of the Funeral of Mary, Queen of England* (Wing R2129B, 1695).
50. L. Schwoerer, 'Images of Queen Mary II, 1689–1694', *Renaissance Quarterly*, 42 (1989), p. 741.
51. Ibid.
52. T. Tension, *A Sermon Preached at the Funeral of Her Late Majesty Queen Mary of Ever Blessed Memory, in the Abbey-Church in Westminster, upon March 5. 1694/5 by His Grace Thomas Lord Arch-Bishop of Canterbury* (Wing T721, 1695), p. 17; Defoe, *The Life of that Incomparable Princess, Mary*, p. 73.
53. Baxter, *William III*, p. 330.
54. Ibid., pp. 333, 337.
55. *Calendar of State Papers Domestic, 1697*, p. 387.
56. Ibid.
57. Ibid., p. 408.
58. Ibid.
59. Ibid., p. 419.
60. Ibid., pp. 432, 441.

61. Ibid., pp. 448–9.
62. Baxter, *William III*, p. 359.
63. G. Burnet, *Bishop Burnet's History of His Own Time* (ESTC T014875, 6 vols, 1724–34), IV, p. 393; M. Routh ed., *Bishop Burnet's History of His Own Time* (6 vols, Oxford, 1833), IV, p. 373.
64. *Calendar of State Papers Domestic, 1697*, p. 432.
65. Ibid., p. 459.
66. *An Account of His Most Excellent Majesty's Splendid Reception into the Famous City of London Together with His Royal Entertainment in and through the Said City, on Tuesday the 16th of this Instant November, 1697* (Wing A204B, 1697), one page.
67. I. Crew, *A Speech Spoken by Isaac Crew an Orphan of the Grammar-school in Christ's-Hospital; To His Majesty King William III. In His Passage through the City of London, Nov. 16. 1697* (Wing C6906, 1697), quotation, p. 2.
68. Ibid., pp. 1–2.
69. *An Account of His Most Excellent Majesty's Splendid Reception.*
70. *Calendar of State Papers Domestic, 1697*, pp. 474–5.
71. Ibid., p. 475.
72. E. N. P., *To the King, on His Peaceable Return, and Magnificent Entry into London By E. N. P* (Wing P20B, 1697), p. 7.
73. *Calendar of State Papers Domestic, 1697*, p. 474.
74. M. Routh ed., *Bishop Burnet's History*, IV, p. 373.
75. *Calendar of State Papers Domestic, 1697*, pp. 477–8.
76. M. Toynbee, 'Sir James Thornhill's Collection', *Burlington Magazine*, 83 (1943), pp. 257–8. From Kneller's state portrait on, William is depicted on canvas and in prints wearing the greater George.
77. E. Ashmole, *The History of the Most Noble Order of the Garter* (ESTC T140592, 1715, p. 539). This is a continuation of Ashmole by an editor.
78. *Calendar of State Papers Domestic, 1696*, p. 293.
79. *Calendar of State Papers Domestic, 1698*, p. 341.
80. *Calendar of State Papers Domestic, 1690–1*, p. 468.
81. *Calendar of State Papers Domestic, 1691–2*, pp. 476–9; *Calendar of State Papers Domestic, 1693*, p. 89.
82. For example, *Calendar of State Papers Domestic, 1689–90*, p. 285.
83. Baxter, *William III*, p. 333.
84. S. van Raaij and P. Spies, *The Royal Progress of William & Mary* (Amsterdam, 1988), p. 133.
85. Ibid.
86. *The Royal Progress; or, A Diary of the King's Journey from His Majesty's Setting Out from Kensington, till His Return* (Wing R2143A, 1695).
87. Robert Spencer, 2nd Earl Sunderland, *ODNB*; see J. P. Kenyon, *Robert Spencer, Earl of Sunderland, 1641–1702* (London, 1958).
88. *The Royal Progress*, p. 5.
89. Ibid., pp. 5–6.
90. Van Raaij and Spies, *The Royal Progress of William & Mary*, p. 137.
91. Ibid., p. 138; *The Royal Progress*, p. 8.
92. Van Raaij and Spies, *The Royal Progress of William & Mary*, pp. 138–9; Newcastle spent £5,612 on the entertainment.
93. Ibid., p. 140; *The Royal Progress*, p. 10.
94. *The Royal Progress*, p. 11.
95. Ibid., pp. 12–13.
96. Ibid., p. 13.
97. Van Raaij and Spies, *The Royal Progress of William & Mary*, p. 141.
98. Ibid.
99. *Royal Progresss*, p. 13; see *Calendar of State Papers Domestic, 1695*, p. 86.
100. Van Raaij and Spies, *The Royal Progress of William & Mary*, p. 144.
101. *Royal Progress*, p. 14.
102. Ibid., p. 15; *Calendar of State Papers Domestic, 1695*, p. 95.
103. Van Raaij and Spies, *The Royal Progress of William & Mary*, p. 145.
104. *Royal Progress*, p. 16.
105. T. Claydon, *William III: Profiles in Power* (Harlow, 2002), p. 44.
106. See R. Sherwood, *The Court of Oliver Cromwell* (London, 1977); cf. Sherwood, *Oliver Cromwell: King in All But Name, 1653–1658* (Stroud, 1997); G. Aylmer, *The State's Servants: The Civil Service of the English Republic, 1649–1660* (London, 1973).

107. J. Sainty and R. Bucholz eds, *Officials of the Royal Household, 1660–1837* (London, 1997), pp. liii–lviii; see also G. Aylmer, *The Crown's Servants: Government and the Civil Service under Charles II, 1660–1685* (Oxford, 2002); A. Keay, *The Magnificent Monarch: Charles II and the Ceremonies of Power* (London, 2008).

108. Above, ch. 7, pp. 298–9. James reduced his household from 1,160 to 780; Sainty and Bucholz eds, *Officials of the Royal Household*, p. lxx.

109. Ibid., p. lx.

110. Ibid., p. lxi.

111. C. Roberts, 'The Constitutional Significance of the Financial Settlement of 1690', *Historical Journal*, 20 (1977), pp. 59–76.

112. Sainty and Bucholz eds, *Officials of the Royal Household*, p.lxiii.

113. Ibid., p. lxi; cf. A. Barclay, 'William's Court as King', in E. Mijers and D. Onnekirk eds, *Refiguring William III: The Impact of the King-Stadtholder in International Context* (Aldershot, 2007), pp. 241–61.

114. Sainty and Bucholz eds, *Officials of the Royal Household*, p.lxi; see *A Collection of Ordinances and Regulations for the Government of the Royal household, Made in Divers Reigns. From King Edward III to King William and Queen Mary* (ESTC T091228, 1790), pp. 380–465.

115. *A Collection of Ordinances*, pp. 418–20.

116. T. Claydon, *William III and the Godly Revolution* (Cambridge, 1996), pp. 93–4.

117. Ibid., p. 92.

118. Below, ch. 12, pp. 488–9.

119. N. Stratford, *Of the Reverence Due to God in His Publick Worship a Sermon Preach'd before the King & Queen, at White-Hall, March 25, 1694* (Wing S5937, 1694), p. 13. Stratford was Bishop of Chester.

120. P. Warwick, *A Discourse of Government as Examined by Reason, Scripture, and Law of the Land* (Wing W991, 1694), p. 76.

121. *A Collection of Ordinances*, p. 418; *Calendar of State Papers Domestic, 1700–1702*, p. 119; D. Doebner, *Memoirs of Mary Queen of England* (1886), *passim*.

122. R. Bucholz, *The Augustan Court: Queen Anne and the Decline of Court Culture* (Stanford, CA, 1993), p. 34.

123. W. Troost, *William III, The Stadholder-king: a Political Biography* (Aldershot, 2005), pp. 215–16; see also E. and M. Grew, *The Court of William III* (London, 1910).

124. Bucholz, *The Augustan Court*, p. 30; Claydon, *William III: Profiles*, p. 44.

125. *Calendar of State Papers Domestic 1689–90*, p. 407; *Calendar of State Papers Domestic 1698*, p. 413; *Calendar of State Papers Domestic, 1699–1700*, pp. 163, 194, 203.

126. For example, Doebner, *Memoirs of Mary Queen of England*, p. 16.

127. *Calendar of State Papers Domestic, 1690–1*, p. 106.

128. Doebner, *Memoirs of Mary Queen of England*, p. 11.

129. Ibid., pp. 29, 36–7, 95 and *passim*.

130. Queen Mary, *ODNB*.

131. R. Gould, *A Poem Most Humbly Offered to the Memory of Her Late Sacred Majesty* (Wing G1429, 1695), p. 10.

132. Above ch. 3, pp. 167–8.

133. Barclay, 'William's Court as King'.

134. T. B. Macaulay, *The History of England, from the Accession of James the Second*, ed. C. H. Firth (6 vols, Oxford, 1914), IV, p. 1,746.

135. *Encyclopaedia Britannica*, 11th edn, vol. 15, p. 817.

136. Bucholz, *Augustan Court*, p. 34.

137. G. Miege, *The New State of England under Their Majesties K. William and Q. Mary in Three Parts* (Wing M2019, 1691), part II, p. 148; E. Bohun, *The Character of Queen Elizabeth* (Wing B3448, 1693), p. 344.

138. See J. Brewer, *The Pleasures of the Imagination: English Culture in the Eighteenth Century* (London, 1997), ch. 1; T. C. Blanning, *Culture of Power and the Power of Culture: Old Regime Europe 1660–1789* (Oxford, 2002), introduction.

139. J. Spurr, *The Restoration Church of England, 1646–1689* (New Haven, CT, and London, 1991), p. 101.

140. C. Rose, *England in the 1690s: Revolution, Religion and War* (Oxford, 1999), p. 157.

141. Ibid., p. 159.

142. Ibid., p. 164.

143. Ibid., pp. 168–70.

144. Spurr, *Restoration Church*, p. 379.
145. Rose, *England in the 1690s*, p. 190.
146. She followed Anglican services when living in the Low Countries; Mary, *ODNB*.
147. Claydon, *William III; Profiles*, pp. 104–5.
148. F. Atterbury, *A Letter to a Convocation-man, Concerning the Rights, Powers, and Priviledges of that Body* (Wing S3652, 1697). On Atterbury, see G. Bennett, *The Tory Crisis in Church and State, 1688–1730: The Career of Francis Atterbury, Bishop of Rochester* (Oxford, 1975).
149. Rose, *England in the 1690s*, pp. 192–3.
150. Claydon, *William III; Profiles*, p. 105. See J. Israel, 'William III and Toleration', in O. Grell, J. Israel and N. Tyacke eds, *From Persecution to Toleration: The Glorious Revolution and Religion in England* (Oxford, 1991), pp. 129–70.
151. T. Browne, *A Congratulatory Poem on His Majesty's Happy Return from Holland* (Wing B5055, 1691), p. 4; Miege, *The New State of England*, II, pp. 66–7.
152. Claydon, *William III; Profiles*, p. 104.
153. Rose, *England in the 1690s*, p. 172; C. Leslie, *Querela temporum, or, The Danger of the Church of England* (Wing L1142, 1694).
154. See, for example, E. Stillingfleet, *A Sermon Preached before the King & Queen at White-Hall on Christmas-Day, 1693 by the Right Reverend Father in God, Edward Lord Bishop of Worcester* (Wing S5665, 1694); T. Sprat, *A Sermon Preached before the King and Queen, at Whitehall, on Good-Friday, April 6, 1694. By the Ld. Bishop of Rochester, Dean of Westminster* (Wing S5063A, 1694).
155. J. Swynfen, *A Sermon Preached at St. Paul's Covent-Garden upon Sunday the Second of December, 1694* (Wing S6289A, 1695), pp. 25–6.
156. Ibid., p. 28.
157. See *The History of the Troubles and Tryal of the Most Reverend Father in God and Blessed Martyr, William Laud, Lord Arch-Bishop of Canterbury* (2 vols, Wing L586, L596, 1695). The year 1695 also saw the publication of George Herbert's sacred poems, *The Temple: Sacred Poems and Private Ejaculations* (Wing H1524,1695).
158. Below, ch. 15, pp. 635–6.
159. Cf. Tillotson's pessimism about the prospect of peace; Rose, *England in the 1690s*, p. 171.
160. Above, ch. 7, p. 303.
161. 1 Will. & Mar. sess. 2 c. 2. This is the full title of what is referred to often as the Bill of Rights, 1689, *Statutes of the Realm* (11 vols, 1810–25), VI, pp. 142–5.
162. Above, ch. 7, pp. 301–3.
163. See John Ashton (1653–1691), *ODNB*.
164. Richard, Viscount Preston, *The Arraignment, Trials, Conviction and Condemnation of Sir Rich. Grahme and John Ashton, Gent. for High Treason against ... King William and Queen Mary at the Sessions ... Holden ... on the 16th, 17th and 19th Days of January, 1690* (Wing A3768, 1690).
165. *A True Account of All Passages at the Execution of John Ashton, Gent Publish'd by Authority* (Wing T2335aA, 1691), p. 1.
166. Ibid., p. 2; *A Copy of Mr. Ashton's Paper, Delivered to the Sheriff at the Place of Execution, January 28, 1690/1* (Wing A3991, 1691), one sheet, two pages.
167. E. Fowler, *An Answer to the Paper Delivered by Mr. Ashton at His Execution to Sir Francis Child ... Together with the Paper Itself* (Wing F1695, 1691). The Answer is thirty-one pages. Fowler, *ODNB*.
168. See *A True Copy of Part of that Paper which Mr. Ashton Left in a Friend's Hands together with the Letter in which He Sent It Enclosed* (Wing A3992, 1691); C. Lawton, *The Vindication of the Dead: or, Six Hours Reflections upon the Six Weeks Labour in Answering Mr. Ashton's Speech Published by Authority* (Wing L739E, 1691), p. 1. Lawton's title mocks the length of the official answer to Ashton's paper. His *Vindication* went to a second edition (Wing S2276aA, 1692).
169. Lawton, *The Vindication*, p. 2.
170. *An Elegy upon the Death of Major John Ashton Who Was Executed for High-treason on Wednesday, the 28th of January, 1691, at Tyburn* (Wing E465A, 1691), broadside.
171. William Anderton (1663–1693), *ODNB*.
172. *An Account of the Conversation, Behaviour and Execution of William Anderton, Printer Who Was Condemned at the Old Baily, on Thursday the 8th of June, for High Treason, and Executed for the Same, at Tybourn on Friday the 16th of June, 1693* (Wing A266, 1693), broadside.
173. *True Copy of the Paper Delivered to the Sheriffs of London and Middlesex by Mr. William Anderton at the Place of Execution, which He Designed there to Have Spoken, but Being Frequently Interrupted*

by the Ordinary, Mr. Samuel Smith, Desired the Said Sheriffs to Publish or Dispose of It as They Should Think Fit, Seeing a Dying Man Was Not Suffered to Speak (Wing A3113, 1693), one page. The last words of the title suggest how the convention of last dying words, which offered opportunities for subversion, was not easily denied.

174. S. Grascome, An Appeal of Murther from Certain Unjust Judges, Lately Sitting at the Old Baily to the Righteous Judge of Heaven and Earth; and to All Sensible English-men, Containing a Relation of the Tryal, Behaviour, and Death of Mr. William Anderton, Executed June 16. 1693. at Tyburn, for Pretended High Treason (Wing G1566, 1693), p. 4; on Grascome, see ODNB.

175. Ibid., p. 28.

176. The Arraignment, Tryal, and Condemnation of Sir John Friend, Knight for High Treason in Endeavouring to Procure Forces from France to Invade this Kingdom and Conspiring to Levy War in this Realm for Assisting and Abetting the Said Invasion, in order to the Deposing of His Sacred Majesty King William, and Restoring the Late King (Wing A3759, 1696), p. 4.

177. The Arraignment, Tryal, and Condemnation of Peter Cooke, Gent. for High-treason, in Endeavouring to Procure Forces from France to Invade this Kingdom (Wing A3757, 1696), p. 71; The Arraignments, Tryals and Condemnations of Charles Cranburne and Robert Lowick for the Horrid and Execrable Conspiracy to Assassinate His Sacred Majesty King William (Wing A3767, 1696), pp. 16, 71.

178. An Account of the Tryal and Conviction of Sir John Friend, for High-treason in Conspiring the Death of His Most Sacred Majesty, King William, and the Subvertion of the Government (Wing A412, 1696), one sheet; T. Percival, The Rye-house Travestie, or, A True Account and Declaration of the Horrid and Execrable Conspiracy Against His Majesty King William and the Government (Wing P1454A, 1696), p. 5. On Friend's and other trials, see J. Garrett, The Triumphs of Providence: The Assassination Plot, 1696 (Cambridge, 1980), part III.

179. Percival, The Rye-house Travestie, pp. 9, 13.

180. Remarks on the Papers Delivered by Sir William Perkins, and Sir John Friend, Kts. at the Place of their Execution (Wing R934, 1696), p. 5.

181. T. Percival, A True and Exact Account of the Rise, Progress, and Contrivance of the Horrid Plot and Conspiracy against the Life of His Most Sacred Majesty King William the Third (Wing P1454B, 1697), pp. 9, 76; The Arraignments, Tryals and Condemnations of Charles Cranburne and Robert Lowick, p. 13.

182. The Last Dying Speech and Behaviour of Capt. Thomas Vaughan Who Was Executed for High-treason, at Execution-dock, on Wednesday, Decemb. the 9th. 1696 (Wing V155, 1696), p. 2.

183. A True Account of the Dying Behaviour of Ambrose Rookwood, Charles Cranburne, and Major Lowick Who Were Executed at Tyburn for High Treason on Wednesday, April 29: with Mr. Cranburn's Speech at the Place of Execution (Wing T2365A, 1696), broadside.

184. Observations upon the Papers Which Mr. Rookwood and Mr. Lowick Deliver'd to the Sheriffs at the Time of Their Execution, April 29, 1696 together with Remarks upon Some Part of Mr. Cranburn's Discourse with the Sheriffs at the Same Time (Wing O123A, 1696), p. 3 and passim.

185. Ibid., p. 16.

186. Ibid., p. 14.

187. Ibid., p. 11.

188. Baxter, William III, p. 337; Remarks on the Papers Delivered by Sir William Perkins, and Sir John Friend, p. 8.

189. The Character of His Royal Highness, William Henry, Prince of Orange. With Allowance (Wing C2017A, 1689).

190. Ibid., p. 7.

191. Ibid.

192. D. Pead, Greatness and Goodness Reprieve Not From Death. A Sermon Occasion'd by the Death of ... William the Third ... Preach'd April the 19th, 1702 (ESTC T 035865, 1702), p. 19.

193. Ibid., p. 20.

194. Baxter, William III, p. 148.

195. Routh ed., Bishop Burnet's History of His Own Time, IV, p. 152.

196. Rose, England in the 1690s, p. 19; Baxter, William III, p. 148.

197. A. Boyer, The History of King William the Third. In III Parts (ESTC T091241, 3 vols, 1702–3), III, p. 519; Baxter, William III, p. 205; Elizabeth Villiers, ODNB.

198. Burnet described her as 'the most universally lamented princess of any person in our age', Routh ed., Bishop Burnet's History of His Own Time, IV, pp. 248–9.

199. Above, ch. 11, p. 468.

200. Routh ed., Bishop Burnet's History of His Own Time, IV, p. 152.

201. W. Sherlock, *A Sermon Preach'd at the Temple-Church, December 30, 1694, upon the Sad Occasion of the Death of Our Gracious Queen ... by William Sherlock* (Wing S3356, 1694), pp. 19–20.
202. T. Tenison, *A Sermon Preached at the Funeral of Her Late Majesty Queen Mary of Ever Blessed Memory in the Abbey-church in Westminster upon March 5, 1694/5* (Wing T721, 1695), p. 17.
203. Cf. Rose, *England in the 1690s*, p. 47.
204. Baxter, *William III*, pp. 380–1.
205. *A Sermon Preach'd on the Occasion of the Death of Our Late Sovereign King William III. of Glorious Memory* (ESTC T094637, 1702), p. 17.
206. Baxter, *William III*, p. 398; Claydon, *William III and the Godly Revolution*, pp. 233–4; Claydon, *William III: Profiles*, pp. 188–9; S. Pincus, *1688: The First Modern Revolution* (New Haven, CT, and London, 2009).

12 Rival Representations

1. See K. Sharpe, *Selling the Tudor Monarchy: Authority and Image in Sixteenth-Century England* (New Haven, CT, and London, 2009), and Sharpe, *Image Wars; Promoting Kings and Commonwealths in England, 1603–1660* (New Haven, CT, and London, 2010).
2. M. Knights, *Representation and Misrepresentation in Later Stuart Britain: Partisanship and Political Culture* (Oxford, 2004), p. 24.
3. T. Long, *A Resolution of Certain Queries Concerning Submission to the Present Government ... by a Divine of the Church of England* (Wing L2980, 1689), sig. A2ᵛ.
4. J. Hartcliffe, *A Sermon Preached Before the Honourable House of Commons, at St. Margaret Westminster, on the Thirtieth of January, 1694/5* (Wing H970, 1695), pp. 8, 25.
5. W. Bewick, *A Sermon Preached at Hexham in Northumberland, upon the Publick Occasion and Fast, Being the 26th of June, 1696* (Wing B2193A, 1696), pp. 18–19.
6. R. Astbury, 'The Renewal of the Licensing Act in 1693 and its lapse in 1695', *The Library*, 33 (1978), pp. 296–322.
7. E. Ward, *The School of Politicks, or, The Humours of a Coffee-house a Poem* (Wing W753B, 1691), pp. 3, 13.
8. Ibid., p. 29.
9. *The History of the Late Revolution in England* (Wing H2166aA, 1689), sigs A2, A4; *Vota Oxoniensia pro serenissimis Guilhelmo rege et Maria regina M. Britanniae &c. nuncupata quibus accesserunt Panegyrica oratio & carmina gratulatoria, comitiis in Theatro Sheldoniano habitis, ipso inaugurationis die XI april, MDCLXXXIX* (Oxford, 1689), sigs Y2ᵛ, Z3.
10. J. Tillotson, *A Sermon Preached at St Mary le Bow Before the Lord Mayor, Court of Aldermen, & Citizens of London, on Wednesday the 18th of June, a Day Appointed by Their Majesties, for a Solemn Monthly Fast* (Wing T1242, 1690), pp. 28–9.
11. S. Slater, *A Sermon Preached on the Thanksgiving Day the 27 day of October, 1692* (Wing S3974, 1693), pp. 8, 31.
12. [D. Defoe], *A Dialogue Betwixt Whig and Tory, aliàs Williamite and Jacobite* (Wing D1361, 1693), p. 1; cf. Defoe, *The Englishman's Choice, and True Interest in a Vigorous Prosecution of the War against France, and Serving K. William and Q. Mary, and Acknowledging their Right* (Wing D831, 1694).
13. R. Fleming, *The Present Aspect of Our Times and of the Extraordinary Conjunction of Things* (Wing F1270, 1694), p. 3.
14. W. Pudsey, *A Political Essay, or, Summary Review of the Kings and Government of England* (Wing P4172, 1698), sig. A6.
15. R. Gould, *A Poem Most Humbly Offered to the Memory of Her Late Sacred Majesty, Queen Mary* (Wing G1429, 1695), p. 9; on Gould, see *ODNB*.
16. V. Alsop, *Duty and Interest United in Prayer and Praise for Kings and All That Are in Authority from I Tim. II. 1,2: Being a Sermon Preach'd at Westminster upon the Late Day of Thanksgiving, Sept. 8, 1695* (Wing A2908, 1695), p. 16; cf. S. Carte, *A Dissuasive from Murmuring Being a Sermon on 1 Cor. X. 10. Preached by Sam. Carte ... May 14. 1694* (Wing C651C, 1694), p. 18: 'what a world of discontent reigns among us'.
17. E. Corp, *The King Over The Water: Portraits of the Stuarts in Exile after 1689* (Scottish National Portrait Gallery, Edinburgh, 2001).
18. *A Full and True Relation of the Death of K. James Who Departed this Life, the 27th of March* (Wing F2320, 1689).

19. *His Majesties Late Letter in Vindication of Himself Dated at St. Germans en Laye, the Fourteenth of this Instant January, 1688/9* (Wing J196, 1689); *His Majesties Letter from St. Germans to the Convention* (Wing J199, 1689).

20. The letter was printed with 'Remarks', pp. 3-4.

21. *His Majesties Letter to Sundry of the Lords, and Others of His Majesties Most Honourable Privy Council, Calling them to Be Witnesses of the Queens Labour* (Wing J204, 1692).

22. *His Majesties Most Gracious Declaration to All His Loving Subjects Commanding their Assistance against the Prince of Orange, and His Adherents* (Wing J216, 1692); *His Majesties Most Gracious Declaration to All His Loving Subjects* (Wing J217A, 1693).

23. *His Majesties Most Gracious Declaration to All His Loving Subjects Commanding their Assistance* [not paginated].

24. James II, *Royal Tracts in Two Parts: the First, Containing all the Select Speeches, Orders, Messages, Letters, &c. of His Sacred Majesty, upon Extraordinary Occasions, Both Before, and Since His Retiring out of England: the Second, Containing Imago Regis, or, The Sacred Image of His Majesty, in His Solitudes and Sufferings, Written During His Retirements in France* (Wing J384, 1692).

25. W. Sherlock, *A Second Letter to a Friend, Concerning the French Invasion in which the Declaration Lately Dispersed under the Title of His Majesty's Most Gracious Declaration to All His Loving Subjects, Commanding their Assistance against the P. of Orange and His Adherents, Is Entirely and Exactly Published, According to the Dispersed Copies: with some Short Observations upon It* (Wing S3339, 1692). This response carried Nottingham's imprimatur; on Sherlock, see *ODNB*.

26. Ibid., pp. 17-19, reveals an anxiety about the response; on Milton's *Eikonoklastes*, see Sharpe, *Image Wars*, pp. 400-3.

27. *The Charge of the Right Honourable Henry Earl of Warrington to the Grand Jury at the Quarter Sessions Held for the County of Chester on the 11th of October, 1692* (Wing D874, 1693), p. 3 and *passim*. Booth himself later advocated the restoration of James, see *ODNB* and M. Knights, 'Uncovering a Jacobite Whig? The Commonwealth Principles of Henry Booth, 1st Earl of Warrington', *Parliamentary History*, 28 (2009), pp. 59-87.

28. *Jacobus Secundus, Dei gratiâ, magnae Britanniae, Franciae & Hiberniae Rex, defensor fidei, omnibus regibus principibus, rebuspublicis &c. postqàm diuturno tamque funesto toti Christianae reipublicae bello Europa conflagravit* (Wing J152, 1697); *The Late King James's Second Manifesto, Directed to the Protestant Princes, Answer'd Paragraph by Paragraph* (Wing L553, 1697).

29. *The Late King James's Second Manifesto*, p. 5.

30. Ibid., p. 14.

31. T. Oates, *Eikon vasilike tetarte, or, The Picture of the Late King James Further Drawn to the Life* (Wing O40, 1697), p. 188.

32. See P. Monod, *Jacobitism and the English People, 1688-1788* (Cambridge, 1989).

33. J. Collier, *The Desertion Discuss'd in a Letter to a Country Gentleman* (Wing C5249, 1689), p. 1 and *passim*.

34. C. Lawton, *The Jacobite Principles Vindicated in Answer to a Letter Sent to the Author* (Wing L739C, 1693), quotation, p. 24.

35. A. Irvine, *A Dialogue Between A. and B. Two Plain Countrey-gentlemen, Concerning the Times* (Wing I1050, 1694).

36. *A Reply to the Answer Doctor Welwood Has Made to King James's Declaration which Declaration was Dated at St. Germaines, April 17th, S.N., 1693* (Wing R1066, 1694), p. 42; Welwood, *An Answer to the Late K. James's Last Declaration*.

37. R. Ferguson, *Whether the Parliament Be Not in Law Dissolved by the Death of the Princess of Orange? and How the Subjects Ought, and Are to Behave Themselves in Relation to those Papers Emitted Since by the Stile and Title of Acts: with a Brief Account of the Government of England: in a Letter to a Country Gentleman* (Wing F765, 1695). Ferguson probably became a Jacobite, *ODNB*.

38. *The Fidelity of a Loyal Subject, of the Kingdom of England: or, An Honest Act of Fidelity to King James, King William, and the Whole Kingdom* (Wing F848, 1698), quotation, p. 2.

39. See K. Sharpe, 'Whose Life Is It Anyway? Writing Early Modern Monarchs and the "Life" of James II', in K. Sharpe and S. Zwicker eds, *Writing Lives: Biography and Textuality, Identity and Representation in Early Modern England* (Oxford, 2008), pp. 233-52.

40. *A Collection of the Several Addresses in the Late King James's Time Concerning the Conception and Birth of the Pretended Prince of Wales* (Wing C5208, 1700); W. Pittis, *Chaucer's Whims: Being Some Select Fables and Tales in Verse, Very Applicable to the Present Times* (ESTC T075499, 1701), p. 2.

41. *On the Tenth of June, MDCCI. Being the Birth-day of his Royal Highness the Prince of Wales* (ESTC T004464, 1701), p. 1.

42. For example, *An Ode on the Death of the Late King James* (ESTC N010449, 1701); *On the Death of King James. By a Lady* (ESTC T058163, 1701); *An Impartial Account of the Life and Actions, of James the Second, Late King of England* (ESTC N007676, 1701).

43. *The Memoirs of King James II. Containing An Account of the Transactions of the Last Twelve Years of His life: with the Circumstances of his Death* (ESTC T039127, 1702); *The Last Dying-Words of the Late King James to His Son and Daughter, and the French King* (ESTC N010923, 1701), one page.

44. *Last Dying Words.*

45. *A Letter to a Minister of State, Concerning the Pretended Prince of Wales's Being Proclaim'd King of England* (ESTC T038069, 1701).

46. *A View of Paris, and Places Adjoining. With an Account of the Court of France; and of the Late King James* (ESTC T063177, 1701), p. 65; G. Hickes, *The Pretences of the Prince of Wales Examin'd, and Rejected. In a Letter to a Friend in the Country* (ESTC T055755, 1701). On Hickes, see *ODNB*.

47. E. Ghest, *An Impartial Disquisition, How Far Conquest Gives the Conqueror a Title* (Wing G634, 1688).

48. *The Price of the Abdication* (Wing P3403, 1693), p. 2.

49. Ibid., p. 1.

50. *An Enquiry into the Nature and Obligation of Legal Rights with Respect to the Popular Pleas of the Late K. James's Remaining Right to the Crown* (Wing I218, 1693), p. 3.

51. *Antiquity Reviv'd: Or The Government of a Certain Island Antiently Call'd Astreada in Reference to Religion, Policy, War and Peace Some Hundreds of Years before the Coming of Christ* (Wing A3510, 1693), p. 56.

52. E. Stillingfleet, *The Case of an Oath of Abjuration Considered and the Vote of the Honourable House of Commons Vindicated in a Letter* (Wing S5564, 1693), p. 30.

53. H. Day, *A Thanksgiving-sermon Preach'd at Sutton in Surrey, April the 16th, 1696 Being the National Thanksgiving Day for His Majesty's Most Happy Preservation from the Most Detestable Assassination, in order to a French Invasion* (Wing H463, 1694), p. 13.

54. W. Atwood, *Reflections upon a Treasonable Opinion, Industriously Promoted, against Signing the National Association and the Entring into It Prov'd to Be the Duty of All Subjects of this Kingdom* (Wing A4179, 1696), epistle dedicatory [n.p.], p. 62.

55. D. Hayton, 'The Country Interest and the Party System, c.1689–1720', in C. Jones ed., *Party and Party Management in Parliament 1660–1784* (Leicester, 1984), pp. 37–85; P. Monod, 'Jacobitism and Country Principles in the Reign of William III', *Historical Journal*, 30 (1987), pp. 289–310; on the pre-civil war Country, see P. Zagorin, *The Court and the Country: The Beginning of the English Revolution* (London, 1969).

56. E. Ward, *The School of Politicks, or, The Humours of a Coffee-house A Poem* (Wing W753A, 1690), pp. 14–15.

57. T. Wagstaffe, *Supplement to His Majesties Most Gracious Speech Directed to the Honourable House of Commons* (Wing W217, 1693), p. 1.

58. Ibid., p. 3.

59. Ibid., p. 7.

60. Ibid., pp. 8–12.

61. Ibid., p. 9.

62. Ibid., p. 11.

63. Ibid., pp. 16–17, 20.

64. Ibid., p. 13.

65. Ibid., p. 18.

66. Ibid.

67. Ibid., p. 22.

68. *The Price of the Abdication.*

69. [W. Anderton], *Remarks Upon the Present Confederacy, and Late Revolution in England* (Wing A3112, 1693), pp. 19, 46 and *passim*. Anderton was likely the author as well as printer, see *ODNB*.

70. S. Grascome, *New Court-contrivances, or, More Sham-plots Still, against True-hearted Englishmen* (Wing G1575, 1693).

71. Anderton, *Remarks upon the Present Confederacy*, p. 21.

72. Ibid., pp. 8, 20.

73. *An Honest Commoner's Speech* (Wing H2580, 1694), p. 3.

74. Ibid., pp. 6, 8.

75. E. Miner, *Poems on the Reign of William III* (Augustan Reprint Society, Los Angeles, CA, 1974), p. ii. Cf. the image of Cromwell altered to depict William III, above, ch. 10, p. 421, fig. 54.

76. *A Parallel Between O.P. and P.O* (Wing P334A, 1694), broadside.
77. E. Stephens, *Old English Loyalty & Policy Agreeable to Primitive Christianity* (Wing S5433, 1695). On Stephens, see *ODNB*.
78. Ibid., pp. 29, 36.
79. J. Whiston, *England's Calamities Discover'd with the Proper Remedy to Restore Her Ancient Grandeur and Policy* (Wing W1686, 1696); on Whiston, see *ODNB*.
80. R. Crosfeild, *Brief Observations Upon the Present Distresses of the Publick, with Some Account of the Causes Thereof, viz. the Corruptions in the Government* (Wing C7241, 1696), p. 1. On Crosfeild's campaign, see M. Knights, 'Parliament, Print and Corruption in Later Stuart Britain', *Parliamentary History*, 26 (2007), pp. 49–61. As Knights argues, Crosfeild is hard to categorize, being neither Whig nor Tory nor using the label 'Country', but was committed to exposing corruption in print.
81. R. Crosfeild, *A Dialogue Between a Modern Courtier and an Honest English Gentleman* (Wing C7242, 1696), p. 8.
82. R. Crosfeild, *Justice the Best Support to Government, or, A Brief Account of Some Publick Transactions During the Late War* (Wing C7246, 1697), p. 22; L. Schwoerer, *No Standing Armies! The Anti-army Ideology in Seventeenth-Century England* (Baltimore, MD, 1974), p. 155.
83. Schwoerer, *No Standing Armies!*, ch. 8. See also C. Levillain, 'William III's Military and Political Career in Neo-Roman Context, 1672–1702', *Historical Journal*, 48 (2005), pp. 321–50.
84. Schwoerer, *No Standing Armies!*, pp. 162–3.
85. J. Trenchard, *An Argument, Shewing That a Standing Army Is Inconsistent with a Free Government and Absolutely Destructive to the Constitution of the English Monarchy* (Wing T2110, 1697); Trenchard, *A Letter from the Author of the Argument Against a Standing Army to the Author of the Balancing Letter* (Wing T2113, 1697); Trenchard, *A Short History of Standing Armies in England* (Wing T2116, 1698); Trenchard, *The Argument Against a Standing Army, Discuss'd by a True Lover of His Country* (Wing A3631, 1698). On Trenchard, see *ODNB*.
86. *Now Is the Time* (Wing N1433, 1689), broadside; J. Milton, *The Readie and Easie Way to Establish a Free Commonwealth* (Wing M2174, 1660), p. 52.
87. M. Zook, *Radical Whigs and Conspiratorial Politics in Late Stuart England* (Philadelphia, PA, 1999).
88. Above, ch. 12, p. 491.
89. N. N., *Some Reasons for Annual Parliaments, in a Letter to a Friend* (Wing N58, 1693), quotation, p. 1.
90. Ferguson, *Whether the Parliament Be Not in Law Dissolved*, pp. 2–3 and *passim*; above, note 37.
91. For late seventeenth-century republicanism, see J. Champion, *Republican Learning: John Toland and the Crisis of Christian Culture, 1696–1722* (Manchester, 2003), ch. 4; B. Worden, 'The Revolution of 1688–1689 and the English Republican Tradition', in J. Israel ed., *The Anglo-Dutch Moment: Essays on the Glorious Revolution and its World Impact* (Cambridge, 1991), pp. 241–77. Champion observes that Williamite republicanism adjusted to monarchy and shared objectives with the Country interest.
92. H. Neville, *Discourses Concerning Government* (Wing N503A, 1698); [Neville], *The Works of the Famous Nicolas Machiavel, Citizen and Secretary of Florence Written Originally in Italian, and from thence Newly and Faithfully Translated into English* (Wing M130, 1694); Schwoerer, *No Standing Armies!*, pp. 173–4. On Neville, see G. Mahlberg, *Henry Neville and English Republican Culture in the Seventeenth Century: Dreaming of Another Game* (Manchester, 2009).
93. *The Oceana of James Harrington and His Other Works, some wherof Are Now First Publish'd from His Own Manuscripts: the Whole Collected . . . with an Exact Account of His Life Prefix'd by John Toland* (Wing H816, 1700).
94. Schwoerer, *No Standing Armies!*, p. 173; *Discourses Concerning Government by Algernon Sidney* (Wing S3761, 1698); *A Complete Collection of the Historical, Political and Miscellaneous Works of John Milton* (Wing M2087, 1698); Milton's *Paradise Lost Imitated in Rhyme* (Wing H2747, 1699).
95. *Saul and Samuel; or, The Common Interest of Our King and Country* (ESTC T203589, 1702), p. 6.
96. *A Dialogue Betwixt Whig and Tory, Alias Williamite and Jacobite* (Wing D1361, 1693), dedication to the king.
97. *The Claims of the People of England, Essayed, In a Letter from the Country* (ESTC T030805, 1701), p. 4.
98. 1700 c.2 12 and 13, Will 3, *Statutes of the Realm* (11 vols, 1810–23), VII, pp. 636–8.
99. See T. Harris, *Politics under the Later Stuarts: Party Conflict in a Divided Society, 1660–1715* (London, 1993); H. Horwitz, *Parliament, Policy and Politics in the Reign of William III* (Manchester, 1977).

100. T. Claydon, *William III: Profiles in Power* (Harlow, 2002), p. 94.
101. Ibid, pp. 112–13.
102. S. Baxter, *William III* (London, 1966), pp. 381–2.
103. Ibid., p. 385.
104. *Four Sermons: I. On the Death of Queen Mary, 1694. II. On the Death of the Duke of Gloucester, 1700. III. On the Death of King William, 1701. IV. On the Queen's Accession to the Throne, in 1703. By William Lord Bishop of St. Asaph* (ESTC N009953, 1712), p. 14.
105. *A Sermon Preach'd on the Occasion of the Death of Our Late Sovereign King William III. of Glorious Memory. By the Author of the Essay for a Comprehension* (ESTC T094637, 1702), p. 15.
106. Ibid.
107. D. Pead, *Greatness and Goodness Reprieve Not From Death. A Sermon Occasion'd by the Death Of that Glorious Monarch William the Third* (ESTC T035865, 1702), p. 10.
108. J. Piggott, *The Natural Frailty of Princes Consider'd; in a Sermon Preach'd the 29th of March, 1702. Upon the Sad Occasion of the Death of . . . William the Third* (ESTC T095223, 1702), p. 17.
109. Ibid., p. 15.
110. T. Goodwin, *A Sermon Preached on the Sad Occasion of the Death of the Best of Kings, William the IIId* (ESTC T060278, 1702), p. 21.
111. J. Jenkins, *A Sermon Preach'd the 22d of March, 1701/2. Upon the Mournful Occasion of the Death of the Late Glorious and Mighty Prince William the Third* (ESTC T106525, 1702), p. 18.
112. W. Tucker, *A Sermon Preached Upon the Much-lamented Death of Our Late Gracious Sovereign, King William III. Of Glorious Memory; at Cobham in Surrey, on Sunday, the 15th day of March, 1701/2. By W. Tucker, Vicar of Cobham, in Surrey* (ESTC T136077, 1702).
113. T. Wise, *A Sermon Preach'd at the Church of Richmond in Surry, Upon the Death of William III. King of Great Britain, France and Ireland, &c. March the 22d, 1701/2. By Thomas Wise M. A. and Fellow of Exeter College in Oxford* (ESTC T114923, 1702), p. 10.
114. Ibid., p. 15.
115. E. Clarke, *A Sermon Preach'd at St. Mary's Nottingham; on Sunday the 15th of March, 1701/2. Upon Occasion of the Death of King William* (ESTC N024816, 1702).
116. S. Chandler, *England's Great Duty on the Death of their Josiah. In a Sermon Preached on the Death of K. William III. of Glorious Memory: at Andover, March 15. 1701/2. and at Portsmouth, April 19. 1702* (ESTC T010776, 1702), pp. 9, 11.
117. R. Norris, *A Sermon Preached on the Death and Funeral of the Late King, William the IIId. Of Glorious Memory* (ESTC T114922, 1702).
118. Ibid., p. 15.
119. W. Bentley, *A Sermon, Occasionally Preached on the Funeral Of Our Late Soveraign William the III. King of England, Scotland, France and Ireland; Who Was Solemnly Interr'd in Henry the 7th. Chappel in the Abby of Westminster. on Sunday April the 12. 1702 By William Bentley* (ESTC T000577, 1702), p. 6.
120. *The Mournful Congress, a Poem, on the Death of the Illustrious King William III. Of Glorious Memory. By a Sincere Lover of His Prince and Country* (ESTC N026288, 1702), pp. 3, 5.
121. *Britannia's Loss. A Poem on the Death of England's Cæsar* (ESTC N032733, 1702), pp. 4, 7 and passim.
122. Smith, *A Pindarique*, p. 7.
123. *Academiae Cantabrigiensis carmina, quibus decedenti augustissimo regi Wilhelmo III. parentat; et succedenti optimis auspiciis serenissimae reginae Annae Gratulatur* (ESTC T001214, 1702); M. Smith, *A Pindarique Poem Sacred to the Glorious Memory of King William III* (ESTC T042302, 1702), p. 4.
124. Smith, *A Pindarique*, pp. 5, 6, 9.
125. *The Mournfull Muse, an Elegy on the Much Lamented Death of King William IIId* (ESTC T170288, 1702), p. 2.
126. J. Oldmixon, *A Funeral-Idyll, Sacred to the Glorious Memory of K. William III* (ESTC T147317, 1702), pp. 7–8.
127. R. Fleming, *Fame's Mausoleum: A Pindarick Poem, with a Monumental Inscription, Sacred to the Glorious Memory of William the Great. Humbly Offered as an Essay* (ESTC T079767, 1702), pp. 8, 15, 18. On p. 18 Fleming pens an inscription for a tomb.
128. Ibid., p. 13.
129. J. Dennis, *The Monument: A Poem Sacred to the Immortal Memory of the Best and Greatest of Kings, William the Third* (ESTC T135780, 1702).
130. Ibid., pp. 2, 10.
131. Ibid., p. 46.

132. G. Burnet, *A Compleat History of the Glorious Life and Actions of That Most Renowned Monarch, William the Third, Late King of England* (ESTC T184740, 1702).

133. Ibid., p. 10.

134. *The Glorious Life, and Heroick Actions of the Most Potent Prince William III. of England, Scotland, France, and Ireland, King* (ESTC T073183, 1702), p. 4.

135. Ibid., pp. 161, 168.

136. J. A., *Princely Excellency: or, Regal Glory. Being an Exact Account of the Most Glorious Heroick, and Matchless Actions, of that Most Serene and Potent Prince, William the Third, Late King of England, Scotland, France, and Ireland* (ESTC T044327, 1702), epistle dedicatory, preface [n.p.].

137. A. Boyer, *The History of King William the Third. In III Parts* (T091241, 1702), part I, preface.

138. Ibid., part III, p. 518.

139. N. Brady, *A Sermon Upon Occasion of the Death of Our Late Sovereign King William; and Her Present Majesty's Happy Accession to the Crown. Preach'd at the Parish-church of Richmond in Surry, on Sunday, Mar. 15. 1701/2* (ESTC T060262, 1702).

140. Dennis, *The Monument*, pp. iii–iv, viii, 22; see also pp. 3, 9, 13, 34, 41, 44, 46–7; E. Lewis, *The Weeping Muse. A Poem. Sacred to the Memory of His Late Majesty* (ESTC T004588, 1702), p. 6; D. Defoe, *The Mock Mourners. A Satyr, by Way of Elegy on King William, the second edition corrected* (ESTC T070835, 1702), p. 14; cf. pp. 2, 4, 6; Brady, *A Sermon Upon Occasion of the Death of Our Late Sovereign*, p. 9 and *passim*.

141. Fleetwood, *Four Sermons*, p. 57.

142. *A Sermon Preach'd on the Occasion of the Death of Our Late Sovereign King William III. of Glorious Memory. By the Author of the Essay for a Comprehension*, p. 20; Goodwin, *A Sermon*, p. 24.

143. Boyer, *The History of King William*, preface.

144. Pead, *Greatness and Goodness*, p. 19; *Mournfull Muse*, p. 3.

145. Lewis, *The Weeping Muse*, p. 7; Dennis, *The Monument*, p. 37.

146. Dennis, *The Monument*, p. 38.

147. Defoe, *The Mock Mourners*, p. 19.

148. Clarke, *Sermon Preach'd at St. Mary's Nottingham*, p. 3.

149. Smith, *A Pindarique Poem*, p. 9.

150. Defoe, *The Mock Mourners*, p. 16.

151. Baxter, *William III*, pp. 400–1 and ch. 27 *passim*.

152. Claydon, *William III: Profiles*, p. 188.

153. J. Israel ed., *The Anglo-Dutch Moment: Essays on the Glorious Revolution and its World Impact* (Cambridge, 1991), p. 42.

154. http://www.bbc.co.uk/history/british/civil_war_revolution/william_iii_01.shtml

155. Baxter, *William III*, p. 398.

156. Claydon, *William III: Profiles*, p. 188.

157. See for example, J. C. D. Clark, *English Society, 1688–1832: Ideology, Social Structure and Political Practice during the Ancien Regime* (Cambridge, 1985); J. P. Kenyon, *Revolution Principles: The Politics of Party, 1689–1720* (Cambridge, 1977). The most recent study revives a Whig interpretation, while emphasizing the radical modernity of the Revolution, S. Pincus, *1688: The First Modern Revolution* (New Haven, CT, and London, 2009).

158. Above, ch. 12, p. 491.

159. See J. Brewer, *The Sinews of Power: War, Money and the English State, 1688–1783* (London, 1989).

160. Above, ch. 11, p. 469.

161. Cf. Claydon, *William III: Profiles*, pp. 102–5.

162. *The Report of the Physicians and Surgeons, Commanded to Assist at the Dissecting the Body of His Late Majesty at Kensington, March the Tenth MDCCI/II* (ESTC T001873, 1702), p. 3 and *passim*.

163. The term 'theology' comes from Kantorowicz's famous study *The King's Two Bodies: A Study in Mediaeval Political Theology* (Princeton, NJ, 1957).

164. Israel ed., *The Anglo-Dutch Moment*, p. 2.

165. K. Sharpe, *Selling the Tudor Monarchy: Authority and Image in Sixteenth-Century England* (New Haven, CT, and London, 2009).

166. J. Habermas, *Strukturwandel der Öffentlichkeit; Untersuchungen zu einer Kategorie der Bürgerlichen Gesellschaft* (Neuweil and Berlin, 1962). This was published in English translation in 1989 as *The Structural Transformation of the Public Sphere: An Inquiry into a Category of Bourgeois Society*. Cf. J. Brewer, *The Pleasures of the Imagination: English Culture in the Eighteenth Century* (London, 1997); T. Blanning, *Culture of Power and the Power of Culture: Old Regime Europe 1660–1789* (Oxford, 2002).

Part IV Prologue: Semper Eadem? Queen Anne

1. E. Gregg, *Queen Anne* (London, 1980). There was not even a new life prepared for the *Oxford Dictionary of National Biography*, Gregg merely reprising his thirty-year-old book.
2. http://www.britannia.com/history/monarchs/mon52.html.
3. http://www.bbc.co.uk/pressoffice/pressreleases/stories/2002/08_august/21/100_britons.shtml
4. Above, ch. 11, p. 469; below, ch. 15, pp. 625–6.
5. Gregg, *ODNB*. Hannah Smith places helpfully greater emphasis on the sacred, '"Last of All the Heavenly Birth": Queen Anne and Sacral Queenship', *Parliamentary History*, 29 (2009), pp. 137–49.
6. Gregg, *Queen Anne*, p. 137.
7. Ibid., p. 141.
8. Below, ch. 13, pp. 546–8.
9. G. Holmes, *British Politics in the Age of Anne* (London, 1967), pp. 6–7.
10. See Mark Knights, *Representation and Misrepresentation in Later Stuart Britain: Partisanship and Political Culture* (Oxford, 2004).
11. K. Sharpe, *Selling the Tudor Monarchy: Authority and Image in Sixteenth-Century England* (New Haven, CT, and London, 2009), epilogue and *passim*.
12. Below, ch. 15, pp. 616–20.

13 A Stuart's Words

1. *Her Majesties Declaration of War against France and Spain* (ESTC T036101, 1702), one page.
2. *A Proclamation Declaring War against France and Spain* (ESTC N012045, 1702).
3. *At the Court at St. James's, the Second Day of May, 1702* (ESTC T022683, 1702); *At the Court at St. James's, the Ninth Day of July, 1702* (ESTC T022684, 1702).
4. See, for example, *By the Queen, A Proclamation. Anne R. Whereas by the Twenty Second Article of the Treaty of Union* (ESTC T019659, 1708); *By the Queen, A Proclamation, Appointing the Distribution of Prizes Taken* (ESTC T019689, 1708).
5. For example, proclamations of 18 May 1702, 23 December 1704, 29 March 1705, 11 April 1708, 23 June, 3 October 1709.
6. Proclamations 26 February 1705 (ESTC N070296); *By the Queen, A Proclamation, for Enforcing the Due Execution of the Act, Intituled, An Act for Establishing a General Post-Office* (ESTC T019479, 1711).
7. For example, 20 July, 30 December 1708, 3 October 1709, 1 March 1710.
8. *By the Queen, A Proclamation, for a General Fast* (ESTC T019708, 1711).
9. Ibid.; *By the Queen, A Proclamation, for a General Fast* (ESTC T019710, 1711).
10. *By the Queen, A Proclamation, Declaring the Suspension of Arms, as well by Sea as Land* (ESTC T019699, 1712); *By the Queen, A Proclamation, Declaring the Continuation of the Cessation of Arms* (ESTC T019698, 1712).
11. *By the Queen, A Proclamation, Against Unlawful Intruders into Churches and Manses in Scotland* (ESTC T019688, 1708).
12. *By the Queen, A Proclamation. Anne R. Whereas by the Twenty Second Article of the Treaty of Union* (ESTC T019659, 1708); *By the Queen, A Proclamation. Anne R. Whereas James Duke of Hamilton Was Duly Elected and Returned to Be One of the Sixteen Peers of Scotland* (ESTC T019683, 1712).
13. See, for example, *A Proclamation Dissolving the Parliament of Scotland* (ESTC N046498, 1707); *A Proclamation Against Such As Have Gone to or Stayed in France since Her Majesties Gracious Indemnity* (ESTC N012053, 1703).
14. *By the Queen, A Proclamation. Anne R. Whereas We Have Received Certain Information, that the Person Who, During the Life of the Late King James the Second, Pretended to be Prince of Wales* (ESTC T019654, 1708).
15. See E. Gregg, 'Was Queen Anne a Jacobite?', *History*, 57 (1972), pp. 358–72.
16. *By the Queen, A Proclamation, for Dissolving this Present Parliament, and Declaring the Speedy Calling Another* (ESTC T019728, 1702).
17. *By the Queen, A Proclamation, for Dissolving this Present Parliament, and Declaring the Speedy Calling of Another* (ESTC T019731, 1708).
18. *By the Queen, A Proclamation, Requiring Quarentine to Be Performed by Ships Coming from the Baltick Sea* (ESTC T019796, 1711).
19. By the Queen (ESTC T190570, 1703).

20. *By the Queen, A Proclamation, for Restraining the Spreading False News, and Printing and Publishing of Irreligious and Seditious Papers and Libels* (ESTC T019760, 1702). Moderate churchmen fought against this move; but Anne evidently favoured at this time the high church party's position; see M. Knights, *Representation and Misrepresentation in Later Stuart Britain: Partisanship and Political Culture* (Oxford, 2006), pp. 266-7. Knights argues that sentiments were put in the queen's mouth. This I think underestimates the extent to which Anne made up her own mind; and pays inadequate attention to the fact that the proclamations, like the speeches, were received as the royal will.

21. *By the Queen, A Proclamation, for Discovering and Apprehending the Author, Printer and Publisher of a Libel, Intituled, Legion's Humble Address to the Lords* (ESTC T019723, 1704); *By the Queen, A Proclamation, for Apprehending John Tutchin, John How, and Benjamin Bragg* (ESTC T019720, 1703).

22. *By the Queen, A Proclamation. Anne R. We Being Informed, that the Streets and Passages Leading through Our Cities of London and Westminster, and Suburbs Thereof, Have Been Filled of Late with Great Numbers of Loose, Idle, and Disorderly Persons* (ESTC T019676, 1710).

23. *By the Queen, A Proclamation, for a General Thanksgiving* (ESTC T019768, 1708).

24. *By the Queen, A Proclamation, for a General Thanksgiving* (ESTC T019767, 1708).

25. *By the Queen, A Proclamation* (ESTC T019669, 1709).

26. Below, ch. 13, pp. 547-9.

27. Letters patent published in the form of a proclamation, 3 November 1704 (ESTC T085384, 1704).

28. *By the Queen, A Proclamation, for Encouraging the Design of Erecting Schools for Propagating the Knowledge of Christ in the Highlands and Islands of Scotland* (ESTC T019747, 1708).

29. *By the Queen, A Proclamation, for the Encouragement of Piety and Virtue, and for the Preventing and Punishing Vice, Profaneness, and Immorality* (ESTC T019784, 1708).

30. *By the Queen, A Proclamation* (ESTC T019667, 1709).

31. See G. Holmes, *British Politics in the Age of Anne* (London, 1967), pp. 66, 75, 375, 514, n. 100.

32. On addresses to Anne, see Knights, *Representation and Misrepresentation*, pp. 117-18, 125-6. Addresses even referred to words in the queen's speeches. Published in the *Gazette*, these loyal addresses became themselves a new feature of royal representation, now constructed as well as affirmed by popular opinion.

33. J. Browne, *The Royal Prophetess: or, Israel's Triumphs over Jabin King of Hazor. An Heroick Poem* (ESTC N012795, 1706), pp. 39-47; J. Bates, *Two (United) Are Better than One Alone. A Thanksgiving Sermon upon the Union of the Two Kingdoms, of England and Scotland, Preach'd at Hackney, May 1. 1707* (ESTC T052158, 1707), p. 13; *Great Britain's Glory: or, the Lives and Glorious Actions of All the Protestant Kings and Queens* (ESTC T183717, 1708); J. Dunton, *A Cat May Look on a Queen: or, a Satyr on Her present Majesty* (ESTC T020329), p. 22. This work was a panegyric not a satire.

34. N.Tate, *A Congratulatory Poem, on Her Majesties Happy Recovery, and Return to Meet Her Parliament. By Mr. Tate, Poet-laureat to Her Majesty* (ESTC N001869, 1714), p. 10.

35. *A Collection of All Her Majesty's Speeches, Messages, &c. From Her Happy Accession to the Throne, to the Twenty First of June 1712* (ESTC T000031, 1712); *A Collection of All Queen Anne's Speeches, Messages, &c. From Her Accession to the Throne, to Her Demise* (ESTC T000034, 1714).

36. *Collection of All Her Majesty's Speeches, 1712*, p. 3.

37. Ibid.

38. *Her Majesties Most Gracious Speech to Both Houses of Parliament, on Wednesday the Eleventh Day of March 1701* (British Library BS 68/28 [41], 1702), one page.

39. *Her Majesties Most Gracious Speech to Both Houses of Parliament, on Munday the Thirtieth Day of March, 1702* (ESTC N007206, 1702), p. 3.

40. Ibid., p. 4.

41. *Her Majesties Declaration of War Against France and Spain* (ESTC T036101, 1702).

42. *Her Majesties Most Gracious Speech to Both Houses of Parliament, On Munday the Twenty Fifth Day of May, 1702* (ESTC N003492, 1702), p. 6.

43. E. Gregg, *Queen Anne* (London, 1980), p. 159.

44. *Her Majesties Most Gracious Speech*, p. 7; Gregg, *Queen Anne*, p. 160.

45. *Her Majesties Most Gracious Speech*, p. 7. Her ministry of May contained nine Tories and three moderate Whigs; G. Holmes, *British Politics in the Age of Anne* (London, 1967), p. 449.

46. *Her Majesties . . . Speech to . . . Parliament . . . the Twenty First Day of October* (Bodleian Pamph. 246 [34], 1702), one page.

47. *Her Majesties Most Gracious Speech to Both Houses of Parliament, On Saturday the Twenty Seventh Day of February, 1702* (ESTC T036112, 1702), p. 3.

48. Gregg, *Queen Anne*, pp. 162-3.

49. *Her Majesties Speech Twenty Seventh Day of February, 1702*, pp. 3-4.

50. Ibid., p. 4.
51. The bill was amended in the Lords and dropped.
52. The suggestion recently made in a paper by Geoff Kemp that, in acting against these libels, Anne was the spokesmen of high church Tories fails to convince, given her stance on toleration.
53. Gregg, *Queen Anne*, p. 172.
54. *Her Majesties Most Gracious Speech to Both Houses of Parliament, on Tuesday the Ninth Day of November, 1703* (ESTC N017485, 1703).
55. *Her Majesties Most Gracious Speech to Both Houses of Parliament, on Friday the Seventeenth Day of December, 1703* (ESTC T085386, 1703), pp. 3-4.
56. *Her Majesties Most Gracious Speech to Both Houses of Parliament, On Munday the Third Day of April, 1704* (ESTC T027228, 1704).
57. On Harley, see B. W. Hill, *Robert Harley: Speaker, Secretary of State and Premier Minister* (New Haven, CT, and London, 1988).
58. *Her Majesties . . . Speech to . . . Parliament . . . the Twenty Fourth Day of October* (Bodleian Pamph. 258 [11], 1704).
59. Gregg, *Queen Anne*, pp. 192-4.
60. *Collection of All Queen Anne's Speeches* (1714), p. 17.
61. Gregg, *Queen Anne*, p. 197.
62. Ibid., p. 208.
63. Ibid., pp. 209-13; Holmes, *British Politics in the Age of Anne*, p. 200.
64. *Collection of All Queen Anne's Speeches* (1714), pp. 17-18.
65. Ibid., p. 19.
66. Ibid.
67. Ibid., p. 20.
68. Gregg, *Queen Anne*, p. 211. Tories objected to her presence.
69. Ibid., pp. 212-14.
70. *Collection of All Queen Anne's Speeches* (1714), p. 22.
71. Gregg, *Queen Anne*, p. 225.
72. *Collection of All Queen Anne's Speeches* (1714), p. 23; *Her Majesty's Most Gracious Speech to Both Houses of Parliament, on Tuesday the Third Day of Decemb. 1706* (ESTC T229694, 1706).
73. *Collection of All Queen Anne's Speeches* (1714), p. 25.
74. Ibid., pp. 25-6: *Her Majesties Most Gracious Speech to Both Houses of Parliament, On Thursday the Sixth Day of March, 1706* (ESTC T013059, 1707).
75. *Collection of All Queen Anne's Speeches* (1714), p. 27; *Her Majesties Most Gracious Speech to Both Houses of Parliament, on Thursday the Twenty Fourth day of April, 1707* (ESTC T036133, 1707).
76. Gregg, *Queen Anne*, p. 240.
77. *Collection of All Queen Anne's Speeches* (1714), pp. 27-9; *Her Majesties Most Gracious Speech to Both Houses of Parliament, on Thursday the Sixth day of November, 1707* (ESTC N007186, 1707), one page.
78. Holmes, *British Politics in the Age of Anne*, pp. 242-3.
79. *Collection of All Queen Anne's Speeches* (1714), pp. 29-30; see *Her Majesties . . . Speech to . . . Parliament . . . the Eighteenth Day of December* (Bodleian Vet. A3 c.43 [15], 1707).
80. *Collection of All Queen Anne's Speeches* (1714), p. 31.
81. Ibid., p. 32; *Her Majesties . . . Speech to . . . Parliament . . . the First Day of April* (Bodleian Vet. A3 c.43 [17], 1708).
82. Gregg, *Queen Anne*, p. 263.
83. Ibid., pp. 263-4.
84. Ibid., p. 269.
85. *Collection of All Queen Anne's Speeches* (1714), pp. 33-4.
86. Ibid., pp. 36-7; *Her Majesties Most Gracious Speech to Both Houses of Parliament, on Tuesday the Fifteenth day of November, 1709* (ESTC N017502, 1709); Gregg, *Queen Anne*, p. 296.
87. For an account, see G. Holmes, *The Trial of Doctor Sacheverell* (London, 1973). Brian Cowan and Mark Knights are preparing new studies of the Sacheverell affair and its ramifications.
88. On Anne's views of Sacheverell, see Holmes, *The Trial of Doctor Sacheverell*, pp. 95, 111, 116, 208, 210-11, 227-8; Gregg, *Queen Anne*, pp. 297-8, 305-7. Observers anxiously watched for clear signs of the conservative Anglican queen's position. Though Anne evidently thought Sacheverell deserved punishment, popular opinion, as well as many Tories, took it that she favoured his cause. Though she came out in support of the impeachment, she later distanced herself from it and also influenced a mild sentence.

89. *Collection of All Queen Anne's Speeches* (1714), pp. 37–8; *Her Majesties . . . Speech to . . . Parliament . . . the Fifth Day of April* (Bodleian Vet. A3 c.43 [20], 1710).

90. Gregg, *Queen Anne*, p. 324.

91. *Collection of All Queen Anne's Speeches* (1714), pp. 38–9; *Her Majesties Most Gracious Speech to Both Houses of Parliament, on Munday the Twenty Seventh day of November, 1710* (ESTC N0050010, 1710).

92. Holmes, *British Politics in the Age of Anne*, pp. 342–3, 454.

93. Gregg, *Queen Anne*, pp. 322–3.

94. Ibid., p. 341.

95. *Collection of All Queen Anne's Speeches* (1714), p. 40; *Her Majesties Most Gracious Speech to Both Houses of Parliament, On Tuesday the Twelfth Day of June, 1711* (ESTC T036137, 1711).

96. Gregg, *Queen Anne*, p. 341.

97. *Collection of All Queen Anne's Speeches* (1714), pp. 41–2, where the speech is erroneously dated 11 December; *Her Majesties . . . Speech to . . . Parliament . . . the Seventh Day of December* (Bodleian Nich. Newspapers 19 [581], 1711).

98. Gregg, *Queen Anne*, pp. 347–8; Holmes, *British Politics in the Age of Anne*, pp. 334–5.

99. Gregg, *Queen Anne*, p. 359.

100. *Collection of All Queen Anne's Speeches* (1714), pp. 43–7; *Her Majesties Most Gracious Speech . . . on Friday the Sixth Day of June, 1712* (BL B.S. 91/8, 1712).

101. *Collection of All Queen Anne's Speeches* (1714), p. 47; *Her Majesties Most Gracious Speech to Both Houses of Parliament, on Saturday the One and Twentieth day of June, 1712* (Bodleian Vet. A3 c.43 [25] 1712).

102. *Collection of All Queen Anne's Speeches* (1714), pp. 48–9; *Her Majesties Most Gracious Speech to Both Houses of Parliament, on Thursday the Ninth Day of April, 1713* (BL 1881.a.5. [6], 1713).

103. See Gregg, *Queen Anne*, pp. 366–7.

104. Ibid., p. 366.

105. *Collection of All Queen Anne's Speeches* (1714), pp. 50–1; *Her Majesties . . . Speech to . . . Parliament . . . the Sixteenth Day of July* (Bodleian Vet. A3 c.43 [27], 1713).

106. *Collection of All Queen Anne's Speeches* (1714), pp. 52–3; *Her Majesties . . . Speech to . . . Parliament . . . the Second Day of March* (Bodleian Vet. A3 c.43 [28], 1714); Gregg, *Queen Anne*, p. 378.

107. *Collection of All Queen Anne's Speeches* (1714), p. 54; *Her Majesties . . . Speech to . . . Parliament . . . the Ninth Day of July* (Bodleian Vet. A3 c.43 [29], 1714). Anne died on 1 August.

108. R. Lloyd, *A Sermon Preach'd at St. Paul's Covent-Garden, on the 30th of January, 1713–14* (ESTC T094188, 1714), p. 15.

109. *A Dialogue Between a New Courtier and a Country Gentleman* (ESTC T132386, 1713), p. 3.

110. Ibid., p. 4.

111. D. Defoe, *A Challenge of Peace, Address'd to the Whole Nation* (ESTC T032976, 1703), sig. A2. Defoe was an agent of Harley's and so *parti pris*; but his view of the queen's speeches is significant.

112. Ibid.; *An Elegy on the Death of Her Most Gracious Majesty Queen Anne* (ESTC T125676, 1714), p. 5.

113. *Dialogue Between a New Courtier and a Country Gentleman*, p. 4.

114. Quoted in Holmes, *British Politics in the Age of Anne*, p. 350; on the influence of a court party in parliament, cf. pp. 350–3, 362–6 *passim*.

115. As before, the services were prepared by bishops but in every case were published by the royal printer and by the queen's special command, and they often bore the royal arms.

116. *A Form of Prayer, To be Used Next after the Prayer in the Time of War and Tumults, throughout the Kingdom of England, Dominion of Wales, and Town of Berwick upon Tweed, in all Churches and Chapels, at Morning and Evening Prayer, as often as There Is Divine Service, during the Time of the War* (ESTC T070795, 1702). The British Library copy has a manuscript date '11 April', probably the date of receipt or purchase, so the prayers must have been issued very soon after Anne's accession on 8 March.

117. Ibid., p. 3.

118. Ibid.

119. *A Form of Prayer, to be Used in all Churches and Chapels . . . on Wednesday the Tenth Day of June, Being the Fast-Day Appointed by Proclamation, to be Observed in a Most Solemn and Devout Manner: for the Imploring of a Blessing from Almighty God upon Her Majesty and Her Allies, Engaged in the Present War against France and Spain. By Her Majesties special Command* (ESTC T070796, 1702), p. 11.

120. Ibid.

121. Ibid., pp. 23, 37.
122. Ibid., pp. 14, 37.
123. *A Form of Prayer, and Thanksgiving to Almighty God; to be Used throughout the Cities of London and Westminster . . . on Thursday the Twelfth Day of this Instant November; and in all other Places . . . on Thursday the Third Day of December next Ensuing. For the Signal Successes Vouchsafed to Her Majesties Forces both by Sea and Land; As also to Those of Her Allies, Engaged in the Present War against France and Spain* (Bodleian Godw. Pamph. 1522 [11], 1702), p. 15.
124. Ibid., p. 20.
125. *A Form of Prayer, To be Used in all Churches and Chapels . . . on Wednesday the Twenty Sixth Day of May, Being the Fast-day Appointed by Proclamation . . . for the Imploring of a Blessing from Almighty God upon Her Majesty, and Her Allies, Engaged in the Present War* (ESTC T070798, 1703), p. 10.
126. Tony Claydon is preparing what will be an invaluable study of the great storm.
127. *A Form of Prayer, to Be Used . . . until the Day of the Publick Fast Appointed to be Kept on Wednesday, Jan. 12. 1703/4* (ESTC T070783, 1703), p. 4.
128. *A Form of Prayer, to be Used . . . on Wednesday the Nineteenth Day of January, Being the Fast-Day . . . for the Imploring of a Blessing from Almighty God upon Her Majesty, and Her Allies, Engaged in the Present War: As also for the Humbling of Our Selves before Him in a Deep Sense of His Heavy Displeasure, Shew'd Forth in the Late Dreadful Storm and Tempest; And in order to the Obtaining the Pardon of Our Crying Sins, the Averting His Judgments, and the Continuance of His Mercies, and . . . that of the Protestant Religion, to us and to our Posterity* (ESTC T070784).
129. Ibid., pp. 19, 24 and *passim*.
130. *A Form of Prayer with Thanksgiving to Almighty God; to Be Used . . . Every Year, upon the Eighth Day of March; Being the Day on which Her Majesty Began Her Happy Reign* (ESTC T070785, 1704), imprimatur.
131. Ibid., sig. A5. The people were also led to pray that private interests not obstruct the queen's care for the national good.
132. *A Form of Prayer and Thanksgiving to Almighty God; to Be Used . . . the Ninth Day of this Instant July, for the Late Great Success Vouchsafed to the Forces of Her Majesty and Her Allies, under the Command of the Duke of Marlborough and Prince Lewis of Baden near Donawert. By Her Majesties Special Command* (ESTC T080021, 1704), p. 4.
133. Ibid., pp. 3–4. 'Not unto us, O Lord . . .'. The text announces that it was 'her majesty's pleasure' that the prayer be used.
134. *A Form of Prayer and Thanksgiving to Almighty God: to Be Used on Thursday the Seventh of September . . . for the Late Glorious Victory Obtained over the French and Bavarians at Bleinheim* (ESTC T066583, 1704).
135. Ibid., sig. A3^v.
136. Ibid., sig. A4^v.
137. M. Astell, *An Impartial Enquiry into the Causes of Rebellion and Civil War in this Kingdom* (ESTC T000820, 1704), p. 33.
138. *A Form of Prayer, to Be Used . . . Wednesday the Fourth Day of April . . . for Imploring the Continuance of a Blessing from Almighty God upon Her Majesty, and Her Allies, Engaged in the Present War: and for Restoring and Perpetuating Peace, Safety and Prosperity to Her and Her Kingdoms, and the Nations and States in Alliance with Her; and Disappointing the Boundless Ambition of France* (ESTC T066588, 1705).
139. Ibid., pp. 11–12, 24–5.
140. *A Form of Prayer, and Thanksgiving to Almighty God: to Be Used on Thursday the Twenty Third of August . . . for the Late Glorious Success in Forcing the Enemy Lines in the Spanish Netherlands, by the Arms of Her Majesty and Her Allies, under the Command of the Duke of Marlborough* (ESTC T070788, 1705).
141. Ibid., p. 4.
142. Gregg, *Queen Anne*, p. 214.
143. *A Form of Prayer, to Be Used . .: on Wednesday the Twentieth Day of March . . . for Imploring the Continuance of Gods Blessing and Assistance on the Arms of Her Majesty, and Her Allies, Engaged in the Present War: And for Restoring and Perpetuating Peace, Safety and Prosperity to Her and Her Kingdoms* (ESTC T070788, 1706).
144. Ibid., pp. 20, 25.
145. Ibid., p. 11.
146. *A Collect to Be Used on Sunday the Nineteenth of this Instant May . . . By Her Majesties Special Command* (ESTC T167237, 1706).

147. *A Form of Prayer and Thanksgiving to Almighty God: to Be Used on Thursday the Twenty Seventh of June . . . for Having Given to the Arms of Her Majesty, in Conjunction with those of Her Allies, under the Command of John Duke of Marlborough, a Signal and Glorious Victory in Brabant, over the French Army; And for Restoring the Greatest Part of the Spanish Netherlands to the Possession of the House of Austria* (ESTC T070790, 1706).

148. Ibid., sigs A3–A3^v.

149. *A Form of Prayer and Thanksgiving, to Be Used on Tuesday the One and Thirtieth Day of December* (ESTC T071329, 1706), quotation, sig. A4.

150. *A Form of Prayer and Thanksgiving, To Be Used on Thursday the First Day of May . . . for Rendring Most Hearty Thanks to Almighty God, for the Wonderful and Happy Conclusion of the Treaty for the Union of Her Majesties Two Kingdoms of England and Scotland; for Imploring His Blessings on the United Kingdom, and on the Arms of Her Majesty and Her Allies* (ESTC T070793, 1707).

151. Ibid., p. 5.

152. Ibid., p. 6.

153. Ibid.

154. Gregg, *Queen Anne*, pp. 261–2.

155. *A Form of Thanksgiving, to Be Used . . . the Eighteenth Day of this Instant April . . . Immediately after the General Thanksgiving, both at Morning and Evening Prayer. By Her Majesties Special Command* (ESTC T069807, 1708), one page.

156. *A Form of Prayer and Thanksgiving, to Be Used on Thursday the Nineteenth Day of August . . . for Rendring Most Hearty Thanks to Almighty God, for the Happy Success of Her Majesties Councils and Forces against the Late Insolent and Unjust Attempt of the Common Enemy and the Pretender, to Invade Her Majesties Kingdom* (ESTC T069783, 1708).

157. Ibid., sig. A3.

158. Ibid., sig. A4.

159. *A Form of Prayer and Thanksgiving, to Be Used on Thursday the Seventeenth Day of February . . . for Rendring Most Hearty Thanks to Almighty God, for Protecting Her Majesty this Year from Many Great Attempts and Treacherous Designs of Her Enemies; and for Blessing the Arms of Her Majesty and Her allies* (ESTC T066589, 1709), sig. A3.

160. Ibid., sig. A3^v.

161. *Prayers to Be Used Next after the Prayer in Time of War and Tumults* (ESTC T070772, 1709), p. 3.

162. *A Form of Prayer, to Be Used . . . on Wednesday the Fifteenth Day of March, Being the Day Appointed for a General Fast* (Bodleian Pamph. 284 [92], 1710); *A Form of Prayer, to Be Used . . . on Wednesday the Twenty Eighth Day of this Instant March* (Bodleian G. Pamph. 1059 [911], 1711), quotation, p. 11.

163. *A Form of Prayer and Thanksgiving, to Be Used on Tuesday the Seventh Day of November* (ESTC T069802, 1710).

164. Ibid., sig. A4.

165. Ibid., sig. A4^v.

166. *By the Queen. A Proclamation for a Publick Thanksgiving 18 May, 1713* (BL 21.h.4 [102], 1713); *By the Queen, a Proclamation, for a Publick Thanksgiving* (ESTC N015703, 1713).

167. *A Form of Prayer and Thanksgiving to Almighty God; to Be Used on Tuesday the Sixteenth Day of June next . . . for the Conclusion of a Just and Honourable Peace* (ESTC T0800830, 1713), sig. A4^v.

168. Ibid., sigs A4^v–B1.

169. Ibid., sig. C4.

170. Astell, *Impartial Enquiry*, p. 33.

171. J. Whittle, *A Thanksgiving-Sermon Preach'd at Foots-Cray in Kent, June the 27th, 1706. for a Signal and Glorious Victory in Brabant, over the French Army* (ESTC T011932, 1706), p. 28.

172. W. Perse, *A Sermon Preached at Malton in Yorkshire. June 27th. 1706* (ESTC T010708, 1706), p. 27.

173. J. Stennett, *A Sermon Preach'd on Thursday the 27th of June 1706* (ESTC T127795, 1706), p. 27.

174. Penelope Aubin, *The Extasy: A Pindarick Ode to Her Majesty the Queen. By Mrs. Aubin* (ESTC T089796, 1708), p. 13.

175. T. Coulton, *Nahash's Defeat, and Jabesh-Gilead's Rescue: A Sermon Preach'd August 19. 1708. On Occasion of the Defeat of the Intended Invasion of North-Britain, and of the French Forces near Audenarde* (ESTC N006023, 1708), p. 18.

176. R. Moss, *A Sermon Preach'd before the Queen at St. James's Chapel, on Wednesday, March 15, 1709/10* (ESTC N023373, 1710), p. 25.

177. S. Wright, *Of Praying for the King. A Sermon Preach'd at Black-Fryars, October 24, 1714. Being the First Lord's-Day after the King's Coronation* (ESTC T085221, 1714), p. 20.

178. On Harley, see J. A Downie, *Robert Harley and the Press: Propaganda and Public Opinion in the Age of Swift and Defoe* (Cambridge, 1979).

179. Cf. A. Williams, *Poetry and the Creation of a Whig Literary Culture* (Oxford, 2005), p. 136.

180. *A New Collection of Poems Relating to State Affairs* (ESTC N005917, 1705), sig. A2ᵛ.

181. J. Chase, *An Ode. on the Success of Her Majesty's Arms* (ESTC N011063, 1706), sig. A2; S. Cobb, *Poems on Several Occasions* (ESTC N020558, 1707), sig. A4.

182. R. Blackmore, *The Kit-cats. A Poem* (ESTC T029486, 1708), p. 6.

183. Cobb, *Poems on Several Occasions*, sig. B1; R. Blackmore, *Advice to the Poets. A Poem. Occasion'd by the Wonderful Success of Her Majesty's Arms* (ESTC T000631, 1706), p. 12.

184. *Whig and Tory: or, Wit on Both Sides. Being a Collection of Poems, by the Ablest Pens of the High and Low Parties* (ESTC T116470, 1712). For opposition verse, see F. H. Ellis ed., *Poems on Affairs of State: Augustan Satirical Verse, 1660-1714. Vol. 6, 1697-1704* (New Haven, CT, and London, 1970); Ellis ed., *Poems on Affairs of State: Augustan Satirical Verse, 1660-1714. Vol. 7, 1704-1714* (New Haven, CT, and London, 1975)

185. *The Church of England's Joy on the Happy Accession of Her Most Sacred Majesty Queen Anne* (ESTC N001645, 1702), p. 4.

186. Ibid., pp. 4, 7.

187. Ibid., p. 6.

188. *The English Muse: or, a Congratulatory Poem. Upon Her Majesty's Accession to the Throne of England* (ESTC N000777, 1702), pp. 5–7.

189. Ibid., p. 7.

190. R. Burridge, *A Congratulatory Poem, on the Coronation of Queen Ann* (ESTC T125564, 1702), pp. sigs A2–A2ᵛ.

191. Ibid., pp. 4–5.

192. Ibid., pp. 6, 19.

193. *England's Triumph, or an Occasional Poem on the Happy Coronation of Anne Queen of England, &c.* (ESTC N000774).

194. J. Shute, *A Pindarick Ode, upon Her Majesties Sending His Grace the Duke of Marlborough to Command the English Forces in Holland* (ESTC N037680), p. 1.

195. Ibid., p. 8.

196. M. Prior, *A Letter to Monsieur Boileau Depreaux; Occasion'd by the Victory at Blenheim* (ESTC T062171, 1704), pp. 5, 7.

197. Ibid., p. 3.

198. J. Dennis, *Britannia Triumphans: or the Empire Sav'd, and Europe Deliver'd* (ESTC T029691, 1704), pp. 21, 69.

199. J. Clare, *The English Hero: or, the Duke of Marlborough. A Poem, Upon the Late Glorious Victory over the French and Bavarians, at Hochstetten* (ESTC T032690, 1704), p. 1; *The Royal Conqueress, a Poem, In Honour of the Late Signal victory over the French and Bavarians* (ESTC T203264, 1704), p. 7.

200. Dennis, *Britannia Triumphans*, pp. 6, 10, 16; J. Oldmixon, *A Pastoral Poem on the Victories at Schellenburgh and Bleinheim* (ESTC T043756, 1704), sig. B1ᵛ.

201. Dennis, *Britannia Triumphans*, p. 69; Clare, *The English Hero*, p. 4; *The Royal Conqueress*, p. 9.

202. D. Defoe, *A Hymn to Victory* (ESTC T068191, 1704), sigs A2, A3ᵛ.

203. Ibid., pp. 14, 35.

204. *The Royal Conqueress*, p. 7.

205. P. Motteux, *Britain's Happiness, a Musical Interlude* (ESTC T068218, 1704), epistle to reader and p. 2.

206. E. Ward, *All Men Mad: or, England a Great Bedlam. A Poem* (ESTC T124432, 1704), p. 3.

207. *Deborah: A Sacred Ode* (ESTC N000332, 1705); S. Wesley, *Marlborough; or, The Fate of Europe: A Poem* (ESTC T038989, 1705), pp. 7, 11; N. Tate, *The Triumph, or Warriours Welcome: A Poem on the Glorious Successes of the Last Year* (ESTC T056172, 1705); J. Addison, *The Campaign, a Poem, to His Grace the Duke of Marlborough* (ESTC N000929, 1705), p. 20.

208. See K. Sharpe, *Selling the Tudor Monarchy: Authority and Image in Sixteenth-Century England* (New Haven, CT, and London, 2009), p. 337.

209. C. Johnson, *The Queen: A Pindarick Ode* (ESTC T014612, 1705), p. 2; E. Settle, *Eusebia Triumphans. The Hanover Succession to the Imperial Crown of England, an Heroick Poem* (ESTC T033552, 1705), p. 27.

210. S. Cobb, *Honour Retriev'd. A Poem. Occasion'd by the Late Victories Obtain'd over the French* (ESTC N007411, 1705), p. 3. Anne was represented on a playing card wearing imperial armour (see BM 1982,U.4619.1–52) in a version of a print representing Elizabeth. I owe this reference to the kindness of Mark Knights.

211. Ibid., p. 14.
212. J. Geree, *A Poem to His Grace the Duke of Marlborough, on the Glorious Successes of the Last Campaign* (ESTC T042565, 1705), p. 12.
213. Tate, *The Triumph*, p. 7.
214. J. Chase, *An Ode. on the Success of Her Majesty's Arms* (ESTC N011063, 1706), pp. 6, 9.
215. C. Johnson, *Ramelies. A Poem* (ESTC T106079, 1706), p. 12.
216. W. Wagstaffe, *Ramelies: a Poem, Humbly Inscrib'd to His Grace, the D. of Marlborough. By W. Wagstaffe, Gent. of Lincoln College Oxon* (ESTC N012719, 1706), p. 9.
217. Johnson, *Ramelies*, p. 12.
218. *England's Glory: A Poem. Perform'd in a Musical Entertainment before Her Majesty, on Her Happy Birth-day* (ESTC T135698, 1706), quotation, p. 5.
219. M. Prior, *An Ode, Humbly Inscrib'd to the Queen. On the Late Glorious Success of her Majesty's Arms. Written in Imitation of Spencer's Stile* (ESTC T041935, 1706), p. 2.
220. J. Oldmixon, *Iberia liberata: A Poem* (ESTC N001473, 1706), p. 5.
221. W. L., *A Pindarick Ode on His Excellency John Duke of Marlborough* (ESTC T173505, 1706), p. 20; P. Aubin, *The Stuarts: A Pindarique Ode* (ESTC T048753, 1707), p. 9.
222. J. Paris, *Ramillies. A Poem, Humbly Inscrib'd to His Grace the Duke of Marlborough* (ESTC N012720, 1706), p. 2.
223. C. Darby, *Union a Poem Humbly Dedicated to the Queen* (ESTC T118345, 1707).
224. *The True-Born Britain. Written by the Author of the True-Born Englishman* (ESTC T195585), pp. 4, 8.
225. E. Settle, *Carmen irenicum. The Union of the Imperial Crowns of Great Britain. An Heroick Poem* (ESTC T086250, 1707), 'To the Patriots'.
226. Ibid., p. 43. See Spenser, *Fairie Queen*, iii, 9; K. Sharpe, *Image Wars: Promoting Kings and Commonwealths in England 1603–1660* (New Haven, CT, and London, 2010), pp. 52, 95, 98.
227. Darby, *Union*, sig. A2.
228. Settle, *Carmen irenicum*, p. 25.
229. Ibid.
230. J. Browne, *The Patriots of Great Britain* (ESTC N010941, 1707), p. 12.
231. Darby, *Union*, p. 7.
232. Settle, *Carmen irenicum*, p. 45.
233. L. Theobald, *A Pindarick Ode on the Union. Written by Lew. Theobald, gent* (T075216, 1707), p. 6; Darby, *Union*, p. 7.
234. Browne, *The Patriots*, pp. 1–2.
235. Settle, *Carmen irenicum*, p. 47.
236. Aubin, *The Stuarts*, p. 10.
237. *The Battel of Audenard. A Poem* (ESTC T062154, 1708), sig. A2.
238. J. Gaynam, *Marlborough Still Conquers: or, Union Hath Got the Day* (ESTC T038990, 1708), p. 10.
239. C. Gildon, *Libertas triumphans: A Poem, Occasion'd by the Glorious Victory Obtain'd near Odenard* (ESTC N003930, 1708), p. 17.
240. *Old England's New Triumph: or, the Battel of Oudenard. A Song* (ESTC N011791, 1708), two pages.
241. On George, see below, ch. 15, pp. 643–4.
242. N. Tate, *A Congratulary [sic] Poem to His Royal Highness Prince George of Denmark, Lord High Admiral of Great Britain. Upon the Glorious Successes at Sea* (ESTC T031194, 1708), pp. 4, 7.
243. P. Aubin, *The Extasy: A Pindarick Ode to Her Majesty the Queen. By Mrs. Aubin* (ESTC T089796, 1708), p. 10.
244. S. Cobb, *The Female Reign: An Ode* (ESTC T035485, 1709), p. [15].
245. *A Letter to a Friend, upon the Successes of the Year M.DCC.VIII* (ESTC N002462, 1709), p. 2.
246. *Alcander: A Poem, Occasion'd by the Victories of His Grace the Duke of Marlborough* (ESTC N015791, 1709), pp. 13–14.
247. Oldmixon, *Iberia Liberata*, p. 3.
248. G. Farquhar, *Barcellona. A Poem. Or, the Spanish Expedition* (ESTC T073087, 1710), pp. 47–8.
249. J. Addison, *The Campaign: A Poem, to His Grace the Duke of Marlborough* (ESTC T019861,1710), p. 8.
250. *The Encomium, a Poem* (ESTC N000772, 1710), p. 5.
251. N. Tate, *The Song for Her Majesty's Birth-day, February the 6th, 1710/11* (ESTC N023793, 1711), p. 2.
252. J. Trapp, *Peace. A Poem: Inscribed to the Right Honourable the Lord Viscount Bolingbroke* (ESTC T095926, 1713); Trapp, *ODNB*.

253. Trapp, *Peace*, pp. 8, 19, 22.
254. M. Smith, *On the Peace: A Poem. Humbly Inscrib'd to the Most Honourable the Earl of Oxford and Mortimer, Lord High Treasurer of Great-Britain* (ESTC N010564, 1713), pp. 15–16.
255. B. Higgons, *A Poem on the Peace: Inscribed to the Most Honble Robert, Earl of Oxford, and Earl Mortimer, Lord High-Treasurer of Great-Britain* (ESTC T062162, 1713), p. 4.
256. Ibid., p. 14.
257. W. Waller, *Peace on Earth. A Congratulatory Poem. By William Waller* (ESTC N046549, 1713), p. 1.
258. Ibid., p. 2.
259. S. Wesley, *An Hymn on Peace. To the Prince of Peace* (ESTC T077119, 1713), pp. 9–11.
260. E. Settle, *Irene Triumphans. The Address of the British Muse to the Peace-makers. An heroick Poem* (ESTC 086272, 1713), 'To the Patriots', p. 9.
261. Ibid., p. 13.
262. Ibid., p. 15.
263. Ibid., pp. 6, 8, 10.
264. For example, *An Anniversary Ode on Her Majesties Birth-day, Being the Sixth day of February, 1702/3* (ESTC N001078, 1703), p. 4; T. Wall, *An Ode for an Entertainment of Musick on Her Majesty's Birth-day* (ESTC T126396, 1703), p. 3; N. Tate, *The Song for New-Years-Day, 1703. Perform'd Before Her Majesty* (ESTC T133793, 1703); E. Fenton, *To the Queen, on Her Majesty's Birth-day* (ESTC T051351, 1712); J. Kusser, *A Serenata. To be Represented on The Birth-Day Of the Most Serene Anne* (ESTC T032954, 1714).
265. *The Church of England's Joy on the Happy Accession of Her Most Sacred Majesty Queen Anne, to the Throne* (ESTC N001645, 1702), p. 6.
266. *Gazette*, 10 August 1704.
267. *Gazette*, 16 May 1706.
268. *Gazette*, 26 July 1708.
269. See Downie, *Robert Harley*, ch. 3, especially pp. 58–60; Downie, 'Periodicals and Politics in the Reign of Queen Anne', in R. Myers and M. Harris eds, *Serials and their Readers, 1620–1914* (Winchester, 1993), pp. 45–61.
270. Downie, *Robert Harley*, p. 71.
271. Ibid., p. 69.
272. *A Relation of the Great and Glorious Success of the Fleet and Forces of Her Majesty and the States General at Vigo* (ESTC T147970, 1702), two pages; cf. *The Glorious Success of Her Majesty's Fleet, and the States General, under the Command of the Honourable, Sir George Rooke, at Vigo* (ESTC T162969, 1702).
273. *A Narrative of Sir George Rooke's Late Voyage to the Mediterranean* (ESTC T000802, 1704), p. 1.
274. Ibid., p. 12.
275. Ibid., pp. 9, 11.
276. Ibid., p. 7.
277. *A Review of the Late Engagement at Sea* (ESTC T000803, 1704), p. 13.
278. Ibid., p. 15.
279. *A Full and Impartial Relation of the Battle Fought on the 13th of August, 1704* (ESTC N001332, 1704), p. 3.
280. F. Hare, *The History of the Campaign in Germany, For the Year 1704* (ESTC T036470, 1705), sig. A2.
281. *This Morning by a Mail from Holland, We Have Advice of the Taking of Landau by Capitulation and the Town of Tarabach and other Particulars* (ESTC N045626, 1704).
282. *A Full Account of the Duke of Marlbrough's Victory over the French, with an Exact List of the Officers Taken Prisoners* (ESTC N001330, 1705).
283. *Whitehall, July 14. 1705. Published by Authority* (ESTC T220336, 1705).
284. *An Exact and Full Account of the Siege of Barcelona* (ESTC T087003, 1706), p. 17.
285. *The History of the Triumphs of Her Majesty's Arms Both by Sea and Land in and about Spain, During this War* (T017791, 1707), pp. 2, 157, 172.
286. *The Life and Glorious Actions of that Right Honourable Sir George Rook, Kt. Sometime Admiral of the English Fleet* (ESTC N047771, 1707); *The Life and Glorious Actions of Sir Cloudesly Shovel, Kt. Admiral of the Consederate Fleet in the Mediterranean Sea* (ESTC T040928, 1707); *An Essay upon the Character of His Grace the Duke of Marlborough* (ESTC N001704, 1707), pp. 16, 25.
287. *An Account of the Glorious Victory Obtained by the Duke of Marlborough over the French. Windsor, July 5th, 1708* (ESTC N029492, 1708).

288. *A Compleat History of the Wars in Flanders, Italy, Spain, Portugal, and on the Rhine* (ESTC T231012); *The History of the Campaign in Flanders, in the Year 1708* (ESTC T036469, 1709), pp. 14, 56.
289. *The History of the Campaign in Flanders, in the Year 1709* (ESTC N017683, 1710), p. 54.
290. Downie, *Robert Harley*, ch. 6.
291. J. Swift, *The Conduct of the Allies, and of the Late Ministry, in the Beginning and Carrying on the Present War* (ESTC N001498, Edinburgh, 1712).
292. See below, ch. 15, p. 640.
293. I owe information on the popularity of sermons to an inaugural lecture by Isabel Rivers delivered at Queen Mary, University of London, 23 May 2007, and to discussions with Dr James Caudle.
294. J. Sharp, *A Sermon Preach'd at the Coronation of Queen Anne, in the Abbey-Church of Westminster, April XXIII. MDCCII* (ESTC T172887, 1702). Sharp was asked to preach by the queen though he was unwell, Sharp *ODNB*.
295. Sharp, *A Sermon*, p. 13.
296. Sharp, *ODNB*.
297. *A Sermon on the Coronation-day, April 23. 1702. Preach'd in the Cathedral Church of Glocester, before the Mayor and Corporation* (ESTC T012040, 1702).
298. Ibid., pp. 14, 20–1.
299. M. Hole, *A Sermon Preach'd on the Day of Her Majesties Coronation: in the Parish Church of Stokegursy in Somersetshire* (ESTC T010728, 1702), p. 18.
300. Ibid.
301. They were of course not always celebrations; see below, ch. 15, pp. 623–4, and A. Kugler, *Errant Plagiary: The Life and Writing of Lady Sarah Cowper, 1644–1720* (Stanford, CA, 2002), pp. 177–9.
302. W. Mynors, *A Sermon Preached May 29. Being the Anniversary of the Restoration of K. Charles II* (ESTC T180536, 1707); R. Phillips, *Religion and Loyalty. A Sermon Preach'd at St. Margaret's Westminster, before the Honourable House of Commons, upon Thursday the 29th of May, 1712* (ESTC T009539, 1712).
303. T. Bisse, *A Sermon Preach'd before the Honourable House of Commons, at St. Margaret's Westminster, On Saturday, May 29. 1714. By Thomas Bisse, D. D. Preacher at the Rolls, and Chaplain in Ordinary to Her Majesty* (ESTC T009524, 1714), p. 21.
304. F. Atterbury, *A Sermon Preached before the Honourable House of Commons, at St. Margaret's Westminster, on Wednesday, March 8. 1703/4. Being The Day of Her Majesty's Happy Accession to the Throne* (ESTC T047686, 1704), pp. 5, 10. Atterbury was a royal chaplain.
305. R. Lloyd, *A Sermon Preached on Wednesday the 8th of March, 1703/4. Being the Day of Her Most Sacred Majesty's Inauguration, at the Parish-church of Epsom in Surrey* (ESTC T010718, 1704), p. 2.
306. B. Hoadly, *A Sermon Preach'd on the Eighth of March, 1704–5. Being the Anniversary Day of Thanksgiving for the Queen's Accession to the Crown* (ESTC T018269, 1705), p. 2; R. Stephens, *The Queen a Nursing Mother. A Sermon Preach'd on Thursday, March the 8th* (ESTC 108060, 1705), pp. 2, 10.
307. O. Blackall, *The Divine Institution of Magistracy, and the Gracious Design of its Institution. A Sermon Preach'd before the Queen, at St. James's, on Tuesday, March 8. 1708* (ESTC T034744, 1709).
308. H. Lambe, *A Good Prince Never Forgotten. A sermon Preach'd at St. Dunstan's in the East, March the 8th 1708/9* (ESTC T068545, 1709).
309. J. Adams, *A Sermon Preach'd before the Honourable House of Commons at St. Margaret's Westminster, on Thursday, March the 8th 1710/11* (ESTC T049107, 1711), pp. 19–21.
310. N. Hough, *A Sermon upon the Anniversary Day of Her Majesty's Happy Accession to the Throne. Preach'd at Kensington-Church, March 8. 1712/13* (ESTC T005085, 1713), p. 5.
311. W. Sutton, *A Sermon Preach'd at the Cathedral-church of Norwich, On Monday, March the 8th 1713/14. Being the Anniversary of Her Majesty's Happy Accession to the Crown. By William Sutton, M. A. and Vicar of Saxthorpe, in Norfolk* (ESTC T060317, 1714); T. Sherlock, *A Sermon Preach'd before the Honourable House of Commons, At St. Margaret's Westminster, On Monday, March 8. 1713/4* (ESTC T008336, 1714), pp. 16–17.
312. Sherlock, *A Sermon*, p. 19.
313. J. Sharp, *The Duty and Advantages of Frequently Receiving the Holy Sacrament. A Sermon Preach'd before the Queen at St. James's Chappel, On Good-Friday, March 26. 1703* (ESTC T035059, 1703); Sharp, *A Serious Exhortation to Repentance and a Holy Life. A Sermon Preach'd before the Queen, at Saint James's Chappel, on Ash Wednesday, Febr. 10. 1702/3* (ESTC T011961, 1703); R. Duke, *A Sermon Preach'd before the Queen, at St. James's. January 9, 1703/4. By R. Duke, Prebendary of*

Glocester, and Rector of Blaby in Leicestershire. Publish'd by Her Majesty's Special Command (ESTC T104687, 1704), p. 23.

314. W. Kennett, *The Duties of Rejoycing in a Day of Prosperity. Recommended in a Sermon Preach'd before the Queen, at Her Royal Chappel in Windsor. On Sunday, June 23. 1706* (ESTC N009032, 1706), p. 14.
315. W. Nicolson, *The Blessings of the Sixth Year. A Sermon Preach'd before the Queen at St. James's Chappel, on Saturday the Eighth of March, 1706/7* (ESTC T056499, 1707), p. 24.
316. T. Manningham, *A Sermon Preach'd before the Queen at Windsor, July the 11th, 1708* (ESTC T012775, 1708), p. 22.
317. G. Stanhope, *A Sermon Preached before the Queen in the Chapel-royal at St. James's; November the 7th 1710. Being the Day of Thanksgiving to Almighty God, for the Successes of this Campaign* (ESTC T067172, 1710), p. 23.
318. Nicolson, *The Blessings of the Sixth Year*, p. 21. See J. Caudle, 'Measures of Allegiance: Sermon Culture and the Creation of a Public Discourse of Obedience and Resistance in Georgian Britain, 1714–60' (Yale University, PhD thesis, 1996).
319. D. Williams, *A Thanksgiving Sermon, for the Success of Her Majesties Forces. Preach'd at Hand-Alley, November 12, 1702* (ESTC T014122, 1702), p. 7.
320. Ibid., pp. 11–12.
321. B. Woodroffe, *A Sermon Preached before the University of Oxford, at St. Mary's Church, Decem. 3. 1702. Being the Day of Thanksgiving, for the Signal Successes, Vouchsafed to Her Majesty's Forces, both by Sea and Land* (ESTC T047842, 1703); H. Prideaux, *A Sermon Preach'd in the Cathedral-church of Norwich, December the 3d, 1702* (ESTC T014071, 1703), p. 15.
322. See R. Fiddes, *A Sermon Preached on the Thanksgiving day: December, 3d. 1702 . . . By Richard Fiddes, Rector of Halsham in Holderness* (ESTC T075694, 1703).
323. W. Elstob, *A Sermon upon the Thanksgiving for the Victory Obtain'd by Her Majesty's Forces, and those of Her Allies, over the French and Bavarians near Hochstet* (ESTC T063882, 1704), p. iii.
324. J. Dubourdieu, *A Sermon Preached on the 7th day of September* (ESTC T104497, 1704), p. 23.
325. J. Evans, *A Sermon Preach'd at Chester and Wrexam. Septemb. 7th. 1704. Being the Day of Publick Thanksgiving for the Glorious Victory at Bleinheim* (ESTC T207098, 1704), p. 6.
326. L. Milbourne, *Great Britain's Acclamation to Her Deborah* (ESTC T011987, 1704), pp. 8, 11, 27 and passim.
327. Ibid., p. 7.
328. Ibid., sig. A2, p. 26.
329. Ibid., p. 24.
330. J. Stennett, *A Sermon Preach'd on Thursday the 7th of September 1704* (ESTC T014094, 1704), p. 12.
331. Ibid., pp. 27, 31.
332. W. Pearson, *A Sermon Preached in the Cathedral and Metropolitical Church of St. Peter in York. Septemb. Vii. 1704* (ESTC T011980, 1704), p. 19.
333. R. Norris, *A Sermon Preach'd on September 7. 1704* (ESTC T049200, 1704), pp. 20–1.
334. Ibid., p. 21.
335. A. Jephson, *A Sermon Preach'd in the Parish-church of Camberwell, on the 7th day of September, 1704* (ESTC T012002, 1705), p. 13.
336. R. Willis, *A Sermon Preach'd before the Queen, at the Cathedral Church of St. Paul, London, on the 23d Day of August 1705. Being the Thanksgiving-day for the Late Glorious Success in Forcing the Enemies Lines in the Spanish Netherlands* (ESTC N000383, 1705), p. 15.
337. F. Atterbury, *A Sermon Preach'd at Whitehall, August the 23d, 1705. Being the Day Appointed for a Publick Thanksgiving for the Late Glorious Success of Her Majesty's Arms* (ESTC T087858, 1705), p. 18.
338. J. Evans, *A Sermon Preach'd May the 19th, 1706. On Occasion of the Surprising Victory Obtain'd at Ramelly in Brabant, May 12* (ESTC T173619, 1706), p. 25.
339. Ibid.
340. G. Stanhope, *A Sermon Preach'd before the Queen at the Cathedral Church of St. Paul, London, the xxviith day of June MDCCVI. Being the Day Appointed for a General Thanksgiving* (ESTC T010693, 1706), p. 26; G. Whittle, *A Thanksgiving Sermon Preached at Foots-Cray in Kent* (ESTC, T011932, 1706), p. 28.
341. J. Wilder, *A Sermon Preach'd on the 27th of June, 1706. Being the Thanksgiving-day* (ESTC T188066, 1706), p. 14.
342. W. Perse, *A Sermon Preached at Malton in Yorkshire. June 27th. 1706. Being the Day of Publick Thanksgiving* (ESTC T010708, 1706), p. 27.

343. G. Burnet, *A Sermon Preach'd before the Queen, and the Two Houses of Parliament, at St. Paul's on the 31st of December, 1706. The Day of Thanksgiving for the Wonderful Successes of this Year* (ESTC T003242, 1707), p. 25.

344. Ibid., pp. 25, 28.

345. W. Ward, *A Sermon Preach'd at Portsmouth, December. 31. 1706* (ESTC T045891, 1707), p. 13.

346. C. Lamb, *England Happy at Home and Abroad. A Sermon Preached in the Parish Church of Enfield, in the County of Middlesex; on December the 31st, 1706* (ESTC T032650, 1707), p. 10.

347. J. Bates, *Two (united) Are Better than One Alone. A Thanksgiving Sermon upon the Union of the Two Kingdoms* (ESTC T052158, 1707); T. Freke, *Union, the Strength of a People. Considered in a Sermon, Preach'd in Bartholomew-Close, On May the First, 1707. Being the Day Appointed by Her Majesty, for a General Thanksgiving for the Happy Union of the Two Kingdoms of England and Scotland, in Great Britain* (ESTC T006395, 1707).

348. R. Davidson, *Brit. Ann. 1a. A Sermon Preach'd on the Thanksgiving-Day, for the Happy Union of Great Britain* (ESTC T012023, 1707).

349. C. Bean, *A Sermon Preach'd before the University of Oxford, on the First of May, 1707. Being the Day Appointed for a General Thanksgiving for the Happy Union* (ESTC T106428, 1707), p. 13.

350. W. Talbot, *A Sermon Preach'd Before the Queen at the Cathedral Church of St. Paul, on May the first, 1707* (ESTC T118675, 1707), p. 13.

351. F. Hutchinson, *A Sermon Preached at St. Edmund's-Bury, on the First of May, 1707* (ESTC T099480, 1707), p. 14.

352. G. Dent, *A Thanksgiving Sermon Preach'd on the First day of May, 1707* (ESTC T107001, 1707), p. 12.

353. P. Dujon, *A Sermon Preached in St. George's Church in Doncaster, May 1* (ESTC T060273, 1707), p. 8.

354. Dent, *A Thanksgiving Sermon*, p. 10.

355. 1 Samuel 11: 1–15.

356. T. Coulton, *Nahash's Defeat, and Jabesh-Gilead's Rescue: a Sermon Preach'd August 19. 1708. on Occasion of the Defeat of the Intended Invasion of North-Britain, and of the French Forces near Audenarde* (ESTC TN006023, 1708), p. 18.

357. T. Knaggs, *A Sermon Preach'd at St. Margarets, Westminster, August the 19th. 1708* (ESTC N022818, 1708), p. 20; M. Stanhope, *God the Author of Victory. A Sermon Preach'd in the Royal-Chappel at White-Hall, on Thursday the 19th of August, 1708* (ESTC N018124, 1708), p. 9.

358. J. Stennett, *A Sermon Preach'd on Thursday, February 17. 1708/9* (ESTC T049210, 1709), p. 19.

359. F. Hare, *A Sermon Preach'd before the Honourable House of Commons, At the Church of St. Margaret Westminster, On Thursday, Feb. 17. 1708/9. Being the Day of Thanksgiving For the Preservation of Her Majesty from the Treacherous Designs and Attempts of Her Enemies this Last Year; And for the Many Great Successes of Her Arms* (ESTC T006578, 1709), p. 10.

360. T. Manningham, *A Sermon Preach'd before the Queen at Saint James's: on Thursday the 17th of February, Being Appointed for a Day of Thanksgiving* (ESTC T024817, 1709), p. 13.

361. T. Masters, *A Sermon Preach'd on November 22. 1709. Being the Day of Thanksgiving for the Successes of the Last Campaign* (ESTC T100548, 1710), p. 15.

362. T. Rivers, *A Sermon Preach'd at the Cathedral-church of Winchester, on Tuesday, Nov. 22. 1709* (ESTC N022918, 1710), p. 13.

363. G. Stanhope, *The Common Obstructions to Faith, and a Good Life Considered. A Sermon Preached in the Chapel-royal at St. James's, Novemb. the 6th, 1709* (ESTC T067035, 1710).

364. R. Altham, *A Sermon Preach'd before the Honourable House of Commons at the Church of St. Margaret Westminster, on Wednesday, Jan. 16. 1711/12. Being the Fast-day for a General Peace* (ESTC T049024, 1712), p. 17 and *passim*.

365. J. Trapp, *A Sermon Preach'd at the Parish-church of St. Martin in the Fields; January the 16th, 1711. Being the Day Appointed by Her Majesty for the General Fast: for Imploring the Blessing of Almighty God upon the Treaty of Peace now in Negotiation* (ESTC T003116, 1712), p. 14.

366. W. Fleetwood, *A Sermon on the Fast-day, January the Sixteenth, 1711/12. Against Such As Delight in War* (ESTC T045871, 1712).

367. Trapp, *A Sermon*, p. 13.

368. E. Chishull, *The Duty of Good Subjects, In Relation to Publick Peace. Being a Sermon Preach'd at the Assizes at Hertford, on August the 11th, 1712* (ESTC T035391, 1712), pp. 12, 21 and *passim*.

369. G. Hooper, *A Sermon Preach'd before both Houses of Parliament, in the Cathedral Church of St. Paul, on Tuesday, July 7. 1713. Being the Day Appointed by Her Majesty for a General Thanksgiving for the Peace* (ESTC T018008, 1713), p. 7.

370. Ibid., pp. 30–1.

371. P. Stubs, *Thankfulness for Peace, the Subjects Duty to God's Vicegerent. A Sermon Preach'd at St James Garlick-Hythe, London* (ESTC T003110, 1713), pp. 16, 24.

372. N. Brady, *A Sermon Preach'd at Richmond in Surrey, upon July the 7th, 1713. Being the Day of Thanksgiving Appointed by Her Majesty for a General Peace* (ESTC T017969, 1713), p. 17.

373. W. Law, *A Sermon Preach'd at Hazelingfield, in the County of Cambridge, on Tuesday, July 7. 1713* (ESTC T066733, 1713), p. 41.

374. Cf. J. C. D. Clark, *English Society, 1660–1832: Religion, Ideology and Politics during the Ancien Regime* (Cambridge, 2000), pp. 109–20.

375. Below, ch. 15, p. 625.

376. *A charge given at the triennial visitation of the diocese of Salisbury, in October 1704* (ESTC T030470, 1704).

377. A. Blackwall, *Duty to God and the Queen. Briefly Expressed in a Sermon Preach'd at St. Mary's Nottingham, March the 17th. 1703/4* (ESTC N009047, 1704).

378. Ibid., p. 5.

379. J. Pierce, *Mercy and Truth, Righteousness and Peace; Treated of as the Glory and Interest of Nations: in an Assize-sermon Preach'd at Northampton, July the 26th, 1704* (ESTC T174694, 1704).

380. L. Beaulieu, *The Reciprocal Duty betwixt Kings and Subjects, Impartially Stated, in a Sermon on Romans xiii* (ESTC T046496, 1706); E. Gibson, *Against Speaking Evil of Princes, and those in Authority under Them: a Sermon Preach'd at the Assizes Held at Croyden in Surrey, March 7th, 1705/6* (ESTC T012014, 1706).

381. B. Hoadly, *The Happiness of the Present Establishment, and the Unhappiness of Absolute Monarchy. A Sermon Preach'd at the Assizes at Hartford, March 22d. 1707/8* (ESTC T018346, 1708).

382. H. Colman, *Government and Obedience. A Sermon Preach'd in the Town of King's-Lynn, Norfolk. September 29. 1711* (ESTC T010753, 1711), p. 31.

383. B. Gatton, *The Doctrine of Non-resistance Stated and Vindicated* (ESTC T034798, 1711); R. Phillips, *Religion and Loyalty. A Sermon Preach'd at St. Margaret's Westminster, before the Honourable House of Commons, upon Thursday the 29th of May, 1712* (ESTC T009539, 1712); B. Carter, *The Duties of Subjects to Princes and Magistrates Stated and Prov'd by the Evidence of Scripture and Reason. A Sermon Preach'd at the Assizes held at Brentwood, for the County of Essex, on Thursday the 14th of August, 1712* (ESTC T214089, 1712).

384. Carter, *The Duties of Subjects*, p. 18.

385. W. Delaune, *A Sermon Preached before the Honourable House of Commons, at St. Margaret's Westminster, January 30. 1702/3* (ESTC T047665, 1703), p. 22.

386. G. Stanhope, *A Sermon Preach'd before the Honourable House of Commons, at St. Margarets-Westminster, on Tuesday the 30th of January, 1704/5* (ESTC T049019, 1705); R. Eyre, *A Sermon Preach'd before the Honourable House of Commons, at Saint Margaret, Westminster, on Friday, Jan. 30. 1707/8* (ESTC T017499, 1708).

387. L. Milbourne, *The Measures of Resistance to the Higher Powers, so far as Becomes a Christian: in a Sermon, Preach'd on January the 30th, 1709/10* (ESTC T142651, 1710), p. 20.

388. *Whigs no Christians. A Sermon Preach'd at Putney, in Surry, Jan. 30. 1712/3* (ESTC N025671, 1713).

389. T. Sherlock, *A Sermon Preach'd before the Queen at St. James's, on Munday [sic] January 31. 1703/4* (ESTC T049065, 1704), p. 11.

390. W. Beveridge, *Submission to Governours. Or, the Doctrine of St. Peter. Concerning Government: Explain'd in a Sermon On the Martyrdom of King Charles I* (ESTC T016430, 1710); W. Fleetwood, *A Sermon Preach'd before the Right Honourable the Lords Spiritual & Temporal, on January the 30th, 1709/10* (ESTC T085529, 1710), p. 18.

391. R. Wynne, *Unity and Peace the Support of Church and State. A Sermon Preach'd before the Honourable House of Commons, on Munday Jan. 31th [sic] 1703/4* (ESTC T050454, 1704). See A. Lacey, *The Cult of King Charles the Martyr* (Woodbridge, 2003), ch. 6, especially pp. 192–204.

392. This is an important, but under-explored subject. See above ch. 1, p. 57; and J. Pocock, *Virtue, Commerce, and History: Essays on Political Thought and History, chiefly in the Eighteenth Century* (Cambridge, 1985), ch. 5.

393. C. Leslie, *A Case of Present Concern, in a Letter to a Member of the House of Commons* (ESTC T082646, 1703), p. 6.

394. A. Fyfe, *The Royal Martyr, K. Charles I. An Opera* (ESTC T045358, Edinburgh, 1705), 'To the Queen', not paginated.

395. *Eikon Basilike* (ESTC T070193, Dublin, 1706), dedication to Ormonde, not paginated.

396. W. Mynors, *A Sermon Preached May 29. Being the Anniversary of the Restoration of K. Charles II* (ESTC T180536, 1707), p. 8.

397. See, for example, M. Astell, *An Impartiall Enquiry into the Causes of Rebellion and Civil War* (ESTC T000820, 1704).

398. H. Gandy, *Some Remarks, or Short Strictures, upon A Compassionate Enquiry into the Causes of the Civil War* (ESTC T049384, 1704), p. 32.

399. *A Satyr upon King William, Being the Secret History of His Life and Reign* (ESTC T073012, 1703), sigs A2ᵛ–A3ᵛ.

400. B. Mandeville, *The Pamphleteers. A Satyr* (ESTC T-71666, 1703), p. 3.

401. J. Tillotson, *A Form of Prayer, Used by His Late Majesty, K. William III* (ESTC T040034, 1704), p. xiii; cf. D. Defoe, *Royal Religion; Being Some Enquiry after the Piety of Princes* (ESTC T032978, 1704); J. Piggott, *A Sermon Preach'd the 7th of September, 1704* (ESTC T014068, 1704), p. 14.

402. D. Defoe, *A Hymn to Victory* (ESTC T068188, 1704), p. 5.

403. A. Jephson, *A Sermon Preach'd in the Parish-church of Camberwell, on the 7th day of September, 1704* (ESTC T012002, 1705), p. 10; B. Hoadly, *A Sermon Preach'd on the Eighth of March, 1704–5. Being the Anniversary Day of Thanksgiving for the Queen's Accession to the Crown* (ESTC T018269, 1705), p. 6.

404. T. Bradbury, *The Divine Right of the Revolution* (ESTC T034758, 1709).

405. Milbourne, *The Measures of Resistance*, pp. 37–8.

406. *Dr. Henry Sacheverell's Speech, Made in Westminster-Hall. On Tuesday, March 7, 1710* (ESTC N065629, 1710), p. 4.

407. See *Advertisement from the Conduit in Cheapside. On this Spot of Ground the Statue of Our Late Glorious King William, Was Design'd to Be Set Up* (ESTC N001802, 1703); *Hannibal at the Gates: or, the Progress of Jacobitism* (ESTC T070826, 1712), p. 34; E. S., *All at Stake: Hannover or Perkin, In a Letter to a Country Clergyman* (ESTC T021222, 1712), pp. 5, 12, 15, 18 and *passim*; F. Squire, *A Brief Justification of the Principles of a Reputed Whigg* (ESTC T107870, 1713), pp. 8–9.

408. Squire, *A Brief Justification*, p. 9.

409. J. Willes, *The Present Constitution, and the Protestant Succession Vindicated* (ESTC T044208, 1714).

410. W. Ayloffe, *A Pocket Companion for Gentlemen and Ladies. Being a True and Faithful Epitomy of the Most Exact and Ample Historians of England* (ESTC T087783, 1703), pp. 122–4.

411. E. Hyde, *The History of the Rebellion and Civil Wars in England, Begun in the Year 1641* (ESTC N009850, 1703), sigs A2–A4ᵛ.

412. T. Rymer, *Foedera, conventiones, literæ, et cujuscunque generis acta publica, inter reges Angliæ* (ESTC T148099, vol. 11, 1703), sig. A3.

413. F. Sandford, *A Genealogical History of the Kings and Queens of England, and Monarchs of Great Britain* (ESTC T147652, 1707).

414. *Great Britain's Glory: or, the Lives and Glorious Actions of all the Protestant Kings and Queens, that ever Reign'd in England* (ESTC T183717, 1708), pp. 20–3.

415. H. Moll, *A History of the English Wars, in France, Spain, Portugal, Netherlands, Germany, &c. Containing all the Sieges and Battles Fought by the English in those Countries, from William the Conqueror, to the Present Time* (ESTC T000697, 1705), sig. A2.

416. T. Blount, *Boscobel: or the Compleat History of His Sacred Majesty Charles II. Most Miraculous Preservation, after the Battle of Worcester* (ESTC T110272, 1709), pp. iii–vi.

417. A. Boyer, *The History of the Reign of Queen Anne, Digested into Annals. Year the First* (ESTC T122946, 1703).

418. A. Boyer, *The History of the Reign of Queen Anne, Digested into Annals. Year the Fifth* (ESTC T122945, 1707), sig. A2.

419. A. Boyer, *The History of the Reign of Queen Anne, Digested into Annals. Year the Tenth* (ESTC T123170, 1712), pp. ii–iii.

420. D. Jones, *A Compleat History of Europe: or, a View of the Affairs thereof, Civil and Military* (ESTC N004961, 1705).

421. Jones and Boyer went to several editions of each year. For a list of stockists, see, for example, the title page of the 1712 edition of Boyer.

422. See below, ch. 15, pp. 623–6, and H. Smith, '"Last of all the Heavenly Birth": Queen Anne and Sacral Queenship', *Parliamentary History*, 28 (2009), pp. 137–49. This essay offers an important corrective to those who dismiss Anne's interest in divine right.

423. W. Baron, *Separation and Sedition Inseparable, whilst Dissenters and Commonwealthsmen Are Permitted to Controll in all Publick Administrations of Church and State* (ESTC T118157, 1703).

424. J. Barnes, *The Good Old Way: or, Three Brief Discourses Tending to the Promotion of Religion, and the Glory, Peace, and Happiness of the Queen, and Her Kingdoms, in Church and State* (ESTC T088705, 1703).

425. *The Source of Our Present Fears Discover'd: or, Plain Proof of Some Late Designs against Our Present Constitution and Government* (ESTC T108540, 1703).

426. *An Essay upon Government. Wherein the Republican Schemes Reviv'd by Mr. Lock, Dr. Blackal, &c. Are Fairly Consider'd and Refuted* (ESTC T094344, 1705), p. 27.
427. Ibid., pp. 55-9.
428. H. Gandy, *Old England: or, the Government of England Prov'd to Be Monarchical and Hereditary, by the Fundamental Laws of England* (ESTC N011019, 1705); W. Prynne, *The Title of Kings Proved to Be jure divino* (ESTC T014234, 1705).
429. For a study, see J. Kenyon, *Revolution Principles: The Politics of Party, 1689-1720* (Cambridge, 1977).
430. F. Atterbury, *To the Wh-Y-s Nineteen Queries, a Fair and Full Answer, by an Honest Torie; Purely for the Publick Good of His Country* (ESTC T051380, 1710). Atterbury became a Jacobite conspirator, *ODNB*.
431. A. R., *Jura regi? majestatis in Anglia: or, the Rights of the English Monarchy* (ESTC T012959, 1711), p. 23.
432. G. Berkeley, *Passive Obedience, or, the Christian Doctrine of Not Resisting the Supreme Power, Proved and Vindicated upon the Principles of the Law of Nature* (ESTC T043742, 1712).
433. H. Bedford, *A Vindication of Her Majesty's Title and Government, from the Dangerous Insinuations of Dr. Higden's View of the English Constitution* (ESTC T178642, 1713). On Bedford, see *ODNB*.
434. W. Robertson, *The Liberty, Property, and Religion of the Whigs. In a Letter to a Whig. Occasion'd by Some Discourse upon the Reverend Dr. Sacheverell's Sermons* (ESTC T082000, 1713).
435. [J. Dunton], *The History of Living Men: or, Characters of the Royal Family* (ESTC N007801, 1702), pp. 13, 28 and *passim*.
436. J. Gordon, *The Character of a Generous Prince Drawn from the Great Lines of Heroick Fortitude* (ESTC N014693, 1703), p. 437.
437. J. Coningham, *A Critical Essay on the Modern Medals* (ESTC T056741, 1704), pp. 65-8.
438. *An Essay upon the Character of His Grace the Duke of Marlborough* (ESTC N001784, 1707), p. 27.
439. *Great Britain's Triumph: or, Her ... Majesty Queen Ann's Title to the Imperial Crown of France Maintain'd by a true Englishman* (Bodleian Vet. A4 e.75 [2], 1707).
440. J. Edwards, *One Nation, and One King. A Discourse on Ezek. XXXVII. 22. Occasion'd by the Happy Union of England and Scotland* (ESTC T006378, 1707), p. 24.
441. *An Oration Sacred to the Imperial Majesty of Anne, Queen of Great-Britain* (ESTC T032952, 1707), pp. 50, 56.
442. Ibid., p. 55.
443. *A Cat May Look on a Queen: or, a Satyr on Her Present Majesty. Attempted by John Dunton, Author of the Satyr on King William* (ESTC T020329, 1708), pp. 44, 46.
444. Ibid., p. 19.
445. Ibid., pp. 60, 71.
446. W. Cockburn, *An Essay upon the Propitious and Glorious Reign of Our Gracious Sovereign Anne, Queen of Great Britain* (ESTC N001543, 1710), p. 38.
447. Ibid., pp. 5, 17.
448. Ibid., p. 59.
449. Ibid., sig. A4^v. See above, ch. 13, p. 566.
450. M. Knights, *Representation and Misrepresentation in Later Stuart Britain: Partisanship and Political Culture* (Oxford, 2004), pp. 113-23.
451. Ibid., pp. 135, 142-8.
452. Ibid., p. 151.
453. A collection of addresses (ESTC N014695, 1710).
454. *A Collection of the Addresses which Have Been Presented to the Queen, since the Impeachment Of the Reverend Dr. Henry Sacheverell* (ESTC T000685, 1710), p. 18.
455. Ibid., p. 13.
456. Ibid., p. 42.
457. *The Following Address was Presented to Her Majesty by Crew Offley, Esq; Accompanied by Several Gentlemen of Cheshire* (ESTC N000145, 1710).
458. *Collection of the Addresses*, p. 8.
459. Ibid., p. 57; cf. p. 32.

14   Re-depicting Female Rule

1. O. Millar, *Tudor, Stuart and Early Georgian Pictures in the Collection of Her Majesty The Queen* (London, 1963), pp. 23-4.

2. See K. Sharpe, *Selling the Tudor Monarchy: Authority and Image in Sixteenth-Century England* (New Haven, CT, and London 2009), ch. 10.
3. Millar, *Tudor, Stuart and Early Georgian Pictures*, p. 143, no. 337.
4. Though see the playing card figuring Anne in imperial armour, above, ch. 13, p. 792, n. 210. Anne was figured as the martial Bellona in a German print (BM Bb, 3.173), but I have seen no English version.
5. J. Dubourdieu, *A Sermon Preached on the 7th Day of September, Being the Day of Thanksgiving* (ESTC T104497, 1704), p. 13.
6. N. Tate, *The Triumph, or Warriours Welcome: A Poem on the Glorious Successes of the Last Year* (ESTC T013846, 1705), p. 15; *Advice to Mr. Vario, the Painter. A Poem* (ESTC N001605, 1709), p. 1.
7. On Monamy see Millar, *Tudor, Stuart and Early Georgian Pictures*, pp. 167–8; F. B. Cockett, *Peter Monamy 1681–1749 and His Circle* (Woodbridge, 2000).
8. Millar, *Tudor, Stuart and Early Georgian Pictures*, p. 139, no. 325.
9. National Gallery of Scotland, Scottish National Portrait Gallery PG 939.
10. National Portrait Gallery, London, NPG 1616; NPG 5227.
11. J. Stewart, *Sir Godfrey Kneller and the English Baroque Portrait* (Oxford, 1983), p. 60; Kneller, *ODNB*.
12. Millar, *Tudor, Stuart and Early Georgian Pictures*, p. 143; see *Calendar of Treasury Books XVIII, 1703*, p. 50.
13. Stewart, *Kneller*, pp. 91–2, nos 47–8; see http://www.innertemplelibrary.org.uk/temple-history/inner-temple-history-the-buildings-hall-treasury.htm
14. Stewart, *Kneller*, p. 92, no. 50, plate 66a.
15. Millar, *Tudor, Stuart and Early Georgian Pictures*, p. 144, no. 340.
16. Ibid., p. 144, no. 399; Stewart, *Kneller*, p. 91, no. 46.
17. Michael Dahl, *ODNB*; Millar, *Tudor, Stuart and Early Georgian Pictures*, p. 151, nos 383–4.
18. NPG 6187; J. Ingamells, *Later Stuart Portraits 1685–1714* (London, 2009), p. 9.
19. Stewart, *Kneller*, p. 73.
20. See N. Tate, *Portrait-Royal. A poem upon Her Majesty's picture set up in Guild-Hall; by order of the Lord Mayor and Court of Aldermen of the City of London. Drawn by Mr. Closterman* (ESTC T133784, 1703), p. 23.
21. NPG 215; Ingamells, *Later Stuart Portraits 1685–1714*, p. 8; Closterman, *ODNB*.
22. Closterman, *ODNB*.
23. Tate, *Portrait-Royal*, pp. 1, 2, 4.
24. Ibid., pp. 6–7, 22.
25. Ibid., p. 8.
26. Ibid., pp. 13–18, 19.
27. Ibid., p. 22; see p. 7.
28. Ibid., pp. 7–8.
29. Ibid., p. 18.
30. Stewart, *Kneller*, pp. 58–9.
31. Ibid., p. 189.
32. D. Green, *Blenheim* (London, 1951), p. 298.
33. Ibid.
34. Stewart, *Kneller*, p. 92, no. 51, plate 58.
35. Green, *Blenheim*, p. 298.
36. Ibid., p. 299.
37. Stewart, *Kneller*, p. 116, no. 467, plate 59; NPG 902; Ingamells, *Later Stuart Portraits 1685–1714*, p. 162.
38. Stewart, *Kneller*, p. 70. These are now in the National Maritime Museum.
39. Boit, *ODNB*.
40. NPG 6282; Ingamells, *Later Stuart Portraits 1685–1714*, p. 8.
41. Royal Collection, RCIN 421497, inscribed by the artist in the enamel on the back: 'Anna D:G: Angl: Scot: Franc: & Hiber: Regina &ct & his Royal Highness George Prince of Denmark C. Boit pinx: Anno 1706'.
42. Royal Collection RCIN 405610; Millar, *Tudor, Stuart and Early Georgian Pictures*, p. 167, no. 488.
43. Royal Collection RCIN 405301.
44. Millar, *Tudor, Stuart and Early Georgian Pictures*, p. 167, no. 489.
45. NPG 1674; Ingamells, *Later Stuart Portraits 1685–1714*, p. 363.
46. These are commonly found in collections of engravings, for example in the British Museum or Huntington Library, Richard Bull Granger; see British Printed Images, http://www.bpi1700.org.uk/jsp/. On Smith, see *ODNB*.

47. NPG D7754; Huntington Library, Bull Granger, 23/1.
48. Huntington Library, Bull Granger, 23/1; BM AN 340958001; see Bridgeman Art Library BAL 72314 for the Lilly canvas at Blenheim.
49. BM AN 217629001.
50. BM AN 399486001.
51. BM AN 485304001.
52. Huntington Library, Bull Granger, 23/4; BM AN 399486001.
53. Huntington Library, Bull Granger, 23/7; NPG D21276.
54. Huntington Library, Bull Granger, 23/4; NPG 31370, 31371; Cf. NPG D21066.
55. BM AN 399522001; BM AN250646001.
56. NPG D19698.
57. NPG D21271.
58. BM AN 399478001.
59. Sharpe, *Selling the Tudor Monarchy*, pp. 399–401.
60. BM AN 164447001; on Overton, see *ODNB*.
61. BM AN 354231001.
62. The impression in the Library of Congress carries the publication line: 'B. Bragge in Paternoster Row against Ivy Lane/Price 6d./1706'.
63. BM AN 353943001.
64. BM AN 35406600.
65. BM AN 35399400, frontispiece to Edward Ward, *The Whigs Unmask'd: Being the Secret History of the Calf's-Head-Club* (ESTC T147726, 1713).
66. BM AN 333791001; BM Satires 1547; F. Stephens and M. George eds, *Catalogue of Political and Personal Satires in the Department of Prints and Drawings in the British Museum* (11 vols, London, 1870), I, no. 1547.
67. BM AN 333793001; Stephens and George eds, *Catalogue of Political and Personal Satires*, I, no. 1549.
68. Mark Knights is conducting a full study of the prints circulating during the Sacheverell affair.
69. *The Picture of Malice, or a True Account of Dr. Sacheverell's Enemies* (ESTC N061445, 1710), p. 20.
70. For example, The Book of Common Prayer (ESTC T182600, 1706); see also G. Brown, *Reformation. A Necessary Companion* (ESTC T013209, 1704).
71. T. Ellis, *The True Royal English School, for Her Majesty's Three Kingdoms* (ESTC N014203, 1709).
72. W. Sherlock, *A Sermon Preach'd before the Queen, at the Cathedral Church of St. Paul, London, on the Seventh of September, 1704* (ESTC T049073, 1704).
73. *The History of England from the Beginning of the Reign of Queen Anne, to the Conclusion of the Glorious Treaty of Union* (ESTC T017551, 1707); *An Oration Sacred to the Imperial Majesty of Anne, Queen of Great-Britain* (ESTC T032952, 1707).
74. G. L., *A Compendious History of the Monarchs of England: From King William the First . . . down to the Eleventh Year of the Reign of Her Present Majesty* (ESTC N027559, 1712); *The Truth's Come Out at Last: or, the Downfall of a Great Favourite* (ESTC N014195, 1712); J. P., *An Antidote Against the Growth of Popery, for the Year 1713* (ESTC T090923, 1713).
75. *England's Triumph, or an Occasional Poem on the Happy Coronation of Anne Queen of England, &c* (ESTC N000774, 1702).
76. Huntington Library, Bull Granger, 24/54, 70–1, 73.
77. T. Bowers, *The Politics of Motherhood: British Writing and Culture, 1680-1760* (Cambridge, 1996), part 1; Bowers, 'Queen Anne Makes Provision', in K. Sharpe and S. Zwicker eds, *Refiguring Revolutions: Aesthetics and Politics from the English Revolution to the Romantic Revolution* (Berkeley, CA, and London, 1998), pp. 57–74.
78. Bowers, 'Queen Anne Makes Provision', p. 70.
79. J. Plunkett, *Queen Victoria: First Media Monarch* (Oxford, 2003).
80. N. Smith, *The Royal Image and the English People* (Aldershot, 2001), p. 134.
81. Smith, *The Royal Image*, pp. 135–6; Bird, *ODNB*.
82. See A. Bolton and H. Hendry, 'Part II: The Minute Book HM Commission for Rebuilding St Paul's Cathedral' (Wren Society, 16, Oxford, 1939), p. 111.
83. *A Well-Timber'd Poem, on Her Sacred Majesty; Her Marble Statue, and its Wooden Enclosure in Saint Paul's Church-Yard* (ESTC T219241, 1712), p. 5.
84. Ibid., p. 7.
85. Ibid., p. 8.
86. J. Trapp, *Peace of Poem: Inscribed to the Right Honorable the Lord Viscount Bolingbroke* (ESTC N020014, 1713), p. 36.
87. Ibid., pp. 34, 36.

88. Smith, *The Royal Image*, p. 135.
89. Ibid.; see BM AN 211166001.
90. BM AN 609926001.
91. Smith, *The Royal Image*, p. 135.
92. Ibid., p. 141, n. 59.
93. A. Brooks and N. Pevsner, *Worcestershire* (New Haven, CT, and London, 2007), p. 721.
94. Public Monument and Sculpture Association National Recording Project, http://pmsa.cch.kcl. ac.uk/LL/CHCT0038.htm. The date mentioned, 1698, is clearly wrong as Anne is depicted in coronation robes.
95. *Southampton City Council – Historic Environment Record Listed Buildings in Southampton* (2009), p. 6.
96. B. Cherry and N. Pevsner, *Devon* (Harmondsworth and Baltimore, 1991), p. 153.
97. *Victoria County History Gloucester*, IV (Oxford, 1988), p. 251.
98. S. Lewis ed., *A Topographical Dictionary of England* (1848), pp. 46–55; K. Esdaile, 'The Royal Sisters: Mary II and Anne in Sculpture', *Burlington Magazine* (1947), pp. 254–7. I am grateful to Theodore Wilkins of the Leeds City Art Gallery for an image and information about this statue.
99. *Victoria County History Hampshire*, V (1912), p. 8, City of Winchester Trust, http://www.cwt. hampshire.org.uk/trust/high/block1.htm.
100. N. Pevsner, *South and West Somerset* (Harmondsworth and Baltimore, MD, 1958), p. 24; Public Monument and Sculpture Association National Recording Project [photograph].
101. For example at Wibtoft, Leicestershire, and at Northampton, see Smith, *The Royal Image*, p. 134.
102. Ibid., p. 135.
103. Above, ch.10, p. 427.
104. *The Church of England's Joy on the Happy Accession of Her Most Sacred Majesty Queen Anne, to the Throne* (ESTC N001645, 1702), p. 7.
105. H. Colvin ed., *The History of the King's Works, V, 1660–1782* (London, 1976), p. 299.
106. *Faction Display'd, in Answer to Faction Display'd, a Poem* (ESTC N005600, 1704), p. 1.
107. Particularly in her modest house at Windsor, see Colvin, *King's Works*, V, p. 333.
108. Ibid., p. 237.
109. Ibid., pp. 239, 253.
110. Ibid., p. 239.
111. Ibid., p. 192.
112. J. Bowack, *The Antiquities of Middlesex* (ESTC T144068, 1705), p. 20.
113. Colvin, *King's Works*, V, p. 194.
114. Ibid., p. 174.
115. S. Thurley, *Hampton Court: A Social and Architectural History* (New Haven, CT, and London, 2003), p. 213.
116. Ibid., pp. 212–13; Colvin, *King's Works*, V, pp. 174–5.
117. Colvin, *King's Works*, V, p. 174.
118. Ibid.
119. Thurley, *Hampton Court*, p. 213.
120. Ibid., pp. 217–18.
121. Ibid., p. 221; Colvin, *King's Works*, V, p. 174.
122. Colvin, *King's Works*, V, p. 333.
123. See C. Morris ed., *The Journal of Celia Fiennes* (London 1947), pp. 276–82.
124. Colvin, *King's Works*, V, p. 334.
125. Morris, *The Journal of Celia Fiennes*, p. 358.
126. Ibid., p. 276.
127. J. Dubourdieu, *A Sermon Preached on the 7th Day of September* (ESTC T104497, 1704), p. 13.
128. E. Fenton, *An Ode to the Sun, for the New-year* (ESTC T042010, 1707), p. 13.
129. Philometrius, *The Country Vicar's Address to Her Majesty* (ESTC N001648, 1707), p. 19.
130. Ibid., p. 20.
131. *A Dialogue between Windsor Castle, and Blenheim House, the Seat of the Duke of Marlborough* (ESTC T112445, 1708).
132. Ibid., p. 8.
133. Ibid., p. 4.
134. Ibid., pp. 5–6.
135. Ibid., p. 8.
136. Ibid.

137. J. Coningham, *A Critical Essay on the Modern Medals. With Some Reflections on the Taste and Judgment of the Ancients* (ESTC T056741, 1704), sig. A6ᵛ.
138. Ibid., p. 37.
139. Ibid., sig. A8.
140. Ibid., p. 66.
141. Ibid., pp. 66, 70.
142. Above, ch.13, pp. 521–2.
143. A. W. Franks and H. A. Grueber, *Medallic Illustrations of the History of Great Britain* (2 vols, 1885), II, p. 228 no. 3; E. Hawkins, *Medallic Illustrations of the History of Great Britain and Ireland to the Death of George II* (1904–11), plate CXV, 1–3.
144. Franks and Grueber, *Medallic Illustrations*, II, p. 228, no. 3; Hawkins, *Medallic Illustrations*, plate CXV, 3.
145. Franks and Grueber, *Medallic Illustrations*, II, pp. 22–9, nos 4–6; Hawkins, *Medallic Illustrations*, plate CXV, 4–6.
146. Bowers, *Politics of Motherhood*, p. 78.
147. Franks and Grueber, *Medallic Illustrations*, II, pp. 229–30, nos 6–9; Hawkins, *Medallic Illustrations*, plate CXV, 8–11.
148. Franks and Grueber, *Medallic Illustrations*, II, p. 233, no. 14; Hawkins, *Medallic Illustrations*, plate CXV, 15–16; Bowers, *Politics of Motherhood*, p. 80.
149. Franks and Grueber, *Medallic Illustrations*, II, p. 236, no. 18; Hawkins, *Medallic Illustrations*, plate CXVI, 4–6.
150. Franks and Grueber, *Medallic Illustrations*, II, p. 241, no. 26; Hawkins, *Medallic Illustrations*, plate CXVII, 1–2.
151. Franks and Grueber, *Medallic Illustrations*, II, p. 246, no. 35; Hawkins, *Medallic Illustrations*, plate CXVIII, 1; Bowers, *Politics of Motherhood*, pp. 78–80.
152. Franks and Grueber, *Medallic Illustrations*, II, pp. 255–6, nos 48–9; Hawkins, *Medallic Illustrations*, plate CXIX, 6–8.
153. Franks and Grueber, *Medallic Illustrations*, II, p. 266, no. 64; Hawkins, *Medallic Illustrations*, plate CXX, 10.
154. Franks and Grueber, *Medallic Illustrations*, II, p. 280, no. 86; Hawkins, *Medallic Illustrations*, plate CXXII, 8–9.
155. Franks and Grueber, *Medallic Illustrations*, II, pp. 284, no. 92; Hawkins, *Medallic Illustrations*, plate CXXIII, 4.
156. Franks and Grueber, *Medallic Illustrations*, II, p. 286, no. 94; Hawkins, *Medallic Illustrations*, plate CXXIII, 7.
157. Franks and Grueber, *Medallic Illustrations*, II, p. 322, no. 148; Hawkins, *Medallic Illustrations*, plate CXXVII, 6.
158. Above, ch.10, p. 425.
159. Franks and Grueber, *Medallic Illustrations*, II, p. 369, no. 213; Hawkins, *Medallic Illustrations*, plate CXXXII, 5.
160. Franks and Grueber, *Medallic Illustrations*, II, pp. 399–400, nos 256–7; Hawkins, *Medallic Illustrations*, plate CXXXV, 10–12. Horace, *Odes*, 4, 14.
161. Franks and Grueber, *Medallic Illustrations*, II, pp. 407–9, nos 270–3; Hawkins, *Medallic Illustrations*, plate CXXXVII, 1–3.
162. J. Conington ed., *The Odes and Carmen Sæculare of Horace* (3rd edn, 1865), p. 124.
163. Franks and Grueber, *Medallic Illustrations*, II, pp. 251–2, nos 43, 44; Hawkins, *Medallic Illustrations*, plate CXIX, 1–2.
164. See K. Sharpe, *Selling the Tudor Monarchy: Authority and Image in Sixteenth-Century England* (New Haven, CT, and London, 2009), pp. 137–8.
165. *Her Majesties Most Gracious Speech to both Houses of Parliament, on Wednesday the Eleventh Day of March 1701* (ESTC T229502, 1702).
166. Franks and Grueber, *Medallic Illustrations*, II, p. 295, no. 107; Hawkins, *Medallic Illustrations*, plate CXXIV, 6–7.
167. Franks and Grueber, *Medallic Illustrations*, II, pp. 296–7, nos 111–13; Hawkins, *Medallic Illustrations*, plate CXXIV, 11–13.
168. Franks and Grueber, *Medallic Illustrations*, II, p. 297, no. 113; Hawkins, *Medallic Illustrations*, plate CXXIV, 13.
169. Franks and Grueber, *Medallic Illustrations*, II, p. 298, no. 115; Hawkins, *Medallic Illustrations*, plate CXXIV, 16.

170. See Wermouth's medal, Franks and Grueber, *Medallic Illustrations*, II, pp. 298-9, no. 116; see also Hawkins, *Medallic Illustrations*, plate CXXIV, 16.

171. For the Danish medals see Franks and Grueber, *Medallic Illustrations*, II, p. 334, nos 163-4; Hawkins, *Medallic Illustrations*, CXXVIII, 7-8.

172. Above, ch. 14, pp. 606-7.

173. Franks and Grueber, *Medallic Illustrations*, II, pp. 367-8, nos 210-12; Hawkins, *Medallic Illustrations*, plate CXXXII, 1-3.

174. C. Oman, *The Coinage of England* (Oxford, 1931), p. 345.

175. Ibid.

176. Ibid.

177. Rooke, *ODNB*.

178. P. Seaby, *The Story of British Coinage* (London, 1985), p. 132.

179. Ibid., p. 133.

180. Oman, *Coinage of England*, p. 346.

181. Seaby, *The Story of British Coinage*, p. 134.

182. http://www.24carat.co.uk/frame.php?url=britannia5frame.html.

15 Stuart Rituals

1. E. Gregg, *Queen Anne* (London, 1980), p. 152.

2. See *Gazette*, 2 April 1702.

3. A. Boyer, *The History of the Reign of Queen Anne, Digested into Annals. Year the first* (ESTC T122946, 1703), p. 22.

4. Ibid., p. 23.

5. T. Claydon, *William III and the Godly Revolution* (Cambridge, 1996), pp. 78-9.

6. *Post Man*, 31 March 1702; *Flying Post*, 11 April 1702; *Post Boy*, 21 April 1702.

7. *Post Boy*, 21 April 1702.

8. Boyer, *The History of the Reign of Queen Anne*, p. 32.

9. *Gazette*, 23 April 1702; *The Form of the Proceeding to the Royal Coronation of Her Most Excellent Majesty Queen Anne, The Twenty Third Day of this Instant April, 1702* (ESTC T040037, 1702).

10. All from *Gazette*, 23 April 1702.

11. See above, ch. 13, pp. 617-18.

12. Ibid. Boyer's account (*History* (1703), pp. 24-7) closely follows the *Gazette*.

13. *The Form of the Proceeding to the Royal Coronation*. See also *Post Man*, 23 April 1702.

14. *Post Boy*, 28 April 1702.

15. *Post Boy*, 28 April 1702, 30 April 1702; *Post Man*, 16 May 1702.

16. *Post Boy*, 12 May 1702.

17. *Post Man*, 5 May 1702.

18. *Post Man*, 21 May 1702.

19. J. Edzard, *God Save the Queen! The Most Hearty Acclamations of the Lutherans in London, Expressed at the Royal Proclamation and Coronation of Her Most Sacred Majesty Queen Anne* (ESTC T104134, 1702), p. 4.

20. Ibid., p. 6.

21. Above, ch. 13, pp. 536-41.

22. R. Bucholz, *The Augustan Court: Queen Anne and the Decline of Court Culture* (Stanford, CA, 1993), p. 207.

23. Boyer, *History* (1703), pp. 141-2.

24. A. Boyer, *The History of the Reign of Queen Anne, Digested into Annals. Year the Third* (ESTC T123171, 1705), pp. 96-7. On this service, see also *The royal triumph: a poem. To Her most excellent Majesty Queen Anne, on her going in state, to St. Paul's Cathedral* (ESTC N012800, 1704).

25. Boyer, *History* (1705), p. 98.

26. Ibid.

27. A. Boyer, *The History of the Reign of Queen Anne, Digested into Annals. Year the Fifth* (ESTC T122945, 1707), pp. 150-1.

28. Bucholz, *Augustan Court*, p. 211.

29. A. Boyer, *The History of the Reign of Queen Anne, Digested into Annals. Year the Seventh* (ESTC T122952, 1709), p. 297.

30. Boyer, *History* (1703), pp. 140-1; Boyer, *History* (1707), p. 152.

31. *Daily Courant*, 29 April, 1707; *Evening Post*, 2 July 1713; Bucholz, *Augustan Court*, p. 345.
32. *Evening Post*, 2 July 1713.
33. Boyer, *History* (1705), p. 98.
34. *View of the Times Their Principles and Practices*, 9 September 1704, a nice instance of the reception of a ritual occasion.
35. Above, ch. 11, p. 462.
36. *Gazette*, 12 March 1702.
37. *English Post*, 12 October 1702.
38. *Gazette*, 6 July 1704.
39. *Diverting Post*, 23 December 1704; see also *The Garter: a Poem on the Six Lords Made Knights-Companions of the Noble Order of the Garter* (ESTC T040534, 1712).
40. *Gazette*, 28 December 1704.
41. For example, *Post Boy*, 18 October 1712; see also *Gazette*, 25 October 1712, 4 August 1713.
42. T. Salmon, *An Historical Account of St. George for England, and the Original of the Most Noble Order of the Garter* (ESTC T017789, 1704); J. Grubb, *The British Heroes: or, a New Ballad in Honour of St. George* (ESTC T095838, 1707); J. Johnston, *The History of the Most Noble Order of the Garter* (ESTC T000680, 1712).
43. *The Garter: A Poem*, p. 6.
44. *The Blue Garter No More a Sign of Honesty than a Gilded Bush is of Good Wine* (ESTC T022923, 1713).
45. National Portrait Gallery, NPG 624. This group portrait by Peter Angelis is thought to show the institution of the new Knights of the Garter at a ceremony held at Kensington Palace on 4 August 1713, the year before the queen's death.
46. Bucholz, *Augustan Court*, p. 213.
47. Boyer, *History* (1703), p. 215; Bucholz, *Augustan Court*, p. 216.
48. Boyer, *History* (1703), p. 215.
49. *British Mercury*, 10 February 1714; Bucholz, *Augustan Court*, pp. 218-19.
50. *Daily Courant*, 6 February 1711.
51. *Post Man*, 10 February 1704; *Post Boy*, 10 February 1713.
52. Bucholz, *Augustan Court*, p. 218.
53. R. Strong, 'The Popular Celebration of the Accession Day of Queen Elizabeth I', *Journal of the Warburg and Courtauld Institutes*, 21 (1958), pp. 86–103; D. Cressy, *Bonfires and Bells: National Memory and the Protestant Calendar in Elizabethan and Stuart England* (London, 1989), ch. 4.
54. *England's Glory: A Poem. Perform'd in a Musical Entertainment before Her Majesty, on Her Happy Birth-day* (ESTC T135698, 1706), p. 2.
55. Ibid., pp. 4–5.
56. Ibid., p. 5.
57. Boyer, *History* (1703), p. 126.
58. Ibid., p. 216.
59. E. Settle, *The Triumphs of London for the Inauguration of the Right Honourable Sir Charles Duncombe, Knight. Lord Mayor of the City of London* (ESTC T086264, 1708), p. 6 and *passim*.
60. See R. Crawfurd, *The King's Evil* (Oxford, 1911); M. Bloch, *The Royal Touch: Sacred Monarchy and Scrofula in England and France* (London, 1973); J. C. D. Clark, *English Society 1688–1832* (Cambridge, 1985), pp. 160–7; Helen Farquhar, 'Royal Charities', *British Numismatic Journal*, II (1916), pp. 39–135; III (1917), pp. 93–163.
61. Above, ch. 11, p. 469.
62. J. Gaynam, *Marlborough Still Conquers: or, Union Hath Got the Day. A poem, upon the Late Victory Obtained by the Prince and Duke of Marlborough; and Union of the Two Kingdoms* (ESTC T038990, 1708), p. 15.
63. T. Fern, *A Perfect Cure for the King's Evil (whether hereditary or accidental) by Effectual Alcalious Medicines* (ESTC T075314, 1709), p. 9.
64. Clark, *English Society*, p. 164.
65. Bucholz, *Augustan Court*, p. 211.
66. Ibid.
67. See, for example, *Gazette*, 29 April 1703, 1 November 1705, 23 June 1709.
68. Bucholz, *Augustan Court*, p. 212.
69. Ibid., p. 224.
70. G. B. Hill ed., *Boswell's Life of Johnson* (revised edn, 6 vols, Oxford 1964), I, pp. 42–3; M. Lane, *Samuel Johnson and His World* (New York, 1975), pp. 18–20; Johnson's touch piece is British Museum AN321812001.

71. Crawfurd, *King's Evil*, p. 153; Bucholz, *Augustan Court*, pp. 211–13.
72. Clark, *English Society*, p. 163.
73. Bloch, *Royal Touch*, pp. 220–3.
74. Above, ch. 3, pp. 168–72.
75. Above, ch. 7, pp. 298–301.
76. Bucholz, *Augustan Court*, p. 26.
77. Above, ch. 11, pp. 466–7; 477–80.
78. Bucholz, *Augustan Court*, p. 44.
79. *Her Majesties Most Gracious Speech to Both Houses of Parliament, on Munday the Thirtieth Day of March, 1702* (ESTC N007206, 1702), p. 4.
80. G. Miege, *The New State of England, under Our Sovereign Queen Anne. In Three Parts* (ESTC T135115, 1703), p. 363.
81. Ibid., pp. 363, 364–76.
82. Boyer, *History* (1703) p. 215.
83. N. Tate, *Portrait-Royal. A Poem Upon Her Majesty's Picture Set Up in Guild-Hall* (ESTC T133784, 1703), p. 16.
84. J. Browne, *The British Court: A Poem. Describing the Most Celebrated Beauties at St. James's, the Park, and the Mall* (ESTC N015571, 1707), pp. 4–5 and *passim*.
85. J. Evans, *A Sermon Preach'd May the 19th, 1706* (ESTC T101954, 1706), p. 15.
86. W. Cockburn, *An Essay Upon the Propitious and Glorious Reign of Our Gracious Sovereign Anne* (ESTC N001543, 1710), p. 73.
87. Ibid., p. 42; *An Oration Sacred to the Imperial Majesty of Anne, Queen of Great-Britain* (ESTC T032952, 1707), pp. 53–4.
88. Bucholz, *Augustan Court*, p. 49.
89. Ibid., p. 57, and tables 2.1, 2.2.
90. *The Leaden-age. A Poem* (ESTC T080394, 1705), p. 14; see also H. Williams ed., *Jonathan Swift: The Journal to Stella* (2 vols, Oxford, 1948), I, pp. 84–5.
91. Bucholz, *Augustan Court*, p. 225.
92. Ibid., p. 154; Williams, *Swift: The Journal to Stella*, II, p. 603.
93. Bucholz, *Augustan Court*, p. 231.
94. Ibid., table 7.5, pp. 231–4.
95. For example, Williams, *Swift: The Journal to Stella*, II, p. 479.
96. Ibid., I, pp. 267, 366; II, pp. 428, 440, 595, 600.
97. Ibid., I, pp. 181, 363; II, pp. 480–1, 485, 507, 615–16.
98. *Occasional Thoughts Concerning Our Present Divisions, and their Remedies* (ESTC T175943, 1704), p. 8.
99. L. Welsted, *A Poem, Occasion'd by the Late Famous Victory of Audenard* (ESTC N011774, 1709), p. 9.
100. See above, ch. 14, pp. 605–6.
101. Bucholz, *Augustan Court*, p. 248.
102. Williams, *Swift: Journal to Stella*, II, p. 522; cf. pp. 585, 600.
103. Bucholz, *Augustan Court*, p. 201.
104. *Historical Manuscripts Commission Fifteenth Report*, part IV (1897) p. 657.
105. Ibid., p. 44.
106. *The Queen's Famous Progress, or; Her Majesty's Royal Journey to the Bath, and Happy Return. With the Most Remarkable Particulars of Her Royal Entertainment at Oxford, and Glorious and Triumphant Reception at the Bath, and All Other Places Going and Coming Thence* (ESTC T046188, 1702).
107. Ibid., p. 2.
108. Ibid., p. 3.
109. Ibid., p. 4.
110. Ibid., p. 5.
111. Ibid.
112. Ibid., p. 6: 'a great many' came to be touched so tickets were needed.
113. Boyer, *History* (1703), p. 99.
114. *The Queen's Famous Progress*, p. 7.
115. Ibid.
116. Ibid., pp. 7–8.
117. Boyer, *History* (1703), p. 78.
118. Ibid.

119. Ibid., pp. 78–9.
120. *The Queen's Famous Progress* was printed for J. W. near Fleet Street and was obviously a commercial venture.
121. Ibid., p. 2.
122. Narcissus Luttrell, *A Brief Historical Relation of State Affaires from September 1678 to April 1714* (6 vols, Oxford, 1857), V, pp. 274, 281.
123. Ibid., pp. 310, 314.
124. Ibid., pp. 319–20.
125. *Gazette*, 19 August 1703.
126. Bucholz, *Augustan Court*, table 7.2, p. 212.
127. Luttrell, *A Brief Historical Relation*, V, pp. 536–7.
128. A. Boyer, *The History of the Reign of Queen Anne, Digested into Annals. Year the Fourth* (ESTC T122948, 1706), p. 10.
129. Ibid., pp. 11–13.
130. Ibid.; *Gazette*, 16 April 1705.
131. Boyer, *History* (1706), p. 13.
132. Luttrell, *A Brief Historical Relation*, V, pp. 578, 586, 589.
133. Boyer, *History* (1706), p. 178.
134. Luttrell, *A Brief Historical Relation*, VI, p. 82; Bucholz, *Augustan Court*, table 7.2, p. 212.
135. Cockburn, *An Essay*, p. 72.
136. Bucholz, *Augustan Court*, p. 225.
137. J. Dunton, *The History of Living Men: or, Characters of the Royal Family* (ESTC N007801, 1702), p. 19.
138. Ibid., p. 20.
139. E. Settle, *Eusebia Triumphans. The Hanover Succession to the Imperial Crown of England, an Heroick Poem* (ESTC T086260, 1704), p. 29.
140. W. Congreve, *A Pindarique Ode, Humbly Offer'd to the Queen* (ESTC T042300, 1706), p. 6.
141. Cockburn, *An Essay*, pp. 25, 50.
142. H. Colman, *Government and Obedience. A Sermon Preach'd in the Town of King's-Lynn, Norfolk. September 29. 1711* (ESTC T010753, 1711), p. 15; F. Yates, 'Queen Elizabeth as Astraea', *Journal of the Warburg and Courtauld Institutes*, 10 (1947), pp. 27–82.
143. *The Tryal and Condemnation of David Lindsay, a Scotch Gent, Late Secretary to the Earl of Melford, for High Treason* (ESTC T000696, 1704).
144. *The Tryal, Examination and Condemnation, of Captain Green of the Worcester* (ESTC N046257, 1704).
145. *Observations Made in England, on the Trial of Captain Green, and the Speech at His Death* (ESTC T092995, Edinburgh, 1705). There were more than a dozen publications relating to this trial in 1704–5; see also Green, *ODNB*.
146. D. Defoe, *The History of the Union Between England and Scotland* (ESTC N052353, 1786/7), p. 82.
147. William Gregg, *ODNB*.
148. *A True Copy of the Paper Left by Mr. William Gregg, who Suffer'd for High-treason the 28th Day of April, 1708* (ESTC N014113, 1708), one page. See also, *The Whole Life and Conversation, Birth, Parentage and Education of Mr. William Gregg. Who was Executed on Wednesday the 28th Day of April, 1708 for High Treason* (ESTC T060021, 1708).
149. G. Holmes, *British Politics in the Reign of Anne* (London, 1967), p. 115.
150. *Observator*, 5 May 1708.
151. *Her Majesties Most Gracious Speech to Both Houses of Parliament, On Munday the Twenty Fifth Day of May, 1702* (ESTC N003492, 1702).
152. *The Humble Address of the Archbishop, the Bishops, and the Rest of the Clergy of the Province of Canterbury, in Convocation Assembled; Presented to Her Majesty At St. James's, On Friday the Sixth Day of November, 1702* (ESTC T036745, 1702).
153. Ibid., p. 4.
154. Ibid.; Boyer, *History* (1703), p. 139.
155. *Her Majesties Most Gracious Speech to both Houses of Parliament, On Saturday the Twenty Seventh Day of February, 1702* (ESTC T036112, 1703).
156. H. Sacheverell, *The Character of a Low-Church-Man: Drawn in an Answer to The true Character of a Church-Man: Shewing the False Pretences to that Name* (ESTC N039677, 1702); Sacheverell, *The Political Union. A Discourse Shewing the Dependance of Government on Religion in General: and of the English Monarchy on the Church of England in Particular* (ESTC T043976, 1702). See also Sacheverell, *ODNB*; G. Holmes, *The Trial of Doctor Sacheverell* (London, 1973).

157. J. Barnes, *The Good Old Way: or, Three Brief Discourses Tending to the Promotion of Religion, and the Glory, Peace, and Happiness of the Queen, and Her Kingdoms, in Church and state . . . III. The Case of the Church of England Truly Represented and Fully Vindicated* (ESTC T088705, 1703); W. Baron, *Separation and Sedition Inseparable* (ESTC T118157, 1703); T. Bennet, *A Defence of the Discourse of Schism* (ESTC T083057, 1703), p. 63 and *passim*.

158. R. Fiddes, *A Sermon Preached on the Thanksgiving Day: December, 3d. 1702* (ESTC T075694, 1703), especially pp. 26–8; B. Hoadly, *The Reasonableness of Conformity to the Church of England, Represented to the Dissenting Ministers* (ESTC T018301, 1703); Hoadly, *ODNB*.

159. D. Defoe, *A Challenge of Peace, Address'd to the Whole Nation* (ESTC T032976, 1703), p. 21.

160. The narrative of the contests in parliament is best followed in Holmes, *British Politics*.

161. H. Mackworth, *Peace at Home: or, a Vindication of the Proceedings of the Honourable the House of Commons, on the Bill for Preventing Danger from Occasional Conformity* (ESTC N010964, 1703).

162. G. Burnet, *The Bishop of Salisbury's Speech in the House of Lords, upon the Bill Against Occasional Conformity* (ESTC N005988).

163. J. Savage, *Security of the Establish'd Religion, the Wisdom of the Nation. A Sermon Preach'd at the Assizes Held at Hertford, August 7. 1704* (ESTC T010321, 1704), quotation, p. 14.

164. D. Defoe, *The Double Welcome a Poem to the Duke of Marlbro'* (ESTC N003822, 1705); cf. Defoe, *Advice to All Parties. By the Author of The True-born English-Man* (ESTC T066298, 1705).

165. R. Willis, *A Sermon Preach'd before the Queen, at the Cathedral Church of St. Paul, London, on the 23d Day of August 1705. Being the Thanksgiving-day* (ESTC N000383, 1705), pp. 4, 7, 15.

166. R. Stephens, *The Queen a Nursing Mother. A Sermon Preach'd on Thursday, March the 8th 1704–5 Being the Anniversary Day of Her Majesty's Happy Accession to the Throne* (ESTC T108060, 1705), p. 10.

167. Ibid., p. 14.

168. 'Violenta non diu continuunt; moderata durant': Philometrius, *The Country Vicar's Address to Her Majesty* (ESTC N001648, 1707).

169. Ibid., p. 5.

170. J. Waller, *Religion and Loyalty, or the Reverence Due Both to Church and State, Asserted in a Sermon, Preach'd at the Parish-church of Bishop-Stortford, in Hertfordshire, Aug. 31. 1708* (ESTC T168694, 1708), p. 19.

171. H. Sacheverell, *The Perils of False Brethren, Both in Church and State* (ESTC T043864, 1709).

172. Ibid., p. 8.

173. Ibid., p. 9.

174. Ibid., p. 18.

175. Ibid., p. 19.

176. For a listing of the literature, see F. Madan, *A Critical Bibliography of Dr. Henry Sacheverell*, ed. W. A. Speck (Lawrence, Kansas, MO, 1978).

177. See Holmes, *Trial of Doctor Sacheverell*. Brian Cowan and Mark Knights are researching new accounts of the trial.

178. T. Knaggs, *A Sermon Preach'd at St. Gyles's Church in the Fields. On Wednesday the 15th Day of March in the Afternoon, 1709/10* (ESTC N0227910, 1710), p. 16.

179. Holmes, *Trial of Doctor Sacheverell*, pp. 115–16, 208–11, 227–8; Anne, *ODNB*.

180. *Her Majesties Most Gracious Speech to both Houses of Parliament, on Wednesday the Fifth Day of April, 1710* (ESTC N017505, 1710).

181. A. B., *A Letter to the Reverend Dr. Henry Sacheverell. On Occasion of His Sermon* (ESTC T013223, 1710), p. 3.

182. R. Blomer, *A Sermon Preach'd in King Henry Vii's Chapel at Westminster, on Thursday the 8th of March, 1710. before the Lower House of Convocation* (ESTC T049150, 1710), pp. 28–9.

183. *Her Majestys Letter to the Arch-bishop of Canterbury* (ESTC T200420, 1711).

184. J. Humfrey, *A Seasonable Suggestion* (ESTC T099870, 1711), p. 17.

185. See W. Fleetwood, *The Thirteenth Chapter to the Romans, Vindicated from the Abusive Senses Put Upon It* (ESTC T039102, 1711), p. 18, for the address of the London clergy on behalf of Hanover.

186. N. Hough, *A Sermon upon the Anniversary Day of Her Majesty's Happy Accession to the Throne. Preach'd at Kensington-Church, March 8. 1712/13* (ESTC T005085, 1713), p. 4.

187. J. Dunton, *A Cat May Look on a Queen: or, a Satyr on Her Present Majesty* (ESTC T020329, 1708), p. 51.

188. A. Boyer, *The History of the Reign of Queen Anne, Digested into Annals. Year the Ninth* (ESTC T122949, 1711), pp. 357, 375; *A Collection of All the Addresses, &c. of the Lords and Commons to the Queen, Since Her Happy Accession to the Throne* (ESTC T128205, 1712), p. 104; B. Loveling, *Peace the Gift of God: Rest, Safety, and Opportunities of Piety, the Fruits of Peace. A Sermon Preach'd*

at Banbury, in Oxford-Shire, on Tuesday the Seventh of July (ESTC T128989, 1713), p. 19; J. Wright, *Phoenix Paulina. A Poem on the New Fabrick of St. Paul's Cathedral* (ESTC T131188, 1709). See M. H. Port ed., *The Commission for Building Fifty New Churches: The Minute Books, 1711–27, A Calendar* (London Record Society, 23, 1986).

189. Hough, *A Sermon upon the Anniversary Day*.
190. Ibid., p. 6.
191. Ibid., p. 9.
192. Ibid., p. 15.
193. *Great Britain's Union, and the Security of the Hanover Succession, Consider'd. In a Letter from Windsor of the 30th of December, 1704* (ESTC T035835, 1705), p. 16.
194. Holmes, *British Politics*, pp. 84–5; Gregg, *Queen Anne*, p. 239.
195. *Her Majesties Most Gracious Speech to Both Houses of Parliament, On Thursday the Sixth Day of March, 1706* (ESTC T031384, 1707).
196. *An Answer to Some Queries, &c. Relative to the Union: in a Conference betwixt a Coffee-master, and a Countrey-farmer* (ESTC T077139, 1706), pp. 11–12; J. Dennis, *The Battle of Ramillia: or, the Power of Union. A Poem. In Five Books* (ESTC T135406, 1706), p. 81.
197. R. Davidson, *Brit. Ann. 1a. A Sermon Preach'd on the Thanksgiving-Day, for the Happy Union of Great Britain. Under Her Sacred Majesty Queen Anne, May the 1st, 1707* (ESTC T012023, 1707), p. 3.
198. G. Dent, *A Thanksgiving Sermon Preach'd on the First Day of May, 1707. On Occasion of the Happy Union between England and Scotland* (ESTC T107001, 1707), p. 12.
199. R. Allen, *A Sermon Preach'd on Thursday the First of May, 1707. Being the Day Appointed for a General Thanksgiving for the Union of England and Scotland* (ESTC 174940, 1707), p. 15.
200. F. Hutchinson, *A Sermon Preached at St. Edmund's-Bury, on the First of May, 1707. Being the Day of Thanksgiving for the Union of England and Scotland* (ESTC T099480, 1707), p. 14.
201. J. Bates, *Two (united) Are Better than One Alone. A Thanksgiving Sermon upon the Union of the Two Kingdoms, of England and Scotland, Preach'd at Hackney, May 1. 1707* (ESTC T052158, 1707), pp. 13, 25.
202. J. Browne, *The Patriots of Great Britain: A Congratulatory Poem* (ESTC N010941, 1707), p. 1.
203. C. Darby, *Union a Poem Humbly Dedicated to the Queen* (ESTC T118345, 1707), p. 7; L. Theobald, *A Pindarick Ode on the Union* (ESTC T075216, 1707), p. 6.
204. E. Settle, *Carmen irenicum. The Union of the Imperial Crowns of Great Britain. An Heroick Poem* (ESTC T086250, 1707), 'To the Queen' and p. 31.
205. N. Tate, *The Triumph of Union: with the Muse's Address for the Consummation of it in the Parliament of Great Britain. Written by Mr. Tate Poet-Laureat to Her majesty* (ESTC T051756, 1707), p. 16.
206. R. Enock, *The Blessed Union: or, a Sermon, Preached on Psalm 133.1. on the First Day of May, 1707. Being the Thanksgiving-day* (ESTC T012018, 1707), p. 26; *The True-Born Britain* (ESTC T195585, 1707), p. 6.
207. *Great-Britain's Happiness: A Poem on the Passing of the Union* (ESTC N000644, 1707).
208. Settle, *Carmen irenicum*, pp. 43, 47.
209. W. Cockburn, *An Essay*, p. 56.
210. *Her Majesties Most Gracious Speech to Both Houses of Parliament, on Wednesday, 5 April, 1710* (ESTC N033129, 1710).
211. Bates, *Two (united)*, p. 29; cf. J. Chamberlayne, *Magnae Britanniæ Notitia: or, the Present State of Great-Britain* (ESTC T054583, 1708), p. vi.
212. N. Brady, *A Sermon upon Occasion of the Death of Our Late Sovereign King William; and Her Present Majesty's Happy Accession to the Crown* (ESTC T060262, 1702), p. 14.
213. Ibid., p. 16.
214. Ibid.
215. F. Hext, *A Funeral Oration* (ESTC N018451, 1702), p. 12; R. Allen, *The Death of a Good King a Great and Publick Loss* (ESTC T121048, 1702), p. 25.
216. J. Dunton, *The History of Living Men: or, Characters of the Royal Family* (ESTC N007801, 1702).
217. Ibid., pp. 3–4, 11, 22, 25.
218. Ibid., p. 28.
219. Ibid., p. 29.
220. *An Oration Sacred to the Imperial Majesty of Anne, Queen of Great-Britain* (ESTC T032952, 1707).
221. *Who Plot Best; the Whigs or the Tories* (ESTC T103622, 1712), p. 11.

222. Dunton, *The History of Living Men*, p. 5.
223. J. Gander, *The Glory of Her Sacred Majesty Queen Anne, in the Royal Navy* (ESTC T102190, 1703), sig. D1.
224. Prince George of Denmark, *ODNB*.
225. *Occasional Thoughts Concerning Our Present Divisions, and their Remedies* (ESTC T175943, 1703), p. 8; C. Johnson, *The Queen: A Pindarick Ode. By Mr. Cha. Johnson* (ESTC N014602, 1705), p. 5.
226. *An Ode to the Queen, on the Death of His Royal Highness George, Hereditary Prince of Denmark* (ESTC N041901, 1708), p. 4.
227. *Exequiae celsissimo principi, Georgio principi Daniæ, ab Oxoniensi Academia solutæ* (ESTC T143001, Oxford 1708), sig. Hh2.
228. D. Sturmy, *A Sermon Preach'd, &c. October the 31st. 1708. on the Death of His Royal Highness the Prince* (ESTC T049145, 1708), p. 13.
229. N. Tate, *Portrait-Royal. A Poem upon Her Majesty's Picture Set Up in Guild-Hall* (ESTC T133784, 1703), sig. A3.
230. George I, *ODNB*.
231. See L. Colley, *Britons: Forging the Nation 1707-1837* (New Haven, CT, and London, 1992).
232. M. Knights, *Representation and Misrepresentation in Later Stuart Britain: Partisanship and Political Culture* (Oxford, 2004), pp. 125, 150-1.
233. L. Theobald, *The Mausoleum. A Poem. Sacred to the Memory of Her Late Majesty Queen Anne. Written by Mr. Theobald* (ESTC T010988, 1714), p. 3.

16 Party Contest and the Queen

1. We recall that Whigs were disreputable Scottish dissenters and Tories dispossessed Irish outlaws.
2. E. Settle, *Eusebia triumphans. The Hanover Succession to the Imperial Crown of England, an Heroick Poem* (ESTC T086260, 1704), preface [not paginated].
3. D. Defoe, *Iure Divino: A Satyr. In Twelve Books. By the Author of The True-Born-Englishman* (ESTC T066292, 1706), p. vi.
4. *A General View of Our Present Discontents* (ESTC N003656, 1710), p. 12.
5. W. Law, *A Sermon Preach'd at Hazelingfield, in the County of Cambridge, on Tuesday, July 7. 1713* (ESTC T066733, 1713), p. 29.
6. B. Hoadly, *A Sermon Preach'd on the Eighth of March, 1704-5. Being the Anniversary Day of Thanksgiving for the Queen's Accession to the Crown* (ESTC T018269, 1705), p. 17.
7. H. T., *Vox Populi, Vox Dei: Being True Maxims of Government* (Bodleian Pamph 282(7), 1709), pp. 10-11; S. Clement, *Faults on Both Sides: or, an Essay upon the Original Cause, Progress, and Mischievous Consequences of the Factions in this Nation* (ESTC T186828, 1710), p. 28.
8. J. Browne, *Liberty and Property. A Satyr* (ESTC N002889, 1705), pp. 15, 18.
9. *Liberty. A Poem* (ESTC N002828, 1705), p. 9; Settle, *Eusebia*, p. 19.
10. H. Lambe, *A Good Prince Never Forgotten. A Sermon Preach'd at St. Dunstan's in the East, March the 8th 1708/9* (ESTC T068545, 1709), p. 9.
11. R. Bucholz, '"Nothing but ceremony": Queen Anne and the Limitations of Royal Ritual', *Journal of British Studies*, 30 (1991), pp. 288-323, quotation, p. 312.
12. Defoe, *Iure Divino*, p. 248.
13. J. Dunton, *A Cat May Look on a Queen* (ESTC T020329, 1708), pp. 22, 34.
14. T. Fern, *A Perfect Cure for the King's Evil* (ESTC T075314, 1709), p.9.
15. Defoe, *Iure Divino*, p. 262.
16. Law, *A Sermon Preach'd at Hazelingfield*, pp. 27, 29; 'we shall be strangers to these impressions of awe and veneration'.
17. P. Bisse, *A Sermon Preach'd before the Right Honourable House of Peers, on Tuesday the 29th of May, 1711* (ESTC T004255, 1711), p. 20.
18. Ibid., p. 21.
19. M. Knights, *Representation and Misrepresentation in Later Stuart Britain: Partisanship and Political Culture* (Oxford, 2004), p. 266.
20. A. Downie, *Robert Harley and the Press: Propaganda and Public Opinion in the Age of Swift and Defoe* (Cambridge, 1979), p. 1.
21. C. Leslie, *A Case of Present Concern, in a Letter to a Member of the House of Commons* (ESTC T082646, 1703), p. 8.

22. *Occasional Thoughts Concerning Our Present Divisions, and Their Remedies* (ESTC T175943, 1704), sig. A2.
23. *Arguments Relating to a Restraint upon the Press* (ESTC T022392, 1712), p. 9.
24. J. How, *Some Thoughts on the Present State of Printing and Bookselling* (ESTC T049409, 1709), p. 11.
25. *Arguments Relating to a Restraint upon the Press*, p. 20.
26. *Some Expedients without which England Cannot Be Happy. Humbly Offer'd to the Consideration of Both Houses of Parliament* (ESTC T074412, 1703), p. 18. The point has been made about the Elizabethan stage; see D. Kastan, 'Proud Majesty Made a Subject: Shakespeare and the Spectacle of Rule', *Shakespeare Quarterly* 37 (1986), pp. 459–75.
27. *Some Expedients*, p. 18.
28. *Aesop the Wanderer: or, Fables Relating to the Transactions of Europe; Occasionally Writ since the Late Battle at Bleinheim* (ESTC T062152, 1704), p. 31.
29. Ibid.
30. W. Dawes, *The Danger of Talking Much, and Wisdom of the Contrary. A Sermon Preach'd before the Queen, Novemb. 1706* (ESTC T067003, 1707), p. 16.
31. *An Antidote Against Rebellion: or, the Principles of the Modern Politician* (ESTC T090298, 1704), p. 31.
32. *Rime and Reason: or, a Word in Season. A satyr* (ESTC T121652, 1705), p. 1.
33. Ibid.
34. T. Knaggs, *A Sermon Preach'd at St. Gyles's Church in the Fields. On Wednesday the 15th Day of March in the Afternoon, 1709/10* (ESTC N022791, 1710), p. 14.
35. *A Letter from a Free-holder of the County of Norfolk, to One of the Knights of the Shire: Occasion'd by Dr. Sacheveralls [sic] Trial* (ESTC T037790, 1710), p. 4.
36. E. Chishull, *The Duty of Good Subjects, In Relation to Publick Peace. Being a Sermon Preach'd at the Assizes at Hertford, on August the 11th, 1712* (ESTC T035391, 1712), p. 14.
37. Law, *A Sermon Preach'd at Hazelingfield*, p. 7.
38. Ibid.
39. Downie, *Robert Harley*, ch. 3; above, ch. 13, *passim*.
40. M. Tindal, *Reasons Against Restraining the Press* (ESTC T066052, 1704), pp. 10, 13.
41. *The Thoughts of a Tory Author, Concerning the Press* (ESTC T008475, 1712), p. 13.
42. W. Clarke, *A Word to the Wise: or, A Hint on the Times, Deliver'd in Three Sermons* (ESTC T052726, 1712), p. 9.
43. Knights, *Representation and Misrepresentation, passim*.
44. See Downie, *Robert Harley*, ch. 8, pp. 190–5; Knights, *Representation and Misrepresentation*, pp. 241–8; also J. Richards, *Party Propaganda under Queen Anne* (Athens, GA, 1972).
45. Knights, *Representation and Misrepresentation*, p. 298.
46. Above, ch. 15, p. 633.
47. *The Interest of England Consider'd, In the Following Questions* (ESTC T017533, 1704), p. iii.
48. *Occasional Thoughts*, p. 20.
49. N. Brady, *A sermon upon Occasion of the Death of Our Late Sovereign King William* (ESTC T047952, 1702), p. 14.
50. Clement, *Faults on Both Sides*.
51. Ibid., p. 14.
52. G. Holmes, *British Politics in the Age of Anne* (London, 1967), p. 139.
53. L. Beaulieu, *The Reciprocal Duty Betwixt Kings and Subjects, Impartially Stated, in a Sermon on Romans xiii. 1. Preach'd in the Cathedral Church of Gloucester at the Assizes, Sunday, July the 14th, 1706* (ESTC T046496, 1706), 'Advertisement'.
54. Defoe, *Iure Divino*, p. 278.
55. J. Oldmixon, *Iberia Liberata: a Poem. Occasion'd by the Success of Her Majesties Arms in Catalonia, Valentia, &c* (ESTC N001473, 1706), p. 9; P. Aubin, *The Stuarts: A Pindarique Ode* (T048753, 1707), p. 11.
56. E. Hyde, *The History of the Rebellion and Civil Wars in England* (ESTC T053942, 1707), p. ix; *An Oration Sacred to the Imperial Majesty of Anne, Queen of Great-Britain* (ESTC T032952, 1707), p. 55.
57. Holmes, *British Politics*, pp. 377–8.
58. *The Danger of Moderation. In a Letter to an Old Parliament-Man in the Country* (ESTC T128204, 1708), p. 4. A contemporary reader of the copy in the British Library has marked this passage for note.
59. For example, *The Politicks of High-church: or, a System of their Principles about Government* (ESTC T043988, 1705); *Advice to the Electors of Great Britain* (ESTC T164739, Edinburgh, 1708); *Republican Queries Answer'd Paragraph by Paragraph* (ESTC N060906, 1710).

60. H. Sacheverell, *The Perils of False Brethren, Both in Church and State* (ESTC T043864, 1709); above, ch. 9.
61. *The New Revolution: or, the Whigs Turn'd Jacobites. A Poem* (ESTC N020060, 1710); B. Hoadly, *The Jacobite's Hopes Reviv'd by Our Late Tumults and Addresses* (ESTC T029030, 1710).
62. W. Bisset, *The Modern Fanatick. With a Large and True Account of the Life, Actions, Endowments, &c. of the Famous Dr. Sa—*(ESTC T041307, 1710), preface.
63. Quotation from *An Elegy on Moderation* (ESTC T032513, 1710), broadside.
64. A. Maynwaring, *A Letter to a Friend Concerning the Publick Debts, Particularly that of the Navy* (ESTC T038023, 1711); W. A. Speck, *Tory and Whig: The Struggle in the Constituencies, 1701–15* (London, 1970), p. 113.
65. For the pro camp, see Defoe and Swift: Defoe, *Reasons Why this Nation Ought to Put a Speedy End to this Expensive War* (ESTC T065915, 1711); Swift, *The Conduct of the Allies, and of the Late Ministry, in Beginning and Carrying on the Present War* (ESTC T031147, 1711). For opposition to peace, see, for example, *A Defence of the Allies and the Late Ministry* (ESTC T167432, 1712); F. Hare, *The Allies and the Late Ministry Defended Against France, and the Present Friends of France. In Answer to a Pamphlet, Entitled, The Conduct of the Allies* (ESTC T021266, 1712); J. Oldmixon, *Remarks upon Remarks: or the Barrier-Treaty and the Protestant Succession Vindicated. In Answer to the False and Treasonable Reflections of the Author of The Conduct of the Allies* (ESTC N026274, 1712).
66. Alexander Justice, *The Interest of Europe, with Respect to Peace and War* (ESTC N017204, 1712), p. 6.
67. *Her Majesty's Most Gracious Speech to Both Houses of Parliament, on Saturday the One and Twentieth Day of June, 1712* (ESTC T229498, 1712); cf. *Grandsire Hambden's Ghost. And Peace, or, No Peace* (ESTC T035820, 1712); *The Supposal: or a New Scheme of Government. Humbly Offer'd to Publick Consideration, by a Lover of Truth and Peace* (ESTC N037615, 1712).
68. *Grandsire Hambden's Ghost*, p. 40; F. Squire, *A Brief Justification of the Principles of a Reputed Whigg. Together with Some Few Remarks on Dr. Sach—l's Late Sermon* (ESTC T107870, 1713), p. 11 and *passim*.
69. E. Gregg, *Queen Anne* (London, 1980), p. 388.
70. Ibid., p. 399.
71. D. Defoe, *The Mock Mourners. A Satyr, by Way of Elegy on King William* ESTC T070835, 1702).
72. See Holmes, *British Politics*, ch. 4.
73. *A Vindication of the Constitution of the English Monarchy, and the Just Rights of the People* (ESTC T102362, 1703), p. 4.
74. Ibid., pp. 11, 14.
75. Ibid., pp. 19–23.
76. R. Crosfeild, *England's Warning-piece. Humbly Offered to the Consideration of the Lords Spiritual and Temporal, and Commons* (ESTC T032672, 1704), pp. 4, 7.
77. *A Letter of Advice to a Friend in London: Written by the Observator in the Country* (ESTC T0004585, 1704), p. 12; E. Ward, *All Men Mad: or, England a Great Bedlam. A Poem* (ESTC T124432, 1704), p. 10.
78. *The Man of Honour or the Character of a True Country Man* (ESTC T038902, ?Edinburgh, 1706), pp. 3, 7.
79. *A New Ballad, Shewing All Shall Be Well One Hundred Years Hence* (ESTC N005349, 1711).
80. *A Dialogue Between a New Courtier and a Country Gentleman* (ESTC T132386, 1713).
81. The assertion of Gregg in both the biography and the life written in 2004 for *ODNB*.
82. *Animadversions Upon a Seditious Libel* (ESTC T073185, 1703), p. 27.
83. H. Care, *English Liberties: or, the Free-born Subject's Inheritance* (ESTC N006537, 1703); L. Schwoerer, *The Ingenious Mr. Henry Care, Restoration Publicist* (Baltimore, MD, 2001).
84. J. Dennis, *Liberty Asserted. A Tragedy* (ESTC N011004, 1704), preface [not paginated] and *passim*.
85. *Rime and Reason*, p. 3.
86. Defoe, *Iure Divino*, p. vi.
87. Ibid., p. 261 and *passim*.
88. F. Higgins, *A Sermon Preach'd at the Royal Chappel at White-Hall; on Ash-Wednesday, Feb. 26. 1706/7* (ESTC N037372, 1707), pp. 8–9; E. Ward, *The Secret History of the Calves-Head Club, or the Republican Unmasq'd* (ESTC T172380, 1704). On the Calves Head Club, see above, pp. 659, 663.
89. *Vox Populi, Vox Dei*, p. 20.
90. *The Judgment of Whole Kingdoms and Nations, Concerning the Rights, Power, and Prerogative of Kings, and the Rights, Priviledges, and Properties of the People* (ESTC T029263, 1710).

91. *All's Come Out: or, their Plot's Discover'd. Being a True Account of a Wonderful Procession that Will Be next Saturday Night, from St. James's to the Royal-Exchange* (ESTC T195167, 1711).
92. *Some Whig-Principles Demonstrated to be Good Sense and Sound Divinity, From their Natural Consequences* (ESTC T026105, 1713).
93. *Her Majesties Most Gracious Speech to both Houses of Parliament, On Saturday the Twenty Seventh Day of February, 1702* (ESTC T036112, 1703).
94. L. Milbourne, *Great Brittains Acclamation to Her Deborah* (ESTC T011987, 1704), p. 18.
95. W. Elstob, *A Sermon Upon the Thanksgiving for the Victory Obtain'd by Her Majesty's Forces, and those of Her Allies, over the French and Bavarians near Hochstet* (ESTC T063882, 1704), p. 11; *King William's Ghost* (ESTC N054983, 1704), p. 31.
96. E. Gibson, *Against Speaking Evil of Princes, and those in Authority under Them: a Sermon Preach'd at the Assizes Held at Croyden in Surrey, March 7th, 1705/6* (ESTC T045828, 1706), p. 29.
97. T. Knaggs, *A Thanksgiving Sermon for Our Many Deliverances* (ESTC T093404, 1709), p. 12; H. Lambe, *A Good Prince Never Forgotten. A Sermon Preach'd at St. Dunstan's in the East, March the 8th 1708/9. Being the Day on which Her Majesty Began Her Happy Reign* (ESTC T068545, 1709), p. 13.
98. *A General View of Our Present Discontents* (ESTC N003656, 1710), p. 4.
99. *A Modest Vindication of the Present Ministry . . . By a Well-wisher to the Peace of Britain* (ESTC N005333, 1707), pp. 12-13.
100. D. Manley, *A True Relation of the Several Facts and Circumstances of the Intended Riot and Tumult on Queen Elizabeth's Birth-day* (ESTC N045508, 1712), p. 7 and *passim*.
101. Sarah Churchill, *ODNB*; Abigail Masham, *ODNB*. See also F. Harris, *A Passion for Government: The Life of Sarah, Duchess of Marlborough* (Oxford, 1991).
102. *The Rival Dutchess: or, Court Incendiary. In a Dialogue Between Madam Maintenon, and Madam M* (ESTC T004547, 1708), p. 6.
103. Ibid., p. 12.
104. *The Perfect Picture of a Favourite: or, Secret Memoirs of Robert Dudley . . . Prime Minister and Favourite of Queen Elizabeth* (ESTC T140916, 1708); see Carole Levin, *'The Heart and Stomach of a King': Elizabeth I and the Politics of Sex and Power* (Philadelphia, PA, 1994), ch. 4.
105. James Drake, *ODNB*.
106. *The Perfect Picture of a Favourite*, sig. a.
107. *The Secret History of the Most Renowned Q. Elizabeth and the E. of Essex* (ESTC T092783, 1708), pp. 2-3.
108. *The Character of an Ill-court-favourite* (ESTC T068292, 1708); *The Character of an Ill-court-favourite* (Wing C2010, 1681).
109. *The Character of an Ill-court-favourite* (1708 edn), p. 17.
110. *The Picture of a Female Favourite* (ESTC N011703, 1708).
111. See E. Gregg, 'Was Queen Anne a Jacobite?', *History*, 57 (1972), pp. 358-75.
112. Holmes, *British Politics*, p. 84.
113. Gregg, *Queen Anne*, pp. 182-4.
114. E. Corp ed., *A Court in Exile: The Stuarts in France, 1689-1718* (Cambridge, 2004); Corp ed., *The Stuart Court in Rome: The Legacy of Exile* (Aldershot, 2003); E. Cruickshanks and E. Corp eds, *The Stuart Court in Exile and the Jacobites* (London, 1995); P. Monod, *Jacobitism and the English People, 1688-1788* (Cambridge, 1989); D. Szechi, *The Jacobites: Britain and Europe, 1688-1788* (Manchester, 1994); R. Sharp, *The Engraved Record of the Jacobite Movement* (Aldershot, 1996), pp. 12, 49, 61.
115. Sharp, *Engraved Record*, p. 57.
116. *An Abridgment of the Life of James II. King of Great Britain, &c. Extracted from an English Manuscript of the Reverend Father Francis Sanders, of the Society of Jesus, and Confessor to His Late Majesty* (ESTC T100280, 1704).
117. *Apotheosis Basilike: or, a Pindarick Ode, Upon the Pious and Blessed Transit Of that Most Excellent Prince James the II. King of Great Britain* (ESTC T053035, 1708), quotation, p. 8.
118. P. Aubin, *The Stuarts: a Pindarique Ode* (ESTC T048753, 1707); *Patience. A Present to the Press-Yard. A Poem* (ESTC N023561, 1706), p. 9.
119. *Patience*, p. 12.
120. R. Ferguson, *The History of the Revolution. By Robert Ferguson* (ESTC T110975, 1706), pp. 5-6; on Ferguson, see *ODNB*.
121. For example, *King William's Affection to the Church of England Examin'd* (ESTC T068173, 1703).
122. *The Late King James His Advice to His Son. Writteu [sic] with His Own Hand, and Found in His Cabinet after His Death* (ESTC T108590, 1703), quotation, p. 6.

123. Ibid., pp. 15–18.
124. *Apotheosis Basilike*, p. 14.
125. J. Cannell, *The Case of the Pretender Stated, and Our Duty on that Occasion. In a Sermon Preach'd at the Parish-Church of St. Nicholas Coleabby, on Sunday March 21. 1707-8* (ESTC T010551, 1708).
126. *The Several Declarations, Together with the Several Depositions Made in Council on Monday Oct. 22. 1688. Concerning the Birth of the Prince of Wales* (ESTC T223115, 1710); *A Plot Discover'd; or, the Protestant Succession in Danger: to which Is Added, a New Character of a Popish Successor* (ESTC N011549, 1711), preface [not paginated].
127. *Observations on the Depositions Concerning the Birth of the Prince of Wales* (ESTC T041784, 1711); *A Full Answer to the Depositions, and to All Other the Pretences and Arguments Whatsoever, Concerning the Birth of the Pretended Prince of Wales* (ESTC T146455, 1711).
128. G. Holmes, 'The Sacheverell Riots: The Crowd and the Church in Early 18th-Century London', in P. Slack ed., *Rebellion, Popular Protest and the Social Order in Early Modern England* (Cambridge, 1984), pp. 232–62.
129. *The History of the Jacobite Clubs* (ESTC T056907, 1712), pp. 10–11.
130. Ibid., pp. 30–3.
131. *Hannibal at the Gates: or, the Progress of Jacobitism. With the Present Danger of the Pretender* (ESTC T070826, 1712), p. 33.
132. D. Defoe, *An Answer to a Question that No Body Thinks of, viz. But What if the Queen Should Die?* (ESTC T056858, 1713), p. 4.
133. D. Defoe, *Reasons Against the Succession of the House of Hanover, with an Enquiry How Far the Abdication of King James, Supposing it to Be Legal, Ought to Affect the Person of the Pretender* (ESTC T065927, 1713), p. 12; see also Defoe, *And What If the Pretender Should Come? Or, Some Considerations of the Advantages and Real Consequences of the Pretender's Possessing the Crown of Great-Britain* (ESTC T056857, 1713).
134. *Protest of the Chevalier St. George; with a Poem Concerning Hereditary Right, Annexed* (ESTC T147438, Edinburgh, 1713), p. 2; J. Asgill, *The Pretender's Declaration Abstracted from Two Anonymous Pamphlets* (ESTC T044259, 1713); above, ch. 13, pp. 533–4.
135. James Francis Edward Stuart, *ODNB*; Gregg, *Queen Anne*, ch. 14.
136. Gregg, *Queen Anne*, pp. 367–8.
137. T. Burnet, *Some New Proofs by Which It Appears that the Pretender is Truly James the Third* (ESTC T146244, 1713), an attack on the Pretender's claims; Asgill, *The Pretender's Declaration Abstracted*.
138. John Viscount Barrington, *A Dissuasive from Jacobitism: Shewing in General what the Nation Is to Expect from a Popish King; and in Particular, from the Pretender* (ESTC N002926, 1713).
139. Ibid., p. 36.
140. Ibid., p. 27.
141. *Characters of the Court of Hannover* (ESTC N000221, 1714), p. 6.
142. See above, note 114.
143. *The Present Danger of Popery in England* (ESTC T093997, 1703), pp. 3–9.
144. J. Webster, *A Letter from One of the Country Party to His Friend of the Court Party* (ESTC N019582, Edinburgh, 1704).
145. Monod, *Jacobitism and the English People*, pp. 167–70.
146. T. Coulton, *Nahash's Defeat, and Jabesh-Gilead's Rescue: a Sermon Preach'd August 19. 1708. on Occasion of the Defeat of the Intended Invasion of North-Britain* (ESTC N006023, 1708), p. 9.
147. D. Szechi, *Jacobitism and Tory Politics 1710-1714* (Edinburgh, 1984), pp. 60–2 and ch. 3 *passim*; Szechi, 'Jacobite Politics in the Age of Anne', *Parliamentary History*, 28 (2009), pp. 41–58.
148. Szechi, *Jacobitism and Tory Politics*, appendix 1.
149. H. Snyder, 'The Last Days of Queen Anne: The Account of Sir John Evelyn Examined', *Huntington Library Quarterly*, 34 (1971), pp. 261–76.
150. Gregg, *Queen Anne*, p. 394.
151. L. Theobald, *The Mausoleum. A Poem. Sacred to the Memory of Her Late Majesty Queen Anne* (ESTC N010988, 1714), p. 1.
152. *A Funeral Oration on the Death of the Incomparable Princess Queen Anne* (ESTC T32955, 1714), p. 22.
153. Theobald, *The Mausoleum*, p. 3; *Funeral Oration*, pp. 14, 18; J. Smith, *The Duty of the Living to the Memory of the Dead. A Sermon Upon the Death of Her Most Sacred Majesty Queen Anne* (ESTC T012873, 1714), p. 15.

154. Smith, *Duty of the Living*, pp. 13–14; *Oration*, p. 14; N. Marshall, *The Royal Pattern: Or, A Sermon Upon the Death of Her Late Most Excellent Majesty Queen Anne: Preach'd in the Parish-Church of Finchley in the County of Middlesex, Upon Sunday August the 8th 1714* (ESTC T168965, 1714), pp. 16, 30.
155. *An Elegy on the Death of Her Most Gracious Majesty Queen Anne, who Dy'd at Her Palace in Kensington, on the First of August 1714* (ESTC T125676, 1714).
156. *Funeral Oration*, p. 14.
157. *An Elegy*, p. 4.
158. *A Collection of All Queen Anne's Speeches, Messages, &c. From Her Accession to the Throne, to Her Demise* (ESTC T000034, 1714).
159. Smith, *Duty of the Living*, p. 13; *Funeral Oration*, p. 7, *Mausoleum*, p. 13.
160. W. Reeves, *A Sermon Preach'd in the Chapel-Royal of Saint James's, on the Eighth day of August 1714* (ESTC T173577, 1714), p. 17.
161. J. Rowden, *A Sermon Upon the Death of Queen Anne, Preach'd at Minching-Hampton in Gloucester-Shire August 8th 1714* (ESTC T053361, 1714), p. 9.
162. Ibid., p. 8.
163. *Funeral Oration*, p. 9; Marshall, *The Royal Pattern*, pp. 14, 18.
164. Reeves, *Sermon*, p. 10; N. Collier, *A Sermon on the Lamented Death of Her Sacred Majesty Queen Anne of Blessed Memory. Preach'd at Harfield in Middlesex. August the 29th* (ESTC T000341, 1714).
165. Theobald, *Mausoleum*, p. 20; *Funeral Oration*, p. 4.
166. *Funeral Oration*, pp. 27, 30.
167. J. Harris, *A Funeral-Pindarique Ode, Sacred to the Happy Memory of Our Late Gracious Sovereign, Queen Anne* (ESTC T003211, 1714), p. 4.
168. Ibid., p. 8.
169. Rowden, *Sermon*, p. 16.
170. *Britannia's Tears: a Satyrical Dirge by Way of a Lamentation on the Deplorable Death of Her Late Gracious Majesty Queen Anne* (ESTC T079208, Dublin, 1714), p. 3.
171. Ibid., pp. 9, 13.
172. Collier, *A Sermon*, p. 6.
173. E. Smith, *A Sermon Preach'd at Wisbeech in the Isle of Ely, August 8. 1714. Being the Sunday after the Death of Queen Anne. Recommending upon that Occasion Suitable Sorrow, Unanimity and Acquiescence in the Present Happy Settlement. With some Arguments, and a Preface Address'd to those who Have Not Yet in Conscience Comply'd with the Government since the Revolution* (ESTC T028225, 1714), p. 6 and *passim*.
174. F. Shaw, *Condolence and Congratulation: a Sermon on the Death of Queen Anne: the Happy Accession of King George to the Throne* (ESTC T120103, 1714), p. 5 and *passim*.
175. *The History of the Life and Reign of Queen Anne* (ESTC N017927, 1714), p. 27.
176. Ibid., p. 28.
177. W. Sellar and R. Yeatman, *1066 and All That* (London, 1930), ch. 39.
178. Ibid., p. 78.
179. G. M. Trevelyan, *England under Queen Anne* (3 vols, London, 1930–4).
180. Ibid., II, p. 307.
181. See the review in *American Historical Review*, 40 (1934), pp. 123–5.
182. G. Clark, *The Later Stuarts, 1660–1714* (Oxford, 1934).
183. G. Clark, *The Later Stuarts, 1660–1714* (Oxford, 1955 edn), p. 220.
184. Ibid., p. 221.
185. D. B. Green, *Queen Anne* (London, 1970).
186. See review (quoted) by Edward Gregg in *European History Quarterly*, 4 (1974), pp. 269–74; cf. review by Henry Horwitz in *American Historical Review*, 77 (1972), p. 137.
187. G. Curtis, *The Life and Times of Queen Anne* (London, 1972), pp. 201, 216 and *passim*. See p. 7 for Antonia Fraser's disparaging remarks on Anne in the preface.
188. J. P. Kenyon, *The Stuarts* (London, 1970), pp. 186–7, 207.
189. Gregg, *Queen Anne* (New Haven, CT, and London, 2001), a reissue of the 1980 book. It is significant that Yale could not commission an entirely new biography.
190. M. Kishlansky, *A Monarchy Transformed: Britain 1603–1714* (London, 1997), pp. 316–17.
191. J. Hoppit, *A Land of Liberty?: England 1689–1727* (Oxford, 2000), pp. 282, 295.
192. L. Colley, review of Gregg, *Queen Anne*, in *Historical Journal*, 24 (1981), p. 972; http://womenshistory.about.com/library/bio/blbio_list_british.htm.
193. http://www.biographyonline.net/british/greatest-britons.html.

194. http://en.wikipedia.org/wiki/Anne_of_Great_Britain; www.historic-uk.com/HistoryUK/England-History/QueenAnne.htm; www.bbc.co.uk/dna/h2g2/A394391; www.who2.com/queenanne.html; www.nndb.com/people/402/000093123.
195. www.nndb.com/people/402/000093123.
196. Queen Anne, *Encyclopædia Britannica*, 2010. *Encyclopædia Britannica* Online, www.britannica.com/EBchecked/topic/26219/Anne.
197. http://www.historic-uk.com/HistoryUK/England-History/QueenAnne.htm.

Epilogue

1. S. Schama, 'The Domestication of Majesty: Royal Family Portraiture, 1500–1850', *Journal of Interdisciplinary History*, 17 (1986), pp. 155–83.
2. L. Colley, review in *Historical Journal*, 24 (1981), p. 972.
3. P. Korshin, 'Figural Change and the Survival of Tradition in the Later 17th Century', in Korshin ed., *Studies in Change and Revolution: Aspects of English Intellectual History, 1640–1800* (Menston, 1972), pp. 99–128.
4. J. Harris, *A Funeral-Pindarique Ode, Sacred to the Happy Memory of Our Late Gracious Sovereign, Queen Anne, &c. With a Congratulary Poem, on Our Present Most Illustrious King George, and His Happy Accession* (ESTC T003211, 1714), p. 8; *A Poem on the Arrival of His Majesty King George* (ESTC T031423, 1714), p. 9; R. Erskine, *A Congratulatory Poem upon the Coronation of His Majesty King George* (ESTC T006528, Edinburgh, 1714).
5. *Characters of the Court of Hannover* (ESTC N000221, 1714), p. 19.
6. *The Welcome. Two Congratulatory Poems, the First, Humbly Inscrib'd to the Most August Monarch George King of Great Britain* (ESTC T114574, Nottingham, 1714), p. 5; E. Smith, *A Sermon Preach'd at Wisbeech in the Isle of Ely, August 8. 1714* (ESTC T028225, 1714), p. 8; S. Gough, *A Sermon Occasion'd by the Happy Accession of King George* (ESTC T045843, 1714), p. 27.
7. *The Welcome*, p. 6.
8. J. Dennis, *A Poem upon the Death of Her Late Sacred Majesty Queen Anne, and the Most Happy and Most Auspicious Accession Of His Sacred Majesty King George* (ESTC T042571, 1714), p. 20.
9. For example, *Poem on the Arrival of His Majesty*, p. 6; J. Owen, *An Occasional Sermon upon the Proclamation of King George, on the First of August, 1714* (ESTC T099404, 1714), p. 17; S. Piers, *George for Britain* (ESTC T040794, 1714).
10. C. Povey, *An Enquiry into the Miscarriages of the Four Last Years Reign* (ESTC T075097, 1714), p. 25.
11. E. Ward, *The Republican Procession, or, the Tumultuous Cavalcade. A Merry Poem* (ESTC T139168, 1714), p. 31.
12. S. Wright, *Of Praying for the King. A Sermon Preach'd at Black-Fryars, October 24, 1714. Being the First Lord's-Day after the King's Coronation* (ESTC T085221, 1714), p. 31.
13. J. Archer, *The Kingdom Turned About. A Sermon Preached at Tunbridge-Wells August 8. 1714. On Occasion of His Present Majesty King George's Happy Accession* (ESTC T029481, 1714), p. 30.
14. Abernethy, *The People's Choice, the Lord's Annointed. A Thanksgiving Sermon for His Most Excellent Majesty King George His Happy Accession to the Throne* (ESTC T086823, Belfast, 1714).
15. Archer, *The Kingdom Turned About*, p. 20.
16. Hannah Smith, *Georgian Monarchy: Politics and Culture, 1714–1760* (Cambridge, 2006), p. 6.
17. George I, *ODNB*.
18. Smith, *Georgian Monarchy*, p. 203.
19. *ODNB*.
20. J. C. D. Clark, *English Society, 1688–1832: Ideology, Social Structure and Political Practice during the Ancien Regime* (Cambridge, 1985).
21. Smith, *Georgian Monarchy*, p. 96.
22. Ibid., p. 95.
23. L. Colley, *Britons: Forging the Nation, 1707–1837* (New Haven, CT, and London, 1992), p. 202.
24. Smith, *Georgian Monarchy*, p. 141.
25. Ibid., p. 61.
26. See K. Sharpe, *Selling the Tudor Monarchy: Authority and Image in Sixteenth-Century England* (New Haven, CT, and London, 2009).
27. For all the above argument, see Sharpe, *Image Wars: Promoting Kings and Commonwealths in England, 1603–1660* (New Haven, CT, and London, 2010).

28. See K. Sharpe, '"Thy longing country's darling and desire": Aesthetics, Sex, and Politics in the England of Charles II', in C. MacLeod and J. Alexander eds, *Politics, Transgression, and Representation at the Court of Charles II* (New Haven, CT, and London, 2007), pp. 1–32.
29. Sharpe, *Selling the Tudor Monarchy, passim.*
30. 'The social imaginary is that common understanding that makes possible . . . a widely shared sense of legitimacy', Charles Taylor, *Modern Social Imaginaries* (Durham, NC, 2004), p. 23.
31. W. Bagehot, *The English Constitution* (1963 edn), p. 88.

INDEX